# CANADIAN CRIMINAL JUSTICE TODAY

SECOND EDITION

**FRANK SCHMALLEGER**

Emeritus, University of North Carolina at Pembroke

DAVID MacALISTER

Simon Fraser University

PAUL F. McKENNA

Public Safety Innovation, Inc.

# CANADIAN CRIMINAL JUSTICE TODAY

PEARSON

Prentice
Hall

Toronto

**National Library of Canada Cataloguing in Publication**

Schmalleger, Frank
    Canadian criminal justice today / Frank Schmalleger, David MacAlister,
Paul F. McKenna. — 2nd ed.

Previous ed. written by Frank Schmalleger ... [et al.].
Includes bibliographical references and index.
ISBN 0-13-039878-0

1. Criminal justice, Administration of—Canada.  I. MacAlister, David, 1959–
II. McKenna, Paul F. (Paul Francis), 1952–

HV9960.C2C36 2004            364.971            C2003-904610-9

0-13-039878-0

Vice-President, Editorial Director: Michael J. Young
Acquisitions Editor: Ky Pruesse
Executive Marketing Manager: Judith Allen
Supervising Developmental Editor: Suzanne Schaan
Production Editor: Charlotte Morrison-Reed
Copy Editor: Susan Marshall
Proofreader: Allyson Latta
Production Manager: Wendy Moran
Page Layout: Susan Thomas/Digital Zone
Art Director: Mary Opper
Interior Design: Lisa Lapointe
Cover Design: Jennifer Stimson
Cover Image: © Judah Harris/Solus Images

6 7 8 9 10      09 10 11 12 13

Printed and bound in the United States of America.

# Contents

# CONTENTS

# PART 2 POLICING   95

# CHAPTER 4  Policing: History and Structure   96

# CONTENTS

# CHAPTER 6   Policing: Legal Aspects   170

# CONTENTS

# CHAPTER 9  Sentencing   281

# CONTENTS

## PART 4 CORRECTIONS 317

## CHAPTER 10 Probation, Parole, and Community Corrections 318

## CHAPTER 11   Correctional Institutions   347

# CONTENTS

# CHAPTER 15  The Future of Criminal Justice   493

# Preface

Criminal justice is clearly a fascinating subject, and Frank Schmalleger's *Criminal Justice Today*, now in its seventh American edition, stands out as an excellent model of the kind of book that will capture and retain a student's interest with many original and dynamic features. The first edition of *Canadian Criminal Justice Today* sought to incorporate the advantages of Professor Schmalleger's approach to a criminal justice text into the Canadian context. It was timely, used highly interesting real-world examples, and had many useful pedagogical features, including boxed features, a glossary, discussion questions, pictures, and graphically pleasing figures and tables. The text clearly filled a need for an accessible and interesting text in the Canadian post-secondary criminal justice arena. The second edition builds on that first effort and offers increased attention to specifically Canadian content. The result is a thoroughly Canadian overview of the criminal justice system.

## New to This Edition

Among the important changes to this edition is the deletion of the chapter "The Search for Causes." This subject is obviously one that is worthy of a book (or more) in itself. Searching for causes of crime is rife with political implications, and requires considerably more attention than can be provided in a single chapter. The typical course on introductory criminal justice does not have sufficient time to allow an adequate analysis of the causes of crime, and most criminology and criminal justice programs devote a separate course or two to the study of crime causation. Accordingly, it is left to others to develop the issues in that area of criminology more fully.

Another significant change affects the look at the law in this text. A chapter entitled "Legal Foundations of Criminal Justice" (Chapter 3) replaces the chapter "Criminal Law" (previously Chapter 4) found in the first edition. As with crime causation, criminal law is a subject worthy of one or more courses in its own right, and a single chapter in an introductory criminal justice text can not do it justice. However, at the introductory level, the student of criminal justice must be aware of the role of law as an aspect of society's formal response to unwanted behaviour. Accordingly, the chapter on legal foundations seeks to give the student a look at the law as a framework within which the criminal justice system operates.

In order to provide a clearer focus on the Canadian criminal justice system, coverage of the U.S. system has been removed from many chapters in the text. To find this information, students may now turn to the chapter on "Multinational Criminal Justice" (Chapter 14), which includes a section on the United States along with a number of other nations.

These are not the only changes to the book. Every chapter in this second edition embodies a significant revision and update. Some of the chapters have been almost completely rewritten. However, while there have been many changes to the second edition, this text retains its commitment to the vision behind the first edition. It still seeks to teach students the fundamental concepts of an evolving discipline. It seeks to impart critical thinking skills allowing students to effectively apply those concepts to the real world, and to apply those concepts and skills to today's problems and to the emerging issues of tomorrow.

## Features

As noted above, this text includes a number of pedagogical features that make the text more dynamic and facilitate learning:

- **Chapter outlines** provide an "at-a-glance" overview of the chapter, along with a list of key concepts and cases.

- *Theory into Practice* **boxes** illustrate how theories of criminal justice can be applied in real life.
- *Policy Issues* **boxes** demonstrate the links between social policy and the teory and practice of criminal justice.
- *Careers in Justice* **boxes** examine the various occupations with the field of criminal justice.
- *Justice in Context* **boxes** highlight important Canadian contributions and events.
- **Figures and tables** offer up-to-date Canadian statistics and information.
- **Definitions of key terms** are placed in the margin for easy reference; a complete glossary can be found at the back of the book.
- **Chapter summaries** recap and ty together the key points of each chapter.
- **Discussion questions** review the chapter content and provide opportunities for critical thinking.
- *Web Links* suggest sites to visit for further reading and research on criminal justice.

## Supplements

*Canadian Criminal Justice Today*, Second Canadian Edition, is accompanied by the following supplements:

- **Instructor's Manual**, providing additional discussion questions, lecture outlines, and teaching tips
- **Test Item File**, offering fill-in-the-blank, true/false, and multiple-choice questions for each chapter
- **Transparency Masters**, incorporating key figures and tables from the text

These supplements can be downloaded from Pearson Education Canada's protected Instructor Central website, at www.pearsoned.ca/instructor.

The "CJ Central" website that accompanies the U.S. edition of *Criminal Justice Today* contains a number of resources of interest to Canadian users, including a "Cybrary," the largest collection of indexed criminal justice, criminology, and criminal law links on the web today. Both instructors and students can visit the site at www.prenhall.com/schmalleger.

# Acknowledgements

Acknowledgments are due to the instructors who provided feedback on the first Canadian edition as well as those who reviewed portions of the manuscript for the new edition:

Reg McIntyre, Durham College

Karin Kaercher, Camosun College

Anthony Micucci, Memorial University of Newfoundland

Donald Pitre, Cambrian College

Lynn Scott, Durham College

Michael Young, Camosun College

Paul Atkinson, Sir Sandford Fleming College

Thanks to the fine staff at Pearson Education who helped to bring this second edition together. In particular, special thanks are owed to Andrew Winton, who has since moved on to begin a new career in the law. He carefully oversaw the initial production of this book. Thanks to John Polanszky, the initial developmental editor, and his successor, Suzanne Schaan. Suzanne diligently persevered in gently cajoling me to submit chapters in a more-or-less timely manner. Without her efforts, I would probably still be rewriting the manuscript. Jessica Mosher, the acquisitions editor, stepped in to handily smooth out problems as they arose. Due to her efforts, her current replacement, Ky Pruesse, has had an easy task with this project. The in-house production editor, Charlotte Morrison-Reed, aptly co-ordinated all efforts at the tail end of the project. I also owe a very special thanks to the copy editor, Susan Marshall, for her thorough and insightful comments on the manuscript. The book is significantly easier to read, and an all around much better product due to her fine efforts.

I continue to learn from those around me every day. A word of thanks goes out to my peers at Kwantlen University College where I worked when this second edition was initiated, and at Simon Fraser University, where I presently work. Simon Fraser University fosters a marvellous environment in which academic writing can become inspired. Over the years, my many students have taught me how to teach. It is primarily for undergraduate students with an interest in criminology that this book was written. I would also like to thank those working in the criminal justice system who continue to share their knowledge and experience with me.

Thanks to Frank Schmalleger, who laid the foundational structure upon which this book is built. Many of his ideas and insights remain ingrained in each of the chapters. I would also like to thank Paul F. McKenna and John Winterdyk for their work on the first edition of this book. Without them, the initial project might never have been completed.

David MacAlister

# About the Authors

**Frank Schmalleger**, Ph.D., is director of the Justice Research Association, a consulting firm focusing on issues of crime and justice. Schmalleger is also founder and co-director of the Criminal Justice Distance Learning Consortium (**cjcentral.com/cjdlc**). He holds degrees from Notre Dame and Ohio State, having earned both a master's (1970) and doctorate in sociology (1974) from Ohio State University with a special emphasis in criminology. From 1976 to 1994 he taught criminal justice courses at The University of North Carolina at Pembroke. For the last 16 of those years he chaired the university's Department of Sociology, Social Work, and Criminal Justice. Schmalleger has also taught in the New School for Social Research's online graduate program. His numerous articles and books including *Criminology Today, Criminal Law Today, Criminal and Justice System in America: An Encyclopedia, Computers in Criminal Justice, Criminal Justice Ethics, Finding Criminal Justice in the Library, A History of Corrections*, and *The Social Basis of Criminal Justice*.

**David MacAlister** is chair of the Criminology Department at Kwantlen University College in British Columbia. His educational background merges criminology with the formal study of law. He holds both a bachelor's and a master's degree in criminology from Simon Fraser University, as well as a law degree from the University of British Columbia. He will complete a Master of Laws degree at Queen's University in 2000.

MacAlister's criminal justice experience has involved him with various police agencies, attitudinal research on corrections, and research consulting work with British Columbia's Ministry of the Attorney General. His current research is in the area of prosecutorial accountability.

# Crime in Canada

*It is better that ten guilty persons escape than one innocent suffer.*

—Sir William Blackstone
Commentaries on the Law of England, vol. iv, 27

*Justice to me is a warm spirit, born of tolerance and wisdom, present everywhere, ready to serve the highest purposes of rational man. To seek to create the just society must be amongst the highest of those human purposes.*

—Pierre E. Trudeau

*The will of the people is the best law.*

—Ulysses S. Grant

The great statesman and orator Daniel Webster (1782–1852) once wrote that "[J]ustice is the great interest of man on earth. It is the ligament that holds civilized beings and civilized nations together." While Webster may have lived in a relatively simple time with few problems and many shared rules, justice has never been easily won. Unlike Webster's era, society today is highly complex and populated by groups with a wide diversity of interests. It is within that challenging context that the daily practice of Canadian criminal justice occurs.

The criminal justice system has three central components: police, courts, and corrections. The history, the activities, and the legal environment surrounding the police are discussed in Part 2 of this book. Part 3 describes courts, and Part 4 deals with prisons, probation, and parole. Part 5 provides a guide to the future of the justice system and of enforcement agencies. We begin here in Part 1, however, with an overview of that grand ideal that we call *justice*—and we consider how the justice ideal relates to the everyday practice of criminal justice in Canada today. To that end, in the three chapters that comprise this section, we will examine how and why laws are made. We will examine the wide array of interests that impinge upon the justice system, and we will examine closely the dichotomy that distinguishes citizens who are primarily concerned with individual rights from those who emphasize the need for individual responsibility and social accountability. In the pages that follow, we will see how "justice" can mean protection from the power of the state for some, and vengeance to others. In this first section, we will also lay the groundwork for the rest of the text by painting a picture of crime in Canada today, showing how policies for dealing with crime have evolved.

As you read about the complex tapestry that is the practice of criminal justice in Canada today, you will see a system in flux, perhaps less sure of its values and purpose than at any time in its history. You may also get the sense, however, that very soon a new and reborn institution of justice may emerge from the ferment that now exists. Whatever the final outcome, it can only be hoped that "justice," as proffered by the Canadian system of criminal justice, will be sufficient to hold our civilization together—and to allow it to prosper well into the current century.

# What Is Criminal Justice?

Canapress/Moe Doiron

**KEY CONCEPTS**

social control
individual rights
  advocates
public order advocates
individual rights
justice
social justice
criminal justice
system of criminal justice
consensus model

conflict model
warrant
summons
booking
bail
information
indictment
preliminary hearing
reasonable grounds

arraignment
trial
consecutive sentence
concurrent sentence
principles of
  fundamental justice
crime control model
due process model
criminology

Guy Paul Morin

# JUSTICE AND CRIMINAL JUSTICE

On the morning of September 11, 2001, two hijacked airliners slammed into the twin towers of the World Trade Center in New York, while a third careened into the Pentagon in Washington, D.C. Then a fourth hijacked airliner crashed into the ground in rural Pennsylvania, as passengers attempted to regain control of their aircraft from its hijackers. On that day, thousands of people were killed in the attacks when the twin towers collapsed, part of the Pentagon burned, and the passengers, crew, and hijackers of all four aircraft met a horrific, fiery death. In moments, all airborne craft had been converted from routine modes of transportation into potential weapons. In response to the risk of ongoing attacks, Canada quickly opened its airports, permitting all U.S.-bound aircraft, from all over the world, to safely land, while authorities grappled with how to respond to the events of that morning. While Canadians viewed the events of September 11 with shock and sympathy for their American neighbours, they also became aware that from that day onward, images of crime and criminal justice throughout North America were irrevocably altered.

People from around the world were directly affected by the September 11 attacks. In the hours that followed the attacks, several world leaders condemned the actions of the terrorists. In Britain, Prime Minister Tony Blair proclaimed, "We can only imagine the terror and carnage there and the many, many innocent people who have lost their lives. This mass terrorism is the new evil in our world today. It is perpetrated by fanatics who are utterly indifferent to the sanctity of life."[1]

In Canada, Prime Minister Jean Chrétien expressed his outrage over the attacks, "There can be no cause or grievance that could ever justify such unspeakable violence. Indeed, such an attack is an assault not only on the targets but an offence against the freedom and rights of all civilized nations …"[2]

It would soon be discovered that 25 Canadians were among those killed in the September 11 attacks. In the days and then weeks that followed that fateful morning, a heightened level of security prevailed. In Canada, CF-18 Hornet jet fighters of the Canadian Armed Forces took to the skies over Toronto and coastal regions to forestall the possibility of an attack on Canada. Many months passed before some semblance of normalcy returned to North America, but no one returned to the sense of complacency that existed prior to September 11. In the investigation that followed, initial suspicions that some of the hijackers had accessed the United States through Canada proved to be unfounded when it was discovered that many of the hijackers had resided in the United States for considerable periods of time, several of them attending flight schools in the United States, an education that aided them in their quest to control the hijacked aircraft.

The events of September 11 were not the first ones to raise the issue of terrorists gaining access to the United States via Canada. While the September 11 attackers appear to have entered the U.S. through different routes, in December 1999, a terrorist was arrested attempting to enter the United States at Port Angeles, Washington, via a ferry from Victoria, British Columbia. Ahmed Ressam, often referred to as the millennium bomber, was arrested by U.S. Customs agents when he tried to enter the United States with more than 59 kilograms of explosives hidden in the trunk of his car. Ressam had lived for several years in Montreal, before travelling to British Columbia in hopes of crossing the border into the United States in order to carry out a terrorist bombing. His plan was to blow up a terminal at Los Angeles International Airport (LAX). He had been denied refugee status in Canada and was travelling under a false passport at the time of his arrest. Subsequent to his 1994 arrival in Canada, Ressam had visited Afghanistan in 1998, receiving terrorist training at one of Osama bin Laden's training camps. Ressam was convicted of terrorist-related offences in the U.S. District Court in Los Angeles on April 6, 2001; however, his sentencing has been delayed until he completes testifying against other suspected terrorists.

AP/Wide World Photos

The 110-story twin towers of the World Trade Center burning after Islamic terrorists commandeered two commercial jetliners and crashed them into the buildings on September 11, 2001. Both buildings collapsed within hours, killing nearly 3,000 people. Another 262 people aboard the airplanes died. Terrorism is a criminal act that may involve mass murder, arson, destruction of property, kidnapping, hijacking, conspiracy, and other offenses.

**social control** The use of sanctions and rewards available through a group to influence and shape the behaviour of individual members of that group. Social control is a primary concern of social groups and communities, and it is the interest that human groups hold in the exercise of social control that leads to the creation of both criminal and civil statutes.

While crime statistics imply that terrorist-related offences, and indeed violent offences in general, are relatively rare, crimes such as the ones described here dramatically highlight the recent concern about terrorist-related and other violent crime facing Canadians and enhance the fear of crime that so many people have come to feel. They also challenge long-cherished beliefs about the extent of **social control** in Canadian society and call into question a number of basic values centred on immigration, violence in the media, and the motivations underlying violent crime. The recent terrorist crimes sent chills up the spines of many Canadians who asked themselves how North America had become a potential target for politically motivated and other violent crime. Seemingly simple standards of decency and responsibility appear to have been lost. Previously accepted arguments that poverty, lack of proper socialization, and society in general are the causes of crime seemed especially ineffective explanations for the events of September 11. Crimes like these have changed the mood of the nation or, perhaps more accurately, have accelerated what was an already changing mood. For many Canadians concerned with crime and justice, and clinging to heartfelt standards of right and wrong, it is as though an age of innocence has ended.

# The Focus of This Book— Individual Rights and Public Order

This book, which is about the Canadian system of criminal justice and the agencies and processes that constitute it, has an orientation that we believe is especially valuable for studying criminal justice today. For the past 20 years, Canada's criminal justice system has struggled to find an identity. The dominant philosophy has been guided in part by the constitutional entrenchment of the *Canadian Charter of Rights and Freedoms*. This document focused on guaranteeing the rights of criminal defendants. This focus has guided our criminal justice system to respect the rights of accused persons. Recently, however, a growing conservative emphasis has focused on the rights and interests of crime victims and collective security, and has called into question some of the fundamental premises upon which the Canadian system of criminal justice operates.

In the aftermath of September 11, Canada enacted the *Anti-terrorism Act*, enhancing the power of the government to deal with suspected terrorists, but also raising questions about the potential impact on individual rights and freedoms. The materials presented in this book are in keeping with the realization that our criminal justice system needs to balance the rights and freedoms accorded to individuals in a free and democratic society with the compelling interests of society in controlling future crime and reducing the harm caused by criminal behaviour.

Most people today who consider the criminal justice system assume either one or the other of these two perspectives. We will refer to those who seek to protect personal freedoms and individual rights within the criminal justice process as **individual rights advocates**. Those who suggest that, under certain circumstances involving criminal threats to public safety, the interests of society (especially crime control) should take precedence over individual rights, will be called **public order advocates**. In this book, we look at ways in which the two perspectives can be balanced to serve both sets of needs.

**individual rights advocates** Those who seek to protect personal freedoms within the process of criminal justice.

**public order advocates** Those who suggest that, under certain circumstances involving criminal threats to public safety, the interests of society should take precedence over individual rights.

Both perspectives have their roots in the values that formed the basis for the system of criminal justice in England, a system from which ours evolved. However, the past 20 years have been especially important in clarifying the differences between the two points of view. The last few years have seen a burgeoning concern with the rights of ethnic minorities, women, the physically and mentally challenged, gays and lesbians, HIV-infected individuals, and many other groups. Following the entrenchment of the *Canadian Charter of Rights and Freedoms* into the Constitution in 1982, an emphasis on equality of opportunity and respect for individuals, particularly in the context of legal rights arising prior to and during trial, has occupied the attention and energies of our courts. Soon a plethora of hard-won individual rights and prerogatives, based on the *Charter of Rights and Freedoms*, were recognized and guaranteed. By the dawning of the new millennium, the individual rights movement had profoundly affected all areas of social life—from religion, through employment, to the activities of the criminal justice system.

This emphasis on **individual rights** was initially accompanied by a significant increase in recorded criminal activity. "Traditional" crimes such as murder, sexual assault, and common assault, as reported by the police, increased notably during the 1980s. Many theories were advanced to explain this rapid increase in observed criminality. A few doubted the accuracy of "official" accounts, claiming that any actual rise in crime was much less than that portrayed in the reports. Some analysts of our culture, however, suggested that increased criminality was the result of new-found freedoms that combined with the long-pent-up hostilities of the socially and economically deprived to produce social disorganization.

The 1990s began with a focus on aboriginal Canadians and Canadian criminal justice. The Mohawk Nation reserve of Kanesatake is adjacent to the town of Oka, near the city of Montreal in Quebec. On March 11, 1990, the Mohawks of Kanesatake erected a barricade in order to stop the city of Oka from enlarging a golf course on land that had been given to the municipality but was claimed by the Mohawks as a sacred burial ground. In the weeks that followed, the Mohawks were joined by other heavily armed Mohawks belonging to a society of Warriors. On July 11, 1990, the Sûreté du Québec (Quebec's provincial police force) attempted to enforce a court injunction granted to the municipality, to evict the Mohawks. Approximately 100 SQ personnel launched an assault on the barricade, but were repelled by gunfire. During the altercation, one officer of the SQ, Corporal Marcel Lemay, was wounded by gunfire during the assault and died a short time later. On the same day, in a show of solidarity, Mohawks of a neighbouring reserve called Kahnawake, blocked the roads leading to the Mercier Bridge, and occupied that bridge, which connected Montreal to the residential area of Châteauguay. Thousands of motorists heading to the city had to be rerouted two hours out of their way for the duration of the crisis. Until the cessation of the occupation of the Mercier Bridge on September 6, 1990 and the surrender of the last of the Warrior Mohawks of Kanesatake on September 26, 1990, numerous incidents of violence erupted as tensions among all of the parties continued to rise. In addition to approximately 1400 to 1800 SQ members in attendance at the crisis, 240 members of the RCMP bolstered the police manpower. Eventually, about 900 soldiers of the Canadian Armed Forces arrived on August 20 to take over the police positions established at Kahnawake and Kanesatake. While the incident ended peacefully, the Oka crisis would set off a wave of aboriginal unrest across the country, manifesting itself in further standoffs between aboriginal groups and Canada's criminal justice system.[3]

By the mid-1990s, however, a strong shift away from the claimed misdeeds of the criminal justice system began, and a new-found emphasis on individual accountability arose among a Canadian public fed up with crime and fearful of their own victimization. Growing calls for enhanced responsibility quickly began to replace the previous emphasis on individual rights.

It was probably the public's perception of growing crime rates, coupled with a belief that offenders frequently went unpunished, or that many received only judicial slaps on the wrists, that led to the burgeoning emphasis on responsibility and punishment. However, a few spectacular crimes that received widespread coverage by the news media heightened the public's sense that crime in Canada was out of hand, and that new measures were needed to combat it.

In 1995, for example, Jean Chrétien, Prime Minister of Canada, and his wife, Aline, had the sanctitude of their home disturbed when André Dallaire, a 34-year-old man from Longueuil, Quebec, entered the Prime Minister's residence at 24 Sussex Drive, armed with a seven-centimetre-long knife. Dallaire had climbed the fence at the Prime Minister's residence, waved at the security cameras, smashed a window, entered the house, and wandered throughout the residence for 30 minutes before being confronted by Aline Chrétien outside the bedroom. She quickly sought refuge in the bedroom, locking the door and telephoning for help while the Prime Minister brandished an Inuit sculpture to defend them should the invader enter the room. The RCMP assigned to protect the Prime Minister took seven minutes to respond to the call for help, and found that Dallaire had put down his knife and appeared to be waiting for their arrival. Dallaire was faced with a charge of attempted murder. In July 1996, the court, after hearing testimony about the man being a paranoid schizophrenic who responded to voices telling him to rid Canada of this Prime Minister, found Dallaire not criminally responsible on account of mental disorder. The incident helped rivet the nation's attention on what appeared to be the increasing frequency of random and senseless violence.[4]

**individual rights** Those rights guaranteed to criminal defendants by the *Charter of Rights and Freedoms* (especially sections 7 through 14) facing formal processing by the criminal justice system. The preservation of the rights of criminal defendants is important to society, because it is through the exercise of such rights that the values of our culture are most clearly and directly expressed.

In that same year, Hubert O'Connor, a Roman Catholic bishop, was found guilty of rape and indecent assault in relation to acts committed in the 1960s against two native women at Cariboo Indian school near Williams Lake, British Columbia. O'Connor became the highest-ranking member of the Roman Catholic Church to be convicted of sex crimes in Canada. O'Connor's conviction served as the pinnacle to a litany of convictions against Roman Catholic clergy in Canada for sex-related crimes.[5] One of Canadian society's most prominent icons of morality had fallen upon difficult times. An institution promoting fundamental values had become tainted in the worst way imaginable. To many Canadians, it became apparent that even the Roman Catholic Church could not be relied upon to consistently promote values respecting the rights of individuals to be free from victimization.[6]

Allegations of physical and sexual abuse in institutions mounted until a Law Commission Report revealed a history of abuse against children that spanned the country. Some of the venerable Canadian institutions that were implicated included the Mount Cashel Orphanage in Newfoundland, the Jericho Hill School for the Deaf, and Maple Leaf Gardens. The list also included residential schools established for aboriginal youth and the children of the Doukhobors in British Columbia, and training schools for boys and girls across the country.[7]

Recently, a landslide of conservative sentiment was ushered in by growing public frustration with the apparent inability of our society and its justice system to prevent crimes and to hold offenders who are identified and then arrested to heartfelt standards of right and wrong. That landslide, when it came in the form of a Reform Party sweep of electoral ridings in Western Canada in 2000, resulted in this opposition party focusing much of

---

BOX 1.1    **Theory into Practice**

## The Post-September 11 Canadian Response to Terrorism

The September 11 terrorist attacks in the northeastern United States caught many terrorist analysts off guard, including those in the RCMP's Criminal Analysis Branch in Ottawa. It is the responsibility of this branch to monitor developing trends in terrorist activity. After the September 11 attacks, the unit assigned six analysts to focus on Islamic extremism, where only one had been assigned to such tasks in the past.

International terrorism has had an impact upon Canada in the past. While most terrorist groups do not consider Canadians primary targets, there is concern over terrorist networks operating in Canada, as well as their raising funds, laundering money, and purchasing arms.

In Canada, the Canadian Security Intelligence Service (CSIS) investigates individuals and groups that pose threats of political violence. In the recent past, this meant the CSIS was investigating about 50 organizations and 350 individual targets, as part of their anti-terrorism program. The groups of interest include Hizballah, Hamas, and numerous Islamic extremist organizations, including Al Qaeda. In addition, the CSIS tracks the activities of the Irish Republican Army (IRA), the Liberation Tigers of Tamil Eelam, the Kurdistan Workers' Party, the Mujahedin e-Khalq, and numerous Sikh terrorist groups.

In the past, there have been several international terrorist acts with a strong connection to Canada. These include incidents involving Sikh extremists, the IRA, and Hizballah.

Following the September 11 attacks, Canada responded to terrorism on a number of fronts. Government expenditures on counter-terrorism activity were increased, and criminal law was altered in order to facilitate the tracking and apprehension of suspected terrorists.

Also, immediately after the September 11 attacks, Canada moved to develop a more comprehensive legal response to terrorism than had previously existed. The two main developments were the passage of the *Anti-terrorism Act* (Bill C-36), which came into force on Christmas Eve of 2001, and the introduction of Bill C-55 (now C-17) to create the *Public Safety Act, 2002*, debated in 2002. The *Anti-terrorism Act* amended the *Criminal Code* to include a definition of terrorist activity in section 83.01 that includes an act or omission committed:

> ... in whole or in part for a political, religious or ideological purpose, objective or cause, and ... in whole or in part with the intention of intimidating the public, or a segment of the public, with regard to its security, including its economic security, or compelling a person, a government or a domestic or an international organization to do or refrain from doing any act ... that intentionally ...

(A)    causes death or serious bodily harm to a person by the use of violence,

Parliament's agenda on targeting seemingly ineffective social programs and the liberal agendas that had built them. Many newly elected public officials stopped asking what society could do to protect individuals accused of crimes and demanded to know instead how offenders could effectively be held accountable for violations of the criminal law.

## Perspectives on Criminal Justice and the Theme of This Book

Realistically, while conservative sentiments still very much influence public policy, it is important to recognize that national feelings, however strong, have historically been somewhat akin to the swings of a pendulum. Hence, while the emphasis on individual rights, which rose to ascendancy 20 years ago, now appears to have been eclipsed by calls for social and individual responsibility, the tension between the two perspectives still forms the basis for most policy-making activity in the criminal justice arena. Rights advocates continue to carry on the fight for an expansion of legal rights, viewing them as necessary to an equitable and just social order. The treatment of the accused, they argue, mirrors basic cultural values. The purpose of any civilized society, they claim, should be to secure rights and freedoms for each of its citizens—including the criminally accused. Rights advocates fear unnecessarily restrictive government action and view it as an assault upon basic human dignity and individual liberty. In defence of their principles, criminal rights activists tend to recognize that it is sometimes necessary to sacrifice some degree of public safety and predictability in

(B)     endangers a person's life,

(C)     causes a serious risk to the health or safety of the public or any segment of the public,

(D)     causes substantial property damage, whether to public or private property, if causing such damage is likely to result in the conduct of harm referred to in any of clauses (A) to (C), or

(E)     causes serious interference with or serious disruption of an essential service, facility or system, whether public or private, other than as a result of advocacy, protest, dissent or stoppage of work that is not intended to result in the conduct or harm referred to in any of clauses (A) to (C) …

The Act also provides for the designation of certain groups as "terrorist groups." Under this Act, it is a crime to collect funds for terrorists or terrorist groups. It is also a crime to contribute to or facilitate the activities of terrorist groups. The Act also enhances police powers with regard to electronic surveillance against terrorist groups, and amends the provisions in a variety of statutes to allow investigative authorities to enhance their monitoring and prosecution of terrorists and their supporters. The proposed *Public Safety, Act, 2002* will further expand the authority of the government over suspected terrorists, particularly with regard to enhancing aviation security. Canada's response to the events on September 11 has also taken on a tactical angle.

In June 2002, Canada moved to integrate its approach to combat terrorism by creating four new Integrated National Security Enforcement Teams (INSET). These multi-agency law enforcement teams are centred in

Vancouver, Toronto, Montreal, and Ottawa. Their common goal is to better track terrorist groups and individuals who pose a threat to Canada's national security. Another goal of these new teams is to apply Canada's new anti-terrorism legislation in order to assist in the early detection of, and to disrupt, any actual or intended terrorist acts. The ultimate aim of these teams is to ensure the safety and security of Canadians.

## QUESTIONS FOR DISCUSSION

1. Should Canada continue to devote the considerable resources that it now does to counter-terrorism activities? Would this money be better spent dealing with other crime prevention programs closer to home?

2. Should customs and immigration officials target individuals fitting an apparent Islamic terrorist profile for strict scrutiny at border crossings? What would be the negative aspects of such "ethnic profiling"?

3. Do you believe Canada to be a potential terrorist target for an extremist group like Al Qaeda? Why or why not?

*Sources:* Canadian Security Intelligence Service. (2001). International Terrorism: The Threat to Canada. *RCMP Gazette*, Vol. 63, No. 6, pp. 5–8; Hamilton, H. (2001). RCMP Analysts Discuss How September 11 Changed the Game. *RCMP Gazette*, Vol. 63, No. 6, pp. 9–10; Steele, K. (2001). RCMP Gets Millions to Help Fight Terrorism. *RCMP Gazette*, Vol. 63, No. 6, pp. 13–14; **www.rcmp-grc. gc.ca/news/nr-03-04.htm** Combined Forces Special Enforcement/Integrated National Security Enforcement Teams Open New Operational Centre. Accessed from RCMP's website July 2003.

order to guarantee basic freedoms. Hence, rights advocates are content with a justice system that limits police powers and holds justice agencies accountable to the highest evidentiary standards.

An example of the kind of criminal justice outcome feared by individual rights advocates can be had in several recent cases. In 1971, Donald Marshall, a Micmac Indian, was convicted of murder in Halifax, Nova Scotia.[8] Marshall consistently maintained his innocence in the killing of his companion, Sandy Seale, and in 1982, after spending 11 years in prison, his lawyer brought forward new evidence that persuaded the federal justice minister (now prime minister), Jean Chrétien, to order the Nova Scotia Court of Appeal to review the case. The review concluded that Marshall had not committed the murder in question.[9] In 1986, the Nova Scotia government appointed a royal commission to review the investigation and prosecution of Marshall. When this royal commission report was released in 1990, it condemned the conduct of individuals connected to the case, and the entire system of criminal justice in Nova Scotia.[10] Under the leadership of Detective Sergeant John MacIntyre, the police investigation resulted in witnesses being intimidated into giving false statements implicating Marshall in the killing. This royal commission report also criticized the prosecution, defence lawyers, the trial judge, and appeal court judges involved in this case at its various stages.

In 1971, David Milgaard was convicted for the 1969 killing of Gail Miller in Saskatoon, Saskatchewan.[11] For 22 years, Milgaard was confined in a penitentiary for a murder he did not commit.

In 1992, Guy Paul Morin was convicted of the murder of nine-year-old Christine Jessop in Queensville, Ontario. In January 1995, the Ontario Court of Appeal acquitted Morin, after DNA evidence excluded him as the person responsible for the offence.[12]

In 2001, a commission of inquiry exonerated Thomas Sophonow in the 1981 killing of 16-year-old Barbara Stoppel who was murdered in a Winnipeg donut shop. Over a 20-year period, Sophonow endured multiple trials and appeals, including spending 45 months in prison.

In January 2002, the federal government appointed former Justice Fred Kaufman to examine an application by Steven Truscott to review his 1959 conviction for the murder of 12-year-old Lynn Harper. Considerable evidence indicates Truscott may not have committed this crime, for which he was sentenced to hang at the age of 14 years. Truscott's sentence was commuted after serving 10 years; however, the fight to clear his name continues.

Individual rights advocates do not confine themselves to citing individual instances of persons being wrongfully convicted of killings. Sometimes, the person does not even make it to trial. In the late 1980s, the provincial government in Manitoba established an inquiry into the justice system's treatment of aboriginal Canadians in that province. One of the incidents prompting this inquiry was the police shooting of John Joseph Harper, a local native leader, on March 9, 1988. Constable Robert Cross of the Winnipeg Police Department had mistaken Harper for a car thief. In fact, Harper was not the man being sought by police. His shooting was subject to an internal investigation and a coroner's inquest, both of which cleared the police of any wrongdoing. Manitoba's aboriginal community reacted with anger, alleging racism on the part of the police. The public outcry resulted in the creation of a commission of inquiry, which handed down its report in 1991.[13] The report concluded that racism played a part in the shooting of Harper and the subsequent mishandling of the internal investigation into the shooting. The Manitoba Aboriginal Justice Inquiry declared police–aboriginal relations in that province to be "seriously deficient."[14]

Individual rights advocates also express concern over Canada's treatment of offenders subsequent to conviction. In 1975, the Federal Court of Canada was asked to evaluate the solitary confinement environment in the B.C. Penitentiary. Several plaintiffs being held in solitary confinement brought forward the action, seeking a declaration that the solitary confinement regime in existence at that time constituted "cruel and unusual punishment." Jack McCann had been kept in solitary confinement in the special correctional unit (SCU) of the B.C. Penitentiary for 754 consecutive days. Several months after release from solitary, McCann escaped from the prison. He was captured several weeks later and returned to solitary, where he stayed for an additional 342 days. During this latter stay, McCann filed his petition with the Federal Court, Trial Division. Six other detainees joined McCann in his challenge to the solitary confinement regime. Between them, they had spent 11.5 years in solitary confinement; McCann had served the longest, with a total of 1471 days.[15] The solitary confinement regime entailed being confined to a cell for 23.5 hours a day, with no outside exercise, sleeping on foam-covered concrete 10 centimetres off the floor with one's head next to a toilet, light burning 24 hours a day, only cold water available in the cells, with no work, no hobbies, no television, no movies, no sports, and no calisthenics.[16] The plaintiffs were successful in that the Federal Court of Canada declared those conditions to be cruel and unusual. Before the decade was out, the B.C. Penitentiary was closed, replaced by Kent Penitentiary, a state-of-the-art maximum-security facility devoid of the Victorian harshness of the B.C. Penitentiary, although some criticism still exists with respect to the solitary confinement regime in the new penitentiary.[17]

The criminal rights perspective allows that it is necessary to see some guilty people go free in order to reduce the likelihood of convicting the innocent.

In the present, rather conservative environment, however, calls for system accountability are often tempered with new demands to unfetter the criminal justice system in order to make arrests easier and punishments swift and harsh. Advocates of law and order, wanting ever-greater police powers, have mounted an effective drive to abandon some of the gains made in support of the rights of criminal defendants over the years. Citing high rates of recidivism, uncertain punishments, and an inefficient courtroom maze, they claim that the criminal justice system has coddled offenders and encouraged continued law violation. Society, they say, if it is to survive, can no longer afford to accord too many rights to the individual or place the interests of any one person over that of the group.

As we begin the twenty-first century, the trick, it seems, will be to balance individual rights and personal freedoms with social responsibility and respect for authority. This text has two basic purposes: (1) to describe in detail the criminal justice system, while (2) helping students develop an appreciation for the delicacy of the balancing act now facing it. The question for the future will be how to ensure the existence of, and effectively manage, a justice system that is as fair to the individual as it is supportive of the needs of society. Is "justice for all" a reasonable expectation of today's system of criminal justice? As the book will show, this question is complicated by the fact that individual interests and social needs frequently diverge, while at other times they parallel one another.

## Social Justice

The well-known British philosopher and statesman Benjamin Disraeli (1804-1881) once defined **justice** as "truth in action." One popular definition of *justice* is "the principle of moral rightness, or conformity to truth."[18] Justice, in the truest sense of the word, is the ultimate goal of criminal justice.

Criminal justice and civil justice are both aspects of a wider form of equity termed **social justice**. Social justice is a concept that embraces all aspects of civilized life. It is linked to notions of fairness and to cultural beliefs about right and wrong. Questions of social justice can be asked about relationships between individuals and between parties (such as corporations and agencies of government), between the rich and the poor, between the sexes, between ethnic groups and minorities, and about social linkages of all sorts. In the abstract, the concept of social justice embodies the highest personal and cultural ideals.

Civil justice concerns itself with fairness in relationships between citizens, government agencies, and businesses in private matters involving contractual obligations, business dealings, hiring, equality of treatment, and so on. **Criminal justice**, in its broadest sense, refers to those aspects of social justice that concern violations of the criminal law. Community interests demand apprehension and punishment of law violators. At the same time, criminal justice ideals extend to the protection of the innocent, fair treatment of offenders, and fair play by the agencies of law enforcement, including the courts and correctional institutions.

Reality, however, typically falls short of the ideal and is severely complicated by the fact that justice seems to wear different guises when viewed from diverse social vantage points. To many people, the criminal justice system and criminal justice agencies often seem biased in favour of the powerful. The laws they enforce seem to emanate more from well-financed, organized, and vocal interest groups than they do from an idealized sense of social justice. Disenfranchised groups—those who do not feel as though they share in the

**justice** The principle of fairness; the ideal of moral equity.

**social justice** An ideal that embraces all aspects of civilized life and is linked to fundamental notions of fairness and to cultural beliefs about right and wrong.

**criminal justice** The criminal law, the law of criminal procedure, and that array of procedures and activities having to do with the enforcement of the criminal law. Criminal justice cannot be separated from social justice because the kind of justice enacted in our nation's criminal courts is a reflection of basic Canadian understandings of right and wrong.

Halifax Mail Star/Ken Jennex

Donald Marshall spent 11 years in prison for the murder of his companion, Sandy Seale, before new evidence was brought forward resulting in his acquittal.

political and economic power of society—are often wary of the agencies of justice, seeing them more as enemies than as benefactors.

On the other hand, justice practitioners, including police officers, prosecutors, judges, and correctional officials, frequently complain of unfair criticism of their efforts to uphold the law. The "realities" of law enforcement, they say, and of justice itself, are often overlooked by critics of the system who have little experience in dealing with offenders and victims.

Whichever side we choose in the ongoing debate over the nature and quality of justice in Canada, we should recognize that the process of criminal justice is especially important

---

## BOX 1.2    Theory into Practice

## Japanese Just Say No to Crime

**W**hile all democratic societies attempt to strike a balance between individual rights and the need for social order, the justice systems of Canada and the United States emphasize individual rights, while Japanese culture has long emphasized group concerns and social order. The impact that such a cultural emphasis has had on crime rates in the United States, Japan, and Canada is eye-opening, as the table shows.

While crime rates have been increasing recently in Japan, they are still well below those in Canada or the United States. Japanese society ostracizes offenders, demanding that they be caught, show remorse, and confess. Japanese prisons are harsh places, where communication between inmates is not permitted and hard work is required. Japanese police have sweeping powers, and civil

### Crime Statistics, 2001
Rate per 100 000 persons

|                    | United States | Japan   | Canada  |
| ------------------ | ------------- | ------- | ------- |
| Murder             | 5.61          | 1.05    | 4.10    |
| Robbery            | 148.50        | 5.02    | 34.00   |
| Aggravated assault | 318.55        | 26.68   | 148.52  |
| Break & enter      | 740.80        | 238.59  | 908.93  |
| Theft              | 3804.58       | 1843.73 | 2758.26 |

liberties, in the sense of Canadian principles of fundamental justice or due process, are far less pervasive in Japan than in Canada or the United States. Police in Japan may detain suspects for up to 21 days before a judicial hearing, and they operate freely of *Charter*-like requirements, often pressuring suspects into confessions.

But the one thing that, more than any other, may account for low rates of crime in Japan is a sense of individual honour and responsibility. For example, a police-run program allows anyone to go to a police station or police call box and borrow money (usually $10–20) at any time on the

in achieving and maintaining social order. From the perspective of social order, law is an instrument of control. Laws set limits on behaviour and define particular forms of social interaction as either acceptable or unacceptable. Laws, including whatever inequities they may embody, are a primary device for the creation of order in any mature society.

## The Justice Ideal: A Modern Conflict

Most of us agree that laws against murder, assault, sexual assault, and other serious crimes are necessary. Certain other laws, such as those against marijuana use, prostitution, gambling, and some "victimless crimes" rest upon a less certain consensus.

Where a near-consensus exists as to the legitimacy of a particular statute, questions may still be raised as to how specific behaviour fits the law under consideration. Even more fundamental questions can centre on the process by which justice is achieved. One case that has received much media attention illustrates these points. On September 22, 1987, Angelique Lyn Lavallee was acquitted at her trial for the murder of her common-law husband, Kevin Rust. Following her acquittal, the Crown won an appeal in the Manitoba Court of Appeal; however, Lavallee's original acquittal was ultimately restored by the Supreme Court of Canada in 1990. The evidence conveyed at trial showed that the couple's relationship was volatile, with frequent violent encounters. Dispute arose on appeal regarding whether evidence of "battered wife syndrome" coming from expert witnesses was admissible with respect to aiding the jury in determining the defendant's state of mind in the context of self-defence.

Almost everyone is in agreement that spousal abuse is a crime that cannot be tolerated. Likewise, most Canadians agree that when a woman is being attacked, she should be able to defend herself, even by using deadly force if no other reasonable means of preserving herself are available. However, Lavallee shot her common-law husband in the back of the head as he was leaving the room she was in. He was not advancing on her in an imminent attack scenario. Few would disagree that spousal abuse is wrong, and most would grant that some form of self-defence is justifiable under certain circumstances, including an imminent attack. The Lavallee situation, however, was complicated by many factors, among them the fact that Lavallee was female, Rust was male; Lavallee was armed, Rust was unarmed. Also, Lavallee failed to testify at her trial, a fact that complicated the evidentiary issues addressed on appeal. The top court ruled that expert evidence of "battered wife syndrome" was admissible at trial. The

honour system. "We can't ask them for I.D. because usually the reason they need to borrow cash is that they've lost their wallet," says Tokio Kunichika, chief of police for the Tokyo subway system. It surprises North Americans to learn that almost all the borrowed money is quickly returned.

Other differences noteworthy between North America and Japan may bear on the incidence of crime. In the United States, more than 30 per cent of children are born to single mothers. In Japan, the figure is around 1 per cent. In Canada, around 11.9 per cent. Also, few Japanese citizens own guns. Official statistics show 425 000 gun owners in Japan (although the figure includes air rifles and "BB" guns), while there are as many as 200 million guns in private hands in the United States. Such data have not been systematically gathered in Canada; however, a survey conducted in 1991 found that 23 per cent of households surveyed had a gun on the premises. Most important of all may be the fact that Japanese children are taught strict values from an early age. As one author puts it, "What Americans call 'family values' are rigorously inculcated in Japan. The value of good behaviour, of fitting into a common society, is drummed into children from the moment they set off to first grade in identical school uniforms."

Not everyone, however, agrees that low crime rates are worth the social cost. "I think that there is a lot that Japan has sacrificed for safety," says Koichi Miyazawa, a professor at Keio University in Tokyo. "Safety has been achieved at the expense of freedom," Miyazawa adds.

## QUESTIONS FOR DISCUSSION

1. Do you agree with Professor Miyazawa that Japan has paid too high a price for reduced rates of crime? Why or why not?

2. Will Canadian and American societies ever be able to reduce crime as the Japanese have? If so, how might that be accomplished?

Sources: Kristof, N.D. (1995, May 14). Japanese Say No to Crime: Tough Methods, at a Price. *The New York Times*, p. 1A; Japan Hangs Three Death Row Convicts. (1995, May 26). Reuters online; Angus Reid Group, Inc. (1991, March). *Firearm Ownership in Canada*, prepared for the Department of Justice; Macionis, J.J., J.N. Clarke, and L.M. Gerber. (1994). *Sociology: Canadian Edition*. (Scarborough: Prentice Hall Canada Inc.); Interpol, International Crime Statistics, online at **www.interpol.int/Default.asp/**

evidence could be admitted to establish the effect of the spousal abuse on her state of mind, and to help the jury to understand why Lavallee chose to shoot her partner in the back of the head rather than leave the home on that evening. The ramifications of the decision are far-reaching. As one commentator on the case has noted, "If there is no duty to leave home rather than use violence, and if a preemptive strike can sometimes be seen as reasonable, this could make it extremely difficult to distinguish between revenge and self-defence."[19]

To many people, the law was clear in this case: Lavallee should not have shot her common-law husband in the back of the head. She should not have shot anyone unless there was an immediate, serious, and demonstrable threat to her safety. Yet while a considerable consensus existed as to the law and the facts of this case, actors in the criminal justice system found themselves embroiled in a raging debate about what an appropriate outcome should be. It may be fruitful to borrow from a famous American legal scholar, analyzing the Bernhard Goetz New York subway shooting case, who referred to Goetz's actions as "a crime of self-defense."[20]

Basic to the Lavallee case is the belief, held by some, including many women in our society, that women and other minorities have historically been both victimized by society, and not fairly represented in the justice process.

Whatever one's opinion of this case, it illustrates the fact that any formal resolution of law violations occurs through an elaborate process. Justice, while it can be fine-tuned in order to take into consideration the interests of ever-wider numbers of people, rarely pleases everyone. Justice is a social product, and, like any product that is the result of group effort, it is a patchwork quilt of human emotions, reasoning, and concerns. One of the major challenges faced by the justice system today comes in the form of disenfranchised groups that are not convinced that they receive "justice" under current arrangements. Was justice done in the Lavallee case? While the question will be debated for years, it is doubtful that an answer acceptable to everyone will ever be found.

# CANADIAN CRIMINAL JUSTICE: THE SYSTEM

## The Consensus Model

**system of criminal justice** The aggregate of all operating and administrative or technical support agencies that perform criminal justice functions. The basic divisions of the operational aspects of criminal justice are law enforcement, courts, and corrections.

To this point, we have described the agencies of police, the courts, and corrections as a **system of criminal justice**.[21] Each of these agencies can, in turn, be described in terms of their subsystems. Corrections, for example, includes federal penitentiaries, provincial prisons, community-based treatment programs such as "halfway houses," and programs for probation and parole. Each subsystem contains still more components. Prisons, for example, can be described in terms of custody levels, inmate programs, health care, security procedures, and so on. Some youth prisons operate as "boot-camp" facilities, designed to "shock" offenders into quick rehabilitation, while other adult facilities are long-term confinement facilities designed for the most hard-core criminals who are likely to return to crime quickly if released. Students of corrections also study the process of sentencing, through which an offender's fate is decided by the justice system, and examine the role of pretrial facilities in holding prisoners prior to conviction and sentencing.

The systems model of criminal justice is characterized primarily by its assumption that the various parts of the justice system work together by design in order to achieve the wider purpose we have been calling "justice." Hence, the systems perspective on criminal justice generally encompasses a larger point of view called the **consensus model**. The consensus model assumes that all the component parts of the criminal justice system strive towards a common goal, and that the movement of cases and people through the system is smooth due to co-operation between the various components of the system.

**consensus model**
A perspective on the study of criminal justice that assumes that the system's subcomponents work together harmoniously to achieve that social product we call "justice."

The systems model of criminal justice, however, is more an analytical tool than it is a reality. Any analytical model, be it in the so-called "hard" sciences or in the social sciences, is simply a convention chosen for its explanatory power. By explaining the actions of criminal justice officials (such as arrest, prosecution, sentencing, and so on) as though they are systematically related, we are able to envision a fairly smooth and predictable process (which is described in more detail later in this chapter), which allows us to describe the totality of criminal justice at a conceptually manageable level.

The systems model has been criticized for implying a greater level of organization and co-operation among the various agencies of justice than actually exists. The word "system" calls to mind a near-perfect form of social organization. The modern mind associates the idea of a system with machine-like precision in which wasted effort, redundancy, and conflicting actions are quickly abandoned and their causes repaired. The justice system has nowhere near this level of perfection, and the systems model is admittedly an oversimplification that is primarily useful for analytical purposes. Conflicts among and within agencies are rife; immediate goals are often not shared by individual actors in the system; and the system may move in different directions, depending upon political currents, informal arrangements, and personal discretionary decisions.

## The Conflict Model

The **conflict model** provides another approach to the study of Canadian criminal justice. The justice system elements, like society as a whole, are said to be rife with conflict and dissension. Different aspects of the system operate at cross-purposes from one another. The conflict model says that criminal justice agency interests tend to make actors within the system self-serving. Pressures for success, promotion, pay increases, and general accountability, according to this model, fragment the efforts of the system as a whole, leading to a criminal justice *non*-system.[22]

Jerome Skolnick's classic study of clearance rates provides support for the idea of a criminal justice non-system.[23] Clearance rates are a measure of crimes solved by the police. The more crimes the police can show they have solved, the happier is the public they serve.

Skolnick discovered an instance in which an individual burglar was caught red-handed during the commission of a burglary. After his arrest, the police suggested that he should confess to many unsolved burglaries that they knew he had not committed. In effect they said, "Help us out, and we will try to help you out!" The burglar did confess—to over 400 other burglaries. Following the confession, the police were satisfied because they could say they had "solved" many burglaries, and the suspect was pleased as well because the police had agreed to speak on his behalf before the judge.

Both models have something to tell us. Agencies of justice with a diversity of functions (police, courts, and corrections) and at all levels (federal, provincial, and local) are linked closely enough for the term "system" to be meaningfully applied to them. On the other hand, the very size of the criminal justice undertaking makes effective co-operation between component agencies difficult. The police, for example, may have an interest in seeing offenders put behind bars. Prison officials, on the other hand, may be working with extremely overcrowded facilities. They may want early-release programs for certain categories of offenders such as those who are judged to be non-violent. Who wins out in the long run could be just a matter of internal politics. Everyone should be concerned, however, when the goal of justice is impacted, and sometimes even sacrificed, because of conflicts within the system.

## CANADIAN CRIMINAL JUSTICE: THE PROCESS

Structurally, as we have seen, the criminal justice system can be described in terms of its component agencies: police, courts, and corrections. Functionally, the components of the "system" may work together well or they may be in conflict. Whether system or non-system, however, the agencies of criminal justice must process cases that come before them. An analysis of case processing within the system provides both a useful guide to this book and a "road map" to the criminal justice system itself. Beginning with the investigation of reported crimes, Figure 1–1 on page 15 diagrammatically shows the processing of a criminal case through the justice system.

**conflict model** A perspective on the study of criminal justice that assumes that the system's subcomponents function primarily to serve their own interests. According to this theoretical framework, "justice" is more a product of conflicts among agencies within the system than it is the result of co-operation among component agencies.

**warrant** Any of a number of writs issued by a judicial officer, which direct a law enforcement officer to perform a specified act and afford protection from damages if he or she performs it.

**summons** An order issued by a judge or justice commanding a person charged with an offence to attend court at a particular time and location in order to be dealt with, according to law.

# Investigation and Arrest

The modern justice process begins with investigation. When a crime has been committed, it is often discovered and reported to the police. On occasion, a police officer on routine patrol discovers the crime while it is still in progress. Evidence will be gathered on the scene when possible, and a follow-up investigation will attempt to reconstruct the likely sequence of activities. A few offenders are arrested or given a notice to appear in court while at the scene of the crime, while some suspects are identified only after an extensive investigation. In such cases, an arrest **warrant** or a **summons** issued by a justice provides the legal basis for an apprehension by police, or compels the attendance of the accused at trial.

An arrest involves taking a person into custody and limits his or her freedom. Arrest is a serious step in the process of justice and involves a discretionary decision made by the police seeking to bring criminal sanctions to bear. Most arrests are made peacefully, but some involve force when the suspect tries to resist. In 2001, only 24 per cent of crime incidents reported to the police resulted in a charge being laid against an offender.[24] Typically, around 60 per cent of cases coming to court result in conviction.[25] This means that less than 15 per cent of incidents reported to the police result in a conviction being registered. During arrest and prior to questioning, defendants are usually advised of their *Charter* rights as enumerated in section 10 of the *Canadian Charter of Rights and Freedoms*. Defendants are told:

(1) The reason for the arrest or detention; (2) The right to have contact with a lawyer in private without delay; (3) The right to access a free legal aid "duty lawyer" who will explain the legal aid program and provide immediate preliminary legal advice, by phone, if such a service is available in the province.[26]

Additionally, accused persons have a right to remain silent, a right which is also protected by the *Charter*. This is one of the most important rights that counsel can tell a client upon being contacted following the client's arrest. Given the importance placed on recognizing this right by the Supreme Court of Canada, the right to silence also is typically stated in express terms by the police officer upon arresting a suspect.

When an officer interrupts a crime in progress, public safety considerations may make it reasonable for the officer to ask a few questions prior to a rights advisement. Many officers, however, feel on sound legal ground only by immediately following arrest with an advisement of rights. Often, an alternative means of securing the accused's attendance in court will be available to the police, in which case an arrest may not be necessary. Investigation and arrest are discussed in detail in Chapter 6, Policing: Legal Aspects.

The Gazette/Allen McInnes

Many arrests are made peacefully, but some involve force when the suspect tries to resist.

## FIGURE 1–1 Criminal Case Processing

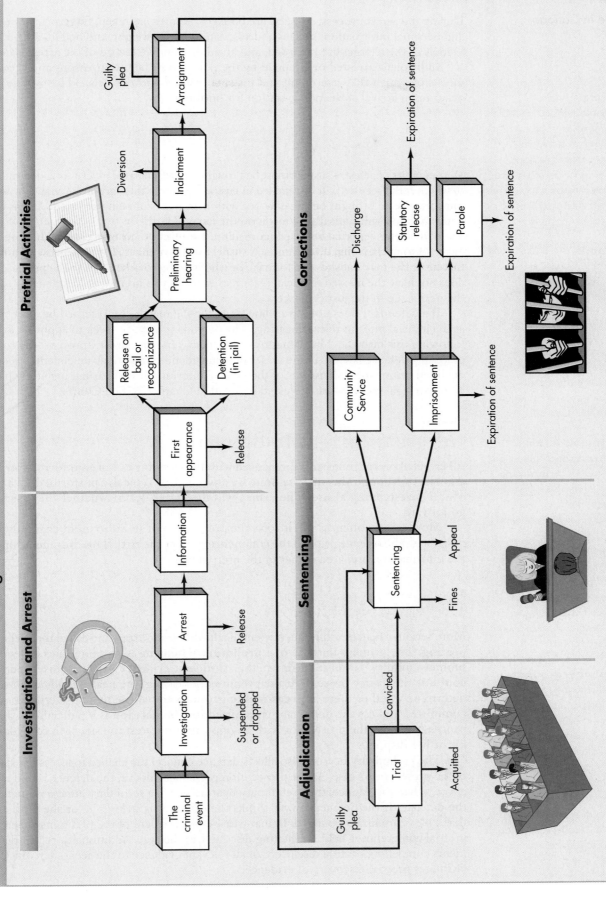

**Investigation and Arrest**

The criminal event → Investigation → Arrest → Information → First appearance

Investigation → Suspended or dropped

Arrest → Release

First appearance → Release

**Pretrial Activities**

First appearance → Release on bail or recognizance → Preliminary hearing

First appearance → Detention (in jail) → Preliminary hearing

Preliminary hearing → Indictment → Arraignment

Indictment → Diversion

Arraignment → Guilty plea

**Adjudication**

Guilty plea → Sentencing

Trial → Convicted → Sentencing

Trial → Acquitted

**Sentencing**

Sentencing → Appeal

Sentencing → Fines

Sentencing → Community Service

Sentencing → Imprisonment

**Corrections**

Community Service → Discharge

Imprisonment → Expiration of sentence

Imprisonment → Statutory release → Expiration of sentence

Imprisonment → Parole → Expiration of sentence

*Source:* Adapted from: U.S. Department of Justice. (1992). *Compendium of Federal Justice Statistics, 1989* (p. 3). Washington, D.C.: Bureau of Justice Statistics.

# Booking

During the arrest process, suspects are booked: pictures are taken, fingerprints are made, and personal information, such as address, date of birth, weight, and height, are gathered. Details of the charges are recorded, and an administrative record of the arrest is created.

Individuals arrested or detained by the police must be given reasons and access to a means by which they can retain and instruct counsel without delay. This will generally occur upon arrival at the police station for **booking**.

# Judicial Interim Release

Within hours of arrest, a suspect must be brought before a judicial official for a determination of whether the accused will be retained in custody, pending the start of the trial. The accused must usually be brought before a justice within 24 hours of being arrested. At this time, a determination will typically be made on the issue of **bail**.

Most defendants are released on recognizance (into their own care or the care of another) during their first appearance. A suspect who is denied release because of a finding that he or she may not show up for trial, or who is going to pose a risk to the public, or who does not have the needed financial resources, is taken to a pretrial holding facility to await the next stage in the justice process.

If a defendant does not have a lawyer, he or she may be represented by duty counsel at the judicial interim release hearing. The defendant may also seek to apply for legal aid following this hearing. The names of assigned lawyers are usually drawn off the roster of practising defence lawyers in the area. Some jurisdictions use public defenders to represent qualified defendants. All aspects of the judicial interim release hearing, including bail and access to legal counsel, are discussed in detail in Chapter 7, The Courts.

# Information and Indictment

All criminal prosecutions are commenced with the swearing out of an **information** before a justice. Although this may be done by anyone, it is typically performed by a police officer investigating a case. The justice will thereafter decide whether the case should go forward.

More serious offences will involve the preparation of an **indictment** charging the accused with the offence prior to the commencement of the trial. This document supplants the information, prepared earlier in the pretrial process.

# Preliminary Hearing

More serious offences will frequently entail a further pretrial hearing called the preliminary hearing. The primary purpose of a **preliminary hearing**, also sometimes called a preliminary inquiry, is to establish whether sufficient evidence exists against a person to continue the justice process. At the preliminary hearing, the hearing judge will seek to determine whether there are **reasonable grounds** to believe that (1) a crime has been committed and (2) the defendant committed it. The decision is a judicial one, but the process provides the prosecutor with an opportunity to test the strength of evidence at his or her disposal.

The preliminary hearing also allows defence counsel the chance to assess the strength of the prosecution's case. As the prosecution presents evidence, the defence is said to "discover" what it is. Hence, the preliminary hearing serves a secondary *discovery* function for the defence. If the defence lawyer thinks the evidence is strong, he or she may suggest that a plea bargain be arranged. In many cases, independent of the preliminary hearing, a pretrial conference is held, facilitating discovery in the case. Additionally, recent developments compelling pretrial disclosure of all relevant evidence to the accused by the Crown facilitates pretrial discovery of evidence.

**booking** A law enforcement or correctional administrative process officially recording an entry into detention after arrest and identifying the person, place, time, and reason for the arrest, and the arresting authority.

**bail** The money or property pledged to the court or actually deposited with the court to effect the release of a person from legal custody.

**information** A document sworn before a judge or justice alleging an offence or offences has/have occurred. The charge document containing specific allegations against the accused.

**indictment** A formal, written accusation submitted to the court by a prosecutor, alleging that a specified person(s) has committed a specified indictable offence(s).

**preliminary hearing** The proceeding before a judicial officer in which it is decided whether there is sufficient evidence to warrant committing a case for trial in a superior court.

**reasonable grounds** A legal criterion residing in a set of facts and circumstances that would cause a reasonable person to believe that a particular other person has committed a specific crime. Reasonable grounds refers to the necessary level of belief that would allow for police seizures (arrests) of individuals and searches of dwellings, vehicles, and possession.

# Arraignment

At **arraignment**, the accused stands before a judge and hears the information or indictment against him or her as it is read. A defendant will be notified of the specific offences, or offences, with which he or she is being charged and will be asked to enter a plea. Acceptable pleas generally include (1) "Not guilty" and (2) "Guilty," although other pleas do arise on rare occasions. Civil proceedings, while not covered in detail in this book, provide an additional avenue of relief for victims or their survivors. Convicted offenders increasingly find themselves facing suits brought against them by victims seeking to collect monetary damages.

Guilty pleas are not always accepted by the judge. If the judge feels a guilty plea was made under duress, or because of a lack of knowledge on the part of the defendant, the plea will be rejected and a plea of "not guilty" will be substituted for it. Sometimes defendants "stand mute"; that is, they refuse to speak or enter a plea of any kind. In that case, the judge will enter a plea of "not guilty" on their behalf. The arraignment process, including pretrial motions made by the defence, is discussed in detail in Chapter 7, The Courts.

**arraignment** The hearing before a court having jurisdiction in a criminal case, in which the identity of the defendant is established, the defendant is informed of the charge(s) and of his or her rights, and the defendant is required to enter a plea.

# Trial

Every criminal defendant facing a possible period of incarceration of five years or more has a right under section 11(f) of the *Charter* to a **trial** by jury. Most criminal trials are not jury trials. For the most part, the criminal courts spend most of their time addressing lesser offences for which jury trials are not available, and trials in which the right to a jury is waived by the accused.

In most jurisdictions, many criminal cases never come to trial. Most are "pled out" (that is, dispensed of as the result of a bargained plea) or dismissed for a variety of reasons. Research conducted in Ontario found that 84 of 101 defendants being followed through the criminal court system were convicted of something, if not of the full offences charged.[27]

In cases that do come to trial, the rules that govern the submission of evidence are tightly controlled by procedural and evidentiary law. Procedural law specifies the way in which trials are conducted, and delineates the powers of the various participants in the criminal trial, while the type of evidence that may be submitted, and what a jury is allowed to hear are governed by evidentiary law, both statute and precedent.

Precedent refers to decisions rendered by courts in previous cases that are cited as the authority for deciding a similar situation in the same manner. Precedent in the law requires judges to decide cases with the same principle, or to reason by analogy from the decision in a prior case.

Trials are expensive and time-consuming. They pit defence lawyers against prosecutors. Regulated conflict is the rule, and the members of a jury are required to decide the facts and apply the law as it is explained to them by the judge. In some cases, however, a jury may be unable to decide. In such cases, it is said to be deadlocked or "hung," resulting in a mistrial being declared. The defendant may then be tried again when a new jury is empanelled. The criminal trial and its participants are described fully in Chapter 8.

**trial** The examination in a court of the issues of fact and law in a case, for the purpose of reaching a judgment of conviction or acquittal of the defendant(s).

# Sentencing

Once a person is convicted, it becomes the responsibility of the judge to impose some form of punishment. The sentence will generally take the form of supervised probation in the community, a fine, a prison term, or some combination of these. Prior to sentencing, a sentencing hearing will be held in which lawyers on both sides present information concerning the defendant. The judge may also request that a pre-sentence report be compiled by a probation officer. The report will contain information on the defendant's family and business situation, emotional state, social background, and criminal history. It will be used to assist the judge in making an appropriate sentencing decision.

Judges traditionally have considerable discretion in sentencing. The *Criminal Code* typically provides high available maximum punishments, and rarely imposes minimum terms. Strict rules governing the selection of a penalty do not exist, resulting in considerable disparity or diversity in sentences being handed out for similar offences. Judges also retain considerable discretion in specifying whether sentences on multiple charges are to run consecutively or concurrently. An offender found guilty of more than one charge may be ordered to serve one sentence after another is completed (a **consecutive sentence**), or be told that his or her sentences will run at the same time (a **concurrent sentence**).

Relatively few sentences are appealed. The appeal process is rather complex, and most courts of appeal have displayed a reluctance to second-guess the decision of the trial judge in selecting the appropriate disposition. Chapter 9, Sentencing, outlines modern sentencing practices and describes the many modern alternatives to imprisonment.

## Corrections

Once an offender has been sentenced, the stage of "corrections" begins. Some offenders are sentenced to prison where they "do time for their crimes." Offenders sentenced to less than two years will be sent to a provincial correctional facility. Offenders sentenced to two years or more will be sent to a federal penitentiary. Once in the correctional system, they are classified according to their security risk and treatment needs, and assigned to confinement facilities and treatment programs. Newer prisons today bear little resemblance to the massive bastions of the past, which isolated offenders from society behind huge stone walls. Many modern prisons, however, still suffer from a "lock psychosis" among top- and mid-level administrators as well as a lack of significant rehabilitation programs. Chapter 11, Correctional Institutions, discusses the philosophy behind prisons and sketches their historical development. Another chapter, Chapter 12, Prison Life, portrays life on the inside and delineates the social structures that develop as a response to the pains of imprisonment.

## Probation and Parole

Not everyone who is convicted of a crime and sentenced ends up in prison. Some offenders are saved from prison by having their sentences suspended and a probationary term imposed. They may also be ordered to perform community service activities as a condition of their probation. During the term of probation, these offenders are required

Queen Elizabeth II signs the *Constitution Act, 1982*, bringing the *Canadian Charter of Rights and Freedoms* into effect on April 17, 1982. This document would dramatically alter the crime control/due process balance in the years to follow.

National Archives of Canada/NAC 14 1503

to submit to supervision by a probation officer and to meet other conditions set by the court. Failure to do so results in revocation of probation and imposition of a prison sentence. Other offenders, who have served a portion of their prison sentences, may be freed on parole. They will be supervised by a parole officer and assisted in their readjustment to society. As in the case of probation, failure to meet the conditions of parole may result in parole revocation and a return to prison. Two chapters deal with the practices of probation and parole and with the issues surrounding them: Chapter 9, Sentencing, and Chapter 10, Probation, Parole, and Community Corrections.

# PRINCIPLES OF FUNDAMENTAL JUSTICE AND INDIVIDUAL RIGHTS

Imposed upon case processing in the criminal justice system are the constitutional requirements of fairness and equity. Guaranteed by section 7 of the *Charter of Rights and Freedoms*, these requirements are referred to as **principles of fundamental justice**. This clause of the *Charter* reads, "Everyone has the right to life, liberty and security of the person and the right not to be deprived thereof except in accordance with the principles of fundamental justice." The constitutional requirement of fundamental justice mandates the recognition of individual rights in the processing of criminal defendants when they are faced with prosecution by the Crown. The guarantee of fundamental justice is found in section 7, but underlies the following six sections in the *Charter*, which are collectively known as the "legal rights."

**principles of fundamental justice**
The basic tenets and principles upon which the legal system is founded.

The fundamental guarantees of the *Charter* have been interpreted and clarified by courts (especially the Supreme Court of Canada) over the last 20 years. The principles of fundamental justice have been interpreted as having far-reaching implications affecting criminal procedure. Principles of fundamental justice require that agencies of justice recognize these rights in their enforcement of the law, and under the court's interpretation of this provision, rights violations may become the basis for the exclusion of evidence or staying of criminal charges. Table 1–1 outlines the basic rights to which defendants in criminal proceedings are generally entitled.

## TABLE 1–1 Individual Rights Guaranteed by the *Canadian Charter of Rights and Freedoms*

A Right to Life, Liberty, and Security of the Person
A Right Against Arbitrary Arrest or Detention
A Right Against Unreasonable Search and Seizure
A Right to Know the Reasons for Arrest or Detention
A Right to Counsel Upon Arrest or Detention
A Right to Challenge the Validity of the Detention by Habeas Corpus
A Right to be Informed of the Specific Offence Charged
A Right to Trial in a Reasonable Time
A Right to Avoid Self-Incrimination
A Right to be Presumed Innocent
A Right to a Trial Before an Independent and Impartial Tribunal
A Right Not to Be Denied Bail Without Just Cause
A Right to a Jury Trial
A Right Against Ex Post Facto Punishments
A Right Against Double Jeopardy
A Right to the Benefit of Lesser Penalties if the Law Lowers a Penalty by Sentencing Time
A Right Against Cruel and Unusual Punishment
A Right to Principles of Fundamental Justice
A Right to an Interpreter at Trial
A Right to Be Treated the Same as Others, Regardless of Race, National or Ethnic Origin, Colour, Religious Preference, Sex, Age, Mental Disability, and Other Personal Attributes

# The Role of the Courts in Defining Rights

Although the Constitution deals with many issues, what we have been calling "rights" are open to interpretation. Many modern rights, although written into the Constitution, would not exist in practice were it not for the fact that the Supreme Court of Canada decided, at some point in history, to recognize them in cases brought before it. The well-known Supreme Court case of *R. v. Hebert*[28] (1990), for example (which is discussed in detail in Chapter 6), found the Court interpreting section 7 of the *Charter* as requiring the recognition of the right to silence. While the courts had always recognized the right of an accused to remain silent, it achieved constitutional status in the *Hebert* decision. On the facts of the case, the Court ruled that the police investigative tactic of placing an undercover officer or agent into a police holding cell to elicit incriminating information from a detainee violates the right to silence where the suspect had indicated a desire to refrain from communicating with the police. After the *Hebert* decision, police investigative tactics had to be altered to give due accord to the rights of the accused to remain silent. It is important to note, however, that while section 7 specifically says that everyone's "life, liberty and security of the person" rights can only be removed through the "principles of fundamental justice," it does *not* say, *in so many words*, that the police are *required to give accord to a right to silence*. Indeed, the right to silence is nowhere mentioned in the *Charter of Rights and Freedoms*. It is the Supreme Court of Canada that, interpreting the Constitution, has said that.

Unlike the high courts of many other nations, the Supreme Court of Canada is very powerful, and its decisions often have far-reaching consequences. The decisions rendered by the justices in cases like *Hebert* become, in effect, the law of the land. For all practical purposes, such decisions often carry as much weight as legislative action. For this reason, some writers speak of "judge-made law" (rather than legislated law) in describing judicial precedents that affect the process of justice.

Rights that have been recognized by Court decisions are often subject to continual refinement. New interpretations may broaden or narrow the scope of applicability accorded to constitutional guarantees. Although the process of change is usually very slow, we should recognize that any right is subject to continual interpretation by the courts—and especially by the Supreme Court of Canada.

## *Crime Control Through Due Process*

**crime control model**

A criminal justice perspective that emphasizes the efficient arrest and conviction of criminal offenders.

Two primary goals were identified at the start of this chapter: (1) the need to enforce the law and maintain social order and (2) the need to protect individuals from injustice. The first of these principles values the efficient arrest and conviction of criminal offenders. It is often referred to as the **crime control model** of justice. The crime control model was first brought to the attention of the academic community in Herbert Packer's cogent analysis of the state of the American criminal justice system in the late 1960s.[29] For that reason, it is sometimes referred to as Packer's crime control model.

**due process model**

A criminal justice perspective that emphasizes individual rights at all stages of the justice system.

The second principle is called the **due process model** for its emphasis on individual rights. Due process is a central and necessary part of Canadian criminal justice. It requires a careful and informed consideration of the facts of each individual case. Under the model, police are required to recognize the rights of suspects during arrest, questioning, and handling. Prosecutors and judges must recognize constitutional and other guarantees during trial and the presentation of evidence. Due process is intended to ensure that innocent people are not convicted of crimes.

Up until now, we have suggested that the dual goals of crime control and due process are in constant and unavoidable opposition to one another. Some critics of criminal justice have argued that the practice of justice is too often concerned with crime control at the expense of due process. Other conservative analysts of the criminal justice scene maintain that our type of justice coddles offenders and does too little to protect the innocent.

While it is impossible to avoid ideological conflicts such as these, it is also realistic to think of the system of justice as representative of *crime control through due process*. It is this model of law enforcement, infused with the recognition of individual rights, which provides a workable conceptual framework for understanding the Canadian system of criminal justice—both now and into the future.

# CRIMINAL JUSTICE AND CRIMINOLOGY

The study of criminal justice as an academic discipline began in the United States in the 1920s when August Vollmer, former police chief of Berkeley, California, persuaded the University of California to offer courses on the subject.[30] Vollmer was joined by his student Orlando W. Wilson and by William H. Parker in calling for increased professionalism in police work through better training.[31] Early criminal justice education was practice-oriented; it was a kind of extension of on-the-job training for working practitioners. In Canada, criminal justice has not developed as an academic discipline much beyond the offering of lower-level undergraduate courses for students planning a career in the criminal justice system. In the early 1990s, the University College of the Fraser Valley in Abbotsford, British Columbia, began an undergraduate degree program in criminal justice. St. Thomas University in Fredericton, New Brunswick, now has a Bachelor of Applied Arts degree program in criminal justice, and in 1999, Mount Royal College in Calgary, Alberta, initiated a Bachelor of Applied Justice Studies degree program.

While criminal justice was often seen as a technical subject, **criminology**, on the other hand, had a firm academic base. Criminology involves the study of the causes of crime and of criminal motivation. It combines the academic disciplines of sociology and psychology in an effort to explore the mind of the offender, the crime phenomenon, and society's response to crime. The study of criminology is central to the criminal justice discipline, and courses in criminology are almost always found in criminal justice programs. Victimology is a subfield of criminology that seeks answers to the question of why some people are victimized while others are not.

**criminology** The scientific study of crime, its causes, its prevention, and society's response thereto, including the rehabilitation and punishment of offenders.

As a separate field of study, criminal justice had fewer than 1000 students before 1950.[32] The turbulent 1960s and 1970s brought an increasing concern with social issues and, in particular, justice. Drug use, social protests, and dramatically increasing crime rates turned the nation's attention to the criminal justice system. During the period, criminology programs developed in numerous university settings across Canada. A centre for criminological research was developed at the University of Montreal in 1960. In 1963, the Centre of Criminology at the University of Toronto was established, providing an interdisciplinary research unit for English-speaking Canada. In the same year, Gwynne Nettler arrived at the University of Alberta and began developing a strong criminology component within the sociology program at that university. A criminology department was developed at the University of Ottawa in 1967, and in 1974, Ezzat Fattah initiated a criminology program at Simon Fraser University in Burnaby, British Columbia. More recently, a School of Human Justice was established at the University of Regina in 1977.[33] The University of Windsor in Southern Ontario has offered an honours degree in criminology through its Sociology/Anthropology Department since 1988. Relative newcomers to the criminology discipline are Carleton University in Ottawa (see box), which opened an Institute of Criminology and Criminal Justice in 1998, and Saint Mary's University in Halifax, Nova Scotia, which initiated a bachelor degree program in criminology in 1999. The future of criminal justice as an independent academic area of study in Canada appears to be reaching a crossroads, with the recent development of the Fraser Valley program, and numerous applied degree programs appearing on the horizon.

# THINGS TO COME: AN OVERVIEW OF THIS BOOK

This textbook is divided into five parts. Part 1, entitled *Crime in Canada*, provides a general introduction to the study of criminal justice, including crime statistics (Chapter 2), and criminal law (Chapter 3).

Part 2 is called *Policing*. Its three chapters focus on the activities of law enforcement agencies. The law enforcement field is described in Chapters 4 and 5, where historical developments are combined with modern studies to depict a dynamic profession. Precedent-setting court cases are introduced in Chapter 6 along with more recent decisions that have refined earlier ones.

BOX 1.3

## Theory into Practice

### Carleton's Most Wanted BA

*By Anita Dolman*

Who said crime doesn't pay? In the four short years since the Institute of Criminology and Criminal Justice was launched, its bachelor of arts program has exploded to become the biggest on campus, with 1082 students enrolled this spring.

"It's become incredibly popular," says Allan Maslove, dean of the Faculty of Public Affairs and Management. "The annual intake is about twice what we predicted it would be when we launched the program. It's very quickly become the largest BA program at Carleton in terms of the number of students."

For years, Carleton offered criminology as a concentration in the law, psychology, or sociology BA programs. In 1998, a new BA in criminology and criminal justice was launched, with concentrations available in law, psychology, or sociology. The institute's faculty is made up entirely of professors from the law, psychology, sociology, and anthropology departments.

Maslove says the institute has been busy recruiting new talent for its related faculties to manage the program's sudden tremendous growth.

"The student numbers have grown much more quickly and to a much higher level than we've anticipated," he says. "I think it's this sort of three-footed discipline base that makes our program so attractive, where the students get a grounding in all three and then choose their concentration in one."

The institute's director, Barry Wright, agrees. "Carleton is unique in its cross-disciplinary approach," he says. "It results in a really comprehensive look at the area."

Just as appealing to some students is getting a shot at one of the institute's coveted placements. Offered to only 80 of the program's top students each year, the one-time placements give third- and fourth-year students a chance to find out what it's like in the real world of criminology.

Field placements include answering phones at a distress centre, working at a correctional facility, training at a parole office, developing forensic psychiatry skills at a hospital, assisting at a law office, or learning first-hand how the system works at the Department of Justice or other government and social service organizations.

"There's a fair bit of competition within the program for the field placement option," says Wright. "It provides students with an opportunity to work in a number of different institutional settings that deal with the administration of criminal justice."

A degree in criminology and criminal justice gives students an understanding of criminal, delinquent and deviant behaviour, criminal law and the criminal justice system, and society's reaction to crime and deviance.

Wright, who is also a law professor, says many students come to the program hoping to move into government someday in law or public policy, while others want to work in corrections, go on to become lawyers, or do graduate work in criminology or one of the three concentrations.

Others apply hoping the BA will give them a leg up when they join the police force.

To help aspiring police officers along the way, the institute has developed a new accelerated degree and diploma program with Algonquin College. Students with the BA can earn credits that will help them fast-track through Algonquin's diploma in police foundations. Likewise, diploma grads can get credits towards an accelerated criminology BA at Carleton.

"Police now are increasingly recruiting university grads," says Wright, who believes a BA gives police an advantage when they first join the force, but also helps them move up the ranks throughout their career.

## QUESTIONS FOR DISCUSSION

1. Does the institution you are attending offer a BA program in criminology or criminal justice? If so, how popular is the program at your institution? If it is popular, why do you think this is the case?

2. Does your institution offer a field placement program? What are the advantages of a field placement program? Do you think the time spent in field placement would be better spent on further academics? Explain.

3. Is there a danger that a multidisciplinary BA program in criminology or criminal justice produces a student who is a "Jack-of-all-trades but master of none"? Why or why not?

*Source: Carleton University Magazine online.* (Spring 2002): http://magazine.carleton.ca/2002_spring/701.htm Reprinted with permission of *Carleton University Magazine.*

Part 3, called *Adjudication*, includes chapters on the courts (Chapters 7 and 8), and sentencing (Chapter 9). Special attention is given throughout Part 4, *Corrections*, to the legal issues surrounding correctional institutions and various forms of criminal punishment. Prisons and penitentiaries (Chapter 11) and prison life (Chapter 12) are discussed in this part, along with probation, parole, and community corrections (Chapter 10).

The final section, Part 5, *Special Issues*, looks at problems facing the justice system today. This part includes a chapter on youth justice (Chapter 13). Chapter 14 provides a cursory overview of criminal justice systems in other nations and points out the need for international understanding. Finally, the challenges and opportunities that the future holds for the practice of Canadian criminal justice, including computer crime and emerging investigative technologies, are discussed in the last chapter (Chapter 15).

Although this book covers many issues, its overall structure is sequential. Consecutive chapters provide a tour of criminal justice agencies and practices as they exist in Canada today. The tour begins in Part 1 with a discussion of crime and the criminal law and ends in Part 4 with a discussion of problems facing the future of criminal justice.

## SUMMARY

In this chapter, the process of Canadian criminal justice and the agencies that contribute to it have been described as a system with three major components: police, courts, corrections. As we have warned, however, such a viewpoint is useful primarily for the reduction in complexity it provides. A more realistic approach to understanding criminal justice may be the non-systems approach. As a non-system, criminal justice is depicted as a fragmented activity in which individuals and agencies within the process have interests and goals that at times coincide, but often conflict.

Defendants processed by the system come into contact with numerous justice professionals whose duty it is to enforce the law, but who also have a stake in the agencies that employ them and who hold their own personal interests and values. As they wend their way through the system, defendants may be held accountable to the law, but in the process they will also be buffeted by the personal whims of "officials" as well as by the practical needs of the system itself. A complete view of Canadian criminal justice must recognize that the final outcome of any encounter with the criminal justice system will be a consequence of decisions made not just at the legislative level, but in the day-to-day activities undertaken by everyone involved in the system. Hence, in a very real sense, justice is a product whose quality depends just as much upon practical considerations as it does upon idealistic notions of right and wrong.

An alternative way of viewing the practice of criminal justice is in terms of its two goals: crime control and due process. The crime control perspective urges rapid and effective law enforcement and calls for the stiff punishment of lawbreakers. Due process, on the other hand, requires a recognition of the defendant's rights and holds the agents of justice accountable for any actions that might contravene those rights.

The goals of due process and crime control are often in conflict. Popular opinion may even view them as mutually exclusive. As we describe the agencies of justice in the various chapters that follow, the goals of crime control and due process will appear again and again. As we will see, the challenge of criminal justice in Canada is to achieve efficient enforcement of the laws while recognizing the rights of individuals. The mandate of crime control through due process ensures that criminal justice will remain an exciting and ever-evolving undertaking.

## DISCUSSION QUESTIONS

1. What are the two models of the criminal justice process that this chapter describes? Which model do you think is more useful? Which is more accurate?

2. What have we suggested are the primary goals of the criminal justice system? Do you think any one goal is more important than another? If so, which one? Why?

3. What do we mean when we say that the "primary purpose of law is the maintenance of order"? Why is social order necessary?

4. Do we have too many criminal laws? Too few? Do we have enough social order, or too little? What more needs to be changed, if anything?

5. What might a large, complex society such as our own be like without laws? Without a system of criminal justice? Would you want to live in such a society? Why or why not?

6. What do we, as individuals, have to give up to facilitate social order? Do we ever give up too much in the interest of social order? If so, when? Have the events of September 11 altered your view of the appropriate balance between individual rights and public order?

# WEBLINKS

www.extension.ualberta.ca/legalfaqs/
### Canadian Legal FAQs
Questions and answers developed by the Legal Studies Program, University of Alberta, including FAQs about the *Criminal Code*.

www.lcc.gc.ca/en/themes/sr/rj/howse/howse_main.asp
### Restorative Justice: A Conceptual Framework
A paper prepared for the Law Commission of Canada about restorative justice, "a process whereby all the parties with a stake in a particular offence come together to resolve collectively how to deal with the aftermath of the offence and its implications for the future."

www.icclr.law.ubc.ca
### International Centre for Criminal Law Reform and Criminal Justice Policy
This Vancouver-based, independent, non-profit institute, officially affiliated with the United Nations, is dedicated to national and international efforts to reduce crime and improve justice. The site contains publications, occasional papers and reports, an events/conference listing, an online forum facility, plus links to partner institutes around the world.

www.attorneygeneral.jus.gov.on.ca
### Ministry of the Attorney General, Ontario: Services
An Ontario government site that provides helpful information about going to court, getting a lawyer, family justice matters, services for crime victims, and more.

# The Crime Picture

RCMP

**KEY CONCEPTS**

violent crime
property crime
clearance rate
murder
sexual assault
date rape
robbery

assault
break and entry
motor vehicle theft
arson
criminal harassment
hate crimes

**KEY CASES**

*R. v. Thatcher*
*R. v. Lelas*
*R. v. Simms*

25

# INTRODUCTION: SOURCES OF DATA

On January 23, 1983, JoAnn Wilson arrived home on Albert Street in Regina, Saskatchewan, after a long day at work. While her husband, daughter, and housekeeper went about their business inside the family home, JoAnn parked her car in the garage. When she emerged from her car, someone approached her in the garage, grabbing her by the throat, while striking her over the head and arms with a meat-cleaver-like object more than 20 times. Her assailant then produced a revolver, probably a .357 magnum, shooting her through the head:

> JoAnn was shot just above the root of the ear. The hollow-point, aluminum-coated, silver-tipped bullet exploded into numerous fragments as it entered her brain. Her face smacked into the garage floor as her body slumped forward.[1]

Statistically, there was little to distinguish her murder from the 682 other homicides that were recorded in Canada that year. JoAnn Wilson (then JoAnn Thatcher) went down in the record books as one more homicide in a country already burdened with news of police shootings, gang-related killings, drug deals gone bad, and homicidal arguments fuelled by liquor and lust.

But there is a story behind every crime statistic, and the Thatcher story is an interesting one. Colin Thatcher, JoAnn's first husband, had met JoAnn while the two of them were attending university in Iowa. Following their marriage, the couple moved to Saskatchewan where JoAnn taught at a high school while Colin ran a ranch. Colin's father, Ross, a well-known politician, became premier of the province in 1964. Following his father's death in 1971, Colin entered the political arena. In 1974, Thatcher took a seat in the provincial legislature.

However, the storybook romance was ending. The couple experienced marital difficulties during the late 1970s, resulting in JoAnn leaving Colin in 1979. The split-up was not amicable. In addition to dispute over custody of the couple's children, a court eventually ordered Colin to pay in excess of $800 000 to his wife. Thatcher's response to the break-up and the impending costs associated with it was to attempt to hire someone to kill JoAnn. In 1980, he offered $50 000 to Gary Anderson, a local small-time offender, to do the killing. Anderson refused the job, but eventually arranged for someone to kill JoAnn. After accepting a sum of money, however, the proposed hit man ended up in jail on unrelated charges. JoAnn had remarried by this time; however, the property distribution from her break-up with Colin was stalled.

In May 1981, Colin and JoAnn were still meeting to effect a property settlement. On May 17, 1981, JoAnn was shot by a rifle while standing in her kitchen washing dishes. Gary Anderson had recently purchased a rifle for Colin Thatcher, delivering it to him at the same time he let Thatcher know the would-be hit man was unavailable as a consequence of being in jail. JoAnn recovered from her wound, but her troubles were not over. In January 1982, while vacationing in Palm Springs, California, Colin Thatcher purchased a .357 magnum revolver. In 1982, Thatcher was re-elected, this time his party formed the government under the leadership of premier Grant Devine. Thatcher was appointed minister of Energy and Mines. The killing of JoAnn Thatcher the following year resulted in heretofore unrealized press coverage. The Crown prosecutors claimed that Colin either killed his wife that winter night, or he hired a contract killer to kill his wife. In the garage where JoAnn was killed, a credit card receipt, signed by Colin Thatcher and dated three days before the killing, was found on the floor, near the body. Colin Thatcher maintains his innocence to this day. He is currently serving a life term for the killing.[2]

This chapter provides a statistical picture of crime in Canada today. It does so by examining information on reported crimes from Statistics Canada's division responsible for collecting crime data, the Canadian Centre for Justice Statistics' (CCJS) *Uniform Crime Reports* (UCR), as well as data from the 1988, 1993, and 1999 General Social Survey (GSS) conducted by Statistics Canada (StatsCan). While reading this chapter, however, it is important to keep in mind that statistical aggregates of reported crime, whatever their source, do not easily reveal the human suffering, cost in lost lives, lessened productivity, and reduced quality-of-life that is caused when an individual falls victim to a crime. Although every murder victim, like JoAnn Wilson, led an intricate life and had a family, dreams, and desires, his or her death at the hands of another person is routinely recorded only as a numerical count in existing statistical

The aging of the prison population is a new phenomenon in Canada's federal penitentiaries. Colin Thatcher (centre) is one of the more famous Canadians who will grow old behind bars.

reports. Such information does not contain details on the personal lives of crime victims but represents merely a compilation of reported law violations.

## Crime Data and Social Policy

Crime statistics do more than provide a picture of crime in this country. If used properly, they can provide one of the most powerful tools available to social-policy decision makers. Decision makers at all levels, including legislators, public officials, and administrators throughout the criminal justice system, rely on crime data to analyze and evaluate existing programs, fashion and design new crime control initiatives, develop funding requests, and plan new laws and crime control legislation. The "get-tough" policies described later in the book, for example, are in large part based upon the public's perception of increasing crime rates and the measured ineffectiveness of existing programs to reduce the incidence of repeat offending.

Governments expend great resources delivering criminal justice services. As shown in Figure 2–1, Canadians annually spend about $10 billion on policing, courts, legal aid, criminal prosecutions, and adult corrections. In order to ensure this money is spent wisely, policy makers require accurate information about the crime picture in Canada. To accomplish this, the Canadian Centre for Justice Statistics routinely collects and disseminates information about crime in Canada.

Some, however, question just how "objective"—and therefore how useful—crime statistics are. Social events, including crime, are complex and difficult to quantify. The Canadian Centre for Justice Statistics regularly publishes bulletins on recently collected crime data called *Juristat*. These publications focus on certain crimes and certain aspects of Canada's system of justice.

Canada's *Juristat* publications attempt to canvass all crimes in their publications. The UCR registers all offences at the point at which the police record a crime as having occurred, regardless of whether an offender is arrested for the incident. All crimes that are reported to the police, and where the police conclude that a crime did in fact occur, are supposed to make their way into the official crime statistics.

## Collecting Crime Data

Crime statistics are difficult to interpret because of the way in which they are collected. Most widely quoted numbers

**FIGURE 2–1 Government Spending on Justice Services, Canada, 2000–01**

Legal Aid 5%
Prosecutions 3%
Courts 9%
Adult Corrections 22%
Policing 61%

Total Expenditures: $9.815 billion
Total Per Capita: $319

*Source:* Adapted from the Statistics Canada publication *Juristat*, Catalogue no. 85-002, Vol. 22, No. 11, October 2002.

purporting to describe crime in Canada come from the Canadian Centre for Justice Statistics' *Uniform Crime Reports* and depend upon reports to the police by victims of crime. One problem with such summaries is that citizens do not always make official reports, sometimes because they are afraid to contact the police, or perhaps because they don't think the police can do anything about the offence. Even when reports are made, they are filtered through a number of bureaucratic levels. As criminologist Frank Hagan points out, quoting an earlier source, "The government is very keen on amassing statistics. They collect them, add to them, raise them to the *n*th power, take the cube root, and prepare wonderful diagrams. But what you must never forget is that every one of these figures comes in the first instance from the *chowty dar* [village watchman], who puts down what he damn pleases."[3]

Another problem is that certain kinds of crimes are rarely reported and are especially difficult to detect. These include "victimless crimes," or crimes that, by their nature, involve willing participants. Victimless crimes include such things as drug use, prostitution-related offences, and gambling. Similarly, white-collar and high-technology offences, such as embezzlement, computer crime, and corporate misdeeds, probably enter the official statistics only rarely. Hence, a large amount of criminal activity goes undetected in Canada, while those types of crimes that are detected may paint a misleading picture of criminal activity by virtue of the publicity accorded to them. (See Figure 2–2.)

A second data-collection format is typified by Statistics Canada's General Social Survey (GSS). This survey relies on personal interpretations of what may (or may not) have been criminal events, and upon quasi-confidential surveys that may selectively include data from those most willing to answer interviewers' questions, and exclude information from less gregarious respondents. Some victims are afraid to report crimes even to non-police interviewers. Others may inaccurately interpret their own experiences or may be tempted

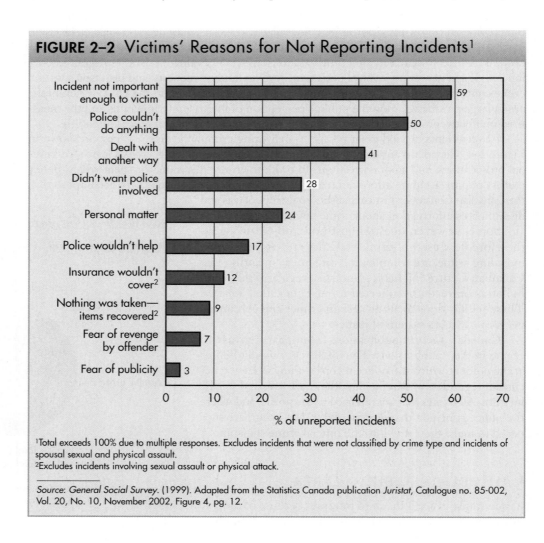

**FIGURE 2–2** Victims' Reasons for Not Reporting Incidents[1]

% of unreported incidents

- Incident not important enough to victim — 59
- Police couldn't do anything — 50
- Dealt with another way — 41
- Didn't want police involved — 28
- Personal matter — 24
- Police wouldn't help — 17
- Insurance wouldn't cover[2] — 12
- Nothing was taken—items recovered[2] — 9
- Fear of revenge by offender — 7
- Fear of publicity — 3

[1]Total exceeds 100% due to multiple responses. Excludes incidents that were not classified by crime type and incidents of spousal sexual and physical assault.
[2]Excludes incidents involving sexual assault or physical attack.

*Source: General Social Survey.* (1999). Adapted from the Statistics Canada publication *Juristat*, Catalogue no. 85-002, Vol. 20, No. 10, November 2002, Figure 4, pg. 12.

to invent victimizations for the sake of interviewers. Since details about the crimes come directly from the victims, and no attempt is made to validate the information against police records or any other source, these data must also be viewed with caution.

Although the UCR and the GSS are the country's major sources of crime data, other regular publications contribute to our knowledge of crime patterns throughout the nation. Available regularly are crime data from the various provincial government ministries responsible for the administration of justice. Such information frequently breaks down crime rates by municipality, giving a look at the local crime picture.

# THE UNIFORM CRIME REPORTS

## Development of the UCR Program

In 1961, Statistics Canada and the Canadian Association of Chiefs of Police entered into a joint effort to begin systematically collecting aggregate crime data at the national level. The result was the UCR survey, which attempted to provide a consistent methodology for counting crimes reported to the police, thereby enabling the police to more effectively allocate their resources, and providing municipalities and provinces with a means to measure their respective crime rates.[4] For the past 35 years, these data have been continuously collected.

In 1985, the Canadian Centre for Justice Statistics (CCJS) began phasing in a new method of collecting the UCR (or UCR2), based on incident information provided by the police as opposed to aggregate information provided by police departments from 1961 onward. The early method of collecting crime data involved the police providing monthly reports on a hard-copy data-collection form submitted to CCJS. These forms contained the number of incidents, the number of crimes cleared (considered solved by the police), and the number of people charged in relation to cleared incidents. This collection of information, while useful in its own right, did not allow for the analysis of specific incidents. Beginning about 18 years ago, those police departments with automated information systems began switching to a revised UCR2 format, that is, from the "aggregate" approach for data collection to an "incident-based" approach, where a separate record or data file was created for each criminal incident. The incident-based approach allowed for significantly greater analytical potential, permitting far more sophisticated analyses of the crime picture in Canada. As of 2002, approximately 123 police departments in Canada had converted to the revised UCR2 format, accounting for approximately 59 per cent of the total volume of crime data in the country.

The collection of UCR data has been aided in Canada by the fact that we have a uniform criminal law that applies nationwide. This means that categories of offences remain uniform, regardless of the jurisdiction collecting the data.

## Historical Trends

Since the UCR Program began, there have been two major trends in crime rates. One occurred during the first 30 years of data collection. During this period, the national overall crime rate grew fairly continuously. This growth manifested itself in the form of violent crime, property crime, and other types of crime. Since a great deal of our crime has historically been committed by our youth, it is possible to attribute much of this increase in crime to World War II. With the end of the war, and the return of thousands of young men to civilian life, birth rates skyrocketed during the period from 1945 to 1955, creating a post-war "baby boom." By 1960, "baby boomers" were entering their teenage years. Such a disproportionate number of young people produced a dramatic increase in most crimes.

Other factors contributed to the increase in reported crime during the same period. Modified reporting requirements, which reduced the stress associated with filing police reports, and the publicity associated with the rise in crime, sensitized victims to the importance of reporting. Coverage by the UCR survey increased from 91.4 per cent of those intended to be captured in the data to 99.4 per cent in 1968. Some of the increase in crime rate during the 1960s may be attributed to the increase in the number of reports filed by police departments over this decade.[5] Increasing crime rates may also be attributable, in part, to new crimes that were added to the *Criminal Code* from the 1960s through the 1980s. Additionally, crimes that may have gone undetected in the past began to figure more prominently in official statistics.

The 1960s witnessed continuing increases in the official crime rate. During this period, large numbers of Canadian youth, born in the post-war baby boom years, matured to the age at which most offenders begin committing crimes (late teens and early twenties). Police agencies grew in size, enhancing the ability of the police to detect and record crimes. Many behaviours, such as impaired driving, spouse assault, and child abuse, that society had tolerated up to that time came to be approached as social problems deserving the attention of the criminal law. Some existing crimes became more strictly enforced, while other behaviours that were not yet defined as crimes became so defined, expanding the scope of conduct that could make its way into the official crime statistics.

Crime rates continued their upward swing with a brief respite in the early 1980s, when post-war boomers began to age out of the crime-prone years. About the same time, however, an increase in drug-related criminal activity may have led to heightened crime rates, especially in the area of violent crime. Since 1991, Statistics Canada's Homicide Survey included a question inquiring into the apparent presence of a drug-related motive for homicide. In 2002, one in eight homicide incidents were reported by police to be gang-related, with most such offences relating to drugs.[6] Crime rates peaked about 1991, with decreases in the rate of most crimes being reported through to 2000. Following nine consecutive years of declining crime rates, the crime rate increased slightly in 2001 and declined slightly in 2002.[7]

## Recent Trends

In 2002, 2.5 million *Criminal Code* incidents were reported in the UCR annual report. Figure 2–3 shows the crime rate in Canada for the period 1962–2002.

Statistics Canada typically divides offences into these groupings: (1) *Criminal Code* violent offences, (2) *Criminal Code* property offences, (3) *Criminal Code* other (non-traffic), (4) *Criminal Code* traffic offences, and (5) other federal offences.

## UCR Terminology

Figure 2–4 illustrates a UCR crime clock that shows crime frequency in Canada. The crime clock was first developed in the FBI's *Uniform Crime Reports*. The FBI used this device to diagram eight serious offences, showing their relative frequency of occurrence.

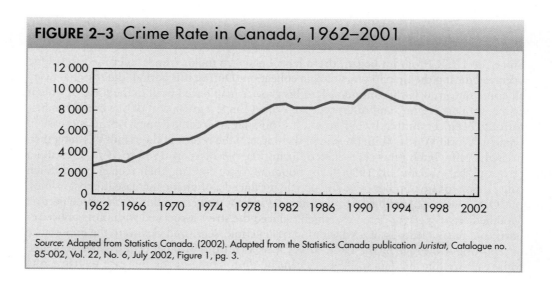

**FIGURE 2–3** Crime Rate in Canada, 1962–2001

*Source:* Adapted from Statistics Canada. (2002). Adapted from the Statistics Canada publication *Juristat*, Catalogue no. 85-002, Vol. 22, No. 6, July 2002, Figure 1, pg. 3.

The crime clock distinguishes between two general categories of crime: **violent crime** and **property crime**. (Violent crime is also referred to as personal crime.) Violent crimes listed here include homicide (including murder, manslaughter, and infanticide), sexual assault, robbery, and aggravated assault. While this list of violent crimes is not exhaustive, it does contain many offences of concern to the typical Canadian. Similarly, the property crimes selected for inclusion are not an exhaustive list of such offences, but rather contain offences of great concern to the average Canadian. The property crimes here include residential break and enter, theft, motor vehicle theft, and arson.

The dichotomy of violent and property offences used here helps us to simplify analysis of the data; however, these data do not typically provide a clear measure of the severity of the crimes being covered.

Crime clock data are based, as are most UCR statistics, upon crimes reported to (or discovered by) the police. For a few offences, the numbers reported are probably close to the numbers that actually occur. Homicide crimes, for example, are crimes that are difficult to conceal because of their serious nature. Even where the crime is not immediately discovered, the victim is often quickly missed by friends and associates, and a "missing persons" report is filed with the police.

**violent crime** An offence category that, according to the *Uniform Crime Reports* (UCR), includes homicide, attempted homicide, sexual assault, other sexual offences, abduction, robbery, and assault. Because the UCR depends upon *reports* (to the police) of crimes, the "official statistics" on these offences are apt to inaccurately reflect the actual incidence of such crimes.

**property crime** An offence category that, according to the UCR Program, includes break and enter, theft, fraud, and possession of stolen property. Since citizen reports of criminal incidents figure heavily in the compilation of "official statistics," the same critiques apply to tallies of these crimes as to the category of violent crime.

**FIGURE 2–4** Crime Clock, 2002, Showing the Frequency of Major Crime Commission

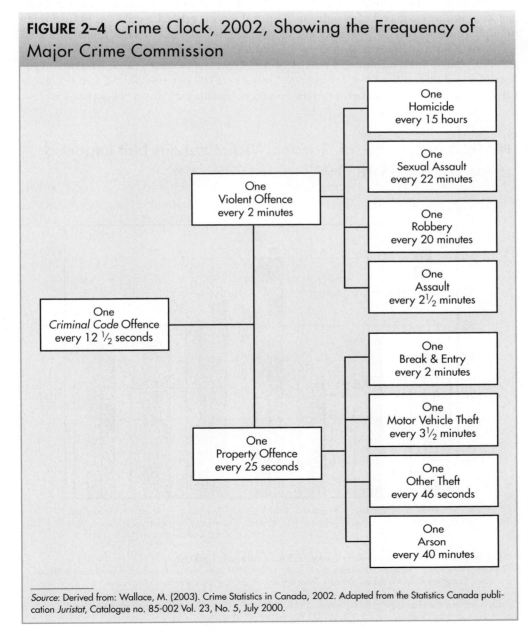

*Source*: Derived from: Wallace, M. (2003). Crime Statistics in Canada, 2002. Adapted from the Statistics Canada publication *Juristat*, Catalogue no. 85-002 Vol. 23, No. 5, July 2000.

Auto theft is another crime that is reported with a frequency similar to its actual rate of occurrence, probably because insurance companies require that a police report be filed before any claims can be collected. Unfortunately, most crimes other than murder and auto theft appear to be seriously under-reported. Victims may not report for various reasons, including (1) the belief that the police can't do anything; (2) a fear of reprisal; (3) embarrassment about the crime itself, or a fear of being embarrassed during the reporting process; and (4) an acceptance of criminal victimization as a normal part of life. Figure 2–5 shows the reasons indicated by respondents for not reporting certain crimes to the police, as reflected in the 1999 Canadian General Social Survey.[8]

UCR data tend to underestimate the amount of crime that actually occurs for another reason: built into the reporting system is the hierarchy rule—a way of "counting" crime reports such that only the most serious out of a series of events is scored. If a man and woman go on a picnic, for example, and their party is set upon by a criminal who kills the man, sexually assaults the woman, steals the couple's car, and later burns the vehicle, the hierarchy rule dictates that only one crime will be reported in official statistics—that of murder. The offender, if apprehended, may later be charged with each of the offences listed, but only one report of murder will appear in the UCR data.

Most UCR information is reported as a *rate* of crime. A rate is computed as the number of crimes *per* some unit of population. National reports generally make use of large units of population, such as 100 000 persons. Hence, the rate of sexual assault reported by the UCR for 2002 was 78 sexual assaults per every 100 000 inhabitants of Canada.[9]

Rates allow for a meaningful comparison over areas and across time. The rate of reported sexual assault for 1989, for example, was about 100 per 100 000.[10] Rates also allow for meaningful comparisons between jurisdictions in Canada with divergent population sizes.

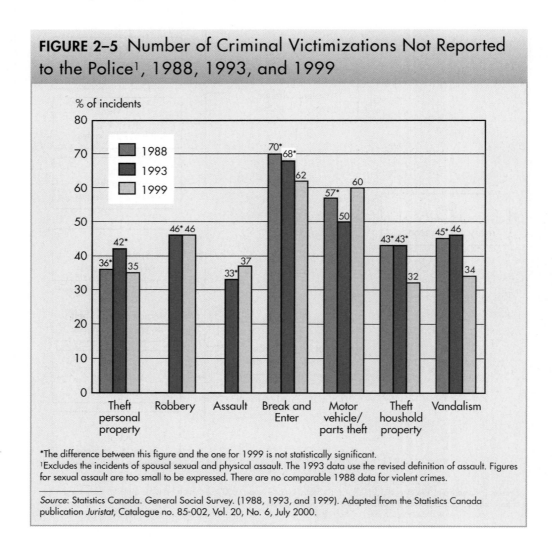

**FIGURE 2–5** Number of Criminal Victimizations Not Reported to the Police[1], 1988, 1993, and 1999

*The difference between this figure and the one for 1999 is not statistically significant.
[1]Excludes the incidents of spousal sexual and physical assault. The 1993 data use the revised definition of assault. Figures for sexual assault are too small to be expressed. There are no comparable 1988 data for violent crimes.

*Source:* Statistics Canada. General Social Survey. (1988, 1993, and 1999). Adapted from the Statistics Canada publication *Juristat*, Catalogue no. 85-002, Vol. 20, No. 6, July 2000.

For example, the 2002 rate of sexual assault in the Nunavut Territory was 961 per 100 000 population (even though fewer than 100 000 people live there). In the province of Quebec, the rate of sexual assault was 56 per 100 000 population. While actual raw numbers reveal many more sexual assaults were recorded in Quebec (4190) than Nunavut (276), we can see that proportionate to the size of the population, the risk of sexual assault appears to be much higher in Nunavut.[11]

We expect the number of crimes to increase as population grows, but rate increases are cause for concern because they indicate that crimes are increasing faster than the population is growing. Rates, however, require interpretation. Although the definition of sexual assault includes both female and male victims, in actuality, between 90 and 96 per cent of sexual assault victims are female.[12] Accordingly, the rate of victimization might be more meaningfully expressed in terms of every 100 000 female inhabitants. Similarly, although there is a tendency to judge an individual's risk of victimization based upon rates, such judgments tend to be inaccurate since they are based purely on averages and do not take into consideration individual life circumstances, such as place of residence, wealth, and educational level. While rates may tell us about aggregate conditions and trends, we must be very careful in applying them to individual cases. The crime clock, itself a useful diagrammatic tool, is not a rate-based measure of criminal activity and does not allow easy comparisons over time.

A commonly used term in today's UCR is **clearance rate**. The clearance rate of any crime refers to the proportion of reported crimes that have been "solved." Clearances are judged primarily on the basis of arrests and do not involve judicial disposition. Once an arrest has been made, a crime is regarded as "cleared" for purposes of reporting in the UCR Program. Exceptional clearances (sometimes called clearances by exceptional means) can result when law enforcement authorities believe they know the identity of the perpetrator of a crime, but cannot make an arrest. The perpetrator may, for example, flee the country, commit suicide, or die.

Table 2–1 shows the crime rate for selected offences in 2002.

**clearance rate** A traditional measure of investigative effectiveness that compares the number of crimes reported and/or discovered to the number of crimes solved through arrest or other means (such as the death of a suspect).

## Homicide

In Canada, "homicide" is a neutral term connoting the causing of death of a human being. Homicides are divided into culpable and non-culpable. Only culpable homicides are considered

**TABLE 2–1** Selected *Criminal Code* Incidents, Canada and the Provinces/Territories, 2002

|  | 2002 | |
|---|---|---|
|  | **Number** | **Rate** |
| **Population** | **31 413 990** | |
| Homicides | 584 | 2 |
| Sexual assaults (levels 1, 2, 3) | 24 350 | 78 |
| Assaults (levels 1, 2, 3) | 235 270 | 749 |
| Robbery | 26 700 | 85 |
| Violent crime – Total | 303 294 | 965 |
| Break & enter | 274 894 | 875 |
| Motor vehicle theft | 161 506 | 514 |
| Other theft | 688 474 | 2191 |
| Property crime – Total | 1 243 945 | 3960 |
| Offensive weapons | 15 834 | 50 |
| Mischief | 332 723 | 1059 |
| Other *Criminal Code* – Total | 837 008 | 2664 |
| *Criminal Code* – Total – without Traffic Offences | 2 384 249 | 7590 |

*Source: Uniform Crime Reporting Survey. CCJS. Adapted from the Statistics Canada publication Juristat, Catalogue no. 85-002, Vol. 23, No. 5, July 2002, Table 3, pg. 16.*

**murder** Usually the intentional killing of a human being. Murder is a generic term that, in common usage, may include first- and second-degree murder.

offences under criminal law. The *Criminal Code* classifies culpable homicide as including murder, manslaughter, and infanticide. **Murder** is classified as first-degree murder and second-degree murder. UCR statistics on homicide describe the yearly number and rate of all incidences of culpable homicide within Canada. Not included in the count are suicides, justifiable homicides (i.e., self-defence), deaths caused by criminal negligence or by accident, and attempts to murder. In 2002, some 582 homicides came to the attention of police departments across Canada.[13]

"First-degree murder" is a term that describes culpable homicide that is planned and deliberate or involves a contract killing, the murder of police officers and prison guards, and murder committed while another serious offence is committed. Examples of such a serious offence would be aircraft hijacking, sexual assault, kidnapping, and hostage taking. Second-degree murder is an intentional and unlawful killing, but one that is generally unplanned. Infanticide entails a new mother killing her child during its first year of life—the killing being caused by an imbalance brought on by the birth. Manslaughter is a category of killings that involves all culpable homicides other than murder and infanticide. Such killings typically involve non-intentional acts either committed in the heat of passion, or where the accused's state of mind was affected by alcohol or drug consumption, or where the accused's state of mind lacked an intention to kill, but he or she was reckless or careless with regard to whether the victim lived or died.

Of all homicides recorded in Canada in 2002, 52 per cent were classified as first-degree murder, 37 per cent were second-degree murder, 10 per cent were manslaughter, and less than 1 per cent were classified as infanticides. These data reflect the tendency of the police to classify homicides at the most serious level possible during the investigatory and charging stages. By the time such cases reach disposition in court, the numbers have changed dramatically, reflecting the effect of plea bargaining, and the partial success of defence arguments at trial of bringing the state of mind of the accused into question.

Figure 2–6 shows the homicide rate over the last 40 years. In recent years, Canada's homicide rate has been very stable. Homicide offences are among the least frequent of all violent offences in Canada. The 2002 homicide rate was 1.85 homicides for every 100 000 persons in the country—up slightly from previous years (up 4 per cent), and a 39 per cent decrease since 1975.

Geographically, homicide rates are highest in Canada's North. While the Yukon Territory had no homicides in 2002, the Northwest Territories had a rate of 9.66 per 100 000, and Nunavut had a rate of 6.97 per 100 000. It should be noted that the northern jurisdictions have relatively small populations, and therefore their homicide rates are dramatically affected by

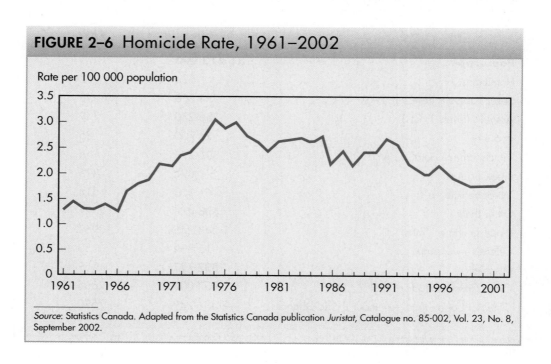

**FIGURE 2–6** Homicide Rate, 1961–2002

Rate per 100 000 population

*Source*: Statistics Canada. Adapted from the Statistics Canada publication *Juristat*, Catalogue no. 85-002, Vol. 23, No. 8, September 2002.

the addition of one or two homicides in any given year. The three northern jurisdictions only had six homicides between them during 2002, with four in the Northwest Territories, and two in Nunavut. While most homicides occur in Canada's two largest provinces, Ontario (178 in 2001) and Quebec (118 in 2001), the actual homicide rates in these provinces are close to the national average (1.47 and 1.58 per 100 000, respectively; the national rate is 1.85). Of the 10 provinces occupying the lower portion of Canada, the Western provinces consistently display the highest homicide rates (3.31 per 100 000 in Manitoba, 2.67 per 100 000 in Saskatchewan, 2.25 per 100 000 in Alberta, and 3.04 per 100 000 in British Columbia). The Western provinces typically show above-average homicide rates, Central Canada around the average, and the Maritime provinces below-average rates. Indeed, Prince Edward Island has averaged only one homicide per year since 1990.

Age is no barrier to homicide. Statistics for 2002 reveal that 44 children (under the age of 12) were victims of homicide, 13 of whom were under one year of age. Of the 44 children killed in 2002, 31 were killed by one of their parents. Additionally, each year a few homicide victims are persons aged 60 and over.[14] The median age of homicide victims is usually 33 to 37. Homicide offenders are most often in the 15–34 age group, with the most common age being in the late twenties.

In the recent past, unlike in the United States where firearms have been the weapon of choice in most homicides, in Canada the most common weapon used was a knife (usually over 30 per cent of all homicides). While in the past, stabbings were the most common cause of death, in recent years firearms and stabbings have been equally common causes of death. Shootings resulted in 149 culpable homicides (25.6 per cent of the total), close to the 182 stabbings (31.3 per cent), 124 beatings causing death (21.3 per cent), 64 strangulations (11 per cent), and the balance primarily involving fire and poisoning. Unlike the United States, Canada has relatively strict gun-control laws that have limited access to firearms, particularly handguns and assault-type weapons. In contrast, the United States is a well-armed

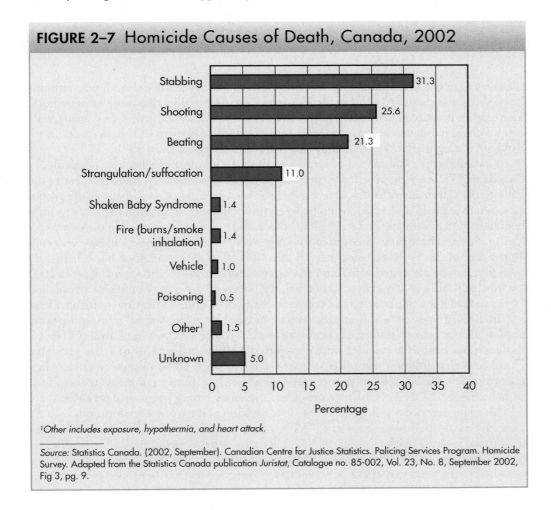

**FIGURE 2–7** Homicide Causes of Death, Canada, 2002

[Bar chart showing Percentage on x-axis (0 to 40):]
- Stabbing: 31.3
- Shooting: 25.6
- Beating: 21.3
- Strangulation/suffocation: 11.0
- Shaken Baby Syndrome: 1.4
- Fire (burns/smoke inhalation): 1.4
- Vehicle: 1.0
- Poisoning: 0.5
- Other[1]: 1.5
- Unknown: 5.0

[1]Other includes exposure, hypothermia, and heart attack.

Source: Statistics Canada. (2002, September). Canadian Centre for Justice Statistics. Policing Services Program. Homicide Survey. Adapted from the Statistics Canada publication *Juristat*, Catalogue no. 85-002, Vol. 23, No. 8, September 2002, Fig 3, pg. 9.

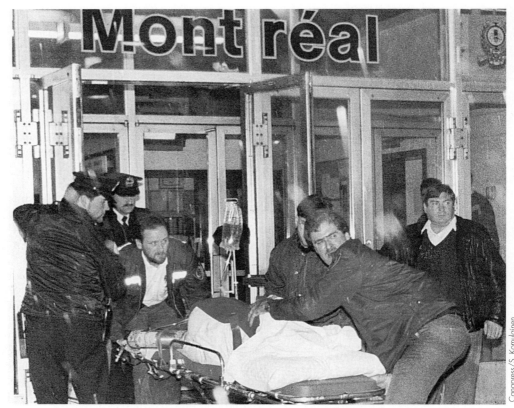

On December 6, 1989, Marc Lepine killed 14 women at the University of Montreal's School of Engineering building, before turning the gun on himself and ending his own life. The Montreal Massacre was the largest mass murder committed on Canadian soil.

society, where guns accounted for 65.6 per cent of all killings in 2000. Handguns outnumbered shotguns by almost 15 to 1 in the U.S. murder statistics, while rifles were a distant third. Knives were used in approximately 13 per cent of all American homicides. In Canada, only recently have handguns become the most common type of firearm used in homicide, with handguns being used more frequently than rifles and shotguns since 1991.

Few killings are committed by strangers. Only 16 per cent of all solved homicides in Canada in 2002 were perpetrated by persons classified as "strangers." In 40 per cent of the killings, the victim and offender were family relatives. In 44 per cent of offences, the parties were acquaintances. The relationship between the victim and offender in the 130 unsolved homicides remains unknown. Over half of all homicide victims were killed in their own residence. Spousal homicides accounted for 20 per cent of all solved homicides, with about 80 per cent of these victims being women. Alcohol and drug consumption has consistently been found to be associated with homicide victims and accused. For those incidents in 2002 for which alcohol consumption was known to the police, 52 per cent of homicide victims and 75 per cent of homicide accused had consumed alcohol or drugs at the time of the incident.

In 2002, 54 per cent of homicides were preceded by an argument. During the same period, 38 per cent of homicides occurred during the commission of another offence. Eighteen per cent of homicides were committed for financial gain or to settle accounts. Homicides that follow from other crimes are more likely to be impulsive rather than planned.[15] Seven killings in 2002 were classified as random murders, three were motivated by hate. Figure 2–7 reveals the proportion of homicides arising from various causes.

Murders may occur in sprees, which "involve killings at two or more locations with almost no time break between murders."[16] Mass murders entail "the killing of four or more victims at one location, within one event."[17] Serial murders happen over time and are officially defined to "involve the killing of several victims in three or more separate events."[18] Days, months, or even years may elapse between the murders. Serial killers have been portrayed frequently in the media. One of the more infamous in recent years is Clifford Robert Olson, who was convicted of killing 11 young victims in 1982. As of the time of writing, Robert William Pickton stands accused of killing 15 women, allegedly depositing their bodies on his farm in Port Coquitlam, British Columbia. Unfortunately, Canadian crime data have not historically been collected in a manner that enables identification of victims of serial killers.[19]

Indeed, the difficulties associated with estimating the number of spree killers, mass murderers, and serial killers in our society at any one time appears to be an insurmountable problem plaguing current methods of collecting data on crime.[20] Because murder is such a serious crime, it consumes substantial police resources. Consequently, over the years the offence has shown an exceptionally high clearance rate. Seventy-seven per cent of all homicides were cleared in 2002.

## Sexual Assault

In 1983, the offences of rape and indecent assault were removed from the *Criminal Code* and replaced with new offences referred to as "sexual assaults." The Supreme Court of Canada ruled in *R. v. Chase* (1988) that the new offence of sexual assault is a broader offence than the old rape law and encompasses all assaults in which the sexual integrity of the victim is violated, even where intercourse does not occur.

**Sexual assault** is the least reported of all violent crimes. According to the Violence Against Women (VAW) Survey conducted by Statistics Canada in 1993, only 6 per cent of all sexual assaults were reported.[21] According to the GSS, conducted in 1999, 78 per cent of sexual assault victims aged 15 or over failed to report the incident to the police. The reasons cited in the VAW survey for not reporting sexual assaults are noted in Table 2–2. In the past, reports of rape were usually taken by seemingly hardened patrol officers or male detectives who may not have been sensitive to the needs of the victim. Historically, the victim's shame and embarrassment played a primary role in explaining the small proportion of rapes reported to the police. In addition, the physical examination that victims had to endure was often a traumatizing experience in itself. Finally, the routine use of the woman's past sexual history, revealed in detail in the courtroom if a trial ensued, led to a large number of such sexual offences going unreported. All of these practices contributed to a considerable hesitancy on the part of rape victims to report their victimizations.

The last decade has seen many changes designed to facilitate accurate reporting of sex offences. Trained female police detectives often act as victim interviewers, physicians have been better educated in handling the psychological needs of victims, and sexual histories are no longer regarded as relevant in most trials.

Sexual assault is a complex crime involving strong emotions and injuries to the victim, which often go beyond the physical. As a consequence, it is not a well-understood offence. Ronald Barri Flowers[22] has identified many cultural myths that surround the crimes of sexual assault and rape. They include the following:

| | | | |
|---|---|---|---|
| Fallacy 1: | Rape cannot occur if the woman resists. | Fact: | Most victims of rape do resist. |
| Fallacy 2: | All women secretly desire to be raped. | Fact: | Although some women may fantasize about rape, none actually want to be raped. |
| Fallacy 3: | The majority of rapes are triggered by women being out alone at night. | Fact: | Most rapes occur following social encounters, such as dates. |
| Fallacy 4: | Rape is a victim-precipitated crime. | Fact: | Rape is an offender-precipitated crime. |
| Fallacy 5: | Only young attractive women are raped. | Fact: | Women of all ages and appearances have been victims of rape. |
| Fallacy 6: | It cannot happen to me. | Fact: | Rape can happen to anyone. |
| Fallacy 7: | Rape is motivated by the need for sexual gratification. | Fact: | Most rapists appear motivated by the need to feel powerful. |
| Fallacy 8: | Most rapes are perpetrated by strangers. | Fact: | Most rapes are committed by acquaintances of the victim. |
| Fallacy 9: | The rapist looks the part. | Fact: | A rapist can be anyone. |
| Fallacy 10: | Rape is an impulsive act. | Fact: | While some rapes are impulsive, many are planned. |

**sexual assault** A form of assault in which the sexual integrity of the victim is violated. This includes, but is not limited to, forcible rape, in which an offender engages in sexual intercourse with a victim, by force and against the will of the victim, or without legal or factual consent.

BOX 2.1 **Theory into Practice**

**Guns, Crime, and Gun Control**

Canada, unlike the United States, does not have anything like the Second Amendment to its Constitution. The Second Amendment guarantees the right to keep and bear arms. Until recent efforts to implement a national firearms registry system, Canada has not had to deal with a gun-control lobby as powerful as the National Rifle Association (NRA) in the United States. However, there is an ongoing debate over the nature of, and limits to, gun control within Canada that is similar to the issue in the United States, in that it pits those who support extensive legislative controls on the sale, ownership, and registration of firearms against those who want as few restraints as possible.

The Canadian Firearms Centre has undertaken a number of research studies dealing with firearms, including their involvement in suicide and domestic homicide. Some of the research findings are as follows:

- In 1995, there were a total of 1125 deaths that involved firearms in Canada. Over the last 10 years, suicides accounted for approximately 80 per cent of all deaths involving firearms.

- In 1995, there were about 4000 suicide deaths in Canada, and of these less, than a quarter involved firearms.

- In the late 1990s, the rate of suicide per 100 000 population was 12.9 in Canada, comparable to the 11.5 rate in the United States. However, Canada's rate of suicide by firearm was only 3.3 per 100 000 population, compared to the U.S. rate of 7.2 per 100 000.

- Between 1975 and 1990, domestic homicides involving firearms accounted for just over one-third of all domestic homicides and 11 per cent of all homicides.

The *Firearms Act*, along with the regulations that relate to this legislation, have been heavily debated in Parliament and in public. The intention of this Act is to foster a culture of safety with respect to the use of firearms. This includes the transportation, storage, and display of firearms, as well as establishing penalties for smuggling and prohibiting military-style assault weapons. The issue of mandatory registration of all firearms has been a particularly contentious issue; however, the *Firearms Act* makes mandatory registration a requirement in order to allow for the tracking of legitimate guns, and to assist police departments. By 2001, all firearms owners in Canada were required to possess a firearms licence. In 2003, the goal to register all firearms in the country was being pursued. Polls conducted in Canada have found that between 70 and 80 per cent of Canadians support some form of gun registration.

## QUESTIONS FOR DISCUSSION

1. Why do you think gun ownership has been such a keenly protected right in the United States, but not in Canada?

2. Do you think gun registration will affect Canada's rate of violent crime? Explain.

*Sources:* Canadian Firearms Centre's website—**www.cfc-ccaf.gc.ca/en/default.asp**; Yvon Dandurand, Y. (1998). Firearms, Accidental Deaths, Suicides and Violent Crime: An Updated Review of the Literature with Special Reference to the Canadian Situation. Vancouver: International Centre for Criminal Law Reform and Criminal Justice Policy.

UCR statistics show 24 350 reported sexual assaults for 2002 (Figure 2–8), virtually unchanged from the number of offences reported for the previous year (24 001). Despite this, the rate of reported sexual assaults has decreased by 35 per cent from eight years ago. Sexual assault is a crime that showed a consistent increase in reported levels from the inception of the new offence in 1983 until 1992. The rate of sexual assaults in 2002 (78 per 100 000) is almost twice the rate of reporting of the offence at its inception in 1983 (41 per 100 000). The criminal law divides sexual assault into three types, referred to by the UCR as Levels I, II, and III. The first level entails the bulk of sexual assaults, the second level involves the presence of a weapon or the causing of bodily harm, while a Level-III sexual assault entails an aggravated offence, including a consequence such as wounding, maiming, disfiguring, or endangering the life of the victim. The increase in reported sexual assaults through the 1980s was found only with respect to Level-I sexual assaults, with the other two offence categories remaining constant.

Most sexual assaults are committed by acquaintances and friends of the victims, and often betray a trust or friendship. In the 1993 VAW Survey, 33 per cent of the women surveyed indicated that they had been sexually assaulted by a date, boyfriend, or other known man (except spouse). **Date rape**, which falls into this category, appears to be far more common than previously believed. In 1997, 28 per cent of sexual assault victims were assaulted by a family member, while overall, 50 per cent of sexual assault victims were assaulted by someone they knew.[23]

Results from the 1999 General Social Survey revealed that of 1.4 million women who had contact with ex-partners over the five-year period being surveyed, 437 000 had

**date rape** Unlawful forced sexual intercourse with a female against her will that occurs within the context of a dating relationship.

**TABLE 2–2** Victims' Reasons for Not Reporting Sexual Assault to Police, Per Cent Distribution, 1993

| Reasons | Total Sexual Assault | Sexual Attack | Unwanted Sexual Touching |
|---|---|---|---|
| Too minor | 44 | 28 | 53 |
| Didn't think the police could do anything | 12 | 14 | 11 |
| Wanted to keep the incident private | 12 | 17 | 8 |
| Dealt with through other channels | 12 | 12 | 12 |
| Shame or embarrassment | 9 | 15 | 6 |
| Didn't want involvement with police or courts | 9 | 12 | 7 |
| Wouldn't be believed | 6 | 8 | 5 |
| Fear of the perpetrator | 3 | 6 | 2 |
| Didn't want him arrested or jailed | 3 | 3 | 2 |
| Didn't want or need help | 2 | —* | 3 |

*Not statistically reliable.
Notes:
[1]Columns do not total 100 per cent because more than one reason could be given.
[2]These data are the most recent available.
*Source*: Adapted from the Statistics Canada publication *Juristat*, Catalogue no. 85–002, Vol. 14, No. 7.

experienced some form of violence at the hands of their ex-partner. Of this group who had experienced such violence, 22 per cent indicated that they had been sexually assaulted by their ex-partner.[24]

Sexual assault is often a planned violent crime that serves the offender's need for power rather than sexual gratification.[25] It is frequently committed by a man known to the victim—as in the case of date rape. Victims may be held captive and subjected to repeated assaults.[26] In the crime of heterosexual sexual assault, any female—regardless of age, appearance, or occupation—is a potential victim. Through personal violation, humiliation, and physical battering, sexual assault offenders seek a sense of personal aggrandizement and feelings of dominance. In contrast, victims of sexual assault often experience a lessened sense of

**FIGURE 2–8** Rates of Sexual Assault Reported to Police per 100 000 Population, 1978–2002

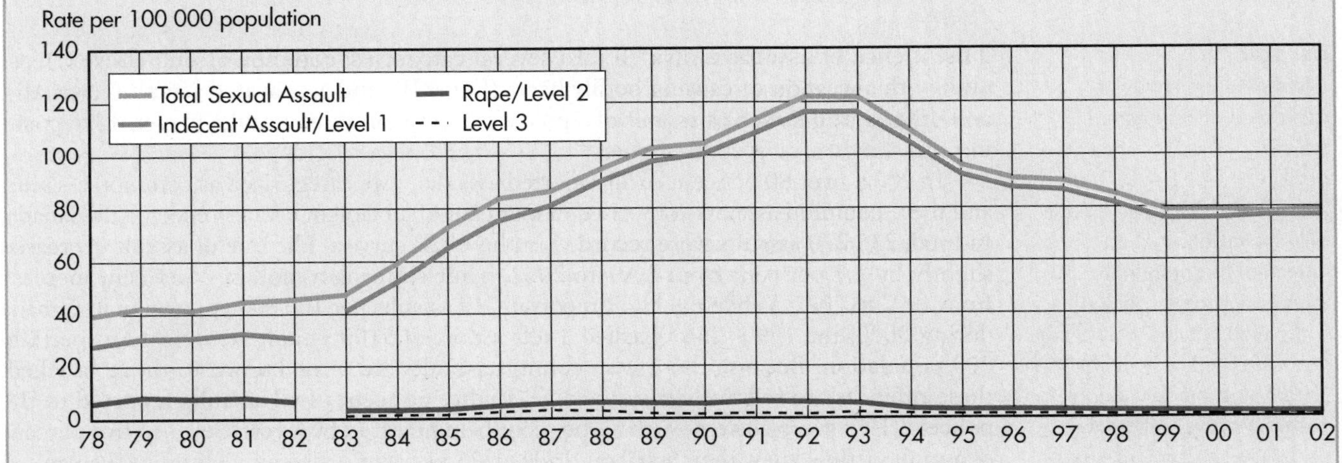

*Source*: Adapted from the Statistics Canada publication *Juristat*, Catalogue no. 85-002, Vol. 17, No. 8, July 1997 and Vol. 22, No. 6, July 2002, Figure 1, pg. 3.

personal worth; increased feelings of despair, helplessness, and vulnerability; a misplaced sense of guilt; and a lack of control over their personal lives.

## Robbery

**robbery** The unlawful taking or attempted taking of property that is in the immediate possession of another, by force or the threat of force. Armed robbery differs from unarmed or strong-armed robbery with respect to the presence of a weapon.

**Robbery**, sometimes confused with burglary, is a personal crime and involves a face-to-face confrontation between victim and perpetrator. Weapons may be used, or strong-armed robbery may occur through intimidation, especially where gangs threaten victims by sheer numbers. Purse snatching and pocket picking are not classified as robbery by the UCR Program, but are included under the category "theft."

In 2002, almost one in ten violent crimes found in the UCR was a robbery. As with most violent crime rates in 2002, the rate of robbery declined slightly (decreasing 3 per cent over 2001), showing an overall decrease in recent years (dropping over 10 per cent from 1997). Interestingly, the use of firearms in robberies has been declining. Firearms were used in 13 per cent of robberies reported in 2002, reflecting a 10 per cent decrease from the preceding year. The number of robberies with firearms declined 64 per cent from 1992 to 2002. In 2001, the primary targets for robbery were individual persons (58 per cent of all robberies). Next in line were commercial establishments such as stores and gas stations (18.5 per cent of all robberies). Non-commercial establishments such as government departments, schools, churches, and hospitals were as likely to be a robbery target (18 per cent) as a commercial establishment, followed, surprisingly, by banks and financial institutions at 2 per cent of all robberies.[27] Only three robberies in that year involved armoured cars as the target. In 2002, 26 700 robberies were reported to the police.

Manitoba, British Columbia, and Saskatchewan display the highest robbery rates in the country, with 142, 111, and 106 robberies per 100 000 population, respectively. The national rate is 85 per 100 000 population. Of the major metropolitan areas in the country, the highest robbery rates were found in Winnipeg (223) and Vancouver (164).[28]

Whenever a robbery occurs, the UCR Program historically scored the event as one robbery, even though there may have been a number of victims who were robbed during the event. With the move towards incident-driven reporting (discussed later in this chapter), however, the UCR is beginning to make data available on the number of individuals robbed in each instance of robbery. Because statistics on crime show only the most serious offence that occurred during a particular episode, robberies are often hidden when they occur in conjunction with other, more serious, crimes. Robbery is primarily an urban offence, and most arrestees are young males who are members of minority groups. The incident-based UCR reports indicate that the robbery rate in large cities is well above the national average. In addition to the high rate noted above for Vancouver, high rates are also regularly found in other urban centres. Ninety-one per cent of individuals accused of robbery in 1993 were male, and 55 per cent were between the ages of 15 and 24.

## Assault

**assault** The unlawful intentional inflicting, or attempted or threatened inflicting, of injury upon a person by another. Historically, "assault" meant only the creation of an imminent threat to inflict injury on another person. A completed act constituted the separate offence of battery. Under most modern penal codes, however, attempted and completed acts are put together under the generic name "assault."

The offence of **assault** is divided into several categories: common assault (Level I), assault with a weapon or causing bodily harm (Level II), and aggravated assault (Level III), and other assaults such as assault of a police officer. Common assaults may involve pushing and shoving, or even fist fights.

In 2002, over 80 per cent of all reported assaults were categorized as common assaults, and these common assaults comprised 62 per cent of all violent crimes reported in Canada. In total, 235 270 assaults were recorded in the UCR survey. The rate of assault decreased slightly by 1.7 per cent from 2001 to 2002, while showing a modest 2 per cent increase from 1992 to 2002. While the UCR reported 749 assaults per 100 000 population in Canada during 2002, the 1999 GSS revealed a self-report of 5100 assault victimizations per 100 000 population. Because those who commit assaults are often known to those attacked, these offences are relatively easy to solve. Eighty per cent of all assaults reported to the police in 1995 were cleared, with 52 per cent being cleared by arrest. Seventy-five percent of assault victims knew their assailant. Indeed, 25 per cent of assault victims were assaulted by their spouse or ex-spouse, and 8 per cent by a close friend, including intimate and ex-intimate relationships. Only 25 per cent of victims were assaulted by strangers in 1995.

## Break and Entry

Although it may carry the potential for personal and even violent confrontations, **break and entry** is primarily a property crime. Burglars are interested in financial gain and usually fence (that is, illegally sell) stolen items to recover a fraction of their cash value. In 2002, 274 894 break and entries were reported to the police. Fifty-nine per cent of these break-ins were of residential properties. The overall rate of break and entries declined by 2.6 per cent in 2002.

Many people fear nighttime burglary of their residence. They imagine themselves asleep in bed as a stranger breaks into their home and then conjure up visions of a violent confrontation. While such scenarios do occur, daytime burglary is more common. Many families now have two or more income earners, and since children are in school during the day, some homes—and even entire neighbourhoods—are virtually unoccupied during daylight hours. This shift in patterns of social activity has led to an ongoing burglary threat against residences during daytime.

Breaking and entering is generally a non-violent crime. In 1999, only 1 per cent of all break-ins involved violence. Residents who were home during a burglary suffered a risk of violence. Statistics Canada does not presently compile data to give an accurate picture of the use of violence during a break-in. However, they recently indicated that a non-representative sample of 106 Canadian police departments, representing 41 per cent of the national crime volume, identified between 1154 and 2449 break-ins entailing a robbery.[29] Accurate numbers do not exist since there is no currently agreed-upon definition of a "home invasion," or break-in combined with a robbery. Property crimes generally involve low rates of clearance. Break and entry is no exception. The clearance rate for break and entry has remained fairly constant over time, and in 2001 was only 16 per cent.[30] Burglars are usually unknown to their victims, and even if known, they conceal their identity by committing their crime when the victim is absent.[31]

## Theft

In Canada, thefts are distinguished by a set dollar amount. Thefts are divided into those for which the value of what is stolen exceeds $5000 and those for which the value is $5000 or below. Categorizing the crime by dollar amount, however, can present unique problems, as during high fiscal inflation periods, when Parliament must enact statutory revisions to adjust the sum differentiating minor crimes from major ones. These revisions occurred in 1995 when the cut-off was raised from $1000 to $5000, and in 1986 when the cut-off was raised from $200 to $1000.

Theft is a kind of "catch-all" category, and reported thefts can involve a diversity of materials with values that range anywhere from pocket change to the stealing of a $100-million aircraft. Specifically excluded from the count of theft for reporting purposes are crimes of motor vehicle theft, fraud, such as embezzlement, and "con" games, and possession of stolen property that are listed as separate offences. Theft has been traditionally thought of as a crime that requires physical possession of the item appropriated. Hence, most computer crimes, including thefts engineered through online access or thefts of software and information itself, have typically not been scored as theft—unless electronic circuitry, disks, or machines themselves were actually stolen.

Reports to the police in 2002 showed 688 474 thefts nationwide. This accounted for almost one-third of all *Criminal Code* incidents reported in 2002, and more than one-half of all property offences. The most common form of theft in recent years has been theft of motor vehicle parts, accessories, and contents. The theft of tires, wheels, stereos, hubcaps, radar detectors, CB radios, cassette tapes, compact discs, and cellular phones accounts for many of the items reported stolen. Forty percent of all thefts are from motor vehicles.

Theft is the most frequently reported major crime according to the UCR. It may also be the UCR's most under-reported crime category because small thefts rarely come to the attention of the police.

## Motor Vehicle Theft

For record-keeping purposes, the UCR Program defines a motor vehicle as an automobile, truck, van, bus, recreational vehicle, tractor-trailer, motorcycle, construction/farm equipment

**break and entry** The unlawful entry of a dwelling house, or other building or structure, railway vehicle, vessel, aircraft or trailer, or a pen or enclosure for fur-bearing animals. Such entry is unlawful if it is for the purpose of committing an indictable offence.

**motor vehicle theft**
The unlawful taking, or
attempted taking, of a self-
propelled road vehicle owned
by another, with the intent to
deprive him or her of it
permanently or temporarily.
The stealing of trains, planes,
boats, construction
equipment, and most farm
machinery is classified as
theft, *not* as motor vehicle
theft, under the UCR
reporting program.

or other motorized land vehicle, go-cart, dune buggy, or snowmobile. Excluded are trains, aircraft, ships, boats, and spacecraft—whose theft would be scored as theft.[32]

**Motor vehicle theft** is a crime in which most occurrences are reported to law enforcement agencies. Insurance companies require police reports before they will reimburse car owners for their losses. Some reports of motor vehicle thefts, however, may be false. People who have damaged their own vehicles in solitary crashes, or who have been unable to sell them, may try to force insurance companies to "buy" them through reports of theft.

In 2002, 161 506 motor vehicles were reported stolen. This number reflects a 5-per cent increase over the previous year, and the first increase in five years. The increasing popularity of minivans and sport-utility vehicles has manifested itself in the motor vehicle theft statistics. Motor vehicle thefts involving vehicles that were identified as trucks, a category that includes minivans and sport-utility vehicles, increased 47 per cent from 1992 to 2002. However, the most popular target for motor vehicle thieves identified by the Vehicle Information Centre of Canada was the late model Hyundai Tiburon. Other late model cars that are frequently stolen include the Acura Integra, the Honda Civic, and the Volkswagen Golf GTI.[33] Theft rates for many late model domestic four-door sedans are very low. Many car manufacturers have begun to install immobilizer devices into new cars in an effort to minimize vehicle thefts. The annual cost of motor vehicle theft is exceptionally high. In 2000, the Insurance Bureau of Canada estimated the value of property stolen or lost through motor vehicle crime was $600 million. The clearance rate for motor vehicle theft was only 13 per cent in 1995, reflecting the lowest clearance rate of all categories identified by Statistics Canada in that year. Many stolen vehicles are routinely and quickly disassembled, with parts being resold through "chop shops." In such shops, stolen vehicles are disassembled, permitting the parts to be sold on the used-parts market. Auto parts are, of course, much more difficult to identify and trace than are intact vehicles. In some parts of the country, chop shops operate like big business, and one shop may strip a dozen or more cars per day. Motor vehicle theft can turn violent in cases of "carjacking"—a crime in which offenders force the occupants of a car onto the street before stealing the vehicle.

Arrest reports for motor vehicle theft show that the typical offender is a young male. Forty per cent of all offenders charged with motor vehicle theft in 2002 were between the ages of 12 and 17. Typically, more than 80 per cent of such offenders are under the age of 25. In 2001, 92 per cent of adult offenders charged with this offence were male.

# OTHER *CRIMINAL CODE* OFFENCES

The "other" category of *Criminal Code* offences does not include traffic offences covered by the *Criminal Code*. However, it does include a variety of offences not neatly included in the violent and property categories outlined above. Of the 2.4 million non-traffic *Criminal Code* offences recorded in 2002, almost 840 000 of them fit into this "other" category. The most frequently reported of such offences is the offence of mischief. In 2002, 332 723 incidents of mischief were recorded. This offence is broadly defined and includes damage to property, interfering with the use of property, and altering or damaging data. This offence is usually hard to prove, with the identity of the offender often remaining elusive. Typically, only about 15 per cent of all mischief offences are cleared, with only a small fraction of these being cleared by charge—usually the worst charge-clearance rate of all offences reported by Statistics Canada.

**Arson** is also included in the "other *Criminal Code*" category. In 2002, 13 192 incidents of arson were recorded. This reflects remarkable stability over the past several years wherein the arson rate has only fluctuated from 42 to 47 incidents per 100 000 population since 1992. Arson clearance rates are also notoriously low, with only 20 per cent of such offences being cleared by the police.

**arson** The burning or
attempted burning of
property with or without intent
to defraud. Some instances of
arson are the result of
malicious mischief, while
others involve attempts to
claim insurance monies.
Still others are committed in
an effort to disguise other
crimes, such as murder,
burglary, and larceny.

Prostitution-related offences showed a 12 per cent increase in 2002 over the preceding year. Despite an increase in 1995, the number and rate of prostitution-related offences still do not match those set in the early 1990s. Indeed, the rate of prostitution offences has declined by 49 per cent since 1992. Prostitution-related offences are rarely reported to the police due to the nature of the incidents, and accordingly, police-recorded levels of prostitution activity reflect the enforcement practices of the police more than the actual amount of prostitution-related activity occurring in Canada.

Court rulings making it easier or more difficult to prosecute prostitutes for soliciting have had a significant impact on prostitution-offence rates in the past, as have changes in the statutory wording governing such prosecutions. Of the 5773 persons charged with prostitution-related crimes recorded in 2002, 47 per cent of them involved male offenders. While many of them were undoubtedly prostitutes or living off the avails of prostitution, most were customers. The willingness and ability of the police to charge such "johns" may reflect the significant proportion of males in the numbers of prostitution-related activities recorded in the UCR data. The 76-per-cent clearance rate for prostitution-related offences recorded in 2001 illustrates the proactive police role in identifying such offences. Typically, a report results from an arrest, not from a member of the public requesting police to investigate.

## Criminal Code *Traffic Offences*

As noted earlier, analysts of Canada's crime picture often rely on Statistics Canada's UCR, which typically looks at the number and rate of *Criminal Code* offences reported to the police, other than traffic-related *Criminal Code* offences. Traffic-related offences are addressed separately since they are associated with activity that typically comes under provincial jurisdiction over motor vehicles and highway traffic. The provincial legislation in the same area permits discretionary police practices across the country to deal with traffic-related matters. The number of offenders charged with impaired driving, for example, does not reflect the actual amount of impaired driving since some jurisdictions encourage the police to deal with impaired driving scenarios through provincial legislation. This often permits temporarily suspending the licence of a suspected impaired driver at the discretion of the police officer at the scene, rather than charging the offender under the *Criminal Code* with an offence.

The rate of impaired driving charges steadily declined until 2001, when the statistics revealed a 7-per-cent increase in impaired driving charges. This increase followed a 20-year decline in the rate of impaired driving charges. In 2002, 80 789 incidents of impaired driving were recorded, reflecting a 3 per cent decrease in the rate of this crime from 2001. Figure 2–9 charts the declining rate of Canadians charged with impaired driving since 1992. Whether these data establish a reduction in the amount of impaired driving is unclear. Without quantifying the numbers of persons checked per year by the police and the extent of the use of roadside suspensions, claims made in this regard remain speculative. Beginning in 2001, the RCMP began including incidents in which roadside suspensions were issued, in the UCR impaired driving data. At least a portion of the apparent increase in impaired driving reported in 2001 is attributable to this change in reporting practices. In 2002, all police agencies in Canada adopted this method of recording impaired driving incidents.

## *Drugs*

In 1997, Canada moved to combine its criminal drug legislation into one act with the passing of the *Controlled Drugs and Substances Act*. Prior to this, the federal government regulated the drug trade through the *Narcotic Control Act*, which dealt with illegal drugs such as marijuana, cocaine, heroin, and its related drugs, and the *Food and Drug Act*, which dealt with restricted and controlled drugs such as LSD, barbiturates, amphetamines, and other chemical drugs. Of the 92 590 drug incidents recorded in 2002, more than 75 per cent of them pertained to marijuana. The number of drug incidents other than marijuana-related offences were fairly constant between 1992 and 2002, while cocaine and heroin-related incidents have consistently declined over this 10-year period. Changes in drug-related crime rates are heavily influenced by changes in police enforcement tactics in the same way that the rates of prostitution and impaired driving offences are affected.[34]

## *Regional Variations*

There is considerable variation in the rate of reported crime in different regions of Canada. Over time, the Maritime provinces consistently have had the lowest rates of crime. The crime rate is somewhat higher in Quebec, higher still in Ontario, increasing through the

Prairie provinces, with the Western provinces typically showing the highest crime rates. Crime rates in the three territories have historically been the highest in the whole country. In 2001, Newfoundland, the eastern-most province, displayed the lowest overall crime rate at 5635 offences per 100 000 population, while Saskatchewan displayed the highest crime rate with 13 458 offences per 100 000 population. Yet the three territories dwarf the provinces by comparison, with rates of 24 865, 30 149, and 24 958 offences per 100 000 population in the Yukon, Northwest Territories, and Nunavut, respectively. The extent to which such regional variations can be explained by the regional differences in rates of unemployment and the numbers of economically marginalized First Nations Canadians in a given area has been the subject of some inquiry,[35] although concrete conclusions in this regard remain elusive. James Hackler speculates that Western Canadians appear to be more willing to engage agencies of social control in response to crime, implying that differences in crime rates across the country are more attributable to variations in such practices than to any real differences in the amount of crime.[36] Table 2–3 shows selected *Criminal Code* incidents according to province and territory.

## Recent and Ongoing Changes in the UCR

Changes are happening to the *Uniform Crime Reports*. Beginning in the early 1980s, Statistics Canada began a switch to the development of an incident-based reporting method. By 2002, 123 police agencies in nine provinces had made the switch to the new method of recording incidents. As of this time, 59 per cent of the total volume of *Criminal Code* incidents was being recorded through the new procedure. The data so generated are not representative of the nation as a whole, and accordingly, one must be careful in making inferences from such data about the nation as a whole. The old system depended upon statistical tabulations of crime data that were often little more than frequency counts. Under the new system, many details are gathered about each criminal incident. Included among them are information on place of occurrence, weapon used, type and value of property damaged or stolen, personal characteristics of the offender and the victim, nature of any relationship between the two, nature of the disposition of the complaint, and so on. The new reporting system will replace the old aggregate UCR survey in time. In the interim, continuity is maintained across the country by converting the incident-based data to aggregate data for the annual reports.

### Self-Report and Victimization Surveys

The UCR Survey provides an inaccurate picture of crime in Canada. Criminologists frequently refer to the loss of data created by the UCR survey's reliance on police-recorded data as the effect produced by a "crime funnel." The crime-funnel analogy shows that the amount of crime recorded by the police is typically less than the amount of crime occurring in the community. Not all crimes that are committed are detected by anyone. For example, many individuals drive home from a night of drinking while impaired without being detected. They wend their way home, where they fall asleep, with the act of impaired driving never being registered as a criminal act. Many crimes are detected, but not reported to the police; for example, a sober person witnesses his or her friend driving while impaired, yet fails to report it to the police.

Many factors impact on the decision to report an offence to the police, such

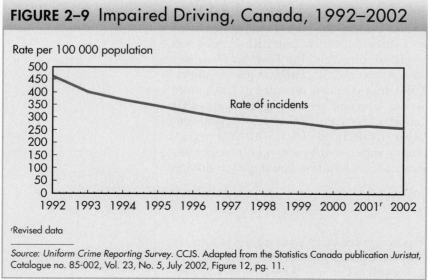

**FIGURE 2–9** Impaired Driving, Canada, 1992–2002

Rate per 100 000 population

Rate of incidents

ʳRevised data

Source: Uniform Crime Reporting Survey. CCJS. Adapted from the Statistics Canada publication *Juristat*, Catalogue no. 85-002, Vol. 23, No. 5, July 2002, Figure 12, pg. 11.

**TABLE 2-3** Selected *Criminal Code* Incidents, Canada and the Provinces/Territories, 2001[1]

| | NL | PE | NS | NB | QC[2] | ON[2] | MB | SK | AB | BC[3] | YK | NT | NU | Canada |
|---|---|---|---|---|---|---|---|---|---|---|---|---|---|---|
| **Population, 2001** | 533 761 | 138 514 | 942 691 | 757 077 | 7 410 504 | 11 874 436 | 1 150 034 | 1 015 783 | 3 064 249 | 4 095 934 | 29 885 | 40 860 | 28 159 | 31 081 887 |
| **Homicides** | | | | | | | | | | | | | | |
| number | 2 | 1 | 9 | 9 | 118 | 178 | 36 | 27 | 70 | 126 | 0 | 4 | 2 | 582 |
| rate | 0.4 | 0.7 | 1.0 | 1.2 | 1.6 | 1.5 | 3.1 | 2.7 | 2.2 | 3.0 | 0.0 | 9.7 | 7.0 | 1.9 |
| % change in rate* | 100.8 | -50.4 | -0.2 | 12.4 | -16.1 | 3.2 | 5.7 | 0.5 | -1.7 | 48.6 | -100.0 | -0.4 | -34.7 | 4.2 |
| **Sexual assaults (1, 2, 3)** | | | | | | | | | | | | | | |
| number | 552 | 147 | 892 | 744 | 4190 | 8282 | 1488 | 1491 | 2591 | 3421 | 97 | 179 | 276 | 24 350 |
| rate | 104 | 105 | 94 | 98 | 56 | 69 | 129 | 147 | 83 | 83 | 324 | 432 | 961 | 78 |
| % change in rate* | -9.1 | 31.5 | 5.9 | -12.2 | 16.4 | -3.6 | 7.7 | 5.0 | -4.2 | -7.9 | 37.8 | 23.8 | 18.5 | 0.3 |
| **Assaults (1, 2, 3)** | | | | | | | | | | | | | | |
| number | 3966 | 987 | 8527 | 5914 | 37 879 | 77 187 | 14 979 | 14 832 | 26 388 | 39 910 | 963 | 2070 | 1668 | 235 270 |
| rate | 746 | 705 | 903 | 782 | 508 | 640 | 1302 | 1466 | 848 | 964 | 3218 | 5000 | 5809 | 749 |
| % change in rate* | 1.5 | 13.2 | 8.2 | 0.3 | 1.4 | -6.1 | 1.4 | 0.4 | -2.1 | -1.0 | 0.8 | 19.5 | 5.6 | -1.7 |
| **Robbery** | | | | | | | | | | | | | | |
| number | 83 | 19 | 557 | 231 | 6887 | 8908 | 1635 | 1068 | 2637 | 4616 | 29 | 21 | 9 | 26 700 |
| rate | 16 | 14 | 59 | 31 | 92 | 74 | 142 | 106 | 85 | 111 | 97 | 51 | 31 | 85 |
| % change in rate* | 24.4 | -21.4 | -11.3 | 34.2 | -3.5 | -2.3 | -10.1 | -1.2 | -4.9 | -1.2 | 8.3 | 23.0 | -26.6 | -3.1 |
| **Violent crime – Total** | | | | | | | | | | | | | | |
| number | 4751 | 1210 | 10 380 | 7373 | 53 625 | 99 990 | 18 925 | 18 331 | 33 539 | 49 641 | 1137 | 2355 | 2037 | 303 294 |
| rate | 894 | 865 | 1099 | 974 | 719 | 829 | 1644 | 1812 | 1077 | 1199 | 3800 | 5688 | 7094 | 965 |
| % change in rate* | -0.1 | 14.6 | 5.9 | -1.7 | 1.5 | -5.3 | 1.5 | 0.5 | -2.1 | -1.4 | 2.3 | 17.2 | 6.3 | -1.6 |
| **Breaking & entering** | | | | | | | | | | | | | | |
| number | 3460 | 966 | 6581 | 4805 | 70 370 | 81 181 | 12 616 | 15 055 | 27 214 | 50 376 | 534 | 907 | 829 | 274 894 |
| rate | 651 | 690 | 697 | 635 | 944 | 673 | 1096 | 1488 | 874 | 1216 | 1785 | 2191 | 2887 | 875 |
| % change in rate* | 8.4 | 29.2 | 0.7 | 0.4 | -5.3 | -2.8 | -5.5 | 0.0 | 4.6 | -3.9 | -12.0 | 27.6 | 16.0 | -2.6 |
| **Motor vehicle theft** | | | | | | | | | | | | | | |
| number | 599 | 244 | 2639 | 1576 | 36 904 | 45 835 | 12 121 | 6904 | 17 948 | 35 980 | 220 | 336 | 200 | 161 506 |
| rate | 113 | 174 | 279 | 208 | 495 | 380 | 1053 | 682 | 576 | 869 | 735 | 812 | 697 | 514 |
| % change in rate* | -5.4 | -11.3 | -3.6 | -9.1 | -10.9 | -8.4 | -8.3 | -13.1 | 1.0 | 7.2 | -7.2 | 16.6 | -19.4 | -5.1 |

**TABLE 2-3** Selected *Criminal Code* Incidents, Canada and the Provinces/Territories, 2001[1]

| | NL | PE | NS | NB | QC[2] | ON[2] | MB | SK | AB | BC[3] | YK | NT | NU | Canada |
|---|---|---|---|---|---|---|---|---|---|---|---|---|---|---|
| **Other theft** | | | | | | | | | | | | | | |
| number | 7567 | 2791 | 19 497 | 12 100 | 119 983 | 219 131 | 29 079 | 29 428 | 82 710 | 163 231 | 1269 | 1074 | 614 | 688 474 |
| rate | 1423 | 1995 | 2064 | 1599 | 1609 | 1816 | 2527 | 2908 | 2656 | 3942 | 4241 | 2594 | 2138 | 2192 |
| % change in rate* | 10.8 | 4.3 | -0.9 | 2.7 | -3.4 | -0.4 | 0.9 | -2.0 | 7.0 | 0.1 | 14.9 | 13.2 | 18.6 | 0.2 |
| **Property crime – Total** | | | | | | | | | | | | | | |
| number | 12 875 | 4483 | 31 385 | 21 280 | 248 896 | 389 947 | 57 277 | 57 447 | 145 175 | 268 699 | 2225 | 2503 | 1753 | 1 243 945 |
| rate | 2422 | 3204 | 3322 | 2812 | 3339 | 3231 | 4977 | 5678 | 4663 | 6488 | 7436 | 6045 | 6105 | 3960 |
| % change in rate* | 5.7 | 8.2 | -2.7 | -0.1 | -4.5 | -1.1 | -3.2 | -3.2 | 5.7 | 0.6 | 3.8 | 16.7 | 10.1 | -0.8 |
| **Offensive weapons** | | | | | | | | | | | | | | |
| number | 214 | 38 | 623 | 397 | 1204 | 4925 | 1112 | 899 | 2113 | 4121 | 60 | 85 | 43 | 15 834 |
| rate | 40 | 27 | 66 | 52 | 16 | 41 | 97 | 89 | 68 | 100 | 201 | 205 | 150 | 50 |
| % change in rate* | 13.7 | -19.7 | 0.1 | 3.0 | -0.7 | -11.7 | -2.9 | 14.8 | 9.7 | 4.8 | 8.1 | -1.6 | -38.1 | -1.2 |
| **Mischief** | | | | | | | | | | | | | | |
| number | 5880 | 1827 | 11 824 | 7510 | 50 070 | 96 243 | 26 335 | 21 061 | 44 019 | 60 621 | 1688 | 3802 | 1843 | 332 723 |
| rate | 1106 | 1306 | 1252 | 993 | 672 | 797 | 2288 | 2082 | 1414 | 1464 | 5641 | 9183 | 6418 | 1059 |
| % change in rate* | 8.0 | 12.3 | 4.0 | 3.4 | -4.0 | -3.9 | 1.6 | 2.5 | -1.1 | -0.3 | 22.4 | 16.0 | 5.8 | -1.1 |
| **Other Criminal Code—Total** | | | | | | | | | | | | | | |
| number | 13 377 | 4980 | 30 125 | 21 348 | 122 211 | 242 993 | 53 733 | 59 484 | 111 159 | 160 007 | 4633 | 8482 | 4476 | 837 008 |
| rate | 2516 | 3559 | 3189 | 2821 | 1639 | 2013 | 4669 | 5879 | 3570 | 3864 | 15 483 | 20 486 | 15 588 | 2664 |
| % change in rate* | 1.8 | 13.9 | 1.8 | 6.6 | 0.5 | -2.9 | 1.1 | 0.8 | -0.1 | 2.2 | 12.6 | 1.1 | 18.3 | 0.1 |
| **Criminal Code—Total without traffic offences** | | | | | | | | | | | | | | |
| number | 31 003 | 10 673 | 71 890 | 50 001 | 424 732 | 732 930 | 129 935 | 135 262 | 289 873 | 478 347 | 7995 | 13 340 | 8266 | 2 384 247 |
| rate | 5832 | 7628 | 7609 | 6608 | 5697 | 6073 | 11 290 | 13 368 | 9310 | 11 551 | 26 718 | 32 220 | 28 786 | 7590 |
| % change in rate* | 3.1 | 11.5 | 0.3 | 2.4 | -2.4 | -2.3 | -0.8 | -1.0 | 2.5 | 0.9 | 8.5 | 6.4 | 13.3 | -0.6 |

*In comparison to the previous year's rate. Percent change based on unrounded rates.

[1] Rates are calculated on the basis of 100 000 population. The population estimates come from the *Annual Demographic Statistics, 2001* report, produced by Statistics Canada. Populations as of July 1: updated postcensal estimates for 2000 and preliminary postcensal estimates for 2001.

[2] OPP data for 2001 were not available due to implementation of a new records management system. As such, 2000 OPP data have been substituted.

[3] Data for 2001 include estimates for 3 months for Vancouver Police and 2 months for Port Moody Police, covering the phase-in period required for a new records management system. In addition, from September 2000 to September 2001, as a result of labour action, there were decreases in the number of crimes reported to the Vancouver Police Department for certain offences. As a result, the number of *Criminal Code* offences reported by Vancouver was affected during this period.

Source: *Uniform Crime Reporting Survey*. CCJS. Adapted from the Statistics Canada publication *Juristat*, Catalogue no. 85-002, Vol. 22, No. 6, July 2002, Table 3, pg. 16.

as the seriousness of the incident, the perception of whether the police can do anything about the offence, and fear of revenge or embarrassment. Of those offences reported to the police, many are lost from the crime data since the complaint takers at police departments will, from time to time, talk victims into finding other ways to resolve their predicaments rather than bring in police involvement. Similarly, police dispatchers must prioritize scarce police resources, further filtering the number of reported offences that eventually proceed further through the crime funnel. Once a decision is made to assign a file number and dispatch a police officer to deal with a call for service, the incident has the potential to make its way into the UCR crime statistics. At this level of analysis, crime data are recorded by the police. This is the point at which the UCR data are generated. Data generated further down the funnel, such as arrest numbers, charged offences, guilty verdicts, or incarceration numbers, are significantly more distant from the actual crime picture than are UCR police-recorded data.

In an effort to obtain a more accurate picture of how much crime is occurring in society, social scientists have resorted to other survey techniques. Potentially, the actual amount of crime occurring in society could be ascertained through self-report surveys. If we could rely on everyone to truthfully answer questions posed to them about their criminal activities, one could theoretically ascertain how many crimes occurred in the past year by asking everyone in Canada about their activities over the past year. Obviously, many people are reluctant to confess to researchers about offences they have committed, particularly if they have not been caught for these offences. Offenders who like to talk about their escapades quickly end up in the criminal justice system. Despite assurances of confidentiality, many people will remain reluctant to confess to offences for which they have thus far evaded detection.

However, such self-report surveys have typically been conducted with youthful offenders. The use of self-report techniques came to prominence with the publication in the U.S. of research findings by Short and Nye in 1958.[37] In Canada, self-report studies have been scant, with one of the few identifiable studies being conducted by Kennedy and Dutton in Alberta in 1989.[38] The authors found that 12.8 per cent of their urban sample and 8.3 per cent of their rural sample reported engaging in acts of spousal assault.[39]

The most effective tool for police agencies in creating good relations is the officers themselves.

# VICTIMIZATION SURVEYS

Victimization surveys represent an effort to uncover what some had been calling the "dark figure" (or unreported offences) of crime. This type of survey avoids some of the problems encountered in self-report surveys. In particular, the problems associated with offenders' reluctance to volunteer information about their past crimes can be avoided by taking a different kind of survey. Rather than surveying individuals to find out about their offending background, surveys have been conducted that inquire into a respondent's victimization background. Presumably, victims are more willing to discuss their experiences than are offenders. Although this method of gathering data takes us one step away from the actual offender, thereby reducing the accuracy of the data to some degree, the willingness of victims to discuss their past victimizations over the willingness of offenders to discuss past offending actions presents a potentially better mechanism for achieving a reasonably accurate picture of the level of crime occurring in society. Of course, many so-called "victimless" crimes will never be identified through victim surveys. Additionally, there is an unknown amount of crime occurring that does not even get detected by the victim and which will not make its way into victimization surveys. However, such incidents will likely be relatively minor in nature, with a consequentially minimal impact on our assessment of the amount of crime suffered by victims in our society.

An effort to identify the amount of crime occurring in Canadian society through the use of a victimization survey was pioneered in 1982 when the federal Ministry of the Solicitor General, in conjunction with Statistics Canada, sponsored a large-scale victimization survey in seven major cities: Greater Vancouver, Edmonton, Winnipeg, Toronto, Montreal, Halifax-Dartmouth, and St. John's.[40] The Canadian Urban Victimization Survey (CUVS) inquired into victimizations endured in 1981, as disclosed in 61 000 telephone interviews. While the methodology of the survey was limited by the non-representativeness of the sample (only urban residents were canvassed), and the small number of different offences being examined (only eight categories of offence were addressed), the survey produced fascinating preliminary findings about the inherent problems in relying on UCR data for an overview of the amount of crime occurring in our society. For example, it was found that of approximately 1.6 million offences endured by this sample, 58 per cent of victimizations were not reported to police. Indeed, personal theft victimizations went unreported 71 per cent of the time. Our official crime data were clearly off the mark as an estimate of the actual amount of crime occurring in Canadian society.[41]

It was also noted in the CUVS that although the survey uncovered more than twice as many crimes as reported in the UCR data, two-thirds of the incidents that went unreported were classified by the victim as "too minor" to require the intervention of the criminal justice system.

## The General Social Survey

In the mid-1980s, Statistics Canada initiated the General Social Survey (GSS) in order to reduce the gaps left by its regular methods of generating statistical data. Although the survey is conducted annually, the survey does not address all issues in each year. The core content varies from year to year and addresses one of health, education, social environment, or personal risk. The third cycle of the GSS occurred in 1988, which was the first year in which personal risk was the core area being surveyed. This was also the core area for the eighth cycle of the survey, conducted in 1993, and the fourteenth cycle in 1999. The survey of personal risk examines the risk of accident and the risk of criminal victimization. No attempt has been made to survey the entire population, but rather a sample of around 26 000 non-institutionalized individuals was drawn in the most recent survey from the target population of all persons aged 15 and older living in the 10 provinces. The survey was conducted by telephone. Given the size of the sample, Statistics Canada has felt comfortable drawing inferences to the population as a whole, and some analysis at the regional level has also been carried out. However, the sample size does not permit analysis at any smaller level of analysis.

The GSS, while drawing a smaller sample than the earlier Canadian Urban Victimization Survey's sample, was designed to draw a representative sample from across the country, including both urban and rural residents. Since the sampling methods for the GSS and the CUVS were different, comparisons between the victimizations encountered in the early 1980s, identified in the CUVS, cannot be made with those identified in the 1988 GSS. However, since the GSS has now been carried out three times on the subject matter of "personal risk" (1988, 1993, and 1999), comparisons of victimization data among these three time periods can now be made. But changes to the 1999 survey with regard to questions about family violence and assault make comparisons with the earlier surveys a bit tricky.

In 1988, 1993, and 1999, the GSS revealed that victimization rates were very similar, with 24 to 25 per cent of Canadians sampled revealing that they had been victimized in a crime or attempted crime during the preceding year.[42] Canada's victimization rate has not changed significantly over the three surveys. Incidents of theft have increased slightly between the 1993 and 1999 surveys. In addition and notably, reporting to the police has declined somewhat according to the most recent survey. Of the eight major crimes assessed in the GSS, only 37 per cent were reported to the police. In contrast, the reporting rate was 42 per cent as recently as 1993. While the GSS showed the overall victimization rate to be constant through the 1990s, the UCR revealed significant decreases in the recorded crime rate during the same period. Many factors can explain the differences in data. The fact that the GSS only targets Canadians aged 15 and older, while the UCR looks at crimes committed against all ages, may contribute to the confusing results. Additionally, the fact that the GSS only inquires into select offences, ignoring, for example, prostitution offences and offences committed against corporations, such as shoplifting, may help to illustrate the difficulty in trying to compare the two measures of criminality.

The 1999 GSS revealed the following information:

- Approximately 7.5 million Canadians per year are touched by crime—or 25 per cent of the population.
- The overall victimization rates for city residents are 40 per cent higher than those experienced by rural residents.
- Residents in Western provinces have a higher risk of victimization than residents in central and eastern Canada.
- Only 37 per cent of all crimes are reported to police.
- Victims of crime are more often women than men. Female personal victimization rate is 5 per cent higher than that for males; the higher rate is largely attributable to a higher sexual assault victimization rate for women.
- Younger people are more likely than the elderly to be victims of crime.
- Young people have the lowest rates of reporting violent victimizations to the police. Only 13 per cent of personal crimes are reported to the police, yet young people are among the highest-risk group for being victimized.
- Violent victimization rates are higher among people in lower-income families.
- The chance of personal criminal victimization is much higher for those individuals participating in evening activities outside the home, particularly if they consume alcohol.
- Seventy-eight per cent of sexual assaults and 63 per cent of other assaults were not reported to police.

## Problems with the GSS

Because most researchers believe that victim surveys provide a more accurate gauge of criminal incidents than do police reports, many tend to accept GSS data over UCR data. The GSS, however, is not without its problems—the primary problem is the potential for false or exaggerated reports. False reports may be generated by overzealous interviewers or self-aggrandizing respondents and are difficult to filter out. There are no reliable estimates as to the proportion of such responses in the GSS totals. Unintentional inaccuracies create other problems. Respondents may suffer from faulty memories, misinterpret events, and ascribe criminal intent to accidents and mistakes. Likewise, the lapse of time between the event itself and the interview may cause some crimes to be forgotten and others to be inaccurately reported.

Just as the UCR is undergoing change, so too is the GSS. The 1999 survey showed some improvement in methodology over the 1993 and 1988 surveys, and we can expect the next survey to reflect ongoing improvements.

### Family Violence and the 1999 GSS

In 1999, the GSS conducted by Statistics Canada was constructed in order to specifically address issues of family violence in Canada. Among the issues addressed were fear of violence, violence experienced by spouses after separation, the effect of exposure to violence on children, and the use of shelters by abused women.

This research revealed that 28 per cent of Canadian women who had contact in the preceding five years with an ex-spouse or ex-partner had endured at least one episode of spousal violence. Of those women experiencing violence from a former partner, 22 per cent indicated experiencing a sexual assault.[43] Indeed, past victimization research revealed that 39 per cent of all women have experienced at least one incident of sexual assault, as defined by our criminal law, since turning 16 years of age. An estimated four million Canadian women have therefore become victims of sexual assault. Of the 39 per cent of women surveyed who indicated they had been sexually assaulted, 79 per cent indicated that they were sexually assaulted by men known to them, as opposed to only 21 per cent who were sexually assaulted by strangers.[44]

According to the 1999 GSS, children witnessed one parent assaulting the other in 461 000 households during the five-year period of the survey. The vast majority of these incidents (70 per cent) involved their mother being abused by a male.[45] From 1999 to 2000, 57 200 women along with 39 200 children were admitted to shelters for abused women across the country. On a single day in April 2000, Canadian shelters turned away 254 women and 222 children, typically due to lack of room.[46]

## Comparisons of the UCR and GSS

Table 2–4 summarizes the differences between the UCR and the GSS, both of which provide estimates of crime in Canada. Both approaches are limited by the type of crimes they choose to measure, by those they exclude from measurement, and by the methods for gathering crime data.

Crime statistics from the UCR and GSS are often used in building explanations for criminal behaviour. Unfortunately, however, researchers often overlook the fact that statistics that are merely descriptive can be weak in explanatory power. For example, GSS data show that "household crime rates" are highest for households (1) headed by younger people, (2) with large numbers of people living in the household, (3) headed by renters, and (4) in central cities.[47] Such findings may lead some observers to conclude that values among certain groups in society both propel them into crime and make them targets of criminal victimization. The truth may be, however, that crime is more complicated than this, and accordingly does not lend itself to such a simple analysis. From simple descriptive statistics, it is difficult to know what causes crime.

## EMERGING PATTERNS OF CRIMINAL ACTIVITY

While it is difficult to predict changes in patterns of crime, we have seen some interesting developments in recent years with regard to patterns in crime. The overall crime rate increased through most of the 1960s, 1970s, and 1980s. The 1990s witnessed a steady decline. In 2001, the official crime rate increased slightly (about 1 per cent). Has the declining crime

## TABLE 2–4  Comparison of the GSS and UCR Surveys

| Survey Characteristics | General Social Survey (GSS) on Victimization | Uniform Crime Reporting (UCR) Survey |
|---|---|---|
| Survey type and coverage | Sample (in 1999) of about 26 000 persons aged 15+ in the 10 provinces | Census of all incidents reported by all police services in Canada |
| Historical data | 1988, 1993, and 1999 | Available continuously since 1962 |
| Source of information | Personal account of criminal victimization incidents, whether reported to police or not | Criminal incidents reported to and recorded by police |
| Scope of survey | 8 categories of criminal offence | Over 100 categories of criminal offence |
| Comparability of offence categories | Sexual assault | Comparable to total sexual assault in UCR |
| | Robbery | Not comparable. UCR includes robberies of businesses and financial institutions |
| | Assault | Comparable to total assault in UCR |
| | Break and enter | Comparable to total assault in UCR |
| | Theft of personal property Theft of household property | Not comparable. UCR does not distinguish between theft of personal and household property |
| | Motor vehicle/parts theft | Comparable to UCR when theft of motor vehicle parts is removed from GSS |
| | Vandalism | Not comparable. UCR has a "mischief" category that includes a broader range of infractions |
| Sources of error | Sampling errors (i.e., differences between estimated values for the sample and actual values for the population) | Public reporting rates to police |
| | Non-sampling errors (e.g., inability of respondents to remember/report events accurately, refusal by respondents to report, errors in the coding and processing of data) | Police discretionary power, changes in policies and practice in relation to capturing all reported incidents |

*Source:* Adapted from the Statistics Canada publication *Juristat*, Catalogue no. 85-002, Vol. 20, No. 10, November 2000, Box 2, p. 4.

rate trend ended? Can we expect to see increases in the year ahead? A significant factor that will affect the crime trend of the future is the demographic makeup of the country.[48] As the proportion of young people making up Canada's population declined, the crime rate declined concomitantly. If future demographic changes produce an increase in the proportion of young people in the population, whether brought about through increased immigration or through a baby-boom echo effect, we may see a trend of increasing crime rates in the country. Figure 2–10 reveals the breakdown of Canadians by age over the last decades. Note the changing numbers found in crime-prone years.

## The Fear of Crime

Although we have learned from the UCR and GSS data that violent street crime is not increasing, many people may not believe it. In fact, some people may be just as afraid as ever. Fear of crime is often out of proportion to the likelihood of criminal victimization. Table 2–5 compares the chance of violent victimization with life chances of other serious events. For most people, the chance of accidental injury at work

Karla Homolka, serving 12 years for manslaughter. The proportion of violent offences being committed by women appears to be increasing.

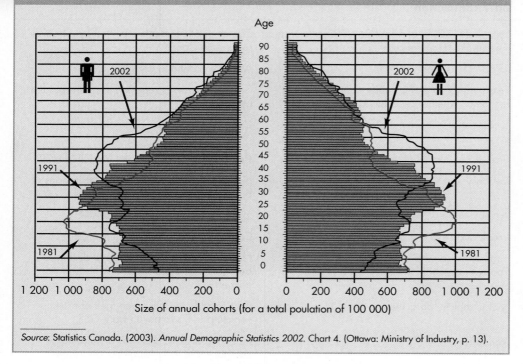

**FIGURE 2–10** Age Pyramid of the Population of Canada, July 1, 1981, 1991, and 2002.

Age

Size of annual cohorts (for a total population of 100 000)

Source: Statistics Canada. (2003). *Annual Demographic Statistics 2002.* Chart 4. (Ottawa: Ministry of Industry, p. 13).

or at home is far greater than the chance of being criminally attacked.

The 1999 GSS has revealed some interesting insights into fear of crime. Twelve percent of Canadians feel somewhat or very unsafe walking alone in their neighbourhoods after dark. Similarly, 20 per cent indicated that they feel very or somewhat worried when home alone in the evening or at night. Feelings of not being safe are highest among women, with 64 per cent feeling somewhat or very worried while awaiting public transportation after dark, and 29 per cent being very or somewhat worried about being home alone at night. Levels of fear were found to be very similar regardless of the age group of the respondent. Overall, 88 per cent of women and 93 per cent of men indicated that they were somewhat or very satisfied with their general level of personal safety.

The analysis of GSS fear-of-crime data shows some measures taken by Canadians as a result of their fear of victimization. Twenty-seven per cent of those surveyed indicated that they had altered their activities or avoided certain places due to their fear of crime. New locks or burglar alarms were installed by 21 per cent of survey respondents. Three per cent obtained a dog for protection, while 3 per cent took a self-defence course. Two per cent of survey respondents changed their phone number due to fear of crime; however, only 0.2 per cent indicated that they had obtained a gun.

## New Crime Concerns

Each year, Parliament addresses matters of public concern through the creation of new laws. With the enactment of criminal legislation, new crimes come into existence. These new crimes become reflected in the official crime picture, adding to existing crimes. Behaviour that may have been tolerated, ignored, or dealt with by other means may come to be prohibited by the criminal law. While each year new crimes are added or existing crimes expanded, we also see old crimes deleted from the criminal law when they no longer comply with the public sentiment regarding the proper scope of the criminal law. In the relatively recent past, offences involving homosexual acts, the seduction of female passengers on board ships, and certain acts previously defined as vagrancy have been deleted from the criminal law. Typically, such acts had ceased to be effectively enforced, and fell into disuse. While a few crimes have been deleted in recent years, others have been added, expanding the scope of the criminal law into new areas.

## Criminal Harassment

**criminal harassment**
Engaging in certain acts that the offender knows, or ought to know, will cause another person to fear for their safety or the safety of another known to them. Relevant acts include following the victim, repeatedly communicating with them, watching their home or place of work, and threatening members of the victim's family. Criminal harassment is commonly referred to as stalking.

In 1993, Canada's Parliament enacted anti-stalking, or **criminal harassment**, provisions under the *Criminal Code.* These included the enactment of a new offence, entitled "Criminal Harassment," which reads in part:

**TABLE 2–5** Life Chances of Serious Events How Do Crime Rates Compare with the Rates of Other Life Events?[1]

| Events | Rate per 1 000 Adults per Year[2] |
|---|---|
| Accidental injury, all circumstances | 242 |
| Accidental injury at home | 79 |
| Personal theft | 72 |
| Accidental injury at work | 58 |
| Violent victimization | 31 |
| Assault (aggravated and simple) | 24 |
| Injury in motor vehicle accident | 17 |
| Death, all causes | 11 |
| Victimization with injury | 10 |
| Serious (aggravated) assault | 9 |
| Robbery | 6 |
| Heart disease death | 4 |
| Cancer death | 2 |
| Rape (women only) | 2 |
| Accidental death, all circumstances | 0.5 |
| Pneumonia/influenza death | 0.3 |
| Motor vehicle accidental death | 0.2 |
| Suicide | 0.2 |
| Injury from fire | 0.1 |
| Homicide/legal intervention death | 0.1 |
| Death from fire | 0.03 |

[1]These rates approximate your chances of becoming a victim of these events. More precise estimates can be derived by taking account of such factors as your age, sex, race, place of residence, and lifestyle.
[2]These rates exclude children from the calculations (those under age 12–17, depending on the series). Fire injury/death data are based on the total population, because no age-specific data are available in this series.
*Source*: National Center for Health Statistics. (1995). Annual Report 1994. Washington, D.C.: USGPO.

s. 264 (1)    No person shall, without lawful authority and knowing that another person is harassed or recklessly as to whether the other person is harassed, engage in conduct referred to in subsection (2) that causes that other person reasonably, in all the circumstances, to fear for their safety or the safety of anyone known to them.

(2)    The conduct mentioned in subsection (1) consists of
  (a) repeatedly following from place to place the other person or anyone known to them;
  (b) repeatedly communicating with, either directly or indirectly, the other person or anyone known to them;
  (c) besetting or watching the dwelling-house, or place where the other person, or anyone known to them, resides, works, carries on business or happens to be; or
  (d) engaging in threatening conduct directed at the other person or any member of their family.

(3)    Every person who contravenes this section is guilty of
  (a) an indictable offence and is liable to imprisonment for a term not exceeding ten years; or
  (b) an offence punishable on summary conviction.

Prior to 1993, the police had to try to fit the offensive behaviour into one of the other existing provisions in the *Criminal Code,* such as threatening an assault, making a harassing

BOX 2.2

## Theory into Practice

## Media Impact on the Public's Fear of Crime

Turn on nightly television in Canada on a typical day and you will see killing after killing, frequent acts of gruesome violence, and murder and mayhem as typical prime-time fare. Only a few specialized forms of programming are relatively violence-free.

Many argue that the networks and cable companies are simply giving viewers what they want. Violence (often tinged with sexuality or combined with explicit sexual behaviour), because it is exciting, attracts audiences. And, of course, large audiences attract advertisers whose fees support the networks.

Not to be outdone by their highly visual counterparts, newspapers and newsmagazines depict real-life episodes of violent crime in every issue. Unfortunately, what some have called the overemphasis on crime and violence, now so characteristic of the media in this country, makes it extremely difficult to separate crime fiction from crime fact. If media emphasis is any guide, it would appear that Canada is awash in crime, especially violent personal crime. The impression given is that crime is likely to strike almost anyone when they least expect it—devastating their lives (should they survive) irreparably. In fact, while there are many victims of violent crime in this country, the media's preoccupation with crime and violence is much overdone. Worse still, such preoccupation had led to an enormous fear of crime among the Canadian public, which, for at least a substantial segment of the population, is probably misplaced.

While widespread concern about crime cannot be doubted, the official crime statistics tell a different story from commonly held beliefs about crime rates. During the 1990s, crime rates steadily declined in Canada. A modest increase in 2001 (+1 per cent) followed nine consecutive years of declining crime rates.[1] Recent crime rates are the lowest since the late 1970s. Some categories of crime that cause grave social concern, such as breaking and entering and impaired driving, have displayed consistent steep declines in recent years. Even youth crime, the cause of much media attention throughout the 1990s, showed steadily declining crime rates throughout the 1990s and into the beginning of this decade.[2]

Realistically, crime—including violent personal crime—has not been on the rise. To the extent that regional variations exist, it should be noted that crime rate increases have occurred in the Prairie provinces and in the North.

Yet, when surveys reporting the fear of crime are examined, Canadians everywhere appear to be on guard. Fear of crime, while apparently declining slightly in recent years, means that frightened Canadians routinely report taking self-protective steps. Statistics from the most recent General Social Survey (1999), which polled[3] fear of crime, for example, show 21 per cent of Canadians have installed security hardware in their homes, and 27 per cent have changed their activities or altered their behaviour as a result of concern over crime. Other surveys, however, have found that those most afraid of crime spend more time watching television than those who are less fearful[4]—lending support to the notion that media portrayals of criminal activity lead to a heightened fear of victimization.

Efforts are currently under way to reduce the degree of crime fear induced by the mass media.[5] The news media have a significant influence on public attitudes and belief about crime. Among the problems, noted in a report by Julian Roberts,[6] are: (1) The media tend not to report or to emphasize declining crime rates. (2) National crime figures, which have been reporting fairly steady declines for the past decade, only come out once a year. Even if these results are reported, this leaves the rest of the year to be filled with an endless stream of reports on individual crimes, often those involving violence, attracting the major headlines. (3) Crime stories are rarely placed into a statistical context. Reports of violent crime rarely include commentary on the extent to which violent crime rates have been changing over time. Unfortunately, no one knows for sure whether television and other media merely broadcast what viewers most want to see, or whether they help to determine what we, as a nation, are becoming.

## QUESTIONS FOR DISCUSSION

1. To what extent does television influence what people think about crime?

2. Does television help shape our culture, or does it merely reflect what we, as a nation, already are?

3. Would you be supportive of more "socially responsible" television news programming? Why or why not? If so, how would you change the content of television news?

---

[1]Savoie, J. (2002). Crime Statistics in Canada, 2001. *Juristat*, Vol. 22, No. 6.
[2]Ibid.
[3]Besserer, S. and Trainor, C. (2000). Criminal Victimization in Canada, 1999. *Juristat*, Vol. 20, No. 10, p. 15.
[4]See Spiegelman, A. (1994, December 15). America's Year in Crime—Enough to Scare Anyone. Reuters wire services.
[5]See Roberts, J.V. (2001). Fear of Crime and Attitudes to Criminal Justice: A Review of Recent Trends, 2001–02. Report for the Ministry of the Solicitor General, pp. 24–26.
[6]Ibid., p. 24.

phone call, or intimidating through threats of violence. The criminal harassment provisions are somewhat broader in scope than the previous provisions in the *Criminal Code*.

Data on criminal harassment offences are only available from those police agencies providing data to the UCR2 survey. In 2001, there were 46 criminal harassment incidents recorded per 100 000 population. This number reflects a 5-per-cent drop from the previous year, but a 40-per-cent increase since 1996.[49] It is difficult to ascertain from the crime statistics whether incidents of this crime increased through the late 1990s, or whether the recorded increases merely reflect increasing awareness of the availability of the provisions on the part of the police and victims.

The highest rates of criminal harassment have been recorded in Saskatoon, Montreal, and Vancouver. Consistently low rates have been reported since 1995 in Calgary and Edmonton.[50] As one might expect, over three-quarters of reported incidents of criminal harassment involve female victims (77 per cent in 1999). The vast majority of accused offenders are male (84 per cent in 1999). Females from 20 to 24 years old are at the greatest risk of being stalked, while males who are 30 to 34 years old are most likely to be accused of stalking. The crime data reveal that women are most likely to be stalked by their ex-partners, while those men who have been stalked are more likely to be stalked by casual acquaintances than by former partners.

## Political and Hate Crimes

In North America, a new era of domestic terrorism may have been ushered in with the terrorist attack on the World Trade Center in 2001. This follows an earlier attack on the World Trade Center in 1993, which left four dead and a more than 30-metre hole through four subfloors of concrete. The 1995 bombing of the Alfred P. Murrah Federal Building in Oklahoma City, Oklahoma, which killed 168 people and injured hundreds more, demonstrated just how vulnerable the United States is to such attacks. Overseas terrorists have made ongoing efforts to invade American population centres, placing "sleeper agents" within the United States, poised to act on the command of distant authorities. Canadians are significantly less concerned with such matters; however, the threat posed by unknown assailants, whether internal or external to our boundaries, is omnipresent.

Worrisome to many enforcement agencies in Canada and the United States are underground survivalist groups with their own vision of a future for our countries. Among them are the White Patriot Party; the Order; Aryan Nations; Posse Comitatus; the Covenant, the Sword, and the Arm of the Lord; the Ku Klux Klan; and umbrella organizations such as the Christian Conservative Church. Described variously as the "radical right," "neo-Nazis," "skinheads," "white supremacists," and "racial hate groups," indications are that these groups are organized, well-financed, and extremely well-armed. John R. Harrell, leader of the Christian Conservative Church in the United States, preaches that the nation is on the eve of destruction. According to some authorities, "Christian patriots" are exhorted to stand ready to seize control of the United States before leadership can fall into the "wrong hands."[51] Such extremist groups adhere to identity theology, a religion that claims that members of the white race are God's chosen people. Identity theology envisions a country ruled exclusively by white people under "God's law."[52]

Just as Hitler's biography *Mein Kampf* served as a call to arms for Nazis in Europe during the 1930s, a novel called *The Turner Diaries* is now used by extremist groups to map their rise to power.[53] *The Turner Diaries* describes an Aryan revolution set in the 1990s in which Jews, blacks, and other minorities are removed from positions of influence in government and society. Some experts believe that the 1995 Oklahoma City bombing was modelled after a similar bombing described in the *Diaries*.

Tom Leyton, reformed neo-Nazi recruiter, shows off some of his racist tattoos at a news conference in Toronto in 1997. Leyton said he planned to have 29 of his hate tattoos removed. He has toured North America to educate teenagers and their parents about racism and skinheads.

*Toronto Star – Richard Lautens*

In 1993, eight men and women were arrested by the FBI and accused of plotting to start a race war in Los Angeles. The plot allegedly involved bombing the prominent 8500-member First African Methodist Episcopal Church in South Central Los Angeles, spraying its members with machine-gun fire, and assassinating Rodney King. Other targets may have included the Reverend Al Sharpton in New York, Nation of Islam Minister Louis Farrakhan, officials of the NAACP, and members of the black rap group Public Enemy. News reports linked groups known as the Fourth Reich Skinheads, the Florida Church of the Creator, and the White Aryan Resistance.[54] In the same year, a confrontation between David Koresh's Branch Davidian followers and federal agents left 91 Davidians and four federal agents dead in Waco, Texas.

The Canadian justice system of today is ill-prepared to deal with the threat represented by supremacist and radical groups. Intelligence-gathering efforts focused on such groups have largely failed. Military-style organization and training are characteristic of the groups that are known, making them difficult to penetrate, and their **hate crimes** correspondingly difficult to prosecute. The armaments at their disposal include weapons of mass destruction, which the firepower and tactical mobility of law enforcement agencies could not hope to match.

**hate crimes** Criminal offences in which there is evidence of prejudice based on race, religion, sexual orientation, or ethnicity.

Confidential research commissioned by the Department of Justice in Ottawa revealed that as many as 9000 hate-inspired crimes occur annually in Canada.[55] The confidential report revealed that as much as 95 per cent of hate crimes are not reported to the police. Of the crimes that are reported, 61 per cent of such hate crimes are said to be motivated by race, 23 per cent by religion, and 11 per cent were against lesbians and gays. However, the true

---

## BOX 2.3    Theory into Practice

## Hate Crimes

In Canadian law, sections 318–319 of the *Criminal Code* deal with matters pertaining to hate crimes. Section 318 deals with "advocating genocide," and anyone who advocates or promotes genocide is guilty of an indictable offence. Section 319 concerns itself with any public incitement of hatred, or wilful promotion of hatred, against any "identifiable group" and is also an indictable offence. The term "identifiable group" is defined as "any section of the public distinguished by colour, race, religion or ethnic origin." A number of highly publicized cases have dealt with hate propaganda issues, including:

*R.* v. *Keegstra* (1990), 61 C.C.C. (3d) 1 (S.C.C.);
*R.* v. *Andrews* (1990), 61 C.C.C. (3d) 490 (S.C.C.)
*R.* v. *Zundel* (1992), 75 C.C.C. (3d) 449 (S.C.C.); and
*R.* v. *Harding* (2001), 160 C.C.C. (3d) 225 (Ont.C.A.)

In the *Keegstra* and *Andrews* cases, the Supreme Court of Canada held that the provisions in the *Criminal Code* prohibiting the dissemination of hate propaganda violated the freedom-of-expression guarantee in the *Canadian Charter of Rights and Freedoms*. However, the Court upheld the law as a reasonable limit on the right to free expression under section 1 of the *Charter*. In doing so, the Court

placed considerable emphasis on the need to view freedom of expression in the context of other rights guaranteed by the *Charter*, such as the right to equality, and the value in promoting a tolerant, multi-cultural society.[1]

In *Harding*, the Ontario Court of Appeal upheld a conviction against an evangelical Protestant who was charged after he distributed anti-Muslim pamphlets outside a Toronto high school. His pamphlets critiqued the school setting aside a room for Muslim prayer, when other forms of religion were barred from being practised inside the school. His pamphlet went on to decry all Muslims as potential terrorists, identifying violent acts committed by Muslims elsewhere in the world, and asserted in part: "The Muslims who commit these crimes are no different than the Muslim believers living here in Toronto. Their beliefs are based on the Koran. They sound peaceful, but underneath their false sheep's clothing are raging wolves seeking whom they may devour. And Toronto is definitely on their hit list." The Supreme Court of Canada declined his application for leave to appeal the conviction further.

In the case of Ernest Zundel, he was charged under section 181 of the *Criminal Code*, which makes it an indictable offence for anyone to publish a statement knowing that it is false and also that it is likely to cause injury or mischief to a public interest. Zundel has published a great deal of material that denies the Holocaust. He was acquitted after the Supreme Court of Canada struck down the false-news provision in the *Criminal Code* as an unjustifiable infringement on the right to freedom of expression. However, in 2001, Zundel left Canada for the United States when the Canadian Human Rights Commission required him to shut down his

extent of hate crimes in Canada remains a mystery since police do not regularly categorize crimes according to their motivation, particularly less serious crimes. For example, a religiously motivated crime involving the desecration of Jewish gravesites with spray-painted swastikas would be recorded as an act of mischief, just like any other wilful damage to property.

The courts, and more recently, Parliament have recognized the need to devote special attention to dealing with hate-motivated crimes. In 1990, the Courts of Appeal in both Ontario and Alberta proclaimed hate-motivation to be an aggravating factor to be used in assessing the appropriate penalty for a given offence. In *R. v. Lelas* (1990),[56] the Ontario Court of Appeal noted that attacks motivated by religious or racial hatred are more heinous, as they attack the very fabric of society, inviting imitation and inciting retaliation. Where the crime involves the desecration of a place of worship, the crime is to be considered even more serious, particularly where it is intended to cause emotional upset or injury to the members of the congregation. In this case, acts of mischief should carry a more severe penalty than acts of mischief carried out merely to damage the property of another. In *R. v. Simms* (1990),[57] the Alberta Court of Appeal proclaimed that sentences for assault should be substantially increased to accommodate the finding that the assaults were racially inspired by the defendants who were found to be either adherents to neo-Nazi organizations or sympathizers to such organizations.

In 1996, Parliament amended the *Criminal Code* by adding section 718.2 that provides in part:

anti-Jewish website. In early 2003, Zundel was returned to Canada from the United States by INS authorities when his U.S. visa expired. Zundel is presently seeking refugee status in Canada. If refugee status is denied, Zundel will be returned to his home country of Germany, where charges of inciting hatred await his return.

The Canadian Association of Chiefs of Police has prepared materials that are designed to grapple with the issue in Canada.[2]

One of their publications identifies the top nine challenges for investigating and prosecuting hate/bias crimes.

### Investigation-related challenges:

- Making the investigating officer conscious of the possibility that the crime is hate/bias motivated.
- Identifying the crime as hate/bias motivated.
- Dealing with the resistance from victims, especially with questions dealing with sexual orientation (fear of intimidation).
- Convincing the potential or actual victim to come forward and report the incident to the police (fear of reprisals) or, when a report is filed, having the victim follow through with court proceedings.
- Determining the motivation; a long process requiring subsequent follow-up interviews by an interviewer.
- Working with victims who destroy evidence because of its offensive nature or with community groups who lack an understanding of hate/bias crimes.

### Prosecution-related challenges:

- Dealing with the lack of awareness and understanding of hate/bias motivated crime on the part of prosecuting attorneys and judges.
- Dealing with the lack of designated prosecuting attorneys dealing with hate/bias crime phenomena.
- Dealing with government's lack of implication and involvement on this important issue.

There is a great deal of concern about the role of the internet in the production and dissemination of hate literature. Law enforcement officials are particularly alarmed at the capacity of certain individuals to communicate on a global basis. Because the internet is blind to international boundaries, this poses a particular challenge for law enforcement agencies and prosecutors.

---

[1]Moran, M. Talking About Hate Speech: A Rhetorical Analysis of American and Canadian Approaches to the Regulation of Hate Speech. In Dyzenhaus, D. and Ripstein, A. (eds.). (2001). *Law and Morality: Readings in Legal Philosophy*, (2nd ed.). Toronto: University of Toronto Press.
[2]Ontario. Ministry of the Solicitor General and Correctional Services. Policing Services Division. (1996). *Police resource package on hate/bias motivated crimes.*

## QUESTIONS FOR DISCUSSION

1. Why do you think the courts upheld the validity of the offence of disseminating "hate propaganda," but struck down the law concerning "spreading false news"?

2. The hate-propaganda provisions require the Attorney General to consent to the initiation of a prosecution. Why do you think this is the case? Should this be the case?

(a) a sentence should be increased or decreased to account for any relevant aggravating or mitigating circumstances relating to the offence or the offender, and, without limiting the generality of the foregoing,

(i) evidence that the offence was motivated by bias, prejudice or hate based on race, national or ethnic origin, language, colour, religion, sex, age, mental or physical disability, sexual orientation, or any other similar factor….

Parliament is sending a clear message to sentencing judges that hate-based motivation is to be treated seriously. All judges are now required to impose stiffer sentences where the evidence supports the contention that the offence is one that was motivated by hatred of persons belonging to any of the categories of persons delineated in the legislative provision.

Canada's method of collecting crime statistics does not allow for the careful analysis of the motivation of many crimes, because the statistics only give numbers, not the reasons why the crimes are committed. It is difficult to determine whether a killing or an act of arson or mischief is motiveless, or is motivated by revenge or even by hatred or political designs. Accordingly, recent concerns about politically motivated acts of terrorism are not directly amenable to statistical analysis through current methods of data collection.

# SUMMARY

Studying the criminal justice system necessarily involves studying the phenomenon of crime. Crime statistics provide a useful but conceptually limited approach to the social reality of crime. Statistics delineate the extent of crime according to the categories they are designed to measure, and they give a picture of victim characteristics through both self-reports and reports to the police. Today's comprehensive program of data gathering allows for a tabulation of the dollar costs of crime and permits a degree of predictability as to trends in crime.

Lacking in most crime statistics, however, are any realistic appraisals of the human costs of crime. The trauma suffered by victims and survivors, the lowered sense of security experienced after victimization, and the loss of human productivity and quality of life caused by crime are difficult to gauge.

On the other side of the balance sheet, statistics fail to identify social costs suffered by offenders and their families. The social deprivation that may lead to crime, the fragmentation of private lives following conviction, and the loss of individuality that come with confinement are all costs to society, just as they are the culturally imposed consequences of crime and failure. Except for numbers on crimes committed, clearance rates, and figures on persons incarcerated, today's data-gathering strategies fall far short of gauging the human suffering and wasted human potential that both causes and follows from crime.

Even where reports do provide quantitative measures, they may still fail to assess some of the objective costs of crime, including lowered property values in high-crime areas and inflated prices for consumer goods caused by the underground economy in stolen goods. White-collar crimes in particular are often well-hidden and difficult to measure, yet many produce the largest direct dollar losses of any type of criminal activity.

Modern crime statistics are useful, but they do not provide the whole picture. Students of criminal justice need to be continually aware of aspects of the crime picture that fall outside of official data.

# DISCUSSION QUESTIONS

1. What are the two major sources of crime statistics for Canada? How do they differ?

2. What can crime statistics tell us about the crime "picture" in Canada? How has that "picture" changed over time?

3. What are the potential sources of error in the major reports on crime? Can you imagine some popular usage of those statistics that might be especially misleading?

4. Why are many crime statistics expressed as a *rate*? How does the use of crime rates improve the reporting of crime data (over a simple numerical tabulation)?

5. What is the difference between the way the UCR traditionally collected crime data, and the direction it has been moving in recent years? Will we lose the ability to compare old crime data with contemporary data once the new scheme for collecting crime statistics is fully implemented?

6. What is the hierarchy rule in crime reporting programs? What purpose does it serve? What do you think of the proposed modifications in the hierarchy rule?

7. What does it mean to say that a crime has been "cleared"? Can you imagine a better way of reporting clearances?

8. What trends do you think are likely to change the crime picture in Canada in the next five years?

# WEBLINKS

http://eir.library.utoronto.ca/library/guide/libraryDetail.cfm?ID=6
**Criminology Information Service & Library**
The CIS at the University of Toronto houses the leading Canadian research collection of criminological material, consisting of more than 25 000 books, journals, government reports, statistics, and other documents, which can be accessed in person or electronically via the internet. The information covers a wide range of subject areas, including public and private policing, violence, deviance and social control, young offenders, criminology, and criminal law.

www.jrsainfo.org
**Justice Research and Statistics Association (U.S.)**
Located in Washington, D.C., the JRSA is an American non-profit organization of state Statistical Analysis Center (SAC) directors, researchers, and practitioners throughout government, academia, and criminal justice organizations. The site provides publications, a calendar of upcoming criminal justice events, two online databases covering a wide range of state criminal justice research and national firearms research, and links to state SACs.

www.statcan.ca/english/Pgdb/justic.htm
**Statistics Canada: Canadian Statistics: The State: Justice and Crime**
Statistics organized under three categories: crimes; victims, suspects, and criminals; and the police and the courts.

www.statcan.ca/cgi-bin/downpub/listpub.cgi?catno=85-002-XIE
**Juristat**
This series of reports, available for $8 apiece, provides detailed statistics and analysis on a variety of topics and issues concerning Canada's justice system.

www.rcmp-grc.gc.ca/organizedcrime/index_e.htm
**RCMP Organized Crime Initiative**
Along with background information and definitions of organized crime, this site offers details about motorcycle gangs, money laundering, white collar crime, Asian gangs, illicit drugs, and prostitution.

# Legal Foundations of Criminal Justice

Canadian Press/Winnipeg Sun/Bruce Rapinchuk

### KEY CONCEPTS

law
statutory law
case law
common law
jural postulates
jurisprudence
criminal law
crime
precedent
civil law

tort
regulations
felonies
inchoate offence
mens rea
defences
mental disorder defence
self-defence
entrapment

### KEY CASES

*R. v. Morgentaler*
*Borowski v. AG for
  Canada*
*Daigle v. Tremblay*
*R. v. Hydro-Quebec*
*R. v. Swain*
*RJR MacDonald Inc. v.
  Canada (Attorney
  General)*
*R. v. Westendorp*
*Doern v. Phillips Estate*
McNaughten's case
*R. v. Daviault*

*R. v. Parks*
*R. v. Stone*
*R. v. Lavallee*
*R. v. Ruzic*
*The Queen v. Dudley and
  Stephens*
*Perka v. The Queen*
*R. v. Shubley*
*R. v. Power*
*R. v. O'Connor*
*R. v. Mack*
*R. v. Askov*
*R. v. Morin*

David Milgaard, shown here with his mother, Joyce, spent 22 years in prison for allegedly killing
Gail Miller in 1969, until DNA evidence proved him innocent and he was released.

# SOURCES OF MODERN LAW

Twenty years ago, as South American jungles were being cleared to make way for farmers and other settlers, a group of mercenaries brutally attacked and wiped out a small tribe of local Indians. About 20 native men, women, and children were hacked to death with machetes or shot. The Indians had refused to give up their land and would not move. At their arrest, the killers uttered something that, to our ears, sounds frightening: "How can you arrest us?" they said. "We didn't know it was illegal to kill Indians!"

These men killed many people. But, they claimed, they were ignorant of the fact that the law forbade such a thing. In this case, these killers didn't consider their victims "human." It may seem obvious to us that what they had done was commit murder, but to them it was something else. Nevertheless, their ignorance of the law was rejected as a defence at their trial, and they were convicted of murder. All received lengthy prison sentences.

The men in this story were hardly literate, with almost no formal education. They knew very little about the law and, apparently, even less about basic moral principles. We, on the other hand, living in a modern society with highly developed means of communications, much more formal schooling, and a large workforce of professionals skilled in interpreting the law, usually know what the law *says*. But do we really know what the law *is?* In this chapter, we will discuss the law both as a product of rule creation and as a guide for behaviour. The criminal justice system is structured and controlled to a large extent by Canada's legal framework. We will examine the constitutional context within which the criminal justice system operates, examine the criminal law in some detail, discuss defences commonly used by defendants charged with violations of the criminal law, and identify key concepts in the areas of criminal procedure and evidence.

## The Nature of Law

Practically speaking, the **law** regulates relationships between people and also between parties (such as agencies of government and individuals). Most of us would probably agree that the law is whatever legislators, through the exercise of their politically sanctioned wisdom, tell us it is. Then we would also expect that the law would be unambiguously specified in a set of books or codes. As we shall see, however, such is not always the case.

The laws of our nation, or of a province, are found in **statutory law** provisions and constitutional enactments,[1] as well as in hundreds of years of rulings by courts at all levels. According to the authoritative *Black's Law Dictionary*, the word *law* "generally contemplates both statutory and **case law**."[2] If "the law" could be found entirely ensconced in written legal codes, it would be plain to nearly everyone, and we would need far fewer lawyers than we find practising today. But some laws (in the sense of precedents established by courts) do not exist "on the books," and even those that do are open to interpretation.

**law** A rule of conduct, generally found enacted in the form of a statute, which proscribes and/or mandates certain forms of behaviour. Statutory law is often the result of moral enterprise by interest groups that, through the exercise of political power, are successful in seeing their valuative perspectives enacted into law.

**statutory law** Written or codified law. The "law on the books," as enacted by a governmental body or agency having the power to make laws.

**case law** That body of judicial precedent, historically built upon legal reasoning and past interpretations of statutory laws, which serves as a guide to decision making, especially in the courts.

## THE DEVELOPMENT OF LAW

Modern law is the result of a long evolution of legal principles (see Table 3–1). To completely and accurately understand contemporary law, you also need to understand both its history and its philosophical foundation. Before discussing further the nature of law, we will examine some of the historical sources of contemporary law.

## Code of Hammurabi

The Code of Hammurabi is one of the first known bodies of law to survive and be available for study today. King Hammurabi ruled the ancient city of Babylon around 2000 B.C. The Code of Hammurabi is a set of laws engraved on stone tablets, which were intended to

**TABLE 3–1** Sources of the Law

| Historical Sources of the Law | Modern Sources of Canadian Law |
| --- | --- |
| Natural law | Canadian Constitution |
| Early Roman law | *Charter of Rights and Freedoms* |
| Common law | Statutes |
| The Old and New Testaments | Case law |
| The Magna Carta | |
| Religious belief and practice | |

establish property and other rights. Babylon was a commercial centre, and the right of private property formed a crucial basis for prosperous growth. Hammurabi's laws spoke to issues of theft, ownership, sexual relationships, and interpersonal violence. Even though Hammurabi's code specified a variety of corporeal punishments, and even death for a number of offences, it standardized the practice of justice in Babylonian society by making punishments predictable. Prior to the Code, captured offenders often faced the most barbarous and capricious of punishments, frequently at the hands of revenge-seeking victims, no matter how minor their offences had been. As Marvin Wolfgang has observed, "In its day, 1700 B.C., the Hammurabi Code, with its emphasis on retribution, amounted to a brilliant advance in penal philosophy mainly because it represented an attempt to keep cruelty within bounds."[3]

## Early Roman Law

The Code of Hammurabi is primarily of archeological importance. Of considerable significance for our own legal tradition, however, is early Roman law. Roman legions under the Emperor Claudius conquered England in the mid-first century. Roman authority over "Britannia" was consolidated by later rulers who built walls and fortifications to keep out the still-hostile Scots. Roman customs, law, and language were forced upon the English population during the succeeding three centuries under the Pax Romana—a peace imposed by the military of Rome.[4]

Roman law derived from the Twelve Tables, written about 450 B.C. The Twelve Tables were a collection of basic rules related to family, religious, and economic life. The Tables appear to have been based upon common and fair practices generally accepted among early tribes, which existed prior to the establishment of the Roman Republic. Unfortunately, only fragments of the Tables survive today.

The best-known legal period of Roman history occurred under Emperor Justinian I, who ruled between A.D. 527 and 565. By the sixth century, the Roman Empire had declined

The Code of Hammurabi, one of the oldest judicial codes known, was discovered inscribed on a stone obelisk, which dates from 1950 B.C. Figures at the top of the stone (a portion of which is shown here) depict King Hammurabi receiving the law from the Babylonian sun god.

Bettmann

substantially in size and influence and was near the end of its life. In what may have been an effort to preserve Roman values and traditions, Justinian undertook the laborious process of distilling Roman laws into a set of writings. The Justinian Code actually consisted of three lengthy legal documents: (1) the Institutes, (2) the Digest, and (3) the Code itself. Justinian's code distinguished between two major legal categories: public and private laws. Public laws dealt with the organization of the Roman state, its senate, and governmental offices. Private law concerned itself with contracts, personal possessions, the legal status of various types of persons (citizens, free persons, slaves, freedmen, guardians, husbands and wives, and so on) and injuries to citizens. It contained elements of both our modern civil and criminal law, and, no doubt, influenced Western legal thought through the Middle Ages.

# Common Law

Common law forms the basis of much of our modern statutory and case law. It has often been called *the* major source of modern criminal law.

**Common law** refers to a traditional body of early unwritten legal precedents, created from everyday English social customs, rules, and practices that were supported by judicial decisions during the Middle Ages. As novel situations arose and were dealt with by British justices, the justices' declarations became the start for any similar future deliberation. These decisions generally incorporated the customs of society as it operated at the time. Eventually, this growing body of judicial pronouncements congealed into a set of legal rules widely accepted as a kind of national law, commonly applied throughout England—and "common law" was born. During this early stage of legal development, judges often took it upon themselves to formally criminalize actions that had previously been regarded as the basis for private disputes. Hence, many acts that we call "crimes" today, such as murder, assault, arson, and burglary, might have remained in the private sphere had it not been for such common-law developments.

Common law was given considerable legitimacy when the English King Edward the Confessor in the eleventh century declared that it was the law of the land. The authority of common law was further reinforced by the decision of William the Conqueror to use popular customs as the basis for judicial action, following his subjugation of Britain in A.D. 1066.

Eventually, court decisions were recorded and made available to barristers (the English word for trial lawyers) and judges. According to Howard Abadinsky, "Common law involved the transformation of community rules into a national legal system. The controlling element (was) precedent."[5]

**common law** A body of unwritten judicial opinion that was based upon customary social practices of Anglo-Saxon society during the Middle Ages.

# The Magna Carta

The Magna Carta (literally, "great charter") is another important source of modern laws and legal procedure. The Magna Carta was signed on June 15, 1215, by King John of England at Runnymede, under pressure from British barons who took advantage of John's military defeats at the hands of Pope Innocent III and King Philip Augustus of France. The barons demanded a pledge from the King John to respect their traditional rights and forced the king to agree to be bound by law.

At the time of its signing, the Magna Carta, although 63 chapters in length, was little more than a feudal document[6] listing specific royal concessions. Its wording, however, was later interpreted during a judicial revolt in 1613 to support individual rights. Sir Edward Coke, chief justice under James I, held that the Magna Carta guaranteed basic liberties for all British citizens and ruled that any acts of Parliament that contravened common law would be void. There is some evidence that this famous ruling became the basis for the rise of Canada's Supreme Court, which has the power to nullify laws enacted by Parliament and the legislatures.[7] Similarly, one specific provision of the Magna Carta, designed originally to prohibit the king from prosecuting the barons without just cause, was expanded into the concept of "due process of law," a fundamental cornerstone of modern legal procedure. Because of these later interpretations, the Magna Carta has been called "the foundation stone of our present liberties...."[8]

# The Canadian Constitution

The Canadian Constitution is one of the most significant wellsprings of our modern law. The written portion of our Constitution was originally created by the Parliament at Westminster in England through a long process of enactments. Since 1982, Canada has possessed the authority to amend its Constitution without recourse to the British Parliament; however, such amendments are bound to be rare indeed. The Constitution is the final authority in all questions pertaining to the rights of individuals, the power of the federal government and the provinces/territories to create laws and prosecute offenders, and the limits of punishments that can be imposed for law violations.

Although the Constitution itself does not contain many specific prohibitions on behaviour, it is the final authority in deciding whether new and existing laws are acceptable, according to the ideals upon which our country is founded. Under the principles of fundamental justice, embodied in section 7 of the *Canadian Charter of Rights and Freedoms* (the *Charter*), the Constitution has served to guide justices in gauging the merits of citizens' claims concerning the handling of their cases by the agencies of justice. As we will soon see, the structure of Canada's criminal justice system is largely dictated by basic constitutional law propositions.

# Natural Law

Some people believe that the basis for many of our criminal laws can be found in immutable moral principles or some identifiable aspect of the natural order. The Ten Commandments, "inborn tendencies," the idea of sin, and perceptions of various forms of order in the universe and in the social world have all provided a basis for the assertion that a "natural law" exists. Natural law comes from outside the social group and is thought to be knowable through some form of revelation, intuition, reason, or prophecy.

Natural law was used by the early Christian church as a powerful argument in support of its interests. Secular rulers were pressed to reinforce Church doctrine in any laws they decreed. Thomas Aquinas (1225–1274) wrote in his *Summa Theologica* that any man-made law that contradicts natural law is corrupt in the eyes of God.[9] Religious practice, which strongly reflected natural law conceptions, was central to early British society. Hence, natural law, as it was understood at the time, was incorporated into English common law throughout the Middle Ages.

Dr. Henry Morgentaler speaking in Toronto at a press conference that was held to mark the 10-year anniversary of Canada's Supreme Court decriminalizing abortion.

The constitution of Canada is built around an understanding of the natural law as reflected by the recognition in the *Charter* of the "supremacy of God" in the preamble to the document.

Students of natural law have set for themselves the task of uncovering just what that law encompasses. The modern debate over abortion is an example of the use of natural-law arguments to support both sides in the dispute. Anti-abortion forces, frequently called "pro-lifers," claim that the unborn fetus is a person and that he or she is entitled to all the protections that we could reasonably and ethically be expected to give to any other living human being. Such protection, they suggest, is basic and humane and lies in the natural relationship of one human being to another. They are striving for passage of a law, or a reinterpretation of past Supreme Court precedent, that would support their position.

Supporters of the present law (which allows abortion upon request under most conditions) maintain that abortion is a "right" of any pregnant woman because she is the one in control of her body. Such "pro-choice" groups also claim that the legal system must address the abortion question, but only by way of offering protection to this "natural right" of women. Keep in mind, however, that what we refer to as "the present law" is not so much a law "on the books," but rather a consequence of a series of decisions rendered by the Supreme Court of Canada in the trilogy of abortion cases in the late 1980s: *R* v. *Morgentaler* (1988),[10] *Borowski* v. *AG for Canada* (1989),[11] and *Daigle* v. *Tremblay*.[12]

## BOX 3.1  Theory into Practice

## The Assault on Abortion: Targeting Doctors

The debate over abortion in Canada has taken a violent turn in some instances; however, not to the degree it has in the United States. Pro-choice and pro-life proponents have put forward determined campaigns to influence public sentiment. Both groups have lobbied Canada's lawmakers to strengthen existing protections for women seeking therapeutic abortions, on one hand, and to establish higher levels of protection for the unborn child, on the other.

In Ontario, the pro-life movement called Linda Gibbons a "prisoner of conscience" for her counselling activities outside of abortion clinics (also referred to as "abortuaries"). Linda, a grandmother of four, was jailed for violating a temporary injunction that banned her from offering counsel to pregnant women. She was released on May 5, 1998.

Certainly, the rate of abortions has increased significantly in Canada over the past 25 years, in both hospitals and clinics. In 1970, there were a total of 11 152 therapeutic abortions among Canadian women, which represents a rate of 3.0 per 100 live births. In 2000, there were 105 669 such abortions among Canadian women. This represents a rate of 32.2 per 100 live births.

In 1996, the Winnipeg Child and Family Services department attempted to place a pregnant mother into a treatment program for her serious solvent abuse problem. The department's order was denied by the courts.

The Canadian Abortion Rights Action League (CARAL) was formed to provide abortion information and to support pro-choice options and legislation. This group, and other pro-choice organizations, point to the problem of extremism associated with the pro-life movement. Since 1994, there have been three abortion-related shootings in Canada. On November 11, 1997, Dr. Jack Fainman, an obstetrician in Winnipeg, was shot while in his home. On November 8, 1994, Dr. Garson Romalis was struck by a bullet in his home in Vancouver. On July 11, 2000, Dr. Romalis was again the target of an anti-abortion activist when he was stabbed outside his clinic. Romalis recovered, and the assailant escaped capture. On November 10, 1995, Dr. Hugh Short, a Hamilton, Ontario doctor was permanently disabled by a sniper's bullet. The similarities in timing, targets, and technique have led some to suggest that this is an attack on women's right to safe, legal abortions.

In 2001, anti-abortion activist James Kopp was arrested in France and subsequently extradited to the Untied States in order to stand trial for the 1998 killing of Barnett Slepian, an abortion doctor in Amherst, New York. On March 19, 2003, Kopp was convicted of that killing. He remains a person of interest to Canadian police, in at least two of the attempts on the lives of Canadian abortion doctors.

## QUESTIONS FOR DISCUSSION

1. What are some of the key points made by those who support pro-life options? Who supports pro-choice?

2. What are the implications of the continuing debate over abortion in Canada for the justice system? How could it impact on Canadian criminal law?

*Sources:* The Canadian Abortion Rights Action League's (CARAL) website: **www.caral.ca**; Birthright's (Toronto, Ontario) website: **www.birthright.org**; Canadian Abortion Statistics: **http://www.webhart.net/vandee/abortstat.shtml**; "Linda Gibbons: Prisoner of Conscience" in Lifesite Canada's website— **www.lifesite.net**; Thompson, C. (2003, March 2003). Judge Finds Anti-abortion Sniper Guilty of Murder. *Globe and Mail*, p. A18.

## Mala in Se/Mala Prohibita

Natural law lends credence to the belief that certain actions are wrong in themselves. These behaviours are called *mala in se*, a Latin term that generally includes crimes against humanity (such as the planned extermination of much of the Jewish population in parts of Nazi-controlled Europe during World War II and the ethnic cleansing in Kosovo), and serious personal crimes including murder, sexual assault, assault, arson, and other crimes of violence.

It is easy to imagine that members of primitive societies, without a system of codified statutes, would still understand that some forms of behaviour are wrong. This intuitive recognition of deviance lends support to the idea of natural law and to the classification of certain offences as *mala in se*.

Crimes that fall outside of the "natural" category are called *mala prohibita*, meaning that they are wrong only because they are prohibited by the law. Poaching on royal land is an example of what was a *mala prohibita* crime under English common law. Most crimes that fall under the heading of "morals offences" today might be called *mala prohibita*. Such offences include prostitution-related crimes, gambling, and illicit drug use.

The distinction between *mala in se* and *mala prohibita* offences derives from common law and was an important consideration in deciding sentences in early England. *Mala prohibita* crimes were tried by justices of the peace and carried penalties that were generally far less severe than those for *mala in se* crimes.

## PURPOSES OF THE LAW

Imagine a society without laws. People would not know what to expect from one another (an area controlled by the law of contracts), nor would they be able to plan for the future with any degree of certainty (civil law); they wouldn't feel safe (criminal law), knowing that the physically more powerful or better-armed could take what they want from the less powerful; and they may not be able to exercise basic rights that would otherwise be available to them as citizens of a free nation (constitutional law). In short, laws channel human behaviour while they simultaneously constrain it, and they empower individuals while contributing to social order.

A few years ago, one of the authors remembers encountering the results of a survey of attitudes among university-age males from across the United States. One of the most surprising of the survey's findings was this: nearly 90 per cent of the young men questioned said they would probably rape a woman if there were no laws against forced sexual behaviour. In other words, they were admitting to strong sexual drives, which they conceded they would attempt to gratify if the threat of legislated sanctions could not be applied to them. While the honesty of those responding to the questionnaire is to be appreciated, this single finding highlights the need for formal rules that put limits on the behaviour of all those who make up any society. Law, and criminal laws in particular, are needed to prevent the victimization of innocents by those seeking purely selfish pleasures. The truth of this assertion is borne out by the lawlessness experienced in war zones, where the number of crimes of all sorts—especially rape and looting—tends to rise dramatically (as happened in Kuwait after Iraqi forces overran the country in 1991, as well as during the recent war in Kosovo).

Max Weber (1864–1920), an eminent sociologist of the early twentieth century, said the primary purpose of law is to regulate the flow of human interaction.[13] By creating enforceable rules, laws make the behaviour of others predictable. This first, and most significant, purpose of the law can be simply stated: laws support social order.

Laws also serve a variety of other purposes. They ensure that the philosophical, moral, and economic perspectives of their creators are protected and made credible. They maintain values and uphold established patterns of social privilege. They sustain existing power relationships, and, finally, they support a system for the punishment and rehabilitation of offenders. Modifications of the law, when gradually induced, promote orderly change in the rest of society.

The question of *what the law does* is quite different from the question of *what the law should do*. Writing in the mid-1800s, for example, John Stuart Mill (1806–1873) questioned the liberal use of the criminal law as a tool for social reform.[14] Mill objected strongly to the use of law as a "way of compulsion and control" for any purpose other than to prevent harm to others. Behaviour that might be thought morally "wrong" should not be contravened by law, said Mill, unless it is also harmful to others. In similar fashion, Nigel Walker, a British criminologist of this century, applied what he called "a sociological eye" to the criminal codes of Western nations and concluded that criminal statutes are not appropriate that seek to contravene behaviour that lacks a clear and immediate harm to others; nor, he said, should laws be created for the purpose of compelling people to act in their own good.[15] In *Our Criminal Law*, the now disbanded Law Reform Commission of Canada (LRCC) adopted a similar approach by declaring that the proper scope of the criminal law is to affirm basic community values by criminalizing "real crimes," with the principal criteria for identifying real crimes as those acts that seriously harm other people:

> Wrongfulness is a necessary, not a sufficient condition of criminality. Before an act should count as a crime, three further conditions must be fulfilled. First, it must cause harm—to other people, to society or, in special cases, to those needing to be protected from themselves. Second, it must cause harm that is serious both in nature and degree. And third, it must cause harm that is best dealt with through the mechanism of the criminal law. These conditions would confine the criminal law to crimes of violence, dishonesty, and other offences traditionally in the centre of the stage. Any other offences, not really wrong but penally prohibited because this is the most convenient way of dealing with them, must stay outside the Criminal Code and qualify as quasi-crimes or violations.[16]

In reality, few legal codes live up to the Walker-Mill criteria, or even the more relaxed LRCC criteria. Most, including our current *Criminal Code*, are influenced strongly by cultural conceptions of right and wrong, and encompass many behaviours that are not immediately and directly harmful to anyone but those who choose to be involved with them. These illegal activities, often called victimless crimes, include drug abuse, certain forms of "deviant" sexuality, gambling, and various other legally proscribed consensual deeds. Advocates of legislation designed to curb these activities suggest that while such behaviour is not always directly harmful to others, it may erode social cohesiveness and ruin the lives of those who engage in it.

Standing in strong opposition to the Walker-Mill perspective are legislators and theorists who purposefully use the law as a tool to facilitate social change. Modifications in the legal structure of a society can quickly and dramatically produce changes in the behaviour of entire groups. A change in the tax laws, for example, typically sends people scrambling to their accountants to devise spending and investment strategies that can take advantage of the change. Our legal system not only condemns interpersonal violence and enforces tax codes, it also serves to support the dominant economic order (capitalism) and to protect the powerful and the wealthy (through an emphasis on private property and the rights that attach to property).

Throughout Canadian criminal law, Judeo-Christian principles hold considerable sway. Concepts such as sin and atonement provide for a view of men and women as wilful actors in a world of personal and sensual temptations. Such ideas have made possible both the legal notion of guilt and corrections-based punishment.

The realization that laws respond to the needs and interests of society at any given time was expressed by the popular American jurist Oliver Wendell Holmes (1809–1894) in an address he gave at Harvard University in 1881. Holmes said, "The life of the law has not been logic; it has been experience. The felt necessities of the time, the prevalent moral and political theories, institutions of public policy, avowed or unconscious, even the prejudices which judges share with their fellowmen have had a good deal more to do than the syllogism in determining the rules by which men should be governed."[17] (The "syllogism," in this sense, refers to abstract theorizing as the basis for law, but Holmes discounted the importance of such "theorizing.")

Once law has been created, it is generally slow to change, because it is built upon years of tradition. The law can be thought of as a force that supports social order, but which is opposed to rapid social change. When law facilitates change, that change usually proceeds in an orderly and deliberate fashion. Revolutions, on the other hand, produce near-instantaneous legal changes, along with massive social disorder.

# Social Engineering

One of the greatest legal scholars of modern times was Roscoe Pound (1870–1964), dean of the Harvard Law School from 1916 to 1936. Pound saw the law as a type of social engineering.[18] The law is a tool, he said, that meets the demands of men and women living together in society. Pound strongly believed that the law must be able to change with the times and to reflect new needs as they arise.

Pound distilled his ideas into a set of **jural postulates**. Such postulates, claimed Pound, form the basis of all law because they reflect shared needs. In 1942, Pound published his postulates in the form of five propositions.[19]

Pound's postulates form a theory of "consensus" about the origins of law—both civil and criminal. He suggests that most laws are the product of shared social needs experienced by the majority of members in the society where they arise. However, a number of writers have criticized Pound for failing to recognize the diversity of society. How, they ask, can the law address common needs in society when society consists of many different groups—each with their own set of interests and needs? As a consequence of such criticism, Pound modified his theory to include a jurisprudence of interest. Whereas the concept of **jurisprudence** refers simply to the philosophy of law or to the science and study of the law, the concept of a "jurisprudence of interest" held that one of the basic purposes of law is to satisfy "as many claims or demands of as many people as possible."[20]

**jural postulates**
Propositions developed by the famous jurist Roscoe Pound, who holds that the law reflects shared needs without which members of society could not co-exist. Pound's jural postulates are often linked to the idea that the law can be used to engineer the social structure to ensure certain kinds of outcomes (such as property rights embodied in the law of theft do in capitalistic societies).

**jurisprudence** The philosophy of law; the science and study of the law.

# Social Conflict

Opposed to Pound's theory of consensus is William Chambliss's view of law as a tool of powerful individuals and groups acting in their own interests, and often in conflict with one another.[21] Conflict theory has its roots in the writings of Karl Marx, who explained all of social history as the result of an ongoing conflict between the "haves" and the "have-nots."

Chambliss believes we should not see the agencies of criminal justice as "neutral." Rather, he says, government is "a weapon of the dominant classes or interest groups in society."[22] Putting it more directly, Chambliss writes, "... in one way or another, the laws which are passed, implemented, and incorporated into the legal system reflect the interests of those groups capable of having their views incorporated into the official (that is legal) views of the society."[23]

# TYPES OF LAW

"Criminal" and "civil" law are the best-known types of modern law. However, numerous distinctions between categories of the law rest upon their source, intent, and application. Laws in Canadian society can be usefully described in terms of the following:

- Public law (including criminal law and constitutional law)
- Private law
- Case law
- Procedural law

We will now discuss each type of law in some detail.

# Public Law

Law may accurately be viewed as a means of regulating the relationships between parties in society. Public law governs the legal relationships in which the society itself or the state is one of the parties to the legal relationship under consideration. Public law can be subdivided further. Constitutional law governs the legal interactions of various parts of government, and sets out the limits of state interference in the lives of the country's citizens. Tax law governs the collection of money for the state, permitting it to operate in a substantive way.

Administrative law governs the conduct of government agencies, in reviewing the many decisions these agencies make on a daily basis, impacting upon the lives of individuals, and the conduct of business throughout society.

# Constitutional Law

The constitutional law of Canada has two major responsibilities. First, it regulates the relationships between the various levels and branches of government. The federal, provincial, and municipal governments all derive their authority from the law of the constitution. Additionally, the executive, legislative, and judicial branches of government are structured according to, and derive their authority to a large degree from, constitutional principles. The second major responsibility of constitutional law has only come to the forefront in the last two decades. This responsibility is the regulation of the power of the state over the individual in society. This aspect of constitutional law is largely governed by the operation of the *Charter of Rights and Freedoms*.

The *Constitution Act, 1867* divides legislative responsibility between the central government in Ottawa and the regional governments or provinces. This statute splits responsibility for the criminal justice system between these two levels of government. In Canada, the two levels of government share responsibility for various aspects of the criminal justice system, with neither level being more important than the other. Sections 91 and 92 of the *Constitution Act, 1867* are the key provisions dividing legislative responsibility between the various levels of government. Section 91 allocates powers to the federal government and includes:

27. The Criminal Law, except the Constitution of Courts of Criminal Jurisdiction, but including the Procedure in Criminal Matters.

28. The Establishment, Maintenance, and Management of Penitentiaries.

In addition, the introductory wording to section 91 allows the federal government to make laws for the "Peace, Order and Good Government of Canada." This authority provides a supplementary or residual power for the federal government to make laws affecting the entire country that do not fit within any more specific heads of power. The federal government's powers in section 91 are supplemented by powers found in the judicature provisions of the *Constitution Act, 1867* (ss. 96–101). These grant the federal government the authority to appoint judges to all of the higher courts in the country, and to create its own courts, including the highest court of appeal for the country: the Supreme Court of Canada. In Canada, the federal government is also responsible for the territories that have not yet attained provincial status. The *Constitution Act, 1871* solidifies the federal responsibility over the territories.

The above-noted powers have resulted in the federal government creating a national police force, the Royal Canadian Mounted Police. The federal government has created a host of criminal laws and other federal statutes, and appointed federal prosecutors to prosecute many of them. It has created courts, and appointed the judges in provincial superior courts, the federal court system, and the Supreme Court of Canada. It has devised a criminal code, set up rules of criminal procedure, and established rules of evidence to be applied in criminal trials. In addition, the federal government has established an elaborate correctional system, with penitentiaries of various levels of security scattered across the country, and a system of parole for the reintegration of offenders back into the community. With such wide-ranging powers, one might at first believe that there is no role left for the provincial and municipal governments to play in the area of criminal justice. This conclusion would be erroneous.

Section 92 of the *Constitution Act, 1867* allocates various powers to the provincial governments. These include the following:

6. The Establishment, Maintenance, and Management of Public and Reformatory Prisons in and for the Province.

7. The Establishment, Maintenance, and Management of Hospitals, Asylums, Charities
   …

8. Municipal Institutions in the Province.
   …

13. Property and Civil rights in the Province.
14. The Administration of Justice in the Province, including the Constitution, Maintenance, and Organization of Provincial Courts, both of Civil and of Criminal Jurisdiction …
15. The Imposition of Punishment by Fine, Penalty, or Imprisonment for enforcing any Law of the Province made in relation to any Matter coming within any of the Classes of Subjects enumerated in this Section.
16. Generally all Matters of a merely local or private Nature in the Province.

Under the provincial heads of power, the *Constitution Act, 1867* has permitted the regional governments to establish and operate many of the key elements in the criminal justice system. The most obviously relevant power is the general assignment of responsibility over the "Administration of Justice" to the provinces. If this provision were to stand alone as the only criminal justice–related provision in the constitution, it would appear to grant plenary jurisdiction to the provinces. However, it must be read in conjunction with the federal powers mentioned above. Through this power, the provinces have established police forces, and Crown Attorney, offices to prosecute criminal (and provincial) offences. Each province has established a court system to deal with criminal trials and appointed judges to the lower courts in the provinces. Through the other provincial powers, the regional governments have established prisons and probation programs for adults and young offenders. They have established forensic psychiatric facilities to house mentally disordered offenders. And they have enacted non-criminal laws and attached penalties to them that make them appear to mimic criminal law in terms of their impact on offenders.

Additionally, the provinces are responsible for municipal institutions. Through this power, each province has established legislation that authorizes the creation of municipal councils. The legislation delegates some of the provincial powers to these municipal councils that are then free to apply these powers in their local contexts. With these powers, municipalities have taken over much of the responsibility for policing in the country, with most major cities creating their own police departments. These police departments typically create prison cells know as "lockups" within the police facilities, which house arrested offenders until they can be taken to court for processing. Municipal councils may also impose prohibitions on conduct and attach penalties, so long as they do not interfere with the federal government's criminal law-making power. The resulting laws, or bylaws as they are generally called, typically carry lesser penalties than those attached to criminal offences. Municipalities even inherit the authority to create municipal courts to deal with such offences.

Canada's constitutional structure has resulted in a fairly complex criminal justice system in which all three levels of government, federal, provincial, and municipal, have an important role to play. The federal government's responsibility over the creation of criminal law and procedure gives it a key responsibility for defining the types of conduct that will be processed through the criminal justice system.

**criminal law** That branch of modern law that concerns itself with offences committed against society, members thereof, their property, and the social order.

**crime** An act committed or omitted in violation of a law forbidding or commanding it for which the possible penalties for an adult upon conviction include incarceration, for which a corporation can be penalized by fine or forfeit, or for which a juvenile can be adjudged delinquent or transferred to criminal court for prosecution.

## Criminal Law

Fundamental to the concept of **criminal law** is the assumption that criminal acts injure not just individuals, but society as a whole. Social order, as reflected in the values supported by statute, is reduced to some degree whenever a criminal act occurs. In England (from which much of Canadian legal tradition devolves) in olden times, offenders were said to violate the "King's Peace" when they committed a **crime**. They offended not just their victims, but also contravened the order established under the rule of the monarch. For this reason, in criminal cases, the state, as the injured party, begins the process of bringing the offender to justice. Even if the victim is dead and has no one to speak on his or her behalf, the agencies of justice will investigate the crime and file charges against the offender. Because crimes injure the fabric of society, the state becomes the plaintiff in criminal proceedings. Court cases reflect this fact by being cited as follows: *R. v. Smith* (1979) (whereby the state is represented by an agent of the Crown, prosecuting under the Latin term for queen, *regina*). In Canada, criminal prosecutions are typically undertaken by agents of the provincial Crown, with the federal Crown prosecutors fulfilling a limited role, despite the federal government's plenary jurisdiction to enact criminal law.

Violations of the criminal law result in the imposition of punishment. Punishment is philosophically justified by the fact that the criminal *intended* the harm and is responsible for it. Punishment serves a variety of purposes, which we will discuss later in the chapter on sentencing (Chapter 9).

Criminal law, which is built upon constitutional principles and operates within an established set of procedures applicable to the criminal justice system, is composed of both statutory and case law. Statutory law is the "law on the books." It is the result of legislative action and is often thought of as the "law of the land." Written laws exist in both criminal and civil areas and are called statutes. Once laws have been written down in an organized fashion, they are said to be "codified." Federal statutes are compiled in the Revised Statutes of Canada (R.S.C.). Provincial statutes and municipal bylaws are also readily available in written, or codified, form. The bulk of the written criminal law in Canada is found in a statute enacted by the federal Parliament called the *Criminal Code*, R.S.C. 1985, c. C-46.

Written criminal law in this country is of two types: substantive and procedural. Substantive law deals directly with specifying the nature of, and appropriate punishment for, particular offences. In Canada, the *Constitution Act, 1867* allocates exclusive authority to make both substantive criminal law and procedural criminal law to the federal Parliament by virtue of section 91(27). In this regard, the *Criminal Code* in our country has laws against murder, sexual assault, robbery, and assault. Additionally, the federal criminal law-making power has been utilized to create offences dealing with drug use in the *Controlled Drugs and Substances Act*, espionage in the *Security of Information Act*, tax evasion in the *Income Tax Act*, terrorism under the *Anti-terrorism Act*, and numerous other offence-containing statutes. Procedural criminal law is largely dealt with in the *Criminal Code;* however, the federal *Youth Criminal Justice Act* contains the procedure to be applied at the trials of young persons, and the *Canada Evidence Act* contains significant provisions governing the conduct of a criminal trial, thereby regulating some aspects of procedure, by dictating the evidence to be admitted at trial. Procedural laws specify acceptable methods for dealing with violations of substantive laws, especially within the context of a judicial setting.

The federal government's legislative responsibility over criminal law is a broad one. In addition to traditional interpersonal violent crimes and property crimes, the criminal law-making power grants the federal Parliament the power to enact environmental protection law,[24] preventive detention of the mentally disordered,[25] and laws prohibiting the advertisement of tobacco products.[26]

While provinces are not granted the authority to create criminal law in Canada, they do have authority granted to them by section 92(15) of the *Constitution Act, 1867* to impose punishment, even including fines and imprisonment, for the violation of their validly enacted legislation. This power has resulted in each of the provinces creating laws governing the use of the highways, the consumption of liquor, the treatment of the mentally disordered, and a variety of other areas, many of which deal with local issues. However, provinces, and the municipalities that inherit their law-making power from the provinces, must be careful not to tread on the ground reserved for the federal government. For example, while provinces and municipalities have the power to legislate with regard to public advertising, an attempt by a municipal council to restrict street prostitutes from advertising the sale of sex for money to potential customers has been found to be too closely related to federal criminal law-making power over soliciting, and not closely enough related to advertising on the streets.[27]

## Case Law

Case law (which comes from judicial decisions) is also referred to as the law of **precedent**. It represents the accumulated wisdom of trial and appellate courts (those that hear appeals) in criminal and civil cases over the years. Once a court decision is rendered, it is written down. Typically, the reasoning behind the decision is recorded as well. Under the rule of precedent, this reasoning should then be taken into consideration by other courts in settling future cases.

**precedent** A legal principle that operates to ensure that previous judicial decisions are authoritatively considered and incorporated into future cases.

Appellate courts have considerable power to influence new court decisions at the trial level. The court with the greatest influence, of course, is the Supreme Court of Canada. The precedents it establishes are guidelines for legal reasoning by which lower courts reach conclusions.

The principle of recognizing previous decisions as precedents to guide future deliberations is called *stare decisis* and forms the basis for our modern "law of precedent." Lief H. Carter has pointed out how precedent operates along two dimensions.[28] He calls them the vertical and the horizontal. The vertical rule requires that decisions made by a higher court be taken into consideration by lower courts in their deliberations. Under this rule, provincial trial courts, for example, should be expected to follow the spirit of decisions rendered by their provincial appellate courts.

---

## BOX 3.2    Theory into Practice

### What Is Crime? The Example of Crimes Against the Environment

In 1985, the Law Reform Commission of Canada released a working paper that dealt with crimes against the environment. At that time, the *Criminal Code* did not have any explicit offences dealing with the natural environment itself, even though the *Code* prohibited offences against persons and property. The Commission supported the idea that some actions, or omissions involving the environment should be viewed as crimes. Reference was made to the "tests" proposed within the Ouimet report,[1] to establish whether a particular offence was a "real" crime or should be reduced to a regulatory offence. Offences should be viewed as real crimes if:

- they contravene a fundamental value;
- they are seriously harmful;
- they are committed with the required mental element;
- the needed enforcement measures would not themselves contravene fundamental values; and
- treating them as crimes would make a significant contribution to dealing with the harms and risks they create.[2]

With growing levels of concern about the possible decline of the environment, including depletion of the ozone layer, global warming, and pollution like that caused by the oil tanker *Exxon Valdez*, there is substantial public support for measures that would allow for the criminal prosecution of offenders. Among the possible sources of harm and catastrophe identified by the Law Reform Commission of Canada are:

- mercury;
- lead;
- polychlorinated biphenyls (PCBs);

- pesticides and herbicides;
- pulp and paper mill effluent;
- hazardous waste;
- chlorine and the transportation of dangerous sub-stances; and
- radiation.

It was noted that as early as 1907, there was a case involving the transportation of dynamite that relied on the *Criminal Code*, even though suitable regulatory remedies existed.[3] This case involved a railway car that was carrying dynamite. Through negligence, the dynamite exploded, killing two people and injuring several others. By proceeding under the *Criminal Code*, the railway was fined $25 000 upon conviction. Under the *Railway Act*, a fine not in excess of $500 would have been available.

In 1997, the Supreme Court of Canada held that a prohibition on the dumping of polychlorinated biphenyls (PCBs) into the environment, set out in interim orders created pursuant to the *Canadian Environmental Protection Act*,[4] was a valid exercise of the federal government's power to enact criminal law.[5] The regulation of the environment is a shared responsibility of the provincial and federal governments.

Legislation is also in place in the United States, Germany, and Japan to criminalize serious environmental pollution, and to place substantial focus on the importance of maintaining public health.

### QUESTIONS FOR DISCUSSION

1. How do environmental crimes differ from other types of crime?

2. What are some other possible areas where lawmakers might consider introducing criminal sanctions in order to protect the environment?

---

[1.]Canadian Committee on Corrections. (1969). *Report of the Canadian Committee on Corrections: toward unity: criminal justice and corrections.* Ottawa: Information Canada.

[2.]Cited in Law Reform Commission of Canada. (1985). *Crimes against the environment (Working paper, no. 44).* Ottawa: Law Reform Commission of Canada, p. 2.

[3.]*R. v. Michigan Central Railway* (1907), 10 O.W.R. 660.

[4.]*Chlorobiphenyls Interim Order,* P.C. 1989-296, s. 6(a), issued under the *Canadian Environmental Protection Act,* R.S.C. 1985, c. 16 (14th Suppl.), ss. 34 and 35.

[5.]*R. v. Hydro-Québec,* [1987] 3 S.C.R. 213.

The horizontal dimension means that courts on the same level should be consistent in their interpretation of the law. The Supreme Court of Canada, operating under the horizontal rule, for example, should not be expected to change its ruling in cases similar to those it has already decided.

*Stare decisis* makes for predictability in the law. Defendants walking into a modern courtroom typically have the opportunity to be represented by lawyers who are trained in legal precedents as well as procedure. As a consequence, defendants will have a good idea of what to expect about the manner in which their trials will proceed.

## Procedural Law

Procedural law is another kind of law, being made up of statutes and case law. It is a body of rules that regulates the processing of an offender by the criminal justice system. Procedural law, for example, specifies in our *Criminal Code* that the testimony of one party to certain crimes, such as perjury and treason, cannot be used as the sole evidence against the other party. General rules of evidence, search and seizure, procedures to be followed in an arrest, and other specific processes by which the justice system operates are contained in procedural law.

As a great jurist once said, however, the law is like a living thing. It changes and evolves over time. Legislatures enact new statutory laws, and justices set new precedents, sometimes overruling established ones. In Canada today, for example, because of the changed role of women in society, our courts allow wives to bring charges of sexual assault against their husbands for acts of rape—an act not subject to criminal prosecution just a few years ago. Similarly, testimony of children may now be given without a judge warning the jury about any inherent dangers in relying on the uncorroborated testimony of a child. Such changes in the law are contrary to years of previously created precedents and statutory enactments.

## Private Law

Private law or **civil law** provides a formal means for regulating non-public relationships between persons, business and other organizations, and agencies of government. The body of civil law contains rules for contracts, divorce, child support and custody, the creation of wills, property transfers, negligence, libel, unfair practices in hiring, the manufacture and sale of consumer goods with hidden hazards for the user, and many other contractual and social obligations. When the private law is violated, a civil suit may follow.

Civil suits seek not punishment, but compensation, usually in the form of property or monetary damages. Civil suits may also be filed in order to achieve an injunction or a kind of judicial cease-and-desist order. A violation of the civil law may be a **tort** (a breach of duty resulting in an injury to an individual), or a contract violation, but it is not a crime. Because a tort is a personal wrong, it is left to the aggrieved individual to set the machinery of the court in motion—that is, to bring a suit.

Civil law is more concerned with assigning "blame" than it is with intent. Civil suits arising from automobile crashes, for example, do not allege that either driver intended to inflict bodily harm. Nor do they claim that it was the intent of the driver to damage either vehicle. However, when someone is injured, or property damage occurs, even in an accident, civil procedures make it possible to gauge responsibility and assign blame to one party or the other. The parties to a civil suit are referred to as the plaintiff (who seeks relief) and the defendant (against whom relief is sought).

In a tragic 1995 case, which provides a good example of civil liability, Douglas Doern, a young man driving home in the early hours one morning, was hit by a vehicle being pursued by the police for a suspicion of impaired driving.[29] In the pursuit, the police had violated numerous police-pursuit policy requirements, some of which would have required termination of the pursuit in question due to the inherent risks in carrying it on. The driver being pursued was also clearly negligent in showing disregard for the safety of the users of the highway by speeding excessively, and running through red lights in a bid to outrun the police. The B.C. Supreme Court found both parties at fault, spreading the blame

**civil law** That portion of the modern law that regulates contracts and other obligations involving primarily personal interests.

**tort** A private or civil wrong or injury. A breach of duty to an individual that results in harm to that person.

25 per cent on the police and 75 per cent on the driver seeking to elude the police. This decision was upheld on appeal to the B.C. Court of Appeal in late 1997. Many Canadian police departments have since undertaken a review of their police-pursuit policies.

Civil law pertains to injuries suffered by individuals that are unfair or unjust according to the standards operative in the social group. Breaches of contract, unfair practices in hiring, the manufacture and sale of consumer goods with hidden hazards for the user, and slanderous comments made about others have all been grounds for civil suits. Suits may, on occasion, arise as extensions of criminal action. Monetary compensation may be sought through our system of civil laws by a victim of a criminal assault, regardless of whether a criminal conviction has been obtained. Civil suits provide a practical means for crime victims to obtain financial compensation for their harm, and may also provide a therapeutic way for crime victims to regain control over their lives.[30]

In recent years, tort damage awards have resulted in developing concern among various segments of society, particularly those most affected by escalating insurance costs associated with covering such damage awards. In particular, the areas of motor vehicle driving and medical malpractice have raised great concern.[31]

A 1993 civil case, which may hold considerable significance for the criminal justice systems in both the United States and Canada, found a Florida jury holding Kmart stores liable for selling a gun to a drunken man. The buyer, Thomas W. Knapp, later used the weapon to shoot his girlfriend, Deborah Kitchen, in the neck—leaving her permanently paralyzed. Kmart was ordered to pay Kitchen $11 million, sending a message to gun retailers across the nation.[32] In 1995, in what may eventually involve a far more massive settlement and have wide-reaching implications, a San Francisco judge ruled that a lawsuit brought by a widow of a man slain by gunfire was based on solid legal principles and could proceed.[33] At issue was whether the handgun maker, Miami-based Navegar, Incorporated, could be sued under a legal theory that holds manufacturers liable for injuries caused by their products. In this case, Michelle Scully sued the gun manufacturer after her husband, John, was killed by an assailant who opened fire on workers in a California law office in 1993. As the shooting started, John Scully threw himself over his wife and shielded her with his body. Some criticized the judge's ruling, saying that it opened a Pandora's box of potential suits against manufacturers of all kinds of products—since lawsuits targeting products that are not defective and which function precisely as intended might result in suits against automobile manufacturers; makers of alcohol, tobacco, and high-cholesterol foods; and even against companies that make knives, gasoline, candles, and other flammable materials when irresponsible individuals choose to use those products to harm others.

Criminal action, not otherwise excusable, will also typically be grounds for a civil suit by the victim against the offender. Many crimes have analogous torts, and provinces typically do not bar recovery through civil law for crimes held accountable through the criminal law. For example, a criminal assault conviction may be followed by a successful civil suit alleging assault and/or battery. A criminal kidnapping conviction may be accompanied by a civil suit for false imprisonment. A breaking-and-entering conviction could be followed by a civil suit for trespass to property. Theft has its analogous civil cause of action in the torts of trespass to chattels, detinue, and conversion.

## Quasi-Criminal Law

**regulations** Enactments of a body subordinate to a legislative body. Such enactments carry the force of law.

Quasi-criminal law refers to the body of laws and **regulations** that have been created by governments to control the activities in everyday life outside the realm of true crimes.[34] Regulation of industry, business, and individuals through tax laws, health codes, restrictions on pollution and waste disposal, vehicle registration, building codes, and the like are examples of quasi-criminal law.

Other quasi-criminal laws cover practices in the areas of customs (imports/exports), immigration, agriculture, product safety, and most areas of manufacturing. Modern individualists claim that overregulation characterizes the Western way of life, although they are in turn criticized for failing to adequately recognize the complexity of modern society. Overregulation has also been used on occasion as a rallying cry for political hopefuls who believe that many Canadians wish to alter Canadian society to a simpler form, characterized by free enterprise and lack of governmental involvement.

Although the criminal law is, for the most part, separate from quasi-criminal regulations, the two may overlap. For instance, the rise in organized criminal activity in the area of toxic waste disposal has led to criminal prosecutions in several provinces.

Regulatory agencies will sometimes arrange settlements that fall short of court action, but which are considered binding on individuals or groups who have not lived up to the intent of federal or provincial regulations. Education, environmental protection, and discriminatory hiring practices are all areas in which settlements have been employed.

# GENERAL CATEGORIES OF CRIME

Violations of the criminal law can be of many different types and vary in severity. Four categories of violation will be discussed in the pages that follow. They are:

- Summary conviction offences
- Indictable offences
- Hybrid offences
- Inchoate offences

## Summary Conviction Offences

Violations of the criminal law can be more or less serious. Summary conviction offences are relatively minor crimes, consisting of offences such as public nudity, causing a disturbance, trespassing at night, vagrancy, communicating for the purposes of prostitution, water skiing at night, taking a motor vehicle without the owner's consent, obtaining food or lodging by fraud, pretending to practise witchcraft, making indecent or harassing phone calls, obtaining transportation by fraud; intimidation, injuring, and endangering or causing unnecessary suffering to animals.

In general, summary conviction offences are punishable by six months in prison or less, and up to a $2000 fine. Corporations convicted of summary conviction offences are liable for up to a $20 000 fine. In fact, many persons convicted of summary conviction offences receive suspended sentences involving a fine and supervised probation. If an "active sentence" is received for a summary conviction offence, it will involve time in a provincial prison or community correctional centre rather than imprisonment in a long-term facility. Some summary conviction offenders have recently been sentenced to conditional sentences to be served in the community and to community service activities as a condition of probation, requiring them to do such things as wash school buses, paint local government buildings, or clean parks and other public areas.

Normally, a police officer cannot arrest a person for a summary conviction offence unless the crime was committed in the officer's presence. If the in-presence requirement is missing, the officer will need to seek an arrest warrant from a justice of the peace or provincial court judge. Once a warrant has been issued, the officer may proceed with the arrest; however, a justice will generally only issue a summons to be served upon the accused, requiring him or her to attend court to deal with the allegation.

## Indictable Offences

Indictable offences are serious crimes and include murder, manslaughter, sexual assault with a weapon, aggravated assault, robbery, theft of an item valued at over $5000, kidnapping, breaking and entering a dwelling house, arson, and so on. Historically, these offences were considered **felonies**, and under common law, felons could be sentenced to death and/or have their property confiscated. Today, persons convicted of indictable offences are

**felonies** Criminal offences punishable by death, or by incarceration in a prison facility for at least one year.

subject to penalties ranging from fines to lengthy prison sentences. The *Criminal Code* specifies the length of prison term available to a sentencing judge for all crimes. Some of the less serious indictable offences carry possible terms of incarceration not exceeding two years: riot, s. 65; permitting an escape, s. 146; keeping a common bawdy house, s. 210(1); abandoning a child, s. 218; and possession of instruments for breaking into coin-operated devices, s. 352. The most serious indictable offences carry a mandatory prison term of life.

# Hybrid Offences

Many offences appear to justify differential treatment due to a variety of circumstances present or absent in a specific case. While a killing is a killing, and should always be treated as a serious offence, some offences appear to be more or less serious, depending on the facts of the case, and should be treated more or less seriously, depending on those facts.

If the crime is a serious matter causing significant injury, the matter should be treated more seriously, with a complex trial procedure ensuring an accurate determination of the issues in the case. Other crimes involving a similar type of act may be committed in circumstances where there is less injury, and where mitigating factors tend to lessen the apparent need to treat the offence as seriously. In such circumstances, a less formal trial may seem appropriate, and the accused should be exposed to lesser penalties. Criminal law in Canada takes these factors into account by making many of the offences "hybrid" offences. These offences are sometimes referred to as "dual procedure" offences, "mixed" offences, or "Crown option" offences. They are offences for which the Crown prosecutor selects whether to have the offence treated as a more serious one (indictable), or a less serious one (summary conviction). If the Crown decides to treat the case as an indictable one, it will expose the accused to a potentially higher penalty, but it will also provide the accused with greater procedural safeguards, often entitling him or her to a jury trial, and to a preliminary hearing before the trial itself is conducted. If the Crown opts to treat the case as a summary conviction offence, the accused will be exposed to a lesser maximum penalty, but he or she will also lose some of the procedural safeguards attached to indictable offences. Such offences are truly a "hybrid," or mixture, of the two primary types of criminal offences. Hybrid offences are readily identifiable by looking at the wording of the *Criminal Code* section identifying the punishment for the offence:

s. 266    Every one who commits an assault is guilty of:

 (a) an indictable offence and liable to imprisonment for a term not exceeding five years; or

 (b) an offence punishable on summary conviction.

# Inchoate Offences

**inchoate offence**  One not yet completed. Also, an offence that consists of an action or conduct that is a step towards the intended commission of another offence.

Another special category of crime is the **inchoate offence**. The word "inchoate" means incomplete or partial, and inchoate offences are those that have not yet been fully carried out. Conspiracies are an example. When a person conspires to commit a crime, the agreement between parties to commit a crime constitutes the crime itself. Provided the parties intend to commit the crime, subsequent actions undertaken in furtherance of the conspiracy are not required for arrest and prosecution. When a conspiracy unfolds, the ultimate act that it aims to bring about does not have to occur for the parties to the conspiracy to be arrested. When people plan to bomb a public building, for example, they can legally be stopped before the bombing.

Another type of inchoate offence is the attempt. Sometimes an offender is unable to complete the crime. Homeowners may arrive just as a burglar is trying to enter their residence. The burglar may drop his tools and run. Even so, this frustrated burglar can be arrested and charged with attempted break and entry.[35]

# GENERAL FEATURES OF CRIME

From the perspective of Western jurisprudence, all crimes can be said to share certain features, and the notion of crime itself can be said to rest upon such general principles. Taken together, these features, which are described in the paragraphs that follow, form the legal essence of the concept of crime.

## The Criminal Act

A necessary first feature of any crime is some act in violation of the law. Such an act is termed the *actus reus* of a crime. The term means a "guilty act." Generally, a person must commit some act before being subject to criminal sanctions. Someone who admits (perhaps on a TV talk show) to being a drug user, for example, cannot be arrested on that basis. To *be something* is not usually a crime—to *do something* is. In the case of the admitted drug user, police who heard the admission might begin gathering evidence to prove some specific law violation in that person's past, or perhaps they might watch that individual for future behaviour in violation of the law. An arrest might then occur. If it did, it would be based on a specific action in violation of the law pertaining to controlled substances.

Vagrancy laws, popular in the early part of the twentieth century, have generally been curtailed by our lawmakers because they did not specify what act violated the law. In fact, the *less* a person did, the more vagrant they were.

An *omission to act*, however, may be criminal where the person in question is required by law to do something. Child-neglect provisions in the *Criminal Code*, for example, focus on parents and child guardians who do not live up to their responsibilities for providing the necessaries of life for their children.

*Threatening to act* can itself be a criminal offence. Telling someone "I'm going to kill you" might result in an arrest based on the offence of "uttering threats" contrary to section 264.1 of the *Criminal Code*.

*Attempted criminal activity* is also illegal. An attempt to murder or sexually assault, for example, is a serious crime, even though the planned act was not accomplished.

As noted above, the conspiracy provisions in the *Criminal Code* do not require any act at all beyond the mere agreement between two or more parties to commit a crime. Similar to the conspiracy offence is the newly enacted anti-stalking law, that is, the offence of *criminal harassment*. Anti-stalking statutes are intended to prevent harassment and intimidation, even when no physical harm occurs. In Canada, rough estimates of the number of stalkers and victims can be gleaned from a Statistics Canada report released in 2000, which revealed data from 106 police agencies in Canada, representing 41 per cent of the national volume of reported crime. While not a representative sample, the data compiled provide some indication of the extent of stalking in Canada. This research showed 5910 victims and 3842 persons accused of criminal harassment in 1999.[36] Stalkers often strike after their victims have unsuccessfully complained to authorities about stalking-related activities such as harassing phone calls and letters. The anti-stalking law, however, still faces a constitutional hurdle of attempting to prevent people not otherwise involved in criminal activity from walking and standing where they wish, and from speaking freely. Ultimately, the Supreme Court of Canada will probably have to decide the legitimacy of this law.

## Mens Rea

**Mens rea** is the second component of crime. It literally means "guilty mind" and recognizes a mental component to crime. The modern interpretation of *mens rea*, however, does not focus so much on whether a person feels guilty about his or her act—but rather looks to whether the act was intended. As the famous American Supreme Court Justice Oliver Wendell Holmes once wrote, "Even a dog distinguishes between being stumbled over and being kicked."[37]

The idea of *mens rea* has undergone a gradual evolution during recent centuries such that today the term can be generally described as signifying *blameworthiness*. Indeed, "moral

**mens rea** The state of mind that accompanies a criminal act. Also, guilty mind.

blameworthiness" is now considered by the Supreme Court of Canada to be a constitutionally mandated prerequisite for conviction.[38] The question asked, at least theoretically, in criminal prosecutions, is whether the person charged with an offence *should be blamed* and held accountable for his or her actions.

*Mens rea* is said to be present when a person *should have known better*, even if the person did not directly intend the consequences of his or her action. A person who acts recklessly, and thereby endangers others, may be found guilty of a crime when harm occurs, even though no negative consequences were intended. For example, a parent who left his or her 15-month-old child alone in the tub can be later prosecuted for criminal negligence causing death or manslaughter by criminal negligence if the child drowns.

It should be recognized, however, that negligence in and of itself is not a crime. Negligent conduct can be evidence of crime only when it falls below some acceptable standard of care. That standard is today applied in courts through the fictional creation of a *reasonable person*. The question to be asked in a given case is whether the behaviour of the accused represents a serious departure from the standard of care that would be exercised by a reasonable person in the same situation. In other words, is it clearly obvious that a person should have known better, and acted differently, than the defendant? The reasonable person criterion provides a yardstick for juries faced with thorny issues of guilt or innocence.

## Concurrence

The concurrence of act and intent is the third component of crime. A person may intend to kill a rival, for example. As she drives to the intended victim's house, gun in hand, fantasizing about how she will commit the murder, the victim may be crossing the street on the way home from grocery shopping. If the two accidentally collide, and the intended victim dies, there has been no concurrence of act and intent.

Some scholars contend that the three features of crime that we have just outlined are sufficient to constitute the concept of crime. Other scholars, however, view modern Western law as more complex. They argue that four additional principles are necessary, including (1) a harm, (2) a causal relationship between the act and the harm, (3) the principle of legality, and (4) the principle of punishment.

## Harm

A harm occurs in any crime, although not all harms are crimes. When a person is murdered or sexually assaulted, harm can clearly be identified. Some crimes, however, have come to be called "victimless." Perpetrators maintain that they are not harming anyone in committing such crimes. Rather, they say, the crime is pleasurable. Prostitution, gambling, "crimes against nature" (some acts of sexual deviance), and drug use are but a few crimes classified as "victimless." People involved in such crimes will argue that, if anyone is being hurt, it is only they. What these offenders fail to recognize, say legal theorists, is the social harm caused by their behaviour. Areas afflicted with chronic prostitution, drug use, sexual deviance, and illegal gambling are usually characterized by depressed property values, disintegrating family life, and the increase of other, more traditional crimes as money is sought to support the "victimless" activities and law-abiding citizens flee the area.

## Causation

Causation refers to the fact that a clear link needs to be identified between the act and the harm occasioned by the crime. A classic example of this principle involves attempted murder. If a person shoots another, but the victim is seriously injured and not killed, the victim might survive for a long time in a hospital. Death may occur, perhaps a year later, because pneumonia sets in or because blood clots form in the injured person from lack of activity. In such cases, defence lawyers will likely argue that the defendant did not cause

Jay Handel was convicted of murdering his six children in October 2003, despite a claim that he was mentally disordered at the time. The defence had argued that he suffered from depression and paranoia, brought about by his disintegrating marriage. Not all mentally disordered offenders succeed in putting forward a defence based upon their mental state at the time of the offence.

the death, but rather the death occurred because of disease. If a jury agrees with the defence's claim, the shooter may go free or be found guilty of a lesser charge, such as assault.

## Legality

The principle of legality is concerned with the fact that a behaviour cannot be criminal if no law exists that defines it as such. It is all right to attempt to commit suicide in so far as our criminal law is concerned, because there is no statute "on the books" prohibiting it. Prior to 1972, the situation was quite different, whereby the *Criminal Code* contained an offence provision making it a crime to attempt to kill oneself. The principle of legality also includes the notion that a law cannot be created tomorrow that will hold a person legally responsible for something he or she does today. These are called *ex post facto* laws. Laws are binding only from the date of their creation or from some specified future date at which they are determined take effect.[39]

## Punishment

Finally, the principle of punishment says that no crime can be said to occur where punishment has not been specified in the law. Theft, for example, would not be a crime if the law simply said, "It is illegal to steal." Punishment needs to be specified, so that if a person is found guilty of violating the law, sanctions can be lawfully imposed.

# ELEMENTS OF A SPECIFIC CRIMINAL OFFENCE

While we can discuss the principles that constitute the general notion of crime, we can also examine specific statutory provisions in order to see what specific elements make up a given crime. The written law specifies exactly what conditions are necessary for a person to be charged in a given instance of crime, and it does so for every offence. The crime of first-degree murder, for example, typically involves four quite distinct elements:

1. A culpable killing;

2. Of a human being;

3. Intentionally;

4. With planning and deliberation (see sections 222, 229, and 231 of the *Criminal Code*).

The elements of any specific crime are the *statutory minimum* without which that crime cannot be said to have occurred. In any case that goes to trial, the task of the prosecution is to prove that all the elements were indeed present and that the accused was ultimately responsible for producing them.

## The *Corpus Delicti* of a Crime

When all of the needed elements are present, we say that the *corpus delicti* of a crime has been established. *Corpus delicti* is a Latin term that refers to the "body of the crime," and means the lawful body or substance, or legal foundation of the offence itself. It does *not* mean the body of the victim, as is sometimes thought. For a criminal definition to be imposed upon a social situation (i.e., to be able to say that a particular crime has occurred), it is necessary that the "body of the crime" be established. The specific statutory elements that constitute a particular type of crime must be shown to be present. *Black's Law Dictionary* puts it another way: "[t]he corpus delicti [of a crime] is the fact of its having been actually committed."[40]

# The Example of First-Degree Murder

Every statutory element in a given instance of crime serves some purpose and is necessary. The crime of first-degree murder, as mentioned earlier, includes *a culpable killing*. Even if all the other elements of first-degree murder are present, the act may still not be first-degree murder if the first element has not been met. In a wartime situation, for instance, killings of human beings occur. They are committed with planning and sometimes with careful deliberation. They are certainly intentional. Yet killing in war is not unlawful, as long as the belligerents wage war according to international conventions.

The second element of first-degree murder specifies that the killing must be *of a human being*. People kill all the time. They kill animals for meat, they hunt, and they practise euthanasia upon aged and injured pets. Even if the killing of an animal is planned, involves deliberation, and perhaps even malice (perhaps a vendetta against a neighbourhood dog that wrecks garbage cans), it does not constitute first-degree murder. Such a killing, however, may violate *Criminal Code* provisions pertaining to cruelty to animals.

The third element of first-degree murder, *intentionality*, is the basis for the defence of accident. An unintentional killing is not first-degree murder, although it may violate some other statute.

Finally, murder has not been committed unless *planning and deliberation* is usually involved. There are different levels of intentionality in our behaviours. Manslaughter provoked by witnessing an act of infidelity on the part of one's spouse involves a deliberate, intended killing in the sense of hatred, anger, or jealousy. A more extreme form of mental state is necessary for a finding of first-degree murder. This extreme kind of moral blameworthiness can be demonstrated by showing that planning and deliberation was involved in the commission of the murder. Often, first-degree murder is described as "lying in wait," a practice that shows that thought and planning went into the illegal killing. Typically, courts require a planned and deliberate killing to show the accused possessed a genuine plan: "a calculated scheme or design which has been carefully thought out, and the nature and consequences of which have been considered and weighed," and that deliberation was present: the act must have been "'considered,' 'not impulsive,' 'slow in deciding,' 'cautious,' implying that the accused must take the time to weigh the advantages and disadvantages of his intended action."[41]

Whether any particular behaviour meets the specific statutory minimums to qualify as a crime may be open to debate. Several years ago, for example, Gerald Smith, of Saskatchewan, was charged with first-degree murder for causing the death of a "drinking buddy" named Darryl Skwarchuk. Mr. Smith, accompanied by friends Skwarchuk and Massier, spent a day eating, drinking, and shooting "birds, ducks, and mailboxes." The threesome came upon an abandoned farmhouse and set about vandalizing it. While Massier was out of sight of the other two, he heard what sounded like an argument between his friends. He thereupon witnessed Smith, shotgun in hand, pointing at Skwarchuk, while Skwarchuk, his gun on the ground, was bleeding from an apparent gunshot in the left elbow, his arm hanging and blood squirting to the ground. It was readily apparent that Smith had just shot their friend. As Skwarchuk screamed to be taken to a hospital, Massier tried to ascertain what was happening. Moments later, Smith reloaded his shotgun. As Skwarchuk turned to run, Smith shot at him again, then again, apparently hitting him in the back. Smith then walked up to Skwarchuk who was sitting with his knees up and his head resting on his knees, put the gun a few centimetres from the back of Skwarchuk's head, and pulled the trigger, delivering a fatal gunshot wound. Based on this horrible recollection of events, a jury convicted Smith on the charge of first-degree murder. However, on appeal to the Saskatchewan Court of Appeal, his conviction was set aside, and a conviction for second-degree murder was substituted, since the Court of Appeal could not find any evidence of planning and deliberation on the part of Smith.[42]

A charge of second-degree murder typically involves an intentional killing of a human being taking place, without the degree of planning and deliberation necessary for it to be classified as first-degree. Manslaughter can be defined simply as the unlawful killing of a human being. Not only is planning and deliberation lacking in manslaughter cases, but the killer may not have even intended that any harm come to the victim. Manslaughter typically necessitates some degree of negligence on the part of the killer, or may involve an intentional killing committed in circumstances of provocation where a normal person would be incapable of resisting the provoking act or insult, acting "on the sudden" upon the provocation. Criminal negligence causing death carries the same penalty as manslaughter and is, for all intents and purposes, indistinguishable from manslaughter, providing what is essentially a subcategory of manslaughter most typically applied in cases of extremely negligent driving resulting in death.[43]

# TYPES OF DEFENCES TO A CRIMINAL CHARGE

When a person is charged with a crime, he or she frequently offers some defence. Our legal system has generally recognized three broad categories of **defences**: personal, situational, and procedural. Table 3–2 lists the various defences typically encountered in Canada's criminal justice system. We will discuss each type of defence.

**defences** (to a criminal charge) include claims based upon personal, special, and procedural considerations that the defendant should not be held accountable for their actions, even though they may have acted in violation of the criminal law.

## Personal Defences

Personal defences are based upon some characteristic of the individual who is charged with the crime. They include the following.

### Age

Age can offer a good defence to a criminal charge, and the defence of "infancy"—as it is known in legal jargon—has its roots in the ancient belief that children cannot reason logically until around the age of seven. Early doctrine in the Christian Church sanctioned that belief by declaring that rationality develops around the age of seven. As a consequence, only children past that age could be held responsible for their crimes.

The defence of infancy today has been expanded to include people well beyond the age of seven. The *Criminal Code* sets the age of criminal responsibility in section 13. It states that "[n]o person shall be convicted of an offence in respect of an act or omission on his part while that person was under the age of twelve years." The *Youth Criminal Justice Act* provides a separate procedure and penalty scheme for persons defined by the Act as a "young person." Section 2 of the Act defines a "young person" as a person 12 years of age or older, but under 18 years of age.

In Canada, children below the age of 12 cannot be charged even with offences under the *Youth Criminal Justice Act*, no matter how serious their actions may appear to others. Below the age of 12, the only recourse for dealing with child offenders is through appropriate provincial child welfare legislation.

### Mental Disorder

Mental disorder is the second form of personal defence. It is important to realize that, for purposes of the criminal law, mental disorder is a legal definition and not a psychiatric one. The legal definition of mental disorder has little to do with psychological or psychiatric understandings of mental illness. Legally defined mental disorder is a concept developed over time to meet the needs of the judicial system in assigning guilt or innocence to particular defendants. It is not primarily concerned with understanding the origins of mental pathology or with treatment, as is the idea of mental illness in psychiatry. As a consequence, medical conceptions of mental illness do not always fit well into the legal categories created by courts and legislators to deal with the phenomenon. The differences between psychiatric and legal conceptualizations of mental disorder often lead to disagreements among expert witnesses who, in criminal court, may appear to provide conflicting testimonies as to the sanity of a defendant.

*The McNaughten Rule*   Prior to the nineteenth century, the mental disorder (or insanity) defence was non-existent. Insane people who committed crimes were punished in the same

## TABLE 3–2 Types of Defences

| Personal (Incapacity) | Situational (Justifications & Excuses) | Procedural/Abuse of Process (including *Charter* violations) |
|---|---|---|
| Age | Self-defence, including | Double jeopardy |
| Mental disorder | defence of others and | Entrapment |
| Intoxication | defence of property | Prosecutorial misconduct |
| Non-insane automatism | Duress (Compulsion under threat) | Unreasonable trial delay |
| | Necessity | |
| | Mistake | |
| | Provocation | |
| | Consent | |
| | Alibi | |
| | Accident | |

way as other law violators. It was Daniel McNaughten (also spelled M'Naghten), a woodworker from Glasgow, Scotland, who, in 1844, became the first person to be found not guilty of a crime by reason of insanity. McNaughten had tried to assassinate Sir Robert Peel, the British prime minister. He mistook Edward Drummond, Peel's secretary, for Peel himself, and killed Drummond instead. At his trial, defence lawyers argued that McNaughten suffered from vague delusions centred on the idea that the Tories, a British political party, were persecuting him. Medical testimony at the trial agreed with the assertion of McNaughten's lawyers that he didn't know what he was doing at the time of the shooting. The judge accepted McNaughten's claim, and the insanity (mental disorder) defence was born. The McNaughten Rule, as it has come to be called, was defined later by the English courts after public outcry following the application of the insanity verdict to McNaughten. This rule still plays a major role in determining insanity in criminal prosecutions in Canada today.

The McNaughten Rule holds that a person is not guilty of a crime if, at the time of the crime, the person either didn't know what he or she was doing, or didn't know that what he or she was doing was wrong. The inability to distinguish right from wrong must be the result of some mental defect or disability. The McNaughten case established a rule for the determination of insanity, which is the basis of section 16 of the *Criminal Code*, delineating Canada's present **mental disorder defence**. The burden of proving insanity falls upon the person raising the defence. Just as defendants are assumed innocent, they are also assumed to be sane at the outset of any criminal trial.

**mental disorder defence** A personal defence that claims that the person charged with a crime did not appreciate what he or she was doing, or that the accused did not know that what he or she was doing was wrong, because the person was suffering from a disease of the mind at the time of the offence.

s. 16 (1) No person is criminally responsible for an act committed or an omission made while suffering from a mental disorder that rendered the person incapable of appreciating the nature and quality of the act or omission or of knowing that it was wrong.

(2) Every person is presumed not to suffer from a mental disorder so as to be exempt from criminal responsibility by virtue of subsection (1), until the contrary is proved on a balance of probabilities.

(3) The burden of proof that an accused was suffering from a mental disorder so as to be exempt from criminal responsibility is on the party that raises the issue.

*Mental Disorder as a Reductionary Defence*   A number of Canadian courts have recognized the ability of mental disorder, falling short of a complete defence under section 16, to constitute a partial defence for the accused. In circumstances where the mental state of the accused renders that person incapable of forming the specific or ulterior intent necessary for complex offences, these courts have said that the accused should not be convicted of such offences due to lack of the requisite *mens rea*. However, in such cases, the accused will inevitably be convicted of a more simple, underlying offence than the offence with which he or she was actually charged. In the case of an accused charged with murder, the use of this defence allows a reduction to the offence of manslaughter, provided the mental disorder impaired the ability of the accused to form the specific intent to kill.[44]

*Mental Disorder and Social Reality*  The mental disorder defence originated as a means of recognizing the social reality of mental disease. Unfortunately, the history of this defence has been rife with change, contradiction, and uncertainty. Psychiatric testimony is expensive, sometimes costing thousands of dollars per day for one medical specialist. Still worse is the fact that each "expert" is commonly contradicted by another.

Some accused who are clearly mentally ill and appear not to be responsible for their crimes fail to fit within the confines of the mental disorder defence and are convicted, often with penalties involving significant time in prison. Other accused who are not mentally disordered appear to be able to take advantage of the mental disorder defence, with the supporting testimony of a forensic psychiatrist, and escape a criminal conviction.[45]

In 1982, John Hinkley was found not guilty by reason of insanity following an assassination attempt on President Ronald Reagan. While the insanity verdict in the case of John Hinkley resulted in calls for the repeal of the mental disorder defence in the U.S., in Canada, the case of André Dallaire provides an interesting point of comparison. Dallaire surreptitiously invaded the prime minister's residence one evening, armed with a knife. He was confronted by Aline Chrétien, the prime minister's wife, and subsequently taken into custody by the RCMP. Dallaire was found not criminally responsible on account of mental disorder (NCRMD) by an Ontario court, and sent to a treatment facility. Dallaire had admitted to police, following the incident, that he wanted to "slit Chrétien's throat." The trial judge declared, "His disorder had cut him off from reality. He had delusions of grandeur, maybe even of a messianic mission. He thought he would be glorified for ridding Canada of this prime minister." Yet, the case had no impact on the mental disorder defence in Canada. There remains no significant movement to curtail or abolish the availability of the defence in Canadian criminal law.[46]

André Dallaire, who invaded Prime Minister Chrétien's residence wielding a knife, was found not criminally responsible on account of mental disorder.

*Consequences of a Mental Disorder Ruling*  The mental disorder defence today is not an "easy way out" of criminal prosecution, as some have assumed. Once a verdict of "not guilty by reason of insanity" is returned, the judge is required to hold a disposition hearing. At this hearing the judge must determine whether to release the accused, release the accused subject to conditions, or order that the accused be detained in a psychiatric facility. Because psychiatrists are reluctant to declare any potential criminal "cured," such a disposition may result in more time spent in an institution than would have resulted from a prison sentence.

## Intoxication

Another personal defence is intoxication. Either drugs or alcohol may produce intoxication. There are several interesting aspects to this defence.

Voluntary intoxication operates as a defence in Canadian criminal law. However, since the accused has made a conscious decision to become intoxicated, the criminal law does not typically allow an outright acquittal to persons who ingest alcohol, knowing full well what they are doing, then committing offences in their intoxicated state. In such circumstances, it flies in the face of logic to allow an outright acquittal, lest everyone get drunk prior to offending in order to escape culpability.

Canadian courts allow a partial or reductionary defence to persons who voluntarily become intoxicated to the point where they no longer are able to form the complex intention necessary to satisfy the *mens rea* requirements of the more complicated offences.[47] For example, a voluntarily intoxicated person who kills another person will have his or her murder charge reduced to manslaughter, provided the accused was sufficiently intoxicated so as to deprive him or her of the ability to form the "intent to kill" necessary for a murder conviction.

Individuals who become voluntarily intoxicated to the extreme may be able to avail themselves of a more expansive intoxication defence. In 1994, the Supreme Court of Canada ruled that in cases of extreme intoxication, akin to a state of mental disorder or an unconscious, involuntary state referred to as automatism, the accused should be entitled to an outright acquittal, regardless of how complex the *mens rea* requirements are for the offence, since the accused would be too intoxicated to have the capacity to form *any* mens rea whatsoever.[48] In *R. v. Daviault* (1994), the Supreme Court of Canada overturned a conviction for sexual assault imposed by the Quebec Court of Appeal, and ordered a new trial in his case, involving the attack of a 65-year-old woman confined to a wheelchair. A pharmacologist testifying at the trial estimated Daviault's blood alcohol level to be between 400 and 600 mg of alcohol per 100 mL of blood, or between five and seven times the legal driving limit. In such a case, the accused may have been acting "involuntarily." The majority of judges on the Supreme Court of Canada ruled that voluntariness (or a conscious willed act) is a fundamental aspect of all crimes.

Following the *Daviault* ruling, Parliament amended the *Criminal Code*, bringing a new provision into effect in 1996 that negates the availability of the extreme intoxication defence in most cases where the offence entails an "interference or threat of interference by a person with the bodily integrity of another person."[49]

## Automatism

A very rare personal defence is automatism or unconsciousness. An individual who is unconscious cannot be held responsible for anything he or she does. Because unconscious people rarely do anything at all, this defence is almost never seen. However, cases of sleepwalking, epileptic seizure, and neurological dysfunction may result in injurious, although unintentional, actions by people so afflicted. Under such circumstances, the defence of unconsciousness might be argued with success.

In *R. v. Parks* (1992), the Supreme Court of Canada applied the defence to acquit a man who had committed a killing during a sleepwalking episode.[50] While asleep in the early hours of May 24, 1987, Mr. Parks, aged 23, arose, apparently in a somnambulistic state and drove 23 kilometres to the home of his mother-in-law and father-in-law, Barbara Ann and Denis Woods. Once there, he proceeded to beat and stab these two victims, causing the death of Barbara Ann Woods and seriously injuring his father-in-law. Testimony called at trial revealed that Mr. Parks was a very deep sleeper who always had trouble waking up. He had experienced severe financial hardship, generally of his own doing, in connection with some unproductive bets on horse races, and a subsequent theft from his employer that resulted in court proceedings against him and the loss of his job. Many of the members of Parks's family also suffered from sleep disturbances, including sleepwalking, adult bedwetting, nightmares, and talking during sleep. The testimony also revealed that he had very good relations with his in-laws, with no animosity or ill-feelings towards them.

Parks was acquitted at trial, a decision that was upheld all the way to the Supreme Court of Canada. The Court ruled that during the entire episode, Parks had been sleepwalking. While asleep, one does not engage in voluntary behaviour. A person in a state whereby he or she is incapable of acting voluntarily cannot be subjected to criminal liability. In *R. v. Stone* (1999), the Supreme Court of Canada recently held that accused offenders will be presumed to act voluntarily, and that an automatism claim must be proved by the defence on a balance of probabilities, with the accused's claim being backed up by supportive psychiatric testimony. The top court is clearly concerned with the possibility of offenders feigning automatism to escape criminal liability.[51]

## Premenstrual Stress Syndrome

The use of premenstrual stress syndrome (PMS) as a defence against criminal charges is very new and demonstrates how changing social conceptions and advancing technology may modify the way in which courts view illegal behaviour. In 1980, British courts heard the case of Christine English, who killed her live-in lover when he threatened to leave her. An expert witness at the trial testified that English had been the victim of PMS for more than a decade. The witness, Dr. Katharina Dalton, advanced the claim that PMS had rendered

Ms. English "irritable, aggressive … and confused, with loss of self-control."[52] The jury, apparently accepting the claim, returned a verdict of "not guilty."

PMS is not yet an officially acceptable defence in Canadian criminal courts. In Canada, the defence could be argued either on its own merits as a new "common law" defence, or it could be argued as an aspect of mental disorder.

### Other Biological Considerations

Modern nutritional science appears to be on the verge of establishing a new category of personal defence related to "chemical imbalances" in the human body produced by eating habits. Strong food allergies, the overconsumption of vitamins or stimulants (including coffee and nicotine), and the excessive ingestion of sugar all will probably soon be advanced by lawyers in defence of their clients. Such a claim could be argued as a separate new common-law defence or as an aspect of intoxication.

The U.S. case of Dan White provides an example of this new direction in the development of personal defences.[53] In 1978, White, a former San Francisco police officer, walked into the office of Mayor Moscone and shot both the mayor and city councilman Harvey Milk to death. It was established at the trial that White had spent the night before the murders drinking Coca-Cola and eating Twinkies, a packaged pastry. Expert witnesses testified that the huge amounts of sugar consumed by White prior to the crime substantially altered his judgment and ability to control his behaviour. The jury, influenced by the expert testimony, convicted White of a lesser charge, and he served a short prison sentence.

The strategy used by White's lawyers has come to be known as the "Twinkie defence." To date, it has not been argued in any reported cases in Canada; however, it may well be characteristic of future defence strategies now being developed in cases across the nation.

## Situational Defences

A defence against criminal charges can be based upon circumstance as well as personal attributes. Defences based upon circumstance take into consideration the situation surrounding a crime. They are typically built around a claim of external pressures, operating at the time the crime was committed, which might have lessened the responsibility or the resolve of the defendant in a way with which the rest of us can sympathize. We will briefly discuss the eight situational defences.

### Self-Defence

**Self-defence** is probably the best known of the situational defences. This defence strategy makes the claim that harm was committed in order to ensure one's own safety in the face of certain injury. A person who harms an attacker can generally use this defence. However, the courts have held that the strict requirements of the *Criminal Code* delineating the defence of self-defence must be met in order for the defence to be available.

Sections 34 through 37 outline the situations in which an individual may use force to defend themselves, while sections 38 through 42 apply to the use of force in the defence of property. Section 34(1) contains the general self-defence provision applicable in most cases:

s. 34 (1)    Every one who is unlawfully assaulted without having provoked the assault is justified in repelling force by force if the force he uses is not intended to cause death or grievous bodily harm and is no more than is necessary to enable him to defend himself.

The extent of the injury inflicted in self-defence must generally be proportionate with respect to the degree of the perceived threat. In other words, a person delivering a repelling blow to a smaller, weaker individual may be justified, but not if the action was in response to a mild slap on the cheek. Where the person acting to defend himself or herself utilizes a level of force approaching deadly force, different considerations apply, and the accused must meet the requirements of section 34(2) to obtain an acquittal on the basis of self-defence:

**self-defence** The protection of oneself or one's property from unlawful injury or the immediate risk of unlawful injury; the justification for an act that would otherwise constitute an offence, that the person who committed it reasonably believed that the act was necessary to protect self or property from immediate danger.

s. 34 (2)   Every one who is unlawfully assaulted and who causes death or grievous bodily harm in repelling the assault is justified if;

(a)   he causes it under reasonable apprehension of death or grievous bodily harm from the violence with which the assault was originally made or with which the assailant pursues his purpose; and

(b)   he believes, on reasonable grounds, that he cannot otherwise preserve himself from death or grievous bodily harm.

The extent of the injury inflicted in self-defence must generally be reasonable with respect to the degree of the perceived threat. In other words, although it may be acceptable for a person to defensively kill someone who is shooting at him, it would be inappropriate to shoot and kill someone who is just gesturing aggressively. Deadly force generally cannot be used to repel non-deadly force.

Self-defence extends to defence of others and to the defence of one's home. A person whose loved ones are being attacked can claim self-defence, under the authority of section 37 of the *Criminal Code*, if the person injures or kills the attacker. Similarly, a person can defend his or her home from invasion or forced entry, even to the point of using deadly force. However, the circumstances that surround the claim of self-defence are limited.

The defence of self-defence is generally useless where the person provoked an attack or where the attacker is justified. In cases of forcible arrest, for example, family members may not intervene to protect their relatives, providing the use of force by the police is legitimate.

Self-defence has been used recently in relation to killings, by wives, of their abusive spouses. Killings that occur while the physical abuse is in process, especially where a history of such abuse can be shown, are likely to be excused by juries as self-defence. On the other hand, wives who suffer repeated abuse but coldly plan the killing of their husbands have not fared well in court.

In *R*. v. *Lavallee* (1990), the Supreme Court of Canada ruled that when a woman kills her unarmed abusive spouse by shooting him in the back of the head as he exits the room, expert testimony regarding "battered wife syndrome" may be admitted by the court in determining whether the use of force was justified under section 34(2) of the *Criminal Code*.[54]

## Duress

Duress or "compulsion under threats" is another of the defences that depends upon an understanding of the situation. Compulsion under threats is defined in the *Criminal Code* in section 17:

s. 17   A person who commits an offence under compulsion by threats of immediate death or bodily harm from a person who is present when the offence is committed is excused for committing the offence if the person believes that the threats will be carried out and if the person is not a party to a conspiracy or association whereby the person is subject to compulsion, but this section does not apply where the offence that is committed is high treason or treason, murder, piracy, attempted murder, sexual assault, sexual assault with a weapon, threats to a third party or causing bodily harm, aggravated sexual assault, forcible abduction, hostage taking, robbery, assault with a weapon or causing bodily harm, aggravated assault, unlawfully causing bodily harm, arson or an offence under section 280 to 283 (abduction and detention of young persons).

A person may act under duress if, for example, he or she steals an employer's payroll in order to avoid being killed by persons threatening to kill that person should he or she fail to deliver the money. Should the person later be arrested for theft or embezzlement, the person can claim that he or she felt compelled to commit the crime to help ensure his or her own safety. A key case, briefly mentioned earlier in the chapter in the context of "moral blameworthiness," has significantly expanded the scope of this defence in Canada. In *R*. v. *Ruzic* (2001), the Supreme Court of Canada decided that the requirement of the threat being of immediate death or bodily harm, in addition to the requirement that the person making the threat be present when the offence is committed, violates constitutional principles. As long as the choice to commit the crime in a duress situation places the accused in a morally involuntary position, the accused will be entitled to an acquittal.[55]

## Accident

The defence of accident claims that the action in question was not intended, but the result of some happenstance. Hunting accidents, for example, rarely result in criminal prosecution because the circumstances surrounding them clearly show the unintentional nature of the shootings. What appear as accidents, of course, may actually be disguised criminal behaviour. In 1957, a hunter in New Brunswick was convicted of criminal negligence in firing a rifle in a manner so as to show wanton or reckless disregard for the lives or safety of other persons.[56] After being warned of boys playing in the bush where he was hunting, the hunter shot at what he claimed was a deer running into the woods. The moving objects turned out not to be deer, but rather four boys, at least two of whom were dressed in red, hurrying along the road. Two of the boys were injured in the shooting. His conviction was upheld in the New Brunswick Court of Appeal, the Court rejecting the apparent reliance on accident as a defence by the accused.

## Mistake

Mistake is a situational defence with two components. One is mistake of law, and the other is mistake of fact. Rarely is the defence of mistake of law acceptable. Most people realize that it is their responsibility to know the law as it applies to them. "Ignorance of the law is no excuse" is an old dictum still heard today. Section 19 of the *Criminal Code* embodies this rule: "Ignorance of the law by a person who commits an offence is not an excuse for committing that offence." On the occasion where a person's error of law is in relation to a "regulatory offence," and that error is brought about by relying on information provided by a government official responsible for the administration and enforcement of that particular law, the defence of ignorance may be successful.[57]

Mistake of fact is a much more useful form of the "mistake" defence. The defence operates in circumstances where a person holds an honest belief that, if it were in fact true, would render the conduct an innocent act. In 1987, Jerry Hall, fashion model and girlfriend of Mick Jagger, a well-known rock star, was arrested in Barbados as she attempted to leave a public airport baggage claim area after picking up a suitcase.[58] The bag contained 10 kilograms of marijuana and was under surveillance by officials who were waiting for just such a pick-up. Ms. Hall defended herself by arguing that she had mistaken the bag for her own, which looked similar. She was released after a night in jail.

## Necessity

Necessity, or the claim that some illegal action was needed to prevent an even greater harm, is a defence that should prove to be useful in cases that do not involve serious bodily harm. However, the defence is rarely, if ever, successful. One of the most famous uses of this defence occurred in *The Queen* v. *Dudley & Stephens* in the late 1800s.[59] The case involved a shipwreck in which three sailors and a cabin boy were set adrift in a lifeboat. After a number of days at sea without rations, two of them decided to kill and eat the cabin boy. At their trial, they argued that it was necessary to do so, or none of them would have survived. The court, however, reasoned that the cabin boy was not a direct threat to the survival of the men and rejected this defence. Convicted of murder, they were sentenced to death, although they were spared the gallows by royal intervention.

Although cannibalism is usually against the law, courts have sometimes recognized the necessity of consuming human flesh where survival was at issue. Those cases, however, involved only "victims" who had already died of natural causes.

In Canada, the defence was discussed at length in *Perka* v. *The Queen* in 1984.[60] This case involved drug smugglers transporting a shipment of marijuana worth more than US$6 million from Colombia, South America, to a point off the coast of Alaska. While en route, the ship experienced mechanical difficulties that worsened as the trip progressed. When the weather worsened, the ship and crew experienced two- to three-metre swells and a rising wind. Faced with the prospect of being lost at sea, the ship put into "No Name Bay" on the west coast of Vancouver Island. While there, the ship ran aground and, running the risk of capsizing, the crew commenced unloading the shipment of drugs onto the shore. At this point, the crew were discovered by the RCMP and they were arrested and charged with importing cannabis into Canada and with possession for the purpose of trafficking.

In their defence, the crew argued that they had no intention of coming into Canada with the drugs; however, the weather and mechanical failures made this course of conduct a necessity. The harm caused by the drugs being temporarily in Canada was less than the harm that would have resulted if the ship remained on the high seas and all were lost to the elements. At trial, the jury accepted the argument of necessity; however, the Crown appealed the acquittals, eventually resulting in a hearing before the Supreme Court of Canada. The top court ordered a new trial, finding that the defence, while valid in Canadian law, contains limitations not put to the jury for consideration at trial. In particular, a major limitation on the defence of necessity is that it will not be available in circumstances where there was a "legal way out." In other words, it is not enough that the circumstances were grave and life-threatening; the jury must go on to consider the alternative courses of conduct. In the fact situation of *Perka*, the jury should have asked themselves why the crew did not throw the drugs overboard prior to entering Canadian waters.

## Provocation

Provocation recognizes that a person can be emotionally enraged by another. Should this person then strike out at his or her tormentor and cause death, the *Criminal Code* indicates the person may not be guilty of any criminality. The defence of provocation is commonly used in bar-room brawls where a person's parentage may have been called into question. It has also been used in some cases where wives have killed their husbands, or children their parents, citing years of verbal and physical abuse. In these latter instances, perhaps because the degree of physical harm inflicted appears to be out of proportion to the claimed provocation, the defence of provocation has not been as readily accepted by the courts.

In Canadian criminal law, the defence of provocation is only available to reduce what would be murder to a conviction for manslaughter. The circumstances under which it is available are also quite limited. Section 232 speaks to the issue of provocation:

s. 232(1)   Culpable homicide that otherwise would be murder may be reduced to manslaughter if the person who committed it did so in the heat of passion caused by sudden provocation.

(2)   A wrongful act or an insult that is of such a nature as to be sufficient to deprive an ordinary person of the power of self-control is provocation for the purposes of this section if the accused acted on it on the sudden and before there was time for his passion to cool.

## Consent

The defence of consent claims that whatever harm was done occurred only after the injured person gave permission for the behaviour in question. Some offences specifically require proof that consent was not present before a conviction can be obtained. Assaultive offences typically entail applying force intentionally to another "without the consent" of that other person. Theft involves taking another person's property without consent.

The *Criminal Code* bars the use of consent as a defence to a homicide offence:

s. 14   No person is entitled to consent to have death inflicted on him, and such consent does not affect the criminal responsibility of any person by whom death may be inflicted on the person by whom consent is given.

The courts have restricted the scope of the consent defence in other circumstances as well. The defence of consent will not be available in an assault involving a fistfight or brawl outside a bar where the parties intend to inflict "non-trivial bodily harm."[61] Fights involving young boys are tolerated by the courts;[62] however, if one of the parties intends to cause serious harm during the fight, the defence of consent will not be available.[63] Fights arising in sporting activities such as boxing matches or hockey games will also be tolerated to some degree by the courts due to the consensual nature of such fights.[64]

## Alibi

A current reference book for criminal trial lawyers says, "Alibi is different from all of the other defenses ... because ... it is based upon the premise that the defendant is truly innocent ..."[65] All the other defences we have discussed are accepted ways to alleviate criminal responsibility. While they may produce findings of "not guilty," the defence of alibi, if believed, should support a ruling of "innocent."

Alibi is best supported by witnesses and documentation. A person charged with a crime can use the defence of alibi to show that he or she was not present at the scene when the crime was alleged to have occurred. Hotel receipts, eyewitness identification, and participation in social events have all been used to prove alibis. Where an accused intends to rely on the alibi defence, the accused must endeavour to reveal it to the police prior to trial. The alibi need not be disclosed to the police at the time of arrest, nor at the earliest opportunity; however, it must be disclosed at a time that allows the police to make a meaningful investigation. Failure to do so will allow the jury to draw an adverse inference.[66]

# Procedural Defences

Chapter 6 describes the legal environment in which the police must operate. When police officers violate constitutional guarantees of proper procedure through improper police conduct, they may create a situation in which guilty defendants can go free. Defences based upon procedure may also occur as a result of actions by prosecutors and judges, and are called procedural defences. In the past, various procedural defences were created on a common-law basis, whereby the courts on their own initiative created procedural bars to prosecuting a case in circumstances that the judges deemed would be unfair or inappropriate. Since the enactment of the *Canadian Charter of Rights and Freedoms* (the *Charter*) in 1982, these defences have typically been subsumed under general procedural guarantees contained in the *Charter*. Included among procedural defences are double jeopardy, *collateral estoppel*, and abuse of process, a broad category that may involve selective prosecution, entrapment, denial of the right to a fair trial, and denial of a speedy trial. Most of these situations are now dealt with by a specific section of the *Charter*, and are discussed in the pages that follow.

## Double Jeopardy

Section 11(h) of the *Canadian Charter of Rights and Freedoms* makes it clear that no person may be tried twice for the same offence. People who have been acquitted of an offence may not be "tried for it again." The same is true of those who have been convicted: they cannot be tried again for the same offence. Cases that are dismissed for a lack of evidence also come under the double jeopardy rule, and cannot result in a new trial.

Double jeopardy does not apply in cases of trial error. Hence, convictions that are set aside because of some error in proceedings at a lower court level (for example, inappropriate instructions to the jury by the trial court judge) will permit a retrial on the same charges. Similarly, when a defendant's motion for a mistrial is successful, or members of the jury cannot agree upon a verdict (resulting in a "hung jury"), a second trial may be held. The double jeopardy rule forbids someone being prosecuted twice for the same offence; however, it does not preclude being subject to administrative proceedings and also being subject to a criminal trial in regard to the same course of conduct. A successful prison disciplinary proceeding did not bar the Crown from also bringing criminal assault charges against an inmate for the same conduct at a later date in *R. v. Shubley* (1990).[67] At common law, the principle of *res judicata* also prohibits multiple convictions for the same *delict* (meaning "wrong"). This bars being convicted, for example, with charges of murder, and manslaughter, and criminal negligence causing death, where a person has killed one person.[68]

## Collateral Estoppel

*Collateral estoppel* is similar to double jeopardy and applies to facts that have been determined by a "valid and final judgment."[69] Such facts cannot become the object of new litigation.

Where a defendant, for example, has been acquitted of a multiple murder charge by virtue of an alibi, it would not be permissible to try that person again for the murder of a second person killed along with the first.

## Abuse of Process

Canadian courts hold a residual discretion to remedy clear cases of an abuse of the court's process by directing the clerk of the court to enter a stay of proceedings on the record of the case. This requires proof of conduct that shocks the conscience of the community, with the proceedings being rendered unfair to the point that they are contrary to the interest of justice. In *R. v. Power* (1994), the Supreme Court of Canada recently declared that the courts must intervene only where there is:

> conspicuous evidence of improper motives or of bad faith or of an act so wrong that it violates the conscience of the community, such that it would genuinely be unfair and indecent to proceed.[70]

Where the prosecution reneges on an agreement to grant immunity to an accused in exchange for that person's co-operation in the prosecution of another person, the circumstances warrant a finding of abuse of process, and the proceedings should be stayed by the court.[71] In *R. v. O'Connor* (1995), the Supreme Court of Canada held that the common-law "abuse of process" doctrine is now totally subsumed for all practical purposes under section 7 of the *Charter*.[72]

Tim Quigley has recently summarized the situations under which abuse of process may successfully be argued. He lists the situations in which decisions made at the prosecutorial stage of a trial amount to an abuse of process as follows:

1. To question the laying of a charge in the first instance;
2. To allege that the Crown has selectively prosecuted one accused out of a group of violators;
3. To challenge the Crown's election on a dual or hybrid offence;
4. To impugn the Crown's refusal to permit a non-jury trial on a section 469 (most serious) offence;
5. To question the Crown's refusal to permit a re-election (to a different mode of trial);
6. To challenge the Crown's insistence upon a jury trial under section 468;
7. To impugn the Crown's motives in entering a stay of proceedings and re-laying the same charge;
8. To question the Crown's supervisory authority over a private prosecution;
9. To allege an improper motive in preferring a direct indictment (thereby by-passing a preliminary inquiry);
10. Where the Crown's failure to provide disclosure has violated the accused's right to make full answer and defence;
11. To assert that police or prosecutorial delay in laying a charge has prejudiced the right to a fair trial;
12. Where the accused, due to mistrials or the ordering of new trials, has been subjected to multiple trials; and
13. To hold the Crown to a plea bargaining arrangement or other undertaking.[73]

Only when the conduct of the state agents amounts to a circumstance that offends the community's sense of justice will the court order a stay of proceedings. In a less serious abuse of process situation, the court may order a less drastic remedy to rectify the wrong.

## Entrapment

**entrapment** An inducement to crime by agents of enforcement.

In addition to prosecutorial misconduct, abuse of process has been used to remedy police misconduct in the form of entrapping behaviour. **Entrapment** has been defined, in

*R.* v. *Mack* (1988),[74] as arising in two sets of situations. First, it arises when the police provide an opportunity to persons to commit an offence without reasonable suspicion that they are already engaging in this type of crime, or the police act with *mala fides*, for dubious motives that are unrelated to the investigation and repression of crime. Second, entrapment occurs where, having reasonable suspicion the accused is enaging in this type of crime, or while engaging in the course of a *bona fide* inquiry, the police go beyond providing an opportunity and actually induce the commission of the offence. A police operation in Vancouver involving undercover officers approaching persons on the Granville Mall, an outdoor shopping district known to be the centre of most of the city's drug trade, and providing them with the opportunity to engage in drug deals, was found to be a *bona fide* inquiry, not giving rise to entrapment.[75] Allegations by the defence that the police were improperly engaging in "random virtue testing" were rejected by the Supreme Court of Canada.

## *Denial of Speedy Trial*

Section 11(b) of the *Charter* guarantees the right to a trial in a reasonable time. The purpose of the guarantee is to prevent unconvicted and potentially innocent people from languishing in jail. Recent judicial pronouncements have attempted to delineate what constitutes "unreasonable delay"; however, it is difficult to find a precise point at which the delay is objectionable. In *R.* v. *Askov* (1990) and *R.* v. *Morin* (1992), the Supreme Court of Canada interpreted section 11(b) of the *Charter* as enabling the courts to define the parameters of what constitutes an acceptable period of pretrial delay.[76] Key factors for determining the extent of acceptable delay are (1) the length of the delay, (2) the explanation for the delay, (3) waiver, and (4) prejudice to the accused. In *Askov*, the top court initially proclaimed that a six-month delay would be the outer bounds of what would typically be considered permissible; however, in the subsequent ruling in *Morin*, the Court noted that it was not setting down a prescribed limitation period, and that on the facts of that case, a delay of more than 14 months did not constitute unreasonable delay.

# Innovative Defences

In recent years, some innovative defensive strategies have been employed, with varying degrees of success, in criminal cases—and it is to these that we now turn our attention. Technically speaking, any defence that is not situational or procedural in nature falls under the category of "personal defence." Hence, the defences discussed in this section may be appropriately listed as personal defences. However, the unique and emerging character of these novel defences makes discussing them in a separate section worthwhile.

In Canada, new defences can arise in several ways. Of course, Parliament may create a new defence by enacting an amendment to the *Criminal Code*, specifying the nature of the defence. Numerous defences referred to above, such as duress, provocation, and mental disorders, are found in the *Criminal Code*. The courts also retain the authority to create new defences on their own initiative. Subsection 8(3) of the *Criminal Code* provides as follows:

ss. 8 (3)   Every rule and principle of the common law that renders any circumstance a justification or excuse for an act or a defence to a charge continues in force and applies in respect of proceedings for an offence under this Act or any other Act of Parliament except in so far as they are altered by or are inconsistent with this Act or any other Act of Parliament.

This provision not only preserves old common-law defences, but also permits the courts to create new common-law defences as the circumstances of particular cases that arise necessitate. Under the authority of this subsection, the Supreme Court of Canada has recognized the defence of intoxication since 1960, the defence of necessity since at least 1984, and the defence of entrapment since at least 1988.

Future years will no doubt hold many surprises for students of the criminal law as defence lawyers become ever more willing to experiment with innovative tactics. As David Rosenhan, a professor of law and psychology at Stanford University, explains it: "We're getting to see some very, very interesting things, and obviously some long shots... There are a terrific number of them."[77] To make his case, Rosenhan points to a number of situations where people who didn't file income taxes in the United States escaped IRS prosecution by arguing that traumatic life experiences gave them an aversion to forms—a condition that their legal counsellors termed "failure to file syndrome." Some defences to even very serious charges seem to border on the ludicrous. In 1995, for example, the state of Texas executed John Fearance, Jr., 40, for stabbing a man 19 times during a burglary, killing him while the man's spouse watched. In his defence, Fearance had claimed that he was temporarily insane at the time of the burglary-murder, saying his "wife had baked a meat casserole" for dinner on the night of the crimes and he "likes his meat served separately."[78]

Canadian lawyers have been less successful than their American counterparts in advancing innovative defences. In 1987, a Canadian armed forces corporal, Marsali Edwards, was convicted of aggravated assault after driving 13 kilometres to the home of her husband, where she stabbed her spouse twice in the back, puncturing a lung in the process. Her defence was that she was suffering from premenstrual syndrome at the time, and therefore was not responsible for her actions on that day. Although convicted by a jury, the judge was sympathetic to her claims, as reflected in a sentence of three years' probation and an order to obtain treatment.[79]

David Paciocco identifies a number of instances where the Canadian courts have not fallen for a "psychobabble" abuse-related defence. In 1989, a Cambodian immigrant to British Columbia attempted to defend himself by claiming an attack on a man with a one-metre machete, severing his hand, was a manifestation of "amok syndrome," defined as a cultural phenomenon witnessed in southeast Asia "in which the individual, with little or no depression, broods over a trivial insult and then, with little or no provocation, suddenly and unexpectedly erupts into an indiscriminate assault on those around him."[80] Similarly, a Vietnamese immigrant named Ly was unsuccessful in advancing a defence based on provocation for killing his unfaithful wife. He wanted the text to be applied in provocation cases to be altered to require the judge to take into account the importance of maintaining honour and saving face prevailing in Vietnamese culture, in determining whether his wife's infidelity should have excused his response, at least to a sufficient degree to warrant reducing his murder charge to one of manslaughter. He was unsuccessful.[81]

However, it is noteworthy that two prison inmates who killed a fellow inmate in Drumheller Penitentiary in Alberta won a new trial in which their defence was that the victim, an enforcer in a rival prison gang, would have killed them if given a chance. Described by one of the Alberta Court of Appeal judges in the matter as a "prison environment syndrome" defence, the majority of that appeal court believed the jury should have been instructed to take into account the "kill or be killed" environment inside a big penitentiary in determining why the killers could have reasonably believed they were left with no choice but to launch a pre-emptive strike in the circumstances.[82]

In an insightful article,[83] Stephen J. Morse, an expert in psychiatry and the law, says that the criminal justice system is now caught in the grips of a "new syndrome excuse syndrome"—meaning that new excuses are being offered on an almost daily basis for criminal activity. Many of these "excuses" are documented in the psychiatric literature as "syndromes" or conditions, and include antisocial personality disorder, posttraumatic stress disorder, intermittent explosive disorder, kleptomania, pathological gambling, postconcussional disorder, caffeine withdrawal, and premenstrual dysphoric disorder (discussed earlier as premenstrual stress syndrome). All these conditions are listed in the American Psychiatric Association's authoritative *Diagnostic and Statistical Manual of Mental Disorders*.[84] Emerging defences, says Morse, include battered women's syndrome, Vietnam syndrome, child sexual abuse syndrome, Holocaust survivor syndrome, urban survival syndrome, rotten social background syndrome, and adopted child syndrome. "Courts," says Morse, "are increasingly inundated with claims that syndromes old and new, validated and unvalidated, should be the basis for two types of legal change:" (1) the creation of new defences to a criminal charge, and (2) "the expansion of old defences: for example, loosening objective standards for justifications such as self-defence." Morse says that the new syndromes tend to work as defences because they describe personal abnormalities, and most people are willing to accept abnormalities as "excusing conditions that bear on the accused's responsibility." The mistake, says Morse, is to think "that if we identify a cause for conduct, including mental or physical disorders, then the conduct is necessarily excused." "Causation," he cautions, "is not an excuse," only an explanation for the behaviour.

Even so, attempts to offer novel defences that are intended to convince jurors that even admitted criminal offenders should not be held responsible for their actions are becoming increasingly characteristic of the American way of justice. Whether such strategies will ultimately provide effective defences may depend more upon finding juries sympathetic to them than it will upon the inherent quality of the defences themselves.

## SUMMARY

The law serves many purposes. Primary among them is the maintenance of social order. Laws reflect the values held by society. The emphasis placed by law upon individual rights, personal property, and criminal reformation and punishment can tell us much about the cultural and philosophical basis of the society of which it is a part. Legal systems throughout the world reflect the experiences of the societies that created them. Islamic law (which is discussed in Chapter 14), for example, has a strong religious component and requires judicial decisions in keeping with the Moslem Koran.

Canadian law developed out of a long tradition of legal reasoning, extending back to the Code of Hammurabi, the earliest known codification of laws. The most recent historical source of modern law has been English "common law." Common law reflected the customs and daily practices of English citizens during the Middle Ages.

Western criminal law generally distinguishes between serious crimes (indictable offences) and those that are less grave (summary conviction offences). Guilt can only be demonstrated if the *corpus delicti* of a crime can be proven in court.

Our judicial system has come to recognize a number of defences to a criminal charge. Mental disorder and self-defence are two of the most important of the modern defences. The mental disorder defence has met with considerable recent criticism. Even as limits are being placed on some traditional defences, however, new and innovative defences continue to emerge.

## DISCUSSION QUESTIONS

1. Name some of the historical sources of modern law.

2. What kinds of concerns have influenced the development of the criminal law? How are social values and power arrangements in society represented in laws today?

3. Do you think there is a "natural" basis for laws? If so, what basis would you think it appropriate to build a system of laws upon? Do any of our modern laws appear to have a foundation in "natural law"?

4. What is "common law"? Is there a modern form of the common law? If so, what is it?

5. Differentiate the powers of the federal, provincial, and municipal governments over criminal justice. Which level of government seems to be the most important in the criminal justice system?

6. What is meant by the *corpus delicti* of a crime? Are there any elements of a particular crime that you might identify as unnecessary? If so, which crime, and what might they be?

7. What is the difference between *mala in se* and *mala prohibita* offences? Do you think this difference is real or only theoretical?

8. Does the mental disorder defence serve a useful function today? If you could create your own rule for determining mental disorder in criminal trials, what would it be? How would it differ from existing rules?

9. Near the end of this chapter, Stephen J. Morse describes many emerging defences, saying that an explanation for behaviour is not the same thing as an excuse. What does he mean? Might an explanation be an excuse under some circumstances? If so, when?

# WEBLINKS

http://canada.justice.gc.ca
### Department of Justice (Canada)
This government site provides information about the ministry and its responsibilities, plus various publications, including "A Guide to the Making of Federal Acts and Regulations."

http://canada.justice.gc.ca/Loireg/charte/const_en.html
### Canadian Charter of Rights and Freedoms
The full text of the *Charter*, which forms Part 1 of the *Constitution Act, 1982*.

www.chrc-ccdp.ca/
### Canadian Human Rights Commission
Established in 1978, the Canadian Human Rights Commission has three main objectives: to promote knowledge of human rights in Canada and to encourage people to follow principles of equality, to provide effective and timely means for resolving individual complaints, and to help reduce barriers to equality in employment and access to services.

http://laws.justice.gc.ca/en/c-46
### *Criminal Code of Canada*
The complete Code, provided by the Department of Justice (Canada).

http://jurist.law.utoronto.ca
### JURIST Canada
JURIST is dedicated to advancing academic, professional, and public legal education by providing resources and ongoing coverage of developments in legal education, law teaching, legal research, legal news and world law

http://wwlia.org/cacrhist.htm
### Canada's *Criminal Code*: A History
An introductory article published by the World Wide Legal Information Association.

# Policing

*Police can be called upon to do practically anything – and at any time of the day, night or year. They are the generalist social intervenors who are constantly nudging society back onto the tracks of civility, order and safety. It is an essential role that no other group in society can fulfil.*

Tonita Murray
Director General, Canadian Police College

The role of the police in contemporary Canadian society has recently been the subject of considerable attention, discussion, and debate. However, Canada's police officers form the front line as the gatekeepers of the criminal justice system. Many police officers view their role in society metaphorically as engaging in a war on crime—engaging in battles that are becoming progressively more sinister each day. It is the police who are called when a crime is in progress, or when one has been committed. The police are expected to objectively and impartially investigate law violations, gather evidence, solve crimes, and make arrests resulting in the successful prosecution of suspects—all the while adhering to strict procedural standards set forth in the Constitution and enforced by the courts. The chapters in this section of *Canadian Criminal Justice Today* provide an overview of the historical development of policing; describe law enforcement agencies at the federal, provincial, and municipal levels; and discuss the legal environments surrounding police activity.

As you will see, while the police are ultimately charged with protecting the public, they often feel that members of the public do not accord them the respect they deserve, and the distance between the police and the public is not easily bridged. Recently, however, a new image of policing has emerged that may do much to heal that divide. This new viewpoint, known as "community policing," goes well beyond traditional conceptions of the police as mere law enforcers and encompasses the idea that police agencies should take counsel from the communities they serve. Under this new model they are expected to prevent crime as well as to solve it, and to help members of the community deal with other pressing social issues.

# Policing: History and Structure

Metropolitan Toronto Police Museum and Discovery Centre

**KEY CONCEPTS**

| | | |
|---|---|---|
| *comes stabuli* | scientific police management | private protective services |
| sheriff | | |
| new police | directed patrol | |

Police ambulance (circa 1905).

# HISTORICAL DEVELOPMENT OF THE POLICE

Many of the techniques used by today's police differ significantly from those employed in days gone by. Read how a policeman, writing 200 years ago, describes the way pickpockets were caught in London around 1800:

> I walked forth the day after my arrival, rigged out as the very model of a gentleman farmer, and with eyes, mouth, and pockets wide open, and a stout gold-headed cane in my hand, strolled leisurely through the fashionable thoroughfares, the pump-room, and the assembly-rooms, like a fat goose waiting to be plucked. I wore a pair of yellow gloves well wadded, to save me from falling, through a moment's inadvertency, into my own snare, which consisted of about fifty fish-hooks, large black hackles, firmly sewn barb downward, into each of the pockets of my brand new leather breeches. The most blundering 'prig' alive might have easily got his hand to the bottom of my pockets, but to get it out again, without tearing every particle of flesh from the bones, was a sheer impossibility … I took care never to see any of my old customers until the convulsive tug at one or other of the pockets announced the capture of a thief. I then coolly linked my arm in that of the prisoner, [and] told him in a confidential whisper who I was …[1]

Although police tactics and strategy have changed substantially since historical times, and while a plethora of police agencies—some of them highly specialized—characterize the modern criminal justice system, the basic purposes of policing in democratic societies remain the same: (1) to prevent and investigate crimes, (2) to apprehend offenders, (3) to help ensure domestic peace and tranquillity, and (4) to enforce and support the laws (especially the criminal laws) of the society of which the police are a part. Simply put, as Sir Robert Peel, founder of the British system of policing, explained it in 1822: "The basic mission for which the police exist is to reduce crime and disorder."[2]

This chapter describes the development of organized policing in Western culture and discusses contemporary Canadian police forces as they function at local, provincial, and federal levels. We give examples of police agencies at each level, and summarize training, professionalism, and employment issues. Finally, we discuss the promise held by private protective services, the rapid recent growth of private security organizations, and the quasi-private system of justice.

## English Roots

The rise of the police as an organized force in the Western world coincided with the evolution of strong centralized governments. While police forces have developed throughout the world, often in isolation from one another, the historical growth of the English police is of special significance to students of criminal justice in Canada, because early Canadian policing was based upon the British model.

English history reveals that at least as early as the time of Alfred the Great (late ninth century), policing was a community responsibility. Formal policing did not exist. Individuals engaged in self-policing, taking care of themselves and others in their local social unit.

Records indicate that efforts at law enforcement in early Britain, except for military intervention in the pursuit of bandits and habitual thieves, were not well-organized until around the year A.D. 1200.[3] When a person committed an offence, and could be identified, he or she was usually pursued by an organized posse. All able-bodied men who were in a position to hear the hue and cry raised by the victim were obligated to join the posse in a common effort to apprehend the offender. The posse was led by the Shire Reeve—"leader of the county"—or by a mounted officer—the **comes stabuli**. Our modern words **"sheriff"** and "constable" are derived from these early terms. The *comes stabuli* were not uniformed, nor were they sufficient in number to perform all the tasks we associate today with law enforcement. This early system, employing a small number of mounted officers, depended for its effectiveness upon the ability to organize and direct the efforts of citizens toward criminal apprehension.

**comes stabuli** Non-uniformed mounted early law enforcement officers in medieval England. Early police forces were small, and relatively unorganized, but made effective use of local resources in the formation of posses, the pursuit of offenders, and the like.

**sheriff** The elected chief officer of a county law enforcement agency, usually responsible for law enforcement in unincorporated areas and for the operation of the county jail.

The offender, knowledgeable of a near-certain end at the hands of the posse, often sought protection from trusted friends and family. As a consequence, feuds developed between organized groups of citizens, some seeking revenge and others siding with the offender. Suspects who lacked the shelter of a sympathetic group might flee into a church and invoke the time-honoured custom of sanctuary. Sanctuary was rarely an ideal escape, however, as pursuers could surround the church and wait out the offender, while preventing food and water from being carried inside. The offender, once caught, became the victim. Guilt was usually assumed, and trials were rare. Public executions, often involving torture, typified this early justice and served to provide a sense of communal solidarity as well as group retribution.

The end of the thirteenth century witnessed the birth of formalized policing in England. As late as A.D. 1275, the *Statute of Westminster* made it clear that policing remained a civic responsibility of all citizens:

> And forasmuch as the Peace of this Realm hath been evil observed heretofore for lack of quick and fresh Suit making after Felons in due Manner and namely because of Franchises, where Felons are received; it is provided, That all generally be ready and apparelled, at the Commandment and Summons of Sheriffs, and at the Cry of the Country, to sue and arrest felons …[4]

In the years that followed, it appears that peace continued to be "evil observed," but a new tactic was employed to enforce criminal apprehension — the use of citizens specifically charged with the responsibility of catching offenders. The *Statute of Winchester*, 1285, stated as follows:

> … in every City Six Men shall keep at every Gate; in every Borough Twelve Men; in every Town Six or Four; according to the Number of the Inhabitants of the Town; and shall watch the Town continually all Night from Sun-setting unto the Sun-rising. And if any Stranger do pass by them, he shall be arrested until Morning … And in every Hundred and Franchise Two Constables shall be chosen …[5]

Over the period of one decade, England moved from a situation where the community policed itself through vigilante-style posses, responding to the raising of the "hue and cry" by aggrieved members of the community, to a situation where the "hue and cry" was supplemented with "night watch" and "constables," who were members of the community charged with the special responsibility of ensuring a law enforcement response to wrongdoers in communities across England.

The development of law enforcement in English cities and towns grew out of an early reliance on bailiffs, or watchmen. Bailiffs were assigned the task of maintaining a night watch, primarily to detect fires and thieves. They were small in number, but served simply to rouse the sleeping population, which could then deal with whatever crisis was at hand. Larger cities expanded the idea of bailiffs by creating both a "day ward" and a "night watch."

British police practices were codified in the *Statute of Winchester*, enacted in 1285. The statute specified (1) creation of the watch and the ward in cities and towns; (2) the draft of eligible males to serve either force; (3) institutionalized use of the "hue and cry," making citizens who disregarded this call for help subject to criminal penalties; and (4) that citizens must maintain weapons in their homes for answering the call to arms.

The *Justices of the Peace Act* of 1361 formally recognized a "keeper of the peace" for each county, an office whose antecedents date back to knights commissioned by Richard I in 1195, responsible for maintaining peace in the realm. The keepers of the peace became formally recognized as justices with the passage of this Act, holding a mixture of police, judicial, and administrative responsibilities. Because their social status was higher than that of other policing roles, the justices supervised the constables and night watch, and were adjudicators in minor matters.[6]

Some authors have attributed the growth of modern police forces to the gin riots that plagued London and other European cities in the 1700s and early 1800s. The invention of gin around 1720 provided, for the first time, a potent and inexpensive alcoholic drink readily available to the massed populations gathered in the early industrial ghettos of eighteenth-century cities. Seeking to drown their troubles, huge numbers of people, far beyond the ability of the local police to control, began binges of drinking and rioting. These binges were a problem for nearly 100 years and created an immense social problem for British authorities. The policing system by this time had evolved into a group of woefully inadequate substitutes, hired to perform their duties in place of the original—and far more capable—draftees. Staffed by incompetents, and unable to depend on the citizenry for help in enforcing the laws, local police became targets of mob violence, and were often attacked and beaten for sport.

## The Bow Street Runners

The early 1700s saw the emergence in London of a large criminal organization led by Jonathan Wild. Wild ran a type of "fencing" operation built around a group of loosely organized robbers, thieves, and burglars, who would turn their plunder over to him. Wild would then negotiate with the legitimate owners for a ransom of their possessions.

The police response to Wild was limited by disinterest and corruption. However, when Henry Fielding, a well-known writer, became the Justice of the Peace of the Bow Street region of London, changes began to happen. Fielding attracted a force of dedicated officers, dubbed the Bow Street Runners, who soon stood out as the best and most disciplined enforcement agents that London had to offer. Fielding's personal inspiration, and his ability to communicate what he saw as the social needs of the period, may have accounted for his success.

In February 1725, Wild was arrested and arraigned on the following charges:

"... 1) that for many years past he had been a confederate with great numbers of highwaymen, pick-pockets, housebreakers, shop-lifters, and other thieves, 2) that he had formed a kind of corporation of thieves, of which he was the head or director ..., 3) that he had divided the town and country into so many districts, and appointed distinct gangs for each, who regularly accounted with him for their robberies ..., 4) that the persons employed by him were for the most part felon convicts ..., 5) that he had, under his care and direction, several warehouses for receiving and concealing stolen goods, and also a ship for carrying off jewels, watches, and other valuable goods, to Holland, where he had a superannuated thief for his benefactor, and 6) that he kept in his pay several artists to make alterations, and transform watches, seals, snuff-boxes, rings, and other valuable things, that they might not be known ...."[7]

Convicted of these and other crimes, Wild attempted suicide by drinking a large amount of laudanum—an opium compound. The drug merely rendered him senseless, and he was hanged the following morning, having only partially recovered from its effects.

In 1754, Henry Fielding died. His brother John took over his work and occupied the position of Bow Street magistrate for another 25 years. The Bow Street Runners remain famous for quality police work to this day.

## The New Police

In 1829, Sir Robert Peel, who was later to become prime minister of England, formed what many have hailed as the world's first modern police force. Passage of the *Metropolitan Police Act* that same year allocated the resources for Peel's force of 1000 uniformed handpicked men. The London Metropolitan Police, also known simply as the "**new police**," soon became a model for police forces around the world.

The Metropolitan Police were quickly dubbed "Bobbies," after their founder. London's Bobbies were organized around two principles: the belief that it was possible to discourage crime and the practice of preventive patrol. Peel's police patrolled the streets, walking beats. Their predecessors, the watchmen, had previously occupied fixed posts throughout the city, awaiting a public outcry. The new police were uniformed, resembling a military organization, and adopted a military administrative style.

London's first two police commissioners were Colonel Charles Rowan, a career military officer, and Richard Mayne, a lawyer. Rowan believed that mutual respect between the police and citizenry would be crucial to the success of the new force. As a consequence, early Bobbies were chosen for their ability to reflect and inspire the highest personal ideals among young men in early nineteenth-century Britain.

**new police** Also known as the Metropolitan Police of London, formed in 1829 under the command of Sir Robert Peel. Peel's police became the model for modern-day police forces throughout the Western world.

BOX 4.1

## Policy Issues

## Peel's Principles of Policing

1. The basic mission for which the police exist is to prevent crime and disorder as an alternative to the repression of crime and disorder by military force and severity of legal punishment.
2. The ability of the police to perform their duties is dependent upon public approval of police existence, actions, behaviour, and the ability of the police to secure and maintain public respect.
3. The police must secure the willing co-operation of the public in voluntary observance of the law to be able to secure and maintain public respect.
4. The degree of co-operation of the public that can be secured diminishes, proportionately, the necessity for the use of physical force and compulsion in achieving police objectives.
5. The police seek and preserve public favour, not by catering to public opinion, but by constantly demonstrating absolutely impartial service to the law, in complete independence of policy, and without regard to the justice or injustice of the substance of individual laws; by ready

offering of individual service and friendship to all members of the society without regard to their race or social standing; by ready exercise of courtesy and friendly good humour; and by ready offering of individual sacrifice in protecting and preserving life.
6. The police should use physical force to the extent necessary to secure observance of the law or to restore order only when the exercise of persuasion, advice, and warning is found to be insufficient to achieve police objectives; and police should use only the minimum degree of physical force which is necessary on any particular occasion for achieving a police objective.
7. The police should at all times maintain a relationship with the public that gives reality to the historic tradition that the police are the public and that the public are the police; the police are the only members of the public who are paid to give full-time attention to duties which are incumbent on every citizen in the interest of the community welfare.
8. The police should always direct their actions toward their functions and never appear to usurp the powers of the judiciary by avenging individuals or the state, or authoritatively judging guilt or punishing the guilty.
9. The test of police efficiency is the absence of crime and disorder, not the visible evidence of police action in dealing with them.

*Source*: Lee, W.L. Melville. (1901). *A History of Police in England*. London: Methuen.

Unfortunately, the new police were not immediately well-received. Some people viewed them as an occupying army, and open battles between the police and the citizenry ensued. The tide of sentiment turned, however, when an officer was viciously killed in the Cold Bath Fields riot of 1833. A jury, considering a murder charge against the killer, returned a verdict of not guilty, inspiring a groundswell of public support for the much-maligned force.

# The Early Canadian Experience

Early Canadian law enforcement efforts were based to a large degree upon the British experience. Towns and cities in colonial Canada depended upon Canadianized versions of the night watch and day ward, but citizens intent on evading their duty dramatically reduced the quality of police service.

The unique experience of the Canadian colonies, however, quickly differentiated the needs of colonists from those of the masses remaining in Europe. Huge expanses of uncharted territory, vast potential wealth, a widely dispersed population involved mostly with agriculture, and a sometimes wild frontier, all combined to mould Canadian law enforcement in a distinctive way. Recent writers on the history of the Canadian police have observed that policing in Canada was originally influenced by two models of policing: the town constable model for urban policing and the mounted constable model for rural expanses of land.[8]

## The Maritimes

The area that was to become known as Canada was first explored by John Cabot in 1497, and then by Jacques Cartier in 1534. Colonization of the area came very slowly, with European attention being initially directed at exploiting the fish resources in the Maritimes.

In an effort to maintain order among the fishermen taking advantage of the lucrative resources swimming in the Grand Banks, British authorities appointed fishing admirals from among the captains of fishing vessels to resolve disputes. It was not until 1729 that a governor for Newfoundland was appointed by the British government and granted authority to appoint justices of the peace and unpaid constables.[9]

Throughout the 1700s and into the 1800s, the coastal areas of the Maritimes came to be patrolled by the British military, while in the towns, the British model of constables and night watch came to be adopted. In less sparsely populated areas, policing was non-existent. In 1871, the military garrison was removed from Newfoundland, and the Newfoundland Constabulary, modelled after the Royal Irish Constabulary, was formed. This police force exercised jurisdiction over the entire island at the time.

## The Frontier

One of the major factors affecting the development of Canadian law enforcement was the frontier, which remained vast and wild until late into the nineteenth century. The backwoods areas remained largely uninhabited at a time when settlement was progressing rapidly in the United States.

In the United States, citizen posses and vigilante groups were often the only law available to settlers on the American frontier. Eventually, formal policing structures emerged, but often not before considerable settlement had already occurred.

By contrast, the Canadian frontier was relatively tame. Throughout the 1700s and 1800s, while settlers of European origin were populating the American West, the chief inhabitants throughout most of what was emerging as Canada remained the indigenous peoples, with the only European presence throughout much of what was to become Western Canada being representatives of the Hudson's Bay Trading Company, exchanging goods for furs among Canada's aboriginal population. Settlement in the West tended to follow after, rather than before, the establishment of a law enforcement presence, as was the case in the United States.

Rural policing in Western Canada was heavily influenced by the model of policing implemented in rural Ireland during the early 1800s. Ireland's countryside was policed by the Royal Irish Constabulary (RIC), an armed, mounted paramilitary police force. This style of policing seemed particularly suited to policing outside urban centres, especially for a large area where there was little formal social control. The paramilitary nature of such a force allowed it to double as a military presence if the need for a military force arose.[10]

Prior to entering Confederation, the Crown colonies of what was to become British Columbia instituted a police force modelled after the RIC.[11] Led by a former RIC officer named Chartres Brew, the B.C. Provincial Police operated in that province until being supplanted by the RCMP in 1950.

The most famous example of RIC-style policing in Canada was the Northwest Mounted Police (NWMP). Formed in 1873, just six years after Confederation, the NWMP was created at the behest of John A. Macdonald, Canada's first prime minister, to police the area known as the Northwest Territories, a vast area of land spanning from Manitoba to the Rocky Mountains.

George Arthur French was the first commissioner of the RCMP. Recruits were enticed to join the force with the prospect of earning one dollar per day in pay, and the promise of a grant of 160 acres (64.75 hectares) of land upon completing their term of enlistment. Undoubtedly, the promise of adventure and excitement were as important to potential recruits as the prospect of financial compensation.

In 1874, 18 officers and 257 men with horses, oxen, and equipment headed west from Dufferin, Manitoba. Before the year was out, the NWMP had established a presence throughout the West, extending from Manitoba to an area comprising the modern-day province of Alberta.

Considerable debate exists regarding the intended role and purpose of the Northwest Mounted Police (see boxed feature next). As a result of the "March West," the NWMP established a law enforcement presence in the Prairies. Settlement of the West followed, with many homesteaders settling around the forts established by the NWMP. The force was also responsible for maintaining law and order in the Yukon during the Klondike Gold Rush of the late 1890s. In recognition of its service to the country, King Edward VII endowed the NWMP with the prefix "Royal" in 1904.

When Saskatchewan and Alberta entered Confederation in 1905 as distinct provinces, the newly formed provincial governments contracted with the RNWMP to provide provincial policing. The RNWMP also assumed policing in northern Manitoba. However, these early efforts at policing for the provinces under contract came to an end in 1917 when the Prairie provinces created their own provincial police agencies.[12] The RNWMP was relegated to federal law enforcement in the remaining northern territories, and a minor federal role elsewhere in the West, confined largely to security-related matters consequent to World War I. The number of mounted police dropped from 1200 to 303 by late 1918.

In 1920, the RNWMP was merged with the Dominion Police, a separate federal force responsible for security of government buildings and other matters within federal jurisdiction in central Canada. This merger resulted in the creation of a police force that was truly national in scope, resulting in the name being changed to the Royal Canadian Mounted Police (RCMP).

The hiatus from provincial contract policing came to an end in 1928 when the RCMP was contracted to provide the province of Saskatchewan with its services. In 1932, the RCMP assumed provincial policing responsibilities in Alberta, Manitoba, New Brunswick, Nova Scotia, and Prince Edward Island. In 1950, provincial policing in British Columbia and Newfoundland was taken over by the RCMP, leaving only Ontario and Quebec with their own autonomous provincial policing agencies—an arrangement that has survived to the present day.[13]

## Policing Canada's Early Cities

Small-scale, organized law enforcement came into being quite early in Canada's larger cities. Canada's first police officers appear to have originated in Quebec City, where in 1651 a form of night watch took to the streets, keeping an eye out for fires and guarding the general safety of residents by night.[14] With the fall of New France to England in 1759, what was to become Canada began to take shape. Following a short period of military rule, the passage of the *Quebec Act* in 1774 ensured that French Canada could maintain much of its original flavour; however, English criminal law was to supplant that portion of the French Civil Code governing such matters, and the English model of justice, which relied on town constables and night watch, who were accountable to a local justice of the peace, was put into place. By 1853, Montreal had developed an armed police force—100 strong, which were staffed, trained, and equipped by a British military garrison at the city.[15]

The new province of Upper Canada, which would eventually become Ontario, officially adopted the English common law in 1792. In the year following, the *Parish and Town Officers Act* of 1793 provided for justices of the peace to appoint high constables and lower constables throughout the region. Likewise, many other parts of the area then known as British North America were adopting British-style policing arrangements.[16]

---

## BOX 4.2　Justice in Context

### Alternative Explanations for the Origins of the NWMP

**Traditional Explanations:**

1. Control of the whisky trade between Americans and the native peoples.
2. Protect the native peoples from unscrupulous fur traders.
3. Establish law and order to foster settlement in the West.

4. Establish sovereignty so as to forestall annexation by the U.S.

**Critical Approaches:**

1. Ensure assimilation of the native peoples into white culture.
2. Guarantee the orderly transfer of land from the native peoples to the government.
3. Protect the interests of central Canadian (Ontario & Quebec) industrialists in the context of their investment and speculation in grain, timber, minerals, and land.

*Note:* An interesting critical account of the origins of the NWMP is provided by Lorne and Caroline Brown in *An Unauthorized History of the R.C.M.P.* (Toronto: James Lewis & Samuel, 1973). This may be contrasted with William Kelly's orthodox account of the origins of the force in *The Royal Canadian Mounted Police: A Century of History* (Edmonton: Hurtig Publishers, 1973).

Peel's new police were closely studied by Canadian leaders, and six years after their creation, in 1835, Toronto implemented a force of six full-time police officers to replace the night-watch system in operation up until that time.

Following Confederation, towns began to appear more rapidly in the West, and police departments were established, employing the British model developed by Peel. One by one, the towns in the West formed their own individual police forces. Since significant settlement was slow in coming to the West, it should come as no surprise that the establishment of police forces did not occur until the late 1800s. Major centres established police forces in the following years:[17]

| | |
|---|---|
| Victoria | 1873 |
| Vancouver | 1886 |
| New Westminster | 1873 |
| Calgary | 1885 |
| Edmonton | 1893 |
| Winnipeg | 1874 |
| Regina | 1908 |

Women did not make their way into police forces until quite late in history.[18] Apparently, Vancouver was the first city in Canada to hire a policewoman—which occurred in 1912.[19] Soon after, major city police departments across Canada began hiring female police officers; however, early duties were largely confined to clerical work, and dealing with women and children. In her review of female police officers in Canada, Jayne Seagrave notes that it was not until 1952 that policewomen in Vancouver began to receive the same training as policemen; however, their duties were still confined to areas perceived at the time to be "appropriate" for women.[20] Seagrave also observes that it was not until 1973 that women were assigned to general patrol duties in Vancouver. This time frame is concurrent with developments occurring elsewhere in Canadian policing. Indeed, it was not until 1974 that women were recruited into the RCMP as regular officers.[21] "The Policewomen's movement was not an isolated phenomenon, but was part of women's movement into other newly created or newly professionalised fields…."[22]

During the early 1900s, automobiles, telephones, and radios all had their impact on the Canadian police. Automobiles, with the affordable era of rapid transportation they created, necessitated police forces with far-reaching powers, high mobility, and the ability to maintain constant communication with enforcement authorities.

Urban police managed to get around on foot or by bicycle, while rural policing relied largely on horses for mobility, with dog sleds being used in the Far North. The large expanses of territory covered by the RCMP necessitated their adoption of suitable transportation devices when the technology became available. Nora and William Kelly have identified the technological milestones impacting on the RCMP throughout its history.[23] The RCMP acquired its first aircraft in 1921, with a full aviation section being established in 1937. An icebreaker, the *St. Roch*, ventured into arctic waters in 1928. Radio communication developed rapidly between 1946 and 1949.

## The Last Half-Century

It was not until 1958 that all RCMP detachments were connected via a national telex system, thereby facilitating a much improved communication network. In 1969, the last of the Arctic dog-sled patrols gave way to motorized snowmobiles. In 1972, the RCMP purchased its first helicopter, and entered the electronic era with the Canadian Police Information Centre (CPIC) coming online to provide all police agencies in Canada with ready access to information about known criminals, stolen vehicles, registered firearms, and stolen property.

The 1980s and 1990s were a time of cultural reflection in Canada, which forever altered the legal and valuative environment in which the police must work. During that period,

Metropolitan Toronto Police Museum and Discovery Centre

Inspection of Toronto Police Officers (circa 1912).

the adoption of the *Canadian Charter of Rights and Freedoms* (CCRF) reflected a burgeoning individual rights movement, accompanied by concerns over national unity and the future role of Canada's indigenous people in our society. The Supreme Court of Canada frequently advanced constitutionally based personal rights for those facing arrest, investigation, and criminal prosecution within the Canadian system of criminal justice. Although a "chipping away" at those rights may have begun in the late 1990s, the earlier emphasis on the rights of defendants undergoing criminal investigation and prosecution will have a substantial impact on law enforcement activities for many years to come.

Police operations were intensely examined during the 1980s through the 1990s, from day-to-day enforcement decisions to administrative organization and police community relations. This re-examination of police operations arose largely from the research conducted primarily in the United States in the 1970s that found the police were often interpersonally isolated from the communities they served.[24]

Traditional policing had evolved into a practice with three cornerstones:[25]

- Random, routine preventive patrol.
- Rapid response to calls for service.
- Follow-up by specialist investigators.

It was assumed that policing was primarily a law enforcement job that could best be performed by having a number of police working at any given time, mobile within their jurisdiction and available to respond to calls instantaneously. This assumption was based on the notion that police in the community had a deterrent effect, controlling crime by their mere presence. However, to be effective, the police had to be randomly travelling throughout the jurisdiction at any time. Accordingly, potential offenders would be deterred from offending by the possibility of police intervention and arrest. To have the desired deterrent effect, police had to be visible. They also could not reduce preventive patrolling, or the deterrent effect would decline.

In the traditional policing model, the police had to respond rapidly to calls for service, based on the assumption that the likelihood of catching an offender is greatest if the police can get to the crime scene as soon as possible, while the offender is still there, or shortly after the offender has left the scene. This rapid-response model required a highly mobile force, and sophisticated communications technology permitting police to respond as quickly as possible to calls received by the police station. Mobility was greatly enhanced by the use of motor vehicles in policing.

BOX 4.3

# Theory into Practice

## Major Government Inquiries into Policing in the 1980s and 1990s

### Commission of Inquiry into Policing in British Columbia (Oppal Commission), 1994

The most recent of the major government inquiries into policing, this commission also possessed the broadest mandate. Justice Oppal's multi-volume report is still having an impact on many aspects of policing, several years later. Oppal's recommendations contributed to changes running all the way from the specific (such as the adoption of the 9-mm semi-automatic handgun by municipal forces) to the more general (such as the wholesale adoption of the community policing philosophy).

### Public Inquiry into the Administration of Justice and Aboriginal People (Manitoba Aboriginal Justice Inquiry), 1991

This inquiry was co-chaired by Associate Chief Justice A.C. Hamilton of the Manitoba Queen's Bench, and Chief Judge C.M. Sinclair of the Manitoba Provincial Court. It was established following the killing of two members of Manitoba's native community. One incident was the death of a young woman, Helen Betty Osborne, at the hands of several young white men, whom many perceived as managing to escape culpability, perhaps due to their race. The other killing involved the police shooting death of J.J. Harper, a prominent man in the local aboriginal community, by a Winnipeg police officer. The inquiry went beyond identifying wrongdoing in the specific incidents leading to the creation of the inquiry, lambasting the criminal justice system and white governments in general for their historical treatment of aboriginal Canadians. The report came out in favour of the creation of a separate aboriginal justice system as the only viable means of dealing with the prevailing problems. The Winnipeg police were specifically criticized for using race as a means to identify suspects, for their lack of cross-cultural training, for inadequate efforts to recruit aboriginal people into police agencies, and for their deficient investigation, and premature exoneration, of the officer-involved shooting of J.J. Harper.

### Policing in Relation to the Blood Tribe (Alberta) Inquiry, 1991

Assistant Chief Judge C.H. Rolf of the Alberta Provincial Court was appointed as a commissioner to conduct a public inquiry into the Blood Tribe of Alberta. The RCMP was criticized for lack of sensitivity to the way in which their interactions with natives were being perceived by natives. The lack of cultural awareness training was identified as a critical deficiency in the police curriculum.

### Royal Commission on the Donald Marshall, Jr., Prosecution (Marshall Commission), 1990

Three superior court justices, headed by Chief Justice Hickman of the Newfoundland Supreme Court, conducted an inquiry into the circumstances surrounding the investigation, prosecution, and subsequent criminal justice system improprieties in dealing with Donald Marshall, Jr., a Micmac native wrongly accused and convicted of killing his friend in 1971. Marshall spent 11 years in a penitentiary for this crime that he did not commit. The commission found the police investigation to be "unprofessional" from the outset. Many recommendations for change were advanced by the Royal commission. Among the most damning indictments of the system was the conclusion that racism in the criminal justice system of Nova Scotia played a significant role in Marshall's arrest and subsequent conviction. Police–aboriginal relations in some areas were so poor that the Royal commission noted some natives characterized their feelings as entailing "mistrust, if not hatred" towards the police.

### Commission of Inquiry Concerning Certain Activities of the RCMP (McDonald Commission), 1981

Justice David McDonald of the Alberta Court of Queen's Bench inquired into wrongdoing within the RCMP, particularly focusing on allegations of wrongdoing by members of the RCMP's intelligence-gathering branch: the Security Service. Members of this branch had been convicted of wrongdoings involving domestic break-ins to gather intelligence of dubious benefit to national security. McDonald's federal inquiry overshadowed a concurrent inquiry by a commission headed by Jean Keable, charged by the Quebec government with inquiring into the same matters. Keable's commission was hamstrung by constitutional considerations of the Supreme Court of Canada that prohibited the commission from inquiring into the "administration and management" of the RCMP as an aspect of interjurisdictional immunity. The McDonald Commission's principal conclusions called for the creation of a civilian intelligence-gathering agency, independent of the RCMP, and organizational reform within the RCMP itself. The major impact of this inquiry was the creation of the Canadian Security Intelligence Service (CSIS) in 1984, with the RCMP forfeiting its national intelligence-gathering function.

The third cornerstone of traditional policing involved follow-up by specialist investigators. It was assumed that specially trained investigators were superior to patrol officers at solving complicated offences. It was also assumed that if patrol officers spent a significant amount of time away from patrol to conduct an investigation, the deterrent effect obtained through preventive patrol would be lessened. Accordingly, a team of detectives was assigned to follow up with calls that patrol officers responded to, but could not resolve immediately, at the scene.

To a large degree, many police agencies in Canada are still modelled on the traditional model of policing. However, the model is based upon several questionable assumptions, and has several negative side effects. The model assumes preventive patrolling is an effective deterrent. The model also assumes (1) that rapid response is a more effective approach to solving crime than routine or delayed response and (2) that detectives are better crime solvers than patrol officers. From the 1970s through to today, all of these assumptions would come under scrutiny, primarily through field research carried out in the United States.

Traditional police-patrol practices also had negative side effects. To create a visible police presence in the community requires the hiring of many police officers at considerable cost to the taxpayers. To provide around-the-clock deterrence, police must work in shifts, including holidays and weekends. Typically, about five police officers must be employed in order to have one available on duty at any given time. The equipment and technology required for rapid deployment adds additional tax burdens. Making the police force mobile and rapid resulted in the widespread use of the automobile for patrol officers, which created a certain distance between police officers and the community being policed.

## Scientific Police Management: Key U.S. Influences

In 1969, the U.S. Congress created the Law Enforcement Assistance Administration (LEAA). The LEAA was charged with combatting crime via the expenditure of huge amounts of money in support of crime prevention and crime reduction programs. In 1982, LEAA expired when the U.S. Congress refused it further funding.

**scientific police management** The application of social scientific techniques to the study of police administration for the purposes of increasing effectiveness, reducing the frequency of citizen complaints, and enhancing the efficient use of available resources.

The legacy of LEAA is an important one for police managers, both in the United States and here in Canada. The research-rich years of 1969–1982, supported largely through LEAA funding, have left a plethora of scientific findings of relevance to police administration and, more importantly, have established a tradition of program evaluation within police management circles. This tradition, which is known as **scientific police management**, is a natural outgrowth of LEAA's insistence that any funded program had to contain a plan for its evaluation. Scientific police management means the application of social scientific techniques to the study of police administration in order to increase effectiveness, reduce the frequency of citizen complaints, and enhance the efficient use of available resources. The heyday of scientific police management occurred in the 1970s, when federal monies in the U.S. were far more readily available to support such studies than they are today.

LEAA was not alone in funding police research during the 1970s. On July 1, 1970, the Ford Foundation announced the start of a Police Development Fund totalling US$30 million, to be spent over the next five years on police departments to support major crime-fighting strategies. This funding led to the establishment of the Police Foundation, which continues to exist today with the mission of "foster[ing] improvement and innovation in American policing."[26] Police Foundation–sponsored studies over the past 20 years have added to the growing body of scientific knowledge on policing.

## The Kansas City Experiment

By far the most famous application of social research principles to police management was the Kansas City Preventive Patrol Experiment.[27] Sponsored by The Police Foundation, the results of this year-long study were published in 1974. The study divided the southern part of Kansas City into 15 areas. Five of these "beats" were patrolled in the usual fashion. Patrol activities were doubled on another five beats, and twice the normal number of patrol officers were assigned to them. The final third of the beats received a novel "treatment" indeed—no patrols were assigned to them and no uniformed officers entered that part of the city unless they were called. The program was kept something of a secret, and citizens were unaware of the difference between the patrolled and "unpatrolled" parts of the city.

The results of the Kansas City experiment were surprising. Records of "preventable crimes," those toward which the activities of patrol were oriented—like burglary, robbery, auto theft, larceny, and vandalism—showed no significant differences in rate of occurrence among the three experimental beats. Similarly, citizens didn't seem to notice the change in patrol patterns in the two areas where patrol frequency was changed. Surveys conducted at the conclusion of the experiment showed no difference among citizens in the three areas as to their fear of crime before and after the study.

The 1974 study can be summed up in the words of the author of the final report: "... the whole idea of riding around in cars to create a feeling of omnipresence just hasn't worked ... Good people with good intentions tried something that logically should have worked, but didn't."[28]

A second Kansas City study focused on "response time."[29] It found that even consistently fast police response to citizen reports of crime had little effect on either citizen satisfaction with the police or on the arrest of suspects. The study uncovered the fact that most reports made to the police came only after a considerable amount of time had passed. Hence, the police were initially handicapped by the timing of the report, and even the fastest police response was not especially effective.

The Kansas City study has been credited with beginning the now-established tradition of scientific police evaluation. Patrick V. Murphy, former police commissioner in New York City and past president of the Police Foundation, said the Kansas City study "ranks among the very few *major* social experiments ever to be completed."[30]

*Effects of the Kansas City Study on Patrol* The Kansas City studies greatly impacted on managerial assumptions about the role of preventive patrol and traditional strategies for responding to citizen calls for assistance. As Joseph Lewis, then director of evaluation at the Police Foundation, said, "I think that now almost everyone would agree that almost anything you do is better than random patrol ...."[31]

While some basic assumptions about patrol were called into question by the Kansas City studies, patrol remains the backbone of police work. New patrol strategies for the effective utilization of human resources have led to various kinds of **directed patrol** activities. One form of directed patrol varies the number of officers involved in patrolling according to the time of day or on the basis of frequency of reported crimes within areas. The idea is to put the most officers where and when crime is most prevalent.

Other cities have prioritized calls for service,[32] ordering a quick police response only when crimes are in progress or where serious crimes have occurred. Less significant offences or certain citizen complaints are handled through the mail or by having citizens come to the police station to make a report.

**directed patrol** A police management strategy designed to increase the productivity of patrol officers through the application of scientific analysis and evaluation of patrol techniques.

## The Rand Study of Detectives

In the mid-1970s, the Rand Corporation undertook a nationwide study in the United States, looking into various aspects of criminal investigation.[33] One major finding of this study was that the initial efforts of the first patrol officer on the scene, responding to a call for service, were crucial in helping to identify a suspect for initial or subsequent arrest. Where no initial suspect was identified, routine post-offence investigative practices were more efficiently performed by patrol officers or clerks rather than by specialist investigators. Finally, "case screening" by follow-up investigators, looking for solvability criteria, i.e., case-related characteristics that indicate a high likelihood the case can be solved, allowed investigators to allocate their time and resources on the cases that were most likely to result in the identification and arrest of a suspect.

The practical result of the Rand Study's findings has been an increased investigative role for patrol officers. The more complex criminal investigations are referred to detectives for follow-up, but the majority of case investigations are conducted by uniformed patrol officers.[34]

## Recent Studies

Recent studies of the police have been designed to identify and probe some of the basic, and often "taken for granted," assumptions that have guided police work throughout this century. The initial response to many of these studies was, "Why should we study that?

Everybody knows the answer already!" The value of applying evaluative techniques to police work, however, can be seen in the following examples:

- The 1994 Kansas City "gun experiment" was designed to "learn whether vigorous enforcement of existing gun laws could reduce gun crime." The Kansas City police department's "weed and seed" program targeted areas designated as "hot spots" within the cities. These were locations identified by computer analysis as having the most gun-related crimes within the metropolitan area. A special gun-detection unit was assigned to the area, and guns were removed from citizens following searches incident to arrest for other (non-gun-related) crimes, traffic stops, and as the result of other legal stop-and-frisk activities. While the program was in operation, gun crimes declined by 49 per cent in the target area, while they increased slightly in a comparison area. Drive-by shootings, which dropped from seven (in the six months prior to the program) to only one (following implementation of the program), were particularly affected.[35]

- The 1984 Minneapolis domestic violence experiment was the first scientifically engineered social experiment to test the impact of the use of arrest (versus alternative forms of disposition) upon crime.[36] In this case, the crime in focus was violence in the home environment. Investigators found that offenders who were arrested were less likely to commit repeat offences than those who were handled in some other fashion. A Police Foundation–sponsored 1992 study of domestic violence in the Metro-Dade (Florida) area reinforced the Minneapolis findings, but found that the positive effect of arrest applied almost solely to those who were employed.

- A third example of modern scientific police management comes from Newport News, Virginia.[37] In the late 1980s, the police in Newport News decided to test traditional incident-driven policing against a new approach called problem-oriented policing. Incident-driven policing mobilizes police forces to respond to citizen complaints and offences reported by citizens. It is what the Newport News police called "the standard method for delivering police services." Problem-oriented policing, on the other hand, was developed in Newport News to identify critical crime problems in the community and to address effectively the underlying causes of crime. For example, one identified problem involved thefts from vehicles parked in the Newport News shipbuilding yard. As many as 36 000 cars were parked in those lots during the day. Applying the principles of problem-oriented policing, Newport News officers explored the problem. After identifying theft-prone lots and a small group of frequent offenders, officers arrested one suspect in the act of breaking into a vehicle. That suspect provided the information that police were seeking: it turned out that drugs were the real target of the car thieves. "Muscle cars," rock-music bumper stickers, and other indicators were used by the thieves as clues to which cars had the highest potential for yielding drugs. The police learned that what seemed to be a simple problem of thefts from cars was really a search for drugs by a small group of "hard-core" offenders. Strategies to address the problem were developed, including wider efforts to reduce illicit drug use throughout the city.

To date, in Canada, there have been no formal evaluations of problem-oriented policing. These and other studies have established a new basis for the use of scientific evaluation in police work today. The accumulated wisdom of police management studies can be summed up in the words of Patrick Murphy, who, now retired as director of the Police Foundation, stated five tenets for guiding North American policing into the next century:[38]

1. Neighbourhood policing programs of all kinds need to be developed, improved, and expanded.

2. More police officers need college- and graduate-level education.

3. There should be more civilians in police departments. Civilian specialists can add to department operations and release sworn officers for enforcement-related duties, leaving administrative tasks to civilian personnel.

4. Departments must continue to become more representative of the communities they serve by recruiting more women and minorities.

5. Restraint in the use of force, especially deadly force, must be increased.

### Canadian Developments

Many of the changes brought about in the U.S. by the adoption of scientific police-management principles were readily adopted in Canada. Major urban police departments, as well as the major provincial police forces and the RCMP, have come to adopt many of the technological and scientific developments pioneered south of the border.

To date, in Canada, there has never been a major infusion of capital dedicated to researching police practices. Individual police departments have endeavoured to develop innovative approaches to old problems in policing, and have, to a large extent, been responsible for evaluating their efforts themselves. The few attempts to evaluate Canadian police agencies are largely confined to recent attempts to implement community policing initiatives, which will be discussed in the next chapter.

# CANADIAN LAW ENFORCEMENT TODAY: FROM THE FEDERAL TO THE LOCAL LEVEL

The organization of Canadian law enforcement is one of the most complex in the world. Each of the three levels of government in Canada—federal, provincial, and local—have created police agencies to enforce their laws. This scheme is complicated by some governmental jurisdictions contracting with agencies from other levels to provide policing services. The matter is complicated still more by the rapid growth of aboriginal police agencies, quasi-private police agencies, and purely private security firms that operate on a profit basis and provide services that have traditionally been regarded as law enforcement activities.

Canada spends almost $10 billion per year on criminal justice services. More than half of this, or almost $6 billion per year, is devoted to the provision of policing by government police agencies.[39] In 1997–98, 74 398 people were employed in Canada's policing agencies.[40] Of these people, 54 719 were actual police officers, with the remaining 19 679 being civilian staff.[41] Most police officers work at the municipal level, either for a local agency, or under contract with the RCMP or the Ontario Provincial Police. In 1997–98, 64 per cent of Canadian police officers provided municipal police services, while 25 per cent provided provincial policing (including RCMP officers working under contract outside Ontario and Quebec).[42] Only 8 per cent of Canadian police officers are RCMP fulfilling federal policing functions, while the remaining 3 per cent of police officers are RCMP officers working in an administrative capacity.[43] Figure 4–2 breaks down the proportion of police officers working at various levels in 2001.

## The Federal Law Enforcement Agency

Unlike the United States, which has 21 separate federal law-enforcement agencies distributed among eight U.S. government departments, in Canada federal policing has been allocated almost exclusively to the Royal Canadian Mounted Police (RCMP). In addition to the RCMP's federal policing role, the Military Police, which is a branch of the Canadian Armed Forces, are responsible for policing military personnel.

The RCMP is the most famous law enforcement agency in the country, and is renowned throughout most of the world, particularly for its early exploits as the NWMP/RNWMP. It is highly regarded by many Canadian citizens, who think of it as an example of what a law enforcement organization should be and who believe that RCMP officers are exemplary police officers. Indeed, the RCMP has become a national symbol. It is difficult to think of any other country in the world where the citizenry view their police agency as a source and symbol of national pride.

BOX 4.4

## Careers in Justice

## Working with the RCMP

The RCMP celebrated its 130th anniversary in 2003 and has a long tradition of service to Canadians in the area of law enforcement. As part of its recruitment process, the RCMP looks for individuals who are community-oriented and who must meet basic qualifications in order to make an application. They must

- be a Canadian citizen;
- be of good character;
- be proficient in either of Canada's official languages;
- be willing to relocate anywhere within Canada;
- be 19 years of age at the time of engagement;
- have a Canadian secondary school diploma or equivalent;
- possess a valid Canadian driver's licence;
- meet the RCMP's medical and physical requirements.

Applicants who wear glasses or contact lenses must also meet minimum vision standards:

- Uncorrected (without eyewear and without squinting): 6/18 (20/60) in each eye, or 6/12 (20/40) in one eye and up to 6/30 (20/100) in the other.
- Corrected (with eyewear): 6/6 (20/20) in one eye and up to 6/9 (20/30) in the other.

Applicants will also be tested for colour vision.

Those who meet the application criteria would be required to attend an information session, write the RCMP Police Aptitude Test (RPAT), partake in a physical fitness and abilities assessment, referred to as the Physical Abilities Requirement Evaluation (PARE), attend an interview (for suitability and security), and write a language test (if necessary). In addition to these procedures, the RCMP would conduct a background investigation, and a medical and psychological evaluation.

Before an individual can enter into a pre-employment agreement with the RCMP, the following prerequisites must be met:

- Keyboarding/typing certificate from an educational institution (minimum 18 words per minute without errors);
- Valid standard first-aid certificate approved under the Canada Occupational Safety and

### Health Regulations, Canada Labour Code

Successful applicants enrol as cadets. All cadets are required to sign a "Cadet Training Agreement" before they begin a challenging academic and physical training program offered through the RCMP's Training Academy in Regina, Saskatchewan. This orientation training is approximately 22 weeks in length and covers a wide range of topics, including basics of Canadian law, problem-solving in community policing, skills development in firearms, driving, tactics, and other matters relating to police and public safety.

For detailed information, applicants should contact their local RCMP recruiting office, which can be found at: **www.rcmp-grc.gc.ca/recruiting/offices_e.htm**.

*The RCMP Today* While the RCMP performs significant duties as a provincial and municipal police force under contractual arrangements, it is also a national police force with responsibilities at the federal level.

The RCMP is an agency organized under the authority of the *RCMP Act*.[44] The federal Solicitor General is the cabinet minister responsible for the RCMP. Under his or her direction, the RCMP is headed by a Commissioner, who is responsible for the "control and management" of the force. Under the Commissioner are four Deputy Commissioners centred at Headquarters in Ottawa. Due to the geographic land mass covered by the RCMP, the organization is divided into 15 regional divisions, separated by province and territory, with Headquarters in Ottawa also making up its own division. Each division is commanded by its own divisional Commanding Officer, and is alphabetically designated (see Figure 4–1). Each division has a headquarters located within the geographic confines of the division, usually in the provincial capital.

These divisions are further subdivided into 52 subdivisions and further into 652 detachments. The RCMP today employs about 21 000 personnel, 15 000 of whom are police officers, operating under an annual budget of $2.3 billion.[45] The RCMP operates a training academy in Regina, Saskatchewan, and the Canadian Police College in Ottawa, Ontario.

Federal law enforcement involves a fairly small but significant number of police personnel. Although more than one-quarter of all police officers in Canada work for the RCMP (15 202 officers), only one-third of RCMP officers work in federal law enforcement (5012); the remainder work under contract for municipal or provincial governments, or are involved in administrative and other service responsibilities.[46]

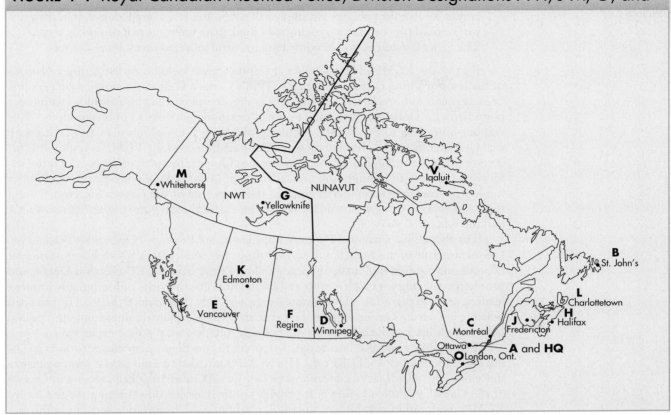

The small number of federal enforcement officers are dispersed across Canada. Much of the work of the RCMP in its federal enforcement capacity is relatively low visibility policing. Approximately 1000 of these officers are assigned exclusively to enforcement of Canada's drug laws. While local law enforcement agencies perform drug law enforcement at the community level, the federal RCMP specifically target international and interprovincial drug trafficking.

The RCMP use a number of tactics to combat the drug trade, including cultivating informants within the drug trade, utilizing undercover agents, engaging in an ongoing coastal/airport watch, providing foreign assistance, providing witness protection, and liaising with foreign drug enforcement agencies in a combined effort to curtail drug use and distribution.

In addition to attempting to control drugs coming into Canada, drug enforcement also attempts to put a lid on drugs being exported to the United States. Police estimate marijuana production in British Columbia alone to top $1 billion in value per year. An estimated $7.8 million worth of high-grade marijuana is exported from that province to the United States every month.[47]

Under the auspices of an Economic Crime Directorate, the federal RCMP also endeavours to control white-collar crime. Such business-related crimes as fraud, false pretenses, theft, breach of trust, secret commissions, offences targeting the federal government, corruption of public officials, tax fraud, computer crime, bankruptcy-related offences, securities fraud, and counterfeiting are the object of the Economic Crime Directorate's efforts to reduce and prevent offences. Recent budget cuts have dramatically affected the RCMP's ability to investigate commercial crime. Indeed, a past commissioner of the RCMP has been quoted as saying:

**FIGURE 4–2** Canadian Police Officers by Level of Policing, 2001

Federal 7.7%
Other 1.9%
Provincial 23.7%
Municipal 66.6%

*Source*: Adapted from the Statistics Canada publication "Police Resources in Canada," Catalogue no. 85-225, December 2002.

The long-term implications clearly are that we're going to end up with two-tier policing with forensic accounting firms dealing with those kinds of [white-collar] crimes because the public purse simply will not be able to accommodate it. In reality, we created a two-tier justice system, and I think that's unfortunate if we end up there. The general public is simply not willing to spend more, to invest more in taxes.[48]

Part of the RCMP's federal policing responsibility includes investigating violations of the law governing customs and excise. While Canada Customs maintains checkpoints at entry points to Canada, Canada Customs agents do not conduct investigations within our boundaries for violations pertaining to the international movement of commodities. This responsibility falls to the RCMP. Similarly, although Canada's borders are staffed with immigration officers, the Immigration and Passport Branch of the RCMP is responsible for investigating the smuggling of illegal aliens into Canada, passport offences, and other offences pertaining to immigration and citizenship. Other federal policing responsibilities range from transportation matters such as those covered by the *Canada Shipping Act*, and the *Aeronautics Act*, through wildlife regulation under the *Migratory Birds Convention Act* and the *Canada Wildlife Act*.

The RCMP has a national International Liaison and Protective Operations Directorate. One central role of this branch is to provide protective services to VIPs such as government officials and foreign diplomats in Canada. The Prime Minister's Protection Detail, and protective policing for major events and the security for the visits of foreign government leaders, are also part of this Directorate's responsibility. Historically, the RCMP provided policing at Canada's major airports; however, this role is rapidly diminishing as the federal government has contracted out airport policing, often to local police departments.

The RCMP must also find budget resources to coordinate activities with foreign police agencies through INTERPOL. The RCMP must also run the recruit training centre in Regina, and an advanced educational facility for all Canadian police agencies in Ottawa at the Canadian Police College. It provides police-service dog training for the entire RCMP organization in Innisfail, Alberta. It coordinates transportation services in the marine, land, and air context. It provides identification services on a national level as well as forensic laboratory services to the nation's law enforcement community. It provides a national computer system accessible by all policing agencies in the country called the Canadian Police Information Centre (CPIC), which is connected to provincial motor vehicle agencies and the U.S. National Crime Information Center (NCIC).

---

## BOX 4.5  Careers in Justice

### Canada Customs Inspectors

TYPICAL POSITIONS: Full-time and part-time inspectors working at various border locations, and airports supporting international travel.

EMPLOYMENT REQUIREMENTS: Open to Canadian citizens and landed immigrants who have successfully graduated from a college or university, or have completed secondary school combined with suitable work experience. Preference is also given to those people with enforcement-related work, investigative experience, information-giving experience, or experience in the management of a commercial enterprise.

OTHER REQUIREMENTS: Each applicant must pass a written Customs Inspector Test. A valid driver's licence or equivalent personal mobility is required. Candidates must pass a valid Enhanced Reliability Check. Prior to applying, potential applicants are encouraged to review the "Customs Inspector Test Information Booklet" at: **www.ccra-adrc.gc.ca/careers/working/customs_inspector-e.pdf**

TRAINING: Successful applicants are required to attend a 14-week in-residence training program at the Rigaud Learning Centre in Quebec. Transportation to and from this training program, and living expenses are paid for by Canada Customs. Upon completion of the training program, new recruits return to their home region to complete a further 38-week on-the-job training program.

SALARY: $43 928 to $48 558 per annum.

DIRECT INQUIRIES TO: Canada Customs and Revenue Agency's "Career Opportunities" website at: **www.ccra-adrc.gc.ca/careers/menu-e.html**

BOX 4.6

# Theory into Practice

## Canadian Police Information Centre (CPIC)

The Canadian Police Information Centre (CPIC) is an integrated, automated system that provides tactical information on crimes and criminals. This computer-based police information system, operational since 1972, is located in the RCMP Headquarters complex at Ottawa, Ontario. Police departments across Canada can immediately access a central computer to operational police information. The CPIC system also has a narrative capability that allows messages to be sent from one terminal to another almost immediately.

In Canada, 15 000 access points allow over 60 000 police personnel working in municipal police departments, federal and provincial agencies, and over 1000 RCMP detachments and specialized units within the RCMP to access the CPIC system.

Beginning in 1999, the RCMP began an extensive $115-million CPIC renewal program to update the entire system and facilitate future changes. The CPIC system contains the following files:

| File | File Data |
| --- | --- |
| **Vehicle** | Vehicles stolen, abandoned, or wanted in connection with crime; stolen licence plates, validation tags, Vehicle Identification Number plates, and parts. |
| **Persons** | Persons wanted by police; parolees; charged, prohibited persons (e.g., drinking, driving, or possessing firearms); missing persons, including children; body marks or scars and descriptions of clothing; unidentified bodies, to which marks, scars, clothing, and dental records can be cross-referenced (also includes body parts, amnesia, and comatose or disaster victims). |
| **Property** | Guns, stolen articles (e.g., VCRs, computers) and securities (e.g., stocks and bonds). |
| **Marine** | Stolen and abandoned boats, stolen boat motors. |
| **Criminal Record Synopsis** | Condensed version of criminal records supported by the submission of fingerprints. The maintenance of this file is the responsibility of Identification Services personnel within the Law Enforcement Services program, RCMP Headquarters, Ottawa. |
| **Dental Characteristics** | Individual dental records are stored in this file, which is a subsystem of the Persons File. It is designed primarily to assist police officers in identifying human remains that may be unidentifiable by normal procedures and techniques, and also to identify amnesia and comatose victims. |
| **Criminal Records** | Full criminal records can be obtained on a query. Maintenance of the file is the responsibility of Identification Services, RCMP HQ, Ottawa. |
| **Inmate File** | Information stored on individuals under the control of Correctional Service Canada, incarcerated or on parole. |

The CPIC system has access to motor vehicle information from each province in Canada, either through an interface with the applicable provincial Motor Vehicle Bureau or because the RCMP is a member of the Centralized Registered Owner System, which duplicates and stores the information in the CPIC online system. Ongoing developments are connected to the firearms registration program and the new national sex offender registry.

CPIC is connected with the U.S. National Crime Information Center (NCIC) and individual state databases through the ACUPIES interface (Automated Canadian United States Police Information Exchange System). This external system interface, controlled by RCMP Interpol Section in Ottawa, operates under ministerial directives and the guidance of the Interpol Charter with respect to the exchange and release of police information to a foreign country. The system provides the ability to send Person, Vehicle, Marine, Property, and Criminal Record queries to the U.S. FBI/NCIC computer system, plus Registered Owner and Driver's Licence checks to each of the 50 states in the U.S. In addition, narrative messages can be passed directly between Canadian and American police agencies through this interface.

The RCMP also provides explosives experts through its Technical Security Branch, and is at the forefront of maintaining criminal intelligence, particularly targeting the analysis of organized crime. It seeks to promote itself and its image through maintaining a 32-officer Musical Ride, performing drills on horseback at major events across Canada and around the world.

In the United States, in addition to the 21 federal agencies whose primary duty is law enforcement, 120 other federal agencies have secondary law enforcement or quasi-enforcement responsibilities. In Canada, the RCMP is the only federal agency performing the enforcement functions fulfilled by these numerous U.S. organizations south of the border.

## Provincial-Level Agencies

The *Constitution Act, 1867* made the "Administration of Justice" a provincial responsibility. This responsibility appears to have clearly granted authority to the provinces to establish their own policing organizations. Despite this granting of authority to the provinces, most provinces were slow to develop formal provincial policing structures. As Curt Griffiths and Simon Verdun-Jones note:

> Legislation authorizing the creation of provincial police forces was passed in Manitoba and Quebec in 1870, British Columbia in 1871, Ontario in 1909, New Brunswick in 1927, Nova Scotia in 1928, and Prince Edward Island in 1930 ... the Royal Newfoundland Constabulary had been operating since 1872 ...[49]

Alberta and Saskatchewan enacted legislation authorizing the creation of provincial forces in 1905; however, the RNWMP policed these provinces under contract until 1917 when these provinces created their own police forces. Such police forces were short-lived, as the RCMP assumed provincial policing responsibilities by contract in Saskatchewan in 1928, and in Alberta in 1932.

Today, only Ontario and Quebec provide their own provincial police forces. All of the other provinces have entered a contract with the federal government to have the RCMP provide the necessary provincial policing. Newfoundland still retains the Royal Newfoundland Constabulary; however, it serves as an urban police force, for all intents and purposes confined to St. John's, while the provincial policing responsibility is provided by the RCMP.

The role of provincial police forces is fairly uniform from province to province. In general, provincial police forces are responsible for providing police services in rural and small-town areas, as well as policing the highways throughout the province. Indeed, provinces typically require municipalities to provide for their own policing upon reaching a given size. In British Columbia, Manitoba, Ontario, and Quebec, a municipality with a population of over 5000 is required to provide its own policing services, while in Alberta this responsibility arises when a municipality's population reaches 2500. In Saskatchewan, a municipality with over 500 inhabitants must provide for its own police force. In New Brunswick and Nova Scotia, every municipality must provide policing services or contract for such services. In Newfoundland and Prince Edward Island, the policing legislation appears to be silent on the matter. For those provinces not requiring the formation of a police service in small towns and villages, the provincial police provide law enforcement.

---

## BOX 4.7  Justice in Context

## The RCMP's Community Policing Emphasis

The RCMP's Community, Contract & Aboriginal Police Services is responsible for promoting and facilitating the implementation of community policing strategies. RCMP community policing is a partnership between the police and the community, sharing in the delivery of police services. As a model of police service delivery, community policing provides for a more collaborative, responsive, and effective approach to public service. The implementation of community policing within the RCMP is a continuing process that started in 1990.

One initiative for implementing community policing within the RCMP has been the development of different "pilot projects" in every division. While the specific programs vary, each project is guided by the same overarching principles:

- Using modern management principles that will foster change.
- Providing the most effective police service that will resolve community problems.
- Consulting with the community.
- Using the newest technology.

These principles have changed detachment structure and culture, and established problem-solving techniques with the community, partners, and the networking process. Successful approaches are characterized as "best practices" community-policing initiatives. Assessment of various practices involves research, with data being collected and analyzed on an ongoing basis.

Provincial police are responsible for enforcing the provincial laws in force in the relevant province, and they enforce the criminal law. Clearly, provincial policing is largely a highway patrol and rural policing enterprise.

## Local Agencies

The term "local police" encompasses agencies of considerable variety and size. Individual municipal departments, contracted municipal detachments, and regionalized police departments may be grouped under the "local" rubric.

Large municipal departments are highly visible because of their huge size, vast budgetary allotments, and innovative programs. Far greater in number, however, are local small-town departments. Some very small communities hire only a few officers, who fill all the roles of administrator, investigator, and night watch—as well as everything in between.

In 1994, there were 578 municipal police agencies in Canada. Of these, 364 were independent police forces, 201 were forces created under contract with the RCMP, and 13 were forces created under contract with the OPP. A 1996 report found that most local police forces are small—with only seven departments found to employ more than 1000 officers. Municipal police forces, including those created under contract, comprise almost 63 per cent of Canada's police strength, and consume over 55 per cent of the $5.78 billion spent annually on policing in this country. Policing is the largest single budgetary expenditure of many Canadian municipalities.

Local police agencies are responsible for enforcing the criminal law, provincial laws, and municipal bylaws in their jurisdictions. Many larger cities and towns have created separate bylaw-enforcement agencies to reduce the onerous enforcement responsibilities placed on local police.[50]

## Vancouver Police Department: Big City Law Enforcement

The Vancouver Police Department serves as a good example of a modern, progressive large-city police agency. Vancouver is a very cosmopolitan city, and Canada's gateway to the Pacific Rim. As such, it is a gathering place for people of all races and nationalities from around the globe. While Vancouver itself is not a large city, with only 514 000 people, the Vancouver metropolitan area is home to around 2 million people. Forty-five percent

The Vancouver Police Department was the first police department in Canada to hire a female police officer. Now there are many women in the Canadian police force. Here, an officer with the Ontario Provincial Police communicates via radio with central dispatch.

of Vancouver residents reported in the last census that they are immigrants. The city displays many ethnic neighbourhoods today, with clearly defined South Asian, East Asian, and Italian areas that make up Vancouver. Preferences in food, style of dress, customs, habits, and even language vary from area to area.

The Vancouver Police Department was formed in April 1886. Initially composed of four police officers, the police department was headed by Chief John M. Stewart.[51] In the year following its official inception, the Vancouver Police Department was taken over by the provincial government in the wake of race riots developing from animosity by the Anglo-settlers against Chinese immigrants. However, by 1888, control of the police department was returned to the city.[52]

Today, the Vancouver Police Department is composed of 1096 police officers.[53] The Commission of Inquiry into Policing in British Columbia found that, in 1992, only 5.7 per cent of the police officers in Vancouver were visible minorities.[54] This number appears to have risen from only 3.8 per cent in 1990.[55] Clearly Vancouver is beginning to put a concerted effort into increasing visible-minority representation on its police force. As of 1992, 10.7 per cent of Vancouver's police officers were women.[56] Financial concerns and organizational restructuring have recently altered the composition of the police department.

### Vancouver Police Department Innovations

The Vancouver Police Department has been a leader in innovative programs. As the largest urban police department in the Lower Mainland area of British Columbia, it provides many specialized police services.

The Vancouver Police Department was the first police department in Canada to hire a female police officer. It was also the first police department to implement a marine squad and the first to introduce mobile data terminals into police cars.

In addition to a regular patrol division, the Vancouver Police has officers working in the following positions:

- Traffic (Motorcycle Squad and Accident Investigation)
- Specialty Investigative Units, including:
  - Homicide
  - Robbery
  - Commercial Crime
  - Vice/Drugs
  - Burglary
  - Stolen Auto
  - Property Crime
  - Sexual Offence Squad
  - Domestic Violence and Criminal Harassment Unit
- Emergency Response Team (Special Weapons and Rescue)
- Forensic Identification
- Criminal Intelligence Section
- Strike Force (Surveillance)
- Crime Prevention (Business Liaison, Block Watch, Personal Safety)
- Marine Squad
- Mounted Squad
- Dog Squad
- Crime Analysis
- School Liaison
- Youth Squad
- Gang Crime

- Police/Mental Health Worker Unit
- Police/Social Worker Unit
- Human Resources Section
- Planning/Research and Audit
- Crime Stoppers
- Secondments to Other Agencies, including:
  - B.C. Police Academy
  - Organized Crime Agency
  - Proceeds of Crime Unit

Starting salary for a probationary constable within the Vancouver Police Department in 2002 was $39 912, with increments running through to the 20th year of service, resulting in an annual salary of $70 608 for a first-class constable. This salary is accompanied by an attractive benefit package. First class sergeants receive an annual salary of $79 812.[57]

## Regionalization

Since the 1960s, local policing in several parts of Canada has been dramatically affected by regionalization of police agencies. Regionalization entails the amalgamation of the police departments of several contiguous municipalities into a single force. In the major cities of many parts of Canada, the surrounding suburbs are composed of individual municipalities attached to the city. In some parts of the country, each of these areas is policed by separate, independent municipal police departments. In other areas, the municipalities in the area surrounding a city are policed by one "regionalized" police department.

On the West Coast, in the two urban centres of Victoria and Vancouver, many municipalities are closely connected to the city, yet each retains its own police department, or a detachment of the RCMP providing municipal policing under contract. In some parts of the country, such as Edmonton and Alberta, the central city is sufficiently spread out to encompass the surrounding suburbs within its territorial jurisdiction, obviating the need for regionalization. In yet other parts of the country, such as in Montreal, Winnipeg, and many parts of southern Ontario, the situation is characterized by regionalized police forces.

### Regional Policing in Southern Ontario: Mega-City Policing

Toronto and its surrounding municipalities constitute the largest urban core in the country. In 1998, Toronto and some of its immediate neighbours merged into one large city. Several of Toronto's other neighbours retained autonomy as separate entities. Policing in the greater Toronto area is performed by the Toronto Police Service in the enlarged City of Toronto, and by regionalized police forces in the areas surrounding it.

Toronto's police service traces its lineage to the hiring of six full-time constables in 1835.[58] Toronto and its surrounding municipalities grew rapidly over time, particularly in the middle of this century. In 1957, in an effort to increase efficiency, the police departments of Toronto and 12 suburban municipalities were combined to form the Toronto Metropolitan Police Department.[59] This represents an example of regionalization, where several departments merged to become one, in the hopes of more effective delivery of police services than would be possible through the operation of small, autonomous police agencies. Today, numerous regionalized police forces exist in southern Ontario.

The area immediately to the west of Toronto is composed of the large urban centres of Mississauga and Brampton, and the town of Caledon. These areas are now policed by the Peel Regional Police Force. Further to the west, Burlington, Milton, and Halton Hills are policed by the Halton Regional Police. To the north of Toronto, Newmarket and its surrounding area is policed by the York Regional Police Force. Regionalized forces may also be found in Hamilton-Wentworth, Durham, and several other communities in southern Ontario. While regionalization appears to be readily accepted as a fact of life in southern Ontario, it is still a contentious issue in other parts of the country.

Regionalization has advantages and also disadvantages. The obvious advantage is the rationalization of resources, resulting in cost savings associated with amalgamation, while

## TABLE 4–1 The Advantages and Disadvantages of Regionalization

**Advantages**

1. Reduced costs of policing brought about by the economies of scale.
2. Elimination of duplication of services.
3. Promotion of equal treatment of all people by the police.
4. Enhanced development of personnel, through wage equity, uniform training, and enhanced promotion opportunity.
5. Increased police capability to deliver specialized services.
6. Increased co-operation between police officers in neighbouring communities.

**Disadvantages**

1. Loss of local control over policing services.
2. High cost associated with initial creation of a regional force.
3. Loss of local identity.
4. Detrimental to the development of community–police links.
5. Police personnel resistance due to possible wage cuts, changes in working conditions, relocation, reallocation of duties, changes in supervisory structures.
6. Loss of resources from the suburbs to the urban core.

*Sources*: Seagrave, J. (1997). *Introduction to Policing in Canada* (pp. 32–35). Scarborough: Prentice Hall; Oppal, W. (1994). *Closing the Gap: Policing and the Community, The Report*. Section D, Regionalization of Police Services. Victoria, B.C.: Attorney General.

the obvious disadvantage involves the loss of local character or commitment to the community being policed by members of a regionalized force. However, the literature reveals many advantages and disadvantages going beyond the obvious (see Table 4–1).

## BOX 4.8 Careers in Justice

### Working with the Canadian Security Intelligence Service

**B**oth the Mackenzie Commission in 1969 and the McDonald Commission in 1977 recommended that the security intelligence functions in Canada should be separated from the RCMP, and that a civilian agency should be established for this purpose. In 1981, the federal government announced the creation of the Canadian Security Intelligence Service (CSIS). The *Canadian Security Intelligence Service Act* was passed by Parliament in 1984.

Initially, CSIS had a staff of 1968, mostly scattered in several locations throughout Ottawa. A study was undertaken in 1987 to ensure that the organization's recruitment, training, development, and personnel management programs were providing CSIS with an appropriate blend of skills, education, and experience to serve Canada's intelligence needs.

Because the CSIS has a range of activities, it is critical that the organization maintain a workforce that is representative and skilled in areas that allow the service to maintain its operational integrity. While the mainstay of CSIS remains the intelligence officer, it also has a need for engineers, translators, technicians, as well as people with financial and computer expertise. Under the *Canadian Security Intelligence Service Act*, the CSIS provides government departments and agencies with security assessments on government employees and contractors, as well as on prospective immigrants to, and citizens in, Canada. In cases where employees or contractors will have access to sensitive information, they must be assessed for reliability and loyalty with relation to national security interests. The Canadian Government Security Policy outlines three levels of security clearance that correspond to relevant degrees of sensitivity:

- Level One (Confidential);
- Level Two (Secret); and
- Level Three (Top Secret).

**FIGURE 4–3** Police Forces in Lower Mainland B.C.

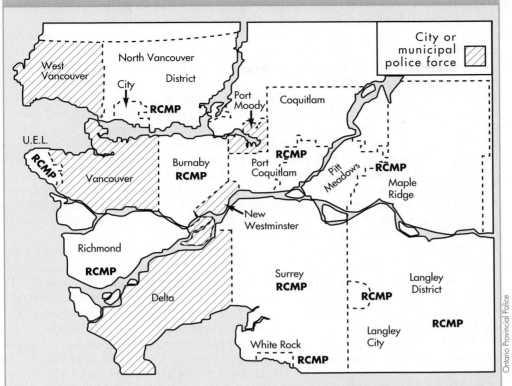

Unlike many urban areas of Canada, the Lower Mainland of B.C. does not use a regionalized police force. Instead, both municipal police agencies and the RCMP working under contract provide police services. In a development akin to regionalization, the RCMP are beginning to share some services among the various detachments.

Checks at each level seek to verify personal, educational, and employment information and references. Criminal records, fingerprints, and credit checks are included in the review. Level One and Two security clearances are valid for a 10-year period. Level Three clearances must be renewed every five years.

### The Intelligence Officer Category

This is the core professional group within CSIS. Intelligence Officers (IOs) are responsible for the collection, analysis, and production of intelligence. To be considered for employment as an IO, an individual must meet the following basic qualifications:

- Canadian citizenship and
- the ability to relocate.

The application process is highly competitive, lengthy, and rigorous. All applicants must undergo extensive security background investigations as part of the process. Proficiency in both official languages is considered an asset, as is proficiency in other languages, and computer skills.

SALARY SCALE: New IOs begin at a salary of $38 670 per annum, progressing to $62 240 over the five-year probationary period.

Canadian citizens interested in career opportunities with CSIS can send their resumés to the attention of CSIS Personnel Services at their local regional office:

- *Atlantic Region* — 1505 Barrington Street, Suite 1901, Halifax, Nova Scotia, B3J 3K5;
- *Quebec Region* — P.O. Box 2000, Station A, Montreal, Quebec, H3C 3A6;
- *Toronto Region* — 277 Front Street West, 10th Floor, Toronto, Ontario, M5V 2X4;
- *Prairie Region* — P.O. Box 105, 10011-109 Street, Edmonton, Alberta, T5J 3S8;
- *British Columbia Region* — P.O. Box 80629, South Burnaby, British Columbia, V5H 3Y1; and
- *National Capital Region* — P.O. Box 9732, Postal Station T, Ottawa, Ontario, K1G 4G4.

*Source*: Canadian Security Intelligence Service Recruitment's website—**www.csis-scrs.gc.ca/eng/employ/employmenu_e.html**

*Contract Policing*

Unlike those in many other countries, policing services in Canada are frequently delivered on a contractual basis by a police agency other than one created by the government level with the constitutional mandate to provide police services. The authority in the federal government to provide police services is not clearly delineated in the distribution of powers in the *Constitution Act, 1867*. Regardless, federal policing is a reality in Canada today. The provinces appear to hold a clear mandate to deliver policing services through their legislative authority over the "Administration of Justice in the Province" granted by section 92(14) of the above-noted constitutional document. Under this authority, provinces have typically delegated authority over local policing down to municipalities, especially in larger centres. Yet, despite the clear mandate for the provinces, their delegates, and the municipalities to provide policing services, many such governments have opted to not create such forces, but rather to contract-in the police work from another agency.

In Ontario, local communities often contract with the Ontario Provincial Police to perform local policing. At present, 100 communities in Ontario contract with the OPP to perform local policing.[60] The OPP and the SQ are two of the largest police agencies in Canada. The OPP presently has 5346 officers, while the SQ has 3817.[61]

The RCMP are involved in contract policing to an even greater extent than the OPP. At present, the RCMP performs municipal policing under contract with the municipalities if the RCMP is already in the province providing provincial policing. The RCMP presently provides provincial policing to eight of the ten provinces, with Ontario (OPP) and Quebec (SQ) as the only two provinces providing for their own provincial policing. The RCMP is the only police force in the territories comprising Canada's Far North.

Of a total of 15 000 RCMP officers, over one-third are working under contract as provincial police officers in the eight contracting provinces. British Columbia absorbs the most of all the contracting provinces, with almost 1400 RCMP officers working as provincially contracted officers (see Figure 4–3). In addition, over 3000 RCMP officers work under contract to municipalities. By far, the majority of these work as municipal police in British Columbia. More than half of the RCMP officers working in Canada are doing so under contract to either a provincial or a municipal government.

# PRIVATE PROTECTIVE SERVICES

**private protective services** Independent or proprietary commercial organizations that provide protective services to employers on a contractual basis. Private security agencies, which already employ about half again as many people as public law enforcement, are expected to experience substantial growth over the next few decades.

Private police constitute a fourth level of enforcement activity in Canada today. **Private protective services**, or private security, has been defined as "those self-employed individuals and privately funded business entities and organizations providing security-related services to specific clientele for a fee, for the individual or entity that retains or employs them, or for themselves, in order to protect their persons, private property, or interests from various hazards."[62] Public police are employed by the government and enforce public laws. Private security personnel work for corporate employers and secure private interests.

According to Statistics Canada's *Juristat Service Bulletin*, "Private Security and Public Policing in Canada,"[63] nearly 121 495 people are employed in private security —more than in all local, provincial, and federal police agencies combined. Employment in the field of private security has expanded at a rapid rate in recent years. Between 1971 and 1991, the number of private investigators in Canada increased by 71 per cent. In the same period, the number of private security guards increased by 126 per cent. During this same 20-year period, public police numbers increased by only 41 per cent. In 1991, there were 115 570 security guards and 5925 private investigators working in Canada, while there were only 56 774 public police officers in the country. It can be expected that private police numbers have continued to grow in the interim, while the number of public police officers has remained relatively constant during the same period.

Private agencies provide tailored policing funded by the guarded organization rather than through the expenditure of public monies. Contributing to this vast expenditure, however, are the various levels of government, which are themselves the main employer of private security personnel, contracting for services that range from guards to highly specialized investigative services.

Major reasons for the quick growth of the proprietary security sector in the United States and Canada include "(1) an increase in crimes in the workplace, (2) an increase in fear (real or perceived) of crime, (3) the fiscal crises of the … [governments, which have] … limited public protection, and (4) an increased public and business awareness and use of more cost-effective private security products and services."[64] In 1990, the influential yearly *Forecast Survey*[65] of private security operations identified substance abuse as the primary concern of security managers throughout American industry—the first time in the survey's 25-year history that property crime was replaced as the industry's front-running concern.

## The Development of Private Policing

Private policing in Canada has a long and rich history. The Hudson's Bay Company used its own personnel to protect the fur trade monopoly held by the company over much of what was to become Canada upon Confederation. Two years after Confederation, the expanse of land held by the Hudson's Bay Company was purchased by Canada, and the Northwest Mounted Police were sent in to replace the private policing that had prevailed up until that point. The first security firms began operation in the mid-1800s, hired mostly by the railway companies that were laying tracks to support the burgeoning nation. Company construction and shipments of supplies, equipment, and money, as well as engineers and company officials, all needed protection from employees prone to theft, various outlaws, and assorted desperadoes.

Guards were hired to stop the theft of railway construction materials in Quebec as early as 1836. The Canadian Pacific Railway had detectives and constables in its employ as early as 1886.[66]

In the United States, Allan Pinkerton opened his Pinkerton National Detective Agency in 1851 with the motto "We Never Sleep."[67] Pinkerton's agency specialized in railway security and would protect shipments as well as hunt down thieves who had made a getaway. The Pinkerton service emblazoned an open eye, to signify constant vigilance, on its office doors and stationery. The term "private eye" is believed to have developed out of the use of this logo. Henry Wells and William Fargo built their still-famous Wells Fargo Company in 1852, and supplied detective and protective services to areas located west of Missouri. Anyone willing to pay their fee could have a force of private guards and investigators working for them. Eventually companies such as Pinkerton and Wells Fargo made their way into Canada—Pinkerton as a detective agency, and Wells Fargo as an armoured car company.

The early days of private security services on both sides of the border led quickly to abuses by untrained and poorly disciplined agents. No licensing standards applied to the private security field, and security personnel sometimes became private "goons," catering only to the wishes of their employers. To cope with the situation, Pinkerton developed an elaborate code of ethics for his employees. Pinkerton's code prohibited his men and women from accepting rewards, from working for one political party against another, or from handling divorce cases (which are a primary source of revenue for private detectives today).

Another firm, the Brink's Company, began as a general-package delivery service in 1859 and grew to a fleet of 85 armoured wagons by 1900. The year 1859 was a busy one for private security, for in that year Edwin Holmes began the first electronic burglar alarm firm in Boston, Massachusetts.

Much has changed since the early days of private policing. Security firms today provide services for hospitals, manufacturing plants, communications industries, retirement homes, hotels, casinos, exclusive communities and clubs, hydroelectric power facilities and nuclear reactors, and many other types of businesses. Physical security, loss prevention, information security, and the protection of personnel are all service areas for private security organizations.

The salaries paid to employees in the private security sector are typically much lower than those in public policing. Statistics Canada reported that in 1991, public police salaries were, on average, 40 per cent higher than those of private investigators ($47 444 versus $33 530), and 123 per cent higher than the average private security guard's salary ($21 263). If training requirements become more rigorous, and recruitment standards are tightened, one might expect this salary disparity to diminish in time.

Mandatory training programs appear to be expanding in this industry. While several U.S. states require mandatory training, this has only recently come to Canada. In 1996, British Columbia adopted a mandatory training program for security guards, offered through the same training institute that provides training to public justice personnel, the Justice Institute of B.C.

Private security agencies have been praised for their ability to adapt to new situations and technology. While most security personnel are poorly paid and perform typical "watch-keeper" roles, the security industry is able to contract with experts in almost any area. Specially assembled teams, hired on a subcontractual basis, have allowed some firms to move successfully into information and technology security. As financial opportunities continue to build in high-tech security, the industry is seeing the creation of a well-educated and highly specialized cadre of workers able to meet the most exacting needs of today's large and multinational corporations.

Security personnel sometimes work undercover, blending with company employees to learn who is pilfering inventories or selling business secrets to competitors. According to the Society of Competitor Intelligence Professionals, over 80 per cent of *Fortune* 1000 companies have regular in-house "snoops" on the payroll.[68] Interestingly, a corporate back-lash is now occurring, which has led to the hiring of even more security specialists by private industry—companies everywhere are becoming concerned with "spookproofing" their files and corporate secrets.[69]

Bodyguards, another area of private security activity, are commonplace among wealthy business executives, media stars, and successful musicians. One of the most respected executive protection programs in the world is offered by Executive Security International (ESI) in Aspen, Colorado. ESI was incorporated in 1981, and its founder, Bob Duggan, built terrorist simulation exercises into most course sequences.[70] Several years ago another firm, the Richard W. Kobetz Company, began an executive protection training program at its North Mountain Pines Training Centre in Berryville, Virginia.[71] Training at Kobetz includes "of-fensive and escort driving techniques," threat assessment education, searches, alarms, weapons, communications, protocol, legal issues, and firearms and defensive techniques. Activities focus on "low-profile" protection, utilizing limited personnel and resources, in contrast to the use of very expensive "high-profile" security as a deterrent technique, which agencies such as the RCMP or the U.S. Secret Service use.[72] The Kobetz Company offers "certification" as a personal protection specialist (PPS) following successful completion of its training.

## The Private System of Justice

Security agencies work for paying clients, while law enforcement agencies are government entities. Differences between the roles of private and public agencies were recently revealed in a U.S. National Institute of Justice–sponsored survey,[73] which showed that security executives order their managerial priorities as follows: (1) the protection of lives and property, (2) crime prevention, (3) loss prevention, (4) fire prevention, and (5) access control. In contrast, public law-enforcement officials list a somewhat different set of priorities: (1) the protection of lives and property, (2) the arrest and prosecution of suspects, (3) the investigation of criminal incidents, (4) the maintenance of public order, and (5) crime prevention.

This difference in priorities, combined with the fact that hired security operatives serve the interest of corporate employers rather than the public, has led to concerns that a private justice system operates next to the official government-sponsored system of criminal justice in Canada. The private system may view behaviour that public police agencies would interpret as a violation of the criminal law, as merely misguided employee activity. Within the private justice system, conflict resolution, economic sanctions, and retraining can supplant criminal prosecution as the most efficacious system for dealing with offending parties. According to a U.S. survey[74] published by the National Institute of Justice, "security managers in all sectors ... report that the most frequently investigated crime is employee theft, and nearly half of them resolve such incidents within their own organizations."

One reason why white-collar and business crimes may be substantially under-reported in official crime statistics is that unofficial resolutions, based upon investigations by proprietary security forces, may be the most frequent method of handling such offences. As some writers have observed, the public justice system may find itself increasingly bypassed by pro-prietary security operations that generally find in the courts "an unsympathetic attitude ... concerning business losses due to crime."[75] The Hallcrest report points out that not only has a "fundamental shift in protection resources ... occurred from public policing to the private sector," but "this shift has also been accompanied by a shift in the character of social control."[76] According to the report, "private security defines deviance in instrumental rather than moral terms: protecting corporate interests becomes more important than fighting crime, and sanctions are applied more often against those who *create* opportunities for loss rather than those who *capitalize* on the opportunity—the traditional offenders."[77]

Hallcrest II identifies the growth of the private justice system as a major source of friction between private security and public law enforcement. According to the report, "(l) law enforcement agencies have enjoyed a dominant position in providing protective services to their communities but now foresee an erosion of their "turf" to private security."[78] Other sources of friction between the two include (1) the fact that "(c)ases brought by private security are usually well developed, putting the law enforcement agency in the thankless position of being an information processor for the prosecutor's office,"[79] and (2) the fact that many cases developed by private security agencies are disposed of through "plea bargaining, which police officers may not understand or support, but which may suit the purposes of a company interested in (deterrence)."[80]

## The Professionalization of Private Security

An issue facing lawmakers across the country today is the extent of authority and the degree of force that can be legitimately used by security guards. Courts have typically interpreted the *Criminal Code* by ruling that private security personnel derive their legitimacy from the same basic authority that an employer would have in protecting his or her own property. In other words, if I have the legal right to use force to protect my home or business, then so do guards whom I have hired to act in my place. The authority to search people is limited to a right to search as an incident to a valid arrest, as necessary to prevent injury or preserve evidence pertinent to the offence for which a person is arrested. According to some courts, private security personnel, because their authority is simply an extension of private rights, are not directly bound by the legal strictures that govern the use of force, the gathering of evidence, and so on

---

### BOX 4.9 Careers in Justice

### Health Care Security

TYPICAL POSITIONS: Full-time and part-time positions, working at various levels from uniformed security guard through mid- and senior-level management. Some health care facilities directly employ their own (proprietary) security, while most contract out security services to a private security company.

EMPLOYMENT REQUIREMENTS: Some provinces, including British Columbia, have legislation governing basic security-training requirements before a licence is issued to a security guard. This training varies in length, but may be as short as one to two weeks in length, and covers diverse subject areas from observation skills to note taking, and includes physical restraint techniques in addition to many other security-related skills. Other basic requirements, while not delineated in legislation, may include (1) an age of 19 years or older, (2) reasonable physical condition, and (3) the ability to pass a thorough background investigation including a criminal records check.

Requirements for mid- and senior-level management positions are more stringent and include experience in the security field, or related work, at a supervisory level, as well as a preference for a BA in a related field such as criminology, or some post-secondary education combined with significant experience in a related field such as policing or corrections.

OTHER REQUIREMENTS: New security guards in hospitals undergo significant orientation in subject areas such as non-violent crisis intervention, fire and first-aid response, and incident/activity documentation. Mid- and senior-management level positions will require training in business and information systems and other administrative functions.

SALARY: Contract security-guard wages can range from about $7 to $12 an hour with contract supervisors making as much as $15 an hour. Proprietary wages are higher with guards making anywhere from $12 to $22 an hour, depending on the province, and supervisors making slightly more. Mid-level managers will earn in the $45 000 to $60 000 range while senior managers can make as much as $90 000, depending on the province.

DIRECT INQUIRIES TO: Any major hospital in Canada and ask for the head of security.

by sworn police officers. Indeed, recent cases suggest that the *Canadian Charter of Rights and Freedoms* only applies to private security personnel when they are making an arrest.

The Oppal report suggests that private security personnel should be bound by the same procedural rules and *Charter* requirements as sworn officers, because they are *perceived* by the public as wielding the authority of public law-enforcement officers.[81] The public should be guaranteed protection from both the public and private police engaged in the law enforcement process.

To ensure at least a minimal degree of competence among private security personnel, most provinces have moved to a licensing process for officers. Most training that does occur is relatively simplistic. Topics typically covered include (1) fire prevention, (2) first aid, (3) building safety, (4) equipment use, (5) report writing, and (6) the legal powers of private security personnel.[82]

Most private security firms today depend upon their own training programs to prevent actionable mistakes by employees. Training in private security operations is also available from a number of schools and agencies. One is the International Foundation for Protection Officers, with offices in Cochrane, Alberta, and Midvale, Utah (U.S.). Following a home study course, successful students are accorded the status of certified protection officer (CPO). In an effort to increase the professional status of the private security industry, the 20 000-member American Society for Industrial Security (ASIS), established in 1955, administers a comprehensive examination periodically in various locations across the country. Applicants who pass the examination win the coveted title of certified protection professional (CPP). CPP examinations are thorough and usually require a combination of experience and study to earn a passing grade. Examination subject areas include[83] (1) security management, (2) physical security, (3) loss prevention, (4) investigations, (5) internal/external relations, (6) protection of sensitive information, (7) personnel security, (8) emergency planning, (9) legal aspects of security, and (10) substance abuse. In addition, candidates are allowed to select from a group of specialized topic areas (such as nuclear power security, public utility security, retail security, computer security, etc.), which pertain to the fields in which they plan to work.

ASIS also functions as a professional association, with annual meetings held to address the latest in security techniques and equipment. ASISNET, an online computer bulletin-board system sponsored by ASIS, provides subscribers with daily security news, up-to-date international travel briefings, and a searchable security-news database. In its efforts to heighten professionalism throughout the industry, ASIS has developed a private-security code of ethics for its members, reproduced in the "Theory into Practice" box on p. 126.

An additional sign of the increasing professionalization of private security is the ever-growing number of publications offered in the area. The *Journal of Security Administration*, published in Miami, Florida, ASIS's *Security Management* magazine, and the *Security Management* newsletter published semi-monthly by the National Foremen's Institute in Waterford, Connecticut, along with the older journal *Security World*, serve the field as major sources of current information.

## Special Provincial Constables

An interesting situation exists in most provinces, whereby special provincial constables are appointed with certain powers to enforce specific statutes pertaining to their area of specialized knowledge or expertise, or to provide policing services in situations that would otherwise require allocation of public police.

In British Columbia, special provincial constables have been identified as working for the following agencies:

- B.C. Securities Commission
- B.C. Transit/Translink
- Canadian National Police
- Canadian Pacific Police
- Coordinated Law Enforcement Unit
- Council of Forest Industries

- Film Classification Branch
- Finance and Corporate Relations
- Greater Victoria Hospital Security
- Insurance Corporation of B.C.
- Labour and Consumer Affairs
- Legislative Buildings
- Ministry of the Environment
- Nanaimo Harbour Commission
- Public Gaming Branch
- RCMP
- Security Programs Division
- Stl'atl'imx National Tribal Police
- Victoria Police Department.[84]

The duties of a special provincial constable will vary, depending upon which organization employs them. In some cases, such as the railway police, transit police, and tribal police, personnel are engaged in duties virtually indistinguishable from those of regular public police. In others, such as film classification, the enforcement powers entail a relatively small aspect of the job. Security personnel at the hospitals in Greater Victoria hold special constable status for the limited purpose of detaining individuals in the facility for the purpose of evaluation under the province's mental health legislation.

## Integrating Public and Private Security

As the private security field grows, its relationship to public law enforcement continues to evolve. Although competition between the sectors remains, many experts now recognize that each can help the other. A U.S. government–sponsored report[85] makes the following policy recommendations designed to maximize the co-operative crime-fighting potential of existing private and public security resources:

1. The resources of proprietary and contract security should be brought to bear in co-operative, community-based crime prevention and security awareness programs.

2. An assessment should be made of (a) the basic police services the public is willing to support financially, (b) the types of police services most acceptable to police administrators and the public for transfer to the private sector, and (c) which services might be performed for a lower unit cost by the private sector with the same level of community satisfaction.

3. With special police powers, security personnel could resolve many or most minor criminal incidents prior to police involvement. State statutes providing such powers could also provide for standardized training and certification requirements, thus assuring uniformity and precluding abuses…. Ideally, licensing and regulatory requirements would be the same for all states, with reciprocity for firms licensed elsewhere.

4. Law enforcement agencies should be included in the crisis-management planning of private organizations…. Similarly, private security should be consulted when law enforcement agencies are developing SWAT and hostage-negotiation teams. The [U.S.] federal government should provide channels of communication with private security with respect to terrorist activities and threats.

5. States should enact legislation permitting private security firms access to criminal history records, in order to improve the selection process for security personnel and also to enable businesses to assess the integrity of key employees.

6. Research should … attempt to delineate the characteristics of the private justice system; identify the crimes most frequently resolved; assess the types and amount of

**Theory into Practice**

## American Society for Industrial Security Code of Ethics

### PREAMBLE

Aware that the quality of professional security activity ultimately depends upon the willingness of practitioners to observe special standards of conduct and to manifest good faith in professional relationships, the American Society for Industrial Security adopts the following Code of Ethics and mandates its conscientious observance as a binding condition of membership in or affiliation with the Society:

### CODE OF ETHICS

I.   A member shall perform professional duties in accordance with the law and the highest moral principles.
II.  A member shall observe the precepts of truthfulness, honesty, and integrity.
III. A member shall be faithful and diligent in discharging professional responsibilities.
IV.  A member shall be competent in discharging professional responsibilities.
V.   A member shall safeguard confidential information and exercise due care to prevent its improper disclosure.
VI.  A member shall not maliciously injure the professional reputation or practice of colleagues, clients, or employers.

### ARTICLE I

A member shall perform professional duties in accordance with the law and the highest moral principles.

Ethical Considerations

I-1  A member shall abide by the law of the land in which the services are rendered and perform all duties in an honorable manner.
I-2  A member shall not knowingly become associated in responsibility for work with colleagues who do not conform to the law and these ethical standards.
I-3  A member shall be just and respect the rights of others in performing professional responsibilities.

### ARTICLE II

A member shall observe the precepts of truthfulness, honesty, and integrity.

Ethical Considerations

II-1  A member shall disclose all relevant information to those having the right to know.
II-2  A right to know is a legally enforceable claim or demand by a person for disclosure of information by a member. Such a right does not depend upon prior knowledge by the person of the existence of the information to be disclosed.
II-3  A member shall not knowingly release misleading information nor encourage or otherwise participate in the release of such information.

### ARTICLE III

A member shall be faithful and diligent in discharging professional responsibilities.

---

Currently in Canada, private security personnel outnumber police officers by more than 2 to 1. While several provinces have initiated regulation over various aspects of private security personnel, the standards are not consistent.

unreported crime in organizations; quantify the redirection of [the] public criminal justice workload … and examine [the] … relationships between private security and … components of the criminal justice system.

7.  A [U.S.] federal tax credit for security expenditures, similar to the energy tax credit, might be a cost-effective way to reduce police workloads.

Contemporary public police and private security agencies are intimately connected through the reliance that private security has developed on the information gathered by the police through their data collection technologies and surveillance abilities. Richard Ericson and Kevin Haggerty refer to this as part of an emerging "risk society" in which knowledge of risk is treated as a commodity that can be applied to control danger.[86]

Ethical Considerations

III-1 A member is faithful when fair and steadfast in adherence to promises and commitments.

III-2 A member is diligent when employing best efforts in an assignment.

III-3 A member shall not act in matters involving conflicts of interest without appropriate disclosure and approval.

III-4 A member shall represent services or products fairly and truthfully.

ARTICLE IV

A member shall be competent in discharging professional responsibilities.

Ethical Considerations

IV-1 A member is competent who possesses and applies the skills and knowledge required for the task.

IV-2 A member shall not accept a task beyond the member's competence nor shall competence be claimed when not possessed.

ARTICLE V

A member shall safeguard confidential information and exercise due care to prevent its improper disclosure.

Ethical Considerations

V-1 Confidential information is nonpublic information, the disclosure of which is restricted.

V-2 Due care requires that the professional must not knowingly reveal confidential information, or use a confidence to the disadvantage of the principal or to the advantage of the member or a third person, unless the principal consents after full disclosure of all the facts. This confidentiality continues after the business relationship between the member and his principal has terminated.

V-3 A member who receives information and has not agreed to be bound by confidentiality is not bound from disclosing it. A member is not bound by confidential disclosures made of acts or omissions which constitute a violation of the law.

V-4 Confidential disclosures made by a principal to a member are not recognized by law as privileged in a legal proceeding. The member may be required to testify in a legal proceeding to the information received in confidence from his principal over the objection of his principal's counsel.

V-5 A member shall not disclose confidential information for personal gain without appropriate authorization.

ARTICLE VI

A member shall not maliciously injure the professional reputation or practice of colleagues, clients, or employers.

Ethical Considerations

VI-1 A member shall not comment falsely and with malice concerning a colleague's competence, performance, or professional capabilities.

VI-2 A member who knows, or has reasonable grounds to believe, that another member has failed to conform to the Society's Code of Ethics shall present such information to the Ethical Standards Committee in accordance with Article VIII of the Society's bylaws.

*Source*: Courtesy of the American Society for Industrial Security. (Online at www.asisonline.org)

# SUMMARY

Today's police departments owe a considerable historical legacy to Sir Robert Peel and the London Metropolitan Police. The "Met," begun in 1829, was the world's first "modern" police force and based its practices upon preventive patrol by uniformed officers. Patrol continues to be the hallmark of police work today, with investigative work and numerous support roles rounding out an increasingly specialized profession. Studies sponsored in the United States by the Police Foundation and the Law Enforcement Assistance Administration during the 1970s and 1980s, however, have brought many of the guiding assumptions of police work under scientific scrutiny.

Canadian policing presents a complex picture, structured as it is along federal, provincial, and local lines. Police agencies function to enforce the statutes of law-making bodies, and legislative authority is naturally reflected in the diversity of police forces that we have in our country today. The RCMP operates as the enforcement arm of the federal government, but also extends its influence to provincial and municipal policing throughout much of the country by policing at these levels through contracts with local and regional governments. Ontario and Quebec have their own provincial police agencies. Municipal policing involves hundreds of police departments ranging from those employing only a handful of officers to regionalized forces employing several thousand officers. Private policing, represented by the recent tremendous growth of for-hire security agencies, adds another dimension to Canadian policing.

Private security is now undergoing many of the changes that have already occurred in other law enforcement areas. Heightened training requirements, legislative regulation, court-mandated changes, and community college–level educational programs in private security are all leading to increased professionalism. Municipal departments may begin efforts to involve private security organizations in their crime detection and prevention efforts, and indications are that private security will soon take a legitimate place alongside other police agencies in the eyes of the public.

## DISCUSSION QUESTIONS

1. What assumptions about police work did scientific studies of law enforcement call into question? What other assumptions are made about police work today that might be similarly questioned and/or studied?

2. What are the three levels of law enforcement described in this chapter? Why do we have so many different types of enforcement agencies in Canada? What problems, if any, do you think are created by such a diversity of levels and agencies?

3. What do you think will be the role of private police services in Canada in the future? How can the quality of such services be assured?

## WEBLINKS

www.rcmp-grc.gc.ca
**Royal Canadian Mounted Police**
The official RCMP site provides details of programs and services, an organizational chart, news releases, recruiting information, and a most-wanted list.

www.rcmpmuseum.com
**RCMP Centennial Museum**
This virtual version of the RCMP Centennial Museum in Regina provides a small sample of historical images and information, as well as the RCMP Veterans' Association page.

www.prospect.org/print/V10/42/stark-a.html
**Arresting Developments: When Police Power Goes Private**
An article in *The American Prospect* (Jan.–Feb. 1999) by Andrew Stark, who teaches management at the University of Toronto.

web.mala.bc.ca/crim/CJS/police/r_peel.htm
**Sir Robert Peel, "Principles of Policing," London, 1829**
Peel's nine original principles.

www.sgc.gc.ca/whoweare/aboriginal/eaboriginal.htm
**Aboriginal Policing Directorate of Solicitor General of Canada**
The Aboriginal Policing Directorate is responsible for administering the First Nations Policing Policy and providing national leadership regarding the delivery of policing services for aboriginal people off-reserve.

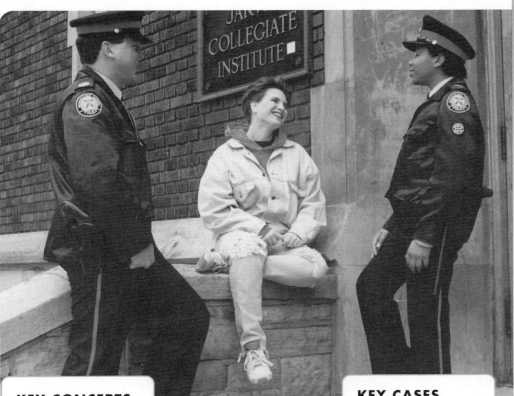

Metropolitan Toronto Police

# Police Management

## KEY CONCEPTS

police management
watchman style
legalistic style
service style
police–community relations
team policing
strategic policing
community policing

police culture
problem-oriented policing
discretion
police working personality
corruption
police professionalism
police ethics

## KEY CASES

Fortey v. Canada (Attorney General)
Vallery v. Poe et al.
Persaud v. Donaldson
Crossman v. The Queen
McTaggart v. Ontario
Klein v. Seiferling
Dix v. Canada

Tennessee v. Garner
Graham v. Connor

# CONTEMPORARY POLICING:
# THE ADMINISTRATIVE PERSPECTIVE

In January 1996, an RCMP Emergency Response Team (ERT) wearing full assault gear, and acting on a tip that a house was being used as a base of operations by three heavily armed suspects known to be actively involved in drug dealing, prostitution, and firearms-related offences, kicked down the doors of the Surrey, British Columbia home of Hank Bramford and Janet Coe. Once inside they took Hank Bramford to the ground, placing him on his stomach and holding a gun to his head. His 53-year-old wife, Janet, had her bedroom door bashed in, as the police barged in, guns in hand. Bamford's 93-year-old mother was also the subject of the police onslaught, when the police broke open her bedroom door and assailed the room, landing on the bed in which she was resting. Apparently, unknown to the police, the suspects being sought had moved from the home several months earlier. Bamford and Coe had only purchased the house four months prior to the aggressive police execution of their search warrant. Police quickly realized that they had outdated information and apologized to the family. The couple soon retained a lawyer to redress their grievance. Said Bamford, "I turned around and there was a heavy calibre handgun in the back of my head. That's a nice thing to wake up to. They had a machine gun on my wife, and they told me to shut the f—up. I thought I was going to get shot. He wasn't in a cop uniform. He was in a balaclava and a dark grey uniform. I thought it was a home invasion—I couldn't believe it. They should have done their homework first."[1]

This case highlights the potentially disastrous consequences of improper police action. Effective **police management**, through which laws are enforced while the rights of suspects and of innocent people are protected, may be the single most important emerging issue facing the criminal justice system in the twenty-first century. As Dan Ogle of the Canadian Police College has noted, "(e)xcessive use of force is one of the greatest difficulties in policing and therefore one of the most important things for a police leader to understand. Well-led police officers understand that they must be prepared at all times to use a tremendous amount of discretion."[2]

**police management**

The administrative activities of controlling, directing, and co-ordinating police personnel, resources, and activities in the service of crime prevention, the apprehension of criminals, the recovery of stolen property, and the performance of a variety of regulatory and helping services.

## Styles of Policing

Police management refers to the administrative activities of controlling, directing, and co-ordinating police personnel, resources, and activities in the service of crime prevention, the apprehension of criminals, the recovery of stolen property, and the performance of a variety of regulatory and helping services.[3] Police managers include any "sworn" police personnel with administrative authority, from the rank of sergeant to inspector, superintendent, or chief—and civilian personnel such as police board chairs, attorneys general, solicitors general, and so on.

While efforts to analyze the evolution of police administration in Canada in terms of distinct eras of development have been less than successful, one can identify general eras in which dominant themes in policing differ. These include the early era (1840s to around 1950), the technological era (1950s to 1970s), the community problem-solving era (1970s to late 1990s), and possibly a current post-modern pluralized risk-management era (2000 to today).

In Canada, the evolution of policing has its own unique history. Canada never experienced the equivalent of the "political era" faced by the Americans. During this period (mid-1800s to late 1920s), Jayne Seagrave identifies Canadian policing developments as encompassing "introduction, expansion, and development" of police agencies, wherein the police initially engaged in a broad array of functions, incorporating "law enforcement, order maintenance, and service functions."[4]

These ideas about the priorities in policing did not die out with the early era, but survive today in what James Wilson calls policing styles.[5] Simply put, a style of policing describes how a particular police agency sees its purpose, and the methods and techniques it undertakes to fulfill that purpose. Wilson's three types of policing—which he did not identify with a particular historical era—are (1) the watchman style (characteristic of an informal style of policing), (2) the legalistic style (professional crime fighting), and (3) the service style (which is becoming more common today). These three styles, taken together, characterize nearly all municipal law-enforcement agencies now operating in this country—although some departments are a mixture of two or more styles.

## The Watchman Style of Policing

Police departments marked by the **watchman style** of policing are primarily concerned with achieving a goal that Wilson calls "order maintenance," by controlling illegal and disruptive behaviour through informal police intervention, including persuasion and threats, or even by "roughing up" a few disruptive people from time to time. Some authors have condemned this style of policing, suggesting that it is unfairly found in lower-class or lower-middle-class communities, especially where interpersonal relations may include a fair amount of violence or physical abuse.

The watchman style of policing appears to be ingrained in many police departments across Canada; however, systematic research attempting to assess the prevalence of this style of policing in Canada has yet to be done.

**watchman style** A style of policing marked by a concern for the maintenance of order. This style of policing is characteristic of lower-class communities, where police informally intervene in the lives of residents in order to keep the peace.

## The Legalistic Style of Policing

Departments operating under the **legalistic style** are committed to enforcing the "letter of the law." Such departments typically expect a high level of training of their officers and compliance to formal policies embodied in rules and regulations structuring the exercise of discretion. Legalistically oriented departments can be expected to routinely avoid involvement in community disputes arising from violations of social norms that do not break the law. Gary Sykes calls this enforcement style "laissez-faire policing," in recognition of its "hands-off" approach to behaviours that are simply bothersome or inconsiderate of community principles.

**legalistic style** A style of policing marked by a strict concern with enforcing the precise letter of the law. Legalistic departments, however, may take a "hands-off" approach to otherwise disruptive or problematic forms of behaviour that are not violations of the criminal law.

## The Service Style of Policing

Departments that stress the goal of service reflect the perceived needs of the community. In service-oriented departments, the police see themselves more as helpers than as embattled participants in a war against crime. Such departments work hand in hand with social service and other agencies to provide counselling for minor offenders and to assist community groups in preventing crimes and solving problems. Prosecutors may support the **service style** of policing by agreeing not to prosecute law violators who seek psychiatric help, or who voluntarily participate in programs such as Alcoholics Anonymous, family counselling, drug treatment, and the like. The service style of policing is commonly found in wealthy neighbourhoods, where the police are well-paid and well-educated. The service style is supported in part by citizens who want to avoid the personal embarrassment that might result from a public airing of personal problems. Such attitudes reduce the number of criminal complaints filed, especially in minor disputes.

**service style** A style of policing that is marked by a concern with helping rather than strict enforcement. Service-oriented agencies are more likely to take advantage of community resources, such as drug treatment programs, than are other types of departments.

## Evolving Styles of Policing

Historically, Canadian police work has involved a fair amount of maintaining order. While research into the development of policing styles in Canada is scant, it is noteworthy that Canada has traditionally embodied a cultural mosaic, consisting of a large number of immigrant communities, socially separated from one another by custom and language. It may be expected that immigrant urban communities in urban areas initially experienced the watchman style of policing. Arrests may have been infrequent but "street justice" was likely imposed on a frequent basis. In these historical settings, the watchman style of policing must have seemed especially appropriate to both the police and many citizens.

As times changed, so too have Canadian communities. Even today, however, it is probably fair to say that the style of policing that characterizes a community tends to flow, at least to some degree, from the lifestyles of those who live there. Rough-and-tumble lifestyles encourage an oppressive form of policing; refined styles produce a service emphasis, with stress on the police and community working together.

## Police–Community Relations

In the 1970s, the legalistic style of policing, so common in Canada until then, began to yield to the newer service-oriented style of policing. Increased understanding about the true nature of typical police work, and concern over the inability of traditional legalistic approaches to deal with developing concerns about street crime, led many police administrators to begin reassessing their approach to the delivery of police services. Police departments across the nation sought ways to understand and deal better with the problems they faced. Policing research of the 1970s, discussed in Chapter 4, caused police administrators to question the emphasis of traditional policing strategies on (1) random routine preventive patrol as a mechanism of deterring crime and disorder on the streets, (2) rapid response to calls for service as a key factor contributing towards the likely apprehension of suspects, and (3) the ritual use of follow-up investigations as the most effective method of resolving unsolved crimes. Along with research revelations about the questionable wisdom of the triumvirate of traditional policing came a revitalization of notions pertaining to the importance of the role played by the public in the policing of communities. Significant outgrowths of this realization were the **police–community relations (PCR)** programs, which many departments created. In this regard, policing in Canada appears to have been strongly influenced by developments south of the border.

Some authors have traced the development of the police–community relations concept to an annual conference begun in the United States in 1955.[6] Entitled the "National

**police–community relations (PCR)** An area of emerging police activity that stresses the need for the community and the police to work together effectively and emphasizes the notion that the police derive their legitimacy from the community they serve. PCR began to concern many police agencies in the 1960s and 1970s.

## BOX 5.1 Theory into Practice

### Policing a Multicultural Society

Members of some culturally diverse groups have backgrounds, values, and perspectives that, while not directly supportive of law-breaking, contrast sharply with those of many police officials. Robert M. Shustra, a well-known writer on multicultural law enforcement, says that police officers "need to recognize the fact of poor police–minority relations historically, including *unequal* treatment under the law."[1] Moreover, says Shustra, "many officers and citizens are defensive with each other because their contact is tinged with negative historical 'baggage.'"

In other words, even though discrimination in the enforcement of the criminal law may not be commonplace today, it was in the past—and perceptions built upon past experience are often difficult to change. Moreover, if the function of law enforcement is to "protect and serve" law-abiding citizens from all backgrounds, then it becomes vital for officers to understand and respect differences in habits, customs, beliefs, patterns of thought, and traditions.[2] Hence, as Shustra says, "The acts of approaching, communicating, questioning, assisting, and establishing trust with members of different groups require special knowledge and skills that have nothing to do with the fact that 'the law is the law' and must be enforced equally. Acquiring sensitivity,

knowledge, and skills leads to [an increased appreciation for the position of others] that will contribute to improved communications with members of all groups."[3]

How can police officers acquire greater sensitivity to the issues involved in policing a diverse multicultural society? Some researchers suggest that law enforcement officers of *all* backgrounds begin by exploring their own prejudices. Prejudices, which are judgments or opinions formed before facts are known and which usually involve negative or unfavourable thoughts about groups of people, can lead to discrimination. Hence, most citizens, including police officers, should be able to reduce their tendency to discriminate against those who are different by exploring and uprooting their own personal prejudices.

One technique for identifying prejudices is cultural awareness training. As practiced in some police departments today, cultural awareness training explores the impact of culture on human behaviour—and especially law-breaking behaviour. Cultural awareness training generally involves four stages:[4]

- *Clarify the relationship between cultural awareness and police professionalism.* As Shustra explains it, "The more professional a peace officer is, the more sophisticated he or she is in responding to people of all backgrounds and the more successful he or she is in cross-cultural contact."[5]

- *Recognize personal prejudices.* In the second stage of cultural awareness training, participating officers are asked to recognize and identify their own personal prejudices and biases. Once officers identify these prejudices, trainers strive to show how such attitudes can affect daily behaviour.

Institute of Police and Community Relations," the meetings were sponsored jointly by the National Conference of Christians and Jews and the Michigan State University Department of Police Administration and Public Safety. The emphasis on police–community relations also benefited substantially from the 1967 report by the U.S. President's Commission on Law Enforcement and the Administration of Justice,[7] which found that police agencies were often socially isolated from the communities they served.

PCR represented a movement away from an exclusive police emphasis on the apprehension of law violators, and meant increasing the level of positive police–citizen interaction. At the height of the PCR movement, city police departments across Canada and the United States began to open storefront centres where citizens could air complaints and easily interact with police representatives. As Egon Bittner recognized,[8] for PCR programs to be truly effective, they need to reach to "the grassroots of discontent," where citizen dissatisfaction with the police exists.

Many contemporary PCR programs involve public relations officers, appointed to provide an array of services to the community. "Neighbourhood Watch" programs, drug awareness workshops, "Operation Identification"—which uses police equipment and expertise to mark valuables for identification in the event of theft—and police-sponsored victims' assistance programs are all examples of services embodying the spirit of PCR. Modern PCR programs, however, often fail to achieve their goal of increased community satisfaction with police services because they focus on providing services to groups that already are well-satisfied with the police. On the other hand, PCR initiatives that do reach disaffected community

- *Acquire sensitivity to police–community relations.* In this stage of training, participating officers learn about historical and existing community perceptions of the police. Training can often be enhanced through the use of carefully chosen and well-qualified guest speakers or participants from minority communities.

- *Develop interpersonal relations skills.* The goal of this last stage of training is to assist officers in developing positive verbal and nonverbal communication skills necessary for their successful interaction with community members. Many trainers believe that participants will continue to develop effective interpersonal skills on the job, because they will quickly begin to see the benefits in terms of reduced interpersonal conflict.

## QUESTIONS FOR DISCUSSION

1. Is there a perception in your community that the police discriminate against ethnic minorities? Do you think the perception is valid?

2. Do your local police have any programs designed to minimize ethnic conflict between the police and the community?

3. Do you think having police officers explore their own prejudices is a useful first step in developing cultural sensitivity? Why or why not?

4. The RCMP sends cadets out to an Indian reserve outside Regina to expose recruits to aboriginal values, beliefs and norms. Do you think field visits such as these are likely to increase cultural sensitivity?

Sources:
[1] Robert M. Shustra et al., *Multicultural Law Enforcements: Strategies for Peacekeeping in a Diverse Society*, 2nd ed. (Upper Saddle River, N.J.: Prentice Hall, 2002), p. 4.
[2] Ibid., p. 16.
[3] Ibid., p. 4
[4] Ibid., pp. 104–106.
[5] Ibid., p. 4.

groups are difficult to manage and may even alienate participating officers. Thus, as Bittner says, "while the first approach fails because it leaves out those groups to which the program is primarily directed, the second fails because it leaves out the police department."[9]

## Team Policing

**team policing** The reorganization of conventional patrol strategies into "an integrated and versatile police team assigned to a fixed district." *Source: Souryal, S. (1977). Police Administration and Management* (p. 261). St. Paul, MN: West.

During the 1970s, a number of communities began to experiment with the concept of **team policing**. An idea thought to have originated in Aberdeen, Scotland,[10] team policing, which in its heyday was defined as the reorganization of conventional patrol strategies into "an integrated and versatile police team assigned to a fixed district,"[11] rapidly became an extension of the PCR movement. Some authors have called team policing a "technique to deliver total police services to a neighbourhood."[12] Others, however, have dismissed it as "little more than an attempt to return to the style of policing that was prevalent ... over a century ago."[13]

Team policing assigned officers on a semi-permanent basis to particular neighbourhoods, where it was expected they would become familiar with the inhabitants and with their problems and concerns. Patrol officers were given considerable authority in processing complaints from receipt through to resolution. Crimes were investigated and solved at the local level, with specialists called in only if the needed resources to continue an investigation were not available locally. Team policing has largely been discarded in Canada, with authors attributing its demise to both resistance from mid-level managers, who were emasculated by the empowerment of line-level patrol officers, and resistance from the patrol officers themselves, who felt that the traditional crime-control mandate (hard policing) was downplayed in favour of a community-relations emphasis (soft policing).[14]

## Community Policing

In the 1990s, the police–community relations concept underwent a substantial shift in emphasis. The old PCR model was built around the unfortunate self-image held by many police administrators of themselves as enforcers of the law who were isolated from, and often in opposition to, the communities they policed. Under such jaded administrators, PCR easily became a shallowly disguised and insecure effort to overcome public suspicion and community hostility.

In contrast, an increasing number of enlightened law enforcement administrators began to embrace the role of service provider. This service-provider orientation has survived into the new millennium in many police agencies. Modern police departments are frequently called upon to help citizens resolve a vast array of personal problems—many of which involve no law-breaking activity. Such requests may involve help for a sick child or the need to calm a distraught person, open a car with the keys locked inside, organize a community crime-prevention effort, investigate a domestic dispute, regulate traffic, or give a talk to a class of young people on the dangers of drug abuse. Calls for service today far exceed the number of calls received by the police that directly relate to law violations. As a consequence, the referral function of the police is crucial in producing effective law enforcement. Officers may make referrals, rather than arrests, for interpersonal problems to agencies as diverse as Alcoholics Anonymous, departments of social service, domestic violence centres, drug rehabilitation programs, and psychiatric clinics.

**strategic policing** A style of policing that retains the traditional police goal of professional crime fighting, but enlarges the enforcement target to include non-traditional kinds of criminals such as serial offenders, gangs and criminal associations, drug distribution networks, and sophisticated white-collar and computer criminals. Strategic policing generally makes use of innovative enforcement techniques, including intelligence operations, undercover stings, electronic surveillance, and sophisticated forensic methods.

In contemporary Canada, police departments function much like business corporations. At least three kinds of "corporate strategies" have guided policing in recent years.[15] They are (1) strategic policing, (2) community policing, and (3) problem-oriented policing.

The first, strategic policing, is something of a hold-over from the technological era of the mid-1900s. **Strategic policing** "emphasizes an increased capacity to deal with crimes that are not well-controlled by traditional methods."[16] Strategic policing retains the traditional police goal of professional crime fighting, but enlarges the enforcement target to include non-traditional kinds of criminals such as serial offenders, gangs and criminal associations, drug distribution networks, and sophisticated white-collar and computer criminals. To meet its goals, strategic policing generally uses innovative enforcement techniques, including intelligence operations, undercover stings, electronic surveillance, and sophisticated forensic methods.

The other two strategies are more closely aligned with the service style described by Wilson.

**Community policing** can be defined as "a collaborative effort between the police and the community that identifies problems of crime and disorder and involves all elements of the community in the search for solutions to these problems."[17] It has also been described as "a philosophy based on forging a partnership between the police and the community, so that they can work together on solving problems of crime, [and] fear of crime and disorder, thereby enhancing the overall quality of life in their neighbourhoods."[18]

Community policing is a concept that evolved out of the early work of Robert C. Trojanowicz and George L. Kelling, who conducted studies of foot-patrol programs in Newark, New Jersey,[19] and Flint, Michigan,[20] showing that "police could develop more positive attitudes towards community members and could promote positive attitudes towards police if they spent time on foot in their neighbourhoods."[21] The definitive work in the area is said by many to be Trojanowicz's book *Community Policing*,[22] first published in 1990.

Community policing attempts to involve the community actively with the police in the task of crime control by creating an effective working partnership between the community and the police.[23] As a consequence, community policing permits community members to participate more fully than ever before in defining the police role. In the words of Jerome Skolnick, community policing is "grounded on the notion that, together, police and public are more effective and more humane co-producers of safety and public order than are the police alone."[24] According to Skolnick, community policing involves at least one of four elements: (1) community-based crime prevention, (2) the reorientation of patrol activities to emphasize the importance of non-emergency services, (3) increased police accountability to the public, and (4) a decentralization of command, including a greater use of civilians at all levels of police decision making.[25] As William Goodbody explains, "Community policing seeks to integrate what was traditionally seen as the different law enforcement, order maintenance and social service roles of the police. Central to the integration of these roles is a working partnership with the community in determining what

**community policing**
A collaborative effort between the police and the community that identifies problems of crime and disorder and involves all elements of the community in the search for solutions to these problems.

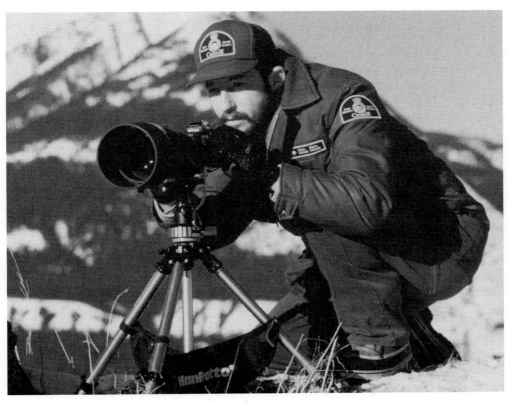

RCMP

Surveillance is a useful tool in numerous forms of criminal investigation.

neighbourhood problems are to be addressed, and how."[26] Table 5–1 highlights the differences between traditional and community policing.

Community policing is a two-way street. It not only requires the police to be aware of community needs, but it also mandates both involvement and crime-fighting action on the part of citizens themselves. As Chris Murphy, a leading academic on community policing in Canada has stated, "Community policing suggests a shift in the authoritative power of the community to control or influence policing by emphasizing that policing is both more effective and legitimate when it responds to community-defined issues."[27]

Creative approaches to policing have produced a number of innovative programs in recent years. In the early 1980s, for example, numerous city departments began experimenting with storefront community policing stations, including in Victoria, British Columbia, and Toronto, Ontario. Chris Braiden began implementing his "village in a city" changes to the way in which policing was carried out in Edmonton in 1986, including the adoption of "ownership" of foot-patrol beats, the development of community police stations, and a philosophical change in the vision of police work throughout the organization. By 1990, Andre Normandeau and Barry Leighton proclaimed in their thoughtful analysis of the topic for the federal Solicitor General, entitled *A Vision of the Future of Policing in Canada: Police-Challenge 2000*: "a growing consensus among police leaders supports the adoption of community policing as the most appropriate police response

## TABLE 5–1 Traditional Versus Community Policing

| Question | Traditional | Community Policing |
|---|---|---|
| Who are the police? | A government agency principally responsible for law enforcement | Police are the public and the public are the police: the police officers are those who are paid to give full-time attention to the duties of every citizen |
| What is the relationship of the police force to other public service departments? | Priorities often conflict | The police are one department among many responsible for improving the quality of life |
| What is the role of the police? | Focusing on solving crimes | A broader problem-solving approach |
| How is police efficiency measured? | By detection and arrest rates | By the absence of crime and disorder |
| What are the highest priorities? | Crimes that are high value (for example, bank robberies) and those involving violence | Whatever problems disturb the community most |
| What, specifically, do police deal with? | Incidents | Citizens' problems and concerns |
| What determines the effectiveness of police? | Response times | Public co-operation |
| What view do police take of service calls? | Deal with them only if there is no real police work to do | Vital function and great opportunity |
| What is police professionalism? | Swift effective response to serious crime | Keeping close to the community |
| What kind of intelligence is most important? | Crime intelligence (study of particular crimes or series of crimes) | Criminal intelligence (information about the activities of individuals or groups) |
| What is the essential nature of police accountability? | Highly centralized; governed by rules, regulations, and policy directives; accountable to the law | Emphasis on local accountability to community needs |
| What is the role of headquarters? | To provide the necessary rules and policy directives | To preach organizational values |
| What is the role of the press liaison department? | To keep the "heat" off operational officers so they can get on with the job | To coordinate an essential channel of communication with the community |
| How do the police regard prosecutions? | As an important goal | As one tool among many |

*Source:* Sparrow, M.K. (1988). *Implementing Community Policing* (pp. 8–9). National Institute of Justice. Washington, D.C.: U.S. Department of Justice.

to crime and disorder problems in modern Canadian society."[28] This view gave further credence to the continuing evolution of service-oriented styles of policing.

Police departments across Canada continued to join the community policing bandwagon through the 1990s. In January 1995, the municipality of Burnaby in British Columbia launched a new comprehensive community policing program referred to as "Ownership Policing." Burnaby is policed by the second-largest municipal RCMP detachment in the country. The Burnaby RCMP plan involves assigning team police officers to permanent beats where they are highly visible throughout the municipality, with the avowed goal of developing and maintaining a much closer relationship with the residents and business-owners in their area. There is also the intention that residents themselves identify their own problems, and establish priorities for dealing with them.

The move towards community policing culminated in the division of the city into four districts, and the creation of community police offices in each district, allowing the police force to develop and maintain close ties with the specific communities being policed.[29]

## BOX 5.2 Theory into Practice

## Community Policing in Calgary, Alberta

The Calgary Police Service has been operating under a community-based policing philosophy since the early 1970s. However, the application of that philosophy has not remained static; as the city has grown and changed, so too has the approach to community-based policing.

In 1989, the Calgary Police Commission gave their new chief of police a mandate to "revitalize Calgary's community-based preventive policing system." In pursuing this mandate, the chief revised the Calgary Police Service's mission statement to include a clear commitment to community-based policing, to increase problem-solving strategies at the front line, and to research and implement a system of differential response to calls for service.

In 1994, the Calgary Police Service undertook a comprehensive organizational review. Senior officers were asked to develop and submit details on initiatives that would address quality of service, effectiveness, and efficiency and human resource development in their respective areas of responsibility. These priorities became the framework for the organization's strategic plan. When the initiatives were reviewed, the following key issues were identified:

- leadership;
- supervision;
- accountability;
- officer development;
- quality of investigations; and
- community involvement.

The features of a Team Deployment model applied in one of the districts of the Calgary Police Service were viewed as being beneficial for the organization when it was assessed according to the following:

- supervision;
- geographic responsibility;
- performance expectations (sergeants and constables);
- problem solving;
- shifts;
- community involvement;
- communication;
- officer development; and
- facilities.

The Calgary Police Service is committed to community policing and views it as an effective and efficient approach to "optimize safety in the City of Calgary." The Calgary Police Service has nurtured a strong partnership with the community in order to address and solve issues relating to crime and social disorder. The citywide transition to the Team Deployment model within the Calgary Police Service took place in 1998 and has been subjected to extensive monitoring and evaluation, and community feedback.

For more information on community policing within the Calgary Police Service, contact:

Bureau of Community Policing Services
Calgary Police Service
133–6th Avenue S.E.
Calgary, Alberta
T2G 4Z1

### QUESTIONS FOR DISCUSSION

1. How does community policing improve the delivery of police services?

2. What are ways in which the Calgary Police Service can determine that community policing is "working" in their community?

3. Are there limits to the extent to which the public can participate in crime prevention and control?

*Source*: Debi Perry, *Structure and Functions of Community Policing in Calgary. An Evolutionary Process.* (Calgary: Calgary Police Services, 1997). Reproduced with permission.

Central to the new community policing program is having the residents themselves identify the most pressing problems facing their communities, and then involving them in working with the police to provide solutions to those problems. In the past, the watch commanders were in charge of supervising the policing of the entire municipality during their assigned watch or shift. Under the new scheme, they were made into district commanders, responsible for the supervision of policing their zone or district.

The emphasis on community policing continues to grow. In addition to the RCMP, which has given some autonomy to the numerous detachments across the country to implement community policing in varied and experimental ways, the Ontario Provincial Police and the Sûreté du Québec have implemented community policing. Across Canada, municipal police agencies quickly jumped on the community-policing bandwagon in the 1990s, to the extent that one author has described it as the "official morality" of policing, although it remains to be seen, in terms of the need to evaluate actual implementation strategies, whether community policing will survive as the dominant paradigm for the delivery of policing services in this country.[30]

## *Critique of Community Policing*

Unfortunately, problems remain in community policing.[31] For one thing, there is evidence that not all police officers or police managers are ready to accept new images of police work. Many are loath to assume new responsibilities as service providers whose role is increasingly defined by community needs, and less by strict interpretation of the law. Mark Dantzker and Michael Mitchell summarized the results of a 1994 survey of RCMP members, looking at their attitudes towards community policing. The analysis of 500 written responses and 300 personal interviews revealed that "a significant number perceive COP (community-oriented policing) to be soft on crime and they don't actually participate in programs like foot patrol."[32] It has been noted in a recent RCMP study that community policing may be criticized as being soft on crime and a waste of resources.[33]

It may be argued that the goals of community policing are impossible to achieve, thereby dooming the undertaking to failure. Police administrators may find the enormity and vagueness of the goals overwhelming, with the result that they may resist attempts at reform. Problems also surround the incorporation of the community into community policing. What/Who are the community? How does one truly get a sense of a community's desires and needs? The notion of allowing the "community" to participate in defining the police role may be ill-conceived, and this notion is the most potentially explosive idea associated with community policing. It has been stated that "if we follow the proposal that the police function is now anything the community defines it to be, it will become virtually impossible for police departments to accomplish any goals."[34] Maintaining community input and interest over extended periods will also arise as a common problem in many community policing initiatives.

Some authors have warned that the **police culture** or **subculture** is so committed to a traditional view of police work, which is focused almost exclusively on crime fighting, that efforts to promote community policing can demoralize an entire department, rendering it ineffective at its basic tasks.[35] It may be argued that too many patrol officers view the public with resentment and hostility, treating the public with rudeness and disrespect.[36] Some analysts warn that only when the formal values espoused by today's innovative police administrators begin to match those of rank-and-file officers can any police organization begin to be high-performing in terms of the goals espoused by community police reformers.[37] In 1991, the newly appointed police chief for Vancouver, William Marshall, began a rapid implementation of a community policing program, modifying shiftwork patterns to enable communities to be better serviced by steady "beat cops."[38]

Shortly after implementing these and other community policing-oriented changes, Marshall became entangled in a conflict with the local police union over contract issues. In 1993, sources internal to the police department informed the media that Marshall had been the acting duty officer in charge of the police cells on an evening when a constable severely beat a handcuffed aboriginal prisoner. Contrary evidence was presented at a formal inquiry, with respect to whether Marshall had complied with regulations governing the reporting of the incident. In the official inquiry's findings, it was held that Marshall had "defaulted in

**police culture** (also **subculture**) A particular set of values, beliefs, and acceptable forms of behaviour characteristic of Canadian police, and with which the police profession strives to imbue new recruits. Socialization into the police subculture commences with recruit training and is ongoing thereafter.

carrying out his responsibility" on the evening in question, with the result that Marshall was forced by the police board to resign in 1994. The case illustrates the problems that may arise when a police chief does not have support for the implementation of community policing initiatives from the rank-and-file officers on patrol.

Public officials are not always ready to accept community policing. Similarly, many citizens are not ready to accept a greater involvement of the police in their personal lives. In *Closing the Gap: Policing and the Community*, Wallace Oppal, the commissioner in charge of inquiring into policing in British Columbia in the early 1990s, reported that opposition to community policing came from a variety of angles.[39] Among the criticisms of community policing presented to the commission, he identified the following:

1. Policing ain't broke, so don't fix it.

2. We do not have the resources necessary to do community-based policing effectively.

3. Community-based policing requires changes that are too complex for traditional police managers.

4. Community-based policing undermines management control, resulting in increased corruption and reduced productivity.

5. The public or community are not actually prepared to become more active in policing.

6. Community-based policing is soft on crime.

7. Expanding the police role in the community undermines community and political authority.[40]

Despite such criticisms, Oppal came out wholeheartedly in favour of a wide-scale move towards community policing in the province.

Some groups remain suspicious of the police. Aboriginal Canadians are very uneasy with the police in various parts of the country.[41] Visible minorities, particularly Africans, have displayed skepticism about police motives in the major urban centres of Quebec and Ontario. No matter how inclusive community policing programs become, it is doubtful that the gap between the police and the public will ever be entirely bridged. The police role of restraining behaviour that violates the law will always produce friction between police departments and some segments of the community.

Despite the criticisms, Paul McKenna argues that it is now clear that community policing is becoming embedded into modern policing, and that its problem-solving form holds the most promise.[42] In his view, a continued commitment to community policing is critical to the stability of Canadian society. Problem-oriented policing (or problem-solving policing) is sometimes viewed as an aspect of community policing, and at other times as a stand-alone policing strategy.

## Problem-Oriented Policing

In 1979, Herman Goldstein published a ground-breaking contribution to police management, in which he coined the term **problem-oriented policing**.[43] Professor Goldstein refined his thesis,[44] and continues to argue that traditional police strategies are ineffective in many cases. Policing has traditionally been incident-driven, in that police are dispatched to respond for a call for service. Traditionally, police have tried to deal with their calls as quickly as possible, in order to be free to engage in preventive patrol, and to be capable of responding to subsequent calls for service. In a sense, this is like putting out fires one after another. The police respond to crisis after crisis, and devote little time to any given crisis. Problem-oriented policing (POP) questions the wisdom of this approach, and encourages the police to look at each call for service as a problem in need of resolution. The best resolution to a problem is often very labour (and time) intensive, and requires a more careful and thoughtful analysis than is typically accorded to a traditional response, which is most concerned with whether a crime has occurred, and if so, who can be charged.

Problem-oriented policing mandates that the police look beyond any given incident in order to fully understand the problem that manifests itself in the call for service. This involves a search for causes, or preconditions, that led to the problem in question. Police

**problem-oriented policing** A style of policing that assumes that many crimes are caused by existing social conditions within the community, and that crimes can be controlled by uncovering and effectively addressing underlying social problems. Problem-solving policing makes use of other community resources such as counselling centres, welfare programs, and job-training facilities. It also attempts to involve citizens in the job of crime prevention through education, negotiation, and conflict management.

must place less emphasis on quickly responding to, and dealing with, incidents in order to take other calls, and instead devote considerable energy towards problem solving. The strategy is generally viewed as being composed of four linked stages of problem resolution, referred to as the SARA model:

**S**canning
**A**nalysis
**R**esponse
**A**ssessment

Scanning involves the identification of a problem. It may involve a police officer thinking in detail about a call for service, asking himself or herself what led to the call for service. Is there some underlying cause or precondition that was not addressed in the traditional police response? Scanning may also arise from a review of local calls for service over time, or in a particular geographic area. Community input may give rise to the identification of a problem as well.

Once a problem is identified, the responsible police officer, or team of officers, will analyze the problem. This analysis includes a search for causes, contributing forces, and an evaluation of the effects and scope of the problem. The parties in the community who are most affected by the problem, and particularly those who hold a stake in the satisfactory resolution of the problem, are identified and brought into the picture.

A response to the problem is the next stage in problem-oriented policing. A logical course of action is, or series of actions are, selected, once what appears to be the best way to resolve the problem has been determined. This may involve mobilizing the community and non-police governmental agencies, as well as police resources, to deal with the matter. Once a response, or a combination of responses, has been selected, it is put into action.

In the fourth stage, the impact of the response is assessed. An evaluation is carried out to determine if the response has had a positive impact on resolving the problem in question. If the problem has not been resolved, the relevant parties gather together and brainstorm for additional possible resolutions to the problem. A new response may be tried, with further assessment.[45]

Many Canadian police agencies have adopted a variation on the problem-oriented SARA model as their strategic focus. The RCMP has formally adopted a strategy referred to as the CAPRA Problem-Solving Model:

**C**lients
**A**cquire/Analyze Information
**P**artnership
**R**esponse
**A**ssessment of Action Taken

This model is taught to all new (training) cadets with the RCMP. It encourages them to employ a problem-solving approach. In this model, police view the people who are affected by the problem as clients. Clients may include suspects, victims, witnesses, local business-owners, various agencies, interest groups, and any others who are drawn into the analysis of the problem. A prominent part of the CAPRA model is partnerships. Relationships with community groups, experts, colleagues, specialized units, and others who can aid in developing or implementing the best possible response to the problem are developed and maintained under this model. In other regards, the CAPRA model embodies the SARA approach inherent in Goldstein's problem-oriented policing approach.

The Ontario Provincial Police have also adopted their own variation on the SARA model, referred to as the PARE approach:

**P**roblem Identification
**A**nalysis
Strategic **R**esponse
**E**valuation

The OPP approach to problem solving is discussed fully in "The How Do We Do It Manual." This approach resembles the Goldstein approach, with additional emphasis placed on the police working in teams, each of which is responsible for a given geographic area.

# Is Policing Entering a New Era?

David Bayley and Clifford Shearing argue that policing has begun to move into a new era.[46] According to these authors, the key characteristics of current policing in Britain, Canada, and the U.S. include a loss of the state's monopoly over policing and a search for a new identity for policing. They discuss these two developments:

> First, policing is no longer monopolized by the public police, that is, the police created by government. Policing is now being widely offered by institutions other than the state, most importantly by private companies on a commercial basis and by communities on a volunteer basis. Second, the public police are going through an intense period of self-questioning, indeed, a true identity crisis. No longer confident that they are either effective or efficient in controlling crime, they are anxiously examining every aspect of their performance—objectives, strategies, organization, management, discipline, and accountability.[47]

The dramatic growth of private policing, discussed below, is seen as pluralizing policing, or making it the responsibility of both public and private agencies. This growth, along with a variety of issues, has resulted in the police searching for a new identity. These issues are said to arise out of the apparent inability of the police to safeguard the public from crime. Traditional strategies seem to have failed at significantly reducing the risk of victimization. Community policing remains as only a portion of what new policing is all about. This new policing also embodies large elements of privatization, civilian participation, and fee-for-service components.

There can be no doubt that policing is experiencing some dramatic changes at the present time. Whether these changes will result in the evolution of a new era of policing, or merely modifications to the recent community-based approach to policing, will remain a matter of some debate for years to come.[48]

One of the best places for police officers to start developing a positive perception of themselves is with children.

# CONTEMPORARY POLICING: THE INDIVIDUAL OFFICER

Regardless of the "official" policing style espoused by a department, individual officers retain considerable **discretion** in what they do. Police discretion refers to the exercise of choice by law enforcement officers in the decision to investigate or apprehend, the disposition of suspects, the carrying out of official duties, and in applying sanctions. As one author has observed, "police authority can be, at once, highly specific and exceedingly vague."[49] The determination to stop and question suspects, the choice to arrest, and many other police practices are undertaken solely by individual officers acting in a decision-making capacity. Kenneth Culp Davis says, "The police make policy about what law to enforce, how much to enforce it, against whom, and on what occasions."[50] The discretionary authority exercised by individual law-enforcement officers is potentially more significant to the individual who has contact with the police than are all department manuals and official policy statements combined.

Patrolling officers will often decide against strictly enforcing the law, preferring instead to handle situations informally. Minor law violations, crimes committed out of the officer's presence where the victim refuses to file a complaint, and certain violations of the criminal law where the officer suspects sufficient evidence to guarantee a conviction is lacking, may all lead to discretionary action short of arrest. Although the widest exercise of discretion is more likely in routine situations involving relatively less serious violations of the law, serious and clear-cut criminal behaviour may occasionally result in an officer using discretion to avoid making an arrest. Drunk driving, possession of controlled substances, and assault are but a few examples of crimes in which on-the-scene officers may decide that warnings or referrals are more appropriate than arrest.

A number of factors influence the discretionary decisions of individual officers. Some of these factors are:

- *Background of the officer.* Police officers bring all of their previous life experiences to their jobs. Values shaped through early socialization in family environments, as well as attitudes acquired from ongoing socialization, affect the decisions that an officer will make. If the officer is prejudiced against certain ethnic groups, it is likely that such prejudices will manifest themselves in enforcement decisions. Officers who place a high value on the nuclear family may handle spouse abuse, child abuse, and other forms of domestic disputes in predetermined ways.

- *Characteristics of the suspect.* Some officers may treat men and women differently. A police friend of one of the authors of this book has voiced the belief that women "are not generally bad ... but when they do go bad, they go very bad." His official treatment of women has been tempered by this belief. Very rarely will this officer arrest a woman, but when he does, he spares no effort to see her incarcerated. Other characteristics of the suspect that may influence police decisions include the suspect's demeanour, style of dress, and grooming. Belligerent suspects are often seen as "asking for it" and as challenging police authority. Well-dressed suspects are likely to be treated with deference, but poorly groomed suspects can expect less exacting treatment. Suspects sporting personal styles with a "message"—biker's attire, unkempt beards, outlandish haircuts, and other non-conformist styles—are more likely to be arrested than are others.

- *Department policy.* Discretion, while not entirely subject to control by official policy, can be influenced by department policy. If a department has targeted certain kinds of offences, or if especially close control of dispatches and communications is held by supervisors who adhere to strict enforcement guidelines, discretionary release of suspects will be quite rare.

- *Community interest.* Public attitudes towards certain crimes will increase the likelihood of arrest for suspected offenders. Contemporary attitudes towards crimes involving children, including child sex abuse, the sale of drugs to minors, domestic violence involving children and child pornography, have all led to increased and strict

**discretion** The exercise of choice, by law enforcement agents, in the disposition of suspects, in the carrying out of official duties, and in the application of sanctions.

enforcement of laws governing such offences across the nation. Communities may identify particular problems affecting them and ask law enforcement to respond. Departments that require officers to live in the areas that they police are operating in recognition of the fact that community interests impact citizens and officers alike.

- *Pressures from victims.* Victims who refuse to file a complaint are commonly associated with certain crimes such as spouse abuse, the "robbery" of drug merchants, and assaults on customers of prostitutes. When victims refuse to co-operate with the police, often little can be done. On the other hand, some victims are very vocal in insisting that their victimization be recognized and dealt with. Modern victim-oriented groups, including Victims of Violence, Mothers Against Drunk Driving, and others, have sought to keep pressure on police departments and individual investigators to ensure the arrest and prosecution of suspects.

- *Disagreement with the law.* Some laws lack a popular consensus. Among them are many so-called "victimless" offences involving acts such as homosexual intercourse, drug use, gambling, pornography, and prostitution. Not all of these behaviours are even crimes in certain circumstances. Gambling is legal in casinos in some provinces. Homosexuality and lesbianism and most forms of sexual behaviour between consenting adults have been legalized, provided they occur in private. Prostitution is officially sanctioned in the context of soliciting participation rather than in the actual act. Recent developments will likely result in some minor drug offences being "decriminalized," with offenders being ticketed rather than arrested. Unpopular laws are not likely to receive much attention from law enforcement officers. Sometimes such crimes are regarded as just "part of the landscape" or as the consequence of laws that have not kept pace with a changing society. When arrests do occur, it may be because individuals investigated for more serious offences were caught in the act of violating an unpopular statute. Offenders arrested pursuant to an arrest warrant for a serious outstanding offence may be "found in possession" of an illegal drug such as a small quantity of a controlled drug, when the police conduct a routine search. Charges may then include "possession of a controlled drug" as well as the substance of the original charge for which the warrant had been issued.

  On the other hand, certain behaviours that are not violations of the law, and which may even be protected by guarantees of free expression, may be annoying, offensive, or disruptive, according to the normative standards of a community or the personal standards of an officer. Where the law has been violated, and the guilty party is known to the officer, the evidence necessary for a conviction in court may be "tainted" or in other ways not usable. Sykes, in recognizing these possibilities, says, "One of the major ambiguities of the police task is that officers are caught between two profoundly compelling moral systems: justice as due process ... and conversely, justice as righting a wrong as part of defining and maintaining community norms."[51] In such cases, discretionary police activity may take the form of "street justice" and approach vigilantism.

- *Available alternatives.* The officer's awareness of alternatives to arrest affects his or her discretion. Community treatment programs, including outpatient drug-and-alcohol counselling, psychiatric or psychological services, domestic dispute resolution centres, and other options may all be kept in mind by officers looking for a "way out" of official action.

- *Personal practices of the officer.* Some officers, because of activities in their personal lives, view potential law violations more or less seriously than other officers do. The police officer who has an occasional marijuana cigarette with friends at a party may be inclined to deal less harshly with minor drug offenders than would non-user officers. The officer who routinely exceeds speed limits while driving the family car may be prone towards lenient action towards speeders encountered while on duty.

# CONTEMPORARY POLICING: ISSUES AND CHALLENGES

A number of issues hold special interest for today's police administrators and officers. Some concerns, such as police stress, danger, and the use of deadly force, derive from the very nature of police work. Others have arisen over the years due to commonplace practice, characteristic police values, and public expectations surrounding the enforcement of laws. Included here are such negatives as the potential for corruption, as well as positive efforts that focus on ethics and recruitment strategies to increase professionalism.

## Police Personality and Culture

In 1966, Jerome Skolnick described what he called the "working personality" of police officers.[52] Skolnick's description was consistent with 1) William Westley's classic study[53] of the police department in Gary, Indiana, in which he found a police culture with its own "customs, laws, and morality," and with 2) Niederhoffer's observation that cynicism was pervasive among officers in New York City.[54] More recent authors[55] have claimed that the "blue curtain of secrecy" surrounding much of police work shields the nature of the police personality from outsiders, and provides police officers with numerous opportunities to engage in acts of corruption and other forms of deviance.

Skolnick found that a process of informal socialization, through which officers learn what is appropriate police behaviour, occurs when new officers begin to work with seasoned veterans. Such informal socialization is often far more important than formal police academy training in determining how rookies will see police work. In everyday life, formal socialization occurs through schooling, religious activities, job training, and so on. Informal socialization is acquired primarily from one's peers in less institutionalized settings and provides an introduction to value-laden subcultures. The information that passes between officers in the locker room, in a police car, over a cup of coffee, or in many other relatively private moments produces a shared view of the world that can be best described as "streetwise." The streetwise cop may know the official department policy, but he or she also knows the most efficient way to get a job done. By the time they become streetwise, rookie officers will know just how acceptable various informal means of accomplishing the job will be to other officers. The police subculture creates few real "mavericks," but it also produces few officers who view their job exclusively in terms of public mandates and official dictums.

Skolnick says that the **police working personality** has at least six recognizable characteristics. Additional writers[56] have identified others. Taken in concert, these characteristics create the picture of the police personality shown in Table 5–2. In Canada, Claude Vincent refers to "occupational identity" in describing the personality of police officers who go beyond a personality displayed on the job to such an extent that their "police" identity extends to all facets of the police officer's life, both on duty and off.[57]

Some components of the police working personality are essential for survival and effectiveness. Officers are exposed daily to situations that are charged with emotions and potentially threatening. The need to gain control quickly over belligerent people leads to the development of authoritarian strategies for handling people. Eventually such strategies become "second nature," and the cornerstone of the police personality is firmly set. Cynicism evolves from a constant flow of experiences that demonstrate that people and events are not always what they seem to be. The natural tendency of most suspects, even when they are clearly guilty in the eyes of the police, is denial. Repeated attempts to mislead the police in the performance of their duty creates an air of suspicion and cynicism in the minds of most officers.

The police personality has at least two sources. On the one hand, some aspects of the world view that comprise that personality can be attributed to the socialization that occurs when rookie officers are inducted into police ranks. On the other, it may be that some of the aspects of the police personality already exist in some individuals and lead them into police work.[58] Supporting the latter view are studies that indicate that police officers who come from conservative backgrounds continue to view themselves as defenders of middle-class morality.[59]

**police working personality** All aspects of the traditional values and patterns of behaviour evidenced by police officers who have been effectively socialized into the police subculture. Characteristics of the police personality often extend to the personal lives of law enforcement personnel.

The socialization process of police officers may be enhanced by the isolation of police officers from others in society, and by the conflicts inherent in the job. Isolation occurs in large part due to the shift work and is exasperated by an "us against them" mentality found among many police officers. Officers who isolate themselves from others in society are likely to be more susceptible to the influences of peers within their police agency.

The socialization process occurs within the context of a job rife with conflict. Curt Griffiths and Simon Verdun-Jones identify three conflicts leading to the development of the working personality.[60] They include living with a discrepancy between what the police actually do, and what they believe they should be doing. Police are often called upon to maintain order and provide social services. Many officers view these functions as less important than crime investigation and enforcement. However, many police officers in various parts of the country seldom engage in enforcement activities. A second source of conflict identified by Griffiths and Verdun-Jones is the uncertain and inconsistent expectations of the community. The public often expects police response to be prompt, and enforcement to be assured; however, these expectations frequently change when the situation comes close to home and involves potential enforcement against a family member or oneself. The third source of conflict is the difficulty experienced by the police attempting to control crime in a system that often seems to be preoccupied with due process concerns. Law enforcement must be carried out while ensuring individual rights are respected, which is often a challenging task for a police officer who knows that every decision may be second-guessed in court at a later date.

Police methods and the police culture are not static. Lawrence Sherman, for example, has reported on the changes in the use of weapons by police that characterized the period from 1970 to the 1980s.[61] Firearms, Sherman tells us, were routinely brought into play 30 years ago. Although not often fired, they would be frequently drawn and pointed at suspects. Few departmental restrictions were placed on the use of weapons, and officers employed them almost as they would their badge in the performance of duties. Today the situation has changed. It is a rare officer who will unholster a weapon during police work, and those who do know that only the gravest of situations can justify the public display of firearms.

Some authors attribute this shift in thinking about firearms to increased training and the growth of restrictive policies.[62] Changes in training, however, are probably more a response to a social revolution about the levels of respect to which citizens are entitled. For example, the widespread change in social consciousness regarding the worth of individuals, which has occurred over the past few decades, appears to have had considerable impact upon police subculture itself.

## Police Deviance

The police role carries considerable authority, and officers are expected to exercise a well-informed discretion in all of their activities. The combination of authority and discretion, however, produces great potential for abuse.

Police deviance has been a problem in our society since the early days of policing. It is probably an ancient and natural tendency of human beings to attempt to placate or "win over" those in positions of authority over them. This tendency is complicated in today's materialistic society by greed and by the personal and financial benefits to be derived from evading

**TABLE 5–2** The Police Personality

Authoritarian
Cynical
Conservative
Suspicious
Hostile
Individualistic
Insecure
Loyal
Efficient
Honourable
Secret
Prejudiced
Machismo

the law. Hence, the temptations towards illegality offered to police range all the way from being offered a free cup of coffee by a small restaurant owner in the thought that one day it may be necessary to call upon the goodwill of the officer, perhaps for something as simple as a traffic ticket, to being offered huge monetary bribes by drug dealers to guarantee that the police will look the other way as an important shipment of contraband arrives.

Exactly what constitutes corruption is not always clear. In recognition of what some have called corruption's "slippery slope,"[63] even the acceptance of minor gratuities is now explicitly prohibited by most police departments.[64] The slippery slope perspective holds that even small "thank-you's" that are accepted from members of the public can lead to a more ready acceptance of larger bribes. An officer who begins to accept, and then expect, gratuities may soon find that his or her practice of policing becomes influenced by such gifts, and that larger ones soon follow. At that point, the officer may easily slide to the bottom of the moral slope—one made slippery by previous small concessions.

Ethicists say that police corruption ranges from minor "offences" to serious violations of the law. Another useful distinction is made by Barker and Carter, who distinguish between *occupational deviance* and *abuse of authority*.[65] Occupational deviance, they say, is motivated by the desire for personal benefit. Abuse of authority, however, occurs most often in order to further the organizational goals of law enforcement—including arrest, ticketing, and the successful conviction of suspects.

Examples of police deviance, ranked in what these authors judge to be an increasing level of severity, are shown in Figure 5–1. Not everyone, however, would agree with this

## FIGURE 5–1 Types of Police Deviance by Category and Example

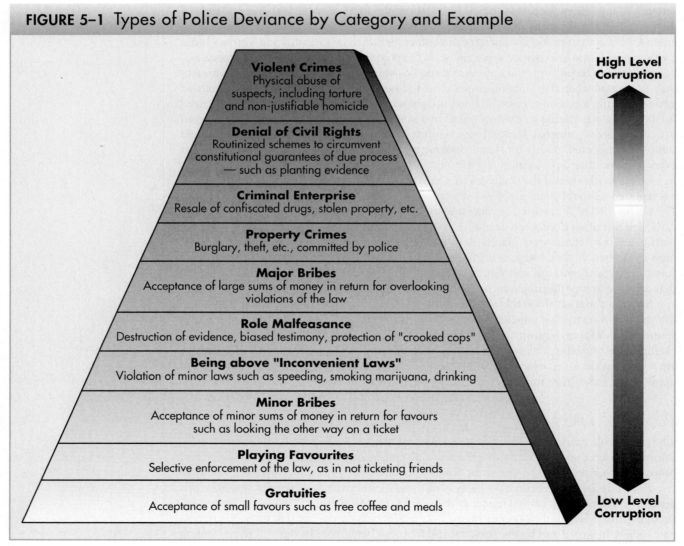

**Violent Crimes**
Physical abuse of suspects, including torture and non-justifiable homicide

**Denial of Civil Rights**
Routinized schemes to circumvent constitutional guarantees of due process — such as planting evidence

**Criminal Enterprise**
Resale of confiscated drugs, stolen property, etc.

**Property Crimes**
Burglary, theft, etc., committed by police

**Major Bribes**
Acceptance of large sums of money in return for overlooking violations of the law

**Role Malfeasance**
Destruction of evidence, biased testimony, protection of "crooked cops"

**Being above "Inconvenient Laws"**
Violation of minor laws such as speeding, smoking marijuana, drinking

**Minor Bribes**
Acceptance of minor sums of money in return for favours such as looking the other way on a ticket

**Playing Favourites**
Selective enforcement of the law, as in not ticketing friends

**Gratuities**
Acceptance of small favours such as free coffee and meals

High Level Corruption

Low Level Corruption

ranking. Many police officers do not view accepting a free meal as a corrupt practice, while some fail to view even the use of excessive force as deviant police behaviour.[66]

Popular books and feature films often tell the story of police misbehaviour. The book *Serpico* was also the subject of a feature film starring Al Pacino. It depicted corruption in New York, and the efforts by one officer to bring that police activity to light. Frank Serpico eventually testified before the Knapp Commission on police corruption in New York City, revealing a complex web of "protection rackets" created by unethical officers.[67] Several years ago, Robert Daley's best-seller *Prince of the City*[68] detailed the adventures of New York City detective Robert Leuci, who walked among corrupt cops with a tape recorder hidden on his body. The more recent bestseller *Buddy Boys*,[69] by Mike McAlary, is subtitled *When Good Cops Turn Bad*. McAlary, an investigative reporter with *New York Newsday*, began his efforts to uncover police corruption with a list of 13 names of officers who had been suspended in New York's 77th precinct. His book describes organized criminal activity among police in the "Big Apple," involving hold-ups of drug dealers, organized burglaries, fencing operations, and numerous other illegal activities conducted from behind the shield. McAlary says New York's criminal officers saw themselves as a kind of "elite" within the department and applied the name "Buddy Boys" to their gang.[70]

In 1993, during 11 days of corruption hearings reminiscent of the Knapp Commission era, a parade of crooked New York police officers testified before the Mollen Commission, headed by former judge and deputy mayor Milton Mollen. Among the many revelations, officers spoke of dealing drugs, stealing confiscated drug funds, stifling investigations, and beating innocent people. Officer Michael Dowd, for example, told the commission that he had run a cocaine ring out of his station house in Brooklyn and bought three homes on Long Island and a Corvette with the money he made. Most shocking of all, however, were allegations that high-level police officials attempted to hide embarrassing incidents in a "phantom file," and that many such officials may have condoned unprofessional and even criminal practices by law enforcement officers under their command. Honest officers, including internal affairs investigators, reported on how their efforts to end corruption among their fellows had been defused and resisted by higher authorities. Spectacular as they were, however, many doubt that the Mollen hearings will have much long-term impact on policing in New York City.

While police corruption scandals of the magnitude experienced in New York City have yet to be uncovered in Canada, we have not been without incidents of corruption in this country. Systematic research on corrupt police activity remains to be carried out in Canada; however, numerous sources provide anecdotal information regarding such activities.

In 1996, Former Staff Sergeant Larry Silzer pleaded guilty to stealing $138 454 from a sum of money turned over to him after it was confiscated in a major heroin arrest. At the time, Silzer was the head of the anti-drug profiteering unit of the RCMP.[71] In 1989, Metropolitan Toronto Police Service Constable Gordon Junger was charged with offences arising out of a set of circumstances whereby he had established a "pay-for-sex escort agency" with a prostitute whom he was living with at the time. The charges against Junger were withdrawn as part of an agreement that resulted in his resigning from the police service.[72]

Parliament's response to police corruption has been to criminalize such conduct pursuant to section 120 of the *Criminal Code*. Section 120 provides:

s. 120.    Every one who

(a)    being a justice, police commissioner, peace officer, public officer or officer of a juvenile court, or being employed in the administration of criminal law, corruptly
   (i)    accepts or obtains,
   (ii)   agrees to accept, or
   (iii)  attempts to obtain, for himself or any other person any money, valuable consideration, office, place or employment with intent
   (iv)   to interfere with the administration of justice,
   (v)    to procure or facilitate the commission of an offence, or
   (vi)   to protect from detection or punishment a person who has committed or who intends to commit an offence, or

(b)    gives or offers, corruptly, to a person mentioned in paragraph (a) any money, valuable consideration, office, place or employment with intent that the person should do anything mentioned in subparagraph (a)(iv),(v) or (vi), is guilty of an indictable offence and liable to imprisonment for a term not exceeding 14 years.

The result need not be an actual interference with the administration of justice. And, an offence need not actually have been procured or facilitated, nor need an offender actually be protected from detection or punishment. As Allan Mewett and Morris Manning note with respect to this section, "The offence under s. 120 is complete where the offer of a bribe has been made or where an officer has agreed to accept or attempted to obtain a preferred bribe where the requisite intent is present."[73]

## *Money—The Root of Police Evil?*

The police personality provides fertile ground for the growth of corrupt practices. Police "cynicism" develops out of continued association with criminals and problem-laden people. The cop who is "streetwise" is also ripe for corrupt influences to take root. Edwin Sutherland years ago applied the concept of differential association to deviant behaviour.[74] Sutherland suggested that continued association with one type of person, more frequently than with any other, would make the associates similar.

Sutherland was talking about criminals, not police officers. Consider, however, the dilemma of the average officer: a typical day is spent running down petty thieves, issuing traffic citations to citizens who try to talk their way out of the situation, dealing with prostitutes who feel "hassled" by the police presence, and arresting drug users who think it should be their right to do what they want as long as it "doesn't hurt anyone." The officer encounters personal hostility and experiences a constant, and often quite vocal, rejection of society's formalized norms. Bring into this environment a perception of being underpaid and the resulting sense that police work is not really valued, and it is easy to understand how an officer might develop a jaded attitude about the double standards of the society that he or she is sworn to protect.

In fact, pay level may be a critical ingredient of the corruption mix. Salaries paid to police officers in the United States have been notoriously low when compared to other professions in the United States involving personal dedication, extensive training, high stress, and the risk of bodily harm. In Canada, the police have typically been more adequately remunerated for their services, which may account for the apparently lower levels of corruption in this country. As police professionalism increases, we may expect to see police salaries rise even further. No matter how much police pay grows, however, it will never be able to compete with the staggering amounts of money to be made through dealing in contraband.

Working hand in hand with monetary pressures towards corruption are the moral dilemmas produced by unenforceable laws that provide the basis for criminal profit. The potential for official corruption is inherent in the legislative taboos on products and services desired by large numbers in society. The demand for prostitution services, gambling, marijuana and other recreational drugs, immense as they are, call into question the wisdom of the law, while simultaneously calling upon the expenditure of significant resources by individuals trying to circumvent the law. As long as substantial segments of the population are willing to make large financial and other sacrifices to feed these trades in illicit goods and services, the pressures on the police to embrace corruption will remain substantial.

## *Building Police Integrity*

High moral standards, embedded into the principles of the police profession, and effectively communicated to individual officers through formal training and peer group socialization, are undoubtedly the most effective way to combat **corruption** in police work. There are, of course, many officers of great personal integrity who hold to the highest of professional ideals, and there is evidence that police training programs are becoming increasingly concerned with reinforcing the high ideals many recruits bring to police work. Police recruit training in the last decade has increasingly incorporated ethics training as an integral component for new officers. Some police departments look for recruits who have some education in ethics. Courses typically expose students to the social and psychological factors

**corruption** Behavioural deviation from an accepted ethical standard.

that lead to police corruption, and then allow students to run through scenarios that expose them to potentially compromising situations. Students who must explain their resolutions to the problems in the classroom context can be expected to internalize some of the ethical principles taught in such classes. It is hoped that addressing such issues as police corruption and police brutality head-on will create a common belief among the new era of police recruits that such practices are unacceptable.

Besides training in ethics, most large law-enforcement agencies have their own Internal Affairs Divisions, which are empowered to investigate charges of wrongdoing made against officers. Where necessary, an external police agency may be called upon to examine reported incidents. The RCMP has periodically been used to conduct investigations into allegations of wrongdoing by a municipal police agency.[75]

Speaking to a group of internal investigators within the RCMP, Rene Marin noted that the internal affairs group is charged with guarding the guardians:

> You are the real guardians: you are the ones who are charged with keeping your colleagues and your force clean. This is not an easy task and I am sure it is sometimes a thankless one. Just as members of the public feel uncomfortable when a police officer starts asking questions, I am sure many of your colleagues feel uncomfortable when you show up and start asking questions, even when your questions are innocent and there is nothing to hide or be afraid of. That is human nature.[76]

More pointedly, such is the concern many police officers have with respect to internal investigations.

Combatting corruption has occupied the attention of many police administrators in recent years. Two major strategies for controlling corruption appear to be relevant for reorganizing Canadian police departments to deal with corruption.[77] The first of these, termed "managerial strategies," involves a four-pronged attack on corruption: (1) New officers are hired and personnel are "turned over," on the theory that corruption cannot survive where the people perpetrating it are removed. (Personnel turnover can also be accomplished by simply shifting officers from one division to another or from one geographical area to another.) (2) "Accountability" is clearly expected of supervisors. Those who will not accept responsibility for combatting corruption are asked to retire early or are removed from their command positions. (3) Closer supervision is required of commanders, especially sergeants, and other "first-line" supervisors. Sergeants are expected to spend more time with their officers, and to create procedures for making any work performed more visible within the context of the department. (4) "Corrupting practices" are ended. Quotas for vice arrests and reimbursements for out-of-pocket, job-related expenses (such as lunches, office supplies, and so on) are eliminated. Drug arrests through "buys" are well-financed, ending the pressure to hold back money from other drug arrests to effect new ones.

A second strategy for reducing corruption is termed "changing the task environment." Government officials make public pleas asking that citizens refrain from offering "gifts" to law enforcement officers. Special teams of officers concentrate on making highly visible arrests of citizens who attempt to bribe the police.

An additional technique often used by departments combatting corruption relies upon "internal policing strategies." Each department either creates an Internal Affairs Division (IAD) or increases the numbers of officers participating in internal investigations. Each department also encourages the Internal Affairs Division to become more active in seeking out information about corruption. Complaints are taken from numerous sources, including citizens who wish to remain anonymous, and former "reactive" strategies are turned into "proactive" efforts to gather information on corruption. Internal Affairs Divisions find wiretaps of known offenders (which sometimes implicate police "on the take") especially useful, as well as "corruption patrolling" (in which IAD agents patrol areas where the potential for police corruption is high), and "integrity tests" (which provide officers with an easy opportunity to commit criminal or corrupt acts).

# The Dangers of Police Work

Police work is, by its very nature, more dangerous than many other occupations. While it is true that most officers throughout their careers never draw their weapons in the line of

Adequate training can offset claims of liability. Here a female police recruit is taught how to restrain a suspect without injuring him.

duty, it is also plain that some officers meet death while performing their jobs. On-the-job police deaths occur from stress, training accidents, and auto crashes. However, it is violent death at the hands of criminal offenders that police officers and their families fear most.

## Violence in the Line of Duty

On December 21, 2001, Constable Dennis Strongquill of the RCMP was shot and killed while attempting to take three armed robbery suspects into custody. Cst. Strongquill and his partner, Cst. Brian Auger, pulled over a pickup truck that had failed to dim its high-beam headlights. The occupants of the vehicle fired on the officers, then chased them as they retreated towards the RCMP detachment headquarters in Russell, Manitoba. There, the suspects rammed the police car and fatally shot Cst. Strongquill. This shooting set off a 14-hour manhunt ending in the death of one of the suspects in a shootout with police outside a motel in Wolseley, Saskatchewan. The other two occupants of the car were arrested and charged with the murder of the police officer.[78] In June 2003, Robert Sand was found guilty of first degree murder in the killing and sentenced to life in prison without parole eligibility for 25 years. The occupant in the car was Sand's girlfriend, Laurie Bell. She was convicted of manslaughter and sentence to 10 years in prison.[79] Concerns over incidents like this haunt many police officers as they perform their routine tasks. However, this type of occurrence is relatively infrequent in Canada.

In 2001, two police officers in Canada were the victims of homicide. In contrast, in the United States, 153 police officers were victims of homicide in 2001, 72 of whom died in the attack on the World Trade Centre.[80] Since 1961, an average of around three officers per year have been killed in Canada while on duty. (See Table 5–3.)

Since 1961, when the Canadian Centre for Justice Statistics began keeping systematic records on justice matters, 117 Canadian police officers have been the victims of homicide while on duty.[81]

Figure 5–2 shows the proportion of officers killed by different circumstances in recent years. Clearly, the majority of police officers who die while on duty are the victims of accidents.[82] Less than one in four dies as a result of gunfire. Whenever a police officer falls victim to an assailant's bullet, it is a tragic and media-grabbing event.

**TABLE 5–3** Canadian Police Officer Victims of Homicide While on Duty, 1961–2003

| Year | Victims | Year | Victims | Year | Victims | Year | Victims | Year | Victims |
|------|---------|------|---------|------|---------|------|---------|------|---------|
|      |         | 1970 | 3       | 1980 | 3       | 1990 | 2       | 2000 | 1       |
| 1961 | 2       | 1971 | 3       | 1981 | 5       | 1991 | 3       | 2001 | 2       |
| 1962 | 11      | 1972 | 3       | 1982 | 1       | 1992 | 1       | 2002 | 2       |
| 1963 | 0       | 1973 | 5       | 1983 | 1       | 1993 | 2       | 2003 | 0       |
| 1964 | 2       | 1974 | 6       | 1984 | 6       | 1994 | 1       |      | (to June) |
| 1965 | 2       | 1975 | 2       | 1985 | 5       | 1995 | 2       |      |         |
| 1966 | 3       | 1976 | 3       | 1986 | 4       | 1996 | 2       |      |         |
| 1967 | 3       | 1977 | 5       | 1987 | 3       | 1997 | 1       |      |         |
| 1968 | 5       | 1978 | 6       | 1988 | 0       | 1998 | 1       |      |         |
| 1969 | 5       | 1979 | 1       | 1989 | 0       | 1999 | 1       |      |         |

*Sources:* Canadian Centre for Justice Statistics. (1992, March). Homicide Project: Police Officers Murdered While on Duty, 1961–1990. Unpublished Report. Ottawa.; *Juristat* reports on Homicide since 1992, and the "Officer Down Memorial Page" on the World Wide Web.

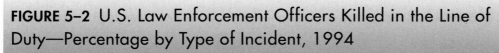

**FIGURE 5–2** U.S. Law Enforcement Officers Killed in the Line of Duty—Percentage by Type of Incident, 1994

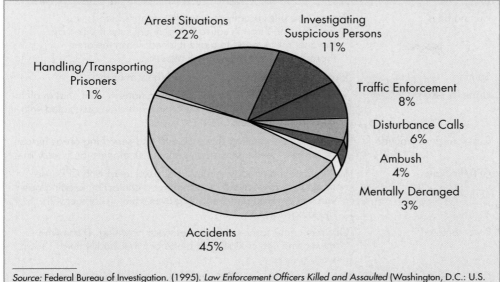

*Source:* Federal Bureau of Investigation. (1995). *Law Enforcement Officers Killed and Assaulted* (Washington, D.C.: U.S. Government Printing Office).

For statistics on police killings to have meaning beyond the personal tragedy they entail, however, it is necessary to place them within a larger framework. There are approximately 55 000 police officers in Canada, yet on average only three are deliberately killed per year. Such numbers demonstrate that the rate of violent death among law enforcement officers in the line of duty is small indeed.

## Risk of Disease and Infected Evidence

Not all the dangers facing law enforcement officers are as direct as outright violence and assault. The increasing incidence of serious diseases that can be transmitted by blood and other bodily fluids, combined with the fact that crime and accident scenes are inherently dangerous, has made "caution" a necessary byword among investigators and "first-on-the-scene" officers. Potential for minor cuts and abrasions abounds in the broken glass and torn metal of a wrecked car, in the sharp edges of weapons remaining at the scene of an assault or murder, and in drug implements such as razor blades and hypodermic needles secreted in vehicles, apartments, and in pockets. Such minor injuries, previously shrugged off by many police personnel, have become a focal point for warnings about the dangers of AIDS (acquired immune deficiency syndrome), hepatitis B, tuberculosis, and other diseases spread through contact with infected blood.

Understandably, there is much concern among officers all over the world regarding how to deal with the threat of AIDS and other blood-borne diseases. However, many police departments maintain that officers have a professional responsibility to render assistance to those who are in need of police services. Persons with infectious diseases must be treated with the same care and dignity shown to all citizens.[83]

Police agencies have also become concerned with the risks involved in using breath-alcohol instruments on infected persons, in handling of evidence of all types, in using seemingly innocuous implements such as staples, in delivering babies in police cars in emergencies, and in being attacked (through being bitten) by infected individuals who are being questioned or who are in custody. The following are among the 16 recommendations made by the FBI as "defences against exposure" to infectious substances (others are listed in Table 5–4):[84]

1. The first line of defence against infection at the crime scene is protecting the hands and keeping them away from the eyes, mouth, and nose.

**TABLE 5–4** Responses to AIDS-Related Law Enforcement Concerns

| Issue/Concern | Educational and Action Messages |
| --- | --- |
| Human bites | Person who bites usually receives the victim's blood; viral transmission through saliva is highly unlikely. If bitten by anyone, milk wound to make it bleed; wash the area thoroughly, and seek medical attention. |
| Spitting | Viral transmission through saliva is highly unlikely. |
| Urine/feces | Virus isolated in only very low concentrations in urine; not at all in feces; no cases of AIDS or AIDS virus infection associated with either urine or feces. |
| Cuts/puncture wounds | Use caution in handling sharp objects and searching areas hidden from view; needle stick studies show risk of infection is very low. |
| CPR/first aid | To eliminate the already minimal risk associated with CPR, use masks/airways; avoid blood-to-blood contact by keeping open wounds covered and wearing gloves when in contact with bleeding wounds. |
| Body removal | Observe crime scene rules: do not touch anything. Those who must come into contact with blood or other bodily fluids should wear gloves. |
| Casual contact | No cases of AIDS or AIDS virus infection attributed to casual contact. |
| Any contact with blood or body fluids | Wear gloves if contact with blood or body fluids is considered likely. If contact occurs, wash thoroughly with soap and water; clean up spills with one part household bleach to nine parts water. |
| Contact with dried blood | No cases of infection have been traced to exposure to dried blood. The drying process itself appears to inactivate the virus. Despite low risk, however, caution dictates wearing gloves, a mask, and protective shoe coverings if exposure to dried blood particles is likely (e.g., crime scene investigation). |

*Source:* National Institute of Justice. (1987, November/December). Report no. 206, p. 6.

2. Any person with a cut, abrasion, or any other break in the skin on the hands should never handle blood or other body fluids without protection.

3. Use gloves, and replace them whenever you leave the crime scene. Wash hands thoroughly.

4. No one at the crime scene should be allowed to smoke, eat, drink, or apply makeup.

5. Use the utmost care when handling knives, razors, broken glass, nails, and the like to prevent a puncture of the skin.

6. If a puncture of the skin does occur, cleanse it thoroughly with rubbing alcohol and wash with soap and water. Then seek immediate medical assistance.

7. When possible, use disposable items at the crime scene, such as pencils, gloves, and throw-away masks. These items should be incinerated after use.

8. Non-disposable items, such as cameras, notebooks, and so on, should be decontaminated using bleach mixed with water.

The National Institute of Justice adds to this list the recommendations that suspects should be asked to empty their own pockets, where possible, and that puncture wounds should be "milked," as in the case of snakebites, in order to help flush infectious agents from the wound.[85] Following an incident in Kingston, Ontario, in which two members of Canada's Military Police Criminal Investigation Section came into contact with the blood of a suspect, the Canadian Military Police adopted a standard operating procedure for such incidents similar to the one advanced by the FBI. In addition, it called for a stringent immunization program to be maintained among officers.[86]

Police departments will face an increasing number of legal challenges in the years to come in cases involving infectious diseases such as AIDS. Some predictable areas of concern will involve (1) the need to educate officers and other police employees about AIDS and other serious infectious diseases, (2) the responsibility of police departments to prevent the spread of AIDS in police lock-ups, and (3) the necessity of effective and non-discriminatory enforcement activities and life-saving measures by police officers in AIDS environments. Few statistics are currently available on the number of officers with AIDS, but public reaction to those officers may be a developing problem area, which police managers will soon need to address.

## Stress Among Police Officers

Perhaps the most insidious and least visible of all threats facing law enforcement personnel today is debilitating stress. While some degree of stress can be a positive motivator, serious stress, over long periods, is generally regarded as destructive, even life-threatening.

Stress is a natural component of police work. The American Institute of Stress ranks policing among the top ten stress-producing jobs.[87] Danger, frustration, paperwork, the daily demands of the job, and a lack of understanding from family members and friends contribute to the negative stresses officers experience. However, it should be noted that some commentators have argued that police work is not any more stressful than other occupations.[88]

Joseph Victor has identified four sources of police stress:[89] (1) external stress, which results from "real dangers," such as responding to calls involving armed suspects; (2) organizational stress, generated by the demands of police organizations themselves, such as scheduling, paperwork, training requirements, and so on; (3) personal stress, produced by interpersonal relationships among officers themselves; and (4) operational stress, which Victor defines as "the total effect of the need to combat daily the tragedies of urban life."

Some of the stressors in police work are particularly destructive. One is frustration brought on by the inability to be effective, regardless of the amount of personal effort expended. From the perspective of the individual officer, the police mandate is to bring about some change in society for the better. The crux of police work involves making arrests based upon thorough investigations that lead to convictions and the removal of individuals who are damaging to the social fabric of the community—all under the umbrella of the criminal law. Unfortunately, reality is often far from the ideal. Arrests may not lead to convictions. Evidence that is available to the officer may not be allowed in court. Sentences that are imposed may seem too "light" to the arresting officer. The feelings of powerlessness and frustration that come from seeing repeat offenders back on the streets, and from seeing injustices done to seemingly innocent victims, may greatly stress police officers and cause them to question the purpose of their professional lives.

Another source of stress—that of living with constant danger—is incomprehensible to most of us, even to the family members of many officers. As one officer says, "I kick in a door and I've gotta talk some guy into putting a gun down.... And I go home, and my wife's upset because the lawn isn't cut and the kids have been bad. Now, to her that's a real problem."[90] Indeed, a survey conducted on a sample of 101 members of the Royal Canadian Mounted Police and their spouses revealed that spouses reported higher stress levels than members, in every area surveyed.[91]

Stress is not unique to the police profession, but because of the "macho" attitude that has traditionally been associated with police work, denial of the stress experience may be found more often among police officers than in other occupational groups. Certain types of individuals are probably more susceptible to the negative effects of stress than are others. The Type A personality was popularized a few years ago as the category of person more likely to perceive life in terms of pressure and performance. Type B personalities were said to be more "laid back" and less likely to suffer from the negative effects of stress. Police ranks, drawn as they are from the general population, are filled with both stress-sensitive and stress-resistant personalities.

*Stress Reduction*  It is natural to try to reduce and control stress. Humour helps, even if it's somewhat cynical. Health care professionals, for example, have long been noted for their ability to joke around patients who may be seriously ill or even dying. Police officers may similarly use humour to defuse their reactions to dark or threatening situations. Keeping an emotional distance from stressful events is another way of coping with them, although such distance is not always easy to maintain. Police officers who have had to deal with serious cases of physical child abuse have often reported on the emotional turmoil they experienced as a consequence of what they saw.

The support of family and friends can be crucial in developing other strategies to handle stress. Exercise, meditation, abdominal breathing, biofeedback, self-hypnosis, guided imaging, induced relaxation, subliminal conditioning, music, prayer, and diet have all been cited as techniques that can be useful in stress reduction. Devices to measure stress levels are available in the form of hand-held heart rate monitors, blood pressure devices, "biodots" (which change colour according to the amount of blood flow in the extremities), and psychological inventories.

Constable Matt Logan of the Headquarters Division of the RCMP has recommended that the RCMP adopt post-recruit training for RCMP officers that would include both the members themselves and their spouses. Among the stress management techniques in his recommendations, we find "self-talk, muscle relaxation, anger management, cognitive restructuring, and understanding emotions."[92] His recommended curriculum includes topics pertaining to police work and family functioning. Training should involve "critical incident stress/post-traumatic stress disorder, issues around grief and loss, conflict resolution, communication in marriage, financial management, and career management."[93]

# Police Civil Liability

An area of growing concern among police managers today is that of civil liability for official misconduct. Police officers may become involved in a variety of situations that create the potential for civil suits against the officers, their superiors, their departments and the government employing them. Major sources of police civil liability are listed in Table 5–5. Swanson says that the most common source of lawsuits against the police involve "assault, battery, false imprisonment, and malicious prosecution."[94]

Civil suits brought against law enforcement personnel are typically brought under the tort law applying in the province where the incident arises. In recent years, damages have been sought by individuals against police officers who have violated their constitutional rights under the *Canadian Charter of Rights and Freedoms*, in what may be referred to as "constitutional tort" actions. Such an avenue of recourse serves to supplement the existing actions in tort, largely embodied in the common law.

## TABLE 5–5 Major Sources of Police Civil Liability

Failure to protect property in police custody

Negligence in the care of persons in police custody

Failure to render proper emergency medical assistance

Failure to prevent a foreseeable crime

Failure to aid private citizens

Lack of due regard for the safety of others

False arrest

False imprisonment

Inappropriate use of deadly force

Unnecessary assault or battery

Malicious prosecution

Violations of constitutional rights

## *Common Sources of Civil Suits*

Of all complaints brought against the police, assault charges are the best known, being, as they are, subject to high media visibility. Less visible, but not uncommon, are civil suits charging the police with false arrest or false imprisonment. Canadian courts have been willing to impose liability in a number of situations where the court has concluded that the amount of force used by the police was excessive in the circumstances.[95]

When an officer makes an arrest without just cause, or simply impedes an individual's right to leave the scene without good reason, he or she may also be liable for the charge of false arrest. Officers who enjoy "throwing their weight around" are especially subject to this type of suit, grounded at it is on the abuse of police authority. Because employers may generally be sued for the negligent or malicious actions of their employees, many police departments are finding themselves named as co-defendants in lawsuits today.

Negligent actions by officers may also provide the basis for suits. High-speed chases are especially dangerous because of the potential for injury to innocent bystanders. Flashing blue and red lights on a police or other emergency vehicle typically *request* only the right-of-way on a highway, they do not demand it. Provincial motor vehicle legislation typically grants only limited immunity to operators of emergency vehicles who violate the rules of the road. Officers who drive in such a way as to place others in danger may find themselves the subject of suits. In the case of *Vallery* v. *Poe et al.* (1971),[96] for example, Ms. Vallery, a pedestrian on a sidewalk, was awarded damages after she was struck and injured by a police car that had collided in an intersection with a car driven by a third party. The officer was found to be 65 per cent at fault,

## BOX 5.3   Theory into Practice

## An Example of Police Civil Liability: The Case of Steven Fortey

On September 28, 1993, at 1:00 A.M., Steven Fortey was staggering home after a night of drinking, when he tripped on the roadway, falling and hitting the back of his head on the ground. Two citizens found him and summoned an ambulance. The ambulance arrived, accompanied by RCMP constable John Dykstra. Fortey was found to have some blood matted in his hair and blood on his shoulder. Both ambulance attendants and Dykstra later described Fortey as drunk, angry, aggressive, profane, and obstinate. The attendants suggested several times to Fortey, both before and after Dykstra arrived, that he should go to the hospital to have his injury checked. Fortey refused angrily. When Dykstra arrived, he heard the attendants tell Fortey he should go to hospital and Dykstra heard him refuse. Dykstra in turn tried to persuade Fortey to go with the ambulance attendants, but he continued to refuse angrily. When the constable asked him what had happened, Fortey replied that he had done nothing wrong. Dykstra gave him three choices: (1) to go to the hospital, (2) to go home, or (3) to be arrested. The constable believed that Fortey was intoxicated in a public place but that Fortey was able to get himself home.

When given the three choices, Fortey walked briskly away. He appeared to be accepting the choice of going home. However, after proceeding a short way, he disappeared off the road. The constable and the attendants drove in search of him, using the spotlights on their vehicles to provide more light, but failed to find him. The ambulance then left, and Dykstra resumed his search. He found Fortey stooping down beside a vehicle in a residential driveway. The constable thought Fortey was trying to hide. The constable again suggested going to the hospital and again Fortey refused. The constable then gave him two choices: (1) go to the hospital, or (2) be arrested. Mr. Fortey again refused hospitalization and was arrested. He was taken to the police cells to sober up, there being no thought of charging him with any offence. Pursuant to the police policy, he was to be released after eight hours, at which time he would be sober.

At the cells, Fortey emptied his own pockets, turned over his personal items rather clumsily, and walked into the drunk tank by himself. No further steps were taken at the police station to get him medical attention. Dykstra instructed the civilian jail guard that Fortey had a head injury and had refused medical attention. The constable told the guard to keep a close watch on him in the cells and to notify the constable if Fortey should change his mind and ask to see a doctor. Fortey was observed in his cell 22 times that morning. In between those observations, Fortey was constantly checked via the television monitor in the guard's station. He was observed to have changed his position several times. After 4.26 A.M., he was thought to be asleep. At 9.50 A.M., when he should have recovered his sobriety, he did not respond to an attempt to rouse him. He was taken to hospital and found at that time to have suffered a depressed skull fracture. Following surgery, Fortey made a slow and partial recovery over a period of seven months until he was discharged to his parents' home. At trial, 51 months after this unfortunate accident, Fortey was left with his right arm almost entirely paralyzed and his right leg was severely restricted. He also had cognitive difficulties, impaired speech, restricted reading skills, and poor word-finding ability; and he experienced intermittent seizures every three or four months. He sued the police for negligent treatment.

The Court found that the refusal of medical attention should be ignored by the police in situations like this where the person cannot make a "rational decision" on the need for medical treatment. As plaintiff, Fortey was found to be partially responsible for his own situation, but the police were found to be 60-per-cent liable for $459 000 in assessed damages.

## QUESTIONS FOR DISCUSSION

1. Do you feel Mr. Fortey should have been compensated for his injuries? Why or why not?

2. Is it just that the police are held accountable for injuries they did not commit? Is it just for the police to be held accountable for harm that results from the in-custody person's refusal to consent to medical care? Why or why not? See also *Lipscei* v. *Central Saanich (District)*, [1995] 7 W.W.R. 582 (B.C.S.C.).

*Source: Fortey v. Canada (Attorney General)* (1997), 45 B.C.L.R. (3d) 264 (S.C.), upheld [1999], B.C.J. No. 1102 (B.C.C.A.).

since he continued to drive in excess of the speed limit, while responding to an accident call, even after learning that an ambulance had been dispatched to the scene and would, in all likelihood, arrive before him.

In many cases, vicarious liability applies where a police officer has engaged in a tort, such that his or her employer, that is, either a municipality, or a board, or the Crown itself, becomes jointly liable for the wrongful actions of the police officer. Departments may endeavour to protect themselves to some degree through regulations limiting the authority of their personnel. Typically, vicarious liability statutory provisions confine liability of the employer to acts done "in the course of employment."

Law enforcement supervisors may find themselves the object of lawsuits by virtue of the fact that they are responsible for the actions of their officers. Where it can be shown that supervisors were negligent in hiring (as when someone with a history of alcoholism, mental problems, sexual deviance, or drug abuse is employed), or if supervisors failed in their responsibility to properly train officers before they armed and deployed them, they may be found liable for damages. In Alberta, the chief of police is vicariously liable for the torts committed by members within his or her police force.

An area that may see some attention is one where an alleged that an alleged "failure to train" forms the basis for legal liability on the part of a municipality, where the failure to train amounts to "deliberate indifference to the rights of persons with whom the police come in contact."[97] In Canada, failure to adequately train police officers has not yet received attention in our courts;[98] however, the future will likely see such matters arising.

## Constitutional Torts

Since the *Canadian Charter of Rights and Freedoms* came into force, many individuals have used the *Charter* to bring police conduct into question. Most often in cases where the defence has argued that the accused's liberties or rights have been violated by the police, the defence has sought to have illegally obtained evidence excluded from trial, or to have the trial process stayed. However, in a handful of cases, the *Charter* has been used as a sword, rather than a shield, because the defence has argued that, because the accused's *Charter*-protected rights and freedoms have been violated by the police, the accused should be awarded financial compensation, or damages.

Section 24. (1) of the *Charter* provides:

s. 24. (1)   Anyone whose rights or freedoms, as guaranteed by this Charter, have been infringed or denied may apply to a court of competent jurisdiction to obtain such remedy as the court considers appropriate and just in the circumstances.

Where the court considers damages to be the appropriate remedy in the circumstances, we may say that the court is dealing with a "constitutional tort." In *Persaud* v. *Donaldson* (1997)[99], the Ontario Court, General Division provided a modest award of $3700 to cover the cost of the legal fees of the applicant who had established a violation of his *Charter*-right to be secure against unreasonable search and seizure. In this case, it was found that the police had engaged in a search based upon a defective warrant. In *Crossman* v. *The Queen* (1984)[100], it was found that a suspect had been denied access to counsel in violation of his rights under section 10(b) of the *Charter*. In this case, the accused had contacted his lawyer by phone from a police station. The lawyer, who informed the police he would be imminently arriving at the police station, was made to wait, when he did arrive at the station, while the suspect was interrogated. The suspect subsequently pled guilty to charges brought by the police; however, he was awarded a meagre $500 for the violation to his right to counsel.

In recent years, judgments for constitutional torts have begun to increase. In *McTaggart* v. *Ontario* (2000), the plaintiff recovered $230 000 in damages against the police because the police withheld exculpatory evidence from the accused, resulting in a wrongful conviction for robbery and a subsequent 20 months spent in prison. In *Klein* v. *Seiferling* (1999), four plaintiffs successfully sued the police for torts entailing *Charter* violations, with each plaintiff receiving between $30 000 and $60 000, following a relatively short two weeks of wrongful incarceration. Most recently, in 2002, Jason Dix was awarded over $750 000 for the conduct of the police and prosecution in Dix's investigation and subsequent trial for murder. Various causes of action were made out, including breaches of the plaintiff's *Charter* rights.[101]

Most departments carry liability insurance to protect them against the severe financial damage that can result from the loss of a large suit. Some officers make it a point to acquire private policies that provide coverage in the event they are named as individuals in such suits. Both types of insurance policies generally provide for a certain amount in legal fees to be paid by the police for defence against the suit, regardless of the outcome of the case. Police departments that face civil suits because of the actions of an officer, however, may find that legal liability and financial liability extend to supervisors, city officials, and the community itself.

## Police Use of Deadly Force

The use of deadly force by police officers is one area of potential civil liability that has received considerable attention in recent years. Historically, the *Criminal Code* has embodied the essence of the fleeing felon rule. It held that officers could use deadly force to prevent the escape of a suspected felon, even when that person represented no immediate threat to the officer or to the public. The fleeing felon rule probably stemmed from early common-law punishments, which specified death for a large number of crimes. Today, however, the death penalty is no longer typically available, even for the most serious offences, and the fleeing felon rule has been called into question.

In 1994, section 25 of the *Criminal Code* was amended to limit the circumstances under which police officers may use deadly force on fleeing suspects:

s. 25. (1)  Every one who is required or authorized by law to do anything in the administration or enforcement of the law

(a)  as a private person,

(b)  as a peace officer, or public officer,

(c)  in aid of a peace officer or public officer, or

(d)  by virtue of his office,

is, if he acts on reasonable grounds, justified in doing what is required or authorized to do and in using as much force as is necessary for that purpose.

A photo promotion showing the effects of Taser International's Advanced Taser®. This less-than-lethal weapon, intended for use in law enforcement and private security, incapacitates potential attackers by delivering an electrical shock to the person's nervous system. The technology is intended to reduce injury rates to both suspects and officers.

(2) Where a person is required or authorized by law to execute a process or to carry out a sentence, that person or any person who assists him is, if that person acts in good faith, justified in executing the process or in carrying out the sentence notwithstanding that the process or sentence is defective or that it was issued or imposed without jurisdiction or in excess of jurisdiction.

(3) Subject to subsections (4) and (5), a person is not justified for the purposes of subsection (1) in using force that is intended or is likely to cause death or grievous bodily harm unless the person believes on reasonable grounds that it is necessary for the self-preservation of the person or the preservation of any one under that person's protection from death or grievous bodily harm.

(4) A peace officer, and every person lawfully assisting the peace officer, is justified in using force that is intended or is likely to cause death or grievous bodily harm to a person to be arrested, if

(a) the peace officer is proceeding lawfully to arrest, with or without warrant, the person to be arrested;

(b) the offence for which the person is to be arrested is one for which that person may be arrested without warrant;

(c) the person to be arrested takes flight to avoid arrest;

(d) the peace officer or other person using the force believes on reasonable grounds that the force is necessary for the purpose of protecting the peace officer, the person lawfully assisting the peace officer or any other person from imminent or future death or grievous bodily harm; and

(e) the flight cannot be prevented by reasonable means in a less violent manner.

(5) A peace officer is justified in using force that is intended or is likely to cause death or grievous bodily harm against in inmate who is escaping from a penitentiary within the meaning of subsection 2(1) of the *Corrections and Conditional Release Act*, if

(a) the peace officer believes on reasonable grounds that any of the inmates of the penitentiary poses a threat of death or grievous bodily harm to the peace officer or any other person; and

(b) the escape cannot be prevented by reasonable means in a less violent manner. R.S., c. C-34, s. 25; 1994, c. 12, s. 1.

The most significant aspect of the amendment restricts the use of deadly force on fleeing suspects to those situations where the officer believes, on reasonable grounds, that the use of deadly force is needed to protect the peace officer or someone else from "imminent or future death or grievous bodily harm" (see above).

This amendment embodies the essence of the 1985 U.S. Supreme Court ruling in *Tennessee* v. *Garner*[102] and perhaps the 1988 U.S. Supreme Court ruling in *Graham* v. *Connor*.[103] While Canadian case law on the use of deadly force is sparse, American courts have devoted considerable attention to this matter in recent years. These U.S. developments have not fallen on deaf ears in Canada. In *Tennessee* v. *Garner*, the Court specified the conditions under which deadly force could be used in the apprehension of suspected felons. Edward Garner, a 15-year-old suspected burglar, was shot to death by Memphis police after he refused their order to halt and attempted to climb over a chain-link fence. In an action initiated by Garner's father, who claimed that his son's constitutional rights had been violated, the Court held that the use of deadly force by the police to prevent the escape of a fleeing felon could be justified only where the suspect could reasonably be thought to represent a significant threat of serious injury or death to the public or to the officer, *and* where deadly force is necessary to effect the arrest. In reaching its decision, the Court declared that "the use of deadly force to prevent the escape of *all* felony suspects, whatever the circumstances, is constitutionally unreasonable."[104]

In 1989, the U.S. Supreme Court, in the case of *Graham* v. *Connor*,[105] established the standard of "objective reasonableness" under which an officer's use of deadly force could be assessed in terms of "reasonableness at the moment." In other words, whether deadly force has been used appropriately should be judged, the Court said, from the perspective of a reasonable officer on the scene, and not with the benefit of "20/20 hindsight." "The calculus of reasonableness," wrote the Justices, "must embody allowance for the fact that police officers are often forced to make split-second judgments—in circumstances that are tense, uncertain, and rapidly evolving—about the amount of force that is necessary in a particular situation." Canadian courts have yet to turn their attention to the new section 25. Accordingly, we must wait to see if the essence of the *Graham* v. *Connor* ruling is to be read into the Canadian provision.

In 1995, following investigations into the actions of federal agents at the deadly siege of the Branch Davidian compound at Waco, Texas, and the tragic deaths associated with a 1992 FBI assault on anti-government separatists in Ruby Ridge, Idaho, the U.S. federal government announced that it was adopting an "imminent danger" standard for the use of deadly force by federal agents. The federal "imminent danger" standard restricts the use of deadly force to only those situations where the lives of agents or others are in danger. As the new standard was announced, federal agencies were criticized for taking so long to adopt them. Morton Feldman, executive vice president of the (U.S.) National Association of Chiefs of Police, said the federal government was finally catching up with policies adopted by state and local law enforcement agencies 17 years previously. "It is totally irresponsible and reprehensible that it took the federal government so long to catch up," said Feldman. "How many hundreds of lives of officers and civilians may have been senselessly lost during the last 17 years because of this reckless, unjustifiable disregard for having an appropriate policy in place?"[106] Under section 25 of the *Criminal Code*, Canadian police are not bound by the "imminent danger" standard, in that they may use deadly force on a fleeing suspect if the officer has reasonable grounds to believe the use of such force is necessary to protect persons from imminent or "future" death or grievous bodily harm. Presumably, this condition would enable a police officer to shoot an escaping serial homicide suspect fleeing the scene of a killing, wherein the suspect could not be stopped by other means. Typically, serial homicide offenders experience a "cooling-off" period between killings, and accordingly would not pose an immediate threat. However, the likelihood of a future offence would allow the police to use deadly force to forestall any future killings by the suspect.

Studies of killings by the police have often focused on claims of discrimination—that is, that black, aboriginal, and other minority suspects are more likely to be shot than whites. Canadian and American research in the area, however, has not provided solid support for such claims. A review of the 13 police shooting deaths in British Columbia between 1970 and 1982 revealed only two of 13 victims to be non-white.[107] In the United States, while individuals shot by police are more likely to be minorities, James Fyfe[108] found that police officers will generally respond with deadly force when mortally threatened and that minorities are considerably more likely to use weapons in assaults on officers than are whites. Complicating the picture further were Fyfe's data showing that minority officers are involved in the shooting of suspects more often than other officers, a finding that may be due to the assignment of such officers to inner-city and ghetto areas. However, a more recent study by Fyfe,[109] which analyzed police shootings in Memphis, Tennessee, found that black property offenders were twice as likely as whites to be shot by police.

Although relatively few police officers will ever feel the need to draw their weapons during the course of their careers, those who do may find themselves embroiled in a web of social, legal, and personal complications. It is estimated that an average year sees around ten suspects killed by gunfire from public police in Canada, while many more are shot and wounded, and even more are shot at and missed.[110]

The personal side of police shootings is well summarized in the title of an article that appeared in *Police Magazine*. The article, "I've Killed That Man Ten Thousand Times,"[111] demonstrates how police officers who have to use their weapon may be haunted by years of depression and despair. Not long ago, according to Anne Cohen, author of the article, all departments did to help officers who had shot someone was to "give him enough bullets to reload his gun." The stress and trauma that result from shootings by officers in defence of themselves or others is only now beginning to be realized, and most departments have yet to develop mechanisms for adequately dealing with it.[112]

Research conducted by Robert Loo looked at post-shooting stress reactions in police officers working for the RCMP. He found that officers experienced most stress reactions within three days of the shooting incident. The average time that elapsed between the shooting and a return to a feeling of normalcy in working, social, and family life was 20 weeks. A summary of the major stress reactions discovered in his research can be found in Table 5–6. His research revealed strong support for services to be provided to officers involved in shooting incidents. Among the possible psychological services that drew support were access to a psychologist in the first few days after the incident, the availability of sick leave following the incident, the availability of psychological services providing counselling, individual therapy, family counselling/therapy, an option to return to work gradually, and the availability of a peer counsellor.[113]

Police have begun to look for options to provide officers with alternatives to the use of deadly force. In 1993, the National Institute of Justice (NIJ) reported on efforts begun in 1987 to develop "less than lethal weapons" for use by law enforcement officers.[114] Questions to be answered include (1) "Can an officer stop a fleeing felon without use of deadly force?" (2) "Are there devices and substances that would rapidly subdue assailants before they could open fire or otherwise harm their hostages?" (3) "Can technology provide devices to incapacitate assailants without also harming nearby innocent hostages and bystanders?" Chemical agents, knock-out gases, stunning explosives, tranquilizing darts, and remote-delivery electronic shocks are all being studied by the agency. NIJ says it is "moving forward with research development and evaluation of devices for use by line patrol officers under a wide variety of circumstances.... [T]he goal is to give line officers effective and safe alternatives to lethal force."[115]

Following a six-month field test in Western Canada, the RCMP approved the M26 Taser for use by RCMP officers across the country.[116] During the trial period, the weapon was used 139 times. In 86 per cent of the cases, the Taser allowed effective control of subjects. Widespread deployment of the Taser within the RCMP awaits adequate training and the necessary funding before the weapon can become part of the RCMP's standard equipment.

## PROFESSIONALISM AND ETHICS

**police professionalism**

The increasing formalization of police work, and the rise in public acceptance of the police that accompanies it. Any profession is characterized by a specialized body of knowledge and a set of internal guidelines that hold members of the profession accountable for their actions. A well-focused code of ethics, equitable recruitment and selection practices, and informed promotional strategies among many agencies contribute to a growing level of professionalism among Canadian police agencies today.

Police administrators have responded in a variety of ways to issues of danger, liability, and the potential for corruption. Among the most significant responses have been calls for increased **police professionalism** at all levels of policing. A profession is characterized by a body of specialized knowledge, acquired through extensive education,[117] and by a well-considered set of internal standards and ethical guidelines that hold members of the profession accountable to one another and to society. Associations of like-minded practitioners generally serve to create and disseminate standards for the profession as a whole.

Contemporary policing has many of the attributes of a profession. Specialized knowledge in policing includes a close familiarity with criminal law, laws of procedure, constitutional guarantees, and relevant court decisions, a working knowledge of weapons and hand-to-hand tactics, driving skills and vehicle maintenance, a knowledge of radio communications, report-writing abilities, interviewing techniques, and media and human relations skills. Other specialized knowledge may include Breathalyzer operation, special weapons firing, polygraph operation, conflict resolution, and hostage negotiation skills. Supervisory personnel require an even wider range of skills, including knowledge of management techniques, personnel administration, and strategies for optimum use of officers and physical resources.

Basic police training requirements vary from organization to organization. While all police organizations in Canada utilize some form of basic training, there is no standard program or curriculum in basic police training in this country. Normandeau and Leighton identify four different models for the delivery of basic police training in Canada.[118] One model involves the separation of police training from the mainstream of adult education. Such a model involves police training of recruits in an institution dedicated exclusively to the training of police officers. The RCMP "Depot" academy in Regina, and the Ontario Police College in Aylmer, Ontario, are examples of this model.

A second model is similar to the first; however, training is carried out on a university campus. Instruction is delivered by police staff who provide the more practical aspects of training, academic staff who teach criminal justice and social service courses, and legal practitioners who teach courses on law. This model is exemplified by the Saskatchewan

**TABLE 5–6** Major Stress Reactions Following Shooting Incident

**Percentage of Members Experiencing
Psychological Impacts from the Shooting Incident with Various Time Frames**

| Stress Reaction | Percentage Experiencing Impacts Time Period | | | |
|---|---|---|---|---|
| | 1† | 2‡ | 3§ | 4" |
| 1. Sleep disturbances | 50 | 13 | 16 | 5 |
| 2. Preoccupation with the accident | 36 | 25 | 16 | 23 |
| 3. Attempts to deny the incident occurred | 13 | 7 | 2 | 0 |
| 4. Headaches | 9 | 4 | 2 | 2 |
| 5. Anger over the incident | 18 | 11 | 11 | 21 |
| 6. If a smoker, increased smoking | 13 | 2 | 0 | 2 |
| 7. Nightmares | 24 | 4 | 0 | 4 |
| 8. Loss of appetite | 18 | 5 | 2 | 5 |
| 9. Depression | 18 | 7 | 7 | 7 |
| 10. Flashbacks to the incident | 27 | 14 | 14 | 11 |
| 11. Wishes that what happened could be undone | 16 | 7 | 9 | 13 |
| 12. Loss of interest in work | 14 | 2 | 4 | 20 |
| 13. Family/marital problems | 2 | 4 | 5 | 9 |
| 14. Increase in alcohol consumption | 9 | 4 | 4 | 7 |
| 15. Guilt feelings | 16 | 11 | 5 | 11 |
| 16. Reconsideration of policing as a career | 13 | 5 | 9 | 14 |
| 17. Irritability | 11 | 7 | 7 | 13 |
| 18. Re-examination of personal values | 18 | 14 | 16 | 27 |

†Occurred within three days of the shooting.
‡Between four days and one week.
§Between eight days and one month.
"After one month.

*Source*: Loo, R. (1986, Spring). Post-Shooting Stress Reactions Among Police Officers. *Journal of Human Stress*, p. 29.

Police College at the University of Regina, and the Atlantic Police Academy at Holland College, Prince Edward Island.

A third model involves the integration of police training with the training of other criminal justice agencies. Training is provided in the same institution as that in which institutional corrections staff, community corrections personnel, and court workers are provided their training. Such a model is used for the provision of training for municipal police in British Columbia at the Justice Institute of British Columbia.

Finally, another model provides police education in the same context as adult education in general. Quebec uses such a model, whereby potential recruits are first put through a 30-month educational program at the college level, from which candidates are selected to move on to a 10-week course at the Quebec Police Institute to learn the more practical aspects of training.

Historically, police training has involved a period of in-class training, followed by a period of field training in which the in-class training is applied. The RCMP still follows such a model, providing six months of basic training at the RCMP Training Depot in Regina, followed by six months of field training at the recruits' first posting. In recent years in Canada, training has become spread out over time, and recruits are provided field training, followed by a return to the classroom to synthesize practical application into classroom learning. Examples of this can be found at the Ontario Police College and the Justice Institute of British Columbia. Basic training at the Ontario Police College involves the following:

Level 1:  1 to 2 weeks of field training carried out at the employing agency
Level 2:  2 months of in-class training
Level 3:  3 months of field training
Level 4:  2 weeks of in-class training
Level 5:  general duties
Level 6:  optional specialized training

Today, training typically involves a wide range of subject areas, although the specifics vary considerably from region to region. Modern subject areas include human relations, firearms and weapons, communications, legal aspects of policing, patrol, criminal investigations, administration, report writing, and criminal justice systems. The array of subjects covered in the RCMP's basic recruit training program may be found in the Theory into Practice box on p. 163.

In-service training for police officers in Canada is provided through a variety of sources. The Canadian Police College in Ontario provides advanced training for all police agencies in Canada. The range of topics covered may also be found in the Theory into Practice box on p. 163. Most other police training institutes in Canada also provide some level of advanced, in-service training.[119]

Police work in Canada is increasingly being guided by an ethical code. This movement originated in the United States in 1956 with the efforts of the Peace Officer's Research Association of California (PORAC), in conjunction with Dr. Douglas M. Kelley of Berkeley's School of Criminology.[120] Eventually, the International Association of Chiefs of Police (IACP) approved and adopted a new *Law Enforcement Code of Ethics* in 1987. (See the Theory into Practice box on page 164.) In Canada, police agencies have increasingly come to adopt a code of ethics. A sampling of **police ethics** codes in Canada has been compiled by Chris Offer, and can be found in the Theory into Practice box on page 164. Ethics training is still not well-integrated into most basic law enforcement training programs, but a movement in that direction has begun and calls for expanded training in ethics are on the increase.

Professional associations abound in police work. The Canadian Association of Chiefs of Police (CACP) has done much to raise professional standards in policing and continually strives for improvements in law enforcement nationwide. Most individual provinces have their own police association or federation that looks after the interests of its members.

Accreditation provides another channel towards police professionalism. The Commission on Accreditation for Law Enforcement Agencies was formed in 1979. Police departments wishing to apply for accreditation through the Commission must meet hundreds of standards relating to areas as diverse as day-to-day operations, administration, review of incidents involving the use of a weapon by officers, and evaluation and promotion of personnel. To date, few police agencies in Canada have become accredited. At present, police agencies in Alberta are at the forefront in this area, with accredited police services in Camrose, Edmonton, and Lethbridge. In Manitoba, the Winnipeg Police Service is also accredited. Two regionalized police agencies, the Peel Regional and the Niagara Regional police services, both in Ontario, have been accredited under the U.S. Commission of Accreditation for Law Enforcement Agencies (CALEA). It is also noteworthy that the Canadian Pacific Railway Police Service became an accredited agency with CALEA in 2002. Although accreditation makes possible the identification of high-quality police departments, it is often undervalued because it carries few incentives. Accreditation is still only the "icing on the cake" and does not guarantee a department any benefits beyond the recognition of peers.

## Educational Requirements

As the concern for quality policing builds, the education of police officers is increasingly emphasized. Historically, many police agencies set their educational requirements at the level of high-school graduation. In recent years, this requirement has been abandoned in favour of requiring some post-secondary education. However, the move towards requiring post-secondary education of potential recruits has been subjected to criticism. As Wallace Oppal noted in his report on policing in British Columbia:

**police ethics** The special responsibility for adherence to moral duty and obligation inherent in police work.

The need for advanced education seems obvious in a career that demands skills ranging from social work, to problem analysis, to an understanding of Canadian law. However, some officers still debate the value of post-secondary education in their profession. These constables, supervisors and managers feel that education gained at a college, technical institute, or university is too theoretical. One officer told the Inquiry that the interpersonal skills his partner learned in the real world, not academic qualifications, might save his life in dangerous real-world situations. Others felt that too much emphasis is being placed on education because it is readily measurable and provides a convenient screening device for recruiters faced with hundreds of applicants.[121]

## BOX 5.4 Theory into Practice

## Police Training: Ontario's Police Learning System

In 1990, the Ontario Ministry of the Solicitor General (now the Ministry of Public Safety and Security) began a thorough review of police training. To accomplish this task, a Strategic Planning Committee on Police Training and Education was appointed with an ambitious mandate to undertake research and develop recommendations for the improvement of police training in Ontario. The committee comprised representatives of policing, education, government, public interest, and community groups, and it devoted a great deal of attention to the substantive issues related to its mandate.

The final report of this committee led to the introduction of the Ontario Police Learning System in early 1996. The research points to the following strategic learning requirements for police constables:

- communication skills;
- interpersonal and sensitivity skills;
- knowledge of human behaviour;
- ability to accept and work with community diversity;
- ability to serve victims;
- ability to initiate, promote, and facilitate community policing;
- ability to use policing-related terminology;
- analytical skills and problem-solving ability;
- knowledge of political systems and processes;
- knowledge of crime prevention strategies;
- personal and organizational development skills;
- knowledge of other agencies;
- team-building skills;
- ability to use crime trend information;
- ability to apply basic police authorities and knowledge of case preparation;

- ability to act ethically and professionally;
- ability to maintain a reasonable level of physical fitness and well-being;
- ability to use force appropriately;
- officer safety skills; and
- conflict avoidance, resolution, and mediation skills.[1]

As a result of this study, work began on the creation of a "Police Foundations" program that would provide candidates with the academic background recommended for employment as a police constable in Ontario. Drawing on the extensive research undertaken by the Strategic Planning Committee on Police Training and Education, a standardized curriculum was recommended. This involves students completing a two-year (four-semester) full-time diploma program, an example of which is provided by Humber College in Toronto. In their first semester, Humber students take courses on the criminal justice system, ethics, aboriginal Canadians, physical fitness, public administration, psychology, and writing skills. The second semester includes courses on criminology, social issues, social services, the *Criminal Code*, sociology, business writing, and more physical fitness. The third semester includes courses on criminal and civil law, police powers, interviewing and investigations, young offenders, community policing, traffic management, lifestyle management, and political science. The final semester includes courses on provincial offences, federal statutes, police powers, investigation and evidence, conflict management, another on community policing, another on lifestyle management, and one on interpersonal and group dynamics.

## QUESTIONS FOR DISCUSSION

1. Does the Ontario model provide a curriculum that appears to be adequate for potential police recruits? If not, what appears to be missing?

2. Would police agencies be better off hiring students educated in the liberal arts and sciences, or students who have taken courses directly oriented to the police job? Explain.

---

1. Ontario Ministry of the Solicitor General. (1992). The Strategic Planning Committee on Police Training and Education. *A police learning system for Ontario: final report and recommendations* (p. 182). Toronto.

BOX 5.5

# Theory into Practice

## Is a Code of Ethics Needed in Policing?

In 1994, Inspector Chris Offer of the Vancouver Police Department embarked upon an inquiry into whether police officers need a code of ethics.[1]

Given the considerable attention paid to police wrongdoing in the media and elsewhere, such a question is certainly worthy of serious consideration.

A common problem in policing is embodied in what has been described as the "Dirty Harry Problem."[2]

The ethical problem pertains to that faced by the fictional movie character portrayed by Clint Eastwood, who found himself in a situation whereby he believed he had to use morally dirty means to achieve a morally good end. What should the police do when they confront a situation where they must break the law in order to achieve some public good? Such ethical dilemmas are regularly encountered in police work.

A code of ethics provides a set of moral standards applicable to all of those belonging to the group asserting the code of ethics. It sets a standard, or lays down principles, often setting an ideal beyond that shared in conventional morality.[3]

The key question appears to be why the police would need a code of ethics when they are already governed by "... police policy manuals, oaths of office and terms of service (that) regulate police conduct."[4]

Is adding a code of ethics nothing more than overkill or window dressing to make the police look good?

Offer argues that the police do indeed need a code of ethics. He argues that "proper and appropriate performance standards need to be made clear to all police officers. Inappropriate and embarrassing performance can be the result of failure to communicate these standards."[5]

It may be argued, as Chris Offer does, that written codes of ethics assist police officers in evaluating difficult ethical dilemmas that are endemic to police work. It can provide a focus for debate on the best way to resolve difficult situations. For those officers who are not ethical, it can even act as a standard of conduct to be used in assessing whether discipline or dismissal is necessary.

A number of ethics codes are presented in Offer's article, among them, the following.

### Code of Ethics—Vancouver Police Department

As a member of the community and as a police officer, I recognize that my fundamental duty is to protect lives and property, preserve peace and good order, prevent crime, detect offenders and enforce the law.

I will faithfully discharge my duties in a just, impartial and reasonable manner, preserving the equality, rights, and privileges of all persons as guaranteed by the *Canadian Charter of Rights and Freedoms*.

I will keep my private life unsullied as an example to all; maintain courageous calm in the face of danger, scorn or ridicule; and be constantly mindful of the welfare of others. Honest in thought and deed in both my personal and official life, I will be exemplary in obeying the laws of the land and the regulations of the Vancouver Police Department.

I will preserve the dignity of all persons. I will be faithful in my allegiance to Her Majesty the Queen and my country. I will honour the obligations of my office and strive to attain excellence in the performance of my duties.

### Winnipeg Police Service—The Police Officer's Code of Ethics

As a police officer, I recognize my primary obligation is to serve the public effectively and efficiently by protecting lives and property, preventing and detecting offences, and preserving peace and order.

I will faithfully administer the law in a just, impartial and reasonable manner, preserving the equality, rights, and privileges of citizens as afforded by law.

I accept that all persons rich or poor, old or young, learned or illiterate, are equally entitled to courtesy, understanding and compassion. I will not be disparaging of any race, creed, or class of people.

In the performance of my duties I acknowledge the limits of my authority and promise not to use it for my personal advantage. I vow never to accept gratuities or favours or compromise myself or the department in any way. I will conduct my public and private life as an example of stability, fidelity, morality, and without equivocation, adhere to the same standards of conduct which I am bound by duty to enforce.

I will exercise self-discipline at all times. I will act with propriety towards my associates in law enforcement and the criminal justice system. With self-confidence, decisiveness, and courage, I will accept all challenges, hardships, and vicissitudes of my profession. In relationships with my colleagues, I will endeavour to develop an "esprit de corps."

I will preserve the dignity of all persons and subordinate my own self-interests for the common good. I will be faithful in my allegiance to Queen and country. I will honour the obligations of my office and strive to attain excellence in the performance of my duties.

## QUESTIONS FOR DISCUSSION

1. Chris Offer argues that a Code of Ethics clearly establishes the police as a self-regulating profession by articulating the standards and values of policing. Do you agree? Why or why not?

2. Which of the above Codes of Ethics do you prefer? Why? Is there anything you would like to add to a police Code of Ethics? Is there anything that should be deleted? Why?

---

[1] Offer, C. (1994). Do the Police Need a Code of Ethics? *RCMP Gazette*, Vol. 56, No. 1, pp. 1-7.
[2] Klockars, C.B. (1980, November). The Dirty Harry Problem. *The Annals of the American Academy of Political and Social Science*, Vol. 452, pp. 33-47.
[3] Offer. Code of Ethics. p. 1.
[4] Ibid.
[5] Ibid.

In his report, Oppal recommends that recruits should be required to have at least one year of post-secondary education prior to being hired. Additional post-secondary education was encouraged in the report.

One report prepared by the U.S. Police Executive Research Forum (PERF) stressed the need for educated police officers, citing the following benefits that accrue to police agencies from the hiring of educated officers:[122] (1) better written reports, (2) enhanced communications with the public, (3) more effective job performance, (4) fewer citizen complaints, (5) greater initiative, (6) a wiser use of discretion, (7) a heightened sensitivity to racial and ethnic issues, and (8) fewer disciplinary problems. On the other hand, a greater likelihood that educated officers will leave police work, and their tendency to question orders and request reassignment with relative frequency, are some education-related drawbacks.

To meet the growing needs of police officers for college-level training, the International Association of Police Professors (IAPP) was formed in 1963. The IAPP later changed its name to the Academy of Criminal Justice Sciences (ACJS) and widened its focus to include criminal justice education. A number of agencies now require the completion of at least some community college courses for officers seeking promotion. The Oppal report recommended that officers taking on the position of a chief officer in a police department hold a university degree.

## Recruitment and Selection

Any profession needs informed, dedicated, and competent personnel. Today, police organizations actively recruit new officers from university campuses, professional organizations, and community colleges and technical institutes that offer two-year programs. Education is an important criterion in selecting today's police recruits. Some police departments require a minimum number of community college credits for entry-level work.

Effective policing, however, may depend more upon personal qualities than it does upon educational attainment. O.W. Wilson once enumerated some of the "desirable personal qualities of patrol officers."[123] They include (1) initiative; (2) the capacity for responsibility; (3) the ability to deal alone with emergencies; (4) the capacity to communicate effectively with persons of diverse social, cultural, and ethnic backgrounds; (5) the ability to learn a variety of tasks quickly; (6) the attitude and ability necessary to adapt to technological changes; (7) the desire to help people in need; (8) an understanding of others; (9) emotional maturity; and (10) sufficient physical strength and endurance.

Standard procedures employed by modern departments in selecting trainees usually include basic skill tests, physical agility measurements, interviews, physical examinations, eye tests, psychological evaluations, and background investigations into the personal character of applicants. After training, successful applicants are typically placed on a one-year probation period. The probationary period in police work has been called the "first true job-related test—in the selection procedure,"[124] providing as it does the opportunity for supervisors to gauge the new officer's response to real-life situations.

## Ethnic and Racial Minorities and Women

In 1995, Harish C. Jain published the results of a survey of visible minorities in various police departments in Canada.[125] He found a marked disparity between the proportion of visible minorities in the labour market and their scant numbers in police officer positions. The proportion of visible minorities in the labour market varied from the upper range of 16.2 to 16.5 per cent in large urban areas (Vancouver and Toronto, respectively), down to a low of less than 1 per cent in New Brunswick, with a national average of 6.3 per cent. Visible minority representation in police organizations ranged from a high of 4.7 per cent in Toronto to 0 per cent in St. Hubert (located east of Montreal), with the RCMP having 0.8 per cent minority representation.[126] Visible minority representation in higher-rank levels is notoriously lacking. While improvement has occurred in this regard in recent years, Jain reports that only one of the 988 sergeants in Montreal is a visible minority.

In recent years, the emphasis placed upon minority recruitment by police agencies has done much to rectify the situation. Jain found only four police organizations in 1987 had visible minority representation above the rank of constable, while by 1990, most of those departments surveyed indicated that they had visible minority representation in such ranks. Many departments, through dedicated recruitment efforts, have dramatically increased their complement of officers from under-represented groups.

The numbers of both women and ethnic minorities have substantially increased in policing.

A 1999 report by the Canadian Centre for Justice Statistics[127] found that women accounted for 13 per cent of all officers in Canadian police departments. However, note that women likely still make up only about 1 per cent of all officer ranks.

A report[128] on female police officers in Canada found that they are subject to a number of barriers: (1) tradition—the "macho" image of what police work entails, (2) credibility—not being taken seriously in the organization, (3) assumptions—being viewed as less committed to the career, pose an increased risk for their partners, are less accepted by the public, (4) self-made—not actively pursuing promotions or offering contributions in the workplace, and (5) isolation—remaining at the periphery of the male-dominated circle or clique.

Recent Canadian research shows that female police officers in the Vancouver Police Department and Lower Mainland RCMP detachments perform with similar abilities and styles when compared to male officers in the same departments.[129] Linden and Fillmore conclude their analysis by commenting on the consistent findings that have shown that female police officers "on patrol consistently show that they are as competent as male officers," and their particular findings that "supervisors and men who have worked with women officers have typically expressed positive attitudes towards their performance."[130] The old stereotypes about women in policing appear to be falling away as research reveals that women in policing are devoted to their work, perform their jobs competently, are accepted by the public and most of their peers, and may even have traits that make them better suited than their male counterparts in many situations commonly encountered in police work. Many women appear to display non-confrontational conflict resolution skills that permit a more satisfactory resolution to potentially volatile situations than a more aggressive response characteristic of many

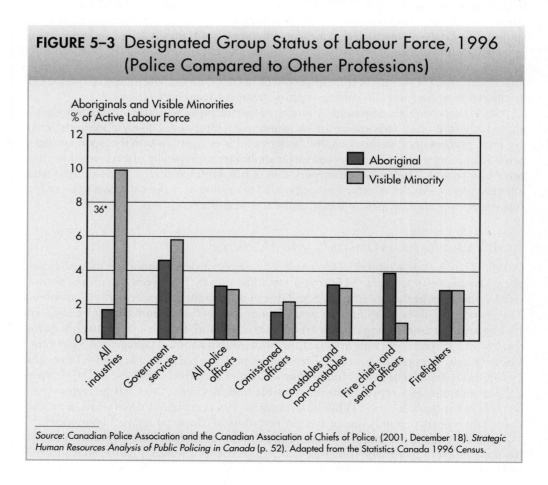

**FIGURE 5–3** Designated Group Status of Labour Force, 1996 (Police Compared to Other Professions)

Aboriginals and Visible Minorities % of Active Labour Force

*Source*: Canadian Police Association and the Canadian Association of Chiefs of Police. (2001, December 18). *Strategic Human Resources Analysis of Public Policing in Canada* (p. 52). Adapted from the Statistics Canada 1996 Census.

male police officers. However, the stress of making inroads into a traditionally male-dominated career has taken its toll on many female police officers. Jayne Seagrave notes that higher rates of attrition exist among female officers than their male counterparts.[131]

For many women in policing, networking may present a potential solution to the stresses encountered by female officers. However, in one study female officers interviewed said that when women get together to solve problems they are seen as "crybabies" rather than professionals. Said one of the women in the study, "[w]e've lost a lot of good women who never should have left the job. If we had helped each other maybe they wouldn't have left."[132]

Networking is a concept that is quickly taking root among women police officers, not only within a given department, but on a wider scale as attested to by the growth of organizations such as the International Association of Women Police. Mentoring, another method for introducing women to police work, has been suggested by some authors.[133] Mentoring would create semi-formal relationships between experienced women officers and rookies entering the profession. Through such relationships, problems could be addressed as they arose, and the experienced officer could serve to guide her junior partner through the maze of formal and informal expectations that surround the job of policing.

Other studies, like those already discussed, have found that female officers are often underutilized and that many departments are hesitant to assign women to patrol and other potentially dangerous field activities. As a consequence, some women in police work experience frustration and a lack of satisfaction with their jobs.[134] Other women are hesitant to consider a police career, and a few departments complain that it is difficult to find significant numbers of well-qualified minority recruits interested in police work. Also, harassment on the job continues to be a reality for some minority and female officers.

Barriers continue to fall. In 1997, for example, the Vancouver Police Department actively recruited homosexuals for its police force. Police hoped that action would result in a reduced fear of reporting crimes among city homosexuals, who for years had been victims of organized assaults by people unwilling to accept their lifestyle. Other barriers are falling as women have begun to enter the ranks of police administration. We are gradually witnessing female police officers enter the upper ranks of police administration in this country.

In a continuing effort to increase the representation of women and ethnic minorities in police work, the Police Foundation recommends (1) involving under-represented groups in affirmative action and long-term planning programs that are undertaken by police departments; (2) encouraging the development of an open system of promotions whereby women can feel free to apply for promotion, and in which qualified individuals of any race or gender will face equity in the promotion process; and (3) using periodic audits to ensure that women officers are not being underutilized by being ineffectively tracked into clerical and support positions.[135]

# THE FUTURE OF POLICING

Future crimes and the future of criminal justice are discussed in detail in Chapter 16. At the close of this chapter, however, it seems appropriate to ask: "What does the future hold for *policing* in Canada?" Anticipated future developments of specific relevance to the police in Canada over the next 10 to 20 years will span a number of changes. An aging population will produce continuing declines in the overall crime rate. Women and ethnic minorities will make up an ever-increasing proportion of Canadian police forces. Technological changes to the police tasks will continue to leave their mark on how policing is carried out. Tensions between increasing concerns over security and ongoing pressures to curb government spending will likely lead to a continued levelling-off of police numbers, or perhaps a small increase in overall police staff levels. As community policing takes its foothold, the range of tasks that are perceived as legitimate forms of police work can be expected to increase. Private police can be expected to fill the gaps, and take on policing in an ever-increasing range of new areas. If the accuracy of these common predictions bears fruit, Canadian law enforcement agencies will face some serious challenges during the coming century.

# SUMMARY

Police work today is characterized by the opportunity for individual officers to exercise considerable discretion, by a powerful subculture that communicates select values in support of a "police personality," and by the very real possibility of corruption and deviance. Opposed to the illegitimate use of police authority, however, are increased calls for an ethical awareness in police work, and continuing growth of the professionalism ideal. Professionalism, with its emphasis on education, training, high ethical values, and personal accountability, should soon lead to greater public recognition of the significance of police work, and to higher salaries for career police personnel. Increased salaries and a clear public appreciation for the police should do much to decrease corruption and deviance in law enforcement ranks.

As the environment surrounding the individual officer changes, so too do cultural expectations for the police profession. The movement away from the maintenance of order in policing, and the new emphasis on community policing, presage continued shifts in the police role.

# QUESTIONS FOR DISCUSSION

1. What are the central features of the police "working personality"? How does the police working personality develop? What programs might be initiated to "shape" the police personality in a more desirable way?

2. Do you think police officers exercise too much discretion in the performance of their duties? Why or why not? If it is desirable to limit discretion, how would you do it?

3. What themes run through the findings of the Knapp Commission? What innovative steps might police departments take to reduce or eliminate corruption among their officers?

4. Is police work a profession? Why do you think it is, or why do you think it is not? What advantages are there to viewing policing as a profession? How do you think most police officers today see their work—as a "profession" or as just a "job"?

5. Reread the *Law Enforcement Code of Ethics* found in this chapter. Do you think most police officers make conscious efforts to apply the code in the performance of their duty? How might ethics training in police departments be improved?

www.cacp.ca
## Canadian Association of Chiefs of Police
Formed in Toronto in 1905, the CACP advocates legislative change and policy reform, community partnerships, and professional and ethical standards.

www.cpc.gc.ca
## Canadian Police College
The CPC teaches courses ranging from computer crime and drugs to executive training and media relations.

www.theiacp.org
## Ethics Training in Law Enforcement
In this international website, you can find, under "Publications," a report by the Ethics Training Subcommittee of the International Association of Chiefs of Police Ad Hoc Committee on Police Image and Ethics. This report identifies problem areas, outlines consequences of unethical behaviour, suggests strategies for implementation of ethics codes, and presents results of a survey of personnel regarding ethics and policing.

www.communitypolicing.ca
## Community Policing Advisory Council of Ontario
The CPAC is a not-for-profit organization with a mandate to foster community policing throughout Ontario.

www.bccla.org
## Policing the Police
In this website, you can find, under "Resources," an archive of press releases and position papers maintained by the British Columbia Civil Liberties Association.

www.sirc-csars.gc.ca
## Security Intelligence Review Committee
SIRC was established in 1984 as an independent body to review the activities of the Canadian Security Intelligence Service (CSIS).

www.blueline.ca
## Blue Line: Canada's National Law Enforcement Magazine
This online version of the print magazine provides feature articles and news briefs, law enforcement links, supplier services, and more.

# Policing: Legal Aspects

Canapress/Ryan Remiorz

**KEY CONCEPTS**

prima facie
discoverability
illegally seized evidence
fruit of the poisoned tree
    doctrine
exclusionary rule
plain view

emergency search
arrest
search incident to an
    arrest
suspicionless search

**KEY CASES**

*Doe* v. *Metropolitan
Toronto Board of
Commissioners of
Police*
*Hunter* v. *Southam*
*R.* v. *Kokesch*
*R.* v. *Evans*
*R.* v. *Godoy*
*R.* v. *Custer*
*R.* v. *Feeney*
*R.* v. *Macooh*
*R.* v. *Collins*
*R.* v. *Burlingham*

*R.* v. *Stillman*
*R.* v. *Clarkson*
*R.* v. *Storrey*
*R.* v. *Oickle*
*R.* v. *Biron*
*Cloutier* v. *Langlois*
*R.* v. *Simpson*
*R.* v. *Hufsky*
*Ibrahim* v. *The King*
*R.* v. *Hebert*
*R.* v. *Mack*
*R.* v. *Manninen*
*R.* v. *Brydges*

# THE ABUSE OF POLICE POWER

In the early hours of February 5, 1987, a 30-year-old unemployed bricklayer named Brian Ethier, while in the company of a friend, Kathleen Balzer, was stopped by Saskatoon police constables Larry Lockwood and Larry Vols for allegedly driving while intoxicated. Police said Ethier's vehicle had been swerving from side to side, and that it had failed to stop at a stop sign. The officers claimed that the vehicle did not stop until travelling three blocks after the activation of their emergency lights, and when the vehicle finally did cease moving, it came to a rest on a sidewalk. The officers noted that Ethier smelled of what they thought to be alcohol, his speech was slurred, and he had bloodshot eyes. Ethier was very upset. By accounts, he was belligerent, used abusive language, and swore at the police officers. After Ethier failed a roadside sobriety test, Constable Lockwood informed Ethier that he was under arrest and demanded that the suspect accompany the police. Ethier objected to the police demand and indicated that he would not come along without a fight.

By this time, a second police vehicle had arrived at the scene, bringing Constables Chatterbok and Peters into the scenario. Peters and Lockwood grabbed Ethier by the arms and pushed his face over the hood of a police car. The officers applied handcuffs to Ethier, subduing his efforts at resistance. Lockwood and Peters maintained their grip on Ethier's arms as they backed him up towards the police car. At this stage, Peters opened the rear door of the police car. Ethier engaged in passive resistance, not making the police officers' job any easier, and he continued in his verbal abuse of the police. This scene could have ended like countless others being carried out across the country had Ethier simply been placed into the car and been driven to the police station where he would likely have provided a breath sample to answer the question over the extent of his state of intoxication. However, the situation did not unfold so smoothly. According to evidence accepted by Justice Sirois of the Saskatchewan Court of Queen's Bench, as Constable Lockwood placed his hand on Ethier's head, pushing it down so he could enter the rear seat of the police car, Constable Vols kicked Ethier in the legs while Ethier had his back to the police car, resulting in knee damage in the form of a tear of the medial collateral ligament. At the police station, Ethier collapsed in an elevator, complaining of a broken leg. Despite this, he was dragged into the cell area and kept in cells overnight. Following his release from the police station the next morning, Ethier reported to a local hospital where, following X-rays, he was transferred to a hospital where his leg was placed in a solid cast for five weeks, to be followed up by a partial cast for a subsequent three weeks. Brian Ethier was described by Sirois J. as "a rugged individual in good physical shape. He was, I believe, insulting, rambunctious, protesting vocally, abusive, uncooperative, threatening but he never struck the police or attempted to do so." For his pain, suffering, and wage loss, Ethier's successful civil suit against the arresting officers resulted in the award of $4545, a paltry sum compared to civil damage awards for police wrongdoing in the United States. However, Sirois J. condemned the actions of the errant police officer in this case:

> A policeman's role is a difficult one and most of the time a thankless one. The police uphold the laws as peace officers and protect citizens from wrongdoers. They often take much abuse while going about their work and they expect this as part of their job, as unpalatable as it might be. They are a friend in need. They have much power that is not to be abused at any time. Otherwise, a police state arises and human rights are no longer respected.[1]

This chapter shows how the police, like everyone else, are not above the law. This chapter describes the legal environment surrounding police activities—from search and seizure through arrest and the interrogation of suspects. As we shall see throughout, this environment is democratically inspired by legal restraints upon the police that help ensure individual freedoms in our society, and that prevent the development of a "police state" in Canada. Like anything else, however, the rules by which the police are expected to operate are in constant flux, and their continuing development forms the meat of this chapter.

# An Evolving Legal Climate

The Constitution of Canada is designed—especially in the legal rights sections of the *Charter of Rights and Freedoms*—to protect citizens against abuses of police power (see Table 6–1). The legal environment surrounding the police in modern Canada is much more complex than it was just 20 years ago. Up until that time, the police operated in a legal environment devoid of a constitutionally enshrined Charter of Rights. In this context, individual rights were largely given only lip service in criminal justice proceedings throughout the country. In practice, law enforcement revolved around tried-and-true methods of search, arrest, and interrogation, which sometimes left little room for recognition of individual rights. Police operations during that period were often far more informal than they are today, and investigating officers frequently assumed that they could come and go as they pleased, even to the extent of invading someone's personal space without the need for a search warrant. Interrogations could quickly turn violent, and the infamous "rubber hose," which was reputed to leave few marks on the body, was probably more widely used during the questioning of suspects than many would like to believe. Similarly, "doing things by the book" could mean beating suspects with thick telephone books, since the books spread out the force of blows and left few visible bruises. Although such abuses were not necessarily day-to-day practices in all police agencies, and while they probably did not characterize the conduct of more than a relatively small proportion of all officers, such conduct pointed to the need for greater control over police activities, so that even the potential for abuse might be curtailed. The *Criminal Code* outlines the responsibilities of peace officers as follows:

"peace officer" includes:

(a) a mayor, warden, reeve, sheriff, deputy sheriff, sheriff's officer and justice of the peace,

(b) a member of the Correctional Service of Canada who is designated as a peace officer pursuant to Part I of the *Corrections and Conditional Release Act*, and a warden, deputy warden, instructor, keeper, jailer guard and any

## TABLE 6–1  Charter Rights Most Directly Affecting Criminal Justice

| | |
|---|---|
| s. 7 | A general right to "life, liberty and security of the person," however this right may be deprived so long as this is done in accordance with "principles of fundamental justice." |
| s. 8 | A prohibition against "unreasonable" search and seizure. |
| s. 9 | A prohibition against "arbitrary" detention or imprisonment. |
| s. 10 | A number of rights arising upon "arrest or detention," including the right to reasons, the right to retain and instruct counsel (and the right to be informed of this right), and the right to challenge the validity of the detention by way of *habeas corpus*. |
| s. 11 | A number of rights ascribed to those persons "charged with an offence," including:<br>• the specific offence being faced<br>• trial in a reasonable time<br>• not to be compelled to testify against oneself<br>• to be presumed innocent, and to be tried before an independent and impartial tribunal<br>• a right to not be denied bail without just cause<br>• a right to a jury if the offence charged carries a possible penalty of 5 years in prison or more<br>• not to be penalized by retroactive penal statutes<br>• a right against being twice put in jeopardy<br>• a right to the benefit of a lesser punishment if the penalty has been varied since the time of the offence |
| s. 12 | A right not to be subjected to "cruel and unusual" treatment or punishment. |
| s. 13 | A right not to have incriminating testimony used against oneself in a subsequent trial. |
| s. 14 | A right to an interpreter. |

other officer or permanent employee of a prison other than a penitentiary as defined in Part I of the *Corrections and Conditional Release Act*,

(c) a police officer, police constable, bailiff, constable, or other person employed for the preservation and maintenance of the public peace or for the service or execution of civil process,

(d) an officer or person having the powers of a customs or excise officer when performing any duty in the administration of the *Customs Act*, or the *Excise Act*,

(e) a person designated as a fishery guardian under the *Fisheries Act* when performing any duties or functions under that Act and a person designated as a fishery officer under the *Fisheries Act* when performing any duties or functions under that Act, or the *Coastal Fisheries Protection Act*,

(f) the pilot in command of an aircraft

    (i) registered in Canada under regulations made under the *Aeronautics Act*, or

    (ii) leased without crew and operated by a person who is qualified under regulations made under the *Aeronautics Act* to be registered as owner of an aircraft registered in Canada under those regulations, while the aircraft is in flight, and

(g) officers and non-commissioned members of the Canadian Forces who are

    (i) appointed for the purposes of section 156 of the *National Defence Act*, or

    (ii) employed on duties that the Governor in Council, in regulations made under the *National Defence Act* for the purposes of this paragraph, has prescribed to be of such a kind as to necessitate that the officers and non-commissioned members performing them have the powers of peace officers; ....

## BOX 6.1    Theory into Practice

## The "Jane Doe" Case

The case of *Doe v. Metropolitan Toronto (Municipality) Commissioners of Police* marks an important development in the law governing the tort liability of public authorities.[1] The police had been investigating a serial rape file involving an unknown offender who targeted women living alone in Toronto apartments that were accessible from a balcony. The group of apartment buildings in which these women lived was in an area close to downtown Toronto. The plaintiff, Jane Doe, had been sexually assaulted by this serial rapist. She advanced both a tort suit and sections 7 and 15 *Charter* claims against the police for their failure to warn her that she was one of a group of women at particular risk from that rapist.

Rather than inform the public, the police continued their investigation with hopes of catching the offender before he struck again. Apparently, police were afraid that informing the public would scare the offender away from the area. MacFarland J. of the Ontario Court, General Division, found in favour of Jane Doe, concluding that the police had used her, and other women in the same position, as bait.

The case is significant for its holding that a public authority, such as the police, can be held accountable in private law for discriminatory attitudes and practices leading to the negligent performance of their duty of care.[2] The case appears to have had a positive effect in making the police more aware of their duty to warn, and it has led to a definite change in police practices in subsequent sexual-assault investigations. Scott Childs and Paul Ceyssens have argued that this case is part of a larger trend of increasing civil liability for the police, suggesting that police officers need more legal training and need to seek out and respond to competent legal advice.[3]

## QUESTIONS FOR DISCUSSION

1. What, in your opinion, is the significance of the Jane Doe case for the Canadian criminal justice system?

2. The material in this Theory into Practice box suggests there is a need for increased formal legal training for police officers. Do you agree?

3. Does the case reflect a system of justice that undervalues women? Are the needs of certain people being denied by the contemporary Canadian criminal justice system?

---

[1.]*Doe v. Metropolitan Toronto Board of Commissioners of Police* (1998), 160 D.L.R. 697 (Ont.Ct.G.D.).

[2.]Randall, M. (2001). Sex Discrimination, Accountability of Public Authorities and the Public/Private Divide in Tort Law: An Analysis of *Doe v. Metropolitan Toronto (Municipality) Commissioners of Police*. *Queen's Law Journal*, 26, pp. 451–495.

[3.]Childs, S. and Ceyssens, P. (1998). *Doe v. Metropolitan Toronto Board of Commissioners of Police* and the Status of Public Oversight of the Police in Canada. *Alberta Law Review*, 36, pp. 1000–1016.

With the enactment of the *Canadian Charter of Rights and Freedoms* on April 17, 1982, Canada entered a new era of legal development. During the mid-1980s, the Supreme Court of Canada embarked on the process of guaranteeing individual rights to individuals who faced criminal prosecution. Since that time, this court's rulings have bound police to strict procedures for investigation, arrest, and interrogation. Recent rulings have scrutinized trial court procedure and enforced humanitarian standards in sentencing and punishment. The top court has recently scrutinized criminal proceedings, imparting its own brand of idealism on the process, showing that it is willing to allow a few guilty people to go free in order to protect the rights of the majority of Canadians.

Higher court decisions and legislative amendments in recent years may be the product of a new and emerging philosophy that attempts to balance individual rights with crime control values. The result may be perceived as a "reversal" of the advances in the area of individual rights developed over the first 15 years of *Charter* interpretation. The Supreme Court has created exceptions to some of its own rules and restraints, and it allows for delay in the implementation of some of its decisions affecting police practice, often suggesting that Parliament bring in legislation balancing the individual interests to be protected with the interests of the society as a whole in effective law enforcement. This situation may represent a changing legal framework that recognizes the realities attending day-to-day police work and the need to ensure public safety. This practical approach to justice is all the more interesting for the fact that it must struggle to emerge from the confines of very recent Supreme Court decisions.

# INDIVIDUAL RIGHTS

Canada's adoption of a constitutionally entrenched *Charter of Rights and Freedoms* has signalled a change from a constitutional system based on the principle of parliamentary supremacy, to one based on the notion of constitutional supremacy. Prior to the adoption of the *Charter*, the Canadian legal system operated on the assumption that Parliament was the supreme lawmaker, and that duly enacted laws were not subject to question. The conduct of government decision makers was not subject to any significant restrictions other than the rule of law. As long as the law was properly enacted, equally applied, and readily ascertainable, it was valid law. Police power, operating under the auspices of such law, was typically free from scrutiny. Under such a system, the interests of the majority, and the interests of those capable of influencing the lawmaking process, were emphasized. Minority interests, other than those of powerful minorities in society, were not well-protected under such a system of government. More importantly, the rights of the individual were also not well-protected under such a system. The *Charter of Rights and Freedoms* was adopted at least partially in hopes of reforming our democratic system of government so that the interests of minorities and individuals as well as collective interests would be protected.

Parliament is no longer considered supreme, and government decision makers now have their conduct subjected to closer scrutiny, to ensure that individual and minority rights are given adequate protection. The result has been a measure of accountability over police conduct, whereby the courts become charged with the role of ensuring that the behaviour of the police, as agents of the government, does not violate minority and individual interests to an unacceptable degree. Without accountability, it is possible to imagine a police state in which the power of law enforcement is absolute and related to political considerations and personal vendettas more than to any objective considerations of guilt or innocence.

Under our system of government, courts become the arena for dispute resolution, not just between individuals, but also between citizens and the agencies of government itself. People who have come into contact with the justice system and who believe that they have not received the respect and dignity due to them under law can appeal to the courts for redress. Such legal efforts are usually based on procedural issues and are independent of more narrow considerations of guilt or innocence of the accused.

In this chapter, we spend a great deal of time on cases where the judgments have clarified constitutional guarantees concerning individual rights and liberties within the criminal justice arena. It is common to hear arrestees today say: "You can't do that! I know my

Many Canadians are unclear as to the precise nature of their rights. In 1993, the Ontario Court of Appeal clarified the basis upon which law enforcement officers, lacking reasonable grounds to arrest, may stop and briefly detain a person for investigative purposes.

rights!" However, many Canadians are often unclear as to the precise nature of their rights. This confusion no doubt arises from the familiarity that most Canadians have with the "rights" of the American criminal justice system, which are regularly depicted in the media, consumed by Canadians as well as Americans. However, minor differences exist between the rights protected in our two countries.

Legal rights are typically concerned with procedure, that is, with how police and other actors in the criminal justice system handle each part of the process of dealing with suspects. Rights violations have often become the basis for a judicial stay of proceedings, the exclusion of evidence resulting in the acquittal of defendants, or the release of convicted offenders after an appeal to a higher court.

## Legal Rights Requirements

As you may recall from Chapter 1, legal rights are embodied in sections 7 to 14 of the *Canadian Charter of Rights and Freedoms*. These rights mandate that justice system officials respect the rights of accused individuals throughout the criminal justice process. The first of the legal rights establishes the general premise that everyone's basic rights to life, liberty, and security of the person are not absolute, but rather may be deprived as long as they are deprived in accordance with the principles of fundamental justice. Among other things, this premise seeks to ensure that the government only allows its agents to deprive Canadians of key fundamental rights in a manner that most people would consider to be procedurally fair. Most legal rights requirements of relevance to the police pertain to three major areas: (1) evidence and investigation (often called "search and seizure"), (2) arrest, and (3) interrogation. Each of these areas has been addressed by an abundance of landmark Supreme Court of Canada decisions. Many of these cases centre around interpreting the meaning of section 7 of the *Charter*, the general legal right:

> Everyone has the right to life, liberty and security of the person and the right not to be deprived thereof except in accordance with the principles of fundamental justice.

Landmark cases are described as such because they produce substantial changes in both the understanding of the requirements of legal rights and in the practical day-to-day operations of the justice system. Another way to think of landmark decisions is that they help significantly in clarifying the "rules of the game"—the procedural guidelines by which the police and the rest of the justice system must abide.

The three areas we are about to discuss have been fairly well-defined by rapidly evolving court precedent. Keep in mind, however, that judicial interpretations of the constitutional requirements contained in the legal rights provisions of the *Charter of Rights and Freedoms* are constantly evolving. As new decisions are rendered, and as the composition of the Court itself changes, additional refinements (and even major changes) may occur. Chapter 13 deals with the law governing the exercise of police powers in relation to young offenders.

## SEARCH AND SEIZURE

Section 8 of the *Charter* declares that "everyone has the right to be secure against unreasonable search or seizure." The language of section 8 is familiar to all of us. The need for warrants, the requirement of reasonable grounds, and the protection of privacy are all derived from this basic right. This section is frequently the subject of commentary by the police, newspaper editorials, television news shows, and daily conversation. The courts' interpretation of this section, however, has given this section the impact it has on the justice system today.

The first landmark case concerning search and seizure was *Hunter* v. *Southam* (1984).[2] The *Edmonton Journal*, a newspaper owned by the Southam newspaper company, was being investigated for possibly engaging in violations of the *Combines Investigation Act*. Federal anti-combines agents went to the business premises of the newspaper to conduct a search in order to examine documents. This search was conducted under the authority of the Director of Investigation and Research of the Combines Investigation Branch. Under the *Combines Investigation Act*, such searches are authorized without a warrant, provided the Director believes that the evidence is relevant to an investigation and the search is supported by a certificate of authorization from a member of the Restrictive Trade Practices Commission. The agents had no search warrant, since at the time the legislation did not require warrants. The agents began their search on the morning of April 20, 1982, three days after the *Charter of Rights and Freedoms* came into force. Southam's attempts to obtain an injunction to stop the search that day were unsuccessful; however, the case eventually made its way up through the appeal process on the basis of a challenge to the constitutional validity of the provisions of the *Combines Investigation Act* that authorized the warrantless search. The appeal eventually reached the Supreme Court of Canada.

The top court ruled that the legislation authorizing the search was of no force or effect due to its inconsistency with section 8 of the *Charter*. Accordingly, the search carried out on the basis of the invalid legislative provisions was not authorized by law, and therefore the government's intrusion into the offices of the *Edmonton Journal* was not supportable.

The Court also ruled that the protection provided by section 8 of the *Charter* goes at least as far as protecting an individual's reasonable expectation of privacy. The purpose of the section is to "[protect] individuals from unjustified state intrusions upon their privacy. That purpose requires a means of preventing unjustified searches before they happen, not simply of determining, after the fact, whether they ought to have occurred in the first place." To ensure such unjustified intrusions do not occur, the police must obtain prior authorization in the form of a warrant before a search will be considered valid: "where it is feasible to obtain prior authorization, I would hold that such authorization is a precondition for a valid search and seizure."

The Supreme Court of Canada requires that, ***prima facie***, the individual seeking to justify a search must establish the following:

1. Prior authorization, usually in the form of a warrant;

2. Issued by a judge or a person capable of acting judicially;

3. The prior authorization, or warrant, should only be issued if the authorizing judge is convinced that the police have established under oath, reasonable and probable grounds to believe an offence has been committed and evidence is to be found at the place to be searched; and

***prima facie*** A Latin term meaning "at first sight" or on the face of the matter. This term indicates that the situation must involve sufficient evidence to establish a fact, absent any evidence to rebut the fact. In essence, the evidence must be the minimum amount of evidence necessary to avoid having a case dismissed.

4. Searches not meeting these requirements will be presumptively invalid; however, special circumstances may necessitate deviating from these requirements.

Entry onto private property by the police, or anyone else, is subject to the tort law applicable in a given jurisdiction, as well as the criminal law governing search and seizure. In particular, the law of trespass to property dictates the legal relationship between the occupier of property and persons entering upon that property. The legal principles applicable in the context of persons treading on the property of another are, to a large degree, delineated in the common law.

Trespass has been defined as both "(1) entering upon the land of another without lawful justification, and (2) placing, throwing, or erecting some material object thereon without any legal right to do so."[3] In the context of police activity, the first definition above covers most situations in which the police may become subject to liability for trespass. For the purposes of occupier liability, the common law has divided categories of people who enter onto property possessed by another as (1) trespassers, (2) licensees, (3) invitees, and (4) contractual entrants.[4] The categories of "invitee" and "contractual entrant" do not commonly arise in the context of normal police duties since they entail situations whereby a person may go upon the land of an occupier as a visitor "from whose visit the occupier stands to derive an economic advantage"[5] (invitee), or from whom a fee has been "paid for the right to enter the premises"[6] (contractual entrant). Most policing situations involve determining whether the police have entered the land of another as a licensee or as a trespasser.

The tort of trespass to land is actionable "without proof of damage,"[7] allowing the occupier to recover damages even in circumstances where it is readily apparent that no loss has been suffered as a consequence of the trespass. Additionally, it is only a voluntary trespass that is actionable. In this context, Klar notes that where a person is startled and thereby inadvertently steps onto the plaintiff's land, a trespass has not occurred.[8] However, Klar also notes that trespass is made out even if the defendant believes he or she was acting in good faith, or was labouring under a mistake.[9]

To escape liability for trespass to land, a defendant must generally show that he or she obtained a licence to enter the property. This requirement may be satisfied by showing the existence of a licence from the lawful occupier of the property, or a licence given by the law, in the form of lawful authority to enter upon the property.[10] Whenever the police contemplate entry onto property, they must be aware of their status prior to entry. In this way, they can be sure to comply with the law, thereby obviating the possibility of a civil suit against themselves and their employer.

If the police enter upon the property of another as a licensee, they should be aware of whether they hold a licence and whether the licence is granted by the occupier or granted by law, since their subsequent status on the land may vary accordingly. A licence granted by the occupier may be withdrawn by the occupier at a moment's notice, while a licence granted by law is not always so easily revoked. In addition to the implications for civil law, the status of the police officer upon entering the property has an impact upon the likelihood of a court also finding that the entry violated section 8 of the *Charter*.

## Express Licence and Implied Licence from the Occupier

An express licence from the occupier of property entails an invitation to enter the property, and includes providing an affirmative response to a request from the person seeking entry for permission to enter. Ceyssens notes "that one of a number of co-occupiers may issue an invitation" and that "a co-occupier cannot unilaterally revoke another's invitation."[11] When seeking entry onto a person's property, a police officer who asks for and receives permission to do so from an occupier of that property is thereby granted a licence to enter the property.

Until recently, drug enforcement officers would commonly get the information necessary to form the reasonable grounds for obtaining a warrant for a search of a home for drug-growing operations by snooping around the house in question. One practice involved a "perimeter search," that is, walking around the outside of a house, looking in the windows, or sniffing at the cracks of doors and windows for the presence of drugs growing inside the premises. A second practice involved a "knock-on" procedure. Here, the police would go to the door of the house, knock on it, and when the resident answered, they would peek into the house or inhale deeply, hoping to get a whiff of drugs growing, or being used, inside the home.

In *R. v. Kokesch* (1990),[12] the Supreme Court of Canada ruled that warrantless perimeter searches are not authorized by statute, and amount to a violation of the right to be secure against unreasonable search and seizure.

An implied licence exists that permits people, including a mail delivery person, a newspaper delivery person, and even police officers, to enter property and approach the front door of a dwelling. The Supreme Court of Canada ruling in *R. v. Evans* (1996)[13] addresses the scope of this implied licence in the context of the police approaching the front door of a dwelling in an effort to apply the "knock-on" procedure. Acting on an anonymous tip, the police found themselves unable to acquire evidence of a marijuana-growing operation through normal investigative practices. In particular, the house in question did not appear to be consuming abnormal levels of electricity, usually a good indicator of a hydroponics-based operation. The officers approached the front door of the house, knocked on it, and when the resident answered the door, the officers were overwhelmed by the aroma of marijuana emanating from inside the dwelling. The officers detained the suspects and secured the premises, following which they obtained a search warrant from a justice. They used their exposure to the smell of marijuana as the basis for reasonable grounds to believe that they could find evidence of a marijuana-growing operation on the premises. A subsequent search resulted in a large quantity of marijuana being seized from the home. At trial, this evidence formed the basis of the prosecution's case, and was successfully introduced against them, resulting in a conviction. While the Supreme Court was unanimous in dismissing the accused's appeal from the conviction imposed by a lower court, the case has significant implications for the police using the same tactics in the future.

Mister Justice Sopinka delivered the majority judgment, with two other justices concurring. While Justice La Forest was in substantial agreement with Sopinka J.'s approach, he wrote his own reasons for judgment. Justice Major delivered a judgment that also dismissed the appeal, but he reached a dramatically different conclusion as to the law governing "knock-on" activities of the police. Sopinka J. and Major J. both traced the implied licence to enter property in order to approach and knock on the door to the English common law in *Robson v. Hallett* (1967).[14] This principle was adopted into Canadian law in *R. v. Bushman* (1968), and *R. v. Johnson* (1994)[15] (as noted by Major J.), and in *R. v. Tricker* (1995)[16] (as noted by Sopinka J.). The two judgments are consonant in noting that while an implied licence to enter the property, approach the door, and knock exists, this licence may be revoked by the property occupier posting a sign to that effect or locking a gate to the property.[17] Additionally, it is noteworthy that the property occupier may lawfully choose to deny entry to the person who is knocking, or to ignore that person and refrain from answering the door.[18]

It is with respect to the scope of the implied licence that Sopinka J. and Major J. differed in their interpretations of the law. According to Sopinka J., the implied licence to approach the door and knock may be viewed as a "waiver" of the right to privacy.[19] He then determined the scope of the waiver contained in the implied licence by looking to the "purpose" behind approaching the door. After noting that the waiver does not authorize burglars approaching a house in order to "case" the location, he relied on *R. v. Bushman* for the proposition that the purpose of the implied invitation is to facilitate communication between the public and the occupant of the dwelling:

> In my view, the implied invitation to knock extends no further than is required to permit convenient communication with the occupant of the dwelling. The "waiver" of privacy rights embodied in the implied invitation extends no further than is required for this purpose. As a result, only those activities that are reasonably associated with the purpose of communicating with the occupant are authorized by the "implied licence to knock". Where the conduct of the police (or any member of the public) goes beyond that which is permitted by the implied licence to knock, the implied "conditions" of that licence have effectively been breached, and the person carrying out the unauthorized activity approaches the dwelling as an intruder.[20]

In the *Evans* case, the police had approached the house with the intent of sniffing for a smell of marijuana once the occupant opened the door, and thereby produced reasonable grounds upon which a warrant to search could be obtained. The objective of the police went beyond communicating with the occupant, going to the point of trying to catch a smell of marijuana coming from the interior of the home once the door was opened. Sopinka J. concluded that the police had accordingly exceeded the scope of the implied licence to approach and knock: "... where the agents of the state approach a dwelling with the intention of gathering evidence against the occupant, the police have exceeded any authority that is implied by the invitation to knock."[21]

Sopinka J. went on to hold that since the police exceeded the bounds of the implied licence, their conduct amounted to a search of the occupant's home (at p. 32), albeit an "olfactory search" (at p. 34). Relying on *Hunter* v. *Southam Inc.* (1984),[22] he concluded that this search, absent a warrant, was *prima facie* invalid. The Crown was unable to rebut this presumption of unreasonableness since the search was not "authorized by law," that is, by the applicable drug legislation in force at the time (which required a warrant to search dwellings for narcotics). Accordingly, the search was found to be in violation of section 8 of the *Charter of Rights and Freedoms*.

Having found the search unreasonable, Sopinka J. declared the warrant, obtained to search the home that was based on the information gathered during the unreasonable search, to be invalid, relying on *R. v. Kokesch* (1990).[23] However, he admitted the evidence gathered from the search of the home since its admission would not, in all the circumstances, bring the administration of justice into disrepute. He held that admission would not render the trial unfair, that the seriousness of the violation was not grave, and that exclusion of the evidence would tarnish the administration of justice more so than would its admission.

The decision of Sopinka J. to admit the evidence in this case should not be taken as a cue to police to continue conducting such "knock-on" searches. Although the evidence was admitted in this case, it is unlikely that this conclusion would be reached again. Sopinka J. noted that the police acted in "good faith" in this situation because the police felt that their conduct was in compliance with *Charter* requirements. Absent this judgment, the police were not aware that their search exceeded their authority. However, that argument is not valid any longer. The Court has pronounced such searches to be unreasonable, and the Court will expect the police to bring their conduct into compliance with the ruling in this judgment in the future.

Major J. concluded that the evidence should also have been admitted, but for different reasons. He found no violation of section 8 of the *Charter* in the conduct of the police in approaching the door to smell for marijuana:

> The police conduct in this case did not constitute a search within the meaning of s. 8 of the Charter. In approaching the front door of the residence in broad daylight and knocking at the door, the police officers were exercising an implied licence at common law. When the door was opened, the observations made by the police officers from this position were simply that: observations of what was in plain view. The appellants could not have any reasonable expectation that no one, including police officers, would ever lawfully approach their home and observe what was plainly discernable from a position where police officers and others were lawfully entitled to be.[24]

Major J. would have held that the actions of the police did not amount to a search, never mind an unreasonable one. After balancing state interests in law enforcement against individual interests in privacy, he found that the threshold for constituting a search is not met in these circumstances:

> To hold that every police inquiry or question constitutes a search under s. 8 would disregard entirely the public's interest in law enforcement in favour of an absolute but unrealistic right of privacy of all individuals against any state incursion however moderate.[25]

The *Evans* case illustrates the scope of the implied licence to approach a door and knock. As a consequence of the majority ruling, the purpose of the police in approaching the door is now a matter of concern. The police must know whether their purpose in approaching a door is to gather evidence (beyond the scope of the licence), or merely to communicate with the occupier (within the scope of the licence). Because the gathering of information in an investigation often produces evidence that can be used against the suspect at trial, in the future the courts will have to determine where to draw the line with regard to identifying the circumstances in which the police cannot be said to hold an implied licence to approach a house.

The implied licence given by the occupier applies in circumstances going beyond approaching the front door for the purposes of communicating with the occupant. In particular, implied licence may justify entry into a building where the conduct of the occupant implies permission to enter. Where an occupant opens the front door and stands aside, these actions may be taken as an implied licence to enter: *Robson* v. *Hallett* (1967).[26] In his summary of the case law, Ceyssens notes that an implied licence has been found to exist in a variety of circumstances:

1. An implied licence exists to come upon a driveway: *Halliday* v. *Nevill* (1984)[27] and *R.* v. *Johnson* (1994).[28]

2. An implied licence exists to enter an enclosed porch where the door to it is left open: *R.* v. *Bushman* (1968).[29]

3. A person other than the occupier answering the door and giving permission to enter provides an implied licence to enter, which can be rebutted by the actual occupier of the dwelling: *Robson* v. *Hallett* (1967).[30]

4. Police responding to a burglar alarm sounding at the police station have an implied licence to enter the premises. This implied licence provides the police with a reasonable period of time to make an investigation: *Kay* v. *Hibbert*.[31]

The existence of an implied licence is excluded by the presence of locked gates, a sign precluding entry, or the presence of guard dogs.[32]

The implied licence to enter property may be revoked by the occupier at any time. A person with the implied authority of the occupier may also revoke the licence: *McArdle* v. *Wallace* (1964).[33] Ceyssens cites numerous authorities that support the notion that when a licence is revoked, the police must leave the premises; failing to do so will result in liability for trespass.[34] Police may not remain in order to make further inquiries. They will be accorded a relatively brief period to depart from the premises. Indeed, an occupier may use reasonable force to eject the police should they fail to leave after the licence is revoked. Only if an independent ground to remain on the property exists will the police be exempt from liability for failing to leave after the grant of a licence has been revoked.[35] These independent grounds to remain on the property will typically entail a justified continued presence through a licence given by law in the form of authority. We will discuss next the circumstances that justify entry onto land or the continued presence of the police through a licence gained by legal authority.

## Licence Gained by Legal Authority

At common law, a duty exists on the police to "protect life and property."[36] This common-law duty carries with it the authority to enter private property without a warrant to protect life and prevent death or serious injury in emergent situations, provided the police properly announce that they plan to enter.[37] Case law has delineated the scope of this duty and the corresponding implied permission to enter a residence to fulfill this duty. Typically, the common law will sanction such entries to prevent serious injuries, not minor ones.[38]

At common law, a duty also exists on the police to "preserve the peace."[39] Prior case law has indicated that a police officer may enter and remain on private premises in order to preserve the peace: *Thomas* v. *Sawkins*.[40] This duty includes gaining entry onto private premises to prevent a breach of the peace from occurring: *McLeod* v. *Commissioner of Police of the Metropolis*.[41] In *R.* v. *Godoy* (1999), the Supreme Court of Canada ruled that the police are entitled to forcibly enter a dwelling in response to an interrupted 9-1-1 call. This power was said to arise at common law and was connected to the police duty to protect life.

Unless the police have a warrant (see Figure 6–1) authorizing them to enter premises to find a person, they typically will be constrained from entering premises in such circumstances. In circumstances where the police seek to make a lawful arrest, they will only have the authority to enter premises to make an arrest in rare circumstances.

In *R. v. Feeney* (1997),[42] the Supreme Court of Canada ruled that a police officer proceeding to effect a warrantless arrest pursuant to the general arrest power in section 495(1)(a) of the *Criminal Code* may not do so, absent exigent circumstances.

In *R. v. Macooh* (1993),[43] Chief Justice Lamer, for the Supreme Court of Canada, confirmed the lawfulness of a police entry onto private premises when the entry is made in hot pursuit, even where the offence for which the person being arrested was not indictable, as long as the police hold the power to arrest for the offence without warrant. This ruling applies even where the offence for which a person is being arrested is a provincial offence. Such circumstances as hot pursuit amount to the type of exigent circumstances justifying warrantless entry to effect an arrest envisioned by the top court in the *Feeney* case.

The most obvious grant of legal authority to enter property is through a search warrant. Where the police seek to gather evidence on a person's property, a search warrant will generally be required. This principle may be traced to the statement of Lord Camden in *Entick* v. *Carrington* (1765)[44]:

> It is very certain, that the law obligeth no man to accuse himself; because the necessary means of compelling self-accusation, falling upon the innocent as well as the guilty, would be both cruel and unjust; and it should seem, that search for evidence is disallowed upon the same principle.[45]

The general provision authorizing the issuance of a search warrant to the police by a justice is found in section 487 of the *Criminal Code*. Section 487.1 of the *Criminal Code* permits the police to obtain a telewarrant, whereby a warrant may be approved by telephone where it is impracticable to appear before a justice in person. Section 103 of the *Criminal Code* provides for a justice to issue a warrant to search and seize "firearms, other offensive weapons, ammunition, or explosive substance" where the interests of safety mandate such action. A warrant to search for incriminating evidence pertaining to a gaming house, bookmaking, a lottery, or a common bawdy house may be issued to the police by a justice in accordance with section 199 of the *Criminal Code*. Under section 462.32, a judge may issue a search warrant in relation to proceeds of crime arising from an enterprise crime or a designated drug offence. A search warrant for precious metals may be issued by a justice in accordance with section 395 of the *Criminal Code*. Section 339(3) permits peace officers to enter any place to ascertain whether lumber bearing a registered timber mark is being held without the knowledge or consent of the owner, as long as the peace officer believes on reasonable grounds it is being kept or detained.

Under section 11(1) of the *Controlled Drugs and Substances Act*, police are able to search any place without warrant, if they believe on reasonable grounds that there is evidence pertaining to an offence under the Act, and they obtain a warrant to search from a justice. A power to search without warrant is granted in section 11(7) for offences under the Act; however, such power may only be exercised in exigent circumstances. Similar powers exist for the search of evidence pertaining to other criminal offences under section 487.11 of the *Criminal Code*.

Under provincial legislation, the police may be granted legal authority to enter premises. Section 67.1 of the B.C. *Liquor Control and Licensing Act* (LCLA) provides for the obtaining of a warrant to search in relation to minors in possession of liquor in a residence. Searches for other offences under the B.C. LCLA are permitted if a warrant is obtained pursuant to section 17 of the B.C. *Provincial Offence Act*. A warrantless power to enter any premises and seize a child in need of protection is governed by provincial child welfare legislation.

Where the licence to enter a place has been obtained through a grant of legal authority, as opposed to an express or implied licence from the occupier to enter the property, the licence cannot be revoked by the occupier of the property. Even in circumstances where the police officer enters the land under a licence, express or implied, from the occupier, he or she is entitled to remain on the property even if subsequently ordered to leave, provided an independent reason to remain on the property exists: *Lamb* v. *D.P.P.* (1989).[46] This entitlement will typically arise from a licence granted by lawful authority.

Most police searches that are carried out under the authority of a warrant flow from the exercise of a power granted to them under the *Criminal Code's* general search warrant provision (see Table 6–2 on page 183). A police officer appearing before a justice of the peace or a Provincial Court judge may request the issuance of a search warrant where the police establish that they have reasonable grounds to believe there is in a "building, receptacle, or place," that is, something specific that pertains to an offence.

Section 488 of the *Code* indicates that warrants are to be executed or carried out by day (defined by the *Code* as running from 6 A.M. to 9 P.M.) unless the warrant specifically authorizes a night search. Additionally, the *Code* provides in section 489 that the persons executing the search warrant may seize things pertaining to offences, even if they are not mentioned in the warrant. After seizing items by warrant, the police officer must either bring the seized items to a justice of the peace, or make a report to the justice indicating what was seized under the warrant.

*The Exclusionary Rule* The exclusionary rule means that evidence seized by the police in a manner that violates a person's rights under the *Charter* cannot be used in a trial if its admission would bring the administration of justice into disrepute. The rule acts as a compromise, balancing a desire to disassociate the criminal justice system from wrongful police conduct, while also admitting as much relevant evidence as can be tolerated without adversely tainting the system with the improper conduct. Exclusion of evidence in the context of *Charter* violations is governed by section 24(2) of the *Charter*:

Enforcement of Guaranteed Rights and Freedoms/Exclusion of evidence bringing administration of justice into disrepute.

ss. 24. (1) Anyone whose rights or freedoms, as guaranteed by this Charter, have been infringed or denied may apply to a court of competent jurisdiction to obtain such remedy as the court considers appropriate and just in the circumstances.

(2) Where, in proceedings under subsection (1), a court concludes that evidence was obtained in a manner that infringed or denied any rights or freedoms guaranteed by this Charter, the evidence shall be excluded if it is established that, having regard to all the circumstances, the admission of it in the proceedings would bring the administration of justice into disrepute.[47]

In *R. v. Therens* (1985),[48] the Supreme Court of Canada first turned its attention to the possibility of excluding evidence under section 24(2) of the *Charter*. The accused lost control of his vehicle and collided with a tree. A police officer arriving at the scene demanded

**FIGURE 6–1** Warrant to Search

**FORM 5**

(*Section 487*)

**Warrant to search**

Canada,
Province of ........................................,
(*territorial division*).

To the peace officers in the said (*territorial division*):

Whereas it appears on the oath of A.B., of ............... that there are reasonable grounds in believing that (*describe things to be searched for and offence in respect of which search is to be made*) are in ............... at ..............., hereinafter called the premises:
This is, therefore, to authorize and require you between the hours of (*as the justice may direct*) to enter into the said premises and to search for the said things and to bring them before me or some other justice.

Dated this ............................ day of ............................ A.D. ........, at ............................ .

..............................................
A Justice of the Peace in and
for ..........................

## TABLE 6–2 Key Warrant Provisions in Statute

**General *Criminal Code* Provisions:**

| | |
|---|---|
| s. 487 | Normal provision to obtain a warrant to search a "building, receptacle or place" for evidence. |
| s.487.01 | Provides for warrants governing the use of a "device or investigative technique" where prior judicial authorization is required to avoid violating s. 8 CCRF. Clearly designed to encompass surreptitious video surveillance. |
| s. 487.05 | Governs warrants for acquiring samples for DNA analysis. |
| s. 487.092 | Governs warrants for dental impressions, hand imprints, and similar bodily impressions. |
| s. 487.1 | Telewarrants. |
| s. 487.11 | Exigent circumstance exemption to warrant requirements. |
| s. 488.1 | Warrants to search a lawyer's office. |
| s. 492.1 | Warrants for use of "tracking devices." |
| s. 492.2 | Authorizes obtaining warrants to install and monitor a telephone number recorder. |

**Miscellaneous *Criminal Code* provisions:**

| | |
|---|---|
| s. 164 | Warrant to seize obscene publications. |
| s. 199 | Warrant to search pertaining to gaming offences. |
| s. 256 | Warrant to obtain blood samples in impaired driving cases. |
| s. 320 | Warrant to seize hate propaganda. |
| s. 395 | Warrant to search for precious metals (violates s. 8 CCRF). |
| s. 462.32 | Warrant to search and seize for property ordered forfeited as the result of its acquisition through an enterprise crime. |
| s. 492 | Seizure and disposal of explosives. |

***Controlled Drugs and Substances Act:***

| | |
|---|---|
| s. 11 | Search and seizure of drugs under warrant. Subsection (7) permits warrantless searches in exigent circumstances. |

**B.C. Legislation (fairly typical of provincial search provisions):**

***Liquor Control and Licensing Act:***

| | |
|---|---|
| s. 67 | Search and seize anywhere (other than a dwelling) without warrant. |
| s. 68 | Search a residence with warrant. |

***Offence Act:***

| | |
|---|---|
| s. 21 | Warrant to search and seize pertaining to provincial offences. |
| s. 22 | Telewarrant to search and seizure pertaining to provincial offences |

***Child, Family and Community Service Act:***

| | |
|---|---|
| s. 17 | Authorizes entry of premises or vessels with judicial authorization to apprehend a child believed to be in need of protection. |

***Firearm Act:***

| | |
|---|---|
| s. 4 | Search without warrant persons and conveyances for firearms violations. |

***Wildlife Act:***

| | |
|---|---|
| s. 93 | Search without warrant persons, conveyances, shops, public markets, storehouses, garages, restaurants, hotels, eating houses and camps for wildlife or fish obtained in violation of the Act. |

that the accused take a Breathalyzer test under the authority of the *Criminal Code*. The accused accompanied the officer to the police station where a sample of breath was provided. At no time was the accused informed of a right to retain and instruct counsel. This was not too surprising. The Supreme Court of Canada had earlier decided in *Chromiak v. R.* (1979) that a person who had been given a Breathalyzer demand was not legally detained, and therefore the right to counsel did not arise at that time.[49] However, in the intervening years, the *Charter of Rights and Freedoms* had come into force. In *Therens*, the Supreme Court ruled that under the *Charter*, the definition of detention must change. Indeed, when an officer requests that a person provide a breath sample, the request contains a sufficient level of psychological pressure to comply with the demand so that courts will infer a detention has occurred. Any "demand or direction which may have significant legal consequences and which prevents or impedes access to counsel" made by an agent of the state will amount to detention. As a result, the rights delineated in section 10 of the *Charter* are triggered by the reading of the Breathalyzer demand. Among these rights are the right to be informed of the right to counsel. Since this right to be informed was violated, the Court turned its attention to the issue of remedy, and found that the exclusion of the Breathalyzer evidence was the most appropriate remedy in the circumstances. However, it was not until a subsequent case that the Supreme Court of Canada clearly articulated a rationale for allowing or not allowing evidence obtained in violation of a *Charter*-protected right into court in accordance with section 24(2) of the *Charter*.

The landmark case delineating the test for the exclusion of evidence under section 24(2) of the *Charter* was *R. v. Collins* (1987).[50] Ruby Collins had been tackled in a bar and subjected to a forceful choking and search of her mouth by drug squad officers who believed that she was carrying narcotics in a balloon in her mouth. Carrying drugs in a balloon in the mouth is a common tactic employed by drug dealers, since they can easily swallow any incriminating evidence upon being approached by a police officer. In fact, Ruby Collins did not have drugs in her mouth, but rather they were eventually found in a balloon in her hand. At her trial and subsequent appeals, the courts found that the police lacked the necessary reasonable grounds to conduct the search, and accordingly, her rights to be secure against unreasonable search or seizure, under section 8 of the *Charter*, were violated. In the Supreme Court of Canada, the main issue centred on whether the evidence found on her person should be admitted or excluded in accordance with section 24(2) of the *Charter*.

In deciding to exclude the evidence and acquit Collins, the Court set out a test for assessing whether the admission of evidence would bring the administration of justice into disrepute. The factors in the test are the following:

1. Would admission of the evidence affect the fairness of the trial? This factor has recently received considerable further attention, as we shall soon see.

2. How serious is the *Charter* violation? A flagrant or serious violation tends to lead towards exclusion, whereas a technical violation, a violation committed inadvertently, a violation motivated by the urgency of the situation, or a violation committed in good faith tend towards admission of the evidence.

3. What effect would "excluding" (as opposed to admitting) the evidence have on bringing the administration of justice into disrepute? A trivial violation resulting in the police finding real evidence establishing a very serious offence would lead to a conclusion that excluding the evidence would cause greater disrepute being brought to the public's perception of the administration of justice than would result from admission of the evidence.

## Discoverability Doctrine

In many cases, the evidence obtained through a *Charter* violation will clearly be excluded on the basis of section 24(2); however, the police investigation (through which the evidence was obtained) may have proceeded in other directions as a result of information gleaned through the illegally obtained evidence, and the police may in fact have uncovered additional evidence, obtained through legitimate means, which is sufficient in itself or in conjunction with other legally obtained evidence to support a conviction. However, a question may arise as to whether the evidence derived from the originally tainted evidence should be admitted, or excluded, due to the evidence being tainted by the illegality of the original evidence.

One of the most famous cases in Canadian criminal law dealt with just such an issue. In 1968, John Wray was interrogated about the murder of Donald Comrie, a 20-year-old gas station attendant who was killed while working for Knoll's Service Station, located east of Peterborough. Wray had been asked by Inspector John Lidstone of the Ontario Provincial Police to accompany him to the station to discuss his activities on the day of the shooting. Upon arriving at the station, Lidstone asked John Wray if he would submit to a polygraph test. Claiming that he had nothing to hide, Wray agreed. Lidstone had already arranged for John Jurems, a private detective from Toronto, to administer the test in his own office. When Wray arrived at Jurems's office, he was not informed that he did not have to take the test nor that Inspector Lidstone would be listening in on the questioning; however, over a five-hour period, Jurems and Lidstone took turns questioning Wray using fairly sophisticated interrogation techniques, and at one point a polygraph test was administered. Eventually, Wray succumbed to Jurems's questioning.

Jurems: Okay, tell us what happened.
Wray:   I went in...
Jurems: You went in, talk a little louder, John.
Wray:   I went in there.
Jurems: Yeah.
Wray:   To Knolls'.
Jurems: Yes, you went in to Knoll's yeah.
Wray:   And the boy —
Jurems: Which boy?
Wray:   There's only one boy.
Jurems: Just the boy that was shot. Yeah, what happened?
Wray:   He came out.
Jurems: Talk a little louder, John.
Wray:   He came out.
Wray:   And asked me what I wanted.
Jurems: He asked you what you wanted.
Wray:   And I told him to open the till.
Jurems: And told him to open the till. Was it closed?
Wray:   Yes.
Jurems: And what did he say?
Wray:   He said, all right.
Jurems: He opened the till, yeah.
Wray:   And then he — he gave me the money.
Jurems: He gave you the money. Well, what the hell did you shoot him for?
Wray:   It was an accident.
Jurems: It was an accident. Sure, you showed it on your check it was an accident.
        All the reactions you gave me when I asked you was the shooting an
        accident, you said, yes, it was an accident. Well, what the hell is wrong
        with that? All they are going to charge you with... You went in there, your
        intentions weren't to do any harm to the man. Where is the gun now?
Wray:   I don't know exactly.
Jurems: Well, where did you drop it, on the way home?
Wray:   No, eh?
Jurems: On the way to Toronto?
Wray:   Yes.
Jurems: Around Oshawa?
Wray:   No.
Jurems: Where?
Wray:   Near Omemee someplace.
Jurems: Where?
Wray:   Omemee.

Jurems: Omemee, in the ditch?
Wray: No.
Jurems: Where?
Wray: In the swamp.
Jurems: In the swamp. Could you, could you show the police where it is?
Wray: Yes.
Jurems: Now you're talking like a man. Jesus Christ, John, because you got to live with it all your life, man, oh, man, you'll never make it if you a person sleeps [sic], hasn't it been bothering you?
Wray: Yes.
Jurems: Have you been sleeping well?
Wray: Yes, fairly well.
Jurems: But it bothers you. A person never lives it down. Now when, now I'll call in the — the Inspector there and you can tell him what happened, okay. Will you tell him?
Wray: Yes.

Inspector Lidstone entered the interview room and informed Wray that he was being charged with murdering Donald Comrie. Wray agreed to show him where the rifle was located. The inspector contacted his office only to find that a lawyer had been retained by Wray's family to represent him, and that this lawyer wanted to speak to Wray. Concerned that such a contact might well result in Wray ceasing his co-operation and refusing to reveal the location of the rifle, Lidstone did not call the lawyer or inform Wray of the lawyer's interest in the case. Within minutes, Wray and the police left the office and headed for the swamp where Wray identified the place where he had disposed of the gun. They searched unsuccessfully for the rifle; however, the next morning the search resumed and a hunting rifle was discovered. A test conducted at the Toronto Centre of Forensic Science revealed that the hunting rifle was indeed the gun that killed Donald Comrie.

At trial, the confession was readily excluded due to inducements offered by the interrogators; however, the central issue in the case rapidly developed into whether the fact that Wray had led police to the murder weapon could be admitted. Although the case was decided well before the implementation of the *Charter*, the trial judge opted to exclude the evidence since its admission would be unfair to the accused given the unacceptable police interrogation. Wray was acquitted. Although the Court of Appeal agreed with this ruling, the Supreme Court of Canada overturned its verdict and ordered a new trial. The top court ruled that even though the confession itself might be inadmissible, the fact that Wray led the police to the real evidence, and the gun itself, should be admitted as long as it was relevant to an issue in the trial. As a result of admitting this derived evidence, Wray was subsequently convicted of murder and sentenced to life in prison.

The *Charter of Rights and Freedoms* has changed the rules of the game in the courtroom. An example of this is found in *R. v. Burlingham* (1995).[51] In 1985, Terrence Burlingham was being questioned by the police about two murders. While he confessed to the first, the police continued to question him with respect to the second murder committed at the same time and in a similar manner to the first. The police interrogated Burlingham for four days, utilizing manipulative techniques. During this interrogation, Burlingham stated that he would not speak without a lawyer present. In response, the police denigrated the integrity of defence counsel, and offered Burlingham a short-fuse plea bargain, whereby they would charge him with only second-degree murder if he identified the location of the gun. However, the police said the deal was only good for the weekend, but the defence counsel was not available during this time. The accused finally gave in, despite a warning from another defence lawyer not to talk to the police. Burlingham confessed to the second killing, took the police to the murder site, and told them where he had thrown the murder weapon. The next morning, Burlingham also told his girlfriend that he had informed the police about where he threw the murder weapon. Later that day, the police informed him that the deal did not consist of accepting a plea to second-degree murder, but rather that they would allow him to plead not guilty to first-degree murder.

During Burlingham's trial for the second murder, the trial judge excluded the confession due to the violation of Burlingham's right to counsel. However, the Court admitted the fact of the gun being found, and Burlingham's statement to his girlfriend that he had informed the police of the location of the weapon. He was convicted of first-degree murder. His appeal to the B.C. Court of Appeal was dismissed. On further appeal to the Supreme Court of Canada, the Court addressed the issue of the admissibility of the derived evidence. The Supreme Court indicated that the evidence of the gun and the statement to the girlfriend should both have been excluded since they were derived from the initial *Charter* breach involving the violation of the accused's right to counsel, and would not have been discovered without this initial *Charter* breach.

Speaking for the majority, Iacobucci J. stated, "I find that the derivative real evidence, the gun, *would not* have been found but for the information improperly obtained through the s. 10(b) [right to counsel] breach." The statement to the girlfriend was also ruled to be derived evidence: "even though the statement may not have been 'caused' directly by the breach, it was certainly made as a result of that breach." Later, he notes "he would have had nothing to say to Hall [the girlfriend] had he been duly advised of his constitutional rights."

The test for determining whether such derived evidence should be admitted is centred on the issue of **discoverability**. Would the police have inevitably discovered the evidence without the violation of the accused's rights? In the *Burlingham* case, the majority concluded that the police would not have discovered the gun without the initial violation of the accused's *Charter* rights. Indeed, the gun was at the bottom of the frozen Kootenay River, and only the accused knew of its whereabouts. Neither would the accused have made the inculpatory statement to his girlfriend had the initial impermissible questioning not occurred: "He would have had nothing to say to Hall had he not been improperly conscripted to provide evidence against himself in the first place by the police." Nor did the police have an independent line of investigation under way that would have uncovered the tainted evidence in question. "Given that no satisfactory indication has been given that, on a balance of probabilities, this evidence would have been found regardless of the unconstitutionally obtained information, it is to be excluded...."

## *The Fruit of the Poisoned Tree Doctrine*

Just as **illegally seized evidence** cannot be used in a trial, neither can evidence that *derives* from an illegal seizure be used. The *Burlingham* case articulated a new principle for assessing whether evidence affects the fairness of a trial. This potentially far-reaching principle may be called the **fruit of the poisoned tree doctrine**. Complex cases developed after years of police investigation may be ruined if defence lawyers are able to demonstrate that the prosecution's case, no matter how complex, was originally based on a search or seizure that violated a basic *Charter* right. In such cases, it is likely that all evidence would be declared "tainted" and become useless.

Canadian courts have addressed the admissibility of derived evidence in the context of whether it affects the fairness of the trial. This issue is connected to the first part of the test developed in *R. v. Collins* for determining admissibility of evidence under section 24(2) of the *Charter*. Where the defence can show that "but for" the actions of the police in violating the accused's *Charter* rights, the evidence would never have been discovered, then the trial judge is required to exclude this evidence from the proceedings since it would adversely affect the fairness of the trial.

This approach to dealing with derived evidence may be viewed as a moderate approach balancing individual rights with the need for social order. The evidence in *Burlingham* would never have been discovered without the *Charter* violation, and therefore the evidence was excluded. The flip side of the coin is that in cases where the Crown can show that the same evidence, on a balance of probabilities, would have been discovered inevitably without the *Charter* violation, the evidence will be ruled admissible.

Although there has been no relevant Canadian case law, this issue arose in the United States in a case resolved by their Supreme Court: *Nix* v. *Williams* (1984).[52] The *Nix* case had its beginnings in 1969 when Robert Anthony Williams was convicted of murdering a 10-year-old girl, Pamela Powers, around Christmas time. Although Williams had been advised of his rights, detectives searching for the girl's body were riding in a car with the defendant when one of them made what has since come to be known as the "Christian burial speech." The detective told Williams that, since Christmas was almost upon them, "the Christian thing to do" would be to give Pamela's body a decent burial, rather than it having to lay in

**discoverability** A test applied to determine whether derived evidence obtained following a *Charter* violation should be admitted. Admission may result if the Crown can show that the police probably would have discovered the evidence regardless of the *Charter* violation.

**illegally seized evidence** Evidence seized in violation of a *Charter*-protected right or freedom. Most illegally seized evidence is the result of police searches conducted without a proper warrant, or of improperly conducted interrogations.

**fruit of the poisoned tree doctrine** A legal principle that excludes from introduction at trial any evidence later developed as a result of an originally illegal search or seizure.

a field somewhere. Williams relented and led detectives to the body. However, because Williams had not been reminded of his right to have a lawyer present during his conversation with the detective in the car, the Supreme Court overturned Williams's conviction. The Court said that the detective's remarks were "a deliberate eliciting of incriminating evidence from an accused in the absence of his lawyer."[53]

In 1977, Williams was retried for the murder, but his remarks that led detectives to the body were not entered into evidence. The discovery of the body was itself used, however, prompting another appeal to the Supreme Court based on the argument that the body should not have been used as evidence since the body was discovered due to the illegally gathered statements. This time the U.S. Supreme Court affirmed Williams's conviction, holding that the body would have been found anyway, since detectives were searching in the direction where it lay when Williams revealed its location. The *Nix* case, as it was finally resolved, is said to have created the "inevitable discovery exception" to the U.S. **exclusionary rule**. In cases such as *Wray* or *Burlingham*, where it can be shown that the police were about to begin dredging the relevant part of the river or the swamp in question, having come across the location by some legitimate means, the resulting evidence, i.e., the discovery of the murder weapon, although obtained through an improperly elicited confession, would nonetheless remain admissible.

**exclusionary rule** The understanding, based on Supreme Court precedent, that incriminating information must be seized according to constitutionally sound procedure, or it may not be allowed as evidence in criminal trials.

## Conscriptive versus Non-conscriptive Evidence

In 1997, the Supreme Court of Canada further clarified the test for exclusion of evidence established in *R. v. Collins*. In determining whether admission of the evidence would adversely affect the fairness of the trial, a court now requires that the evidence in question be determined as "conscriptive" or "non-conscriptive." This distinction was clearly articulated in *R. v. Stillman*.[54]

Stillman was the last person seen with a murder victim while she was still alive. The victim's body was found in a river. The autopsy revealed that she had been killed by a blow to the head, and that there was semen in her vagina and a bite mark on her abdomen. Stillman was arrested for murder. Under threat of force, the police took bodily samples from the accused, including hair, pubic hair, and teeth impressions. The police also surreptitiously obtained bodily samples from mucous in a tissue left behind in a washroom garbage can by the accused during a break in interrogation. Although the accused had retained counsel, all of the above samples were collected after the lawyer had left. The fact situation in *Stillman* would not likely arise today given amendments to the *Criminal Code* that facilitate the police obtaining the type of evidence in question.

Stillman was released without being charged; however, once the lab results on the DNA and odontology analysis were received, Stillman was rearrested. At trial and on appeal, the defence raised issues concerning the search and seizure of samples and impressions, and the admissibility of the evidence. At trial, the evidence was admitted in its entirety, and the accused was convicted of first-degree murder. The Supreme Court of Canada decided that the determination of admissibility, beginning with an assessment of the impact on trial fairness, requires a court to classify the evidence as either "conscriptive" or "non-conscriptive," based on the manner in which the evidence was obtained. The Supreme Court held:

> If the evidence, obtained in a manner that violates the Charter, involved the accused being compelled to incriminate himself either by a statement or the use as evidence of the body or of bodily substances it will be classified as conscriptive evidence.... On the other hand, if the evidence, obtained in a manner that violates the Charter, did not involve the accused being compelled to incriminate himself either by a statement or the use as evidence of the body or of bodily substances it will be classified as non-conscriptive evidence.

The Court also noted that where the evidence is found to be non-conscriptive, its admission will not typically render the trial unfair, and therefore the court should move on to the second branch of the test developed in *R. v. Collins* and assess the seriousness of the violation. On the other hand, where the evidence is conscriptive in nature, a court should then determine whether the evidence would have been discovered without the *Charter* violation (as in *Burlingham*). Where the accused has been compelled to participate in the creation or discovery of the evidence, and where it would not have been discovered by the police through other investigation methods, then this evidence would adversely affect the fairness of the trial, and it must be excluded.

## Problems with Precedent

Although the cases dealing with the exclusion of evidence for a *Charter* violation have evolved significantly since the earliest cases under the *Charter*, even the first cases showed the problems with precedent concerning police powers. The *Therens* case demonstrates the power of the Supreme Court in *enforcing* what we have called the "rules of the game." It also lays bare the much more significant role that the Court plays in rule creation. Until the *Therens* case was decided, law enforcement officers had little reason to think they were acting in violation of basic rights. Common practice had not required that they inform suspected impaired drivers that they could contact a lawyer before taking a breath test. Typically, a suspected impaired driver was either released to a friend or took a cab ride home. Alternatively, a suspected impaired driver would be temporarily housed in a "drunk tank" overnight, since releasing this person would be the same as releasing an intoxicated person into the public. Under most provincial liquor legislation, an intoxicated person in public should be arrested and detained until he or she sobers up. The rule that resulted from *Therens*, requiring police to advise drivers being given a Breathalyzer demand about their right to retain and instruct counsel, was a new one, and it would forever alter the enforcement activities of police officers. Yet the *Therens* case was also retroactive, in the sense that it was applied to Therens himself.

There is a problem in the way in which our system generates and applies principles of fair process, which may be obvious from our discussion of the *Therens* case. The problem is that the present appeals system, focusing as it does upon the "rules of the game," presents a ready-made channel for the guilty to go free. There can be little doubt that Therens had violated the *Criminal Code*. The Breathalyzer evidence clearly implicated him in the offence with which he was charged. Yet he escaped punishment because of the unconstitutional behaviour of the police—behaviour that, until the Supreme Court ruling, had not been viewed as anything but legitimate.

Even if the police knowingly violate the principles of fundamental justice, which they sometimes do, our sense of justice is compromised when the guilty go free. Famed U.S. Supreme Court Justice Benjamin Cardozo (1870–1938) once complained, "The criminal is to go free because the constable has blundered."

Students of criminal justice have long considered three possible solutions to this problem. The first solution would be to suggest that rules of fundamental justice, especially when newly articulated by the courts, should be applied only to future cases, but not to the initial case in which they are stated. The justices in the *Therens* case, for example, might have said, "We are creating a definition of the term 'detention' based upon our realization in this case. Police officers are obligated to use it as a guide in all future searches. However, insofar as the guilt of Mr. Therens is concerned, it will be decided under rules of evidence existing at the time, and we will let whatever decision results stand."

A second solution would be to punish police officers or other actors in the criminal justice system who act illegally, but not allow the guilty defendant to escape punishment. This solution would be useful in applying established precedent where officers and officials had the benefit of clearly articulated rules and should have known better. Under this arrangement, any officer today who intentionally violates constitutional guarantees might be suspended, reduced in rank, docked pay, or fired. If the police conduct itself constitutes a crime, then the officer should be charged, as well as the accused in the case.

A third possibility would be to allow the Supreme Court to address more theoretical questions involving issues of fundamental justice, by way of a reference. Concerned police supervisors and officials could ask how the Court would rule "if...." As things now work, the Court can only address references forwarded by the federal or provincial cabinets. Perhaps an expansion of the reference power would answer more questions about current or proposed police practices before they result in litigation.

The obvious difficulty with these solutions, however, is that they would substantially reduce the potential benefits available to defendants through the appeals process and, hence, would effectively eliminate the process itself. The expansion of the reference power may also result in an already overworked court being subjected to even greater demands.

## A Move Towards Crime Control?

Professor Don Stuart, an ardent critic of recent Supreme Court of Canada case law, has identified a number of cases that tend to show that the recent decisions of the Supreme Court of Canada have opted for crime control values over those of due process.[55]

Early *Charter* cases dealing with the section 8 protection from unreasonable search or seizure had asserted that the section protects an individual's reasonable expectation of privacy, for example, *Hunter* v. *Southam*. In the 1996 decision of *R.* v. *Edwards*,[56] the top court refused to hold that a suspected drug possessor had a privacy interest in his girlfriend's apartment. Accordingly, a search of her apartment in apparent violation of section 8 of the *Charter* (the right to be secure against unreasonable search or seizure) did not give rise to a violation of the accused's rights. In the subsequent case of *R.* v. *Lawrence and Belnavis*,[57] the same court held that a passenger in a vehicle normally has no privacy interest in a vehicle that belonged to someone else. In *R. v M.(M.R.)*,[58] the Supreme Court of Canada held that students in schools have a diminished expectation of privacy, to the extent that school authorities are permitted to search students suspected of drug trafficking without the need for a warrant. In other words, our right to be free from unreasonable search and seizure is a right not to have our privacy invaded by police or other government searches, but only where our expectation of privacy is a reasonable one. In addition to an apparent lack of willingness on the part of the Supreme Court to find violations of the right to be free from unreasonable search or seizure, Stuart indicates that the recent cases have also frequently resulted in the admission of evidence even where a *Charter* breach is established.

If the police acted in good faith, the search occurred outside of the accused's home, or the offence is serious, Professor Stuart argues that the evidence is likely to be admitted against the accused. While advocates of public order would argue that these are welcome changes to the Supreme Court's approach to balancing individual rights and the need for public protection, advocates of individual rights are wary that these changes signal a fundamental shift back to the pre-*Charter* approach in the courts.

## The Plain View Doctrine

**plain view** A legal term describing the ready visibility of objects that might be seized as evidence during a search by police in the absence of a search warrant specifying the seizure of those objects. In order for evidence in plain view to be lawfully seized, officers must have a legal right to be in the viewing area and must have cause to believe that the evidence is somehow associated with criminal activity.

Police officers have the opportunity to begin investigations or confiscate evidence, without the need for a warrant, based on what they find in **plain view** and open to public inspection. The plain view doctrine was stated in the New Brunswick Court of Appeal case of *R.* v. *Ruiz* (1991).[59] This principle involves a common-law power that can be applied in a situation where the police are lawfully in a location from which they can view a particular area. The officer must discover the incriminating evidence "inadvertently," without prior knowledge of the location of the evidence. Additionally, it must be immediately apparent to the police that the items they observe pertain to a crime. Since this power permits the police to seize the suspicious object, as Joan Brockman and V. Gordon Rose indicate, the power does not really entail a power to search, but rather a power to seize.[60]

Common situations in which the plain view doctrine is applicable include emergencies such as crimes in progress, fires, and accidents. A police officer responding to a call for assistance, for example, might enter a residence intending to provide aid to an injured person and find drugs or other contraband in plain view. If so, the officer would be within his or her legitimate authority to confiscate the materials and effect an arrest if the owner of the substance could be identified.

The plain view doctrine applies only when the police see something under legal circumstances—that is, in places where the police have a legitimate right to be, and typically only if the sighting was coincidental. Similarly, the incriminating nature of the evidence seized must have been "immediately apparent" to the officers making the seizure.[61] If officers conspired to avoid the necessity for a search warrant by helping to create a plain view situation through surveillance, duplicity, or other means, the doctrine would likely not apply.

## Emergency Searches of Property

Certain emergencies may justify a police officer in searching a premises, even without a warrant. Recent amendments to section 487.11 of the *Criminal Code* have resulted in such a

BOX 6.2

## Theory into Practice

## Canadian Law of Search and Seizure: The *Feeney* Case

In Canada, a peace officer has the statutory authority to search for and seize objects that may have been used in the commission of a criminal offence, or that will provide evidence with respect to such an offence. The key powers of search and seizure are included in section 487 of the *Criminal Code*. This section deals with the information required for the endorsement of a search warrant. Of course, the law on search and seizure in Canada became significantly more complicated with the introduction of the *Canadian Charter of Rights and Freedo*ms, particularly in light of section 8 of the Charter, which amounts to a constitutional protection against unreasonable search and seizure.

A relatively recent landmark decision by the Supreme Court of Canada highlights the complexity of this issue. In *R. v. Feeney* (1997), 115 C.C.C. (3d) 129 (S.C.C.), the Court allowed the accused's appeal on a murder conviction and excluded evidence obtained in violation of section 8 of the *Charter*. In this case, police entered Feeney's trailer, without grounds or a warrant. When they observed blood on him, the police arrested him for murder. The Court held that both the entry and arrest in *Feeney* were unlawful and violated the *Charter*.

This ruling created some confusion with respect to the enforcement of warrants and prompted some uncertainty in the police community about attempting to effect an arrest of a suspect in a dwelling house. In 1997, Parliament remedied the situation by enacting section 529.1 of the *Criminal Code*, which reads in part:

A judge or justice may issue a warrant ... authorizing a peace officer to enter a dwelling-house described in the warrant for the purpose of arresting or apprehending a person identified or identifiable by the warrant if the judge or justice is satisfied by information on oath that there are reasonable grounds to believe that the person is or will be present in the dwelling-house and that ... (b) grounds exist to arrest the person without warrant ...

This clarifies some of the procedural elements highlighted in *Feeney*. Warrants must have specific authorization for the police to enter a dwelling house for the purpose of arrest. The legislative amendments also provide a power for the police to enter and arrest in exigent circumstances without a warrant (s. 529.3):

... the peace officer may enter the dwelling-house for the purpose of arresting or apprehending a person, without a warrant ... if the peace officer has reasonable grounds to believe that the person is present in the dwelling-house, and the conditions for obtaining a warrant ... exist but by reason of exigent circumstances it would be impracticable to obtain a warrant."

Examples of exigent circumstances provided in the *Code* include (1) having reasonable grounds to suspect entry is necessary to "prevent imminent bodily harm or death" (s. 529.3(2)(a)) and (2) to "prevent the imminent loss or imminent destruction of evidence" (s. 529.3(2)(b)).

## QUESTIONS FOR DISCUSSION

1. What would be a "dwelling house" for the purpose of this, or related, circumstances?

2. Why does the *Charter* provide protection against search and seizure?

3. What would happen if a police officer with a warrant learned that the suspect was in a dwelling house other than the one identified in the warrant?

4. Note that a warrant may be dispensed with in "exigent circumstances." Can you think of other exigent circumstances, besides those mentioned in the *Code*, that would justify warrantless entry to arrest or apprehend?

Sources: Gold. A. (1997). *Annual Review of Criminal Law 1997* (pp. 14–15). Toronto: Carswell; Department of Justice, Feeney Amendments fact sheet, **canada.justice.gc.ca/en/news/nr/1997/feprs.html**.

search being called an exigent circumstances search or an **emergency search**. The newness of this amendment and the absence of case law on the matter makes it difficult to determine what types of searches can be justified under this provision:

**Where warrant not necessary.**

s. 487.11    A peace officer, or a public officer who has been appointed or designated to administer or enforce any federal or provincial law and whose duties include the enforcement of this or any other Act of Parliament, may, in the course of his or her duties, exercise any of the powers described in subsection 487(1) or 492.1(1) without a warrant if the conditions for obtaining a warrant exist but by reason of exigent circumstances it would be impracticable to obtain a warrant.

**emergency search**
A search conducted by the police without a warrant, which is justified on the basis of some immediate and overriding need—such as public safety, the likely escape of a dangerous suspect, or the removal or destruction of evidence.

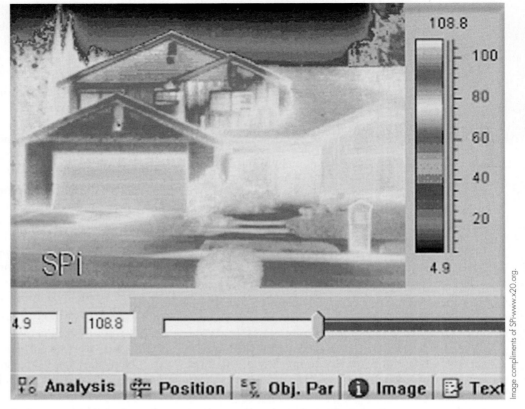

Image compliments of SPi-www.x20.org.

A photo created by a thermal imaging device. The photo shows "hot spots" in a suspected marijuana grower's home that might be produced by lights used to grow the plants indoors. In *R. v. Tessling* (2003), the Ontario Court of Appeal held that the police may not use such devices without a search warrant.

Perhaps some instruction may be obtained in this regard from recent U.S. developments. According to the Legal Counsel Division of the FBI, there are three threats that "provide justification for emergency warrantless action."[62] They are clear dangers: (1) to life, (2) of escape, and (3) of the removal or destruction of evidence. Any one of these situations may create an exception to the requirement of a search warrant. Where emergencies necessitate a quick search of premises, however, law enforcement officers are responsible for demonstrating that a dire situation existed that justified their actions. Failure to do so successfully in court, will, of course, taint any seized evidence and make it unusable.

In *R. v. Godoy*,[63] the Supreme Court of Canada recognized that a power exists for the police to enter a residence in order for them to investigate an interrupted 9-1-1 call. The common-law duty of the police to preserve life is engaged when an apparently distressed 9-1-1 caller is cut off. In *Godoy*, when the police arrived at the place from which the call originated, they were denied entry by a male occupant of the home. The police forced entry of the apartment in order to locate the caller and determine the reason for her call to 9-1-1. The Court found this forced entry to be a justifiable use of police powers in the circumstances.

## ARREST

Police officers seize not only property, but also persons—a process we refer to as an "**arrest**." Most people think of arrest in terms of what they see on popular television crime shows. The suspect is chased, subdued, and "cuffed" after committing some loathsome act in view of the camera. Some arrests do occur that way. In reality, however, most instances of arrest are far more mundane.

**arrest** Taking a suspect into physical custody by authority of law, usually for the purpose of charging the person with a criminal offence. Technically, an arrest occurs whenever a person's freedom to leave is curtailed by a law enforcement officer.

An arrest, and the decision to enforce it, typically evolves as the situation between the officer and suspect develops. The situation usually begins with polite conversation and a request by the officer for information. Only when the suspect tries to leave, and tests the limits of the police response, may the suspect discover that he or she is really in custody.

An arrest that follows the questioning of a suspect is probably the most common type of arrest. When the decision to arrest is reached, the officer has concluded that a crime has been committed and that the suspect is probably the one who committed it. The presence of these mental elements constitutes the reasonable grounds needed for an arrest. Reasonable grounds are the basic minimum requirements for an arrest under any circumstances.

In *R. v. Storrey*,[64] the Supreme Court of Canada commented on the need for the police to have reasonable grounds in order to effect an arrest. Clearly, this requirement imposes on the police a need to consider more than personal hunches about the guilt of a suspect before making an arrest. The *Criminal Code* requires that an arresting officer have subjective reasonable grounds on which to base the arrest. Those grounds must, in addition, be objectively justifiable. That is to say, a reasonable person placed in the position of the officer must be able to conclude that there were indeed reasonable grounds for the arrest. On the other hand, the police need not demonstrate more than reasonable grounds. Specifically, they are not required to establish a *prima facie* case for conviction before making an arrest.[65]

These requirements seem to support earlier case law that ruled that the police have the power to arrest if they believe a person is "apparently" committing an offence. These appearances must also be readily apparent to a neutral observer in the same position as the police officer. Simply acting on a hunch will not satisfy the need for reasonable grounds for arresting a suspect. However, the police need not be satisfied that a basic case can be made out against the suspect before acting.

Arrests may also occur when the officer comes upon either a crime in progress or an evolving disturbance. Such situations often require apprehension of the offender to ensure the safety of the public. Most arrests made during such volatile circumstances are based, as we will soon see, on the police officer's power to arrest for a "breach of the peace" rather than for a specific offence, which may be relatively minor or non-existent at the time of the arrest. In fact, the *Criminal Code* does not allow arrest for a minor offence such as a summary conviction offence unless it is committed in the presence of an officer. In any event, crimes in progress clearly provide the reasonable grounds necessary for an arrest.

The fact that both statute law and common law govern police powers of arrest, e.g., search and seizure, makes it difficult to ascertain the precise nature of police powers in Canada. Both the public at large, and the police in the performance of their duty, find it also difficult to comprehend the full extent of the existing statute law, and even more so, the immense body of case law that governs the scope of police powers. As the Law Reform Commission of Canada notes:

> The absence of statutory guidance in certain areas of police powers means that police and suspects are often uncertain of their rights and duties. It is only through lengthy and costly litigation that greater certainty is provided in these areas and, then, only with respect to the specific fact situation before the court.[66]

A complete understanding of the nature and extent of police powers of arrest demands an analysis of both the statute law and the case law governing police practice.

The *Criminal Code* and some provincial legislation outlines arrest powers. While provincial legislation varies from place to place, the *Criminal Code* provisions provide uniformity nationwide for some of the major arrest powers exercised by the police. However, since one of the most frequently exercised arrest powers is found under provincial legislation, these too must be addressed.

The *Criminal Code* arrest powers have evolved from the English notion that the police are members of the public, with the rights and obligations incumbent on all members of the public.[67] However, the police are members of the public specifically charged with enforcing the law. As such, the structure of the *Criminal Code* is understandable because the *Code* provides powers of arrest available to everyone. The Code also provides additional powers that are available only to the police. Accordingly, the police powers are an extension of the individual's powers of arrest.

RCMP 1992-009(A15)

Police officers seize not only property, but also persons—a process we refer to as an "arrest."

# Defining Arrest and Detention

The definition of arrest is elusive.[68] The *Criminal Code* is silent on the definition of an arrest; however, Canada's courts have applied a liberal definition. In *R. v. Whitfield* (1970),[69] the Supreme Court of Canada adopted the definition of arrest outlined in *Halsbury's Laws of England*:

> Arrest consists of the actual touching of a person's body with a view to his detention. The mere pronouncing of words of arrest is not an arrest, unless the person sought to be arrested submits to the process and goes with the arresting officer. An arrest may be made either with or without a warrant.[70]

The Law Reform Commission of Canada has taken this definition to imply that police in Canada can effect an arrest in one of two ways: "(i) touching with a view to detention, even where the suspect may not submit voluntarily; or (ii) stating that the suspect is under arrest where the suspect submits."[71] These two methods of effecting an arrest are consonant with the view advanced by Roger Salhany,[72] who reviewed the English and Canadian case law dating back to the eighteenth century.

Distinguishing between an arrest and a detention is, at times, a difficult task. The Law Reform Commission of Canada turned its attention to the dicey problem of defining "detention":

> There is a good deal of truth in the common sense observation that in ordinary usage, "detention" seems to connote a broad range of limitations on liberty from the relatively short-lived, trivial and unofficial on the one hand, to the official imposition of a period of incarceration on the other. The common law, of course, did not countenance any interference with individual liberty other than through lawful arrest. Forms of lawful detention short of arrest are thus creatures of statute. The common thread binding these categories of detention, from the most trivial to the most intrusive, is the notion that the restraint on one's liberty or freedom of movement is compulsory, not voluntary.[73]

A person who voluntarily co-operates with the police by inviting them into his or her home to conduct an interview,[74] or who voluntarily accompanies the police to the police station in order to answer police questions[75], is not considered in law to be detained. The case law appears to support Allman's conclusion that "... there is no presumption that every citizen being asked questions by the police is detained."[76] Clearly, the police have a right to question all witnesses and suspects in conducting an investigation.[77] Canadian courts have recently gone so far as to justify short-term detention in circumstances not justifying an arrest so that the police can begin their investigation. This so-called "investigative detention" constitutes a significant inroad into individual liberty.

Determining whether a person has been detained by the police is crucial in Canadian law, since certain rights are granted to persons arrested or detained by the police. In particular, an accused is entitled to reasons for the arrest or detention, and to the right to retain and instruct counsel. The following list of factors is used in determining whether a person being questioned at a police station by the police should, in law, be considered to be detained:

1. The precise language used by the police officer in requesting the person to come to the police station and whether the person was given a choice or expressed a preference that the interview be conducted in the police station rather than at his or her home;

2. Whether the accused was escorted to the police station by a police officer or came himself or herself in response to a police request;

3. Whether the accused left at the conclusion of the interview or whether he or she was arrested;

4. The stage of the investigation; that is, whether the questioning was part of the general investigation of a crime or whether the police had already decided that a crime had been committed and that the accused was the perpetrator or was involved in its commission, and the questioning was conducted for the purpose of obtaining an incriminating statement;

5. Whether the police had reasonable and probable grounds to believe the accused had committed the offence;

6. The nature of the questions, whether they were questions of a general nature designed to obtain information, or whether the accused was confronted with evidence pointing to his guilt;

7. The subjective belief by an accused that he or she was detained, although relevant, is not decisive because the issue is whether he or she reasonably believed that he or she was detained. Personal circumstances relating to the accused such as low intelligence, emotional disturbance, youth, and lack of sophistication are circumstances to be considered in determining whether he or she had a subjective belief that he was detained: *R. v. Moran* (1987);[78] *R. v. Voss* (1989).[79]

## Arresting Offenders Without Warrant

### The Criminal Code

The *Criminal Code* provides the powers of arrest, with and without warrant, applicable to all criminal offences. The availability of these powers varies, depending upon the type of offence and the legal status of the person who is endeavouring to effect the arrest.

The *Criminal Code* sets out powers in section 494 that allow any person, whether or not the person is a peace officer, to arrest another person without warrant in different circumstances. First, if a person is found committing an indictable offence, he or she may be arrested without warrant by any other person:

s. 494. (1) Any one may arrest without warrant
    (a) a person whom he finds committing an indictable offence; or
    (b) a person who, on reasonable grounds, he believes
      (i) has committed a criminal offence, and
      (ii) is escaping from and freshly pursued by persons who have lawful authority to arrest that person.

    (2) Any one who is
    (a) the owner or a person in lawful possession of property, or
    (b) a person authorized by the owner or by a person in lawful possession of property, may arrest without warrant a person whom he finds committing a criminal offence on or in relation to that property.

(3) Any one other than a peace officer who arrests a person without warrant shall forthwith deliver the person to a peace officer.

A person who is not a peace officer may also arrest another person without warrant if he or she has reasonable grounds for believing the other person has committed a criminal offence and has escaped from, and is being freshly pursued by, persons with the lawful authority to make an arrest. Any person other than a peace officer who exercises his or her power to arrest under section 494 must deliver the person as soon as is reasonably practicable in the circumstances to a peace officer.[80]

In addition to the general power to arrest conferred on all persons under section 494, the *Criminal Code* provides additional arrest powers to peace officers. These powers are found in section 495. Note that the police are granted additional discretion to arrest under this section; however, this discretion is limited as a result of an amendment to this section brought about by the *Bail Reform Act* in 1970:

**Peace Officer Arrest Power**

(1)     A peace officer may arrest without warrant
    (a)   a person who has committed an indictable offence or who, on reasonable grounds, he believes has committed or is about to commit an indictable offence;
    (b)   a person whom he finds committing a criminal offence; or
    (c)   a person in respect of whom he has reasonable grounds to believe that a warrant of arrest or committal, in any form set out in Part XXVIII in relation thereto, is in force within the territorial jurisdiction in which the person is found.

(2)     A peace officer shall not arrest a person without warrant for
    (a)   an indictable offence mentioned in section 553,
    (b)   an offence for which the person may be prosecuted by indictment or for which he is punishable on summary conviction, or
    (c)   an offence punishable on summary conviction,
in any case where
    (d)   he believes on reasonable grounds that the public interest, having regard to all the circumstances including the need to
        (i)    establish the identity of the person,
        (ii)   secure or preserve evidence of or relating to the offence, or
        (iii) prevent the continuation or repetition of the offence or the commission of another offence,
may be satisfied without so arresting the person, and
    (e)   he has no reasonable grounds to believe that, if he does not so arrest the person, the person will fail to attend court in order to be dealt with according to law.

While section 494 generally confers the power to arrest for serious offences (indictable and hybrid) actually found in progress (finds committing), section 495 provides police officers more latitude to arrest without warrant for any indictable offence, including those offences that are completed (has committed), and offences that have not yet occurred (is about to commit). These powers allow the police officer to go beyond dealing with present-tense crimes and arrest for crimes that occurred in the past, and those that the police officer reasonably believes are about to occur in the immediate future.

The ability of the police to arrest under section 495 also encompasses a broader ability to deal with offences occurring at the moment. Under section 494, persons could only arrest for "indictable offences" found occurring. But under section 495, a peace officer can arrest a person found committing[81] any criminal offence, even a less serious summary conviction offence. A person must be found apparently committing a summary conviction offence for the peace officer to be able to make a valid arrest. A person is not liable to arrest under this section even if the peace officer has reasonable grounds to believe a summary conviction offence has been, or is about to be committed. In such circumstances, the offender, or potential offender, remains immune from police arrest.[82]

Section 495 contains the primary arrest power for peace officers. However, it also limits the ability of peace officers to exercise that power. Peace officers are directed by section 495(2) not to arrest persons for offences other than the more serious, purely indictable offences.

This subsection requires the police to refrain from arresting a suspect unless the "public interest" requires that the police arrest in the circumstances. Of course, if the police are dealing with a suspect in a serious indictable offence such as a murder, a robbery, or an aggravated sexual assault, the discretion to arrest is not fettered by section 495(2). Presumably, the public interest will always mandate an arrest in such circumstances. Should a peace officer opt to arrest the suspect, the law will not interfere with the exercise of the police officer's discretion.

Where a peace officer encounters an individual whom the officer believes should be compelled to attend court, arrest is clearly not always the best option for securing such attendance. Indeed, in the circumstances set out in section 495(2), arrest is prohibited. Where the offence is less serious (summary, Crown election, or within the absolute jurisdiction of a Provincial Court Judge), arrest must not occur unless the "public interest" requires arrest. This requirement arises in the following circumstances:

**F**  The accused will likely **fail** to appear in court, so arrest is necessary in order to secure the accused's attendance.

**I**  The **identity** of the accused remains a mystery to the police; accordingly, there is a need to arrest, at least until the accused's identity is secured.

**S**  There is a need to **secure** or preserve evidence, often arising where the police see a need to have the accused attend the police station in order to provide a sample of their breath in a case of suspected impaired driving.

**P**  There is a need to **prevent** the continuation or repetition of the offence, or to stop the accused from committing a new offence.

If the above criteria are satisfied, the public interest mandates that attendance in court be secured through alternative means.

The *Criminal Code* also provides arrest powers in circumstances that are not related to securing a person's attendance to deal with a particular offence at trial. Individuals and the police are granted special powers to arrest, not for an offence, per se, but where a situation is actually or potentially volatile. As with the power to arrest for particular offences, this additional power is granted not only to all individuals but also to peace officers. Such powers are found in sections 30 and 31, respectively, of the *Criminal Code*:

s. 30.  Every one who witnesses a breach of the peace is justified in interfering to prevent the continuance or renewal thereof and may detain any person who commits or is about to join in or to renew the breach of the peace, for the purpose of giving him into the custody of a peace officer, if he uses no more force than is reasonably necessary to prevent the continuance or renewal of the breach of the peace or than is reasonably proportioned to the danger to be apprehended from the continuance or renewal of the breach of the peace.

s. 31. (1)  Every peace officer who witnesses a breach of the peace and every one who lawfully assists the peace officer is justified in arresting any person whom he finds committing the breach of the peace or who, on reasonable grounds, he believes is about to join in or renew the breach of the peace.

(2)  Every peace officer is justified in receiving into custody any person who is given into his charge as having been a party to a breach of the peace by one who has, or who on reasonable grounds the peace officer believes has, witnessed the breach of the peace.

These sections do not create an offence of "breaching the peace"; they merely provide an arrest power. A person arrested under this power will generally be released shortly thereafter, once the police are satisfied that a breach of the peace will not recur. Police utilize this handy power very frequently; most patrol officers use it on a regular basis to deal with rapidly evolving situations calling for immediate action, often to prevent violence from occurring. Often, those engaging in, or those who have engaged in, a breach of the peace are driven some distance from the location of the breach and released to go about their business.

The courts have been reluctant to precisely define a breach of the peace. The lack of a definition presumably allows the police to rely on their power to deal with rapidly emerging, potentially difficult situations through arrest and to defuse a situation without worrying over the possibility that the courts may second-guess their decisions at a later date.

In *R. v. Lefebvre* (1982),[83] Wetmore J. noted the difficulty in defining a breach of peace: "the difficult line is between those matters of annoyance and nuisance in a public sense and those matters more serious, but falling short of a riot."[84] However, he accepts the definition outlined in the English case of *R. v. Howell* (1981):[85]

> We are emboldened to say that there is a breach of the peace whenever harm is actually done or is likely to be done to a person or in his presence to his property or a person is in fear of being so harmed through an assault, an affray, a riot, unlawful assembly or other disturbance.

This definition attempts to outline the scope of the breach of the peace arrest power without overly narrowing its scope. However, this definition envisions a fairly serious incident. Given that the exercise of the power to arrest without warrant entails denying a person's liberty, one can understand why a fairly high standard involving the potential for serious harm was accepted.

Conduct that amounts to a breach of the peace will often also amount to an offence under the *Criminal Code*. For example, section 175 creates an offence of "causing a disturbance," which captures many of the situations also covered by "breach of the peace." When someone causes a disturbance, the police may arrest that person for a breach of the peace, or arrest that person under section 495, provided the FISP grounds require an arrest. Often, the public interest will mandate an arrest to prevent the continuation or repetition of the offence.

While the *Criminal Code* provisions refer to breaches of the peace found in progress, the B.C. Court of Appeal has ruled that the arrest powers under the *Code* are supplemented by a common-law power to arrest without warrant, where a police officer honestly and reasonably believes that a breach of the peace will be committed in the immediate future.[86] Clearly, this arrest power shows that taking someone into custody for a breach of the peace is a preventive remedy rather than a process that would initiate a prosecution.

In *Lefebvre*, it was noted that, as a preventive remedy, persons arrested for breach of the peace should not be held for longer than 24 hours. However, there appears to be no reason why a person, so arrested, could not be made the subject of a peace bond requiring that person to "keep the peace and be of good behaviour."[87] Failure to comply with the peace bond leaves the person liable to imprisonment.

## Searches Incident to an Arrest

The Supreme Court of Canada has established a clear rule that police officers have the right to conduct a search of a person being arrested, and to search the area constituting

Detector dog sniffing for narcotics or firearms.

Department of National Revenue, Customs and Excise, Canada

the immediate surroundings of that person, in order to guarantee the safety of the police and the accused, to prevent the accused's escape, and to provide evidence against the accused: *Cloutier* v. *Langlois* (1990).[88] This rule holds even if the officer lacks reasonable and probable grounds to believe that the suspect possesses a weapon or evidence.

This "rule of the game" was recognized at least as far back as 1921 in *Gottschalk* v. *Hutton* (1921).[89] This rule became firmly established in other cases involving personal searches, such as *R.* v. *Morrison* (1987)[90] and *R.* v. *Miller* (1987).[91] However, it was the *Cloutier* case that clearly articulated the position of Canada's top court on the **search incident to an arrest** power. While the Court upheld the officer's right to conduct a search without a warrant for the officer's personal protection, and to use the fruits of such a search when it turns up evidence, the power to search does not impose a duty to search. The search must be for a valid objective or for a purpose related to the objectives of the proper administration of justice. The search power must not be used to "intimidate, ridicule or pressure" the accused in order to facilitate confessions. The search must not be carried out in an abusive fashion. The use of physical or psychological constraint should be in proportion to the objectives and the circumstances of the particular case.

The Court's decision in *Cloutier* clearly pertains to searches carried out on persons subjected to a valid arrest. Canadian law does not permit the police to frisk or conduct a "pat down" search of persons stopped on the street. While U.S. law permits the police to "stop and frisk" persons found in suspicious circumstances, Canadian law does not allow this.

In *R.* v. *Caslake*,[92] the police impounded a car belonging to a suspected drug offender at the time he was arrested. When the car was impounded, it was subjected to a search by the police, ostensibly to conduct an inventory of its contents in accordance with police policy. A search of the vehicle produced a sum of money and a quantity of marijuana, subsequently used as evidence at trial, resulting in a conviction. The Supreme Court of Canada held that the police may conduct a vehicle search that is incident to a lawful arrest, provided the vehicle is searched for one of the purposes outlined in *Cloutier*, as follows:

1. ensuring the safety of the police and the public;
2. protecting evidence from destruction; and
3. discovering evidence.

Although the vehicle in this case was searched according to the police inventory policy rather than for one of the above three grounds, the evidence was nonetheless ruled to be properly admissible for a number of reasons. The Court held that (1) the search was not particularly intrusive, (2) there is a diminished expectation of privacy in vehicles, (3) the search was carried out in good faith according to the police policy, (4) the police held reasonable and probable grounds to conduct the search, and (5) the *Charter* violation was not particularly serious.

## Detention Under Articulable Cause

In 1993, the Ontario Court of Appeal, in the case of *R.* v. *Simpson*,[93] clarified the basis upon which law enforcement officers, lacking reasonable grounds to arrest, may stop and briefly detain a person for investigative purposes. In *Simpson*, the Court ruled that the legitimacy of such a stop must be evaluated according to a "totality of circumstances" criterion—in which all aspects of the defendant's behaviour, taken in concert, may provide the basis for a legitimate stop. In this case, the defendant, Simpson, appeared suspicious to police because he had just left a suspected "crack house," getting into a vehicle parked in the driveway. The person sitting in the driver's seat of the car was a woman. Once the vehicle pulled out of the driveway and headed down the street, the police followed. After following the vehicle a short way, the officer put on his vehicle's flashing lights, directing the other vehicle to pull over. After stopping the vehicle, the officer ordered the two occupants out of the vehicle. Spotting a bulge in the pocket of Simpson's coat, the officer asked him to remove the object, which he did. The object was a small plastic bag containing cocaine. The officer testified that he did not have reasonable grounds to arrest the suspect prior to that time. He indicated that he stopped the vehicle in the hope of getting the occupants to explain themselves, hoping that they would trip themselves up and give him grounds to arrest.

While the trial judge allowed the evidence and convicted the accused of possession of cocaine for the purpose of trafficking, the Ontario Court of Appeal allowed the accused's

**search incident to an arrest** A warrantless search of an arrested individual that is conducted to ensure the safety of the arresting officer(s), the public, to prevent escape, and to secure evidence. Because an individual placed under arrest may be in the possession of weapons or aids to escape, courts have recognized the need for arresting officers to protect themselves and others by conducting an immediate and warrantless search of an arrested individual and the immediate surrounding area without the need for a warrant. Because evidence may be disposed of by a suspect, a power to search the arrestee and the immediate area for evidence also arises at the time of arrest.

appeal, acquitting him. However, the Appeal Court clearly recognized that the police retain a power derived from the common law that permits them to stop persons for investigative purposes, provided the circumstances are appropriate. The circumstances in this case were not appropriate. The court noted that:

> Where an individual is detained by the police in the course of efforts to determine whether that individual is involved in criminal activity being investigated by the police, that detention can only be justified if the detaining officer has some 'articulable cause' for the detention.[94]

The Court went on to draw on the American case law to suggest that the police must have "a number of objectively discernable facts," giving the detaining officer reasonable cause to suspect the suspect is involved in the type of criminal activity under investigation. A **suspicionless search**, or "hunch" based on "intuition gained by experience," is not enough. Accumulating facts for reasonable cause is the first step in looking at the "totality of the circumstances" that must be comprehensively assessed in determining if the detention is justified in the circumstances.

In 1996, in the case of *R. v. Lal,*[95] the B.C. Supreme Court indicated that an officer has the authority to stop a person for investigative detention. Two officers guarding a Vancouver home belonging to a member of a drug gang involved in ongoing altercations with a rival gang, stopped a unique car (an Acura NSX with a custom-ordered canary-yellow paint job) driven by a known member of the rival gang within a few blocks of the guarded residence. Officers stopped the vehicle and conducted a search, revealing a handgun. The accused was charged with carrying a concealed weapon and possession of a restricted weapon. The Court accepted the notion that the police had articulable cause to conduct the detention and search. The *Simpson* and *Lal* cases appear to create a power in the police to engage in an investigative detention; however, the scope of the power remains unclear. The *Lal* case appears to extend the power beyond merely detaining a suspicious person long enough to find out what is going on, and includes an authority to carry out a search of the person. This extension is indeed an expansion of police powers akin to the "stop and frisk" powers held by U.S. police, arising out of the ruling in *Terry* v. *Ohio*. While Canadian courts have been creating police powers in this regard, U.S. courts have been seeking to put limits on the "stop and frisk" powers of the police.

In a recent U.S. case, Timothy Dickerson, who was observed leaving a building known for cocaine trafficking, was stopped by Minneapolis police officers after they noticed him acting suspiciously. The officers decided to investigate further and ordered Dickerson to submit to a pat-down search. The search revealed no weapons, but the officer conducting it testified that he felt a small lump in Dickerson's jacket pocket, believed it to be a lump of crack cocaine upon examining it with his fingers, and then reached into Dickerson's pocket and retrieved a small bag of cocaine. Dickerson was arrested, tried, and convicted of possession of a controlled substance. His appeal, which claimed that the pat-down search had been illegal, eventually made its way to the U.S. Supreme Court.

The high court ruled that "if an officer lawfully pats down a suspect's outer clothing and feels an object whose contour or mass makes its identity immediately apparent, there has been no invasion of the suspect's privacy beyond that already authorized by the officer's search for weapons." However, in *Dickerson*, the Justices ruled, "the officer never thought that the lump was a weapon, but did not immediately recognize it as cocaine." The lump was determined to be cocaine only after the officer "squeezed, slid, and otherwise manipulated the pocket's contents." Hence, the Court held, the officer's actions in this case did not qualify under what might be called a "plain feel" exception. In any case, said the Court, the search in *Dickerson* went far beyond what is permissible under *Terry*—where officer safety was the crucial issue. The Court summed up its ruling in *Dickerson* this way: "While *Terry* entitled [the officer] to place his hands on [the] respondent's jacket and to feel the lump in the pocket, his continued exploration of the pocket after he concluded that it contained no weapon was unrelated to the sole justification for the search under Terry," and the search was therefore illegal.

## Vehicle Stops

Vehicles present a special law-enforcement problem. They are highly movable, and, when a driver or an occupant is arrested, the need to search the vehicle may be immediate. The

**suspicionless search**
A search conducted by law enforcement personnel without a warrant and without suspicion. Suspicionless searches are only permissible if based on an overriding concern for public safety.

police may stop a vehicle in a variety of contexts. Most provinces have motor vehicle legislation that (1) permits the police to stop a vehicle and demand that the driver show his or her licence and proof of insurance and (2) that permits the police to set up roadside breath checks or roadblocks in order to randomly stop vehicles to assess the sobriety of drivers.

The first significant Supreme Court case involving the question of whether random motor vehicle stops constitute an arbitrary detention in contravention of section 9 of the *Charter* was that of *R. v. Hufsky*,[96] in 1988. In the *Hufsky* case, the Court ruled that a fixed checkpoint established for the purposes of checking drivers' licences, insurance and registration, the mechanical fitness of vehicles, and driver sobriety, was an arbitrary detention infringing section 9 of the *Charter*. However, the practice was ruled to be justifiable under section 1 of the *Charter* given the importance of maintaining safety on the highways, and the limited nature and scope of the intrusion expressly authorized under the Ontario motor vehicle legislation. Two years later, in *R. v. Ladouceur*,[97] the limits of permissible vehicle stops were expanded to permit random roving vehicle stops, as long as they were made for the same purposes outlined in *Hufsky*. In *R. v. Mellenthin*,[98] the Supreme Court of Canada indicated that the police must confine the aims of their random vehicle stops, under the auspices of motor vehicle legislation, to vehicle and driving issues. The Court also noted that a visual inspection "into" the vehicle is legitimate for ensuring the safety and protection of those carrying out the check stops. However, in such circumstances, the vehicle stop amounts to a detention, wherein the accused typically feels compelled to comply with police questioning and, therefore, there will be no valid consent where, as in this case, the officer asked the driver to reveal the contents of a bag within the vehicle. A consent to disclose the contents of a bag in the car would only be valid if the accused was informed by the police of his or her right to refuse to reveal the contents. In *Mellenthin*, the Court excluded the evidence of drugs. The police officer had asked the driver to disclose the contents of a gym bag on the front seat of the car, without advising him that he was under no obligation to do so. When the bag was opened, drugs were revealed. This general approach to the limited scope of vehicle stops was recently affirmed by the Saskatchewan Court of Appeal decision in *R. v. Ladouceur*.[99] The Court held that a fixed checkpoint could only be used for legitimate motor-vehicle-related matters. It may not be used for other investigative purposes, such as looking for vehicles carrying contraband.

## THE INTELLIGENCE FUNCTION

The police role includes the need to gather information through the questioning of both suspects and informants. Even more often, the need for information leads police investigators to question potentially knowledgeable citizens who may have been witnesses or victims. Data gathering is a crucial form of intelligence, without which enforcement agencies would be virtually powerless to plan and effect arrests.

The importance of gathering information in police work cannot be overemphasized. Studies have found that the one factor most likely to lead to arrest in serious crimes is the presence of a witness who can provide information to the police. Undercover operations, neighbourhood watch programs, "crime stopper" groups, and organized detective work—all contribute information to the police.

## Informants

Information gathering is a complex process, and many ethical questions have been raised about the techniques that police use. Using paid informants, for example, concerns ethicists who believe that informants are often paid to get away with crimes. The police practice (endorsed by some prosecutors) of agreeing not to charge one offender in a group of offenders if he or she will "talk," and testify against the others, is another concern of students of justice ethics.

As we have seen, reasonable grounds are an important aspect of both police searches and legal arrests. The courts have consistently emphasized the need for the police to have reasonable grounds for believing a suspect has committed an offence, before powers of arrest will become available or before issuing a warrant for conducting a search. The case of *R. v. Debot* (1986)[100] analyzed the extent to which the information obtained from confidential informants can be used, and established a two-pronged test for deciding whether the information provided by an informant could be used to establish reasonable grounds:

- The totality of the surrounding circumstances permit a justice to verify the accuracy of an informant's allegation.

- The standard of reasonable probability is met.

This two-pronged test of *R. v. Debot* was intended to prevent the issuance of warrants on the basis of false or fabricated information. A mere statement by the police officer that he or she has been told by a reliable informer that, for example, a certain person is carrying on criminal activity, or that contraband can be found at a particular location, will not be sufficient basis for a justice to issue a warrant. The underlying circumstances that led the informer to this conclusion must be set out, so the justice can evaluate whether the necessary reasonable grounds exist. A justice must be satisfied that the grounds stated for obtaining a warrant are current, and that there is a "nexus" or connection between the grounds for believing that an offence has been committed, and that evidence of the commission of the offence will be found at the location the police wish to search: *R. v. Turcotte* (1987).[101]

Information provided by unnamed confidential informers will not be sufficient basis for issuing a warrant, where there is no evidence to substantiate the accuracy of the informers' information, no information about how the informers came upon their information, and no independent evidence to support their allegations: *R. v. Berger* (1989).[102]

The identity of informants may be kept secret if they have been explicitly assured of confidentiality by investigating officers, or if a reasonably implied assurance of confidentiality has been made. The Supreme Court of Canada has indicated in *Bisaillon* v. *Keable* (1983) and *R. v. Scott* (1990)[103] that a common-law privilege protects the identity of an informer, whereby the identity of the informer may only be revealed in the narrow circumstances of ensuring full answer and defence by an accused, or to challenge the validity of a search warrant. ("Full answer and defence" is a legal phrase that indicates the guaranteed right of an accused at the close of the Crown's case to present a defence in answer to the charge. This right is protected by sections 276(3)(a), 650(3), and 802(1) of the *Code*. In *R. v. Leipert* (1997),[104] the Supreme Court of Canada noted that the informer's identity may only be revealed in the challenge to a search warrant where this is essential to a fair trial.

## Police Interrogation

At common law, the police have a clear right to ask questions while conducting an investigation: *R. v. Bazinet* (1986).[105] However, no one is under an obligation to answer police questions, indeed we need not even identify ourselves when requested to do so: *Koechlin* v. *Waugh and Hamilton* (1957).[106] If a person refuses to answer police questions, the police must decide either to arrest the person if they already have the grounds to do so, detain the person if they have a reasonable suspicion based on articulable cause, or allow the person to walk away. Once arrested or detained, a person acquires certain informational rights under the *Charter*. The person must be given the reason for being held, and be informed of his or her right to retain and instruct counsel:

s. 10 Everyone has the right on arrest or detention
    (a) to be informed promptly of the reasons therefor;
    (b) to retain and instruct counsel without delay and to be informed of that right; and
    (c) to have the validity of the detention determined by way of *habeas corpus* and to be released if the detention is not lawful.

The courts have long held that strict rules apply for determining whether the incriminating statements that the accused makes to the police will be admissible against the accused at a subsequent trial. If a person says something to another person that is incriminating, and the other person recounts these statements later in court, then these statements are actually a form of hearsay. However, the common law has long held that an exception to the hearsay rule exists that justifies admitting such evidence as an admission or confession.

Admissions are statements that are adverse in interest to the accused's innocence. In essence, admissions are incriminating statements wherein the accused admits all or part of the case for the Crown against the accused. When the accused makes an incriminating statement to anyone, other than a person in authority, that person may be required to subsequently appear in court and recount the statement for the court. In such a way, if a suspect tells a neighbour, friend, or complete stranger that an offence was committed, that person can be brought into court to retell the story.

Where an admission is made to a person in authority, the common-law confession rule applies. This rule requires that strict conditions be attached to the admission of the statement in court. The general rule was succinctly stated in *Ibrahim* v. *The King*:[107]

> It has long been established as a positive rule of English criminal law that no statement by an accused is admissible in evidence against him unless it is shown by the prosecution to have been a voluntary statement in the sense that it has not been obtained from him either by fear of prejudice or hope of advantage exercised or held out by a person in authority.

While the term "person in authority" is a fairly broad concept, it is clear that a police officer will always be considered a person in authority, and therefore the confession rule applies in the context of the police questioning a suspect. The rule requires that any statement to the police, if it is to be admissible, must be free from "fear of prejudice or hope of advantage." In essence, the statement must be free and voluntary. It must not be the result of inducements such as promises of leniency or threats of harm (see Table 6–3).

## Operating Mind

Canadian courts have supplemented the Ibrahim Rule with a requirement that a confession, to be admissible, must be the product of an operating mind. In the first of two significant cases, *R.* v. *Ward*, (1979),[108] the Supreme Court of Canada upheld excluding a confession where the accused made the statement in a dazed state and could not recall the circumstances surrounding the statement. Ward had been involved in a car crash in which he was discovered unconscious. His female companion was found dead outside the vehicle. He was immediately revived at the scene, at which time he denied driving the car; however, a short while later and again at the hospital five or six hours later, he admitted to being the driver of the vehicle. At trial, facing a charge of criminal negligence, Ward indicated that he had no memory of what happened between being at a hotel prior to the accident and the afternoon or evening following the accident. A doctor who treated him at the hospital

---

BOX 6.3 **Theory into Practice**

**Public Interest and the Right To Privacy**

Police in the City of Guelph, Ontario, videotaped sexual activity in a public washroom. The defendants were charged and convicted of gross indecency. On appeal, they argued that the videotaping violated section 8 of the *Canadian Charter of Rights and Freedoms*, which guarantees freedom from unreasonable search and seizure. The Court dismissed the appeal and in their judgment included the following observations:

> In our opinion the appellant had no reasonable expectation of privacy. The police surveillance established that this public washroom had become the meeting-place for this group of men—for the practice of homosexual acts. The conduct offended s. 157 of the *Criminal Code*. Accordingly, there being no reasonable expectation of privacy on the part of either of the appellants, the electronic surveillance by video camera carried out by the police did not violate their rights under s. 8 of the *Charter*.

### QUESTIONS FOR DISCUSSION

1. Under what circumstances should there be a right to privacy?

2. What are other situations where a person's right to privacy may be reasonably limited by the state?

*Source: R. v. LeBeau and Lofthouse* (1988), 41 C.C.C. (3d) 163 (Ont.C.A.).

**TABLE 6–3** Examples of Threats and Inducements Rendering Confessions Inadmissible

***Threats:***

"It would be better for you if you told us what happened"

"You will be arrested if you do not tell us where the stolen goods are"

"You had better tell the truth"

"It is necessary to give an explanation"

***Inducements:***

A reply of "yes" to the suspect's question: "If I give a statement, will I be released?"

"The investigating officer, during his interrogation of the accused, told him that he believed that what the boys were saying was true, but that he wanted to help the accused, and the accused could help himself by speaking about the incidents. The accused did not ask what kind of help the officer meant, but proceeded to give a statement"

"I will do anything I can to help you out"

"You will get a light sentence if you confess"

Source: Salhany, R.E. (1997). *The Police Manual of Arrest, Seizure & Interrogation* (7th ed.). Toronto: Carswell. With permission of Carswell, a division of Thomson Canada Limited.

supported his argument by indicating that Ward was unable at that time to explain what had happened. Since his incriminating statements were not the result of an operating mind, the Supreme Court held that the statements were properly excluded at trial.

The operating mind requirement was further discussed in *R. v. Horvath* (1979).[109] In this case, Horvath, a suspect in killing his mother, voluntarily submitted to a polygraph test. The questioning lasted for four hours, during which numerous breaks occurred. During one of these breaks, while being watched by the police, Horvath admitted to himself out loud that he had killed his mother. He also admitted the killing under further questioning by the police. However, the trial judge refused to accept the confession after accepting the testimony of a psychiatrist that Horvath had been in a "hypnotic state" for much of the interview, this state being brought on by the skilful questioning of the police investigators. The Supreme Court of Canada accepted this explanation, ruling the evidence involuntary.

Interrogation not only must be free of coercion and hostility, but also it cannot involve sophisticated trickery designed to ferret out a confession. While interrogators do not necessarily have to be scrupulously honest in confronting suspects, and while the expert opinions of medical and psychiatric practitioners may be sought in investigations, the use of professionals skilled in psychological manipulation to gain confessions will be subject to close scrutiny by a trial judge.

While the above cases seem to mandate the exclusion of a confession that an accused makes while the accused is unaware of what he or she is saying, the Supreme Court of Canada appears to extend the operating mind concept a little further in relation to intoxicated persons. In *R. v. Clarkson* (1986),[110] the Court upheld excluding a woman's confession to murdering her husband because she was intoxicated when she confessed. Because she was intoxicated at the time of the act, she lacked the mental capacity to be aware of the consequences of making the statement.

## Informed Choice to Confess

A fairly recent ruling of the Supreme Court of Canada indicates that the assessment of the decision to confess should be subjected to even closer scrutiny than that required by *Ibrahim* and the "operating mind" cases. In *R. v. Whittle* (1994),[111] it was held that in addition to assessing whether the suspect had an operating mind, a trial judge must go on to determine the effect of the police conduct on the decision of the suspect to speak. If the police conduct deprived the suspect of making an informed and effective choice by reason of trickery, coercion, misinformation, or lack of information, then such a finding could lead to the exclusion of the incriminating statement.

The Supreme Court of Canada's most recent statement on the voluntariness of confessions is found in *R. v. Oickle*,[112] where the Court appeared to indicate a tolerance of police tactics that some could argue affect the voluntariness of a confession. The accused, who was an arson suspect, was given a polygraph examination by the police and was told that he had failed it. The police exaggerated the reliability of the results of this test. The police also promised psychiatric help, minimized the importance of the accused's confessing to multiple fires as opposed to just one, and threatened to interrogate the accused's fiancée during the interrogation of the accused. The majority of the court showed little concern for the police use of trickery and questionable tactics to obtain a confession.

## Jailhouse Informants

In 1990, the Supreme Court of Canada, in the case of *R. v. Hebert*,[113] threw a dampening blanket over the use of sophisticated techniques to gain a confession. Hebert was arrested on robbery charges, and after consulting with counsel, he told the police that he did not want to make a statement. He was placed in a cell, and an undercover police officer was placed in the same cell. Hebert made incriminating statements to the officer, not knowing his true identity. The Supreme Court noted that the accused has a right to silence under section 7 of the *Charter* and that where the accused indicates he or she is exercising his or her choice not to speak to the police, the authorities are prohibited from using subterfuge to interrogate the accused by eliciting statements against his or her wishes.

In the subsequent year, in *R. v. Broyles* (1991),[114] the Supreme Court of Canada extended the rationale in the *Hebert* case to cover the conduct of agents of the state, such as prisoners acting as police informers. Where such persons elicit information from their jailhouse companions who have asserted their right to silence, the subsequent statements will be in violation of section 7 of the *Charter*. Where a suspect offers incriminating statements to a jailhouse companion, without that companion eliciting the statement from the suspect, the use of the statement as evidence will not run afoul of section 7 of the *Charter*. The right to silence is not violated where a prison inmate who is not acting as an agent of the state goes to the police with incriminating statements overheard while the inmate was in the suspect's cell: *R. v. Gray* (1991).[115]

Where the suspect is not arrested or detained, the use of a "target plant" investigation technique appears to be legitimate. Such investigations involve the police posing as criminals, becoming friends with the target, and gaining his or her confidence. In such relationships, the undercover officer typically discloses details of criminal activity that he or she has engaged in and expects the target to do the same in return in order to prove the target's validity as a criminal. Such disclosures are then used directly against the offender in court, or they form the basis of further investigative inquiries. A number of provincial courts of appeal have approved the use of such tactics in recent years.[116]

### *Entrapment*

Both section 7 of the *Charter* and the common law prohibit the police from using entrapping tactics to capture suspected offenders. The rationale behind a prohibition on entrapment is a concern that the police may entice or procure people, who would otherwise not commit an offence, into offending. Numerous cases have arisen in this regard in the context of undercover operations in the area of drug enforcement. Catching drug dealers is a difficult task for various reasons. Unlike other crimes, the parties involved in drug transactions are consensual. Such so-called "victimless" crimes do not have victims or complainants calling the police to report offences. Also, all of the parties to drug transactions make a tremendous effort to ensure that the police do not find out that such transactions are occurring. The result is that police engage in proactive efforts to become involved in the trade themselves to a sufficient degree that they can generate enough evidence to obtain a conviction against suspected traffickers.

In *R. v. Mack* (1988),[117] the Supreme Court of Canada set a number of limits on police conduct with respect to such undercover tactics. (See Table 6–4.)

Permissible police behaviour with respect to catching offenders is limited to offering the party an opportunity to commit an offence. If at any time the police go beyond providing an opportunity and actually induce the commission of the offence, then this action will amount to entrapment. Additionally, the police are prohibited from providing an opportunity to persons whom the police do not reasonably suspect are already engaged in the type of criminal activity in question, unless the police are engaged in a "bona fide" inquiry. (See Table 6–5.)

### TABLE 6–4 Entrapment in Canadian Law: *R. v. Mack* (1988), 44 C.C.C. (3d) 513 (S.C.C.)

| | Providing an opportunity to commit an offence | Going beyond providing an opportunity and inducing the commission of the offence |
| --- | --- | --- |
| Police have reasonable suspicion that this suspect is engaged in criminal activity | not entrapment | entrapment |
| Police have no reasonable suspicion that this suspect is engaged in criminal activity; however, the police are engaged in a *bona fide* inquiry[1] | not entrapment | entrapment |
| Police have no reasonable suspicion that this suspect is engaged in criminal activity, and the police are not engaged in a *bona fide* inquiry[2] | entrapment | entrapment |

[1.] An example of a *bona fide* inquiry was identified by the court in *R. v. Barnes* (1991), 63 C.C.C. (3d) 1 (S.C.C.), wherein the police randomly asked people associated with an area of the city well-known for drug trafficking if those people were willing to sell drugs.
[2.] The absence of a *bona fide* inquiry will involve the police in the practice of "random virtue testing."

### TABLE 6–5 Inducing the Commission of an Offence: *R. v. Mack* (1988), 44 C.C.C. (3d) 513 (S.C.C.)

*Factors to be taken into account:*

1. The type of crime being investigated and the availability of other investigative techniques for the police detection of its commission.
2. Would an average person in the position of the accused have been induced to commit the offence?
3. The persistence and number of attempts made by the police before the accused agreed to committing the offence.
4. The type of inducement used by the police including deceit, fraud, trickery, or reward.
5. The timing of the police conduct, in particular, whether the police have instigated the offence or simply become involved in ongoing criminal activity.
6. Whether the police conduct involved the exploitation of human characteristics such as the emotions of compassion, sympathy, and friendship.
7. Whether the police appear to have exploited a particular vulnerability of a person such as a mental handicap or a substance addiction.
8. The proportionality of the police involvement as compared to the accused, including an assessment of the degree of harm caused or risked by the police, as compared to the accused, and the commission of any illegal acts by the police themselves.
9. Whether the police or their agents made any threats, implied or express, to the accused.
10. Whether the police conduct is directed at undermining other constitutional values.

In *R. v. Barnes* (1991),[118] the Court found that a "bona fide" inquiry was justification for the police in Vancouver to target a six-block area of the open-air Granville Mall for drug enforcement. The police randomly provided an opportunity for those associated with the area to engage in the drug trade. Prior to this operation, the police had discovered that a significant proportion of the city's drug arrests were made at this shopping mall. The reasonable suspicion of the police regarding the extent of the criminal activity occurring in this area separated this crackdown from "random virtue testing" that would not be condoned by the courts.

In recent years, undercover police operations took a new twist when the police began engaging in "reverse sting" operations. A reverse sting involves the police offering to deliver drugs to suspected drug purchasers, rather than attempting to purchase drugs from drug suppliers, which was the type of scenario encountered in *Mack*. Recent court criticism regarding such practices led the federal government to provide legislative guidance on the subject. The *Controlled Drug and Substances Act (Police Enforcement) Regulations* now provide exemptions for police to engage in reverse sting operations for drug enforcement. Under these regulations, the police may offer drugs for sale to potential purchasers without being considered to have unlawfully engaged in drug trafficking themselves. No doubt we will see case law in the near future addressing the legitimacy of such exemptions.

## The Right to Counsel

Section 10(b) of the *Charter* guarantees the right to retain and instruct counsel upon being arrested or detained. It also contains the right to be informed of that right. The Supreme Court of Canada ruled in *R. v. Manninen* (1987),[119] that two further duties are imposed on the police by section 10(b). These require:

- The detained or arrested person be given a reasonable opportunity to contact counsel if he or she wishes to do so.
- Suspend questioning until the accused has been given a reasonable opportunity to retain and instruct counsel.

In 1990, in the case of *R. v. Brydges*,[120] the Supreme Court of Canada interpreted section 10(b) to also mean that the police should inform the accused of any available legal aid or duty counsel system in the jurisdiction, including 24-hour access to free legal advice by telephone, if it exists.

---

BOX 6.4 **Theory into Practice**

## Individual Rights versus Group Interests: Police Spot Checks

The law that relates to motor vehicles in Canada impacts on a great number of people, because so many members of the public rely on cars and other vehicles for their work and leisure activities. Also, individuals who operate such vehicles are subject to federal and provincial legislation. There is a substantial public interest in reducing the number of persons who drive while impaired. The cost in human lives as a result of impaired driving is too high, and measures that address the incidence of drunk driving have strong public support.

Police departments have introduced spot checks to reduce impaired driving. Such programs allow an officer to stop a vehicle at random in order to determine the driver's sobriety. An officer can stop a vehicle without the officer having any grounds for the belief that the driver may be impaired. For example, the Metropolitan Toronto Police have operated a spot-check program since 1977. Programs such as RIDE (Reduce Impaired Driving Everywhere) are effective tools for combatting and controlling impaired driving.

In a series of Supreme Court of Canada cases, the use of "arbitrary" roadside checks for sobriety, while violating section 9 of the *Charter*, were upheld as constitutionally permissible under section 1 of the *Charter*. The courts have also ruled that roadside tests that help an officer determine someone's coordination are permissible under section 1 of the *Charter*. This section deals with those limits that may be justified in a free and democratic society.

*Sources: R. v. Dedman,* [1985] 2 S.C.R. 2; *R. v. Hufsky,* [1988] 1 S.C.R. 621; *R. v. Ladouceur,* [1990] 1 S.C.R. 1257; *R. v. Mellenthin,* [1992] 3 S.C.R. 615.

It is perhaps noteworthy that the police are not obligated under the *Charter* to inform a suspect of his right to remain silent. A suspect who exercises the right to counsel in a diligent manner will almost certainly be told by his or her legal counsel that he or she should not communicate with the police.

## Waiver of Rights by Suspects

Suspects in police custody may legally waive their *Charter* rights to retain counsel or remain silent through a *voluntary* "aware of the consequences" waiver. A waiver based upon an *awareness of the consequences* can only be made if a suspect has been advised of his or her rights, and was in a condition to understand the advisement. Where the suspect is intoxicated, the Crown is under a particularly heavy burden to establish the validity of the waiver: *R. v. Clarkson* (1986).[121] A suspect must be able to understand the consequences of not invoking the *Charter* rights. This understanding requires an awareness of the extent of his or her jeopardy. In the case of *R. v. Black* (1989),[122] the Supreme Court of Canada indicated that when the circumstances change while the suspect is in custody, and the extent of jeopardy has increased, the suspect must again be informed of his or her right to retain and instruct counsel and be given an opportunity to do so. In the *Black* case, the suspect was being held for an attempted murder, whereupon the victim died and the reason for the arrest of the suspect changed to murder. The Supreme Court ruled that a duty rests on the police at that point to re-inform the suspect of his or her right to counsel and give the suspect a reasonable opportunity to contact counsel before continuing questioning.

While the *Charter* gives an arrested or detained person the right to retain counsel, this right does not give him or her the right to free or state-funded counsel: *R. v. Matheson* (1994).[123] The Supreme Court of Canada ruled that governments are not obligated to provide a free lawyer to suspects; however, state agents must give detained persons a reasonable opportunity to contact counsel. During this time, they must refrain from eliciting incriminating information from the detained person. What constitutes a reasonable opportunity will depend on the specific circumstances and will be affected by the presence of duty counsel schemes in the relevant jurisdiction. The term during which police must "hold off" from questioning might extend to the time at which the local legal-aid office opens for business if there is no 24-hour-a-day legal-aid service or duty counsel available.

## Body Cavity and Strip Searches

Body cavity searches are among the most problematic for police today. "Strip" searches of convicts in prisons, including the search of body cavities, have generally been held to be permissible. The Ontario Court of Appeal in *R. v. Morrison* (1987)[124] indicated that the power of the police to search the person as an incident to a lawful arrest even justifies a strip search of an accused who has been placed under arrest for theft and possession of stolen property. However, police must ensure that they have reasonable and probable grounds necessitating a strip search that go beyond the grounds justifying an arrest. In *R. v. Golden* (2001),[125] the Supreme Court of Canada ruled that the only valid purposes for a strip search incidental to a lawful arrest are (1) to discover weapons in the detainee's possession, (2) to ensure the safety of the detainee, the police, or others, and (3) to discover evidence or to preserve and prevent its disposal. Strip searches should not be carried out as a matter of routine, and police must ensure that the searches are carried out in a reasonable manner. To protect the detainee's dignity, such searches should typically be carried out at the police station. Searches conducted at the border are permitted to be somewhat more intrusive than is tolerated in regular law enforcement since people crossing the nation's borders expect to be subjected to greater scrutiny. Judicial tolerance of increased levels of scrutiny at the border can be expected given the events of September 11, 2001.

The 1990 Supreme Court case of *R. v. Greffe*[126] focused on the issue of "alimentary canal smuggling," in which the suspect typically swallows condoms filled with cocaine or heroin and waits for nature to take its course to recover the substance.

In the *Greffe* case, a suspect believed to be a "balloon swallower" arrived in Canada. He was detained by customs officials, had his luggage searched, and was given a "pat-down" search by a customs agent. The suspect was not informed of his right to retain and instruct counsel, and was not informed of his right under the *Customs Act* to have the proposed search reviewed by a senior official or a justice of the peace. Having found no drugs, the customs officials turned the suspect over to the RCMP, who arrested him and informed him of his right to retain and instruct counsel without delay and that he need not say anything to them. The police told Greffe that he was being arrested on outstanding traffic warrants. He was informed that he would be taken to a hospital and subjected to a rectal exam. At the hospital, a doctor, using a sigmoidoscope, conducted the rectal exam and recovered two condoms containing nearly a quarter of a million dollars' worth of heroin. At his trial for possession of heroin for the purpose of trafficking, the accused was acquitted due to discrepancies in the testimonies and notes of the officers involved, and the spurious reason given to the accused at the airport that his arrest was based on traffic warrants, rather than the actual reason for arresting him, which was the suspicion of the police that he was importing heroin. Had proper procedure been followed by the officers involved, the rectal search would no doubt have been reasonable in the circumstances.

In *R. v. Monney* (1999),[127] the Supreme Court of Canada assessed the practice of customs agents holding suspected drug couriers until their bodily waste had been excreted and

---

BOX 6.5  **Theory into Practice**

**Public Interest and the Right to Privacy: Diminishing Protection Against Searches**

The right to privacy is a fundamental value protected by the *Canadian Charter of Rights and Freedoms*.[1] Most of us would probably agree that privacy is also a basic human need. Our legal system, on the other hand, has long recognized that the right to privacy must be limited in cases where individuals are reasonably suspected of having committed crimes. Arrest warrants, search warrants, and orders permitting electronic surveillance may be issued by courts if there are reasonable grounds that evidence will be found on a "credibly based probability." Canadian courts zealously protected the privacy interest during the *Charter*'s first decade. In recent years, however, the Supreme Court has rendered decisions that may be construed as backing away from the importance of individual privacy.

In *R. v. Edwards*, (1996),[2] the top court upheld a conviction against an accused drug trafficker. The drug evidence was found in the apartment of Edwards's girlfriend. The police had entered the apartment without a warrant, gaining entry through the accused's girlfriend's co-operation, which was obtained by a series of lies and half-truths. The police seized the drugs in the apartment. In upholding the admissibility of the drug evidence, the Court held that the accused had no reasonable expectation of privacy in his girlfriend's apartment because he was no more than a "privileged guest." As such, the right to be free from unreasonable search or seizure was not infringed by the police conduct.

In the second case, *R. v. M.(M.R.)* (1998),[3] the Court ruled that a high-school vice-principal could search a student suspected of drug dealing at a school dance with the police present. The Court also ruled that students have a "significantly diminished" expectation of privacy in the school environment. The position of trust in which school officials find themselves was used to support the holding that teachers and school administrators must be granted flexibility to deal with discipline problems at their schools. Standards for searches that are considered "reasonable" in a school setting are different from those for searches in other contexts. The Court ruled that the courts should typically defer to the judgment of school officials in determining whether they believed the officials had reasonable grounds to conduct a search of a student.

Both decisions in *R. v. Edwards* and *R. v. M.(M.R.)* were decried by civil libertarians, because they indicated a dangerous change in high court direction. The Supreme Court's new willingness to permit searches in circumstances falling short of the *Hunter* standard were criticized as an "unfortunate dilution" of section 8 protection, infringing on the rights of presumptively innocent citizens.[4]

## QUESTIONS FOR DISCUSSION

1. Can you think of any instances, other than those mentioned here, where a "compelling interest" might justify the search of persons where a diminished expectation of privacy may be construed to apply? If so, what might they be?

2. Do you think school searches should apply different standards than those applicable elsewhere? Why or why not?

---

[1]The right to "privacy" has been found to be the core value underlying the right to be secure from "unreasonable search or seizure," as protected by section 8 of the *Charter*. See *Hunter* v. *Southam Inc.*, [1984] 2 S.C.R. 145.
[2]*R. v. Edwards*, [1996] 1 S.C.R. 128.
[3]*R. v. M.(M.R.)*, [1998] 3 S.C.R. 393.
[4]Stuart, D. (1999). The Unfortunate Dilution of Section 8 Protection: Some Teeth Remain. *Queen's Law Journal*, 25, p. 65.

searched for drugs. The Court held that a passive "bedpan vigil" does not violate the right to be free from unreasonable search or seizure. While such a procedure may be embarrassing, the court ruled it was no more invasive than a strip search. Certainly, international travellers can be expected to welcome the adoption of such practices by customs agents over the use of rectal cavity examinations.

## Electronic Eavesdropping

Modern technology makes increasingly complex forms of communication possible. From fibre-optic phone lines, microwave and cellular transmissions, and fax machines, to computer communications involving modems and databases, today's global village is a close-knit weave of flowing information.

In 1974, the *Criminal Code* was amended, making it an offence to unlawfully intercept a private communication by electronic means. However, the legislation permitted such interceptions to be made in certain limited circumstances, most notably, where one of the two parties to a communication consents to the interception and in circumstances where judicial authorization has been obtained. The Supreme Court of Canada ruled in *R. v. Duarte* (1990)[128] that the interception of private communications by an agency of the state amounts to an unreasonable search and seizure where prior judicial authorization has not been approved. Accordingly, the one-party consent option has been eliminated as an investigative tool for the police. Recent amendments to sections 184.1, 184.2, and 184.4 of the *Criminal Code* permit wearing a body pack, or otherwise allowing for the interception of private communications with one-party consent where there is believed to be a risk of bodily harm to the undercover agent or others. (A body pack, or "wire," is an electronic voice transmission device that is taped to an undercover agent.) Information obtained from a body pack, where no warrant has been obtained, will not be admissible in court, except in limited circumstances where the offence in question arises out of an attack on the undercover officer.

To get a wiretap authorization, agents of the prosecutorial authorities, both federal and provincial, must typically apply to a superior court judge for authorization to eavesdrop with respect to certain listed serious offences. Such applications are supported by affidavits containing specific information establishing reasonable and probable grounds for the authorization being sought. Such authorizations must be in the "best interests of justice" and will only be allowed where it is established that other investigative tactics have been tried and have failed, or are unlikely to succeed, or are impractical due to the urgency of the situation.

## SUMMARY

The principles of individual liberty and social justice are the cornerstones of the Canadian way of life. Ideally, the purpose of the criminal justice system is to ensure justice while guarding liberty. Liberty and justice are dual threads that weave throughout the tapestry of the justice system—from the simplest daily activities of police on the beat, to the often complex and lengthy renderings of the Supreme Court of Canada.

For the criminal justice system, the question becomes "How can individual liberties be maintained in the face of the need for official action, including arrest, interrogation, incarceration, and the like?" The answer is far from simple, but it begins with a recognition of the fact that "liberty" is a double-edged sword, entailing obligations as well as rights. For police action to be "just," it must recognize the rights of individuals, while simultaneously holding citizens accountable to the social obligations defined by law.

# DISCUSSION QUESTIONS

1. Which Supreme Court decisions discussed in this chapter do you see as most important? Why? Are there any Supreme Court decisions discussed in this chapter with which you disagree? If so, which ones? Why do you disagree?

2. Do you agree with the theme of this chapter's summary, that "for police action to be just, it must recognize the rights of individuals, while simultaneously holding citizens to the social obligations defined by law"? What is the basis for your agreement or disagreement?

3. What do the *principles of fundamental justice* mean to you? How do you think we should try to ensure fundamental justice in our legal system?

4. According to an old saying, "The criminal is to go free because the constable has blundered." Can we afford to let some guilty people go free in order to ensure that the rights of the rest of us are protected? Is there some other (better) way to achieve the same goal?

# WEBLINKS

www.acjnet.org
### Access to Justice Network: Canadian Law and Justice
*ACJNet* is a resource site for Canadian justice and legal information and services, including legislation, people and organizations, publications, databases, and discussion forums on justice and legal issues.

www.culturalrenewal.ca/lex/lex-8.html
### Charter Violations and the Exclusion of Evidence
Summary and discussion of a Supreme Court of Canada decision concerning search and seizure.

www.gov.pe.ca/photos/original/section24.pdf
### The Supreme Court of Canada on Excluding Evidence Under s. 24(2) of the Charter
A detailed digest of Supreme Court of Canada case law pertaining to the exclusion of evidence for violations of *Charter*-protected rights and freedoms, prepared by Gerard Mitchell.

www.rcmp-learning.org/fr-welc.htm
### Powers of Arrest Exercise
This website is designed to facilitate the training of RCMP officers. By linking through "Learning for Jobs" to "General Duty Police Investigator" then "Resources/Activities" followed by "Online Resources," you can scroll down an alphabetical list to find "Powers of Arrest Exercise." This allows you to test your understanding of police arrest powers. Answers to the scenario questions are provided on the website.

www.cppa-acpp.ca/index-english.htm
### Canadian Professional Police Association
This website is for the newly formed national police association composed of the Canadian Police Association (CPA) and the National Professional Police Association (NAPP).

# Adjudication

*To hear patiently, to weigh deliberately and dispassionately, and to decide impartially; these are the chief duties of a judge.*

—Albert Pike (1809–1891)

*A jury consists of 12 persons chosen to decide who has the better lawyer.*

—Robert Frost

The well-known British philosopher and statesman Benjamin Disraeli (1804–1881) once defined justice as "truth in action." The study of criminal case processing by courts at all levels provides perhaps the best opportunity available to us from within the criminal justice system to observe what should ideally be "truth in action." The courtroom search for truth, which is characteristic of criminal trials, pits the resources of the accused against those of the state. The ultimate outcome of such procedures, say advocates of our adversarial-based system of trial practice, should be both truth and justice.

Others are not so sure. British novelist William McIlvanney (1936–) once wrote: "Who thinks the law has anything to do with justice? It's what we have because we can't have justice." Indeed, many critics of the present system claim that courts at all levels have become so concerned with procedure and with sets of formalized rules that they have lost sight of truth.

The chapters that make up this section of *Canadian Criminal Justice Today* provide an overview of Canadian courts, including their history and present structure, and examine the multi-faceted roles played by both professional and lay courtroom participants. Sentencing, the practice whereby judges impose sanctions on convicted offenders, is covered in the concluding chapter of this section. Whether Canadian courts routinely uncover truth and therefore dispense justice, or whether they are merely locked into a pattern of hollow procedure which does little other than mock the justice ideal, will be for you to decide.

# The Courts

Canapress/Jonathan Hayward

## KEY CONCEPTS

criminal court system
jurisdiction
original jurisdiction
appellate jurisdiction
provincial/territorial
  court systems
appeal
Chief Justice
dispute resolution centres

federal court system
judicial review
reference power
first appearance
recognizance
surety
plea
plea bargaining

## KEY CASES

*R. v. Morales*
*R. v. Pearson*

The Supreme Court of Canada sits in Ottawa, hearing cases of national importance, including many cases dealing with the operation of the criminal justice system.

# INTRODUCTION

Between the often-enthralling police quest for suspects and the sometimes hopeless incarceration of offenders stands the**criminal court system**. Courts at all levels dispense justice on a daily basis and work to ensure that all official actors in the justice system carry out their duties in recognition of the rule of law.

At many points in this book, and in three specific chapters (Chapter 6, Policing: Legal Aspects; Chapter 10, Probation, Parole, and Community Corrections; Chapter 12, Prison Life), we take a close look at court precedents that have defined the legality of enforcement efforts and correctional action. In Chapter 3, Legal Foundations of Criminal Justice, we explored the law-making function of courts. This chapter describes the Canadian court system at both the provincial and federal levels. Then in Chapter 8, we will look at the roles of courtroom actors—from lawyers to victims, and from jurors to judges—and examine each step in a criminal trial.

**criminal court system**
The court system that entails lower-level provincial trial and appellate courts, and the Supreme Court of Canada.

# CANADIAN COURT HISTORY

Two court systems coexist in Canada today: (1) provincial/territorial courts and (2) federal courts. Figure 7–1 outlines the structure of today's federal court system, while Figure 7–2 diagrams the provincial/territorial court system. This court system, which is a dual court system in some aspects, but unified in others, is the result of a historical balance between the need for a strong influence from the central government to ensure consistency, predictability, and stability, and the need for regional autonomy, due to the vast geographic and cultural differences that characterize Canada. The two major influences on Canada's court structure are that of Britain, which is unitary in nature, and the United States, which is a dual court system. The lines of precedent and the lines of appeal run vertically in unitary court systems. Appeals typically ascend to a single court at the top of the court hierarchy. Dual court systems are more autonomous, with lines of precedent and appeal terminating within a given court system, allowing other court systems to operate independently.

The last 135 years have seen a slow ebbing of the central government's power relative to the power of the provincial governments. Ever since Confederation, however, federal courts have not heard cases involving offences that make up the bulk of the criminal law. Indeed, at the time of Confederation, there was no federal court, as we know it today, and the Supreme Court of Canada did not come into existence until 1875, more than 10 years after Confederation. Even though the federal government has exercised its power over the making of criminal law, by enacting a criminal code shortly after Confederation, it has been left to the provincial/territorial courts to try criminal law cases, with very few exceptions.

This chapter describes both federal and provincial/territorial court systems in terms of their historical development and current structure. Because the large majority of criminal cases originate within the provincial courts, we turn our attention first to them.

## Provincial Court Development

Each of the original British North American colonies had its own court system for resolving disputes, both civil and criminal. As early as 1752, Nova Scotia had turned its "General Court," composed of the governor-in-council, into a Supreme Court of Judicature, mirroring the role played by the Royal Courts of Justice in England. The General Court had been a combination of legislature and court that made laws, held trials, and imposed sentences.[1] (Governor-in-council now refers to the cabinet or executive

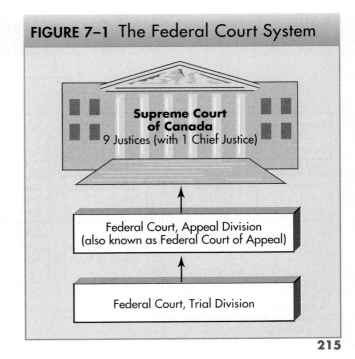

**FIGURE 7–1 The Federal Court System**

**Supreme Court of Canada**
9 Justices (with 1 Chief Justice)

Federal Court, Appeal Division
(also known as Federal Court of Appeal)

Federal Court, Trial Division

of government, composed of either a premier or the prime minister and all the cabinet ministers of either a provincial or the federal government. Pre-Confederation, the governor-in-council was the Governor of the Crown colony and his cabinet ministers. It is this body that doubled as a court in early Nova Scotia.) By the late 1700s, most of the Crown colonies had established a superior Court of Judicature, exercising civil and criminal jurisdiction.[2]

Quebec fell to the British conquest in 1760; however, it was not until the Royal Proclamation of 1763 that the common law of England was introduced in Quebec. A Court of King's Bench was established, exercising authority over both criminal and civil jurisdiction in the colony. In 1774, the passage of the *Quebec Act* by the British Parliament restored French civil law to Quebec, retaining the criminal law of England in that colony as in all others. Civil and criminal jurisdiction were divided between the Court of Common Pleas for civil cases and the Court of King's Bench, which had jurisdiction over criminal matters. The *Constitution Act* of 1791 split the colony of Quebec into Upper and Lower Canada, a recognition of the large number of English settlers in the region that became Upper Canada. Upper Canada's *Judicature Act* of 1794 created a centralized King's Bench court with both civil and criminal jurisdiction, while Lower Canada retained its more decentralized system.[3]

While the Maritime provinces and central Canada had established their court systems during the late 1700s, the West would not see court systems established until the next century due to the lack of significant colonization prior to that time. In 1853, Governor Douglas established a Court of Common Pleas on Vancouver Island. In 1858, Matthew Baillie Begbie, known as the "hanging judge," began functioning as a superior court judge on the mainland of British Columbia. With the political union of Vancouver Island and the mainland in 1866, the Supreme Court of British Columbia was formed.[4] Superior courts were not created in the Prairie provinces until after Confederation.[5]

In the Prairies, the Hudson's Bay Company held a royal Charter from 1670 until just before Confederation. This royal Charter gave the company the authority to make and enforce laws for the region that comprised a huge portion of what is today Central and Western Canada. In this area, the Hudson's Bay Company exerted tremendous influence over everyone in the region. The company's "chief factors" had the authority to conduct trials and punish offenders at the company's trading posts.[6] Typically, fines were imposed for most infractions. Serious offences were dealt with by sending the offender back to Upper or Lower Canada, or in some cases, England, for trial and punishment. The high cost of sending offenders to England for trial resulted in the termination of this practice and a reliance on conducting trials in British North America from 1803 onward.[7]

## FIGURE 7–2 Provincial/Territorial Court Systems

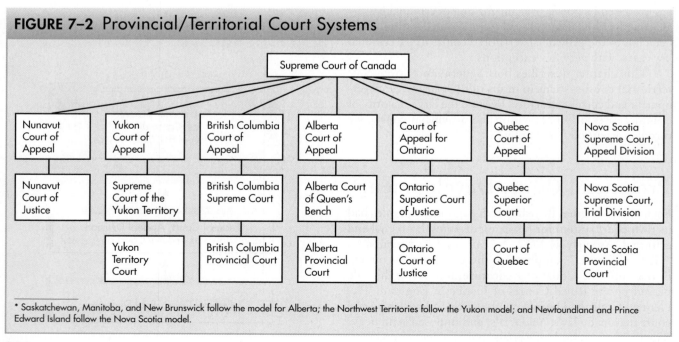

* Saskatchewan, Manitoba, and New Brunswick follow the model for Alberta; the Northwest Territories follow the Yukon model; and Newfoundland and Prince Edward Island follow the Nova Scotia model.

Each of the Crown colonies, other than Quebec, developed a court system that borrowed heavily from the court system prevailing in England.[8] Typically, each colony had a superior court analogous to the English High Court. On the next level down was a county or district court with more limited **jurisdiction**, both territorially and with respect to subject matter. At the bottom of the hierarchy were inferior courts whose jurisdiction was confined to minor criminal matters and small civil claims. Such courts were staffed by justices of the peace or magistrates.

Historically, justices of the peace fulfilled a multitude of roles, making them responsible for adjudicating minor matters in court, supervising police action through the issuance of warrants, and also performing local government functions such as tax collecting. Indeed, higher-ranking officers in the Northwest Mounted Police were also designated as justices of the peace, thereby permitting them to hold court with respect to minor matters arising in the territories being policed by the force.[9] In contrast to the higher courts, justices and magistrates in the lower courts were typically laypersons with no legal training. This situation slowly began to change, as evidenced by the introduction of a bill to the Nova Scotia Legislative Assembly in 1824, requiring that appointees to the inferior courts be "professional men," thereby mandating that lawyers supervise even the lowest courts in the colony.[10]

As time went by, the role of the justice of the peace eventually began to centre on pretrial activities such as conducting bail hearings and issuing warrants to the police, while magistrates became more professional and more tightly allied with the trial function. Also eventually, the magistrate's court would evolve in the late twentieth century into the provincial court,[11] a tribunal charged with the vast bulk of the trial work in Canada's criminal justice system.

While the higher courts were always friendly environments for lawyers, the same could not be said at times with respect to the inferior courts in years gone by. D. Owen Carrigan recounts a story of one police magistrate who worked in Toronto from 1877 until 1920:

> Lawyers citing legal precedents particularly annoyed him. According to the learned magistrate they wasted his time. "Why read me another judge's opinion?" he asked. "If it agrees with my view, what is the object? If it takes a different view why should I follow another man's mistakes?"[12]

Prior to Confederation, all Canadian colonies had established fully functioning court systems. The practice of law, however, was substantially inhibited by a lack of trained lawyers. Despite such an obstacle, the courts developed along the lines of British courts, developing complex rules and procedures, mirroring the intricacies of English common law and procedure.[13] Also prior to Confederation, courts in Canada were typically trial courts, or courts of **original jurisdiction** (which can be defined as the lawful authority of a court to hear cases that arise within a specific geographic area, or which involve particular kinds of law violations). Courts with **appellate jurisdiction** (that is, the lawful authority of a court to review a decision made by a lower court) were virtually absent. The few appeals that did arise were dealt with by the executive branch of government, or in the most serious cases, the Privy Council in England.[14]

By the time of Confederation, most colonies in Canada had established a two- or three-tiered court system of (1) inferior courts of limited jurisdiction, using justices or magistrates, (2) intermediate trial courts of limited jurisdiction, such as a county or district court (absent in some jurisdictions), and (3) superior courts of general jurisdiction, such as a King's Bench or Supreme Court.

## Provincial/Territorial Court Systems From Confederation

The passage of the *British North America Act* of 1867 (since renamed the *Constitution Act, 1867*) provided for the structure of courts under the new Dominion of Canada. The Act by no means represents a blueprint for a court structure, but rather provides for the court structure prevailing in Canada today. Under this Act, Canada's court structure developed with both unitary and dual characteristics.

Section 92(14) provided that the provinces were responsible for the "Constitution, Maintenance, and Organization of Provincial Courts, both of Civil and of Criminal Jurisdiction ...," thereby allowing the provinces to retain authority for setting up a general

**jurisdiction** The territory, subject matter, or persons over which lawful authority may be exercised by a court or other justice agency, as determined by statute or constitution.

**original jurisdiction** The authority of a given court over a specific geographic area or over particular types of cases. We say that a case falls "within the jurisdiction" of the court.

**appellate jurisdiction** The lawful authority of a court to review a decision made by a lower court.

system of courts. Under this authority, provinces typically maintained their magistrates courts, county or district courts, and superior courts, including an appellate division or court in some cases. However, the Act interestingly declined to grant the provinces the authority to select the judges for the higher levels of courts created by the provinces. In sections 96 to 100, the federal government was given responsibility for appointing and paying the judges of the "Superior, District, and County Courts in each Province ... ." This left the provinces with the limited power of judicial appointment, confined to the lowly magistrates courts.

Upon Confederation, the creation of "criminal law" fell to the federal government under section 91(27) of the *Constitution Act, 1867*. However, the enforcement of that law fell to the provinces under the authority of the "Administration of Justice" in section 92(14). This authority was taken to include not only a significant provincial role in law enforcement but also responsibility for conducting criminal prosecutions in court. Such prosecutions were carried out in the **provincial/territorial court systems**, since these systems were deemed to be the venue for criminal trials under the plain wording of section 92(14).[15]

In recent years, magistrates courts have been renamed as provincial courts in all provinces, for example. Proponents of court reform sought to unify redundant courts, which held overlapping jurisdictions. The most significant development in this regard has been the amalgamation of intermediate trial-level courts into a superior court in each province. This amalgamation has left the county court as a piece of Canada's history. The provincial superior court is now composed of two courts, a trial court and an appellate court, or in some cases, the same result is achieved by having a trial division and an appellate division of the superior court.

Even after Confederation, appeals were still being taken from the top levels of the provincial court structure to the Judicial Committee of the Privy Council in England. This committee was a court composed of judges typically drawn from the Law Lords in the House of Lords. (The House of Lords is composed of Lords Spiritual [senior bishops], Lords Temporal [hereditary peers and appointed life peers], and Law Lords [appointed senior judges].) Shortly after Confederation, the federal government created a Supreme Court for the country; however, for most of Canada's history, one could appeal the Supreme Court's decisions to the Privy Council, and even bypass the Supreme Court of Canada in favour of a direct appeal to the Privy Council. Indeed, it was not until 1949 that appeals to the Privy Council from Canada were brought to an end, with the last Canadian case being decided by that body in 1959.[16]

## Provincial/Territorial Court Systems Today

The provinces and territories today have similar court systems; however, individual differences do exist. Within the constitutional structure mandated by the *Constitution Act, 1867*, a move has been under way to simplify provincial court structures. However, the push towards amalgamation has brought forward the issue of whether we would be better off with a single unified criminal court, reducing what were once three levels of trial court into a single trial court responsible for all criminal trials. This change would alter the prevailing trial court system that utilizes inferior (provincial) courts for many criminal trials, but preserves the superior (Supreme or Queen's Bench) court as the exclusive venue for trying the most serious cases,[17] by having one court responsible for all trials. Nunavut is the first jurisdiction in Canada to adopt a unified single-level trial court.

The court reform movement is still ongoing today. Ontario has been particularly active in trying to reform its court system in order to have one trial court and one appeal court.[18] A major impediment to this reform has been the limitation imposed by the constitutional division of responsibility over courts set out in the *Constitution Act, 1867*. While the provinces have control over their provincial court structures, the federal government retains the authority to appoint all judges of the higher courts in the provinces. At present, the inferior provincial court judges are appointed by the province; however, the superior court judges, at both the trial and appellate levels, are appointed by the federal government. The question is then "Who would appoint the judges to a unified trial court?" This power would require either a constitutional amendment granting the judicial appointment power to one level of government, or a measure of federal-provincial co-operation on such matters, the likes

**provincial/territorial court systems** Provincial judicial structures. Most provinces have at least three court levels, generally referred to as lower level provincial courts, superior courts, and a provincial court of appeal.

of which are unlikely in this era of competition between the federal and provincial governments over various aspects of authority.

All jurisdictions in Canada provide for a final avenue of appeal to the Supreme Court of Canada. Regardless of whether the issue to be resolved is one of federal or provincial law, the appeal may ultimately be resolved in this top national court. In this way, Canada's court system has a uniquely unitary flavour for a federated country. The central national Supreme Court of Canada, with its federally appointed judges, is the ultimate arbiter of issues arising in any part of the country.

# Provincial Courts

Provincial courts are where criminal cases begin. Provincial courts conduct arraignments, set bail, take pleas in most cases, oversee Crown disclosure, oversee the selection of mode of trial, conduct preliminary hearings, and conduct many trials. (We will discuss each of these separate functions in more depth below.) If the defendant is found guilty at this level (or pleads guilty), this lowest of trial courts imposes sentence. In the past, the inferior or lower courts were authorized to hear only less serious criminal cases, usually involving summary conviction offences, or to hear special types of cases, such as traffic violations and other provincial offences, family disputes, small claims, and so on. Today, such courts are also empowered to hear many serious offences, including such indictable offences as manslaughter and robbery, where the accused elects to be tried in a provincial court.

Provincial courts do not hold jury trials, depending instead on the hearing judge to determine both fact and law. Lower courts are much less formal than are courts of general jurisdiction. In an intriguing analysis of court characteristics in the United States, Thomas Henderson[19] found that lower-level courts process cases according to what he called a "decisional model." The decisional model, said Henderson, is informal, personal, and decisive. It depends on the quick resolution of relatively uncomplicated issues of law and fact.

In a sample of cases decided in Canadian lower provincial criminal courts between 2000 and 2001, it was found that common assault and impaired driving were the most commonly encountered offences.[20] Of the cases captured in the sample, 61 per cent resulted in the accused being convicted.[21]

Superior courts of criminal jurisdiction, variously called Queen's Bench courts, Supreme Courts, or Superior Courts, that perform trials are authorized to hear any criminal case. These courts are also the appellate courts for provincial courts that try cases involving summary conviction and provincial offences. Such superior courts are capable of sitting with or without a jury and typically will have a jury present during a trial of the most serious offences.

Henderson[22] describes courts of general jurisdiction according to a procedural model. Such courts, he says, make full use of juries, prosecutors, defence lawyers, witnesses, and all the other actors usually associated with complex trials. The procedural model, which is far more formal than the decisional model, is fraught with numerous court appearances for the defendant, which are necessary to ensure that all of a defendant's due process rights are protected. The procedural model makes for a long, expensive, relatively impersonal, and highly formal series of legal manoeuvres, involving many professional participants. The formal trappings of trials conducted in provincial superior courts have a lengthy history, and while judges and lawyers no longer wear wigs, lawyers are required to appear in black gowns and may be required to address the judge as "My Lord" or "My Lady," as the case may be.

Trial courts of general jurisdiction operate within a fact-finding framework called the adversarial process. That process pits the interests of the state, represented by Crown lawyers or prosecutors, against the professional skills and abilities of defence lawyers. The adversarial process is not a free-for-all, but is, rather, constrained by procedural rules specified in law and sustained through tradition. While the adversarial process also technically exists at the provincial court level, the constraints imposed by high caseloads often result in the appearance of a decreased level of formality.

## *Provincial Appellate Courts*

All provinces today have an appellate division or an Appeal Court as part of their "Superior Court of Criminal Jurisdiction," consisting of a panel of judges who conduct appeal hearings,

## TABLE 7–1  Criminal Court Systems

### Supreme Court of Canada

- Final Appeal Court, hearing appeals from the Courts of Appeal in all jurisdictions in Canada.
- The Supreme Court is composed of a Chief Justice who is also the Chief Justice for Canada and eight puisne Justices who make up the balance of the court.
- Sits with a panel of judges when hearing appeals. There may be 5, 7, or 9 judges at a time.
- Generally hears appeals in criminal cases only after granting the appellant leave to appeal. Appeals on indictable offences may be heard without leave where there was a dissenting opinion in the Court of Appeal.

### Provincial/Territorial Court of Appeal

- Highest Court of Appeal in the province.
- The Chief Justice of this court is also the Chief Justice of the province.
- Hears appeals on summary conviction matters that have already been appealed to the provincial superior court. Hears all indictable offence appeals, regardless of the court in which the offence appeals and regardless of the court in which the offence was tried.
- Sits with a panel, which is often composed of 3, 5, or in some jurisdictions on serious matters, 7 judges.
- Typically the last level of appeal for sentence appeals.

### Provincial/Territorial Superior Court

- Sits as both a trial level court and an appeal court.
- The only level of court that may have a jury (generally an option when sitting as a trial court).
- Sits with one judge at a time.
- The only level of court that can try the most serious offences (e.g., murder, see s. 469).
- Hears appeals on summary conviction matters tried in the court below.

### Provincial/Territorial Court

- The workhorse of the criminal justice system, hearing over 90 per cent of cases.
- A trial level court, this court hears all summary conviction matters and many indictable offences (including all of those in s. 553, and many other electable offences are heard here).
- Unlike all of the above courts, judges at this level are provincial appointees.
- All criminal cases start out at this level with the accused's arraignment. Bail is also typically set here.
- Those indictable offence cases that will be tried in the superior court will typically be preceded by a preliminary inquiry in this court.
- Trial of young people under the *Youth Criminal Justice Act*.

but not trials. There are no juries at this level. Judges must sit as a panel, which is typically composed of three or five judges (always an odd number), who will question the lawyers arguing the case and render a decision after discussing the case with one another in a private meeting and voting on the outcome. The outcome of any case is determined by a majority vote, with the decision of the majority of the judges reflecting the opinion of the court, and those in disagreement, if any, providing a dissent.

An **appeal** by a convicted defendant asks that a higher court review the actions of a lower one. Courts of Appeal, once they accept to hear an appeal, do not conduct a new trial. Instead, they provide a review of the case on the record. In other words, appellate courts examine the written transcript of lower court hearings to ensure that those proceedings were carried out fairly and in accordance with proper statutory and case law. They also allow brief

**appeal** Generally, the request that a court with appellate jurisdiction review the judgment, decision, or order of a lower court and set it aside (reverse it) or modify it.

oral arguments to be made by lawyers for both sides and will generally consider other briefs or information filed by the appellant (the party initiating the appeal) or respondent (the side opposed to the appeal).

Most convictions are affirmed upon appeal.[23] Occasionally, however, an appellate court will determine that the trial court erred in allowing certain kinds of evidence to be heard, or that it failed to interpret properly the significance of a relevant statute. When that happens, the verdict of the trial court will be reversed, and the case may be remanded, or sent back for a new trial, or the conviction will be overturned and an acquittal substituted. Provincial courts of appeal fulfill an important role in reviewing the sentence imposed by a trial court. Sentences being reviewed by a provincial court of appeal may be affirmed or rejected. If a sentence is rejected, an alternative disposition may be imposed. Where an acquittal is overturned by an appellate court, or where there is a dissent at the provincial court of appeal level, an appeal on a question of law will typically be available as the accused's right to appeal to the Supreme Court of Canada on a question of law. In other cases, leave may be granted by the Supreme Court of Canada to allow an appeal to that level.

## The British Columbia Court System: An Example

British Columbia provides an example of a typical province's court structure. Prior to a 1989 reorganization, British Columbia had a typical three-tiered court system in which criminal trials could be conducted in the lowest B.C. provincial court, in the intermediate B.C. county court, or in the superior court, that is, the B.C. Supreme Court. The choice of court was dictated by a combination of the following: Crown selection, the seriousness of the offence, the choice of some defendants, and the administrative necessity dictated by court caseload.

Today, the British Columbia system, which is diagrammed in Figure 7–3, reflects a fairly typical court structure. At the top of this court system's hierarchy is the B.C. Court of Appeal, entailing 15 justices including the **Chief Justice** of the Court of Appeal who is also the Chief Justice of British Columbia.[24] An additional four judges sit as Court of Appeal justices on a supernumerary basis, handling any excess in workload. This court was established in 1907 and has been in continuous operation since that year. The Court of Appeal sits regularly in Vancouver, and periodically in Victoria, Kamloops, and Kelowna.

The B.C. Supreme Court is the historical mainstay of justice in the province. Although it is not the largest court in terms of case volume, it is the traditional court of inherent jurisdiction. This means that the court is presumed to have the jurisdiction to hear a case at trial unless the jurisdiction has been taken away by statute. Under the *Criminal Code*, the B.C. Supreme Court is the superior court of criminal jurisdiction for the province, meaning that this court is presumed to have jurisdiction unless such jurisdiction is expressly taken away. By virtue of section 468 of the *Criminal Code*, this court has jurisdiction over indictable offences. Although this provincial court has been granted jurisdiction under the *Code* to try some indictable offences, this jurisdiction is only held in concurrence with the Supreme Court, which can, in the right circumstances, be in a position to exert jurisdiction over any indictable offence.

In British Columbia, there are about 100 Supreme Court judges. Many provinces keep their superior court in the provincial capital, often requiring judges of that court to reside in that city. In such provinces, the court sits in the capital and periodically travels, holding court outside the capital in what are referred to as "assizes." In British Columbia, this problem is minimized by factors associated with its history. The historic presence of two urban centres, one on Vancouver Island (Victoria) and one on the mainland (Vancouver), affected the structure of the Supreme Court in B.C., creating a more decentralized structure than exists in some other provinces and much more so than in England. Indeed, as far back as 1897, Supreme Court judges in B.C. have resided in New Westminster, Clinton, Vancouver, Kamloops, and Victoria.[25] With the merger of the County Court into the Supreme Court in 1990, the Supreme Court became even more decentralized, with judges residing in far-flung parts of the province such as Dawson Creek in the north, and the towns of Nelson and Cranbrook in the east. Even now, the majority of the Supreme Court judges reside in Vancouver. The administrative head of the B.C. Supreme Court holds the title of the Chief Justice of the B.C. Supreme Court. In addition to judicial administration responsibilities, the Chief Justice of the Court also hears cases at trial.

**Chief Justice** Court administrators acting as coordinating personnel who dictate budgeting of operating funds, and court docket administration.

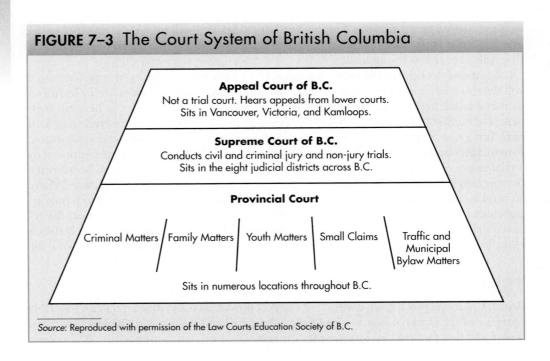

FIGURE 7–3 The Court System of British Columbia

**Appeal Court of B.C.**
Not a trial court. Hears appeals from lower courts.
Sits in Vancouver, Victoria, and Kamloops.

**Supreme Court of B.C.**
Conducts civil and criminal jury and non-jury trials.
Sits in the eight judicial districts across B.C.

**Provincial Court**

Criminal Matters | Family Matters | Youth Matters | Small Claims | Traffic and Municipal Bylaw Matters

Sits in numerous locations throughout B.C.

*Source:* Reproduced with permission of the Law Courts Education Society of B.C.

Like Court of Appeal justices, Supreme Court justices are appointed by the federal government. The federal Minister of Justice is responsible for such appointments in accordance with the federal *Judges Act*. A Commissioner for Federal Judicial Affairs receives nominations for appointment to the provincial superior courts. Statutory criteria mandate that a potential appointee be a member of the B.C. Bar Association and have at least 10 years' experience as a practising lawyer and/or judge. The Commissioner determines whether the nominee meets the statutory criteria for appointment[26] and then refers the name to an assessment committee in B.C., which has the responsibility for screening the names of prospective candidates. This committee is composed of:

1. A nominee from the B.C. Law Society;
2. A nominee of the B.C. Branch of the Canadian Bar Association;
3. A federally appointed judge nominated by the Chief Justice of B.C.;
4. A nominee of the B.C. Attorney General; and
5. Three nominees of the federal Minister of Justice.

The committee classifies the nominees as "recommended," "highly recommended," and "unable to recommend." The results of this assessment are returned to the Commissioner for Federal Judicial Affairs who retains the nominees' names on file for up to two years, during which time the federal Justice Minister may select from the recommended and highly recommended groups.[27] The elevation of a judge from a lower court appointment to a new position as a judge of the B.C. Court of Appeal is not referred to these committees. Such decisions are made by the Federal Justice Minister in consultation with the Attorney General and the Chief Justice of the province.[28] This process of appointment is the same as that for appointing superior court judges in all of the other provinces. Superior court judges currently earn a salary of around $210 000 per year, with the Chief Justices of the Supreme Court and the Court of Appeal each earning an additional $18 000 annually. Superior court judges hold office under "good behaviour" with security of tenure until they reach the retirement age of 75.

The Supreme Court has general trial jurisdiction over matters not assigned by statute to the provincial courts or the Federal Court of Canada, and also hears appeals from the provincial courts on summary conviction and provincial offence cases. Thus, the Supreme Court is simultaneously the highest trial court and the lowest appellate court in British Columbia's judicial system. The trial jurisdiction of the British Columbia Supreme Court includes, among other matters, original jurisdiction over civil disputes involving $10 000 or more; controversies involving the estates of decedents, minors, and persons adjudicated to be incompetent; cases relating to the review of government decision making; criminal prosecutions for serious indictable offences; constitutional disputes; divorce; and actions to determine the title and boundaries of real property.

Provincial courts represent the lowest trial court level in British Columbia. Provincial court judges reside in 36 communities scattered throughout the province. The number of judges in each provincial court varies with the population and caseload of the jurisdiction. Currently, there are 145 full-time provincial court judges in B.C., and an additional 10 judges working as ad hoc or part-time judges. To be eligible for the office of provincial court judge in B.C., a person must have been a member of the B.C. Bar for five years. Judges at this level hold office until reaching the age of 70. The trial jurisdiction of the provincial court is established by statute. The jurisdiction of the provincial court extends to small-claim civil disputes involving less than $10 000; family law matters such as custody and access to children; and the division of family property on the breakdown of a relationship. Young offenders are almost always tried by this court, and provincial offences are also dealt with in this court. Most criminal trials in British Columbia take place before a judge sitting as a judge of the provincial court. The county courts are sometimes referred to as "the people's courts," probably because a large part of the court's work involves high-volume citizen disputes, such as traffic offences, all summary conviction criminal matters, and relatively small monetary disputes. Provincial court judges in British Columbia recently received a pay increase, bringing their salary to around $160 000 per year.[29]

In British Columbia, justices of the peace also sit as trial judges in relation to minor matters such as traffic offences. Throughout the provinces, justices of the peace have historically been available to review the application by the police for warrants and to receive charges being laid by the police. Warrants typically require a judicial signature, a role that justices of the peace may fulfill with regard to most matters. Charges laid by the police are usually received by a justice of the peace who then exercises discretion about whether to compel an accused person to attend court to answer to the charge. Additionally, justices of the peace have conducted bail hearings. The availability of justices of the peace alleviates the need for judges being called out on weekends and evenings.[30] While the salary of a justice of the peace is on average about half of that of a provincial court judge, justices of the peace are responsible for many of the same duties. It has been claimed that justices of the peace are overworked, underpaid, and inadequately trained.[31] In many parts of Canada, justices of the peace may be laypersons, with no law degree required, yet their role is very demanding, freeing up provincial court judges for more onerous tasks. Alberta recently amended its law to require all justices of the peace exercising judicial functions to be members of the law society with at least five years' experience. This change was upheld by a Supreme Court of Canada ruling in *Ell* v. *Alberta* (2003).[32] British Columbia has recently moved to increase the level of independence and security of tenure for justices of the peace performing judicial roles (now known as Judicial Justices of the Peace), but this province does not yet require a formal law degree or bar admission as an employment prerequisite.

## Provincial Court Administration

To function efficiently, courts require uninterrupted funding, adequate staffing, trained support personnel, a well-managed case flow, and coordination between levels and among jurisdictions. To oversee these and other aspects of judicial management, power is divided between senior judicial officials and the Attorney General's Ministry. The provinces utilize a combination of Chief Justices in the various Superior Trial Courts and Courts of Appeal, and Chief Judges in the various provincial courts. Additionally, the Attorney General's Ministry for each province ensures adequate staffing of court personnel, construction and maintenance of courthouse buildings, and other related matters. A few years ago, the system of judicial administration in Canada was criticized by Perry Millar and Carl Baar as

> a somewhat ramshackle and outmoded conglomerate of diverse systems, the legacy of an unsophisticated social era. It is unschooled in modern management methods, lacking in modern business technology and equipment, and unalerted to the task of administering a highly complex and self-contradicting organization.[33]

In Canada, a growing realization that some form of coordinated management was necessary for effective court operation eventually led most jurisdictions to create administrative offices of court administrators. The following tasks are typical of the responsibilities of provincial court administrators across the country today:[34]

1. The preparation, presentation, and monitoring of a budget for the court system;

2. The analysis of case flows and backlogs to determine where additional resources such as judges, prosecutors, and other court personnel are needed;

3. The collection and publication of statistics describing the operation of courts;

4. Efforts to streamline the flow of cases through individual courts and the system as a whole;

5. Service as a liaison between the legislature and the court system;

6. The development and/or coordination of requests for funding;

7. The management of court personnel, including promotions for support staff and the handling of retirement and other benefits packages for court employees;

8. The creation and the coordination of plans for the training of court personnel (in conjunction with local chief judges and training institutes; and

9. The assignment of judges to judicial districts.

In Canada, the fact that the Attorney General's ministry retains some administrative control over courts is viewed as a problem, given that Crown counsel, as agents of the Attorney General, are one of the major parties regularly appearing before the courts.[35] This "inherent conflict" creates the appearance that the courts are too tightly connected to the executive branch of government, thereby lacking the necessary level of administrative independence. However, the Court Services Branch in most provincial ministries of the Attorney General is largely responsible for the smooth functioning of the criminal court process. In British Columbia, for example, court services were instrumental in bringing a new case-tracking system into full operation in 2001.

The Justice Information System (JUSTIN) allows electronic access to various criminal justice agencies, permitting them to track the progress of cases through to disposition. The result of this technology is a provincewide database that is accessible from any court location. Information about a case is entered only once, but this information can be updated or accessed at any time by various agencies and personnel, such as Crown Counsel offices, court registry offices, and in the offices of trial schedulers, as the case moves through the court system. Various documents, such as the "Police Report to Crown Counsel, Accused History Report, Notification letters, caution letters, alternative measures packages, Informations, Indictments, Warrants and Summons,"[36] are automatically generated in JUSTIN. The system expedites the ongoing flow of cases through the courts by eliminating the need for duplicating work through allowing information to be updated and eliminating the need for the same data to be generated or inputted in any case. For example, there is no need to repeatedly have criminal records checked by police, Crown, etc. The system's automation eliminates manual procedures employed in the past, and also allows for improved court scheduling.

## Alternative Dispute Resolution

Some communities have begun to recognize that minor disputes may be resolved without the need for formal court hearings. The functions of **dispute resolution centres** and victim-offender reconciliation programs are to hear victims' claims of minor wrongs, such as passing bad cheques, shoplifting, and other minor theft, and attempt to mediate the situation between the victim and the offender. Frequently staffed by volunteer mediators, such programs work to resolve disagreements (in which minor criminal offences might otherwise be charged) without the need to assign blame. Victim-offender reconciliation programs began in the mid-1970s, with the earliest Canadian program commencing in Kitchener, Ontario, in 1974. Following the lead of this program, numerous jurisdictions in the country adopted similar programs, culminating in the province of British Columbia

**dispute resolution centres** Informal hearing infrastructures designed to mediate interpersonal disputes without need for the moral formal arrangements of criminal trial courts.

## FIGURE 7–4 Adult Court Processing of Federal Statute Cases in Provincial and Selected Superior Courts, Ten Provinces and Territories in Canada, 2001–02

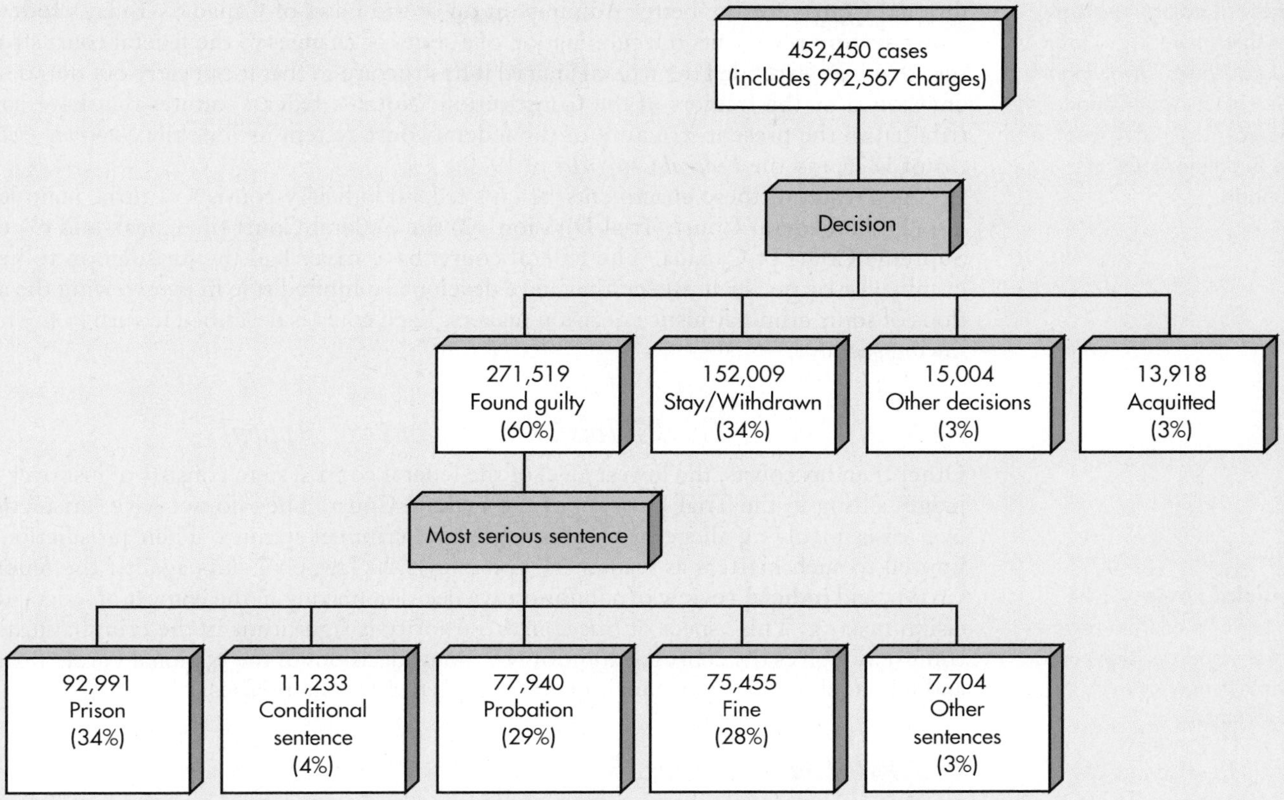

```
                          ┌───────────────────────────┐
                          │      452,450 cases        │
                          │ (includes 992,567 charges)│
                          └───────────────────────────┘
                                      │
                          ┌───────────────────────────┐
                          │         Decision          │
                          └───────────────────────────┘
                                      │
        ┌──────────────┬──────────────┼──────────────┬──────────────┐
  ┌───────────┐  ┌───────────┐  ┌───────────┐  ┌───────────┐
  │  271,519  │  │  152,009  │  │  15,004   │  │  13,918   │
  │Found guilty│ │Stay/Withdrawn││Other decisions││Acquitted │
  │   (60%)   │  │   (34%)   │  │   (3%)    │  │   (3%)    │
  └───────────┘  └───────────┘  └───────────┘  └───────────┘
        │
  ┌───────────────────┐
  │Most serious sentence│
  └───────────────────┘
        │
  ┌───────────┬───────────┬───────────┬───────────┬───────────┐
┌────────┐ ┌────────┐ ┌────────┐ ┌────────┐ ┌────────┐
│ 92,991 │ │ 11,233 │ │ 77,940 │ │ 75,455 │ │  7,704 │
│ Prison │ │Conditional││Probation││  Fine  │ │ Other  │
│ (34%)  │ │sentence │ │ (29%)  │ │ (28%)  │ │sentences│
│        │ │  (4%)  │ │        │ │        │ │  (3%)  │
└────────┘ └────────┘ └────────┘ └────────┘ └────────┘
```

*Notes:* Found guilty decisions include absolute and conditional discharges. Stay/Withdrawn includes cases stayed, withdrawn, dismissed and discharges at preliminary inquiry. Other decisions include final decisions of found not criminally responsible, waived in province/territory, and waived out of province/territory. This category also includes any order where a conviction was not recorded, the court's acceptance of a special plea, cases that raise Charter arguments and cases where the accused was found unfit to stand trial. The sentence was not known in approximately 2 per cent of convicted cases in 2001/02. Conditional sentencing data was not collected in Québec for 2001/02, resulting in an undercount of conditional sentences. Probation total includes mandatory probation for cases given a conditional discharge (approximately 5 per cent of cases with a guilty finding) or a suspended sentence (approximately 10 per cent of cases with a guilty finding). Adult Criminal Court Survey data are not reported by Manitoba, Northwest Territories, and Nunavut.

*Source:* Statistics Canada. Adult Criminal Court Survey. Canadian Centre for Justice Statistics. In *Juristat*, Catalogue no. 85-002, Vol. 23, No. 2.

adopting alternatives to court, such as victim-offender mediation, as a systemwide approach to dealing with non-recidivist minor offenders.

Some centres work only with referrals ordered by Crown counsel, diverting offenders charged with offences away from a trial. Others receive police agency referrals, that is, cases in which no one has been charged with an offence. It is obvious that dispute resolution programs will never entirely supplant the formal criminal justice mechanism, and a person who is charged with a crime but appears before a mediator first may later be prosecuted for the crime if this person fails to reach, or fulfill, a deal to resolve the dispute in question.

Dispute resolution centres have been criticized for the fact that they typically work only with minor offences, thereby denying the opportunity for mediation to victims and offenders in more serious cases, and for the fact that they may be viewed by defendants as just another form of criminal sanction, rather than as a true alternative to criminal justice system processing.[37] Other critics claim that community dispute resolution centres do little more than provide a forum for shouting matches between the parties involved.

# The Federal Courts and the Criminal Justice System

As we have seen, provincial courts had their origins in early colonial arrangements. Federal courts, however, were created by virtue of authority granted to the central government by the *Constitution Act, 1867*. Section 101 of that Act provides for the federal government to establish "a General Court of Appeal for Canada, and for the establishment of any additional Courts for the better Administration of the Laws of Canada." Today's **federal court system** represents the culmination of a series of changes to the federal court structure that have expanded the federal judicial infrastructure so that it can carry out duties not envisioned by the framers of the Constitution. Notable federal statutes that have contributed to the present structure of the federal court system include the *Supreme Court Act* of 1875 and the *Federal Court Act* of 1970.

As a result of these enactments, today's federal judiciary consists of three main levels: (1) the Federal Court, Trial Division, (2) the Federal Court of Appeal, and (3) the Supreme Court of Canada. The federal courts have never had the jurisdiction to hear criminal cases, per se; however, they have developed a limited role in overviewing the actions of some criminal-justice decision makers. Each court is described in turn in the following sections.

## Federal Courts: Trial Division and Court of Appeal

Other than tax courts, the lowest level of the federal court system consists of just over 20 judges sitting in the Trial Division of the Federal Court. They do not have jurisdiction over cases involving alleged violations of federal criminal statutes. Their jurisdiction is limited to such matters as trademark and copyright law, civil suits against the federal Crown, and **judicial review** of administrative decision making in the context of federal decision making. This aspect of this court's authority is significant in the criminal justice context as it gives the court the authority to review decisions of the National Parole Board, and inmate disciplinary tribunals operating in federal penitentiaries.

## Federal Court of Appeal

The appellate court in the federal judicial system is the Federal Court of Appeal. Only about 12 judges sit at this level. The Federal Court of Appeal has national jurisdiction over appeals from the Trial Division of the Federal Court. Some boards and tribunals have their decisions appealed directly to this court rather than to the Trial Division.

While the federal courts (Trial Division and Appeal Division) have seen their caseloads grow and their importance in Canada's legal system increase in recent years, it would be inappropriate to compare the extent of their authority to that of the federal courts in the United States. Canadian federal courts lack the authority to conduct criminal trials, with the odd exception such as income tax evasion. In the United States, federal courts retain the jurisdiction to try matters arising out of all federal law. Although most criminal law in the United States is a matter of state law, there is still a large area of criminal law dealt with by the federal government, and therefore the federal courts. In Canada, all criminal law is enacted by the federal government, but historically, the fact that the administration of the criminal law is a provincial matter has dictated that criminal trials be carried out in the provincial/territorial court systems.

## The Supreme Court of Canada

At the apex of the federal court system, and indeed all of the provincial/territorial court systems, stands the Supreme Court of Canada. The Supreme Court is located in Ottawa, the national capital. The Court consists of nine justices, eight of whom are referred to as puisne justices. The ninth presides over the Court as the Chief Justice of Canada. (See Table 7–2.) Supreme Court justices are selected by the Prime Minister upon consultation with the federal Minister of Justice and the federal cabinet. Upon taking office, justices serve until reaching the age of 75 unless they take retirement at an earlier date. Lengthy terms of service are a tradition among justices.

**TABLE 7–2** Justices of the Supreme Court of Canada

| Justice | Entered Duty | Province |
|---|---|---|
| **Chief Justice** | | |
| Beverley McLachlin* | 1989 | British Columbia/Alberta |
| **Puisne Justices** | | |
| Frank Iacobucci | 1991 | Ontario |
| John Major | 1992 | Alberta |
| Michel Bastarache | 1997 | New Brunswick |
| W. Ian C. Binnie | 1998 | Ontario |
| Louise Arbour | 1999 | Ontario |
| Louis LeBel | 2000 | Quebec |
| Marie Deschamps | 2002 | Quebec |
| Morris J. Fish | 2003 | Quebec |

*Appointed Chief Justice January 2000.

The Supreme Court of Canada wields immense power. The Court's greatest authority lies in its capacity for judicial review of lower-court decisions arising out of both the provincial/territorial and federal court systems. By exercising its power of judicial review, the Court decides what laws and lower-court decisions are in keeping with the intent of the common law and the Constitution. The power of judicial review is not explicit in the Constitution, but was likely anticipated by its framers, since most federated states such as Canada and the United States need a forum to iron out disputes between the two levels of government in each country.

In the early years, the Supreme Court of Canada was not highly influential in developing legal doctrine, since, as noted above, appeals could go on, or even bypass, the Supreme Court

The Supreme Court of Canada hands down a decision, which is binding on all other courts in the country.

and go directly to the Privy Council in England. Accordingly, it was not until the 1950s that the Supreme Court of Canada began to exert itself as the final arbiter of legal issues in this country.

*Increasing Complexity and the Supreme Court*   The evolution of the Supreme Court of Canada provides one of the most dramatic examples of institutional development in Canadian history. Sparsely described in the Constitution, the Court has grown from a repository of political appointees into a modern organization that wields tremendous legal power over all aspects of Canadian life. Much of the Court's growth has been due to its increasing willingness to mediate fundamental issues of law and to act as a resort from arbitrary and capricious processing by the justice systems of the provincial/territorial and national governments.

The decisions handed down by the Court since the adoption of the *Canadian Charter of Rights and Freedoms* in 1982, described earlier in Chapter 6, established the Court as a mighty force in our political system by virtue of the power of judicial review. As we discussed at length in Chapter 6, the Court began to apply that power in the mid-1980s to issues of crime and justice at the national and local levels. You may recall that the Court signalled its change in orientation in the earliest cases under the *Charter* by developing the exclusionary rule as a remedy for violation of a *Charter*-protected right. From that time forward, the Court's workload became increasingly heavy and even today shows few signs of abatement.

*The Supreme Court Today*   The Supreme Court has limited original jurisdiction and does not conduct trials, except in the most exceptional of cases, as in situations where all appeals have been exhausted and a federal Minister of Justice orders that a case be reopened and tried by a court of his or her choosing as an aspect of the royal prerogative of mercy. The Court, rather, reviews the decisions of lower courts and may accept cases from both the Federal Court of Appeal and provincial courts of appeal. For a case to be heard, typically an application for leave to appeal must be heard by at least three justices, a majority of whom must vote in favour of a hearing. When the Court agrees to hear a case, it will review the records of the case, and entertain written and oral arguments from the parties directly affected, and even intervenors, or other parties concerned in the outcome of the case.

Although the Supreme Court may review any decision appealed to it that it decides is worthy of review, in fact, the Court elects to review only cases that involve a substantial question of national importance. Of several hundred requests for review received by the Court yearly, only about 120 are actually heard.

Decisions rendered by the Supreme Court are rarely unanimous. Instead, opinions that a majority of the Court's justices agree upon become the judgment of the Court. Justices who agree with the Court's judgment, but for a different reason, or because they feel that they have some new light to shed on a particular legal issue involved in the case, write concurring opinions. Justices who do not agree with the decision of the Court write dissenting opinions. Those dissenting opinions may offer new possibilities for successful appeals made at a later date.

In addition to the Supreme Court's role as a reviewer of lower-court decisions, the Court also has an important power to hand down reference opinions. Under the *Supreme Court Act*, the federal executive may ask the Supreme Court for its opinion on a constitutional question. This permits the government to resolve questions surrounding the constitutionality of a proposed legislative or policy scheme without actually putting the scheme into action. In this way, expensive start-up costs can be avoided if it turns out that the proposed course of action is constitutionally impermissible. Similar powers exist for provincial governments to pose constitutional questions to their respective courts of appeal, and typically, with a further review at the Supreme Court of Canada level. This **reference power** clearly places the Supreme Court in a pivotal position with respect to politics and law in Canada.[38]

While all of the judges on the Supreme Court of Canada are appointed by the federal government, over the years some formal and some informal rules have constrained the federal government in its choice of candidates for the Supreme Court. The *Supreme Court Act* requires that three of the nine justices come from the province of Quebec. This ensures that at least some of the judges on the top court will be familiar with the unique civil law aspects of the Quebec legal system. Over the years, Ontario has secured an equal number of positions on the top bench. With six of the nine positions taken up by jurists from Central Canada, this only leaves three justices, one of whom is typically drawn from the Maritimes, and two from the West.

**reference power**   The ability of a court to answer questions pertaining to the constitutional validity of laws or policy when requested to do so by the executive branch of government.

Current Canadian Supreme Court Justices.

*Ideas for Change* Increasing caseloads at the Supreme Court level, particularly due to the increased number of cases dealing with interpretations of the *Charter*, and concerns over the exclusive and unsupervised federal role in appointing justices to the top court, have led to proposals to restructure the Supreme Court. Recent proposals have involved entrenching the authority of this court in the Constitution, providing for a role for the provinces in the appointment process, and increasing the size of the court, perhaps to accommodate more judges from Quebec.[39] Despite calls for reform, it appears unlikely that significant changes will occur in the near future.

## PRETRIAL ACTIVITIES

In the next chapter, we will discuss typical stages in a criminal trial, as well as describe the many roles assumed by courtroom participants such as judges, prosecutors, defence lawyers, victims, and suspects. A number of court-related pretrial activities, however, routinely take place before a trial can begin. Those activities are described in the pages that follow.

## First Appearance or Arraignment

Most defendants do not come into contact with an officer of the court until their **first appearance** (also **initial appearance**) before a provincial court judge to deal with the offence. The vast majority of offenders are permitted to remain in the community, pending the hearing of their cases. If an accused is arrested following the commission of a crime, he or she will typically be released by the police shortly thereafter and be required to attend court at a later date.

## Pretrial Release by the Police

When the police deal with offenders, they want as few people as possible being detained, pending their trial. Police powers of arrest are somewhat restrictive. In many situations, the police will be required to release the person (even though he or she will be charged), and

**first appearance**
(also **initial appearance**)
An appearance before a provincial court judge that entails the process whereby the charge is read to the accused. At this stage in the criminal justice process, bail may be set or pretrial release arranged.

secure his or her attendance at court through some mechanism other than arresting and holding that person. In many cases, police officers will release the person with an "appearance notice." This notice tells the suspect when to show up for his or her initial appearance in court, and whether he or she must also report to the police station before this time in order to be fingerprinted. These appearance notices, if subsequently confirmed by the justice, constitute a valid form of process to compel the accused's attendance in court. By the time the accused shows up for court, a charge will also have been laid.

The police also have the option of not arresting a suspect, but as long as they can identify the suspect, they may allow the suspect to first go free, and then subsequently charge the suspect, eventually requesting that the justice receiving the charge issue a "summons" or "arrest warrant," either of which is a valid form of process to compel an accused's attendance in court.

Where the police arrest a suspect, they must be mindful of whether the suspect should be subsequently released before appearing before a justice. If the grounds that justified arresting rather than securing some other form of process have subsequently disappeared (such as the police now know the identity of the suspect), the suspect may be released on an appearance notice, or released with a view to the police securing a summons at a later time. In some circumstances, the suspect will be released by the officer-in-charge of the police department or detachment where the suspect is being held (see *Code* ss. 495-498). It is generally those suspects charged with the more serious offences who cannot benefit from this form of early release. If a suspect is not released by the arresting officer or the officer-in-charge, the suspect will be brought before a justice for a judicial interim release hearing, typically within 24 hours. Those suspects charged with the most serious offences are brought before a superior court judge for a judicial interim release hearing.

If an accused is arrested by the police, but is not released by law enforcement authorities, he or she will encounter a judicial officer prior to answering any charges being brought against him or her. The rationale underlying the initial appearance is to present the accused with the allegations. Typically, the accused will be called forward, the charge will be read to the accused, and the accused will be asked whether the charge is understood. Typically, these three steps will be the extent of matters covered in the initial appearance, as the case will typically be adjourned to permit the accused to access legal counsel to represent him or her.

Where the accused has counsel present, a number of matters may also be dealt with at the time of the initial appearance. With respect to hybrid offences, the Crown will usually indicate at this time how it intends to proceed. If the case involves a summary conviction matter, the accused will be asked to plead to the offence. Similarly, if the offence is a minor indictable (s. 553) offence, a plea will be taken. If a plea of not guilty is entered, a date for trial will be set. If the offence is a section 469 offence (like murder), a date for the preliminary hearing may be set. If the offence is any other indictable offence, the accused will be asked to elect the mode of trial in accordance with section 536(2). This allows the accused to elect trial by a provincial court judge, trial by a superior court judge sitting alone, or trial by a superior court judge with a jury. In the former case, a plea may be taken. In the latter two circumstances, a date for the preliminary inquiry may be set. Table 7–3 provides a summary of the process for identifying the mode of trial.

Where the accused has been held in custody, the *Criminal Code* requires a justice to determine whether there is just cause to detain the suspect.

## Judicial Interim Release

Prior to reforms in the 1970s, a suspect was typically arrested by the police and detained in custody, pending his or her trial. Martin Friedland found (in 1965) that a sample of 6000 cases going through courts in Toronto revealed that 92 per cent of accused persons were compelled to attend court by way of police arrest, and of those arrested, 84 per cent remained in custody until their first appearance.[40]

Today, if the police have detained a suspect in custody, the decision to do so is quickly reviewed by a judicial officer. This review is referred to as a judicial interim release hearing, and may be carried out by a justice of the peace or a provincial court judge in most cases.

Form/Formulaire 9     (Secs./Art. 496, 497)
PCR 059                     Rev./Rev. 09/94

**APPEARANCE NOTICE ISSUED BY A PEACE OFFICER**
**CITATION À COMPARAÎTRE DÉLIVRÉE**
**PAR UN AGENT DE LA PAIX**
(To a person not yet charged with an offence)
(À une personne qui n'est pas encore inculpée d'infraction)

**CANADA.** PROVINCE OF BRITISH COLUMBIA/PROVINCE DE LA COLOMOBIE-BRITANNIQUE

To/À _____

of/de _____
_____

**You are alleged to have committed** *(set out substance of offence)*
**Il est allégue que vous avez commis** *(indiquer l'essentiel de l'infraction)*

1. You are required to attend Court on/Vous être présent(e) au tribunal le
_____ at/à _____ M., in the

Provincial Court located at/heures, à la Cour provinciale située à _____
_____

**and to attend thereafter as required by the Court, in order to be dealt with according to law, to answer to the charge set out above, any included charge, or any charge or charges disclosed by the evidence.**
et d'être présent(e) par la suite selon les exigences du tribunal, afin d'être traité(e) selon la loi, de répondre à l'infraction énoncée ce-dessus, à toute inculpation incluse, ou à toute inculpation ou toutes inculpations dont les preuves font état.

2. You are also required to appear on/Vous êtes en outre requis(e) de comparaître le
_____ at/à _____ M., at the/heures, à
_____
(Police station/Poste de police)
_____
(Address/Adresse)
for the purpose of the *Identification of Criminals Act* (ignore if not filled in).
pour l'application de la Loi sur l'identification des criminels. (Ne pas tenir compte de cet alinéa sin, est pas rempli.)

    You are warned that failure, without lawful excuse, to appear for the purpose of the *Identification of Criminals Act* or to attend court in accordance with this appearance notice is an offence under subsection 145 (5) of the *Criminal Code*.

    Vous êtes averti(e) que l'omission de comparaître, sans excuse légitime, pour l'application de la *Loi sur l'identification des criminels* ou d'être présent(e) au tribunal en conformité avec la présente citation à constitue une infraction en vertu du paragraphe 145 (5) du *Code criminel*.

(see reverse of form for subsection 145(5) and (6) and section 502 of the *Criminal Code*)
(voir au verso du formulaire pour les paragraphes 145(5) et (6) et l'article 502 du *Code criminel*)

Issued at/Délivré à _____ M./heures

on/le _____, at/à

_____
in the Province of British Columbia.
dans la province de la Colombie-
Britannique.

_____
*Signature of Peace Officer/*
*Signature de l'agent de la paix*

P.C. No.
N° de l'A.P. _____
Det. or Force
Dét. ou Force _____

_____
*Signature of Accused/Signature de l'inculpé*

**TABLE 7–3** Determining Mode of Trial

| Summary Conviction Offences (Including hybrid offences being treated by the Crown as Summary Conviction offences) | Indictable Offences (Including hybrid offences being treated by the Crown as Indictable Offences) | | |
|---|---|---|---|
| | **Absolute Jurisdiction Offences** | **Electable Offences** | **Superior Court Judge and Jury Offences** |
| e.g., soliciting (s. 213) | Listed in *Code* s. 553<br><br><br>e.g., theft under $5000 (s. 334) | Not listed but negatively defined in *Code* s. 536 (2) as those indictable offences not listed in s. 553, s. 469<br><br>e.g., robbery (s. 344) | Listed in *Code* s. 469<br><br><br>e.g., murder (s. 235) |
| Trial: Provincial Court (*Code* Part 27) | Trial: Provincial Court (*Code* Part 19) | **Accused elects one of 3 modes of trial:**<br><br>**1**   **2**   **3**<br>Trial:  Prelim:  Prelim:<br>Prov. Ct.  Prov. Ct.  Prov. Ct.<br>(Pt 19)  (Pt 18)  (Pt 18)<br><br>     Trial:  Trial: Sup.<br>     Sup. Ct.  Ct. judge<br>     judge  and jury<br>     alone  (Pt 20)<br>     (Pt 19) | Preliminary Inquiry: Provincial Court (*Code* Part 18)<br><br>Trial: Superior Court Judge and Jury Trial* (*Code* Part 20)<br><br><br>*jury may be dispensed with if both the AG and accused consent (*Code* s. 473) |
| Appeal: Superior Court (*Code* Part 27) | Appeal: Court of Appeal (*Code* Part 21) | | |

This hearing seeks to balance the need to protect society from offenders who have finally been brought into custody by the state and the need to protect the rights of individuals to be presumed innocent until convicted by a court.[41]

For typical offences, the justice's review of the police decision to detain proceeds in a relatively informal fashion, with the judge seeking to decide whether, at that time, the circumstances necessitate ongoing detention. At this stage in the criminal justice process, the suspect generally is not given an opportunity to present evidence on the offence. Suspects without their own legal counsel will typically be represented by duty counsel—lawyers who typically receive remuneration under the province's legal aid scheme and who speak for all suspects who are unrepresented at this stage.

According to the procedural rules set out in the *Criminal Code* (s. 503), defendants who have been taken into custody must be brought before a justice "without unreasonable delay," and where a justice is available, no later than 24 hours after being brought into custody. For other than the most serious offences, such as murder, the accused is entitled to a presumption that favours release. If the Crown does not "show cause" as to why continued detention is required, the judge orders the release of the accused. For this reason, these hearings are often referred to as "show cause" hearings; however, they are sometimes referred to by their more formal name of "judicial interim release hearings," or the less formal name of "bail hearings."

The criteria applied at a show cause hearing are provided in section 515 of the *Criminal Code*. If an accused is to be detained, the Crown must establish that detention is justified on specific grounds:

A trial jury. The Crown may bypass a preliminary hearing completely and commit a case to trial in a superior court by filing a direct indictment.

s. 515(10)    ... the detention of an accused in custody is justified only on one or more of the following grounds:

(a)    where the detention is necessary to ensure his or her attendance in court in order to be dealt with according to law;

(b)    where the detention is necessary for the protection or safety of the public, including any victim of or witness to the offence, having regard to all the circumstances including any substantial likelihood that the accused will, if released from custody, commit a criminal offence, or interfere with the administration of justice; and

(c)    on any other just cause being shown and, without limiting the generality of the foregoing, where the detention is necessary in order to maintain confidence in the administration of justice, having regard to all the circumstances, including the apparent strength of the prosecution's case, the gravity of the nature of the offence, the circumstances surrounding its commission and the potential for a lengthy term of imprisonment.

If the Crown opts not to show cause, the suspect is ordered released on an "undertaking to appear" without any conditions attached. This undertaking is effectively a signed promise to show up in court at a later date. If the Crown gives the justice cause for concern, but has not justified detention, various options are open to the justice at the show cause hearing. These options are, in escalating level of severity, as follows:

1. Undertaking to appear, with conditions such as refraining from contacting the complainant, or from possessing firearms;

2. A **recognizance**, which is a signed promise to appear in court and a recognition that failure to appear will create a debt of a pre-set amount of money, which the Crown can collect following the failure of the accused to show up in court. Conditions may also be attached to the recognizance;

3. A recognizance with a **surety**, which is the same as a simple recognizance, however, also requires that the accused have one or more other people, such as family or friends, sign the release document creating a debt in their names should the accused fail to appear in court. Conditions may also be attached to the release;

4. A recognizance with a deposit, where the prosecutor consents. This type of recognizance is the classic form of bail, whereby the suspect must put up some money, or

**recognizance** Refers to the pretrial release of a criminal defendant on their written promise to appear. No cash bail is required; however, a debt to the Crown is created should the accused fail to attend court for trial.

**surety** The requirement that a person other than the accused sign for the accused's release, thereby indebting that individual to the Crown should the accused fail to appear for court.

other valuable security, before being granted release. Conditions may also be at-tached; and

5. A recognizance with a deposit, with or without a surety, and with or without condi-tions. This type of recognizance is only available where the accused resides outside the province or more than 200 kilometres from the place in which the accused is in custody.

This scheme essentially sets up a ladder going from the least restrictive alternative to the most restrictive. Judges must work their way up the ladder, imposing the least re-strictive option that is applicable in the circumstances.

An accused may have to face a reverse onus situation at his or her bail hearing in a few exceptional cases such as those found in sections 515(6) and 522(2) of the *Criminal Code*. Where an individual has been charged with an indictable offence, other than a sec-tion 469 offence, alleged to have been committed while the accused was at large on some form of pretrial release with respect to another indictable offence, the accused carries the burden of showing why he or she should be released. This situation also prevails where a person is charged with an indictable (but non–s. 469) offence and is a non-resident of Canada, where the accused is charged with failure to appear or breach of bail conditions, where the accused is charged with a terrorism offence, and where the accused is charged with certain *Controlled Drugs and Substances Act* offences, such as (1) possession for the purpose of trafficking, (2) trafficking, (3) importing and exporting, (4) possession for the pur-pose of exporting, and (5) producing certain controlled drugs. In such circumstances, the accused will be presumptively ordered detained unless the accused can show cause why he or she should be released. In such circumstances, the judge applies the ladder outlined above, but in reverse. The most severe restrictions are to be presumed to apply unless it can be shown that lesser restrictions are justified in the circumstances.

Where an accused is charged with one of the most serious indictable offences such as murder (and the others listed in s. 469), the accused will be remanded by a justice into cus-tody until the accused applies for a show cause hearing before a superior court judge. Only a judge of a superior court can order such offenders released on bail, and the reverse onus situation applies. These reverse onus situations have so far been upheld by the Supreme Court of Canada, in *R. v. Morales* (1992) and *R. v. Pearson* (1992), as not infringing on an in-dividual's right "not to be denied bail without just cause" under section 11(e) of the *Charter*.[42]

Unlike the situation in the United States, professional bail bondsmen are illegal in Canada.[43] Canadians seeking release do not usually need to put up money to guarantee their return for trial. The legislative scheme in this country emphasizes releasing as many sus-pects pending trial as possible. Indeed, the legislative scheme anticipates that most suspects arrested by the police will be released even prior to a bail hearing. However, in analyzing 100 cases going through a court system in Ontario, Richard Ericson and Patricia Baranek found that the police frequently used their discretion to either detain a suspect or release a sus-pect prior to a show cause hearing to threaten the suspect into giving a statement to them, lest the suspect be detained and subjected to the whims of a judge at a bail hearing.[44]

While the goals of the policy underlying the "judicial interim release" provisions in the *Criminal Code* are laudable, the scheme has not been without its critics. Reading letters to the editor in any local newspaper will quickly reveal the concern that many members of the public have over the release of suspected offenders back into the community. Concerns of the offenders absconding or reoffending are often well-placed. Civil libertarians are concerned with the consistent research findings that denial of bail is strongly correlated with subsequent conviction, likelihood of incarceration, and length of incarceration.[45] Social justice advocates express concern when the implications of this research are applied to the fact that women, aboriginals, blacks, and immigrants are more likely to be detained pend-ing their trial.[46]

The Manitoba Aboriginal Justice Inquiry found that charged individuals who were also aboriginal were 1.34 times more likely than non-aboriginals to be held in detention prior to trial. Of all adult males between the ages of 18 and 34, aboriginals spent 1.5 times longer in pretrial detention. Women in the same age category spent 2.4 times longer in pre-trial detention. In Winnipeg, aboriginal persons being detained while pending trial spent more than twice as long in pretrial detention as non-aboriginals. Aboriginals in the

Manitoba justice system were found to be 2.5 times more likely to receive incarceration than non-aboriginals.[47]

Where bail has been denied and the trial does not commence against the accused on short order, an automatic "delayed trial bail review" occurs after 30 days on summary conviction offences, and 90 days on indictable offences (s. 525). The conditions of bail carry through until the end of a trial, and if convicted, until sentence is imposed (s. 523). Provisions also exist in the *Criminal Code* to allow for variation of bail conditions, bail review by a higher court, and release on bail pending an appeal.[48]

## The Preliminary Inquiry

Although the preliminary hearing is not nearly as elaborate as a criminal trial, it has many of the same characteristics. Not all offences will carry with them the right to a preliminary inquiry. All summary conviction offences are tried in a provincial court and do not entail a preliminary hearing. The least serious indictable offences listed in section 553, such as theft, possession of stolen property, and fraud, are likewise tried in provincial court without the benefit of a preliminary inquiry. The most serious offences (listed in s. 469) will, almost without fail, involve a preliminary hearing. All of the other indictable offences (those not listed in ss. 553 or 469) may have a preliminary hearing, provided the accused elects to be tried in a superior court.

The main purpose underlying the preliminary inquiry is to determine whether there is sufficient evidence to justify committing the case to trial in the higher court. This rationale ensures that time will not be wasted in the higher courts, and that accused persons will not unnecessarily be required to endure the trauma of a criminal trial when the case against them is weak. The defendant is taken before a provincial court judge, and events unfold in much the same manner as they would in a trial. The prosecution presents witnesses and offers evidence in support of the complaint. The defendant is afforded the right to cross-examine the Crown witnesses, and may even testify and also call witnesses on his or her own behalf, following the close of the Crown's submissions. The outcome of the hearing will turn on a determination of whether there has been any evidence provided, upon which a reasonable jury, properly instructed by the judge, might convict.[49]

At this stage of the criminal justice process, the defendant's guilt need not be proved beyond a reasonable doubt. All that is required is a demonstration of some evidence on each and every element of the offence. If the judge finds enough evidence to justify a trial, the defendant is committed to trial. If the complaint against the defendant cannot be substantiated, the defendant is ordered discharged. Even if the defendant is discharged, the Crown may commit the case to trial by using a "direct indictment," which is authorized by the provincial Attorney General or his or her deputy.[50] In fact, the Crown may bypass the preliminary inquiry completely and commit a case to trial in a superior court by filing a direct indictment.

By the mid-1980s, every jurisdiction in Canada had abolished the grand jury. A grand jury was composed of private citizens who heard evidence presented by the prosecution, voting on the indictment or charges presented to them by the prosecution. If the majority of the grand jury agreed to forward the indictment to the trial court, it became a "true bill" upon which further prosecution would turn. With the abolition of the grand jury system in Canada, the preliminary hearing became the method for weeding out the weakest cases from the trial docket. Recent meetings between federal and provincial justice ministers have recognized a developing consensus among many provinces and territories for the elimination of the preliminary inquiry.[51] Various jurisdictions are now investigating ways to reduce the use of preliminary inquiries and to minimize the number of offences for which they will be available.

### Plea Bargaining

A guilty **plea** is often not as straightforward as it might seem to be and is typically arrived at only after complex negotiations known as **plea bargaining**. Plea bargaining is a process of negotiation that usually involves the defendant, prosecutor, and defence counsel. This process may be viewed as being founded upon the mutual interests of all three parties involved.

**plea** In criminal proceedings, a defendant's formal answer in court to the charge contained in information, or an indictment that he or she is guilty or not guilty of the offence charged, or has a special plea to make to the offence.

**plea bargaining** The negotiated agreement between defendant and prosecutor, as to what an appropriate plea and associated sentence should be in a given case. Plea bargaining circumvents the trial process and dramatically reduces the time required for the resolution of a criminal case.

Defence lawyers and their clients will agree to a plea of guilty when they are unsure of their ability to win acquittal at trial. Prosecutors may be willing to bargain because the evidence they have against the defendant is weaker than they would like it to be. From the prosecutorial perspective, plea bargaining results in a quick conviction, without the need to commit the time and resources necessary for trial. Benefits to the accused include the possibility of reduced or combined charges, reduced defence costs, and a lower sentence than might otherwise have been anticipated. Indeed, researchers in the field, such as Simon Verdun-Jones and Alison Hatch,[52] and Stanley Cohen and Anthony Doob,[53] have identified these concessions that may be obtained through plea bargaining:

(a) A reduction in the charge against the accused;

(b) A withdrawal or stay of charges;

(c) A promise not to proceed on other charges;

(d) A recommendation or promise as to the type of sentence to be expected;

(e) A recommendation as to the severity of sentence;

(f) A Crown election to proceed by summary conviction rather than indictment where the offence involved is a hybrid offence;

(g) A promise not to seek a sentence of preventive detention by withholding a Dangerous Offender Application;

(h) A promise not to seek a Long Term Offender Declaration;

(i) A promise not to seek an enhanced penalty where the *Code* allows for one in the event of a prior conviction for the same offence;

(j) A promise not to charge other persons;

(k) A promise concerning the nature of any submission to be made to the sentencing judge, (such as not mentioning aggravating circumstances);

(l) A promise not to compel a jury trial through resort to a preferred indictment or by means of the power given under section 568 of the *Code*;

(m) A recommendation or promise as to the place of incarceration or arrangements concerning early release;

(n) An arrangement for the sentencing to take place before a particular judge;

(o) A promise not to appeal the sentence imposed; and

(p) A promise not to object to the defence's submissions with respect to sentencing.

Public opinion on plea bargaining is generally fairly negative. When Karla Homolka received a 12-year prison sentence on a guilty plea for manslaughter, in exchange for testimony implicating her husband in a first-degree murder allegation, the public became incensed at the result when it became apparent during the trial that Homolka and Bernardo were a sadistic killing team. Research conducted for the Law Reform Commission of Canada found that over 79 per cent of respondents with an opinion on the practice of plea bargaining expressed "strong or general disapproval of the practice...."[54]

In Canada, judges are not involved in the plea bargaining process. Although judges are unwilling to become involved so as to guarantee a sentence before a plea is entered, most prosecutors and criminal trial lawyers know what sentences to expect for typical pleas. Cohen and Doob's research indicates that the public may be more willing to accept the practice of plea bargaining if the process is more open and accountable.[55] They indicate that this acceptance may require some judicial involvement in the plea bargaining process, providing the necessary oversight that the public associates with legitimizing the plea bargaining process.

Plea bargaining, though common over the years, has generally been veiled in secrecy. However, it is manifestly clear that an inequality of bargaining positions exists between the defence and Crown counsel in plea negotiations. Pleas struck as the result of so-called bargains seem to arise out of the state's coercive power to encourage the defendant's co-operation. Richard Ericson and Patricia Baranek advanced the argument that only about a quarter of those lawyers entering into plea discussions on behalf of their clients believed that the result was really a bargain for the accused.[56] Clearly, the plea bargaining process, while widespread, may not result in an abundance of offenders "getting off too light," as public opinion appears to hold.

The disposition of criminal charges by agreement between the prosecutor and the accused could be said to be an essential component of the smooth functioning of the administration of justice. If every criminal charge were subjected to a full-scale trial, the legal system would need to multiply the number of judges and court facilities by many times. Today, bargained pleas are commonplace. Some surveys have found that 90 per cent of all criminal cases prepared for trial are eventually resolved through a negotiated plea.[57]

Prosecutors who regularly engage in the practice of plea bargaining rarely advertise it. Often unrealized is the fact that plea bargaining can be a powerful prosecutorial tool. Power carries with it, however, the potential for misuse. Plea bargains, because they circumvent the trial process, can be abused by prosecutors and defence lawyers who are more interested in a speedy resolution of cases than they are in seeing justice done. Carried to the extreme, plea bargaining may result in defendants being convicted of crimes they did not commit. It is conceivable that innocent defendants (especially those with prior criminal records) who—for whatever reason—think a jury will convict them, may plead guilty to lessened charges in order to avoid a trial, although this probably happens only rarely.

# SUMMARY

Throughout Canada there are two sets of court systems. One consists of provincial courts, where there are lower-level trial courts that deal with a broad array of matters, including criminal trials, and appeal courts to deal with errors made at the trial level. The other court system is the federal court system, created by statute to deal with a number of matters, few of which pertain to the criminal justice system.

Provincial courts have virtually unlimited power to decide nearly every type of case, subject only to limitations imposed by statute. Lower-level provincial courts are located in almost every town across the nation, and are the courts with which citizens usually have contact. These courts handle most criminal matters and the great bulk of legal business concerning family matters, small civil disputes, young offenders, and the criminal law.

Superior courts in the provinces present an intriguing contrast. They exude an aura of highly formalized judicial procedure. A court at this level in one jurisdiction may be called a Queen's Bench Court, while in other jurisdictions, it may be referred to as a Supreme Court or a Superior Court.

Federal courts have the power to decide only those cases over which the *Federal Court Act* gives them authority. These courts are located principally in the largest cities in the country. Only carefully selected types of cases may be heard in federal courts. The highest federal court, the Supreme Court, is located in Ottawa, and is perhaps better referred to as a "national" Court than a "federal" Court, since it hears appeals from the provincial courts of appeal in addition to appeals from the Federal Court of Appeal.

In this chapter, we described pretrial practices; in the next chapter, we will look at trial-related activities. Prior to trial, courts often act to shield the accused from the punitive power of the state through pretrial release. In doing so, they must balance the rights of the unconvicted defendant against the potential for future harm that that person may represent. A significant issue facing pretrial decision makers is how to ensure that all defendants, rich and poor, are afforded the same degree of protection.

# DISCUSSION QUESTIONS

1. What is the "unitary court system"? How does it contrast with the dual court system in America? How has Canada developed a system that fits between the two concepts? Could the drive toward even greater court unification eventually lead to a monolithic court system? Would such a system be effective?

2. This chapter says that 90 per cent of all criminal cases carried beyond the initial stages are finally resolved through bargained pleas. What are some of the problems associated with plea bargaining? Given those problems, do you believe that plea bargaining is an acceptable practice in today's criminal justice system? Give reasons for your answer.

3. People who are accused of crimes are often granted pretrial release. Do you think all defendants accused of crimes should be so released? If not, what types of defendants might you keep in jail? Why?

4. What inequities exist in today's system of pretrial release? How might the system be improved?

5. Should we eliminate the use of the preliminary inquiry? Should some other mechanism exist to filter cases headed for trial in the superior courts?

# WEBLINKS

www.duhaime.org
**Canadian Law: A History**
A history of Canadian law, written by Lloyd Duhaime, a lawyer and author who lives and works in Victoria, B.C.

http://canada.justice.gc.ca/Loireg/index_en.html
**Laws of Canada**
This Department of Justice Canada's website provides online access to Canadian statutes and regulations, constitutional documents, and other publications.

www.scc-csc.gc.ca
**Supreme Court of Canada**
This site provides information about the court, research information, and free access to all Supreme Court of Canada decisions (since January 1993).

http://canada.justice.gc.ca
**Canada's System of Justice**
This publication describes an overview of Canada's justice system, published by the Department of Justice Canada.

www.fja.gc.ca
**Office of the Commissioner for Federal Judicial Affairs**
This page provides access to Canadian Federal Court decisions.

# The Courtroom Work Group and the Criminal Trial

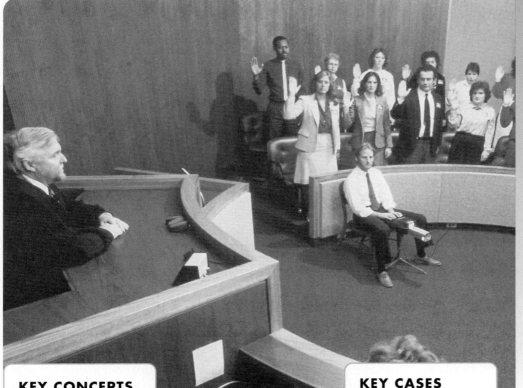

Canadian Press/Felicity Don

**KEY CONCEPTS**

courtroom work group
judge
security of tenure
prosecutor
prosecutorial discretion
abuse of process
defence counsel
public defender
bailiff
expert witness
lay witness
subpoena
victim assistance programs
juror
rules of evidence

adversarial system
jury selection
peremptory challenge
scientific jury selection
sequestered jury
opening statements
evidence
direct evidence
circumstantial evidence
real evidence
testimony
perjury
hearsay
hearsay rule
closing argument
verdict

**KEY CASES**

*Woolmington v. D.P.P.*
*R. v. Stinchcombe*
*R. v. Boucher*
*R. v. S.(F.)*
*Nelles v. Ontario*
*R. v. Mohan*
*Dagenais v. Canadian Broadcasting Corporation*
*Canadian Broadcasting Corporation v. New Brunswick (Attorney General)*
*R. v. Askov*
*R. v. Morin*

*R. v. Collins*
*R. v. Sharma*
*R. v. Pelfrey*
*R. v. Sherratt*
*R. v. Williams*
*R. v. Parks*
*R. v. Crosby*
*R. v. Avon*
*R. v. Levogiannis*
*R. v. Khan*
*R. v. B.(K.G.)*
*R. v. U.(F.J.)*
*R. v. Conway*
*R. v. G. (R.M.).*

# INTRODUCTION

Canada's legal aid system is in crisis. In 2001, the provincial government of British Columbia announced that it was intending to slash the legal aid budget of the Legal Services Society of British Columbia. The government announced a plan to reduce legal aid funding by 38.8 per cent over three years, from $88 million in 2001-02 to less than $54 million in 2004-05.[1] In early 2002, after the Legal Services Society had twice refused to pass a budget reflecting the government's desired cuts, the board of directors of the society was dismissed, and a trustee was appointed to operate the society during the funding cut period. Headlines about legal aid in the country's newspapers speak loud and clear, for example: "Why We Must Save Legal Aid."[2] This article reveals that Ontario's legal aid system, after suffering several years of cuts, was recently (2002) in a position where there were 23 per cent fewer lawyers delivering legal aid than there were in 1997, while the caseload for legal aid work has increased over 50 per cent during the same period. In the five years prior to 1996, the legal aid schemes in Canada had seen unprecedented growth. In 1994-95, legal aid costs accounted for 7 per cent of total spending for public-sector justice services in Canada. In that same fiscal year, 3 per cent of public-sector justice services spending was allocated to prosecutions; however, 58 per cent was absorbed by policing costs. In 1990-91, the federal government capped its contribution to criminal legal aid across the country at approximately $86 million per year.[3] In recent years, this budget has declined to less than $82 million per year.[4] Despite declining crime rates in the 1990s, a number of changes placed an increasing burden on the ability of the legal aid plans to meet the needs of those seeking free legal advice.[5] These changes included an increasing number of court-directed cases mandating the provision of legal aid, rising fees for legal aid lawyers, and perhaps even a slowdown in the economy.

Lack of adequate funding for legal aid has the potential of taking away from the ideal of a criminal trial process that reflects any sense of equality between the parties involved. To the public eye, criminal trials generally appear to be well-managed and even dramatic events. Like a play on a stage, a criminal trial involves many participants playing many different roles. Parties to the event can be divided into two categories: "professionals" and "outsiders." The "professional" category includes official courtroom actors, well-versed in criminal trial practice, who set the stage for and conduct the business of the court. Judges, Crown lawyers (or Crown counsel), private defence lawyers, public defenders, and others who earn a living serving the court fall into this category. Professional courtroom actors are also called the **courtroom work group**. Some writers[6] have pointed out that, aside from statutory requirements and ethical considerations, courtroom interaction among professionals involves an implicit recognition of informal rules of civility, co-operation, and shared goals. Hence, even within the adversarial framework of a criminal trial, the courtroom work group is dedicated to bringing the procedure to a successful close.[7]

In contrast, "outsiders" are generally unfamiliar with courtroom organization and trial procedure. Most outsiders visit the court temporarily to provide information or to serve as members of the jury. Similarly, because of their temporary involvement with the court, the defendant and victim are also outsiders, even though they may have more of a personal investment in the outcome of the trial than anyone else.

This chapter continues to examine trial court activities, building on the pretrial process described in the last chapter. In order to place the trial process within its human context, however, we will first discuss the various roles of the many participants in a criminal trial.

**courtroom work group**
Professional courtroom actors, including judges, prosecuting lawyers, private defence counsel, public defenders, and others who earn a living serving the court.

# THE COURTROOM WORK GROUP: PROFESSIONAL COURTROOM ACTORS

## The Judge

### Role of the Judge

The trial **judge** is probably the figure most closely associated with a criminal trial. The judge has the primary duty of ensuring justice. In the courtroom, the judge holds ultimate

**judge** An appointed public official who presides over a court of law and who is authorized to hear and sometimes to decide cases and to conduct trials.

authority, ruling on matters of law, weighing objections from either side, deciding on the admissibility of evidence, and disciplining anyone who challenges the order of the court. Judges also sentence offenders after a verdict has been returned, and in most criminal trials, judges decide the guilt or innocence of defendants who either have no access to, or waive, a jury trial.

Each trial court level in each jurisdiction has a chief judge or chief justice who, besides serving on the bench as a trial judge, must also manage the court system. Management includes assigning judges to special committees, assigning cases to judges, adjusting the scheduling of trials, and coordinating activities with other courtroom actors. Chief judges usually assume their positions by virtue of executive decree and rarely have any formal training in management. Hence, the managerial effectiveness of a chief judge is often a matter of personality and dedication more than anything else.

## Judicial Selection

As we discussed in Chapter 7, judges at the federal level are selected by the federal Minister of Justice and take their place on the bench without confirmation or oversight by any external body. At the provincial level, things work somewhat differently. Superior court judges in any particular province are appointed by the federal Minister of Justice, but only from a pool of candidates deemed by a committee, in that province, to be qualified to hold such judicial office. Provincial court judges are selected by the provincial Attorney General, with the process varying from province to province. Several provinces now utilize a screening body, such as a judicial council, to either prepare pools of potential appointees, or to review candidates selected for possible appointment.

The judicial appointment system has been criticized because it has political overtones at both the federal and provincial levels. Under the appointment systems, judicial hopefuls may have to remain in favour with incumbent politicians in order to receive appointments. Even with the presence of screening committees, judicial candidates must receive the endorsement of the politicians in office if they are to have much hope of receiving a judicial position. Peter Russell and Jacob Ziegel found that of 228 judicial appointments made during the four-year tenure of Progressive Conservative Prime Minister Brian Mulroney, 47.4 per cent of appointees had affiliations with the Progressive Conservative party.[8] While most of the appointees are considered to be "good to excellent" by the profession, Russell and Ziegel's research revealed that of those appointees rated fair or weak, 76.9 per cent had political connections to the government. Because partisan politics plays a role in each system, critics have claimed that sitting judges can rarely be as neutral as they should be.

## Canadian Judicial Council

In 1971, the federal *Judges Act* was amended to authorize the creation of the Canadian Judicial Council. The Council is composed of 35 members, including

- the Chief Justice of Canada, Chair;
- the Chief Justice and Associate Chief Justice, plus the Chief Judge and Associate Chief Judge of the federal courts, including the Tax Court and the Court Martial Appeal Court;
- the Chief Justice and Associate Chief Justice of all federally appointed provincial courts; and
- the Senior Judge of each of the Territorial Superior Courts.

This body is charged with dealing with such matters as continuing education for judges, handling complaints about judicial misconduct, and developing consensus among the judiciary regarding matters involving the administration of justice.[9]

Historically, very little attention has been devoted to judicial training. It seems to have been tacitly assumed that if a person was a competent lawyer, then he or she would also be a competent judge, with no regard being attached to the differences in these two roles. Through coordination with the National Judicial Institute (NJI), the Canadian Judicial Council has sought to improve the educational opportunities available to judges.

The NJI's mandate is to develop and deliver continuing education courses for both federally and provincially appointed judges. At present, judges are encouraged to devote 10 days per year to continuing education. In addition to a seminar for newly appointed judges, the NJI also offers seminar courses on such matters as "Social Context Education," "Criminal Jury Trials," "Genetics, Ethics and Property," "Appellate Courts," "Criminal Law," "Family Law," and "Settlement Conferences."[10]

With nearly 1000 federally appointed judges in Canada, the Canadian Judicial Council has its hands full trying to ensure that as many judges as possible receive adequate ongoing education. Many of the seminars attract 20 to 30 judges at a time. One seminar on criminal jury trials, held in 2001, attracted 78 federal and provincial judges.[11]

## Judicial Misconduct

In December 1995, Mr. Justice Jean Bienvenue of the Quebec Superior Court pushed at the boundaries of appropriate judicial behaviour when, during a woman's murder trial, he remarked that "... when women ascend the scale of virtues they reach higher than men ..." but "... when they decide to degrade themselves, they sink to depths to which even the vilest men could not sink."[12] He was referring to the accused, a woman who had allegedly murdered her husband by slashing his throat. He also referred to the Nazi Holocaust when, during sentencing, he noted that "even the Nazis did not eliminate millions of Jews in a painful or bloody manner. They died in the gas chambers, without suffering." When the jury found the woman guilty of second-degree murder, rather than the more serious offence of first-degree murder, he noted to an officer of the court that the jurors were "idiotic and incompetent." The Canadian Judicial Council received a complaint with respect to the judge's conduct from the Quebec Minister of Justice, the Minister of Justice for Canada, and about 100 members of the public. At a hearing conducted by the Canadian Judicial Council, evidence came forward that this same judge had been noted for making racist slurs, making inappropriate comments about a female juror, a female reporter's attire, and others. A bailiff also testified that the judge had asked him to get him a bottle of vodka from his car while a jury was in deliberations.[13]

To date, Canada has never thrown a superior court judge out of office.[14] Such judges hold office with **security of tenure**, during what is referred to as "good behaviour."[15] To remove a superior court judge from office requires an Action by Parliament. The first stage in this process is an investigation by an inquiry committee, followed by a recommendation by the Canadian Judicial Council for the judge's removal.[16] It appeared that Canada was on its way to removing its first superior court judge with the *Bienvenue* case; however, the judge resigned from office and the proceedings against him were terminated before such action could be contemplated any further.[17]

While most judges are highly professional, in and out of the courtroom, some judges occasionally overstep the limits of "good behaviour." Poor judgment may result from bad taste, insensitivity, or archaic attitudes, as in the case of B.C. County Court judge Peter Van der Hoop, who in 1989 described a three-year-old girl as "sexually aggressive," after sentencing her attacker to 18 months probation for sexual interference.[18] In that case, the Canadian Judicial Council found the judge's choice of words unfortunate, but concluded that his comments did not warrant a formal investigation.

The federal *Judges Act* sets out the criteria under which the Canadian Judicial Council will recommend removal of a judge from office:

**security of tenure**

The protection of judicial independence, embodying the notion that judges cannot be removed from office except in cases of judges breaking the "good behaviour" requirement.

s. 65 (2)   Where, in the opinion of the Council, the judge in respect of whom an inquiry or investigation has been made, has become incapacitated or disabled from the due execution of his office by reason of:

(a)   age or infirmity,

(b)   having been guilty of misconduct,

(c)   having failed in the due execution of his office, or

(d)   having been placed, by his conduct or otherwise, in a position incompatible with the due execution of his office,

the Council, in its report to the Minister under subsection (1), may recommend that the judge be removed from office.

This provision gives some, but not sufficient, scope to the concept of "good behaviour." It is noteworthy that bad behaviour, not a bad decision, will justify recommending the removal of a judge. When a judge renders a bad decision, the decision may be appealed. But when a judge behaves badly, the decision as to whether a judge should continue in office can only be made through an inquiry. Gerald Gall has provided an excellent summary of examples of bad behaviour on the part of judges.[19] He concludes that "it takes a very dramatic malfeasance before the removal provisions are brought into force."[20]

Lower-court judges have been ordered removed from office, for example, for issuing bad cheques and drunkenness, "ticket fixing," extreme sexist commentary, and sexual impropriety.[21] Each province has its own scheme for dealing with the impropriety of lower provincial court judges by typically establishing a judicial council that investigates wrongdoing, but the power of removal generally rests with the provincial cabinet.[22] Rather than endure the humiliation associated with the formal removal process, judges who have been investigated for engaging in bad behaviour frequently take early retirement or resign from office.

## The Crown Prosecutor

The prosecuting lawyer, called variously the "Crown attorney," "**Crown prosecutor**," "**Crown counsel**," or "public prosecutor," is responsible for presenting the state's case against the defendant. Since crimes are offences against the people as embodied in the state, technically speaking, the prosecuting lawyer is the primary representative of the people, as formally embodied in the Crown. Prosecutions are carried out on behalf of the provincial Crown as well as the federal Crown. Federally, and in all provinces except Nova Scotia, the prosecuting lawyer acts directly as an agent of the Attorney General.

Prosecutions in relation to provincial offences, municipal bylaws, and virtually all offences under the *Criminal Code* are carried out by agents for the provincial Attorney General. However, the prosecution of federal offences, other than *Criminal Code* offences, is carried out by agents of the federal Attorney General. Accordingly, one will frequently see provincial Crown counsel carrying out the bulk of prosecutions in our criminal courts, with the periodic appearance of a federal prosecutor to handle such offences as drug possession and trafficking.

The Attorney General fulfills many duties, whether it be at the federal or provincial level. The federal Attorney General is a member of cabinet and the legal advisor to the government. The Attorney General's ministry is involved in drafting legislation for the government. As noted earlier, the Attorney General has a key role in overseeing the courts and the selection of judges. In most provinces, the Attorney General also oversees the provision of police and correctional services. With so many roles, it is no surprise that the Attorney General hires lawyers to act as agents in conducting criminal prosecutions.

Joan Brockman and V. Gordon Rose note that there are typically three different employment relationships between the government and the lawyers that act as prosecutors on their behalf.[23] First, each Attorney General has a staff of "full-time employees" who work for a regular salary, with benefits typically associated with a full-time regular job. Second, an Attorney General may hire full-time or part-time "contract prosecutors." These are lawyers, typically hired for a limited period of time, who perform prosecutorial services. Their contracts are often renewable. The federal government frequently hires a lawyer or law firm to provide prosecutorial services in relation to non–*Criminal Code* federal offences, such as drug offences, that is, in areas that do not warrant a full-time staff to deal with such matters. The third type of employment relationship involves hiring "ad hoc prosecutors." Private lawyers are sometimes hired on such a basis either to determine whether charges should be laid in the circumstances, or to actually carry out the prosecution. This employment relationship permits the government to hire someone outside the agency in cases that are politically charged, for example, in a case where a member of government is being investigated for wrongdoing. The use of ad hoc prosecutors also allows the government to hire lawyers who are experts in a particular area of concern, without retaining staff on a full-time basis.

In addition to the job of prosecuting cases, the Crown prosecutor in many provinces is also the legal advisor to local police departments. Because prosecutors are sensitive to the

**Crown prosecutor**
(also **Crown counsel**)
A public official, licensed to practise law, whose job it is to conduct criminal proceedings on behalf of the Crown against an accused person. Also called a Crown attorney.

kinds of information needed for conviction, they may help guide police investigations and will exhort detectives to identify usable witnesses, uncover additional evidence, and the like. This role is limited, however. Police departments are independent of the administrative authority of the prosecutor, and co-operation between them is based more on the common goal of conviction than on any kind of supervisory control.

While the criminal trial is typically described as an adversarial process, the Crown prosecutor is not simply a partisan advocate. Philip Stenning notes that prosecutors have typically been viewed as "ministers of justice" and "officers of the court."[24] He translates from Mr. Justice Taschereau of the Supreme Court of Canada:

> The situation which the Crown occupies is not that of an advocate in a civil case. His functions are quasi-judicial. He should not so much seek to obtain a verdict of guilty as assist the judge and jury to render the most complete justice. Moderation and impartiality should always characterize his conduct before the court. He will in fact have honestly fulfilled his duty and will be beyond all reproach if, putting aside any appeal to emotions, in a dignified manner consistent with his role, he exposes the evidence to the jury without going beyond what it actually reveals.[25]

Stenning notes numerous cases to similar effect, where the Crown prosecutor has a special position, and indeed also notes that the *Code of Professional Conduct* of the Canadian Bar Association speaks to the matter, placing the prosecutor in a special position of ensuring fairness in the proceedings, rather than being a true adversary. As a barrister, the Crown prosecutor is also acting as "officer of the court." In this sense, Crown prosecutors are charged with preserving the integrity of the court process in all of their dealings in court.

Once a trial begins, the job of the prosecutor is to present the evidence gathered by the state in relation to the offence charged. Prosecutors introduce evidence against the accused, steer the testimony of witnesses "for the Crown," and argue in favour of conviction if that is what the evidence logically leads towards. Since defendants are presumed innocent until proven guilty, the burden of demonstrating guilt beyond a reasonable doubt rests with the prosecutor. The English House of Lords noted this responsibility in *Woolmington* v. *D.P.P* (1935):

> Throughout the web of the English Criminal Law one golden thread is always to be seen, that it is the duty of the prosecution to prove the prisoner's guilt subject to what I have already said as to the defence of insanity and subject also to any statutory exception. If, at the end of and on the whole of the case, there is a reasonable doubt, created by the evidence given by either the prosecution or the prisoner ..., the prosecution has not made out the case and the prisoner is entitled to an acquittal. No matter what the charge or where the trial, the principle that the prosecution must prove the guilt of the prisoner is part of the common law of England, and no attempt to whittle it down can be entertained.[26]

## *Prosecutorial Discretion*

**prosecutorial discretion**
The decision-making power of prosecutors, based upon the wide range of choices available to them, in handling of criminal defendants, scheduling cases for trial, accepting bargained pleas, and so on. The most important form of prosecutorial discretion lies in the power to authorize a charge, or not to authorize a charge, against a suspect.

Prosecutors occupy a unique position in the nation's criminal justice system by virtue of the considerable **prosecutorial discretion** they exercise. They have very broad powers, which are not constrained by many controls.[27] Before a case comes to trial, prosecutors may decide to accept a plea bargain, divert suspects to a public or private social-services agency, or dismiss the case entirely for lack of evidence or for a variety of other reasons. In some provinces, Crown counsel must approve any charges being laid by the police.[28] Recent research has shown that one-third of all cases are stayed or withdrawn by the prosecution prior to the end of the trial.[29] The rate of refusal to approve charges in those provinces using a charge approval process remains an area in need of research; however, it is likely that the charge approval standard being applied in any given province affects the approval rate. For example, in British Columbia, a province using a charge approval process, Crown counsel are required by the Attorney General (as outlined in the AG's policy manual) to apply a stringent standard in authorizing prosecutions to go ahead:

Charge Standard:

Allegations must be examined to determine whether there is a substantial likelihood of conviction; and if so, whether the public interest requires a prosecution of the accused.[30]

In other provinces, and federally, the charge approval standard is set at a lower level, such as whether there is a "reasonable prospect of conviction."[31] A lower charge approval standard likely results in fewer cases being screened out by prosecutors prior to trial.

In preparation for trial, the prosecutor may decide what charges are to be brought against the defendant, and then examines the strength of incriminating evidence and decides what witnesses to call. An important Supreme Court of Canada decision has held that the duty of the prosecution is, in effect, to assist the defence in building its case by making available any evidence in its possession. In this case, *R. v. Stinchcombe* (1991),[32] the Court held that the prosecution is required to disclose to the defence any evidence in its possession that is relevant to the case, whether or not it intends to use it, and whether the evidence is inculpatory (tending to prove guilt) or exculpatory (tending to prove innocence). Although

## BOX 8.1  Theory into Practice

## When the Crown Goes Bad

Prosecutions in Canada are carried out in the name of the Crown. Prosecutors act as agents for the provincial Attorney General in most criminal cases. The role of the prosecutor is unique. On the one hand, a prosecutor is required to operate in an adversarial system, representing the state in a case that usually has real, tangible victims who would like to see the accused convicted. On the other hand, the prosecutor has considerable discretion with regard to the conduct of a criminal prosecution, and the courts are often reluctant to interfere with a prosecutor's decision-making process.

However, the Crown is not an ordinary advocate. The Crown is variously described as possessing a "ministerial" or "quasi-judicial" role. In *R. v. Boucher* (1955),[1] the Supreme Court of Canada described the Crown's role in the following terms:

> It cannot be over-emphasised that the purpose of a criminal prosecution is not to obtain a conviction; it is to lay before a jury what the Crown considered to be creditable evidence relevant to what is alleged to be a crime. Counsel have a duty to see that all available legal proof of the facts is presented: it should be done firmly and pressed to its legitimate strength, but it must also be done fairly. The role of the prosecutor excludes any notion of winning or losing; his function is a matter of public duty than which in civil life there can be none charged with greater personal responsibility. It is to be efficiently performed with an ingrained sense of the dignity, the seriousness and the justness of judicial proceedings (per Rand J.) ...
>
> The position held by counsel for the Crown is not that of a lawyer in civil litigation. His functions are quasi-judicial. His duty is not so much

to obtain a conviction as to assist the judge and jury in ensuring that the fullest possible justice is done. His conduct before the court must always be characterised by moderation and impartiality. He will properly have performed his duty and will be beyond all reproach if, eschewing any appeal to passion, and employing a dignified manner suited to his function, he presents the evidence to the jury without going beyond what it discloses (per Taschereau J.).

In recent years, many Crown counsel appear to prefer a more adversarial role than that envisioned by the top court in *Boucher*. In *R. v. S.(F.)* (2000),[2] the Ontario Court of Appeal rebuked the performance of Crown counsel in a trial where the prosecutor personalized his role, explaining to the jury that his role was to "obtain a conviction." The prosecutor repeatedly referred to the complainant as "notre victime" (our victim), as if she were the client of the Crown prosecutor. In his cross-examination of the accused, the Crown was sarcastic, flippant, and disrespectful towards the accused. He inaccurately summarized the accused's testimony to the jury, ridiculed the accused's explanation professing innocence, and misled the jury with regard to a Supreme Court of Canada judgment from which he read excerpts to the jury.

The Court of Appeal ruled that the accused could not receive a fair trial in such an atmosphere. Crown counsel had breached every aspect of the Supreme Court's classic articulation of the Crown's role in *Boucher*. In order to remedy the serious prejudice, the Court set aside the conviction and ordered a new trial.[3]

## QUESTIONS FOR DISCUSSION

1. If you were a crime victim, what kind of Crown would you like to see prosecute the person who victimized you? How would you feel if you were the defendant facing the prosecutor in *R. v. S.(F.)*?

2. Do you think head prosecutors in Canada should be elected as they are in the United States?

[1] *R. v. Boucher*, [1955] S.C.R. 16.
[2] *R. v. S.(F.)* (2000), 31 C.R. (5th) 159 (Ont.C.A.)
[3] For further discussion of the case, see: Calarco, P. (2000). *S.(F.): When Crowns Go Bad (Again!)*. *Criminal Reports*, 5th, 31, pp. 173–176.

the Crown retains some discretion not to disclose to the accused, such as in cases where it is necessary to protect witnesses from harassment or danger, or where a privilege exists, this discretion may be reviewed by a judge prior to trial. Indeed, some jurisdictions have established special disclosure courts to provide a regular forum in which judges may review why Crown counsel decides not to disclose information to the defence.

One special decision that the prosecutor makes concerns the filing of separate or multiple charges. The decision to try a defendant simultaneously on multiple charges can allow for the presentation of a considerable amount of evidence and permit an in-court demonstration of a complete sequence of criminal events. Such a strategy also has a practical side; it saves time and money by substituting one trial for what might otherwise be any number of trials if each charge were to be brought separately before the court. From the prosecutor's point of view, however, trying the charges one at a time carries the advantage of allowing for another trial on a new charge if a "not guilty" verdict is returned the first time.

The activities of the prosecutor do not end with a finding of guilt or innocence. Following conviction of the accused, prosecutors are allowed to make sentencing recommendations to the judge. They can be expected to argue that aggravating factors (which we will discuss in Chapter 9, on sentencing), prior criminal record, or especially heinous qualities of the offence in question call for strict punishment. When convicted defendants appeal, prosecutors may need to defend their own actions and to argue, in factums filed with appellate courts, that convictions were properly obtained.

Until relatively recently, it has generally been held that prosecutors enjoyed much the same kind of immunity against liability in the exercise of their official duties that judges do. However, the 1989 Supreme Court of Canada case of *Nelles* v. *Ontario*[33] provided that an absolute immunity is not justified in the interests of public policy. In particular, a person must have the right to sue where a prosecutor has acted maliciously and thereby caused damage to the victim. Such suits may not be brought where a person has been convicted. It has been noted that the ability to bring a suit against a prosecutor for malicious prosecution is unlikely to produce an effective remedy and is marred by considerable hurdles.[34] Among the problems noted by Don Stuart are the high costs of such litigation, and in the absence of a remedy for incompetent or negligent conduct on behalf of a prosecutor, the plaintiff must establish actual malicious behaviour. In the *Nelles* case, the suspect had been prosecuted through to the end of a preliminary inquiry on the allegation that she had killed children while working as a nurse in Toronto. Although discharged at the preliminary hearing, her suit against the Crown in Right of Ontario was unsuccessful as she could not establish the necessary malicious conduct on the part of the Attorney General or his agents on the facts of her case.

## The Abuse of Discretion

Because of the large amount of discretion prosecutors wield, the potential for them to abuse it is considerable. For example, a prosecutor may decide not to prosecute friends or political cronies, or to accept guilty pleas to drastically reduced charges for personal considerations. These kind of discretionary decisions are always inappropriate and potentially dangerous. On the other hand, Crown prosecutors, seeking heightened visibility in order to support grand political ambitions, may prosecute overzealously. This is also another source of abuse. Some forms of abuse may be unconscious. At least one study conducted in the United States suggests that some prosecutors may have a built-in tendency towards leniency where female defendants are concerned, but tend to discriminate against minorities in deciding whether to prosecute.[35]

Although prosecutors must answer to their supervisors in the Attorney General's ministry, and ultimately to the Attorney General, it has been noted "that there is little effective legal, political, or administrative accountability for prosecutors."[36] Unlike the situation in the United States, local prosecutors are not subject to periodic re-election by the populace. Gross misconduct by a prosecutor may be addressed in several ways: (1) the prosecutor's conduct may be scrutinized by the Attorney General, (2) the Attorney General may have to answer for the prosecutor's conduct in a legislature, (3) by action on the part of the Law Society, and (4) by judicial review.[37] Short of criminal misconduct, however, most of the options available to either the court or the Attorney General are limited.

The *Canadian Charter of Rights and Freedoms* has given the courts a renewed opportunity to bring prosecutorial conduct under scrutiny. Where the conduct of a prosecutor can be characterized as an **abuse of process**, a court may intervene to stay the prosecution of a case, or provide a different remedy if the court considers it appropriate. An abuse of process may arise either where the conduct of the prosecution renders a trial unfair, or where the conduct, by its very nature, usurps the integrity of the judicial process itself.[38] Courts have recently been concerned with allegations of judge shopping, discriminatory prosecution, and personal vendettas as conduct relevant to an abuse of process inquiry.[39]

## The Prosecutor's Professional Responsibility

As members of the legal profession, prosecutors are subject to the Canadian Bar Association's (CBA) *Code of Professional Conduct*. Serious violations of the code may result in a prosecutor being disbarred from the practice of law. The duties imposed by the Bar Association on a prosecutor today are as follows:

> When engaged as a prosecutor, the lawyer's prime duty is not to seek a conviction, but to present before the trial court all available credible evidence relevant to the alleged crime in order that justice may be done through a fair trial upon the merits. The prosecutor exercises a public function involving much discretion and power and must act fairly and dispassionately. The prosecutor should not do anything that might prevent the accused from being represented by counsel or communicating with counsel and, to the extent required by law and accepted practice, should make timely disclosure to the accused or defence counsel (or the court if the accused is not represented) of all relevant facts and known witnesses, whether tending to show guilt or innocence, or that would affect the punishment of the accused.[40]

The duty of the prosecutor is to seek justice, not merely to obtain a conviction. Hence, a prosecutor is barred by the standards of the legal profession from advocating any fact or position that he or she knows is untrue.

# Defence Counsel

## Role of the Defence Lawyer

The **defence counsel** is a trained lawyer who may specialize in the practice of criminal law. The task of the defence lawyer is to represent the accused as soon as possible after arrest

The defence counsel is a trained lawyer who may specialize in the practice of criminal law. Above are two defence lawyers who represented Paul Bernardo at his trial.

**abuse of process** The use of powers, legitimately conferred on an individual, for purposes other than those originally intended, such as for personal gain. It may also include the illegitimate use of powers granted to the individual to achieve organizational goals such as detaining and prosecuting offenders.

**defence counsel**
(also **defence lawyer**)
A licensed trial lawyer hired or appointed to conduct the legal defence of an individual accused of a crime and to represent him or her before a court of law.

BOX 8.2

# Theory into Practice

## The Law Society of Upper Canada: Rules of Professional Conduct

The conduct of lawyers is very important to the effectiveness of the criminal justice system in Canada. Accordingly, rules of professional conduct exist in order to ensure public confidence in the administration of justice and in the legal profession. While the Canadian Bar Association has developed certain guidelines for its members, individual provinces have established specific rules to set out precise parameters of conduct. For example, as of 2000, the Law Society of Upper Canada in Ontario has rules for governing the lawyer's relationships with clients, for governing the practice of law in general, for setting out a lawyer's responsibilities to the court and other members of the legal system, for governing the lawyer's interaction with articling students and employees, and for governing relations with other lawyers and with the law society itself.

Each set of rules contains a variety of more specific rules, with relevant commentary that explains the operation of the rules. For example, under the main rule governing the lawyer's relationship to the administration of justice, the first rule and commentary pertain to the lawyer's role as an advocate:

4.01 (1) When acting as an advocate, a lawyer shall represent the client resolutely and honourably within the limits of the law while treating the tribunal with candour, fairness, courtesy, and respect.

Under the attached commentary, a lawyer's duties extend still further, requiring a lawyer to:

… raise fearlessly every issue, advance every argument and ask every question, however distasteful, which the lawyer thinks will help the client's case and to endeavour to obtain for the client the benefit of every remedy and defence authorized by law …

Since the legal system is adversarial, lawyers are given specific guidance for working in an adversarial atmosphere:

In adversary proceedings the lawyer's function as advocate is openly and necessarily partisan. Accordingly, the lawyer is not obliged (save as required by law or under these rules and subject to the duties of a prosecutor set out below) to assist an adversary or advance matters derogatory to the client's case.

In adversary proceedings that will likely affect the health, welfare, or security of a child, a lawyer should advise the client to take into account the best interests of the child, where this can be done without prejudicing the legitimate interests of the client.

When acting as an advocate, a lawyer should refrain from expressing the lawyer's personal opinions on the merits of a client's case.

For defence counsel, here is the specific commentary that discusses the unique ethical situations attendant to defending criminally accused persons:

Rule 4.01 When defending an accused person, a lawyer's duty is to protect the client as far as possible from being convicted except by a tribunal of competent jurisdiction and upon legal evidence sufficient to support a conviction for the offence with which the client is charged. Accordingly, and notwithstanding the lawyer's private opinion on credibility or the merits, a lawyer may properly rely on any evidence or defences including so-called technicalities not known to be false or fraudulent.

Admissions made by the accused to a lawyer may impose strict limitations on the conduct of the defence, and the accused should be made aware of this. For example, if the accused clearly admits to the lawyer the factual and mental elements necessary to constitute the offence, the lawyer, if convinced that the admissions are true and voluntary, may properly take objection to the jurisdiction of the court, or to the form of the indictment, or to the admissibility or sufficiency of the evidence, but must not suggest that some other person committed the offence or call any evidence which, by reason of the admissions, the lawyer believes to be false. Nor may the lawyer set up an affirmative case inconsistent with such admissions, for example, by calling evidence in support of an alibi intended to show that the accused could not have done or, in fact, has not done the act. Such admissions will also impose a limit on the extent to which the lawyer may attack the evidence for the prosecution. The lawyer is entitled to test the evidence given by each individual witness for the prosecution and argue that the evidence taken as a whole is insufficient to amount to proof that the accused is guilty of the offence charged, but the lawyer should go no further than that.

The lawyer should never waive or abandon the client's legal rights, for example, an available defence under a statute of limitations, without the client's informed consent.…

*Source*: Law Society of Upper Canada. (2002). *Rules of professional conduct (as amended to June 22, 2002)*. LSUC's Website: **www.lsuc.on.ca/services/ RulesProfCondpage_en.jsp**

and to ensure that the individual rights of the defendant are not violated through processing by the criminal justice system. Other duties of the defence counsel include testing the strength of the prosecution's case, being involved in plea negotiations, and preparing an adequate defence to be used at trial. In the preparation of a defence, criminal lawyers may enlist private detectives, experts, witnesses to the crime, and character witnesses. Some criminal lawyers will perform aspects of the role of private detective or investigator themselves. They will also review relevant court precedents to determine what the best defence strategy might be.

Defence preparation may involve intense communications between lawyer and defendant. Such discussions are recognized as privileged communications, which are protected by solicitor–client confidentiality. In other words, a defence lawyer cannot be compelled to reveal information that his or her client has confided to the lawyer.[41]

If his or her client is found guilty, a defence lawyer will be involved in arguments at sentencing, may be asked to file an appeal, and will probably counsel the defendant and the defendant's family as to what civil matters (payment of debts, release from contractual obligations, and so on) may need to be arranged after sentence is imposed. Hence, the role of the defence lawyer encompasses many aspects, including attorney, negotiator, confidant, family and personal counsellor, social worker, investigator, and, as we shall see, bill collector.

## The Private Criminal Lawyer

Three major categories of defence lawyers assist criminal defendants in the United States: (1) private criminal lawyers; (2) judicare counsel; and (3) public defenders.

Private criminal lawyers (also called "retained counsel") either have their own legal practices or work for law firms in which they may be partners or associates. As those who have had to hire defence lawyers know, the fees of private lawyers can be high. Most privately retained criminal lawyers charge in the range of $100 to $200 per hour. Included in the bill is the time it takes to prepare for a case, as well as time spent in the courtroom. "High-powered" criminal defence lawyers who have established a regional or national reputation for successfully defending their clients can be far more expensive. A few such lawyers, such as Edward "Eddie" Greenspan, Brian Greenspan, Morris Manning, Clayton Ruby, and Alan Gold, have become household names by virtue of their association with famous defendants and well-publicized trials. Fees charged by famous criminal defence lawyers may run into the hundreds of thousands of dollars—and sometimes exceed $1 million—for handling just one case!

Clearly, the profit motive has turned the practice of law into a business, leaving many lawyers dissatisfied and perhaps less trusted by their clients than was true in the past. Lawyers are indoctrinated into the profession as articling students with a need to generate "billable hours" so that their law firms can bring in enough money to keep the business solvent, and hopefully expanding. Today, the profit margin seems to be a major cause for concern in law firms, more so than in the past. The practice of law is today at least as much a business as it is a profession.

Although there are many high-priced criminal defence lawyers in the country, the high cost of retaining a lawyer is most evident in the context of lawyers specializing in civil causes of action, many of whom take a large portion of the monetary awards that they win for their clients. Few law students actually choose to specialize in criminal law, even though the job of a criminal lawyer may appear glamorous. Some begin their careers immediately following law school, while others seek to gain experience working as prosecutors or public defenders for a number of years before going into private practice. In contrast to criminal lawyers whose names are household words, the collection of fees can be quite difficult for other defence lawyers. Most defendants are poor. Those who aren't are often reluctant to pay what may seem to them to be an exorbitant fee, and woe betide the defence lawyer whose client is convicted before the fee has been paid!

### Criminal Defence of the Poor

In 2001-02, total government spending hit $593 million to provide legal representation, primarily for criminal defendants unable to afford their own.[42] (See Figure 8–1.) In the

1990s, government spending on legal aid went through significant cutbacks. However, in recent years (2000-01 and 2001-02), government spending on legal aid has increased.

Legal aid schemes in Canada fit into one of three models: (1) the judicare model, (2) the public defender model, and (3) the combined model. Unlike the situation in the United States, where a series of decisions in U.S. Supreme Court cases have guaranteed that defendants unable to pay for private criminal-defence lawyers will receive court-appointed and paid legal representation, the schemes for indigent defence developed along a different line in Canada.

Instead of court-appointed defence lawyers, whose fees are paid at a rate set by the state or local government, Canadian jurisdictions typically used a system of legal aid whereby a government-subsidized non-profit society, such as a legal services society, maintained a pool of funds from which money would be dispersed to lawyers acting on behalf of needy clients who qualified under criteria established by the society. This was the model of legal aid that had prevailed in England, and continues in many jurisdictions today, frequently referred to as the judicare model.[43]

As the name implies, the judicare model is analogous to a medicare model in the provision of medical services. In each scheme, the client is allowed to select the professional of his or her choice, at least from those who are willing to work for the fee contained in the tariff set by the scheme. This element of choice is perhaps the best part of the judicare model. Clients like to have the freedom to select a lawyer of their choice. This model also seems to be more like the traditional lawyer-client relationship rather than the alternative, that is, the **public defender** model, where the client loses control over choice.

Whereas judicare lawyers are typically private lawyers who periodically, or even almost exclusively, work for the legal aid tariff, public defenders are lawyers who are kept on staff and paid a regular salary to provide criminal defence representation to anyone who is looking for it. This model is like the typical American model of indigent legal representation. People who cannot afford a lawyer go to a public defender's office, and if they qualify for representation, they are provided with a lawyer from the team of lawyers on staff in that office. Such offices are typically attached to a particular courthouse. Lawyers are assigned to cases on a first-come basis, so clients have no say in their choice of lawyer.

Since staff lawyers, or public defenders, are paid a regular salary, there is less room for financial abuse by lawyers in such a system. Regardless of the caseload, a lawyer working under such a scheme receives the same rate of pay. There is no financial incentive to take a case to trial rather than to reach a plea agreement. In contrast, the judicare schemes typically pay lawyers a fee for service. Just as the Canadian medical system has been criticized for financially rewarding doctors for doing unnecessary tests, and encouraging excessive office visits, the judicare model has been criticized for rewarding lawyers with additional fees for trials over what they would get for simply making sentencing submissions following a guilty plea. Similarly, taking a case on appeal will be more financially rewarding

**public defender** A lawyer employed by a government agency or sub-agency, or by a private organization under contract to a unit of government, for the purpose of providing defence services to indigents.

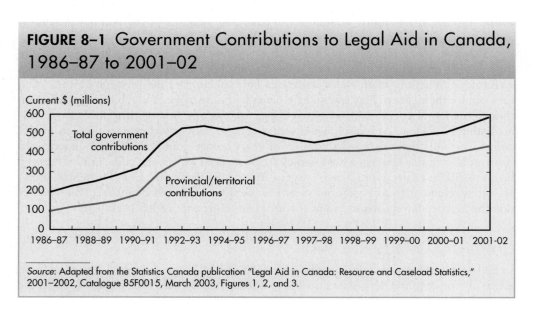

**FIGURE 8–1** Government Contributions to Legal Aid in Canada, 1986–87 to 2001–02

Source: Adapted from the Statistics Canada publication "Legal Aid in Canada: Resource and Caseload Statistics," 2001–2002, Catalogue 85F0015, March 2003, Figures 1, 2, and 3.

than allowing the client to simply serve out his or her sentence, without challenging the decision of the judge at trial. Accordingly, the judicare model has been viewed by many as an inefficient way of delivering legal aid to the poor.

Critics charge that public defenders, because they are government employees, are not sufficiently independent from prosecutors and judges. For the same reason, clients may be suspicious of public defenders, viewing them as state functionaries. Finally, the huge caseloads typical of public defenders' offices create pressures towards an excessive use of plea bargaining.

In Canada, some provinces have opted for the public defender model in recent years. Others have retained the judicare model. Most provinces have chosen a combined model. The province of Ontario has resorted to this approach only recently. While much has been said about the relative costs of each model, Table 8–1 shows no clear advantage to either model.

The assumption that the public defender model is more cost efficient than the judicare model has led many provinces to move towards this model in recent years. While there has been considerable research and debate in recent years over the relative merits of each system,[44] it appears that the two models provide similar rates of conviction.[45] Debate rages over whether public defender systems are actually more cost-efficient than judicare systems. One problem with free counsel, whether judicare or staff, concerns degree of effort. Although most legal aid lawyers probably take their jobs seriously, some feel only a loose commitment to their clients. Paying clients, in their eyes, deserve better service, and they are apt to get it.

Critics of the current system of indigent defence point out that the system is woefully underfunded. Because of limited funding, legal services societies are required to set low income threshold points beyond which an accused will be unable to obtain funded counsel. In British Columbia, a member of a family of four will be unable to obtain legal aid if their family income exceeds $1792 per month; neither can an accused own anything, such as a car, worth more than $5000.[46]

A recent development that appears to target middle-income earners is the concept of prepaid legal insurance. Under such plans, the individual pays an annual premium to an insurance company, which then pays for any legal fees incurred by an individual should the subscriber later require the services of a lawyer. While such schemes are still quite rare, it is a new direction in legal services likely to see continued development in the future.[47]

## The Ethics of Defence

As we have discussed, the job of defence counsel at trial is to prepare and offer a vigorous defence on behalf of the accused. A proper defence often involves the presentation of evidence and the examination of witnesses, all of which requires careful thought and planning. Good lawyers, like quality craftspeople everywhere, may find themselves emotionally committed to the outcome of trials in which they are involved. Beyond the immediacy of a given trial, lawyers also realize that their reputations can be influenced by lay perceptions of their performance and that their careers and personal financial success depend upon consistently "winning" in the courtroom.

The nature of the adversarial process, fed by the emotions of the participants, conspires with the often privileged and extensive knowledge that defence lawyers have about a case to tempt the professional ethics of some counsellors. Because the defence counsel may often know more about the guilt or innocence of the defendant than anyone else prior to trial, the defence must be careful of ethical and procedural considerations. Lawyers violate both law and the standards of their own profession if they knowingly misrepresent themselves or their clients.

**TABLE 8–1 Per-Capita Spending by Province/Territory, 2001–02**

| Jurisdiction | Per-Capita Expenditure | % Change from Previous Year |
|---|---|---|
| **Primary Judicature** | | |
| New Brunswick | $7.18 | 32 |
| Ontario | $24.72 | 21 |
| Alberta | $10.59 | 19 |
| **Primary Staff** | | |
| Newfoundland | N/A | N/A |
| Prince Edward Island | $5.61 | 6 |
| Nova Scotia | $13.78 | 18 |
| Saskatchewan | $11.72 | 8 |
| **Mixed** | | |
| Quebec | $15.95 | 15 |
| Manitoba | $16.99 | 8 |
| British Columbia | $21.96 | 3 |
| Northwest Territories | $91.61 | 7 |
| Yukon | $37.16 | 8 |
| Nunavut | $124.08 | 23 |
| **Canada** | **$19.42** | **16** |

*Source:* Adapted from the Statistics Canada publication "Legal Aid in Canada: Resource and Caseload Statistics," 2001–2002, Catalogue 85F0015, March 2003, Table 4.

To help lawyers know what is expected of them, ethical standards abound. The Canadian Bar Association and each provincial law society have established the main sets of standards.

## *The Canadian Bar Association's Code of Professional Conduct and the Law Society of Upper Canada's Rules of Professional Conduct*

In order to practise law, a lawyer must be a member of the provincial law society in the province where he or she works. As the governing bodies of the legal profession, each provincial law society sets rules regulating the conduct of its members. The CBA's *Code of Professional Conduct* is not binding on any lawyers unless the province's law society incorporates the code into its own rules. Since the CBA's *Code* is largely based on the Law Society of Upper Canada's rules, which are in force in Ontario, the two sets of standards in that province overlap substantially. Even if the CBA's *Code* has not been adopted by a law society, the *Code* provides a set of guidelines to which lawyers ought to conform. Each set of standards is revised periodically. Rule 9 of the CBA's *Code of Professional Conduct* governs the lawyer's role as an advocate, speaking directly to the proper ethical conduct expected of a lawyer who appears in court on behalf of a client. This rule is identical to Rule 10 in the Law Society of Upper Canada's (LSUC) *Rules of Professional Conduct*. In British Columbia, a *Code of Professional Conduct* sets out the main canons of ethics covered by the CBA's and LSUC's rules. Chapter 1 of the *Code of Professional Conduct* sets out the general ethical obligations of a lawyer to

1. the state;

2. courts and tribunals;

3. the client;

4. other lawyers;

5. oneself.

Subsequent chapters of the *Code* provide more detailed guidance to lawyers faced with ethical issues. Chapter 8 deals with the lawyer's duties as an advocate. According to the first set of rules in this chapter, a lawyer must **not**:

(a) abuse the process of a court or tribunal by instituting or prosecuting proceedings which, although legal in themselves, are clearly motivated by malice on the part of the client and are brought solely for the purpose of injuring the other party;

(b) knowingly assist the client to do anything or acquiesce in the client doing anything which the lawyer considers to be dishonest or dishonourable;

(c) appear before a judicial officer, when the lawyer, the lawyer's associates or the client have business or personal relationships with such officer that may reasonably be perceived to affect the impartiality of that officer;

(d) attempt or acquiesce in anyone else attempting, directly or indirectly, to influence the decision or actions of a court or tribunal or any of its officials by any means except by open persuasion as an advocate;

(e) knowingly assert something for which there is no reasonable basis in evidence, or the admissibility of which must first be established;

(f) deliberately refrain from informing the tribunal of any pertinent authority directly on point and which has not been mentioned by the opponent;

(g) dissuade a material witness from giving evidence, or advise such a witness to be absent;

(h) knowingly permit a witness to be presented in a false or misleading way, or to impersonate another person; or

(i) appear before a court or tribunal while impaired by alcohol or a drug.

A lawyer acting in the capacity of defence counsel must give the client the best defence possible, even though the lawyer may have personal doubts about the client's innocence. Rules 3(5) and 3(6) in Chapter 1 of the *Code* provide:

(5) A lawyer should endeavour by all fair and honourable means to obtain for a client the benefit of any and every remedy and defence which is authorized by law. The lawyer

must, however, steadfastly bear in mind that this great trust is to be performed within and not without the bounds of the law. The office of the lawyer does not permit, much less demand, for any client, violation of law or any manner of fraud or chicanery. No client has a right to demand that the lawyer be illiberal or do anything repugnant to the lawyer's own sense of honour and propriety.

(6) It is a lawyer's right to undertake the defence of a person accused of crime, regardless of the lawyer's own personal opinion as to the guilt of the accused. Having undertaken such defence, the lawyer is bound to present, by all fair and honourable means and in a manner consistent with the client's instructions, every defence that the law of the land permits, to the end that no person will be convicted but by due process of law.

However, once a client has confessed guilt to a lawyer, the lawyer's conduct is affected from that point onward. If the client shows an intention to take the stand to make false statements, the lawyer is duty-bound to take action. Counsel must advise his or her client against such action. If the client persists, the lawyer is duty-bound to withdraw from the case. Chapter 8, Rules 2 through 5, govern such circumstances:

2. Where a client advises the lawyer that the client intends to offer false testimony in a proceeding, the lawyer shall explain to the client the lawyer's professional duty to withdraw if the client insists on offering, or in fact does offer, false testimony.

3. Where a client who has been counselled in accordance with Rule 2 advises the lawyer that the client intends to offer false testimony in a proceeding the lawyer shall, in accordance with Chapter 10, withdraw from representing the client in that matter.

4. A lawyer who withdraws under Rule 3 shall not disclose to the court or tribunal, or to any other person, the fact that the withdrawal was occasioned by the client's insistence on offering false testimony.

5. A lawyer shall not call as a witness in a proceeding a person who has advised the lawyer that the witness intends to offer false testimony.

Once representation has been undertaken, the functions and duties of defence counsel are the same whether defence counsel is privately retained, or serving in a legal aid or public defender program.

Even with these rules, however, defence lawyers are under no obligation to reveal information obtained from a client without the client's permission. At common law, a solicitor-client privilege extends to include all forms of communication made for the purpose of obtaining or providing legal advice with respect to a matter on which a client has contacted a lawyer. Sometimes, however, the rules may create a situation that places the lawyer in a difficult ethical dilemma in which the lawyer's duty to the court and the due administration of justice is pitted against the lawyer's duty to maintain confidentiality.[48]

Many lawyers strongly committed to the defence perspective are unwilling to engage in balancing acts that may imperil their client's best interests. Famous criminal defence lawyer Edward Greenspan strongly stated this opinion:

I can only hope that the best interests of the accused do result in the best interests of society, but, if in fact they do not, it is not my client who must suffer. I can not agree that my representations of my client must be affected by considering society's interests — that is not my function. Let justice be done, all right, but *for my client* [his emphasis].[49]

## The Bailiff

Each court has an officer variously referred to as a **sheriff**, a court officer, or the **bailiff**, who is another member of the professional courtroom work group. The bailiff is responsible for ensuring order in the courtroom, calling or finding witnesses in the courthouse, and preventing the escape of the accused (if the accused has not been released on bail). The bailiff also supervises the jury, from the initial calling-up of potential jurors, through to protecting their privacy during deliberations.

Courtrooms can be dangerous places. Periodically, disgruntled clients of the justice system decide to exact revenge, either against a judge, or against those with whom they have

**bailiff** (also **sheriff**)
The court officer whose duties are to keep order in the courtroom and to maintain physical custody of the jury.

been embroiled in a legal dispute. Additionally, prisoners periodically seize the opportunity to make an escape from a courtroom, whose security is less stringent than that of a high-security prison facility. In these cases, the bailiff or sheriff takes on a law enforcement responsibility as the preserver of order in the court.

## Local Court Administrators

Many provinces now employ trial court administrators whose job it is to facilitate the smooth functioning of courts, in particular, judicial districts or areas. Court administrators and trial schedulers provide uniform court management, assuming many of the duties previously performed by chief judges, prosecutors, and court clerks. Where court administrators operate, the ultimate authority for running the court still rests with the chief judge. Administrators, however, are able to relieve the judge of many routine and repetitive tasks, such as record keeping, scheduling, case flow analysis, personnel administration, space utilization, facilities planning, and budget management. They may also serve to take minutes at meetings of judges and their committees.

Effective court administrators are able to track lengthy cases and identify bottlenecks in court processing. They then suggest strategies to make the administration of justice increasingly efficient for courtroom professionals and more humane for lay participants.

## The Court Recorder

Also called the court stenographer or court reporter, the recorder creates a record of all that occurs during trial. Accurate records are very important in criminal trial courts because appeals may be based entirely upon what occurred in the courtroom. Especially significant are all verbal comments made in the courtroom, including testimony, objections, the rulings of the judge, the judge's instructions to the jury, arguments made by lawyers, and the results of rulings by the judge on objections raised by counsel. Occasionally, the judge will rule that a statement should be "stricken from the record" because it is inappropriate or unfounded. The official trial record, often taken on a stenotype machine or audio recorder, may later be transcribed in manuscript form and will become the basis for any appellate review of the trial. Today's court stenographers often employ computer-aided transcription software (CAT), which translates typed stenographic shorthand into complete and readable transcripts.

## Clerk of Court

The duties of the clerk of court extend beyond the courtroom. The clerk maintains all records of criminal cases, including all pleas and motions made both before and after the actual trial. The clerk also prepares any subpoenas for witnesses for both the prosecution and defence, and acts on the judge's order to issue bench warrants. During the trial, the clerk (or an assistant) marks physical evidence for identification as instructed by the judge and maintains custody of such evidence. The clerk also swears in witnesses and performs other functions as the judge directs.

In most provinces, acting as a clerk of the court is an important stepping stone towards achieving the position of justice of the peace. A clerk of court's many years of experience in court leaves him or her quite well-prepared for the judicial functions carried out by justices today.

## The Expert Witness

**expert witness** A person who has special knowledge and skills recognized by the court as relevant to the determination of guilt or innocence. Expert witnesses may express opinions or draw conclusions in their testimony—unlike lay witnesses.

Most of the "insiders" we've talked about so far are either employees of the state or have ongoing professional relationships with the court (as in the case of defence counsel). An **expert witness**, however, typically does not have that kind of status. Expert witnesses are recognized for specialized skills and knowledge in an established profession or technical area. They must demonstrate their expertise through education, work experience, publications, and awards. By testifying at a trial, they provide an effective way of introducing scientific evidence in such areas as medicine, psychology, psychiatry, ballistics, crime scene analysis, photography, and many other disciplines. An expert witness, like the other courtroom "actors" described in this chapter, is generally a paid professional. And, like all other witnesses, they are subject to cross-examination. Unlike other ("lay") witnesses, however, they are allowed to express opinions and draw conclusions, but only within their particular area of expertise. Expert witnesses may be veterans of many trials. Some well-known expert witnesses traverse the country and earn very high fees by testifying at one trial after another.

Expert witnesses have played significant roles in many well-known cases. The 1995 decision of the Ontario Court of Appeal to acquit Guy Paul Morin of the murder of Christine Jessop in Queensville, Ontario, was based on expert evidence on the analysis of human DNA. In the same year, in the United States, the criminal trial of O. J. Simpson became a stage for a battle between experts in the analysis of human DNA, while expert testimony in the trial of John Hinckley resulted in a finding of "not guilty by reason of insanity" for the man accused of shooting then president Reagan. Similarly, the evidence of psychiatric experts was an important factor in the 1987 trial of Ken Parks. Parks drove 22 kilometres from Pickering, Ontario to Scarborough, where he killed his mother-in-law and wounded his father-in-law, while apparently in a sleepwalking state. Parks' acquittal was upheld by the Supreme Court of Canada.[50] An important Supreme Court of Canada case addressing the admissibility of expert witness testimony is *R. v. Mohan*[51] (1994), which is discussed in greater detail in Chapter 15.

One of the difficulties with expert testimony is that it can be confusing to the jury. Sometimes the trouble is due to the nature of the subject matter and sometimes to disagreements between the experts themselves. Often, however, the difficulty arises because the law requires that the expert testimony be confined to clearly articulated legal issues. The difference between medical and legal definitions of mental disorder, for example, points to a divergence in both history and purpose between the law and science. Courts that attempt to apply criteria, such as the Canadian variation on the McNaughten rule (discussed earlier in Chapter 3), in deciding claims of "mental disorder" or "disease of the mind" often find themselves faced with the testimony of psychiatric experts who refuse even to recognize the terminology. Such experts may prefer, instead, to speak in terms of psychosis and anxiety disorders—words that have no place in judicial jargon. Legal requirements, because of the uncertainties they create, may pit experts against one another and confuse the jury.

Even so, most authorities agree that expert testimony is usually perceived by jurors to be more trustworthy than other forms of evidence. In a study of scientific evidence, one prosecutor commented that if he had to choose between presenting a fingerprint or an eyewitness at trial, he would always go with the fingerprint.[52] Some authors have called attention to the difficulties surrounding expert testimony. Procedural limitations often severely curtail the kinds of information that experts can provide. Psychiatric experts operate with different fundamental assumptions about human behaviour than the law does, resulting in further problems with the tendering of expert evidence in criminal trials.[53]

Expert witnesses can earn substantial fees. DNA specialist John Gerdes, for example, was paid $100 per hour for his work in support of the defence in the O. J. Simpson criminal trial, and New York forensic pathologist Michael Baden charged $1500 per day for time spent working for Simpson in Los Angeles. Even Canadian experts had their hand in the *Simpson* case, with renowned spousal abuse expert Donald Dutton, from the University of British Columbia, attending at the Simpson hearings.

# OUTSIDERS: NON-PROFESSIONAL COURTROOM PARTICIPANTS

A number of people find themselves either unwilling or unwitting participants in criminal trials. Into this category fall defendants, victims, and most witnesses. Although they are "outsiders" who lack the status of paid professional participants, these are precisely the people who provide the "grist" for the judicial mill. Without them, trials could not occur, and the professional roles described earlier would be rendered meaningless.

**lay witness** An eyewitness, character witness, or any other person called upon to testify who is not considered an expert. Lay witnesses must testify to facts alone and may not draw conclusions or express opinions.

**subpoena** An order issued by a court requiring an individual to appear in court and to give testimony. Some subpoenas mandate that books, papers, and other items be surrendered to the court.

**victim assistance programs** Organized programs that offer services to victims of crime, for example, crisis intervention and follow-up counselling, and that help victims secure their rights under the law.

**juror** A member of a jury, selected for jury duty, and required to serve as an arbiter of the facts in a court of law. Jurors are expected to render verdicts of guilt or innocence as to the charges brought against an accused, although they may sometimes fail to do so (as in the case of a hung jury).

# Lay Witnesses

A non-expert witness, otherwise known as a **lay witness**, may be called by either the prosecution or defence. Lay witnesses may be eyewitnesses, who saw the crime being committed or who came upon the crime scene shortly after the crime had occurred. Another type of lay witness is the character witness, who provides information about the personality, family life, business acumen, and so on of the defendant in an effort to show that the defendant is not the kind of person who would commit the crime that he or she is charged with. Rules of court typically put considerable restrictions on the use of character witnesses prior to the sentencing phase. Of course, the victim may also be a witness, providing detailed and sometimes lengthy testimony about the defendant and the event in question.

Witnesses are officially notified that they are to appear in court to testify by a document called a **subpoena**. Subpoenas are generally "served" by a process server. Both sides in a criminal case may subpoena witnesses and might ask that persons called to testify bring with them books, papers, photographs, videotapes, or other forms of physical evidence. Witnesses who fail to appear when subpoenaed may face contempt-of-court charges.

A witness is responsible for providing accurate testimony concerning only those things of which he or she has direct knowledge. Normally, witnesses will not be allowed to repeat things told to them by others unless it is necessary to account for certain actions of their own. Since few witnesses are familiar with courtroom procedure, the task of testifying is fraught with uncertainty and can be traumatizing.

Anyone who testifies in a criminal trial must do so under oath, or by taking a solemn affirmation, for those who find either "swearing" or a reference to God objectionable. All witnesses are subject to cross-examination, a process that will be discussed in detail later in this chapter. Lay witnesses may be surprised to find that cross-examination can force them to defend their personal and moral integrity. A cross-examiner may question a witness about prior bad acts, criminal acts, or poor reputation, even where such matters have never been the subject of a criminal proceeding.[54] As long as the intent of such questions is to demonstrate to the jury that the witness may not be a person who is worthy of belief, those questions will normally be permitted by the judge.

Witnesses have traditionally been shortchanged by the judicial process. Subpoenaed to attend court, they have often suffered from frequent and unannounced changes in trial dates. A witness who promptly responds to a subpoena to appear by appearing in court on the date and time specified may find that legal manoeuvring has resulted in unanticipated delays. Strategic changes by either side may make the testimony of some witnesses entirely unnecessary, and people who have prepared themselves for the psychological rigours of testifying often experience an emotional letdown.

To compensate a witness for his or her time, and to make up for lost income, most provinces pay witnesses for each day that they spend in court. Payments typically range from $20 to $30 per day, which rarely recompenses a witness for his or her time; however, it provides some indication of support for the role of the witness in the criminal proceeding.

In another move to make the job of witnesses less onerous, most jurisdictions have taken to using **victim assistance programs** (also called victim/witness assistance programs), described shortly, in Crown counsel offices. Such individuals are usually trained volunteers who notify witnesses and victims of scheduling changes and cancellations in criminal proceedings. In British Columbia, the *Victims of Crime Act* gives a victim the right to information about his or her case, from the police investigatory stage through to the prosecution of the case.

# Jurors

Section 11(f) of the *Canadian Charter of Rights and Freedoms* provides that "[a]ny person charged with an offence has the right ... to the benefit of trial by jury where the maximum punishment for the offence is imprisonment for five years or a more severe punishment." The makeup of a criminal trial jury can be determined from the *Criminal Code* and provincial legislation. A jury is composed of 12 people. If a **juror** is unable to continue being on the jury during a trial due to accident, illness, or personal emergency, a judge may discharge the juror. However, a jury cannot have less than 10 jurors, or the judge must declare a mistrial.[55]

Jury duty is regarded as a responsibility of citizenship. Other than youths, the mentally and physically infirm, and certain people such as police personnel, lawyers, prison guards, and government officials, persons called for jury duty must serve unless they can convince a judge, or other court official, that they should be excused for overriding reasons. Aliens, people convicted of a serious offence, and citizens who have served on a jury within the past two years are excluded from jury service in most jurisdictions.[56] The names of prospective jurors are often gathered from the voter registration rolls of a province or municipality.

Ideally, the jury should be a microcosm of society, reflecting the values, rationality, and common sense of the average person. The *Criminal Code* outlines a scheme for selecting a jury that is indifferent towards each side in the case, and is representative of the community from which the accused has come. The Supreme Court of Canada has held that a criminal defendant has the right to have his or her case heard before an impartial and representative jury.[57] Ideally, a jury is composed of a representative cross-section of the community in which the alleged crime has occurred and where the trial is to be held. The idea of a jury of one's peers stems from the Magna Carta's original guarantee of jury trials for "freemen." "Freemen" in England during the thirteenth century, however, were more likely to be of similar mind than is a cross-section of Canadians today. Hence, although the duty of the jury is to deliberate upon the evidence and, ultimately, to determine guilt or innocence, social dynamics may play just as great a role in a jury's verdict as do the facts of a case.

In a 1998 case, *R. v. Williams*,[58] the Supreme Court of Canada clarified the notion that an impartial and representative jury entails a right of the accused to minimize the likelihood of bias or prejudice. While it is not necessary for every jury to have representatives of every conceivable racial, ethnic, religious, gender, and economic group in the community, the possibility of racial prejudice may now be brought out through questioning in the process of empanelling the jury. Where it is established by expert evidence, or by a judge accepting an obvious assertion by counsel, that there is widespread prejudice in a community against members of the accused's race, counsel for the accused is entitled to ask the potential jurors a few relevant questions in this regard. Potential jurors may be asked if they are prejudiced in a way that could affect their partiality, and if so, whether they are capable of setting aside that prejudice if they sit as a juror. Canadian lawyers may not ask extensive questions of a juror; neither can they ask jurors to answer extensive questionnaires as jurors do in many U.S. states.

## The Role of the Victim in a Criminal Trial

Not all crimes have clearly identifiable victims. Some, like murder, do not have victims who survive. Where there is an identifiable surviving victim, however, he or she is often one of the most forgotten people in the courtroom. Although the victim may have been profoundly affected by the crime itself, and is often emotionally committed to the proceedings and trial outcome, he or she may not even be permitted to participate directly in the trial process. Although a powerful movement to recognize the interests of victims has begun (and is discussed in detail in the next chapter), it is still not unusual for crime victims to be totally unaware of the final outcome of a case that intimately concerns them.[59]

Hundreds of years ago the situation surrounding victims was far different. During the early Middle Ages in much of Europe, victims, or their survivors, routinely played a central role in trial proceedings and in sentencing decisions. They testified, examined witnesses, challenged defence contentions, and pleaded with the judge or jury for justice, honour, and often revenge. Sometimes they were even expected to carry out the sentence of the court, by flogging the offender or by releasing the trapdoor used for hangings. This "golden age" of the victim ended with the consolidation of power into the hands of monarchs who declared that vengeance was theirs alone.

Today, victims, like witnesses, experience many hardships as they participate in the criminal court process. Some of the rigours they endure are

1. Uncertainties as to their role in the criminal justice process;
2. A general lack of knowledge about the criminal justice system, courtroom procedure, and legal issues;

3. Trial delays that result in frequent travel, missed work, and wasted time;

4. Fear of the defendant or of retaliation from the defendant's associates; and

5. The trauma of testifying and of cross-examination.

The trial process itself can make for a bitter experience. If victims take the stand, defence lawyers may test their memory, challenge their veracity, or even suggest that they were somehow responsible for their own victimization. After enduring cross-examination, some victims report feeling as though they, and not the offender, have been portrayed as the criminal to the jury. The difficulties encountered by victims have been compared to a second victimization at the hands of the criminal justice system. Additional information on victims and victims' issues, including victims' assistance programs, is provided in the next chapter.

## The Role of the Defendant in a Criminal Trial

Generally, a defendant must be present at his or her indictable offence trial. The *Criminal Code* permits an accused on a summary conviction matter to be represented by an agent; however, for indictable offences, "an accused other than a corporation shall be present in court during the whole of the accused's trial."[60] Sections 803 and 475 of the *Criminal Code* empower a court to try an accused in absentia if the accused fails to appear for trial, or absconds during the course of the trial.

Most criminal defendants are poor, uneducated, and often alienated from the underlying philosophy of the Canadian justice system. The defendant in a criminal trial is commonly perceived as a relatively powerless person at the mercy of judicial mechanisms. Many defendants are just that. However, such an image is often far from the truth. Defendants, especially those who seek an active role in their own defence, choreograph many courtroom activities. Experienced defendants, notably those who are career offenders, may be well-versed in courtroom demeanour.

Defendants in criminal trials have a right to represent themselves and need not retain counsel. Such a choice, however, may not be in their best interests. Research conducted by Renner and Warner in Halifax found that those who do not have legal representation fare somewhat worse than their legally represented counterparts in criminal court.[61] Indeed, as might be expected, they found that those accused pleading guilty were twice as likely to be unrepresented as those pleading not guilty. Those accused who were represented by legal counsel and pleaded guilty were found to be more likely to receive a lenient disposition from the court than those who were not represented.

Even without self-representation, every defendant who chooses to do so can substantially influence events in the courtroom. A defendant can exercise choice in (1) deciding whether to testify personally, (2) selecting and retaining counsel, (3) planning a defence strategy in coordination with his or her lawyer, (4) deciding what information to provide to (or withhold from) the defence lawyer, (5) deciding what plea to enter, and (6) determining whether to file an appeal, if convicted.

Nevertheless, even the most active defendants suffer from a number of disadvantages. One disadvantage is the tendency of others to assume that anyone on trial must be guilty. Although a person is "innocent until proven guilty," the very fact that he or she is accused of an offence casts a shadow of suspicion that may foster biases in the minds of jurors and judges. Another disadvantage lies in the often-substantial social and cultural differences that separate the offender from the professional courtroom staff. While lawyers and judges tend to identify with upper-middle-class values and lifestyles, few offenders do. The consequences of such a gap between defendant and courtroom staff may be insidious and far-reaching.

## The Press in the Courtroom

Often overlooked, because they do not have an official role in courtroom proceedings, are spectators and the press. At any given trial, both spectators and media representatives may be present in large numbers. Spectators include members of the families of both victim and defendant, friends of either side, and curious onlookers—some of whom are avocational court watchers.

Newswriters, television reporters, and other members of the press are apt to be present at "spectacular" trials (those involving some especially gruesome aspect or famous personality) and at those in which there is a great deal of community interest. The right of reporters and spectators to be present at a criminal trial, while not specifically mentioned in the *Charter of Rights and Freedoms*, was ruled by the Ontario Court of Appeal to be an "integral and implicit part" of the guarantee of freedom of expression that includes freedom of the press and other media of communication.[62]

Press reports at all stages of a criminal investigation and trial often create problems for the justice system. Significant pretrial publicity about a case may make it difficult to find jurors who have not already formed an opinion as to the guilt or innocence of the defendant. News reports from the courtroom may influence or confuse non-sequestered jurors who hear them, especially when they contain information brought to the bench, but not heard by the jury.

The need to balance the right to a fair trial against the need for freedom of the press has been dealt with somewhat differently in Canada than in the United States. The U.S. Supreme Court has ruled that trial court judges cannot legitimately issue gag orders, preventing the pretrial publication of information about a criminal case, as long as the defendant's right to a fair trial and an impartial jury could be ensured by traditional means. These means include (1) a change of venue, whereby the trial is moved to another jurisdiction less likely to have been exposed to the publicity; (2) trial postponement, which would allow for memories to fade and emotions to cool; and (3) jury selection and screening to eliminate biased persons from the jury pool. In Canada, courts have not traditionally been willing to rely on such means of protecting the fairness of a trial; instead they more readily impose limitations on the press. At common law and in statute, the courts have the discretion to place a ban on publication.[63]

In 1994, the Supreme Court of Canada case of *Dagenais* v. *Canadian Broadcasting Corporation*,[64] looked at the tension between guaranteeing the right to a fair trial and the right

Cameras are still not permitted during criminal trials in Canada. Artists continue to render drawings of court proceedings.

of the media to freedom of the press. The Court upheld the discretionary power arising at common law with respect to ordering a publication ban, but it placed limits on the exercise of this discretion. The discretion may only be exercised to protect against real threats to the fairness of a trial, and only where the beneficial effects outweigh the harmful effects on freedom of expression. A publication ban should only be imposed where there is a real and substantial risk to the fairness of the trial, wherein reasonably available alternative measures will not prevent the risk, and the beneficial effects of the publication ban outweigh the harmful effects. The Court refused to say that the *Charter* contained a hierarchy of rights in which fairness of the trial overrode freedom of expression, but stated that a "balance" should be achieved that respects the importance of both rights.[65]

Publication bans under statute are guided by section 486(3) of the *Criminal Code*, which states that a court dealing with an offence listed in the section, which deals mainly with sexual offences, may order a ban on publication of the identity of the complainant or other witness, or any other information that may disclose the complainant's identity. Section 486(1) goes further and actually permits a judge to conduct a trial while "all or any members of the public" are excluded from the courtroom. The Supreme Court of Canada in *Canadian Broadcasting Corporation* v. *New Brunswick (Attorney General)* (1996)[66] ruled that a court must carefully exercise its discretion under this provision. The party seeking an order excluding the public from the courtroom must displace the presumption that the courtroom is to be open, showing the order (1) is necessary for the "proper administration of justice," (2) is as limited as possible, and (3) that the negative effects of the order do not outweigh its beneficial effects.

Typically, members of the press as well as radio and television reporters are allowed into courtrooms. Although 47 U.S. states now allow courtroom cameras,[67] Canadian courts have generally been unwilling to permit cameras in the courts. Ontario legislation permits the presence of cameras if all parties to the proceedings consent to their presence; however, the norm remains that cameras are not found in the courts.[68]

While the U.S. Supreme Court has been less favourably disposed to television coverage than have state courts, the Supreme Court of Canada has permitted access to the television media to the court for the past several years. Canada's parliamentary television channel frequently carries coverage of legal arguments being presented in cases before the Supreme Court of Canada. While some would argue that television coverage of court proceedings allows a greater proportion of the public to access the events unfolding in our judicial system, others would argue that the media's presence detracts from the dignity and decorum of the courtroom, leading to a circus-like atmosphere. The O.J. Simpson criminal trial of 1995 renewed debate over the merit of television in the courtroom. In 1981, a Florida defendant appealed his burglary conviction to the U.S. Supreme Court,[69] arguing that the presence of television cameras at his trial had turned the court into a circus for lawyers and made the proceedings more a sideshow than a trial. The Supreme Court, recognizing that television cameras have an untowards effect upon many people, agreed. In the words of the Court, "Trial courts must be especially vigilant to guard against any impairment of the defendant's right to a verdict based solely upon the evidence and the relevant law."[70]

The Canadian Judicial Council, in its 1994-95 annual report, seems to agree with those opposed to television in the courtrooms. After serious debate on the merits, the Council reaffirmed a resolution passed in 1983 formally opposing televising court proceedings, with its recommendation against such television coverage not applying to the Supreme Court of Canada, thereby permitting the top court to continue to allow televised coverage of its hearings.[71]

# THE CRIMINAL TRIAL

From arrest through sentencing, the criminal justice process is carefully choreographed. Arresting officers must follow proper procedure in the gathering of evidence and in the arrest and questioning of suspects. Judges, prosecutors, jailers, and prison officials are all subject to similar strictures. Nowhere, however, is the criminal justice process more closely circumscribed than at the stage of the criminal trial.

Procedures in a modern courtroom are highly formalized. **Rules of evidence**, which govern the admissibility of evidence, and other procedural guidelines determine the course of a criminal hearing and trial. Rules of evidence are partially based on tradition. All criminal trials are subject to rules of evidence embodied in the common law and in formalized rules of evidence found in the *Canada Evidence Act*.

Trials are also circumscribed by informal rules and professional expectations. An important component of law school education is the teaching of rules that structure and define appropriate courtroom demeanour. Courts have begun to promulgate case-flow management rules to increase the efficiency of the criminal courts. These rules facilitate the smooth functioning of the criminal process by ensuring the necessary parties appear at relevant points in the process, and that the parties are prepared to move ahead at the various stages in the proceedings.[72] In addition to statutory rules, law students are thoroughly exposed to the ethical standards of their profession as found in the Canadian Bar Association's standards and other writings.

In the next few pages, we will describe the chronology of a criminal trial and comment on some of the widely accepted rules of criminal procedure. Before we begin the description, however, keep two points in mind. One is that the primary purpose of any criminal trial is the determination of the defendant's guilt or innocence. In this regard, it is important to recognize the crucial distinction that scholars make between legal guilt and factual guilt. Factual guilt deals with the issue of whether the defendant is actually responsible for the crime of which he or she stands accused. If the defendant "did it," then he or she is, in fact, guilty. Legal guilt is not so clear. Legal guilt is established only when the prosecutor presents sufficient evidence to convince the judge (where the judge determines the verdict) or jury that the defendant is guilty as charged. The distinction between legal guilt and factual guilt is crucial because it points to the fact that the burden of proof rests with the prosecution, and it indicates the possibility that guilty defendants may, nonetheless, be found "not guilty."

The second point to remember is that criminal trials under our system of justice are built around an adversarial system and that central to such a system is the advocacy model. Participating in the adversarial system are advocates for the Crown (the public prosecutor, Crown counsel or Crown attorney) and for the defendant (defence counsel, public defender, and so on). The philosophy behind the adversarial system holds that the greatest number of just resolutions in all foreseeable criminal trials will occur when both sides are allowed to argue their cases effectively and vociferously before a fair and impartial arbiter. The system requires that advocates for both sides do their utmost, within the boundaries set by law and professional ethics, to protect and advance the interests of their clients (that is, the defendant and the Crown). The advocacy model makes clear that it is not the job of the defence lawyer or the prosecution to judge the guilt of any defendant. Hence, even a defence lawyer who is convinced that his or her client is factually guilty is still exhorted to offer the best possible defence and to counsel the client as effectively as possible.

The **adversarial system** has been criticized by some thinkers who point to fundamental differences between law and science in the way the search for truth is conducted.[73] While proponents of traditional legal procedure believe that truth can best be uncovered through an adversarial process, scientists adhere to a painstaking process of research and replication to acquire knowledge. Most of us would agree that scientific advances in recent years may have made factual issues less difficult to ascertain. For example, some of the new scientific techniques in evidence gathering, such as DNA fingerprinting (discussed in detail in Chapter 15), are now able to unequivocally link suspects to criminal activity. Whether scientific findings should continue to serve a subservient role to the adversarial process itself is a question now being raised. The ultimate answer will probably be couched in terms of the results that each process is able to produce. If the adversarial model results in the acquittal of too many demonstrably guilty people because of legal "technicalities," or the scientific approach inaccurately identifies too many suspects, either could be restricted.

We turn now to a discussion of the steps in a criminal trial. Jury trials are, of necessity, more complex than non-jury trials. As Figure 8–2 shows, the jury trial chronology consists of seven stages:

**rules of evidence** Rules of court that govern the admissibility of evidence at a criminal hearing and trial.

**adversarial system** The two-sided structure under which Canadian criminal trial courts operate, which pits the prosecution against the defence. In theory, justice is done when the most effective adversary is able to convince the judge or jury that his or her perspective on the case is the correct one.

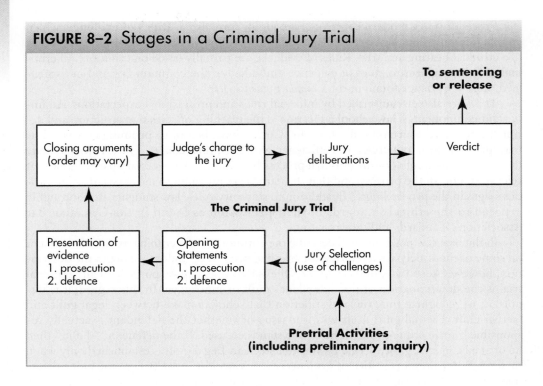

**FIGURE 8–2** Stages in a Criminal Jury Trial

- Jury selection
- Opening statements
- Presentation of evidence
- Closing arguments
- Judge's charge to the jury
- Jury deliberations
- Verdict

For purposes of brevity, jury deliberations and the verdict will be discussed jointly. If the defendant is found guilty, the judge will impose a sentence at the conclusion of the trial. Sentencing is discussed in the next chapter.

## Trial Initiation

As we mentioned in Chapter 7, section 11(b) of the *Canadian Charter of Rights and Freedoms* guarantees that everyone charged with an offence is entitled "to be tried in a reasonable time." Clogged court calendars, limited judicial resources, and general inefficiency, however, often combine to produce what appears to many to be unreasonable delays in trial initiation. The attention of the Supreme Court was brought to bear on trial delays in three precedent-setting cases: *R. v. Askov* (1990),[74] *R. v. Morin* (1992),[75] and *R. v. Collins* (1995).[76] The *Askov* case involved a number of co-accused being tried together for offences involving extortion and various weapons offences. Askov was an associate of his co-accused, Melo, Hussey, and Gugliotta. Melo was engaged in the business of supplying exotic dancers to bars in the Toronto area. Another supplier of exotic dancers, Belmont, who had supplied strippers in the Toronto area in the past, but was at the time engaged in this enterprise in Montreal and areas of Ontario outside Toronto, expressed a desire to engage in this business in the Toronto area once again. Melo took this as an invasion of his territory, and, according to Belmont, Askov and the others had demanded that he pay a substantial commission for the privilege of operating in the Toronto area. Eventually, the four co-accused were arrested following an incident in which Melo and Askov threatened Belmont with a sawed-off shotgun, in November 1983.

Three of the accused were held in custody for almost six months without bail. Eventually, all were released on recognizances. The preliminary hearing was not completed until September

1984, some 10 months after the initial arrests. Following the preliminary inquiry, a trial date was set for October 1985; however, when that time arrived, it was apparent that the trial could not go ahead, and consequently a trial date for September 1986 was set as the earliest available date. At the outset of the trial in September 1986, lawyers for the accused successfully moved for a stay of proceedings because the pretrial delay had been unreasonable.

The stay of proceedings was the subject of a successful Crown appeal; however, the issue ultimately ended up in the Supreme Court of Canada for resolution. There, the Court asserted that the right to a trial in a reasonable time is a fundamental guarantee of the *Charter*, which was violated on the facts of this case. Drawing heavily on U.S. cases, Mr. Justice Peter Cory spoke for the majority of the Supreme Court of Canada in identifying the factors for determining if pretrial delay had been excessive (see the Theory into Practice box, "Acceptable Pretrial Delay").

The court in which Askov and his associates would appear for trial was located in Brampton, Ontario. Research by Professor Carl Baar indicated that the length of delay in this jurisdiction was perhaps the worst in the country.[77] Cory J. concluded that even in a worst-case scenario, such as that prevailing in Brampton, the delay between committal for trial (the end of a preliminary inquiry) and the onset of trial should not exceed six to eight months.[78]

In the weeks that followed the *Askov* ruling, it was reported by *The Lawyers Weekly* that a "shock wave" was sent through the criminal justice system of Ontario because of the

## BOX 8.3  Theory into Practice

### Acceptable Pretrial Delay

Mr. Justice John Sopinka explained the criteria for determining the outer bounds of acceptable pretrial delay:

(i)  The length of the delay.

This factor looks at the length of time from the charge to the end of the trial. The longer the delay, the more difficult it should be for a court to excuse it. Very lengthy delays may be such that they cannot be justified for any reason.

(ii)  Waiver of time periods.

If the length of the delay warrants further inquiry, the court should look at whether the accused has waived a trial in a reasonable time. If the accused waives his or her rights by consenting to, or concurring in, a delay, this waiver must be taken into account. However, for a waiver to be valid it must be informed, unequivocal, and freely given. An example of a waiver or concurrence that could be inferred is the accused's consent as communicated to his or her counsel to a fixed date for trial.

(iii)  The reasons for the delay.

(a)  Inherent time requirements

The complexity of a case will affect the length of the delay. This will result in more delay in some cases than others. For example, cases involving a preliminary inquiry must be expected to have a longer delay than those which do not.

(b)  Actions of the accused.

Where the accused engages in significant pretrial strategies and tactics that result in delay, these actions will be taken into account in determining if the delay is unreasonable.

(c)  Actions of the Crown.

Delays attributable to the action of the Crown or officers of the Crown will weigh in favour of the accused. Excessive adjournments, delayed disclosure, motions to change venue, and similar practices may result in excessive delay.

(d)  Limits on institutional resources.

This is the most common source of delay. Delay attributable to this cause arises when the parties are ready for trial, but the system is unable to accommodate them. A court should recognize that some delay is inevitable from time-to-time. However, administrative guidelines may be issued regarding the appropriate length of acceptable delay attributable to scarce resources. Delays in the range of six to eight months between committal for trial at a preliminary inquiry and the start of a trial in a superior court are not unreasonable. A delay of eight to ten months for trial in provincial court would not be unreasonable.

(iv)  Prejudice to the accused.

Considerable emphasis is placed on the need for the accused to show the delay has prejudiced them if they are to obtain a remedy. Prejudice arises in many ways, but will be present where an accused wishes to put the case behind them, but is subjected to the ill-effects of ongoing delay. An accused remanded into custody pending trial is prejudiced by delay. Accused who are subjected to strict bail conditions are also significantly prejudiced by delay. It will also prejudice the accused if the delay has resulted in the memories of witnesses fading, or evidence otherwise being lost through the passage of time.

*Source: R. v. Morin*, [1992] 1 S.C.R. 771.

number of cases being stayed by the courts for exceeding the six- to eight-month limit apparently imposed by *Askov*.[79] According to Mr. Justice John Sopinka, writing in a subsequent case,[80] the fallout of the *Askov* case was that the Crown in Ontario stayed or withdrew over 47 000 cases because of excessive delay. While the perceived initial impact of *Askov* was that a number of accused persons escaped conviction on what many would perceive to be a "technicality," the ultimate impact of the case may not be as simple as it first appears. Michael Mandel notes that following the case, millions of dollars were poured into the Ontario criminal justice system to eliminate the backlog of cases.[81] More courtrooms, more judges, more prosecutors, and ultimately more prison space were the real results flowing from *Askov*, so "the system could now process and imprison more people faster."[82]

Seventeen months after its *Askov* ruling, the Supreme Court of Canada re-entertained the issue of pretrial delay in *R. v. Morin* (1992). In *Morin* and its companion case *R. v. Sharma* (1992), the Supreme Court of Canada ruled that 14-month and 13-month respective delays did not amount to an unreasonable pretrial delay. The time limits perceived to flow from *Askov* were said by the Court in these subsequent cases to reflect "administrative guidelines" rather than strict limitation periods.

In *R. v. Collins* and *R. v. Pelfrey*, the Supreme Court looked at a situation in which two persons, accused of murder, had been detained in custody for 22 months. Collins and

---

## BOX 8.4   Theory into Practice

### Pretrial Motions and Preliminary Applications

A motion is defined by the *Pocket Dictionary of Canadian Law*[1] as "[a]n oral or written application that the court rule or make an order before, during or after a trial." Written motions are called applications. This box lists the typical kinds of motions that may be made by both sides in a criminal case before and after trial.

### Motion for Discovery

A motion for discovery, filed by the defence, asks the court to allow the defendant's lawyers to view the evidence that the prosecution has under its control. Physical evidence, lists of witnesses, documents, photographs, and so on, which the prosecution plans to introduce in court, will usually be made available to the defence as a result of such a motion.

### Motion to Exclude Evidence

In the preliminary hearing, or through pretrial discovery, the defence may learn of evidence that the prosecution intends to introduce at the trial. If some of that evidence has been, in the opinion of the defence counsel, unlawfully acquired, a motion to have the evidence excluded may be filed with the trial court.

### Motion to Quash the Indictment/Information

A variety of circumstances may result in the filing of a motion to quash the indictment. They include an opinion, by defence counsel, (1) that the indictment contains an offence not known to the law; (2) that the indictment is void because it is vague; or (3) that the charge is duplicitous (containing more than one allegation in a count). Courts typically give the Crown considerable latitude to amend the defect of which the defence complains.

### Motion for an Adjournment

This motion seeks a delay in the start of the trial, or an interruption in the course of the trial. Motions for an adjournment are often based on the inability to locate important witnesses, the illness of a witness, or a change in defence counsel immediately prior to or during the trial. Most adjournments are requested with the consent of both parties.

### Motion for Change of Venue

In well-known cases, pretrial publicity may lessen the opportunity for a case to be tried before an unbiased jury. A motion for a change in venue asks that the trial be moved to some other area where prejudice against the defendant is less likely to exist.

### Motion for Severance of Counts

Defendants charged with a number of crimes may ask to be tried separately on all or some of the charges. Although consolidating charges for trial saves time and money, some defendants may think that it is more likely to make them appear guilty.

### Motion for Severance of Defendants

Similar to the preceding motion, this request asks the court to try the accused separately from any co-defendants. Motions for severance are likely to be filed where the defendant believes that the jury may be prejudiced against him or her by evidence applicable only to other defendants.

Pelfrey were acquitted at trial; however, the Crown successfully argued for a new trial in the Court of Appeal. At the new trial, the accused attacked the Crown on the grounds that the length of pretrial delay was unreasonable. The trial judge directed a stay of proceedings; however, the Crown successfully appealed yet again, and a new trial was ordered. That decision was appealed to the Supreme Court of Canada, where a majority upheld the trial judge's order for a stay of proceedings, ultimately freeing the accused. In its ruling, the Court held that much of the delay could be attributable to the Crown, being brought about by the Crown's requests for adjournments and its late disclosure to the accused. Clearly, the courts will consider cases on a case-by-case basis to determine whether a delay is unreasonable, rather than relying on specific limitation periods.

In 1994, the Law Reform Commission of Canada published its final working paper prior to being disbanded. In this paper, the Commission made several recommendations for pretrial delay reform.[83] In its paper, the Commission recommended a multi-pronged approach to deal with excessive delay. It also recommended that improved case-flow management be combined with statutorily prescribed limitation periods for trial initiation, along with improvements to the system of pretrial procedure that would simplify and streamline the process of getting cases to court.

## Motion to Determine Fitness to Stand Trial

"Unfitness to stand trial," even though it may be no defence against the criminal charge, can delay trial. A person cannot be tried, sentenced, or punished while insane. If a defendant is insane at the time a trial is to begin, this motion may halt the proceedings until treatment can be arranged.

## Motion for Particulars

This motion asks the court to order the prosecutor to provide detailed information about the charges which the defendant will be facing in court. A defendant charged with a number of offences, or with a number of counts of the same offence, may make such a motion. He or she may, for example, seek to learn which alleged instances of an offence will become the basis for prosecution or which specific items of contraband allegedly found in his or her possession are held to violate the law.

## Motion for a Mistrial

A mistrial may be declared at any time, and a motion for mistrial may be made by either side. A mistrial is likely to be declared where highly prejudicial comments are made by either attorney. Defence motions for a mistrial do not provide grounds for a later claim of double jeopardy.

## Motion for Arrest of Judgment

After the verdict of the jury has been announced, but before sentencing, the defendant may make a motion for arrest of judgment. Such a motion means the defendant believes that some legally acceptable reason exists as to why sentencing should not occur. Defendants who are seriously ill, hospitalized, or who have gone insane prior to judgment being imposed, may file such a motion.

## Motion to Ban Publication

Prior to the onset of proceedings, either side may request that the court ban the media from publishing the identity of the complainant or another witness or other information that might reveal such information, under section 486 of the *Criminal Code*. A motion to ban publication of any information presented at trial may also be granted through the court's common law power.

## Motion to Close the Trial to the Public

A court may be requested by either side to order that the trial be conducted in camera, or behind closed doors. While there is a presumption that trials will be open to the public, section 486 of the *Criminal Code* allows such an order in exceptional circumstances.

## Application for an Interpreter

Lawyers for either side may apply to the court to have an interpreter appointed where a witness is not proficient in the language of the trial, or where a sign language interpreter is required by someone with a hearing impairment.

## Application for Exclusion of Witnesses

A routine application, ordered in virtually every criminal case, whereby the court on its own motion, or at the request of either side, will order all witnesses who will be giving evidence in a trial to be excluded from the courtroom until they are to take the stand. In this way, it is believed that witnesses will be less likely to alter their testimony to bring their statements into conformity with what other witnesses are heard saying.

[1]Dukelow, D.A. and Nuse, B. (1991). *Pocket Dictionary of Canadian Law.* Toronto: Carswell.

**jury selection** The process whereby, according to law and precedent, members of a particular trial jury are chosen.

**peremptory challenge** A means of removing unwanted potential jurors without the need to show cause for their removal. Prosecutors and defence lawyers routinely use peremptory challenges in order to eliminate from juries individuals who, although they express no obvious bias, may be thought to hold the potential to sway the jury in an undesirable direction.

# Jury Selection

As we mentioned in our discussion of the role of the jury in a criminal trial, section 11 of the *Charter* also guarantees the right to a trial by jury with respect to the more serious offences. Clearly, this right entails **jury selection** to ensure a right to a jury that is impartial to both parties. An impartial jury is not necessarily an ignorant one. In other words, jurors will not always be excused from service on a jury if they have some knowledge of the case that is before them.[84] Jurors, however, who have already formed an opinion as to the guilt or innocence of a defendant are likely to be excused.

Anyone who has ever been called as a juror knows that some prospective jurors try to get excused and others who would like to serve are excused because they are not judged to be suitable. Prosecution and defence counsel use challenges to ensure the impartiality of the jury that is being empanelled. Three types of challenges are recognized in criminal courts: (1) a challenge to the array, (2) a challenge for cause, and (3) a **peremptory challenge**.[85]

A challenge to the array (section 629) entails an assertion, generally by the defence lawyer, that the pool from which potential jurors are to be selected is not representative of the community or is biased in some significant way. In essence, it involves a challenge against the entire group of potential jurors subpoenaed to attend court for jury duty. A challenge to the array is argued before the trial judge before jury selection begins. Challenges must be put in writing and allege either partiality, fraud, or wilful misconduct on the part of the person responsible for preparing the array or jury panel.

During the jury selection process, the judge, prosecution and defence counsel, and the potential jurors themselves play an important role in a process known as *empanelling* the jury. Jurors are expected to be unbiased and free of preconceived notions of guilt or innocence. The names, address, and number on the panel of each potential juror in the array are written on a separate card. All of the cards are placed in a box by the court clerk who shakes the box and then randomly draws one card at a time, calling out the name of

---

## BOX 8.5 Theory into Practice

### Challenges for Cause and Race

During the process of empanelling a jury, each party is entitled to challenge the potential makeup of the jury through procedures established in the *Criminal Code*. Usually a large pool of potential jurors has been summoned to court by a court official. If the entire pool is suspect, both the accused and the Crown are entitled to challenge the array (ss. 629–630). These challenges are rarely successful, requiring fraud, partiality, or wilful misconduct. The prosecution and accused are entitled to a number of peremptory challenges. These allow for the exclusion of witnesses without providing a reason. Each party is allowed 20 such challenges in murder cases, 12 for all other offences carrying a maximum penalty exceeding five years in prison, and four peremptory challenges in all other cases (s. 634).

In addition to peremptory challenges, the Crown and defence are entitled to make any number of challenges for cause (s. 638). Challenges for cause usually entail an accusation that a potential juror is not impartial to the outcome. Normally, Canadian courts have been reluctant to permit extensive questioning of potential jurors by lawyers

in the case. This situation began to change several years ago when Mr. Justice Doherty on the Ontario Court of Appeal held that a trial judge may permit counsel for the accused, who was black and charged with killing a white man, to ask questions about prejudice or partiality of potential jurors, at least in the racially charged environment of greater Toronto.[1]

Following this ruling, the Supreme Court of Canada unanimously ruled that if the accused can establish that there is a realistic potential for partiality, the accused is permitted to challenge a potential juror for cause.[2] *R. v. Williams* (1998) involved a native man on trial for the robbery of a pizza parlour. Where the potential for partiality arises from claims of widespread racial prejudice in the community, the trial judge should exercise his or her discretion to permit challenges for cause based on racial bias.

### QUESTIONS FOR DISCUSSION

1. Do you agree with the Court's reasoning that challenges for cause based upon race should be permitted in the selection of criminal trial juries? Why or why not?

2. Why is the accused entitled to fewer peremptory challenges for less serious offences? Could this likely be challenged under the *Canadian Charter of Rights and Freedoms*?

---

[1] *R. v. Parks* (1993), 24 C.R. (4th) 81 (Ont.C.A.).
[2] *R. v. Williams*, [1998] 1 S.C.R. 1128.

the prospective juror. This is repeated until the judge believes that a group large enough for counsel to select a jury has been drawn, taking into account that some will be challenged or stood aside. Those whose names are drawn are then subject to being challenged by the Crown or defence, or being stood aside by the judge.

The judge may stand aside (section 633) a juror whose name has been called because of personal hardship or other reasonable cause. Such individuals remain, and may be called upon, if there are not sufficient remaining numbers in the array to prepare a jury.

Counsel for both Crown and defence have equal authority to challenge potential jurors. The challenge may either be "for cause" (ss. 638–640), or be a "peremptory" challenge (s. 634). Each side has an unlimited number of challenges for cause, and the number of peremptory challenges is limited by the seriousness of the offence (20 for first-degree murder, 12 for offences punishable by over five years' imprisonment, and four for any other offence). If a challenge for cause is made, the judge must select two persons who have already been sworn for the jury (or two other potential jurors if two have not yet been sworn), in order to have them determine whether the challenge for cause should succeed.[86]

The Supreme Court has addressed the significant concern that jurors may be biased when they are exposed to news media stories about a case when these stories appear before the start of trial. In *R. v. Sherratt* (1991),[87] the Supreme Court approved questioning about the impact of pretrial publicity on a potential juror's impartiality, where the particular publicity and notoriety of the accused, as developed in pretrial publicity, could potentially have the effect of destroying a potential juror's indifference between the accused and the Crown. There must be an "air of reality" to the ground for the challenge.

Potential racial bias has been identified by the courts as an area of major concern. The issue came to a head in *R. v. Parks* (1993),[88] where the Court of Appeal ruled that defence lawyers were permitted to ask a question about racial prejudice, given the facts of the case involving an interracial homicide where a black person had been accused of killing a white victim during an illegal drug transaction. It had been well-documented that extensive and intensive racist beliefs could be found in Canada, particularly in Metropolitan Toronto where the trial was set.[89]

The third kind of challenge, the peremptory challenge, effectively removes potential jurors without the need to give a reason. Peremptory challenges, used by both the prosecution and defence, are limited in number, and therefore are generally used as a last resort where a challenge for cause has proven to be unsuccessful.

A developing field, which seeks to take advantage of peremptory challenges, is **scientific jury selection**. Scientific jury selection relies on social-scientific techniques to gauge the

**scientific jury selection**
The use of social-scientific techniques to gauge the likelihood that potential jurors will vote for conviction or acquittal.

The six-man, six-woman jury that took five and a half days to reach a verdict in the Alison Parrott murder case. In Canada, a Supreme Court decision recently opened the door to increased use of the challenge procedure to select juries more predisposed to decide a case one way or the other.

likelihood that potential jurors will vote for conviction or acquittal. This method allows predictions to be based on the economic, ethnic, and other personal and social characteristics of each member of the juror pool. Traditionally, Canadian lawyers have known very little about potential jurors prior to the jury being empanelled. Questioning potential jurors was historically severely curtailed in contrast to extensive questioning carried on in most American courts. The recent decision of the Supreme Court of Canada in *R. v. Williams* (1998)[90] appears to have opened the door to using the challenge procedure to select a jury more predisposed to decide a case one way or another. Questions about prejudice may move beyond the racial area, to include questions about potential jurors' prejudices towards gays or lesbians, towards accused child molesters, or other matters pertinent to the case at hand. Perhaps questioning in the future will go beyond prejudice in the community and touch on other factors that might make the potential juror less than desirable to one side or the other in a particular case.

Criticisms of intensive jury selection techniques have focused on the result of the process. Such techniques generally remove potential jurors who have any knowledge or opinions about the case to be tried. Also removed are persons trained in the law or in criminal justice. Anyone working for a criminal justice agency or anyone who has a family member working for such an agency or for a defence lawyer will likely be dismissed through peremptory challenges on the chance that they may be biased in favour of one side or the other. Scientific jury-selection techniques may result in the additional dismissal of educated or professionally successful individuals, to eliminate the possibility of such individuals exercising undue control over jury deliberations. The result of the jury selection process may be to produce a jury composed of people who are uneducated, uninformed, and generally inexperienced at making any type of well-considered decision. Some of the jurors may not understand the charges against the defendant or comprehend what is required for a finding of guilt or innocence. Likewise, some selected jurors may not even possess the span of attention needed to hear all the testimony that will be offered in a case. As a consequence, decisions rendered by such a jury may be based more upon emotion than upon findings of fact.

After wrangling over jury selection has run its course, the jury is sworn in. At this point the judge will decide whether the jury is to be sequestered during the trial. Members of a **sequestered jury** are not permitted to have contact with the public and are often housed in a motel or hotel until completion of the trial. Anyone who attempts to contact a sequestered jury or to influence members of a non-sequestered jury may be held accountable for jury tampering. In Canada, section 647 of the *Criminal Code* permits a judge to allow a jury to separate, and accordingly, they may return to their own homes each night in such circumstances. In practice, most Canadian jury trials are conducted in this way, with sequestration being the exception rather than the rule. Following jury selection, the stage is set for opening arguments[91] to begin.

**sequestered jury** A jury that is isolated from the public during the course of a trial and throughout the deliberation process.

## Opening Statements

**opening statement** The initial statement of a lawyer (or of a defendant representing himself or herself) made in a court to a judge, or to a judge and jury, describing the facts that he or she intends to present during trial in order to prove his or her case.

The presentation of information to the jury begins with **opening statements**, or opening addresses, made by the prosecution and defence. Non-jury trials may follow this same procedure,[92] and accordingly one frequently sees opening statements made to a judge sitting alone. The purpose of opening statements is to advise the jury of what the lawyers intend to prove and to describe how such proof will be offered. Evidence itself is not offered during opening statements. Eventually, however, the jury will have to weigh the evidence presented during trial and decide between the effectiveness of the arguments made by both sides. When a defendant has little evidence to present, the main job of the defence lawyer will be to dispute the veracity of the prosecution's version of the facts. Under such circumstances, defence counsel may choose not to present any evidence or testimony at all, focusing instead on the burden-of-proof requirement facing the prosecution. Such plans will generally be made clear during opening statements. At this time the defence counsel is also likely to stress the human qualities of the defendant and to remind jurors of the significance of their task.

Lawyers for both sides are bound by a "good faith" ethical requirement in their opening statements. That requirement limits the content of such statements to mentioning only that evidence that the lawyers actually believe can and will be presented as the trial progresses. Allusions to evidence that a lawyer has no intention of offering are regarded as unprofessional and could well be defined as "professional misconduct." When material alluded to in an opening statement cannot, for whatever reason, later be presented in court, it may offer opposing counsel an opportunity to discredit the other side.

## The Presentation of Evidence

The crux of the criminal trial is the presentation of evidence. The Crown is first given the opportunity to present evidence intended to prove the defendant's guilt. After prosecutors have rested their case, the defence is afforded the opportunity to provide evidence favourable to the defendant.

**Evidence** is of two general types: direct and circumstantial. **Direct evidence**, if believed by the judge or jury, proves a fact without needing to draw inferences. Direct evidence may consist, for example, of the information contained on a photograph or videotape. It might also consist of testimonial evidence provided by a witness on the stand. A straightforward statement by a witness, such as "I saw him do it!" is a form of direct evidence.

**Circumstantial evidence** is indirect. It requires the judge or jury to make inferences and draw conclusions. At a murder trial, for example, a person who heard gunshots and moments later saw someone run by with a smoking gun in hand might testify to those facts. Even though there may have been no eyewitness to the actual homicide, the jury might later conclude that the person seen with the gun was the one who pulled the trigger and committed the homicide. Contrary to popular belief, circumstantial evidence is sufficient to produce a verdict and conviction in a criminal trial. In fact, some prosecuting lawyers claim to prefer working entirely with circumstantial evidence, weaving a tapestry of the criminal act in their arguments to the jury.

**Real evidence** consists of physical material or traces of physical activity. Weapons, tire tracks, ransom notes, and fingerprints all fall into the category of physical evidence. Real or physical evidence is introduced into the trial process by means of exhibits. Exhibits are objects or displays that, once formally accepted as evidence by the judge, may be shown to members of the jury. Documentary evidence is another type of real evidence that includes writings such as business records, journals, written confessions, and letters. Documentary evidence can extend beyond paper and ink to include magnetic and optical storage devices used in computer operations and video and voice recordings.

One of the most significant decisions a trial court judge makes is deciding what evidence can be presented to the jury. In making that decision, judges will examine the relevance of the information in question to the case at hand. Relevant evidence is that which has a bearing on the facts at issue. For example, a decade or two ago, it was not unusual for a woman's sexual history to be brought out in rape trials. Under "rape shield provisions," the *Criminal Code* today will not typically allow such a practice, recognizing that these details often have no bearing on the case.[93] Although Canada's last attempt at structuring a comprehensive rape-shield statute was struck down for overly infringing on the rights of an accused at trial,[94] recent Supreme Court of Canada decisions, including the 1995 case of *R. v. Crosby*,[95] indicate that the new provision is valid in permitting a trial judge to inquire whether the probative value of evidence regarding prior sexual behaviour between the accused and the complainant outweighs the prejudicial impact that such evidence might have on the trier of fact.

In evaluating evidence, judges must weigh the probative value of an item of evidence against its potential inflammatory or prejudicial qualities. Evidence has probative value when it is useful and relevant. Even useful evidence, however, may unduly bias a jury if it is exceptionally gruesome or presented in such a way as to imply guilt. For example, gory photographs, especially in full colour, may be withheld from the jury's eyes. In one recent case, a new trial was ordered when 35-mm slides of the crime scene were projected on a wall over the head of the defendant as he sat in the courtroom. The appellate court found that this action prejudiced the jury.

On occasion, some evidence will be found to have only limited admissibility. Limited admissibility means that the evidence can be used for a specific purpose, but that it might not be accurate in other details. Photographs, for example, may be admitted as evidence for the narrow purpose of showing spatial relationships between objects under discussion,

**evidence** Anything useful to a judge or jury in deciding the facts of a case. Evidence may take the form of witness testimony, written documents, videotapes, magnetic media, photographs, physical objects, and so on.

**direct evidence** Evidence that, if believed, directly proves a fact. Eyewitness testimony (and, more recently, videotaped documentation) account for the majority of all direct evidence heard (or viewed) in the criminal courtroom.

**circumstantial evidence** Evidence that requires interpretation or which requires a judge or jury to reach a conclusion based on what the evidence indicates. From the close proximity of a smoking gun to the defendant, for example, the jury might conclude that she pulled the trigger.

**real evidence** Evidence consisting of physical material or traces of physical activity.

even though the photographs themselves may have been taken under conditions that did not exist (such as daylight) when the offence was committed.

When judges err in allowing the introduction of evidence that may have been illegally or unconstitutionally gathered, grounds may be created for a later appeal if the trial concludes with a "guilty" verdict. Even when evidence is improperly introduced at trial, however, the *Criminal Code* provides that there may be no grounds for an effective appeal where there would be "no substantial wrong or miscarriage of justice"[96] in leaving the trial verdict undisturbed. Sometimes called the "harmless error" rule, this provision has been applied by courts, much to the chagrin of many accused persons, who technically win on appeal but find the conviction against them undisturbed. If there is a "reasonable possibility" that the verdict against the accused would have been different, then the court of appeal should not apply the provision.[97]

## The Testimony of Witnesses

**testimony** Oral evidence offered by a sworn witness on the witness stand during a criminal trial.

Witness **testimony** is generally the chief means by which evidence is introduced at trial. Witnesses may include victims, police officers, the defendant, specialists in recognized fields, and others with useful information to provide. Some of these witnesses may have been present during the commission of the alleged offence, while most will have had only a later opportunity to investigate the situation or to analyze evidence.

Before a witness will be allowed to testify to any fact, the questioning lawyer must establish the person's competence. Competency to testify requires that witnesses have personal knowledge of the information they will discuss and that they understand their duty to tell the truth.

One of the defence lawyer's most critical decisions is whether to put the defendant on the stand. Defendants have a right to remain silent and to refuse to testify in proceedings against them, protected both by the common law and section 11(c) of the *Charter*. In section 4(6) of the *Canada Evidence Act*, we find that "the failure of the person charged, or the wife or husband of that person, to testify shall not be made the subject of comment by the judge or by counsel for the prosecution." Interestingly, in the precedent-setting case of *R. v. Avon* (1971),[98] the Supreme Court of Canada looked at a case in which the accused did not testify, and the trial judge made the following comment to the jury:

> The accused did not testify. Evidently, he could have done so. He is not obliged to do so. I must tell you immediately, ... it is not because the accused did not testify that you should believe that he could be guilty.... Actually, you have merely the Crown's evidence. The defence did not call witnesses, and the accused did not testify: he did not have to. It is up to the Crown to prove its case.[99]

Chief Justice Gérald Fauteux, speaking for a majority of the court wrote:

> I would say that the language used ... is a "statement" of an accused's right not to testify, rather than a "comment" on his failure to do so. In my opinion, the instructions complained of cannot be construed as prejudicial to the accused or such to suggest to the jurors that his silence was used to cloak his guilt.[100]

The Court declared that if a defendant refuses to testify, prosecutors and judges are enjoined from even commenting on this fact, other than to instruct the jury that such a failure cannot be held to indicate guilt.

Direct examination of a witness takes place when a witness is first called to the stand. If the prosecutor calls the witness, the witness is referred to as a witness for the prosecution. Where the direct examiner is a defence lawyer, witnesses are called witnesses for the defence.

The direct examiner may be granted some latitude to ask questions that require a "yes" or "no" answer, but typically the examiner employs narrative questions that allow the witness to tell a story in his or her own words. During direct examination, courts generally prohibit the use of leading questions, or those that suggest answers to the witness.[101] Accordingly, counsel must be careful with questions leading to a "yes" or "no" response, as many such questions will be interpreted by the court as leading the witness into an answer, being inherently suggestive.

Cross-examination refers to the examination of a witness by anyone other than the direct examiner. Anyone who offers testimony in a criminal court has the duty to submit to cross-examination.[102] The purpose of cross-examination is to test the credibility and memory of a witness, and elicit testimony favourable to the party conducting the cross-examination.

Unlike the law in most states in the United States, Canadian law does not restrict the scope of cross-examination to material covered during direct examination. Questions about any matter relevant to facts in issue before the court may be the subject of cross-examination. Leading questions, generally disallowed in direct examination, are regarded as the mainstay of cross-examination. Such questions allow for a concise restatement of testimony that has already been offered, and serve to focus efficiently on potential problems that the cross-examiner seeks to address.

Some witnesses offer perjured testimony, or statements that they know to be untrue. Reasons for perjured testimony vary, but most witnesses who lie on the stand probably do so in an effort to help friends accused of crimes. Witnesses who perjure themselves are subject to impeachment. To impeach a witness, either the defence counsel or prosecution must demonstrate that the witness has intentionally offered false testimony. One way to demonstrate false testimony is to show that the witness's previous statements and recent declarations are inconsistent with testimony provided in court. If it can be proven that the false testimony was knowingly offered while under oath, and the witness held an

## BOX 8.6 Theory into Practice

## Canadian Law and Self-Incrimination

In the United States, anyone testifying in court, whether he or she is an ordinary witness or the accused, may refuse to answer questions on the grounds that the person testifying has a right not to incriminate himself or herself. In the O.J. Simpson case, this right came into effect when LAPD detective Mark Fuhrman exercised his right, under the fifth amendment to the U.S. *Bill of Rights*, to refuse to answer questions put to him about his past.

In Canada, the accused in his or her own trial has the right to refuse to take the stand to answer questions as part of the common-law privilege against self-incrimination. The common-law position is bolstered by one of the rights found in the *Charter of Rights and Freedoms*:

s. 11     Any person charged with an offence has the right ...
          (c)   not to be compelled to be a witness in proceedings against that person in respect of the offence ...

While this right protects an accused person from having to take the stand at his or her trial, it does not apply to other witnesses. In Canadian law, the Mark Fuhrman type of situation (the position of a non-accused called to testify), is handled somewhat differently. Under the *Canada Evidence Act*, one finds the following provision:

s. 5(1)   No witness shall be excused from answering any question upon the ground that the answer to such question may tend to incriminate him, or may tend to establish his liability to a civil proceeding ...

Clearly, in the Canadian context, the option of refusing to answer questions as a witness at a trial does not present itself. If subpoenaed to testify, witnesses must attend court, take the stand, and answer questions put to them. However, witnesses do not end up in a position whereby they will be incriminating themselves by virtue of the operation of another provision in the *Charter of Rights and Freedoms*:

s. 13     A witness who testifies in any proceedings has the right not to have any incriminating evidence so given used to incriminate that witness in any other proceedings, except in a prosecution for perjury or for the giving of contradictory evidence.

A relatively recent ruling in the Supreme Court of Canada[1] has found that any evidence derived from, or obtained as a result of, the testimony given by a witness in court may not be used against that person in a subsequent trial for whatever wrongdoing has been revealed through his or her testimony in court. While such a situation is not directly dealt with by section 13 of the *Charter*, the "principles of fundamental justice" enshrined in section 7 of the *Charter* require this conclusion.

## QUESTIONS FOR DISCUSSION

1. Does the American approach concede too much to the interests of the individual rights, or the "due process" perspective, by making the protection of the guilty paramount to the interests of the state in getting to the truth? Explain your answer.

2. Does the Canadian approach concede too much to the interests of the crime control value system, in producing efficient trials that ensure a maximum number of convictions, at the expense of individual liberty? Explain your answer.

[1] *R. v. S.(R.J.)* (1995), 96 C.C.C. (3d) 1 (S.C.C.).

**perjury** The intentional making of a false statement as part of the testimony by a sworn witness in a judicial proceeding on a matter relevant to the case at hand.

intention to mislead the court, the witness commits an act of perjury. **Perjury** is a serious offence in its own right, and dishonest witnesses may face fines or jail time.[103] When it can be demonstrated that a witness has offered inaccurate or false testimony, the witness has been effectively impeached.

At the conclusion of the cross-examination, the direct examiner may again question the witness. This procedure is called "redirect examination," and may be followed by a re-cross-examination and so on, until both sides are satisfied that they have exhausted fruitful lines of questioning.

## Children as Witnesses

An area of special concern involves children as witnesses in a criminal trial, especially where the children may have been victims. Currently, in an effort to avoid what may be traumatizing direct confrontations between child witnesses and the accused, the *Criminal Code* permits the use of closed-circuit television that allows the child to testify out of the presence of the defendant, or to testify from behind a one-way screen, whereby the accused can see the witness, but the accused is not visible from the witness stand.[104] Section 715.1 of the *Criminal Code* also allows the use of videotaped testimony made shortly after the alleged offence, provided the witness takes the stand and confirms the content of the videotape is accurate.

In 1991, the Supreme Court of Canada, in the case of *R. v. Levogiannis*,[105] ruled that a courtroom screen, used to shield child witnesses from visual confrontation with a defendant in a child sex-abuse case, does not violate the rights of an accused under either section 7 or section 11(d) of the *Charter*. Using a courtroom screen is not to be confined to cases of exceptional or inordinate stress on the child, but rather should be used in any case where the trial judge believes that this measure is necessary to obtain a "full and candid account of the acts complained of."[106] The judge may consider the capabilities and demeanour of the child, the nature of the allegations, and the circumstances of the case in deciding whether to permit a screen or closed-circuit testimony.

Although a face-to-face confrontation with a child victim may not be necessary in the courtroom, until 1990 the Supreme Court of Canada had been reluctant to allow into evidence descriptions of abuse and other statements made by children, even those made by children to child-care professionals, when those statements are made outside of the courtroom. The Court, in *R. v. Khan* (1990),[107] looked at a case involving a doctor charged with sexual assault. A patient of the doctor, a three-and-a-half-year-old girl (T.), was alone with the doctor in his office for what was supposed to be a routine examination. Fifteen minutes after leaving the doctor's office with her mother (Mrs. O.), the child had the following conversation:

> *Mrs. O.:* So you were talking to Dr. Khan, were you? What did he say?
> *T.:* He asked me if I wanted a candy. I said "Yes." And do you know what?
> *Mrs. O.:* What?
> *T.:* He said, "Open your mouth." And do you know what? He put his birdie in my mouth, shook it and peed in my mouth.
> *Mrs. O.:* Are you sure?
> *T.:* Yes.
> *Mrs. O.:* You're not lying to me, are you?
> *T.:* No. He put his birdie in my mouth. And he never did give me any candy.

The mother testified before the trial judge that the word "birdie" meant penis to the child. The trial judge ruled that the child, just over four-and-a-half years old at the time, could not testify, either sworn or unsworn. The trial judge also ruled that the mother could not testify since her evidence would be entirely hearsay. On appeal, Madam Justice Beverley McLachlin, writing for the Court, indicated that both the child's evidence and the evidence of the mother should have been admitted. The mother could testify in court to what the child had told her following the office visit under an exception to the hearsay rule. Where the evidence meets the test of "necessity and reliability," it may properly be admitted into evidence.

## The Hearsay Rule

The *Khan* case gives rise to one aspect of witness testimony that bears special mention. **Hearsay** is anything not based on the personal knowledge of a witness. A witness may say, for example, "John told me that Fred did it!" Such a witness becomes a hearsay declarant, and, following a likely objection by counsel, the trial judge will have to decide whether the witness's statement will be allowed to stand as evidence. In most cases, the judge will instruct the jury to disregard such comments from the witness, thereby enforcing the **hearsay rule**. The hearsay rule does not permit the use of "second-hand evidence."

There are some exceptions to the hearsay rule, however, that have been established by both precedent and tradition. One is the dying declaration. Dying declarations are statements made by a person who is about to die. When heard by a second party, they may usually be repeated in court, providing that certain conditions have been met. Dying declarations are generally valid exceptions to the hearsay rule when they are made by someone who knows that he or she is about to die and when the statements made relate to the cause and circumstances of the impending death.[108]

Spontaneous statements provide another exception to the hearsay rule. Statements are considered spontaneous when they are made in the heat of excitement before the person has time to make them up. For example, a defendant who is just regaining consciousness following the occurrence of a crime may say something that could later be repeated in court by those who heard it.

Out-of-court statements made by a witness, especially when they have been recorded in writing or by some other means, may also become exceptions to the hearsay rule. The use of such statements usually requires the witness to testify that the statements were accurate at the time they were made. This "past recollection recorded" exception to the hearsay rule is especially useful in drawn-out court proceedings that occur long after the crime has occurred. Under such circumstances, witnesses may no longer remember the details of an event. Their earlier statements to authorities, however, can be introduced into evidence as past recollection recorded.

## K.G.B. Statements

These are not statements made to the Russian secret police. *K.G.B.* statements arise in the context of a statement made to the police, under conditions that guarantee the trustworthiness of the statement, that are subsequently recanted by the witness. A witness may make a statement during a police investigation that implicates a friend in a crime, but when the witness realizes the impact of the statement that he or she has made, the witness may wish to take it back, or refuse to testify to the same effect in open court, out of fear that his or her friend will be convicted. In such cases, the Supreme Court of Canada declared, in *R. v. B.(K.G.)* (1993),[109] that the prosecution may tender the initial statement at trial as proof that the statement is true if certain preconditions are met: (1) the statement is made under oath or solemn affirmation, following a warning as to the existence of sanctions for telling a lie and a caution about the significance of an oath or affirmation, (2) the statement is videotaped in its entirety, and (3) the opposing party has a full opportunity to cross-examine the witness about the statement. Following *R. v. B.(K.G.)*, many police departments began installing video equipment in interview rooms at police stations, and used commissioners for the taking of oaths from witnesses, before taking statements from witnesses in important cases. However, this cumbersome process was not practical in all circumstances, and the Supreme Court of Canada subsequently held in *R. v. U.(F.J.)* (1995) that one or more of the strict requirements of the *K.G.B.* case could be dispensed with if the requirements of "necessity" and "reliability" could still be assured.[110] Despite the loosening of the rules brought about by *F.J.U.*, many courts will be reluctant to admit prior inconsistent statements that fail to meet the *K.G.B.* criteria, unless special circumstances exist.[111]

# Closing Arguments

At the conclusion of a criminal trial, both sides have the opportunity for a final, narrative presentation to the jury in the form of a **closing argument**. This summation provides a review

**hearsay** Something that is not based on the personal knowledge of a witness. Witnesses who testify, for example, about something they have heard are offering hearsay by repeating information about a matter of which they have no direct knowledge.

**hearsay rule** The long-standing evidentiary rule is that hearsay cannot be used in court. Rather than testimony based upon hearsay being accepted, the trial process asks that the person who was the original source of the hearsay information be brought into court to be questioned and cross-examined. Exceptions to the hearsay rule may occur when the person with direct knowledge is dead or otherwise unable to testify.

**closing argument** An oral summation of a case presented to a judge, or to a judge and jury, by the prosecution or by the defence in a criminal trial.

and an analysis of the evidence. Its purpose is to persuade the jury to draw a conclusion that is favourable to the presenter. Testimony can be quoted, exhibits referred to, and attention drawn to inconsistencies in the evidence that has been presented by the other side.

The order of closing arguments is affected by whether the defence has called any evidence. Where the defence has called evidence, the defence will then present its closing arguments to the jury before the prosecution makes its final points. Where no evidence has been called by the defence, the Crown will be required to provide closing arguments first, and the defence will get the last word with the jury.[112]

Some specific issues may need to be addressed during summation. If, for example, the defendant has not taken the stand during the trial, the defence counsel's closing argument will inevitably stress that this failure to testify cannot be regarded as indicating guilt. Where the prosecution's case rests entirely upon circumstantial evidence, the defence can be expected to stress the lack of any direct proof, while the prosecutor is likely to argue that circumstantial evidence can be stronger than direct evidence, since it is not as easily affected by human error or false testimony.

## The Judge's Charge to the Jury

After closing arguments, the judge will charge the jury to "retire and select one of your number as a foreman (or forewoman) and deliberate upon the evidence that has been presented until you have reached a **verdict**." The words of the charge will vary somewhat among judges, but by virtue of section 650.1 of the *Criminal Code*, a judge may hold a conference between the accused and the prosecutor to go over what should be contained in the charge to the jury. All judges will remind members of the jury of their duty to consider objectively only the evidence that has been presented and of the need for impartiality. The differing roles of judge and jury will be explained, along with the burden of proof resting on the Crown. The judge will remind jury members of the statutory elements of the alleged offence, of the defences available to the accused, and of alternative verdicts that the jury can return.

**verdict** In criminal case processing, a formal and final finding made on the charges by a jury and reported to the court, or by a trial judge when no jury is used.

After deliberating upon the evidence in the Alison Parrott murder case, the jury prepares to deliver its verdict. Francis Roy, pictured in the prisoner's box, was found guilty.

Toronto Star/Paul McCusker

In their charge, many judges will also provide a summary of the evidence presented, usually from notes they have taken during the trial, as a means of refreshing jurors' memories of events. The judge will typically outline the theories advanced by each side. Juries will be informed of the need to return a unanimous verdict. Following the charge, the jury will be removed from the courtroom and permitted to begin its deliberations. Juries are sequestered at this time.

# Jury Deliberations and the Verdict

In cases where the evidence is either very clear or very weak, jury deliberations may be brief, lasting only a matter of hours or even minutes. Some juries, however, deliberate for days or sometimes weeks, carefully weighing all the nuances of the evidence they have seen and heard. A jury may require further instructions or guidance from the judge, which will result in a re-charge. Additionally, counsel for either side may raise objections to the way in which the jury was charged to begin with, resulting in the judge bringing the jury back into the courtroom to be re-charged.

Some juries are unable to agree upon any verdict. When a jury is deadlocked, it is said to be a hung jury. Since a unanimous decision is required, a jury may be deadlocked by the strong opposition of only one member to a verdict agreed upon by all the others.

If after considerable effort to reach a verdict, the jury is still unable to reach one, section 653 of the *Criminal Code* permits the judge to discharge the jury and direct that a new jury be empanelled. A judge is allowed to help, with an appropriate exhortation, a jury that has reached an impasse. The rules governing an appropriate exhortation were recently set down by the Supreme Court of Canada in the 1996 case of *R. v. G. (R.M.).*[113] The exhortation, as it is known, should avoid introducing factors that are extraneous or irrelevant to the jury's task of reaching a verdict. Jurors should not be pressured to abandon an honestly held view of the evidence. Factors such as the expense of the trial, the inconvenience of a new trial, or the hardships caused by leaving the issues raised by the trial unresolved for a further period of time are inappropriate points to discuss. The judge must encourage the jurors to once again reason together. A juror should not be encouraged to change his or her mind simply for the sake of conforming to the majority opinion. Additionally, the trial judge should not impose a time deadline for reaching a verdict.

## *Problems with the Jury System*

U.S. Judge Harold J. Rothwax, a well-known critic of the jury system, tells the tale of a rather startling 1991 case over which he presided. The case involved a murder defendant, a handsome young man who had been fired by a New York company that serviced automated teller machines (ATMs). After being fired, the good-looking defendant intentionally caused a machine in a remote area to malfunction. When two former colleagues arrived to fix it, he robbed them, stole the money inside the ATM, and shot both men repeatedly. One of the men survived long enough to identify his former co-worker as the shooter. The man was arrested and a trial ensued; but after three weeks of hearing the case, the jury deadlocked. Judge Rothwax later learned that the jury had voted 11 to 1 to convict the defendant, but the one holdout jury member just couldn't believe that "someone so good-looking could commit such a crime."[114]

Many everyday cases, like those seen routinely by Judge Rothwax, and some highly publicized cases, such as the murder trial of O.J. Simpson, which the whole world watched, have called into question the ability of the jury system to do its job—that is, to sort through the evidence and accurately determine a defendant's guilt or innocence. Because jurors are drawn from all walks of life, many cannot be expected to understand modern legal complexities and to appreciate all the nuances of trial court practice. Some instructions to the jury are probably poorly understood and rarely observed by even the best-intentioned jurors.[115] In highly charged cases, emotions are often difficult to separate from fact, while during deliberations, juries are probably dominated by one or two forceful personalities. Jurors may also become confused over legal technicalities, suffer from inattention, or be unable to understand fully the testimony of expert witnesses or the significance of technical evidence.

BOX 8.7

## Theory into Practice

## What Will Courtrooms of the Future Be Like?

Recently, the College of William & Mary (located in Williamsburg, Pennsylvania, and the second oldest college in the U.S.), in conjunction with the National Center for State Courts (NCSC), unveiled Courtroom 21, the most technologically advanced courtroom in the United States. Courtroom 21, located in the McGlothlin Courtroom of the College of William & Mary, offers anyone concerned with the future of trial practice and with courtroom technology a glimpse at what courtrooms may be like in the mid-twenty-first century. Courtroom 21 includes the following integrated capabilities:

1. Automatic video recording of proceedings using ceiling-mounted cameras with voice-initiated switching. A sophisticated voice-activation system directs cameras to tape the person speaking, to record what is said, and to tape evidence as it is being presented.

2. Recorded televised evidence display with optical disk storage. Documentary or real evidence may be presented to the judge and jury via television through the use of a video "presenter," which also makes a video record of the evidence as it is being presented for later use.

3. Text-, graphics-, and TV-capable jury computers. Courtroom 21's jury box contains computers for information display and animation so that jury members can easily view documents, live or pre-recorded video, and other graphics such as charts, diagrams, and pictures. TV-capable jury computers also allow for the remote appearance of witnesses—that is, for questioning witnesses who may be unable or unwilling to physically appear in the courtroom and for the display of crime scene re-enactments via computer animation.

5. Access for judge and lawyers to online legal research databases. Available databases contain an extensive variety of statutes, case law, and other precedents, allowing judges and lawyers to find answers to unanticipated legal questions which arise during trial.

6. Built-in video playback facilities for out-of-court testimony. Because an increasing number of depositions are being recorded on video by attorneys in preparation for trial, Courtroom 21 has capabilities for video deposition playback. To present expert witness testimony or to impeach a witness, video depositions can be played on court monitors.

7. Information storage with software search capabilities. Integrated software programs provide text-searching capabilities to courtroom participants. Previously transcribed testimony can be searched and reviewed.

8. Concurrent (real-time) court reporter transcription, including the ability for each lawyer to mark an individual computerized copy for later use. A court reporter uses a self-contained computer for real-time capture of testimony in the courtroom. When the reporter writes, the computer translates strokes into English transcripts, which are immediately distributed to the judge and counsel via their personal computers. Using this technology, the judge and lawyers can take a copy of the day's testimony with them on their laptop computer for evening review and trial preparation.

The technology now being demonstrated in Courtroom 21 suggests many possibilities. For one thing, court video equipment could be used by lawyers for filing remote motions and other types of hearings. As one of Courtroom 21's designers puts it, "Imagine the productivity gains if lawyers no longer need to travel across a city ... for a ten-minute appearance."

Courtroom 21 designers also suggest that the innovative use of audio and video technology can preserve far more evidence and trial detail than written records, making a comprehensive review of cases easier for appellate judges. Video court records, analysts say, "might also improve the performance of attorneys and judges. By preserving matters not now apparent on a written record, such as facial expressions, voice inflections, body gestures, and the like, video records may cause trial participants to be more circumspect in their behaviour than at present." High technology can also be expected to have considerable impact on the trial itself. The technology built into Courtroom 21 readily facilitates computer animations and crime scene re-enactments. While Courtroom 21 shows what a typical courtroom of the near future may be like, it also raises questions about the appropriate use of innovative courtroom technologies. As one of Courtroom 21's designers points out, "Modern technology holds enormous promise for our courts. We must recognize, however, that technology's utility often depends upon how people will use it ... we must be sensitive to technology's impact and work to recognize and minimize any negative consequences it might have on our system of justice."

The Technology of Justice Task Force in its 1997 draft report to the Pennsylvania Futures Commission predicted that by the year 2020, "There will be 'virtual courtrooms,' where appropriate, to provide hearings without the need for people to come to a physical courthouse." Trials via teleconferencing, public internet access to many court documents, and payments of fines by credit card are all envisioned by the Task Force.

## QUESTIONS FOR DISCUSSION

1. How might technologies such as those discussed in this box affect the outcome of criminal trials, if at all? Are there dangers in allowing high-technology courtrooms? What might they be?

2. Can you imagine criminal trials in which the use of high-technology courtrooms might not be appropriate? If so, what might they be?

Sources: Court Technology Bulletin, Vol. 6, no. 1, January/February 1994; Court Technology Bulletin, Vol. 6, no. 1, March/April 1994; the National Center for State Courts World Wide Web site on the internet (from which some of the material in this box is taken); and the Technology of Justice Task Force Draft Report to the Pennsylvania Futures Commission, February 21, 1997.

Many such problems became evident in the trial of Raymond Buckey and his mother, Peggy McMartin Buckey, who were tried in Los Angeles for allegedly molesting dozens of children at their family-run preschool.[116] The trial, which involved 65 counts of child sexual molestation and conspiracy and 61 witnesses, ran for more than three years. Many jurors were stressed to the breaking point by the length of time involved. Family relationships suffered as the trial droned on, and jurors were unable to accompany their spouses and children on vacation. Small-business owners, who were expected to continue paying salaries to employees serving as jurors, faced financial ruin and threatened their absent employees with termination. Careers were put on hold, and at least one juror had to be dismissed for becoming inattentive to testimony. The trial cost taxpayers more than US$16 million, but it was nearly terminated as jury membership and the number of alternative jurors declined due to sickness and personal problems. Ultimately, the defendants were acquitted.

Another trial in which the defendants were similarly acquitted of the charges against them involved the murder prosecution of Peter Gill, Bindy Johal, Ho-Sik Kim, and Michael Budai, charged with the murder of brothers Jim and Ron Dosanjh, apparent rivals in the Vancouver cocaine trade. Gill and his associates were the subject of the longest-running and most costly murder trial in B.C.'s history.[117] Following the not-guilty verdict against Gill and his co-accused, evidence came to light revealing that Gillian Guess, one of the jurors in the trial, had been having a sexual affair with Peter Gill during the course of the trial. Jurors from the Gill trial became witnesses in the subsequent "obstruction of justice" trial against Guess, where they indicated that she had apparently decided rather early in the trial that the accused were not guilty.

## BOX 8.8   **Theory into Practice**

## The Juror's Role: The Gillian Guess Case

Trial by jury is an honoured component of our justice system and was established in Canada during the colonial times as part of the English common law. Lord Devlin noted that each jury was "a little parliament" and its function was to demonstrate the freedom of the people. However, trial by jury is not without its critics. It is claimed that the laypersons who make up a jury lack the qualifications necessary to make findings of fact in either criminal or civil cases. Regular citizens are simply not able to understand the detailed complexities of the modern legal system. E.N. Griswold, dean of Harvard Law School, observed:

> The jury trial is the apotheosis of the amateur. Why should anyone think that 12 persons brought in from the street, selected in various ways, for their lack of general ability, should have any special capacity for deciding controversies between persons?[1]

In Canada, a recent case has highlighted some of the negative elements of trial by jury. A woman, Gillian Guess, was charged with obstruction of justice as a result of a sexual relationship she had with one of the accused killers, while she was sitting on the jury. Gillian Guess admitted,

during wiretapped telephone conversations, that she did indeed have an affair with Peter Gill, a defendant in the murder trial. Gill and five other men were accused of the murders of Ron and Jimmy Dosanjh during a cocaine turf war in downtown Vancouver, B.C. The jury in this trial, which included Gillian Guess, took seven days to arrive at a verdict acquitting all six accused. The Crown prosecutor referred to Guess as the "antithesis" of what a suitable juror should be, largely due to her intense relationship with Gill. On June 19, 1998, Gillian Guess became the first juror in North America to be convicted of obstructing justice for engaging in a personal relationship with an accused whose case she was hearing. On August 24, 1998, she was sentenced to 18 months' incarceration, but was released after 3 months and became a key witness in the obstruction of justice charge against her former lover, Peter Gill. In July 2002, he was sentenced to prison for 5 years and 10 months for his part in the obstruction of justice. It has been suggested that this case will result in changes to the instructions that are given to jury members by judges. Such changes could include an explicit statement from the trial judge instructing jurors not to have any contact with the accused. For her part, Ms. Guess remains convinced that her only crime was that of "falling in love."

---

[1]As cited in Hans & Vidmar. *Judging the Jury* (p. 114). New York: Plenum Press.

*Sources:* MacIntosh, D.A. (1989). *Fundamentals of the Criminal Justice System* (pp. 381-386). Toronto: Carswell; Juror and Accused Killer had Affair, Court Hears. *Toronto Star* online. (1998, May 12); Sankar, C. (1998, June 20). Guess Found Guilty. *Globe and Mail* online; Man Who Had Sex with Juror Sentenced. (2002, July 2). CBC News online.

Opponents of the jury system have argued that it should be replaced by a panel of judges who would both render a verdict and impose sentence. Regardless of how well considered such a suggestion may be, such a change could not occur without modification to section 11(f) of the *Charter*.

An alternative suggestion for improving the process of trial by jury has been the call for professional jurors. Professional jurors would be paid by the government, as are judges, prosecutors, and public defenders. Their job would be to sit on any jury, and they would be expected to have the expertise to do so. Professional jurors would be trained to listen objectively and would be schooled in the kinds of decision-making skills necessary to function effectively within an adversarial context. They could be expected to hear one case after another, perhaps moving between jurisdictions in cases of highly publicized crimes.

The advantages of a professional jury system would be:

*Dependability*. Professional jurors could be expected to report to the courtroom in a timely fashion and to be good listeners, since both would be required by the nature of the job.

*Knowledge*. Professional jurors would be trained in the law, would understand what a finding of guilt requires, and would know what to expect from other actors in the courtroom.

*Equity*. Professional jurors would understand the requirements of due process and would be less likely to be swayed by the emotional content of a case, having been schooled in the need to separate matters of fact from personal feelings.

A professional jury system would not be without difficulties. Jurors under such a system might become jaded, deciding cases out of hand as routines lead to boredom, and categorizing suspects according to whether they "fit the type" for guilt or innocence, the types being developed on the basis of the jurors' previous experiences. Job requirements for professional jurors would be difficult to establish without infringing on the jurors' freedom to decide cases as they understand them. For the same reason, any evaluation of the job performance of professional jurors would be a difficult call. Finally, professional jurors might not truly be peer jurors, since their social characteristics might be skewed by education, residence, and politics.

# IMPROVING THE ADJUDICATION PROCESS

Courts today are coming under increasing scrutiny, and media-rich trials, such as that of Gillian Guess, have heightened the awareness of problems with the Canadian court system. One of today's most important issues involves reducing the number of court levels by unifying courts. The current multiplicity of courts frequently leads to what many believe are avoidable overlaps and duplication of services in the handling of criminal defendants. Problems are exacerbated by the split in judicial authority between federal and provincial levels of government. Proponents of unification suggest the elimination of overlapping jurisdictions, the creation of special-purpose courts, and the formulation of administrative offices to achieve economies of scale.[118]

Court-watch citizens groups are also rapidly growing in number. Such organizations focus on the trial court level, but they are part of a general trend towards seeking greater openness in government decision making at all levels.[119] Court-watch groups monitor court proceedings on a regular basis and attempt to document and often publicize inadequacies. They frequently focus on the handling of indigents, fairness in the scheduling of cases for trial, unnecessary court delays, the reduction of waiting time, the treatment of witnesses and jurors, and the sentencing practices of different judges.

The statistical measurement of court performance is another area that is receiving increased attention. Research has looked at the efficiency with which prosecutors schedule cases for trial, the speed with which judges resolve issues, the amount of time judges spend on the bench, and the economic and other costs to defendants, witnesses, and communities involved in the judicial process.[120] Statistical studies of this type often attempt to measure elements of court performance as diverse as sentence variation, charging accuracy, fairness in plea bargaining, even-handedness, delays, and attitudes towards the court by lay participants.[121]

In 1996, the Canadian Judicial Council, which is the research, education, and coordinating agency of federally appointed judges, published an annual report, in which it summarized the major issues currently facing the judiciary.[122] The report covered a wide range of issues, including some of the following: (1) principles governing judicial conduct; (2) the number of judges in the various courts; (3) principles governing independence and accountability of the judiciary; (4) electronic citation of judgments; and (5) updating the jury system, particularly by allowing extra jurors for long trials in order to accommodate the loss of jurors along the way. Clearly, the Canadian court system has many topical issues that will keep critics and reformers busy for years to come.

# SUMMARY

This chapter discussed activities and personnel characteristics of today's criminal courts. Although many individualized courtroom roles can be identified, the criminal trial stands as the hallmark of Canadian criminal justice. The criminal trial owes its legacy to the development of democratic principles in Western society and builds upon an adversarial process that pits prosecution against defence.

Trials have historically been viewed as peer-based fact-finding processes intended to protect the rights of the accused while sifting through disputed issues of guilt or innocence. The adversarial environment, however, that has served Canadian courts since Confederation, is now being questioned. Well-publicized trials of the last decade or two have demonstrated apparent weaknesses in the trial process. Moreover, a plethora of far-reaching social and technological changes have recently transpired that might at least partially supplant the role of advocacy in the fact-finding process. In many cases, new technologies (such as DNA fingerprinting, which is discussed in detail in Chapter 15), which were unanticipated by the framers of our present system, hold the promise to closely link suspects to criminal activity. Today's electronic media can rapidly and widely disseminate investigative findings. This combination of investigative technologies and readily available public information may eventually make courtroom debates about guilt or innocence obsolete. Whether the current adversarial system can continue to serve the interests of justice in an information-rich and technologically advanced society will be a central question for the twenty-first century.

# DISCUSSION QUESTIONS

1. We described participants in a criminal trial as working together to bring about a successful close to courtroom proceedings. What do you think a "successful close" might mean to a judge? To a defence lawyer? To a prosecutor? To the jury? To the defendant? To the victim?

2. What is a dying declaration? Under what circumstances might it be a valid exception to the hearsay rule? Why do most courts seem to believe that a person who is about to die is likely to tell the truth?

3. Do you think the present jury system is outmoded? Might "professional jurors" be more effective than the present system of "peer jurors"? On what do you base your opinion?

4. What is an expert witness? A lay witness? What different kinds of testimony may both provide? What are some of the difficulties in expert testimony?

5. What are the three forms of legal aid defence used throughout various regions of Canada? Why might defendants prefer private lawyers over public counsel?

WEBLINKS

cba.org/abc
**Canadian Bar Association**
CBA.org is an information service for the association, offering news and publications, mailing lists, discussion groups, event listings, legal links, and more.

www.cjc-ccm.gc.ca/english
**Canadian Judicial Council**
A website dedicated to improving the quality of judicial service in courts with federally appointed judges in Canada. The site includes annual reports and the results of inquiries into allegations of judicial misconduct.

www.acjnet.org/capcj
**Canadian Association of Provincial Court Judges**
The CAPCJ site provides information about the jurisdiction, size, and operations of Canada's 14 courts of first instance, organized under subject headings such as Canada's Court System, Criminal Jurisdiction, Youth Court, and Family Court.

www.jurist.law.utoronto.ca
**Jurist Canada**
The best legal website in Canada. This site keeps you up-to-date on Canadian law by providing access to the full text of important court and administrative tribunals' decisions, links to other relevant websites, links to current news media accounts of legal issues, and more.

www.iap.nl.com
**International Association of Prosecutors**
The IAP is a non-governmental, non-political organization formed in 1995 by the United Nations.

# Sentencing

Toronto Star/Paul McCusker

## KEY CONCEPTS

retribution
just deserts
incapacitation
deterrence
specific deterrence
general deterrence
rehabilitation
restoration
structured sentencing
indeterminate
determinate sentencing
structured sentencing

determinate sentencing
aggravating
    circumstances
mitigating circumstances
pre-sentence report
restorative justice
victim impact statements
capital punishment
determinate sentencing

## KEY CASES

*R. v. Latimer*

*R. v. Luxton*

*R. v. Goltz*

*R. v. Morissey*

*R. v. Wust*

*R. v. Proulx*

*R. v. Knoblauch*

*Kindler* v. *Canada
    (Minister of Justice)*

*U.S.A.* v. *Burns*

# CRIME AND PUNISHMENT: INTRODUCTION

In 1993, Saskatchewan farmer Robert Latimer took his 12-year-old daughter for one last walk. Tracy suffered from a severe case of cerebral palsy, and exhibited severe physical disability and constant pain, brought about by her condition. The last walk was out to the garage, where Latimer placed his daughter into the cab of his truck, left the vehicle with the engine running and the exhaust piped into the cab, and returned to his house. A short while later, he removed his daughter's now-limp body, brought it back to the house, and called an ambulance.

Latimer's situation re-sparked debate from coast to coast on the question of whether persons who engage in mercy killing should be subject to the same rigours of the criminal law as those who intentionally kill for less malevolent reasons. After a trial, and appeals that reached the Supreme Court of Canada, Latimer was subjected to a retrial in 1997. In November of that year, the jury returned a verdict of guilty of second-degree murder. Because the jury found the requisite "intent to kill" was present, there was no room for the jury to return a verdict on a lesser offence such as manslaughter. Under Canadian law, the jury has no role in selecting the sentence of an offender, unless the person is convicted of second-degree murder. In the case of a second-degree murder conviction, the jury is required to recommend a mandatory minimum period of incarceration during which the offender is ineligible to be released on parole. This mandatory minimum period is from 10 to 25 years. However, when the jury was informed of its role in selecting the minimum parole eligibility date, several jurors wept—indicating that they did not know about the 10-year minimum.[1]

The jury retired to consider its most difficult task. When it returned, it presented the judge with a recommendation that completely ignored the law. The jury said that Latimer should be eligible for parole after serving one year. With this recommendation, Justice Noble of the Saskatchewan Court of Queen's Bench invoked section 12 of the *Charter of Rights and Freedoms*—the prohibition against the imposition of cruel and unusual treatment or punishment. According to Noble J., to force Latimer to endure a 10-year minimum period of incarceration would not be acceptable in light of the jury's recommendation and the facts of the case:

> I find that Mr. Latimer's section 12 Charter right has been violated and that he be granted a constitutional exemption from the sentence. Mr. Latimer was motivated solely by his love and compassion for Tracy and the need—at least in his mind—that she should not suffer any more pain.

Noble J. then sentenced Latimer to two years less a day, with one year to be served in jail, and a recommendation for parole during the second year of his sentence.

In November 1998, the Saskatchewan Court of Appeal overturned this sentence, ruling that the law as it stands must be applied.[2] A final appeal by Latimer to the Supreme Court of Canada was unsuccessful, and he was sentenced in 2001 to life in prison, without parole eligibility for 10 years.[3] This case illustrates one of the great dilemmas in sentencing: how does one develop and apply the law so as to treat everyone equally, yet at the same time ensure that justice is done in individual cases?

Sentencing is the imposition of a penalty upon a person convicted of a crime. Sentencing decisions are made by judges, although as noted above, a jury has a limited role in second-degree murder cases. The sentencing decision is one of the most difficult made by any judge. Not only does it involve the future, and perhaps the integrity, of the defendant, but society looks to sentencing to achieve a diversity of goals—some of which may not be fully compatible.

This chapter examines sentencing in terms of both philosophy and practice. We will describe the goals of sentencing as well as the historical development of various sentencing models in Canada. We will also discuss the role of victims in contemporary sentencing practices. This chapter contains a detailed overview of victimization and victims' rights in general—especially as they relate to courtroom procedure and to sentencing practice. Finally, we will describe the significance of pre-sentence investigations.

# THE PHILOSOPHY OF CRIMINAL SENTENCING

Traditional sentencing options have included imprisonment, fines, probation, and—in the past, for very serious offences—death. Limits on the range of options available to sentencing authorities are generally specified by law. Historically, those limits have shifted as understanding of crime and the goals of sentencing have changed. Sentencing philosophies, or the justifications upon which various sentencing strategies are based, are manifestly intertwined with issues of religion, morals, values, and emotions.[4] Philosophies that gained ascendancy at particular times in history were likely to be reflections of more deeply held social values. The mentality of centuries ago, for example, held that crime was due to sin, and suffering was the culprit's due. Judges were expected to be harsh. Capital punishment, torture, and painful physical penalties served this view of criminal behaviour.

An emphasis on deterrence through rational punishment became more prevalent around the late eighteenth and early nineteenth centuries, brought about, in part, by Enlightenment philosophies. An offender came to be seen as a highly rational being who, more often than not, intentionally and somewhat carefully chose his or her course of action. Sentencing philosophies of the period stressed the need for sanctions that outweighed the benefits to be derived from making criminal choices. Severity of punishment became less important than quick and certain penalties.

## BOX 9.1 Theory into Practice

## Purpose and Principles of Sentencing

### Criminal Code

718. The fundamental purpose of sentencing is to contribute, along with crime prevention initiatives, to respect for the law and the maintenance of a just, peaceful and safe society by imposing just sanctions that have one or more of the following objectives

  (a) to denounce unlawful conduct;

  (b) to deter the offender and other persons from committing offences;

  (c) to separate offenders from society, where necessary;

  (d) to assist in rehabilitating offenders;

  (e) to provide reparations for harm done to victims or to the community; and

  (f) to promote a sense of responsibility in offenders, and acknowledgment of the harm done to victims and to the community.

718.1 A sentence must be proportionate to the gravity of the offence and the degree of responsibility of the offender.

718.2 A court that imposes a sentence shall also take into consideration the following principles:

  (a) a sentence should be increased or reduced to account for any relevant aggravating or mitigating circumstances relating to the offence or the offender, and, without limiting the generality of the foregoing,

  (i) evidence that the offence was motivated by bias, prejudice or hate based on race, national or ethnic origin, language, colour, religion, sex, age, mental or physical disability, sexual orientation, or any other similar factor,

  (ii) evidence that the offender, in committing the offence, abused the offender's spouse or common-law partner or child,

  (iii) evidence that the offender, in committing the offence, abused a position of trust or authority in relation to the victim,

  (iv) evidence that the offence was committed for the benefit of, at the direction of or in association with a criminal organization, or

  (v) evidence that the offence was a terrorism offence

  shall be deemed to be aggravating circumstances;

  (b) a sentence should be similar to sentences imposed on similar offenders for similar offences committed in similar circumstances;

  (c) where consecutive sentences are imposed, the combined sentence should not be unduly long or harsh;

  (d) an offender should not be deprived of liberty, if less restrictive sanctions may be appropriate in the circumstances; and

  (e) all available sanctions other than imprisonment that are reasonable in the circumstances should be considered for all offenders, with particular attention to the circumstances of aboriginal offenders.

By the beginning of the twentieth century, rehabilitation became a dominant rationale for sentencing, based largely on Positivist philosophies. Offenders were viewed as people who engaged in criminal behaviour because something was causing them to behave that way. Such theories assumed that these causative forces were typically beyond an individual's control, whether it be an impoverished childhood or defective brain functioning that caused a person to act in a certain way. Treatment-oriented penalties were believed to be the best means of dealing with offenders.

Recent thinking has emphasized the need to limit offenders' potential for future harm by separating them from society. We also still believe that offenders deserve to be punished, and we have not entirely abandoned hope for their rehabilitation. Modern sentencing practices are influenced by five goals, which weave their way through widely disseminated professional and legal models, continuing public calls for sentencing reform, and everyday sentencing practice. Each goal represents a quasi-independent sentencing philosophy, since each makes distinctive assumptions about human nature and holds implications for sentencing practice. The five goals of contemporary sentencing are:

1. Just Deserts;

2. Incapacitation;

3. Deterrence;

4. Rehabilitation; and

5. Restoration.

## Just Deserts

**retribution** The act of taking revenge upon a criminal perpetrator.

**Retribution** is a call for punishment predicated upon a felt need for vengeance. Retribution is the earliest known rationale for punishment. Most early societies punished offenders whenever they could catch them. Early punishments were swift and immediate—often without the benefit of a hearing—and they were often extreme, with little thought given to whether the punishment "fit" the crime. Death and exile, for example, were commonly imposed, even on relatively minor offenders. In contrast, the Old Testament dictum of "An eye for an eye, a tooth for a tooth"—often cited as an ancient justification for retribution—was actually intended to reduce the severity of punishment for relatively minor crimes.

**just deserts** As a model of criminal sentencing, one which holds that criminal offenders deserve the punishment they receive at the hands of the law, and that punishments should be appropriate to the type and severity of crime committed.

In its modern guise, retribution corresponds to the **just deserts** model of sentencing. The just deserts philosophy holds that offenders are responsible for their crimes. When they are convicted and punished, they are said to have received their "just deserts." Retribution sees punishment as deserved, justified, and even required[5] by the offender's behaviour. The primary sentencing tool of today's just deserts model is imprisonment, but in the past, extreme cases were seen to merit capital punishment (that is, death) as the ultimate retribution. Today, the maximum penalty for any offence in Canada is life in prison, without eligibility for parole for 25 years. This penalty is reserved for the most serious offences in our *Criminal Code*.[6] From a just deserts perspective, all other penalties for all other offences must be scaled down from this, and kept in proportion to the seriousness of the harm flowing from the offence.

Although it may be an age-old goal of criminal sentencing, deserts-oriented retribution is very much in the forefront of public thinking and political policy making today. Within the last few years, as society's perspective has emphasized the individual, public demands for retribution-based criminal punishments have been loud and clear. In 1997, for example, the federal Parliament amended the *Criminal Code* to incorporate a fundamental principle to guide sentencing judges in section 718.1: "A sentence must be proportionate to the gravity of the offence and the degree of responsibility of the offender." Proportionality of punishment to the degree of harm is the essence of just deserts. Recent moves to make prison life less soft are also part of the retributive approach to justice.

In recent years, many vocal members of the public have called for harsher prison conditions, and a return to the chain gang. With public anti-crime sentiment at what may be an all-time high, says Jonathan Turley, director of the Prison Law Project, "It's difficult to imagine a measure draconian enough to satisfy the public desire for retribution."[7] As critics say, however, the fact that none of these measures will likely deter crime is beside the point. The goal of retribution, after all, is not deterrence, but satisfaction.[8]

However, just deserts operates to limit the amount of punishment that can be imposed. Philosophically, the only punishment that may be meted out is that which is truly deserved. Desert is limited by the degree of harm caused by the crime. Any punishment that exceeds the degree of harm caused is disproportionate and unjustified. So, rather than operating as a justification for extreme penalties, just deserts operates to limit and constrain the amount of punishment imposed upon an offender. Of course, many people differ in their view of what amount of punishment is proportionate to the harm caused. In this sense, we each have our own sense of the range of appropriate punishments.

Just deserts must also wrestle with the need for parity among punishments. Since courts now use a variety of punishments, like fines, imprisonment, community service orders, and the like, adherents of just deserts sentencing want to ensure equal treatment of offenders who commit the same type of crimes in similar situations. Once the system strays away from the sole use of imprisonment, it becomes difficult to ascertain the penal bite, or harshness, of any given penalty on any given offender. For example, a modest fine has more penal bite on a homeless person than on a wealthy individual.

## Incapacitation

**Incapacitation**, the second goal of criminal sentencing, seeks to protect innocent members of society from offenders who might do them harm if they were not prevented in some way. In ancient times, mutilation and amputation of the extremities were sometimes used to prevent offenders from repeating their crimes. A variety of cultures has also banished offenders to faraway lands to render them incapable of committing further harms to the community. Modern incapacitation strategies separate offenders from the community in order to reduce opportunities for further criminality. Incapacitation is sometimes called the "lock 'em up approach" and forms the basis for the movement towards prison "warehousing," discussed later in Chapter 11.

Both incapacitation and retribution are used as justifications for imprisonment. One significant difference between the two perspectives lies in the fact that incapacitation requires only restraint—and not punishment. Hence, advocates of the incapacitation philosophy of sentencing are sometimes also active prison reformers, seeking to humanize correctional institutions. Since imprisonment is costly, the key to a sound incapacitation strategy is to identify those offenders who are most likely to reoffend, and to isolate them only as long as is necessary to provide societal protection. This task has proven to be virtually impossible to accomplish with any level of efficiency. At the forefront of technology, confinement innovations are now offering ways to achieve the goal of incapacitation without the need for imprisonment. Electronic confinement (discussed shortly) and biomedical intervention (such as "chemical castration") may be able to achieve the goals of incapacitation without the need for imprisonment.

Just deserts justifies the imposition of a sentence of punishment by looking back in time to the offence that occurred and the need to account for (or compensate for) the harm caused to the victim. This accounting is accomplished by imposing a similar level of harm on the offender as that inflicted on the victim. In contrast, incapacitation justifies the imposition of a sentence by looking to the future and envisioning the crimes that will not be committed in the future because the offender is behind bars, unable to inflict harm on anyone except other inmates. The penalty that is justifiably imposed may indeed be the same under either desert or incapacitation—that is, lengthy confinement. Indeed, as we will soon see, many of the other justifications for sentencing can result in the imposition of similar types of penalties.

## Deterrence

**Deterrence** uses punishment as an example to convince people that criminal activity is not worthwhile. Its overall goal, like that of incapacitation, is crime prevention. It is based on the

CHAPTER 9
Sentencing

**incapacitation** The use of imprisonment or other means to reduce the likelihood that an offender will be capable of committing future offences.

**deterrence** A goal of criminal sentencing that seeks to prevent others from committing crimes similar to the one for which an offender is being sentenced.

285

**specific deterrence**

A goal of criminal sentencing that seeks to prevent a particular offender from engaging in repeat criminality.

**general deterrence**

A goal of criminal sentencing that seeks to prevent others from committing crimes similar to the one for which a particular offender is being sentenced, by making an example of the person sentenced.

simple psychological principle that an organism (including a person) is less likely to repeat a behaviour that is associated with the infliction of a painful stimulus.[9] **Specific deterrence** seeks to reduce the likelihood of recidivism (repeat offences) by convicted offenders, by imposing punishment in order that they learn that criminal behaviour will result in the imposition of painful stimuli. In this way, the offender is expected to learn not to reoffend in order to avoid the pain of punishment. **General deterrence** strives to influence the future behaviour of people who have not yet been arrested and who may be tempted to turn to crime. General deterrence operates on principles commonly understood as social learning. An individual can learn to avoid the punishment that follows undesirable behaviour by seeing that other people are being punished for such behaviour, including criminal behaviour.[10]

Deterrence is one of the more "rational" goals of sentencing. This goal is rational because it is easily articulated, and also because the amount of punishment required to effect deterrence can be investigated objectively. From the late eighteenth century to the early nineteenth century, English philosopher and legal scholar Jeremy Bentham (1748–1832) argued that deterrence should guide penal policy. From the time of Jeremy Bentham, criminologists have attempted to develop a calculus, or mathematical formula, for how harsh punishments need to be in order to deter effectively. Deterrence is based on the assumption that the individual exercise of free will leads people to avoid crime where the benefit to be derived from committing crime is outweighed by the pain of punishment. It is generally agreed today that harsh punishments can virtually eliminate many minor forms of criminality.[11] Few traffic tickets would have to be written, for example, if minor driving offences were punishable by death. A free society such as our own, of course, is not willing to impose extreme punishments on petty offenders, and even harsh punishments are not demonstrably effective in reducing the incidence of serious crimes such as murder and drug running.

Deterrence is compatible with the goal of incapacitation, since at least specific deterrence can arguably be achieved through incapacitating offenders. Both deterrence and incapacitation seek to curb the amount of future crime. Hugo Bedau,[12] however, points to significant differences between retribution and deterrence. Retribution is oriented towards the past, says Bedau. It seeks to redress wrongs already committed. Deterrence, in contrast, is a strategy for the future because it aims to prevent new crimes. But as H.L.A. Hart has observed,[13] retribution can be the means through which deterrence is achieved. By serving as an example of what might happen to others, punishment may have an inhibiting effect.

Aboriginal Ganootamaage Justice Services of Winnipeg volunteers take part in a healing circle for a 20-year-old shoplifter, not shown in photo, at the Aboriginal Center. It was the first sentence handed down by a healing circle under a new provincial program for aboriginal offenders.

Winnipeg Free Press/Joe Bryksa

# Rehabilitation

Rehabilitation seeks to bring about fundamental changes in offenders and their behaviour. As with deterrence and incapacitation, the ultimate goal of rehabilitation is to reduce the number of future criminal offences. Whereas deterrence depends upon a "fear of the law" and the consequences of violating it, rehabilitation generally works through medical and psychological treatments to reduce the likelihood of future criminality.

The term *rehabilitation*, however, may actually be a misnomer for the kinds of changes that its supporters seek. Rehabilitation literally means to return a person (or thing) to their previous condition. Hence, medical rehabilitation programs seek to restore functioning to atrophied limbs, rejuvenate injured organs, and mend shattered minds. In the case of criminal offenders, however, it is unlikely that restoring many to their previous state will result in anything other than a more youthful type of criminality.

In the past, rehabilitation as a sentencing strategy, if it existed at all, was primarily applied to youths. One of the first serious efforts to reform adult offenders was begun by the Pennsylvania Quakers, who initiated the development of the late-eighteenth-century penitentiary. The penitentiary, which attempted to combine enforced penance with religious instruction, proved to be something of an aberration. Within a few decades, it had been firmly supplanted by a retributive approach to corrections.

It was not until the 1930s that **rehabilitation** achieved a primary role in the sentencing of adult offenders in Canada. At the time, the psychological world view of therapists such as Sigmund Freud became popular. Psychology held out, as never before, the possibility of a structured approach to rehabilitation through therapeutic intervention. The rehabilitative approach of the mid-1900s became known as the medical model of corrections, since it was built around a prescriptive approach to the treatment of offenders that provided at least the appearance of clinical predictability.

The primacy of the rehabilitative goal in sentencing fell victim to a "nothing works" philosophy in the late 1970s. The nothing-works doctrine was based upon studies of recidivism rates, which consistently showed that rehabilitation was more an ideal than a reality. With as many as 90 per cent of former convicted offenders returning to lives of crime following release from prison-based treatment programs, public sentiments in favour of incapacitation grew. Although the rehabilitation ideal has clearly suffered in the public arena, some emerging evidence has begun to suggest that effective treatment programs do exist and may even be growing in number.[14]

**rehabilitation** The attempt to reform a criminal offender. Also, the state in which a reformed offender is said to be.

# Restoration

Victims of crime or their survivors are frequently traumatized by their experiences. Some are killed, and others receive lasting physical injuries. For many, the world is never the same. The victimized may live in constant fear—reduced in personal vigour and unable to form trusting relationships. **Restoration** is a sentencing goal that seeks to address this damage by making the victim and the community "whole again."

A report for the Solicitor General of Canada indicates that the impetus for a restorative approach comes from at least two sources. First, empirical evidence indicates that criminal justice sanctions have little impact on recidivism. Second, people are concerned that the system's focus on the offender has betrayed and abandoned the victim. Accordingly, the criminal justice system has begun to turn to the restorative approach.[15]

A report by the U.S. Department of Justice explains restoration in this way:

**restoration** A goal of criminal sentencing that attempts to make the victim "whole again."

> Crime was once defined as a "violation of the State." This remains the case today, but we now recognize that crime is far more. It is—among other things—a violation of one person by another. While retributive justice may address the first type of violation adequately, restorative justice is required to effectively address the lat[t]er…. Thus (through restorative justice) we seek to attain a balance between the legitimate needs of the community, the … offender, and the victim.[16]

The "healing" of victims involves many aspects, ranging from victim assistance initiatives to legislation supporting victim compensation. Sentencing options that seek to restore the victim to his or her state before the crime occurred have focused primarily on restitution payments that offenders are ordered to make, either to their victims or to a general fund, which may then go to reimburse victims for suffering, lost wages, and medical expenses. In support of these goals, the 1995 amendments to the *Criminal Code* imposed a requirement

BOX 9.2    **Theory into Practice**

## Aboriginal Healing Circles and Sentencing

One attempt to embrace restorative justice in the sentencing process has been to use sentencing circles. This idea is built upon the notion of healing circles found in some aboriginal communities. After spending several years working as a Crown prosecutor in northwestern Ontario, Rupert Ross wrote about his experiences with aboriginal healing circles and aboriginal culture in *Return to the Teachings: Exploring Aboriginal Justice.*[1] In this book, he uses anecdotal material to allow the reader to see through the eyes of aboriginal people who come into contact with the criminal justice system, allowing a different view of the legal process. This process starts with the commission of a crime, through the healing circle, and eventually to the point of healing.

Healing circles, or sentencing circles as they are sometimes called when integrated into the formal court sentencing process, typically means that a group of chairs in the courtroom are arranged, with permission of the sentencing judge, in a circle. The seats are taken up by the judge, the victim(s), the offender, the defence lawyer, the prosecutor, police officers, family members, and interested members of the community. Rather than conducting an adversarial hearing into the most appropriate sentence, the judge facilitates discussion among all of the parties, trying to reach a consensus as to how best to deal with the offender. The overriding goal is restorative, that is, finding a means to reintegrate the offender into the community and undo the harm caused through the commission of a crime. While the judge makes the final disposition, the wishes of all affected parties can be taken into account through such a sentencing process.

Here are some of the advantages in using circle sentencing:[2] First, the monopoly on the process is taken away from the lawyers and judges, and shared with those most directly affected by the sentencing decision, encouraging lay participation. Second, it enhances the type and amount of information available to the sentencing decision maker. Third, it fosters a creative search for new disposition options. Fourth, it promotes a sharing of the responsibility for the successful completion of the sentence. Fifth, it emphasizes constructive rather than punitive solutions.

Circle sentencing has become popular among aboriginal communities, particularly those in the Far North. In 1992, Judge Stuart of the Yukon Territorial Court was one

of the first to employ the process in *R.* v. *Moses.*[3] Since then, courts across the country have employed circle sentencing. In recent years, courts have sought standards to determine when circle sentencing should be used rather than a conventional sentencing hearing. Appeal courts have called upon trial courts to outline the rules and standards to be applied in determining which cases should go before a sentencing circle, and the applicable procedures.[4] Saskatchewan provincial court judges have outlined criteria for using sentencing circles that have attracted some support:

1. The accused must agree to be referred to the sentencing circle.
2. The accused must have deep roots in the community in which the circle is held and from which the participants are drawn.
3. That there are elders or respected non-political community leaders willing to participate.
4. The victim is willing to participate and has not been subjected to coercion or pressure in so agreeing.
5. The court should try to determine beforehand, as best it can, if the victim is subject to battered spouse syndrome. If she is, then she should have counselling made available to her and be accompanied by a support team in the circle.
6. Disputed facts have been resolved in advance.
7. The case is one in which a court would be willing to take a calculated risk and depart from the usual range of sentencing.[5]

Not all requests for the use of circle sentencing will be approved by the court.[6]

## QUESTIONS FOR DISCUSSION

1. Can you think of some disadvantages to using circle sentencing? Can you think of some advantages not outlined above?

2. Does the Saskatchewan approach to the availability of circle sentencing provide adequate criteria? Are there too many factors here? Not enough? Should it be available to non-aboriginal offenders?

3. Does circle sentencing provide an overly romanticized view of aboriginal culture? Does it cast a wide variety of diverse cultures as singular and coherent in a way that is contrary to reality?

---

[1]Ross, R. (1996). *Returning to the Teachings: Exploring Aboriginal Justice.* Toronto: Penguin Canada.
[2]*R.* v. *Moses* (1992), 11 C.R. (4th) 357 (Yuk.Terr.Ct.).
[3]Ibid.
[4]*R.* v. *B.L.,* [2002] A.J. No. 215 (Alta.C.A.), *R.* v. *Johns,* [1996] 1 C.N.L.R. 172 (Yuk.Terr.C.A.), *R.* v. *Morin,* [1995] S.J. No. 457 (Sask.C.A.).
[5]*R.* v. *Joseyounen,* [1995] 6 W.W.R. 438 (Sask.P.C.).
[6]*R.* v. *Cheekinow* (1993), 80 C.C.C. (3d) 143 (Sask.Q.B.).

that courts consider any "victim impact statement" submitted to the court (s. 722), and require courts to give priority to the payment of restitution by a victim over the payment of fines or any forfeiture orders imposed by the court.

Winnipeg's Restorative Resolutions program provides one example of a strategy to utilize restitution as an alternative to prison.[17] This program takes cases in which the Crown recommends a sentence of at least nine months in prison, the offender agrees to plead guilty, and the offender presents evidence of being willing to participate in a community-based plan that includes meeting with the victim and attending programs. Evaluation of this program reveals that it is successful in providing lower rates of recidivism than were found in two comparison groups—one composed of prison inmates and the other composed of probationers.[18] One must consider these findings with caution, as minor differences did exist between the group exposed to restorative sanctioning and the comparison groups. These differences, rather than the different correctional approaches, may have caused the variations in the results.

Some advocates of the restoration philosophy of sentencing point out that restitution payments and work programs that benefit the victim can also have the added benefit of rehabilitating the offender. The hope is that such sentences may teach offenders personal responsibility through structured financial obligations, job requirements, and regularly scheduled payments.

# CANADA'S SENTENCING APPROACH

While the *philosophy* of criminal sentencing is reflected in the goals of sentencing we have just discussed, different sentencing *practices* have been linked to each goal. During most of the twentieth century, for example, the rehabilitative goal has been influential. Since rehabilitation required that individual offenders' personal characteristics be closely considered in defining effective treatment strategies, judges were generally permitted wide discretion in choosing from among sentencing options. Although incapacitation is increasingly becoming the public's sentencing strategy of choice, the *Criminal Code* still allows judges to impose fines, probation, or widely varying prison terms, all for the same offence. These sentencing practices, characterized primarily by vast judicial choice, constitute a diverse approach to sentencing.

The sentencing approach in Canada relies heavily upon judges' discretion to choose among types of sanctions and set upper and lower limits on the length of prison stays. The *Criminal Code* rarely sets lower limits to penalties, typically leaving the judge to select a penalty within a range that usually has no lower limit, but a fairly high maximum, presumably to be reserved for the worst-case scenario. Even when a judge selects a particular length of prison sentence, it is possible that the offender will not serve the full sentence due to the availability of conditional release.

Conditional release operates for both federal and provincial inmates, and allows an inmate to obtain release long before the expiration of his or her sentence, imposed by the sentencing judge. Inmates may find themselves released on one form of conditional release or another even before one-sixth of the sentence imposed by the court has been served. Full parole is typically possible after serving one-third of the sentence imposed by the court. In this sense, a judicial sentence of, for example, nine years in a penitentiary effectively becomes a sentence of no more than nine years, and no less than three years, although the inmate will even be eligible for more restrictive forms of conditional release even sooner.

Judicial discretion under Canada's sentencing approach also extends to the imposition of concurrent or consecutive sentences, where the offender is convicted on more than one charge. Consecutive sentences are served one after the other, while concurrent sentences expire simultaneously. Judges have some latitude in determining whether multiple sentences run together or one after the other.

Our sentencing model was created to take into consideration detailed differences in degrees of guilt. Under this model, judges could weigh minute differences among cases, situations, and offenders. All of the following could be considered before sentence was passed: (1) whether the offender committed the crime out of a need for money, for the thrill it afforded, out of a desire for revenge, or for the "hell of it"; (2) how much harm the offender intended; (3) how much the victim contributed to his or her own victimization; (4) the extent of the damages inflicted; (5) the mental state of the offender; (6) the likelihood of successful rehabilitation; (7) the degree of the offender's co-operation with authorities; and (8) a near infinity of other individual factors (see the Theory into Practice box "Aggravating and Mitigating Factors" on page 292).

Under our current sentencing model, the inmate's behaviour (while incarcerated) is a primary determinant of the amount of time served. Parole boards wield great discretion under the model, acting as the final arbiters of the actual sentence served.

## Problems with the Canadian Sentencing Model

**indeterminate** Refers to a model of sentencing that allows for subsequent discretion regarding the eventual release date. Release is contingent upon the offender's eventual rehabilitation, which is thereby promoted through this sentencing approach.

**Indeterminate** sentencing is still the rule in all Canadian jurisdictions. By the 1970s, however, the model had come under fire for contributing to inequality in sentencing.[19] Critics claimed that the approach allowed divergent judicial personalities, and the often too-personal philosophies of judges, to produce a wide range of sentencing practices from very lenient to very strict. The "hanging judge," a type of judge that still presides in some jurisdictions today, was depicted as tending to impose the maximum sentence allowable under law on anyone who came before the bench, regardless of circumstances. Worse still, the broad discretion built into the Canadian sentencing model was criticized for perpetuating a system under which offenders might be sentenced, at least by some judges, more on the basis of social characteristics, such as race, gender, and social class, than on culpability.

Because of the personal nature of judicial decisions, offenders often depend upon the advice and ploys of their lawyers in hopes of appearing before a judge who is believed to be a good sentencing risk. Requests for delays are a common defence strategy in sentencing matters. A request for a delay is an attempt to manipulate the selection of judicial personalities involved in sentencing decisions.

Another charge levelled against the current approach to sentencing is that it tends to produce dishonesty in sentencing. Because of sentence cutbacks for good behaviour and other reductions available to inmates through involvement in work and study programs, punishments rarely mean what they say. An apparently punitive sentence of five years, for example, might actually see an inmate released, at least on day parole, in a matter of months after a calculation of conditional release eligibility dates is completed. To ensure appropriate prison terms in Canada, legislative amendments have resulted in the courts being granted the authority (1) to require certain offenders, convicted of serious indictable offences, to serve at least 50 per cent of their sentence before being eligible for conditional release (s. 743.6 in the *Criminal Code*), and (2) to allow for the detention of other offenders believed to be at serious risk of reoffending by causing death or serious bodily harm, until the expiration of their full sentence (*Corrections and Conditional Release Act*).

In some U.S. indeterminate jurisdictions, some court officials have been led to extremes. In 1994, for example, a judge in Oklahoma, a state where indeterminate sentencing is practised, followed a jury's recommendation and sentenced convicted child molester Charles Scott Robinson, aged 30, to 30 000 years in prison.[20] Judge Owens, complying with the jury's efforts to ensure that Robinson would spend the rest of his life behind bars, sentenced him to serve six consecutive 5000-year sentences. Robinson had 14 previous felony convictions. Such sentences are not possible in Canada due to the effect of the "totality principle," the "restraint principle," and the "proportionality principle,"[21] all of which combine to require sentencing judges to limit the upper boundary of their sentences.

Due largely to the uncertain nature of sentencing practices, time served in prison is generally far less than sentences would seem to indicate. A 1997 report by the Correctional Service of Canada revealed that an inmate typically became eligible for full parole after serving only one-third of the sentence imposed by the court, and that over 40 per cent of inmates applying for full parole were granted release in 1996-97.[22] Inmates rarely served more than two-thirds of a sentence imposed by the court for two years or more.

## THE RISE OF STRUCTURED SENTENCING

In recent years, Canada's sentencing scheme has come under considerable scrutiny. In 1987, the Canadian Sentencing Commission produced a report recommending a main overhaul of Canada's approach to criminal sentencing.[23] One of the recommendations was that the process should be made more "fair and equitable" by giving judges meaningful guidance in the selection of an appropriate sentence, and the elimination of full parole for most offences.

This call for action echoed developments that had occurred over the preceding decade in the United States. Until the 1970s, all 50 states used a form of sentencing similar to that in Canada. Soon, however, calls for equity and proportionality in sentencing, heightened by claims of racial disparity in the sentencing practices[24] of some judges, led many states to move towards closer control over their sentencing systems.

Critics of the indeterminate model have called for the recognition of three fundamental sentencing principles: proportionality, equity, and social debt. Proportionality refers to the belief that the severity of sanctions should bear a direct relationship to the seriousness of the crime committed. Equity is based upon a concern with social equality and means that similar crimes should be punished with the same degree of severity, regardless of the general social or personal characteristics of offenders. According to the principle of equity, for example, two bank robbers in different parts of the country, who use the same techniques and weapons, with the same degree of implied threat, even though they are tried under separate circumstances, should receive roughly the same kind of sentence. The equity principle needs to be balanced, however, against the notion of social debt. In the case of the bank robbers, the offender who has a prior criminal record can be said to have a higher level of social debt than the one-time robber, where all else is equal. Greater social debt, of course, would suggest a heightened severity of punishment or a greater need for treatment, and so on.

Beginning in the 1970s, a number of U.S. states moved to address these concerns by developing a different model of sentencing known as **structured sentencing**. One form of structured sentencing, called **determinate sentencing**, requires that a convicted offender be sentenced to a fixed term that may be reduced by good time or earned time. Good time, sometimes referred to as earned time, refers to the amount of time deducted from time to be served in prison on a given sentence as a reward for the inmate's good behaviour. In the U.S., determinate sentencing eliminates parole and creates explicit standards that set the appropriate punishments for offences. Determinate sentencing practices also specify an anticipated release date for each sentenced offender.

In structured sentencing, the jurisdiction typically abolishes the parole release decision and replaces the parole-controlled penalty structure with a fixed (flat) sentence that could be reduced by a significant good-time provision. Only Arizona has adopted such a structured sentencing scheme in recent years.[25] In three other states (California, Illinois, and Indiana), the legislators provide presumptive ranges of confinement.[26]

In response to the growing determinate sentencing movement, a few U.S. states have developed voluntary/advisory sentencing guidelines. Such guidelines consist of recommended sentencing policies that are not required by law. They are usually based on past sentencing practices and serve as guides to judges. Another model of structured sentencing employs commission-based presumptive sentencing guidelines. This model differs from both determinate and voluntary/advisory guidelines in several respects. Most importantly, presumptive sentencing guidelines were not developed by the legislature but by a sentencing commission that often represented a diverse array of criminal justice and sometimes private citizen interests. As with other structured approaches, the major concern is to reduce disparity, increase certainty, and maintain proportionality.[27]

Presumptive sentencing guidelines generally allow for "aggravating" or "mitigating" factors—indicating greater or lesser degrees of culpability—which judges can take into consideration in imposing a sentence somewhat at variance from the presumptive term. **Aggravating circumstances** are those that appear to call for a tougher sentence and may include especially heinous behaviour, cruelty, injury to more than one person, and so on.

**Mitigating circumstances**, or those that indicate that a lesser sentence is called for, are generally similar to legal defences, although in this case they only reduce criminal responsibility, not eliminate it. Mitigating factors include such things as co-operation with the investigating authority, surrender, good character, and so on. Common aggravating and mitigating factors are listed in the Theory into Practice box on the next page.

**determinate sentencing** (also called **structured sentencing**) A model for criminal punishment that sets one particular punishment, or length of sentence, for each specific type of crime. Under the model, for example, all offenders convicted of the same degree of burglary would be sentenced to the same length of time behind bars.

**aggravating circumstances** Those elements of an offence or of an offender's background that could result in a harsher sentence under the determinate model than would otherwise be called for by sentencing guidelines.

**mitigating circumstances** Those elements of an offence or of an offender's background that could result in a lesser sentence under the determinate model than would otherwise be called for by sentencing guidelines.

# Critiques of Structured Sentencing

Structured sentencing models, which have generally sought to address the shortcomings of indeterminate sentencing by curtailing judicial discretion in sentencing, are not without their critics. Detractors charge that structured sentencing is (1) overly simplistic, (2) based on a primitive concept of culpability, and (3) incapable of offering hope for rehabilitation and change. For one thing, they say, structured sentencing has built-in limitations, which render it far more difficult for a sentencing judge to select a sentence that adequately reflects the blameworthiness of individual offenders. Legislatures and sentencing commissions, say critics, simply cannot anticipate all the differences that individual cases can present. The application of aggravating and mitigating factors, while intended to cover most circumstances, will inevitably shortchange some defendants who don't fall neatly into the categories provided.

A second critique of structured sentencing is that while it may reduce judicial discretion substantially, it may do nothing to hamper the huge discretionary decision-making power of prosecutors.[28] In fact, U.S. federal sentencing reformers, who have adopted a structured sentencing model, have specifically decided not to modify the discretionary power of prosecutors, citing the large number of cases that are resolved through plea bargaining. Such a shift in discretionary authority, away from judges and into the hands of prosecutors, say critics, may be misplaced.

Another criticism of structured sentencing questions its fundamental underlying purpose. Advocates of structured sentencing inevitably cite greater equity in sentencing as the primary benefits of such a model. Reduced to its essence, this means that "those who commit the same crime get the same time." Others, however, have pointed out that the

## BOX 9.3  Theory into Practice

### Aggravating and Mitigating Circumstances

Allan Manson (2001)[1] summarizes the circumstances that could be considered aggravating or mitigating in Canadian law. Aggravating factors are those that will make the court view the offence as more serious and worthy of higher penalty, while mitigating factors will be used by a court to lower the penalty that an offender would otherwise receive.

The *Criminal Code* outlines some aggravating factors. These include spouse or child abuse, evidence that a position of trust was violated, and evidence that the offence was committed for a criminal organization (s. 718.2). The courts have identified other aggravating factors, as follows:

1. Previous convictions.
2. Actual or threatened use of violence or use of a weapon.
3. Cruelty or brutality.
4. Offences committed while subject to conditions.
5. Multiple victims or multiple incidents.
6. Group or gang activity.
7. Impeding victim's access to the justice system.
8. Substantial economic loss.
9. Planning and organization.
10. Vulnerability of victim.
11. Status or role of victim.
12. Deliberate risk taking.

With regard to mitigating circumstances, the judge may look to the following factors:

1. First-time offender.
2. No prior record advanced.
3. Prior good character.
4. Guilty plea and remorse.
5. Evidence of impairment.
6. Employment record.
7. Collateral or indirect consequences.
8. Post-offence rehabilitative efforts.
9. Unrelated meritorious conduct.
10. Acts of reparation or compensation.
11. Provocation and duress.
12. Delay in prosecution or sentencing.
13. Gap in criminal record.
14. The test case scenario.
15. Disadvantaged background.
16. Mistaken belief in the nature of a prohibited substance.

## QUESTIONS FOR DISCUSSION

1. What aggravating circumstances, if any, would you add to the list cited in this box? Why?

2. What mitigating circumstances, if any, would you add to this box? Why?

---

[1]Manson, A. (2001). *The Law of Sentencing.* Toronto: Irwin Law.

philosophical underpinnings of the movement may be quite different. Albert Alschuler,[29] for example, suggests that structured sentencing is a regressive social policy that derives from American weariness with considering offenders as individuals. Describing this kind of thinking, Alschuler writes: "Don't tell us that a robber was retarded. We don't care about his problems. We don't know what to *do* about his problems, and we are no longer interested in listening to a criminal's sob stories. The most important thing about this robber is simply that he *is* a robber."[30]

A different line of thought is proposed by Christopher Link and Neal Shover,[31] who found in a study of state-level economic, political, and demographic data that structured sentencing may ultimately be the result of declining economic conditions and increasing fiscal strain on state governments rather than any particular set of ideals.

A fifth critique of structured sentencing centres on its alleged inability to promote effective rehabilitation. Under indeterminate sentencing schemes, an offender has the opportunity to act responsibly and thus to participate in his or her own rehabilitation.[32] However, lack of responsible behaviour results in denial of parole and extension of the sentence. And, structured sentencing schemes, by virtue of dramatic reductions through good-time allowances and parole opportunities, leave little incentive for an offender to participate in educational programs, to take advantage of opportunities for work inside of correctional institutions, to seek treatment, or to contribute in any positive way to his or her own change.

While these critiques may be valid, they will probably do little to stem the rising tide of structured sentencing. The growth of structured sentencing over the past few decades represents the ascendancy of the "just deserts" perspective over other sentencing goals. In a growing number of jurisdictions, punishment, deterrence, and incapacitation have replaced rehabilitation and restitution as the goals that society seeks to achieve through sentencing practices. In Canada, in the year (1989) following the release of the Canadian Sentencing Commission's recommendation that Canada adopt a guideline system of sentencing, the House of Commons Standing Committee on Justice and the Solicitor General also released a report backing away from a highly structured approach to sentencing, recommending instead that Canada adopt a system of "advisory guidelines."[33] It also recommended that Canada retain parole. But recent sentencing amendments have failed to incorporate either mandatory or advisory guidelines into our criminal law. Developments in the United States and recent proposals for a form of guideline sentencing scheme in the United Kingdom may foster changes in this direction in Canada's future. If the justice system in Canada does not adopt a sentencing guideline system, it may still be influenced by other recent sentencing developments in the U.S.: mandatory sentencing and truth-in-sentencing initiatives.

# MANDATORY SENTENCING AND TRUTH IN SENTENCING

Mandatory sentencing, which is actually another form of structured sentencing,[34] deserves special mention. Mandatory sentencing is just what its name implies—a structured sentencing scheme that allows no leeway in the nature of the sentence required and under which clearly enumerated punishments are mandated for specific offences or for habitual offenders convicted of a series of crimes. Mandatory sentencing, because it is truly *mandatory*, differs from presumptive sentencing (discussed earlier), which allows for at least a limited amount of judicial discretion within ranges established by published guidelines. Some mandatory sentencing laws in place in the United States require only modest mandatory prison terms (for example, three years for armed robbery), while others are much more far-reaching.

Typical of far-reaching mandatory sentencing schemes are three-strikes laws, discussed in the Theory into Practice box on the next page. Three-strikes laws (and, in some jurisdictions, two-strikes laws) require mandatory sentences (sometimes life in prison without the possibility of parole) for offenders convicted of a third serious offence (typically a felony). Such mandatory sentencing enhancements are aimed at deterring known and potentially violent offenders and are intended to incapacitate convicted criminals through long-term incarceration.

Three-strikes laws impose longer prison terms than most earlier mandatory minimum sentencing laws. California's three-strikes law, for example, requires that offenders who are convicted of a violent crime and who have had two prior convictions serve a minimum of 25 years in prison. The law doubles prison terms for offenders convicted of a second violent felony.[35]

By passing mandatory sentencing laws, U.S. legislators attempt to convey the message that certain crimes are deemed especially grave and that people who commit them deserve, and may expect, harsh sanctions. These laws are sometimes passed in response to public outcries following heinous or well-publicized crimes.

Mandatory sentencing has had significant consequences that deserve close attention. Among them are its impact on crime and the operation of the criminal justice system. The possible consequences for certain groups of people also bears examination. While some studies have found mandatory sentencing to be an effective deterrent,[36] others have not,[37] and yet others have produced mixed results.[38] None of the studies, however, examined the incapacitation effects of these laws on individual offenders.

Mandatory sentencing has also been evaluated in terms of its impact on the criminal justice system. Traditionally, criminal courts have relied on a high rate of guilty pleas to speed

## BOX 9.4 Theory into Practice

### Three Strikes and You're Out: Should the Tough New Movement in American Criminal Sentencing Come to Canada?

In the spring of 1994, California legislators passed the state's now-famous "three strikes and you're out" bill. Amid much fanfare, Governor Pete Wilson signed the "three-strikes" measure into law, calling it "the toughest and most sweeping crime bill in California history."[1]

California's law, which is retroactive (in that it counts offences committed before the date the legislation was signed), requires a 25-year-to-life sentence for three-time felons with convictions for two or more serious or violent prior offences. Criminal offenders facing a "second strike" can receive up to double the normal sentence for their most recent offence. Parole consideration is not available until at least 80 per cent of the sentence has been served.

Today, about half the American states have passed three-strikes legislation. And other states are still considering it. At the federal level, the U.S. *Violent Crime Control and Law Enforcement Act* of 1994 contains a three-strikes provision, which mandates life imprisonment for federal criminals convicted of three violent felonies or drug offences.

Questions remain, however, as to the effectiveness of three-strikes legislation, and many are concerned about its

impact on the U.S. justice system. One year after it was signed into law, the California three-strikes initiative was evaluated by the RAND Corporation.[2] RAND researchers found that, in the first year, more than 5000 defendants were convicted and sentenced under the law's provisions. The large majority of those sentenced, however, had committed non-violent crimes such as petty theft and drug possession, causing critics of the law to argue that the law was too broad. Eighty-four per cent of "two-strikes" cases, and nearly 77 per cent of "three-strikes" convictions resulted from non-violent, drug, or property crimes.

A similar 1997 study of three-strikes laws in 22 states, conducted by the Campaign for an Effective Crime Policy (CECP), concluded that such legislation results in clogged court systems and crowded correctional facilities while encouraging three-time felons to take dramatic risks to avoid capture.[3] A 1998 study found that only California and Georgia were making widespread use of three-strikes laws.[4] Other states, the study found, have narrowly written laws that are applicable to repeat offenders only in rare circumstances.

A 2001 study of the original California legislation and its consequences concluded that three-strikes laws are overrated.[5] According to the study, "California's three-strikes law has increased the number and severity of sentences for nonviolent offenders, but has had no significant effect on the state's decline in crime." The study found that declines in California crime rates that were often attributed to the legislation were consistent with nationwide declines in the rate of crime and would most likely have occurred without the law. "Crime had been declining for several years prior to the enactment of the three-strikes law, and what's happening in California is very consistent with what's been happening nationally, including in states with no three-strikes law," said Marc Mauer, an author of the study.

Supporters of three-strikes laws argue that those convicted under them are career criminals who will be denied the opportunity to commit more violent crimes. "The real story

up case processing and to avoid log-jams. Through plea bargaining, prosecutors have been able to offer inducements (by way of lowered sentences) to defendants. However, mandatory sentencing laws can disrupt established plea bargaining patterns by preventing a prosecutor from offering a short prison term in exchange for a guilty plea. But, unless policy makers enact long-term mandatory sentences that apply to many related categories of crimes, prosecutors can usually shift strategies and bargain on charges rather than on sentences—thus retaining plea bargaining as a valid option in most courtrooms.

An alternative to mandatory minimum sentencing, which would protect sentencing policy, preserve legislative control, and still toughen sentences for repeat violent offenders, is presumptive sentencing. Other possibilities include (1) directing mandatory sentencing laws at only a few especially serious crimes and requiring "sunset" provisions (for example, requiring geriatric inmates who have reached a specified age to be released after serving a certain minimum); (2) subjecting long mandatory sentences to periodic administrative review to determine the advisability of continued confinement in individual cases; (3) building a funding plan into sentencing legislation to ensure awareness of and responsibility for the costs of long-term imprisonment; and (4) developing policies that make more effective and systematic use of intermediate sanctions.

here is the girl somewhere that did not get raped," said Mike Reynolds, a Fresno, California photographer whose 18-year-old daughter was killed by a felon on parole. "The real story is the robbery that did not happen," he added.[6]

Practically speaking, California's three-strikes law has had a dramatic impact on the state's criminal justice system. By 1999, more than 40 000 people had been sentenced under the law. But the law has its critics. " 'Three strikes and you're out' sounds great to a lot of people," says Alan Schuman, president of the American Probation and Parole Association. "But no one will cop a plea when it gets to the third time around. We will have more trials, and this whole country works on plea bargaining and pleading guilty, not jury trials," Schuman said at a meeting of the association.[7] Some California district attorneys have responded by choosing to prosecute fewer misdemeanants in order to concentrate on the more serious three-strikes defendants. According to RAND, full enforcement of the law could cost as much as US$5.5 billion annually, or US$300 per California taxpayer.

Researchers at RAND concluded that while California's sweeping three-strikes legislation could cut serious adult crime by as much as one-third throughout the state, the high cost of enforcing the law may keep it from ever being fully implemented. In 1996, the California three-strikes controversy became even more complicated following a decision by the state supreme court (in *People* v. *Superior Court of San Diego-Romero*[8]) that allowed California judges to retain the discretion of reducing three-strikes sentences and of refusing to count previous convictions at sentencing "in furtherance of justice." The legislation remains firmly in place today, but proposals to amend it have been made. Some want the law more strongly worded so that judges would be required to follow it, while others suggest that three-strikes sentences should only be imposed on offenders who commit violent crimes, such as murder, rape, armed robbery, and certain types of arson.

On March 5, 2003, the U.S. Supreme Court ruled that California's three-strikes law does not amount to the imposition of cruel and unusual punishment. In that case,[9] the Court found the mandatory 25-year minimum before parole eligibility was not offensive to constitutional principles, even though the offender, with two prior felony convictions, had only been convicted of stealing three golf clubs, a third felony.

## QUESTIONS FOR DISCUSSION

1. Do you think "three-strikes" laws serve a useful purpose? If so, what is that purpose? Might other sentencing arrangements meet that same purpose? If so, what arrangements might those be?

2. How will "three-strikes" laws impact government spending on the criminal justice system? Do you think that such shifts in spending can be justified? If so, how?

3. Should Canada adopt a version of the three-strikes law? How should it operate if it is adopted here?

[1] Miller, M. (1994, March 7). California Gets "Three Strikes" Anti-Crime Bill. Reuters wire services.
[2] Nissenbaum, D. (1995, March 6). Three-Strikes First Year Debated. United Press online, northern edition.
[3] Campaign for an Effective Crime Policy. (1997). *The Impact of Three Strikes and You're Out Laws: What have we Learned?* Washington, DC: CECP.
[4] Dickey, W. and Stiebs Hollenhorst, P. (1998, December). Three Strikes Laws: Massive Impact in California and Georgia, Little Elsewhere. *Overcrowded Times*, Vol. 9, No. 6, pp. 2–8.
[5] Lewin, T. (2001, August 23). 3-Strikes Law is Overrated in California, Study Finds. *The New York Times*.
[6] Smith, B. (1995, January 11). Crime Solutions. The Associated Press online.
[7] King, R.S. and Mauer, M. (2001, August). *Aging Behind Bars: "Three Strikes" Seven Years Later*. Washington, DC: The Sentencing Project.
[8] *People* v. *Superior Court of San Diego-Romero*, 13 Cal. 4th 497, 917 P.2d 628.
[9] *Ewing* v. *California*, 123 S.Ct. 1179 (2003).

# Truth in Sentencing

More recently, the movement towards "truth in sentencing," an area of sentencing reform, in the United States has accelerated. Truth in sentencing, which has been described as "a close correspondence between the sentence imposed upon those sent to prison and the time actually served prior to prison release,"[39] has become an important policy focus of many American state legislatures and the U.S. federal Congress. The *Violent Crime Control and Law Enforcement Act* of 1994 set aside US$4 billion in federal prison construction funds (called "Truth in Sentencing Incentive Funds") for states that adopt "truth in sentencing" laws and are able to guarantee that certain violent offenders will serve 85 per cent of their sentences. By 1996, three states—Arizona, California, and Illinois—had legislatively embraced the 85-per-cent requirement. A recent report by the Bureau of Justice Statistics[40] found that although many other states are moving towards practices that support truth in sentencing, most will need to greatly accelerate that trend if they are to be eligible for available federal monies.

Some American states have chosen to approach "truth in sentencing" in another way. In 1994, for example, the New Jersey Supreme Court imposed a "truth in sentencing" rule on New Jersey judges, which, although it doesn't require lengthened sentences, mandates that judges publicly disclose how much time a convicted defendant is likely to spend behind bars. Judges must also state when a defendant can be released from prison on good behaviour. "Under the truth-in-sentencing policy, the public will not be left with the mistaken impression that the sentence imposed is what the defendant will actually serve," the state's high court said. Robert Egles, executive director of the New Jersey State Parole Board, called the court's decision a good one. "This is a good decision, especially for victims and crime victims' families," Egles said. "The issue didn't seem to be how long the sentences were, but about the honesty of the system. If it's a 10-year sentence, but the defendant can get out in two years, it should be said," concluded Egles.[41]

# THE SENTENCING ENVIRONMENT

A number of studies have attempted to investigate the decision-making process that leads to imposition of a particular sentence. Early studies[42] found a strong relationship between the

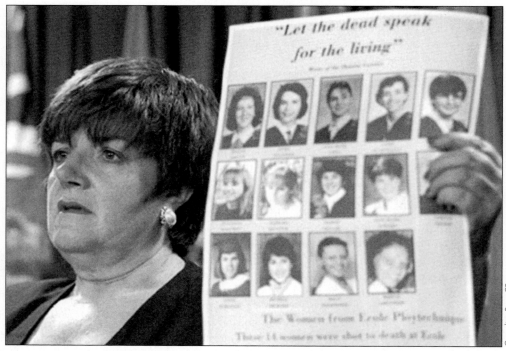

Community interests demand apprehension and punishment of law violators. Here, the president of Canadians Against Violence Everywhere Advocating its Termination (CAVEAT) holds up a photo of the 14 women killed by gun violence at the École Polytechnique in Montreal.

informal influence of members of the courtroom work group and the severity, or lack thereof, of sentences imposed. A number of studies suggested that minorities ran a much greater risk of imprisonment.[43] Other studies have found that sentencing variations arise from extra-legal conditions[44] and that public opinion can influence the type of sentence handed down.[45]

The complexity of the sentencing process was articulately depicted in John Hogarth's analysis of lower court judges in Ontario.[46] Hogarth found that such factors as background characteristics of judges, penal philosophy, and judicial attitudes had an enormous impact on sentencing decisions, concluding:

> In fact, only about 9 per cent of the variation in sentencing could be explained by objectively defined facts, whilst over 50 per cent of such variation could be accounted for simply by knowing certain pieces of information about the judge himself.[47]

Research conducted in structured sentencing jurisdictions in the United States have begun to show that sentences in a number of jurisdictions are becoming more objective and, hence, predictable.[48] An Ontario study of racial equity in sentencing,[49] which looked at prison admissions from 1986-87 to 1992-93, found the following:

- The proportion of blacks being admitted to prison increased from 7 per cent of the total to 15 per cent of the total over the six years studied;
- The greatest increase in admissions of blacks were found for drug trafficking and drug importing offences;
- The proportion of black admissions to an all-female institution increased from 14 per cent to 54 per cent over the six years studied;
- Aboriginal Canadians were also overrepresented in prison admissions;
- A sample of convicted black offenders were more likely to receive custodial sentences than a comparable sample of convicted white offenders;
- Black accused were less likely to plead guilty;
- Black accused were more likely to be proceeded against by indictment rather than by summary conviction, and the reverse was true for white accused; and
- Black men sentenced to incarceration were more likely than white men sentenced to incarceration to have been denied bail during their trials.[50]

Research has consistently shown that aboriginal Canadians have been overrepresented in prison populations.[51] This overrepresentation is consistent across the country, but is most pronounced in the Prairie provinces.[52] While it has been asserted that the overrepresentation of aboriginals in Canadian prisons reflects discrimination by actors in the criminal justice system, a recent assessment of the plight of aboriginal Canadians in the context of sentencing indicates that it may be too soon to say that actual bias exists.[53] Public support for giving aboriginal offenders special consideration in order to decrease their numbers in prison is generally lacking. However, once the public is made aware of the extent of aboriginal overrepresentation and the poor financial situation of Canada's aboriginal people, public support for sentencing concessions tends to increase.[54]

Sentencing research in Canada was pioneered by John Hogarth's landmark study in 1972. His findings of disparity and the influence of extra-legal factors on decision making were echoed in the simulated case research undertaken by Palys and Divorski in 1986.[55] Recent efforts to analyze sentencing in Canada found significant disparities across the country; however, the results of the study were based on an aggregate database, which did not permit the researchers to draw any inferences about the cause of such disparities in sentencing decisions.[56]

# THE PRE-SENTENCE REPORT

Before imposing sentence, a judge may request information on the background of a convicted defendant. Traditional wisdom has held that certain factors increase the likelihood of rehabilitation and reduce the need for lengthy prison terms. These factors include a good

**pre-sentence report**
The examination of a convicted offender's background prior to sentencing. Pre-sentence examinations are generally conducted by probation/parole officers and submitted to sentencing authorities.

job record, satisfactory educational attainment, strong family ties, church attendance, an arrest history of only non-violent offences, and psychological stability.

Information about a defendant's background often comes to the judge in the form of a **pre-sentence report**. The task of preparing pre-sentence reports falls to the probation office. A pre-sentence report is typically a detailed written report on the defendant's personal and criminal history, including an assessment of present conditions in the defendant's life. A pre-sentence report is much like a résumé, except that it focuses on what might be regarded as negative as well as positive life experiences.

A typical pre-sentence report is divided into 10 major informational sections, as follows: (1) personal information that identifies and describes the defendant; (2) a chronology of the current offence and circumstances surrounding it; (3) a record of the defendant's previous convictions, if any; (4) home life and family data; (5) educational background; (6) health history and current state of health; (7) military service; (8) religious preference; (9) financial condition; and (10) sentencing recommendations made by the probation/parole officer who is the author of the report.

The data on which a pre-sentence report is based come from a variety of sources. Since the 1970s, modern computer-based clearing houses of criminal information, such as the RCMP's Canadian Police Information Centre (CPIC), have simplified at least part of the data-gathering process. CPIC became operational in 1972 and has information on people wanted for criminal offences throughout Canada. Individual jurisdictions also maintain criminal records repositories that are able to provide comprehensive files on the criminal history of persons processed by the justice system.

In a pre-sentence report, almost any third-party data are subject to ethical and legal considerations. The official records of almost any agency or organization, while they may prove to be an ideal source of information, are often protected by privacy requirements.

Sometimes the defendant is a significant source of much of the information that appears in the pre-sentence report. When such is the case, efforts are usually made to corroborate the information provided by the defendant. Unconfirmed data will generally be marked on the report as "defendant-supplied data" or simply "unconfirmed."

The final section of a pre-sentence report is usually devoted to the investigating officer's (IO) recommendations. The IO may recommend split sentencing, a term of imprisonment, or any other sentencing options available for the offence in question. The IO may also recommend that the probationer participate in community service programs or in drug or substance abuse programs. Some analysts have observed that a "judge accepts an officer's recommendation in an extremely high percentage of cases."[57] Most judges are willing to accept the report writer's recommendation because they recognize the professionalism of pre-sentence investigators and because they know that the investigator may well be the supervising officer assigned to the defendant should a community alternative be the sentencing decision.

Pre-sentence reports may be useful sentencing tools. Many officers who prepare them take their responsibility seriously. A recent study,[58] however, shows a tendency among pre-sentence investigators to satisfy judicial expectations about defendants by tailoring reports to fit the image the defendant projects. The prior criminal record of an offender and the present offence may influence the interpretation of all the other gathered data.[59]

# THE VICTIM—FORGOTTEN NO LONGER

Thanks to a grassroots resurgence of concern for the plight of victims, which began in this country in the 1970s and continues to grow, the sentencing environment now frequently considers the needs of victims and survivors.[60] Unfortunately, in times past, the concerns of victims were often forgotten. Although victims might testify at trial, other aspects of the victimization experience were frequently downplayed by the criminal justice system—including the psychological trauma engendered by the victimization process itself. That changed in the 1990s as Parliament began to amend the criminal law to take the interests of the victim into account, and efforts to enshrine a "Victim's Bill of Rights" into our law began to attract serious attention. The 1990s witnessed the widespread expansion of victim assistance programs and other victim-oriented developments. Victim assistance programs today tend to offer services in the areas of crisis intervention and follow-up counselling, and to help victims secure their rights under the law.[61] Following successful prosecution of an offender, some victim assistance programs also advise victims in the filing of civil suits that would allow the victim to recoup financial losses directly from the offender. Canada has witnessed an increase in the number of crime victims who sue offenders, and in many cases significant damage awards have resulted.[62] The majority of individuals seeking civil redress are victims of domestic assault or sexual assault.

Although a victims' rights amendment to the Constitution is not yet a reality, most provinces have passed their own victims' rights legislation. This legislation typically imposes a surcharge on fines levied against persons committing provincial offences. These amounts are then used to fund victim services in the province. Some provinces, like British Columbia and Ontario, have established a toll-free telephone line to provide information to victims of crime.

Much of the philosophical basis of today's victims' rights movement can be found in the restorative justice model, which was discussed briefly earlier in this chapter. **Restorative justice** emphasizes offender accountability and victim reparation. Restorative justice also provides the basis for victim compensation programs—which are another means of recognizing the needs of crime victims (see Table 9–1 for a comparison of restorative justice with retributive justice). Many provinces have legislation providing for monetary payments to victims of crime. Such payments are primarily designed to compensate victims for medical expenses and lost wages. All existing programs require that applicants meet certain eligibility criteria, and most set limits on the maximum amount of compensation that can be received. Generally disallowed are claims from victims who are significantly responsible for their own victimization.

Not everyone agrees that the contemporary victims' rights movement is as valuable as it might seem. Robert Elias, whose book *Victims Still: The Political Manipulation of Crime Victims* provides one opposing view, argues that the movement "has supported progressively conservative legislation that attacks constitutional rights, and has adopted a retributive

**restorative justice**
A sentencing model that builds upon restitution and community participation in an attempt to make the victim "whole again."

## TABLE 9–1 Differences between Retributive and Restorative Justice

| Retributive Justice | Restorative Justice |
|---|---|
| Crime is an act against the state, a violation of a law, an abstract idea. | Crime is an act against another person or the community. |
| The criminal justice system controls crime. | Crime control lies primarily with the community. |
| Offender accountability is defined as taking punishment. | Accountability is defined as assuming responsibility and taking action to repair harm. |
| Crime is an individual act with individual responsibility. | Crime has both individual and social dimensions of responsibility. |
| Victims are peripheral to the process. | Victims are central to the process of resolving a crime. |
| The offender is defined by deficits. | The offender is defined by the capacity to make reparation. |
| Emphasis is on adversarial relationships. | Emphasis is on dialogue and negotiation. |
| Pain is imposed to punish and deter/prevent. | Restitution is a means of restoring both parties; goal of reconciliation/restoration. |
| Community is on sidelines, represented abstractly by the state. | Community is facilitator in restorative process. |
| Response is focused on offender's past behaviour. | Response is focused on harmful consequences of offender's behaviour; emphasis on the future and on reparation. |
| Dependence is upon proxy professionals. | There is direct involvement by both the offender and the victim. |

*Source*: Adapted from the following: Bazemore, G. and Umbreit, M.S. (1994, October). *Balanced and Restorative Justice: Program Summary* (p. 7). Washington, D.C.: OJJDP.

philosophy against offenders who themselves are victims of a repressive system."[63] Elias cites, for example, what he calls "the war on drug victims" (drug users), as symptomatic of the unfortunate policies inherent in conservative approaches to crime control.

## Victim Impact Statements

**victim impact statements** The court may use this victim- or survivor-supplied information to make a sentencing decision.

Another consequence of the victims' rights movement has been a call for the use of **victim impact statements** prior to sentencing. A victim impact statement is generally a written document that describes the losses, suffering, and trauma experienced by the crime victim or the victim's survivors. Each province dictates the precise nature of this form. Judges are required to consider such statements, if filed with the court, in arriving at an appropriate sanction for the offender.

There is little information to date on what changes, if any, the use of victim impact statements at sentencing is having on the length or type of sentence imposed by a court. Canadian courts have ruled that victims do *not* have a right to orally comment in court on the sentence that they believe would be appropriate for an offender. Their comments, written or oral, must be confined to explaining the impact the crime has had on them.[64] While victims may make oral presentations at sentencing hearings, it is not likely that allowing victims to speak at sentencing hearings affects many case outcomes in Canada. In the U.S., victims can speak at sentencing hearings in some states. At least one study in California found that fewer than 3 per cent of California victims chose to appear or testify at sentencing hearings after that state's victims' rights law was enacted.[65]

Receiving impact statements from victims, however, does not guarantee that a sentencing court will be sympathetic. On April 3, 1995, for example, a court in Berlin, Germany, refused to imprison Guenter Parche—the unemployed German machinist who stabbed 19-year-old tennis superstar Monica Seles in the back with a kitchen knife at the 1993 Hamburg Open. Even though Seles told the court that Parche "ruined my life" and ended her career "as the world's best tennis player,"[66] the judge ruled that a suspended sentence was appropriate because the man apparently had not intended to kill Seles—only to disable her so that German star Steffi Graf could regain the number-one world ranking in women's tennis. At the hearing, Seles' psychologist had testified that Seles "felt like a bird trapped in a cage and was terrified that Parche would strike again."[67] Seles was not able to play professional tennis for more than two years following the attack, and never regained championship standing.

One 1994 study of the efficacy of victim impact statements in the United States found that sentencing decisions were rarely affected by them. In the words of the study: "These statements did not produce sentencing decisions that reflected more clearly the effects of crime on victims. Nor did we find much evidence that—with or without impact statements—sentencing decisions were influenced by our measures of the effects of crime on victims, once the charge and the defendant's prior record were taken into account."[68] The authors concluded that victim impact statements had little effect upon courts because judges and other "officials have established ways of making decisions which do not call for explicit information about the impact of crime on victims."

Changes to section 722 of Canada's *Criminal Code*, brought about in 1999, permit crime victims to read their victim impact statements aloud in court at the sentencing hearing. Alternatively, victims may submit a written victim impact statement to the judge.

## COMMON SENTENCING OPTIONS

Sentencing is fundamentally a risk management strategy designed to protect the public while serving the goals of rehabilitation, deterrence, incapacitation, just deserts, and restoration. Because the goals of sentencing are difficult to agree upon, so too are the sanctions. Lengthy prison terms do little for rehabilitation, while community release programs can hardly protect the innocent from offenders who are determined to commit crimes.

Assorted and sometimes opposed sentencing philosophies continue to exist in the criminal justice system. But the law is sufficiently open as to allow differing approaches to be taken by different sentencing judges, depending upon their own personal philosophy of sentencing.

Judges may select from a variety of sentencing options. These include traditional, common sentencing options. Other sentencing options supplement these traditional sentencing choices, which are:

- Imprisonment;
- Probation; and
- Fines.

In a variety of cases, the three options are widely available to judges. The option selected generally depends upon the severity of the offence and the judge's best guess as to the likelihood of future criminal involvement on the part of the defendant. Sometimes two options are combined, as when an offender might be fined and sentenced to prison, or placed on probation and fined, or ordered to make restitution payments.

While the federal government has set down the general sentencing scheme in the *Criminal Code*, some variation in sentencing occurs from province to province. Jurisdictions that operate under presumptive sentencing rules generally limit the judge's choice to only one option and often specify the extent to which that option can be applied. Dollar amounts of fines, for example, are pre-set, and prison terms are specified for typical examples of each type of offence. The Alberta Court of Appeal has committed itself to a "starting point approach."

Under this approach, the Alberta Court of Appeal has precisely specified the appropriate sentence for a typical case, but permits trial courts to deviate from this sentence if the particular facts of the case before a court contain aggravating or mitigating circumstances. While some other provinces, such as Manitoba, have warmed up to the idea of a starting point approach to sentencing, others, such as Ontario, have rejected the notion.[69]

## Imprisonment

Recently, the Canadian Centre for Justice Statistics reported on the sentencing practices of nine Canadian jurisdictions.[70] The report examined sentencing practices in adult provincial courts. It did not address youth court sentencing, nor did it look at sentencing in the superior courts, that is, those courts tending to deal with the most serious offences. Accordingly, this report does not provide a complete picture of sentencing in Canada. However, it should be noted that the report indicated that more than 90 per cent of criminal cases are resolved at the provincial court level.[71] Highlights of the sentencing study showed that provincial courts deal with a wide range of criminal offences, many of them quite minor in nature. Of these:

- 27 per cent of the cases that resulted in a single conviction for an offender also resulted in the offender being sentenced to an active prison term.
- 45 per cent of the cases involving a single charge resulted in the imposition of a fine, the most frequently imposed sanction.
- 40 per cent of offenders were sentenced to probation (often with fines or other special conditions).
- The average prison sentence imposed for a single charge was just 94 days.
- Prison sentences varied with the severity of the offence, such that the average sentence for manslaughter was around 68 months, the average sentence for robbery was 17 months, and the average sentence for break-and-enter was seven months.

The same survey revealed that the offences most likely to result in imprisonment are homicide offences, which resulted in incarceration 90 per cent of the time. However, other serious offences are less likely to result in imprisonment. The offence of arson resulted in incarceration in only 39 per cent of cases, and the offence of theft over $5000 resulted in a prison sentence in only 43 per cent of cases.

In Canada, the type of offence dictates the maximum length of incarceration. Summary conviction offences typically carry a maximum period of imprisonment of six months. A few summary conviction offences permit a higher maximum term of up to 18 months in prison. These offences include the following hybrid offences, which may be tried as summary conviction offences if the Crown so chooses: threatening to cause death or bodily harm (s. 264.1(1)(a)), assault causing bodily harm or with a weapon (s. 267), unlawfully causing bodily harm (s. 269), sexual assault (s. 271), forcible confinement (s. 279(2)), and failing to comply with a probation order (s. 733.1). Maximum terms are typically reserved for the worst cases of such crimes. A typical case is associated with a lesser period of incarceration, usually in keeping with other cases displaying similar facts to the case before the court. Summary conviction offences typically do not carry a minimum period of incarceration, thereby permitting the sentencing judge to impose alternative sentences such as fines or probation. An exception is a case involving a second-time impaired driver, who could face a minimum period of incarceration of 14 days, and a minimum of 90 days for a third conviction (s. 255).

The maximum periods of incarceration for indictable offences in Canada are indicated in the penalty provision pertaining to each offence. The maximum periods are typically 2 years, 5 years, 10 years, 14 years, or life in prison. A judge may impose a lesser penalty than the maximum, and usually will unless the case is perceived to be a worst-case scenario.

## Consecutive and Concurrent Sentencing

For an offender who is guilty of multiple offences, the judge may decide that the corresponding sentences should run one after the other, or that the sentences should all run at the same time, beginning from a common starting date. Consecutive sentencing requires the offender to serve the sentences one at a time. Accordingly, three consecutive one-year sentences would require the offender to face a three-year sentence. Concurrent sentencing of three one-year sentences produces a different result. All three one-year sentences run together, so the offender is really only facing a one-year sentence.

Judges have discretion in determining whether to order that sentences be served consecutively or concurrently. This arises where an offender is convicted of multiple offences tried together. Generally, the discretion to order sentences to run concurrently or consecutively is guided by determining whether the acts associated with the offences are part of a common transaction, and if so, the result is concurrent sentencing, or the acts are discrete, and if so, the result is consecutive sentencing. When an offender gets consecutive sentencing for interconnected offences, he or she is, in effect, getting a bulk discount from the sentencing judge.

## Mandatory Minimums

In a few cases, the *Criminal Code* imposes mandatory minimum terms for indictable offences, such as the mandatory one-year minimum sentence for first-time firearms-related offences (ss. 85, 86(2)), and a 14-day minimum for second-time gaming offenders (ss. 202, 203), and second-time alcohol-related driving offences (s. 255), a four-year minimum for wounding with intent (s. 244), and extortion using a firearm (s. 346(1)(1.1)(a)), and kidnapping (s. 279), and a five-year minimum for persons living off the avails of a prostitute under the age of 18 (s. 212 (2.1)). A life sentence is a mandatory minimum (and maximum) penalty for persons convicted of a murder offence (s. 235). Other homicide offences, such as manslaughter involving the use of a firearm (s. 236) or criminal negligence causing death involving the use of a firearm (s. 220(a)), carry a maximum sentence of life, but a minimum sentence of four years in prison. Other manslaughter offences carry a maximum term of life, but no minimum period of incarceration.

In 1990, the Supreme Court of Canada ruled in *R. v. Luxton* that the 25-year parole ineligibility rule that applies to offenders convicted of first-degree murder does not amount to cruel and unusual treatment or punishment, thereby not contravening section 12 of the *Charter of Rights and Freedoms*.[72] In this case, the mandatory life term and period of parole ineligibility was held not to be excessive, and did not "outrage" our standards of decency. In 1991, in *R. v. Goltz*, the top court held that a mandatory seven-day period of imprisonment for driving while under suspension also did not violate section 12 of the *Charter*.[73] Such a penalty was deemed not to be so excessive or grossly disproportionate as to outrage standards of decency. Similarly, in the more recent case of *R. v. Morissey* (2000), the Supreme Court of Canada ruled that the mandatory four-year period of imprisonment imposed on those convicted of criminal negligence causing death with a firearm did not offend the constitutional prohibition on cruel and unusual treatment or punishment.[74]

The Supreme Court of Canada's most recent pronouncement on mandatory minimum punishments was made in the 2001 case of *R. v. Latimer*.[75] Robert Latimer was convicted of the second-degree murder of his 12-year-old daughter, Tracy. The only sentence available under the *Criminal Code* for such an offence is a mandatory life term, with parole eligibility to be set at between 10 and 25 years. The jury appears to have been persuaded that Mr. Latimer killed his daughter in an act of mercy for the incredible pain she had to endure as a result of her debilitating disease. Accordingly, it asked that parole be set at one year, a sentence not permitted by law. The trial judge, taking the jury's sentiments into account, sentenced Latimer to one year in prison plus one year of probation, yet again a sentence not permitted by the existing law. On appeal, both the Saskatchewan Court of Appeal and the Supreme Court of Canada overturned the trial judge's sentencing ruling. It was ultimately held that a life sentence must be imposed and that parole eligibility should be dealt with after Latimer had served ten years in prison. The top court rejected requests from Mr. Latimer's counsel that it grant a constitutional exemption to permit an earlier review of parole eligibility. The Court ruled that the gravity of the offence was not outweighed by the individual circumstances, and there remained a need for denunciation in this case.

## Two-Year Rule

Offenders sentenced to prison terms in Canada are subject to the two-year rule. This rule mandates that all offenders sentenced to imprisonment of two years or longer (including life) serve that time in a federal penitentiary. Offenders whose sentences are under two years must serve the sentences in provincial prisons. The sentence of two years less a day is the most severe sentence that may be imposed on an offender without that offender having to go to a federal institution.

When an inmate serves time in a provincial (or territorial) prison, the inmate can be closer to his or her community contacts. Family and friends are more likely to be in the area, and thereby maintain relationships interrupted by life in prison. Additionally, the typical offender in a provincial prison tends to be a bit less "hard core" than the inmates serving lengthy sentences in federal penitentiaries. However, federal prisons typically have a greater array of programs for inmates. Rehabilitation and educational facilities are also typically more extensive and better developed in federal institutions than in provincial prisons.

## Pre-Sentence Custody

Offenders who are detained in custody without judicial interim release usually seek credit for time served prior to sentencing. Section 719(3) of the *Criminal Code* entitles the sentencing judge to take such time into account in calculating the eventual sentence. The Supreme Court of Canada recently indicated in *R. v. Wust* (2000) that this discretion should typically be exercised, and may even result in an offender being sentenced to less than the statutorily imposed minimum sentence, as long as the pre-sentence custody and the sentence term comply with statutory criteria.[76] Since (1) conditions in remand (custody) are more stark than those of sentenced confinement, (2) there are fewer programs in remand, and (3) the offender is not eligible for conditional release in remand, the Court in *Wust* indicated the credit for time served could be calculated using a "two for one" formula. Accordingly, an offender who spends six months awaiting trial and sentence in remand could get a year knocked off the eventual sentence that the court considers appropriate.

## Dangerous and Long-Term Offenders: Indeterminate Sentencing

Indeterminate sentencing relies on the belief that convicted offenders are more likely to participate in their own rehabilitation if they can reduce the amount of time they have to spend in prison. Inmates with good behaviour are more likely to be released early, while a recalcitrant inmate will likely remain in prison until the end of his or her term. For that reason, parole generally plays a significant role in an indeterminate sentencing model.

Canada has adopted a purely indeterminate sentencing model for offenders declared by the courts to be dangerous offenders. Such offenders are sentenced to an indeterminate period of incarceration, with no release date. Their eventual return to the community is completely in the hands of the parole authorities. If not granted parole, such offenders will serve out the rest of their lives in prison, as if doing a life sentence.

While the general sentencing provisions are indeterminate in the sense that the exact release date for an offender is unknown at the time of sentencing because parole is unavailable, the judge will set a warrant expiry date (WED) as the expiration of the sentence. No offender may be held beyond this date. However, in Canada, a judge may not set an ultimate release date for offenders who are specifically declared as "dangerous offenders," following a special sentencing hearing. Additionally, under recent legislative amendments, some offenders will be subjected to lengthy periods of supervision following their release from prison.

The dangerous offender designation is governed by Part 24 of the *Criminal Code*. Under these provisions, a person convicted of a "serious personal injury offence" (defined in s. 752) and who poses a future threat (see s. 753) may be designated as a dangerous offender at a special sentencing hearing. The Crown must make a specific application for such a hearing, and notify the offender that it will occur. Two types of serious personal injury offences trigger the application of these provisions. The first are serious offences that carry long penalties under normal sentencing provisions, that entail violence or attempted violence (or conduct), and that are actually or likely to endanger life or safety or likely to inflict severe psychological harm. The second category of offences includes, sexual assault offences. Committing one of these offences is not enough for the offender to be declared dangerous. The prosecution must make the appropriate application, with the consent of the Attorney General, and provide adequate notice to the offender of the application (see s. 754). The Crown may order the offender be subjected to a custodial remand for assessment (see s. 752.1). To be successful, the Crown must go on to prove that additional factors relating to the underlying offence are present.

The additional burden on the prosecution is to prove that the offender poses some future threat, thereby warranting the dangerous offender designation. If the offender has committed one of the violence-related triggering offences mentioned above, the Crown must go on to establish one of the following:

(i) a pattern of repetitive behaviour by the offender, of which the offence for which he or she has been convicted forms a part, showing a failure to restrain his or her behaviour and a likelihood of causing death or injury to other persons, or inflicting severe psychological damage on other persons, through failure in the future to restrain his or her behaviour,

(ii) a pattern of persistent aggressive behaviour by the offender, of which the offence for which he or she has been convicted forms a part, showing a substantial degree of indifference on the part of the offender respecting the reasonably foreseeable consequences to other persons of his or her behaviour, or

(iii) any behaviour by the offender, associated with the offence for which he or she has been convicted, that is of such a brutal nature as to compel the conclusion that the offender's behaviour in the future is unlikely to be inhibited by normal standards of behavioural restraint.

Where the offence relied on by the Crown is a sexual assault offence, the Crown must also prove the following:

... the offender, by his or her conduct in any sexual matter including that involved in the commission of the offence for which he or she has been convicted, has shown a failure to control his or her sexual impulses and a likelihood of causing injury, pain or other evil to other persons through failure in the future to control his or her sexual impulses.

If the offender is found to be dangerous, the court will impose a sentence of detention in a federal penitentiary for an indeterminate period of time. In such a case, the offender will not be eligible for parole for seven years. Courts will hear evidence from at least one mental health expert in determining whether to declare an offender a dangerous offender.

Such an expert is typically a psychiatrist or a clinical psychologist who evaluates an offender through a risk assessment. In order that such an assessment be carried out, the court will typically remand the offender to a mental health facility. Most dangerous offender hearings involve offenders whose criminal records show a repeated pattern of predatory offending, and their risk assessments show that the offender is at a high risk of reoffending violently and/or sexually in the future. Indeed, the vast majority (over 80 per cent) of Canada's current 313 declared dangerous offenders have prior convictions for sexual offences. If a dangerous offender application is unsuccessful, the court may declare the offender to be a long-term offender.

Where a dangerous offender application has been unsuccessful, or where the Crown has decided that such a declaration is not necessary, but the normal sentencing regime is inadequate, the Crown may choose to seek to have the offender declared a long-term offender. Again, the offender must have committed a serious personal injury offence, and application must be made. The court may declare an offender to be a long-term offender if a sentence of two years or more is appropriate, the risk of the offender reoffending is substantial, and the possibility of eventually controlling the risk posed by the offender in the community is reasonable (s. 753.1(1)). The risk of the offender reoffending will be substantial where the offender will likely cause death or injury or inflict severe psychological harm, or where the offender will likely cause injury, pain, or other evil through the commission of similar sexual offences (s. 753.1(2)). If the court declares the offender to be a long-term offender, the court will impose a sentence of at least two years in prison, to be followed by a further period of community supervision of up to 10 years in duration (ss. 753.1(3) and 753.2).

Since a life sentence in Canada carries no numeric equivalent, it too is an indeterminate sentence. Offenders sentenced to life in prison are at the mercy of the parole authorities. They may be released at their parole eligibility date, or at some subsequent date, but this release is by no means guaranteed. If the parole board deems the offender to be a sufficient risk, the offender serving a life sentence will spend the remainder of his or her life behind bars.

## Fines

The fine is one of the oldest forms of punishment, predating even the Code of Hammurabi.[77] Until recently, however, the use of fines as criminal sanctions suffered from built-in inequities and a widespread failure to collect them. Inequities arose when offenders with vastly different financial resources were fined similar amounts. A fine of $100, for example, can place a painful economic burden upon a poor defendant but is only laughable when imposed on a wealthy offender.

Today, fines are once again receiving attention as serious sentencing alternatives. One reason for the renewed interest is the stress placed upon government resources by the welfare state. The extensive imposition of fines not only results in less crowded prisons but can also contribute to government coffers and lower the tax burden of law-abiding citizens. Other advantages of using fines as criminal sanctions include the following:

- Fines can deprive offenders of the proceeds of criminal activity;
- Fines can promote rehabilitation by enforcing economic responsibility;
- Fines can be collected by existing criminal justice agencies and are relatively inexpensive to administer; and
- Fines can be made proportionate to both the severity of the offence and the ability of the offender to pay.

The recent nine-jurisdiction sentencing study by the Canadian Centre for Justice Statistics found that 39 per cent of convicted defendants in the courts surveyed received fines as sentences, some in combination with another penalty.[78] This figure reflects a decline in the use of fines since 1995-96, when 45 per cent of conviction cases resulted in the imposition of a fine.

Fines are often imposed for relatively minor law violations, such as impaired driving, dangerous operation of a vehicle, causing a disturbance, or obstructing the police. Judges in many courts, however, order fines for relatively serious violations of the law, including assault, theft with a value exceeding $5000, fraud, and the sale and possession of various drugs. There have even been cases where the most severe disposition faced by an offender for the offences of manslaughter, robbery, and sexual assault was the imposition of a fine.[79] Fines are much more likely to be imposed where the offender has both a clean record and the ability to pay.[80]

Opposition to the use of fines is based upon the following arguments:

- Fines may result in the release of convicted offenders into the community but do not impose stringent controls on their behaviour;

- Fines are a relatively mild form of punishment and are not consistent with the "just deserts" philosophy;

- Fines discriminate against the poor and favour the wealthy;

- Indigent offenders are especially subject to discrimination since they entirely lack the financial resources with which to pay fines; and

- Fines are difficult to collect.

A number of these objections can be answered where judges have complete financial information on defendants. However, in reality, judges often lack concrete information on an offender's economic status. Perhaps as a consequence, judges themselves are often reluctant to impose fines. Two of the most widely cited objections of judges to fines are (1) fines allow more affluent offenders to "buy their way out" and (2) poor offenders cannot pay fines.[81]

A solution to both objections can be found in the Scandinavian system of day fines. The day-fine system is based upon the idea that a fine should be proportionate to the severity of the offence but the fine also needs to take into account the financial resources of the offender. A day fine is computed by first assessing the seriousness of the offense, the defendant's degree of culpability, and his or her prior record as measured in "days," that is, the number of days in an equivalent prison sentence. The number of days is then multiplied by the person's daily wages. Hence, if two persons were sentenced to a five-day fine, but one earned only $20 per day, and the other $200 per day, the first would pay a $100 fine, and the second would pay $1000.

In Canada, the least serious criminal offences, or summary conviction offences, carry a typical maximum fine of $2000, or $25 000 where the defendant is a corporation. The summary conviction offence of charging a criminal interest rate (s. 347) carries a maximum fine of $25 000. An indictable offence does not carry a maximum fine penalty; however, a judge will have to consider the ability of the offender to pay in assessing the appropriate financial penalty.

An offender who defaults in the payment of a fine is liable to spend time in prison for the default (s. 734(5)). The length of prison time is calculated by taking the amount of the fine remaining unpaid, adding to it the cost of conveying the offender to prison, and dividing this amount by eight times the provincial minimum hourly wage. For example:

$$\frac{\$1000 \text{ unpaid fine} + \$400 \text{ cost of conveyance}}{7.00 \ (\$7.00/\text{hour min. wage}) \times 8 \ (8\text{-hour workday})} = 1400/56 = 25 \text{ days}$$

This allows a uniform calculation of the appropriate period of time an offender must spend in prison in lieu of paying the fine imposed by the court.

In some provinces, offenders who are unable or unwilling to pay a fine to pay off their debt to society can instead engage in community work (s. 736). The offender earns credits that go towards "paying off" the fine imposed by the court.

## Miscellaneous Sentencing Options

While the most commonly encountered sentencing options are the fine, incarceration, and probation (to be discussed in the next chapter), there are other sentencing options available under Canadian criminal law. These options give the sentencing judge the ability to select the sentence that particularly fits the offence and/or the offender in question.

## Absolute and Conditional Discharge

These sentencing options can apply in the anomalous situation where an offender has pleaded guilty (or been found guilty), but is deemed not to have been convicted of the offence in question. Such a disposition allows the offender to escape the debilitating aspects of a criminal record, although a record is kept to ensure that the recipient of a discharge is not perpetually treated as a first-time offender.

There are two types of discharge: absolute and conditional. An absolute discharge results in the accused being released with no further obligation to the justice system. A conditional discharge results in the offender being placed under a probation order for a period of time, during which he or she must fulfill the conditions imposed by the court (such as performing a service, or paying a sum of money to the victim). Section 730 of the *Criminal Code* only permits a discharge where there is no minimum penalty for the offence in question, and the maximum penalty is less than 14 years or life imprisonment. That such a penalty be imposed must be in the best interests of both the accused and of the public.

## Restitution

Restitution involves the offender paying a sum of money to the victim, in order to restore the victim to his or her pre-offence position. Restitution fulfills a function similar to that of a damage award in the civil law of torts. Restitution may be ordered as a condition of a probation order, or independently under section 738 of the *Criminal Code*. The sentencing judge may order restitution to anyone who has suffered loss or damage to property, or bodily injury resulting from the offence, or the arrest or attempted arrest of the offender.

Where other financial penalties (such as a fine) are also imposed against the offender in addition to restitution, the restitution order takes precedence. If the offender fails to pay the restitution order, the victim may register the order as a judgment in civil court, permitting the use of a civil process, such as execution or garnishment, to recover the money.

## Prohibition and Forfeiture Orders

Various provisions in the *Criminal Code* permit a sentencing judge to order an offender to refrain from doing certain things as a penalty, or requiring the offender to turn something over to the court.

The most commonly encountered prohibition orders are those that follow convictions for impaired driving and related offences. Section 259 of the *Code* requires a prohibition from driving for between three months and three years for a first conviction on a drinking-and-driving offence. The minimum length of the driving prohibition increases for subsequent convictions.

Prohibition orders must be issued under section 100 of the *Code* to those convicted of certain violent offences listed in section 85, and other offences carrying lengthy penalties. These orders prohibit the offender from possessing firearms, ammunition, or explosives. Firearm prohibition orders may also be issued for those convicted of other less serious offences. Section 446 authorizes prohibition orders in relation to the possession of animals for those convicted of offences pertaining to cruelty to animals.

Numerous provisions in the *Code* authorize forfeiture orders against offenders. These orders require offenders to turn over an object to the court, relinquishing possession of the object. Through forfeiture, people who are guilty of possessing things like obscene publications, explosives, and prohibited weapons not only suffer a penalty for the act but also must relinquish the offending item. *Criminal Code* provisions also authorize the forfeiture of the proceeds of crime in certain circumstances.

## Conditional Sentencing

If an offence does not carry a minimum prison sentence and the judge feels that a sentence of less than two years is appropriate, he or she may sentence the offender to a period of less than two years to be served in the community, so long as the judge believes that this sentence would not constitute an undue risk to the community (see ss. 742–742.7

of the *Code*). The offender will be subjected to restrictions while serving his or her time in the community.

In *R. v. Proulx*, the Supreme Court of Canada ruled in 2000 that the conditional sentence can be broadly applied, even for very violent offences, as long as the statutory criteria are satisfied.[82] Where trial judges impose a conditional sentence, the top court ruled, appeal courts should be reluctant to interfere. In *R. v. Knoblauch* (2000), the Supreme Court of Canada went so far as to permit a conditional sentence. The trial judge ordered this sentence for a mentally disordered offender, imposing a condition that the sentence be served in a mental health facility.[83] This situation appears to stretch the notion of the conditional sentence as a non-custodial alternative to incarceration to its limits.

# A Penalty From Canada's Past: The Death Penalty

Some crimes are especially heinous and seem to cry out for extreme punishment. While Canada has abolished the death penalty, many U.S. states today have statutory provisions that provide for a sentence of **capital punishment** for especially repugnant crimes. The death penalty itself, however, has a long and gruesome history. Different civilizations have historically put criminals to death for a variety of offences. As times changed, so did accepted methods of punishment, and even methods of execution. Under the Davidic monarchy, biblical Israel institutionalized the practice of stoning convicts to death.[84] In that practice, the entire community could participate in dispatching the offender. As an apparent aid to deterrence, the convict's deceased body could be impaled on a post at the gates of the city or otherwise exposed to public view.[85]

Athenian society, around 200 B.C., was progressive by the standards of its day. The ancient Greeks restricted the use of capital punishment and limited the suffering of the condemned through using poison derived from the hemlock tree. Socrates, the famous Greek orator, accused of being a political subversive, died this way.

The Romans were far less sensitive. They used beheading most often, although the law provided that arsonists should be burned alive and false witnesses thrown from a high rock.[86] Suspected witches were clubbed to death, and slaves were strangled. Even more brutal sanctions included drawing and quartering, and social outcasts, Christians, and rabble rousers were thrown to the lions or crucified. Although many people think that crucifixion was a barbarous practice that ended around the time of Christ, it survives to the present day. In 1997, for example, courts in Yemeni (a country at the southern tip of the Arabian peninsula) sentenced two convicted murderers to be publicly crucified. It was the second time in three months that Yemeni courts, in an effort to combat a spate of violent crimes, imposed crucifixion sentences.[87]

After the fall of the Roman Empire, Europe was plunged into the Dark Ages, a period of superstition marked by widespread illiteracy and political turmoil. The Dark Ages lasted from A.D. 426 until the early thirteenth century. During the Dark Ages, executions were institutionalized through ordeals that were designed to both judge and punish. Suspects were submerged in cold water, dumped in boiling oil, crushed under huge stones, forced to do battle with professional soldiers, or thrown into bonfires. Theological arguments prevalent at the time held that innocents, protected by God and heavenly forces, would emerge from any ordeal unscathed, while guilty parties would perish. Trial by ordeal was eliminated through a decree of the Fourth Lateran Council of 1215, under the direction of Pope Innocent III, after later evidence proved that many who died in ordeals could not have committed the crimes of which they were accused.[88]

Following the Fourth Lateran Council, trials, much as we know them today, became the basis for judging guilt or innocence. The death penalty remained in widespread use. As recently as a century and a half ago, 160 crimes were punishable in England by death.[89] The young received no special privilege. In 1801, a child of 13 was hanged in Tyburn, England, for stealing a spoon.[90]

Techniques of execution became more sophisticated by the nineteenth century. One engine of death was the guillotine, invented in France around the time of the French Revolution. The guillotine was described by its creator, Dr. Joseph-Ignace Guillotin, as "a cool breath on the back of the neck"[91] and was widely used to eliminate opponents of the Revolution.

Ted Mathias/Wide World Photos

A guerney used in lethal injections. Most American states still retain capital punishment, and the large majority of those authorize execution through lethal injection.

In Canada, as in Britain and the United States, hanging became the preferred mode of execution. By the early 1890s, electrocution had replaced hanging as the preferred form of capital punishment in the United States, while Canada and Britain carried on with hanging until the eventual abolition of the death penalty. The appeal of electrocution was that it stopped the heart without visible signs of gross bodily trauma.

Since before Confederation, hundreds of people have been put to death. Indeed, Canada's hangman from 1913 until around 1940 went by the name of Arthur Ellis and was responsible for executing 549 people.[92] Although capital punishment was widely used throughout the eighteenth and nineteenth centuries, the twentieth century witnessed a constant decline in the number of persons legally executed in Canada. The last person executed in Canada was put to death in 1962. All subsequent death sentences were commuted to life in prison, with the last being commuted upon the formal abolition of capital punishment in 1976.

## Executions in the United States: The Grim Facts

While the number of executions in the United States has declined over previous centuries, execution of offenders continued with only minimal interruption in the late 1960s and early 1970s. Between 1930 and 1967, when the U.S. Supreme Court ordered a nationwide stay of pending executions, nearly 3800 persons were put to death. The years 1935 and 1936 were peak years, with nearly 200 legal killings each year. Executions declined substantially every year thereafter. Between 1967 and 1977, a *de facto* moratorium existed, with no executions carried out in any U.S. jurisdiction. Following the lifting of the moratorium, executions increased. A modern record for executions was set in 1997, with 74 executions—37 in Texas alone. In 2001, 66 legal executions were carried out in the United States.

In 1995, the state of New York reinstated the death penalty after a 30-year hiatus. Today, 38 of the 50 states and the U.S. federal government have capital punishment laws.[93] All states but New York permit execution for first-degree murder, while treason, kidnapping, the murder of a police or correctional officer, and murder while under a life sentence are punishable by death in selected jurisdictions.[94] New York allows for the imposition of a death sentence in cases involving the murder of law enforcement officers, judges, and witnesses and their families, and applies this punishment to serial killers, terrorists, murderers-for-hire, and those who kill while committing another felony such as robbery or rape.

The number of crimes punishable by death under U.S. federal jurisdiction increased dramatically with the passage of the *Violent Crime Control and Law Enforcement Act* of

1994—and now includes a total of about 60 offences. State legislators are also moving to expand the types of crime for which a sentence of death can be imposed. In 1997, for example, the Louisiana Supreme Court upheld the state's year-old death penalty statute for the rape of a child. This statute allows for the imposition of a capital sentence when the victim is under 12 years of age. The case involved an AIDS-infected father who raped his three daughters, aged five, eight, and nine years old. In upholding the father's death sentence, the Louisiana court ruled that child rape is "like no other crime."[95]

A total of 3717 persons were under sentence of death throughout the United States on July 1, 2001. The latest statistics show that 98 per cent of those on death row are male, 46 per cent are classified as white, 9 per cent are Hispanic, 43 per cent are African-American, and 2 per cent are of other races (mostly Native American and Pacific Islander).[96] Finally, methods of imposing death vary by state. Most death penalty states authorize execution through lethal injection. Electrocution is the second most common means of dispatch, while hanging, the gas chamber, and firing squads have survived, at least as options available to the condemned, in a few states.

The legal process through which a capital sentence is carried to conclusion is fraught with problems. The main difficulties are the automatic review of all death sentences by appellate courts and constant legal manoeuvring by defence counsel, because these often lead to a dramatic delay between the time when the sentence is passed and the time when it is carried out. Today, an average of 10 years passes between the time when a sentence of death is imposed and the time when it is carried out.[97] Such lengthy delays, compounded with uncertainty over whether a sentence will ever be imposed, directly contravene the generally accepted notion that punishment should be swift and certain.

In a move to reduce delays in the conduct of executions, the U.S. Supreme Court, in the case of *McCleskey* v. *Zandt* (1991),[98] limited the number of appeals a condemned person may lodge with the courts. Saying that repeated filings for the sole purpose of delay promotes "disrespect for the finality of convictions" and "disparages the entire criminal justice system," the Court established a two-pronged criterion for future appeals. According to *McCleskey*, in any petition beyond the first, filed with a federal court, capital defendants must demonstrate (1) good cause why the claim now being made was not included in the first filing and (2) how the absence of that claim may have harmed the petitioner's ability to mount an effective defence. Two months later, the Court reinforced *McCleskey*, when it ruled in *Coleman* v. *Thompson* (1991)[99] that state prisoners could not cite "procedural default," such as a defence lawyer's failure to meet a state's filing deadline for appeals, as the basis for an appeal to the federal court.

In 1995, in the case of *Schlup* v. *Delo*,[100] the U.S. Supreme Court continued to define standards for continued appeals from death-row inmates, ruling that before appeals based upon claims of new evidence could be heard, "a petitioner must show that, in light of the new evidence, it is more likely than not that no reasonable juror would have found him guilty beyond a reasonable doubt." A "reasonable juror" was defined as one who "would consider fairly all of the evidence presented and would conscientiously obey the trial court's instructions requiring proof beyond a reasonable doubt."

Opportunities for U.S. federal appeals by death-row inmates were further limited by the *Antiterrorism and Effective Death Penalty Act* of 1996, which set a one-year post-conviction deadline for state inmates filing federal *habeas corpus* appeals. The deadline is six months for state death-row inmates who were provided a lawyer for *habeas* appeals at the state level. The Act also (1) requires federal courts to presume that the factual findings of state courts are correct, (2) does not permit state-court misinterpretations of the U.S. Constitution to be used as a basis for *habeas* relief unless those misinterpretations are "unreasonable," and (3) requires that all petitioners must show, prior to obtaining a hearing, sufficient facts to establish by clear and convincing evidence that no reasonable fact-finder would have found the petitioner guilty without the constitutional error. Finally, the Act also requires initial approval from the panel that there is indeed sufficient new evidence warranting a second appeal by a three-judge panel before an inmate can file a second federal appeal raising newly discovered evidence of innocence. In 1996, in the case of *Felker* v. *Turpin*,[101] the U.S. Supreme Court ruled that limitations on the authority of federal courts to consider successive *habeas corpus* petitions imposed by the *Antiterrorism and Effective Death Penalty Act* of 1996 were permissible since they did not deprive the U.S. Supreme Court of its original jurisdiction over such petitions.

Some observers have objected that recent legislation, combined with the U.S. Supreme Court's own spate of decisions limiting the opportunity of convicted offenders to appeal, would swiftly and dramatically increase the rate of executions across the nation and prevent thousands of inmates, including those not on death row, from receiving a fair hearing on valid appeals. "There will be many injustices which will not be corrected," warned Stephen Bright of the Southern Center for Human Rights, following passage of the 1996 *Antiterrorism Act*. "We'll see a lot of people in this country executed despite fundamental violations of the Constitution and despite innocence," said Bright.[102]

## The Impact of America's Death Penalty on Canadians

Texas is particularly active in executing offenders. One death-row inmate who recently died at Texas' Walls Unit in Huntsville, Texas, was a Canadian, Joseph Stanley Faulder. Faulder was convicted for the 1975 killing of an elderly widow in the Texas oil-town of Gladewater.[103] After his marriage fell apart in the early 1970s, Faulder had become a drifter. He ended up in a bar, hustling pool in a small town in Texas and meeting up with a woman going by the name of Stormy Summers. Evidence indicates that the two decided to break into the home of an elderly woman who reputedly kept valuables in a safe in her home. When the robbery turned up nothing of value, the victim ended up dead with a knife in her chest. Following two trials and numerous appeals, Faulder was convicted of her killing and sentenced to death. Summers escaped with a plea bargain resulting in immunity and parole. On December 10, 1998, just 15 minutes before Faulder's scheduled execution, he learned that the U.S. Supreme Court had granted a temporary stay of execution.[104] However, the stay was short-lived, and as a new execution approached, it became apparent that Faulder would have to pay the ultimate price for the allegations against him. On June 17, 1999, Faulder was executed by lethal injection.

Stan Faulder's case is not the only capital punishment case that has drawn attention in Canada. Several cases have arisen as a result of extradition of offenders from Canada to the United States where they may face the death penalty. Article 6 of the *Extradition Treaty Between Canada and the United States of America*, C.T.S. 1976/3 provides, "When the offence for which extradition is requested is punishable by death under the laws of the requesting State and the laws of the requested State do not permit such punishment for that offense, extradition may be refused unless the requesting State provides such assurances as the requested State considers sufficient that the death penalty shall not be imposed, or if imposed, shall not be executed." Frequently, the Canadian Minister of Justice authorizes extradition without seeking assurances that the death penalty will not be imposed.

In 1991, the Supreme Court of Canada entertained two appeals, one involving Joseph Kindler, wanted for murder in Pittsburgh, and the other involving Charles Ng, the infamous alleged serial killer who, along with Leonard Lake, is said to have kidnapped, tortured, raped, and killed dozens of people at a ranch located 240 kilometres northeast of the San Francisco Bay area, in Calaveras County. The cases involving Kindler and Ng are unrelated except in that both were fugitives from American justice, hiding out in Canada when they were caught by the police. Both fought their extradition back to the United States on the grounds that they would face the death penalty upon their return to their respective states. They argued that since Canada had abolished the death penalty, it had recognized that the imposition of the death penalty constitutes cruel and unusual punishment, prohibited by section 12 of the *Charter of Rights and Freedoms*. If the Court ordered extradition, the Court would, in effect, bring about their deaths unless the Canadian Minister of Justice obtained assurances from the U.S. states that the death penalty would not be imposed. In these cases, the Minister of Justice at the time, John Crosby, neither sought nor obtained such assurances.

In rejecting the appeals of both Kindler and Ng, the Supreme Court of Canada authorized the extradition of the two men to the United States, with the possibility that they would face the death penalty. The top court ruled that although the imposition of the death penalty by a Canadian court may constitute cruel and unusual punishment, no such imposition occurred in these cases. It is the U.S. courts that would impose the penalty. All that the Canadian courts must do is ensure that the requirements for extradition are present.[105] Likewise, extradition to face the death penalty does not offend section 7 of the *Charter of Rights and Freedoms* unless the penalty imposed in the requesting state shocks the Canadian conscience. Returning the Americans to their home country to meet the possibility of the death penalty for brutal and shocking murders committed in the United States does not meet that test. The Supreme Court appeared, at least in part, to be concerned with the possibility of Canada becoming a safe haven for fugitive offenders from the United States, who were facing the death penalty at home.[106]

In 2001, the Supreme Court of Canada reached a different conclusion in a case involving Canadian nationals.[107] Two teenagers, Glen Sebastian Burns and Atif Rafay, allegedly carried out a plan to travel from their West Vancouver home to the home of Rafay in Bellevue, Washington, and kill Rafay's parents in hopes of receiving a $350 000 inheritance.[108] On July 12, 1994, Rafay and Burns were said to have killed Tariq and Sultana Rafay, and their autistic daughter, Basma, by bludgeoning them to death with a baseball bat. A few days after the killings, Burns and Rafay returned to West Vancouver, not even returning to Washington state for the Rafays' funeral. Within a year, the RCMP completed an undercover investigation on the two young men, culminating in charges being laid against them for aggravated first-degree murder in Bellevue, a capital crime in Washington state.

This time, the Canadian courts were faced with a situation in which Canadian citizens were about to be surrendered to a foreign state where they would quite possibly be put to death. In a unanimous decision, the Supreme Court of Canada ruled that extraditing Canadians in these circumstances violates their rights under section 7 of the *Charter of Rights and Freedoms* to "life, liberty and security of the person" in a manner "not in accordance with the principles of fundamental justice."[109] The Court noted that the act of surrendering the fugitives in this

---

**BOX 9.5    Theory into Practice**

**The Death Penalty— Justice Cory's Declaration**

In Canada, the death penalty has not existed since 1976. In 1987, Parliament entertained a free vote to determine whether to reinstate the death penalty, defeating this proposal by a fairly narrow margin (148 to 127). While many Canadians wonder whether the death penalty will ever be reinstated in Canada, debate about the value of the penalty has been a largely intellectual exercise on this side of the Canada-U.S. border. The debate, however, has taken on a practical context in situations involving the decision by Canada's Attorney General on whether to seek assurances that persons being extradited to the U.S. to possibly face the death penalty will, in fact, be spared this penalty.

In 1994, two Canadians, Glen Sebastian Burns and Atif Rafay, travelled to the Washington state town of Bellevue, where they allegedly murdered the family of one of the boys and then returned to Canada. When American authorities identified the boys as their prime suspects, they sought their extradition to face trial for the capital crimes. The Attorney General of Canada has discretion, under our extradition treaty with the United States, to make extradition contingent on the U.S. providing assurances that the death penalty will not be applied. In this case, the Attorney General ordered extradition without seeking such assurances. The two young men appealed this decision to the Supreme Court of

Canada. The Court blocked the extradition until the Attorney General sought the necessary assurances from American authorities.[1] Assurances that the death penalty would not be applied were eventually provided, and the Canadians were extradited to Washington, where they still await trial as of early 2003. In the process of ruling on the extradition, the top court commented on the problems associated with the death penalty, as follows:

> The recent and continuing disclosures of wrongful convictions for murder in Canada, the United States and the United Kingdom provide tragic testimony to the fallibility of the legal system, despite its elaborate safeguards for the protection of the innocent. When fugitives are sought to be tried for murder by a retentionist state, however similar in other respects to our own legal system, this history weighs powerfully in the balance against extradition without assurances.

In an earlier pair of companion cases, dealt with by the Supreme Court of Canada in 1987,[2] Justice Cory took advantage of the opportunity to declare that Canada will not entertain a return of the death penalty:

> ... some punishments or treatments will always be grossly disproportionate and will always outrage our standards of decency: for example the infliction of corporal punishment, such as the lash, irrespective of the number of lashes imposed, or, to give examples of treatment, the lobotomisation of certain dangerous offenders or the castration of sexual offenders. From this decision two principles emerge. First, punishments must never be grossly disproportionate to that

case, that is, without assurances that the death penalty would not be imposed, could result in a final, irreversible, arbitrary punishment wherein the deterrent value was doubtful. It also noted that Canada's Parliament has soundly rejected the death penalty. At that time, incidents of wrongful conviction contributed to the Court's concern that the possibility of capital punishment being imposed on an innocent person was a grave risk. Accordingly, extradition without assurances was rejected. In the months following the Supreme Court's decision, Washington state granted assurances the death penalty would not be imposed, and the young men were extradited to face trial. Their trial was scheduled to begin in mid-2003.

## Opposition to Capital Punishment

Canada abolished its death penalty in 1976. Abolition was achieved despite public opinion at the time, which pollsters indicated still favoured retention of the death penalty.[110] In 1987, Parliament re-entertained the death penalty issue with a free vote in the House of Commons on whether capital punishment should be reinstated. Despite public opinion, which still appeared to favour the death penalty, Parliament voted to continue its abolitionist stance. Whether Canada will return to the death penalty remains an open issue.[111] The United States appears unwilling to part company with capital punishment despite considerable opposition to the death penalty from a variety of sources.

Because of the strong emotions that are associated with state-imposed death, many attempts have been made to abolish capital punishment in the United States. Michigan,

which would have been appropriate to punish, rehabilitate or deter the particular offender or to protect the public from that offender. Second, and more importantly for the purposes of this case, punishments must not in themselves be unacceptable no matter what the crime, no matter what the offender. Although any form of punishment may be a blow to human dignity, some form of punishment is essential for the orderly functioning of society. However, when a punishment becomes so demeaning that all human dignity is lost, then the punishment must be considered cruel and unusual. At a minimum, the infliction of corporal punishment, lobotomisation of dangerous offenders and the castration of sexual offenders will not be tolerated.

...

A consideration of the effect of the imposition of the death penalty on human dignity is enlightening. Descriptions of executions demonstrate that it is state-imposed death which is so repugnant to any belief in the importance of human dignity. The methods utilized to carry out the execution serve only to compound the indignities inflicted upon the individual.

Cory J. then reviewed the pain and suffering entailed in several forms of capital punishment, and assessed the constitutionality of capital punishment in the context of the prohibition against cruel and unusual treatment or punishment under section 12 of the *Charter*:

What is acceptable as punishment to a society will vary with the nature of that society, its degree of stability and its level of maturity ...

If corporal punishment, lobotomy and castration are no longer acceptable and contravene s. 12 then the death penalty cannot be considered to be anything other than cruel and unusual punishment. It is the supreme indignity to the individual, the ultimate corporal punishment, the final and complete lobotomy and the absolute and irrevocable castration.

As the ultimate desecration of human dignity, the imposition of the death penalty in Canada is a clear violation of the protection afforded by s. 12 of the Charter. Capital punishment is per se cruel and unusual.

## QUESTIONS FOR DISCUSSION

1. Do you agree with Cory J.'s assessment of the death penalty as "the ultimate desecration of human dignity"? Why or why not?

2. If the imposition of the death penalty is such an affront to human dignity, is there any way in which it could be made less so?

3. Was the Court correct to impose a moratorium on extraditions without assurances regarding the death penalty in the *Burns* case? What would happen if the U.S. reneged on its assurances, and applied the death penalty in the *Burns* case?

---

[1] *U.S.A.* v. *Burns*, [2001] 1 S.C.R. 283.
[2] *Kindler* v. *Canada (Minister of Justice)*, [1991] 2 S.C.R. 779 and *Reference re Ng Extradition (Canada)*, [1991] S.C.R. 858.

widely regarded as the first abolitionist state, joined the Union in 1837 without a death penalty. A number of other states, including Massachusetts, West Virginia, Wisconsin, Minnesota, Alaska, and Hawaii, have since spurned death as a possible sanction for criminal acts. Many western European countries have also rejected the death penalty. As noted earlier, it remains a viable sentencing option in 38 of the states and all U.S. federal jurisdictions. As a consequence, arguments continue to rage over its value.

Today, there are six main rationales for abolishing capital punishment:

1. The death penalty can, and has been inflicted on, innocent people;

2. Evidence has shown that the death penalty is not an effective deterrent;

3. The imposition of the death penalty is, by the nature of our legal system, arbitrary;

4. The death penalty discriminates against certain ethnic and racial groups;

5. Imposition of the death penalty is far too expensive to justify its use; and

6. Human life is sacred, and killing at the hands of the state is not a righteous act, but rather one which is on the same moral level as the crimes committed by the condemned.

The first five abolitionist claims are pragmatic; that is, they can be measured and verified (or disproved) by looking at the facts. The last claim is primarily philosophical and therefore not amenable to scientific investigation.

---

## BOX 9.6　Theory into Practice

### The Death Penalty— LaForest Leaves the Door Open

Cory J. was in the dissent in the *Kindler* and *Ng* cases. The majority was represented by two different opinions, one written by Justice McLachlin, and the other by Justice LaForest. While McLachlin J. went out of her way to avoid passing judgment on the constitutionality of the death penalty itself, LaForest J. hinted that there might be some room to preserve a reinstatement of the death penalty in Canada in some circumstances. He began by assessing whether the imposition of the penalty would "shock the conscience" of Canadians. After noting the closeness of the free vote in Parliament on reinstatement in 1987 (148 to 127), he went on to address the issue in the following way:

> There are, of course, situations where the punishment imposed following surrender—torture, for example—would be so outrageous to the values of the Canadian community that the surrender would be unacceptable. But I do not think the surrender of fugitives who may ultimately face the death penalty abroad would in all cases shock the conscience of Canadians.

In his discussion of the imposition of the death penalty by governments beyond our borders, he seems to imply that he believes Canadians would tolerate the use of the death penalty in some circumstances. He makes this point clearer later in the judgment:

> There is strong ground for believing that having regard to the limited extent to which the death penalty advances any valid penological objectives and the serious invasion of human dignity it engenders that the death penalty cannot, except in exceptional circumstances, be justified in this country. But that, I repeat, is not the issue.

McLachlin J.'s majority opinion said the issue of whether the death penalty amounts to cruel and unusual punishment need not be addressed in the cases under review since the punishment of death was not being imposed by the government of Canada, but by a government in the foreign state, to whom the *Canadian Charter of Rights and Freedoms* does not apply.

### QUESTIONS FOR DISCUSSION

1. What kind of "exceptional circumstances," if any, do you believe would be acceptable situations in which the death penalty is justified? What do you think LaForest J. envisioned as exceptional circumstances?

2. In the United States, Supreme Court Justice Antonin Scalia has been quoted as saying "justice requires ... brutal deaths to be avenged by capital punishment." Do you agree? Why or why not?

3. Given the Canadian Supreme Court's concern over the possibility of executing the wrongly convicted, do you think Canada could ever entertain reinstatement of the death penalty?

## *The Future of the Death Penalty*

Because of the nature of the positions that both sides advocate, there is little common ground even for discussion between retentionists and abolitionists. Foes of the death penalty hope that its demonstrated lack of deterrent capacity will convince others that it should be abandoned. Their approach, based as it is upon statistical evidence, appears on the surface to be quite rational. However, it is doubtful that many capital punishment opponents could be persuaded to support the death penalty even if statistics showed it to be a deterrent because of the strong emotional response. Likewise, the tactics of death penalty supporters are equally instinctive. Retentionists could probably not be swayed by statistical studies of deterrence, no matter what they show, since their support is bound up with emotional calls for retribution.

The future of the death penalty, both in Canada and the United States, rests primarily with the legislatures. Canada's Parliament decided in 1998 to abolish the last vestiges of the death penalty by seeking to amend the *National Defence Act* to eliminate the last remaining military offences, such as espionage and mutiny with violence, carrying the death penalty. In both countries, supreme court intervention may have an impact on any law allowing the imposition of the death penalty. A return to the death penalty in Canada would almost certainly see challenges to the penalty brought under the *Charter of Rights and Freedoms*.

## SUMMARY

The goals of criminal sentencing are many and varied, and include retribution, incapacitation, deterrence, rehabilitation, and restoration. The just deserts model, with its emphasis on retribution and revenge, is the ascendant sentencing philosophy in Canada today. Many citizens, however, still expect sentencing practices to provide for other general sentencing goals. This ambivalence towards the purpose of sentencing reflects a more basic cultural uncertainty regarding the root causes of crime, the true nature of justice, and the fundamental goals of the criminal justice system.

Canada's sentencing structure reflects an eclectic approach to the topic. Typically, judges are given wide discretion to select what they deem to be an appropriate sentence in the circumstances of a particular case. In recent years, some structure has managed to creep in, with provisions for mandatory minimum sentencing for a few offences appearing in the *Criminal Code*. Recent efforts to find appropriate intermediate sanctions, between prison and probation, have garnered considerable attention, as courts increasing rely on conditional sentencing and consider other alternatives.

Structured sentencing, an approach gathering acceptance in the United States, and perhaps in the United Kingdom, and as embodied in sentencing guidelines, is a child of the just deserts philosophy. The structured sentencing model, however, while apparently associated with a reduction in the biased and inequitable sentencing practices that had characterized previous sentencing models, may not be the panacea it once seemed. Inequitable practices under the indeterminate model may never have been as widespread as opponents of that model claimed them to be. Worse still, the practice of structured sentencing may not reduce sentencing discretion but merely move it out of the hands of judges and into the ever-widening sphere of plea bargaining. Doubly unfortunate, structured sentencing, by its de-emphasis of parole, weakens incentives among the correctional population for positive change and tends to swell prison populations until they are overflowing. Even so, as society-wide sentiments and the social policies they support swing further in the direction of social responsibility, the interests of crime victims and the concerns of those who champion them will increasingly be recognized.

## DISCUSSION QUESTIONS

1. Outline the various sentencing rationales discussed in this chapter. Which of these rationales do you find most acceptable as the primary goal of sentencing? How might your choice of rationales vary with type of offence? Can you envision any other circumstances that might make your choice less acceptable?

2. In your opinion, is the return to just deserts consistent with a structured sentencing model? Why or why not?

3. Trace the differences between structured and indeterminate sentencing. Which model holds the best long-term promise for crime reduction? Why?

# WEBLINKS

www.parl.gc.ca/InfoComDoc/36/1/JURI/Studies/Reports/jurirp14-e.htm
**Victims' Rights: A Voice, not a Veto**
Report of the Standing Committee on Justice and Human Rights, October 1998.

www.acjnet.org
**ACJNet Publications: Sentencing in Canada**
This publication, published by the John Howard Society of Alberta, explains the purpose and principles of sentencing, as defined by the *Criminal Code*, and describes the various types of sentencing.

www.chebucto.ns.ca/Law/PLENS/sentence.html
**Sentencing—Public Legal Education Society of Nova Scotia**
Published by the Public Legal Education Society of Nova Scotia, this pamphlet provides general information about sentencing, from legal definitions to advice on finding a lawyer and how to act in court.

www.csc-scc.gc.ca
**Implementing the Life Line Concept**
Report of the Correctional Service of Canada's Task Force on Long-Term Offenders, February 1998.

www.sentencingproject.org
**The Sentencing Project**
Located in Washington, D.C., the Sentencing Project is an independent source of criminal justice policy analysis, data, and program information for the public and policy makers. The site provides resources and information for the news media and a public concerned with criminal justice and sentencing issues, as well as information about the National Association of Sentencing Advocates and about the Campaign for an Effective Crime Policy.

# Corrections

*Punishment—that is justice for the unjust.*

—St. Augustine

The great Christian apologist C.S. Lewis (1898–1963) once remarked that if satisfying justice is to be the ultimate goal of Western criminal justice, then the fate of offenders cannot be dictated merely by practical considerations. "The concept of desert is the only connecting link between punishment and justice," Lewis wrote. "It is only as deserved or undeserved that a sentence can be just or unjust," he concluded.

Once a person has been arrested, tried, and sentenced, the correctional process begins. Unlike that which Lewis exhorts, however, the contemporary Canadian correctional system—which includes probation, parole, jails, prisons, strict discipline, and many innovative alternatives to traditional sentence— is tasked with far more than merely carrying out sentences. We also expect our correctional system to ensure the safety of law-abiding citizens, that it select the best alternative from among the many available for handling a given offender, that it protect those under its charge, and that it guarantee fairness in the handling of all with whom it comes into contact.

This section of *Canadian Criminal Justice Today* details the development of probation, parole, community corrections, and imprisonment as correctional philosophies; describes the nuances of prison and jail life; discusses special issues in contemporary corrections (including AIDS, geriatric offenders, and famle inmates); and summarizes the legal environment that both surrounds and informs the modern-day practice of corrections. Characteristic of today's correctional emphasis is a society-wide push for harsher punishments. The culmination of that strategy, however, is dramatically overcrowded correctional institutions, the problems of which are also described. As you read through this section, encountering descriptions of various kinds of criminal sanctions, you might ask yourself: "When would a punishment of this sort be deserved?" In doing so, remember to couple that thought with another question: "What are the ultimate consequences (for society and for the offender) of the kind of correctional program we are discussing here?" Unlike Lewis, you may also want to ask: "Can we afford it?"

# Probation, Parole, and Community Corrections

Canadian Press/Bob Wilson

**KEY CONCEPTS**

community corrections
probation
conditional sentence
parole
restitution
parole revocation
revocation hearing
caseload

split sentence
shock probation
shock incarceration
intermittent sentence
intensive probation supervision
home confinement

**KEY CASES**

R. v. Proulx
R. v. Knoblauch
Re Nicholson and Halidimand-Norfolk Board of Police Commissioners
Ex Parte McCaud
R. v. Robinson

R. v. Moore; Oag v. R.
R. v. Wilmott
Swan v. Attorney General of British Columbia
Howarth v. National Parole Board

# INTRODUCTION TO COMMUNITY CORRECTIONS

During the evening of June 17, 1988, 11-year-old Christopher Stevenson was abducted at knifepoint from a mall in Brampton, Ontario. Investigations led to the arrest of Joseph Roger Fredericks by Peel Regional Police. Fredericks confessed to the boy's abduction and led investigators to his body. Fredericks was charged, tried, and convicted of first-degree murder. He was diagnosed as being a severe psychopath and pedophile with homosexual tendencies. Fredericks had been incarcerated for most of his life and was identified by a psychiatrist as being part of a small group of dangerous, high-risk sexual predators who could have been expected to reoffend.[1] On January 3, 1992, Fredericks was himself murdered while serving his sentence in the Kingston Penitentiary. The inquest following Fredericks's death in custody made 71 recommendations for improvements in four general areas:

- Keeping dangerous offenders in custody;
- Improving the sharing of information;
- Providing more resources and staff training for treatment programs; and
- Ensuring more visible accountability.

In July 1985, Celia Ruygrok, the night supervisor in a community residential centre in Ottawa, was murdered by a resident who was on parole for an earlier murder conviction. A coroner's inquest into Ruygrok's murder was held in 1987. This inquest made several recommendations with respect to sentencing, conditional release, information sharing, and cooperation among the various elements of the criminal justice system. The recommendations were significant to a task force established by the federal Solicitor General to examine the policy implications of the Ruygrok inquest. In attempting to come to terms with his daughter's murder, Gerald Ruygrok became personally involved in criminal justice issues as a community volunteer.[2]

Offences like these have cast a harsh light on the early release of criminal offenders. This chapter takes a close look at the realities behind the practice of what we call "community corrections." **Community corrections**, also called **community-based corrections**, is a sentencing style that represents a movement away from traditional confinement options and an increased dependence upon correctional resources that are available in the community. Community corrections can best be defined as court-ordered sanctions that permit convicted offenders to remain in the community under conditional supervision as an alternative to prison sentences. Community corrections includes sentencing options such as probation, conditional sentencing with home confinement, the electronic monitoring of offenders, and other new and developing programs—all of which are covered in this chapter. Another sentencing alternative under community corrections is the offender's conditional release from prison prior to the expiration of the offender's sentence.

**community corrections** (also called **community-based corrections**) A sentencing style that represents a movement away from traditional confinement options and an increased dependence upon correctional resources that are available in the community.

## WHAT IS PROBATION?

**Probation**, which is one aspect of community corrections, is "a sentence served while under supervision in the community."[3] Like other sentencing options, probation is a court-ordered sanction. Its goal is to allow for some degree of control over criminal offenders while using community programs to help rehabilitate them. Most of the alternative sanctions discussed later in this chapter are, in fact, predicated upon probationary sentences in which the offender is first placed on probation and then ordered to abide by certain conditions while remaining free in the community—such as participation in a specified drug or alcohol program. Most probationers have their sentences to any other dispositions suspended by the court and are then placed on probation. However, an inmate who is sentenced to a short period of incarceration, to be served on weekends, is placed on probation during the week, when he or she is out of custody.

Probation has a long and diverse history. By the 1300s, English courts had established the practice of "binding over for good behaviour,"[4] under which offenders could be placed in

**probation** A sentence of imprisonment that is suspended. Also, the conditional freedom granted by a judicial officer to an adjudicated adult or juvenile offender, as long as the adult or juvenile meets certain conditions of behaviour.

## FIGURE 10-1 Overview of Events in the Adult Correctional System

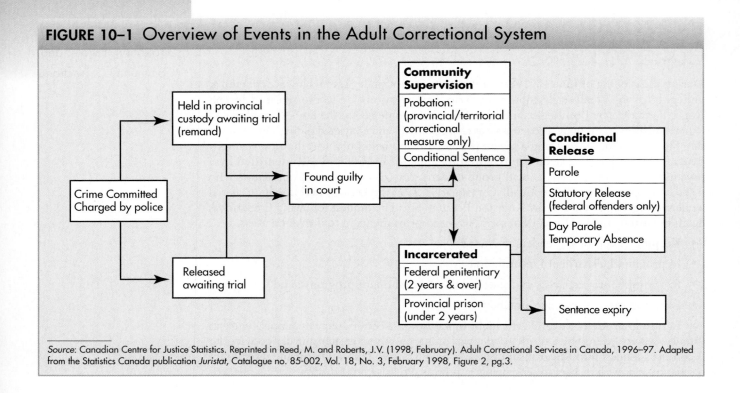

*Source*: Canadian Centre for Justice Statistics. Reprinted in Reed, M. and Roberts, J.V. (1998, February). Adult Correctional Services in Canada, 1996–97. Adapted from the Statistics Canada publication *Juristat*, Catalogue no. 85-002, Vol. 18, No. 3, February 1998, Figure 2, pg.3.

the custody of willing citizens. John Augustus (1784–1859), however, is generally recognized as the world's first probation officer. Augustus, a Boston shoemaker, attended sessions of criminal court in the 1850s and would offer to take carefully selected offenders into his home as an alternative to imprisonment.[5] At first, he supervised only drunkards, but by 1857 Augustus was accepting many kinds of offenders and devoting all his time to the service of the court.[6] Augustus died in 1859, having bailed out more than 2000 convicts during his lifetime.

Probation in Canada got off to a relatively slow start.[7] The first legislation to come into force was in 1889, and was based on the *British Probation of First Offenders Act* (1887). The federal government made provisions for probation supervision in 1921 and, in 1927, the law was consolidated in the *Criminal Code* of Canada. Ontario was the first province to introduce legislation providing for the appointment of probation officers, with British Columbia following suit in 1946. However, it is generally held that Canada did not have a truly effective system of probation in place until 1951. This is particularly interesting in light of the fact that the Royal Commission to Investigate the Penal System of Canada (1938) recommended that trained social workers should be engaged in support of a national probation service.

## The Extent of Probation

Today, probation is one of the most common forms of criminal sentencing in Canada. In 1999–2000, 40 per cent of all persons found guilty of a single offence, in a sampling of nine Canadian jurisdictions, were sentenced to probation.[8] Figure 10–2 shows the proportion of single-conviction cases involving a variety of offences that resulted in the imposition of a probation sentence.

Even serious offenders stand a good chance of receiving a probationary term. As noted in Figure 10–2, 78 per cent of those convicted of assault with a weapon received a probation term in 1999–2000. Similarly, 76 per cent of those convicted of sexual assault received a probationary sentence, as did 73 per cent of those convicted of kidnapping. Indeed, of the 83 single-conviction homicide cases caught in the review, 12 cases resulted in a probation sentence.[9] The average length of a probation sentence was 434 days in 1999–2000; the *Criminal Code* sets the maximum period of probation that may be imposed by a court

**FIGURE 10–2** Single-Conviction Offences Frequently Receiving a Probation Sentence in Nine Provinces and Territories in Canada, 1999–2000

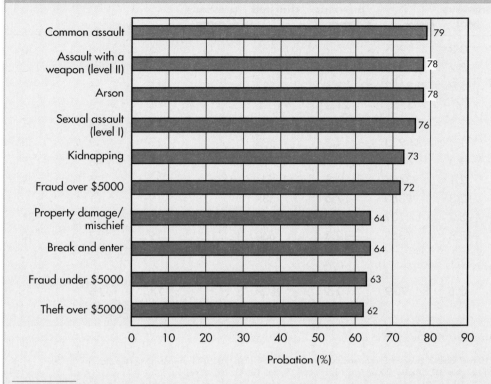

Source: Statistics Canada. Adult Criminal Court Survey. Canadian Centre for Justice Statistics. Figure 6. Single-conviction Offences Frequently Receiving a Probation Sentence Nine Provinces and Territories in Canada, 1999/2000. In *Juristat*, Vol. 21, No. 10, p. 10.

at three years.[10] Table 10–1 shows the average count number (as a "count") of probationers in Canada in 2000–01.

Individual jurisdictions, however, made greater or lesser use of probation. Prince Edward Island, with the smallest probationary population, supervised only 632 people on an average day in 2000–01, while Ontario reported 52 181 persons on probation.[11] Of course, the size of the population in these two provinces varies greatly. Looking at the rate of persons on probation per 100 000 adults, one finds probation is used least frequently in Quebec, with only 135 per 100 000 adult population on probation on an average day, while Manitoba has the highest rate of any province, with 752 per 100 000 on probation. The highest rate of probation reported in Canada in 2000–01 was in the Yukon Territory, with 1660 per 100 000 on probation, although this actually amounts to only 917 actual probationers.[12]

## Probation Conditions

Offenders sentenced to probation must agree to abide by court-mandated conditions of probation. Such conditions are of two types: general and specific. General conditions applying to all probationers include requirements that the probationer "keep the peace and be of good behaviour," "appear before the court when required to do so by the court," and "notify the court or the probation officer in advance of any change of name or address, and promptly notify the court or the probation officer of any change of employment or occupation."[13] Judges use a standardized form to outline general conditions of probation. Many

**TABLE 10–1** Average Count and Number of Probation Admissions in Canada, 2000–01

| Jurisdiction | Average monthly probation count | % change from previous year | Number of admissions | % change from previous year | Rate per 100 000 adults charged | % change from previous years | % female | % aboriginal | Median age |
|---|---|---|---|---|---|---|---|---|---|
| Newfoundland | 2338 | 3.3 | 1906 | 5.2 | 557 | | 15 | 8 | 30 |
| Prince Edward Island | 661 | −8.2 | 533 | −10.0 | 632 | | .. | .. | .. |
| Nova Scotia | 4365 | −5.9 | 3653 | −3.6 | 597 | | 15 | 6 | 30 |
| New Brunswick | .. | .. | 1733 | 21.3 | .. | | 16 | 8 | .. |
| Quebec | 7813 | −2.3 | 7704 | 8.5 | 135 | | 13 | 8 | 31 |
| Ontario | 52 181 | −1.4 | 34 920 | 4.5 | 583 | | 17 | 9 | 33 |
| Manitoba | 6440 | 6.8 | 6811 | .. | 752 | | 15 | 46 | 29 |
| Saskatchewan | 3803 | 2.1 | 3457 | 6.6 | 504 | | 20 | 65 | 29 |
| Alberta | 8696 | 2.3 | 9360 | 7.5 | 387 | | 19 | 21 | .. |
| British Columbia | 13 854 | −5.3 | 11 509 | −6.3 | 438 | | 16 | 18 | 31 |
| Yukon | 375 | −13.8 | 353 | −12.8 | 1660 | | 19 | 57 | 30 |
| Northwest Territories | .. | .. | · | · | ·· | | · | · | • |
| Nunavut | .. | .. | · | · | ·· | | · | · | • |
| **Provincial/ Territorial Total** | **100 526** | **−3.5** | **81 939** | **3.2** | **425** | | **17** | **15** | • |

· not available for any reference period
·· not available for specific reference period

*Source*: Statistics Canada. (2002). Text Table 10 and Table 3. Selected Characteristics of Probation Admissions, 2000/01. Adapted from the Statistics Canada publication *Juristat*, Catalogue no. 85-002, Vol. 22, No. 10, October 2002, pgs. 13, 18, and 19, and Vol. 18, No. 3, pg. 10.

probationers are also required to pay a fine to the court, usually in a series of installments that are designed to reimburse the justice system for its costs.

Additional conditions may be mandated by a judge who feels that the probationer is in need of particular guidance or control. A number of special conditions are routinely imposed upon sizable subcategories of probationers, and these conditions are presented in Table 10–2. An additional, frequent condition is that the probationer must report to a probation officer as frequently as the probation officer directs. Refraining from the consumption of drugs or alcohol is also a frequent condition for offenders with substance abuse problems. A community service order is a popular condition, requiring the offender to provide up to 240 hours of service in his or her community. The judge may add special conditions that are tailored specifically to individual probationers, such as requiring the probationer to attend a drug or alcohol treatment program. However, a probationer may only be subjected to a condition of involvement in a general treatment or rehabilitation program if the offender agrees to do so. Of course, if a convicted offender is presented with this alternative to imprisonment, consent to a treatment condition can be expected to be forthcoming.

# WHAT IS CONDITIONAL SENTENCING?

**Conditional Sentencing** is a relatively new community-based sanction whereby an offender is sentenced to a period of imprisonment that can be served in the community subject to conditions imposed by the court.[14] This sentence differs from probation in that the sentence is not suspended, but rather is actually imposed, although by allowing the sentence to be served in the community, this sentence tends to "mimic" probation. The conditional sentence must be less than two years, and the conditions that may be imposed can be more restrictive than those applying to probation orders.

**conditional sentencing**
Sentencing an offender, who is deemed not to be a danger to the community, to a period of imprisonment for less than two years, to be served in the community rather than in a provincial prison. Such sentences place strict conditions on the offender, such as requiring them to remain in their home for the duration of the sentence.

## TABLE 10–2 Probation Conditions

According to section 732.1(2) of the *Criminal Code*, all probation orders must contain the conditions that the offender:

(a) keep the peace and be of good behaviour;

(b) appear before the court when required to do so by the court; and

(c) notify the court or the probation officer in advance of any change of name or address, and promptly notify the court or the probation officer of any change of employment or occupation.

In addition, under s. 732.1(3), a sentencing judge may attach some or all of the following conditions, as appropriate:

(a) report to a probation officer
    (i) within two working days, or such longer period as the court directs, after the making of the probation order, and
    (ii) thereafter, when required by the probation officer and in the manner directed by the probation officer;

(b) remain within the jurisdiction of the court unless written permission to go outside that jurisdiction is obtained from the court or the probation officer;

(c) abstain from
    (i) the consumption of alcohol or other intoxicating substances, or
    (ii) the consumption of drugs except in accordance with a medical prescription;

(d) abstain from owning, possessing or carrying a weapon;

(e) provide for the support or care of dependants;

(f) perform up to 240 hours of community service over a period not exceeding eighteen months;

(g) if the offender agrees, and subject to the program director's acceptance of the offender, participate actively in a treatment program approved by the province;

(g.1) where the lieutenant governor in council of the province in which the probation order is made has established a program for curative treatment in relation to the consumption of alcohol or drugs, attend at a treatment facility, designated by the lieutenant governor in council of the province, for assessment and curative treatment in relation to the consumption by the offender of alcohol or drugs that is recommended pursuant to the program;

(g.2) where the lieutenant governor in council of the province in which the probation order is made has established a program governing the use of an alcohol ignition interlock device by an offender and if the offender agrees to participate in the program, comply with the program; and

(h) comply with such other reasonable conditions as the court considers desirable, subject to any regulations made under subsection 738(2), for protecting society and for facilitating the offender's successful reintegration into the community.

In 2000, the Supreme Court of Canada decided in *R. v. Proulx* that conditional sentencing is designed to fulfill punitive as well as rehabilitative goals.[15] Accordingly, courts frequently impose severe restrictions such as house arrest and strict curfews on offenders. Judges must rule out the need for a penitentiary term (two years or longer) and for noncustodial terms before choosing a conditional sentence. However, judges must also take into account whether the safety of the community would be endangered before opting for a conditional sentence rather than a short jail term.

## The Extent of Conditional Sentencing

Conditional sentencing is meant to provide an alternative to incarceration. It is not meant to be a more punitive form of probation. As Table 10–3 reflects, jurisdictions across the country have typically shown declining rates of imprisonment since the conditional sentencing provisions were brought into force in 1996 (*Juristat*, Vol. 22, No. 11, pp. 18–19). Conditional sentences are handed out in about 3.5 per cent of cases across the country.[16] Analysis of provincial variation in the use of conditional sentencing reveals that Saskatchewan has adopted the sentencing alternative wholeheartedly, with 133 per 100 000 population on a conditional sentencing at any given time. In 2000–02, this province had more offenders serving a conditional sentence (1006) than serving a provincial custodial sentence (826), as did Quebec, British Columbia, and the Yukon Territory.[17]

Judges appear to be gradually warming up to the conditional sentencing alternative. In 2000–01, there were 17 084 conditional sentence program admissions, reflecting a 17-per-cent increase when compared to the same admissions in 1997–98.[18] Despite this, custodial admission rates rose by almost 4.5 per cent over the same period.[19] Conditional sentencing holds out some promise as an alternative to high rates of incarceration, particularly among aboriginal offenders in Canada's Prairie provinces.

**TABLE 10–3** Average Daily Count[1] Sentenced Custody, 1995–96 to 2000–01

| | 1995–96 | 1996–97 | 1997–98 | 1998–99 | 1999–2000 | 2000–01 |
|---|---|---|---|---|---|---|
| Newfoundland | 319 | 275r | 248 | 258r | 222 | 225 |
| Prince Edward Island | 96 | 71r | 79 | 73 | 71 | 73 |
| Nova Scotia[2] | 346 | 318r | 299 | 285 | 247 | 222 |
| New Brunswick[3, 4] | 353 | 339 | 319 | 274 | 244 | 204 |
| Quebec | 2303 | 2267 | 2117 | 2102 | 1993r | 2011 |
| Ontario | 4690 | 4819 | 4631 | 4441 | 4003 | 3737 |
| Manitoba | 696 | 639 | 570 | 615 | 603 | 596 |
| Saskatchewan | 1088 | 980 | 958 | 955 | 854 | 826 |
| Alberta | 2084 | 1825 | 1463 | 1601 | 1430 | 1323 |
| British Columbia | 1933 | 1626 | 1525 | 1513 | 1467 | 1476 |
| Yukon | 63 | 53 | 60 | 52 | 43 | 35 |
| Northwest Territories[5] | 278 | 311 | 304 | 309 | 207 | 163 |
| Nunavut | … | … | … | … | 36 | 63 |
| **Provincial/ Territorial Total** | 14 249 | 13 522 | 12 573 | 12 478 | 11 421 | 10 953 |

r revised

… not applicable

[1] Counts are reported as average daily counts.

[2] Nova Scotia's sentenced custody is reported as an average monthly count.

[3] New Brunswick probation and conditional sentence counts are estimates in 1999–2000.

[4] Data for 2000–01 are from a new operational system; caution is recommended when comparing 2000–01 to previous years.

[5] Figures reported by the Northwest Territories after 1998–99 no longer include figures reported by Nunavut.

*Source*: Statistics Canada. Adult Correctional Services Survey. Canadian Centre for Justice Statistics. Table 3. Average Daily Count and Rate per 100,000 Adults, Selected Sentences, 1995/96 to 2000/01. In *Juristat*, Catalogue no. 85-002, Vol. 22, No. 10, p. 18.

# Conditional Sentencing Conditions

Conditional sentencing orders carry the same mandatory conditions as probation orders, plus a reporting requirement and travel restriction must be imposed.[20] Optional conditions that the court may impose are similar to those for probation orders, and include the option of court-ordered treatment attendance, even without the offender's consent. In *R. v. Knoblauch* (2000), the Supreme Court of Canada ruled that the conditional sentencing scheme is sufficiently flexible to permit a court to sentence an offender to a conditional sentence to be served in a custodial psychiatric facility if this is considered an appropriate setting for rehabilitative treatment. In this case, the accused advocated the use of a lock-up psychiatric facility as an alternative to incarceration. It remains to be seen whether courts may impose such a condition against the will of the accused.[21]

# WHAT IS PAROLE?

**Parole** is the supervised early release of inmates from correctional confinement. The National Parole Board (Canada) refers to it as "a carefully constructed bridge between incarceration and return to the community."[22] It differs from probation in both purpose and implementation. Cole and Manson (1990) provide an interesting insight into the origin of the word:

> Parole was originally the word of honour given by a prisoner of war of the officer class not to escape or commit an act of hostility to the forces of his captors. In return, he was allowed to live at large in a certain place, or even to visit his home, until he was exchanged or released on cessation of hostilities.[23]

In Canada, three provinces (British Columbia, Ontario, and Quebec) operate their own parole boards with jurisdiction over all inmates in their own institutions. The National Parole Board has jurisdiction over all offenders serving sentences of two years or more, as well as offenders serving sentences in provincial and territorial correctional facilities where there are no provincial boards of parole.[24] Whereas probationers generally avoid serving time in prison, offenders who are paroled have already been incarcerated. While probation is a sentencing option available to a judge who determines the form probation will take, parole, in contrast, results from a careful review of information regarding the offender, as well as an assessment of the risk of returning the offender to the community before the end of the sentence of incarceration. Included in the information reviewed by a parole board are the following:

- The offence;
- The offender's criminal history;
- The offender's social problems, including alcohol and/or drug abuse and incidence of family violence;
- The offender's mental status, particularly if it may influence the possibility of further crime;
- The offender's performance during earlier release sessions;
- Information about the offender's relationships and employment;
- Psychiatric and psychological reports;
- Professional opinions and reports from others such as judges and police, which might address any undue risk from the offender's release; and
- Victim information.

Once the parole board has examined this preliminary information, the board members then consider the probability that the inmate will reoffend, on a statistical basis. Specific factors that the board considers include:

- Offender behaviour in the institution;
- Information supplied by the offender that shows change in behaviour (e.g., ability to manage impulses) or insight into criminality;

**parole** The status of an offender conditionally released from a prison by discretion of a paroling authority prior to expiration of sentence, required to observe conditions of parole, and placed under the supervision of a parole agency.

- Indication of benefits from programs undertaken by the offender (e.g., substance abuse counselling, literacy training);

- Information relating to treatment for any disorder diagnosed by relevant professionals; and

- Offender's release plan.

In Canada, as in several other jurisdictions, conditional release programs (i.e., parole) have become part of the criminal justice system. Parole is based on a belief that offenders should be given a gradual, supervised release into the community in order to allow them to reintroduce themselves into society. Several studies support this belief. The *Corrections and Conditional Release Act* outlines six principles that relate directly to boards of parole:

- Protection of society is the most important consideration in any conditional release decision.

- All relevant information must be considered.

- Parole boards enhance their effectiveness through the timely exchange of relevant information among criminal justice components and by providing information about policies and programs of offenders, victims, and the general public.

- Parole boards will make the least restrictive decision consistent with the protection of society.

- Parole boards will adopt and be guided by appropriate policies, and board members will be given appropriate training.

- Offenders must be given relevant information, reasons for decisions, and access to the review of decisions to ensure a fair and understandable conditional release process.

The National Parole Board has exclusive authority under the *Corrections and Conditional Release Act* to function as an administrative tribunal that can grant, deny, cancel, or terminate parole. It can also order the detention of offenders who are subject to statutory release under certain circumstances. The National Parole Board makes conditional release decisions for offenders in federal and territorial institutions as well as parole decisions in provinces and territories that do not maintain their own parole boards, and for all offenders in the territories. It is important to note that the National Parole Board does not have responsibility for young offenders (i.e., those under 18 years of age, as established by the *Youth Criminal Justice Act*) unless they have been tried as adults in an adult court.

The use of parole in Canada began in 1899, when Parliament passed the *Ticket of Leave Act*. This legislation established conditional release and introduced a system of supervised freedom for offenders. Initially, the Act did not set out any limits on eligibility for parole, and conditional release could be granted to anyone by the Governor General of Canada. In 1901, a new position was created for a "Dominion Parole Officer." The function of these parole officers was to interview inmates to assess their plans upon release. This function coincides with that of a case manager in the current context.

Penal reformers in the 1930s began to question the whole orientation of the Canadian penitentiary system and argued for less punitive approaches. As noted above, the Royal Commission to Investigate the Penal System of Canada (1938) was instrumental in making recommendations to improve this system and placed greater emphasis on rehabilitation over punishment. The National Parole Board, the creation of a federal committee of inquiry in the 1950s, was perceived as a "logical" step in the process of providing for the rehabilitation and reformation of prisoners. The *Parole Act* of 1959 established the National Parole Board as an independent, administrative entity. In 1966, the *Department of the Solicitor General Act* made the Solicitor General responsible for the overall management and direction of reformatories, prisons, penitentiaries, parole, remissions, and the Royal Canadian Mounted Police (RCMP).[25] Included within the current federal Ministry of the Solicitor General are the National Parole Board, RCMP, Correctional Service of Canada, and Canadian Security Intelligence Service.

The National Parole Board undertook steps to increase the openness and accountability of its policies in the 1980s and, in 1992, the federal government passed the *Corrections and Conditional Release Act* under which the board now operates. The mission statement of the National Parole Board is as follows:

**FIGURE 10–3** Full Parole Grant Rate of Provincial Parole Boards as Compared to that of the National Parole Board

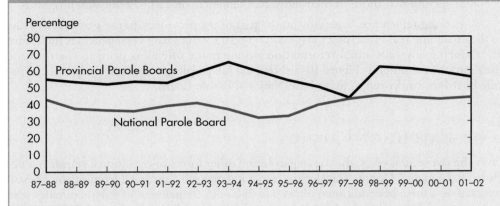

Source: Reprinted in Reed, M. and Roberts, J.V. (1998, February). Adult Correctional Services in Canada, 1996–97 (p. 10). *Juristat*, Vol. 18, No. 3; Government of Canada. (2002). National Parole Board. Performance Measurement Division. Grant Rates for Full Parole, p. 52. Adapted from the Statistics Canada publication *Juristat*, Catalogue no. 85-002, Vol. 18, No. 3, February 1998, pg. 10.

The National Parole Board, as part of the criminal justice system, makes independent, quality conditional release and pardon decisions and clemency recommendations. The Board contributes to the protection of society by facilitating, as appropriate, the timely integration of offenders as law-abiding citizens.

As you may recall from Chapter 9, indeterminate sentences are a key part of a philosophy that stresses rehabilitation. The indeterminate sentence was made possible by an innovative New York law following the call of leading correctional innovators. Parole was a much-heralded tool of nineteenth-century corrections, whose advocates had been looking for a behavioural incentive to motivate youthful offenders to reform. Parole, through its promise of earned early release, seemed the ideal innovation.

In Canada, there are basically four types of conditional release:

*Temporary absence.* This is usually the first type of release an offender will be granted. It may be with or without escort, and can be granted for several purposes, including work on community service projects, contact with family, personal development, or for medical reasons. Escorted temporary absences (ETAs) are available to inmates upon entering prison. For federal inmates, unescorted temporary absences (UTAs) are generally available at one-half of the full parole eligibility term, that is, after one-sixth of the sentence has been served. However, these federal inmates are never eligible for day parole until at least six months of their sentence has been served. Federal offenders classified as maximum-security inmates are not eligible for release on a UTA. A provincial inmate in Ontario is also eligible for a UTA after serving one-sixth of his or her sentence;

*Day parole.* This allows the prisoner to participate in community-based activities that may prepare the offender for release on full parole or for statutory release. An offender who is on day parole must return to his or her institution or a halfway house at night. A federal offender typically becomes eligible for day parole six months before becoming eligible for full parole. A provincial inmate in B.C. is eligible for day parole after serving one-sixth of his or her sentence. There is no provincial day parole in Ontario or Quebec;

*Full parole.* This allows prisoners to serve the remainder of their sentences under supervision within the community. Most federal offenders, and all provincial offenders serving over six months, become eligible for release on full parole after serving one-third of their individual sentences; and

*Statutory release/Earned remission.* Most federal inmates must, by law, be released under supervision, once they have completed two-thirds of their individual sentences. This release is referred to as statutory release. It does not apply to offenders who are serving life or indeterminate sentences. Provincial inmates in Quebec, British Columbia, and Ontario who do not apply for parole are released without supervision after serving two-thirds of their individual sentences on earned remission programs.

A growing reluctance, especially on the part of the provinces, to use parole seems due to the expanding realization that today's correctional routines have been generally ineffective at producing any substantial reformation among many offenders prior to their release back into the community. Figure 10–3 shows the full parole grant rate of the provincial parole boards as compared to that of the National Parole Board.

## The Extent of Parole

Over the last several years, the use of parole and other forms of conditional release has declined in Canada.[26] Despite this decline, most inmates who are freed from prison are still released on a form of conditional release. In 2000–01, 95 per cent of federal inmates who were released from custody did so on some form of conditional release. Day parole release accounted for 29 per cent of the releases. Three per cent of the released offenders were granted full parole, while 63 per cent were released on statutory release.[27] Table 10–4 shows, from 1997–98 until 2000–01, the National Parole Board (Canada) decisions made with respect to the granting of conditional release.

Adult corrections costs have remained relatively stable in recent years. In 2000–01, $2.5 billion was spent on adult corrections. This spending reflects a modest 1-per-cent increase over spending in the previous year,[28] which suggests that correctional supervision is considerably more cost efficient than custodial supervision. The federal government estimates the average annual cost of holding a federal inmate in custody to be $66 381. By contrast, an inmate on parole supervision is estimated to cost $16 800 per year. Clearly, even modest increases in the use of community corrections, if accompanied by a decline in the use of custodial detention, can produce significant cost savings.[29]

In Canada, there were 119 900 offenders on probation or on some form of conditional release in the community in 2000–01.[30]

In 2000–01, approximately 83 per cent of day parolees successfully completed their day parole, while about 12 per cent were returned to prison for parole violations and another 5 per cent went back to prison for new offences committed during their day-parole period. Inmates on full parole successfully completed their parole 74 per cent of the time, while

### TABLE 10–4 Grant Rates for Federal and Provincial Day Parole by Race and Gender

| Year | Aboriginal | | Non-Aboriginal | | Male | | Female | |
|---|---|---|---|---|---|---|---|---|
| | Fed. (%) | Prov. (%) | Fed. (%) | Prov. (%) | Fed. (%) | Prov. (%) | Fed. (%) | Prov. (%) |
| 1997–1998 | 71 | 35 | 73 | 43 | 72 | 40 | 86 | 92 |
| 1998–1999 | 73 | 60 | 75 | 66 | 74 | 63 | 89 | 81 |
| 1999–2000 | 70 | 76 | 73 | 76 | 72 | 74 | 85 | 97 |
| 2000–2001 | 74 | 71 | 71 | 70 | 71 | 69 | 89 | 94 |
| 2001–2002 | 75 | 57 | 71 | 66 | 71 | 62 | 87 | 82 |
| **5-Year Average** | **73** | **57** | **73** | **63** | **72** | **60** | **87** | **83** |

*Source:* Government of Canada. (2002). National Parole Board. Performance Measurement Division. Table 37. Grant Rates for Federal and Provincial Day Parole by Race and Gender (%), p. 45.

16 per cent were returned to prison for violating parole conditions and 10 per cent had their parole revoked for committing new offences. Of the 162 offenders on full parole whose parole was revoked in 2000–01, 137 of them had committed non-violent offences.[31]

## Parole Conditions

The conditions of parole remain very similar to the conditions agreed to by probationers.[32] The general conditions of parole require that the parolee obey the law and keep the peace, report to his or her parole supervisor as instructed by the parole supervisor, and immediately report to this supervisor any change of address, change of employment, or change of financial situation. A parolee is required to remain in Canada, and to carry his or her release certificate and identity card, and is also prohibited from possessing weapons. A parolee must periodically report to parole officers, or to the local police if he or she is travelling, and parole officers may visit a parolee at his or her home and place of business—often arriving unannounced.

The successful and continued employment of parolees is one of the major concerns of parole boards and their officers, and studies have found that successful employment is a major factor in reducing the likelihood of repeat offences.[33] The importance of employment is stressed in pre-release parole planning.

In the United States, special parole conditions may also be added to parole. For example, a parolee may be required to pay a "parole supervisory fee of $15" every month, a requirement now being routinely imposed in some jurisdictions (although monetary amounts may vary). A relatively new innovation, parole supervision fees shift some of the expenses of community corrections to the offender.

# PROBATION, CONDITIONAL SENTENCING, AND PAROLE: THE PLUSES AND MINUSES

## Advantages of Probation and Parole

Probation is used to meet the needs of offenders who require some correctional supervision short of imprisonment, while also providing a reasonable degree of security to the community. Conditional sentencing provides a genuine intermediate disposition between probation and incarceration, in which a prison sentence may be served in the community under even greater restrictions than one would find under probation. Parole fulfills a similar purpose for offenders released from prison. Probation, conditional sentencing, and parole provide a number of advantages over imprisonment, including:

*Lower Cost.* Imprisonment is expensive. Studies have consistently found that the cost of incarcerating an offender is approximately five to ten times the cost of intensive community supervision.[34] Not only do probation and parole directly save money, they may indirectly provide cost savings by reducing the likelihood of the families of offenders relying upon social assistance. Additionally, the offenders may obtain employment and make restitution payments to their victims. Inmates cost well in excess of $100 per day to house in most institutional environments.[35] Some jurisdictions require that offenders pay a portion of the costs associated with their own supervision. For example, in the state of Texas, in an innovative program that uses market-type incentives to encourage probation officers to collect fees,[36] the state has been able to annually recoup more than half of the total that it spends on probation services.

*Increased Employment.* Few people in prison have the opportunity to engage in meaningful work. Work release programs, correctional industries, and inmate labour programs operate in most jurisdictions, but they usually provide only low-paying jobs and require few skills. At best, such programs engage only a small portion of the inmates in any given facility. Probation, conditional sentencing, and parole, on the other hand, make it possible for offenders under correctional supervision to work full-time at jobs in the "free" economy. They can contribute to their

**restitution** A court requirement that an alleged or convicted offender pay money or provide services to the victim of the crime or provide services to the community.

own and their families' support, stimulate the local economy by spending their wages, and support government through the taxes they pay.

*Restitution.* Offenders who are able to work are candidates for court-ordered restitution. Society's interest in **restitution** (sometimes called "making the victim whole again") may be better served by a probationary sentence or parole than by imprisonment. Restitution payments to victims may help restore their standard of living and personal confidence while teaching the offender responsibility.

*Community Support.* The decision to either release a prisoner on parole or sentence a convicted offender to a probationary term is often partially based on considerations of the offender's family and other social ties. Such decisions are made in the belief that offenders will be more subject to control in the community if they participate in a web of positive social relationships. An advantage of both probation and parole is that they allow the offender to continue personal and social relationships. Probation and conditional sentencing avoid splitting up families, while parole may reunite family members who were separated when the offender went to prison.

*Reduced Risk of Criminal Socialization.* Prison has been called a "school in crime." Probation and conditional sentencing insulate adjudicated offenders, at least to some degree, from the kinds of criminal values that permeate prison. Parole, by virtue of the fact that it follows time served in prison, is less successful than probation in reducing the risk of criminal socialization.

*Increased Use of Community Services.* Probationers, offenders who have received conditional sentencing, and parolees can take advantage of services offered through the community, including psychological therapy, substance abuse counselling, financial services, support groups, church outreach programs, and social services. While a few similar opportunities may be available in prison, the community environment itself can enhance the effectiveness of treatment programs by reducing the stigmatization of the offender and allowing the offender to participate in a more "normal" environment.

*Increased Opportunity for Rehabilitation.* Probation, conditional sentencing, and parole can all be useful behavioural management tools. They reward co-operative offenders with freedom and allow for the opportunity to shape the behaviour of offenders who may be difficult to reach through other programs.

## Disadvantages of Probation, Conditional Sentencing, and Parole

Any honest appraisal of probation, conditional sentencing, and parole must recognize that they share a number of strategic drawbacks, such as:

*A Relative Lack of Punishment.* The "just deserts" model of criminal sentencing insists that punishment should be a central theme of the justice process. While rehabilitation and treatment are recognized as worthwhile goals, the model suggests that punishment serves both society's need for protection and the victim's need for revenge. Probation, however, is seen as virtually no punishment whatsoever and is coming under increasing criticism as a sentencing strategy. Conditional sentencing allows for more punitive conditions, including house arrest, but is also criticized for being an overly lenient response to crime. Parole is likewise criticized because (1) it releases some offenders early, even when they have been convicted of serious crimes, while other, relatively minor offenders, may remain in prison, and (2) it is dishonest because it does not require completion of the offender's entire sentence behind bars.

*Increased Risk to the Community.* Probation, conditional sentencing, and parole are strategies designed to deal with convicted *criminal* offenders. The release into the community of such offenders increases the risk that they will commit additional offences. Community supervision can never be so complete as to eliminate such a possibility entirely, and studies on parole have pointed to the fact that an accurate assessment of an offender's potential to do harm is beyond our present capability.

A 1998 study for the Canadian Centre for Justice Statistics found that a large percentage of those who serve the balance of their sentences in the community on parole do so without violating the conditions of their parole.[37] In 1996–97, less than 2 per cent of all federal **parole revocation**s were related to a violent criminal charge. During the same period, 75 per cent of all provincial full paroles were successfully completed.[38]

*Increased Social Costs.* Some offenders placed on probation and parole will effectively and responsibly discharge their obligations. Others, however, will become social liabilities. Of course, released offenders are at increased risk of committing new crimes. Since they have few marketable job skills, they could also end up on social assistance.

**parole revocation**
The administrative action of a parole board removing a person from parole status in response to a violation of lawfully required conditions of parole.

---

## BOX 10.1   Justice in Context

## Working in Parole in Canada

In Canada, the National Parole Board is responsible for parole services for federally sentenced offenders and for provincially sentenced offenders in all provinces except British Columbia, Ontario, and Quebec, which have their own parole boards. Recently, the National Parole Board reviewed its mission and mandate and developed core values to guide its efforts. Core Value 3 is set out below:

> We believe that the contribution of qualified and motivated individuals is essential to promoting the achievement of the Parole Board's Mission.

### Operating Principles

> The Parole Board is a results-driven and value-based organization, dedicated to the achievement of its Mission and committed to seeking improvement in the performance of all its responsibilities. We believe all personnel, be they Board members or staff at any level or location within the organization, contribute to the achievement of the Board's Mission through the effective and efficient performance of their work.
>
> The Board should be comprised of people who have a good understanding of the principles of the criminal justice system, will support attainment of the Board's Mission and have gained their place in the organization on the basis of a selection process that recognizes merit and competence.

> The Board values all of its personnel and promotes collegiality and cooperation in all facets of its operations. The work of Board members and staff is mutually complementary and it is the responsibility of each individual to promote a working environment characterized by mutual trust and respect.
>
> We provide direction to all employees through policy or other means that conveys a clear understanding of the requirements and the results to be attained from their implementation. We also recognize a responsibility to provide training to the Board's personnel in order that they may achieve the results and expectations of their work.
>
> We believe that individuals shall effectively carry out their responsibilities and shall be accountable for their actions.
>
> The Board encourages a healthy and secure environment which is conducive to the achievement of our Mission. We value communication, openness and flexibility and we support new opportunities to bring about improvements. Individuals must be supported and encouraged in the exercise of their responsibilities, and recognized for their accomplishments.
>
> We recognize that we rely on, and benefit from, close associations with a variety of criminal justice system partners, such as the Correctional Service of Canada, to maximize collective performance. We work cooperatively with a broad range of individuals and groups who can either assist our efforts or provide independent support for the attainment of the Board's Mission.

*Source:* National Parole Board's website accessible at time of printing at **www.npb-cnlc.gc.ca/about/corev_e.htm**

# THE LEGAL ENVIRONMENT

Several especially significant Canadian court decisions provide a legal framework for probation and parole supervision. By way of administrative law, the case *Re Nicholson and Haldimand-Norfolk Regional Board of Commissioners of Police* is important in addressing the duty to act fairly. This case has been cited in many cases dealing with probation and parole. Nicholson was a probationary constable in the town of Caledonia. He was promoted to second-class constable in March 1974, following his 12-month probation period, and became a member of the then recently formed Haldimand-Norfolk Regional Police. In June 1974, Nicholson received a letter informing him that the Board of Commissioners of Police had approved the termination of his services. He was not provided with a hearing in the matter of his termination, nor was he given reasons for the termination. Nicholson sought judicial review of the administrative decision to terminate him, and succeeded in the lower courts. Eventually, the case was appealed to the Supreme Court of Canada. The Court found that the duty to act fairly had not been observed in this case. The duty to act fairly now also applies to parole granting and revocation hearings.

Other court cases focus on the conduct of a parole or probation **revocation hearing**. Revocation, or revoking probation or parole, is a common procedure. Revocation of probation or parole may be requested by the supervising officer if a parolee or probationer has allegedly violated the conditions of community release or has committed a new crime. The most frequent violations for which revocation occurs are (1) failing to report as required to a probation or parole officer, (2) failing to participate in a stipulated treatment program, and (3) abusing alcohol or drugs while under supervision. In the context of probation, a revocation hearing occurs in court where a judge may order that a probationer's suspended sentence be made "active," sending the offender to prison. The parole board holds a parole revocation hearing, and has the authority to grant release, or the board may order that a parolee return to prison to complete his or her sentence in confinement.

*Ex Parte McCaud* is still an important case involving revocation, and was also the first important "prisoner's rights" case to appear before the Supreme Court of Canada.[39] Norman Douglas McCaud had been released from the Kingston Penitentiary on parole in October 1961. He had been serving a sentence of 10 years' imprisonment. On June 6, 1963, he was taken into custody and informed that his parole had been revoked. McCaud complained that he had never been informed of the reason for his parole's revocation. He was also not given an opportunity to be present at his hearing. His lawyers argued that McCaud's treatment was a violation of the *Canadian Bill of Rights*, especially section 2(e). Spence J. stated in his judgment that:

> The question of whether that sentence must be served in a penal institution and subject to the conditions of parole is altogether a decision within the discretion of the Parole Board as an administrative matter and is not in any way a judicial determination.

The case of *Re Moore and the Queen*[40] deals with the parole board's powers to suspend an inmate's release under mandatory supervision. Marlene Moore's mandatory supervision was immediately suspended upon her release from prison and she was recommitted to custody. This practice became known as "gating," where an inmate is released from prison and returned to custody immediately after leaving the gates of the prison. In Moore's case, the National Parole Board based its decision on a belief that recommitting Moore to custody was necessary to prevent a breach of the terms of her release. However, the Court in *Re Moore and the Queen* ruled that the National Parole Board had only the power to revoke or suspend mandatory supervision because of the inmate's post-release conduct. Moore, therefore, was entitled to be released and the National Parole Board had no authority to deny her that right.

The case of *R. v. Wilmott* (1967)[41] dealt with the relationship of the parole system to sentencing in Canada. In this case, a 17-year-old convent student who worked at a museum was on her way to work when she broke a heel on her shoe. Two youths, one being Wilmott, offered her a ride. She asked to be taken to the museum but was driven into the country and attacked by Wilmott's companion. Wilmott then sexually assaulted the girl. The trial judge imposed a sentence of 12 years' imprisonment, noting that, had it not been for the statutory remission, which allowed for a reduction in the length of a sentence that was

**revocation hearing**

A hearing held before a legally constituted hearing body (such as a parole board) in order to determine whether or not a probationer or parolee has violated the conditions and requirements of his or her probation or parole.

automatically granted after time served, and the operation of the parole system, he would have given Wilmott a sentence of six to eight years. On appeal, it was held that the trial judge "… ought not to have allowed his sentence to be influenced by his conception of the parole system." However, McLennan J.A., in the judgment of the appeal court, makes the following important observation:

> The function of a Court in imposing a sentence of imprisonment and of the Board in reviewing the case of a prisoner for the purpose of granting or refusing parole, in my opinion, cannot be isolated one from the other, but the two functions are part of one process designed and intended by Parliament to be complimentary one to the other in the field of correction. (p.183)

In the case of *Swan* v. *Attorney General of British Columbia*, the court made an effort to move above and beyond the normal approach to parole cases, which Allan Manson has characterized in his annotation to this case as normally "characterized by overly technical and narrow inquiries into the statutory structure of the parole process."[42] This case allowed the judge to examine a decision by the parole board to revoke parole in light of the *Canadian Charter of Rights and Freedoms*, particularly sections 7 and 9, and to reflect on some procedural obligations of the National Parole Board. McEachern C.J.S.C. also dealt with important considerations of fairness and fundamental justice.

A decision to "suspend" parole is typically made by a parolee's parole supervisor. Suspension grants law enforcement authorities the power to arrest and detain the parolee until a decision is made by the parole supervisor to order the offender's subsequent release or recommend that the parole board order reconfinement. The decision to suspend a parolee was subject to a post-suspension hearing at the time of Swan's case. The decision to terminate parole and order the offender be returned to prison is referred to as parole revocation. This decision can only be made by the parole board, and was not subject to review at the time of Swan's case.

In 1977, Swan was sentenced to six years' imprisonment. In 1980, he was released on parole, with the usual reporting requirements. In 1982, there was some confusion about the prisoner's whereabouts, because the parole officer said that he did not know where the parolee was, although Swan indicated that he had provided this information to the parole officer. In November 1982, Swan's parole was suspended by a "warrant of apprehension and suspension of parole." In February 1983, a special report was prepared by the same parole officer noting that this warrant was still outstanding and recommending revocation of parole. This recommendation was supported by the National Parole Board. Swan was eventually arrested on a driving charge and held in custody. At Swan's trial, the judge found that the prisoner was entitled to a hearing with normal "natural justice safeguards" upon the suspension of his parole. The parole board was not justified in providing less "protection" to the prisoner after his parole was revoked, that is, less protection than he would have if he desired a hearing to review the initial decision to suspend his parole. The Court reserved its decision on the release of Swan, pending a post-revocation hearing at which the prisoner would not only be present, but also have an opportunity to understand and answer all matters.

Another interesting parole case is *Howarth* v. *National Parole Board*[43] (1974). Lenard John Howarth was held in close custody in the Joyceville Institution, sentenced in 1969 to a term of seven years for armed robbery. In 1971, he was granted parole and during the academic years 1971–72 and 1972–73, he was enrolled at the Faculty of Social Work, Queen's University. Otherwise, Howarth was gainfully employed during most of the period of his release on parole. However, in August 1973, his parole was suspended and he was arrested on a charge of indecent assault. In September 1972, this charge was withdrawn. Howarth was advised that his parole had been revoked, and the parole board contended that it was under no obligation to enlighten him regarding this revocation, nor to give him an opportunity to be heard. Howarth's appeal was dismissed by the court. In his dissent, Dickson J. offers the following interesting observations:

> The gravity of the impact of revocation upon the rights of a parolee requires no emphasis. Upon revocation he is reincarcerated. He loses the statutory remission standing to his credit at the time of his release on parole (210 days in the case of Mr. Howarth) and gets no credit for time served while on parole (779 days in the case of Mr. Howarth).

In short it does not seem to me that one need not [sic] look far to find within the function of the National Parole Board, having regard to the nature of its duties and the disciplinary effect of its order, identifiable judicial features.[44]

A recently emerging legal issue in the United States relates to the potential liability of probation officers, parole boards, and the boards' representatives for the criminal actions of offenders whom they supervise or have released. Some U.S. courts have held that officers are generally immune from suit because they are performing a judicial function on behalf of the state.[45] Other courts, however, have indicated that parole board members who do not carefully consider mandated criteria for judging parole eligibility could be liable for injurious actions committed by parolees.[46] In general, however, most experts agree that parole board members cannot be successfully sued unless release decisions are made in a grossly negligent or wantonly reckless manner.[47] Discretionary decisions of individual probation and parole officers that result in harm to members of the public, however, may be more actionable under civil law, especially where their decisions were not reviewed by judicial authority.[48] Legislation in Canada endeavours to protect parole board authorities from civil liability.

Parole work in Canada is founded upon a professional relationship with the parole officer's clients (i.e., offenders) including a thorough assessment of the risk factors inherent in each offender's criminal history. Parole officers ensure that offenders follow their "correctional plans" through such things as visits with the offender, with or without warning; meetings with family, police, and/or employers; and discussions with individuals assisting the offender through a program. The parole officer may take disciplinary measures if the offender does not meet the conditions of parole. A disciplinary measure may extend to the point of sending the offender back to prison.

Parole officers must adhere to established rules and standards in the performance of their duties. They are required to prepare reports on the progress of offenders under their supervision and are expected to discuss cases with their own supervisors. Probation officers work closely with many community agencies to assist their clients with issues that will impact their abilities to make the transition back to society. In Canada, an individual parole officer typically carries a caseload of 25 to 30 offenders.

The tasks performed by the probation officer and parole officer are often quite similar. Some jurisdictions combine the roles of both officers into one job. This section describes the duties of both probation and parole officers, whether separate or performed by the same individuals. Probation/parole work consists primarily of four functions: (1) presentence investigations, (2) intake procedures, (3) needs assessment and diagnosis, and (4) the supervision of clients.

Some of the normal duties associated with being a probation and/or parole officer include:[49]

- Interviewing offenders to prepare pre-sentence reports and assess the offender's prospects for successful reintegration into the community;
- Planning rehabilitation programs with offenders, establishing rules of conduct, goals, and objectives;
- Referring offenders to community and social service programs, as required;
- Supervising the terms of a probation order;
- Interviewing probationers and parolees regularly to evaluate their progress in accomplishing goals and maintaining the terms specified in their probation contracts and rehabilitation plans;
- Recommending necessary remedial action or beginning court action when there has been a failure to comply with the terms of probation or parole;
- Interviewing inmates to assess their adjustment problems and to develop appropriate rehabilitation programs;
- Preparing classification reports recommending type of incarceration and the types of interventions considered applicable for the rehabilitation of the inmates;
- Planning rehabilitation programs with offenders, identifying needs and establishing goals and objectives;

- Liaising with the inmate's family and contacts in the community to maintain established links outside of the institution; and

- Advising and counselling inmates regarding their problems and to evaluate individual progress.

Entry requirements for this type of position could include:

- A bachelor's or master's degree in social work, criminology, psychology, or other related social science discipline; and

- For parole officers, several years of experience as a correctional officer and successful completion of a university equivalency test may be substituted for formal educational requirements.

The Canadian Criminal Justice Association, through its Standards and Accreditation Development Committee, developed a series of "manuals of standards" in areas relevant to criminal justice. The manual dealing with parole field services includes a section regarding "personnel and training." It sets out the following standards dealing with parole staff development:[50]

The parole service has policy and standards that specify minimum training and qualifications for every position. The training needs are defined for each position with relation to the following areas:

- Correctional theories and philosophy;

- The legal framework of corrections;

- Correctional programs and resources;

- All policies and procedures applicable to the employee's job description;

- Authority, accountability and responsibilities associated with the employee's position;

- Skills required to work with clients including special groups within the parole service;

- Communication skills; and

- Security.

Where probation is a possibility, an intake procedure may include a pre-sentence investigation (the first function), described in Chapter 9, in which the offender's background is examined in order to provide the sentencing judge with the facts needed to make an informed sentencing decision. An intake procedure may also involve a dispute settlement process, during which the probation officer works with the defendant and victim to resolve the complaint prior to sentencing. Intake duties tend to be more common for juvenile probation officers than they are for probation officers who appear in adult criminal court, but all officers may find themselves in the position of having to recommend to the judge what sentencing alternative would best answer the needs of the case.

Diagnosis (in the third function) refers to the psychological assessment of the probation/parole client, which may be done formally through using written tests administered by certified psychologists, or informally through the observations of the officer. Needs assessment, another area of the probation/parole officer's responsibility, extends beyond the psychological needs of the client to a cataloguing of the services necessary for a client's successful experience on probation or parole.

Supervision of sentenced probationers or released parolees is the most active stage of the probation/parole process, involving months (and sometimes years) of periodic meetings between the officer and client and an ongoing assessment of the success of the probation/parole endeavour in each individual case.

One special consideration affecting the work of all probation/parole officers is the need for confidentiality. The details of the pre-sentence investigation, psychological tests, needs assessment, conversations between the officer and client, and so on should not be public knowledge. On the other hand, courts have generally held that communications between the officer and client are not privileged, as they might be between a doctor and patient. Hence, incriminating evidence related by a client can be shared by officers with the appropriate authorities.

## *Difficulties with the Parole/Probation Officer Job*

Perhaps the biggest difficulty that probation and parole officers face is their need to walk a fine line between two conflicting sets of duties, one of which is to provide quasi social work services and the other of which is to handle custodial responsibilities. In effect, two conflicting images of the officer's role coexist. The social work model stresses a service role for officers and views probationers and parolees as "clients." Officers are seen as "caregivers," who attempt to assess accurately the needs of their clients and, through an intimate familiarity with available community services—from job placement, indigent medical care, and family therapy, to psychological and substance abuse counselling—match clients and community resources. The social work model depicts probation/parole as a "helping profession," wherein officers assist their clients in meeting the conditions imposed upon them by their sentences.

The other model for officers is correctional. It views probation/parole clients as "wards" whom officers are expected to control. This model emphasizes community protection, which officers are supposed to achieve through careful and close supervision. Custodial supervision means that officers will periodically visit their charges at work and at home, often arriving unannounced. It also means that they will be ready and willing to report clients for new offences and for violations of the conditions of their release.

Most officers, by virtue of their personalities and experiences, probably identify more with one of these two models than with the other. They think of themselves either primarily as caregivers or as correctional officers. Regardless of the emphasis that appeals most to individual officers, however, demands of the job are bound to generate role conflict at one time or another.

A second problem in probation/parole work is high caseloads. The U.S. President's Commission on Law Enforcement and the Administration of Justice recommended that the average probation/parole **caseload** should be about 35 clients per officer.[51] However, a caseload of 250 clients is common in some U.S. jurisdictions. Various authors have found that high caseloads, combined with limited training, and time constraints forced by administrative and other demands, culminate in stop-gap supervisory measures.[52] "Postcard probation," in which clients mail in a letter or card once a month to report on their whereabouts and circumstances, is an example of one stop-gap measure that harried agencies with large caseloads use to keep track of their wards. In Canada, on average, an individual parole officer will be responsible for approximately 25 to 30 offenders. However, these caseloads will be significantly lower if the offenders require intensive supervision. Alternatively, these caseloads may be higher if a portion of the day-to-day supervision of the offender is undertaken by a contracted agency such as the John Howard Society or the Salvation Army. The contracted approach to supervision is used extensively in isolated areas in Canada, and Correctional Services Canada uses such contracts to supervise 20 per cent of the 10 000 offenders under its jurisdiction.[53]

Another difficulty with probation/parole work is the lack of opportunity for career mobility.[54] Probation and parole officers are generally assigned to small agencies, serving limited geographical areas, with one or two lead officers (usually called chief probation officers). Unless retirement or death claim the supervisors, there will be little chance for other officers to advance.

**caseload** The number of probation or parole clients assigned to one probation or parole officer for supervision.

# INTERMEDIATE SANCTIONS

Significant new sentencing options have become available to judges in innovative jurisdictions over the past few decades. Many such options are called "intermediate sanctions" because they are sentencing alternatives that fall somewhere between outright imprisonment and simple probationary release back into the community. They are also called "alternative sentencing strategies." Michael J. Russell, former director of the U.S. National Institute of Justice, says that "intermediate punishments are intended to provide prosecutors, judges, and corrections officials with sentencing options that permit them to apply appropriate punishments to convicted offenders while not being constrained by the traditional choice between prison and probation. Rather than substituting for prison or probation, however, these sanctions—which include intensive supervision, house arrest with electronic monitoring, and shock incarceration—bridge the gap between those options and provide innovative ways to ensure swift and certain punishment."[55]

A number of citizen groups and special interest organizations are working to widen the use of sentencing alternatives. One U.S. organization of special note is the Washington, D.C.–based Sentencing Project. The Sentencing Project was formed in 1986 through support from foundation grants. The Project is dedicated to promoting a greater use of alternatives to incarceration and provides technical assistance to public defenders, court officials, and other community organizations. In Canada, there are several jurisdictions that are looking at similar measures, including restorative justice programs that seek to divert offenders from correctional institutions.

The Sentencing Project, and other groups like it, have contributed to the development of over 100 locally based alternative sentencing service programs in the U.S. Most alternative sentencing services work in conjunction with defence lawyers to develop sentencing plans. Such plans include well-considered citizen suggestions as to what appropriate sentencing in a given instance might entail. Plans are often quite detailed, and may include letters of support from employers, family members, the defendant, and even victims. Sentencing plans may be used in plea-bargaining sessions or presented to judges following trial and conviction. A decade ago, for example, U.S. lawyers for country and western singer Willie Nelson successfully proposed an alternative option to tax court officials, which allowed the singer to pay huge past tax liabilities by performing in concerts for that purpose. Lacking such an alternative, the tax court might have seized Nelson's property or even ordered the singer confined to a federal facility.

The basic philosophy behind intermediate sanctions is this: When judges can choose well-planned alternatives to imprisonment, the likelihood of a prison sentence can be reduced. An analysis of alternative sentencing plans such as those sponsored by the Sentencing Project shows that they are accepted by judges in up to 80 per cent of the cases in which they are recommended, and that as many as two-thirds of offenders who receive alternative sentences successfully complete them.[56]

Intermediate, or alternative, sanctions have three distinct advantages:[57] (1) They are less expensive to operate on a per-offender basis than imprisonment; (2) they are "socially cost effective," because they keep the offender in the community, thus avoiding both the breakup of the family and the stigma of imprisonment; and (3) they are flexible in terms of resources, time of involvement (in terms of arranging something like community service to be done at times that will not interfere with the offender's regular employment), and place of service. Some of these new options are described in the paragraphs that follow.

## Split Sentencing

In jurisdictions where a **split sentence** is an option, judges may impose a combination of a brief period of imprisonment and probation. Defendants who receive split sentences are often ordered to serve time in a local jail rather than in a long-term confinement facility. "Ninety days in jail, together with two years of supervised probation" would be a typical split sentence. Split sentences are frequently used with minor drug offenders, and serve notice that continued law violations may result in imprisonment for much longer periods. Section 731(1)(b) of the *Criminal Code* limits the incarceration portion of a split sentence to two years or less, if incarceration is to be followed by supervised probation.

## Shock Probation/Shock Parole

Some American jurisdictions have experimented with **shock probation**, which is very similar to split sentencing. Again, the offender serves a relatively short period of time in custody and is released on probation by court order. The difference is that under shock probation, an offender must *apply* for probationary release from confinement, which may or may not be granted by the court. And in response to this application, the court in effect makes a re-sentencing decision. The reality of probation is that it is only a statutory possibility, and often little more than a vague hope for the offender as imprisonment begins.

**split sentence** A sentence explicitly requiring the convicted person to serve a period of confinement in a local, state, or federal facility followed by a period of probation.

**shock probation** The practice of sentencing offenders to prison, allowing them to apply for probationary release, and enacting such release in surprise fashion. Offenders who receive shock probation may not be aware of the fact that they will be released on probation, and may expect to spend a much longer time behind bars.

If probationary release is ordered, it may well come as a "shock" to the offender who, facing a sudden reprieve, may forswear future criminal involvement. Shock probation was first begun in Ohio in 1965[58] and is used today in about half the United States.[59] Canadian law does not currently permit the use of shock probation.

## Shock Incarceration

**shock incarceration**

A sentencing option that makes use of "boot-camp"–type prisons in order to impress upon convicted offenders the realities of prison life.

**Shock incarceration**, which became quite popular in the U.S. in the 1990s, utilizes military-style "boot-camp" prison settings to provide a highly regimented program involving strict discipline, physical training, and hard labour. Shock incarceration programs are, typically, of short duration, lasting for only 90 to 180 days. Offenders who successfully complete these programs are generally placed under community supervision. Program "failures" may be moved into the general prison population for longer terms of confinement. A study of these types of programs was undertaken by the Ontario Ministry of the Solicitor General and Correctional Services in 1996.[60]

In the United States, the first shock incarceration program began in Georgia in 1983.[61] Since then, other programs have opened in Alabama, Arkansas, Arizona, Florida, Louisiana, Maryland, Michigan, Mississippi, New Hampshire, New York, Oklahoma, South Carolina, Texas, Massachusetts, and other states. New York's program is the largest, with capacity for 1602 participants, while Tennessee's program can handle only 102. About half of the programs provide for voluntary entry. A few allow inmates to decide when and whether they want to quit. Although most U.S. jurisdictions allow judges to place offenders into such programs, some delegate that authority to corrections officials. In two U.S. jurisdictions, Louisiana and Texas, judges and corrections personnel have joint authority in the decision-making process. Some jurisdictions, such as Massachusetts, have begun to accept some specific female inmates into boot-camp settings. The Massachusetts program, which first accepted women in 1993, requires female inmates to undergo nearly four months of pre-program training.

The most comprehensive study of boot-camp prison programs to date examined shock incarceration programs in eight U.S. jurisdictions: Florida, Georgia, Illinois, Louisiana, New York, Oklahoma, South Carolina, and Texas. The report,[62] which was issued in 1995, found that boot-camp programs were especially popular because "they are perceived as being tough on crime," and "have been enthusiastically embraced as a viable correctional option." The report concluded, however, that "the impact of boot camp programs on offender recidivism is at best negligible." A U.S. national study, focusing on the correctional treatment of juvenile offenders, compared 27 boot camps to 22 traditional institutions.[63] The study's findings were reported in 2001:

- Despite their growth in popularity in the 1990s, correctional boot camps remain controversial. Critics question whether their military-style methods are appropriate to managing and treating juvenile delinquents and whether these methods positively affect juvenile behaviour while the delinquents are confined and after their release. Boot-camp advocates contend that the facilities' program structure gives staff more control over the participants and provides the juveniles with a safer environment than do traditional facilities.

- Juvenile boot camps more frequently report positive responses to their institutional environments than do institutions providing more traditional settings. Boot-camp juveniles said they were better prepared for release, were given more therapeutic programming, experienced more structure and control, and were more active than were youths in traditional facilities. The one exception was that boot-camp youths were more likely to report feeling that they were in danger from the staff.

- Staff in boot camps more frequently reported favourable perceptions of their institutional environments, where the perceptions involved a caring and just environment and more structure and control, than did staff in traditional facilities. Boot-camp staff also more frequently reported favourable working conditions, such as less personal stress and better communication among staff.

- Initial levels of anxiety were slightly higher for boot-camp participants; initial levels of depression were higher for juveniles in traditional facilities. Anxiety and

A boot camp in Barrie, Ontario. Shock incarceration utilizes military-style "boot-camp" prison settings to provide programs for young, first offenders that involve strict discipline, physical training, and hard labour.

depression decreased over time for juveniles in both facilities. Social bonding with family, school, and work decreased for juveniles in both types of facilities while they were institutionalized.

- In general, boot camps were more selective about the juveniles admitted to the facility than were traditional institutions. Boot camps admitted fewer juveniles who had psychological problems or were suicide risks, and the boot camps required psychological, medical, and physical evaluations before allowing juveniles to enter. In 25 per cent of the boot camps studied, participants had to volunteer to enter the program.

In Canada, Ontario has taken a step towards the introduction of this approach. The "strict discipline" program for young offenders was introduced by the Solicitor General and Minister of Correctional Services in 1996 as a result of recommendations from a task force. The main objective of the program is to enhance community safety by reducing the reoffence rate of young persons. This type of program features an intensive, highly structured routine that includes work sessions, self-discipline, life skills, and academic elements. Selected young offenders serve an initial sentence in a secure-custody primary facility. This is followed by a session in an open-custody secondary facility.

The first secure-custody facility in Ontario is known as Project Turnaround and is located on the site of a former correctional centre in Medonte Township near Barrie. Figure 10–4 details the "strict and structured regime" that characterizes a proposed new approach to young offender behaviour management and compares it with the present system in place.

More limited studies, such as one that focused on shock incarceration in New York state, have found that boot-camp programs save money in two ways: "first by reducing expenditures for care and custody" (since the intensive programs reduce time spent in custody, and participation in them is the only way New York inmates can be released from prison before their minimum parole eligibility dates) and "second, by avoiding capital costs for new prison construction."[64] A 1995 study of Oregon's Summit boot-camp program reached a similar conclusion. Although they did not study recidivism, Oregon researchers found that "the Summit boot camp program is a cost-effective means of reducing prison overcrowding by treating and releasing specially selected inmates earlier than their court-determined minimum period of incarceration."[65]

**FIGURE 10–4** Present System at Project Turnaround and the New Stricter Regime

| Present System | Strict and Structured Regime |
|---|---|
| **7:00 a.m. to 1:00 p.m.** | **6:45 a.m. to 1:00 p.m.** |
| • wake-up call | • lights on, wake up, chores assigned |
| • second wake-up call | • beds made to standard |
| • get up | • breakfast, hygiene parade |
| • shower, get ready for breakfast | • breakfast inspection |
| • breakfast | • study time, get ready for school |
| • tidy up bunk/cell area | • dress code in effect, school or work |
| • free time | • school over for morning |
| • telephone, TV, rest | • lunch, hygiene parade |
| • morning school program, if enrolled | • midday inspection |
| • school over from morning | • recreation, if earned |
| • TV, get ready for lunch | • no electronic video games |
| • eat lunch, get ready for recreation | • no unearned privileges |
| • young offenders go for recreation | |
| | |
| **1:00 p.m. to 7:00 p.m.** | **1:00 p.m. to 7:00 p.m.** |
| • afternoon school, if enrolled | • school or work, dress code in effect |
| • after-school free time | • special privileges only if earned |
| • TV, video games | • supper |
| • board games, cards, telephone, ping pong, pool table | • supper inspection |
| • supper | • recreation or programs if earned |
| • recreation or programs start | • mandatory homework period |
| | • no electronic video games, no unearned privileges |
| | |
| **7:00 p.m. to 11:00 p.m.** | **7:00 p.m. to 11:00 p.m.** |
| • evening programs | • evening programs if earned |
| • TV, Nintendo, board games, cards, telephone, ping pong, pool table | • special privileges only if earned |
| • free time | • evening snack, evening chores assigned |
| • evening snack | • end of day inspection |
| • unit lockup/bedtime, lights out | • unit lockup/bedtime per standing on incentive day |
| | • lights out, no electronic games, no unearned privileges |

Source: Ontario Ministry of the Solicitor General and Correctional Services. (1998). Present System at Project Turnaround and the New Stricter Regime. *Backgrounder: Strict and Structured Regime* (Toronto: MSGCS, 1998), p.4. Courtesy of the Ontario Ministry of the Solicitor General and Correctional Services.

## Intermittent Sentencing and Community Service

**intermittent sentence**
One which requires that a convicted offender serve weekends (or other specified periods of time) in a confinement facility, while undergoing probation supervision in the community.

An **intermittent sentence** requires that an offender serve weekends in jail and receive probation supervision during the week. The *Criminal Code* mandates that such a sentence not exceed 90 days of incarceration.[66] Such a sentence has the advantage of allowing an offender to continue working or to attend vocational training, while allowing the court to send a strong denunciatory message in the form of genuine jail time. A problem with the extensive use of intermittent sentencing is the overcrowding that can occur in prisons during weekends, which disrupts prison staff schedules.

# Intensive Supervision

**Intensive probation supervision** (IPS) has achieved considerable attention in the United States, where it was first implemented by Georgia in 1982. It has been described as the "strictest form of probation for adults in the United States."[67] The Georgia program involves a minimum of five face-to-face contacts between the probationer and supervising officer per week, mandatory curfew, required employment, a weekly check of local arrest records, routine and unannounced alcohol and drug testing, 132 hours of community service, and automatic notification of probation officers via the State Crime Information Network whenever an IPS client is arrested.[68] The average IPS caseload is much lower than the national average. Georgia officers work as a team with one probation officer and two surveillance officers supervising approximately 40 probationers.[69] IPS is designed to achieve control in a community setting over offenders who would otherwise have gone to prison.

North Carolina's Intensive Supervision Program follows the model of the Georgia program and adds a mandatory "prison awareness visit" within the first three months of supervision. North Carolina selects candidates for the Intensive Supervision Program on the basis of six factors: (1) the level of risk the offender is deemed to represent to the community; (2) assessment of the candidate's potential to respond to the program; (3) existing community attitudes towards the offender; (4) the nature and extent of known substance abuse; (5) the presence or absence of favourable community conditions, such as positive family ties, the possibility of continuing meaningful employment, constructive leisure-time activities, and adequate residence; and (6) the availability of community resources relevant to the needs of the case (such as drug treatment services, mental health programs, vocational training facilities, and volunteer services).[70] Some jurisdictions have extended intensive supervision to parolees, allowing the early release of some who would otherwise serve lengthy prison terms.

# Home Confinement and Electronic Monitoring

**Home confinement**, also referred to as house arrest, has been defined as "a sentence imposed by the court in which offenders are legally ordered to remain confined in their own residences."[71] These offenders may leave only to attend to medical emergencies, go to their jobs, or buy household essentials. House arrest has been cited as offering a valuable alternative to prison for offenders with special needs. However, not everyone believes house arrest is a suitable alternative to prison. David Daubney, the current General Counsel of the Canadian Department of Justice's Sentencing Reform Team, chaired a Parliamentary standing committee on justice and the solicitor general in the mid-1980s. This committee was charged with reviewing sentencing, conditional release, and related aspects of corrections, and published a report on sentencing reform in 1988. The Daubney Committee was not convinced that house arrest would be successfully in getting offenders to accept responsibility for their behaviour.[72] Yet pregnant women, geriatric convicts, offenders with special disabilities, seriously or terminally ill offenders, and people with developmental disabilities might all be more appropriately supervised through home confinement than through traditional incarceration.

Alberta requires that offenders placed in their house-arrest program complete community service work. Known as the Community Surveillance Supervision program, it allows offenders to serve their sentences while remaining in the community.[73] Saskatchewan Corrections developed its Intensive Supervision/Electronic Monitoring Program in order to manage offenders in the community. Newfoundland and Labrador have formulated the framework for a Monitored Conditional Release Program that would release low-risk/high-need offenders from secure custody in order for them to participate in community-based programs.[74]

Florida's Community Control Program, authorized by the state's *Correctional Reform Act* of 1983, is the most ambitious home-confinement program in the United States.[75] On any given day in Florida as many as 5000 offenders are restricted to their homes and supervised by community control officers who visit unannounced. Candidates for the program are required to agree to specific conditions, including (1) restitution, (2) family support payments, and (3) supervisory fees (around $50 per month). Offenders in this program must

**intensive probation supervision** A form of probation supervision involving frequent face-to-face contacts between the probationary client and probation officers.

**home confinement** House arrest. Individuals ordered confined to their homes are sometimes monitored electronically to be sure they do not leave during the hours of confinement (absence from the home during working hours is often permitted).

Commonly called "house arrest," the electronic monitoring of convicted offenders appears to have the capacity to dramatically reduce correctional costs for nondangerous offenders.

also complete daily logs about their activities. Community control officers have a minimum of 20 contacts per month with each offender. The officer also talks with the offender's neighbours, spouses, friends, landlords, employers, and others in order to detect the signs of possible program violations or renewed criminality.

Florida's most serious home-confinement offenders are monitored via a computerized system of *electronic bracelets*. When an offender receives a telephone call from an officer, the offender inserts a computer chip, worn in a wristband, into a specially installed modem in the home, verifying his or her presence. (The telephone calls are random.) More modern units make it possible to record the time a supervised person enters or leaves the home, to tell whether the phone line or equipment has been tampered with, and to send or receive messages.[76] Electronic monitoring of offenders has undergone dramatic growth both in Florida and across the United States. A survey by the National Institute of Justice in mid-1987,[77] just as the use of electronic monitoring was beginning, showed only 826 offenders being monitored electronically. By 1989, only two years later, the number had jumped to around 6500, while by the end of 1997, it stood at 21 375.[78] Of these offenders, 15 373 were serving probationary sentences, and 6002 were parolees. In Canada, the impact of overcrowding has led to the serious consideration of electronic monitoring.[79]

The estimated cost of electronic monitoring is approximately $47 per day for each offender in Canada. In British Columbia, the electronic monitoring program was originally intended to monitor offenders who were required to serve drinking-and-driving sentences intermittently on weekends. Presently, the program may be used for any adult offender who is serving a continuous sentence and who meets the following criteria:[80]

- Poses no threat to the community;
- Has no pattern of violence in his or her history;
- Is serving a short (i.e., four months or less) sentence, or is nearing the end of a longer sentence;
- Is willing to obey the rules of the program and accept its restrictions;
- Is suitable in terms of his or her home situation; and
- Has a good reason for staying in the community (e.g., job, schooling, treatment program, or child-care obligations).

In British Columbia, the B.C. Corrections Branch or the sentencing judge can make recommendations for electronic monitoring; however, the final decision remains with the Corrections Branch.[81]

Many jurisdictions in the United States view house arrest as a cost-effective response to the rising expense of imprisonment. Estimates show that traditional home confinement programs cost about US$1500 to US$7000 per offender per year, while electronic monitoring increases the costs by at least US$1000.[82] Advocates of house arrest argue that it is also socially cost-effective, as it provides no opportunity for the kinds of negative socialization that occur in prison. Opponents have pointed out that house arrest may endanger the public, that it may be illegal,[83] and that it may provide little or no punishment.

As prison populations continue to rise, some suggest that alternative sentencing strategies will become increasingly attractive. Many questions remain to be answered, however, before most alternative sanctions can be employed with confidence. Joan Petersilia has succinctly phrased these questions in a Rand Corporation study[84] as follows:

- Do alternative sentencing programs threaten public safety?

- How should program participants be selected?

- What are the long-term effects of community sanctions on people assigned to them?

- Are alternative sanctions cost-effective?

- Who should pay for alternative sanctions?

- Who should manage stringent community-based sanctions?

- How should program outcomes be judged?

- What kinds of offenders benefit most from alternative sanctions?

  Unfortunately, few definitive answers to these questions are yet available.


# THE FUTURE OF PROBATION AND PAROLE

Parole has been widely criticized in recent years. Citizen groups claim that it unfairly reduces prison sentences imposed on serious offenders. Academics allege that parole programs can provide no assurance that criminals will not commit further crimes. Media attacks upon parole have centred on recidivism and have highlighted the so-called "revolving prison door" as representative of the failure of parole.

In 1990, the case of Robert Owens caused a great deal of controversy in British Columbia. Owens was a convicted pedophile who had been released from the federal Mountain Institution in Agassiz, B.C., and had gone to live in a quiet North Vancouver neighbourhood. Once news of Owens' presence became known, residents of the community held rallies and mounted letter-writing campaigns to their local MLAs. Fear for the safety of their children was the key motivating factor behind the reaction to Owens and his presence in their midst.

An article dealing with this case[85] points out the dilemma within the criminal justice system. If, as a sexual offender, Owens had been released from prison under the supervision of a probation officer, the fears of the community might not have been so strong. However, prisoners like Owens, who are at the greatest risk of reoffending, are somehow able to slip through the cracks. Because they do not qualify for parole and the attached restrictions, they are able to move into any community once their sentences have been served, and pose a potential threat. Unlike the approximately 80 per cent[86] of sexual predators who qualify for parole, Owens was not successful because he failed to receive any program of treatment approved by the parole board. In 1994, the provincial parole board confirmed Owens' detention because it believed that he would commit some offence causing serious harm or death before the end of this sentence. Of course, at the end of his sentence, Owens had to be released into the community. In spite of the fact that he has been described as a "regressed pedophile with a specific sexual arousal to prepubescent females" who remained at risk of reoffending, Owens was essentially a free man. Eventually and of his own accord, he left the North Vancouver area that had lobbied so hard to have him removed, but the issue remains unresolved.

Official attacks upon parole have come from some powerful corners. Parolees have complained about the unpredictable nature of the parole experience, citing their powerlessness in the parole contract. Against the pressure of official attacks and despite cases like that of Owens, parole advocates struggle to clarify and communicate the value of parole in the correctional process.

As more and more jurisdictions move towards the elimination of parole, other voices call for moderation. Since most offenders will eventually regain their freedom, we need to ask ourselves whether we want individuals who have been detained in prison for lengthy periods to return to the streets "cold turkey," or would we prefer some model of gradual reintegration under supervision? A 1995 report concluded that those U.S. jurisdictions that have eliminated parole "have jeopardized public safety and wasted tax dollars." In the words of the report, "Getting rid of parole dismantles an accountable system of releasing prisoners back into the community and replaces it with a system that bases release decisions solely on whether a prison term has been completed."[87]

Probation, although it has generally fared better than parole, is not without its critics. The primary purpose of probation has always been rehabilitation. Probation is a powerful rehabilitative tool because, at least in theory, it allows the resources of a community to be focused on the offender. Unfortunately for advocates of probation, however, the rehabilitative ideal holds far less significance today than it has in the past. The contemporary demand for "just deserts" appears to have reduced the tolerance society feels for even relatively minor offenders. Probation advocates themselves have been forced to admit that probation is not a very powerful deterrent because it is far less punishing than a term of imprisonment. Arguments in support of probation have been weakened because some of the positive contributions probation had to offer are now available from other sources. Victims' compensation programs, for example, have taken the place of probationers' direct restitution payments to victims.

Acknowledging the complexities of the present situation, Vincent O'Leary has identified six trends that are bound to affect the future of both probation and parole:[88]

1. Increasing pressure to ensure that community supervision reflects the goals that society has established for the handling of offenders;

2. The acknowledgment of risk control as an important function of the criminal justice system and the need to recognize that errors can be made in assessing risks;

3. The increased use of a variety of supervisory methods and variation in the size of caseloads supervised by one officer;

4. Clarification of the process by which offenders are moved from one level of supervision to another;

5. Greater emphasis on the accountability of individual officers as to the specific behavioural objectives to be achieved in working with clients; and

6. Creation of information systems useful in judging effectiveness and in providing feedback on specific supervisory practices.

Probation will probably always remain a viable sentencing option if only because there will always be minor offenders for whom imprisonment is hard to justify. The limited space available in our nation's prisons will also probably work in favour of parole and other forms of conditional release. The relatively new community disposition of conditional sentencing offers considerable promise for the future. Conditional sentencing avoids many of the pitfalls of probation without the costly and debilitating effects of incarceration. If combined with house arrest, and where the offender can be monitored by electronic supervision, conditional sentencing provides a rational alternative to incarceration in many cases.

# SUMMARY

Probation, conditional sentencing, and parole are three of the most recent large-scale innovations in the long history of correctional supervision. Each can be viewed as either a blessing or a curse, depending upon which of their attributes are emphasized. All three provide opportunities for the reintegration of offenders into the community, or the maintenance of offenders in the community, through the use of resources not readily available in institutional settings. Unfortunately, however, increased freedom for criminal offenders also means some degree of increased risk for other members of society. Until and unless these alternatives solve the problems of accurate risk assessment, reduced recidivism, and adequate supervision, they will continue to be viewed with suspicion by clients and citizenry alike.

# DISCUSSION QUESTIONS

1. Probation is a sentence served while under supervision in the community. Do you believe that a person who commits a crime should be allowed to serve all or part of his or her sentence in the community? If so, what conditions would you impose on the offender?

2. Can you think of any other "general conditions" of probation or parole that you might add to the list of those found in the *Criminal Code* in this chapter? If so, what would they be? Why would you want to add them?

3. Do you believe that ordering an offender to make restitution to his or her victim will teach the offender to be a more responsible person? Support your opinion.

4. Do you believe that "role conflict" is a real part of most probation and parole officer's jobs? If so, do you see any way to reduce the role conflict experienced by probation and parole officers? How might you do it?

5. Do you think home confinement is a good idea? What do you think is the future of home confinement? In your opinion, does it discriminate against certain kinds of offenders? How might it be improved?

# WEBLINKS

www.operb.gov.on.ca
**Ontario Parole and Earned Release Board**
The Ontario Parole and Early Release Board is the agency responsible for the early release of inmates into the community from provincial institutions in that province.

www.msp.gouv.qc.ca/reinsertion/reinsertion_en.asp?ndn=03&txtSection=commqueb
**The commission québécois des libérations conditionelles**
The Quebec Parole Board is responsible for the conditional release of inmates from provincial institutions in the province of Quebec.

www.csc-scc.gc.ca/text/faits/facts07_e.shtml
**Basic Facts about Federal Corrections**
A publication by the Correctional Service of Canada.

www.johnhoward.ca
**John Howard Society of Canada**
The John Howard Society of Canada is an organization of provincial and territorial societies whose goal is to understand and respond to problems of crime and the criminal justice system, through research, advocacy, community education, and coalition building.

www.npb-cnlc.gc.ca
**National Parole Board**
Canada's National Parole Board, as part of the criminal justice system, makes independent decisions on conditional release and pardons. In addition, it makes clemency recommendations.

www.gov.bc.ca/bcparole
**Board of Parole for the Province of British Columbia**
The government agency in B.C. responsible for conditional release of inmates from provincial institutions.

# Correctional Institutions

Myrleen Ferguson Cate/Photo Edit Inc.

## KEY CONCEPTS

| | | |
|---|---|---|
| prison | work release | design capacity |
| Pennsylvania style | recidivism | dissociation |
| Auburn system | warehousing | direct supervision |
| medical model | nothing works doctrine | |
| community-based corrections | rated capacity | |
| | operational capacity | |

**prison** A state or federal confinement facility having custodial authority over adults sentenced to varying terms of confinement.

# EARLY PUNISHMENTS

In the history of criminal justice, the current era may be remembered as the time of imprisonment. Prior to the development of the **prison**, early punishments were often cruel and torturous. An example is found in the graphic and unsettling description of a man broken on the rack in 1721, which is provided by Camden Pelham in his *Chronicles of Crime*.[1] The offender, Nathaniel Hawes, a domestic servant in the household of a wealthy nobleman, had stolen a sheep in order to entertain a woman friend. When the "overseer" of the household discovered the offence, Hawes "shot him dead." Pelham's description of what happened next follows: "For these offences, of course, he was sentenced to be broken alive upon the rack, without the benefit of the *coup de grace*, or mercy-stroke. Informed of the dreadful sentence, he composedly laid himself down upon his back on a strong cross, on which, with his arms and legs extended, he was fastened by ropes. The executioner, having by now with a hatchet chopped off his left hand, next took up a heavy iron bar, with which, by repeated blows, he broke his bones to shivers, till the marrow, blood, and splinters flew about the field; but the prisoner never uttered a groan nor a sigh! The ropes being next unlashed, I imagined him dead … till … he writhed himself from the cross. When he fell on the grass … he rested his head on part of the timbar, and asked the by-standers for a pipe of tobacco, which was infamously answered by kicking and spitting on him. He then begged his head might be chopped off, but to no purpose." Pelham goes on to relate how the condemned man then engaged in conversation with onlookers, recounting details of his trial. At one point, he asked one of those present to repay money he had loaned him, saying, "Don't you perceive, I am to be kept alive." After six hours, Pelham says, Hawes was put out of his misery by a soldier assigned to guard the proceedings. "He was knocked on the head by the … sentinel; and having been raised upon a gallows, the vultures were busy picking out the eyes of the mangled corpse, in the skull of which was clearly discernible the mark of the soldier's musket."

This gruesome tale may seem foreign to modern readers—as though it describes an event that happened in a barbarous time long ago, or in a place far away. However, physical punishments, often resulting in death, were commonplace a mere 200 years ago. Today, when we think of criminal punishment, we routinely think of prisons. We tend to forget that prisons, as correctional institutions, are relatively new. Prior to the emergence of imprisonment, convicted offenders were routinely subjected to fines, physical punishment, and often death. Corporal punishment was the most common form of criminal punishment, and generally fit the doctrine of *lex talionis* (the law of retaliation: "an eye for an eye, and a tooth for a tooth"). Under *lex talionis*, the convicted offender was sentenced to suffer a punishment that was very much like the original injury. Hence, if a person blinded another, he or she was blinded in return. Murderers were themselves killed, with the form of execution sometimes being tailored to fit the method the murderer had used in committing the crime. The short story by Franz Kafka entitled *In the Penal Colony* provides a brutally graphic extension of the notion of making the punishment fit the crime, aided by the frightening efficiency of technology.[2]

## Flogging

Historically, the most widely applied physical punishment was flogging.[3] The Bible mentions instances of whipping, and Christ was himself scourged. Whipping was widely used in England throughout the Middle Ages, and some offenders were said to have been beaten as they ran through streets and towns, hands tied behind their backs. English colonists carried the practice of flogging with them to Canada. The first *Criminal Code* passed in Canada in 1892 prescribed punishment by whipping for a variety of offences. Even in the 1950s, whipping was available for the following offences under the *Criminal Code*:

- Assault on the sovereign: 7 years' imprisonment plus whipping

- Strangling to commit an indictable offence: life imprisonment plus whipping

- Indecent assault on a female, wife beating, beating a female: 2 years' imprisonment plus whipping

- Rape: death, or life imprisonment with or without whipping
- Attempts to commit rape: 7 years' imprisonment plus whipping
- Carnal knowledge of a girl under 14 years of age: 2 years' imprisonment plus whipping
- Attempt to have carnal knowledge of a girl under 14: 2 years' imprisonment plus whipping
- Indecent assault on a male: 10 years' imprisonment plus whipping
- Burglary while armed with an offensive weapon: life imprisonment plus whipping
- Assault with intent to rob: 3 years' imprisonment plus whipping

Initially, the cat-o'-nine tails was used for whipping. The cat-o'-nine tails was made of at least nine strands of leather or rope instead of the single strip of leather, which makes up most modern-day whips. Eventually, a strap or paddle came to be used as the preferred instrument for the infliction of corporal punishment in Canadian prisons. In 1954, whipping was removed as a penalty for "assault on the sovereign," "acts of gross indecency," and "assaults on wife or other females." However, it was retained and used for other offences, particularly rape offences, and to maintain prison discipline until 1968. Corporal punishment was formally abolished in Canadian penitentiaries in 1972.[4]

The practice of whipping, however, is still with us elsewhere in the world. Amnesty International reports its use in various parts of the world for political and other prisoners. In 1994, the flogging in Singapore of Michael Fay, an American teenager convicted of spray-painting parked cars, caused an international outcry from opponents of corporal punishment. The Fay flogging (called "caning" in Singapore, because it was carried out with a bamboo rod) led to a rebirth of interest in physical sanctions in this country, especially for teenagers and vandals. In recent years, the use of corporal punishment by parents and teachers, rather than the criminal justice system, has drawn attention from our courts.

In 2000, the Ontario Superior Court of Justice ruled in *Youth and the Law* v. *Canada (Attorney General)* that the *Criminal Code* provision (s. 43) allowing the use of "force by way of correction" by school teachers, parents, and individuals standing in the place of a parent to be constitutionally valid. Parents and teachers must be granted the authority for a "limited domain of physical discipline" to carry out their responsibilities over children. The Court viewed the legislation as striking the correct balance between protecting children from child abuse and protecting parents from unwarranted criminal prosecution for assault.

However, in 2002 in *R.* v. *Poulin*, the Prince Edward Island Supreme Court found that a woman who cared for children in a residential centre, while standing in the place of the parents of child residents, could not avail herself of the protection offered by section 43 of the *Criminal Code*. The woman had used a rod to discipline a number of children under her care. The Court ruled that the force used must be objectively reasonable, and on the facts of the case, the level and frequency of the use of force was excessive and unreasonable.[5] Canada has not introduced any legislation authorizing the use of corporal punishment as a mode of punishment in the criminal justice system.

# Mutilation

Flogging is a painful punishment, so much so that the memory of having received it might deter repeat offences. Mutilation, on the other hand, was primarily a strategy of specific deterrence that made it difficult or impossible for individuals to commit future crimes. Throughout history, various societies have amputated the hands of thieves and robbers, blinded spies, and castrated rapists. Blasphemers have had their tongues ripped out, and pickpockets have suffered broken fingers. Extensive mutilation, which included blinding, cutting off the ears, and ripping out the tongue, was instituted in eleventh-century Britain and imposed upon hunters who poached on royal lands.[6]

Today, some countries in the Arab world, including Iran and Saudi Arabia, still rely upon the limited use of mutilation as a penalty to incapacitate selected offenders. Mutilation also creates a general deterrent by providing potential offenders with walking examples of the consequences of crime.

# Branding

In some societies, branding has been used as a lesser form of mutilation. Prior to modern technology and mechanized record keeping, branding served to readily identify convicted offenders and to warn others, with whom they might come into contact, of their dangerous potential.

The Romans, Greeks, French, British, and many other societies have all used branding at one time or another. In France, in the early 1800s, the skin of prisoners condemned to forced labour often carried the letter "T" (for *travaux forcés*) while thieves would be marked with the letter "V" (for *voleur*).[7] It was not until 1829 that the British Parliament officially eliminated branding as a punishment for crime, although the practice had probably ended somewhat earlier.

Barnes and Teeters, early writers on the history of the criminal justice system, report that branding in the American colonies was customary for certain crimes, with first offenders being branded on the hand and repeat offenders receiving an identifying mark on the forehead.[8] Women were rarely marked physically, although they may have been shamed and forced to wear marked clothing. Nathaniel Hawthorne's story of *The Scarlet Letter* describes that practice, where the central figure is required to wear a red letter "A," embroidered on her dress, signifying adultery.

# Public Humiliation

A number of early punishments were designed to humiliate offenders in public, and to allow members of the community an opportunity for vengeance. The stocks and pillory were two such punishments. The pillory closed over the head and hands and held the offender in a standing position, while the stocks kept the person sitting with the head free. A few hundred years ago, each town had its own stocks or pillory, usually located in some central square or alongside a major thoroughfare.

Offenders sent to the stocks or pillory found themselves captive and on public display. They could expect to be heckled and spit upon by passersby. Other citizens might gather to throw tomatoes or rotten eggs. On occasion, citizens who were particularly outraged by the magnitude or nature of the offence would substitute rocks for other less lethal missiles and end the offender's life. Retribution remained a community prerogative, and citizens wielded the power of final sentencing. The pillory was still used in Prince Edward Island as late as 1876.[9]

The brank and ducking stool provided other forms of public humiliation. The brank was like a bird cage and it was fit over the offender's head. On the brank was a small door that, when closed, caused a razor-sharp blade to be inserted into the mouth. The ducking stool looked like a see-saw. The offender was tied to it and lowered into a river or lake, turning him or her nearly upside down in the water. Both devices were used in colonial times to punish gossips and were designed to fit that crime by teaching the offender to keep a shut mouth or a still tongue.

# Workhouses

The sixteenth century was a time of economic upheaval in Europe, caused partly by wars but also by the stirrings of the industrial revolution, which would soon sweep the continent. By mid-century, thousands of unemployed and vagrant people were scouring towns and villages, seeking food and shelter. It was not long before they depleted the financial reserves of churches, which were the primary social relief agencies of the time.

In the belief that poverty was caused by idleness, governments were quick to create workhouses designed to instill "habits of industry" in the unemployed. The first workhouse in Europe opened in 1557 in a former British palace called Saint Bridget's Well. The name was shortened to "Brideswell," and brideswells became a synonym for workhouses. Brideswells taught work habits, not specific skills. Inmates were made to fashion their own furniture, build additions to the facility, and raise gardens. When the number of inmates exceeded the volume of useful work to be done, "make-work" projects, including building treadmills and cranks, were invented to keep them busy.

Workhouses were judged successful, if only because they were constantly filled. By 1576, the British Parliament decreed that every county in England should build a workhouse. Although workhouses were forerunners of our modern prisons, criminal offenders were not incarcerated in them—only vagrants and the economically disadvantaged. Nor were they designed to punish convicts, but served instead to reinforce the value of hard work. The first workhouse in Nova Scotia was constructed in 1754.[10]

## Exile

The ancient Hebrews periodically forced a sacrificial goat, symbolically carrying the tribe's sins, into the wilderness, a practice that has given us the modern word "scapegoating." Since then, many societies have banished "sinners" directly. The French sent criminal offenders to Devil's Island, and the Russians used Siberia for centuries for the same purpose.[11]

England sent convicts to the American colonies beginning in 1618. The British program of exile, known as "transportation," served the dual purpose of providing a captive labour force for the development of the colonies while assuaging growing English opposition to corporal punishments. In 1776, however, the American Revolution forced the practice to end, and British penology shifted to using aging ships, called hulks, as temporary prisons. Hulks were anchored in harbours throughout England and served as floating confinement facilities even after transportation (to other parts of the globe) resumed.[12]

In 1787, only 17 years after Captain Cook had discovered the continent, Australia became the new port of call for English prisoners. The name of Captain William Bligh, governor of the New South Wales penal colony, survives to the present day as a symbol of the difficult conditions and rough men and women of those times.

## The Emergence of Prisons

The identity of the world's first true prison may never be known, but we do know that at some point, penalties for crime came to include incarceration. During the Middle Ages, "punitive imprisonment appears to have been introduced into Europe … by the Christian Church in the incarceration of certain offenders against canon law."[13] Similarly, debtors' prisons existed throughout Europe during the 1400s and 1500s, although they housed inmates who had violated the civil law rather than criminals. John Howard, an early prison reformer, mentions prisons that housed criminal offenders in Hamburg, Germany; Berne, Switzerland; and Florence, Italy, in his 1777 book, *State of Prisons*. As J. Semple points out, Howard's work was extremely important because it provided:

> … a vast compendium in which information was systematically set out and facts and figures were carefully tabulated to enable comparisons to be made between different gaols in different counties. Howard was the harbinger of social science.[14]

Some early efforts to imprison offenders are reflected in the Hospice of San Michele, a papal prison that opened in 1704, and the Maison de Force, begun at Ghent, Belgium, in 1773. The Hospice was actually a residential school for delinquent boys and housed 60 youngsters at its opening. Both facilities stressed reformation over punishment, and their services were early alternatives to physical and public punishments.[15]

Well-known British moral and political philosopher Jeremy Bentham contributed substantially to what may be called the "philosophy" of prisons, in his fascinating panopticon writings.[16] Originally produced as a series of letters written between 1787 and 1791, this work provides substantial detail on a complex plan for the construction of a model prison. Furthermore, they offer an insight into Bentham's theory of power. Semple provides a thorough examination of Bentham's lifelong campaign to have his panopticon model put into practice and reveals the importance of his thinking in many subsequent designs for penal institutions.[17] Semple notes that Michel Foucault placed Bentham's panopticon at the centre of his interpretation of penal history:

In his [Foucault's] thesis Bentham's panopticon is the prototype of a sinister instrument in this new physics of power making possible a furtive exercise of authority to control and subjugate.[18]

Bentham's panopticon writings, even though underestimated for a considerable period, offer an interesting focus for research in prison theory and design.[19] Bentham's ideas are evident in such institutions as the Western Penitentiary in Pittsburgh (built between 1820 and 1826), and the Stateville Penitentiary, constructed in 1916 in Joliet, near Chicago.[20] Indeed, Semple points out that modern historians have taken Bentham's ideas more seriously in terms of their impact on penal history.[21]

Near the end of the eighteenth century, the concept of imprisonment as punishment for crime reached its fullest expression in the United States. Soon after they opened, U.S. prisons came to serve as models for European reformers searching for ways to humanize criminal punishment. For that reason, and in order to better appreciate how today's prisons operate, it is important to understand the historical development of the prison movement in the United States. Table 11–1 depicts the stages through which Canadian prisons progressed following introduction of the concept of incarceration as a punishment for crime in the 1830s.

## The American Influence

In 1790, Philadelphia's Walnut Street Jail was converted into a penitentiary by the Pennsylvania Quakers. The Quakers, following the legacy of William Penn, intended to introduce religious and humane principles into the treatment of offenders. They saw in prisons the opportunity for penance—and viewed them as places wherein offenders might make amends to society and accept responsibility for their misdeeds. The philosophy of imprisonment begun by the Quakers, heavily imbued with elements of both rehabilitation and deterrence, carries over to the present day.[22]

Inmates of the Philadelphia Penitentiary were held in solitary confinement and were expected to wrestle with the evils they harboured. Penance was the primary vehicle through which rehabilitation was anticipated, and Bible study was strongly encouraged. Solitary

### TABLE 11–1 Evolution of Prisons in Canada

| Time Period | Era | Major Developments |
|---|---|---|
| 1830s–1867 | Pre-Confederation punishment era | Gradual shift from physical punishments towards the use of incarceration as punishment begins. Workhouses exist, the penitentiary is "born," and local prisons are built. |
| 1867–1900s | Post-Confederation punishment era | Federal/provincial split of jurisdiction, major expansion of penitentiary construction occurs. |
| 1930s–1940s | Early reform era | Gradual improvement in some prison conditions occurs, and prison industry takes root. |
| 1940s–1970s | Rehabilitation and reintegration era | Medical model of crime is adopted, concomitantly, rehabilitation is given emphasis and release success is linked to successful reintegration back into the community. |
| 1980s–1990s | Inmate opportunities era | Inmates are provided opportunites for reform, and a variety of programs are developed and offered. |
| 1990s–today | Risk management and control era | Program opportunities are continued, with an emphasis on protection of the community through assessing and controlling the risk of reoffending. |

confinement was the rule, and the penitentiary was architecturally designed to minimize contact between inmates, and between inmates and staff. Exercise was allowed in small, high-walled yards attached to each cell. Eventually handicrafts were introduced into the prison setting, permitting prisoners to work in their cells.

Fashioned after the Philadelphia model, the Eastern Penitentiary (1829) opened in Cherry Hill, Pennsylvania, and the Western Penitentiary (1826) in Pittsburgh. Solitary confinement and individual cells, supported by a massive physical structure with impenetrable walls, became synonymous with the Pennsylvania system of imprisonment. Supporters heralded the **Pennsylvania style** as one that was both humane and provided inmates with the opportunity for rehabilitation. Many well-known figures of the day spoke out in support of the Pennsylvania style, among them Benjamin Franklin and Benjamin Rush—both of whom were influential members of the Philadelphia Society for Alleviating the Miseries of Public Prisons.[23]

As prison populations began to grow, solitary confinement became prohibitively expensive. One of the first large prisons to abandon the Pennsylvania model was the New York State Prison at Auburn. Auburn introduced the congregate but silent system, under which inmates lived, ate, and worked together in enforced silence. This style of imprisonment, which came to be known as the **Auburn system**, relied on group workshops rather than solitary handicrafts and reintroduced corporal punishments into the handling of offenders. Whereas isolation and enforced idleness were inherent punishments under the Pennsylvania system, Auburn depended upon whipping and hard labour to maintain the rule of silence.[24]

Since even then, as now, there were competing ideas about which style of prison worked best and was most humane. Auburn prison was the site of an experiment in solitary confinement—which was the basis of the Pennsylvania style. Eighty-three men were placed in small solitary cells on Christmas Day of 1821 and released in 1823 and 1824. Five of the 83 died, one went insane, another attempted suicide, and the others became "seriously demoralized."[25] Although the Auburn experiment did not accurately simulate the conditions in Pennsylvania (no handicrafts or exercise were allowed and prisoners were placed in tiny

**Pennsylvania style** (also **penitentiary**) A form of imprisonment developed by the Pennsylvania Quakers around 1790 as an alternative to corporal punishments. The style involved solitary confinement and encouraged rehabilitation.

**Auburn system** (also **congregate but silent system**) A form of imprisonment developed in New York state around 1820 that depended upon prisons with large populations, where prisoners were held as a group, and required to be silent. This style of imprisonment was a primary competitor with the Pennsylvania style.

---

## BOX 11.1  Theory into Practice

### American Notes by Charles Dickens, 1868

In 1842, the famous English author Charles Dickens made a tour of North America. Along the way, he visited Canada, staying for a short while in Kingston, the home of Canada's first penitentiary, which was under construction during his visit. These are a few of his comments:

> Indeed, it may be said of Kingston, that one half of it appears to be burnt down, and the other half not to be built up. The Government House is neither elegant nor commodious, yet it is almost the only house of any importance in the neighbourhood. There is an admirable gaol here, well and wisely governed, and excellently regulated in every respect. The men were employed as shoemakers, ropemakers, blacksmiths, tailors, carpenters, and stone-cutters; and in building a new prison, which was pretty far advanced towards completion. The female prisoners were occupied in needlework. Among them was a beautiful girl of twenty, who had been there

> nearly three years. She acted as bearer of secret dispatches for the self-styled Patriots on Navy Island during the Canadian Insurrection: sometimes dressing as a girl, and carrying them in her stays; sometimes attiring herself as a boy, and secreting them in the lining of her hat. In the latter character she always rode as a boy would, which was nothing to her, for she could govern any horse that any man could ride, and could drive four-in-hand with the best whip in those parts. Setting forth on one of her patriotic missions, she appropriated to herself the first horse she could lay her hands on; and this offence had brought her where I saw her. She had quite a lovely face, though, as the reader may suppose from this sketch of her history, there was a lurking devil in her bright eye, which looked out pretty sharply from between her prison bars.

### QUESTIONS TO CONSIDER

1. The gaol (jail) at Kingston appears to have housed young and old, male and female. Why is the later separation of offenders by gender and by age considered to be a mark of progress?

2. Should political prisoners be housed with regular inmates? When should prisoners be considered political prisoners?

cells), it provided an effective basis for condemnation of the Pennsylvania style. Partly as a result of the experiment, the Reverend Louis Dwight, an influential prison reformer of the time and leader of the prestigious Prison Discipline Society of Boston, became an advocate of the Auburn system, citing its lower cost[26] and humane conditions.[27] Lower costs resulted from the simpler facilities required by mass imprisonment, and from group workshops that provided economies of scale unachievable under solitary confinement. Dwight also believed, in large part due to the experiment in solitary confinement, that the Pennsylvania style of imprisonment was unconscionable and inhumane. As a consequence of criticisms fielded by Dwight and others like him, most American prisons built after 1825 followed the Auburn architectural style and system of prison discipline.

The Auburn model, after much debate and deliberation, was also found to be suited to the Canadian experience.[28] For example, a proposal for the construction of what would become the Kingston Penitentiary was put forward by H.C. Thomson, editor of the *Upper Canadian Herald*. He was appointed as chair of a select committee to design the prison and, in 1831, he visited the Bridewell Prison in Glasgow and examined the Auburn system in New York.[29] Kingston Penitentiary, which opened in 1835, was a maximum-security facility that held men, women, children, and the mentally disabled. It remains an important institution in the history and development of corrections in Canada.[30]

At about the same time, however, a number of European governments sent representatives to study the virtues of the two American systems. Interestingly, most concluded that the Pennsylvania style was more conducive to reformation than was Auburn, and many European prisons adopted a strict separation of inmates. Two French visitors, Gustave de Beaumont and Alexis de Tocqueville, stressed the dangers of what they called "contamination," whereby prisoners housed in Auburn-like systems could negatively influence one another.[31]

The penitentiary at Kingston pre-dated Confederation by over 30 years. It contained about 150 cells, each 0.77 metres wide and 2.4 metres long.[32] Each cell contained a bed, which was nothing more than a metal rack hinged to the wall, that was folded down in the evening for sleep. Toilet facilities were nothing more than a bucket. Discipline was severe, and a regime of silence was imposed. Despite the harsh conditions, Charles Dickens offered words of support for the institution following his visit to Kingston, Ontario, in the winter of 1842:

> There is an admirable jail here, well and wisely governed, and excellently regulated, in every respect. The men were employed as shoemakers, ropemakers,

Kingston Penitentiary, which opened in 1835, was a maximum-security facility that held men, women, children, and the mentally disabled.

Correctional Services of Canada Museum Collection

blacksmiths, tailors, carpenters, and stonecutters; and in building a new prison, which was pretty far advanced towards completion.[33]

In the years to follow, the Kingston Penitentiary would not draw much praise from commentators. In 1848, a royal commission chaired by George Brown, editor of *The Globe* newspaper in Toronto, found the warden was mismanaging the prison, and the inmates were subjected to abuse. The report led to the removal of the warden and minor improvements in prison conditions; however, the regime remained substantially intact.[34]

## Irish and Australian Influences

The negative effects of life in early penitentiaries was moderated to some extent by the emergence of a reformatory influence, which grew out of practices innovated by two outstanding correctional leaders of the mid-1880s: Captain Alexander Maconochie and Sir Walter Crofton.

### Captain Alexander Maconochie and Norfolk Island

During the 1840s, Maconochie served as the warden of Norfolk Island, a prison off the coast of Australia for "doubly condemned" inmates. English prisoners sent to Australia, who committed other crimes while there, were taken to Norfolk so that they would be segregated from less recalcitrant offenders in Australia. Prior to Maconochie's arrival, conditions at Norfolk had been atrocious. Disease on the island was rampant, fights between inmates left many dead and more injured, sanitary conditions were practically non-existent, and physical facilities were not conducive to good supervision. Maconochie immediately set out to reform the island prison. He is still remembered for saying, "When a man keeps the key of his own prison, he is soon persuaded to fit it to the lock."[35] In that belief, he worked to create conditions that would provide incentives for prisoners to participate in their own reformation.

Maconochie developed a system of marks, through which prisoners could earn enough credits to buy their freedom. Bad behaviour removed marks from the inmate's ledger, while acceptable behaviour added to the number of marks earned. The mark system made early release possible and led to a recognition of the indeterminate sentence as a useful tool in the reformation of offenders. Prior to Maconochie, inmates had been sentenced to

## BOX 11.2 Theory into Practice

### Convict Labour in an Early Ontario Prison

Joseph Gondor Berkovits (1994)[1] cites a brief letter by one Henry Howell, an 18-year-old inmate in the Ontario Central Prison, which was closed down in 1915, that highlights the rather poor conditions of the prison:

> Sir, Mr. Massie, I cannot understand it. I've been in trouble ever since you sent me in the Brick yard. Mr. Massie it's just like this. After I have been weeling about two hours, my feet get sore & my legs get weak & commences to pain me in the knee joint & then I walk kind of lame, & when night come I am played clean out, & when I come up to my cell, I take a couple of mouths full of Bread & sip of tea & then I undress my self & get into Bed, & I am sound a-sleep before I know it, but I most allways wake up about one or two o'clock in the morning, & then I feel all Broke up, my legs pain me all over, & my feet feels sore, & the cords or sinuses each side & around my neck feels sore & I feel all still ... in my knee, my legs are all stiffened up & I can scarcely turn my head around, because it is so stiff in the mornings. That rope I have around my neck seems to tear my neck all to pieces ... Mr. Massie, I hope you will not have any more hard feelings against me. I've only got 32 more days, so I ask you will you be so kind as to give me another job ... [J]ust give me an other job & try me, & see if I can't keep my word. (Just give me one chance & I shall be the best boy in the prison.)

---
[1]Berkovits, J.G. (1994). Prisoners for Profit: Convict Labour in the Ontario Central Prison, 1874–1915. In Phillips, J., Loo, T., and Lewthwaite, S. (eds.). *Crime and Criminal Justice: Essays in the History of Canadian Law* (Vol. V, pp. 478–515, at p. 499). Toronto: The Osgoode Society.

determinate sentences specifying a fixed number of years they had to serve before release. The mark system squarely placed responsibility for winning an early release upon the inmate. Because of the system's similarity to the later practice of parole, it won for Maconochie the title "father of parole." Maconochie returned to Britain and was afforded an opportunity to apply his penal system within the new Birmingham Prison.[36]

Opinion leaders in England, however, saw Maconochie's methods as too lenient. Many pointed to the fact that the indeterminate sentence made new lives possible for criminals in a world of vast opportunity (the Australian content) at the expense of the British empire, while many good citizens had to live out lives of quiet desperation and poverty back home. Amid charges that he coddled inmates, Maconochie was relieved of his duties as warden in 1844.

Maconochie's innovations had come to the attention of Sir Walter Crofton, head of the Irish Prison System. Crofton adapted the idea of early release to his program of progressive stages. Inmates who entered Irish prisons had to work their way through four stages. The first, or entry level, involved solitary confinement and dull work. Most prisoners in the first level were housed at Mountjoy Prison in Dublin. The second stage assigned prisoners to Spike Island, where they worked on fortifications. The third stage placed prisoners in field units that worked directly in the community on public service projects. Unarmed guards supervised the prisoners. The fourth stage depended upon what Crofton called the "ticket of leave." The leave ticket allowed prisoners to live and work in the community under the occasional supervision of a "moral instructor." The ticket could be revoked at any time up until the expiration of the offender's original sentence.

Crofton was convinced that convicts could not be rehabilitated without successful reintegration into the community. His innovations were closely watched by reformers across Europe. Unfortunately, a wave of violent robberies swept England in 1862 and led to passage of the 1863 *Garrotters Act*, which mandated whipping for robberies involving violence and longer prison sentences for many other crimes—effectively rolling back the clock on Crofton's innovations, at least in Europe.

In the late 1800s, Ontario's prison inspector, John Woodburn Langmuir,[37] studied examples of different reformatory prisons and launched a determined, one-man campaign to bring a reform approach to his province. These efforts resulted in the opening of the Andrew Mercer Ontario Reformatory for Females in Toronto, in 1880.[38] Shortly after Confederation

Archives of Ontario

The Andrew Mercer Reformatory for Women, which opened in Toronto in 1880. Throughout the 1870s, in Canada, there was a significant expansion of the federal penitentiary system.

and throughout the 1870s in Canada, there was a significant expansion of the federal penitentiary system. Prisons were built in Montreal, Quebec (1873), Stony Mountain, Manitoba (1876), and New Westminster, British Columbia (1878). Two prisons (in St. John and Halifax) were closed in 1880 with the construction of a prison in Dorchester, New Brunswick.[39]

With the limited success of the reformatory style of prison, concerns over security, discipline, and the need to develop a work ethic appear to have become dominant in Canadian prisons.[40]

# KEY ISSUES IN CANADIAN CORRECTIONS

Most police departments, operating at all levels, have cells in which they can hold arrested individuals for short periods of time. People who have been taken into custody are typically brought before a justice or a judge within 24 hours, when a decision is made about releasing the person pending trial or remanding them into custody. If remanded, the accused is generally conveyed to a provincial remand centre where he or she will stay until the court process is complete. Upon sentencing, and if incarceration is ordered by the judge, the offender will move into the correctional system.

Canada's correctional system entails provincial and federal elements. Short sentences are served in provincial institutions, while longer sentences put the offender under federal control. Similar issues arise in relation to both federal and provincial corrections, although some matters have more influence on one part of the system than do others. All prisons must contend with large numbers of individuals with a lot of time on their hands. Should they be engaged in work? Should treatment be provided? What happens when too many inmates are kept in one institution? Should solitary confinement be used to maintain discipline in the institution? These are some of the issues that we will discuss in this chapter.

## The Prison Industry

Prison industry has had an interesting history in Canada. In the earliest years, prisoners were essentially leased out to provide labour for private enterprise. Throughout most of Canada's history, inmates did little work of any real value. In 1938, another royal commission on prisons, the Archambault Commission, looked into Canada's prison system and concluded that the prisons system should do more than merely contain prisoners; it should seek to reform and rehabilitate inmates and provide education and vocational training.[41]

In Kingston, where the new penitentiary was being built at that time, local tradespeople were opposed to the teaching of trades to inmates, who were to help build the prison, on the grounds that doing so would threaten their economic welfare.[42] Only recently has the historical use of convicts as a cheap source of labour been researched to any extent.[43] Workhouses in pre-Confederation Nova Scotia attempted to ingrain a Protestant work ethic in offenders by assigning laborious tasks to them. Early uses of inmate labour, in that province, included cutting granite and laying road bed. From the early 1800s, concerns about inmates providing free labour surfaced. Labour unions became very well-organized and powerful by the early part of the twentieth century. The Great Depression of the 1930s, in which jobs were scarce, brought with it a call for an end to the cheap labour supplied by the prisons.

In Canada, the potential to more fully develop the prison industry was not realized until the MacGuigan Subcommittee recommended in 1977 that the *Penitentiary Act* be amended to permit the products of inmate labour to be available on the open market and that a prison industries corporation be established.[44] Gandy and Hurl have considered the involvement of inmates in prison industries in Canada, and identify several concerns expressed by the labour unions. These concerns include (1) government employees being made redundant by prison labour, (2) the potential for private industry to exploit inmate workers, and (3) the very real possibility that inmate labour could take jobs away from non-inmate workers.[45] Despite these concerns, the CORCAN Corporation was created in 1980 to operate as a production and marketing agency for the Canadian Penitentiary Service.[46] The corporation currently operates in over half of the federal penitentiaries and employs

5100 offenders.[47] It currently is involved in agriculture, construction, manufacturing, services, and textiles.[48]

CORCAN has been plagued by operating deficits and high production costs.[49] However, Macdonald argues that these types of programs can be made viable, if properly managed.[50] Indeed, CORCAN's Annual Report for 2001–2002 shows a modest profit for the year. The mandate of CORCAN is "to aid in the safe reintegration of offenders into Canadian society by providing employment and training opportunities to offenders incarcerated in federal penitentiaries and, for brief periods of time, after they are released into the community."[51]

CORCAN is designated as a "Special Operating Agency" with the Correctional Service of Canada, which grants it more autonomy than would otherwise be the case. In addition to providing inmates with skills training, the corporation also aims to reduce the costs of running the federal correctional system. Specific service areas that reflect a modern focus include:

- Computer repair;
- Data entry;
- Digital imaging;
- Micrography;
- Printing;
- Telemarketing; and
- Warehousing and distribution.

Inmates engaged in CORCAN programs can earn up to $6.90 per day. In order to address concerns that CORCAN does not adversely affect the private sector, it has been structured and designed with controls in place that limit its market. Accordingly, CORCAN generally sells to the public sector (i.e., federal, provincial, and municipal governments, schools, hospitals, and registered charities).[52] A recent study suggests that continuous offender participation in CORCAN prison industry programs immediately prior to release may have a positive impact on post-release recidivism.[53]

It is reasonable to expect that inmates who have developed work-related skills in prison transfer some of those skills and a pro-employment attitude to life on the outside after release. Pre-release employment appears linked to post-release success.[54] In an analysis of inmate work programs, C. Gillis found that several factors influence the success of inmates securing work after release from prison:[55]

- The unemployment rate affects the likelihood of inmates obtaining employment upon release, with low unemployment rates increasing the likelihood of released inmates securing work;
- The offender's associations with individuals involved in crime decreased the likelihood of the released inmate finding quality employment opportunities;
- A positive attitude increased the likelihood of securing employment post-release; and
- The level of work-related skills prior to incarceration was the most significant factor in determining the quality of post-release employment. Accordingly, work-related training may not be as important for inmates with significant pre-admission skills.

In recent years, through CORCAN, inmates have been involved in significant work projects. This has allowed many inmates to develop marketable job skills, and it has provided goods and services for the market. In the future, private enterprise will likely renew its interest in using inmate labour.[56] The private sector will not take long to realize that using economical inmate labour could help to minimize production costs. In the current era of accountability, it is foreseeable that inmates will be expected to pay for their stay in prison out of the money made through their involvement in prison industry.

The popularity of prison industry reflects the Correctional Service of Canada's emphasis on providing "program opportunities."[57] Rather than warehousing (i.e., idle confinement) or inflicting ongoing punishment, this opportunity approach to prison administration seeks to make relevant programs available to inmates.[58] Another aspect of the programs' opportunity approach to running a prison is providing treatment programs for inmates.[59]

# Treatment in Prisons

By the late 1940s, Canada's prisons began to entertain high hopes for rehabilitating prisoners. A new interest in "corrections" and reformation combined with the latest in behavioural techniques to usher in an era of medical and behavioural treatment built around what was then a prevailing psychiatric model. Inmates came to be seen more as "clients" or "patients" than as offenders, and terms like "resident" or "group member" replaced the "inmate" label. Inmates were provided with various forms of psychotherapy and behaviour modification techniques in an effort to restore pro-social attitudes. This era was based on a **medical model** of corrections—one that implied that the offender was sick and that rehabilitation was only a matter of finding the right medical treatment.[60]

Ekstedt and Griffiths have noted the movement to a treatment model that focused substantially on inmate rehabilitation. This included vocational training and therapeutic intervention techniques (e.g., group counselling and individual therapy). Also consistent with the medical model was the hiring of correctional staff trained in psychiatric and psychological treatment.[61] In 1948, Canada's first prison psychiatric hospital was opened in Kingston, complete with electroshock therapy equipment.[62] As Ekstedt and Griffiths point out: "Adoption of the medical model had a substantial impact on the Canadian correctional system, and throughout the 1950s and 1960s, there was increased involvement of behavioural science professionals in correctional programs."[63]

While American correctional systems began to downplay programming in the 1970s, Canada has retained a policy that promotes the availability of a range of programs in its federal correctional system. Ekstedt and Griffiths provide the following list of correctional treatment "modalities" that have been applied in the Canadian context:

- Individual and group psychotherapy;
- Reality therapy;
- Transactional analysis;
- Erhard Seminar Training (EST);
- Transcendental meditation (TM);
- Psychodrama;
- Client-centred therapy;
- Behaviour modification; and
- Therapeutic community.[64]

Over the years, various therapies were used in prisons, including behavioural therapy, chemotherapy, aversion therapy, sensory deprivation, and neurosurgery. Behavioural therapy is based on providing rewards for approved behaviour, while punishing undesirable behaviour. Examples of rewards in prisons are better housing conditions, canteen allotments, or TV privileges. Chemotherapy involved drugs, especially tranquilizers, to modify behaviour. Neurosurgery, including the now-notorious frontal lobotomy, was performed on some highly aggressive inmates to control their destructive urges. Sensory deprivation sought to calm disruptive offenders by denying them the stimulation that might set off outbursts of destructive behaviour through isolating inmates in a quiet, secluded environment. In aversion therapy, drugs or electric shocks were administered in an attempt to teach the offender to associate pain and displeasure with specific stimuli, which previously led to criminal behaviour. Homosexual child abusers, for example, were shown pictures of nude children and simultaneously given shocks, often in especially sensitive parts of their anatomy.

A 1953 Committee of Inquiry, chaired by Supreme Court Justice Gérald Fauteux, formally introduced the medical model into the federal correctional system.[65] However, inmates have not always been happy with this model. In the 1970s, riots erupted in Canadian prisons, whereby inmates called for changes throughout the prison system.[66] By the end of the 1970s, therapeutic rehabilitation had entrenched itself in Canadian prison systems, which was part of the reason for the development of specialized psychiatric treatment for a variety of inmate needs and the construction of regional psychiatric centres (or regional health centres).[67]

The treatment era suffered from attacks upon the medical model on which it depended. Academics and legal scholars pointed to a lack of evidence in support of the

the **medical model**
A theoretical framework for the handling of prisoners, which held that offenders were "sick" and could be "cured" through behavioural and other appropriate therapies.

model[68] and began to stress the teaching of individual responsibility rather than treatment in the handling of offenders.

Although one could identify the late 1970s as the end of the treatment era in the U.S., many correctional rehabilitation programs continue to survive in Canada and new ones are constantly being developed.

# Programs in Federal Institutions

The majority of Canada's inmates are serving time in provincial institutions. In a "one-day snapshot" of correctional facilities in Canada on October 5, 1996, some 23 679 of a total of 37 541 inmates were housed in provincial institutions.[69] Ten per cent of these provincial inmates were serving intermittent sentences, usually on weekends. Twenty-five per cent were on remand awaiting trial or appeal. Of the remainder, 45 per cent were serving sentences of six months or less. Since provincial inmates serve such a short time, programs are quite scant. On the day of the "snapshot," 13 862 inmates were serving federal sentences of two years or longer. It is these inmates who receive the majority of prison programs in Canada.

Federal corrections operates under a number of different laws and policies. Perhaps most important is the *Corrections and Conditional Release Act*, which has guided federal corrections since 1992. Under this legislation, the Correctional Service of Canada (CSC) seeks to ensure a "just, peaceful and safe" society by carrying out the sentence of the court, and assisting inmates in their "rehabilitation" and "reintegration" back into the community as law-abiding members of society. The CSC seeks to accomplish these goals through a variety of programs.[70]

## *Counter-Point Program*

One of the Correctional Service's programs is called the "Counter-Point Program." Theory and research provide information that can guide efforts in the prevention and treatment of criminal behaviour and thus help to identify and minimize the risk factors in offender recidivism. These factors include (1) the offender's attitudes, values, and beliefs that permit the offender to excuse, minimize, or condone criminal behaviour; and (2) skill deficits in areas such as self-monitoring and self-management. Helping the offender to correct his or her attitudes, values, and beliefs and build skills in self-monitoring and self-management appear to reduce the likelihood of recidivism.

The underlying philosophy of the Counter-Point Program is derived from social learning theory. Consistent with this theoretical model, cognitive-behavioural strategies are introduced to provide the offender with the tools needed for change. There are four main goals of the program. The first goal is to enhance the offender's willingness to alter criminal attitudes and behaviours by way of motivational interviewing techniques. A second goal is to provide participants with the skills necessary to identify and change pro-criminal attitudes. Third, the program seeks to provide participants with self-regulation and self-management skills to ensure continued changes in attitude and behaviour. Fourth, the program seeks to assist inmates in identifying high-risk situations and aid them in developing the necessary resources to prevent future criminal behaviour.

The Counter-Point Program addresses these major issues by teaching the offender to identify, change, and replace pro-criminal beliefs with pro-social beliefs. Offenders are also taught about the skills necessary to maintain pro-social attitudes and behaviours. The Counter-Point Program has three processes: intake, intervention, and closure.

The intake process is aimed at orientation, assessment, and goal setting (via motivational interviewing techniques). The function of the closure stage is to review with the inmate his or her final progress report, and to involve a parole officer for an analysis of the inmate's relapse-prevention plan.

## *Education and Job Training*

The Correctional Service of Canada seeks to provide a variety of educational programs in order to allow inmates to upgrade their education and thereby be more competitive for jobs once they are released. Educational programs are provided at institutions of all security levels. The various programs include adult basic education, courses that allow inmates to complete their secondary education, vocational training, and post-secondary education. Each program hopes to provide offenders with opportunities to acquire the education appropriate to their present needs, past achievements, and academic abilities.

At the time of admission to federal corrections, 65 per cent of offenders show an educational level below grade 8, and 82 per cent have an educational level lower than grade 10. The Correctional Service sponsored a 1992 report called "Can Educating Adult Offenders Counteract Recidivism?" that concluded that specific intellectual skills gained through adult basic education (ABE) may equip offenders to deal more effectively with problems encountered in daily life in the community. The sense of achievement that flows from successfully completing an ABE program helps to bolster the confidence of inmates, encouraging them to make further positive changes in their lives. The ABE program allows inmates to upgrade their academic skills to a grade-10 level, providing a basis for further education or skills training.

Approximately 40 per cent of the inmates enrolled in an educational program are in the ABE program, making it a high priority with the Correctional Service. Successful completion of the secondary education program leads to graduation with a high-school diploma at the grade-12 level. Approximately 25 per cent of the participation in Correctional Service education programs occurs at this level. Inmates are well aware that a secondary-school diploma has become a prerequisite for securing lasting employment and for entering a variety of training opportunities.

Post-secondary education offers offenders the opportunity to acquire a trade or university-level education, as well as updating or enhancing trade qualifications prior to their release from prison. Less than 10 per cent of inmates participating in educational programs are involved in post-secondary education.

Vocational programs are the choice of approximately 25 per cent of all inmates seeking education or training. These programs provide training in a range of job-related skills that are relevant to employment opportunities, both in the institutions and in the community. Some of the subjects currently offered by the Correctional Service's vocational programs are

- welding and metal trades,
- hairdressing,
- small engine repair,
- auto mechanics and auto body repair,
- electronics,
- carpentry and cabinet making,
- upholstery,
- plumbing,
- cooking, and
- computer programming.

The vocational education programs also include a generic skills component that addresses industrial and shop safety, as well as personal and interpersonal skills related to success in any workplace.

## Family Violence Program

The Family Violence Program focuses on male offenders who have been abusive in their family relationships, have a history of committing intra-familial assaults, or have been identified as at "high risk" of committing such acts of abuse. Programs are also available for female inmates, where the emphasis is on issues affecting the victims of sexual abuse.

The Correctional Service's Family Violence Program teaches offenders that violence is a response learned through direct experience or imitation. The program provides information while teaching specific skills, and typically consists of three elements: education, skill development, and relapse prevention. While a low-intensity program contains only the educational component, moderate- and high-intensity programs contain all three elements. Changing attitudes requires considerable time, so a continuum of treatment is provided, running from the institution to the community. Offenders in the high-intensity program are provided with additional monitoring while in the institution and also after conditional release.

In addition to the Family Violence Program, rehabilitation is available for inmates who have already committed at least two violent offences or who are considered at "high risk," based on an actuarial risk assessment, to commit violent crimes. The Violence Prevention Program also includes a Segregation Program. The Violence Prevention Program is an intensive reintegration program based upon contemporary theory and research, and delivered by a mental health professional and a program officer.

Since aggression and violent behaviour are multi-dimensional, the targets of change (i.e., the foci of the intervention or treatment, what it is that needs to be altered) are usually complex and multiple. Accordingly, the Violence Prevention Program integrates a variety of rehabilitative approaches. The conceptual model focuses on preventing violent criminal activity and interpersonal aggression that are not exclusively based on anger or emotional control problems. The primary intervention approach emphasizes relapse prevention. These techniques are reinforced by emphasizing education, self-control, social problem solving, role-playing, and homework assignments.

This program is four months long, involving group sessions, with each group having a maximum of 12 participants. The program also includes a few individual sessions directed at the specific needs of the participants, and two testing sessions. The main modules include:

1. Making Change: Orientation and the process of change;

2. Violence Awareness: Examining the personal origins of violence;

3. Anger Control: Basic skills for controlling anger and managing stress;

4. Solving Problems: Social problem-solving and information-processing skills;

5. Social Attitudes: Examining and reformulating the beliefs supporting violence;

6. Positive Relationships: Reducing victimization and intimate violence;

7. Resolving Conflicts: Communication and negotiation skills;

8. Positive Lifestyles: Restructuring the lifestyle triggers of violence;

9. Self-Control: Developing short-term and long-term direction;

10. Violence Prevention: Developing a comprehensive violence prevention plan.

A key objective of the Violence Prevention Program is for each participant to develop, articulate, and manage a comprehensive violence relapse prevention plan. This plan is based on the offender's understanding of how prior actions were aggressive and of recognizing high-risk circumstances that may result in further aggression. Institutional and community prevention programs assist participants to apply their violence prevention plan to their individual environment and circumstances through group, and individual sessions that focus on adapting and modifying relapse prevention efforts.

A recent violence prevention initiative is oriented towards dealing with inmates who are behavioural management problems within the institution. Such inmates are frequently segregated from other inmates to minimize the harm they might inflict on the general prison population. This initiative is referred to as the Segregation Program, which is also delivered by a mental health professional and a program officer. The goal of this program, which deals with inmates currently in segregation units, is to return as many inmates as possible to the general population of Canada's prisons. In addition to providing a means to return offenders to the general population as early as possible, this initiative also seeks to provide rehabilitative programs to offenders who have no short-term alternatives to segregation.

The segregation program has three distinct phases. The initial phase is assessment. Here, the inmate is introduced to the segregation program, and the reason for segregating the offender is identified. The goal is to produce an individualized program plan that will allow the offender to return to a less restrictive setting. The program also provides mechanisms for appropriate referrals to mental health specialists and case management officers.

Phase two is the problem-solving phase, designed to occur within the first month of segregation. At this stage, motivational and social problem-solving strategies are provided to assist the inmate to cope with a return to general population. The goal of this crisis-oriented intervention phase is to quickly engage the offender in developing strategies to recognize and change the behaviour that prompted segregation. This phase may involve active mediation on the part of the program officer in negotiations with offender representatives, transfer boards, and existing institutional services. The basic techniques of cognitive change and self-monitoring are introduced at this phase.

The third and last phase is cognitive change. This phase is also a follow-up to the motivational and problem-solving techniques introduced in the second phase. Participants are instructed in basic cognitive change processes, altering the way offenders mentally approach problems, and relapse-prevention techniques.

## Living Skills Programs

Numerous Living Skills programs are offered in federal institutions. These programs provide inmates with strategies for dealing with many situations that arise in daily living. They seek to fill gaps in the coping skills that many inmates display.

One such program is the Cognitive Skills Program. This is a core component of the Living Skills programs. It focuses on the development of interpersonal reasoning skills to modify the inmate's egocentric, impulsive, illogical, and rigid thinking. This program helps inmates to calculate the consequences of their behaviour, recognize problems as they arise, and be flexible in their thinking.

A related program is the Boosting Cognitive Skills Program designed for the inmate to review and maintain the skills learned in the Cognitive Skills Program. These functions are particularly appropriate for inmates who completed the Cognitive Skills Program early in their sentence, and who are on the verge of receiving conditional release.

An Anger and Emotions Management Program is another Living Skills program, addressing needs faced by a large number of offenders. The anger management program seeks to train offenders in the skills necessary to manage anger and other emotions associated with acts of aggression or other anti-social behaviour. There is also a Boosting Anger and Emotions Management Program, giving inmates the opportunity to review and practise skills learned earlier.

Other Living Skills programs include a Living Without Violence in the Family Program, a Parenting Skills Program, a Leisure Skills Program, and a Community Integration Program.

Specific programs have been developed for different offender groups. Offenders with a history of sexual offences are given the opportunity to be assessed for sexual offender programs. Such programs focus on identifying the nature and pattern of sexual-offending behaviour, and developing strategies to reduce the risk of reoffending.

## Sexual Offender Programs

In this program, sexual offenders will undertake a therapeutic and semi-structured program that seeks to foster self-management. This program deals with cognitive distortions, deviant sexual arousal and deviant fantasies, social competence enhancement, anger and emotional management, and empathy and awareness of victims.

Sexual offender programs emphasize the need for offenders to take responsibility for their actions, to recognize the behaviours that precede and follow sexual offences, to identify situations that place them at risk of reoffending, and to assist them to develop recidivism prevention strategies. Reducing the risk of sexual offending through a combination of self-management and external control is also emphasized.

As with other programs, offenders who have participated in a sexual offender program may also participate in a follow-up maintenance program, which is provided in both institutional and community settings. The goal of this program is to maintain the gains that were made in the sexual offender program, to monitor risk level, and to further develop skills that will enhance effective self-management.

## Ethno-cultural Programs

Because Canada's multicultural makeup has been expanding in recent years, the range of ethnic minorities is likely to increase in our prisons. The Correctional Service seeks to provide culturally appropriate programs in its institutions. As might be expected, this goal has resulted in programs oriented towards the high proportion of aboriginal offenders found in federal institutions, but it also manifests itself in programs for offenders belonging to other cultural groups. The Correctional Service also seeks to recognize and accommodate different religions in prison, and to promote awareness and tolerance of cultural diversity. Numerous institutions have also adopted culturally and spiritually appropriate treatments for aboriginal sexual offenders.

## Substance Abuse Programs

The majority of offenders have problems associated with alcohol and drugs that appear to be connected to their criminal activity. The Correctional Service administers a Computerized Lifestyle Assessment Instrument (CLAI) as the primary method of identifying substance-abuse problems in offenders. Information collected by the CLAI allows case management officers to make appropriate treatment decisions. This data, combined with other assessment measures, can be used in the development of an individualized correctional plan that takes into account the severity of the substance abuse problem and the appropriate treatment.

Over the years, the Correctional Service has developed and implemented a range of substance abuse programs to match the offenders' treatment needs in an effort to maximize effectiveness. Ongoing efforts result in the modification of programs, embodying emerging findings in the fields of substance abuse theory, research, and clinical practice.

The Correctional Service's current substance abuse programs include an induction and orientation program for all newly admitted offenders, an intermediate intensity program for offenders with serious problems, an intermediate intensity program for long-term offenders, a program in development to address the specific needs of female offenders, a community-based relapse prevention program, and programs in development to specifically target substance abuse among aboriginal offenders. The Correctional Service is evaluating the effectiveness of these programs on an ongoing basis, but claims considerable success for several of their programs.

# The Community-Based and Reintegrative Format

Beginning in the 1960s, the realities of prison crowding, combined with a renewed faith in humanity and the treatment era's belief in the possibility of behavioural change, inspired a movement away from institutionalized corrections and towards the creation of opportunities for reformation within local communities. The transition to **community-based corrections** (also variously called "deinstitutionalization" and "decarceration") was based on the premise that rehabilitation could not occur in isolation from the free social world to which inmates must eventually return. Advocates of community corrections portrayed prisons as dehumanizing, claiming they further victimized offenders who had already been negatively labelled by society. In 1959, the passage of the *Parole Act* led to the formation of the National Parole Board, whose purpose is to oversee the early release of inmates who have been rehabilitated back into Canadian society. The Canadian understanding of the aims and objectives of community-based corrections was advanced by the work of a task force chaired by William Outerbridge.[71] Ekstedt and Griffiths offer three key justifications for this approach as a result of their examination of the literature:[72]

**community-based corrections** A sentencing style that represents a movement away from traditional confinement options and an increased dependence upon correctional resources that are available in the community.

- Community-based programs are more humane than incarcerating offenders in correctional institutions;
- Community-based programs are less costly than institutional services; and
- Community-based programs increase the chances of the successful reintegration of the offender into the community.

Two of the goals of the Correctional Service of Canada (the CSC) are to enhance the efforts of professionals in community-based programs and to promote public understanding of community corrections.[73] The CSC has made the following commitments to the Canadian public in the area of community corrections:

- Assess each offender to determine the level of risk to the public and problem areas to be addressed;

- Prepare a Correctional Treatment Plan with each offender to ensure that he or she has the supervision, training, and programming needed to reduce the risk to reoffend;

- Suspend the release of any offender believed to be at risk of criminal involvement;

- Ensure that information about particular offenders is made available … to police, victims, and other legitimate partners in the supervision area;

- Supervise each offender by seeing him or her at the offender's home and in CSC offices at a frequency that complies with CSC standards for supervision; and

- Document each offender's case according to CSC policy.

Decarceration, which built upon many of the alternative or intermediate sanctions discussed in the last chapter, used a variety of programs to keep offenders in contact with the community and out of prison. Among these programs were halfway houses, **work release** programs, and open institutions. Halfway houses have sometimes been called "halfway-in" or "halfway-out" houses, depending upon whether offenders were being given a second chance prior to incarceration or were in the process of gradual release from prison. Some early halfway houses were begun in Canada at the beginning of the 1900s, being operated by the Salvation Army.[74] It was not until the late 1960s and early 1970s that halfway houses became widespread, under the continuing involvement of the Salvation Army and the efforts of the John Howard Society and the St. Leonard's Society.[75]

Today's work release programs house offenders in traditional correctional environments—usually minimum security prisons—or in residential-type facilities, but permit them to work at jobs in the community during the day and return to the prison at night. These programs may be run by the Correctional Service, or by a private agency.[76] Work release for federal prisoners is authorized by the National Parole Board, where the risk to public safety is deemed not to be serious.[77] As work release programs grew, study release—whereby inmates attend local colleges and technical schools—was initiated in most jurisdictions as an adjunct to the work release programs. In Canada, work release programs are usually available to federal and provincial inmates through temporary-absence and day parole programs.[78]

Work release programs are still very much a part of modern corrections. Many inmates work in the community as they approach the end of their sentences. Unfortunately, work release programs are not without their social costs. Some inmates commit new crimes while in the community, and others use the opportunity to effect escapes.

The community-based format led to innovations in the use of volunteers and to the extension of inmate privileges. Open institutions routinely provided inmates with a number of opportunities for community involvement and encouraged the community to participate in the prison environment. Most open institutions, for example, made training available to citizens who wished to sponsor prisoners on day trips into the community for recreation, meals, and the like. Other open institutions allowed weekend passes or extended visits by family members and friends, while others have permitted conjugal visiting. Conjugal visits between male inmates and their spouses take place in motel-like environments constructed on the prison grounds. Most federal inmates are eligible for conjugal visits.[79] In a 1995 survey of federal inmates in Canada, 6 per cent of inmates reported having sex with another inmate.[80] Conjugal visits may have a role to play in minimizing unwanted sexual aggression in prisons.

## Warehousing/Overcrowding: A Future Direction?

During the late 1970s and into the 1990s, public disappointment, fuelled by perceptions of high **recidivism**[81] rates, coupled with dramatic news stories of inmates who committed

**work release** A prison program in which inmates are temporarily released into the community in order to meet job responsibilities.

**recidivism** The repetition of criminal behaviour. In statistical practice, a recidivism rate may be any of a number of possible counts or instances of arrest, conviction, correctional commitment, and correctional status changes, related to counts of repetitions of these events within a given period of time.

CHAPTER 11
Correctional Institutions

BOX 11.2 **Theory into Practice**

## Inside the SHU— Canada's Special Handling Unit

Directly north of the islands of Laval and Montreal in Quebec, near the centre of a large, treeless parcel of land, sits a group of buildings that house federal correctional facilities administered by CSC. These facilities include the Regional Reception Centre (RRC) for the Quebec Region of CSC. The RRC is a multi-level security facility that receives all offenders recently given a federal sentence in Quebec.

Located within the RRC is the SHU, since 1997 the only unit of its kind operated by CSC for the very small percentage of inmates who require its special handling procedures and the constant vigilance of its staff.

The SHU has the same maximum-security designation as all of the other maximum-security institutions operated by CSC. Almost all of the SHU's inmates arrive from other maximum-security institutions located across the country.

"They have been transferred to the SHU because they each jeopardized the safety of staff and other inmates in those institutions and they need special handling," says Denis Cloutier, who was the RRC warden and the person responsible for day-to-day operations at the SHU until June 2000.

Of the inmates transferred to the SHU, over 80 per cent were placed there following incidents of aggressive behaviour towards staff or other inmates, including murder, sexual assault, and hostage-taking. The remainder were placed at the SHU for escape attempts or institutional disturbances.

"By placing these inmates in an institution with security measures that are stricter than those in a regular maximum-security facility, we not only protect our staff, but the inmates feel more secure as well," says Mr. Cloutier.

"In a regular, maximum security institution, there may be 30 or more inmates in a common area. Here at the SHU, no more than eight or nine inmates are permitted to congregate in a common area at any one time."

All maximum-security institutions have detention units where inmates can be kept for a time. In these units, inmates are confined to their cells for up to 23 hours a day. At the SHU, inmates are able to spend more time out of their cell, but their movements and actions are closely monitored and strictly controlled.

Mr. Cloutier points out that "at the SHU, we are able to concentrate our resources to accomplish this, to provide a better and more secure environment for both staff and inmates." About 90 staff members work at the SHU, with an average of 15 to 20 correctional officers working each day shift.

While the CSC has jurisdiction over almost 13 000 inmates in custody, the inmate population of the SHU currently stands at 75 or approximately half of one per cent of all inmates in CSC custody. Clearly, getting transferred to the SHU is an exceptionally rare occurrence.

People enter the RRC, which houses the SHU, through a series of sliding gates and security checks and past four-metre high fences topped with coils of razor wire. Entry occurs under the scrutiny of a large watchtower that surveys the treeless approaches much like an airport control tower peers out over a long stretch of runways.

Inside the RRC, inmates can be seen cleaning, working at different tasks, or perhaps walking to a program—scenes familiar to anyone who has toured or worked in any of Canada's 52 federal correctional facilities.

Across the RRC, a seemingly endless and whitewashed tunnel leads to another series of security checks and locked doors protecting the entrance to one of Canada's most secure prison units.

Inside the SHU, the greyness of the day beyond the walls blends with the artificial light of the unit, leaving the central area clearly lit but with few shadows.

The SHU has five cell blocks, each including a small, triangular exercise yard. These cell blocks fan out around a central control post equipped with tinted windows. Inside this control post, correctional officers monitor all inmate activity and control all cell doors and the barriers that mark each range.

When an inmate moves off a cell block to attend a visit or a program, for example, that inmate's cell is unlocked

---

**warehousing** A policy of keeping offenders locked up in prison, usually for lengthy periods of time, without providing any form of treatment or using their labour productively.

gruesome crimes while in the community, led many to call for legislatures to curtail the most liberal aspects of educational, rehabilitative, and work release programs. Media descriptions of institutions where inmates lounged in supposed luxury with regular visits from spouses and lovers, and took frequent weekend passes infused the popular imagination with images of "prison country clubs." The perceived failure of the rehabilitative ideal in community-based corrections, however, was due as much to changes in the individual sentencing decisions of judges as it was to citizen outrage and restrictive legislative action. In the U.S., evidence points to the fact that many judges came to view rehabilitation programs as failures and decided to implement what we have earlier called the just deserts model[82] of criminal sentencing. The just deserts model, as discussed in Chapter 9, built upon a renewed belief that offenders should "get what's coming to them," and quickly led to a policy of **warehousing** serious offenders for the avowed purpose of protecting society—and to a rapid

individually from the central control post. The inmate advances to the barrier at the end of the cell block. There, he is handcuffed, the barrier is opened, and he is escorted to his destination by the officers.

In the SHU, inmates moving from one area of the facility to another are handcuffed and escorted by two or three correctional officers. All visits, all programs, and all interviews by staff are conducted through a clear Plexiglas barrier. SHU inmates have no direct contact with anyone except other inmates unless they are handcuffed and accompanied by correctional officers. Given that these inmates are some of the most dangerous in Canada, and have proven so in regular maximum-security institutions, the strict security of life at the SHU is hardly surprising. What may surprise visitors is the veneer of calm masking the underlying tension. Each day, SHU staff members must manage that tension while working in one of CSC's most secure correctional units.

In addition to the exercise yards, there are four common rooms and a gymnasium where inmates are allowed to mingle. Inmates do not need to be handcuffed to go to the common rooms, which they can access without coming into direct contact with staff.

While all of this takes place, security cameras and watchful correctional officers on a catwalk overhead and in the central control post monitor the activities and actions of the inmates on the floor.

About 39 per cent of the inmates transferred to the SHU are serving life sentences. However, over 60 per cent of them are serving determinate sentences that will end one day, most within several years. CSC's role is to administer these federal sentences bearing in mind that some offenders will eventually return to the community. To this end, CSC tries to get SHU inmates into programs and safely return them to a regular, maximum-security institution as soon as acceptable.

"The challenge is balancing security concerns with the delivery of programs so we can get most of these guys back down to a regular maximum-security institution," says Mr. Cloutier. In fact, most of the inmates will not spend a great deal of their sentences at the SHU. Of the 75 inmates at the SHU, 58 had been there for less than two years and only 10 had been there for more than five years.

## Role of the National Review Committee

While the day-to-day operation of the SHU is the warden's responsibility, the authority to transfer inmates in and out of the SHU is delegated to a National Review Committee (NRC) comprising the heads of Canada's maximum security institutions, and other correctional officials.

When an inmate is confined under the strict security measures of the SHU, his case is systematically reviewed to determine whether or not he could be transferred to a regular maximum-security institution. In fact, the NRC is required to review each inmate at the SHU at least once every four months.

Every two months, members of the NRC meet to review half of the facility's inmate population, carefully listening to the opinions of SHU staff about these inmates.

During each NRC review, all SHU inmates under consideration have an opportunity to make their own submissions.

The NRC, whose members have decades of correctional experience and expertise, ensures that inmates who should be at the SHU remain there, and that others are placed in a maximum-security institution whenever possible.

Together, the NRC and the staff of the SHU help CSC fulfill its Mission of protecting Canadian society by "exercising reasonable, safe, secure and humane control."

## QUESTIONS FOR DISCUSSION

1. It may be asserted that the SHU is a monument to the thesis that some criminals cannot be reformed and should be repressed and disciplined by absolute inflexibility. Is this true? If so, what type of offenders should be held in the SHU?

2. Will we always have a need for prisons like the one described here? Why or why not?

decline of the deinstitutionalization initiative. Canadian judges also became aware of community concern about community corrections' failures.

Recidivism rates are widely quoted in support of the drive to warehouse offenders. One U.S. study, for example, showed that nearly 70 per cent of young adults paroled from prison in 22 states during 1978 were rearrested for serious crimes one or more times within six years of their release.[83] The 1978 study group was estimated to have committed 36 000 new felonies within the six years following their release, including 324 murders, 231 rapes, 2291 robberies, and 3053 violent assaults.[84] Worse still, observed the study's authors, was the fact that 46 per cent of the recidivists would have been in prison at the time of their readmission to prison if they had fully served the maximum term to which they had been originally sentenced.[85] Those with long prior-arrest records (six or more previous adult arrests) were rearrested 90 per cent of the time following release, and the younger the parolee was at first arrest, the greater the chance of a new crime violation. Equally intriguing was the finding that "[t]he length of time that a parolee has served in prison had no consistent impact on recidivism rates."[86] While Canada's National Parole Board claims modest recidivism rates, the public and the judiciary remain concerned with the failures that occur. The National Parole Board recently reported 83-per-cent successful non-recidivism for its day parolees, and 70-per-cent successful non-recidivism for its full parolees.[87] However, the public is more likely to focus on the 17 and 30 per cent of failed recidivists, respectively.

The failure of the rehabilitative model in corrections was proclaimed emphatically by Robert Martinson in 1974.[88] Martinson and his colleagues had surveyed 231 research studies conducted to evaluate correctional treatments between 1945 and 1967. The researchers were unable to identify any treatment program that substantially reduced recidivism. Although Martinson argued for fixed sentences, a portion of which would be served in the community, his findings were often interpreted to mean that lengthy prison terms were necessary to incapacitate offenders who could not be reformed. About the same time, the prestigious National Academy of Sciences released a report in support of Martinson, saying "we do not now know of any program or method of rehabilitation that could be guaranteed to reduce the criminal activity of released offenders."[89] This combined attack on the treatment model led to the **nothing works doctrine**, which, beginning in the late 1970s, cast a pall of doubt over the previously dominant treatment philosophy. However, Martinson's work did not go unchallenged. The first sustained response was mounted by Ted Palmer who critiqued Martinson's findings on methodological grounds.[90] This challenge was taken up in Canada by Gendreau and Ross when they evaluated 95 treatment programs, primarily dealing with young offenders.[91] They concluded that Martinson's claim was premature, and that additional quality research was required before any such conclusions could be drawn.

As a consequence, from 1980 to 1995, the Canadian prison population grew dramatically (see Figure 11–1), and prisons everywhere became notoriously overcrowded, whether crime rates were rising, as they did in the 1980s, or declining, as they did throughout the 1990s.[92] The average daily count in Canadian prisons increased 50 per cent between 1980 and 1995; however, there have been modest annual declines since that year.[93] Despite this gradual decline, overcrowding in prisons remains one of the most serious problems facing the criminal justice system today. In the 1980s and 1990s, many new prisons were built across the country, at both the federal and provincial level, yet many inmates remain "double-bunked," the term used to describe the holding of two inmates in a single cell.[94] A review of institutional profiles shows most federal institutions use double-bunking to some degree[95] (see also Figure 11–1).

**nothing works doctrine**
The belief, popularized by Robert Martinson in the 1970s, that correctional treatment programs have little success in rehabilitating offenders.

### FIGURE 11–1 Average Daily Number of Offenders in Canada, 1987–88 to 2000–01

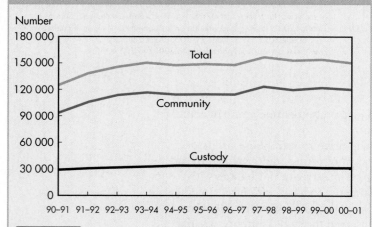

*Source:* Reprinted in Reed, M. and Roberts, J.V. (1998, February). Adult Correctional Services in Canada, 1996-97. In *Juristat*, Vol. 18, No 3, p. 1; Statistics Canada. Canadian Centre for Justice Statistics, Adult Correctional Services Survey. Adapted from the Statistics Canada publication *Juristat*, Catalogue no. 85-002, Vol. 18, No. 3, February 1998, pg.1, and Vol. 22, No. 10, October 2002, p. 16.

While prison incarceration rates have declined slightly in recent years, ongoing increases in the number of charged offenders who are remanded into custody pending their trial accounts for a significant portion of the overcrowding problem. A 2002 report[96] by the Canadian Centre for Justice Statistics, for example, reveals that admissions to remand increased by 8 per cent in 2000–01 over the previous year. This increase is part of an ongoing trend in recent years, occurring at a time when the number of offenders charged with offences has been relatively stable or declining.[97]

### The Dimensions of Overcrowding

Even though new prisons were quickly being built throughout Canada over the last two decades, prison overcrowding is still very much a reality today. A 1995 report[98] by the Correctional Service of Canada found that over 26 per cent of federal inmates reported being double-bunked. Of these, 12 per cent felt threatened by their cell mate. Experts agree that prison crowding can be measured in several ways, including:[99]

- Space available per inmate (such as square metres of floor space);
- How much time inmates are confined in cells or housing units (versus time spent on recreation, and so on);
- Living arrangements (i.e., single- versus double-bunking); and
- Type of housing (use of segregation facilities, tents, and so on, in place of general housing).

Complicating the density picture still further is the fact that prison officials have developed three definitions of prison capacity. **Rated capacity** refers to the size of the inmate population a facility can handle, according to the judgment of experts. **Operational capacity** is the number of inmates that a facility can effectively accommodate based on an appraisal of the institution's staff, programs, and services. **Design capacity** refers to the inmate population for which the institution was originally built to handle. Rated capacity estimates usually yield the largest inmate capacities, while design capacity (upon which observations in this chapter are based) typically shows the highest amount of overcrowding.

Whether prison overcrowding amounts to cruel and unusual treatment or to punishment has not been authoritatively determined in Canada. Crowding by itself is not cruel and unusual punishment, according to the U.S. Supreme Court in *Rhodes* v. *Chapman* (1981),[100] which considered the issue of double-bunking among other alleged forms of "deprivation" at the southern Ohio correctional facility. The Ohio facility, built in 1971, was substantially overcrowded according to the original housing plans on which it was constructed. Designed to house one inmate per cell, the cells were small (only seven square metres of floor space on the average). However, at the time the suit was filed, the facility held 2300 inmates, 1400 of whom were doubled-celled. Kelly Chapman, an inmate serving a sentence as an armed robber and prison escapee, claimed that his portion of a cell was too small—smaller even than the space recommended by the Ohio State Veterinarian Services for a five-week-old calf. Thirty-six states joined the case in support of the Ohio practice of double-celling, while the American Medical Association and the American Public Health Association took Chapman's side.[101] The Court, reasoning that overcrowding is not necessarily dangerous if other prison services are adequate, held that prison housing conditions may be "restrictive and even harsh," for they are part of the penalty that offenders pay for their crimes.

The John Howard Society of Alberta[102] has identified some of the negative effects associated with prison overcrowding:

- Since there are fewer resources to go around, the opportunities for inmates to engage in self-improvement and rehabilitative programs are lessened;
- The lack of inmate opportunities leads to idleness and related discontent and disruptive behaviour; and
- The lack of access to regular resources, such as washrooms, the library, and television-lounge seating leads to frustration and associated conflict and competition that may result in aggression and violence.

Overcrowding is the legacy of a warehousing orientation. Warehousing, a strategy that continues to be advocated by many, has produced inordinately high prison populations.[103] While the debilitating effects of prison overcrowding remain to be challenged as being truly cruel and unusual punishment, our courts have entertained the question of whether solitary confinement could amount to cruel and unusual punishment.

## Solitary Confinement

The Canadian experience has indicated that, in certain circumstances, solitary confinement or "dissociation" does constitute "cruel and unusual punishment."[104] Two cases deal with this matter in differing ways.

In a 1977 case, *Magrath* v. *The Queen*,[105] an inmate of the Mountain Institution in British Columbia was transferred to the maximum-security facility in New Westminster for a "flagrant or serious disciplinary offence" and given 10 days' **dissociation** punishment. His claim was that this was cruel and unusual punishment; however, the Court held that this was not the case. In *McCann et al.* v. *The Queen et al.*,[106] a group of inmates argued that

**rated capacity** The size of the inmate population a facility can handle, according to the judgment of experts.

**operational capacity** The number of inmates a prison can effectively accommodate based upon management considerations.

**design capacity** The number of inmates a prison was architecturally intended to hold when it was built or modified.

**dissociation** Isolating a prison inmate within the penal setting, often referred to as solitary confinement. Dissociation may be used as punishment to maintain discipline within the institution (punitive dissociation), or administratively as a prison management tactic to protect an inmate from the general population or to insulate the general prison population from an inmate's influence (administrative dissociation).

their dissociation within the New Westminster, B.C. institution was cruel and unusual punishment. Here, there was evidence that the inmates were held in small cells, measuring four metres by two metres, with cement slabs 10 centimetres off the ground covered by a sheet of plywood and a foam mattress for a bed. These cells were illuminated 24 hours a day and the inmates were only allowed to leave their cells for meals and a daily half-hour of exercise in the corridor of their cell block. This case is interesting in that it provides insight into expert testimony offered by penologists and psychiatrists with respect to these conditions. It was found that the circumstances did indeed amount to cruel and unusual punishment and constituted a form of torture. One of the inmates, McCann, was in this type of cell for 754 days continuously, and between January 1967 and May 1974 he spent a total of 1471 days in dissociation.

Research on solitary confinement appears to be contradictory. Some evidence indicates it is harmful to inmates, while other evidence suggests it is not. A recent analysis suggests the mental health and psychological functioning of inmates subjected to 60 days of segregation does not deteriorate.[107] Others have cited anecdotal evidence contradicting this finding,[108] and call for further research before definitive conclusions can be drawn.[109] Among the symptoms identified in the literature on solitary confinement are the following:[110]

- Perceptual distortions and hallucinations;

- Massive free-floating anxiety;

- Impaired concentration and memory;

- Persecutory thoughts, at times reaching delusional proportions;

- Acute confusional states, at times associated with dissociation, mutism, and partial amnesia;

- Impulsive behaviour, for example, sudden mutilation or violence;

- Aggressive fantasies;

- Fatigue, insomnia, loss of appetite, nausea, headaches, and depression.

In Canadian prisons, solitary confinement takes on two forms: punitive dissociation and administrative dissociation. Punitive dissociation involves placing inmates into solitary confinement as a form of punishment. It may only be imposed following a disciplinary hearing at which principles of fairness must be followed. Administrative dissociation involves inmates being sent into solitary confinement at the direction of the prison authorities. This occurs at the request of some inmates who do not want to remain in the general population. Inmates who were police officers prior to being sent to prison and inmate informants typically request isolation from the general population. However, periodically, an inmate will be segregated into solitary confinement against his or her will at the discretion of the prison administration. This occurs where the administration believes solitary confinement is necessary in the best interests of the institution. A task force of the Correctional Service of Canada found in 1997 that about one-half of the 722 inmates in administrative segregation in federal penitentiaries at the time were involuntarily segregated.[111] The reasons for administrative segregation vary widely, but inmates are administratively segregated when the administration believes the inmate is going to harm or intimidate other inmates, and when the administration fears the inmate in question will engage in other unlawful or disruptive behaviour. Professor Michael Jackson has studied the process for many years, and concludes that Canada's use of solitary confinement continues to run counter to human rights principles.[112]

Recent years have witnessed a shift in public attitudes in favour of the just deserts model of corrections. Such a view downplays reform or rehabilitation in favour of ensuring that prisons punish offenders, giving them what is believed to be their deserved punishment. Symptomatic of this view is the popularity of conservative Canadian critics in Canada's West. These critics would like to see a clampdown on prison comforts such as "pizza and pornography" parties; inmates sharing child pornography materials; miniature golf courses; prisons with horses, mountain bikes, and ceramic studios; and other comforts perceived to be excessive.[113]

Other get-tough initiatives can be seen in the "three strikes and you're out" laws now appearing before state legislatures throughout the United States. "Three-strikes" legislation[114] mandates lengthy prison terms for criminal offenders convicted of a third violent crime or felony. While "three-strikes" laws have either been enacted or are being considered in more than 30 states and by the U.S. federal government (which requires life imprisonment for federal criminals convicted of three violent felonies or drug offences), critics of such laws say that these laws will not prevent crime. Jerome Skolnick, of the New York University School of Law, for example, criticizes three-strikes legislation because, he says, while it may satisfy society's desire for retribution to "lock 'em up and throw away the key,"[115] such a practice will almost certainly not reduce the risk of victimization—especially the risk of becoming a victim of random violence. That is so, says Skolnick, because most violent crimes are committed by young men between the ages of 13 and 23. "It follows," according to Skolnick, "that if we jail them for life after their third conviction, we will get them in the twilight of their careers, and other young offenders will take their place." Three-strikes programs, says Skolnick, will lead to creation of "the most expensive, taxpayer-supported middle-age and old-age entitlement program in the history of the world," which will provide housing and medical care to older, burned-out law violators. However, others contend that this type of legislation is highly effective in reducing violent crime.[116]

Proponents of today's get-tough policies, while no doubt interested in personal safety, lower crime rates, and balanced budgets, are keenly focused on retribution. And where retribution fuels a correctional policy, then deterrence, reformation, and economic considerations play only secondary roles. The real issue for the advocates of retribution-based correctional policies is not whether these policies deter crime or lower crime rates, but rather the overriding conviction that criminals *deserve* punishment. As more and more U.S. states continue to enact three-strikes and other get-tough legislation, prison populations across the United States will swell even more. The new just deserts era of correctional philosophy, however, provides what has become for many an acceptable rationale for prison expansion. Canadian lawmakers are under continuing pressure to stiffen penalties and consider making prisons a much less hospitable environment in which to live. California officials estimate that three-strikes legislation "will account for over 50 per cent of the prison population" in that state by 2004.[117] Given projections like these, many now claim that the new retribution-based "lock 'em-up" philosophy may bode ill for the future of corrections.

## Selective Incapacitation—A Strategy to Reduce Overcrowding

Some authors have identified the central problem of the present era as one of selective versus collective incapacitation.[118] Collective incapacitation is a strategy that would imprison almost all serious offenders and is still found today in jurisdictions that rely upon lengthy predetermined, or fixed, sentences for given offences or for a series of specific offences (as in the case of three-strikes legislation just discussed). Collective incapacitation is, however, prohibitively expensive as well as unnecessary in the opinion of many experts.

Prison contraband on display in a supervisor's office. Note the handmade quality and concealability of most of the weapons.

Not all offenders need to be imprisoned, because not all represent a continuing threat to society—but those who do are difficult to identify.[119]

In many jurisdictions where the just deserts initiative holds sway, selective incapacitation is rapidly becoming the rule. Selective incapacitation seeks to identify the potentially most dangerous criminals with the goal of selectively removing them from society. Repeat offenders with records of serious and violent crimes are the most likely candidates for incapacitation—as are those who will probably commit such crimes in the future even though they have no records. But potentially violent offenders cannot be readily identified, and those thought likely to commit crimes cannot be sentenced to lengthy prison terms for things they have not yet done.[120]

In support of selective incapacitation, many U.S. states have enacted career offender statutes, which attempt to outline criteria for accurately identifying potentially dangerous offenders out of known criminal populations. However, efforts at selective incapacitation have been criticized for yielding a rate of "false positives" of over 60 per cent,[121] and some authors have been quick to call selective incapacitation a "strategy of failure."[122] In any event, as the just deserts model matures, it is likely that we will see clear-cut targeting of violent offenders and the exclusion of offenders who commit minor drug crimes, property crimes such as the burglary of an uninhabited dwelling or business, and other non-violent offences. Canada's dangerous offender legislation, set out in sections 752–761 of the *Criminal Code*, and the provisions that allow authorities to hold high-risk offenders until their sentences expire reflect this country's efforts to selectively incapacitate offenders who are believed to constitute the highest risks.[123]

# PRISONS TODAY IN CANADA

Today, the Correctional Service of Canada is responsible for 53 federal institutions, 17 community correctional centres, 71 parole offices, and 19 district offices.[124] Table 11–2 shows how these federal correctional facilities are presently classified.

The offender population in Canada's federal institutions as of April 29, 2001, was 12 815. Of that total, 97 per cent (12 430) were men, and 3 per cent (385) were women. In 2000–01, there were a total of 235 000 adults sentenced to correctional institutions in Canada (this includes all provincial and territorial prisons as well as federal institutions).[125] This figure calculates to a rate of adult imprisonment in Canada of 133 per 100 000 adult population. There are more offenders in provincial and territorial prisons than there are in federal penitentiaries at any given time. The average daily count for offenders sentenced to provincial/territorial institutions was 10 953 inmates in 2000–01, while a further 7428 were remanded in custody pending trial.

**TABLE 11–2** Classification of Correctional Service of Canada Institutions

| Level of Security | Region | | | | | |
|---|---|---|---|---|---|---|
| | **Atlantic** | **Quebec** | **Ontario** | **Prairies** | **Pacific** | **Total** |
| Maximum Security | 1 | 3 | 2 | 1 | 1 | 8 |
| Medium Security | 2 | 5 | 5 | 4 | 4 | 20 |
| Minimum Security | 1 | 3 | 4 | 7 | 2 | 17 |
| Multi-level | 1 | 1 | 2 | 3 | 1 | 8 |
| Community Corr. Ctr. | 4 | 6 | 3 | 3 | 1 | 17 |
| **Total** | **9** | **18** | **16** | **18** | **9** | **70** |

*Source*: "Basic Facts About Corrections in Canada: Facilities." (2003, February). © Her Majesty the Queen in Right of Canada. All rights reserved. *Let's Talk*, Volume 25, No. 3, Correctional Services of Canada. 2000. Reproduced with permission of the Minister of Public Works and Government Services Canada, 2003. Accessible at time of writing at **www.csc-scc.gc.ca/text/faits/facts07-content04_e.shtml**. Reproduced with permission of Correctional Service of Canada.

Federal institutions house inmates for considerably longer periods of time than do provincial institutions. The "two-year rule" dictates that sentences shorter than two years are to be served in a provincial facility, while sentences of two years or longer are served in the federal system.[126] Accordingly, the vast majority of prison admissions (over 90 per cent) are received by the provincial system, for relatively short sentences.[127] Nearly three-quarters of offenders sentenced to serve time in provincial facilities were granted a sentence of three months or less in 2000–01.[128] In fact, almost one-half (48 per cent) of provincial prison admissions were for one month or less. In federal institutions, almost one-half (47 per cent) of sentence admissions were for a duration of between two and three years. Only 4 per cent of federal admissions were for life sentences.[129]

In the United States, there are approximately 1500 state and 84 federal prisons in operation today, although more are quickly being built, as both the state and federal governments scramble to fund and construct new facilities. America's prison population more than quadrupled in the 20 years following 1980, and by January 2001, America's prisons (combined state and federal populations) held 1 381 892 inmates.[130]

Prisons in the United States are even more crowded than those in Canada. The incarceration rate for U.S. state and federal prisoners serving a sentence of more than one year is currently about 480 prisoners per every 100 000 U.S. residents.[131] Racial disparity is quite marked in the U.S.: the rate of incarceration for whites is 1108 per 100 000 white men in their late twenties, the rate for blacks is 9749 per 100 000 black males.[132]

Most people sentenced to Canadian federal penitentiaries have been convicted of violent crimes (53 per cent), while property crimes (18 per cent) are the second most common category for which inmates have been sentenced, and drug crimes are the reason for which 17 per cent of federal sentences are imposed.[133] In contrast, prisoners sentenced for property crimes are usually the single largest group of provincial inmates (e.g., 27 per cent of admissions in B.C., and 28 per cent in Ontario), while violent offence rates among provincial prison admissions vary quite widely, ranging from only 5 per cent in Quebec to up to 46 per cent in Manitoba.[134] The imprisonment of drug offenders accounted for less than 10 per cent of provincial prison admissions in 2000–01.[135] In Canada, the breakdown of most serious offences committed on admission to custody is reflected in Figure 11–2.

The inmate populations in both Canada[136] and the United States, in general, suffer from a low level of formal education, come from a socially disadvantaged background, and lack significant vocational skills.[137] Most adult inmates have served some time in juvenile correctional facilities.[138]

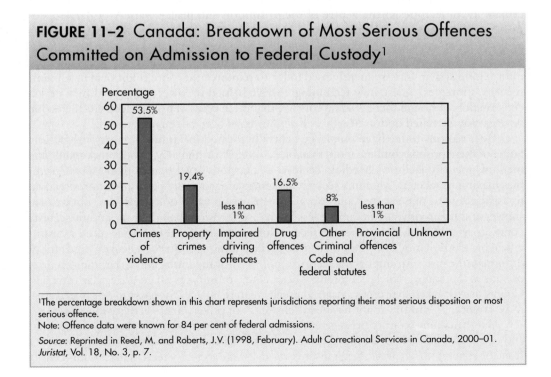

**FIGURE 11–2** Canada: Breakdown of Most Serious Offences Committed on Admission to Federal Custody[1]

[1]The percentage breakdown shown in this chart represents jurisdictions reporting their most serious disposition or most serious offence.

Note: Offence data were known for 84 per cent of federal admissions.

*Source:* Reprinted in Reed, M. and Roberts, J.V. (1998, February). Adult Correctional Services in Canada, 2000–01. *Juristat*, Vol. 18, No. 3, p. 7.

# Federal Penitentiaries

The size of prison facilities varies greatly. There are currently eight maximum-security institutions in the federal penitentiary system, each with an average population of over 200 inmates. The populations of several institutions exceed that figure; for example, Kingston Penitentiary currently houses 372 inmates.

At the federal level, the Correctional Service of Canada (CSC) employed more than 15 000 people in 2001. This figure does not include the approximately 10 000 volunteers who are actively involved in CSC activities such as tutoring, inmate literacy training, visitation programs, social, recreational, multicultural activities, and substance and alcohol abuse programs,[139] with the majority performing direct custodial tasks in state institutions. In Canada, in 1997, females represented 37.3 per cent of those employed by the CSC.[140]

The CSC has divided Canada into five regions: Pacific, Prairies, Ontario, Quebec, and Atlantic. Each region has a headquarters, which is responsible for administering the facilities in the region, and has similar characteristics, typically consisting of the following:

- One or more high-security penitentiaries for long-term, high-risk cases;
- Two or more medium-security institutions for the bulk of offenders who are not high risks;
- One institution for adult women, or facilities within a male prison to separately house female offenders;
- One specialized mental health–type security prison, referred to as a Regional Psychiatric Centre or Regional Health Centre, for mentally ill prisoners and offenders with psychiatric treatment needs; and
- Two or more community correctional centres for low-risk offenders.

# Security Levels

Maximum-security prisons are the institutions most often portrayed in movies and on television. They tend to be either massive old prisons with high stone walls, or recently constructed facilities with cell blocks surrounded by high, chain-link fencing and guard towers. The newer facilities incorporate advances in prison architecture to provide tight security without sacrificing building aesthetics. Maximum-custody prisons tend to locate cells and other inmate living facilities at the centre of the institution and place a variety of barriers between the living area and the institution's outer perimeter. Technological innovations such as electric perimeters, laser motion detectors, electronic and pneumatic locking systems, metal detectors, X-ray machines, television surveillance, radio communications, and computer information systems are frequently used today to reinforce the more traditional maximum-security strategies. These new technologies have helped to lower the cost of new prison construction, although there is some concern that these types of prison electronic detection devices may be relied on too heavily before they have been adequately tested.

Most regions today have one large centrally located maximum-security institution. Some of these prisons combine more than one custody level and may be both maximum- and medium-security facilities. Medium security is a custody level that in many ways resembles maximum security. Medium-security prisoners are generally permitted more freedom to associate with one another and can go to the prison yard, exercise room, library, and shower and bathroom facilities under less intense supervision than their maximum-security counterparts. Indeed, the perimeter security of a medium-level facility is often indistinguishable from that of a maximum-security facility, although internal security precautions differ significantly. An important security tool in both medium- and maximum-security prisons is the count, which is literally a head count of inmates taken at regular intervals. Counts may be taken four times a day and usually require inmates to report to designated areas to be counted. Until the count has been "cleared," all other inmate activity must cease.

Many medium-security prisons tend to be smaller than maximum-security institutions and often have barbed-wire-topped chain-link fences; however, others use the more secure stone or concrete-block walls, being institutions that were formerly used as maximum-security facilities. In the more modern facilities, cells and living quarters tend to have more windows and are often located closer to the perimeter of the institution than is the case in maximum security. Dormitory-style housing, where prisoners live together in "ward"-like arrangements, may be employed in medium-security facilities. Medium-security facilities generally have more prison programs and opportunities for inmates to participate in recreational and other programs than do maximum-custody facilities.

Minimum-security institutions do not fit the stereotypical conception of prisons. Minimum-security inmates are generally housed in dormitory-like settings and are free to walk the yard and visit most of the prison facilities. Some newer prisons provide minimum-security inmates with private rooms, which they can decorate (within limits) according to their tastes. Inmates usually have free access to a "canteen," which sells personal products like cigarettes, toothpaste, and chocolate bars. Minimum-security inmates often wear their own clothes rather than uniforms worn by those inmates in higher custody levels. They work under only general supervision and usually have access to recreational, educational, and skills-training programs on the prison grounds. Guards are unarmed, gun towers do not exist, and fences, if they are present at all, are usually low and sometimes even unlocked. Many minimum-security prisoners participate in some sort of work or study release program, and some have extensive visitation and day parole privileges. Counts may still be taken, although most minimum-security institutions keep track of inmates through daily administrative work schedules. The primary "force" holding inmates in minimum-security institutions is their own restraint. Inmates live with the knowledge that minimum-security institutions are one step removed from close correctional supervision and that if they fail to meet the expectations of administrators, they will be transferred into more secure institutions, which will probably delay their release. Inmates returning from assignments in the community may be frisked for contraband, but body cavity searches are rare in minimum custody, being reserved primarily for inmates suspected of smuggling.

When offenders enter the prison system, most jurisdictions assign prisoners to initial custody levels based upon their perceived dangerousness, escape risk, and type of offence. The initial offender-intake assessment is performed at a regional reception centre, where all inmates being taken into the system are housed together for a short period to assess their level of risk and their individual needs. After assessment, some inmates may be placed at the medium- (or even minimum-) custody level. Inmates move through custody levels according to the progress they are judged to have made in self-control and demonstrated responsibility. Serious, violent criminals and, in particular, all offenders convicted of murder begin their prison careers with lengthy sentences in maximum-security custody. They will eventually have the opportunity, in most cases, to work their way down to minimum security, although the process may take a number of years. Those who "mess up" and represent continuous disciplinary problems are returned to higher custody levels. Minimum-security prisons, as a result, house inmates convicted of all types of criminal offences.

The security level at a typical Canadian penitentiary today is either medium or minimum. Medium- and minimum-security institutions house the bulk of the country's federal prison population (over 85 per cent), and offer a number of programs and services for rehabilitating offenders and for creating the conditions necessary for a successful re-entry of the inmate into society. Most prisons offer psychiatric services, academic education, vocational education, substance abuse treatment, health care, counselling, recreation, library services, religious programs, and industrial and agricultural training. The Correctional Service of Canada is responsible for approximately 12 500 inmates on any particular day.[141]

Table 11–3 provides a listing of federal facilities across Canada.

## The Provincial Prison System

At the time of Confederation, responsibility over "public and reformatory prisons" passed to the provinces, while the federal government took over the responsibility for penitentiaries. This split in jurisdiction persists to the present day, with provinces being responsible for "public and reformatory prisons," housing inmates sentenced to less than two years, and the federal government exercising control over "penitentiaries," housing inmates whose aggregate sentence is two years or longer. In 2002, the Canadian Centre for Justice Statistics

## TABLE 11–3 The Correctional Service of Canada's Facilities across Canada in 1986

| Region | Security Level | Rated Capacity | Year Opened |
|---|---|---|---|
| **Atlantic Region** | | | |
| Atlantic Institution | Max. | 240 | 1987 |
| Dorchester Penitentiary | Med. | 298 | 1880 |
| Nova Institution for Women | Min./Med. | 24 | 1995 |
| Springhill Institution | Med. | 374 | 1967 |
| Westmorland Institution | Min. | 237 | 1975 |
| **Quebec Region** | | | |
| Reg. Rec. Centre | Max. | 90 | 1984 |
| Archambault Institution | Med. | 285 | 1969 |
| Leclerc Insitution | Med. | 482 | 1961 |
| Cowansville Institution | Med. | 427 | 1966 |
| Drummond Institution | Med. | 252 | 1984 |
| Federal Training Ctr. | Min. | 377 | 1932 |
| Joliette Institution for Women | Min./Med. | 105 | 1997 |
| La Macaza Institution | Med. | 240 | 1978 |
| Montée-St-François Institution | Min. | 243 | 1963 |
| Sainte-Anne-des-Plaines Institution | Min. | 180 | 1970 |
| Donnacona Institution | Max. | 359 | 1986 |
| Port-Cartier Institution | Max. | 236 | 1988 |
| **Ontario Region** | | | |
| Kingston Penitentiary | Max. | 431 | 1835 |
| Regional Treatment Centre | Max. | 157 | 1959 |
| Grand Valley Inst. for Women | Med./Min. | 72 | 1997 |
| Millhaven Institution | Max. | 276 | 1971 |
| Collins Bay Institution | Med. | 462 | 1930 |
| Joyceville Institution | Med. | 453 | 1959 |
| Warkworth Institution | Med. | 523 | 1967 |
| Bath Institution | Med. | 309 | 1972 |
| Beaver Creek Institution | Min. | 160 | 1961 |
| Fernbrook Institution | Med. | 194 | 1998 |
| Frontenac Institution | Min. | 193 | 1962 |
| Pittsburgh Institution | Min. | 182 | 1963 |
| **Prairie Region** | | | |
| Bowden Institution | Med. | 495 | 1974 |
| Reg. Psychiatric Centre | Multi. | 194 | 1978 |
| Saskatchewan Pen. | Max./Med. | 64/499 | 1911 |
| Edmonton Institution | Max. | 216 | 1978 |
| Edmonton Institution for Women | Med./Min. | 45 | 1996 |
| Stony Mountain Institution | Med. | 490 | 1876 |
| Drumheller Institution | Med. | 585 | 1967 |
| Grande Cache Institution | Min. | 440 | 1983 |
| Rockwood Institution | Min. | 168 | 1962 |
| Grierson Centre | Min. | 64 | 1972 |
| Pê Sâkâstêw Centre | Min. | 40 | 1997 |
| Riverbend Institution | Min. | 102 | 1962 |
| Willow Cree Healing Lodge | Min. | 40 | 2003 |
| **Pacific Region** | | | |
| Regional Health Centre | Max. | 153 | 1972 |
| Kent Institution | Max. | 215 | 1979 |
| Kwìkwèxwelhp Institution | Min. | 87 | 1975 |
| Matsqui Institution | Med. | 284 | 1966 |
| Mountain Institution | Med. | 320 | 1962 |
| Mission Institution | Med. | 230 | 1977 |
| William Head Institution | Med. | 225 | 1959 |
| Ferndale Institution | Min. | 134 | 1973 |

*Source:* The Correctional Service of Canada. "Organization" and "Regions and Facilities," accessible at time of writing at **www.csc-scc.gc.ca/text/region/regions_e.shtml**

released data on provincial and federal facilities in Canada, noting that more than one-half (60 per cent) of all incarcerated individuals in Canada are currently being held in provincial correctional facilities.[142] However, they note that of the 31 500 offenders in custody in Canada, 7428 of them are being held on remand, and are therefore not under sentence. Of the sentenced offenders, 10 953 were sentenced to provincial facilities, and 12 732 were committed to federal custody. While the rate of offenders sentenced to both federal and provincial custody has declined in recent years, the rate of remand has increased significantly, offsetting those declines. The result is a relatively stable incarcerated population in this country.

Inmates serving time in provincial prisons are housed for relatively short durations. While every day probably seems like an eternity for those sitting behind bars, it is noteworthy that almost one-half of provincially sentenced inmates are committed to a sentence of one month or less. Only 8 per cent of provincial inmates are serving a sentence of one year or longer.

Each province and territory is responsible for the maintenance and administration of its correctional facilities. Provincial/territorial correctional facilities include remand centres that house the accused who are awaiting trial and facilities that house convicted offenders sentenced to less than two years in prison. In addition to providing the above facilities, the provinces and territories also provide youth custody facilities (discussed in Chapter 14) and custodial facilities for inmates found unfit to stand trial and not criminally responsible on account of mental disorder. So there can be a variety of different kinds of institutions in each province or territory. Accordingly, there is considerable regional variation in the provision of correctional services to short-term offenders. For example, in Nova Scotia, the Department of Justice's Correctional Services Division is responsible for adult correctional institutions, young offender custody services, and community corrections. Presently, this province maintains nine adult provincial correctional facilities,[143] three young offender facilities, and seventeen community corrections offices.

The security ratings and programs are different for each type of institution. For example, facilities for inmates who suffer from mental disorders are typically secure psychiatric facilities, which may also be used for pretrial and pre-sentence mental health assessments. Generally, provincial facilities provide fewer programs than do federal institutions, due in large part to the shorter duration of detention.

The provinces and territories have historically managed to house provincial/territorial inmates at a lower cost than has the federal government, although the cost of maintaining correctional facilities is still considerable, even at the local level. The present scheme allows for the spreading of the correctional expense between the provincial and federal governments. Pre-Confederation, several of the British North American colonies had even constructed penal facilities. Some of these facilities, such as Ontario's provincial gaols (the traditional term for jails) in Cornwall (built in 1835), Chatham (1849), Brantford (1852), and Pembroke (1867), are still in operation as provincial prisons. Others, like the Kingston Penitentiary (1835), were taken over by the federal government. Beginning in the late 1990s, many provinces, particularly Ontario, began to identify the older facilities that were in need of replacement, and began a program of decommissioning the older facilities, replacing them with modern ones. In recent years, provincial expenditures on correctional facilities have remained relatively stable in constant dollar terms, while similar federal government expenditures have continued to increase. Since pre-Confederation, each provincial or territorial jurisdiction has had its own story to tell with respect to the growth and development of its correctional system.[144]

When riots, disturbances, or suspicious deaths occur at prisons, the government responds by conducting inquiries, reviews, and inquests. These examinations generate a significant amount of detailed insight on individual institutions.[145] The results of these examinations have often precipitated changes in other correctional facilities.[146] For example, in Ontario, which has had a long tradition of public scrutiny directed at its prisons, jails, and reformatories,[147] the Royal Commission on the Toronto Jail provided an important insight into the need for reform and change in Canadian jails and custodial services.[148] Additionally, such inquiries have had an impact on prison management and frequently generate a considerable amount of research and documentation that provides solid background for students and policy makers alike.[149]

Aboriginal offenders make up a disproportionate number of inmates in both federal and provincial institutions, but more so in provincial prisons in Canada's West and North. According to the 1996 census, only 2 per cent of Canada's adult population were aboriginal people; however, 17 per cent of federal admissions and 19 per cent of provincial admissions to custody were aboriginal. In the Yukon, 17 per cent of the adult population were aboriginal, yet 72 per cent of sentenced admissions to the territorial facilities were aboriginal. In Manitoba, 9 per cent of the population were aboriginal, while 64 per cent of provincial prison admissions were aboriginal. In Saskatchewan, the results were similar, with 8 per cent of the population being aboriginal and 76 per cent of the provincial prison admissions being aboriginal, respectively.

## Recent Improvements

Canada's prison system is in continual transition. This system has also undergone considerable scrutiny over the years. Many inquiry commissions and court challenges have identified problems in various penal institutions across Canada. While the negative aspects of prisons have been readily emphasized over the years, rarely has the system received any commendation for the improvements that have been made. In the midst of frequent lawsuits, court-ordered changes in prison administration, and overcrowded conditions, the development of outstanding prison facilities rarely has been recognized. Those institutions which have provided positive environments are frequently not even given any positive recognition within the prison system itself.

In the United States, there has been a move towards accreditation of correctional facilities. The American Correctional Association Commission on Accreditation has developed a set of standards that correctional institutions can use in self-evaluation. Those institutions that meet the standards can apply for accreditation under the program. Unfortunately, accreditation of prisons has few "teeth." Although unaccredited universities would not be in business for long, few prisoners can choose the institution to which they will be sentenced. However, Canada took a small step towards accreditation when, in 1985, the Canadian Criminal Justice Association published a series of manuals that contain standards for various areas of relevant activity within the criminal justice system (i.e., prisons, central agencies, parole authorities, probation services, parole field services, community residential centres, and community correctional centres). The manual of standards on prisons contains a wealth of important data that outlines a potential basis for accreditation of Canadian adult corrections, covering the following topics:[150]

- Organization;
- Food services;
- Personnel and training;
- Security and control;
- Financial management;
- Use of force;
- Protection of rights;
- Discipline and segregation;
- Information systems;
- Health care services;

- Facility;
- Psychological services;
- Orientation and classification;
- Conditional release;
- Prisoner communication;
- Community interaction;
- Programs—general, employment, education, library, recreation, counselling, religion;
- Fire, safety, and occupational health.

In Canada, the federal government supports a significant amount of research through the Correctional Service of Canada. This department undertakes important research studies and publishes the results for the wider correctional community.[151] Such research produces information that should be used to form the basis of correctional reform throughout the country. The federal government has attempted to incorporate the latest research findings into its prison-related policy and legislative amendments.

In 1998, Parliament began a comprehensive review of the *Corrections and Conditional Release Act*. This legislation is the foundation of the Canadian correctional system, and the federal government has committed itself to an open dialogue on the effectiveness of this legislation. In order to generate discussion with respect to the Act, the Solicitor General of Canada's office has released a consultation document.[152] This report found that the policies embodied in the Act had a significant impact on facilitating the reintegration of offenders into society. The review indicates that efforts to improve public safety through correctional reform remain on going.

## Women and Prison

Although women account for less than 10 per cent of the prison population in Canada,[153] their presence has been slowing increasing in our prisons.[154] As of April 1, 2001, only

3 per cent of inmates sentenced to federal incarceration were women.[155] Jailed women face a number of special problems. As a result of their relative scarcity in prison populations, particularly at the federal level, resources for them are often lacking.[156] Not all jurisdictions today even provide separate facilities for female inmates. Educational levels are very low among jailed women, and few are high-school graduates.[157] Pregnancy is another problem. Across the United States, 4 per cent of female inmates are pregnant at the time they come to jail,[158] but as many as 40 per cent of the population of federally sentenced women in Canada already have children when they go to prison.[159] As a consequence, jailed mothers are frequently separated from their children.

The issue of women in jails in Canada has proven to be a difficult one. At the federal level, prior to the mid-1990s, the Correctional Service of Canada only provided one institution, the Kingston Prison for Women, for all federally sentenced women. Problems at that institution resulted in strong recommendations and a decision to close down that facility. Madam Justice Louise Arbour conducted a detailed inquiry into events at this facility in 1994. It began with the airing of a videotape that showed members of the CSC emergency response team dealing with female inmates in a manner that shocked the Canadian public.[160] Arbour's report, and the recommendations it contained, had far-reaching implications for the treatment of female offenders in Canada's prisons and jails.[161] In 1994, the *Forum on Corrections Research*, published by the Correctional Service of Canada, devoted an entire issue to topics related to "Women in Prison."[162] This area of concern has been long neglected; however, the appearance of several essays, articles, and studies has begun to correct this oversight.[163]

Between 1995 and 1997, the federal government opened up five new multi-security-level institutions across the country to house federally sentenced women. These institutions, located in Alberta, Saskatchewan, Ontario, Quebec, and Nova Scotia, allowed female inmates the benefit of residing in an institution that may be closer to their homes, thereby fostering visits from family and friends. These facilities are also much more hospitable than the old Kingston Prison for Women. The living quarters provide communal living space, with shared kitchen, dining, laundry, and bathroom facilities. The new design was envisioned as a way to allow the women to regain control over their lives, and to encourage them to work together as a community.

In 2000, the Kingston Prison for Women was finally closed, with the last remaining inmates being sent to the various new institutions across the country. However, problems persisted. The multi-security-level facilities were not considered adequate for handling some of the more difficult inmates in the federal system. As a result, a number of the maximum-security female inmates were moved into male institutions, where they were provided separate facilities. The Correctional Service of Canada is still in the process of dealing with this situation by modifying some of the new female institutions to accommodate the increased regimentation required of higher security classified women.

Drug abuse is another significant source of difficulty for jailed women. A significant proportion of women who are admitted to jail, perhaps as high as 70 per cent, have a substance abuse problem at the time of admission.[164] Adding to the problem is the fact that substantive medical programs for female inmates, such as obstetrical and gynecological care, are often lacking. In planning adequate future medical services for female inmates, some writers have advised jail administrators to expect to see an increasingly common kind of inmate: "[a]n opiate-addicted female who is pregnant with no prior prenatal care having one or more sexually transmitted diseases, and fitting a high-risk category for AIDS (prostitution, IV drug use)."[165]

Female inmates are only half the story. Women working in corrections are the other. In a recent study,[166] Linda Zupan, one of the new generation of outstanding jail scholars, found that women were disproportionately employed in jobs at the lower ranks. Although 60 per cent of all support staff (secretaries, cooks, and janitors) in her study were women, only one in every ten chief administrators was female. Zupan explains this pattern by pointing to the "token-status" of women staff members in some of the nation's jails.[167]

Canada recently appointed a female Deputy Commissioner of Corrections in an effort to begin to redress the glass ceiling that has historically prevented women from assuming senior administration positions in corrections. In 1996, Nancy Stableforth was appointed Deputy Commissioner for Women in the CSC. In 2002, she was also made Deputy Commissioner for the entire Ontario region of the federal Correctional Service. As of 1998, there were no less than 13 federal institutions headed by female wardens.[168] Despite the lack of women among the senior staff in most correctional systems, Zupan found that women correctional employees in the U.S. were significantly committed to their careers and that attitudes of male workers towards female co-workers in jails were generally positive.[169] As Zupan notes, "[a]n obvious problem associated with the lack of female officers in jails housing females concerns the potential for abuse and exploitation of women inmates by male staff."[170]

Women have been employed by Canada's federal Penitentiary Service since the opening of the Prison for Women in 1934. However, in 1978, female correctional officers began to be employed in all-male institutions. By 1998, 22 per cent of staff in federal prisons were women. Jails that do hire women generally accord them equal footing with male staffers. Although cross-gender privacy is a potential area of concern, few jails limit the supervisory areas that may be visited by female officers working in male facilities. In three-quarters of the U.S. jails studied by Zupan, women officers were assigned to supervise male housing areas.[171] Only one in four jails that employed women restricted their access to unscreened shower and toilet facilities used by men and/or to other areas such as sexual offender units.

## Direct Supervision Jails

Some authors have suggested that the problems found in many jails today stem from "mismanagement, lack of fiscal support, heterogeneous inmate populations, overuse and misuse of detention, overemphasis on custodial goals, and political and public apathy."[172] Others propose that environmental and organizational elements inherent in traditional jail architecture and staffing have given rise to today's difficulties.[173] Traditional jails, say these observers, were built upon the assumption that inmates are inherently violent and potentially destructive. Hence, most of today's jails were constructed to give staff maximum control over inmates—through the use of thick walls, bars, and other architectural barriers to the free movement of inmates. Such barriers, however, also limit the correctional staff's visibility and access to many confinement areas. As a consequence, the barriers tend to encourage the kinds of inmate behaviour that jails were meant to control. Inefficient hallway patrols and expensive video technology help in overcoming the limits that old jail architecture places on supervision.

In an effort to solve many of the problems that have dogged jails in the past, a new jail management strategy emerged during the 1980s. Called **direct supervision** (or podular/direct supervision, or PDS), this contemporary approach "joins podular/unit architecture with a participative, proactive management philosophy."[174] Often built as a system of "pods," or modular self-contained housing areas linked to one another, direct supervision jails eliminate the old physical barriers that separated staff and inmates. Gone are bars and isolated secure observation areas for officers, replaced by an open environment, in which inmates and correctional personnel mingle with relative freedom. In a growing number of such "new-generation" jails, large reinforced Plexiglas panels have supplanted walls and serve to separate activity areas, such as classrooms and dining halls, from one another. Soft furniture is often found throughout these institutions, and individual rooms take the place of cells, allowing inmates at least a modicum of personal privacy. In today's direct supervision jails, 16 to 46 inmates typically live in one pod, with correctional staffers present among the inmate population on an around-the-clock basis.

The first direct supervision jail opened in the 1970s in Contra Costa County, California. This 386-bed facility became a model for other new-generation jails. In Canada, this model has been adopted in many recently constructed facilities, such as those in British Columbia and Ontario.

Direct supervision jails have been touted for their tendency to reduce inmate dissatisfaction, and for their ability to deter rape and violence among the inmate population. By eliminating architectural barriers to staff/inmate interaction, direct supervision facilities are said to place officers back in control of institutions. While these innovative facilities are still too new to assess fully, a number of studies have already demonstrated their success at reducing the likelihood of inmate victimization. One such study,[175] published in 1994, found that staff morale in direct supervision jails was far higher than in traditional institutions,

**direct supervision**
Describes temporary confinement facilities that eliminate many of the traditional barriers between inmates and correctional staff. Physical barriers in direct supervision jails are far less common than in traditional jails, allowing staff members the opportunity for greater interaction with, and control over, residents.

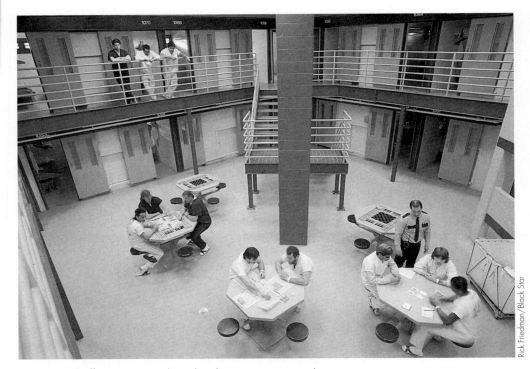

Inmates and officers can mingle in this direct supervision jail.

while inmates reported reduced stress levels, and fewer inmate-on-inmate and inmate-on-staff assaults occurred in podular jails. Similarly sexual assault, jail rape, suicide, and escape have all been found to occur far less frequently in direct supervision facilities than in traditional institutions.[176] Significantly, new-generation jails appear to reduce substantially the number of lawsuits brought by inmates and lower the incidence of adverse court-ordered judgments against jail administrators.

The most comprehensive study of direct supervision jails to date, which reported its results in April 1995, found that 114 confinement facilities across the United States could be classified as direct supervision facilities.[177] The study, which attempted to survey all such jails, found that direct supervision jails:

1. Range in size from small jails with 24 inmates (and 12 officers on staff), to large facilities with 2737 (and 600 correctional officers);

2. Average 591 inmates and employ 148 officers, with an inmate-to-officer ratio of 16.8:1 during a given shift;

3. Are podular in design, with an average of 47 inmates and one officer per pod at any given time;

4. Hold local, state, and U.S. federal prisoners. About 45 per cent of the institutions surveyed held only local inmates, while the rest held mixed groups of inmates;

5. Varied by security level. The majority (about 59 per cent) were mixed-security levels, while 26 per cent were maximum security jails. About 13 per cent described themselves as medium-security facilities, and another 2 per cent fit within the minimum-security category; and

6. Were usually unionized. About 70 per cent of direct supervision jails reported unionized staffs.

While the number of direct supervision jails seems to be rapidly growing, such facilities are not without their problems, particularly in the United States. In 1993, for example, the 238-bed Rensselaer County PDS jail in Troy, New York, experienced a disturbance "that resulted in a total loss of control … removal of officers from the pods—and the escape of two inmates."[178] Sometime later, the 700-bed San Joaquin County Jail in Stockton, California, experienced numerous problems, including the escape of seven inmates.

Some authors[179] have recognized that new-generation jails are too frequently run by old-style managers and that correctional personnel sometimes lack the training needed to make the transition to the new style of supervision. Others[180] have suggested that managers of direct supervision jails, especially those at the mid-level, could benefit from clearer job descriptions and additional training. In the words of one Canadian advocate of direct supervision,[181] "training becomes particularly critical in direct supervision jails where relationships are more immediate and are more complex." Finally, people who hire prison staff recommend[182] that potential new staff members be psychologically screened and that pre-employment interviews be emphasized, to determine the suitability of applicants for correctional officer positions in direction supervision jails.

## Jails and the Future

In contrast to more visible issues confronting the justice system, such as gun control, the fiscal crisis, and youth gangs, jails have received relatively little attention from the media and have generally escaped close public scrutiny. Efforts, however, to improve the quality of jail life are under way. Some changes involve adding crucial programs for inmates. A recent American Jail Association study of drug treatment programs in jails, for example, found that "a small fraction (perhaps fewer than 10 per cent) of inmates needing drug treatment actually receive these services."[183] Follow-up efforts were aimed at developing standards to guide jails administrators in increasing the availability of drug treatment services to inmates.

Accommodating the needs of Canada's large aboriginal population has become, and will remain, a focal concern for institutional corrections in Canada. Many institutions have been developed as aboriginal healing lodges. These institutions typically employ staff of aboriginal decent, and bring in aboriginal Elders and Native Liaison Workers to deal with the special needs of aboriginal inmates. Aboriginal teachings, ceremonies, and other cultural elements are worked into the lives of the inmates in these institutions. Even existing penitentiaries have begun to incorporate aboriginal healing elements into their programs for native inmates. The future will likely bring increased efforts to accommodate the special needs of aboriginal offenders in both federal and provincial institutions.

Jail industries are another growing area in programs. The best of them serve the community while training inmates in marketable skills.[184] This trend will likely combine with private enterprise moving into prisons to capitalize on the large pool of inmate labour that is still relatively underdeveloped.[185] Inmate labour is inexpensive compared to labour on the free market, and is likely to be exploited both for profit and as a means of developing increased accountability of inmates. The high cost of housing inmates could be offset if inmates were able to pay a portion of their upkeep from the money made producing goods via prison industries. We are likely to see ongoing privatization of prisons, and increased privatization of services within existing public prisons in the years ahead.

Other innovative programs operate by using citizen volunteers. Today, many volunteers work in correctional facilities—many of them as tutors in general education programs. Others offer substance abuse counselling, marriage counselling, and chaplain's services. Citizen volunteers contribute countless hours of service time each year. Jail boot camps, like those in Ontario for youthful offenders, are also growing in popularity. The experiments in Ontario are being closely observed.

One final element in the unfolding saga of jail development should be mentioned: the emergence of jail standards. In Ontario, the Ministry of the Solicitor General and Correctional Services has established standards for police organizations that have lock-up facilities for the holding of prisoners. In the United States, the Commission on Accreditation for Corrections, operated jointly by the American Correctional Association and the U.S. federal government, has developed its own set of jail standards,[186] as has the National Sheriff's Association. Both sets of standards are designed to ensure a minimal level of comfort and safety in local lock-ups. Increased standards, though, are costly. Local jurisdictions, already hard-pressed to meet other budgetary demands, will probably be slow to upgrade their jails to meet such external guidelines, unless forced to. Ken Kerle, in a study[187] of 61 U.S. jails that was designed to test compliance with National Sheriff's Association's guidelines, discovered that in many standards areas—especially those of tool control, armory planning, community resources, release preparation, and riot planning—most jails were sorely out of compliance. Lack of a written plan was the most commonly cited reason for failing to meet the standards.

In what may be one of the best sets of recommendations for the development of jails that can serve into the current century, Joel A. Thompson and G. Larry Mays[188] suggest that:

- Higher level governments should provide financial aid and/or incentives to local governments for jail construction and renovation;

- All jurisdictions must develop mandatory jail standards;

- Mandatory jail inspections should become commonplace in the enforcement of standards;

- Citizens should be educated about the function and significance of jails to increase their willingness to fund new jail construction;

- All jails need to have written policies and procedures to be used in training and to serve as a basis for a defence against lawsuits; and

- Communities should explore alternatives to incarceration since most jail detainees are not threats to society and should not occupy scarce and expensive cell space.

# PRIVATE PRISONS

Some jurisdictions have begun to supplement their prison resources through contracts with private firms to provide custodial and other correctional services. The goal is to reduce over-crowding and to lower operating expenses. Corrections Corporation of America (CCA) was one of the first companies to offer privately operated correctional facilities to different states. In 2001, Management and Training Corporation was contracted by the government of Ontario to operate the Central North Correctional Facility at Penetanguishene. It was allotted a five-year contract at a cost of just over one-half of the amount spent by the government to operate a facility by itself. In 2002, the Ontario government contracted out the production of food services at the Maplehurst Correctional Complex in Milton to a private corporation. The movement towards privatization of prisons rests on sound historical ground. However, beyond Ontario, the Canadian experience has not yet fully embraced privatization of prisons. There has been some interest shown in the area of facilities for young offenders, as noted in Chapter 10. In Ontario, the strict discipline program is operated by a private organization that contracts with the provincial government for this purpose.

Many hurdles remain before the privatization movement can effectively provide large-scale custodial supervision. The Theory into Practice box on the next page addresses some of the questions about the movement towards private prisons. One of the most significant barriers to privatization lies in the efforts of public employee unions to keep prison jobs within the public sector. Other practical hurdles exist. Jurisdictions that do contract with private firms may face the spectre of strikes by guards, who do not come under public-sector employee laws restricting the ability of such employees to strike. Moreover, since responsibility for the protection of inmates' rights still lies with the government, the jurisdictions' liability will not transfer to private corrections.[189] In today's legal climate, it is unclear whether a jurisdiction can shield itself or its employees through private prison contracting, but it would appear that such shielding is unlikely to be recognized by the courts. To limit liability, governments will probably have to oversee private operations as well as set standards for training and custody.

Opponents of the movement towards privatization claim that cost reductions can only be achieved through lowered standards for the treatment of prisoners. They fear a return to the inhumane conditions of early jails, as private firms seek to turn prisons into profit-making operations. For jurisdictions that do choose to contract with private firms, the U.S. National Institute of Justice recommends a "regular and systematic sampling" of former inmates to appraise prison conditions, as well as "on-site inspections at least every year" of each privately run institution. Government personnel serving as monitors should be stationed in large facilities, and a "meticulous review" of all services should be conducted prior to the contract renewal date.[190]

- Can the government delegate its powers to incarcerate persons to a private firm?
- Can a private firm deprive persons of their liberty and exercise coercive authority, perhaps through use of deadly force?
- Who would be legally liable in the event of lawsuits?
- Who would be responsible for maintaining the prison if the private employees go on strike?
- Would a private company have the right to refuse to accept certain types of inmates, for example, those with AIDS?

- If a private firm went bankrupt, who would be responsible for the inmates and the facility?
- Could a private company reduce staff salaries or hire non-union members as a way of reducing costs?
- Would the "profit motive" operate to the detriment of the government or the inmates, either by keeping inmates in prison who should be released or by reducing services to a point at which inmates, guards, and the public were endangered?
- What options would a government with no facility of its own have if it became dissatisfied with the performance of the private firm?
- Is it appropriate for the government to circumvent the public's right to vote to increase its debt ceiling?

*Source*: Bureau of Justice Statistics. (1988). *Report to the Nation on Crime and Justice* (2nd ed.). Washington, D.C.: U.S. Department of Justice.

## SUMMARY

Modern prisons are the result of historical efforts to humanize the treatment of offenders. "Doing time for crime" has become society's answer to the corporal punishments of centuries past. Even so, questions remain about the conditions of imprisonment in contemporary prisons and penitentiaries, and modern corrections is far from a panacea. The security orientation of correctional staff and administration tends to downplay the importance of treatment programs. Existing prisons are overcrowded, and new ones are expensive to build. An end to crowding is nowhere in sight, and a new just deserts era is influencing today's prison policy, characterized by a "get-tough" attitude that continues to maintain prison populations even as it reduces inmate privileges, and expands the range of sentencing alternatives open to the courts. Studies demonstrating the likelihood of recidivism among prior correctional clients have called the whole correctional process into question, and the just deserts era may reflect a strategy of frustration more than one of hope.

Prisons today exist in a kind of limbo. As prison populations remain high, uncertainties about the usefulness of treatment have left few officials confident of their ability to rehabilitate offenders. The return of prison industries, the interest in efficient technologies of secure imprisonment, and court-mandated reforms are all signs that society has given up any hope of large-scale reformation among inmate populations.

## DISCUSSION QUESTIONS

1. Trace the historical development of imprisonment, in Canada, beginning with the introduction of the Auburn system in Kingston. Why has the prevalent style of imprisonment in Canada changed over time? What changes do you see coming?

2. In your opinion, would a return to physical punishments and public humiliation be effective deterrents of crime in today's world? Why or why not?

3. What do you think is the future of prison industries? Describe the future you envision. On what do you base your predictions?

4. What do you see as the role of private prisons? What will be the state of private prisons two decades from now?

5. Explain the pros and cons of the just deserts model of corrections. Do you believe that new rehabilitative models will be developed that will make just deserts a thing of the past? If so, on what will they be based?

6. What solutions, if any, do you see to the present overcrowded conditions of many prison systems? How might changes in the law help ease overcrowding? Are such changes a workable strategy? Why or why not?

# WEBLINKS

www.mpss.jus.gov.on.ca/english/english_default.html
**Ontario Ministry of Public Safety and Security**
The official Ontario government's website, containing information about the history and present-day operation of provincial corrections in that province.

www.csc-scc.gc.ca
**Correctional Service of Canada**
This government website contains information about the *Corrections and Conditional Release Act*, community operations, sex offender programs, women in prison, and other topics, as well as numerous CSC publications.

www.cbc.ca/prison/index.html
**Inside Canada's Prisons**
Excerpts of written summaries and video clips from a joint CBC/*Maclean's* documentary investigation into the federal penitentiary system in Canada.

www.icpa.ca
**International Corrections and Prisons Association**
ICPA provides a forum for criminal justice professionals to join in a dialogue and to share ideas and practices aimed at advancing professional corrections.

http://laws.justice.gc.ca/en/C-44.6/index.html
**Consolidated Statutes—C-44.6—Corrections and Conditional Release Act**
Legislation governing corrections in Canada.

www.csc-scc.gc.ca/bprisons/text/forum/bprisons/main_e.shtml
**Beyond Prisons Symposium—Kingston, Ontario**
This international symposium, held in Kingston, Ontario, in March 1998, was hosted by the Correctional Service of Canada in collaboration with the Canadian International Development Agency, and focused on the increasing reliance on incarceration as a means of addressing crime, and the resulting growth in prison populations.

www.corrections.com
**The Corrections Connection**
News and resources for the U.S. corrections industry.

# Prison Life

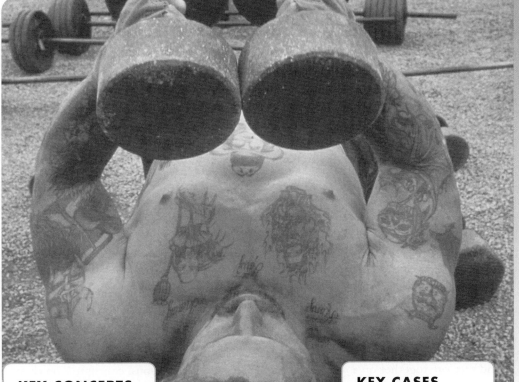

Sipa Press/Amineh Johannes

## KEY CONCEPTS

total institutions
prison subculture
prisonization
prison argot
hands-off doctrine

civil death
writ of *habeas corpus*
writ of *certiorari*
grievance procedure

## KEY CASES

*Solosky* v. *The Queen*
*R.* v. *Miller*
*Cardinal* v. *Director of
Kent Institution*
Re Maltby et al. and AG
Saskatchewan et al.

*Bryntwick* v. *Yeomans
and Rousseau*
*R.* v. *Olson*
*Weatherall* v. *Canada
(Attorney General)*

# REALITIES OF PRISON LIFE: THE MALE INMATE'S WORLD

For the first 150 years of their existence, prisons and prison life could be described by the phrase "out of sight, out of mind." Very few citizens cared about prison conditions, and those unfortunate enough to be locked away were regarded as lost to the world.[1] By the mid-1900s, however, beginning with the treatment era, such attitudes started to change. Concerned citizens began to offer their services to prison administrations, neighbourhoods began accepting work-release prisoners and halfway houses into their communities, and social scientists initiated the serious study of prison life.

This chapter describes the realities of prison life today, including prisoner lifestyles, prison subcultures, sexuality in prison, prison violence, and inmates' "rights" and grievance procedures. We will discuss both the world of the inmate and the staff world. A separate section on women in prison details the social structure of women's prisons, daily life in such facilities, and the various types of female inmates. We turn now to early research on prison life and will quickly move on to a discussion of the inmate world.

## Research on Prison Life—Total Institutions

Hans Reimer, then chairman of the Department of Sociology at Indiana University, set the tone for studies of prison life in 1935 when he voluntarily served three months in prison as an incognito participant observer.[2] Reimer reported the results of his studies to the American Prison Association, stimulating many other, albeit less spectacular, efforts to examine prison life. Other early studies include Donald Clemmer's *The Prison Community* (1940),[3] Gresham M. Sykes's *The Society of Captives: A Study of a Maximum Security Prison* (1958),[4] Richard A. Cloward et al.'s *Theoretical Studies in Social Organization of the Prison* (1960),[5] and Donald R. Cressey's *The Prison: Studies in Institutional Organization and Change* (1961).[6]

These studies and others focused primarily on maximum-security prisons for men. They treated correctional institutions as formal or complex organizations and employed the analytical techniques of organizational sociology, industrial psychology, and administrative science.[7] As modern writers on prisons have observed, "[t]he prison was compared to a primitive society, isolated from the outside world, functionally integrated by a delicate system of mechanisms, that kept it precariously balanced between anarchy and accommodation."[8]

Another approach to the study of prison life was developed by Erving Goffman, who coined the term **total institutions** in a 1961 study of prisons and mental hospitals.[9] Goffman described total institutions as places where the same people work, play, eat, sleep, and recreate together on a daily basis. Such places include prisons, concentration camps, mental hospitals, seminaries, and other facilities in which residents are cut off from the larger society either forcibly or willingly. Total institutions are small societies. They evolve their own distinctive values and styles of life and place pressures on residents to fulfil rigidly proscribed behavioural roles.

Generally, the work of prison researchers built upon findings of other social scientists who discovered that any group with similar characteristics, subject to confinement in the same place at the same time, develops its own subculture with specific components that govern hierarchy, behavioural patterns, values, and so on. Prison subcultures, described in the next section, also provide the medium through which prison values are communicated and expectations made known.

**total institutions**
Enclosed facilities, separated from society both socially and physically, where the inhabitants share all aspects of their lives on a daily basis.

## Prison Subcultures

Two social realities coexist in prison settings. One is the official structure of rules and procedures put in place by the wider society and enforced by prison staff. The other is the more informal, but decidedly more powerful, inmate world. The inmate world, best described by its pervasive immediacy in the lives of inmates, is controlled by **prison subculture**. The realities of prison life—including a large and often densely packed inmate population that

**prison subculture**
The values and behavioural patterns characteristic of prison inmates. Prison subculture has been found to have surprising consistencies across the country.

must look to the prison environment for all its needs—mean that prison subculture is not easily subject to the control of prison authorities.

Prison subcultures develop independently of the formal plans of prison administrators. Inmates entering prison discover a social world not mentioned in the handbooks prepared by correctional staff. The different concerns, values, roles, and even language of inmates weave a web of social reality into which new inmates step, and in which they must participate. Those who try to remain aloof soon find themselves subjected to dangerous ostracism and may even be suspected of being in league with the prison administration.

The socialization of new inmates into the prison subculture has been described as a process of prisonization.[10] **Prisonization** refers to the learning of convict values, attitudes, roles, and even language. When the process is complete, new inmates have become "cons." The values of the inmate social system are embodied in a code. When inmates violate this code, the violations can produce sanctions ranging from ostracism and avoidance to physical violence and homicide.[11] Sykes and Messinger[12] recognize five elements of the prison code:

1. Don't interfere with the interests of other inmates. Never rat on a con.

2. Don't lose your head. Play it cool and do your own time.

3. Don't exploit inmates. Don't steal. Don't break your word. Be right.

4. Don't whine. Be a man.

5. Don't be a sucker. Don't trust the guards or staff.

Stanton Wheeler closely examined the concept of prisonization in a study of the Washington State Reformatory.[13] Wheeler found that the degree of prisonization experienced by inmates tends to vary over time. He described the changing levels of an inmate's commitment to prison norms and values by way of a "U-shaped" curve. When an inmate first enters prison, Wheeler said, the conventional values of outside society are of paramount importance. As time passes, the lifestyle of the prison is adopted. However, within the half-year prior to release, most inmates begin to demonstrate a renewed appreciation for conventional values.

Different prisons share aspects of a common inmate culture,[14] so that prison-wise inmates who enter a new facility far from their homes will already know the ropes. **Prison argot**, or language, provides one example of how widespread prison subculture can be. The terms used to describe inmate roles in one institution are generally understood in others. The word "rat," for example, is prison slang for an informer. Popularized by crime movies of the 1950s, the term "rat" is understood today by members of the wider society. Other words common to prison argot are shown in the Theory into Practice box "Prison Argot: The Language of Confinement," on the next page.

Some criminologists have suggested that inmate codes are simply a reflection of general criminal values. If so, they are brought to the institution rather than created there. Either way, the power and pervasiveness of the inmate code require convicts to conform to the world view held by most prisoners.

## The Evolution of Subcultures

Prison subculture is constantly changing. Like any other North American subculture, it evolves to reflect the concerns and experiences of the wider culture, reacting to new crime control strategies and embracing novel opportunities for crime and its commission. The AIDS epidemic of the last two decades, for example, has brought about changes in prison sexual behaviour, at least for a segment of the inmate population, while the emergence of a high-tech criminal group has further differentiated convict types. Because of such changes, John Irwin, by the time he was about to complete his now-famous study entitled *The Felon* (1970), expressed worry that his book was already obsolete.[15] *The Felon*, for all its insights into prison subculture, follows in the descriptive tradition of works by Clemmer and Reimer. Irwin recognized that by 1970 prison subcultures had begun to reflect cultural changes sweeping North America. A decade later, other investigators of prison subculture were able to write, "It was no longer meaningful to speak of a single inmate culture or even subculture. By the time we began our field research—it was clear that the unified, oppositional convict culture, found in the sociological literature on prisons, no longer existed."[16]

**prisonization** The process whereby newly institutionalized individuals come to accept prison lifestyles and criminal values. While many inmates begin their prison experience with only a modicum of values supportive of criminal behaviour, the socialization experience they undergo while incarcerated leads to a much wider acceptance of such values.

**prison argot** The slang characteristic of prison subcultures and prison life.

Stastny and Tyrnauer, describing prison life at Washington State Penitentiary in 1982, discovered four clearly distinguishable subcultures: (1) official, (2) traditional, (3) reform, and (4) revolutionary. Official culture was promoted by the staff and by the institution's administrative rules.[17] Enthusiastic participants in official culture were mostly correctional officers and other staff members, although inmates were also well aware of the normative expectations official culture imposed on them. Official culture impacted the lives of inmates primarily through the creation of a prisoner hierarchy based upon sentence length, prison jobs, and the "perks" that co-operation with the dictates of official culture could produce. Traditional prison culture, described by early writers on the subject, still existed, but its participants spent much of their time lamenting the decline of the convict code among younger prisoners. Reform culture was unique at Washington State Penitentiary. It was the result of a brief experiment with inmate self-government during the early 1970s. Some elements of prison life that evolved during the experimental period survived the termination of self-government and were eventually institutionalized in what Stastny and Tyrnauer call reform culture. Such elements included inmate participation in civic-style clubs, citizen involvement in the daily activities of the prison, banquets, and inmate speaking tours. Revolutionary culture built upon the radical political rhetoric of the disenfranchised and found a ready audience among minority prisoners who saw themselves as victims of society's basic unfairness. Although they did not participate in it, revolutionary inmates understood traditional prison culture and generally avoided running afoul of its rules.

## The Functions of Prison Society

How do social scientists and criminologists explain the existence of prison societies? Although people around the world live in groups and create their own cultures, in few

BOX 12.1 **Theory into Practice**

## Prison Argot: The Language of Confinement

Writers who have studied prison life often comment on the use by prisoners of a special language or argot. This language generally refers to the roles assigned by prison culture to types of inmates as well as to prison activities. Slang varies from country to country and from region to region. Some terms are considered fairly universal.

| | |
|---|---|
| Bird: | A young offender. |
| Boss/Bull: | Prison guard. |
| Buggin' Out: | Going ballistic, losing one's mind or going crazy. |
| Bullet: | A one-year prison sentence. |
| Cherry (or Cherrie): | The female inmate who has not yet been introduced to lesbian activities. |
| Deuce less: | A sentence of two years less a day — the maximum provincial sentence. |
| Diddler (or baby diddler): | One who sexually assaults children. |
| Dime: | Ten, as in a 10-year sentence, or $10. |
| Fag: | The male inmate who is believed to be a "natural" or "born" homosexual. |
| Fish: | The newly arrived inmate. |
| Fluff: | The female inmate who plays the female role during lesbian relations. |
| Jackrabbit Parole: | Escaping after serving a long sentence. |
| Max Out: | To serve one's full sentence. |
| Rat: | An inmate who squeals (provides information about other inmates to the prison administration). |
| Screw: | Guard. |
| Seg: | Segregation – sometimes called Ad Seg. |
| Skinner: | Sex offender. |
| Snitch: | Informant. |
| Switch: | Sandwich. |
| Wolf: | The male inmate who assumes the aggressive masculine role during homosexual relations. |

Source: *A Prisoner's Dictionary from the Other Side of the Wall.* Accessible at time of writing at **http://dictionary.prisonwall.org**

cases does the intensity of human interaction approach the level found in prisons. As we discussed in Chapter 11, today's prisons are often overcrowded places, where inmates can find no retreat from the constant demands of staff and the pressures brought by fellow prisoners. Prison subculture, according to some authors, is fundamentally an adaptation to deprivation and confinement. This subculture is a way of addressing the psychological, social, physical, and sexual needs of prisoners living within the context of a highly controlled and regimented institutional setting. Others have noted the dangers that may result from prisoners who are given access to several programs that develop their physical strength and tactical knowledge.[18]

What are some of the deprivations that prisoners experience? In *The Society of Captives*, Gresham Sykes calls these deprivations the "pains of imprisonment."[19] The pains of imprisonment—the frustrations induced by the rigours of confinement—form the nexus of a deprivation model of prison culture. Sykes said that prisoners are deprived of (1) liberty, (2) goods and services, (3) heterosexual relationships, (4) autonomy, and (5) personal security, and that these deprivations lead to the development of subcultures intended to ameliorate the personal pains that accompany them. Inmates must grapple with a variety of intense pressures that are imposed by imprisonment.[20]

In contrast to the deprivation model, the importation model of prison culture suggests that inmates bring with them values, roles, and behaviour patterns from the outside world. Such external values, second nature as they are to career offenders, depend substantially upon the criminal world view. When offenders are confined, these external elements shape the inmate social world.

The social structure of the prison, a concept that refers to accepted and relatively permanent social arrangements, is another element that shapes prisoner subculture. Donald Clemmer's early prison study recognized nine structural dimensions of inmate society. He said that prison society could be described in terms of:[21]

1. The prisoner/staff dichotomy;

2. The three general classes of prisoners;

3. Work gangs and cellhouse groups;

4. Racial groups;

5. Type of offence;

6. The power of inmate "politicians";

7. Degree of sexual abnormality;

8. The record of repeat offences; and

9. Personality differences due to pre-prison socialization.

Clemmer's nine structural dimensions are probably still descriptive of prison life today. When applied in individual situations, they designate an inmate's position in the prison "pecking order" and create expectations of the appropriate role for that person. Prison roles serve to satisfy the needs of inmates for power, sexual performance, material possessions, individuality, and personal pleasure—and to define the status of one prisoner relative to another. For example, inmate leaders, sometimes referred to as "real men" or "toughs" by prisoners in early studies, offer protection to those who live by the rules. They also provide for a redistribution of wealth inside of prison and see to it that the rules of the complex prison-derived economic system—based on barter, gambling, and sexual favours—are observed.

## Homosexuality in Prison

Homosexual behaviour inside of prisons is an important area that is both constrained and encouraged by prison subculture, and Sykes' early study of prison argot found many words describing homosexual activity. Among them were the terms "wolf," "punk," and "fag." Wolves were aggressive men who assumed the masculine role in homosexual relations. Punks were forced into submitting to the female role, often by wolves. Fags described a special category of men who had a natural proclivity towards homosexual activity. While both wolves and punks were fiercely committed to their heterosexual identity and participated in

A group of male inmates dressed as women. Homosexuality is common in both men's and women's prisons.

homosexuality only because of prison conditions, fags generally engaged in homosexual lifestyles before their entry into prison and continued to emulate feminine mannerisms and styles of dress once incarcerated.

Prison homosexuality depends to a considerable degree upon the naïveté of young inmates experiencing prison for the first time. Older prisoners looking for homosexual liaisons may ingratiate themselves with new arrivals by offering cigarettes, money, drugs, food, or protection. At some future time these "loans" will be "called in," with payoffs demanded in sexual favours. Because the inmate code requires the repayment of favours, the "fish" who tries to resist may quickly find himself face to face with the brute force of inmate society.

Prison rape represents a special category of homosexual behaviour behind bars. Estimates of the incidence of prison rape are both rare and dated. Estimates based on the results of studies vary considerably. One such study found 4.7 per cent of inmates in the Philadelphia prison system willing to report sexual assaults.[22] Another survey found that 28 per cent of prisoners had been targets of sexual aggressors at least once during their institutional careers.[23]

Rape in prison is often the result of gang activity, or of inmates working together to overcome the victim. While not greatly different from other prisoners, a large proportion of sexual aggressors are characterized by low education and poverty, are products of a broken home headed by the mother, and possess records for violent offences. Victims of prison rape tend to be physically slight, young, white, non-violent offenders from non-urban areas.[24] Lee Bowker, summarizing studies of sexual violence in prison,[25] provides the following observations:

1. Most sexual aggressors do not consider themselves to be homosexuals;
2. Sexual release is not the primary motivation for sexual attack;
3. Many aggressors must continue to participate in gang rapes in order to avoid becoming victims themselves; and
4. The aggressors have themselves suffered much damage to their masculinity in the past.

As in cases of heterosexual rape, sexual assaults in prison are likely to leave psychological scars long after the physical event is over.[26] The victims of prison rape live in fear, may feel constantly threatened, and can turn to self-destructive activities.[27] At the very least, victims question their masculinity and undergo a personal devaluation. In some cases, victims of prison sexual attacks turn to violence. Frustrations, long bottled up through abuse and fear, may explode and turn the would-be rapist into a victim of prison homicide.

## Prison Lifestyles and Inmate Types

Prison society is strict and often unforgiving. Even so, inmates are able to express some individuality through the choice of a prison lifestyle. John Irwin was the first well-known author to describe prison lifestyles, viewing them (like the subcultures of which they are a part) as adaptations to the prison environment.[28] Other writers have since elaborated on these coping mechanisms. In Canada, perhaps the best-known prison writer is Roger Caron, whose story is told in *Go-boy!*, which won a Governor General's award for literature.[29] Listed in the pages that follow are some of the types of prisoners described by commentators.

*The Mean Dude.* Some inmates adjust to prison by being mean. They are quick to fight, and when they fight, they fight like wild men (or women). They give no quarter and seem to expect none in return. Other inmates know that such prisoners are best left alone. The mean dude receives frequent write-ups and spends much time in solitary confinement.

The mean dude role is supported by the fact that some prisoners occupy it in prison as they did when they were free.[30] Similarly, certain personality types, such as the psychopath, may feel a natural attraction to this role. On the other hand, prison culture supports the role of the mean dude in two ways: (a) by expecting inmates to be tough, and (b) through the prevalence of a type of wisdom that says that "only the strong survive" inside prison.

A psychologist might say that the mean dude is acting out against the fact of captivity, striking out at anyone he or she can. This type of role is more common in male institutions and in maximum-security prisons. It tends to become less common as inmates progress to lower security levels.

*The Hedonist.* Some inmates build their lives around the limited pleasures that can be had within the confines of prison. The smuggling of contraband, homosexuality, gambling, drug running, and other officially condemned activities provide the centre of interest for prison hedonists. Hedonists generally have an abbreviated view of the future, living only for the "now." Such a temporal orientation is probably characteristic of the personality type of all hedonists and exists in many persons, incarcerated or not.

*The Opportunist.* The opportunist takes advantage of the positive experiences that prison has to offer. Schooling, trade training, counselling, and other self-improvement activities are the focal points of the opportunist's life in prison. Opportunists are the "do-gooders" of the prison subculture. They are generally well-liked by prison staff, but other prisoners shun and mistrust them because they come closest to accepting the role that the staff defines as "model prisoner." Opportunists may also be religious—a role adaptation worthy of a separate description (see below).

*The Retreatist.* Prison life is rigorous and demanding. Badgering by the staff and actual or feared assaults by other inmates may cause some prisoners to attempt psychological retreat from the realities of imprisonment. Such inmates may experience neurotic or psychotic episodes, become heavily involved in drug and alcohol abuse, or even attempt suicide. Depression and mental illness are the hallmarks of the retreatist personality in prison. The best hope for the retreatist, short of release, is protective custody combined with therapeutic counselling.

*The Legalist.* The legalist is the "jail house lawyer." Just like the mean dude, the legalist fights confinement. The weapons in this fight are not fists or clubs, however, but the legal "writ." Convicts facing long sentences, with little possibility for early release through the correctional system, are most likely to turn to the courts in their battle against confinement.

*The Radical.* Radical inmates picture themselves as political prisoners. Society, and the successful conformists who populate it, are seen as oppressors who have forced criminality upon many "good people" through the creation of a system that distributes wealth and power inequitably. The radical inmate speaks a language of revolution and may be versed in the writings of the "great" revolutionaries of the past.

The inmate who takes on the radical role is unlikely to receive much sympathy from prison staff. Radical rhetoric tends to be diametrically opposed to staff insistence on accepting responsibility for problematic behaviour.

*The Colonist.* Some inmates think of prison as their home. They "know the ropes," have many "friends" inside, and may feel more comfortable institutionalized than on the streets. They typically hold positions of either power or respect (or both) among the inmate population. These are the prisoners who don't look forward to leaving prison. Most colonizers grow into the role gradually, and only after already having spent years behind bars. Once released, some colonizers have been known to attempt new crimes in order to return to prison.

*The Religious.* Some prisoners profess a strong religious faith. They may be "born-again" Christians, committed Muslims, or even Hare Krishnas. Religious inmates frequently attend services, may form prayer groups, and sometimes ask the prison administration to allocate meeting facilities or create special diets to accommodate their claimed spiritual needs.

While it is certainly true that some inmates have a strong religious faith, staff members are apt to be suspicious of the overly religious prisoner. The tendency is to view such prisoners as "faking it" in order to demonstrate a fictitious rehabilitation and thereby gain sympathy for an early release.

*The Realist.* The realist is a prisoner who sees confinement as a natural consequence of criminal activity. Time spent in prison is an unfortunate "cost of doing business." This stoic attitude towards incarceration generally leads the realist to "pull his or her own time" and to make the best of it. Realists tend to know the inmate code, are able to avoid trouble, and continue in lives of crime once released.

# REALITIES OF PRISON LIFE: THE STAFF WORLD

The flip side of inmate society can be found in the world of the prison staff, which includes many more people and professions than guard. Staff roles encompass those of warden, psychologist, counsellor, area supervisor, program director, instructor, and correctional officer—and, in some large prisons, physician and therapist. Officers, generally seen as at the bottom of the staff hierarchy, may be divided into cellblock and tower guards, while some are regularly assigned to administrative offices where they perform clerical tasks.

Like prisoners, correctional officers undergo a socialization process that helps them to function by the official and unofficial rules of staff society. Lucien Lombardo has described the process by which officers are socialized into the prison work world.[31] Lombardo interviewed 359 correctional personnel at New York's Auburn Prison and found that rookie officers had to quickly abandon preconceptions of both inmates and other staff members. According to Lombardo, new officers learn that inmates are not the "monsters" that much of the public makes them out to be. On the other hand, rookies may be seriously disappointed in their experienced colleagues when they realize that ideals of professionalism, often stressed during early training, are rarely translated into reality. The pressures of the institutional work environment, however, soon force most correctional personnel to adopt a united front in relating to inmates.

One of the leading formative influences on staff culture is the potential threat that inmates pose. Inmates far outnumber correctional personnel in any institution, and the hostility they feel for guards is only barely hidden even at the best of times. Correctional personnel know that however friendly inmates may appear, a sudden change in institutional climate—as can happen in anything from simple disturbances on the yard to full-blown riots—can quickly and violently unmask deep-rooted feelings of mistrust and hatred.

As in years past, prison staffers are still most concerned with custody and control. Society, especially under the emerging just deserts philosophy of criminal sentencing, expects correctional staff to keep inmates in custody as the basic prerequisite of successful job performance. Custody is necessary before any other correctional activities, such as instruction or counselling, can be undertaken. Control, the other major staff concern, ensures order, and an orderly prison is believed to be safe and secure. In routine daily activities, control over almost all aspects of inmate behaviour becomes paramount in the minds of most correctional officers. It is the twin interests of custody and control that lead to institutionalized procedures for ensuring security in most facilities. The use of strict rules, body and cell searches, counts, unannounced shakedowns, the control of dangerous items, materials, and contraband, and the extensive use of bars, locks, fencing, cameras, and alarms all support the human vigilance of the staff in maintaining security.

## Types of Correctional Officers

Staff culture, in combination with naturally occurring personality types, gives rise to a diversity of officer "types." Like the inmate typology we've already discussed, correctional staff can be classified according to certain distinguishing characteristics. Among the most prevalent types are the following:

*The Dictator.* Some officers go by the book; others go beyond it, using prison rules to enforce their own brand of discipline. The guard who demands signs of inmate subservience, from constant use of the word "sir" or "ma'am" to frequent free shoeshines, is one type of dictator. Another goes beyond legality, beating or "macing" inmates even for minor infractions or perceived insults. Dictator guards are bullies. They find their counterpart in the "mean dude" inmate described earlier.

Dictator guards may have sadistic personalities and gain ego satisfaction through the feelings of near omnipotence that come from the total control of others. Some may be fundamentally insecure and employ a false bravado to hide their fear of inmates. Officers who fit the dictator category are the most likely to be targeted for vengeance should control of the institution temporarily revert to the inmates.

*The Friend.* Friendly officers try to fraternize with inmates. They approach the issue of control by trying to be "one of the guys." They seem to believe that they can win inmate co-operation by being nice. Unfortunately, such guards do not recognize that fraternization quickly leads to unending requests for special favours—from delivering mail to bending "minor" prison rules. Once a few rules have been "bent," the officer may find that inmates have the upper hand through the potential for blackmail.

Many officers have amiable relationships with inmates. In most cases, however, affability is only a convenience that both sides recognize can quickly evaporate. Friendly officers, as the term is being used here, are *overly* friendly. They may be young and inexperienced. On the other hand, they may simply be possessed of kind and idealistic personalities built on successful friendships in free society.

*The Merchant.* Contraband could not exist in any correctional facility without the merchant officer. The merchant participates in the inmate economy, supplying drugs, pornography, alcohol, and sometimes even weapons to inmates who can afford to pay for them.

Probably only a very few officers consistently perform the role of merchant, although a far larger proportion may occasionally turn a few dollars by smuggling some item through the gate. Low salaries create the potential for mercantile corruption among many otherwise "straight-arrow" officers. Until salaries rise substantially, the merchant will remain an institutionalized feature of most prisons.

*The Indifferent.* The indifferent type of officer cares little for what goes on in the prison setting. Officers who fit this category may be close to retirement, or they may be alienated from their jobs for various reasons. Low pay, the view that inmates are basically "worthless" and incapable of changing, and the monotonous ethic of "doing time" all combine to numb the professional consciousness of even young officers.

Inmates do not see the indifferent officer as a threat, nor is such an officer likely to challenge the *status quo* in institutions where merchant guards operate.

*The Climber.* The climber is apt to be a young officer with an eye for promotion. Nothing seems impossible to the climber, who probably hopes eventually to be warden or program director or to hold some high-status position within the institutional hierarchy. Climbers are likely to be involved in schooling, correspondence courses, and professional organizations. They may lead a movement towards unionization for correctional personnel and tend to see the guard's role as a "profession" that should receive greater social recognition.

Climbers have many ideas. They may be heavily involved in reading about the latest confinement or administrative technology. If so, they will suggest many ways to improve prison routine, often to the consternation of other complacent staff members.

Like the indifferent officers, climbers turn a blind eye towards inmates and their problems. They are more concerned with improving institutional procedures and with their own careers than they are with the treatment or day-to-day control of inmates.

*The Reformer.* The reformer is the "do-gooder" among officers, the person who believes that prison should offer opportunities for personal change. The reformer tends to lend a sympathetic ear to the personal needs of inmates and is apt to offer "arm-chair" counselling and suggestions. Many reformers are motivated by personal ideals, and some of them are highly religious. Inmates tend to see the reformer guard as naive, but harmless. Because the reformer actually tries to help, even when help is unsolicited, he or she is the most likely of all the guard types to be accepted by prisoners.

# The Professionalization of Correctional Officers

Expectations of correctional officers have never been high. Prison staffers are generally accorded low status in occupational surveys. Guard jobs require minimal formal education and hold few opportunities for professional growth and advancement. They are low-paying, frustrating, and often boring. Growing problems in North American prisons, including emerging issues of legal liability, however, require a well-trained and adequately equipped professional guard force.[32] As correctional personnel become more and more proficient, the old concept of guard is being supplanted by that of a professional *correctional officer*.[33]

Most jurisdictions make efforts to eliminate individuals with potentially harmful personalities from correctional officer applicant pools, and several locations make use of some form of psychological screening in assessing candidates for prison jobs.[34]

Although only a few jurisdictions utilize psychological screening, all make use of training programs intended to prepare successful applicants for prison work. In British Columbia, those intending to work as correctional officers in provincial institutions are required to complete a pre-employment training program, run by the Justice Institute of British Columbia.[35] The program requires six weeks of full-time training, and includes a variety of teaching methods. Candidates are required to pass a screening process and must pay $1800 for their own training. Completion of the program results in the candidate being put on a list for call-out work. Eventually, as full-time positions open up, they are then invited to apply for them. In Ontario, correctional officers must complete a similar program, at their own expense, prior to being put on a call-out list for jobs.

## BOX 12.2 Theory into Practice

### Ethics for Correctional Officers: Ideas from John Jones

Dr. John Jones of the Law and Justice Centre, Sir Sandford Fleming College, in central Ontario, provides many ideas for correctional officers to deal with ethical issues in their daily routines. He provides seven tools to aid correctional officers in making the right decisions:

- Setting Limits: Informing colleagues ahead of time about one's own personal limits.
- Application of Ethical Principles: Basing one's decisions on either (1) a utilitarian calculus, through choosing a course of conduct that will produce the greatest good for the greatest number of people (benefit maximization), or (2) choosing conduct that provides everyone with the respect they deserve as humans (equal respect).
- The Bell, the Book, and the Candle: Before making a decision, ask oneself (1) Are warning bells going off? (2) Is there any written guidance to help (laws, regulations, codes of ethics)? and (3) How will the decision appear in the light of day?
- The Imaginary Video Camera: Imagine that your behaviour is always being recorded for future review.

- Critical Thinking: Refrain from taking any point of view at face value, and think for yourself, weighing the merits and demerits of any idea and being sure to look at all sides of an issue before embarking on a course of conduct.
- The Other Person's "Moccasins": Try to look at situations from the perspective of other stakeholders in the situation.
- Moral Stages: Lawrence Kohlberg's theory of moral development suggests that we operate at various stages of moral development, generally progressing to higher stages in later life. Then, according to this theory, before making a decision, we should ask ourselves if we are operating at a middle stage, that is, going with the flow, or a higher stage of moral development, displaying courage and principled behaviour.

## QUESTIONS FOR DISCUSSION

1. Why are there inherent dangers in applying only one principle or tool in making ethical decisions?

2. Is it realistic to expect new correctional officers to keep all of these tools in mind at all times? Is it more difficult for more seasoned officers? Why?

*Source:* Jones, J.R. (2000). *Reputable Conduct: Ethical Issues in Policing and Corrections,* Second Edition © 2000, Pearson Education Canada Inc.

The Correctional Service of Canada provides its new recruits with a 12-week Correctional Training Program, which combines classroom instruction and self-directed learning.[36] At the federal level, training is delivered at regional staff colleges. Initial training includes:[37] (1) learning the mission statement and core values; (2) developing interpersonal and communication skills; (3) security procedures and strategies; (4) self-defence; and (5) basic case management, for those who are appointed as institutional or community-based case management officers.

The Correctional Service of Canada has also developed the "Correctional Career Management Program." This program has been in operation since 1993 and represents a competency-based approach to the management of human resources. A single process has been streamlined to combine staffing, performance management, developmental training, and career planning. Core competencies have been identified to support this program. The following positions within the corrections system are included in the program:

- Correctional Officer (Levels I and II);
- Case Management Officer (Institutional and Community);
- Correctional Supervisor;
- Unit Manager;
- Area Director and Director, Community Corrections Centre;
- Coordinator, Case Management;
- Coordinator, Correctional Operations;
- Security Maintenance Officer;
- Institutional Preventive Security Officer; and
- Admission and Discharge Officer.

# PRISON RIOTS IN CANADA

The 10 years between 1970 and 1980 have been called the "explosive decade" of prison riots.[38] The decade began with a massive uprising at Attica Prison in New York state in September 1971.[39] The Attica riot resulted in 43 deaths, and more than 80 men were wounded. The "explosive decade" soon spread to Canada, where a number of prison riots erupted in the mid-1970s. They reached a climax when the B.C. Penitentiary suffered a hostage taking that resulted in a staff member's death, followed by a riot nine months later that destroyed a significant portion of the prison.

Prison riots did not stop with the end of the explosive 1970s. In April 1996, Headingley Correctional Institution, a provincial facility in Manitoba, was the scene of a riot that lasted two days, resulting in correctional officers and other inmates being beaten, and fires being set. The beating of protective custody inmates was particularly brutal, with fingers being severed, and one inmate falling victim to an attempted castration. The riot did not subside for 24 hours, and it resulted in damage worth $3.5 million.[40] In November 2001, inmates at the penitentiaries in Drumheller and Edmonton rioted. The Drumheller riot resulted in the killing of a 21-year-old inmate, whose body was paraded through the prison by other inmates. All of this followed an earlier riot in May of 2001, producing over $1 million in property damage at Drumheller Institution.[41] Before the riot erupted, staff had no idea that a riot was impending.[42]

Prison riots appear to be both the cause, and the result, of significant levels of stress within institutions.[43] In Canada, prison disturbances are frequently the result of what would appear to be minor restrictions placed on the inmates by prison authorities, for example, the withdrawal of television privileges, or other activities that cause prison tensions to escalate rapidly and unexpectedly.

## Causes of Riots

It is difficult to explain satisfactorily why prisoners riot, despite study groups that have attempted to piece together the "facts" leading up to an incident.[44] After the riot at Attica, the New York State Special Commission of Inquiry filed a report that recommended the creation of inmate advisory councils, changes in staff titles and uniforms, and other institutional improvements. The report emphasized "enhancing (the) dignity, worth, and self-confidence" of inmates. The New Mexico attorney general, in a final report on the violence at a prison in Santa Fe, blamed a breakdown in informal controls and the subsequent emergence of a new group of violent inmates among the general prison population.[45]

A number of authorities[46] have suggested a variety of causes for prison riots. Among them are the following:

1. An insensitive prison administration and neglected inmates' demands. Ignoring calls for "fairness" in disciplinary hearings, better food, more recreational opportunities, and the like may lead to riots.

2. The street lifestyles with which most inmates are familiar. It should be no surprise that prisoners use organized violence when many of them were violent people before they entered prison.

3. Dehumanizing prison conditions. Overcrowded facilities, the lack of opportunity for individual expression, and other aspects of total institutions culminate in explosive situations of which riots are but one form.

4. The way that riots regulate inmate society and redistribute power balances among inmate groups. Riots provide the opportunity to "cleanse" the prison population of informers and rats and to resolve struggles between power brokers and ethnic groups within the institution.

5. "Power vacuums" created by changes in prison administration, the transfer of influential inmates, or court-ordered injunctions that significantly alter the informal social control mechanisms of the institution.

Although riots are difficult to predict in specific institutions, some prison systems appear ripe for disorder. Situations where prisons are overcrowded and where prisons house a significant number of gang members can easily result in violence and eventual rioting. Gang membership among inmates in the Canadian prison system, practically non-existent in years past, is now a major problem for prison administration.[47] The Headingley riot, for example, has been attributed in part to tensions between two aboriginal street gangs with a significant number of members in the prison.[48] While the gang presence inside Canadian prisons is not as pronounced as it is in many American prisons, it is clearly a factor that prison officials must address. Relatively little has been written about gangs in the Canadian prison system; however, the gang presence has been identified on two fronts: aboriginal gangs and biker gangs. Aboriginal gangs behind bars include the Manitoba Warriors, the Indian Posse, Red Alert, and the Native Syndicate. Biker gangs include the Hell's Angels, and their rivals in Quebec, the Bandidos, which recently absorbed the Rock Machine motorcycle gang. A recent court ruling found an inmate not guilty of carrying a concealed weapon after he convinced the Court that he needed to carry a shank (homemade knife) on his person in order to protect himself from gang violence within the maximum-security Edmonton Institution.[49] Clearly, the presence of gangs within a prison adds to the level of tension, increasing the potential for a riot.

The "real" reasons for any riot are probably institution-specific and may not allow for easy generalization. However, it is no simple coincidence that the "explosive decade" of prison riots coincided with the growth of revolutionary prisoner subcultures referred to earlier. As the old convict code began to give way to an emerging perception of social victimization among inmates, it was probably only a matter of time until those perceptions turned to militancy. Seen from this perspective, riots are more a revolutionary activity undertaken by politically motivated cliques than spontaneous and disorganized expressions stemming from the frustrations of prison life. A number of official studies have explored these occurrences in detail and attempted to present recommendations for their avoidance in the future.[50]

## Stages in Riots and Riot Control

Generally speaking, rioting cannot be predicted.[51] Riots are usually unplanned and tend to occur spontaneously, the result of some relatively minor precipitating event. Once the stage has been set, prison riots tend to evolve through five phases:[52] (1) explosion, (2) organization (into inmate-led groups), (3) confrontation (with authority), (4) termination (through negotiation or physical confrontation), and (5) reaction and explanation (usually by investigative commissions). Donald Cressey[53] points out that the early explosive stages of a riot tend to involve "binges" during which inmates exult in their new-found freedom with virtual orgies of alcohol and drug use or sexual activity. Buildings are burned, facilities are wrecked, and old grudges between individual inmates and inmate groups are settled, often through violence. After this initial explosive stage, leadership changes tend to occur. New leaders emerge who, at least for a time, may effectively organize inmates into a force that can confront and resist the officials' attempts to regain control of the institution. Bargaining strategies then develop and the process of negotiation begins.[54]

In the past, many correctional facilities depended upon informal procedures to quell disturbances—and often drew upon the expertise of seasoned correctional officers who were veterans of past skirmishes and riots.[55] Given the large size of many of today's institutions, the rapidly changing composition of inmate and staff populations, and increasing tensions caused by overcrowding and the movement towards reduced inmate privileges, the "old guard" system can no longer be depended upon to quell disturbances. Hence, most modern facilities have incident management procedures and systems in place that are designed to be implemented in the event of disturbances. Such systems remove the burden of riot control from the individual officer, depending instead upon a systematic and deliberate approach developed to deal with a wide variety of correctional incidents.

# REALITIES OF PRISON LIFE: WOMEN IN PRISON

Throughout Canada,[56] about 5 per cent of the total prison population are women. Women serving federal sentences in Canada made up 385 (3 per cent) of the total federal offender population of 12 815 inmates in April 2001.[57] A recent survey of correctional facilities in Canada found that 9.1 per cent of new admissions involving offenders sentenced to provincial custody were women, while 5 per cent of federally sentenced offenders were women.[58] Most female inmates are housed in centralized facilities known as "women's prisons," which are dedicated exclusively to the holding of female felons. Many jurisdictions, however, particularly those with small populations, continue to keep women prisoners in special wings of what are otherwise institutions for men.

While there are still far more men than women imprisoned across Canada (approximately 19 men for every woman in Canada), the number of female inmates appears to be rising.[59] While female prison admissions have accounted for around 9 per cent of all prison admissions since 1991, the number of federally sentenced women in custody increased from 329 in 1996 to 385 in 2001. It would appear that female inmates are not being released at the same rate at which they are being brought into the federal prison system. However, as the Arbour Commission of Inquiry points out, the increase in women's involvement in violent crime may be more apparent than real.

The conclusions are conflicting and complicated by the fact that dealing with small numbers of women artificially inflates any real increase when simple percentages are employed. For example, one additional federally sentenced woman incarcerated for sexual assault would represent a 100 per cent increase in the total number of women for such offences, as there is currently only one.[60]

Women's prisons are frequently overcrowded, as are men's. At the federal level, this has been alleviated with the construction of several new institutions for female offenders across the country. However, a review of recent levels of occupation shows about one-half of the

The number of women in prison is growing steadily.

federal institutions are housing inmates beyond their rated capacity.[61] Overcrowding often leads to feelings of intense hostility, frustration, and anger.

Professionals working with imprisoned women attribute the rise in female prison populations largely to drug offences. Table 12–1 shows the proportion of men and women imprisoned for various kinds of offences in Canada in 1999–2000. As one might expect, 80 per cent of females convicted and sentenced for homicide received jail time for the offence. However, women rarely commit this serious offence. Indeed, only five women were convicted of homicide offences in this time period, and four of these were sentenced to imprisonment. It is interesting to note that women are less likely than are men to be sentenced to imprisonment in virtually every offence category. Women are slightly more likely than men to receive a prison term for weapons offences and for being unlawfully at large. They are much more likely than men to receive jail time for sexual morals offences, particularly those pertaining to prostitution. In addition, the "Other Federal Statute" category, which typically includes drug offences, reveals that women are slightly more likely than men to receive jail time upon conviction for these offences.[62]

One reason for the growth in the number of women behind bars may be the demise, over the last decade or two, of the "chivalry factor." The chivalry factor, so called because it was based upon an archaic cultural stereotype that depicted women as helpless or childlike compared to men, allegedly lessened the responsibility of female offenders in the eyes of some male judges and prosecutors—resulting in fewer active prison sentences for women involved in criminal activity. Recent studies show that the chivalry factor is now primarily of historical interest. In jurisdictions examined, the gender of convicted offenders no longer affects sentencing practices except insofar as it may be tied to other social variables. B. Keith Crew,[63] for example, in a comprehensive study of gender differences in sentencing, observes, "[a] woman does not automatically receive leniency because of her status of wife or mother, but she may receive leniency if those statuses become part of the official explanation of her criminal behavior (e.g., she was stealing to feed her children, or an abusive husband forced her to commit a crime)."

Although there may be no one "typical" prison for women, and no perfectly "average" female inmate, from a Canadian context, one study revealed that two-thirds of all federally sentenced women are mothers, and 70 per cent of that number are single parents all, or part, of the time, 68 per cent were physically abused (this number climbing to 90 per cent in the case of aboriginal women inmates), 53 per cent of all federally sentenced women were sexually abused (61 per cent of the aboriginal women were sexually abused), fewer than one-third of these women inmates had any formal job qualifications beyond basic education, and two-thirds were never employed on a steady basis.[64] A recent survey of incarcerated federally sentenced women revealed some interesting characteristics:[65]

1. Over one-half fit into the younger age category (18–34 years);

2. 61.7 per cent are unmarried;

3. 19.1 per cent are serving sentences for murder;

4. Just over one-third (34.9 per cent) are serving a short federal sentence (2–3 years); and

## TABLE 12–1 Single-Conviction Cases Resulting in Imprisonment[1] by Gender, Selected Incidents, 1999–2000

Each number is a percentage of all convictions per offence type that resulted in a sentence of imprisonment.)

| | Gender | |
| --- | Males | Females |
| | % | % |
| Homicide | 91 | 80 |
| Attempted Murder | 67 | — |
| Common Assault | 20 | 8 |
| Assault with Weapon | 36 | 16 |
| Aggravated Assault | 59 | 34 |
| Sexual Assault (Level 1) | 43 | 29 |
| Sexual Assault (Levels 2 & 3) | 61 | — |
| Sexual Abuse | 43 | 27 |
| Abduction | 40 | 8 |
| Kidnapping | 49 | — |
| Robbery | 72 | 63 |
| **Violent Crime—Total** | **28** | **13** |
| Breaking and Entering | 52 | 22 |
| Possess Stolen Property | 38 | 23 |
| Fraud Over $5000 | 19 | 9 |
| Fraud $5000 and Under | 26 | 12 |
| Theft Over $5000 | 47 | 19 |
| Theft $5000 and Under | 33 | 16 |
| Mischief | 17 | 12 |
| Arson | 44 | 22 |
| **Property Crime—Total** | **33** | **16** |
| Morals — Sexual | 11 | 42 |
| Unlawfully at Large | 87 | 89 |
| Offensive Weapons | 18 | 21 |
| Failure to Appear | 54 | 45 |
| Impaired Driving | 15 | 6 |
| **Criminal Code—Total** | **31** | **19** |
| **Other Federal Statute** | **17** | **19** |

[1]Represents all persons sentenced in nine jurisdictions in Canada.

*Source:* Belanger, B. (2001). Sentencing in Adult Criminal Courts, 1999/00. Adapted from the Statistics Canada publication *Juristat, Catalogue no. 85-002,* Vol. 21, No. 10, December 2001, Fig. 6, pg. 10.

5. Almost one-fifth (19.4 per cent) are serving life sentences.

The survey also found that more than one-third of incarcerated offenders were visible minorities.[66] Often these women have been physically and/or sexually abused in the past, have low levels of educational achievement, have a poor employment history, and have a history of substance abuse.[67]

Since a large proportion of women entering prison are mothers, and many of those women retain custody of their children at the time of prison admission, the Correctional Service of Canada has implemented a Mother-Child Program that allows female inmates to keep their children in the institution with them, for some or all of the time. Critics charge that women inmates face a prison system designed for male inmates and run by men. Hence, pregnant inmates, many of whom are drug users, malnourished, or sick, often receive little prenatal care—a situation that risks additional complications. Separation from their children is a significant deprivation facing incarcerated mothers. Although husbands and/or boyfriends may assume responsibility for the children of imprisoned spouses/girlfriends, such an outcome is the exception to the rule. Historically, a large proportion of children are released by their imprisoned mothers into foster care or put up for adoption.

The Correctional Service of Canada has instituted core programs to provide female inmates with life skills, substance abuse, and literacy training.[68] Some institutions offer facilities as diverse as play areas complete with toys, while others attempt to alleviate difficulties associated with mother-child visits. As part of the five-year review of the Canadian *Corrections and Conditional Release Act*, it was noted that some of the following programs should be made available, and designed specifically, for women:

- Abuse/trauma issues;
- Education and employment skills;
- Substance abuse; and
- Parenting.

The Arbour Commission of Inquiry and other inquiries have placed a significant emphasis on the special needs of aboriginal women offenders. For example, the programming available at the Okimaw Ohci Healing Lodge was studied for its value in this context.[69]

Other meaningful prison programs for women are often lacking[70]—perhaps because the ones that are in place were originally based upon traditional models of female roles that left little room for substantive employment opportunities.[71] Many trade-training programs still emphasize low-paying jobs such as cook, beautician, or laundry machine operator.[72] Classes in homemaking are not uncommon. However, as Morton (1997) exemplifies, serious attention is now being given to the development and exploration of better programming for female offenders.[73] As part of the five-year review of the *Corrections and Conditional Release Act* focusing on women offenders, an effort was made to consider some innovative programs offered through the Nova Institution for Women in Atlantic Canada, the Okimaw Ohci Healing Lodge, and the Burnaby (B.C.) Correctional Centre for Women. A sample of these programs is found in Table 12–2.

## Social Structure in Women's Prisons

Most studies of women's prisons have revealed a unique feature of such institutions:[74] the way that women inmates construct organized families.[75] Typical of such studies are Ward and Kassebaum's *Women's Prison: Sex and Social Structure*,[76] E. Heffernan's *Making It in Prison: The Square, The Cool, and the Life*,[77] and Rose Giallombardo's *Society of Women: A Study of Women's Prisons*.[78] From a Canadian perspective, Margaret Shaw's examination, *Paying the Price: Federally Sentenced Women in Context*[79] is useful, as is Bonny Walford's study, *Lifers: The Story of Eleven Women Serving Life Sentences for Murder*.[80]

Giallombardo, for example, examined the Federal Reformatory for Women at Alderson, West Virginia, spending a year in gathering data (1962–63). Focusing closely on the formation of families, she wrote about the homosexual alliance as a marriage unit, devoting a chapter in her book to this topic. In this chapter, she describes in great detail the sexual identities assumed by women at Alderson and the symbols they chose to communicate those roles. Hair style, dress, language, and mannerisms were all used to signify "maleness" or "femaleness." Giallombardo details "the anatomy of the marriage relationship from courtship to 'fall out,' that is, from inception to the parting of the ways, or divorce."[81] Romantic love at Alderson was seen as of central importance to any relationship between inmates, and all homosexual relationships were described as voluntary. Through marriage, the "stud broad" became the husband and the "femme" the wife.

Studies attempting to document the extent of inmate involvement in prison "families" produce varying results. Some have found as many as 71 per cent of women prisoners involved in the phenomenon, while others have found none.[82] The kinship systems described by Giallombardo and others, however, extend beyond simple "family" ties to the formation of large, intricately related groups involving a large number of non-sexual relationships. In these groups, the roles of "children," "in-laws," "grandparents," and so on

**TABLE 12–2** Sampling of Innovative Programs for Women Offenders in Canada

| Nova Institution for Women | Okimaw Ohci Healing Lodge | Burnaby Correctional Centre for Women |
|---|---|---|
| **Core Programs** <br>• Substance Abuse <br>• Cognitive Living Skills <br>• Community Integration <br>• Survivors of Abuse and Trauma <br>• Parenting Skills | **Core Programs** <br>• Cognitive Skills for Women <br>• Society of Aboriginal Addictions Recovery (SOARR) <br>• Relapse Prevention <br>• Parenting Skills <br>• Positive Emotions | |
| **Personal Development Programs** <br>• Addictions Recovery Group <br>• Conflict Resolution Skills <br>• Black Focus Group <br>• Native Liaison Worker <br>• Native Sisterhood <br>• Individual Psychotherapy | **Culturally-Specific Programs** <br>• Sacred Circle <br>• Sweat Lodge Ceremony/ Healing Ceremony <br>• Sun Dance Ceremony <br>• Traditional Teaching/Skills <br>• Native Studies <br>• Positive Aboriginal Lifestyles | **Personal Development/ Therapeutic Programs** <br>• Education <br>• Music Therapy <br>• Chaplaincy <br>• Elizabeth Fry Society Programs <br>• Living Skills Programming <br>• Parenting Course <br>• Aboriginal Programs <br>• Health and Psychological Services <br>• Mother-Child Program |
| **Educational & Vocational Programs** <br>• Educational Upgrading <br>• Canine Program ("Pawsitive" Directions) <br>• Horticulture Program <br>• Microsoft "Word" and "Excel" <br>• Cleaning Work Program | **Education Programs** <br>• School Levels 1–4 <br>• College <br>• Peer Tudor <br>• Standard First Aid and CPR | **Occupational/Vocational Programs** <br>• Tailor Shop <br>• Flower Shop <br>• Horticulture Program <br>• Canine Program <br>• Building Maintenance <br>• Non-traditional Trades Training |
| **Spirituality Programs** <br>• Values <br>• Women's Spirituality | **Employment Programs** <br>• Kitchen Worker <br>• Janitor <br>• Maintenance Worker <br>• Ceramic Shop <br>• Library Worker <br>• Mother-Child Program | |
| **Health and Wellness Programs** <br>• Leisure <br>• Self-image/Self-concept <br>• Stress Management <br>• Wellness | | |
| **Creativity and Self-Expression Programs** <br>• Art Expression <br>• Arts & Crafts | | |

*Source:* Solicitor General of Canada. (1998). *Women Offenders: CCRA 5 Year Review* (pp. 22–34). Ottawa: Solicitor General of Canada. Reproduced with permission.

may be explicitly recognized. Even "birth order" within a family can be become an issue for kinship groups.[83] Kinship groups sometimes occupy a common household—usually a prison cottage or dormitory area. The description of women's prisons provided by authors like Giallombardo show a closed society in which social interaction—including expectations, normative forms of behaviour, and emotional ties—is regulated by an inventive system of artificial relationships that mirror the outside world.

Some authors have suggested that this emphasis on describing family structures in women's prisons is unfortunate because it tends to deny other structural features of those institutions.[84] The family emphasis may, in fact, be due to traditional explanations of female criminality that were intertwined with narrow understandings of the role of women in society.

## Types of Female Inmates

As in institutions for men, the subculture of women's prisons is multi-dimensional. Esther Heffernan, for example, found that three terms used by women prisoners she studied—the "square," the "cool," and the "life"—were indicative of three styles of adaptation to prison life.[85] Square inmates had few early experiences with criminal lifestyles and tended to sympathize with the values and attitudes of conventional society. Cool prisoners were more likely to be career offenders. They tended to keep to themselves and were generally supportive of inmate values. Women who participated in the "life" subculture were familiar with lives of crime. Many had been arrested repeatedly for prostitution, drug use, theft, and so on. "Life" group members were full participants in the economic, social, and familial arrangements of the prison. Heffernan believed that "the life" offered an alternative lifestyle to women who had experienced early and constant rejection by conventional society. Within "the life" women could establish relationships, achieve status, and find meaning in their lives. The "square," the "life," and the "cool" represented subcultures to Heffernan, because individuals with similar adaptive choices tended to closely relate to one another and to support the lifestyle characteristic of that type.

"Square" inmates are definitely in the minority in prisons for both men and women. Perhaps for that reason they have rarely been studied. In an insightful self-examination, however, one such inmate, Jean Harris, published her impressions of prison life after more than seven years in the maximum-security Bedford Hills (New York) Correctional Facility. Harris was convicted of killing the "Scarsdale Diet Doctor," Herman Tarnower, over a romance gone sour. A successful socialite in her early fifties at the time of the crime, Harris had an eye-opening experience in prison. Her book, *They Always Call Us Ladies*,[86] argues hard for prison reform. Sounding like the "square" she was, Harris says other inmates are "hard for you and me to relate to"[87] and describes them as "childlike women without social skills."[88] Speaking to a reporter, Harris related, "There's really nobody for me to talk to here."[89] Harris was granted clemency by New York Governor Mario Cuomo on December 29, 1992—after serving 12 years in prison.[90]

Recently, the social structure of women's prison has become dichotomized by the advent of "crack kids," as they are called in prison argot. "Crack kids," whose existence highlights generational differences among female offenders, are streetwise young women with little respect for traditional prison values, for their elders, or even for their own children. Known for frequent fights, and for their lack of even simple domestic skills, these young women quickly estrange many older inmates, some of whom call them "animalescents."

## Violence in Women's Prisons

Some authors have suggested that violence in women's prisons is less frequent than it is in institutions for men. Bowker observes that "[e]xcept for the behavior of a few 'guerrillas,' it appears that violence is only used in women's prisons to settle questions of dominance and subordination when other manipulative strategies fail to achieve the desired effect."[91] It appears that few homosexual liaisons are forced, perhaps representing a general aversion among women to such victimization in wider society. At least one study, however, has shown the use of sexual violence in women's prisons as a form of revenge against inmates who are overly vocal in their condemnation of such practices among other prisoners.[92]

Not all abuse occurs at the hands of inmates. On April 22, 1994, following a violent, though brief, confrontation between inmates and correctional staff at the Prison for Women in Kingston, Ontario, the inmates involved were placed in the segregation unit of that institution. On April 26, the warden of the Prison for Women ordered that the all-male "Institutional Emergency Response Team" (IERT) from the neighbouring Kingston Penitentiary conduct a cell extraction and strip-search of eight female inmates in segregation. These events, and the resulting public outcry that followed the airing of a videotape by the CBC current affairs program *The Fifth Estate*, brought about a Commission of Inquiry under the Honourable Louise Arbour. This inquiry undertook a broad-ranging examination of the measures in place in the Prison for Women for responding to incidents, the adequacy and appropriateness of the actions taken in response to specific incidents, and other issues relating to the treatment of inmates in this institution. The Commission's report and recommendations make for important reading in the area of corrections and women offenders. Indeed, the Commission found the contents of the videotape that recorded some of the actions taken by the IERT to be so powerful that it recommended that the Secretariat of the Ministry of the Solicitor General make it available to the public free of charge, upon request.

The Commission of Inquiry into Certain Events at the Prison for Women in Kingston made 14 key recommendations, including:[93]

- Create a position within the Correctional Service of Canada of Deputy Commissioner of Women;

- Give priority to work programs that have a vocational training component, provide a pay incentive, and constitute a meaningful occupation;

## BOX 12.3 Theory into Practice

## Prisons from the Prisoner's Perspective

While sociologists, criminologists, and professional administrators have devoted considerable attention to prisons and prison life, the subject matter cannot be understood without becoming aware of the perspectives of those who are confined behind prison walls day after day. Yet, as a group, prisoners have not traditionally had many opportunities to let their voices be heard. In an effort to partially remedy this situation, the *Journal of Prisoners on Prisons* publishes material written by only prisoners and former prisoners. In one issue, the following statement appears:

> With all our boasted reforms, pretensions of social change, and far-reaching technological advancements, we still allow human beings to be the scapegoats for our guilt-ridden consciences. As long as a powerless and voiceless "cannon fodder" is available, we will have backs to stand on to elevate our misguided sense of self-worth. Ten, fifteen, twenty-five year sentences are handed out in our courts like vitamins. We condemn the victims of our materialistic folly to hell-holes named Millhaven, Stony Mountain, and Archambault. In an effort to promote the modern advancements in penology, we have replaced hard labour and corporal punishment with warehousing, inordinate sentences, and psychological labeling. Degradation and cruelty have not ceased, they have just been disguised. So we lock up, pervert, and turn bitter our social blemishes so that society may be protected from the phantoms of its own making.[1]

One of the points being made in this excerpt is that society has abdicated its role in dealing with widespread social problems by placing far too many citizens into prison rather than developing sound social policies to deal with the factors that lead to crime in the first place. While sociologists have presented such arguments before, they become more compelling from the perspective of someone who has truly experienced the impact of society's formal social-control efforts, rather than from the scientific observer's perspective.

### QUESTIONS FOR DISCUSSION

1. In what ways can the prisoner's perspective enlighten us as to the role of prisons and the realities of prison life? Can social scientists ever hope to grasp these insights without having the personal experience of the inmate?

2. Are prison tours a valuable part of a criminology student's education? How do you think they appear from the inmate's perspective?

[1]McCormick, J.E. (1993). Two Kinds of Prisons. *Journal of Prisoners on Prisons*, 5(1), p. 24.

- Establish explicit protocols dealing with the access of male staff in the female living units and to ensure that male IERTs not be deployed in an institution for women;

- Introduce the Healing Lodge for aboriginal women inmates;

- Create sanctions for correctional interference with the integrity of a sentence;

- Strictly monitor any instances of administrative segregation; and

- Provide proper education of CSC staff and employees with respect to the rights of incarcerated offenders.

The U.S. Task Force on the Female Offender[94] also recommended a number of changes in the administration of prisons for women. Among them were the following:

1. Substance abuse programs should be available to women inmates;

2. Women inmates need to acquire greater literacy skills, and literacy programs should form the basis upon which other programs are built;

3. Female offenders should be housed in buildings independent of male inmates;

4. Institutions for women should develop programs for keeping children in the facility in order to "fortify the bond between mother and child"; and

5. To ensure equal access to assistance, institutions should be built to accommodate programs for female offenders.

# PRISONERS' RIGHTS

Until the 1970s, Canadian courts took an essentially neutral approach—commonly called the **hands-off doctrine**—towards the running of prisons. Judges assumed that prison administrators were sufficiently professional in the performance of their duties to balance institutional needs with humane considerations. The hands-off doctrine rested upon the belief that defendants lost most of their rights upon conviction, suffering a kind of **civil death**. Many jurisdictions defined the concept of civil death through legislation that denied inmates the right to vote, hold public office, or even marry.

The hands-off doctrine ended in 1975 when a federal court declared that the solitary confinement regime at the B.C. Penitentiary amounted to cruel and unusual punishment (discussed in Chapter 11).[95] The Court's decision resulted from what it judged to be inhospitable conditions and poor treatment of the inmates by the custodial staff. Stories about the system by long-time inmates claimed that a number of other inmates had been driven mad by the treatment and conditions in the infamous "Penthouse."

Detailed media coverage of the trial, plus the death of prison employee Mary Steinhouser and a large-scale riot at the B.C. Penitentiary foreshadowed the demise of the institution, with its eventual closure that accompanied the opening of Kent Penitentiary as a replacement maximum-security facility for Western Canada in 1979. Within a few years, courts began to intervene in the running of Canada's prisons. In the 1979 precedent-setting decision of *Solosky* v. *The Queen*, the Supreme Court of Canada declared that it was willing to second-guess institutional practice, and it issued guidelines for institutional staff in their dealings with inmates.[96] In that case, the Court issued these guidelines to govern the examination of inmate correspondence with their solicitor, so as to give effect to the sanctity of the solicitor–client relationship. While the appellant lost his case in *Solosky*, the case is important because it signalled a willingness on the part of the courts to at least review the actions of prison authorities.

## The Legal Basis of Prisoners' Rights in Canada

The best source for detailed background information on the legal basis of prisoners' rights in Canada is John Conroy's *Canadian Prison Law*.[97] Conroy points out that

> [t]he coming into force of the Canadian Charter of Rights and Freedoms … on April 17, 1982 and its equality section (s. 15) on April 17, 1985 … compels a

**hands-off doctrine**
An historical policy of non-intervention with regard to prison management, which American courts tended to follow until the late 1960s. For the past 30 years, the doctrine has languished as judicial intervention in prison administration has dramatically increased, although there is now growing evidence of a return to a new hands-off doctrine.

**civil death** The legal status of prisoners in some jurisdictions who are denied the opportunity to vote, hold public office, marry, or enter into contracts by virtue of their status as incarcerated felons. While civil death is primarily of historical interest, some jurisdictions still place limits on the contractual opportunities available to inmates.

completely fresh analysis of the rights of individuals and the use and abuse of power in Canadian society.[98]

Prisoners' rights, because they are constrained by the legitimate needs of imprisonment, are more conditional rights than they are absolute rights.[99] Conditional rights, because they are subject to the exigencies of imprisonment, bear a strong resemblance to privileges, which should not be surprising since "privileges" were all that inmates officially had until the modern era. The practical difference between a privilege and a conditional right stems from the fact that privileges exist only at the convenience of the institutions that grant them and can be revoked at any time, for any reason. The rights of prisoners, on the other hand, have a basis in law that is external to the institution.[100] Although the institution may change these rights for legitimate correctional reasons, they may not be infringed upon without good cause that can be demonstrated in a court of law.[101]

The past two decades have seen many lawsuits brought by prisoners. In Canada, many lawsuits have challenged the constitutionality of some aspect of their confinement. A suit filed by a prisoner with a court, seeking their release, is generally a **writ of *habeas corpus***. It formally requests that the person detaining a prisoner bring the prisoner before a judicial officer to determine the lawfulness of imprisonment. In addition, a **writ of *certiorari*** has been used to aid such an application, as it enables the court to review the decision of a governmental decision maker, and quash the decision if an error of law is found. Aside from appeals by inmates that question the propriety of their convictions and sentences, such constitutional challenges represent the bulk of legal action initiated by those imprisoned.

**writ of *habeas corpus***
The writ that directs the person detaining a prisoner to bring the prisoner before a judicial officer in order for the officer to determine the lawfulness of the imprisonment.

**writ of *certiorari*** The writ that allows a court to review the record of a decision handed down by an inferior court or tribunal, typically looking for an error of law.

## Precedents in Inmate Rights

Courts continue to consider cases that address issues relating to inmate rights, at various levels in Canada. A number of particularly significant decisions are discussed in the pages that follow.

---

**BOX 12.4** **Theory into Practice**

## Administrative Segregation in the Correctional Service of Canada

For most of his academic career, Professor Michael Jackson of the Law Faculty at the University of British Columbia has examined the rights of prisoners under the regime established by the federal correctional authorities. An area of particular concern for him has been the use of administrative segregation.

Segregation, or solitary confinement, is either punitive or administrative. Punitive segregation involves inmates being sent into solitary confinement as a punishment for infringing the prison rules, as decided by an institutional disciplinary board. In contrast, administrative segregation involves a decision by the prison administration to isolate a prisoner because it is believed to be in the best interests of prison management. In recent years, the process of detention and review for administrative purposes has gone through considerable change:

> The current framework sets out detailed, structured review and accountability mechanisms involving the Segregation Review Board, the warden, and Regional Headquarters. There are requirements for hearings at which a prisoner has the right to make representations; to make that right effective, the prisoner must be given three days' advance notice, in writing, of the hearing and the information that the Board will be considering at the hearing. There is a further requirement that a plan be developed to resolve the situation that led to the segregation and, in cases of extended segregation, that a plan be developed within sixty days which addresses in detail the schedule of activities regarding a prisoner's case management services and his access to spiritual support, recreation, psychological counselling, administrative education and health care services.

Indeed, many of the recent changes in administrative segregation came out of the indictment and recommendations for reform advanced by Professor Jackson in the

## Communications

Rights that are accorded to persons in custody must be balanced against the need for security, order maintenance, and the ability to satisfy the treatment needs of inmates in the institution in which they are being held. In the Supreme Court of Canada, it has been held that institutional interests in protecting the public and ensuring the rehabilitation of offenders can, in fact, abbreviate the presumption that the solicitor–client communication is to remain beyond the supervision of the correctional authorities. In the case of *Solosky* v. *The Queen* (1979),[102] the Court ruled that a prisoner's mail may be censored if censoring is necessary for the purposes of institutional security. On the other hand, mere institutional convenience cannot provide a sufficient basis for the denial of rights.

## Religious Practice

Courts will generally uphold the principle that inmates should be given a "reasonable opportunity" to pursue their faith, even when the religious practice associated with a particular faith is different from traditional forms of worship. Inmate rights to freedom of religion under section 2(a) of the *Charter of Rights and Freedoms* are the same as the rights allotted to non-inmates. Meeting facilities should be provided for religious use when those same facilities are made available to other groups of prisoners for other purposes;[103] however, it is unlikely that any group could claim exclusive use of a prison area for religious reasons. The right to assemble for religious purposes may be denied, however, if such meetings are used to plan escapes or to dispense contraband. Also, prisoners in segregation do not have to be given an opportunity to attend group religious services.

In an interesting example at the extreme margins of this issue, a U.S. federal court held that an inmate who claimed to practise witchcraft must be provided with the artifacts necessary to conduct his service of worship. The items included sea salt, sulphur, a quartz clock, incense, candles, and a white robe.[104] However, drugs and other dangerous substances are not considered permissible even when the prisoner (or defendant) claims that they are essential elements of a religious service. In *Re Maltby et al. and AG*

1980s. However, a key reform that Professor Jackson had called for has not been implemented: the independent review of a decision to segregate an inmate. Since the management's decision to segregate and maintain an inmate in segregation is reviewed by Correctional Service agents, there would be a natural tendency to protect the decisions of fellow-workers, without opening up such decisions to the clear light of independent reassessment:

> The pressure against second-guessing your colleague in a work situation may be very strong when that colleague is someone you have known for twenty-five years and with whom you and your family have ties of affection and respect.
>
> It might be suggested that the same is true for judges. They also move within a circle involving recurring contact and ongoing professional, social, and personal relationships. The difference is that within the judiciary — recognizing that individual judges have personal and ideological biases — there is a long and well-entrenched tradition of independence; furthermore, the transparency of published reasons for decisions is buttressed by an independent bar asserting and defending the competing interests

at stake. It is the absence of this tradition and these same hallmarks of justice within the prison that anchors the case for independent adjudication of those decisions that critically affect the rights and liberties of prisoners.

While considerable changes have been made to the plight of inmates, the quest to ensure that the "rule of law" is upheld behind prison walls continues.

## QUESTIONS FOR DISCUSSION

1. Should inmates receive the same rights as non-incarcerated citizens, except for the obvious loss of the right to liberty? If not, how do we decide the rights that should not be available to inmates?

2. Can any arguments be advanced against the call for independent review of administrative segregation decisions? Do these arguments have merit?

*Source:* Jackson, M. (2002). *Justice Behind the Walls: Human Rights in Canadian Prisons.* Vancouver: Douglas & McIntryre. Also available in its entirety online and accessible at time of writing at **www.justicebehindthewalls.net/02_publications _00.html**

*Saskatchewan et al.* (1983),[105] it was held that limiting access to chaplains and religious ceremonies in provincial remand centres did not violate the right to freedom of religion. It was found that, under the circumstances, the limits were reasonable for reasons of institutional security.

## Visitation

Visitation and access to the news media are other areas that have come under court scrutiny. Maximum-security institutions rarely permit "contact" visits, and some have, on occasion, suspended all visitation privileges. In one Canadian case, *Bryntwick* v. *Yeomans and Rousseau* (1983),[106] a prisoner's visiting rights with his common-law wife were indefinitely suspended because she refused to be subjected to a nude search. However, no grounds were provided by the institution to support the search; therefore, the Court ordered that the visitation rights be restored. In an American case, the U.S. Supreme Court upheld a policy within the Los Angeles County Central Jail that prohibited all visits from friends and relatives. Here, the Court agreed that the security of the jail could be jeopardized by the combination of a large jail population and the conditions under which visits might take place.[107] The case of *R.* v. *Olson* (1996)[108] deals with the matter of an inmate's right to maintain contact with the media. Beyond this case, efforts have been made in the House of Commons to introduce a private member's bill that would prevent serial killers and rapists (such as Clifford Olson and Paul Bernardo) from writing or collaborating on books dealing with their horrific crimes.[109]

## Legal Access to the Courts

A well-established right of prisoners is access to the courts and to legal assistance. The right of Canadian prisoners to petition the court has arisen in a variety of cases. The case of *R.* v. *Miller* (1985),[110] a far-reaching Supreme Court of Canada decision, established that aggrieved federal inmates may launch claims for relief in either the provincial courts or the federal courts. The Court clearly wanted to ensure that inmates had access to remedies in the courts. The decision also provided a broad role for the prerogative remedies of *habeas corpus* and *certiorari*, allowing them to be used to challenge, not just the detention itself, but the form of detention. Accordingly, inmates may now use these remedies to challenge the decision of prison administrators to transfer an inmate to a more secure special handling unit, or to administrative segregation.

The Supreme Court of Canada subsequently held in *Cardinal* v. *Director of Kent Institution* (1985) that the prison administration is under a duty to act fairly in deciding to commit an inmate to administrative segregation,[111] and in its decision to keep an inmate in administrative segregation after a Segregation Review Board has recommended the inmate's return to the general population.[112]

In a case noted earlier, *Solosky* v. *The Queen*, the Supreme Court indicated that inmates must be free to consult with their counsel in anticipation of legal action against institutional authorities. Such letters, however, may be opened and inspected for contraband[113] by prison authorities. Also, the right to meet with hired counsel for reasonable periods of time will be upheld by the courts.[114]

## Medical Care of Prisoners

The federal government has committed itself to providing adequate health care to inmates housed in its institutions. The Regulations of the *Corrections and Conditional Release Act*[115] provide that every inmate shall be provided with "essential health care" conforming to "professionally accepted standards," as well as non-essential mental health care that will contribute to the inmate's rehabilitation and reintegration into the community. U.S. courts have intervened to establish a duty to provide medical care in the absence of such regulations. In *Estelle* v. *Gamble* (1976), the U.S. Supreme Court concerned itself with "deliberate indifference" on the part of the staff towards a prisoner's need for serious medical attention. "Deliberate indifference" can mean a wanton disregard for the health of inmates. Hence, while poor treatment, misdiagnosis, and the like may constitute medical malpractice, they do not necessarily constitute deliberate indifference.[116]

More recently, in *Farmer* v. *Brennan* (1994),[117] the U.S. Supreme Court clarified the concept of "deliberate indifference" by holding that it required both actual knowledge and disregard of risk of harm. The case involved Dee Farmer, a preoperative transsexual with obvious feminine characteristics who had been incarcerated with other males in the federal prison system. Farmer was sometimes held in the general prison population but was more often in segregation. While mixing with other inmates, however, Farmer was beaten and raped by a fellow prisoner. Subsequently, he sued correctional officials, claiming that they had acted with deliberate indifference to his safety because they knew that the penitentiary had a violent environment as well as a history of inmate assaults, and because they should have known that Farmer would be particularly vulnerable to sexual attack.

The Court sent Farmer's case back to a lower court for rehearing, after clarifying what it said was necessary to establish deliberate indifference. "Prison officials," wrote the justices, "have a duty under the Eighth Amendment to provide humane conditions of confinement. They must ensure that inmates receive adequate food, clothing, shelter, and medical care and must protect prisoners from violence at the hands of other prisoners. However, a constitutional violation occurs only where—the official has acted with 'deliberate indifference' to inmate health or safety." The Court continued: "A prison official may be held liable under the Eighth Amendment for acting with 'deliberate indifference' to inmate health or safety only if he knows that inmates face a substantial risk of serious harm and disregards that risk by failing to take reasonable measures to abate it."[118]

Two other U.S. cases, *Ruiz* v. *Estelle* (1982)[119] and *Newman* v. *Alabama* (1972),[120] have had substantial impact concerning the rights of prisoners to medical attention. In *Ruiz*, the Texas Department of Corrections was found lacking in its medical treatment programs. The Court ordered an improvement in record keeping, physical facilities, and general medical care, while it continued to monitor the progress of the department. In *Newman*, Alabama's prison medical services were found so inadequate as to be "shocking to the conscience." Problems with the Alabama program included:[121]

* Insufficient medical personnel;
* Poor physical facilities for medical treatment;
* Poor administrative techniques for dispersal of medications;
* Poor medical records;
* A lack of medical supplies;
* Poorly trained or untrained inmates who provided some medical services and performed minor surgery; and
* Medically untrained personnel who determined the need for treatment.

## Privacy

Inmates cannot have a reasonable expectation of privacy while incarcerated.[122] In the case of *Weatherall* v. *Canada (Attorney General)* (1993), the Supreme Court of Canada addressed the issue of privacy expectations of inmates.[123] In *Weatherall*, a prison inmate challenged the constitutionality of frisk searching and patrolling of cell ranges, in a male facility, by female guards. Frisk searching consisted of a hand search of a clothed inmate from head to foot. The inmate objected to "cross-gender touching" and the possible viewing of inmates while they were undressed. This appeal was dismissed because it was determined that frisk searches, counts, and unannounced patrols are necessary practices consistent with the security of the prison. It is expected that there will be a "substantially reduced level of privacy" in the prison and a prisoner "cannot hold a reasonable expectation of privacy with respect to these practices." As a result, section 8 (unreasonable search and seizure) of the *Canadian Charter of Rights and Freedoms* is not called into play.

## Disciplinary and Grievance Procedures

Today, all prisons have an established **grievance procedure**, whereby an inmate files a complaint with local authorities and receives a mandated response. Modern grievance procedures range from a hearing with a hearing board, composed of staff and inmates, to a hearing with a single staff appointee charged with the resolution of complaints. Inmates who are dissatisfied with the handling of their grievance can generally appeal beyond the level of the local prison unit.

**grievance procedure**
Formalized arrangements, usually involving a neutral hearing board, whereby institutionalized individuals have the opportunity to register complaints about the conditions of their confinement.

BOX 12.5

## Theory into Practice

## Inmate Grievances and the Correctional Service of Canada

Grievances of all types are bound to exist among the prison population. Whether those grievances are justified or not, they require to be dealt with so that order and morale of the institution can be maintained. At present, we heard that such grievances can only be resolved, if at all, when an inmate's only avenue of complaint is the very administration which is frequently the source of his dissatisfaction. It is perfectly evident that at Kingston Penitentiary the total absence of any formula by which such matters could be effectively aired was a factor in the disturbance itself.

- Swackhamer Commission Report on the 1971 Riot at Kingston Penitentiary

In response to the finding that there was no fair mechanism in place to deal with inmate grievances in the federal penitentiary system, the federal government created the Office of the Federal Correctional Investigator in 1973. In the months that followed, a new grievance procedure was put in place. Since those early reform efforts, the Correctional Investigator's role has become more clearly institutionalized, and the grievance procedure has become more streamlined.

In 1992, the federal *Corrections and Conditional Release Act* came into force. It altered numerous aspects of federal prison policy. Part of the changes involved implementing a new grievance procedure, contained in the Regulations to the new Act. The new procedure emphasizes both informal resolution of grievances and informal mediation among the parties. The process involves a prisoner filing a grievance with the supervisor of the staff member responsible for dealing with the grievance, sometimes with the assistance of a grievance clerk who is a fellow-prisoner. Then informal mediation is attempted through the supervisor. If informal mediation fails, the complainant is referred to a grievance committee if there is one in the institution. The committee consists of equal numbers of staff and prisoners, who convene a hearing and hear the submissions from the prisoner and the staff. The committee will either resolve the matter or refer it to the warden. If the prisoner disagrees with the committee's decision or recommendation, he or she can appeal the matter to the warden. If the prisoner is dissatisfied with the warden's decision, the matter is then referred to an outside review board. The outside review board consists of members of the community. The decision of the outside review board, where such review is invoked, is only advisory. Where the institutional head chooses to disregard the recommendations of the review board, the prisoner's only remedy is to appeal the decision to the next level of the grievance process, to the head of the region. If still not satisfied, the offender may ultimately appeal to the Commissioner of Corrections. For further details, see the *Corrections and Conditional Release Regulations*, S.O.R./92-620, ss. 74–82.

## QUESTIONS FOR DISCUSSION

1. Does the grievance procedure satisfy your conception of fairness? Is there any aspect of the grievance procedure that you think should be changed? Why?

2. Should outside review boards have the ability to force the warden to make changes inside the institution? What problems might flow from such a reform?

So that inmates can know what is expected of them as they enter prison, inmates are typically given a rulebook that contains all chargeable offences, ranges of penalties, and disciplinary procedures.

In Canada, beyond the *Charter of Rights and Freedoms*, federal statutes that serve to protect the rights of offenders include the following: *Criminal Code of Canada*, *Corrections and Conditional Release Act*, *Criminal Records Act*, *Transfer of Offenders Act*, *Access to Information Act*, *Privacy Act*, and the *Canadian Human Rights Act*.

There exists, within the federal correctional system, a complaint and grievance procedure that affords offenders an opportunity to file complaints informally, or in writing. Offenders are entitled to a response to such grievances. In 2001–02, the federal Office of the Correctional Investigator received 7993 complaints arising from federal institutions. The Correctional Investigator recently noted that the Solicitor General's Ministry, which is responsible for running the Penitentiary Service, has largely ignored the observations and recommendations made by the Investigator in the recent past.[124]

At the federal level, in Canada, the Correctional Investigator was first appointed as a Commissioner under Part II of the *Inquiries Act* in 1973. The Correctional Investigator's mandate was to independently investigate inmate complaints and report on the problems of federal inmates. Part III of the *Corrections and Conditional Release Act* clarified that the role of the Correctional Investigator was that of an ombudsperson for federal corrections, implying independence, unrestricted access to information when conducting investigations, and scope to publicly report his or her recommendations. Table 12–3 shows a breakdown of the complaints received by the Office of the Correctional Investigator during 1996–97.

## ISSUES FACING CANADIAN PRISONS TODAY

Prisons are society's answer to a number of social problems. They house outcasts, misfits, and some highly dangerous people.[125] While prisons may provide a part of the answer to the question of crime control, they also face problems of their own. A few of those special problems are described below.

**TABLE 12–3** Office of the Correctional Investigator Complaints— 2000–01

| Type | # | Type | # |
|---|---|---|---|
| Administrative Segregation | 418 | Mental Health | 39 |
| a) Placement 321 | | a) Access | 27 |
| b) Conditions | 97 | b) Programs | 12 |
| Case Preparation | 731 | Official Languages | 15 |
| a) Conditional release | 280 | Operation/Decisions of the OCI | 48 |
| b) Post-suspension | 74 | Penitentiary Placement | 151 |
| b) Temporary absence | 136 | Programs | 247 |
| c) Transfer | 241 | a) Access | 220 |
| Cell Effects | 371 | b) Quality/Content | 27 |
| Cell Placement | 85 | Release Procedures | 36 |
| Claims Against the Crown | 152 | Request for Info | 102 |
| a) Decisions | 60 | Safety/Security of Offender(s) | 165 |
| b) Processing | 92 | Search and Seizure | 31 |
| Community Programs/Supervision | 18 | Security Classification | 209 |
| Conditions of Confinement | 228 | Sentence Administration – Calculation | 77 |
| Correspondence | 83 | SHU – NRC Reviews | 18 |
| Death or Serious Injury | 3 | | |
| Decisions (General) – Implementation | 34 | Staff | 281 |
| Diet | 63 | Staff Responsiveness | 427 |
| a) Religious | 31 | | |
| b) Medical | 32 | | |
| Discipline | 102 | | |
| a) ICP decisions | 126 | Telephone | 169 |
| b) Minor Court Decision | 19 | Temporary Absence Decision | 147 |
| c) Procedures | 57 | Transfer | 761 |
| Discrimination | 38 | a) Decision – Denials | 230 |
| Employment | 130 | b) Implementation | 140 |
| Transfer | 312 | c) Involuntary | 391 |
| a) Decision | | | |
| b) Involuntary | 254 | | |
| File Information | 397 | Urinalysis | 40 |
| a) Access – Disclosure | 126 | | |
| b) Correction | 271 | | |
| Financial Matters | 178 | Use of Force | 36 |
| a) Access to Funds | 66 | Visits | 506 |
| b) Pay | 112 | a) General | 315 |
| Food Services | 35 | b) Private family visits | 191 |
| Grievance Procedure | 218 | | |
| Grievance Procedure Processing | 126 | **Total** | **7993** |
| Health Care | 987 | | |
| a) Access | 645 | | |
| b) Decisions | 342 | | |

*Source*: Office of the Correctional Investigator Database. (1998). Adapted from Solicitor General of Canada. *Towards A Just, Peaceful and Safe Society: The Corrections and Conditional Release Act Five Years Later: Consultation Paper*(pp. 36–37). Ottawa: Public Works and Government Services Canada. Reproduced with permission.

# AIDS

An earlier chapter discussed the steps being taken by police agencies to deal with health threats represented by AIDS. In 2002, the Canadian HIV/AIDS Legal Network reported that the number of confirmed HIV/AIDS cases among federal inmates in Canada rose from 14 in 1989 to 217 in 2000[126]—an increase of more than 15-fold in a little over 10 years. By the time of the survey, it was found that the incidence of HIV infection in prison exceeded that in the general population by between six and seventy times. Several inmates have died as a result of HIV/AIDS and hepatitis C, which can be transmitted to people in a way similar to HIV/AIDS.[127] A survey conducted in the United States in 1995 estimated the number of HIV-infected inmates in that nation's prisons at much higher levels—perhaps as high as 80 000 inmates.[128] The Correctional Service of Canada has responded to the situation by introducing a methadone maintenance program to allow addicted prisoners access to a sterile substitute to contraband drugs and shared needles within prisons. Switzerland, Germany, and Spain have initiated needle exchange programs in their prisons. Canadian prisons still do not provide needle exchange programs; however, bleach has been made available in many prisons for sterilizing needles. Some prisons have begun to distribute condoms to inmates, in an effort to minimize the transmission of HIV/AIDS through sexual intercourse.

While more male inmates are affected by HIV/AIDS, the percentage of the population of female inmates affected by HIV/AIDS is significantly higher. According to the *Action on AIDS in Prison* report, it is estimated that 1.66 per cent of male inmates in the federal system are infected by HIV/AIDS, while as many as 11.94 per cent of the female inmates in the Edmonton Institution for Women are HIV/AIDS positive. The incidence of HIV/AIDS infection among the general population stands at 1 case per 600 cases, according to the recent report. In the United States, HIV/AIDS has become the leading cause of death among prison inmates. The fact that inmates tend to have histories of high-risk behaviour, especially intravenous drug use, probably explains the huge difference in infection rates.

Contrary to popular opinion, AIDS transmission inside of prisons appears minimal. In a test of inmates at a U.S. Army military prison, 542 prisoners who, upon admission had tested negative for exposure to the AIDS virus (HIV), were retested two years later. None showed any signs of exposure to the virus.[129] On the other hand, some authorities suggest that it is only a matter of time before intravenous drug abuse and homosexual activity inside of prisons begin to make a visible contribution to the spread of AIDS.[130] Similarly, prison staffers fear infection from AIDS through routine activities, such as cell searches, responding to fights, performing body searches, administering CPR, and confiscating needles or weapons.

A recent report by the U.S. National Institute of Justice[131] suggests that there are two types of strategies available to correctional systems to reduce the transmission of AIDS. One strategy relies upon medical technology to identify seropositive inmates and segregate them from the rest of the prison population. Mass screening and inmate segregation, however, may be prohibitively expensive. These methods may also be illegal. Some states in the U.S. specifically prohibit HIV-antibody testing without the informed consent of the person tested.[132] The related issue of confidentiality may be difficult to manage, especially where the purpose of testing is to segregate infected inmates from others. In addition, civil liability may result where inmates are falsely labelled as infected or where inmates known to be infected are not prevented from spreading the disease. Although, as of 1995, only two U.S. state prison systems[133] segregated all known HIV-infected inmates, more limited forms of separation can be practised. In 1994, for example, a U.S. federal appeals court upheld a California prison policy that bars inmates who are HIV-positive from working in food-service jobs.[134]

Many U.S. state prison systems routinely deny jobs, educational opportunities, visitation privileges, conjugal visits, and home furloughs to HIV-positive inmates, causing some researchers to conclude that "inmates with HIV and AIDS are routinely discriminated against and denied equal treatment in ways that have no accepted medical basis."[135] Theodore Hammett, a leading researcher on AIDS in prison, says, "the point is, people shouldn't be punished for having a certain medical condition."[136]

The second strategy is one of prevention through education. Educational programs teach both inmates and staff members about the dangers of high-risk behaviour, and offer suggestions on how to avoid HIV infection. An NIJ model program[137] recommends the use of simple straightforward messages presented by knowledgeable and approachable trainers. Alarmism, says NIJ, is to be avoided. A 1994 survey[138] found that 98 per cent of state and federal prisons in the U.S. provide some form of AIDS/HIV education, and that 90 per cent of jails do as well—although most such training is oriented towards correctional staff, rather than inmates.

In anticipation of court rulings that could prohibit the mass testing of inmates for the AIDS virus, the second strategy seems best. A third, but controversial, strategy involves issuing condoms to prisoners. Although this alternative is sometimes rejected because it implicitly condones sexual behaviour among inmates, six correctional systems within the United States report that they make condoms available to inmates upon request,[139] and the practice is becoming widespread in Canadian prisons.

## Elderly Offenders

As the just deserts model takes greater hold, and more and more criminals are sentenced to longer prison terms, there will be increasing numbers of older prisoners among the

---

**BOX 12.7 Justice in Context**

### Race and Justice: Commission on Systemic Racism in the Ontario Criminal Justice System

In October 1992, the Ontario government appointed a commission to consider the question of "systemic racism" in the province's criminal justice system. Because the Canadian constitutional and legal framework supports fairness and equality, it was seen as important that the framework supported non-discriminatory practices. In Ontario prisons, the Commission's interim report noted that inmates from a diversity of ethnic and racial backgrounds could be disadvantaged by the existing programs and services that were designed and delivered to meet the needs of the dominant culture. Through extensive consultation, the Commission found that:

- It is clear from the evidence that racist language and attitudes plague the environments of many Ontario prisons. It is not a few individuals but the culture of corrections that must change.
- The disregard of the problem by managers, their silence, and their failure to take preventive action contribute to the maintenance of racially poisoned environments.
- One of the limitations of existing management practice is that racism is simply not defined as a significant problem. Instead, it is tolerated as an assumed price that must be paid in order to maintain peace and order.
- There is no evidence that racist practices are necessary to maintain order in prisons. On the contrary, the negative

feelings, adversarial relationships, and hostility generated by such practices can only contribute to dissension, conflict, unrest, and instability.

- In spite of these findings, we believe that among the existing management of prisons in Ontario, there are women and men who are capable of rising to the challenge of eliminating racism. What is required is "aggressive commitment" to this goal.
- Some prisons in Ontario tolerate and encourage racial segregation in the allocation of prisoners among living units. In many prisons for sentenced offenders, this practice is linked to rehabilitation programs.
- The rehabilitation services available to black and other racial minority prisoners are inadequate. Too many ministry staff need to be reminded that rehabilitation is supposed to meet the programming and treatment needs of individual prisoners. It is incorrect to believe that equality means that all prisoners, whatever their race or cultural heritage, should receive identical services.
- The Ontario prison system principally caters to white, Euro-Canadian norms; many of the service needs of black and other racial minority prisoners remain either unacknowledged or dismissed.
- Many institutions operated by the correctional ministry in Ontario fail to recognize the "inherent dignity and worth" of prisoners or to "treat prisoners as individuals." Available services are often inaccessible to black or other racial minority or linguistic minority prisoners, or are inappropriate to their needs. Prisoners from these communities who struggle to receive services that match those routinely provided for white prisoners of Euro-Canadian heritage face the risk that they will be viewed as over-assertive or as "trouble-makers."

---

*Source:* Ontario. (1994). Commission on Systemic Racism in the Ontario Criminal Justice System. Interim Report. *Racism Behind Bars: The Treatment of Black and Other Racial Minority Prisoners in Ontario Prisons* (pp. ii–iii). Toronto: Queen's Printer. © Queen's Printer for Ontario, 1994. Reproduced with permission.

general prison population. Although some prisoners grow old behind bars, others are old at the time they enter prison. Canadian prisons, serving an aging population, are seeing more elderly prisoners than ever before. A 1996 report estimated that 9.3 per cent of federally sentenced prisoners were 50 years old or older.[140] Notably, this percentage reflects a 10-per-cent growth from 1993 in the number of offenders in that age category.

The "greying" of North America's prison population is due to a number of causes: (1) increasing crime among those over 50; (2) the gradual aging of the society from which prisoners come; (3) a trend towards longer sentences, especially for violent offenders with previous records; and (4) the gradual accumulation of older individuals serving life sentences or indeterminate sentences.[141]

Interpersonal crimes are what bring most older inmates into the federal correctional system. According to one study, 38 per cent of inmates who were over the age of 50 had committed sex-related offences.[142]

Julius Uzuoba identifies three categories of older offenders in Canada's federal prisons. First, there is the offender who was sentenced to prison while relatively young, but who has a very lengthy or indeterminate sentence. This type of offender makes up approximately 10 per cent of the older offenders in prison. This offender is typically serving his or her first sentence of incarceration, and poses little risk if eventually released. The second category of older offenders is represented by the offender who has been in and out of prison for much of his or her life, adopting a criminal career lifestyle, in which time in prison is every bit as much a part of his or her life as time spent outside of prison. This type of offender typically adjusts well to prison, and, unlike the first type, views himself or herself as a criminal. Uzuoba estimates about 17 per cent of older offenders fall into this category. The third category includes those offenders who are serving their first period of incarceration relatively late in life. Members of this group led for the most part a law-abiding life, until they committed a serious offence at some point late in their lives. This group contains the largest proportion of all older offenders, estimated to be about 73 per cent of all older offenders.

Uzuoba's research on older offenders in federal custody revealed that they have similar levels of academic achievement and job skills, in the same way that younger offenders do. Family relation factors appear to be similar between younger and older offenders. However, older offenders are (1) more likely to have experienced sexual dissatisfaction in their personal relationships, (2) more likely to have a history of alcohol abuse, and (3) were prone to a more aggressive behavioural orientation, and to be less adept at coping with stress.

According to Uzuoba, life in prison presents a unique set of problems for older offenders. Health care is more critical for offenders over age 50. The health of an inmate relative to that of a person on the outside is said to reflect a 10-year differential. Accordingly, a typical 50-year-old inmate may reflect the health of a typical 60-year-old living outside of prison. Further, older offenders are more likely to develop a dependency on the institution. Institutional programming presents unique problems for older offenders. Educational and vocational training programs have considerably less relevance for the older offender. Perhaps some program staff hold the view that "you cannot teach old dogs new tricks," thereby reducing the impetus to create programming tailored to the older offender.

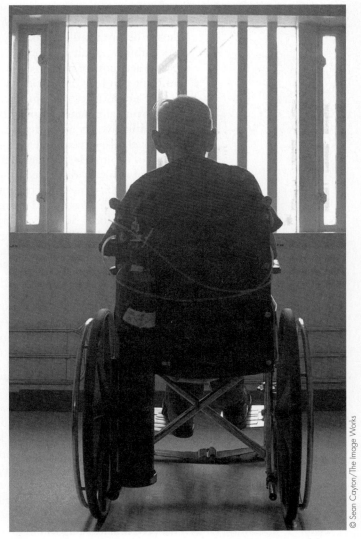

Geriatric inmates are becoming an increasingly large part of the prison population.

© Sean Cayton/The Image Works

Long-termers and geriatric inmates have special needs. They tend to suffer from handicaps, physical impairments, and illnesses not generally encountered among their more youthful counterparts. Unfortunately, few prisons are equipped to deal adequately with the medical needs of aging offenders. Some large facilities have begun to set aside special sections to care for elderly inmates with "typical" disorders such as Alzheimer's disease, cancer, or heart disease. Unfortunately, such efforts have barely kept pace with problems. The number of inmates requiring round-the-clock care is expected to increase significantly over the next two decades.[143]

Unique approaches to housing and programming for older offenders need to be considered. What kinds of programs are most likely to be useful in providing the older inmate with the needed tools for success on the outside? Which counselling strategies hold the greatest promise for introducing socially acceptable behaviour patterns into the long-established lifestyles of elderly offenders about to be released? There are few answers to these questions. To date, with the exception of Uzuoba's work, no in-depth studies to answer such questions have been conducted that might help prepare Canada's prison system for handling the needs of older inmates.[144]

## Mentally Ill Inmates

Inmates with mental illnesses are another inmate category with special needs. Some inmates suffer from anxiety-related disorders or have personality problems that increase tension in prison. Others have serious psychological disorders that may have escaped earlier diagnosis (before trial) or that did not provide a legal basis for the reduction of criminal responsibility. A fair number of offenders develop psychiatric symptoms while in prison. Some accounts of modern prisons have focused squarely on the problem, identifying significant numbers of individuals in prisons who have experienced a major mental disorder.

The incidence of major mental disorders among prison inmates is startling. One study of provincial inmates found that about 25 per cent had experienced a psychotic or significant affective disorder at some point in their lives.[145] A study of federal inmates revealed that over 84 per cent had a diagnosis of a mental disorder at some point in their lives.[146]

Unfortunately, few jurisdictions have any substantial capacity for the psychiatric treatment of mentally disturbed inmates. In 1982, Hans Toch described the largely ineffective practice of bus therapy, whereby disturbed inmates were shuttled back and forth between mental health centres and correctional facilities.[147] Through its ongoing research efforts, the Correctional Service of Canada has sponsored several valuable studies that have examined mental health issues relative to Canadian inmates.[148] Matters of health care (i.e., medical, dental, and mental health care provided by registered health care professionals) are covered under sections 85 to 89 of the *Corrections and Conditional Release Act* at the federal level. This legislation defines mental health care as:

> ... the means of care of a disorder of thought, mood, perception, orientation or memory that significantly impairs judgment, behaviour, the capacity to recognize reality or the ability to meet the ordinary demands of life.

The Correctional Service of Canada is required to provide universal access to essential health services for inmates, but the responsibility of making pro-health choices lies with the offender.

Mentally deficient inmates constitute still another group with special needs. Some studies estimate the proportion of mentally deficient inmates at about 10 per cent.[149] Mentally deficient inmates are less likely to successfully complete training and rehabilitative programs than are other inmates. They also have difficulty in adjusting to the routines of prison life. As a consequence, they are likely to exceed the average in the proportion of sentence they are likely to serve.[150]

While some mentally disordered offenders are accommodated within the Correctional Service of Canada through the Service's Regional Psychiatric Centres, many mentally disordered inmates languish in prison cells without treatment. The Supreme Court of Canada recently approved of applying conditional sentencing, where the sentence is to be partly served in a provincial psychiatric facility, to accommodate the needs of mentally disordered offenders in conflict with the law.[151]

## SUMMARY

Prisons are small societies. Various studies of prison life have detailed the pre-eminence of prison subcultures, replete with inmate values, social roles, and lifestyles. Prison subcultures have a profound influence on both inmates and staff and must be reckoned with by everyone involved in the criminal justice system.[152]

Complicating life behind bars are the numerous conflicts of interest between inmates and staff. Lawsuits, riots, violence, and frequent formal grievances are symptoms of these differences. The conditional rights of prisoners, which have been defined by the high courts in Canada, mandate professionalism among prison administrators and require vigilance in the provision of correctional services.

Problems that exist in conventional society are internalized, and often intensified, by the closed society of prison. HIV-infected inmates, elderly offenders, women offenders, and

---

BOX 12.8 **Policy Issues**

### The Office of the Federal Correctional Investigator: Recommendations Falling on Deaf Ears?

In 1973, the office of the Correctional Investigator was established to investigate allegations of wrongdoing inside the federal penitentiary system. The Correctional Investigator conducts investigations and makes recommendations for change. An annual report is published, outlining the past year's activities of the Investigator, which are like that of an ombudsperson. There is no power to force changes, only to bring matters of maladministration to light. It is then up to the government to take the initiative to reform any process or redress any wrongdoing that has occurred. Since there is no enforcement mechanism, there is always a risk that the government will ignore the recommendations of the Correctional Investigator, and wrongdoing will go unaddressed.

In the Annual Report of the Correctional Investigator for 2001–02, the following assertion was made:

> The observations and recommendations detailed in last year's Report have in large part been ignored.

The Executive Director, who reviewed the response of the Correctional Service to the 2000–01 Annual Report, then sent a letter to the Senior Deputy Commissioner of Corrections, stating in part:

> I am quite frankly disappointed with the Service's response. As you know we were initially advised in early July of this year that the Service's response would be finalized by the end of August. To be provided with a copy of the response on the same day that the Annual Report was tabled has served no one well.
>
> With respect to the substance of the response, I readily accept the fact that there are and will continue to be issues where our respective positions are fundamentally different. What I find difficult to accept is a response which in large part, fails to reasonably address the specifics of either the issues or the recommendations and continues to ignore past commitments.

For the 2001–02 report, the Correctional Service of Canada published its response to the Correctional Investigator's Report online. You can view both the report and the response online at : **www.oci-bec.gc.ca/ereports.asp**

### QUESTIONS FOR DISCUSSION

1. Do you think the Correctional Investigator should have the power to force change within the correctional system? If not, is there a way in which we can make sure the recommendations are not buried or ignored by bureaucrats?

2. If you have looked at the current report and the Correctional Service's response to the report, do you think the Correctional Service adequately responded to the recommendations of the Correctional Investigator? Is there more that the Correctional Service could be doing? Explain.

inmates with mental illnesses all constitute special groups within the inmate population that require additional care.

Crime does not stop at the prison door, nor does rehabilitation begin automatically. If we expect prisons to meet the demands of rehabilitation and reformation, in addition to those of retribution, punishment, and deterrence, we must be willing to solve the problems of prisons first.

## DISCUSSION QUESTIONS

1. Explain the concept of prison subcultures. What purpose do you think such subcultures serve? Why do they develop?

2. What does "prisonization" mean? Describe the U-shaped curve developed by Wheeler as it relates to prisonization. Why do you think the curve is U-shaped?

3. What are the primary concerns of prison staff? Do you agree that those concerns are important? What other goals might staff focus on?

4. Does the claim that "the rule of law does not run behind prison walls" adequately describe the situation in Canadian prisons? What do you think might be the future of prisoners' rights in this country?

5. Explain the "balancing test," established by the Canadian Supreme Court in *Solosky* v. *The Queen*, for deciding issues of prisoners' rights. How might such a test apply to the emerging area of inmate privacy?

6. What are some of the special problems facing prisons today that are discussed in this chapter? What new problems do you think the future might bring?

## WEBLINKS

www.csc-scc.gc.ca/text/pblct/rights/human/toce_e.shtml
**Human Rights and Corrections: A Strategic Model**
The Working Group on Human Rights was established in May 1997 to review the Correctional Service of Canada for compliance with the rule of law in human rights matters, for both inmates and employees, and to provide a general strategic model for evaluating compliance within any correctional context.

www.jpp.org/fulltext-v2/jppv2n1-b.html
**The Canadian Penal Press: A Documentation and Analysis**
An article by Robert Gaucher about publications produced in Canadian prisons.

www.elizabethfry.ca
**Canadian Association of Elizabeth Fry Societies (CAEFS)**
CAEFS is a federation of autonomous societies that works with, and on behalf of, women involved with the justice system, particularly women in conflict with the law. Elizabeth Fry Societies are community-based agencies dedicated to offering services and programs to marginalized women, advocating for legislative and administrative reform, and offering public forums.

www.elizabethfry.ca/p4w/2percent.htm
**CSC and the 2 Per Cent Solution (The P4W Inquiry)**
A report by Kim Pate about the 1996 Commission of Inquiry into Certain Events at the Prison for Women at Kingston.

www.csc-scc.gc.ca/text/rsrch/reports/r70/r70e_e.shtml
**Managing Older Offenders: Where Do We Stand?**
The full report by Julius Uzoaba for the Correctional Service of Canada that surveys the situation of older offenders serving federal time in Canada.

home.istar.ca/~ccja/angl/overc.html
**Prison Overcrowding and the Reintegration of Offenders**
An in-depth analysis and discussion guide published by the Canadian Criminal Justice Association.

# Special Issues

*The best thing about the future is that it comes one day at a time.*

—Abraham Lincoln

No one can truly say what the future holds. Will the purveyors of individual rights or social order advocates ultimately claim the day? We cannot say for sure. This much is certain, however: things change. The Canadian system of criminal justice in the next century, and the century after that, will not be quite the same system we know today. Many of the coming changes, however, are now discernible—and hints at what is to come appear on the horizon with increasing frequency and growing clarity. Some of the more obvious of the coming changes are already upon us. They include (1) a restructuring of the juvenile justice system in the face of growing concerns about violent juvenile crime and spreading youth gang warfare; (2) the increased bankruptcy of a war against drugs whose promises seem increasingly hollow; (3) a growing recognition of Canada's international role as both victim and purveyor of worldwide criminal activity; and (4) the quickly unfolding potential of cybercrimes—those which both employ high-technology in their commission and target the fruits of such technology.

This, the last part of *Canadian Criminal Justice Today* discusses each of these issues in the chapters that follow. It also draws your attention back to the bedrock underlying the Canadian system of justice—the Constitution, the *Charter of Rights and Freedoms*, and the demands of due process, all of which can be expected to continue to structure the justice system well into the future.

# Youth Criminal Justice

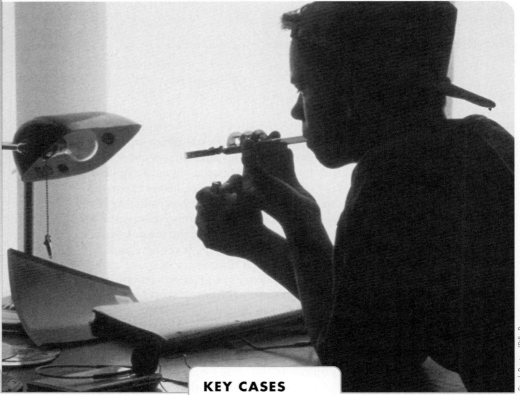

Stock Boston/Billy Barnes

## KEY CONCEPTS

| | |
|---|---|
| youth justice system | status offenders |
| delinquency | status offences |
| parens patriae | social ecology |
| due process | social disorganization |
| delinquent children | opportunity theory |
| undisciplined children | cohort |
| dependent children | normlessness |
| neglected children | youth justice philosophy |
| abused children | |

## KEY CASES

| | |
|---|---|
| Re Gault | *R. v. M.(M.A.)* |
| *Williams v. Garcetti* | *R. v. S.(S).* |

# INTRODUCTION

On November 2, 1998, 16-year-old Clayton McGloan was stabbed at a house party in an upscale community in northeast Calgary. Two brothers, aged 15 and 17, were initially charged with aggravated assault and assault with a weapon. Young McGloan died two days later after his parents consented to remove their son from life support. The brothers were subsequently charged with second-degree murder. After the new charges were laid, the Crown applied to have both boys transferred to adult court.

Several weeks later, Clayton's parents and girlfriend, along with a group of approximately 60 teenagers and parents, marched and petitioned outside the Calgary youth court building, calling for government officials to toughen the *Young Offenders Act* (YOA) by moving more violent youths into adult court and ensuring stiffer penalties.[1]

In 2003, Canada replaced the YOA with a new *Youth Criminal Justice Act* (YCJA), seeking to treat serious young offenders more seriously, and to find alternative ways of responding to less serious youth offenders. Clayton McGloan's case is neither an isolated example of senseless youth violence nor of public outcry. Increasingly, we hear examples of crimes, among both young males and females, that reflect a capacity for cold, calculated acts of violence. A 1993 *Juristat* report noted that "firearms were involved in a higher percentage of violent crimes among youth than among adults."[2] Another recent case that attracted a public outcry for the replacement of the *Young Offenders Act* occurred in 1997 when several youth bullied and beat 14-year-old Reena Virk. Following the initial beating of the Victoria, B.C. resident, a second beating by one of the seven girls and a boy who was involved in the initial beating resulted in Reena Virk eventually being drowned.[3]

These sad cases appear to reflect much of what faces Canadian youngsters today. All too many of our nation's children live as outcasts in a society that has neglected its responsibility for the care and training of its young, and has left them to grow up—often far too fast—as best they can. On the other hand, some children appear to be willing participants in criminal activity, and crime statistics show that a significant proportion of all illegal activity today is committed by young persons. Only 8 per cent of the population of Canada are youths. However, in Canada, almost one-half of all crimes committed by youths are property-related (approximately 44 per cent), and 2001 data indicate that persons aged 12 to 17 committed approximately 27 per cent of all property crimes that resulted in charges being laid,[4] and 16 per cent of all violent crimes. However, the overall rate of youths charged with *Criminal Code* offences dropped in eight of the past ten years. In fact, property crimes committed by youths have declined steadily since 1991 (see Figure 13–1). The rate of violent crimes committed by youths declined in the late 1990s; however, in both 2000 and 2001, this rate increased (7 per cent and 2 per cent, respectively).

As David Foot noted in his book *Boom, Bust and Echo* (1996), however, the drop in crime rate during the 1990s was attributable to a shift in demographics. Foot refers to those youth born between 1980 and 1995 as the "baby-boom echo," because they are the children of the baby-boom generation. At their peak in 1990, baby boomers produced 406 000 children, as compared to 479 000 children born in late 1957, another baby-boom year.[5] The proportion of youths in Canada's total population steadily declined between the early 1980s and the mid-1990s, and this decline coincided with declining crime rates. Once the children of the baby-boom echo begin to hit their crime-prone years (15–24) in 2005 to 2014, it should not come as a surprise that youth crime will appear to be increasing. But there are conflicting views as to whether young persons are committing more crimes today. As we will see throughout this chapter, many elements contribute to our understanding of delinquency and youth crime. We will begin by summarizing some recent data from Statistics Canada. Table 13–1 shows *Juristat* statistics on the numbers of young persons arrested for selected offences.

Statistics Canada reported the following findings in various 2001 and 2002 *Juristat* reports:

- The overall police-reported crime rate increased slightly in 2001 after decreasing for nine years in a row.

- The rate of youths charged with property crimes declined 3 per cent, reflecting 10 consecutive years of declining property crime rates for youths. Break-ins accounted for the largest decline (6 per cent).

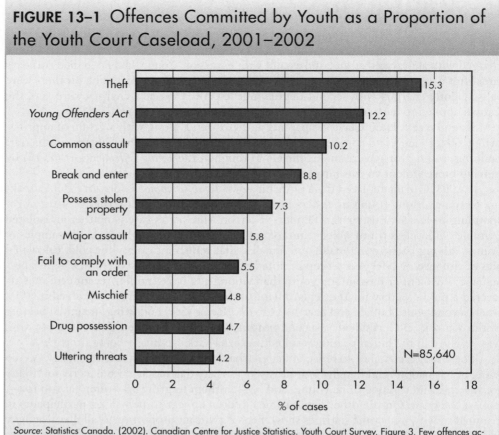

**FIGURE 13–1** Offences Committed by Youth as a Proportion of the Youth Court Caseload, 2001–2002

*Source:* Statistics Canada. (2002). Canadian Centre for Justice Statistics. Youth Court Survey. Figure 3. Few offences accounted for a large proportion of the youth court caseload. Adapted from the Statistics Canada publication *Juristat*, Catalogue no. 85-002, Vol. 23, No. 3, June 2003, Figure 3, p. 4.

- The rate of youths charged with violent crimes increased 2 per cent, following a 7-per-cent increase in the preceding year. These recent increases followed four consecutive years of decline. The overall increase in youth violent crime was fuelled by a 10-per-cent increase in the number of youths charged with robbery, and a dramatic 35-per-cent increase in the number of robberies committed by youths with a firearm.

- Thirty youths were accused of homicide—13 fewer than in 2000. The 10-year annual average (1991–2001) is 48. The 2001 youth homicide rate was the lowest in over 30 years.

- In 2001, 76 per cent of youths charged with *Criminal Code* offences were male. The same gender breakdown applies to violent crime as well as to property crime.

- In self-report findings, only 44 per cent of male youths reported that they did not engage in aggressive behaviour, while 71 per cent of female youths reported that they did not engage in aggressive acts.

- In 2001, almost 2.5 million youths were between the ages of 12 through 17 (8 per cent of the population of Canada).

As noted, a number of researchers have attempted to downplay the seriousness of youth crime, yet it is well-documented that many adults involved in criminal acts began their illegal activities while young. Therefore, if we

**TABLE 13–1** Rate of Youths Charged

| Selected Offences | Youth Charged | Adults Charged |
|---|---|---|
| **Total violent** | **20%** | **30%** |
| Assaults | 15% | 26% |
| Robbery | 3% | 2% |
| **Total property** | **53%** | **38%** |
| Theft | 26% | 19% |
| Breaking and entering | 15% | 7% |
| Theft motor vehicle | 6% | 2% |
| **Total other *Criminal Code*** | **27%** | **32%** |
| Mischief | 6% | 4% |
| **Total *Criminal Code*** | **100%** | **100%** |

*Source:* Adapted from *Juristat*, Catalogue no. 85-002, Vol. 10, No. 2.

Sister Lesley Sacouman, a Roman Catholic nun, helped to establish Rossbrook House—a year-round open refuge for street kids—in Winnipeg.

are truly interested in reducing the crime rate, we must understand why and how young persons commit crimes.

This chapter has four purposes. First, we will describe the **youth justice system** from its historical beginnings to the present. The youth justice system has its roots in the adult system. In the young offenders' system, however, we find a more uniform philosophical base, and a generally clear agreement about the system's purpose. Both may be due to the system's relative newness and to the fact that society generally agrees that young people who have gone wrong are worthwhile salvaging. However, as a box in this chapter shows, the philosophy that underlies the youth justice system in Canada is being constantly called into question by "get-tough" advocates of law and order, many of whom are fed up with violent crime by young persons.

Our second purpose will be to compare the youth and adult systems as they currently operate. On April 1, 2003, Canada's new *Youth Criminal Justice Act* (YCJA) came into force, replacing the *Young Offenders Act* that governed youth justice between 1984 and 2003. The philosophy behind the youth justice system has led to administrative and other procedures that are not found in the adult system. The youth justice process, for example, is frequently not as open as the adult system. Although the current legislation has opened the courtroom doors, at the judge's discretion, hearings may be held in secret. With a few exceptions, the names of offenders are not published.

Our third focus will be to describe in detail the agencies, processes, and problems of the youth justice system itself. Although each province and territory may have variations, a common system structure is shared by all.

Of course, the youth justice system is not without its critics. Just as the adult criminal justice system has not been able to eliminate adult criminality, the young persons' system has been unable to entirely curb youth crime. Hence, near the end of this chapter, we will turn to our fourth focus and consider issues raised by critics of the youth justice system.

**youth justice system**
Government agencies that function to investigate, supervise, adjudicate, care for, or confine youthful offenders and other children subject to the jurisdiction of the Youth Justice Court.

# YOUTH JUSTICE THROUGHOUT HISTORY

## Earliest Times

The history of the Western world reveals that children who committed crimes in past centuries could expect no preferential treatment because of their youth. They were adjudicated and

**delinquency**  A pejorative term that refers to young persons' actions or conduct in violation of criminal law, status offences, and other misbehaviour.

**parens patriae**  A common-law principle that allows the state to assume a parental role and to take custody of a child when he or she becomes delinquent, is abandoned, or is in need of care that the natural parents are unable or unwilling to provide.

punished alongside of adults. The laws of King Aethelbert, the earliest legal document written in the English language (circa A.D. 600), made no special allowances for the age of the offender. Recorded cases reveal that children as young as six or eight were hanged or burned at the stake. Children were also imprisoned along with adults because segregated facilities did not exist for young persons. Neither the development of gaols (an old word for jails) in the thirteenth century nor the early English prisons provided any leniency on the basis of age.[6] Similarly, little distinction was made between criminality and **delinquency** or other kinds of undesirable behaviour. Problems such as epilepsy, insanity, retardation, or poverty were seen in the same light as crime,[7] and people suffering from these conditions were shut away in facilities shared by young and adult offenders.

Court philosophy in dealing with juveniles derived from an early Roman principle called *patria postestas*. Under Roman law (circa 753 B.C.), the father of a family had absolute control over his children, and they in turn had an absolute responsibility to obey his wishes. The power of the father extended to issues of life and death for all members of the family, including slaves, spouses, and children.[8] Roman understanding of the social role of children strongly influenced English culture, and eventually led to development of the legal principle of **parens patriae**. *Parens patriae* allowed the king, or the English state, to take the place of parents in dealing with children who broke the law. *Parens patriae* held that the king was the father of the country and thus had parental rights over all his citizens.

By the Middle Ages, social conceptions of children had become strongly influenced by Christian churches. Church doctrine held that children under the age of seven had not yet reached the age of reason and therefore could not be held liable for spiritual transgressions. In adopting the perspective of the Church, English law of the period excepted children under the age of seven from criminal responsibility. Young persons aged 7 to 14 were accorded a special status, being tried as adults only if it could be demonstrated that they fully understood the nature of their criminal acts.[9] Adulthood was considered to begin at age 14, when marriage was also allowed.[10]

Early English institutions placed a large burden of responsibility on the family, and especially the father, who, as head of the household, was held accountable for the behaviour of all family members. Children, and even wives, were almost totally dependent upon the father and had a status only slightly above that of personal property. When the father failed in his responsibility to control family members, the king, through the concept of *parens patriae*, could intervene.

The inexorable power of the king, often marked by his personal and unpredictable whims, combined with a widespread fear of dismal conditions in English institutions, forced many families to hide their kin who had problems. The retarded, insane, and epileptic were kept in attics or basements, sometimes for their entire lives. Delinquent children were confined to the home or, if the family from which they came was wealthy enough, sent overseas to escape the conditions of asylums and gaols.

## Juveniles in Frontier Canada

Early Canadian solutions to the problems of delinquency were much like those of the English. Puritan influence in the colonies, with its heavy emphasis on obedience and discipline, frequently led to both juveniles and adults being jailed for a wide variety of offences. Legislation reflected the biblical Ten Commandments and often provided harsh punishments for transgressors of almost any age. For example, in 1649, a 15- or 16-year-old girl was charged in a town in Quebec for theft. Her punishment—hanging. Although hanging was not a common punishment, children were prosecuted essentially in the same manner as adults. However, they were also tried for such minor offences as throwing stones and petty theft.[11] Severe punishment was consistent with Puritan beliefs that unacknowledged social evils might bring the wrath of God down upon the entire colony.

By the end of the eighteenth century, social conditions in Europe and Canada began to change. The Enlightenment, a highly significant intellectual and social movement, focused on human potential, and generally rejected previously held supernatural explanations in favour of scientific ones. It was accompanied by the growth of an industrialized economy, and a move away from farming. Ineffective laws, lower infant death rates, and the social innovations introduced during the Enlightenment led to a reassessment of the place of children in society. In this new age, society became increasingly concerned about the well-being of children. One of the first Canadians to express reformist ideas about the handling of delinquents was the physician Charles Duncombe. In the 1840s, he became an advocate for penal reform and argued that municipal governments and the local community had an obligation to protect the welfare of neglected and misguided youth.

## The Institutional Era: Pre-Confederation

The nineteenth century was a time of rapid social change in Canada. The population was growing dramatically, towns were burgeoning, and the industrial era was in full swing. Industrial tycoons, the new rich, and frontier-bound settlers lived elbow-to-elbow with immigrants eking out a living in the sweatshops of the new mercantile centres. In this environment, children were a source of cheap labour. They worked on assembly lines and in shops. Parents were gratified by the income that their offspring earned. On the frontier, settlers and farm families put their children to work clearing land and seeding crops.[12]

Unfortunately, economic opportunities were not equally favourable to all. Some families who moved or settled in cities became victims, living in squalor and being unable to meet the needs of their children. Many families, seeing only the economic opportunities represented by their children working at an early age, neglected to provide them with anything but a rudimentary education. Children who did work laboured for long hours, and had little time for family closeness. Other children, abandoned by families unable to support them, were forced to live on the streets, where they formed tattered gangs, surviving off the refuse of the glittering cities.

### The House of Refuge

A few years after a New York report that called for the development of "houses of refuge," the Brown Commission, in 1849, paved the way for the construction of houses of refuge in Canada. It was suggested that Montreal, Quebec City, Toronto, or Hamilton establish such houses. Houses of refuge were to be places of care and education where children could learn positive values towards work.

The Brown Commission marked a formal shift in the treatment of young offenders. While the Commission dealt more generally with the operation and management of provincial penitentiaries, it also addressed the treatment of young persons in houses of refuge. The Commission noted that "in waging war with crime, there is no department so satisfying, so encouraging, as the rescue and reformation of the young; and there it is the battle should be fought with utmost warmth."[13]

The Commission recommended that a house of refuge should be divided into two departments. One should deal with the neglected or undisciplined, and the other should accommodate those convicted of a crime. Consistent with the philosophy of the new reform, the Commission argued that children in the care of a house of refuge should be provided with educational and vocational instruction. In this manner, they would be prepared to serve as apprentices in the trades or businesses related to their acquired skills.

This time period has also been referred to as the "socialization mode." During this period, parents focused on training their children, acting as guides and treating their children more equally.[14]

Interest in the "socialization mode" was not embraced by all segments of society. For example, the Roman Catholic Church was concerned that the houses of refuge would become "nurseries of crime."[15] Nevertheless, prison inspectors such as Andrew Dickson were instrumental in the establishment of a juvenile detention centre. He even suggested that farms be attached to the centre. In this way, young offenders could learn about farming and be apprenticed to local farms.

Hence, with these initiatives, the welfare movement began to take shape. As a result of the recommendations set out by the Brown Commission, young offenders were kept separate from adult offenders and their needs given greater attention through a variety of treatment initiatives. In addition, the reform movement slowly gave way to other developments such as compulsory education, industrial schools, and reformatory schools.

## The Chicago Reform School: The Child Savers

By the mid-1800s, the child savers movement began. Child savers espoused a philosophy of productivity and eschewed idleness and unprincipled behaviour. Anthony Platt,[16] a modern writer who recognized the significance of the child savers movement, suggests that the mid-1800s provided an ideological framework combining Christian principles with a strong emphasis on the worth of the individual. Child savers held that children were to be guided and protected. Its advocates came mostly from the middle and upper social classes.

One product of the child savers movement was the reform school—a place for delinquent youth that embodied the atmosphere of a Christian home. By the middle of the nineteenth century, the reform school approach to handling juveniles was well under way. The Chicago Reform School, which opened in the 1860s, provided an early model for the reform school movement. The movement focused primarily on pre-delinquent youth who showed tendencies towards more serious criminal involvement. Reform schools attempted to emulate wholesome family environments in order to provide the security and affection believed to be necessary in building moral character.

The reform school movement also emphasized traditional values and the worth of hard work. The movement tended to idealize country living, apparently in the belief that the frantic pace of city life made the transition from child to adult difficult. Some early reform schools were built in rural settings and many were farms. A few programs even developed that tried to relocate problem children to the vast, open expanses of Western Canada.

The reform school movement was not without its critics. As one modern-day observer writes, "If institutions sought to replicate families, would it not have been better to place the pre-delinquents directly in real families?"[17] As with houses of refuge, reform schools soon became overcrowded. What began as a meaningful attempt to help children ended in routinized institutional procedures devoid of the reformer's original zeal. A friction also emerged between those who supported the industrial schools and those who favoured a non-institutional approach—a clash between a judicial philosophy and the social welfare approach.

John Joseph Kelso became one of the pioneers of the child savers movement in Canada. He was instrumental in the establishment of the Humane Society in Toronto in 1887, as well as in the formation of the Toronto Children's Aid Society in 1889, and he became an advocate of foster home care.[18]

As a news reporter in Toronto, Kelso saw first-hand the plight of neglected and wayward children. It became his life's mission to help these children. Kelso and many of his supporters were able to persuade provincial and federal politicians that humanitarian reforms were needed in the handling of juveniles. Although various provinces had begun to introduce legislation reflecting a humanitarian orientation, it was not until July 1894 that Parliament passed the first piece of federal legislation on juvenile delinquency. It was known as the *Youthful Offenders Act*, which is very similar to the 1984 Act. The passing of this legislation marked a dramatic step towards formal state intervention and control of delinquent youth. The Act dealt with such issues as arrest, imprisonment, and trial proceeding for juveniles. The passage of the Act also set the stage for the introduction of the first juvenile court.

## The Era of the Juvenile Delinquents Act

An expanding recognition of the needs of children, along with several developments in the 1800s, led to Canada treating youthful offenders differently from adults. In 1857, the first juvenile institution in Canada was opened at Penetanguishene, Ontario. With the passage of the *Youthful Offenders Act* (similar to the *Young Offenders Act* in name only), and the 1891 Report of the Commissioners Appointed to Inquire into the Prison and Reformatory System of Ontario, strong support for separate juvenile courts developed. Segregating youth from adults was considered to be a more effective and humanitarian way of dealing with delinquent and wayward youth. This development was influenced, in part, by the "discovery" of childhood, the efforts of the child savers movement, and a philosophical and practical shift in a more benevolent attitude towards the use of penal measures.[19]

The transition to youth courts was not immediate. Differences of opinion between the provinces on how juveniles should be dealt with delayed the process until the passage of the *Juvenile Delinquents Act* (JDA) in 1908. In that year, the first juvenile court opened in Winnipeg, Manitoba. Kelso played a major role by lobbying politicians at all levels for the creation of juvenile courts. Another strong advocate and supporter was W.L. Scott, a lawyer and president of the Ontario Children's Aid Society. It was Scott who mounted a compelling lobby to amend the *Youthful Offenders Act* so that it would avail the opportunity for the creation of children's courts. Yet resistance came from such prominent officials as Inspector David Archibald of the Toronto police, who thought young offenders were more in need of strict discipline and accountability than treatment as misguided and misdirected innocent souls.[20] However, the social and political climate had shifted towards a welfare-oriented model, and Kelso and his supporters' ideas prevailed.

The juvenile court movement and the JDA were based on a number of philosophical principles that can be summarized as follows:

1. The belief that the state is the "higher or ultimate parent" of all the children within its borders. This underlying philosophy was known as *parens patriae*.

2. The belief that children are worth saving, and that non-punitive procedures should be used to save the child. To this end, the JDA granted judges wide discretion in the handling of cases and youth could be punished for both criminal offences and status offences—offences for which only young persons could be sanctioned (e.g., truancy).

3. The belief that children should be nurtured. While the nurturing process is under way, they should be protected from the stigmatizing impact of formal adjudicatory procedures. Court hearings for young persons should be heard in private and neither the names of those youth involved nor their identities should be released.

4. The belief that justice, to accomplish the goal of reformation, must regard the individual; that is, each child is different, and the needs, aspirations, living conditions, and so on, of each child must be known if the court is to be truly helpful.

5. The belief that non-criminal procedures are in the best interests of the child. The denial of **due process** could be justified in the face of constitutional challenges because the court acted not to punish, but to help.[21] The JDA stated that delinquents could not be detained in the same facilities as adults.

While the JDA could be praised for its attempts to provide the state with an opportunity to deal with delinquents firmly and yet in an understanding manner, the Act came under increasing scrutiny towards the end of the 1950s. Child advocates and probation officers, who supported the child-welfare model of juvenile justice, argued that the system simply was not working. The primary criticisms focused on the unbridled power granted to the court in dealing with juveniles and the system's apparent inefficiency in rehabilitating young offenders and preventing young offenders from committing further crimes. In addition, the informal nature of court proceedings was criticized. Juvenile court proceedings were seen as a fundamental violation of young persons' rights. For example, section 20 of the JDA enabled the courts to decide indeterminate sentences that far exceeded the discretion that was possible under the adult system (see also below).

Further impetus for reform came as a result of the *Re Gault* decision in 1967 in the United States. The landmark case involved Gerald Gault, a 14-year-old boy who was charged with making an obscene phone call. The case eventually made it to the Supreme Court of the United States, which ruled that "juveniles have a right to receive counsel, to confront and to cross-examine witnesses, to remain silent, to be given a transcript of the hearing, and the right to appeal."[22] The decision impacted the reform of juvenile justice not only in the United States but also internationally, including Canada.[23]

While criticism was mounting, politicians and scholars could not agree on the direction in which reform needed to proceed.[24] Two opposing models emerged: the welfare model and the justice model.[25]

**due process** A legal principle that requires fair procedure to be applied in judicial proceedings, sometimes referred to as procedural due process. The legal principle is capable of a broader meaning that allows judges to require the content of the law to be fair, sometimes referred to as substantive due process.

**delinquent children**
Under the JDA, children who had engaged in activities that would be considered crimes if the children were adults. Under the YCJA, the term "young person" is applied to such a child in order to avoid the stigma that comes from application of the term "delinquent."

**undisciplined children**
Children who were beyond parental control, as evidenced by their refusal to obey legitimate authorities such as school officials and teachers.

**dependent children**
Children who have no parent(s) or whose parent(s) is (are) unable to care for them.

**neglected children**
Children who are not receiving the proper level of physical or psychological care from their parent(s) or guardian(s), or who have been placed up for adoption in violation of the law.

**abused children** Children who have been physically, sexually, or mentally abused. Most provinces also consider that a child is abused when they are forced into delinquent activity by a parent or guardian.

**status offenders** In the past, children who committed an act that was contrary to the law by virtue of the young persons' status as children. Purchasing cigarettes, buying alcohol, and truancy were examples of such behaviour.

**status offences** Acts or conduct declared by statute to be offences, but only when committed by or engaged in by a young person. Current legislation has moved away from the notion of status offences, penalizing acts that would be crimes if committed by an adult.

The JDA was based on the welfare model, which in turn is based on the paternalistic philosophy. Advocates of this model argued that the JDA was ineffective because the juvenile criminal system lacked sufficient resources to work properly. Proponents of the welfare model believed that intervention strategies needed to be tailored to the specific needs of young persons. They felt that a balance between addressing the specific needs of young persons and respecting the rights of young persons was possible.

By contrast, the justice model was based in the classical school of criminology. It maintained that people are essentially hedonistic beings who seek to maximize their pleasure and minimize their pain. Behaviour was believed to be a function of free will and crimes involved calculated risks by certain people who wished to maximize their pleasure with minimal pain. Proponents of this model called for demanding greater accountability of young offenders while offering them certain legal rights.

In the 1970s, while the debate was raging, youth crime apparently increased, the youth unemployment rate increased, and Canada experienced a recession. Canadians became increasingly disenchanted and began to campaign for a law-and-order approach. Hence, the government began to embrace aspects of a "get tough" approach, balancing these with a new interest in individual rights brought about by the adoption of the *Canadian Charter of Rights and Freedoms* in 1982. At the same time, the government tried to retain elements of the former welfare-based model, creating the *Young Offenders Act* in 1984. The *Youth Criminal Justice Act* of 2003 continues to embody the spirit of the justice model first embodied in the YOA almost 20 years earlier.

## Categories of Children in the Youth Justice System

By the time of the Great Depression, most provinces had expanded the definition of "child" in juvenile statutes to include six categories of children that are still used today in many jurisdictions to describe the variety of children subject to youth court jurisdiction:

1. **Delinquent children** were those who violated the criminal law. If they were adults, the word "criminal" would have been applied to them.

2. **Undisciplined children** were said to be beyond parental control, as evidenced by their refusal to obey legitimate authorities such as school officials and teachers. They needed state protection.

3. **Dependent children** typically had no parents or guardians to care for them, had been abandoned, or had been placed for adoption in violation of the law.

4. **Neglected children** were those who did not receive proper care from their parents or guardians. They had suffered from malnutrition, had not been provided with adequate shelter, or had not received a proper upbringing.

5. **Abused children** included those who suffered physical abuse at the hands of their custodians; a category that was later expanded to also include emotional and sexual abuse.

6. **Status offenders**, a special category that was to lead to many later disputes, embraced children who violated laws written only for children.

**Status offences** included behaviour such as truancy, vagrancy, running away from home, and incorrigibility. The youthful "status" of young persons was a necessary element in such offences. Adults, for example, could decide to run away from home and not violate any law. Because provincial laws required that children be subject to parental control at home, children who ran away were subject to apprehension and then appearance before youth court.

Status offences were a natural outgrowth of the old juvenile court philosophy. As a consequence, however, young persons in need of help often faced procedural dispositions that treated them as though they were delinquent. As a result, rather than lowering the rate of incarceration, the juvenile court movement led to its increase. Critics of the juvenile court movement quickly focused on the abandonment of due process rights, especially in the case of status offenders, as a major source of problems. Detention and incarceration, they argued, were inappropriate options where children had not committed crimes.

BOX 13.1 **Theory into Practice**

## Prince George Youth Custody Facility

The *Youth Criminal Justice Act* came into force in 2003. This Act replaced the *Young Offenders Act*, which had been in force since 1984, which in turn replaced the *Juvenile Delinquents Act*, in force from 1908–84. The ultimate sanction in all forms of youth justice law in Canada has been detention in a secure facility. Each province and territory is responsible for creating and maintaining its own youth detention facilities. In British Columbia, there are several facilities providing secure custody for young offenders. One of these is found in Prince George, the largest city in the central part of the province.

Prince George Youth Custody Centre is a secure facility providing a range of programs that allow youths to make constructive use of their time while in custody. All youths admitted to the Centre are between 12 and 17 years of age. Prince George is one of four secure-custody centres in B.C. It is both open- and secure-custody-based, and is responsible for the custody arrangements for the entire interior region of the province.

Upon a youth's admission to the facility, the case management coordinator conducts an interview and assigns a living unit based upon custodial disposition, background information, and case management principles. A case manager is assigned to all residents staying longer than 30 days. The case manager assists each resident in developing and achieving goals and objectives for his or her stay. The case manager also assists in planning and advocating applications for transfer to open custody, temporary absences and/or early release, as considered appropriate.

The centre's daily routine is structured around educational and recreational programs. The residents are responsible for their chores, laundry, and personal hygiene. The educational curriculum at the centre includes academic courses, life-skills training, and education taught by seven full-time teachers. Woodwork and metalwork are taught as part of that component. Evening programs include visits, education, arts and crafts, hobbies, athletics, life skills, substance abuse, and other programs. On weekends, school is replaced by a variety of programs with an emphasis upon special events involving outside community groups.

The residents maintain a website that outlines the various programs and gives an overview of the residents' daily routine. For example, a typical Tuesday involves the following:

07:00 – Room doors are enabled. Each youth has an alarm clock and is responsible to be ready for breakfast at 08:00.
08:00 – Breakfast: youths are responsible for chores and clean-up. These tasks are assigned by the youths themselves.
09:00 – 12:00 – All youth attend school (Monday to Thursday)
12:00 – 13:00 – Lunch
13:00 – 15:00 – Street Theatre
15:00 – 16:00 – Yoga
16:00 – 17:00 – Supper
17:00 – 17:30 – Free time
17:30 – 19:30 – Al-Anon (offsite)
19:30 – 20:00 – Free time/unit activities

Each day, the available activities change. Some of the programs currently available are violent offenders' treatment program, native dancing/family night, women-only Bible study, anger management, self-esteem program, violence against women, Alateen, street theatre, adventure-based learning, yoga, cultural awareness, sexually transmitted diseases, cooking program, workout program, hobbies, folk art program, sexually exploited youth, parenting support group, drug and alcohol, horticultural program, sewing/quilting program, dating/relationships program, and Girl Guides.

Many of the residents are aboriginal and come from the northern part of the province. An effort is maintained to accommodate their cultural heritage, and to deal with the most pressing and particular issues for this significant portion of the resident population.

Discipline within the facility varies, depending upon the seriousness of the incident. Fighting will result in a 24- to 72-hour lockdown. An argument may result in being locked in one's room for an hour, or the rest of the night. If chores are not completed correctly, then the result is lockdown or early bedtime, or youths may even get extra duties involving additional chores.

*Source:* With permission of Prince George Youth Custody Centre's website. Accessible at time of writing at **www.members.pgonline.com/~pgycc/**

# EXPLANATIONS OF YOUTH CRIME

"By the year 2010, Canada will have 180 000 more youth in the at-risk age group."[26]

One of the first comprehensive social scientific explanations for delinquency, advanced by Clifford Shaw and Henry McKay[27] in the 1920s, was known as **social ecology**. The social ecology approach focused on the misbehaviour of lower-class youth, and saw delinquency primarily as the result of **social disorganization**. Whereas social order is the condition of a society characterized by social integration, consensus, smooth functioning, and

**social ecology** An approach that focused on the misbehaviour of lower-class youth, and saw delinquency primarily as the result of social disorganization.

**social disorganization**
A condition that is said to exist when a group is faced with social change, uneven cultural development, maladaptiveness, disharmony, conflict, and lack of consensus.

**opportunity theory**
A perspective that sees delinquency as the result of limited legitimate opportunities for success available to most lower-class youth.

**cohort** A group of individuals sharing similarities of age, place of birth, and residence. Cohort analysis is a social scientific technique by which such groups are tracked over time in order to identify unique and observable behavioural traits that characterize them.

lack of interpersonal and institutional conflict, social disorganization exists when a group is faced with social change, uneven development, maladaptiveness, disharmony, conflict, and lack of consensus. Geographic areas characterized by economic deprivation were said to have high rates of population turnover and cultural heterogeneity, both of which were seen as contributors to social disorganization. Social disorganization weakened otherwise traditional societal controls, such as family life, church, jobs, and schools, making delinquency more likely in such areas.

Because of their influence on policy makers of the 1930s, the first large-scale delinquency prevention program grew out of the work of Shaw and McKay. Known as the Chicago Area Project, the program developed self-help neighbourhood centres staffed by community volunteers. Each centre offered a variety of counselling services, educational programs, camps, recreational activities, and discussion groups. Programs were intended to reduce social disorganization by bringing members of the community together to work towards common goals, and by providing community members with the skills needed for success.

The approach of Shaw and McKay was replaced in the 1960s by a perspective known as **opportunity theory**. Opportunity theorists saw delinquency as the result of the lack of legitimate opportunities for success available to most lower-class youth. Richard A. Cloward and Lloyd E. Ohlin[28] described the most serious delinquents as facing limited opportunities due to their inherent alienation from middle-class institutions. Others have claimed that delinquency is a natural consequence of participation in lower-class culture. Even stable lower-class communities, these authors suggest,[29] produce delinquency as a matter of course. A combination of both approaches is found in the work of Albert K. Cohen,[30] who held that delinquency, especially gang-related activity, is a response to the frustration that lower-class youth experience when they find they cannot share in the rewards of a middle-class lifestyle. According to Cohen, vengeance and protest are major motivators among deprived youth and may account for vandalism and other seemingly senseless acts.

Opportunity theory gave rise to treatment models designed to increase chances for legitimate success among lower-class youth. Programs such as New York City's Mobilization for Youth provided education, skills training, and job placement services to young men and women. Mobilization for Youth, through the federal funds it received, hired hundreds of unemployed neighbourhood youths to work on community projects such as parks conservation and building renovation.

Gresham M. Sykes and David Matza[31] at least partially recognized the role of individual choice in delinquent behaviour in their description of the neutralization of responsibility as a first step towards law violation. The delinquent, according to Sykes and Matza,[32] typically drifts between conformity and law violation and will choose the latter when social norms can be denied or explained away.

**Cohort** analysis is a useful technique for identifying the determinants of delinquency. Cohort analysis involves a group of people that share common characteristics. The analysis usually begins when the individuals are born and traces the development of the group until its members reach a certain age. Since the only major cohort study conducted in Canada is still in its early stages (see discussion in relation to violent youth below), we will summarize some of the major American and European studies that have been useful in illuminating the picture of youth crime.

One well-known analysis of a birth cohort, undertaken by Marvin Wolfgang during the 1960s, found that a small nucleus of chronic juvenile offenders accounted for a disproportionately large share of all juvenile arrests.[33] Wolfgang studied males born in Philadelphia in 1945 until they reached age 18. He concluded that a relatively small number of violent offenders were responsible for most of the crimes committed by the cohort. Eighteen per cent of cohort members accounted for 52 per cent of all arrests in the Philadelphia cohort. A follow-up study found that the seriousness of offences committed by members of the cohort increased once they reached adulthood, but that the actual number of offences decreased as the cohort aged.[34] Wolfgang's analysis has since been criticized for its lack of a second cohort, or "control group," against which the experiences of the cohort under study could be compared.[35]

Perhaps the most comprehensive study to date that has attempted to unveil the underlying causes of crime committed by young persons was begun in 1986, with early results reported in 1994 and 1995. The study, named the Program of Research on the Causes and Correlates of Juvenile Delinquency,[36] was sponsored by the U.S. Department of

Justice's Office of Juvenile Justice and Delinquency Prevention (OJJDP). The study drew together data on 4000 youths from three distinct but coordinated projects: (1) the Denver Youth Survey, conducted by the University of Colorado; (2) the Pittsburgh Youth Study, undertaken by University of Pittsburgh researchers; and (3) the Rochester Youth Development Study fielded by professors at the State University of New York at Albany. The survey sampled youngsters at high risk for serious delinquency and drug use and found that (1) "the more seriously involved in drugs a youth was, the more seriously that juvenile was involved in delinquency," (2) "greater risks exist for violent offending when a child is physically abused or neglected early in life," (3) "students who were not highly committed to school had higher rates of delinquency," (4) "poor family life exacerbates delinquency and drug use," and (5) affiliation with street gangs and illegal gun ownership are both predictive of delinquency. The study also found that "peers who were delinquent or used drugs had a great impact on [other] youth." Perhaps the most significant result of the study was the finding that three separate developmental pathways to delinquency exist. The pathways identified by the study were:

1. The *authority conflict pathway*, down which subjects appeared to begin quite young (as early as three or four years of age). "The first step," said the study authors, "was stubborn behaviour, followed by defiance around age 11, and authority avoidance—truancy, staying out late at night, or running away."

2. The *covert pathway*, which begins with "minor covert acts such as frequent lying and shoplifting, usually around age 10." Delinquents following this path quickly progressed "to acts of property damage, such as fire-starting or vandalism, around age 11 or 12, followed by moderate and serious forms of delinquency."

3. The *overt pathway*, in which the first step was marked by minor aggression such as "annoying others and bullying—around age 11 or 12." Bullying was found to escalate into "physical fighting and violence as the juvenile progressed along this pathway."

The study also identified youth who, although being at risk of delinquency, did not engage in delinquent behaviour. The research points to five factors that characterize these juveniles. These factors, called protective factors, are the following:

1. Commitment to school;

2. Achievement at school;

3. Continuance of education (no dropping out);

4. High levels of parental supervision;

5. High levels of attachment to parents; and association with conventional peers and peers approved of by their parents.

As part of the Cambridge Study of Delinquent Development, one of the most comprehensive English cohort studies involved 396 boys from a working-class area of London. The cohort were all born between 1951 and 1954, and were tracked up to their 25th birthday. The study focused on chronic and indictable offences.

Among the more important findings, the researchers found that approximately 6 per cent of the offenders with six or more convictions accounted for the majority of offences. These offenders tended to be convicted at an earlier age than non-chronic offenders, came from low-income families, had low IQ and attainment, and had older siblings who had been convicted. And while the researchers were unable to predict the type of offences, they observed that the risk of becoming a chronic offender increased significantly if the youth had been convicted for the first time between the ages of 10 and 13.[37]

Other studies have also indicated the importance of regular school attendance and commitment to success at school. A 1996 American report by the U.S. Office of Juvenile Justice and Delinquency Prevention (OJJDP), for example, found that "chronic absenteeism is the most powerful predictor of delinquent behaviour." A comprehensive 1997 task force report by the American Society of Criminology similarly concluded that "strong evidence links early problem behaviour to later adolescent delinquency and serious adult criminality" and suggested that early intervention is the key to preventing the development of chronic patterns of criminal behaviour. Authors of the task force report wrote that

Canadian Press/Nick Procaylo

Some names and comments written in a guestbook at a memorial service held for slain teenager Reena Virk. The case was one of a number of cases that attracted a public outcry for changes to the *Young Offenders Act.*

"[T]here is clear indication that problem behaviour often begins early in life, and there is strong evidence of substantial continuity between problem behaviour in early childhood and later adolescent delinquency and serious adult criminality. 'An ounce of prevention is worth more than a pound of cure' is more than an old adage. Not only can early prevention and intervention reduce future crime and delinquency, but waiting until the mid-to-late teenage years to intervene in serious, persistent delinquency commonly results in an uphill and all too frequently fruitless battle."[38]

In order to prevent youth crime, we need to understand it. In this section, we have highlighted but a few of the more common approaches to explaining youth crime. However, there is no one specific cause of delinquency. Human behaviour is simply too complex. In the late 1980s, a number of explanations that attempted to adopt an integrated and multidisciplinary approach began to emerge. Recent research suggests that we are on the verge of a paradigm shift that may hold new promise for understanding and ultimately responding to youth crime.[39] An integrated and interdisciplinary approach to the study of criminal (delinquent) behaviour combines elements of many fields of study (e.g., sociology, political science, natural sciences, economics, and psychology) in an effort to better understand the nature of crime, justice, and law. Michael Gottfredson and Travis Hirschi have taken steps in this direction by expanding upon Hirschi's "social bond" theory to incorporate concepts from bio-social, psychological, routine activities, and rational choice theories to develop a general theory of crime.[40]

## THE PROBLEMS OF CHILDREN TODAY

Besides delinquency, but in some ways contributing to it, there are an array of other problems that face children today. Many of these problems are quite different from those that existed when the juvenile court was formed. Today's youth have to deal with an increasing number of social and personal stresses that did not exist at the turn of the twentieth century. Many feel a lack of purpose and that their voices are not heard or respected by society. This feeling is reflected in some of the senseless crimes that some youth have committed. In 1993, for example, two Canadian girls, aged 12 and 13, were arrested after a high-speed chase. In court, the judge described them as appearing "to be totally out of everyone's control … They're a danger to be at large."[41] John Dilulio, Jr., co-director of the Foundation for the American Family, suggests that the increase in violent and senseless youth crime is a by-product of growing up in an environment of increasing "moral poverty."[42] In the same article, Helen Jones, co-founder of the Ontario Association of Parent Support Groups, criticizes social workers and police officers who encourage young people to move out if life at home is too difficult.

Young persons' comments on a variety of issues show they are subjected to considerable stress and pressure while growing up.[43] Young persons who have been in the youth justice system have expressed "tragic frustration about both the processes and institutions."[44] How is it that the youth of today appear more angry and frustrated? Over half a century ago, many of the problems encountered by young persons grew out of their value as inexpensive labour in the "sweatshops" and factories of the industrial evolution that was sweeping North America. The economic prosperity that followed World War II, however, was based on a less labour-intensive form of production. Complicating matters still further was the need for the national economy to absorb millions of women who were entering the labour force. Young persons, no longer needed for their labour, were thrown into a cultural limbo. Some, unable to meaningfully participate in the long educational process that was becoming increasingly necessary for future success, turned to delinquency and vandalism. For these disenfranchised youth, criminal activity became an alternative avenue to excitement and some limited sense of purpose.

By the 1960s, a self-indulgent ethic had replaced the sense of personal responsibility among a good proportion of North American youth. For lower-class youth, the ethic led to violence, theft, and increased participation in gangs. Middle-class youth, because they were more affluent, focused on what some authors at the time called the "automobile-alcohol-sex combination,"[45] rejecting middle-class values of social duty and personal restraint.

While much of the literature of delinquency focuses on the criminality of lower-class youth, there is evidence that middle- and upper-class youths today commit a fair number of delinquent acts. A recent American study of the "lifetime delinquency" of Ivy League college students, for example, found "substantial levels of involvement in a variety of serious offences."[46] According to the study, 167 students admitted to 4100 past offences ranging from public intoxication to forcible rape.

Regardless of class background, a number of common problems face juveniles today. Each is described in the sections that follow.

# Drug and Alcohol Abuse

Since the late 1960s and early 1970s, many of today's adolescents have experimented with illegal drugs. Adolescents are, by nature, experimental. And while it remains a serious problem behaviour, substance abuse among young persons has dropped since the mid-1980s. However, among high-risk youths, the use of drugs has significantly increased and is becoming commonly linked to law-breaking behaviour.

Before we review some of the data, it is necessary to distinguish between abuse and experimentation. Numerous surveys show that most youth have been occasional users of some type of legal and/or illicit drug. However, investigators are less clear about what constitutes drug abuse. For example, in one study, researchers found that after following a group of adolescent problem drinkers over a seven-year period, most were judged not to be problem drinkers in their adult years. It was suggested that as a result of the aging process, many adolescent substance abusers did not continue to be abusers or become adult criminals.[47]

Nevertheless, it is well-documented that many youth charged with violent crimes had consumed some type of drug on the day the offence was committed. After many years of declining drug use in the 1980s, drug use among high-school students in Ontario increased in the 1990s, but eventually levelled off in recent years.[48] A survey of Ontario high-school students, conducted in 2001, revealed that alcohol consumption was fairly high among teens (65.6 per cent admitted to consuming it in the past year); however, the majority of teens did not use illegal drugs like marijuana and cocaine. Nonetheless, the study confirmed that more high-school students consumed marijuana in that year (29.8 per cent) than consumed ordinary tobacco cigarettes (23.6 per cent). Many students appear to have accepted the message that soft drug use is okay or trendy. The survey also found that while overall drug use among high-school students was fairly stable, the use of marijuana appeared to be gradually increasing, and the use of ordinary cigarettes, solvents, and LSD declined.[49] Inhalants (e.g., glue, butyl nitrite, paint thinner, and aerosol cans) are likely to be the first chemicals used by youth, especially native youth. They have been described as the "gateway drugs" for native drug users. Solvents appear to be popular because of their cost effectiveness, availability, and rapid mood elevation.[50] Chronic use of some inhalants has been associated with neurological, kidney, and liver damage.

The Centre for Addiction and Mental Health (CAMH) studies high-school drug use every two years in Ontario. The consumption of some drugs has increased significantly in recent years. Between 1993 and 2001, consumption of marijuana rose, as did consumption of Ecstasy (MDMA), PCP, hallucinogens, cocaine, and solvents.[51] Consumption of inhalants has always been highest among younger students, particularly those in grades 7 through 9.[52] Table 13–2 shows a breakdown in drug use among surveyed students in 2001. The CAMH reports that there has been a significant fluctuation in drug use since it began collecting data in 1977; however, the pattern of drug use has stabilized in recent years.

More than one-third (39 per cent) of students surveyed in the 2001 study reported being exposed to drug selling in their neighbourhood during the preceding year. Perceived availability has been linked to rates of drug use.[53]

Drug abuse may also lead to other types of crime. One recent study found that seriously delinquent youth were regular drug users.[54] But, more alarmingly, unlike adults, adolescent substance abusers are more inclined to mix drugs and risk becoming poly-substance abusers.[55] And as the American Bureau of Justice Statistics concludes: "The involvement of adolescent users in other destructive behaviour is strongly associated with the number and types of harmful substances they use; the more substances they use, the greater their chance of being involved in serious destructive or assaultive behaviour."[56] While drug abuse and delinquency can technically exist without each other, the fact that the correlation between them is very strong speaks to greater social and cultural concerns that must be addressed within society.

Although highly controversial, other countries handle the drug problem in different ways. The Netherlands, for example, has attempted to remove the "glamour" of drugs by legalizing various soft drugs. In that country, there are approximately 1200 legal drug outlets. In addition to being able to reduce the price of soft drugs, the Dutch are also able to monitor the quality of these drugs. And while the legal selling of otherwise illegal drugs might appear to be counterintuitive, the crime rate in the Netherlands declined 25 per cent between 1993 and 1997.[57] Since drugs have been around since ancient times, the Canadian criminal justice system might want to explore different options.

## Violence

Observers of the national scene have recently reported an apparent epidemic of violence among the nation's teenagers. At the beginning of this chapter, we read about the 16-year-old Calgarian youth Clayton McGloan, who was stabbed to death on Halloween night in 1998 for trying to prevent a party at his parents' home from getting out of control. In the same year, also in Calgary, a 17-year-old was stabbed to death by two teens after a dispute between the victim and the young killers. Newspapers regularly provide accounts of violence perpetrated by youthful offenders.

We must be careful not to conclude from these accounts that teen violence is on the increase. It is possible that what was once sloughed off as schoolyard antics or bullying is now being reported as assaultive behaviour to the police. Currently, as the public pleas for greater accountability, and a greater willingness to report delinquent incidents to authorities develops, the criminal justice system has taken a tougher stance against delinquency. So, while official data suggest that violent youth crime rates increased in 2000 and 2001,[58] these rates may simply reflect increased reporting by citizens and stronger enforcement practices by the police. As the esteemed sociologist Robert Merton once suggested, apparent increases in delinquency may simply be the result of a self-fulfilling prophecy. Yet, in the face

**TABLE 13-2** Summary of Findings from the Student Drug Use Survey in Ontario, 2001

(Percentage using drugs during the past 12 months by total, sex, and grade)

| | Total | M | F | G7 | G8 | G9 | G10 | G11 | G12 | OAC |
|---|---|---|---|---|---|---|---|---|---|---|
| Cannabis | 29.8% | 33.7% | 26.0% | 5.1% | 12.0% | 28.8% | 39.0% | 45.7% | 43.5% | 43.0% |
| Glue | 3.0 | 3.7 | 2.3 | 3.9 | 5.7 | 3.8 | 2.7 | 1.2 | 1.8 | — |
| Solvents | 5.7 | 5.5 | 6.0 | 9.7 | 9.3 | 7.6 | 3.8 | 2.3 | 3.9 | — |
| Barbiturates (M) | 11.8 | 12.5 | 11.1 | 7.6 | 10.9 | 12.8 | 16.1 | 9.8 | 12.5 | 11.2 |
| Barbiturates (NM) | 3.9 | 3.5 | 4.3 | 2.3 | 3.0 | 2.9 | 8.1 | 2.9 | 4.0 | 2.0 |
| Heroin | 1.0 | 1.4 | 0.7 | 0.9 | 0.9 | 2.2 | 1.2 | 0.5 | — | — |
| Methamphetamine | 3.8 | 5.0 | 2.7 | 1.2 | 1.4 | 3.7 | 6.8 | 4.9 | 5.0 | 2.5 |
| Stimulants (M) | 7.0 | 8.7 | 5.4 | 4.6 | 8.3 | 8.3 | 7.1 | 8.3 | 8.9 | 1.5 |
| Stimulants (NM) | 6.4 | 4.8 | 8.0 | 1.9 | 3.3 | 5.5 | 7.8 | 10.3 | 10.4 | 7.4 |
| Tranquillizers (M) | 3.2 | 4.0 | 2.4 | 1.2 | 3.7 | 2.3 | 2.6 | 5.4 | 5.9 | 2.1 |
| Tranquillizers (NM) | 2.2 | 2.8 | 1.7 | 0.6 | 2.1 | 1.4 | 2.7 | 3.3 | 4.2 | 1.9 |
| LSD | 4.5 | 6.0 | 3.1 | 0.9 | 2.5 | 4.6 | 8.0 | 5.0 | 7.8 | 1.4 |
| Other Hallucinogens | 11.4 | 13.2 | 9.6 | 0.9 | 3.8 | 9.7 | 15.2 | 19.2 | 20.5 | 14.4 |
| Cocaine | 4.3 | 4.6 | 3.9 | 2.4 | 3.2 | 3.2 | 6.5 | 7.0 | 3.5 | 2.6 |
| Crack Cocaine | 2.0 | 2.4 | 1.6 | 0.5 | 1.7 | 3.7 | 1.4 | 2.6 | 2.9 | 0.5 |
| PCP | 2.7 | 3.2 | 2.2 | 0.8 | 1.2 | 3.8 | 3.7 | 2.9 | 4.4 | 1.3 |
| Ice | 0.6 | 0.7 | — | 0.6 | 1.0 | — | 0.6 | 1.2 | — | 0.5 |
| Ecstasy (MSMA) | 6.0 | 6.7 | 5.4 | 0.9 | 3.0 | 7.2 | 6.8 | 9.5 | 9.2 | 6.8 |
| Rohypnol | 2.9 | 3.3 | 2.6 | 1.6 | 2.6 | 5.2 | 3.0 | 1.2 | 5.4 | 0.9 |
| GHB | 1.2 | 1.7 | 0.8 | 0.6 | — | 1.2 | 3.6 | — | 1.2 | 0.9 |
| Ritalin | 2.8 | 3.8 | 1.7 | 4.2 | 4.2 | 2.4 | 2.7 | 1.8 | 2.0 | 0.9 |

*Source:* Drug Use Among Ontario Students 1997–1999: Findings from the OSDUS (Toronto: CAMH Research Document No. 5, 1999). © 1999 Centre for Addiction and Mental Health. Reprinted with permission from Centre for Addiction and Mental Health.

of the sheer number of anecdotal accounts, it would appear inappropriate to brush off such accounts as simple media sensationalism.

Official crime data reveal that the rate of violent incidents among young persons decreased for four consecutive years (1996–99) before increasing in 2000 and 2001. The rate of homicides committed by young persons has declined dramatically in recent years, with the lowest youth homicide rate in over 30 years in 2001.[59] However, there has been a sharp increase in the number of major assaults and armed robberies committed by youth during the same time. In addition, recent public surveys indicate that citizens believe youth violence increasingly "appears to be unprovoked, random, and increasingly unpredictable."[60] Even the police lend support to such perceptions. In 1992, the head of the youth division for the Halifax Regional Police said, "There's no question that youth criminal activity is up. Each generation they get was a little more sophisticated, a little more violent. And it's unexplainable, needless violence."[61] Perhaps the most dramatic examples of "needless violence" in recent years were the 1999 gun-and-bomb killing in a local high school in Littleton, Colorado, followed a few weeks later by the copycat killing in the small southern Alberta community of Taber. However, we must be careful not to conclude from these dramatic incidents, extensively covered in the media, that youth violence is spiralling out of control, because, other than the recent increase in youth robberies, recent youth crime data largely mimics that of adults in Canada.

Statistics Canada and Human Resources Development Canada have recently commenced a National Longitudinal Survey of Children and Youth, seeking to track children from early life up to the age of 25. Data collection for this cohort survey began in 1994, and will continue for many years to come. *Juristat* released results from the second cycle of the survey (1996–97), relevant to delinquency in youth in 2001.[62] Results showed that 56 per cent of boys aged 12 to 13 reported engaging in some type of aggressive behaviour, such as threatening someone or getting into fights. Girls reported a much lower rate of 29 per cent. The majority of aggressive acts reported were relatively minor. Youth who did not report being aggressive at ages 10 and 11 appear to have remained non-aggressive as they entered adolescence, with only 5 per cent of them reporting high frequencies of aggression when they reached 12 and 13. However, not all youth who reported high levels of aggression at ages 10 and 11 remained aggressive. Only 55 per cent of this highly aggressive group reported any aggression at ages 12 and 13. Youth who are aggressive (1) are victims of bullying, (2) experience high levels of punitive parenting and low parental nurturing, and (3) tend to be depressed.

Another possible explanation for the alleged increase in youth violence may be the apparent increase in the number of weapons in the hands of teens. As indicated in the media accounts above and in official police statistics, the number of youth charged with weapons-related offences has steadily increased in recent years.

Yet another factor that may account for increased youth violence is the rapid growth of youth gangs (see below) and an increase in hate crimes initiated by young persons. Although a subject direly lacking in research in Canada, in the 1998 movie *American History X*, "Danny's role offers some insight into the life of a young skinhead." Finally, although the incident rate of youth crime declined in the mid- to late 1990s, this decline was largely due to a drop in the number of adolescents in the Canadian population. And while property crime rates account for most of the decline, violent crime rates among young persons have increased. As stated earlier, these trends cannot be so readily dismissed as social and political artifacts.

## Gangs

Historic accounts show that juvenile gangs have been an inner-city phenomenon since the turn of the century. One of the first reported youth gangs in Canada dates back to 1890 when five boys were arrested in Toronto for committing 20 break-and-enters.[63] However, definitions of "youth gang" are somewhat nebulous. For example, it is not uncommon to see youth "hanging out" in malls, around street corners, or in schoolyards. In fact, young people have always had an affinity for congregating for social reasons. The degree to which such youth are closely affiliated may or may not constitute a gang or a law-violating youth group, as American sociologist Walter Miller suggested in the 1970s. However, when a group of youth engages in criminal activities, they risk being identified as a gang.

Recent gang activities differ substantially from those in the early twentieth century. Whereas membership in early gangs served to provide some sense of personal identity in the immigrant's culturally diverse world, many of today's youth gangs have developed into financial enterprises. Like other aspects of youth crime, modern variations of youth gangs began to appear in the 1960s and 1970s. Current youth gang activities may centre on the acquisition and sale of stolen goods, drug running, petty crime, rowdyism, and the sex trade. In some instances, they use ruthless violence to protect financial opportunities.

A Canadian study found that punk gangs do not fit the typical mould. Only when confronted with verbal abuse or instigation would they react with violence when they felt they needed to protect themselves.[64] By contrast, in the late 1990s, native youth gangs were becoming a serious concern in some parts of Canada. For example, in April 1997, Winnipeg introduced anti-gang legislation directed at the growing native youth (and adult) gang problem. In November 1998, the Winnipeg police made their first major arrest of nearly 40 street-gang members. Similar measures have been taken in Alberta and Quebec in an effort to curb gang and organized crime activities.[65] In addition, various cities across the country have established special youth gang squads to monitor and control the problem.

As with youth violence, some have raised questions about the true extent to which youth gang activity has increased. As noted above, youth by nature prefer to associate in groups, and accounts of some groups engaging in gang-type behaviour date back to the early 1800s. There are even early accounts of females being involved in gang activities. One of the earliest studies of female gang activity found that young females have also been involved in gangs since the early 1800s and that traditionally they have been, and largely continue to be, affiliated with male gangs.[66] Contemporary studies indicate, however, that female gangs are becoming more common as a result of changes in the social and cultural makeup of society.

While the existence of youth gangs may not be in dispute, it appears that gang-related activity has increased. Whereas earlier gangs evolved around issues of loyalty and protection of territory, increasingly modern gangs are involved in the sale of illegal drugs, extortion, and other serious criminal activity. Where once gangs relied on knives, chains, and baseball bats, today's gangs are increasingly better organized, using guns and other deadly weapons. Furthermore, because of social dislocation and economic pressures, gang activity has escalated. In the United States, for example, such gangs as the Crips and Bloods have drawn international attention and have even been the focus of several movies. Canadian youth gangs by contrast, while less notorious, have left their mark on the fabric of Canadian society. There have been accounts of extortion, drive-by shootings, and even violence among different youth gangs. Cities such as Vancouver, Montreal, and Toronto have experienced problems with young Asian immigrant gangs, in addition to native gang groups. One media account claimed that more than 180 youth gangs were present in Greater Toronto schools.[67] Of course, many of these so-called gangs were nothing more than groups of young people who associated with one another and thought up names to attach to their individual groups. However, a 1998 survey, conducted by the *Toronto Star*, of over 1000 high-school students in the Toronto area found that one in ten claimed to belong to a gang, and 53 per cent of students said there were gangs in their schools. Many students reported being fearful and feeling intimidated by the presence of gangs in their schools.

In Western Canada, much of the media's concern over youth gangs has concentrated on Asian gangs. In the Vancouver area, the extent to which gang activity is connected to Asia has received some attention in recent years. While a preliminary analysis of youth gangs, which looked at incarcerated gang members in Greater Vancouver, found that only 34 per cent of the members were of Asian origin, the study also found that 40 per cent of the members were of European extraction.[68] More recent research indicates that youth gangs in Greater Vancouver are made up of different youth groups, only some of whom can be aptly classified as actual street gangs.[69] Many so-called "wanna-be" groups coexist with the more organized, profit-oriented street gangs. Robert Gordon's research of Vancouver-area street gangs revealed that 85 per cent of his small sample (n=35) of street gang members were visible minorities, the majority of whom (60 per cent) were born in Canada.[70] These gang members came from a variety of ethnic backgrounds, including Indo-Canadian, Hispanic, and Iranian, as well as Vietnamese and Chinese. The biggest single ethnic group among the "wanna-be" group members were Canadian-born individuals of European descent.[71] Michael Young's study of the history of gangs in Vancouver revealed that gang activity has appeared in wave-like patterns over time, with the last "wave" beginning in 1985 and dwindling off in the mid-1990s.[72]

Just as society has evolved, so has the image and nature of gang activity. Although still predominantly centred in large urban areas, gangs are appearing in smaller communities. Female gangs are becoming more common, and gang activities are generally becoming more violent. Explanations of why youths join gangs include the following: (1) rational choice (i.e., to benefit from law-violating careers—quick money and excitement), (2) to arise from the social blight of certain urban areas (e.g., ethnic groups), and (3) because the gang's activities serve as an outlet for some types of personalities (e.g., hate groups). A recent U.S. study reported that gang membership "increases the likelihood and frequency that members will commit serious violent crimes" and that criminal behaviour among gang members is significantly more likely to be violent and involve drugs than criminal behaviour among non-gang members.[73]

Efforts to control youth gangs include youth service programs, police gang-detail units, legislative measures, and community-based efforts. However, because we still do not understand all of the root causes of gangs, most initiatives to address the problem have come up short. For example, Huff found that, contrary to popular belief, "youth can resist overtures to join a gang without serious reprisals from members."[74]

# Runaways and Homeless Youth

Several years ago, a television documentary referred to runaways as the "lost tribe." And while "street kids" are not a recent phenomenon, society has only recently paid attention to their growing numbers. In the United States, the Office of Juvenile Justice and Delinquency Prevention sponsored a major survey of missing, abducted, runaway, and thrown-away children that estimated the number of children who go missing each year at over 1.3 million.[75] Meanwhile, in Canada, the issue of missing children has been addressed by a multi-agency government initiative entitled "Our Missing Children."[76] Based on RCMP data, the number of missing children was estimated at approximately 67 000 in 2001.[77] Of this number, the RCMP reported that approximately 80 per cent were runaways and less than 1 per cent involved abductions. Most children, approximately 73 per cent, who run away have run away before. Although the Canadian data reveal a considerably smaller number of missing children than in the United States, the number of children who run away is increasing, and given the risk that runaways pose to themselves and to society at large, this increase cannot be ignored.

**normlessness** A criminological term first developed by Emile Durkheim, it refers to a pervasive sense in a society that the traditional norms and values have broken down and that society is lacking in cohesion and necessary regulation by formal and informal control mechanisms.

Children run away for a variety of reasons. Some come from homes where there is little love and affection. Others may feel over-controlled, choosing to escape from feelings of oppression and **normlessness**. Some clash with their parents over disputed activities within the home, problems in school, and because of difficulties with friends. For example, throwaways are those youth who are asked to leave home by their parents. Others are lured away from home by the promise of drugs or the money that drugs might bring. Official statistics show that almost 95 per cent leave home because of an argument, while 66 per cent leave because of physical or sexual abuse, and 33 per cent leave because of emotional abuse.[78]

Whatever the reason, the number of runaway children has become a problem of near-epidemic proportions. The American Office for Juvenile Justice and Delinquency Prevention estimates that the vast majority of those children "who remain at large for a few weeks will resort to theft or prostitution as a method of self-support"; however, only approximately 20 per cent will ever come into official contact with police or social service agencies.[79] Yet, the risks of being on the street are significant. Based on his review of Canadian literature, MacLaren observed that mental health issues resulting from life on the street, prostitution, HIV/AIDS, drug use and abuse, and criminal involvement are common among street youth.[80] Referring to a national survey study by Fisher, MacLaren notes that 80 per cent of the sample reported some involvement in criminal activities. Of those young persons who had run away, nearly 70 per cent had suicidal thoughts or attempts, and one-third of female runaways relied on prostitution for money.

While the young offender system and the *Criminal Code* have provisions to address abductions, the system is hampered by the associated statutes in its ability to deal effectively with runaways. Running away from home is not a criminal act. Under the *Youth Criminal Justice Act*, "runners," as they are often referred to, can only be charged if they breach a court order. As a result, although a runaway child may be placed in an unguarded group home by police officers and social service workers, neither shelter workers nor the police have any legal authority to force the child to stay in the facility. If a young person is a runaway and commits a minor offence such as shoplifting, he or she is unlikely to be detained, hence adding to the potential risk of the youth's safety should he or she choose not to return home.

Children are prone to victimization and exploitation. Accordingly, the need to find runaway children quickly is obvious. The sooner they are found, the less likely they are to fall prey to the uncertainties of life on the run. Short-term solutions to the runaway problem are being sought in clearing houses that catalogue and disseminate information about missing and located children. When a young person is reported missing to the police, a record is entered into the Canadian Police Information Centre (CPIC). In addition, the RCMP Missing Children's Registry receives all such information as well as information about why the young person may be missing, e.g., parents are divorced, or the child recently may have experienced problems at home or at school. The essence of these informational strategies is speed. The fast dissemination of information, and the rapid reunion of family members with runaway children may provide the best hope that distraught children can be persuaded to return home.

Until the *Youth Criminal Justice Act* or provincial welfare legislation is amended to provide the provinces and local jurisdictions with the needed authority to take runaway children into custody and safely control them, the problem of runaways will remain. And while the U.S. Attorney General's Advisory Board on Missing Children has called for just such a change,[81] there is no indication that such steps are being taken in Canada. Until such time, they will remain the "lost tribes."

## Sexual Abuse

As Florence Rush observed in her book *The Best Kept Secret*, the recognition of and response to the problem of child sexual abuse has evolved slowly.[82] In fact, it was not until the late nineteenth century that society appeared to be concerned. Even then the response was not so much out of concern for children but "the widespread anxiety over an outbreak of venereal disease related to flourishing (child) prostitution."[83]

It was not until the Canadian government established a special committee to examine the growing concern of child sexual abuse more closely that it became a public issue. In 1984, the Report of the Committee on Sexual Offences Against Children and Youth, also known as the Badgley Report, confirmed the extent of the problem. Depending on the issue being examined, the committee found that nearly half of all females and about one-third of all young males had been victims of one or more unwanted sexual acts. Based on the recommendation of the Badgley Report, the government moved to amend criminal law to make it easier to prosecute child sex offenders.

In 1988, federal legislation was passed, circumscribing the procuring of minor children for sexual performances. Despite these new measures, the sexual and physical abuse of children continues to make media headlines. Canadian society has been shocked by charges against former training school teachers, day-care centre operators, and public-school teachers. While such stories tend to capture the attention of the media, in 1996, family members, not outsiders, were responsible for 20 per cent of cases involving physical assault against children and nearly 35 per cent of cases of sexual assault. However, parents accounted for 64 per cent of the cases of physical abuse and 43 per cent of the cases of sexual abuse (see Table 13–3).[84] Increasingly, efforts are also being made to prepare children to face the eventuality that they do find themselves away from the care of their parents. Today, many elementary schools routinely train young children to resist and report the inappropriate advances of adults. It is interesting to note that a child's age as defined in provincial child protection legislation varies from 16 (i.e., Newfoundland, Nova Scotia, Ontario, and Saskatchewan) to under 18 in most other provinces except for British Columbia, which defines a child in need of protection as any youth under the age of 19. Public concern over the mobility of the sexual abusers of children, and their relative invisibility in residential neighbourhoods, led to the development of sexual offender registries in several provinces at the turn of the millennium. Ontario and Nova Scotia created such registries, and British Columbia passed legislation authorizing a registry that has not yet (2003) been proclaimed in force.[85]

At a meeting of the federal-provincial-territorial ministers responsible for justice, held in Calgary in November 2002, the ministers agreed on the high priority of protecting young persons and other vulnerable groups from sexual offenders. At the meeting, the federal Solicitor General announced the federal government was planning to institute a national sexual offender registry system. This new system would be based on the Canadian Police Information Centre (CPIC) system. Draft legislation that would authorize this national registry was introduced to Parliament in December 2002.[86] This legislation would require convicted offenders to register within 15 days of being released from prison, and to re-register with every change of address. This registry will also allow police to identify registered sexual offenders living in a particular area, through a query on the new Sex Offender Database accessible through the CPIC. Until the federal legislation comes into effect, provincial legislation provides the basis for the primary means of determining the whereabouts of potential offenders. In addition, most provinces have legislation that makes reporting

In recent years, the number of runaway children has become a problem of near-epidemic proportions. This adolescent runaway lives under a highway overpass.

**TABLE 13–3  Assaults against Children and Youth in the Family, 1996.**

| Accused-Victim Relationship | | Sexual Assault | | | | | | | Physical Assault | | | | | | |
|---|---|---|---|---|---|---|---|---|---|---|---|---|---|---|---|
| | | Age of Victim | | | | | | | Age of Victim | | | | | | |
| | | Total | <3 | 3–5 | 6–8 | 9–11 | 12–14 | 15–17 | Total | <3 | 3–5 | 6–8 | 9–11 | 12–14 | 15–17 |
| Total | Number | 6 481 | 164 | 867 | 1 026 | 1 101 | 1 805 | 1 518 | 16 371 | 342 | 509 | 961 | 1 997 | 5 465 | 7 097 |
| | Percentage[1] | 100 | 100 | 100 | 100 | 100 | 100 | 100 | 100 | 100 | 100 | 100 | 100 | 100 | 100 |
| Acquaintance | Percentage | 49 | 25 | 41 | 46 | 47 | 56 | 51 | 53 | 17 | 25 | 40 | 54 | 60 | 52 |
| Stranger | Percentage | 13 | 6 | 5 | 8 | 13 | 14 | 21 | 22 | 4 | 9 | 15 | 21 | 21 | 26 |
| Unknown | Percentage | 6 | 12 | 7 | 5 | 5 | 5 | 6 | 5 | 10 | 8 | 7 | 5 | 4 | 5 |
| **Family total** | Percentage | 32 | 57 | 48 | 42 | 36 | 25 | 21 | 20 | 69 | 58 | 38 | 20 | 15 | 17 |
| Spouse | Percentage | — | — | — | — | — | 1 | — | 2 | — | — | — | — | — | 4 |
| Parent | Percentage | 14 | 30 | 20 | 15 | 16 | 11 | 10 | 13 | 58 | 49 | 33 | 15 | 10 | 7 |
| Other immediate family | Percentage | 9 | 9 | 12 | 13 | 11 | 7 | 6 | 4 | 6 | 6 | 3 | 3 | 4 | 5 |
| Extended family | Percentage | 9 | 18 | 16 | 14 | 9 | 6 | 4 | 1 | 5 | 4 | 2 | 2 | 1 | 1 |

—Nil or zero.

[1]Figures may not add up to 100 per cent due to rounding.

*Source*: Adapted from the Statistics Canada publication *Juristat,* Catalogue no. 85-002, Vol. 17, No. 11, November 1997.

a situation in which you have reason to believe that a child or young person has been abused or neglected. The penalties for not reporting include a fine (usually up to $5000) and/or a jail term of up to six months. The issue with this type of legislation is that it is only a responsive legal measure and not a preventive one; by the time a case is reported, the young person may have already been victimized.

# Other Forms of Abuse

Most forms of child abuse are crimes that adults commit against children. For that reason, we will not discuss them in detail in this chapter. All forms of abuse, however, are damaging to children and should be prosecuted. Some forms of abuse, such as sexual procurement, may lead to the child's involvement in delinquency. Parental encouragement of delinquency is a problem that young persons sometimes encounter if they come from families already engaged in criminal activities. Prostitutes, for example, sometimes encourage their daughters to learn the profession. In families where the theft and sale of stolen goods is a way of life, children may be recruited for shoplifting or for burglaries that require wiggling into tight spaces where an adult might not fit.

Research has shown that children who are encouraged in delinquency by adults tend to become criminals when they reach maturity. More surprising, however, is the finding that abused children have a similar tendency towards adult criminality.[87] A recent study by the American National Institute of Justice found that children "who had been abused or neglected … were more likely to be arrested as juveniles, as adults, and for a violent crime."[88] Another recent study[89] has found that the strength of the relationship between maltreatment and delinquency in a child is moderated by differences in the levels of the enzyme monoamine oxidase A (MAO-A), a natural chemical that is found in different levels in different people. The influence of maltreatment on a young person's subsequent offence behaviour appears to be least pronounced in males with high levels of MAO-A activity. MAO-A levels appear to be intertwined with maltreatment. If this relationship is valid, early intervention into abusive environments may be particularly important in leading to an overall reduction in future criminality among those individuals with comparatively low levels of MAO-A.

Curbing the mistreatment of children through police intervention is clearly an important criminal justice goal. Unfortunately, however, some studies show that police officers

BOX 13.2 **Theory into Practice**

**M**any crime victims have been searching for ways to obtain recompense for harm they have experienced. Many pretrial division programs and even youth court sentencing decisions embody some form of financial compensation, or work equivalent, to be paid by the youthful offender to the victim. However, most young people have little or no financial resources to compensate victims in any meaningful way. As a result, victims have begun to demand that the parents of victims be held accountable for the wrongs committed by their children.

A number of jurisdictions have responded with laws placing responsibility for a child's behaviour squarely on his or her parents. In the U.S., California's *Street Terrorism Enforcement and Prevention Act* subjects parents of wayward youths to arrest. Gloria Williams, the first person arrested[1] under the law, was charged with neglecting her parental duties after her 15-year-old son was charged with rape. Police said photo evidence proved she had known her son was a gang member. Charges against her were dropped when she was able to show that she had taken a parenting course in an effort to gain better control over her son.

Canadian parental responsibility laws do not go as far as some of their American counterparts, but they have started to fill the gap that has existed in this area. In British Columbia, the *School Act*[2] provides that parents should be financially responsible for the damage caused to school property by their children:

s. 10   If property of a board or a francophone education authority is destroyed, damaged, lost or converted by the intentional or negligent act of a student or a francophone student, that student and that student's parents are jointly and severally liable to the board or francophone education authority in respect of the act of that student.

In addition, the provinces of Manitoba, Ontario, and British Columbia have enacted broader legislation, imposing financial obligations on parents for the damage caused by their children. For example, the Ontario *Parental Responsibility Act* provides as follows:

Parents' liability

2.   (1)   Where a child takes, damages or destroys property, an owner or a person entitled to possession of the property may bring an action in the Small Claims Court against a parent of the child to recover damages, not in excess of the monetary jurisdiction of the Small Claims Court,

(a) for loss of or damage to the property suffered as a result of the activity of the child; and

(b) for economic loss suffered as a consequence of that loss of or damage to property. 2000, c. 4, s. 2 (1).

(2)   The parent is liable for the damages unless the parent satisfies the court that,

(a) he or she was exercising reasonable supervision over the child at the time the child engaged in the activity that caused the loss or damage and made reasonable efforts to prevent or discourage the child from engaging in the kind of activity that resulted in the loss or damage; or

(b) the activity that caused the loss or damage was not intentional.

For the purposes of determining whether a parent exercised "reasonable supervision" over a child or made "reasonable efforts to prevent or discourage the child from engaging in the kind of activity that resulted in the loss or damage," the courts are entitled to consider factors such as the child's age, prior behaviour, the danger inherent in the activity, the child's physical and mental states, whether the parent made a reasonable effort to have the child supervised if not under the parent's immediate control, whether the parent has sought courses on parenting skills or professional assistance for the child.

Supporters of the new laws say they are trying to force parents to be responsible parents. But critics claim that the statutes go "well beyond the pale of traditional law."[4] It may be argued that the new laws make people responsible for the wrongs committed by someone else. Will we soon make it a crime to have a child who commits a crime? How the new laws will fare in court is not known. In 1993, however, the California Supreme Court, in the case of *Williams* v. *Garcetti*,[5] unanimously upheld California's parental responsibility statute. Whether or not the new U.S. or Canadian laws ultimately survive challenges to their constitutionality—which are bound to continue—they represent, for the moment at least, society's interest in using the familial bond as a mechanism of social control.

## QUESTIONS FOR DISCUSSION

1. Do you agree with the basic philosophy of parental responsibility laws, that is, that parents can and should be punished for the misdeeds of their children who are minors? Does it send a message to teens that they are not responsible for their wrongdoings? Might youth who want to get back at their parents vandalize property, knowing their parents will have to pay for the damage? Why or why not?

2. Should Canada adopt American-style parental responsibility statutes that attach criminal responsibility for a child's wrongdoing to the child's parents? Do you believe that parental responsibility laws such as the one in California would be effective in reducing the incidence of youthful offending in Canada? Why or why not?

[1] Now, Parents on Trial. (1989, October 2). *Newsweek*, pp. 54–55.
[2] *School Act*, R.S.B.C. 1996, c. 412.
[3] *Parental Responsibility Act*, S.O. 2000, c. 4.
[4] Now, Parents on Trial. p. 55.
[5] *Williams* v. *Garcetti*, 5 Cal. 4th 561 (1993) (Calif.S.C.).

called to the scene of situations involving child abuse are reluctant to make an arrest or even to report these cases to social service agencies.[90] In an effort to support vigorous prosecution of child abuse cases, in 1998 Alberta enacted the *Protection of Children Involved in Prostitution Act*. This statute allows police officers and child welfare workers to apprehend underage prostitutes without a court order. While a provincial court ruling in Alberta declared the entire legislative scheme unconstitutional in 2000,[91] the Alberta Court of Queen's Bench overturned that decision, finding the scheme to be constitutionally sound later in the same year.[92]

## Teen Suicide

Children today face many stresses that were unheard of years ago. Drugs, peer pressure, abuse (sexual and otherwise), violent and broken homes, and parents' insistence on success lead some children to take their own lives. In late 1997, 17-year-old Kenneth Au Yeung, a choirboy, committed suicide by jumping off a viaduct in Toronto. He was a gifted student with an IQ of 144, who, other than being somewhat quiet, showed no visible signs of distress. Kenneth and several other students from the school served on the yearbook committee. When the school yearbook came out, school staff discovered some of the content was not what had been expected. On December 10, Kenneth and several of his friends were called into the principal's office and confronted with an inappropriate reference to the Maple Leaf Gardens sex abuse scandal that appeared in the yearbook. Fearing that a confession might affect their chances of getting into university, all the boys denied any involvement. A police investigation ensued and the possibility of filing charges was discussed with the boys at the school. Kenneth and a friend confessed to participating in the prank of altering the yearbook to include inappropriate comments. Later the same day, Kenneth committed suicide. Inside his coat pocket, police found two pieces of paper—a photocopy of the altered message and a suicide note that read "I'm sorry for everything."[93] An inquiry later suggested that teens should be aware of the right to contact their parents when serious disciplinary matters arise at school, and that the police should be better trained to understand the potential for teen suicide in such situations.[94]

Suicide among teenagers is a quickly growing phenomenon. In 1998, Canada had the third-highest teen suicide rate in the world. A high-school survey found that in an average class of 30 students, four will attempt suicide while nearly three-quarters will think about it. In the United States, 16 teens commit suicide every day. Although no one is certain why suicide rates are on the increase, various support and crisis agencies have identified some warning signals as follows: (1) abrupt changes in personality; (2) eating disturbances or significant weight loss; (3) changes in sleep patterns; (4) withdrawal from friends, family members, and school activities; (5) hostile behaviour; (6) running away; (7) substance abuse; (8) disregard for personal hygiene; (9) neglect of academic work; (10) frequent headaches, fatigue, and stomachaches; (11) constant boredom; (12) giving away possessions; and (12) verbal clues, such as "this is the last time we will be together."[95]

## What Can Be Done about Youth Crime?

Although the problems facing children today are many and varied, some believe that children in trouble share some common characteristics. Broken homes, little parental supervision, poor role models, conduct disorders, poor interpersonal relationships, lack of educational opportunity, and poverty, and even neuropsychological indicators are factors contributing to delinquency and later criminality. However, over the years, the one prevailing relationship is that between problem families and delinquency (and youth crime). Both the Ministry of the Solicitor General of Canada and the American Office of Juvenile Justice and Delinquency Prevention (OJJDP) have suggested that effective programs intended to reduce both the problems faced by children and the incidence of juvenile delinquency "must emphasize opportunities for healthy social, physical and mental development." "Such programs," said OJJDP, "must involve all components of the community, including schools, healthcare professionals, families, neighbourhood groups, law enforcement and community-based organizations."[96] Meanwhile, the Ministry of the Solicitor General observed that consistent parental supervision and a stable family lower the risk of delinquency.[97]

Some also suggest that the time has come for a re-evaluation of the basic philosophy underlying the legislation governing young offenders. Although this legislation will be discussed in greater detail towards the end of this chapter, briefly, in light of a growing concern about youth violence, the law is considered too lenient and in need of reform. Opinion is divided, but the decision by the federal government to repeal the YOA and replace it with the *Youth Criminal Justice Act* that promises to be harder on serious young offenders shows an acceptance of the crime control approach to youth crime.

Most who have studied solutions to the problems of young persons, however, come back to basics such as the quality of family life, economic conditions within neighbourhoods, proper socialization, and supportive social institutions. In 1994, for example, the American Office of Juvenile Justice and Delinquency Prevention published a "Policymaker's Guide," based on the findings of a metastudy,[98] which summarized many other studies that have been conducted over decades. The report concluded that (1) there is "a positive relationship between parental conflict and delinquency," (2) "the effect of broken homes on delinquency is real and consistent," (3) the tendency towards delinquency and other problems is enhanced for children living in low-income families, (4) "physical abuse of children leads them into violence later in life," and (5) "children who have criminal parents are at greater risk of becoming delinquent themselves." The report also suggested that "a healthy home environment, one in which parents and children share affection, cohesion, and involvement, reduces the risk of delinquency," and the risk of other childhood problems within both one- or two-parent families. Additionally, the report notes that "parental rejection. appears to be one of the most significant predictors of delinquency." The report concluded that "parents play a critical role in moral development," and "the quality of [parental] supervision is consistently and strongly related to delinquency" and other childhood problems. As a consequence, said the authors, "parents must adequately monitor their children's behaviour, whereabouts and friends," and they "must reliably discipline their children for antisocial and prohibited behaviour, but must do so neither rigidly nor severely."

The above observations likely have an intuitive appeal to most of us. A review of the sociological and psychological literature tends to support the contention that family, and specifically our parents, play a critical role in our socialization process. However, in recent years, some have begun to question the integrity of these findings. Perhaps the most recognized critic of the "parent/family matters" is Judith Rich Harris. In her much-publicized book *The Nurture Assumption*,[99] Harris reviews an extensive body of interdisciplinary literature and concludes that parents, broken homes, and family socialization matter less than one's peer groups. Her group socialization theory asserts that what appears to be familial influence may simply be genetic (direct and indirect) heritability. Based on her extensive reviews of behavioural genetic research, Harris argues that perhaps half the variation in personalities can be attributed to heredity. The other half of our personalities comes from our interaction with our peers. She notes, for example, that psychologists tend to focus on humans as individuals but we are, by nature, social creatures. So while parents might impact our behaviour at home, once children step out the front door it is their friends who forge their behaviour. For example, when you were young, how many of you started drinking, smoking, skipping classes, using certain language, and so on, because your parents encouraged it?

Although in its relative infancy, the implications of Harris's theory are profound. Researchers will undoubtedly subject the group socialization theory to scientific inquiry. And as criminological inquiry becomes more interdisciplinary in its approach,[100] these and related findings may forge a new way of looking at why young persons (and adults) do what they do. These are exciting and dynamic times for criminology and youth (criminal) justice.

# SIGNIFICANT COURT DECISIONS AFFECTING YOUNG OFFENDERS

Since the concept of youth crime is dependent on a legal definition, every country's youth justice system has been influenced by significant cases and legislative reform that forge the manner in which society deals with young offenders. These legal developments are sometimes influenced by social, economic, public, and/or political factors. As was noted earlier in this chapter, Canada's youth justice system has evolved considerably since the *Juvenile Delinquents Act* was introduced in 1908. Some of the impetus for change has come from a growing concern for individual rights, as manifested in significant cases, particularly in the U.S., and most importantly, the advent of the *Charter* era in this country. Some of the U.S. cases that have had an indirect influence on the Canadian juvenile justice system include *Kent v. U.S.* (1966), which recognized the need for at least minimal due process in juvenile court hearings,[101] and *Re Gault* (1967), which focused on the right for a young offender to be informed about the charges against him or her, the right to obtain counsel, the right to cross-examine witnesses, protection against self-incrimination, and the right to appeal.[102]

In Canada, the biggest impetus for change came in the early 1980s, when the *Charter of Rights and Freedoms* came into force. The *Charter* did not differentiate between youth and adult rights, so the *Young Offenders Act* (YOA) embodied many of the basic due process rights outlined in the *Charter*, so as to ensure the youth justice process complied with *Charter* requirements. Although not to the same magnitude as in the U.S., Canada has had its share of significant youth justice cases over the years. Many of those cases dealt with the interpretation and application of provisions in the old *Juvenile Delinquents Act* and the new *Young Offenders Act*. With the replacement of the pre-existing youth criminal justice regime by the *Youth Criminal Justice Act* (YCJA), many of the old cases are no longer relevant. As with the YOA, the YCJA attempts to give due accord to the individual rights of accused young persons coming before the courts.

# CHANGING YOUTH JUSTICE LAW

The philosophy of the 1908 *Juvenile Delinquents Act* (JDA) was governed by a "welfare model."[103] Youth were seen to be in need of care and guidance. The courts have historically exercised a *parens patriae* jurisdiction that allows them to act as surrogate parents, making decisions seen to be in the best interests of the child. Criminal acts by young people were viewed as symptomatic of a need for regulation and control. The state intervened through youth courts to provide dispositions that might remedy the child's delinquent state, and mould him or her into a law-abiding young adult.

The American decisions outlined above had an influence on Canadian legal developments. The Canadian JDA was criticized for failing to give due recognition to the due process rights of young people. Accordingly, in 1984, the JDA was repealed and the *Young Offenders Act* (YOA) was brought in to replace it. This new Act was built to a large degree on a "justice model" that guaranteed due process safeguards for youth, and started a movement towards adult-style accountability. Lawyers played a larger role in juvenile justice, and youth court trials began to resemble adult criminal trials. The goal was to hold young people accountable for their actions, but to continue to recognize that their youthful status required more lenient treatment than would prevail in adult court. However, the most serious cases would result in being transferred to adult court and the possibility of more punitive dispositions.

The adoption of the *Youth Criminal Justice Act* (YCJA) continued the move away from the welfare model towards a model with mixed philosophies. On the one hand, many of the due process values initiated by the YOA continue in the YCJA. In addition, the new act embodies the philosophy of restorative justice, particularly in relation to less serious offending. Additionally, however, the YCJA provides a punitive, accountability-based model, particularly for dealing with serious violent offending. In many ways, the youth justice system now reflects a "crime control" model. More adult sanctions may be applied, and more punitive sanctions may be ordered for the more serious youth offences. However, the YCJA also reflects more of an restorative justice approach than was possible under the YOA.[104] Table 13–4 compares the differing approaches to youth justice that have occurred over time under the JDA, YOA, and YCJA.

**Youth justice philosophy** is outlined clearly at the opening of the YCJA. Among the declared principles in section 3 are the following: (1) objectives to prevent crime, rehabilitate and reintegrate young offenders, and ensure meaningful consequences for their offences;

**youth justice philosophy**
A way of thinking about the approach society should take to responding to crime committed by young people. The philosophy of a youth justice system may be embodied in its guiding principles.

**TABLE 13–4** Canada's Youth Justice Statutes Over Time: A Comparison of the *Youth Criminal Justice Act*, the *Young Offenders Act*, and the *Juvenile Delinquents Act*

| | *Youth Criminal Justice Act,* 2003–present | *Young Offenders Act,* 1984–2003 | *Juvenile Delinquents Act,* 1908–84 |
|---|---|---|---|
| Operating Principles | • Statement of principles declared in preamble and statute itself<br>• Specific principles to guide police, prosecutors, judges, and others at various stages of the process<br>• Includes protection of society, accountability, social values, proportionality of sentences, rehabilitation and reintegration, protection of the rights of youths, and respect for victims | • Similar themes to those of YCJA<br>• Principles declared in the statute<br>• No overriding or principal goal for the system<br>• Contained inconsistent and competing principles<br>• Due process and justice orientation | • No statement of principles, but based on a *parens patriae* or welfare model |
| Diversion Outside of the Court Process | • Encourages measures other than court proceedings when these measures would be adequate to hold offender accountable<br>• Authorizes warnings, cautions, and referrals to community programs<br>• Sets out objectives for diversion | • Permitted alternative measures, but did not formalize police or prosecutorial recourse to non-court alternatives<br>• Little guidance on alternatives to formal process | • No provision for diversion<br>• Only possible through informal efforts of police or prosecution |
| Court Jurisdiction | • Governs 12–17-year-olds | • Governed 12–17-year-olds | • Governed juveniles who are at least 7 years old. Maximum age varied from province to province, and ranged from 15–17 years. At times, the maximum ages were different for boys and girls. |
| Offence Categories | • Violations of any federal statute are processed under the YCJA.<br>• Act sets out special procedure for youth | • Violations of any federal statute were processed under the YOA; a procedural statute<br>• Provincial violations processed under provincial YOAs | • "Delinquency" created as a special offence when a child violated any federal, provincial, or municipal law, or for a child who was found guilty of any "sexual immorality" or "vice"<br>• "Juvenile delinquent," a status attached to a child who committed a delinquency; viewed as a condition or a state of being |
| Court Procedures | • Due process followed<br>• Legal aid to provide counsel<br>• Trials in open court | • Due process followed<br>• Right to counsel<br>• Trials in open court | • Informal procedure; diversity in practices across the country<br>• Trials held in camera<br>• Use of lawyers discouraged |
| Youth Sentences | • Clear purpose and principles<br>• Least restrictive alternative — limited use of custody<br>• Rehabilitation to be a key factor<br>• Intensive supervision and intensive custody options<br>• Maximum fine: $1000 | • No clear guidance to judges on sentencing<br>• Open and secure custody options<br>• Maximum fine: $1000 | • Committed the child to an industrial school<br>• Maximum fine: $25<br>• Probation was a common sentence |

**TABLE 13–4** Canada's Youth Justice Statutes Over Time: A Comparison of the *Youth Criminal Justice Act*, the *Young Offenders Act*, and the *Juvenile Delinquents Act* (cont.)

| | Youth Criminal Justice Act, 2003–present | Young Offenders Act, 1984–2003 | Juvenile Delinquents Act, 1908–84 |
|---|---|---|---|
| Adult Sentences | • Youth Justice Court empowered to impose adult sentences, eliminating need for transfer hearing<br>• Age for presumptive adult sentences lowered to 14<br>• Presumptive adult sentences extended to punish a pattern of repeat, violent offences | • Transfer hearing required to place the youth into adult court<br>• Age for presumptive offences set at 16<br>• Transfer to adult court presumptively available for murder, manslaughter, attempted murder, and aggravated sexual assault<br>• Transfer also used for many non-violent offenders<br>• If offender convicted, an adult sentence was imposed | • Transfer to adult court possible for those 14 or older who committed acts that would be indictable offences if the offender were an adult — must be for the good of the child and the interests of the community must demand it |
| Victims | • Victim's interests enshrined in principles<br>• Victim entitled to access to youth records<br>• Role for victim in diversion and community-based measures encouraged | • No formal recognition of the victim's role<br>• Victim must ask for access to youth records | • No mention of victims |
| Custody and Supervision | • Custody to be used as a last resort<br>• Custody must be followed up by community supervision<br>• Maximum probation period: 2 years | • Maximum custody term: usually 2 years<br>• Maximum probation period: 2 years | • No maximum custody term<br>• No maximum probation period |

(2) an acceptance that youths lack the maturity of adults, which means an impact on accountability, a need for enhanced procedural protections, special emphasis on rehabilitation and reintegration, and a recognition of the importance of timely intervention; (3) intervention is to be fair and in proportion to the seriousness of the offence; (4) intervention should reinforce respect for societal values, encourage the repair of harm done, be meaningful to the offender, and respect the cultural background of the offender; (5) special guarantees for individual rights, but also a recognition of the role of victims, and a role for parents to be informed, including an opportunity for victims and parents to participate.[105] This combination of principles and due-process requirements has created a unique justice system for young persons that takes into consideration the special needs of young people while attempting to offer reasonable protection to society.

The principles found in the YCJA may at times be conflicting. For example, seeking the goal of rehabilitation will not always coincide with striving to mete out proportionate penalties. There will be times when what might be perceived as too lenient a sentence, compared to that given to an adult offender who committed a similar crime, will be the most appropriate to foster reform of that young person. Similarly, the due process principles will often come into conflict with restorative goals. A due process orientation demands that the state has the task of proving guilt beyond a reasonable doubt, using only evidence that is properly deemed admissible, and following procedures that comply with the rules of natural justice. A young person who demands that the state fully comply with all due-process safeguards will not be in a state of mind to engage in an open dialogue centred around accepting responsibility for his alleged actions. Similarly, balancing the due process rights of accused young persons, which entitle them to provide a full answer to the allegations against them, and the opportunity to develop and present whatever defence he or she believes justifies or excuses their actions, against the claims of victims, including their desires for compassion and respect for their dignity will not be an easy task in real-world situations.

## Youth Criminal Justice Act

### How the System Works

On April 1, 2003, the *Youth Criminal Justice Act* (YCJA) came into force.[106] The Act defines the minimum age as 12 and the maximum age as 17. The jurisdiction of youth justice courts is no longer valid on a person's 18th birthday.[107] The provisions of the Act deal with

---

**FIGURE 13–2A** Continuum of Juvenile Justice Models

| | Participatory | Welfare | Corporatism | Modified Justice | Justice | Criminal Control |
|---|---|---|---|---|---|---|
| **General Features** | Informality | Informality | Administrative decision-making | Due process informality | Due process | Due process discretion |
| | Minimal formal intervention | Generic referrals | Offending | Criminal offences | Criminal offences | Offending/ discretion |
| | Resocialization | Individualized sentencing | Diversion from court/custody programs | Bifurcation: soft offenders diverted, hard offenders punished | Least restrictive alternative | Punishment |
| | | | | | Determinate sentences | Determinate sentences |
| **Key Personnel** | Educators | Childcare experts | Juvenile justice specialists | Lawyers/ childcare experts | Lawyers | Lawyers/ justice actors |
| **Key Agency** | Community agencies/citizens | Social work | Interagency structure | Law/ social work | law | law |
| | School and community agencies | | | | | |
| **Tasks** | Help and education team | Diagnosis | Systems intervention | Diagnosis/ punishment | Punishment | Indeterminate sentencing |
| **Understanding of Client Behaviour** | People basically good | Pathology/ environmentally determined | Unsocialized | Diminished individual responsibility | Individual responsibility | Responsibility/ accountability |
| **Purpose of Intervention** | Re-education | Provide treatment (*parens parriae*) | Retrain | Sanction behaviour/ provide treatment | Sanction behaviour | Protection of society/ retribution deterrence |
| **Objectives** | Intervention through education | Respond to individual needs/ rehabilitation | Implementation of Policy | Respect individual rights/responds to "special" needs | Respect individual rights/punish | Order maintenance |
| **Countries** | Japan | Australia The Netherlands | England/Wales Hong Kong | Canada | Italy Germany Russia | USA Hungary |

*Source:* Winterdyk, J. (1997). *Juvenile Justice Systems: International Perspectives* (pp. xi–xii). Toronto: Canadian Scholars' Press. Used by permission of Canadian Scholars Press (**www.cspi.org**).

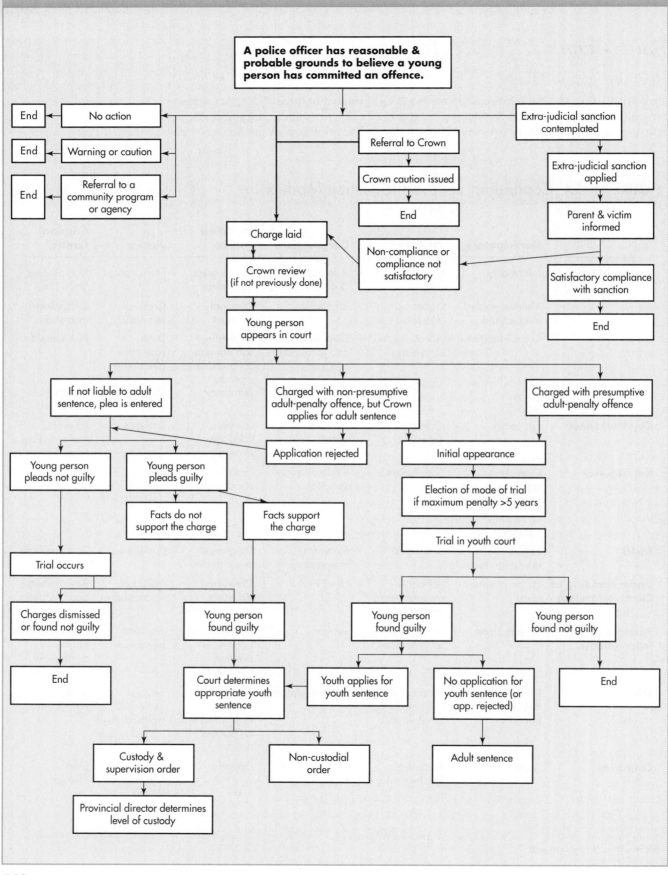

**FIGURE 13–2B** The Youth Criminal Justice Process

young offenders in conflict with the law. Its major sections concern guiding principles, diversion, youth justice court procedure and evidence, sentencing, imposition of adult sentences for the most serious offences, custody and supervision, and records.

### Arrest and Pretrial Detention

Young people in conflict with the law may come to the attention of the police or youth justice court authorities. Young people are guaranteed the same rights as adults against unreasonable search and seizure (section 8 of the *Charter*); the right not to be arbitrarily detained or imprisoned (section 9), and the right to retain and instruct counsel and to be informed as to the charge (section 10).

In addition to these rights under the *Charter*, there are also special provisions in the YCJA that pertain to youth in police custody. Section 25 of the YCJA guarantees the right of a young person to retain and instruct counsel upon being arrested or detained, a right that continues throughout the proceedings. Section 146 is intended to ensure that young persons have their rights respected when questioned by the police or other authorities. Given that young persons can be readily influenced by adults, it is important that these particular rights are protected. Section 146 also states that any statement must be given voluntarily, and a young person has the right to consult another person before providing a statement. In *R. v. M.(M.A.)* (1986),[108] the B.C. Court of Appeal addressed a similar provision under the old *Young Offenders Act* (YOA). In this case, a youth in B.C., who had a learning disability, was charged with gross indecency. Even though the police read him his rights and informed him about the right to consult counsel and/or an adult, the youth waived his rights. Upon appeal, the Court ruled that the police simply reading the relevant section of the YOA to the offender was not sufficient to guarantee the offender's understanding. Instead, an attempt should be made in any case to ensure that the young person reflects an appreciation of the consequences of the choices he or she makes.

Hence, in accordance with due process, a young person upon being arrested or detained must have his or her rights read to him or her (s. 25) and a parent/guardian must be notified "as soon as possible" of the young person's arrest (s. 26). Section 113 of the YCJA grants the authority for the police to take fingerprints and photographs of the accused, provided the young person is charged with an indictable or hybrid offence. Records of fingerprints may be retained for a period of time by the authorities after a conviction, with the time period varying and depending upon the seriousness of the offence. Convictions for the more serious offences may result in fingerprint records being retained for up to five years after the sentence has been served (s. 119(2)(h)).

Most major police departments have special youth divisions with officers specially trained in dealing with young persons. Because of the emphasis on restorative justice, on rehabilitation, and on the special needs that characterize the juvenile justice process, as well as on special legal considerations, youth division officers usually can choose from a number of discretionary alternatives in the form of special programs, especially in the handling of non-violent offences.

Even youth who are eventually diverted from the system may spend some time in custody. Section 30(3) of the YCJA requires that young persons ought to be held separate and apart from adults. As in the adult system, jail is not seen as the primary alternative for young persons awaiting a first appearance; however, the use of secure detention for young persons is acceptable if it is justified under the same grounds that apply to adults in the *Criminal Code*. All pretrial detention hearings are conducted by the youth justice court.

## Extra-Judicial Measures

The YCJA promotes measures that will divert non-violent offenders into non-court-based programs, many of which operate on restorative justice principles (ss. 8–12). Although the YCJA is a federal Act, the provinces have a certain degree of discretion in implementing the YCJA. The federal government is currently attempting to reduce the resulting interprovincial variations in diversionary programs through increased funding to the provinces to enable the provinces to create common programs. However, interprovincial variations will undoubtedly continue to exist. This problem was quite pronounced under the YOA with regard to "alternative measures." In 1990, the province of Ontario was challenged under section 15 (equality rights) of the *Charter* for failing to provide alternative measures that were available in some other provinces. A landmark case in that year was *R. v. S.(S).*,[109] which addressed Ontario's failure to develop alternative measures. The Supreme Court of Canada overturned a decision of the Ontario Court of Appeal that had held that the failure of the province to implement section 4 of the YOA, calling for the provision of alternative measures for young offenders, was a violation of section 15 of the *Charter*. The Supreme Court of Canada held that provinces "may" develop alternative measures programs, but are not required to do so. While this case was decided under the predecessor legislation to the YCJA, the same issue could arise under the new legislation. Under the YCJA, the statute requires all provinces to have "extra-judicial measures" in place, although provinces will retain control over the nature and scope of such programs. It remains to be seen whether all provinces comply with this requirement.

All young persons found guilty of an offence under the YCJA are subject to receive a "youth sentence." The parameters of the youth sentences are defined in section 42 of the Act, and the principles to be applied to their determination are found in sections 38 and 39.

Extra-judicial measures will take on different forms in different jurisdictions. Police discretion may result in youthful offenders being diverted out of the formal youth court system. Section 6 authorizes the police to issue cautions to young offenders, rather than to charge them. Local communities may establish Youth Justice Committees (s. 18, YCJA) that may play a role in arranging for the support or supervision of youth in conflict with the law. Sections 18 and 41 of the YCJA allow an offender to be sent to a Youth Justice Conference, where diverted offenders may meet with victims and community members in an attempt at restoration as an alternative to formal court proceedings. The concept of a Youth Justice Conference is derived from the notion of a "family group conference," which evolved in New Zealand as a diversionary, restorative justice initiative.

While many provinces operate pre-charge extra-judicial measures programs, others offer post-charge programs in which the Crown exercises its discretion not to proceed with a charge so long as the youth agrees to become involved in an approved program. A youth who attends one of these restorative justice programs will be required to commit to some form of accountability or reparation. The YCJA refers to these as "extrajudicial sanctions" (s. 10). Failure to comply with extra-judicial sanctions may result in the youth appearing in youth justice court to be dealt with according to law. The emphasis on extra-judicial measures is a welcome change to critics who believed the formal youth justice system was overused in responding to less serious cases. Now, many less serious cases can be dealt with outside of the formal court process.

## *Youth Justice Court Proceedings*

Where extra-judicial measures are inappropriate, the YCJA provides a mechanism for the Crown to proceed to trial with a formal charge against the young person. Unlike in the United States and several other countries,[110] young persons tried in youth court are not typically entitled to a preliminary inquiry. Proceedings under the YCJA require that young persons are tried in youth justice court.

Section 142 of the YCJA stipulates that the court proceedings in youth court should be like the court proceedings governing "summary conviction offences" in adult court. In this way, the proceedings are intended to be less complex and more expeditious than for indictable offences. For example, trials are almost always conducted by a judge alone, and there is no jury or preliminary inquiry. It is only if the young accused is facing a possible sentence of five years or longer that the YCJA permits a preliminary inquiry and a jury trial. In such cases, the trial will be before a superior court judge. The fact that a young person is not usually entitled to trial by jury or a preliminary hearing is not likely to be considered a violation of the *Charter of Rights and Freedoms*. Rulings based on the YOA found that the *Charter* was not violated in denying the right to a jury for offences that if committed by adults would result in a jury trial.[111]

Many cases that formally go to youth justice court do not result in trials. Many youthful offenders plead guilty. In 2000–01, 60 per cent of young people appearing in youth court either were found guilty or pleaded guilty.[112] The corresponding conviction rate for adult offenders was 61 per cent.[113] If a youth pleads guilty, section 32 of the YCJA requires the judge to ensure the youth understands the consequences of pleading guilty or not guilty, and the right to legal representation, if the accused is unrepresented. In a case involving a guilty plea, the Crown simply reads a summary of the offence before the court. If the judge, in accordance with section 36 of the YCJA, is satisfied that the summary supports the charge, then the court will find the youth guilty and entertain a sentence. If, however, the judge is not satisfied with the summary, a not-guilty plea is entered and a trial must ensue.

Should the case go to trial, the young person is entitled to the presumption of innocence that can only be rebutted if the Crown proves its case beyond a reasonable doubt. Section 25 of the YCJA requires that as soon as the youth is arrested or appears in court, the youth be advised he or she has a right to counsel. If the young person is unable to obtain counsel, the judge of youth justice court "shall" refer the youth to the local legal-aid office to determine if legal aid can be provided. If the youth wishes to obtain legal counsel, but has been denied legal aid, the court is required to order that the young person be granted legal representation under section 25(4)(b). Since few young persons can afford to retain private counsel, they often must rely on legal aid. It is possible for the accused to appear unrepresented; however, the philosophy of the YCJA is that this is generally not considered to be fair or in the best interests of a young person.

Another consideration of the court process is the special provisions intended to protect the privacy of young persons. The YCJA generally prohibits the publication of the names and other information that could identify young offenders (s. 110). It is assumed that this restriction will help to reduce the stigma that attaches to the formal legal process.[114]

Exceptions to the no-publication rule arise in a variety of contexts. The name of a young person can be published if the young person has been given an adult sentence for a serious offence (s. 110(2)(a)).[115] Finally, section 132 states that while youth justice court proceedings are generally open to the public, at the discretion of the judge, members of the public may be excluded if their presence would be "seriously injurious or seriously prejudicial" to the young person accused of an offence, or to a young witness.

## Sentencing

Once a young person has been convicted under the YCJA, the judge can deliver a sentence. Part 4 of the Act gives judges considerable guidance in sentencing young offenders, as do the overall principles declared in section 3 of the Act (see box on Youth Sentencing Principles). For relatively straightforward and minor offences, the sentencing hearing may flow immediately after an adjudication of guilt. For more complicated cases, a separate sentencing hearing is held. Section 40 allows the youth justice court judge to order that a pre-sentence report be prepared. A report is always required if the Crown is seeking a custodial term (s. 39(6)). The range of sentences are outlined in section 42 of the Act. They include:

- a reprimand;
- an absolute discharge—no further consequences for the young person, available if it is in the best interests of the young person and not contrary to the public's interest;
- a conditional discharge—with specific conditions, which may include a reporting requirement;
- a fine of up to $1000—the court takes into account the youth's ability to pay;
- compensation for loss or damage to property, or for loss of income or support;
- restitution for lost property or the loss of a property interest;
- compensation by way of personal services;
- community service;
- prohibition, seizure, and forfeiture orders;
- up to two years' probation;
- enrolment in an intensive support and supervision program;
- attendance at a non-residential program for up to 240 hours;

BOX 13.4 **Theory into Practice**

## Society's Response to the "Squeegie Kid" Phenomenon

Canada's homeless population includes a significant number of youth; however, there are no accurate statistics on the number of homeless in this country. Barbara Murphy's look at the homelessness situation in Canada addresses the problem of trying to ascertain the number of homeless:

> … estimating the number of homeless nationwide is a process full of pitfalls. If the focus is on the number who are literally homeless, that is, people who sleep in shelters provided for homeless people or in other places most of us do not consider dwellings, the task is next to impossible. Census counts in most countries assume that everyone has an address, making the normal type of census of little use in estimating the number of homeless.[1]

Murphy concludes that in 2000 there were approximately 35 000 to 40 000 homeless people in Canada. There were, sleeping in shelters or on the street, up to 10 000 people in Montreal and a similar number in Toronto. Vancouver had up to 5000, and there were anywhere from 1000 to 2000 in each of the following major cities: Edmonton, Calgary, Ottawa, Winnipeg, Hamilton, Halifax, Saskatoon, and Regina. These estimates do not include the tens of thousands of people who live in substandard accommodations that fall short of most people's standards of "housing."

While numerous private agencies, individuals, and government entities have recognized and responded to the growing problem of homelessness, some groups and governments responded to growing public irritation, which emerged in the 1990s, with the whole issue of homelessness youth, with a call for legislative action. New, intolerant attitudes towards the homeless first appeared in a few American cities, taking the form of bylaws that restricted public begging and the washing of automobile windshields by the homeless (squeegie kids). While the stated reason for enacting these bylaws was typically concern for public safety, Murphy believes that this was not the real reason. She claims that the true rationale behind such laws was concern over the adverse impact that panhandling could have on tourists.

Tougher attitudes also began appearing in Canadian cities during the late 1990s. Some government officials, reflecting the attitudes of downtown business owners in many major cities, began to openly refer to the homeless as "pests," "intimidators," and "thugs."[2] In 1995, Winnipeg was the first city to turn hardened attitudes into tougher legislation through the enactment of a bylaw restricting public begging. Violating the bylaw carried a fine up to $1,000 or up to six months in prison. Winnipeg's bylaw became a model for the rest of the country, with other cities creating similar enactments in the latter part of the 1990s.

Toronto's city council came under pressure to pass a similar bylaw; however, after considerable debate, the city council voted against such an approach in 1998. The city's lawyers suspected that "the city had no legal authority to regulate panhandling and might even be violating the *Canadian Charter of Rights*."[3] The following year, the province of Ontario provided an alternative approach in the form of the *Safe Streets Act*.[4] This imposed restrictions on aggressive panhandling throughout the province of Ontario, rather than through a local bylaw:

### Safe Streets Act, 1999

1.  In sections 2 and 3,
    "solicit" means to request, in person, the immediate provision of money or another thing of value, regardless of whether consideration is offered or provided in return, using the spoken, written or printed word, a gesture or other means.
2.  (1) In this section, "aggressive manner" means a manner that is likely to cause a reasonable person to be concerned for his or her safety or security.
    (2) No person shall solicit in an aggressive manner.
    (3) Without limiting subsection (1) or (2), a person who engages in one or more of the following activities shall be deemed to be soliciting in an aggressive manner for the purpose of this section:
    1.  Threatening the person solicited with physical harm, by word, gesture or other means, during the solicitation or after the person solicited responds or fails to respond to the solicitation.
    2.  Obstructing the path of the person solicited during the solicitation or after the person solicited responds or fails to respond to the solicitation.

- deferred custody and supervision—like a conditional sentence for adults served in the community—for less than six months' duration;
- a custody and supervision order, with custody to be followed by community supervision for one-half of the custody period. Detention is for up to two years for most offences, and three years if the available punishment for an adult is life in prison. Convictions for attempted murder, manslaughter, and aggravated assault carry the

3. Using abusive language during the solicitation or after the person solicited responds or fails to respond to the solicitation.

4. Proceeding behind, alongside or ahead of the person solicited during the solicitation or after the person solicited responds or fails to respond to the solicitation.

5. Soliciting while intoxicated by alcohol or drugs.

6. Continuing to solicit a person in a persistent manner after the person has responded negatively to the solicitation.

...

3. (2) No person shall,
(a) solicit a person who is using, waiting to use, or departing from an automated teller machine;
(b) solicit a person who is using or waiting to use a pay telephone or a public toilet facility;
(c) solicit a person who is waiting at a taxi stand or a public transit stop;
(d) solicit a person who is in or on a public transit vehicle;
(e) solicit a person who is in the process of getting in, out of, on or off a vehicle or who is in a parking lot; or
(f) while on a roadway, solicit a person who is in or on a stopped, standing or parked vehicle.

...

4. (2) No person shall dispose of any of the following things in an outdoor public place:
1. A used condom.
2. A new or used hypodermic needle or syringe.
3. Broken glass.

(3) It is a defence to a charge under subsection (2) for the person who disposed of the condom, the needle or syringe or the broken glass to establish that he or she took reasonable precautions to dispose of it in a manner that would not endanger the health or safety of any person.

5. (1) Every person who contravenes section 2, 3 or 4 is guilty of an offence and is liable,
(a) on a first conviction, to a fine of not more than $500; and
(b) on each subsequent conviction, to a fine of not more than $1,000 or to imprisonment for a term of not more than six months, or to both.

(2) For the purpose of determining the penalty to which a person is liable under subsection (1),
(a) a conviction of the person of a contravention of section 2 is a subsequent conviction only if the person has previously been convicted of a contravention of section 2 or 3;
(b) a conviction of the person of a contravention of section 3 is a subsequent conviction only if the person has previously been convicted of a contravention of section 2 or 3; and
(c) a conviction of the person of a contravention of section 4 is a subsequent conviction only if the person has previously been convicted of a contravention of section 4.

6. A police officer who believes on reasonable and probable grounds that a person has contravened section 2, 3 or 4 may arrest the person without warrant if,
(a) before the alleged contravention of section 2, 3 or 4, the police officer directed the person not to engage in activity that contravenes that section; or
(b) the police officer believes on reasonable and probable grounds that it is necessary to arrest the person without warrant in order to establish the identity of the person or to prevent the person from continuing or repeating the contravention.

This statute has been challenged as infringing on various rights protected by the *Canadian Charter of Rights and Freedoms*.[5] So far, the challenge has been unsuccessful.

## QUESTIONS FOR DISCUSSION

1. Do you believe that homeless youths ought to be prohibited from cleaning car windows for money? Why or why not?

2. Notice that section 5 of the Act allows for an escalating scale of penalties, rising with each subsequent conviction. Does this make sense in a statute aimed at controlling the behaviour of the destitute homeless?

[1] Murphy, B. (2000). *On the Street: How We Created Homelessness* (p. 10). Winnipeg: J. Gordon Shillingford Publishing.
[2] Murphy. *On the Street* (pp. 15–17).
[3] Murphy. *On the Street* (p. 17).
[4] *Safe Streets Act, 1999,* S.O. 1999, c. 8.
[5] *R. v. Banks,* [2001] O.J. No. 3219 (Ont.C.J.).

three-year maximum penalty, but longer periods of supervision are permitted. Murder convictions carry a mandatory detention and supervision order that may extend to ten years—up to six in custody—for first-degree murder, and seven years for second-degree murder—up to four of which are to be served in custody;

- an intensive rehabilitative custody-and-supervision order—where serious violent offences have been committed, involving mentally disordered offenders for whom a treatment plan has been developed.

BOX 13.5 **Theory into Practice**

## Youth Sentencing: Purpose and Principles

***Youth Criminal Justice Act*, 2002, sections 3 and 38**

3. (1) The following principles apply in this [the YCJA] Act:

(*a*) the youth criminal justice system is intended to

(i) prevent crime by addressing the circumstances underlying a young person's offending behaviour,

(ii) rehabilitate young persons who commit offences and reintegrate them into society, and

(iii) ensure that a young person is subject to meaningful consequences for his or her offence in order to promote the long-term protection of the public;

(*b*) the criminal justice system for young persons must be separate from that of adults and emphasize the following:

(i) rehabilitation and reintegration,

(ii) fair and proportionate accountability that is consistent with the greater dependency of young persons and their reduced level of maturity,

(iii) enhanced procedural protection to ensure that young persons are treated fairly and that their rights, including their right to privacy, are protected,

(iv) timely intervention that reinforces the link between the offending behaviour and its consequences, and

(v) the promptness and speed with which persons responsible for enforcing this Act must act, given young persons' perception of time;

(*c*) within the limits of fair and proportionate accountability, the measures taken against young persons who commit offences should

(i) reinforce respect for societal values,

(ii) encourage the repair of harm done to victims and the community,

(iii) be meaningful for the individual young person given his or her needs and level of development and, where appropriate, involve the parents, the extended family, the community and social or other agencies in the young person's rehabilitation and reintegration, and

(iv) respect gender, ethnic, cultural and linguistic differences and respond to the needs of aboriginal young persons and of young persons with special requirements; and

(*d*) special considerations apply in respect of proceedings against young persons and, in particular,

(i) young persons have rights and freedoms in their own right, such as a right to be heard in the course of and to participate in the processes, other than the decision to prosecute, that lead to decisions that affect them, and young persons have special guarantees of their rights and freedoms,

(ii) victims should be treated with courtesy, compassion and respect for their dignity and privacy and should suffer the minimum degree of inconvenience as a result of their involvement with the youth criminal justice system,

(iii) victims should be provided with infor-

Judges under the YOA could sentence a youth to secure custody or to open custody, depending on what the judge deemed to be the most appropriate in the circumstances, unless a province had set up a provincial director to determine the appropriate level of custody (ss. 24.1(2) and (3), YOA). Open custody took the form of a community residential centre, while closed custody resembled a prison, with tight perimeter security. Under the YCJA, the two levels of custody remain. However, the Act grants the discretion to determine the appropriate level of custody to the provincial director (s. 83(3)), taking this decision out of the hands of the sentencing judge who is presumably most familiar with the facts of the case. This transfer of discretion may result in increased regional disparity between treatments as directors in different provinces may take contrary views of appropriate custody levels for different types of offenders. If left in the hands of the courts, one would expect the prospect of appellate review to ensure greater consistency, particularly if the Supreme Court of Canada were to issue guidelines to sentencing judges in youth cases.

As might be expected, most judges decide not to sentence juveniles to confinement. The YCJA is designed to minimize the incarceration of youthful offenders, reserving it for the

mation about the proceedings and given an opportunity to participate and be heard, and

    (iv) parents should be informed of measures or proceedings involving their children and encouraged to support them in addressing their offending behaviour.

(2) This Act shall be liberally construed so as to ensure that young persons are dealt with in accordance with the principles set out in subsection (1).

    ...

38. (1) The purpose of sentencing under section 42 (youth sentences) is to hold a young person accountable for an offence through the imposition of just sanctions that have meaningful consequences for the young person and that promote his or her rehabilitation and reintegration into society, thereby contributing to the long-term protection of the public.

(2) A youth justice court that imposes a youth sentence on a young person shall determine the sentence in accordance with the principles set out in section 3 and the following principles:

(a) the sentence must not result in a punishment that is greater than the punishment that would be appropriate for an adult who has been convicted of the same offence committed in similar circumstances;

(b) the sentence must be similar to the sentences imposed in the region on similar young persons found guilty of the same offence committed in similar circumstances;

(c) the sentence must be proportionate to the seriousness of the offence and the degree of responsibility of the young person for that offence;

(d) all available sanctions other than custody that are reasonable in the circumstances should be considered for all young persons, with particular attention to the circumstances of aboriginal young persons; and

(e) subject to paragraph (c), the sentence must

(i) be the least restrictive sentence that is capable of achieving the purpose set out in subsection (1),

(ii) be the one that is most likely to rehabilitate the young person and reintegrate him or her into society, and

(iii) promote a sense of responsibility in the young person, and an acknowledgement of the harm done to victims and the community.

(3) In determining a youth sentence, the youth justice court shall take into account

(a) the degree of participation by the young person in the commission of the offence;

(b) the harm done to victims and whether it was intentional or reasonably foreseeable;

(c) any reparation made by the young person to the victim or the community;

(d) the time spent in detention by the young person as a result of the offence;

(e) the previous findings of guilt of the young person; and

(f) any other aggravating and mitigating circumstances related to the young person or the offence that are relevant to the purpose and principles set out in this section.

## QUESTIONS FOR DISCUSSION

1. Do any of the sentencing principles conflict with one another? Explain your answer.

2. As a youth sentencing judge, would you feel comfortable sentencing a youthful offender with these principles (and knowledge of the statutorily available penalties) as your only guidance? What additional guidance would you desire, if any?

most problematic, violent offenders. The most common youth sentence is probation (48 per cent).[116] Probationary disposition usually means that the young person will be released into the custody of a parent or guardian and ordered to undergo some form of training, education, or counselling. Of those receiving a probation sentence, 22 per cent receive probation for a period of six months or less, 56 per cent for a period of seven through 12 months, and 22 per cent for 12 months or more. The median length of probation is one year.[117] As in the adult system, young offenders placed on probation may be ordered to pay fines or make restitution. Because young persons rarely have financial resources or jobs, most economic sanctions take the form of court-ordered work programs, such as service to parks and recreation departments, assisting at food banks and other charitable organizations, or to the community in general.

## Adult Sentences

Under the YOA, committing a serious offence could result in a youth being transferred to adult court, where he or she would be subjected to more severe penalties. The YCJA

**Theory into Practice**

## Canada is Not Immune from the "School Shooter" Phenomenon

In 1999, merely eight days following the now infamous school massacre at Columbine High in Colorado, a 14-year-old male in Taber, Alberta, shot two high-school students, killing one and seriously wounding the other.[1] Shootings of this nature raise the question of how schools should respond to threats of violence.

The FBI has compiled a treatment assessment model for the purposes of assessing and evaluating threats, including identifying the key warning signs, with an aim toward intervention and future prevention of the school shooter phenomenon.[2]

The "Threat Assessment Perspective" was designed for educators, mental health professionals, and law enforcement agencies. This model provides a four-pronged assessment approach. In this approach, the student's personality traits and behaviour, family dynamics, school dynamics, and social dynamics are assessed to evaluate the potential of a threat in a spoken, symbolic, or written form. The model also provides a method for examining the student making the threat, and assessing the risk associated with the threat. This process takes a great deal of time, during which the student may be suspended from school.

Janet Reno, the United States Attorney General in the late 1990s, stressed that because there is the risk of unfairly labelling and stigmatizing children, a threat assessment model must be used judiciously. In the Taber, Alberta incident, the shooter was no longer a student in the high school, so the FBI model, and others like it, would not have helped. However, in 2001, the Calgary Board of Education responded to a situation in which a student used threatening language by immediately suspending the student from attending school until an evaluation of the risk associated to the threat could be completed. This process was lengthy, and therefore the ensuing suspension resulted in the student falling behind in his school work. In addition, the procedure resulted in the student being stigmatized as a result of being labellled as a "potential shooter" among fellow students.

### QUESTIONS FOR DISCUSSION

1. Will Canadian schools be likely to invest the time and effort to apply the FBI's model of assessment? Should an in-depth risk assessment be performed at every hint that someone may become a "school shooter"?

2. Should schools respond to any indication of a threat by suspending a student until the risk associated with the threat is assessed? What are the risks associated with suspension, pending a risk assessment?

---

[1]Purvis, A. (1999, May 10). Tragedy in Taber. *Time Magazine*.
[2]O'Toole, M.E. (2000). *The School Shooter: A Threat Assessment Perspective*. Quantico, Virginia: FBI Academy. Accessible as at time of writing at **www.fbi.gov/publications/school/school2.pdf**

---

eliminates the procedure for transferring young offenders to adult court, but permits the application of adult sentences where the circumstances warrant. The determination of whether an adult sentence is justified only arises after a finding of guilt. A youth may be subjected to an adult sentence if he or she is 16 years or older, unless a province decides to adopt a lower-age limit, which may be as low as 14 years. A young person given an adult sentence is presumed to serve his or her sentence in a youth facility.

Sections 61 to 81 of the YCJA outline the circumstances in which a young person may be subjected to an adult penalty. A court may consider an adult sentence if (1) the youth has been convicted of an offence for which an adult could receive a sentence of more than two years, and (2) the youth meets the minimum-age requirements. The YCJA creates a presumption in section 62 that an adult sentence will attach to certain particularly serious offences. The Act (in section 2) divides relevant presumptive offences into three groups: (a) specified offences: murder, attempted murder, manslaughter, and aggravated assault, and (b) repeat serious violent offences. In addition, there is a range of offences for which no presumption arises, but for which the Crown may apply for the court to entertain an adult penalty (s. 64).

Where an accused is facing an offence for which a presumptive adult sentence applies, the youth may still apply

## TABLE 13–5 Youth Court Dispositions—2000–01

| Disposition | Percentage of Cases |
| --- | --- |
| Other | 3 |
| Absolute discharge | 2 |
| Community service order | 7 |
| Fine | 6 |
| Probation | 48 |
| Open custody | 17 |
| Secure custody | 17 |

Note: These dispositions were made under the YOA. The YCJA offers a differing array of sentencing options.

*Source:* Adapted from the Statistics Canada publication *Juristat*, Catalogue no. 85–002, Vol. 22, No. 3, March 2002, p. 12.

to court to have a youth sentence applied. The onus rests on the young person to convince the court that a youth sentence will suffice in his or her case.

In 1996, the Manitoba Justice Minister introduced Bill 58, the *Parental Responsibility Act*, which allows victims of vandalism and other forms of delinquency to pursue perpetrators' parents in small claims court for damages of up to $5000. Interestingly, the burden of proof of innocence rests with the parents. The Act is novel in that it bridges criminal and civil law measures. Ontario joined the Manitoba initiative in 2000 and British Columbia enacted similar legislation that came into force in 2002.[118] The B.C. Act provides in part:

3.          Subject to section 6 ... if a child intentionally takes, damages or destroys property of another person, a parent of the child is liable for the loss of or damage to the property experienced as a result by an owner and by a person legally entitled to possession of the property.

6   (1).     ... if either an owner of property or a person legally entitled to possession of property suffers property loss, the owner, the person legally entitled to possession of the property or both may commence a civil action under this Act against a parent of a child who caused the property loss to recover damages, in an amount not exceeding $10 000, excluding interest and costs, in respect of the property loss.

A child is defined in the Act as "a person who is under the age of 18 years."[119] It remains to be seen whether these civil and criminal measures will facilitate a restoration of parental responsibility and parental authority. Research will also need to explore at what point such measures represent unfair punishment of parents and at what age youths begin to bear the liability for their actions. For example, since many young offenders come from single-parent families and/or the lower socio-economic ranks, fining and punishing parents may worsen family problems. To what extent does such an Act undermine the intention of the YCJA, which states that young persons are required to be held accountable for their actions and a growing body of research that suggests that one's peers may have a more critical influence on a youth's behaviour than his or her parents?[120]

# CUSTODY FOR YOUNG PEOPLE

The YCJA calls for provinces to have at least two levels of custody, differentiated by the degree of restraint placed on the youth. Young people who evidence the potential for serious new offences may be ordered to participate in rehabilitative programs within a secure environment such as a youth centre or training school. Less restrictive options must be available for those youth who can adequately be dealt with in a more open custody setting. *Juristat* reports that in 2000–01, there were 14 909 young people sentenced to custodial supervision.[121] Slightly more than half of these (53 per cent) were sentenced to open (less secure) custody, with the balance being sentenced to secure custody. During the same period, an additional 9362 young people were admitted to custody on remand. The majority of youth sentences (36 509 cases) involve probation rather than custody.

Most provinces have a variety of secure facilities for young offenders. They range from formal detention centres that on the outside resemble adult institutions, to boot camps, ranches, forestry camps, wilderness programs, and group homes, as well as provincially hired private facilities that also hold a proportion of the total number of young people reported under custody. For example, starting in 1994, all youths placed in secure custody in Manitoba are required to participate in programs and lifestyles that closely resemble the structure of the popular boot camps in the United States. The model focuses on confinement, Spartan conditions, and highly structured activities. In 1997, Ontario opened a similar secure boot-camp facility near Barrie, known as Project Turnaround. The program lasts 16 days and is highly regimented. However, in addition to a rigorous physical fitness program, the project addresses vocational, education, and life skills.[122] The program received national attention when, within the first week of opening, five youths escaped. Security has since been re-evaluated and addressed. The facility was closed, at least temporarily, in February of 2003, when an unacceptable level of mould was found there.[123]

Boot camps have not met with significant success. In a major report on youth violence, carried out by the U.S. Surgeon General, boot camps were found to be ineffective at preventing future crime:

> Compared to traditional forms of incarceration, boot camps produced no significant effects on recidivism in three out of four evaluations and trends towards increased recidivism in two. The fourth evaluation showed significant harmful effects on youths, with a significant increase in recidivism.[124]

Young people confined to secure custody usually receive relatively short sentences. In 2000–01, 48 per cent of young offenders released from custody had served less than one month in confinement.[125] A further 44 per cent served between one month and six months. In recent years, the rate of sentenced custody admissions has been declining. This reflects a trend, which began in the 1990s, towards greater application of alternative measures. But it may also be partly to blame for public outcry against the perceived leniency of the young offender system.

The operative philosophy of custodial programs for young people focuses predominantly on the rehabilitative ideal. Young offenders are usually committed to secure facilities with the hope of treatment being provided. Release is often timed to coincide with the beginning or end of the school year.

## SUMMARY

Children are the future hope of each mature generation, and under today's laws they occupy a special status. That status is tied closely to cultural advances that occurred in the Western world during the past 200 years, resulting in a re-evaluation of the child's role. Many children today lead privileged lives that would have been unimaginable a few scant decades ago.

Others are not so lucky, and the problems they face are as diverse as they are staggering. Some problems are a direct consequence of increased national wealth and the subsequent removal of children from the economic sphere, which have lessened expectations for responsible behaviour during the childhood years. Others grow from the easy availability of illicit drugs—a fact that has dramatically altered the early life experiences of many children. Finally, the decline of traditional institutions and the seeming plethora of broken homes throughout our country have all combined with the moral excesses of adult predators interested in the acquisition of sexual services from children, to lead to a quick abandonment of innocence by many young people today. Gang involvement, child abuse and neglect, young runaways and suicides, and serious incidents of delinquency have been the result.

In the face of these massive challenges, the youth justice system's commitment to a philosophy of protection and restoration has been subjected to many challenges. The present system, for the most part, still differs substantially from the adult criminal justice system in the multitude of opportunities it provides for diversion, and in the emphasis it places on rehabilitation rather than punishment. The professionalization of delinquency, however, the hallmark of which is repetitive and often violent criminal involvement of young people, represents a major new challenge to the idealism of the youth justice system. Addressing that challenge may well prove to be the most significant future determinant of system change.

# DISCUSSION QUESTIONS

1. How does the philosophy and purpose of the youth justice system differ from that of the adult system of criminal justice? In your opinion, should children continue to receive what many regard as preferential treatment from the court? Why or why not?

2. What was the general impact of *Gault* on youth justice? Has the *Gault* decision had an impact on the Canadian approach to youth justice? Why does it appear that, by comparison, Canadian cases have a less significant impact on the young offenders' system than the American cases discussed?

3. Describe the principles of youth justice that set up a guiding philosophy for the YCJA. Do some of the principles appear to be inconsistent? If so, which ones? If not, how is the Act able to adequately respond to the differing problems presented by illicit drug use by young people as well as the repetitive and apparently vicious delinquency of urban gang members?

4. In your opinion, are status offences still a useful concept in our system of youth justice? Should laws that circumscribe status offences be retained or abandoned? Why?

5. One reason given in this chapter for youth crime is the lack of meaningful roles for young people in modern society. Do you agree with this explanation? Why or why not?

6. One problem with secrecy in youth justice court hearings and records is that others in society are not protected from continued youth crime. Do you think the publication of case facts and/or young people's names in the youth justice system is justified? Or do you think that those who stand to be injured by the future delinquency of adjudicated offenders should be warned? Why or why not?

7. What do you think of the parental-responsibility laws described towards the end of this chapter? Do you think such laws are useful? Are they fair? Can they achieve their desired results? Would you change them in any way? If so, how?

# WEBLINKS

qsilver.queensu.ca/law/papers/papers.htm
**Professor Nicholas Bala's Recent Papers**
A collection of papers, written by Nicholas Bala, a Queen's University law professor who specializes in youth and family law. In particular, note the papers dealing with criminal behaviour of children under 12, and his brief to the Senate Committee looking at the YCJA.

www.youthincare.ca
**National Youth in Care Network**
Founded in 1986 by a group of young people dedicated to the idea of youth empowerment, NYICN is a non-profit, charitable organization run by and for young people, aged 14 to 24, who are, or have been, in the care of child welfare authorities across Canada.

www.juvenilejustice.com
**Juvenile Justice Magazine**
Juvenile Justice is an online, bimonthly magazine serving juvenile justice professionals in the U.S.

canada.justice.gc.ca/en/dept/pub/ycja/youth.html
***Canada's Youth Criminal Justice Act – A New Law, A New Approach***
The federal Department of Justice's website provides documents explaining the operation of the new *Youth Criminal Justice Act*, as well as a link to the full text of the YCJA.

www.csc-scc.gc.ca/text/pblct/forum/v11n2/indexe_e.shtml
**Youth and Corrections**
Articles about youth and justice from the May 1999 issue of *Forum*, a Correctional Service of Canada online journal.

# Multinational Criminal Justice

The Image Works/Larry Mulvehill

## KEY CONCEPTS

| | | |
|---|---|---|
| comparative criminologists | procuratorate | *tazirt* crimes |
| comparative criminal justice | Mediation Committees | Parliament |
| | Islamic law | INTERPOL |
| ethnocentrism | *Hudud* crimes | Europol |

# THE INTERNATIONAL PERSPECTIVE

Japan greeted the year 2000 by enacting three crime bills that gave law enforcement officials limited power to wiretap phones, stiffened penalties for organized criminal activity, and increased protections for witnesses.[1] For the most part, the new laws were directed against the yakuza, Japan's organized crime syndicates. The laws, however, were also a sign that Japan is facing more crime than ever before and that its citizens are becoming increasingly concerned about violent crime.

Until recently, Japan had been regarded as an optimistic and relatively crime-free country. Less than a decade ago, Japan seemed safe from violent crime, and fear of crime was at the bottom of citizens' concerns. Japanese crime rates had been the lowest among developed countries since the end of World War II.

The Japanese sense of security largely disappeared in 1995, when Shoko Asahara, leader of the 10 000-member Aum Shinri Kyo (Supreme Truth) sect, was arrested and charged with masterminding a nerve gas attack on a Tokyo subway station. The attack left 12 dead and more than 5500 injured. Intense Japanese media coverage of Asahara's arrest and pending trial made the event in some ways the Far Eastern equivalent of the 1995 O.J. Simpson trial, which received extensive coverage in the American media.

Two years after the gas attacks, Japan was forced to come to terms with another shocking crime when police arrested a 14-year-old boy who confessed to beheading a fellow student and drinking the victim's blood.[2] The head of 11-year-old victim Jun Hase was discovered by a custodian at the gate of a junior high school in the city of Kobe. Hase's eyes had been gouged out, and his mouth had been slashed from ear to ear. In place of his tongue, police found a taunting note, which called investigators "fools" and boasted that the killer enjoyed seeing people die.[3] The suspect in the case, whose name was not released, told police he killed Hase, brought the severed head home, washed it in a bathroom, and hid it overnight in the attic above his room. The next morning, he carved the head while sitting at his desk, then placed it near the school. Police who later searched the boy's room found horror videos, knives, and a book about the Zodiac serial killings that took place in San Francisco in the 1960s. Investigators also reportedly found notebooks recording details of other attacks, and the boy then confessed to two assaults on young girls and to two other attacks in which one girl was beaten to death and another was stabbed.

The gruesome murder of young Hase had an especially demoralizing effect on many Japanese. Mootoo Sakai, 34, a Kobe hotel doorman, was one of many upset by the beheading. "I'm worried that more and more crimes are being committed by youngsters. I just wonder where Japanese society is headed,"[4] he said. Two years later, Sakai's words were supported by the annual crime statistics released by the Japanese government. The official 2002 statistical report showed that—in contrast to reported crime in Canada—the number of crimes in Japan had reached new heights. Most of the increase came from crimes such as muggings (up 15 per cent in one year), nighttime store robberies (up 24 per cent), and various property crimes (with increases ranging from 10 to 25 per cent).[5]

To most Japanese, violent crimes seemed to be everywhere. Newsworthy crimes that occurred in Japan over 2002 include the gang rape and brutal beating of a 20-year-old university student by five students from the medical school at Tokyo's prestigious Keio University; the arrest of a 16-year-old boy from the town of Takane for beating his father to death; the robbery of a Tokyo jewellery store by a 14-year-old boy; the tossing of a 6-year-old boy from a condominium window by a 20-year-old man running a test in preparation for his own suicide; the arrest of a 19-year-old man for stabbing his mother to death following a discussion about his fiancée: and the arrest of a 23-year-old female teacher in Nagoya for having had sex with a 14-year-old student — all of which sound very much as if they could be crimes lifted from the pages of American tabloids.[6] Local commentators in Japan have attributed the rise in violence to children being spoiled, schools being too lax, and a "pressure cooker" society that frowns upon failure.[7]

As Japanese citizens began adjusting to a lessened sense of personal security, some suggested that officials there could learn something from the experience of other industrialized countries in which criminality is rampant. A few even suggested that comparing Japanese troubles with understandings of what had historically contributed to high crime rates in America might produce effective strategies to head off further crime and social disorder in Japan.

Criminologists who study crime and criminal justice on a cross-national level are referred to as **comparative criminologists**, and their field is called comparative criminology or **comparative criminal justice**. Comparative criminal justice is becoming increasingly valued for the insights it provides. By comparing institutions of justice in different countries, procedures and problems that have been taken for granted under one system can be re-evaluated in the light of world experience. As communications, rapid travel, and other technological advances effectively "shrink" the world, we find ourselves in a nearly ideal situation of being able to learn first-hand about the criminal justice systems of other countries, and to use that information to improve our own. This chapter explains the value of comparative criminology for students of criminal justice, points to the problems that arise in comparing data among and between nations, and explores four criminal justice systems in other parts of the world: those of China and England, the United States, and Islam (the Muslim world). International police agencies are also described, and the role of the United Nations in the worldwide fight against crime is discussed.

## Ethnocentrism and the Study of Criminal Justice

Like most other human beings, we often assume that the way we do things is the best way to do them. Such provincial attitudes are probably part of human nature. As a consequence of this attitude, however, the study of criminal justice in Canada, and elsewhere, has been largely ethnocentric. The word "ethnocentric" literally means centred on one's own culture. Because people are socialized from birth into a particular culture, they tend to prefer their own culture's way of doing things over that of any other. Native patterns of behaviour are seen as somehow "natural," and therefore better, than foreign ones. The same is true for values, beliefs, and customs. People tend to think that the religion they were born into holds a spiritual edge over other religions, that their values and ethical sense are superior to those of others, and that the fashions they wear, the language they speak, and the rituals of daily life in which they participate are somehow better than comparable practices elsewhere. Ethnocentric individuals rarely stop to think that people elsewhere in the world probably cling to their own values, beliefs, and standards of behaviour with just as much fervour as they do. Hence, **ethnocentrism** is not a uniquely Canadian phenomenon.

Only in recent years have students of criminal justice begun to examine the justice systems of other cultures. Unfortunately, not all cultures are equally open, and it is not always easy to explore them. In some societies even the *study* of criminal justice is taboo. As a result, data-gathering strategies taken for granted in Western culture may not be well received elsewhere. One author, for example, speaking about China, has observed, "The seeking of criminal justice information through face-to-face questioning takes on a different meaning in Chinese officialdom than it does generally in the Western world. While we accept this method of inquiry because we prize thinking on our feet and quick answers, it is rather offensive in China because it shows lack of respect and appreciation for the information given through the preferred means of prepared questions and formal briefings."[8] Hence, most of the information available about Chinese criminal justice comes from officials and "routine." Western social science practices such as door-to-door interviews, participant observation, and random surveys might produce substantial problems for researchers who attempted to use such techniques in China.

## Problems with Data

Similar difficulties arise in the comparison of crime rates from one country to another. The crime rates of different nations are difficult to compare[9] because of (1) differences in the way a specific crime is defined, (2) diverse crime reporting practices, and (3) political and other influences on the reporting of statistics to international agencies.

Definitional differences create what may be the biggest problem. For cross-national comparisons of crime data to be meaningful, it is essential that the reported data share conceptual similarities. Unfortunately, that is rarely the case. Nations report offences according to the legal criteria by which arrests are made and under which prosecution can occur. Switzerland, for example, includes bicycle thefts in its reported data on what we call "auto theft" because Swiss data gathering focuses more on the concept of personal transportation than it does upon the type of vehicle stolen. The Netherlands has no crime category for "robberies," counting them as thefts. Japan classifies an assault that results in death as "assault," or "aggravated assault," not homicide. Greek rape statistics include crimes of sodomy, "lewdness," seduction of a child, incest, and prostitution. Communist China reports only robberies and thefts that involve the property of citizens, since crimes against state-owned property fall into a separate category.[10]

Social, cultural, and economic differences between countries compound the difficulties we have identified. Auto theft statistics, for example, when compared between countries like Canada and China, need to be placed in an economic as well as demographic context. While Canadians have two automobiles for every three people, China has only one car per 100 citizens. For the Chinese auto theft rate to equal that in Canada, every automobile in China would have to be stolen nearly twice each year!

Reporting practices vary substantially between nations. The International Police Organization (INTERPOL) and the United Nations are the only international organizations that regularly collect crime statistics from a large number of countries.[11] Both agencies can only request data, and have no way of checking on the accuracy of the data reported to them. Many countries do not disclose the requested information, and those that do often make only partial reports. In general, small countries are more likely to report than large ones, and non-socialist countries are more likely to report than socialist nations.[12]

International reports of crime are often delayed. Completely up-to-date data are rare, since the information made available to agencies like the United Nations and INTERPOL is reported at different times and according to schedules that vary from nation to nation. In addition, official United Nations world crime surveys are conducted only infrequently. To date, seven such surveys have been undertaken.

Crime statistics also reflect political biases and national values. Some nations do not accurately admit to the frequency of certain kinds of culturally reprehensible crimes. Communist countries, for example, appear loath to report property crimes such as theft, burglary, and robbery because the very existence of such offences demonstrates perceived inequities within the communist system. After the break-up of the Soviet Union, Alexander Larin, a criminal justice scholar who worked as a Russian investigator during the 1950s and 1960s, revealed that "inside the state security bureaucracy, where statistics were collected and circulated, falsification of crime figures was the rule, not the exception." The practice was "self-perpetuating," said Larin. "Supervisors in the provinces were under pressure to provide Moscow with declining crime rates. And no self-respecting investigator wanted to look worse than his neighbour…. From the top to the bottom, the bosses depended on their employees not to make them look bad with high crime statistics."[13]

On the other hand, observers in democratic societies showed similar biases in their interpretation of statistics following the end of the Cold War. Some Western analysts, for example, reporting on declines in the prison populations of Eastern and Central Europe during that period, attributed the decline to lessened frustration and lowered crime rates brought about by democratization (in one country, Hungary, prison populations declined from 240 inmates per 100 000 persons in 1986 to 130 per 100 000 in 1993, with similar decreases in other nations).[14] The more likely explanation, however, appears to have been the wholesale post-Soviet release of political dissidents from prisons formerly run by communist regimes.

# THE CHINESE JUSTICE SYSTEM

The People's Republic of China (PRC), with a land area of 9 561 000 square kilometres and a population of more than 1.2 billion people, is arguably the largest nation on earth. Some people predict that in the twenty-first century, as the Chinese economy awakens and its massive military might makes itself felt, it will become the world's most important nation. For that reason students of criminal justice should have some understanding of the Chinese justice system and of the cultural assumptions that underlie it.

In the spring of 1989, the world focused its attention on China, where students and workers supported mass demonstrations favouring freedom and democracy. Tiananmen Square, in the centre of Beijing, became the rallying point for protesters. The huge and famous portrait of Mao Tse-tung, China's revolutionary communist leader, which overlooks the square, was defaced with paint. Students even constructed a small replica of the Statue of Liberty on the bricks of the square. As the world looked on, the Chinese Red Army, acting on orders of party leader Deng Xiaoping and members of the Chinese Communist Party Central Committee, moved decisively to end the demonstrations. On June 4, 1989, at least 800 people died in a hail of rifle fire directed at the protesters. It is estimated that thousands more perished in the weeks that followed.[15] Some were victims of government action to suppress continuing demonstrations, while others were summarily tried and executed for inciting riots and for plotting against the government. While the Chinese democratic revolution of 1989 did not succeed, this revolution is evidence of the sense of single-minded purpose so characteristic of Chinese society. It is that shared sense of purpose that underlies the Chinese legal system today.

## Maoist Justice

Under party Chairman Mao Tse-tung, criminal justice in the PRC was based upon informal societal control. Mao abhorred bureaucratic agencies and procedures and, during his reign, accused offenders found themselves turned over to the populace for a hearing and punishment.[16] The infamous Chinese Cultural Revolution, which began in 1966 and lasted until 1973,[17] was intended to integrate Maoist teaching and principles into Chinese society. During the revolutionary period Mao called upon his hordes of fanatical followers known as Red Guards to "smash the police and the courts." One of Mao's most popular sayings intoned: "Depend on the rule of man, not the rule of law."[18] Because of Maoist thinking, the PRC had no criminal or procedural legal codes, no lawyers, and no officially designated prosecutors until after 1978. Under Mao, the police were replaced by military control with arrest powers residing in the People's Liberation Army.

According to the concept of "class justice," taught by the Cultural Revolution, the severity of punishment an offender received depended upon his or her social and political identity. Consistent with the tenor of the times, a Chinese textbook of the late 1960s proclaimed, "the point of our criminal law is chiefly directed towards the enemies of socialism."[19] Wealthy, successful, and educated people, because of their high status under previous regimes, were automatically suspected of crimes, and were often summarily tried and severely punished for the vaguest of allegations. Following Mao's death, the Cultural Revolution was denounced by the Central Committee of the Chinese Communist party as "responsible for the most severe setback and the heaviest losses suffered by the party, the state and the people since the founding of the People's Republic."[20]

## The Chinese Justice System Today

In 1978, two years after the death of Chairman Mao, another wave of reform swept China. This time a

---

**BOX 14.1  Theory into Practice**

### Individual Rights Guaranteed Under the Constitution of the People's Republic of China

**(Adapted December 4, 1982 by the Fifth National People's Congress, Beijing)**

| Right | Guaranteed by |
|---|---|
| 1. Equality Before the Law | Article 33 |
| 2. Freedom from Unlawful Detention | Article 37 |
| 3. Right Against Unlawful Personal Searches | Article 37 |
| 4. Protection from Unlawful Arrest | Article 37 |
| 5. Right Against Unlawful Searches of a Residence | Article 39 |
| 6. Right to a Public Trial | Article 126 |
| 7. Right of Defence in a Criminal Trial | Article 126 |
| 8. A Right to Use One's Native Spoken and Written Language in Court | Article 134 |

formalized legal system, based upon codified laws, was created and a radically revised Constitution was given life on December 4, 1982. Predictability and security, especially for the potentially most productive members of society, became the goal of the new National People's Congress. The Congress sought to ensure internal stability, international commerce, and modernization through legislation. The Chinese Constitution now contains 24 articles on the fundamental rights and duties of citizens[21] and guarantees equality before the law for everyone.

The modern Chinese justice system is structured along jurisdictional lines similar to those in Canada. At the highest level, the Chinese justice system is built around four national offices: the Ministry of Public Security (comparable to the Department of the Solicitor General of Canada), the Supreme People's Court (like our Supreme Court of Canada), three levels of the People's Court (like our provincial court system), and the Ministry of Justice (similar to our federal Ministry of Justice). Article 5 of the Chinese constitution specifies that the **procuratorate** is directly responsible for supervising the administration of criminal justice throughout the country, including the investigation of crimes, the activities of the courts, the police and correctional institutions, and to initiate prosecution.

Chinese police agencies, which fall under the authority of the Ministry of Public Security, are often regarded as technologically backward. Some, however, are beginning to apply twenty-first-century technology in the fight against crime. In 1995, for example, Chinese officials announced[22] that police forces in more than 20 provinces had begun to use DNA fingerprinting as a method of criminal identification. Also in 1995, the China Criminal Information Center, a computerized national network designed to provide police forces throughout China with rapid interprovincial information on criminal offenders, began operating in 11 provinces along China's east coast. Officials said they hoped that the new computer system will allow for improved control over China's huge migrant population,[23] estimated at between 60 and 80 million people—especially members of that group who are involved in criminal activity.

As in Canada, courts in China are hierarchically organized (see Figure 14–1). The Supreme People's Court is the highest court in China. It deals with cases that may have an impact on the entire country.[24] The Supreme People's Court has absolute autonomy and is not subject to interference by any individual, administrative body, or organization. Most cases come before the Court on appeal, but it will hear cases submitted for trial by people's courts at lower levels. The Court is divided into three sections: criminal court, which deals with felony violations of the law, mostly on appeal, and death penalty reviews; civil affairs court; and economic court.

At the opposite judicial extreme, the Primary People's Court (or Basic People's Court) operates at the county level as the court with original jurisdiction over most criminal cases. Two judicial levels—the Intermediate People's Court, and the Higher People's Court, stand between the Basic Court and the Supreme People's Court. Both function as courts of appeal, although intermediate courts have original jurisdiction in criminal cases with the potential for sentences involving death or life imprisonment. The intermediate courts also hear criminal charges brought against foreigners.

Defendants may choose to be represented in Chinese courts by a lawyer, a relative, or a friend, a citizen recommended by a people's organization or the institution that employs them, or they may choose to represent themselves. If they desire, a lawyer will be appointed for them. Lawyers in China, however, have a far different role from that of their Canadian counterparts. While they work to protect the rights of the defendant, Chinese lawyers have a responsibility to the court that transcends their duties to the accused. Defence lawyers are charged with helping the court render a just verdict.[25] The Chinese believe that vigorous defence strategies such as those found in the adversarial framework of Western justice can lead to criminals escaping responsibility.[26]

**procuratorate**
(also **procuracy**) A term used in many countries to refer to agencies with powers and responsibilities similar to those of prosecutors' offices in Canada.

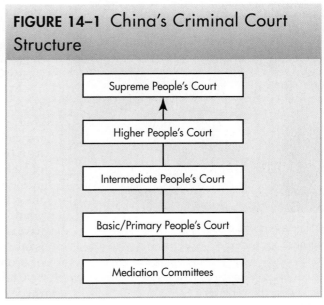

**FIGURE 14–1** China's Criminal Court Structure

- Supreme People's Court
- Higher People's Court
- Intermediate People's Court
- Basic/Primary People's Court
- Mediation Committees

A visit by a delegation of the American Bar Association to Shanghai determined that 78 per cent of the workload of Chinese lawyers consisted of defending accused criminals. The remaining 22 per cent was divided about equally between family practice (wills, divorces, adoptions, inheritance, and so on) and civil suits.[27] The legal profession in China is not, on the whole, well-trained. While most lawyers probably have some formal legal education, many simply meet the conditions of Article 8 of the Chinese constitution, which requires persons who wish to engage in the practice of law to "have the cultural level of graduates of institutions of higher learning, and be suitable to be lawyers."

The Chinese justice system has a built-in system of checks and balances that, in theory, operates to prevent abuses of power. Arrests made by the police, for example, must be approved by the local procuratorate's office. If a decision is made to prosecute, the court may conduct its own investigation prior to the start of trial to determine whether prosecution is warranted.

The official Chinese crime rate is astonishingly low—only 56 crimes per every 100 000 citizens in 1995 (compared to 8913 per 100 000 people in 1995 for Canada), with only 1 690 000 major crimes (including murder, assault, rape, robbery, and abducting and trafficking in human beings) throughout the country.[28] However, official crime rates may be little more than fabrications designed for the foreign media. Asian experts say that China is now experiencing a crime wave unprecedented since the communist revolution in 1949.[29] Drug crimes are especially problematic, with narcotics seizures in 1998 reported to be the highest in the history of communist China. Much crime may be due to high unemployment rates. Eleven per cent of the Chinese urban workforce was unemployed in 1999.[30]

One special area of concern to outsiders has been China's wholesale violation of intellectual property rights by profiteers who reproduce foreign movies, compact discs, tapes, and software, and resell them in China and throughout Asia without paying permission fees or royalties. North American industry spokespersons estimate that Chinese copyright, trademark, and patent violations cost American companies alone up to US$1.5 billion a year in lost sales.[31] In response to stiff international pressure, China has recently taken steps to criminalize such activities, including the establishment of special courts to prosecute those who violate laws governing intellectual property,[32] and the enforcement of new anti-piracy laws seems to be speeding up.

Organized crime is another problem in China. Chinese gang roots can be traced to secret societies, called triads, that fought to restore the Ming Dynasty, which was overthrown in 1644. Beginning in the early 1900s, the triads that still survived became increasingly involved in criminal activities. In 1949, after the communist takeover, China's gangs and underworld secret societies were either eradicated or forced into hibernation. In recent years, these "black societies" have made a strong comeback, manufacturing and selling guns, running illegal gambling operations, smuggling, forcing women into prostitution, and fighting gun battles with local police. In 1995, Chinese officials announced a major crackdown on organized crime throughout the country, vowing to execute any gang bosses who could be identified. Military Police Colonel Zhang Dingxing was blunt in his assessment of the situation. "All leaders of black societies will be executed without exception,"[33] he said, announcing the crackdown.

Once arrested, suspects face a high likelihood of conviction. Records show a 99-per-cent conviction rate in Chinese criminal courts (versus 61 per cent in Canada).[34] A crime problem of growing concern to the Chinese is youth offending. Juvenile gang activity is on the increase, with gang members often coming from families of high Communist Party functionaries.[35] Youthful offenders are seen by local Chinese experts to be experiencing a moral vacuum, whereby the official party view of one's role in society is in conflict with what youth see going on around them in the real world.[36] Some officials have also suggested that international gang-related drug trafficking is on the rise in the PRC. However, although China has had a history of problems with opium abuse, actual consumption of illicit drugs by Chinese citizens probably occurs at a rate much lower than that of the Western world.[37]

Office of International Criminal Justice

A Chinese police officer lectures a young man. Chinese society expects conformity in ways foreign to the Western mind, permitting police officers to act as the conscience of the community even when no law has been broken.

## Mediation Committees

One reason for the low official crime rate is the Chinese system of People's **Mediation Committees**. By virtue of the large number of cases they resolve, mediation committees may be the most important component of justice in modern China. A mediation committee generally consists of five to seven people, with judicial assistants assigned to the committee by the Bureau of Justice, the courts, and the procuratorates.[38] Mediation committees are officially guided by law and government policy. Their power, however, comes from the force of public opinion.[39] Education and persuasion are their primary tools.[40]

Committees function informally based on the belief that minor disputes and misdemeanour offences such as minor assaults, thefts, and vandalism can be best handled at local levels without unnecessary protocol. Mediation committees are also believed to play a significant role in crime prevention by resolving disputes before they evolve into serious altercations. That is why housing disputes, divorce cases, and land-sharing problems also commonly come before such committees. Agreements reached must be based on voluntary consent and must conform with the law.

People's Mediation Committees are everywhere in China—in factories, on farms, in schools, and in businesses. According to some authorities, over 800 000 Chinese mediation committees, functioning on a regular basis, handle over eight million cases per year.[41] In contrast, only 3000 regular courts are in existence at all levels throughout the entire country.[42] Mediation committees serve to divert a large number of people from processing by county and provincial courts. They also serve to dramatically lower the number of officially reported offences throughout China.

One item of special interest in international criminal justice circles involves the reversion of Hong Kong to China in 1997. Despite objections from London, Chinese officials created a new Supreme Court of Hong Kong. The new court, called the Court of Final Appeal for Hong Kong, replaced London's Privy Council as the territory's supreme judicial agency.

## Chinese Criminal Punishments

The punishment of offenders in China can be severe in cases that go beyond mediation and enter the court system. Thirty-eight per cent of convicted offenders in China are sentenced to more than five years in prison,[43] and repeat offenders are subject to harsh punishments. Widespread use of the death penalty, usually carried out with a single bullet to the back of the head, is characteristic of contemporary China. Executions are often preceded by a public rally during which the prisoner's name, crime, and punishment are announced to the crowd, while the prisoner is forced to stand with head bowed and hands tied. After the execution, the offender's family is routinely ordered to pay for the cost of the bullet used in the execution. The number of people executed each year is secret, according to a Chinese Supreme Court official. Amnesty International, however, says that more people are executed in China each year than in all of the rest of the world. The organization estimates that China's Strike Hard (Against Crime) campaigns, which began in 1983 and are revived periodically, have led to at least 19 446 executions between 1990 and 2000—an execution rate around 35 times that of the United States.[44] Amnesty International also says that a recent *Yanda*, or anti-crime campaign aimed at combatting major crimes, such as murder and robbery, led to 1014 death sentences between April and June of 1996—resulting in over 800 immediate executions.[45]

In China, capital punishment can be imposed for a wide variety of crimes. One man executed in 1995, for example, was condemned for publishing pornographic books; four others for faking tax receipts. "The death penalty is apparently used to deter people from actions that interfere with economic development," said one Western observer.[46] Widespread use of the death penalty, while expected to deter others, is admittedly not based upon studies of the punishment's effectiveness as a deterrent. As one Chinese diplomat said, "We don't feel the death penalty is based on research but on common-sense arguments and primal response."[47] Although death sentences must be reviewed by the Supreme People's Court, the Court may rule on the legality of a case before a defendant is sentenced, which clears the way for speedy executions.

According to authorities there, Chinese prisons hold 1.28 million inmates in 685 prison units. Western authorities, however, doubt that official Chinese statistics are correct.

**Mediation Committees**
Chinese civilian dispute resolution groups found throughout the country. Mediation Committees successfully divert many minor offenders from handling by more formal mechanisms of justice.

Independent research into Chinese arrest and sentencing patterns, and accounts by former prisoners, lead some to conclude that as many as 16 to 20 million people are confined in 990 labour reform prisons—that is, prisons set aside for inmates whose only crime may be speaking out against the dictatorial aspects of Chinese government.

Many Chinese prisons are notoriously primitive. Typical cells, which range in size from 36 to 50 square metres, hold 30 to 50 inmates, who sleep on hard woven mats covering the floor. Cells, which are unheated in the winter, are fitted with only one latrine and are lit with a single light bulb.

For all its seeming harshness, the Chinese justice system is based upon a strong cultural belief in personal reformation. As one author has observed, "Repentance, which means reclaiming individuals for society, is at the heart of Chinese justice."[48] Confucius taught that "Man is at birth by nature good,"[49] and Chinese authorities seek to build opportunities into their criminal justice system that allow offenders to change for the better. Even a person sentenced to death is generally granted a two-year period during which he or she may repent and attempt to demonstrate that he or she has changed. If the offender can successfully convince the court that he or she has reformed, his or her sentence will be commuted.[50]

Violation of prison rules may result in extended incarceration, solitary confinement, or "group criticism." The study of communist policy, according to official Chinese interpretation, is required of all inmates. Such study is the focal point of prison treatment programs.[51] Political prisoners are subjected to *laogai*,[52] or "thought reform through labour," and are required to work at prison farms, factories, and the like.

Official parole eligibility comes only after the offender has shown repentance and has performed "meritoriously" while in prison. In practice, however, parole may be granted routinely after half the sentence has been served (specifically 10 years for life sentences).[53] Chinese parole follows the institutional model, in which individual confinement facilities recommend parole to the court, which then makes the final decision. Parole officers are unknown in China, but parolees are supervised by local police agencies and by citizens groups.

The philosophy that underlies Chinese corrections is well summed up in the words of a Western observer who recently visited prisons there: "Inmates are expected to conform not to benefit themselves, but to benefit their families, villages, and even their country. Crime is not a reflection of individual failure, but instead is considered a reflection of the family, the community, and even the larger society. It is for the good of society, it is for the good of the communist structure that one must reform one's self. The individual is punished, but he is punished as a member of the group."[54] Faith in repentance, a fundamental doctrine in Chinese corrections, is apparently well-placed. The official rate of recidivism in China is only 4.7 per cent for serious offenders.[55]

In 1994, China's legislature, the National People's Congress, passed the National Prison Reform Law. The law guarantees prisoners dignity, safety, the right to a legal defence, the right of appeal, and freedom from physical abuse. The law also prohibits forced confessions and the illegal confiscation of property, and holds prison officials responsible for ensuring that inmates serve their full sentences. The 1994 law officially codified a decade-old set of Chinese administrative guidelines for prisons. The guidelines, originally approved in 1982, had been largely ignored by prison administrators and remained unenforced—allowing Chinese prisons to become the target of international human rights groups that have strongly criticized prisons there.

## ISLAMIC CRIMINAL JUSTICE

Islamic law has been the subject of much discussion in the world since the September 11, 2001 terrorist attacks on the World Trade Center and the Pentagon, and the resulting destruction of the Taliban regime in Afghanistan by Western military forces. It is important for Western students of criminal justice to recognize, however, that Islamic law refers to legal ideas (and sometimes entire legal systems) based on the teachings of Islam—and that it bears no intrinsic relationship to acts of terrorism committed by misguided zealots with Islamic backgrounds. Similarly, Islamic law is by no means the same thing as "jihad" (Muslim holy war) or Islamic fundamentalism. Although the subject of much curiosity, justice in Islamic countries is often not well-understood by Westerners. Various interpretations of Islam still form the basis of laws in many countries, and entire legal systems of some nations are based on Islamic principles. Islamic law holds considerable sway in a large number of countries, including Syria, Iran, Iraq, Pakistan, Afghanistan, Yemen, Saudi Arabia, Kuwait, the United Arab Emirates, Bahrain, Algeria, Jordan, Lebanon, Libya, Ethiopia, Gambia, Nigeria, Oman, Qatar, Senegal, Tunisia, Tajikistan, Uzbekistan, and Turkey (which practises official separation of church and state).

Criminal justice professor Sam Souryal and his co-authors describe four aspects of justice in Arab philosophy and religion. Islamic justice, they say, means:[56]

- A sacred trust, a duty imposed on humans to be discharged sincerely and honestly. As such, these authors say, "Justice is the quality of being morally responsible and merciful in giving everyone his or her due."

- Mutual respect of one human being by another. From this perspective, a just society is one that offers equal respect for individuals through social arrangements made in the common interest of all members.

- An aspect of the social bond that holds society together and transforms it into a brotherhood in which everyone becomes a keeper of everyone else and each is held accountable for the welfare of all.

- A command from God. Whosoever violates God's commands should be subject to strict punishments, according to Islamic tradition and belief.

As Souryal and his co-authors observe, "The third and fourth meanings of justice are probably the ones most commonly invoked in Islamic jurisprudence," and form the basis of criminal justice practice in many Middle Eastern countries.

# The *Hudud* Crimes

**Islamic law** (or *Shari'ah* in Arabic, which means "path of God") forms the basis of theocratic judicial systems in Kuwait, Saudia Arabia, the Sudan, Iran, and Algeria. Other Arabic nations, such as Egypt, Jordan, and Iraq, recognize substantial elements of Islamic law in their criminal justice systems, but also make wide use of Western and non-theocratic legal principles. Islamic law is based upon four sources. In order of importance, these sources are (1) the Koran (also spelled "Quran" and "Qur'an"), or Holy Book of Islam, which Muslims believe is the word of God, or "Allah"; (2) the teachings of the Prophet Mohammed; (3) a consensus of the clergy in cases where neither the Koran nor the prophet directly address an issue; and (4) reason or logic, which should be used when no solution can be found in the other three sources.[57]

Islamic law recognizes seven *Hudud* (sometimes called *Hodood* or *Huddud*) crimes—or crimes based on religious strictures. ***Hudud* crimes** are essentially violations of "natural law" as interpreted by Arab culture. Divine displeasure is thought to be the basis of crimes defined as *Hudud*, and *Hudud* crimes are often said to be crimes against God (or, more specifically, "God's rights"). Four *Hudud* crimes for which punishments are specified in the Koran are (1) making war upon Allah and His messengers, (2) theft, (3) adultery, and (4) false accusation of fornication or adultery. Three other *Hudud* offences are mentioned by the Koran, for which no punishment is specified—(1) "corruption on the earth," (2) drinking of alcohol, and (3) highway robbery, and the punishments for these crimes are determined by tradition.[58] The seven *Hudud* offences, and associated typical punishments, are shown in Table 14–1. "Corruption on Earth" is a general category of religious offence, not well understood in the West, which includes activities such as embezzlement, revolution against lawful authority, fraud, and "weakening the society of God."

The religious aspect of Islamic law makes for strict punishment of moral failure. Sexual offenders, even those who engage in what may be considered essentially victimless crimes in Western societies, are subject to especially harsh treatment. The Islamic penalty for fornication, for example, is 100 lashes. Men are stripped to the waist, women have their clothes bound tightly, and flogging is carried out with a leather whip. Adultery carries a much more severe penalty: flogging and stoning to death.

**Islamic law** A system of laws, operative in some Arab countries, which is based upon the Muslim religion and especially the holy book of Islam, the Koran.

***Hudud* crimes** Serious violations of Islamic law regarded as offences against God. *Hudud* crimes include such behaviour as theft, adultery, sodomy, drinking alcohol, and robbery.

469

## TABLE 14–1  Crime and Punishment in Islamic Law: The Iranian Example[1]

Islamic law looks to the Koran and the teachings of the Prophet Mohammed to determine which acts should be classified as crimes. The Koran and tradition specify punishments to be applied to designated offences, as the following verse from the Koran demonstrates: "The only reward of those who make war upon Allah and His messenger and strive after corruption in the land will be that they will be killed or crucified, or have their hands and feet on alternate sides cut off, or will be expelled out of the land" (Surah V, Verse 33). Other crimes and punishments include the following:

| Offence | Punishment |
|---|---|
| Theft | Amputation of the hand |
| Adultery | Stoning to death |
| Fornication | One hundred lashes |
| False accusation (of adult fornication) | Eighty lashes |
| Corruption on earth | Death by the sword or burning |
| Drinking alcohol | Eighty lashes; death if repeated three times |
| Robbery | Cutting off of hands and feet on alternate sides |

[1]For more information, see the following: Souryal, S.S. and Potts, D.W. (1994). The Penalty of Hand Amputation for Theft in Islamic Justice. *Journal of Criminal Justice*, Vol. 22, No. 3, pp. 249–265; Saney, P. (1983). Iran. In Johnson, E.H. (ed.). *International Handbook of Contemporary Developments in Criminology* (pp. 356–369). Westport, CT: Greenwood.

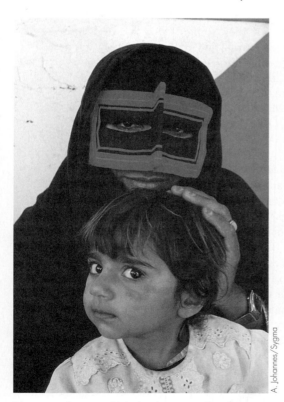

Islamic tradition and Muslim law strongly influence the style of dress worn by this woman in Oman. Islamic law is based on the teachings of the Koran and the sayings of the Prophet Mohammed.

Under Islamic law, even property crimes can be firmly punished. Thieves who are undeterred by less serious punishments may eventually suffer amputation of the right hand. In a reputedly humane move, Iranian officials recently began the use of an electric guillotine, specially made for the purpose, which can sever a hand at the wrist in one-tenth of a second. For amputation to be imposed, the item stolen must have value in Islam. Pork and alcohol, for example, are regarded as being without value, and their theft is not subject to punishment. Islamic legal codes also establish a minimum value for stolen items that could result in amputation being imposed. Likewise, offenders who have stolen because they are hungry, or are in need, are exempt from the punishment of amputation and receive fines or prison terms.

Slander and the consumption of alcohol are both punished by 80 lashes. Legal codes in strict Islamic nations also specify whipping for the crimes of pimping, lesbianism, kissing by an unmarried couple, cursing, and failure of a woman to wear a veil. Islamic law provides for the execution, sometimes through crucifixion, of robbers. Laws stipulate that anyone who survives three days on the cross may be spared. Depending upon the circumstances of the robbery, however, the offender may suffer the amputation of opposite hands and feet, or simply exile.

Rebellion, or revolt against a legitimate political leader or established economic order, which is considered an aspect of "corruption on earth," is punishable by death. The offender may be killed outright in a military or police action or, later, by sentence of the court. The last of the *Hudud* crimes is rejection of Islam. The penalty, once again, is death, and can be imposed for denying the existence of God or angels, denying any of the prophets of Islam, or rejecting any part of the Koran.

In 1995, a court in Tehran, Iran, sentenced a man to death for what is believed to be the biggest bank fraud case in Iranian history.[59] The defendant, Fazel Khodadad, was convicted of embezzling US$21.7 million from state-run Bank Saderat. Khodadad was sentenced under Islamic laws, which allows capital punishment for "sabotaging the country's economic system." Khodadad was also sentenced to 50 lashes for other illegal activities, including drug abuse, and 99 lashes for an illegal sexual relationship with a woman involving "touching, kissing and lying next to each other." The woman, identified only as M.H., received a sentence of 99 lashes, which was suspended for two years.

*Hudud* crimes can be severely punished, Souryal observes, because "punishment serves a three-tiered obligation: (1) the fulfilment of worship, (2) the purification of society, and (3) the redemption of the individual." However, Souryal adds, the interests of the individual are the least valuable component of this triad, and may have to be sacrificed "for the wholesomeness and integrity of the encompassing justice system."[60]

## The *Tazir* Crimes

All crimes other than *Hudud* fall into an offence category called *tazirat*. A **tazir** crime is regarded as any action not considered acceptable in a spiritual society. *Tazir* crimes include crimes against society and against individuals, but not against God. *Tazir* crimes may call for *Quesas* (retribution) or *Diya* (compensation or fines). Crimes requiring *Quesas* are based on the Arabic principle of "an eye for an eye, a nose for a nose, a tooth for a tooth," and generally require physical punishments, up to and including death. *Quesas* offences may include murder, manslaughter, assault, and maiming. Under Islamic law, such crimes may require the victim or his representative to serve as prosecutor. The state plays a role only in providing the forum for a trial and in imposing punishment.

## Islamic Courts

Islamic courts typically exist on three levels.[61] The first level hears cases involving the potential for serious punishments, including death, amputation, and exile. The second level deals with relatively minor matters, such as traffic offences, and violations of city ordinances. Special courts, especially in Iran, may hear cases involving crimes against the government, narcotics offences, state security, and corruption. Appeals within the Islamic court system are only possible under rare circumstances and are by no means routine. A decision rendered by second-level courts will generally stand without intervention by higher judicial authorities.

Under Islamic law, men and women are treated very differently. Testimony provided by a man, for example, can be heard in court. The same evidence, however, can only be provided by two virtuous women—one female witness will not be sufficient to have the evidence heard.

While Islamic law may seem barbaric to many Westerners, Islamic officials defend their system by pointing to low crime rates at home and by alleging near-anarchy in Western nations. An early criticism of Islamic law was offered by Max Weber at the start of the twentieth century.[62] Weber said that Islamic justice is based more upon the moral conceptions of individual judges than it is upon any rational and predictable code of laws. He found that the personality of each judge, what he called "charisma," was more important in reaching a final legal result than was the written law. Weber's conclusion was that a modern society could not develop under Islamic law because enforcement of the law was too unpredictable. Complex social organizations, he argued, could only be based upon a rational law, which is relatively unchanging from place to place and over time.[63]

More recent observers have agreed that "Islamic justice is based on philosophical principles that are considered alien, if not unconscionable, to the Western observer." However, these same writers note, strict punishments such as hand amputation "may not be inconsistent with the fundamentals of natural law or Judeo-Christian doctrine. The imposition of the penalty in specific cases and under rigorous rules of evidence—as the principle requires—may be indeed justifiable, and even necessary, in the Islamic context of sustaining a spiritual and peaceful society."[64]

# CRIMINAL JUSTICE IN ENGLAND AND WALES

The country of England is quite small—only a little larger than the island of Newfoundland, but with a population of around 49 million people—considerably more than all of Canada.

**tazir crime** A minor violation of Islamic law, regarded as an offence against society, not God.

**TABLE 14–2** Notifiable Offences and Changes in Reporting—England and Wales (12 months: from September 2001 to September 2002)

| Offence Group | Number of Offences | | % Change |
|---|---|---|---|
| | 12 months to Sep 2001 | 12 months to Sep 2002 | |
| Violence against the person | 624 300 | 742 900 | 18.9 |
| Sexual offences | 38 700 | 45 700 | 18.1 |
| Robbery | 105 400 | 120 700 | 14.5 |
| Total violent crime | 768 400 | 909 300 | 18.3 |
| Break and enter | 414 600 | 447 100 | 7.8 |
| Theft of and from vehicles | 965 100 | 998 400 | 3.5 |
| Other thefts and handling | 1 210 700 | 1 363 500 | 12.6 |
| Fraud and forgery | 321 400 | 326 300 | 1.5 |
| Criminal damage | 1 010 300 | 1 089 500 | 7.8 |
| Total property crime | 4 356 600 | 4 688 100 | 7.6 |
| Drug offences | 115 900 | 130 200 | 12.3 |
| Other offences | 63 400 | 69 500 | 9.6 |
| **Total of all reported offences** | **5 304 200** | **5 797 100** | **9.3** |

*Source*: Povey, D., C. Ellis, and S. Nicholas (2003). *Crime in England and Wales: Quarterly Update, 12 months to September 2002*. Home Office Statistical Bulletin 02/03. London:, Home Office. See also **www.homeoffice.gov.uk/rds/pdfs2/ hosb203.pdf**, accessible at time of writing.

One of the original participants in the industrial revolution, it remains a highly industrialized nation. England is linked closely to its neighbours—Wales, Scotland, and Northern Ireland—an alliance that created the political entity of "the United Kingdom of Great Britain and Northern Ireland."

Our Canadian heritage, both legal and cultural, has been strongly influenced by Britain. Chapter 3 described the way in which British common law formed the basis of our own legal traditions, and Chapter 4 showed how Canadian police forces and other criminal justice agencies in their formative periods drew upon earlier English experience. Because England is a much more open society than either China or most Islamic countries, a far greater amount of descriptive detail is available about the criminal justice system there.

# Rates of Crime[65]

British crime surveys mirror their Canadian counterparts, and the Research and Statistics Department of the Home Office makes reports of crime freely available to researchers.[66] Major crimes in England and Wales are termed "notifiable offences," the counterpart of "*Criminal Code* offences" or "Uniform Crime Data" in Canada. In recent years, public opinion polls have identified crime as the number one concern of the British voting public. By any measure, crime would appear to be high in England (see Table 14–2). From September 2001 to September 2002, for example, approximately 5.8 million criminal offences were recorded by police forces throughout England and Wales—one for every nine members of the population. Another 6.5 million crimes went unreported, according to data gathered by the British Crime Survey (BCS). In 2001–02, the BCS estimated there were 16.4 million crimes against people. While personal crimes reported in the BCS victimization survey reflected a 2-per-cent drop over the previous year, crimes reported to the police showed a slight increase. Reported crimes included 1 million burglaries (i.e., break and enter), 1.3 million household thefts, and just under 1 million thefts of, or from, private motor vehicles. Between September 2001 and September 2002, 81 per cent of reported crimes in England and Wales were against property, while 12.8 per cent were violent crimes and 2.2 per cent were drug offences.

## The British Political System

England is a country without a formal written constitution. The legal basis of English government, however, can be found in at least three significant documents: (1) the *Magna Carta*, (2) the *Bill of Rights*, and (3) the *Act of Settlement*. The *Magna Carta*, written in 1215, was forced upon the king by English nobility and the upper classes. It guarantees a number of legal rights to British citizens accused of crimes, including the right to due process of law and a hearing before one's peers. The English *Bill of Rights*, passed by **Parliament** in 1688, established the two houses of Parliament (the House of Lords and the House of Commons), guaranteed free elections, and placed parliamentary authority in statutory matters over that of the sovereign. Therefore, although modern England still has a royal family whose members perform ceremonial functions, the real power to make laws and run the nation lies in the hands of the two houses of Parliament and the Prime Minister. In 1700, the *Act of Settlement* reinforced the powers of Parliament and made clear the authority of judges and other officials.

While we have inherited many of our criminal justice practices from the British, since Confederation in 1867 and the signing of the *British North America Act* in that year, Canada has forged several major differences that make our system unique from our colonial ancestors. These differences are significant for the administration of criminal justice:

- The British system, unlike the Canadian, makes no provision for judicial review of parliamentary action. Acts of Parliament are the law of the land and cannot be overruled by any court.

- Britain is a unitary state where parliamentary law applies at both the national and local level, while Canada has both federal and provincial laws.

- Canada has laws that apply beyond the reach of either the federal Parliament or the provinces. These conditions and procedures are prescribed in the *Constitution Act, 1982*.

- In Britain, a unity of powers, rather than a separation of branches, characterizes the government. Executive, legislative, and judicial authorities all ultimately rest in Parliament.

- The British political system is essentially a *flexible* system because no one document can be referred to as representing the constitution.

In Canada, the Constitution reflects a modification of the English political system, altered to allow a federal system of government and also altered to incorporate substantial written elements into the Constitution.

## Modern Criminal Law in England

In 1967, the English Parliament passed the *Criminal Law Act*, a sweeping piece of legislation that substantially altered English criminal procedure. The old distinction between "felonies" and "misdemeanours" was eliminated in favour of two new offence categories: "arrestable" (or indictable) and "non-arrestable" (or summary) offences. Under English common law, the arrest powers of the police without a warrant were limited to treason, felonies, and breaches of the peace. The *Criminal Law Act* broadened arrest powers in the absence of a warrant to all offences "for which [a] sentence is fixed by law," and to attempts to commit such offences. The 1967 Act also gave private citizens the power to arrest offenders they caught engaging in criminal activity or whom they had reasonable suspicion to believe had committed an arrestable offence.

In November 1994, a powerful nationwide conservative emphasis led to passage of the *Criminal Justice and Public Order Act* (1994). This Act (CJA) marked a return to a get-tough English anti-crime policy. British Home Secretary Michael Howard explained why

**Parliament** The British legislature; the highest lawmaking body of the United Kingdom composed of the House of Commons and the House of Lords.

the bill was passed in these words: "In the last 30 years the balance in the criminal justice system has been tilted too far in favour of the criminal and against the protection of the public. The time has come to put that right."[67]

The CJA selectively criminalized what had previously been especially serious violations of the civil law, made it easier to catch and convict criminals, made it harder for repeat offenders to get bail, and restricted, at least to some degree, the rights of criminal defendants. Prior to the new legislation, for example, police officers in England were required to caution detained persons with the admonishment: "You do not have to say anything unless you wish to do so, but anything you say may be given as evidence." Criticisms of the British right to silence were effectively promoted in the national media by law enforcement agencies, which cited difficulties in obtaining convictions when a suspect's silence went unquestioned. Such criticisms found their way into the 1994 legislation, and English courts are now permitted to draw "such inferences as are appropriate" from a suspect's silence.

Today, an English police officer arresting someone is required to say: "You do not have to say anything, but it may harm your defence if you do not mention when questioned, something which you later rely on in court. Anything you say may be used as evidence." When preparing to question a suspect, officers are enjoined to admonish: "I must warn you that if from now on you refuse to account for a fact, a court may draw their own conclusions why you have not done so." Hence, under modern British law, a suspect's refusal to answer questions (specifically to account for one's presence at a given location or to account for the possession of objects, substances, and bodily injuries) can be used later by a court to infer his or her guilt. The CJA also gives British courts wider powers to sentence persistent offenders between the ages of 12 and 14 and effectively doubles the maximum possible sentence youthful offenders can receive.

The *Sex Offenders Act* of 1997 imposed a registration requirement on newly convicted offenders, including those supervised in the community or released from prison. The duration of the registration requirement depends on sentence length, type of offence, age of the offender, and age and gender of the victim. Under the Act, a convicted sex offender is required to keep the police informed of his current address.

In 1998, the *Crime and Disorder Act*, passed by the British Parliament, received royal assent. The purpose of the Act, in the words of the British Home Office, "is to tackle crime and disorder and help create safer communities."[68] The Act builds upon the theme of establishing local partnerships between the police and the local community to cut crime. The Act also places a statutory obligation on local authorities and the police to conduct a "crime audit" of levels and patterns of crime in their area, to analyze the results of audits, to hold consultations on the results, to prepare a strategy to reduce levels of crime and disorder, to implement and monitor the effectiveness of that strategy, and to repeat the process every three years.

Finally, in 2001, the English Parliament passed the *Anti-terrorism, Crime and Security Bill*, which became law after receiving royal assent shortly afterward. The wide-ranging legislation, modelled, in part, after the 2001 *USA Patriot Act*, includes (1) new police powers for the purpose of monitoring terrorist groups, (2) a provision for detention without trial for suspected international terrorists even when they cannot be deported (British law, like Canada's, does not allow deportation of criminal suspects to countries with the death penalty), and (3) a new offence of knowingly causing a nuclear explosion.[69] Like its Canadian and American counterparts, the *Anti-terrorism, Crime and Security Act* contains a sunset provision, meaning that some significant provisions of the law will have to be periodically renewed by Parliament.

## Police in England

The historical development of police forces in nineteenth-century Britain is described in Chapter 4. By World War II, 183 police departments—some large, some very small—existed throughout England and Wales.[70] Each was headed by a chief constable, and jurisdictional disputes between departments were common. Major efforts to consolidate police departments culminated in the *Police Acts* of 1946 and 1964, to which contemporary British policing owes its structure. The *Local Government Act* of 1972 further reduced the number of police forces throughout England and Wales until the combined forces numbered just

"British "Bobbies." Uniformed English police officers have a recognizable appearance rooted in the time of Sir Robert Peel.

43. The smallest police agency in Britain today has over 600 officers—a good-sized department by Canadian standards. On March 31, 2002, some 129 603 sworn police officers were employed throughout England and Wales, and 58 909 full- and part-time civilians served police forces there. There are an average of 240 police officers per 100 000 population, and 18 per cent of the police force is composed of female officers.[71]

The police of Britain are subject to civilian control through local commissions called police authorities. Two-thirds of each police authority are elected civilians, while one-third of the authority's members are judicial officers elected by fellow magistrates. Each police authority appoints a local chief constable, with overall authority for the daily operations of the police, and an assistant chief constable. In 1994, Parliament passed the *Police and Magistrates Courts Act*, legislation that emphasizes the important role that local communities play in setting the goals of police service. In tones reminiscent of the American emphasis on community policing, British Home Secretary Michael Howard described the new law this way: "I believe that an active partnership between government, the public, and the police is the way forward. The *Police and Magistrates Courts Act* gives us the framework for the future."[72]

Beyond the local level, the British Home Secretary has statutory authority to intervene in police administration, police discipline, and suspected cases of corruption and mismanagement. The Home Secretary also provides for the coordination of police services throughout Britain, runs the police college and local police training centres, maintains forensic laboratories, and is ultimately responsible for information management, including national databases and telecommunications.

Britain does not have a national police force.[73] The Metropolitan Police District, with 26 000[74] members, however, serves many centralized functions. The Metropolitan Police District encompasses 32 boroughs and portions of four counties surrounding London. Headquartered at New Scotland Yard, perhaps the most famous address of any police force in the world, the Metropolitan Police District serves as a national repository for information on crime statistics, criminal activity, fingerprints, missing persons, and wayward and delinquent juveniles. The agency also maintains links with INTERPOL and handles requests for information from police agencies in other countries.

In 1992, the National Criminal Intelligence Service (NCIS), charged with intelligence gathering and record keeping, began operation in England.[75] Likened by some to the American FBI, few real similarities exist—primarily because NCIS agents do not have an operational role but function only as staff officers to exchange information on criminal activity with other police agencies throughout England.

In 1948, the Police College opened at Ryton-upon-Dunsmore. The Police College was designed to enhance professionalism among the nation's constables. The training it provided made possible professional advancement within police ranks. In 1960, the college relocated to Bramshill. Known today by its new name, the Police Staff College at Bramshill serves as an international model for police management training.[76]

Traditionally, British police officers have gone on patrol unarmed, except for a nightstick or billy club. Events in the 1980s, especially terrorist attacks on civilian targets including London's Heathrow Airport, led to a reassessment of traditional policy. That reassessment continues today, although most beat constables remain unarmed. Weapons are kept

## BOX 14.2    Theory into Practice

## Arming the British Police

In a tradition dating back to the days of the "Wild West," North American law enforcement officers routinely carry guns. Expertise with a handgun or rifle has long been regarded as a sign of accomplishment among police ranks. The development of a well-financed and often brutal drug subculture,[1] however, has left many police officers feeling outgunned. In a tragic Florida shootout several years ago, three FBI agents were killed by heavily armed bank robbers. The agents' traditional revolver-type sidearms were no match for the robbers' automatic pistols and machine guns. Since then, most law enforcement agencies have increased the "firepower" available to their agents by issuing 9-mm semi-automatic pistols. This change has occurred simultaneously in the United States and in Canada. As a consequence, Canadian law enforcement officers today are routinely well-armed.

In contrast to the Canadian situation,[2] the police of England (with the exception of those guarding international airports, a few highly sensitive locations, and some violence-prone inner-city neighbourhoods) do not carry weapons beyond a simple "billy club." The typical British municipal police department maintains several handguns under lock and key for use only in emergencies.[3] In fact, only recently have British officers been authorized to use a weapon under any circumstances, and firearms practice was not a routine part of law enforcement training until recently in England.

Today, all British police forces have firearms units, and the deployment of armed officers has increased in recent years. The London Metropolitan Police introduced Armed Response Vehicles (ARVs) in 1991, and many police forces have followed its lead. In London, each ARV contains three uniformed officers, who are members of the elite SO19 Tactical Firearms section. They continually patrol areas of the city where they are most likely to be needed. The officers carry both Glock 17 semi-automatic handguns, and Heckler & Koch MP5 9-mm carbines. According to the SO19 webpage, weapons were called into service 1440 times in 1999, an increase of 990 per cent over their first year of operation.[4]

The 1993 opening of the "Chunnel," a tunnel linking France and England under the English Channel, became another focus for the British aversion to armed police. Under an agreement between the two countries, French police, typically armed, may not carry weapons on tunnel trains and are permitted to have weapons only in a controlled zone at the tunnel's mouth. They have to surrender their weapons if they leave the area.[5]

There are a number of significant reasons for the British reluctance to arm their police. Of greatest significance may be the fact that British citizens are themselves unarmed. The "right to bear arms" is foreign to English law, and very few guns are in private hands in any part of the country.

## Death Rate (per 100 000 population) from Firearms—1994[6]

| | |
|---|---|
| Australia | 2.65 |
| Sweden | 1.92 |
| England and Wales | 0.41 |
| Canada | 4.31 |
| Japan | 0.05 |
| Switzerland | 5.31 |
| United States | 14.24 |

## QUESTIONS FOR DISCUSSION

1. What might happen if Canadian police were unarmed? Would there be more crime? More violence? Why or why not?

2. Do you think it will be necessary for most British police officers to eventually carry handguns? Why or why not?

---

[1]See: Oscapella, E. (1998). *The Relationship Between Illegal Drugs and Firearms: A Literature Review Conducted for the Department of Justice*. Ottawa: Department of Justice.
[2]In 1998, the Royal Newfoundland Constabulary became the last major North American police force to add sidearms to their uniform. Prior to this, sidearms were kept at the police station or in the trunk of their patrol vehicles.
[3]CBS Early Morning News. (1989, March 17).
[4]Available at the time of writing at **www.met.police.uk/so19/so19_armed_ response.htm**
[5]Chunnel Patrol. (1992, March/April). *Criminal Justice Europe*, p. 3.
[6]Krug, E.G., Powell, K.E., and Dahlberg, L.L. (1998). Firearm-Related Deaths in the United States and 35 Other High- and Upper-middle-income Countries. *International Journal of Epidemiology*, 27(2), pp. 214–221.

on hand in local police stations and can be issued upon the order of senior police personnel. Officers who routinely patrol highly congested areas, including those with considerable international traffic such as major airports, are now armed with handguns and automatic weapons as a precaution against terrorist attack. In emergencies, local chief constables are authorized to call on the military for armed assistance. Even so, support continues to grow for British police to routinely carry sidearms as part of their everyday equipment. Yet, former Scotland Yard chief Ken Hyder warns that "carrying guns as a normal part of equipment will lead to accidental shootings of bystanders as well as suspects." "Arming the police in a routine way," says Hyder, "would have two other effects—it would distance them from the public, whom they need to provide them with information and support, and it would encourage more villains to arm themselves."[77]

Evidentiary standards, such as the Canadian exclusionary rule, do not apply to the British police. British courts have not utilized precedent-setting decisions to carve out individual rights for citizens who face apprehension and criminal prosecution to the same extent as Canadian courts. What they have done, through judicial conferences, is to draw up "directions" for acceptable police procedure. A key document to emerge from such conferences was the *Judges' Rules and Administrative Directions*, drawn up in 1964. Rules such as the ones contained in this document have the weight of law even though they are technically only administrative regulations. Although offenders may not be released when incriminating evidence is gathered inappropriately, as may happen in Canada, improper actions by police officers can be grounds for reprimand or dismissal.

In 1995, British police began using the world's first national DNA database. It was hailed as "the biggest advance in the fight against crime since the use of fingerprints." As of February 2003, the database held 1.7 million records; however, the plan is to expand this database to 2.6 million records by 2004.[78] The 1994 CJA gives police officers the authority to collect and retain "non-intimate" biological specimens without the consent of anyone charged with a crime. Records in the database are based on information about convicted criminals and unsolved crimes; however, the database may also include information about investigations other than criminal investigations.

## Courts in Britain

Given our historical ties to England, it is not surprising that the British court system and our two models of the judiciary share many common characteristics, and yet there are a number of contrasts between the actual Canadian and English judicial processes (see Figure 14–2). For example, Canadians visiting the Old Bailey, the major court in London, will be struck by by the differences in style and in some of the differences in court procedure. Yet, the hierarchical and interrelated natures of the Canadian and English systems are very similar. For example, both systems share a clear distinction between the *trial* and the *appellate* functions of the court. In addition, in Canada we have a distinction between *provincial* and *federal* courts that does not exist in the British court system.

In England, at the lowest level of the criminal justice system, are the approximately 900 *magistrates' courts*—similar to our provincial/territorial criminal courts. Magistrates' courts are staffed by unpaid lay justices who are not required to have formal training in the law. Unlike in Canada, magistrates sit as a body, usually a group of three, and hear cases without a jury. While they are unpaid, they are compensated for expenses and loss of earnings. Alternatively, a magistrates' court may sit with a District Judge, who is a lawyer by training, and is paid by the state to sit as a magistrate. District judges usually decide more complex summary matters. The use of lay magistrates reflects the historical and continued influence of laypersons in the British judiciary system.

The physical layout in a magistrates' court is structured but more informal than in the higher courts.

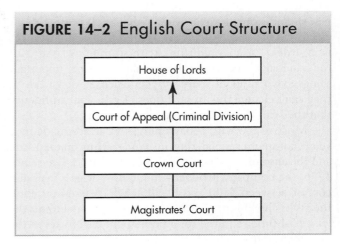

**FIGURE 14–2 English Court Structure**

House of Lords

↑

Court of Appeal (Criminal Division)

Crown Court

Magistrates' Court

Magistrates wear formal attire but do not wear the wigs or gowns found in the higher courts. A magistrates' court could be described as the "people's court," where verbal protocol and decorum are more relaxed than in the higher courts.

While magistrates' courts generally try less serious cases in the same way that summary offences are tried in Canada, criminal defendants charged with certain major crimes may waive the right to trial by jury and be tried at this level. It has been estimated that magistrates' courts handle 95 to 98 per cent of all criminal cases in England and Wales.[79] In Canada, it is estimated that provincial courts handle approximately 90 per cent of all criminal cases. Within the magistrates' courts, certain courts are designated "Youth Courts," and these courts process the majority of youthful offenders (ages 12 to 18) who are apprehended for criminal law violations.

Although English common law originally provided for hearings before a grand jury, the grand jury system was abolished by parliamentary action in 1933. Magistrates' courts have taken over some of the functions of the grand jury, including that of binding over serious offenders for trial by higher courts. Magistrates are limited in their sentencing authority to a maximum of six months' imprisonment. In serious cases, however, they are able to refer convicted defendants to higher courts for sentencing.

Persons charged with major offences may be bound over for trial in a *Crown court* after an initial hearing (called a preliminary inquiry) by a magistrate. Created in 1971,

---

BOX 14.3 **Theory into Practice**

## Tradition in English Courts

The handmade, curled horsehair and silk wigs that English judges and barristers wear while in courtrooms first became fashionable in the 1680s. Many traditionalists claim that wigs lend authority to practitioners of the law, while others say that they're mere remnants of a bygone formal era and should be discarded. Like most social institutions in Britain, however, the legal profession is steeped in tradition, and tradition dictates that—in addition to wigs—gowns, robes, breeches, stockings, court shoes, and buckles must be worn by criminal court judges.

A recent poll of British jurors found that most feel more confident about judicial proceedings when they see wigs worn by officials in court. Even so, many now suggest that it is time for courtroom personnel to adopt modern forms of dress. Still others suggest that a shift of focus is in order. "You would think with so much wrong with the criminal justice system they would have more important things to worry about," says barrister Michael Mansfield. "If they can't change the dress, it doesn't give you confidence that they can change anything else," he adds.

Most of the wigs today's judges wear are made by a small company specializing in handcrafting named Ede and Ravenscroft. Located in London's Chancery Lane since 1726, the company produces about 1000 wigs a year at a cost of between $500 and $2,500 each, depending upon the style. Techniques for making the wigs, including the length of time required for a permanent curl to set in the horsehair, remain closely guarded secrets.

QUESTIONS FOR DISCUSSION

1. If you were a British citizen, do you think you would vote to retain traditional modes of dress for British judges and barristers? Why or why not?

2. Superior courts in Canada typically require lawyers and judges to appear in robes. Lower courts merely require somewhat formal attire, but robes are not to be worn. Could Canadian courts benefit from greater formality—perhaps following the English example of wigged justices? On the other hand, might less formality in all Canadian courtrooms be better? Why?

In keeping with tradition, British judges still wear the obligatory "wig" when sitting on the bench.

Crown courts are headed by justices appointed by the king or queen on the recommendation of the Lord Chancellor. Twelve-member juries hear Crown court cases. As in Canada, but unlike the United States, jury selection tends to be quick and jurors are seldom challenged. Each side is only permitted three peremptory challenges. Canadian prosecutors and defence are allowed up to 20 peremptory challenges. Conviction requires only a majority consensus, not unanimous agreement among jurors.

Tradition dictates considerable formality at all court levels. Crown court judges and counsel both wear powdered wigs, gray and curled, and black flowing robes. The wigs for the lawyers sit like modest hats on the back of their heads while judges wear a fuller wig that extend, down to their shoulders. Verbal give and take is highly structured and polite. Judges are addressed as "my Lord" or "your Lordship" and they sit in a high position. Sharp exchanges between the bench and counsel almost never occur, and lawyers are expected to treat one another with respect.

Unlike in Canada, the accused does not sit with his or her lawyer but in the "dock," which is elevated so that he or she can be seen by all. The accused is accompanied by a uniformed police officer. The defendant's lawyer sits at a separate table near the centre of the courtroom.

Crown courts also hear appeals from magistrates' courts. Appeals are heard without a jury. Petitions from magistrates' courts that concern questions of law sometimes go directly to an appellate court called the high court. The high court has three divisions: (1) the Queen's Bench, (2) Family Court, and (3) the Chancery. The Chancery Division deals with matters of inheritance, trusts, property, and so on, while the Family Court concerns itself with marriages, divorces, adoption, and the like. The section of the high court that focuses on criminal matters is the divisional court of the Queen's Bench. Like other divisions of the high court, the Queen's Bench sits without a jury when hearing criminal appeals.

Another intermediate appellate court occupies a level above the high court. Called the *Court of Appeal*, it has two divisions: one civil and one criminal. The Court of Appeal consists of 16 lord justices of appeal and is headed by a judge called the *Master of the Rolls*. Criminal appeals not resolved by the high court may go to the Court of Appeal. Appeals involving the sentencing decisions made by the magistrates' or Crown courts can go directly to the criminal division of the Court of Appeal.

At the apex of the appellate process stands the *House of Lords*. While the House of Lords sits as one of the houses of Parliament, a subset of the House contains the 12 Law Lords. The House of Lords may hear appeals from both the Queen's Bench and the criminal division of the Court of Appeal. An appeal to the House will be heard only by those members who specialize in the appeals process. Although the House of Lords is the highest appellate court in Britain, it has nothing like the power of the Canadian Supreme Court. Acts of Parliament are inviolate and cannot be "struck down" or significantly modified by judicial interpretation. In fact, while the right to appeal exists, appeals are rarely heard at this level and convictions are rarely overturned.

## Corrections in England

The British correctional system operates under the *Prison Act* of 1964 and the *Young Offenders Institution Statutory Instrument*, passed in 1988. The correctional system is under the administrative control of the Home Secretary who makes appointments to the national Prison Board, which in turn sets policy for the Prison Department. The Prison Department oversees the activities of the nation's prisons, the parole board, and probation and after-care services. A separate agency, the Board of Visitors, permits lay volunteers to serve on hearing boards attached to individual prisons. Each Board of Visitors is empowered to hear alleged violations of prison regulations and is expected to prepare a yearly report on prison conditions.

Three kinds of prisons exist in England: short-term, medium-term, and long-term. Short-term institutions house offenders serving less than 18 months, while medium-term institutions hold persons sentenced to between 18 months and four years. Long-term prisons hold prisoners sentenced to more than four years. Inmates in all British prisons are expected to work, although meaningful work programs are not available for everyone.[80]

Since the 1970s, Britain's penal system has been regularly criticized for its handling of prisoners. In fact, Fairchild reports the United Kingdom has been involved in more cases

**FIGURE 14–3** International Incarceration Rates, Selected Countries, 2003.

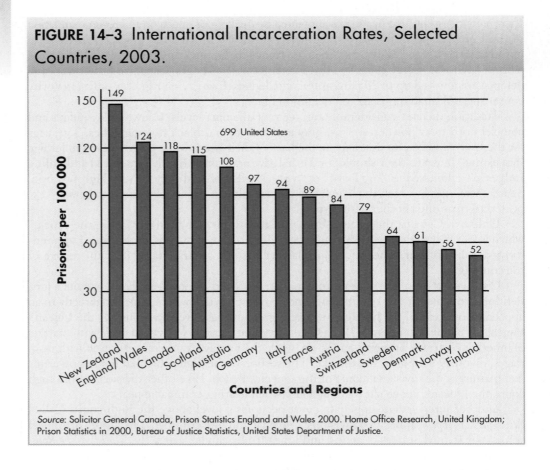

*Source*: Solicitor General Canada, Prison Statistics England and Wales 2000. Home Office Research, United Kingdom; Prison Statistics in 2000, Bureau of Justice Statistics, United States Department of Justice.

appearing before the European Court of Human Rights than any other country.[81] Furthermore, in the face of growing crime fears, members of Parliament have come under increasing pressure to require longer and more frequent prison sentences for many offenders. Growing crime rates, high levels of unemployment, increased drug use, and the development of poverty-ridden ghetto-like areas in many of the nation's large cities have all contributed to a public perception of unnecessary leniency in the criminal justice system. (See Figure 14–3 for 2003 international incarceration rates in selected countries.) The 1994 CJA, passed in response to growing public concerns about crime, mandated increased sentences for a variety of crimes, and the building of six new privately run prisons to handle the increase in prison populations expected to result.

As in Canada, the call for longer sentences has come up against the reality of prison overcrowding. The British prison population as of January 31, 2003, was about 70 909 inmates (including 3618 women)—an approximately 7-per-cent increase over the previous year.[82] The recent growth in the prison population reflects an ongoing trend of increasing numbers dating back to at least 1991.[83]

While an active prison reform movement exists in Britain, it faces many barriers. Many British prisons are antiquated, and some have been described as "… dilapidated to the point of hazardousness."[84] Unfortunately, the financial crisis that the country has experienced for the past few decades provides little hope for widespread and extensive modernization of existing prisons.

# THE UNITED STATES CRIMINAL JUSTICE SYSTEM

The United States is Canada's closest neighbour, and its strongest cultural influence. Developments in the criminal justice system of the United States typically have a significant influence on developments arising in Canada. The similarities between the two systems are quite striking. However, notable differences also exist.

Both Canada and the United States are federal jurisdictions, with responsibility for criminal justice in each country divided between the federal and regional governments. Both jurisdictions have inherited the English common-law legal system, and both countries sport a judiciary that oversees the justice system through the application of a bill of rights.

## Crime Rates: The Results of a 2000 Study

A *Juristat* comparison of police-reported crime rates between Canada and the United States revealed that, in 2000, the rates of violent crime were much higher in the U.S., while the rates of property crime were generally higher in Canada.[85] The national homicide rate in Canada in that year was 1.8 homicides per 100 000 citizens, while the U.S. homicide rate was three times higher at 5.5 homicides per 100 000. Similarly, the aggravated assault rate in the U.S. was more than twice that in Canada. The robbery rate in the U.S. was 65 per cent higher than that in Canada. On the other hand, there were 30-per-cent more burglaries and motor vehicle thefts per 100 000 citizens in Canada than in the United States. The arson rate was also 40 per cent higher in Canada than in the U.S. The only property offence category showing more per capita offending in the United States was theft.

The number of arrests for drug offences, impaired driving, and prostitution are also significantly higher in the U.S. A comparison of crime rates in large metropolitan areas in the two countries showed higher homicide rates in almost all the major American centres studied, while in Vancouver and Winnipeg, the rates of break-and-enter offences and motor vehicle thefts were higher than in any of the nine major U.S. centres included in the study.

## Modern Criminal Law in the United States

While Canada has a uniform criminal code enacted by the federal government, and that applies across the entire country, most criminal law in the U.S. is created and enforced by state jurisdictions. Each state has enacted its own penal code. The *United States Code* (USC) embodies the federal criminal law.

American criminal law maintains a distinction between felonies and misdemeanours, a distinction long since abandoned in Canadian criminal law. Felonies are serious crimes. This category includes offences such as murder, rape, aggravated assault, robbery, burglary, and arson. People convicted of felonies are usually subject to a more severe range of penalties than those convicted of lesser offences.

Misdemeanours are relatively minor crimes, consisting of offences such as petty theft, simple assault, breaking and entering, the possession of burglary tools, disorderly conduct, disturbing the peace, filing a false crime report, and writing bad cheques. Offences that are misdemeanours in some jurisdictions may be felonies in others. Typically, people who commit misdemeanours are subject to lesser penalties, including shorter maximum periods of incarceration, typically one year or less in duration. In actuality, most misdemeanants receive an alternative sentence such as a fine or probation. Normally, a police officer cannot arrest a person for a misdemeanour unless the crime was committed in the officer's presence.

# The Police in the United States

The historical development of the police in the U.S. mirrors that in Canada to a significant degree. However, some differences have arisen between the two countries. Policing reflects the division of responsibilities among the federal, state, and local authorities in the U.S. The variety of police agencies is even more diverse than that found in this country.

## Federal Policing

There are 21 separate federal law enforcement agencies distributed among eight U.S. government services. The best known of the federal police agencies is the Federal Bureau of Investigation (FBI). The FBI began in 1908 as the Bureau of Investigation, tasked with the investigation of antitrust violations, bankruptcy fraud, and the pursuit of federal fugitives. However, under the directorship of J. Edgar Hoover, the Bureau expanded its mandate, taking control of the identification of criminals, the development of a national crime laboratory, and eventually taking on a lead role in the war against gangsters during the 1920s and 1930s.

Today, the FBI fulfills a variety of investigative and support functions. The Counterterrorism Division consolidates all FBI counterterrorism initiatives. It acts as the lead agency in investigating major national terrorist incidents, such as the September 11, 2001 attacks, and the Oklahoma City bombing. The FBI also has a Criminal Investigation Division that investigates organized crime, but this division also becomes involved in investigating violent crimes and property crimes of an interstate nature, as well as kidnappings and bank robberies. In addition to these direct investigatory divisions, the FBI has a Laboratory Division, and a Criminal Justice Information Services Division that provides services to police agencies across the United States. The Training Division is responsible not only for training FBI agents, but also for providing training that is accessed by police agencies throughout the U.S. and around the world.

The FBI runs 56 field offices, and employs 27 800 people, including 11 400 special agents. With an annual budget of US\$3.5 billion per year, the FBI's jurisdiction extends to more than 200 specific crimes and certain broad areas of criminal activity.[86] Recruitment and training standards are very high.

## State Level and Local Agencies

State law enforcement agencies can be divided generally into two types. In some states, a centralized model is employed whereby the tasks of criminal investigations are combined with the patrol of state highways. These centralized agencies assist local law enforcement agencies when requested to do so, operate identification bureaus, maintain a criminal record repository, patrol the highways, and provide training for municipal and county police agencies. A second model of state policing is a decentralized model, where, typically, a clear distinction is drawn between traffic enforcement on state highways and other state-level law enforcement functions through the creation of at least two separate agencies. Under the decentralized model, a state highway patrol agency confines itself to traffic enforcement on the state's freeways and other major thoroughfares, while a separate bureau of investigation has a range of investigative responsibilities throughout the state. Many jurisdictions also have separate state law enforcement agencies responsible for such matters as wildlife laws and park policing.

As in Canada, most policing occurs at the local level in the U.S. Major municipalities have their own police agencies, and each country typically has an elected local sheriff who operates a department responsible for unincorporated areas and the county jail. While some municipalities have huge police agencies, like New York's Police Department with 37 000 officers, others employ only one or two officers.[87]

## American Criminal Courts

Two types of courts function in the American criminal justice system: (1) state courts and (2) federal courts. The state courts hear cases involving violations of state law. Federal courts typically hear issues involving federal law, but they also hear cases involving conflict between local or state statutes and constitutional guarantees, especially those found in the American *Bill of Rights*.

Since most criminal law involves state law, it is the state courts that carry the bulk of criminal case processing. Most states employ two levels of trial court, one deciding less serious matters, or handling misdemeanour cases, while another acts as a superior trial court of general jurisdiction, handling more serious cases. Many states have an intermediate appellate court (often called a court of appeals), and all have a supreme court that sits at the top of the state court hierarchy. While some lower-court judges are elected in some states, all higher-court and federal judges are appointed.

The apex of the American criminal justice system is the U.S. Supreme Court. It is composed of nine judges nominated by the President of the United States and confirmed by the Senate. The Court hears appeals arising from the U.S. courts of appeals, and from the state supreme courts. In reality, very few appeals are actually heard by the top court. Of approximately 5000 requests for review received by the Court each year, only about 200 are actually heard.

The prosecution of cases in state courts is carried out by prosecuting attorneys, known also as district attorneys, solicitors, state's attorneys, county attorneys, or commonwealth attorneys. Federal prosecutions are carried out by U.S. attorneys who are appointed to their positions. Except for these U.S. attorneys, and the solicitors in four U.S. states, the typical prosecutor is an elected official.[88] Generally, the district attorney employs a staff of deputy district attorneys to carry out the day-to-day business of prosecuting cases in court. Defence lawyers are either attorneys in private practice, court-appointed counsel, or public defenders.

## Sentencing and Corrections

American courts have opted for greater structure in sentencing than have Canadian courts. Numerous jurisdictions have adopted highly restrictive sentencing guidelines. These guidelines are usually in grid form, whereby the sentencing judge simply lines up the offence with the number of prior convictions and is then provided with an appropriate sentence (or narrow range of permissible sentences). Some jurisdictions have adopted other forms of mandatory sentencing, including three-strikes laws that require a life (or other lengthy) sentence for a third conviction for a serious or violent crime.

One American sentencing option that is rare to the Western world is the death penalty. Today, 38 of the 50 states and the federal government have capital punishment laws.[89] Most capital cases are first-degree murder cases. However, enactment of the *Violent Crime Control and Law Enforcement Act* of 1994 plus the 2001 *USA Patriot Act* resulted in a significant increase in the number of federal offences punishable by death. The list now includes a total of about 60 offences. On October 1, 2002, a total of 3697 offenders were under sentence of death in the United States.[90] The latest statistics show that 98.5 per cent of those on death row are male, 45 per cent are white, 9 per cent are Hispanic, 45 per cent are African American, and 2 per cent are of other races (mostly Native American and Pacific Islander).[91]

There are approximately 84 federal prisons, 1500 state prisons, and a further 3365 locally operated jails in the United States today. Combined, these institutions housed 1 962 220 inmates on December 31, 2001.[92] The United States has the highest incarceration rate of any Western nation. American prisons are very large by Canadian standards. One out of every four state institutions is a large maximum-security prison with a population approaching 1000 inmates. As might be expected, prison overcrowding is an even greater problem in the United States than it is in Canada.

The move towards a retributive penal policy has been even more pronounced in the United States than in Canada. This has resulted in massive increases in the American prison population in recent years. In 2001, there were 470 inmates per 100 000 U.S. residents.[93] This figure is up from 292 per 100 000 as recently as 1990. In Canada, there were 133 inmates per 100 000 citizens in 2001.[94] The result of recent "get tough" attitudes that are so pervasive throughout the U.S. has been a de-emphasis of probation and parole, and an increased reliance on incarceration.

# INTERNATIONAL CRIMINAL JUSTICE ORGANIZATIONS

The first international conference on criminology and criminal justice met in London in 1872.[95] The London conference evolved out of emerging humanitarian concerns about the treatment of prisoners. Human rights, the elimination of corporal punishment, and debates over capital punishment occupied the conference participants. Although other meetings were held from time to time, little agreement could be reached among those in the international community on criminal etiology, justice paradigms, or the philosophical and practical bases for criminal punishment and rehabilitation. Finally, in 1938 the International Society for Criminology (ISC) was formed to bring together people from diverse cultural backgrounds who shared an interest in social policies relating to crime and justice. In its early years, membership in the ISC consisted mostly of national officials and academicians with close government ties.[96] As a consequence, many of the first conferences (called International Congresses) sponsored by the ISC strongly supported the status quo and were devoid of any significant recommendations for change or growth.

Throughout the 1960s and 1970s, the ISC was strongly influenced by a growing worldwide awareness of human rights. About the same time, a number of international organizations began to press for an understanding of the political and legal processes through which deviance and crime came to be defined. Among them were the Scandinavian Research Council for Criminology (formed in 1962), the Criminological Research Council (created in 1962 by the Council of Europe), and other regional associations concerned with justice issues.

A number of contemporary organizations and publications continues to focus world attention on criminal justice issues. Table 14–3 lists some of the better-known organizations. Perhaps the best-known modern centre for the academic study of cross-national criminal justice is the International Centre of Comparative Criminology at the University of Montreal. Established in 1969, the centre serves as a locus of study for criminal justice professionals from around the world and maintains an excellent library of international criminal justice information. The University of Illinois at Chicago's Office of International Criminal Justice has also become a well-known contributor to the study of comparative criminal justice. In conjunction with the University's Center for Research in Law and Justice, the office publishes the newsletter *Criminal Justice International* and sponsors study tours of various nations.

There are many sources of contemporary information on criminal justice agencies and activities around the world. They include (with their sponsor/publisher) *International Annals of Criminology* (ISC), *International Review of Criminal Policy* (United Nations), *International Journal of Criminal Policy* (United Nations), *International Journal of Penal Law* (International Association of Penal Law), *International Journal of Comparative and Applied Criminal Justice* (Wichita State University), *International Journal of Criminology and Penology* (Academic Press), *Victimology: An International Journal* (National Institute of Victimology), *Howard Journal of Criminal Justice* (Howard League for Penal Reform), *International Review of Criminal Police* (INTERPOL), and *International Security* (UNISAF Publications Ltd.).

**TABLE 14–3** Historical and Modern International Criminal Justice Organizations

The International Society of Criminology
The International Federation of Senior Police Officers
Scandinavian Research Council for Criminology
Criminological Research Council (Council of Europe)
International Association of Youth Magistrates
International Commission of Jurists
International Association of Penal Law
International Society of Social Defense
Amnesty International
International Chiefs of Police
International Criminal Police Organization (INTERPOL)
International Prisoners Aid Association
Howard League for Penal Reform
United Nations Crime Prevention and Criminal Justice Program
Europol

In 1995, the Mitre Corporation in McLean, Virginia, began an internet service on the World Wide Web to provide information about the United Nations Crime Prevention Branch. Called UNOJUST, for United Nations Online Justice Information System, the service holds much promise as an online provider of international criminal justice information. Similarly, the International Centre for Criminal Law Reform and Criminal Justice Policy is a UN-affiliated institute that operates a website that allows access to publications and information about programs involving criminal justice and criminal law reform throughout the world.

## The Role of the United Nations in Criminal Justice

The United Nations (UN), composed of 185 member states and based in New York City, is the largest and most inclusive international body in the world. From its inception in 1945, the UN has been very interested in international crime prevention and world criminal justice systems. A UN resolution entitled the *International Bill of Human Rights* supports the rights and dignity of all persons who come into contact with the criminal justice system.

One of the best-known specific United Nations' recommendations on criminal justice is its Standard Minimum Rules for the Treatment of Prisoners, adopted in 1955 at the first United Nations Congress on the Prevention of Crime and the Treatment of Offenders. The Rules call for the fair treatment of prisoners, and include recognition of the basic humanity of all inmates and specific standards for housing, nutrition, exercise, and medical care. Follow-up surveys conducted by the UN have shown that the Rules have considerably influenced national legislation and prison regulations throughout the world.[97] Although the Rules do not have the weight of law, unless adopted and enacted into local legislation, they carry the strong weight of tradition, and at least one expert claims that "there are indeed those who argue that the Rules have entered the *corpus* of generally customary human rights law, or that they are binding … as an authoritative interpretation of the human rights provisions of the United Nations charter."[98]

A more recent, but potentially significant, set of recommendations can be found in the UN Code of Conduct for Law Enforcement Officials. The Code calls upon law enforcement officers throughout the world to be cognizant of human rights in the performance of their duties and specifically proscribes the use of torture and other abuses. In late 1997, Secretary-General Kofi Annan received approval of his visionary plan for restructuring and reorienting the UN. One of the plans approved was the creation of a new, cabinet-level "Office" that would be responsible for "all matters concerned with crime prevention, criminal justice, and international control of narcotics."[99]

The United Nations World Crime Surveys provide a global portrait of criminal activity. Seen historically, the Surveys have shown that crimes against property are most characteristic of nations with developed economies (where crimes against property constitute 82 per cent of all reported crime), while crimes against the person occur much more frequently in developing countries (where crimes against the person account for 43 per cent of all crime).[100]

Through its Crime Prevention and Criminal Justice Program, the United Nations continues to advance the cause of crime prevention and to disseminate useful criminal justice information. The Program's 40-member State Commission on Crime Prevention and Criminal Justice, and its secretariat, the Crime Prevention and Criminal Justice Branch of the United Nations Offices at Vienna, provide forums for ongoing discussions of justice practices around the world. The Program has regional links throughout the world, sponsored by supportive national governments that have agreed to fund the Program's work. The European Institute for Crime Prevention and Control (HEUNI), for example, provides the Program's regional European link in a network of institutes operating throughout the world. Other network components include the United Nations Interregional Crime and Justice Research Institute (UNICRI), which moved its operations from Rome to Turin, Italy, in 1998; an Asian regional institute (UNAFEI) in Tokyo, Japan; ILANUE, based in San Jose, Costa Rica, which focuses on crime problems in Latin America and the Caribbean; an African institute (UNAFRI) in Kampala, Uganda; Australia's AIC in Canberra; an Arabic institute (ASSTC) in Riyadh, Saudi Arabia; and other centres in Siracusa, Italy, and in Vancouver and Montreal (see above).[101]

At its formation, the Crime Prevention and Criminal Justice Program announced as its goals:

> 1) the prevention of crime within and among states; 2) the control of crime both nationally and internationally; 3) the strengthening of regional and international co-operation in crime prevention, criminal justice and the combating of transnational crime; 4) the integration and consolidation of the efforts of member states in preventing and combating transnational crime; 5) more efficient and effective administration of justice, with due respect for the human rights of all those affected by crime and all those involved in the criminal justice system; and 6) the promotion of the highest standards of fairness, humanity, justice and professional conduct.[102]

In 1995, the United States signed an agreement with the United Nations Crime Prevention and Criminal Justice Branch. The intention of the agreement was to facilitate the international sharing of information and research findings. According to Jeremy Travis, Director of the National Institute of Justice, the agreement would boost "international co-operation on dissemination of knowledge on crime and justice."[103] Under the agreement, the NIJ would join 11 other criminal justice research organizations throughout the world as an associate UN institute.

Continuing a tradition begun in 1885 by the former International Penal and Penitentiary Commission, the United Nations holds an international congress on crime every five years. The first UN crime congress met in Geneva, Switzerland, in 1955. Crime congresses provide a forum via which member states can exchange information and experiences, compare criminal justice practices between countries, find solutions to crime, and take action at an international level. The Tenth UN Congress on the Prevention of Crime and the Treatment of Offenders was held in Vienna, Austria, in 2000. Topics discussed at the meeting included (1) promoting the rule of law and strengthening the criminal justice systems of various nations, (2) the need for international co-operation in combatting transnational crime, and (3) the need for a fair, ethical, and effective system of criminal justice in the promotion of economic and social development.

## Transnational Crime

Transnational crime, or transnational organized crime, and the internationally organized criminal groups that support it promise to be one of the most pressing challenges of the early twenty-first century. In a recent conference in Seoul, Korea, U.S. Assistant Attorney General Laurie Robinson addressed the issue of transnational crime, saying, "The United States recognizes that we cannot confront crime in isolation.... It is clear crime does not respect international boundaries. It is clear crime is global. As recent economic trends demonstrate, what happens in one part of the world impacts all the rest. And crime problems and trends are no different."[104]

The post–Cold War world is more dangerous and less stable than when power was balanced among the superpowers. The power vacuum created in many parts of the world by the fall of the Soviet Union has led to a number of new threats. According to Robert Gelbard, U.S. Assistant Secretary for International Narcotics and Law Enforcement Affairs:

> The main threat now is transnational organized crime. It comes in many forms: drug trafficking, money laundering, terrorism, alien smuggling, trafficking in weapons of mass destruction, fraud and other forms of corruption. These problems all have one critical element in common. They threaten the national security of all states and governments—from our closest allies to those that we find most repugnant. No country is safe. International criminal organizations all seek to establish pliant governments that can be manipulated through bribery and intimidation. They respect no national boundaries and already act with virtual impunity in many parts of the world.[105]

Worse still, entire nations may become rogue countries, or quasi-criminal regimes, where criminal activity runs rampant and wields considerable influence over the national government. In recent years, Russia, for example, appears to be quickly approaching this status through an intertwining of the goals of organized criminal groups and official interests that run to the top levels of government. The number of organized criminal groups operating in Russia is estimated at over 12 000.[106] Emilio Viano, professor of criminology at the American University and an expert on Russian organized crime, notes that "what we have is an immense country practically controlled by organized crime. These groups are getting stronger and stronger and using Russia as a base or their global ventures taking over everything from drugs and prostitution to currency exchange and stealing World Bank and IMF (International Monetary Fund) loans."[107] In 1999, the U.S. federal authorities discovered that more than US$10 billion had passed through the Bank of New York in a major money-laundering scheme run by Russian organized crime.[108] Much of the money may have come from loans paid to Russia that were tied to the IMF almost a year earlier.

The globalization of crime has necessitated the enhanced coordination of law enforcement efforts in different parts of the world and the expansion of local law enforcement activities beyond national borders. Canadian and American police agencies routinely send agents to assist law enforcement officers in other countries that are involved in transnational investigations. Another tool in the fight against transnational crime is extradition. Not all countries, however, are willing to extradite suspects wanted in Canada.

## INTERPOL and Europol

The International Criminal Police Association (**INTERPOL**), headquartered in Lyon, France, traces its origins to the first International Criminal Police Congress of 1914, which met in Monaco. The theme of that meeting was international co-operation in the investigation of crimes and the apprehension of fugitives. INTERPOL, however, did not officially begin operations until 1946, when the end of World War II brought about a new spirit of international harmony.

Today, 176 nations belong to INTERPOL. Canada joined INTERPOL in 1949 after the federal Ministry of Justice assigned the RCMP as the National Central Bureau (NCB) for INTERPOL. As a member of the organization, INTERPOL Ottawa performs a number of functions, including the collection of documents and information from various sources pertaining to international law enforcement and forwarding them to other NCBs and the INTERPOL General Secretariat. In addition, INTERPOL Ottawa works closely with other NCBs to facilitate the tracking and apprehension of criminals who might be operating at an international level. This close co-operation has significantly helped the

**INTERPOL** An acronym for the International Police Association. INTERPOL began operations in 1946 and today has 137 member nations.

BOX 14.5 **Theory into Practice**

## Russian Organized Crime: The Vory v Zakone

"Toronto is considered one of the current strongholds of the Russian mob. The strongest group, according to a confidential report by Canadian intelligence, should be connected to the most powerful organizations, those of Yaponchik, the Taiwanese, and Mogielevitch."[1] On June 8, 1995, Vyacheslav Kirillovich Ivankov (known in Russian as "Yaponchik," or "The Jap") was arrested by the FBI in New York City. Ivankov is reputed to be Russia's most influential *vor*, or organized crime boss. His presence in New York was one of a number of signs that Russian organized crime has rapidly become a major international force. Another was a 1994 visit to Moscow by FBI Director Louis J. Freeh, who used the occasion to announce that Russian organized crime had become a new top priority for U.S. law enforcement agencies.[2]

Russian organized crime, under the leadership of *vory* (the plural form of the word "*vor*"), has existed since at least the eighteenth century. With the dissolution of the Soviet Union, however, organized crime in Russia has flourished. In a speech to the Russian parliament, then Russian leader Boris Yeltsin told legislators, "As the major crime networks … have grown more and more impudent, the law enforcement agencies have virtually assumed a policy of noninterference!"[3] Yeltsin charged that rampant corruption among law enforcement officials had led to the problem.

Visitors to Russia report that organized crime controls large sectors of Russian society—selling everything from bootlegged vodka on city street corners to stolen nuclear weapons across international borders. Bribery is a way of life in modern Russia, and interference from the police is rare. The salary of a criminal investigator is about $160 a month—less than that of a city bus driver. Many experienced police officers have left for jobs in private security, since most of Russia's new entrepreneurs willingly pay high prices for protection for themselves and the goods they manufacture. Bandits are common, and shipments of manufactured goods must be protected by armed men as they wend their way west to European borders.

Organized crime in Russia bears striking resemblances to crime families in the West. At the uppermost level of Russian organized crime are the *vory v zakone*, a Russian phrase meaning "thieves professing the code." The *vory* are the godfathers of Russian organized crime. There are said to be about 387 *vory* throughout Russia (about 100 of whom are currently serving prison sentences). In 1994, the Russian Ministry of Internal Affairs (MVD) detained 45 *vory* for questioning. Since the *vory* are leaders and organizers, and do not commit crimes themselves, however, Russian law rarely applies to them. Russian criminal law remains virtually unchanged since the Soviet days, and Russian police and prosecutors are not able to rely upon American anti-Mafia laws, such as the *Racketeer Influenced and Corrupt Organization Act* (RICO). As Russian police Lt. Col. Nikolai Aulov, an anti-organized crime official in St. Petersburg, puts it, "It's very difficult to convict someone who wasn't doing something with his own hands. The laws are imperfect."[4]

Like Mafia families, Russian organized crime groups are hierarchies. With the *vor* as head, a second-level trusted advisor, or *sovetnik*, channels information between the *vor* and the group's members (*gruppa obespechenie*). The lowest-level group operatives are called *shestiorka*, or bag men and errand boys. They are often recruited from among prisoners and known street hoods, and are charged with carrying out the group's dirty work. Like Mafia bosses, the *vor* live by a strict code.

Until Russian social disorganization is under control, it is likely that Russian organized crime will continue to flourish. Recently, U.S. State Department spokesperson Christine Shelly cautioned law enforcement personnel on the dangers of Russian organized crime. "The rise in organized crime, financial crime, nuclear materials smuggling and drug trafficking are all aspects of that problem … which give us great concern," said Shelly. "The negative effect which crime can have on democratic and economic reform movements not only in Russia but also in the new independent states of the former Soviet Union and the potential that that has for the average citizen to equate crime with a kind of market economy—those are all serious implications of the growing crime problem," she said.[5]

## QUESTIONS FOR DISCUSSION

1. What similarities does organized crime in Russia share with its counterpart in the West? Why do such similarities exist?

2. How might Russian organized crime impact on Canada? What steps can Canadian law enforcement agencies take to prevent Canadian victimization by Russian criminals and their activities?

[1]Nicaso, A. (2001). Le Mafie – Part 14 – Flirting with Power: The Russian Mob is Spreading its Wings in Canada and the U.S. *Tandem – Online Magazine*. Accessed March 16, 2003 at **www.tandemnews.com/viewstory.php?storyid=95&page=3**
[2]Finkenauer, J.O., and Voronin, Y.A. (2001). *The Threat of Russian Organized Crime*. Washington, DC: U.S. Department of Justice.
[3]Hockstader, L. (1995, February 27). Russia's War on Crime: A Lopsided, Losing Battle. *The Washington Post* online.
[4]Ibid.
[5]U.S. Concerned About Russian Crime. (1995, March 6). Reuters online.

RCMP in dealing with offences varying from hostage taking to economic and financial crimes, and to drug trafficking.[109]

To further facilitate its involvement in INTERPOL, the RCMP has liaison officers posted at 19 embassies or high commissions. The officers provide assistance to law enforcement agencies across Canada who might be seeking information on criminal activity in foreign countries. This Foreign Services Directorate also serves to locate victims or witnesses outside of Canada and/or apprehend those who have fled Canadian jurisdiction. For example, INTERPOL Ottawa played a key role in the 1996 capturing of Albert Walker, who embezzled millions of dollars from Canadian clients while posing as a financial advisor in Paris, Ontario, and then fled with his daughter to England. There he attempted to assume a new identity after killing another man. He was eventually caught and convicted in 1998. As of late 1998, he was attempting to be returned to Canada to serve out his sentence and stand trial for 37 counts of fraud and theft. He is still suspected of having hidden vast sums of money, which he is using to try to negotiate a lighter sentence. In addition, he is also appealing his murder conviction of former associate Richard Platt.[110]

INTERPOL's primary purpose is to act as a clearing house for information on offences and suspects who are believed to operate across national boundaries. The organization is committed to "promot(ing) the widest possible mutual assistance between all criminal police authorities within the limits of laws existing in … different countries and in the spirit of the Universal Declaration of Human Rights."[111] INTERPOL does not intervene in religious, political, military, or racial disagreements in participant nations. As a consequence, a number of bombings and hostage situations were not officially investigated until 1984, when INTERPOL pledged itself to the fight against international terrorism. More recently, the world traffic in illegal drugs has also become a major focus of INTERPOL's efforts; however, the new methods of smuggling pose major challenges for INTERPOL. A former British police officer informed an anti-drug conference in Doha, Qatari, that "Interpol spends 60 per cent of its time and resources fighting drug trafficking … trade in illegal drugs is estimated to be second only to the international arms trade, in financial terms … "[112]

In late 2001, INTERPOL's Seventieth General Assembly unanimously adopted the Budapest Anti-terrorism Resolution. The resolution calls for greater police co-operation in fighting international terrorism. As a follow-up to the resolution, INTERPOL's Sixteenth Annual Symposium on International Terrorism took place at the organization's headquarters.

INTERPOL does not have its own field investigators. It draws, instead, upon the willingness of local and national police forces to lend support to its activities. The headquarters staff of INTERPOL consists of around 250 individuals, many with prior police experience, who direct data-gathering efforts around the world and who serve to alert law enforcement organizations to the movement of suspected offenders within their jurisdiction.

The members of the European Union agreed to the establishment of the European Police Office (Europol) in the Maastricht Treaty of February 7, 1992. Based in the Hague, the Netherlands, **Europol** started limited operations in 1994 in the form of the Europol Drugs Unit. Over time, other important law enforcement activities were added to the Europol agenda. The Europol Convention was ratified by all member states in 1998, and Europol commenced full operations the next year. Europol's mission is to improve the effectiveness and co-operation of law enforcement agencies within the member states of the European Union with the ultimate goal of preventing and combatting terrorism, illegal drug trafficking, illicit trafficking in radioactive and nuclear substances, illegal money laundering, trafficking in human beings (including child pornography), and other serious forms of international organized crime. Europol and INTERPOL are committed to inter-agency co-operation, and they work with one another in developing information on international terrorism, drug trafficking, and trafficking in human beings.[113]

# The International Criminal Court

On July 1, 2002, the *Rome Statute of the International Criminal Court* (ICC) entered into force. This statute is an international document signed by nations from around the world, including Canada. Created under the auspices of the United Nations, the ICC is intended

**European Police Office (Europol)** The integrated police-intelligence gathering and dissemination arm of the member nations of the European Union.

to be a permanent criminal court for trying individuals (not countries) who commit the most serious crimes of concern to the international community, such as genocide, war crimes, and crimes against humanity, including the wholesale murder of civilians, torture, and mass rape. The ICC is a global judicial institution, with international jurisdiction, complementing national legal systems around the world. Support for the ICC was developed through the United Nations where, at present, 88 countries have ratified the court's creation. The court officially came into existence after 60 countries ratified the statute in early 2002.

The ICC initiative began after World War II, after unsuccessful efforts to establish an international tribunal to try individuals accused of war crimes.[114] In lieu of such a court, military tribunals were held in Nuremberg, Germany, and Tokyo, Japan, to try those accused of war crimes. Although the 1948 genocide convention[115] called for an international criminal court, efforts to establish a permanent court were delayed for decades by the Cold War and by the refusal of some national governments to accept the court's proposed international legal jurisdiction.

In December 1948, the UN General Assembly (GA) adopted the *Universal Declaration of Human Rights* and the *Convention on the Prevention and Punishment of the Crime of Genocide*. It also called for criminals to be tried "by such international penal tribunals as may have jurisdiction." A number of member states soon asked the United Nations International Law Commission (ILC) to study the possibility of establishing an international criminal court. Development of the ICC was delayed by the Cold War, which took place between the world superpowers — none of which were willing to subject their military personnel or commanders to international criminal jurisdiction in the event of a "hot" war. In 1981, however, the UN General Assembly asked the ILC to consider the creation of an international code of crimes.

The 1992 war in Bosnia-Herzegovina, which involved clear violations of the Genocide and Geneva conventions,[116] heightened world interest in the establishment of a permanent ICC. A few years later, 160 countries participated in the UN Diplomatic Conference of Plenipotentiaries on the Establishment of an International Criminal Court,[117] which was held in Rome. At the end of that conference, member states voted overwhelmingly in favour of the Rome statute, calling for establishment of an ICC.

The United States, however, has rejected the jurisdiction of the ICC, claiming that members of the American military could unjustly become subject to ICC jurisdiction. This concern resulted in the passage of the *American Servicemembers' Protection Act* of 2002 (ASPA), which was brought into force when President Bush signed the *USA Patriot Act* in August 2002. The legislation authorizes the president to use "all means necessary and

International Criminal Court

Canadian Press/Dusan Vranic

appropriate" to release U.S. or Allied personnel from detention by the Court. European leaders have expressed strong disapproval of the American legislation.

Prior to the existence of a true international criminal court, the United Nations established ad hoc tribunals to prosecute officials accused of war crimes. This resulted in the creation of the International Criminal Tribunal for the Former Yugoslavia (ICTY), and an ad hoc tribunal for the prosecution of war crimes committed in Rwanda. At present, former president Slobodan Molosevic of the former Yugoslavia is being tried for alleged war crimes committed during his time in power in the ICTY.

In 2003, the states that ratified the Rome statute elected the judges to sit on the new International Criminal Court. Canada's nominee, Philippe Kirsch, was selected, and now sits as one of the 18 judges.

# SUMMARY

The international perspective has much to contribute to the study of Canadian criminal justice. Law enforcement agencies, court personnel, and correctional officials in Canada can benefit from exposure to innovative crime prevention and investigative and treatment techniques found in other parts of the world. Policy makers, through a study of foreign legal codes and the routine practice of criminal justice in other countries, can acquire a fresh perspective on upcoming decisions in the area of law and justice.

A number of barriers, however, continue to limit the applicability of cross-national studies. One is the continuing unavailability of sufficiently detailed, up-to-date, and reliable international information on crime rates, victimization, and adjudication. Another, more difficult limit is imposed by ethnocentrism. Ethnocentrism, a culturally determined hesitancy on the part of some people to consider any personal or professional viewpoints other than their own, reduces the likelihood for serious analysis of even the limited international information that is available in the area of criminal justice.

Given enough time, most barriers can be overcome. Although political, economic, and ideological differences will remain dominant throughout the world for many years, the globe is shrinking. Advances in communications, travel, and the exchange of all types of information are combining with an exponential growth in technology to produce a worldwide interdependence among nations. As new international partnerships are sought and formed, barriers to understanding will fall. However, part of the challenge will be to balance civil and human rights against crime control efforts.

# DISCUSSION QUESTIONS

1. What benefits can be had from the study of criminal justice systems in other countries? Are there any potential negative consequences of such a study?

2. If you were to study the criminal justice systems of other countries, which nations would you select for analysis? Why?

3. What is "ethnocentrism"? Where does it come from? What purpose does it serve? How can it be overcome? Should it be?

4. It was suggested that the effectiveness of any criminal justice system is less dependent on the model of justice or constitutional law than it is on "the issue of social justice in the application of any set of laws." Do you agree? What issues might we want to explore in light of the statement?

5. What are some of the limitations facing the serious international study of criminal justice today? Do you see any way in which those limitations can be overcome?

6. Do you think the practice of criminal justice in England could benefit from the creation of a precedent-setting exclusionary rule by the courts? Why or why not? How might British courts create such a rule?

# WEBLINKS

www.icpsr.umich.edu/NACJD
## National Archive of Criminal Justice Data
NACJD, a branch of the Inter-university Consortium for Political and Social Research at the University of Michigan, acquires, archives, processes, and provides free access to more than 550 computer-readable criminal justice data collections for research and instruction.

www.csis-scrs.gc.ca
## Canadian Security Intelligence Service
As Canada's national intelligence organization, the fundamental mission of the CSIS is the protection of Canada's national security interests and the safety of Canadians.

www.interpol.com
## INTERPOL (International Criminal Police Organization)
The Interpol website is a virtual reference library and exhibition, providing information on Interpol and what it does—dispelling the myth of the organization as being a top-secret police group—as well as a profile of goods and services designed to assist law enforcement officers in combatting crime.

www.ifs.univie.ac.at/~uncjin/uncjin.html
## UN Crime and Justice Information Network
UNJIN is a global crime prevention and criminal justice information network, which provides a central clearing house for input from non-governmental organizations and scientific institutions.

www.amnesty.org
## The Death Penalty in China: Breaking Records, Breaking Rules
An Amnesty International report, released August 1997.

www.ifs.univie.ac.at/uncjin/mosaic/wcs.html
## Global Report on Crime and Justice
The data sets of the First through Fifth United Nations Surveys of Crime Trends and Operations of Criminal Justice Systems (1970–94) are available from this site.

www.info.gov.hk/police
## Hong Kong Police Force
Homepage of the Hong Kong Police Force, one of the most technologically advanced police forces in the world.

www.ncis.co.uk
## National Criminal Intelligence Service (NCIS)
NCIS develops intelligence on serious and organized crime in the U.K. and throughout the world, and works with both national and international law enforcement agencies and governments.

www.crime-prevention-intl.org
## International Center for the Prevention of Crime
Headquartered in Montreal, ICPC is an international non-governmental organization, created to assist cities and countries in reducing crime and insecurity. The site contains a wealth of information and articles from around the world dealing with such topics as community-based policing, problem solving, partnerships, and prevention strategies and practices.

www.police.uk
## UK Police Service
This site provides links to constabularies in Scotland and Northern Ireland, North England, Wales and South West England, and South East England.

# The Future of Criminal Justice

AP/Wide World Photos

## KEY CONCEPTS

criminalistics
criminalists
ballistics
forensic anthropology
DNA profiling
cybercrime
white-collar crime
occupational crime

corporate crimes
computer crimes
hacker
high-technology crimes
data encryption methods
computer viruses
terrorism

## KEY CASES

*R. v. McNally*
*R. v. F.(S.)*
*R. v. Sharpe*
*R. v. Tessling*

# INTRODUCTION

On February 7, 2002, police descended on a pig farm in Port Coquitlam, a Vancouver suburb, armed with a search warrant. In the months that followed, police would investigate the farm, an area of about 4047 square metres, with a fine-tooth comb. Heavy excavation equipment was brought in and the top layers of soil were sifted. In the end, over 3000 pieces of evidence were obtained from the farm's dirt. Between February and October of 2002, as police gathered more evidence, Robert William Pickton, the owner of the farm, was charged with a total of 15 counts of murder. The Pickton case has become the largest serial-murder investigation in Canadian history. More than 50 women, many of them sex-trade workers, have vanished from Vancouver streets in recent years. The apparent discovery of DNA evidence at the Pickton farm helped resolve the question of where many of these missing women ended up. The search for fragments that would reveal the DNA of victims required painstaking analysis of tons of earth. At its peak, the investigation involved over 90 people, including 30 to 40 police officers, 52 forensic and archaeological experts, as well as numerous archaeology students. Forensic experts helped to identify the victims and to reconstruct the crime scene. The ability to turn what appeared to be a large muddy farm into a rich field of forensic evidence reflects the extent of the changes that have occurred in forensic sciences in recent years. The future will no doubt bring continued advances in the field of criminal investigation.[1]

Breakthroughs in DNA and other forms of forensic analysis are not confined to aiding prosecutorial teams. Donald Marshall, David Milgaard, Richard Norris, and Guy Paul Morin are among the growing number of Canadians who have been exonerated thanks to modern technology.

Emerging technology will change many of the practical aspects of the criminal justice system in this century—from the way in which evidence is gathered to the development of innovative forms of sentencing. Even so, the criminal justice system of the future will probably be much like the system we know today. It will rest upon constitutional mandates and will be responsive to court precedents. The system itself will remain recognizable through its backbone of subsystems: the police, courts, and corrections. Deterrence, apprehension, and reformation will continue to guide the day-to-day operations of criminal justice agencies. New issues will arise, but most of them will be resolved within the context of the question that has guided Canadian criminal justice since its inception: how to ensure public safety while guaranteeing justice in a free society.

Future changes in the fabric of society will also change aspects of the criminal justice system. Changes in demography, ideology, and behaviour, such as illegal drug use, smuggling, organized crime, computer crimes, terrorism, and a greater social acceptance of certain victimless crimes (e.g., gambling), have already occurred and are now firmly rooted in substantial segments of Canadian society.

It is never easy to anticipate future changes. This chapter attempts to identify some of these, and to predict what impact they will have on Canadian criminal justice. Perhaps the two most significant sources of change will be technology and the continuing evolution of society. Throughout history, scientific advances often came before society was ready for them. And when they did, they were denied or suppressed. Today, however, the situation is reversed. Technology is now often the prime mover, forcing social change when new developments occur. Because technology is an important harbinger of change in the modern world, this chapter focuses on the opportunities and threats that technology represents to the justice system.

# TECHNOLOGY AND CRIMINAL JUSTICE

Only a few years ago, such organizations as Crime Stoppers, Neighbourhood Watch, and other crime prevention–based programs relied on community-level co-operation in order to combat crime in their community. Today, many of these grassroots organizations have websites on the internet because the internet has become an inexpensive medium for rapid communication and promotion. On the other hand, online computer services have also become increasingly susceptible to crime. Just as quickly as technology changes, so does the face of crime.

Few would dispute the observation that we live in a world governed by rapid change. Technology and science are the modern-day engines of change, and they continue to run relentlessly forward. The impact of technological and scientific changes on all areas of human life has been dramatic. The automobile and the aircraft have made the world a smaller place, and journeys that would have required months a century ago can now be made in a day. Radio and television have transformed the planet into a "global village," in which every human being can be in touch with events of importance immediately as they happen anywhere around the globe. Computers have dramatically altered the rate at which information is being produced, so much so that storing information has become more important than using it. Future computers, it is hoped, will sort through the accumulated information, allowing us to quickly distinguish the significant from the mundane.

Advancing technology, along with the legislation designed to control it, will create crimes never before imagined. The future will see a race between technologically sophisticated offenders and law enforcement authorities as to who can wield the most advanced skills on either side of the age-old battle between crime and justice.

Technological advances signal both threats and opportunities for the justice field. By the turn of the twentieth century, police callboxes became standard features in many cities, utilizing the then new technology of the telephone to pass along information on crimes in progress or to describe suspects, who had escaped arrest, and their activities. A few years later, police departments across the nation adapted to the rapid growth in the number of private automobiles and the laws governing their use. Motorized patrol, radar, police helicopters, and aircraft allowed police to rapidly respond to criminal activity. Today's citizens' band radios, often monitored by local police and highway patrol agencies in some provinces, and cellular car telephones with direct numbers to police dispatchers, are examples of the continuing trend of police adapting to advances in communications technology.

Technology impacts on criminal justice in many areas. In the United States, the National Law Enforcement Technology Center (NLETC), formerly known as the Technology Assessment Program Information Center (TAPIC), of the National Institute of Justice's Office of Science and Technology, performs yearly assessments of key technological needs and opportunities facing the justice system. The Center is responsible for helping to identify, develop, manufacture, and adopt new products and technologies designed for law enforcement, corrections, and other criminal justice applications.[2] NLETC concentrates on four areas of advancing technology: (1) communications and electronics, (2) forensic science, (3) transportation and weapons, and (4) protective equipment.[3] The Center refers new hardware testing to the Law Enforcement Standards Laboratory (LESL)—a part of the US National Bureau of Standards.

The technological focus of the NLETC is facilitating suspect apprehension and protecting enforcement personnel. But others have pointed to the potential of emerging technologies to treat offenders. Simon Dinitz, for example, has suggested that novel forms of biomedical intervention could serve as innovative treatments, building upon the earlier practices of castration, psychosurgery, and drug treatment.[4] The possibilities are limited only by the imagination,[5] including chemical substances to reform the offender, drugs to enhance the memories of witnesses and victims, and the alteration of the personality through microchip implants.[6] In 2002, for example, a pharmaceutical-medical journal reported results from a test for the effectiveness of the drug Ritalin (methylphenidate) as a means to provide treatment for cocaine addiction.[7] Although the research is in its early stages, the drug holds out promise as a future therapy for cocaine addiction. The potential for scientific advancements that will have an impact on crime prevention and control has never been greater.

# CRIMINALISTICS: PAST, PRESENT, AND FUTURE

The use of technology in the service of criminal investigation is a subfield of criminal justice referred to as **criminalistics**. Criminalistics is the application of scientific techniques to the detection and evaluation of criminal evidence. Police crime scene analysts and laboratory

**criminalistics** The use of technology in the service of criminal investigation; the application of scientific techniques to the detection and evaluation of criminal evidence.

**criminalists** The term applied to police crime scene analysts and laboratory personnel versed in criminalistics.

personnel versed in criminalistics are referred to as **criminalists**. Modern criminalistics began with the need to specifically identify individuals. Early methods of personal identification were notoriously inaccurate. In the 1800s, for instance, one day of the week was generally dedicated to a "parade" of newly arrested offenders during which experienced investigators from distant jurisdictions would scrutinize the convicts, looking for recognizable faces.[8] By the 1840s, the Quetelet system[9] of anthropometry became popular. The Quetelet system depended on precise measurements of various parts of the body to give an overall "picture" of a person for use in later identification.

The first "modern" system of personal identification was created by Alphonse Bertillon.[10] Bertillon was the director of the Bureau of Criminal Identification of the Paris Police Department during the late 1800s. The Bertillon system of identification was based on the idea that certain bodily aspects, such as eye colour, skeletal size and shape, and ear form, did not change substantially after physical maturity had been reached. This sytem combined physical measurements with the then emerging technology of photography. Although photography had been used previously in criminal identification, Bertillon standardized the technique by putting measuring guides beside suspects so that their physical dimensions could be calculated from their photographs and by photographing both front views and profiles of suspects. By using photographs, he could expand his sample without actually having to see these people. He took real-life measurements too, but much of his work involved using photos to look at as many offenders as possible in a short time.

Fingerprints, produced by contact with the ridge patterns in the skin on the fingertips, became the subject of intense scientific study in the mid-1840s. While their importance in criminal investigation today seems obvious, it was not until the 1880s that scientists began to realize that each person's fingerprints were unique and unchangeable over a lifetime. Both discoveries appear to have come from the Englishmen William J. Herschel and Henry Faulds, when they were working in Asia.[11] Some writers have observed that Asiatic lore about finger ridges and their significance extends back to antiquity and suggest that Herschel and Faulds must have been privy to such information.[12] As early as the Tang Dynasty (A.D. 618–906), inked fingerprints in China were being used as personal seals

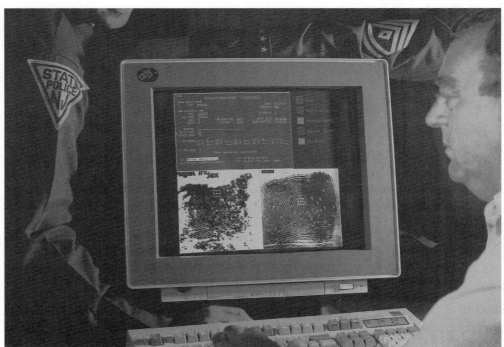

An automated fingerprint ID system in operation. Technology has been a boon to police investigations, although high-tech criminals have often more than kept pace with advances in investigative technology.

on important documents. There is some evidence that the ancient Chinese had classified patterns of the loops and whorls found in fingerprints, and were using them for the identification of criminals as far back as 1000 years ago.[13]

Identifying offenders by their fingerprints was popularized by Sir Francis Galton[14] and officially adopted by Scotland Yard in 1901 and in Canada in 1911. By the 1920s, police departments everywhere were identifying criminals by their fingerprints, and Bertillon's system was quickly replaced. Suspects were fingerprinted and their prints were compared with those lifted from a crime scene. The comparisons typically required a great deal of time and a bit of luck to produce a match. Over time, the fingerprint inventories in Canada became very large, including those of all persons in the armed services and certain branches of federal employment, and the entire inmate population of Canada. So researchers were looking constantly for an efficient way to rapidly compare large numbers of prints. Until the 1980s, the most effective comparisons depended upon classification methods that first automatically eliminated large numbers of prints. As late as 1974, one author lamented: "Considering present levels of technology in other sciences … [the] classification of fingerprints has profited little by technological advancements, particularly in the computer sciences. [Fingerprint comparisons are] limited by the laborious inspection by skilled technicians required to accurately classify and interpret prints. Automation of the classification process and potentially comparison as well would open up fingerprinting to its fullest potential."[15]

Fingerprints remain one of the best types of evidence for placing an individual at a crime scene. Police officers trained in identification gather such evidence. Once the fingerprints are lifted and analyzed, the information can be entered into the national Automated Fingerprint Identification System (AFIS). The system contains fingerprints for some 2.7 million individuals and 70 000 unidentified latent fingerprints from unsolved crimes.[16] The latest technology employs electro-optical scanning systems that digitize live fingerprints, eliminating the need for traditional inking-and-rolling techniques.[17] Other advances in fingerprint identification and matching are also being made. The use of lasers in fingerprint lifting, pioneered in the United States, for example, recently allowed the FBI to detect a 50-year-old fingerprint of a Nazi war criminal on a postcard.[18] Computerization and digitization improve accuracy and reduce the incidence of "false positives" in ongoing comparisons.[19] In 1997, the Ontario Provincial Police (OPP) Forensic Identification Service pioneered the first Argon laser detection of fingerprints. The OPP also became the first police force to introduce the Mobile Crime Unit. Today, the OPP can transport this hi-tech laboratory to the crime scene.[20]

The ability to computerize fingerprint identification systems represents a major step forward for evidence-gathering technology, making it possible for different automated fingerprint identification systems to exchange data. Prior to computerization, the comparison of fingerprint data between AFIS systems was often difficult or impossible. But now police agencies across the nation can share and compare fingerprint information over telephone lines linking their AFIS systems.[21]

Modern criminalistics also depends heavily upon **ballistics**, to analyze weapons, ammunition, and projectiles; medical pathology, to determine the cause of injury or death; **forensic anthropology**, to reconstruct the likeness of a decomposed or dismembered body; forensic entomology, to determine issues such as the time of death; forensic dentistry, to help identify deceased victims and offenders; the photography of crime scenes (now often done with video cameras); plaster and polymer casting of tire tracks, boot prints, and marks made by implements; polygraph (the "lie detector") and voice-print identification; as well as myriad other techniques. Many criminal investigation practices have been thoroughly tested and are now accepted by most courts for the evidence they offer (polygraph and voice-print identification techniques are still being refined and have not yet won the wide acceptance of the other techniques mentioned).

In 2003, there were six RCMP forensic crime laboratories across Canada. The laboratories are staffed by experts who are trained in a variety of the emerging forensic analysis techniques such as biology, counterfeits, chemistry, documentation, firearms, photography, toxicology, and serology.[22]

**ballistics** The analysis of firearms, ammunition, projectiles, bombs, and explosions.

**forensic anthropology** The application of anthropological principles and techniques in the service of criminal investigation.

BOX 15.1 **Justice in Context**

## The Most Pressing Problems Facing the Criminal Justice System Today

Each year, the cabinet ministers at the federal, provincial, and territorial levels, who hold primary responsibility for the justice system, meet in order to set priorities and exchange concerns regarding criminal justice matters. In November 2002, these cabinet ministers addressed many important issues at a meeting in Calgary. Here is an edited version of the subsequent press release:

### Legal Aid

While the provincial and territorial ministers called upon the federal government to return to 50/50 cost sharing for criminal legal aid, the federal government committed to a fair and equitable allocation of legal aid funding. It also agreed to provide resources for criminal legal aid, to develop a mutually agreeable solution for dealing with court-ordered counsel and fees, and to address innovative ways to deliver legal aid services.

### Preliminary Inquiries

There was strong support among many provinces and territories for the elimination of preliminary inquiries. Recognizing that some governments wished to retain the procedure, all governments agreed to examine alternatives to preliminary inquiries and to minimize the number of offences for which they are available.

### Intermittent Sentences

The provincial and territorial Ministers of Justice called on the federal government to amend the *Criminal Code* to more clearly define when intermittent sentences can be imposed and to allow the provinces and territories to establish an alternative to custodial intermittent sentences, whereby intermittent sentences could be served by participation in a non-custodial program.

### Conditional Sentences

A major concern is the application of conditional sentences in inappropriate circumstances, such as for serious violent and sexual offences and particularly offences against children. The House of Commons Standing Committee on Justice and Human Rights is expected to issue a report pertaining to conditional sentencing next year.

### Protection of Children

All governments concede that better protection of children from sexual exploitation, including child pornography, is needed. Concern exists over current laws that deal with written child pornography and the defence of artistic merit. Some believe that the age of sexual consent should be raised to protect children from sexual predators. The child pornography provisions of the *Criminal Code* may be reformed, and a new offence may be created to deal with the sexual exploitation of youth under 18.

### Intoxicating Inhalants

A federal/provincial/territorial working group will address this issue and consider whether creating a new criminal offence pertaining to the sale of intoxicating inhalants would be an effective deterrent.

### Cross-examination by Self-represented Accused

All criminal justice ministers were supportive of Manitoba's proposal to limit the right of self-represented accused to personally cross-examine victims of criminal harassment. The federal Minister of Justice said an amendment addressing this issue could be included in forthcoming legislation dealing with children and other vulnerable witnesses.

### Victims of Crime

Ministers stressed the need to examine all avenues to protect victims and asked the federal/provincial/territorial working group to explore the advantages and practical implications of proposed options.

### *Youth Criminal Justice Act*

Provincial and territorial ministers, with the exception of Quebec, expressed concern about the cost and time frame of implementing the Act. The provinces and territories also expressed concern about the level of federal contribution to youth justice funding.

### Spousal Abuse

Several government innovations have played a key role in supporting the implementation of the spousal abuse policies to ensure the system is sensitive to the unique realities of victims of spousal abuse. Recent innovations include the creation of specialized courts, expedited processes, and early treatment programs. Issues pertaining to manslaughter in domestic violence cases will be referred to officials for further research and action.

## Mega Cases

The Quebec courts have experienced challenges in managing large and complex trials. Quebec suggested (1) that the minimum number of jury members in a mega case could be reduced from 10 to 8 and (2) that if the original judge steps down, the judge appointed as a replacement would be obliged to continue the trial at the point at which the original judge stepped down. Ministers agreed that the two changes proposed by Quebec would be significant to the current system and, as such, deserve thorough study.

## Aboriginal Justice

Working and funding relationships are critical in this area. A working group is currently dealing with the issue of dividing new allocations. The federal Minister of Justice commented on the recent statements in the Throne Speech about commitment to strengthen aboriginal self-governance and to help build strong and safe communities.

## Voyeurism

The federal Department of Justice has consulted with the public on the creation of the new criminal offences of sexual voyeurism and distribution of voyeuristic materials. There will soon be *Criminal Code* amendments introduced to create these offences.

## Sex Offender Registration

A joint federal-provincial-territorial effort has developed a model of a sex offender registration system. Concern exists that this registry will not include offenders currently under sentence. Future enhancements will include photos of all offenders in the RCMP data system (known as CPIC). Provision for geo-mapping may be included in future enhancements. Legislation to support the new system is expected to be introduced by year-end.

## Anti-Terrorism

In November 2001, an examination of the impact and costs of anti-terrorism and public safety legislation and initiatives in response to the events of September 11 was initiated to address concerns and to identify possible solutions.

## Organized Crime

Organized crime remains a top priority of both levels of government. A National Agenda on Organized Crime was adopted in 2000. Street gangs were added to the list of common policy priorities, which now includes: illegal drugs, outlaw motorcycle gangs, economic crime, high-tech crime, money laundering, illegal migration, corruption, and street gangs. Organized crime activity at ports was also added to a list of pressing concerns that already includes the following: intimidation of public officials, gaming, auto theft, and organized crime activity in diamond mining. Marijuana-growing operations are recognized as a major funding source for a range of other organized criminal activity, and immediate action, including investigation and deterrence, is required for effective measures in these cases. Outlaw motorcycle gangs remain a major concern.

## Integrated Justice Information

Ministers supported the national adoption of the Canada Public Safety Information Network data standards. Without national standards, the sharing of public safety information between criminal justice systems is at risk of not being understandable, reliable, or accurate.

## Parole Issues

Changes to the National Parole Board policy will ensure that all provincial applications for parole will be heard by a two-member panel. Concern surrounds parole eligibility rules for offenders who have taken a life or killed a police officer or a correctional officer.

## Streamlining the Justice System

Greater efficiencies within the justice system are required to reduce costs and delays, to better respect victims and witnesses, and to better protect children. Further discussions will examine ways to improve the efficiency and effectiveness of, and access to, the justice systems, including structural and administrative reforms.

## QUESTIONS FOR DISCUSSION

1. Do the issues addressed at the 2002 first ministers' meeting deal with issues that you would consider to be the most pressing problems facing the criminal justice system today? Is there anything you would add to their next agenda?

2. It has been argued by some critics that the division of legislative and policy responsibility among the various levels of government leads to an inefficient criminal justice system. Do you believe meetings of the type discussed above enhance or reduce that problem?

*Source:* Canadian Intergovernmental Conference Secretariat, accessible at time of writing at **www.scics.gc.ca/cinfo02/830768004_e.html**

# Emerging Technologies in Criminalistics

The future will see criminalistics aided by a number of technologies now in their infancy. They include:

- DNA profiling and new serological/tissue identification techniques;
- Online databases and clearing houses for the sharing of criminal justice information;
- Electronic ion mobility spectrometry to detect traces of controlled substances;
- Computer-generated psychological profiles and computer-aided crime scene analysis;
- Computer enhancements of photographs, images, and other types of evidence;
- Forensic animation (computer simulations of criminal activity); and
- Chemical and microscopic examination of fibres and other materials using advanced techniques.

A brief description of these technologies, including their current state of development and the implications they hold for the future, is provided in the paragraphs that follow.

## DNA Profiling

**DNA profiling** Using biological residue found at the scene of a crime to make genetic comparisons, with the ultimate goal of identifying criminal suspects.

**DNA profiling**, also termed DNA (deoxyribonucleic acid) fingerprinting, relies on the detection of human DNA for identification. The technique was "discovered" by Dr. Alec Jeffery from Britain in 1985. Since its discovery, Canadian police have been quick to embrace the technology, while the courts have adopted a more conservative approach to accepting forensic DNA analysis as admissible and reliable evidence. However, with the 1995 amendment to *Criminal Code* section 487.04, police are now allowed to obtain bodily substances for DNA analysis (see below). A warrant is required to obtain such evidence, and only for such offences as assault, sexual assault, sexual exploitation, manslaughter, murder, and several other specifically identified crimes.

DNA is a nucleic acid found in the centre of cells. It is the principal component of chromosomes, the structures that transmit hereditary characteristics between generations. Each DNA molecule is a long, two-stranded chain of subunits, called nucleotides, coiled in the form of a double helix. Because genetic material is unique to each individual (except in the case of identical twins), DNA can provide a highly reliable source of suspect identification. The Ontario case of *R. v. McNally* (1989) represented the first case in which DNA evidence was used to convict the accused, who had sexually assaulted an elderly woman.[23] Since that landmark case, most other provinces have successfully used DNA evidence to convict a growing number of offenders. In 2000, Canada launched its National DNA Data Bank, which contains DNA profiles derived from biological samples. The data bank contains two key components, (1) an index of convicted offenders, with the DNA profiles of offenders who have been required by law to surrender a DNA sample following conviction for a designated offence, and (2) a crime scene index, with DNA profiles from evidence left behind at crime scenes. By early 2003, the National DNA Data Bank contained 34 103 samples in its convicted offenders index, and 7782 in its crime scene index. This data bank had been accessed in 524 investigations by the end of January 2003, resulting in 545 "offender hits," each hit involving the matching of a crime scene to an offender.[24]

DNA profiling requires only a few human cells for comparison purposes. One drop of blood, a few hairs, a small amount of skin, or a trace of semen usually provide sufficient genetic material for comparison purposes. Because the DNA molecule is very stable, genetic tests can be conducted on evidence taken from crime scenes long after fingerprints have disappeared. The process, diagrammed in Figure 15–1, involves a highly technical procedure called electrophoresis, which has been more readily embraced in Canadian courts than in such countries as Australia, the United Kingdom, and the United States.[25]

Over the years, the impact of scientific evidence has increased substantially with the introduction of DNA evidence. However, DNA evidence may not be accepted as either absolute or certain. In the widely publicized case of Guy Paul Morin, in the mid-1990s, it was revealed that DNA evidence has limitations. Accused of killing a nine-year-old neighbour girl in 1992, Morin was convicted on sloppy police work and evidence gathering—including DNA evidence. The use of DNA evidence was still in its infancy during the

**FIGURE 15–1** The DNA Fingerprinting Process

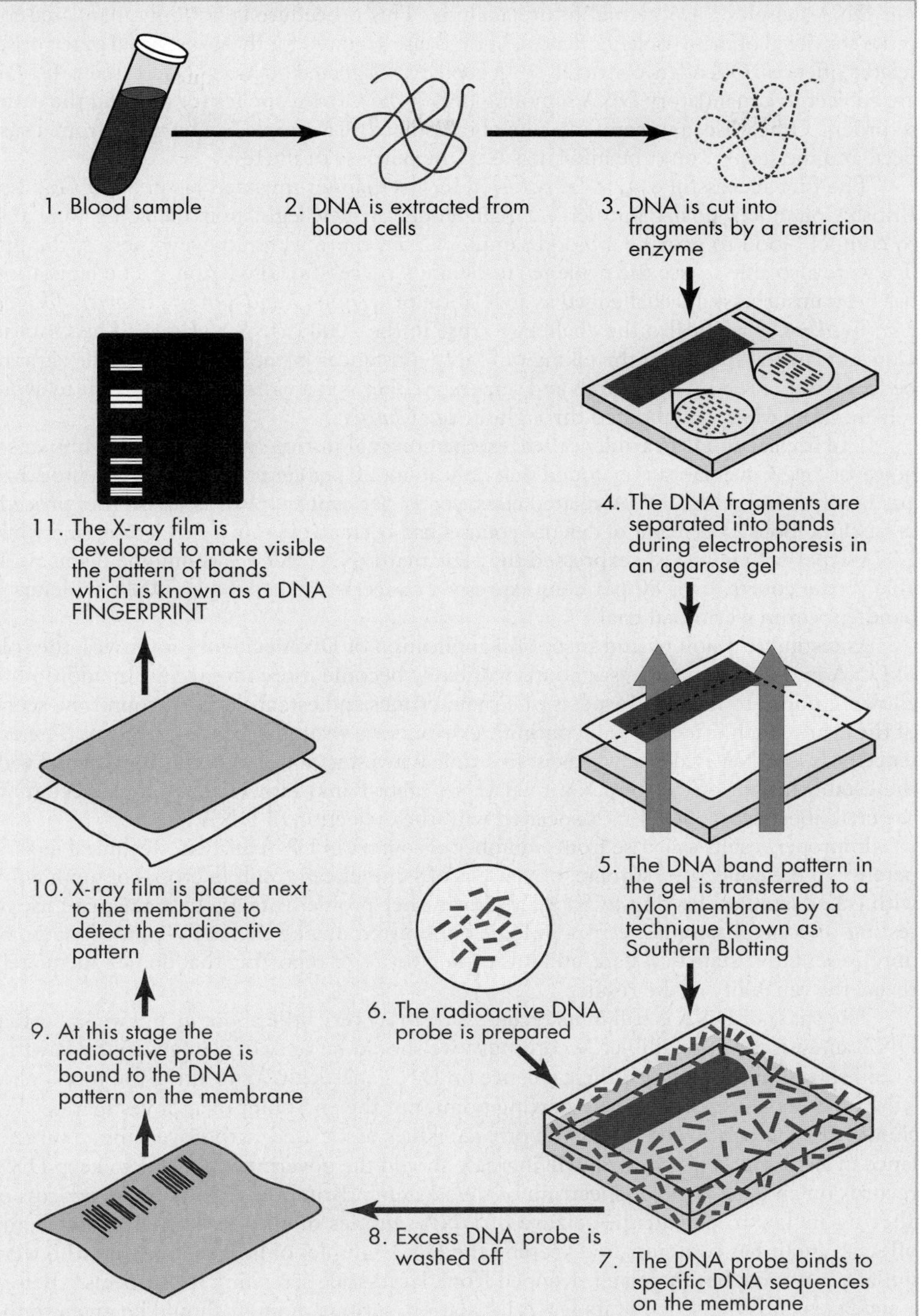

1. Blood sample

2. DNA is extracted from blood cells

3. DNA is cut into fragments by a restriction enzyme

4. The DNA fragments are separated into bands during electrophoresis in an agarose gel

5. The DNA band pattern in the gel is transferred to a nylon membrane by a technique known as Southern Blotting

6. The radioactive DNA probe is prepared

7. The DNA probe binds to specific DNA sequences on the membrane

8. Excess DNA probe is washed off

9. At this stage the radioactive probe is bound to the DNA pattern on the membrane

10. X-ray film is placed next to the membrane to detect the radioactive pattern

11. The X-ray film is developed to make visible the pattern of bands which is known as a DNA FINGERPRINT

*Source:* Cellmark Diagnostics, Division of ICI Americas, Inc. Reprinted with permission.

investigative stages of Christine Jessop's murder. Had Morin's DNA not ultimately been tested outside of Canada, he could still be serving a life sentence. The case was instrumental in forcing laboratories to improve the testing methods as well as to raise some caution about the fallibility of scientific evidence.

In July 1995, the government passed amendments to the *Criminal Code*, which established the procedures for DNA testing in relation to many crimes such as incest, kidnapping, murder, other homicide offences, and sexual assault. In addition, the provisions included safeguards in an effort to prevent the abuse of DNA evidence gathering. Offenders convicted of "primary designated offences" (see s. 487.04 of the *Criminal Code*) are generally required to submit DNA samples for potential future analysis. This procedure is not only mandated for those convicted of many violent offences, but it is also required for those convicted of terrorist-related offences. Offenders convicted of "secondary designated offences" (again, see s. 487.04) are subject to a mandatory DNA sampling only if the Crown applies for one and the court so orders. Otherwise, a warrant must be obtained before a sample can be taken from a suspect, and the suspect must be informed as to the purpose of the test.

The first successful case to be resolved in this manner involved Jason Scott Good of British Columbia who had murdered a man. Under the new legislation, the police were able to compel Good to provide a blood sample. Given there were no eyewitnesses, the police were also able to use the evidence to obtain a successful conviction.[26] The legislation has been unsuccessfully challenged as a violation of sections 7 and 8 of the *Charter of Rights and Freedoms.* Specifically, the challenge arose in the 2000 case *R.* v. *F.(S.)*[27] The Ontario Court of Appeal ruled that the taking of bodily substances is not a violation of the right to be free from unreasonable search and seizure; neither is it a violation of the right to avoid self-incrimination as embodied throughout the *Charter*.

The impact of DNA evidence within the criminal justice system has been immense; however, one Canadian survey found that only about 20 per cent of Crown prosecutors had any involvement with a DNA-related class, yet 57 per cent support its use in trial procedures. Only about 23 per cent of defence counsel had been involved in a DNA case. And while DNA experts unanimously expressed the view that DNA evidence should be made available to the courts, over 80 per cent expressed concern about the way DNA evidence is handled within a criminal trial.[28]

As testing technology and successful application of DNA evidence improves, the role of DNA in the criminal investigations will likely become more important. In addition to allowing police to identify suspects of certain crimes and establish facts around the scene of the crime, such evidence will continue to exonerate wrongly accused suspects. The extent to which DNA evidence will assist in criminal investigations has been strengthened with the establishment of the new National DNA Data Bank. However, we must recognize the civil liberties implications associated with the collection of DNA.

Improper results can arise from a number of sources in DNA analysis. Technical incompetence in the collection, storage, or analysis of samples can result in cross-contamination with other samples, leading to faulty results. Other problems relate to inadequate use or testing of control samples, errors in logic committed during the analysis, inadequate or unrepresentative statistical data, and misleading forms of reporting that do not adequately reveal the reliability of the results.[29]

The study of DNA is still in its infancy. We know very little about it, and we know that DNA analysis is not infallible. Accordingly, we should be wary of changes to the law that would allow police to expand their reliance on DNA analysis as a substitute for good police work. DNA analysis should be a starting point, not the end point of an investigation. We should also be concerned about the privacy issues associated with government surveillance in any form. This concern will increase should the government decide to keep DNA records on an even broader spectrum of the citizenry. Britain is already in the process of altering its law to permit the seizure of DNA samples of all people charged with any offence, and it has contemplated keeping the DNA samples of innocent people who were initially included, but then later dropped from, large-scale screening for suspects.[30] Before Canada expands the scope of its DNA legislation, serious thought should be given to the civil liberty issues associated with this technology.

## *Online Databases and Clearing Houses*

As we have seen in earlier chapters, computers are already an integral part of most police departments. They are a tool for performing such routine tasks as word processing, filing, record keeping, printing reports, and scheduling human resources and facilities. Computers that serve as investigative tools, however, have the greatest potential to impact criminal justice in the near future. The automated fingerprint technology discussed earlier is but one example of information-based systems designed to help in identifying offenders and solving crimes. Other systems include criminal personality profiling, geographic profiling, and Violent Crime Linkage Analysis System (ViCLAS). Combining findings from behavioural research with modern computer technology, ViCLAS is designed to construct profiles on all homicides that are sexual or predatory in nature as well as several other types of violent criminal behaviour. The system is based on the assertion that repeat offenders tend not only to follow similar patterns of behaviour but also to exhibit identifiable and predictable characteristics and motivation.[31] Until the Bernardo/Homolka case, use of ViCLAS was left to the discretion of the investigator. However, as a result of a number of difficulties in investigating this case and based on an inquiry chaired by Mr. Justice Archie Campbell of the Ontario Court General Division in 1996, the police investigation in this case was severely criticized. Among the report's recommendations was one by Campbell J. calling for mandatory ViCLAS reporting by all police sources as well as an expansion of the DNA laboratory, strengthening the coroner's system, and improving the capacity for electronic information sharing.[32]

## Geographic Profiling: Computer-Aided Investigation

One of the earliest schools of criminological thought involved the studies of human ecology. This line of inquiry stemmed from the works of Darwin and his followers who studied plant and animal ecology, geography, and the spatial distribution of social phenomena in the late nineteenth century. Sociologists Park and Burgess adapted the concept of human ecology to the study of human behaviour. In the ensuing decades, human ecology has evolved into the sub-discipline of *environmental criminology*. Several Canadian researchers and practitioners have become leaders in this field. Of particular interest has been the pioneering work done by Kim Rossmo, a former Detective Inspector with the Vancouver Police Department.

Having studied under Paul and Patricia Brantingham at Simon Fraser University, Rossmo became keenly interested in geographic profiling. Geoprofiling, as it is also known, involves the analysis of human behavioural patterns in relation to the physical environment. Research has shown that, like animals, humans travel in relatively predictable patterns and that most crimes occur in relative proximity to an offender's place of residence. Different crimes tend to have different distances between the offender's home and the location of the crime, with violent crimes being committed closer to the offender's home than property offences. The more seasoned an offender, the greater the likelihood that he or she will travel farther to commit an offence.

Using sophisticated computer technology, investigators rely on a geographic information system to identify the possible location of the offender. In order to generate a geographic profile, the investigator enters information into this system about the locations where crimes were committed, data on the victims, and a variety of other relevant variables. Then the system generates three-dimensional computer maps that indicate the most likely area where the offender might reside, and his or her work site, social venues, and travel routes of the offender.[33]

Another innovative computer-based aid has been the ORION system, pioneered by the Vancouver City Police Department's now defunct Geographic Profiling Unit. This system integrates "psychological profiles, photos, postal codes, motor vehicle licensing information, letters criminals have sent to taunt police or victims, census data, and land-use records."[34] Once this information is entered, the program produces a *jeopardy surface*—a three-dimensional multicoloured map that reflects an optimal search path for the area. The map can be used to more efficiently and effectively deploy patrol cars, and focus searches in target areas. In addition, the ORION system is compatible with ViCLAS, and has been implemented to help successfully solve a number of crimes. Such technology holds much promise for criminal investigative procedures and should aid the police and criminal justice system in fighting crime.

## Computer-Based Training

Computers provide an ideal training medium for criminal justice agencies. They allow users to work at their own pace, and they can be available around the clock to provide instruction on-site to personnel whose job requirements make other kinds of training difficult to implement. Computer-based training (CBT) is already well-established as a management training tool, but it is now being developed for specific applications in the field of law enforcement.[35]

Some of the more widely used computer-training programs include shoot/no-shoot decision-based software and police pursuit driving simulators. The Atari Mobile Operations Simulator (AMOS), firearms training simulation (FATS), and ROBBEC'S JUST (Judgment Under Stress Training) are just a few of the contemporary products available to police training divisions. Recent innovations in the field of virtual reality (a kind of high-tech-based illusion) have led to the creation of realistic computer-based virtual environments in which law enforcement agents can test their skills.[36] Other high-technology-based training is available via the Law Enforcement Satellite Training Network (LESTN), a privately owned company operating out of Carrollton, Texas.

We have mentioned some of the most prominent technologies in criminal justice, but these are by no means all of them. Laser fingerprint-lifting devices, space-age photography, video camera–equipped patrol cars, satellite mapping, advanced chemical analysis techniques, and hair and fibre identification are all sophisticated, expensive crime-fighting techniques. Refinements in technology, lower costs, and better training will see many of these technologies become common investigative tools. Field test kits for drug analysis, chemical sobriety checkers, and hand-held ticket-issuing computers have already made the transition from high technology to widespread application. As one expert has observed, "police agencies throughout the world are entering an era in which high technology is not only desirable but necessary in order to combat crime effectively."[37]

The National Center for Missing and Exploited Children

Computer-aged image of a missing child. The child, Autumn Jade Young, is shown in the upper left photo at the time of her disappearance when she was three years old. Computer imaging updated her appearance in the upper right photo, to what she might be expected look like at age nine. Shortly after the image was released, Autumn was returned to her family.

# Problems in Implementation

All technological innovations, however, do not represent entirely smooth sailing, for several reasons. First, the speed with which justice agencies successfully adapt to the opportunities brought by technology may be limited. Some writers have observed that "law enforcement has been slow to utilize new technology,"[38] and a study by the International Association of Chiefs of Police found that only 10 per cent of American police departments are innovative in their use of computers.[39] As anyone knows who has bought a computer recently, technology changes rapidly, making equipment quickly obsolete. Just the sheer amount of choice involved may also be daunting, as can the dependability of some high-technology vendors' claims about their products. And line staff and decision makers within police departments may lack the personal experience and knowledge to use technology effectively. Equally significant, the future legal implications and social acceptability of specific technologies is uncertain.[40]

A second area of concern arises from the "super-sleuth" capabilities of some high-technology items. As high-tech gadgetry becomes more commonplace in criminal justice agencies, we can be sure that the courts will watch for potential violations of individual rights. New photographic techniques developed for the space program, for example, which permit enlargement of details never before thought possible, or the use of super-listening devices, such as those now used to isolate and amplify the voices of referees and quarterbacks on weekend television, may extend investigative capabilities beyond previous understandings of limited search and seizure.

Finally, it must be recognized that the investigative and other opportunities created by technology for the agents of criminal justice have their flip side in the threats represented by the products of modern science in the hands of criminals.

# Cybercrime: The New White-Collar Crime

The down side of high technology, as far as the justice system is concerned, is the potential it creates for lawbreakers to commit old crimes in new ways, or to commit new crimes never before imagined. Sometimes in today's high-tech world it's even difficult to tell when a crime has occurred. At the XIIIth Annual Symposium on Criminal Justice in 1998, experts from around the world addressed a number of growing **cybercrime** issues such as information assurance, child pornography on the internet, investigative and prosecutor concerns, security implications, and cyber-terrorism.[41]

In 1995, for example, University of Michigan student Jake A. Baker, 20, became the first person ever indicted for writing something on the internet, when he was arrested by the FBI and charged with five counts of interstate transmission of threats.[42] Baker had posted a series of stories on the internet about his fantasy of torturing, raping, and murdering a female classmate. One of his messages contained the phrase, "Just thinking about it anymore doesn't do the trick. I need to do it." Another note read: "Torture is foreplay, rape is romance, snuff (killing) is climax."[43]

Although he could have sentenced Baker for up to five years in prison, Detroit U.S. District Judge Avern Cohn threw out the charges after Baker had spent 29 days in jail.[44] Cohn ruled that Baker's violent internet writings were protected under the free-speech clause of the U.S. Constitution. In contrast, the government had argued that true threats are not so protected and maintained that Baker's naming of a specific woman had raised the threats to the level required for violation of federal criminal law. Under the law, however, federal prosecutors would have had to prove that Baker intended to carry out his threats—something the judge did not believe could be done.

At the other end of the spectrum, in 1998, Dan Blackett, a London, Ontario college student, discovered an information site listing hundreds of pages of personal and credit card information. Blackett had been doing research for his computer science course about on-line security when he came across the site. The site had names of people from all corners of the world, and was accessible without the use of a password or access name. Being an ethical and law-abiding student, Blackett contacted the FBI and offered them the information. However, because he resides in Canada, Blackett was told to give his information to the

**cybercrime** Crime committed via computers. Another term for computer crime.

RCMP. Officials acknowledged that online security is still a major problem for internet servers and that "credit card companies don't really seem to care that their customers' private information is unprotected."[45]

The extent to which cybercrimes exist is unknown; however, there is growing evidence that they are pervasive in society. As organized crime groups and terrorist groups become increasingly involved in computer crime, the threat of new and more harmful forms of crime presents new challenges to the criminal justice system. Current efforts to investigate and combat computer-related crimes are hindered by what a member of the RCMP Technological Crime Section in Ottawa refers to as a "gap in domestic law and in international co-operation" that hinders detection, prosecution, and investigation.[46]

## White-Collar Crime

**white-collar crime**
Non-violent crime for financial gain committed by means of deception by persons having professional status or specialized technical skills during the everyday pursuit of their business endeavours.

Because of the skill and knowledge required by their crimes, most, but not all, of today's high-tech offenders can aptly be labelled white-collar criminals. The term **white-collar crime** was coined by Edwin Sutherland in his 1939 presidential address to the American Sociological Society.[47] Sutherland later defined the term to include crimes committed by persons in authority during the normal course of their business transactions. White-collar crimes include embezzlement, bribery, political corruption, price-fixing, misuse and theft of company property, corporate tax evasion, fraud, and money laundering (which obscures the source of funds earned through illegal activities, allowing them to enter the legitimate financial arena). White-collar crimes tend to be committed by financially secure, well-educated, middle- or upper-class persons. Sutherland claimed that the prevalence of white-collar crimes shows that "the theories of criminologists that crime is due to poverty or to psychopathic and sociopathic conditions statistically associated with poverty are invalid."[48] Anyone, said Sutherland, is capable of committing a crime, but many crimes are overlooked when committed by powerful people.

A broad, and somewhat more modern, definition of white-collar crime might be "non-violent crime for financial gain committed by means of deception by persons having professional status or specialized technical skills during the everyday pursuit of their business endeavors."[49] The insider-trading scam of stock market tycoon Ivan Boesky, which netted an estimated US$400 million[50] for Boesky and his friends, and securities fraud perpetrated by junk-bond king Michael Milken, which cost him an estimated $400-million fine, provide two recent examples of white-collar crime.

Another example of white-collar crime can be found in the savings and loan fiasco (S&L) of the late 1980s and early 1990s, which has been called "the biggest white-collar crime in history."[51] The S&L disaster was a long time in the making. While the boom days following World War II were lucrative for the savings and loan industry, hard times set in during the 1970s, when low-interest long-term housing loans made by member institutions were costing the industry more than it could earn. Then, falling interest rates and a surge in land development combined with decreased federal regulation to produce a climate in which savings and loan institutions could quickly turn big profits by signing increasingly risky loans. Following deregulation, made possible in part by Congress' passing of the *Depository Institutions Deregulation and Monetary Control Act* of 1980, organized criminal groups began working the S&L market. As Frank Hagan notes, "[t]he S&L scandal reflected increased criminal opportunity due to an economic crisis that was taken advantage of by greedy insiders who collectively looted financial institutions and left the bill to the U.S. taxpayers."[52]

Closer to home, white-collar crime appears to have been involved in the bankruptcy of Canadian gold prospector Bre-X Minerals Ltd. In the mid-1990s, Bre-X officials claimed that assayed ore from the company's Busang mine in Indonesia proved that the company owned what was likely to be the world's largest gold reserve. In what some have called the greatest stock fraud of the century, shares of the company's stock soared from pennies to a value of $206 each. After a number of debacles, including the suspicious death of the company's chief geologist who fell from a helicopter over the Indonesian jungle, the company admitted in 1997 the truth of an independent report that showed that the company's claim was based on falsified data.[53] Bre-X shareholders were left with worthless stock certificates, while the company's vice-president of exploration filed for residency status in the Cayman Islands, where he owns an $8-million beachfront home. David Walsh, the owner of Bre-X, retired from the company in November 1997 and then, at the age of 52, died the following year, leaving trustees to deal with more than 50 000 creditors.[54]

White-collar criminals tend to be punished less severely than other offenders. In the 1930s and 1940s, Edwin Sutherland studied the 70 largest corporations of his time and found that 547 adverse court and regulatory agency decisions had been made against them—an average of 7.8 decisions per corporation.[55] Although this should have been evidence of routine corporate involvement in white-collar criminality, almost no corporate executives were sentenced to prison. More recent studies have shown that about 40 per cent of convicted federal white-collar offenders are sentenced to prison versus 54 per cent of non-white-collar criminals.[56] When prison sentences are imposed, white-collar offenders are sentenced to only 29 months on average, versus 50 months for other offenders. In the 1980s, when Canadian-based Stone Consolidated Inc. was finally charged with spilling PCB-laced transformer oil, the company was fined a mere $35 000.[57] As other authors have noted, "[f]or some reason our system has seen nothing unjust in slapping an 18-year-old inner-city kid with a 20-year prison sentence for robbing a bank of a couple of thousand dollars while putting a white-collar criminal away for just two years in a 'prison camp' for stealing $200 million through fraud."[58]

Today, occupational crimes pervade society. The economic, social, and political impact and implications are often far-reaching and yet our efforts to control such crimes have been limited.

## Occupational Crime

Criminologists were quick to realize that if persons of high socio-economic status could commit crimes during the course of their business, then so could persons of lower social standing.[59] The term "**occupational crime**" was coined to describe the on-the-job illegal activities of employees. Thefts of company property, vandalism, the misuse of information, software piracy that occurs in the workplace, and many other activities come under the rubric of occupational crime. The employee who uses company phones for personal calls, the maintenance worker who steals cleaning supplies for home use, and the store clerk who lifts items of clothing or jewellery provide other examples of occupational criminality. The American Council of Better Business Bureaus estimates that one-third of all plant and office workers steal from their employers.[60] Total losses are said to be in the range of US$14 to US$28 billion per year.[61] The Council believes that one-third of all business failures are directly attributable to employee crime.[62]

In a recent book on occupational crime,[63] Gary S. Green defines occupational crime as "any act punishable by law which is committed through opportunity created in the course of an occupation that is legal."[64] Green has developed the following typology that considerably broadens the classification of occupational criminality: "(a) crimes for the benefit of an employing organization (organizational occupational crime); (b) crimes by officials through the exercise of their state-based authority (state authority occupational crime); (c) crimes by professionals in their capacity as professionals (professional occupational crime); and (d) crimes by individuals as individuals (individual occupational crime)."[65]

James Coleman provides a further distinction between types of white-collar crime.[66] Coleman points out that some white-collar crimes affect only property, while others endanger the safety and health of people. The knowing sale of tainted food products or medicine are examples of the latter type of crime. Coleman has also suggested that the term "organizational crime" distinguishes offences designed to further the goals of corporate entities from business-related crimes committed by individuals to further their own desires.[67] Organizational crimes are the "crimes of big business." Sometimes, however, it pays to remember that all crimes are committed by people and not by institutions.

Some authors maintain that occupational and **corporate crimes** are a way of life in North American businesses.[68] Examples abound. The *Multinational Monitor*, an American publication, publishes articles that focus on corporate crime. Every year, they produce their list of top "ten worst corporations." In 1997, the list included such notable companies as Nike, the Philip Morris tobacco company, and Decoster egg farms.[69] In other years, a variety of Canadian companies have also made the list.

White-collar crime, occupational crime, and corporate crime, although typically committed by businesspersons, lawyers, politicians, and criminal justice officials, share many

**occupational crime**
Any act punishable by law that is committed through opportunity created in the course of an occupation that is legal.

**corporate crimes**
Violations of a criminal statute by a corporate entity or by its executives, employees, or agents acting on behalf of and for the benefit of the corporation, partnership, or other form of business entity.

characteristics of organized crime. Unlike organized crime offenders, white-collar offenders do not see themselves as criminals, and rationalize their activities as being affected by the corporate environment and its market demands. And despite their pervasive presence, there continues to be a lack of information on the former types of crime. It was not until 1998 that the first institute on organized crime and corruption (the Nathanson Centre) was established at York University in Toronto. Its director, Margaret Beare, is a recognized expert in the field and has produced a number of significant publications on the subject. However, few other Canadian criminologists have studied corporate or occupational crime. Part of the problem is attributable to the lack of funds and limited official data sources. In addition, co-operation among corporations may not be readily forthcoming.[70] Nevertheless, given the growing awareness of their social, economic, and political impact, Canadian criminologists and criminal justice agencies would do well to direct more attention to these forms of criminal activity.

## Computer and High-Technology Crime

During Sutherland's time, political corruption and corporate bribery were serious concerns. Although both exist as offences today, computer crimes are rapidly becoming the white-collar crime *par excellence* in the modern world. **Computer crimes**, which some experts refer to as cybercrime, are committed using computers and computer technology. Thefts of computer equipment, although sometimes spectacular, are not computer crimes, but are instead simply theft. In 1995, for example, armed robbers clad in sports coats and ties robbed Centon Electronics, a computer-chip distributor based in California's Silicon Valley, of more than US$12 million in computer chips, after tying up employees.[71] At the time of the heist, the stolen chips, consisting primarily of 32-megabyte memory modules, were worth more per pound than gold.

"True" computer criminals, however, go beyond the theft of hardware, focusing instead on the information stored in computer systems and manipulating it in a way that violates the law. In 1995, for example, the arrest of computer expert Kevin Mitnick, known as the "FBI's most wanted **hacker**," alarmed security experts because of the potential harm represented by Mitnick's electronic intrusions. The 31-year-old Mitnick allegedly broke into an internet service provider's computer system and stole more than 20 000 credit card numbers. Although Mitnick appears to have been arrested before the numbers were sold or clandestinely distributed, experts feared that others with similar high-tech skills might be tempted to enact copycat schemes—costing companies that issue credit cards millions of dollars. Mitnick was caught with the help of Tsutoma Shimomura, whose home computer Mitnick had also attacked, and who assisted FBI experts in tracking him through telephone lines and computer networks to the computer in his Raleigh, North Carolina apartment.[72]

Cybercrime is very expensive. Former RCMP security specialist Doug Dzurko informed the Vancouver chapter of the Information Systems Audit and Control Association of the following findings: theft of proprietary information ($33 million), telecommunications fraud ($17 million), and financial fraud ($11 million). Meanwhile, an American survey found that 64 per cent of the companies surveyed reported security breaches of their computers systems in the course of a year.[73] Cybercrime not only costs companies millions of dollars, but also, experts note, it is difficult to detect and because of its international nature is difficult and costly to prosecute.

Another form of cybercrime, the unauthorized copying of software programs, also called software piracy, appears rampant. According to the Software Publishing Association (SPA), global losses from software piracy totalled US$15.4 billion in 1996.[74] According to the SPA, 46 per cent of all software in use in the world has been copied illegally. Some countries have especially high rates of illegal use. Of all the computer software in use in Vietnam, for example, it is estimated that 99 per cent has been illegally copied. On a dollar basis, most piracy occurs in Asia and Pacific Rim countries, while Western Europe and North America also account for substantial losses.

## Prosecution of Computer and High-Tech Crime

As recently as the early 1970s, computer crimes were virtually unheard of, and until the early 1980s, there were virtually no computer crime laws. Crimes committed using computer

**computer crimes**
Any crimes that take advantage of computer-based technology in its commission. This definition highlights the manner in which a crime is committed, more than it does the target of the offence. Hence, the physical theft of a computer, or of a floppy disk, would not be a computer crime, while the use of computer software to analyze a company's security operations prior to committing a robbery might be.

**hacker** A computer hobbyist or professional, generally with advanced programming skills. Today the term "hacker" has taken on a sinister connotation and includes those hobbyists who are bent on illegally accessing the computers of others, or who attempt to demonstrate their technological prowess through computerized acts of vandalism.

BOX 15.2 **Theory into Practice**

## The Terminology of Computer and High-Technology Crime

### Software

Computer programs or instructions to machines that control their operations. Software is generally found in magnetic storage media, but can be reproduced on paper or held in either machine or human memory.

### Hardware

Computer machinery, including keyboards, disk or tape drives, optical scanners, "mice," video monitors, printers, central processing units, modems, terminals, add-on boards, peripherals, and so on.

### CPU

Central processing unit. That part of the computer that houses the microprocessor and performs data manipulations.

### Modem

A telecommunications device used to link computers. A modem is generally used by hackers to gain illegal access to other computers.

### Hackers

Computer hobbyists or professionals, generally with advanced programming skills. The term "hackers" often describes computer operators involved in "computer trespass."

### Internet

The world's largest computer network. The internet permits access to the World Wide Web (www) and to many other forms of data exchange.

### Copying

The duplication of software or the transfer of data from one storage media to another. One of the most prevalent problems in computer crime is the unauthorized duplication of copyrighted software.

### Illegal Access

Unauthorized entrance into a computer's files or operating system. Access is possible through private information (a password), physical trespass, or electronically via a modem and software. In legal terminology, illegal access is often referred to as "computer trespass."

### Theft by Computer

The illegal use of a computer to transfer money, valuables, software, data, or other property from one account or machine to another.

### Theft of Computer Services

The illegal use of computer time or of information or other services available online or directly. Employees of computer-based industries may use machines for personal purposes (such as cheque-book balancing, games, and so on), while hackers may acquire online services illegally by circumventing security and fee systems.

### Virus

A computer program designed to secretly invade systems and modify either the way in which they operate or alter the information they store. Viruses are destructive software that may effectively vandalize computers of all sizes. Other destructive programs include *logic bombs*, *worms*, and *Trojan horse* routines, which hide inside seemingly innocent software or disks.

---

technology had to be prosecuted, if at all, under laws intended for other purposes. Property offence laws were sometimes applied to prosecute illegal entry into computer systems, laws against theft were applied to the stealing of digitized information, and embezzlement statutes were applied to illegal electronic fund transfers. Today, sections 342.1, 342.2, and 430 of the *Criminal Code* are intended to combat computer crime. The sections pertain to the destruction or altering of data; rendering data meaningless; and/or interfering with someone using legitimate data. These are all hybrid offences, but the "unauthorized use of a computer" offence in section 342.1 carries a penalty of a possible maximum of ten years in prison if prosecuted by indictment. The other offences carry a maximum imprisonment term of two years if prosecuted by indictment.

In spite of new laws, as noted above, the detection, apprehension, and prosecution of offenders is very difficult. Most law enforcement agencies have limited resources. For example, there are only about 170 RCMP officers (less than one-half of 1 per cent of the total force) who are trained in computer-related crime detection techniques. Of these members, only about one-half are assigned to commercial crime units across the country. But, as one former RCMP security specialist noted, as of 1998 there has only been one documented case of online bank robbery. The crime involved Vladimir Levin of St. Petersburg, Russia. He siphoned Citibank for US$500 000 in 1994 "and might have gotten away with $10 million if he hadn't been betrayed by an accomplice."[75]

To further complicate the ability to prosecute such offenders, officials who predominately operate in a reactive mode can only react to, instead of anticipating, cybercrime. In 1998, the RCMP announced that they were ill-equipped to fight white-collar crime. Between 1997 and 1998, the RCMP's economic crime branch lost nearly 30 positions, further limiting its ability to effectively combat computer and other **high-technology crimes**.[76] This unfortunate trend is happening in an area of crime where the offenders are usually one step ahead in their level of sophistication and technology. Unless resources can be found to assist law enforcement agencies, high-tech bandits will continue to pose a serious threat to society.

**high-technology crimes** Violations of the criminal law whose commission depends upon, makes use of, and often targets, sophisticated and advanced technology.

## Types of Computer Crime

One problem in the development of comprehensive computer crime laws is the lack of legislative appreciation for the potentially wide variety of crimes that can be perpetrated using a computer. While a comprehensive typology of computer-based crime has yet to be developed,[77] the categories that follow probably encompass most such offences today.

*Unauthorized Access to Data*  An old adage says that "knowledge is power." Information stored in today's magnetic and laser-read media is often sensitive (like personnel records) or necessarily secret (such as corporate marketing plans or the detailed technical description of a new product). Unauthorized access to data can lead to lawsuits over patent infringements, loss of a competitive edge, and the need to redo many hours or even months of work. The frequent need for access to computer-based data, and the routine use of telephone lines for data transfer, make such information particularly susceptible to snooping. Four techniques are used today to prevent the compromise of sensitive data:

**data encryption methods** Methods used to encode computerized information.

- *Physical security*. Locked disk files, key-operated hard disks, removable storage media, and limited-access computer rooms are all physical measures that can be taken to thwart the potential viewing or theft of information.

  - *Passwords or other forms of identification*. Individual computers and networks sometimes require users to properly enter a password or other form of identification to gain access. Some advanced systems use optical imaging to recognize the unique network of blood vessels on the retina of a user requesting access to highly secure computer networks. "Eyeball scanners," voice-recognition units, hand geometry scanners, keyboard rhythm recognition units, and other high-technology gadgetry, known in the trade as biometric security devices, are not readily available to most businesses because of cost.

The 15-year-old Montreal computer hacker, known as "Mafiaboy," was responsible for shutting down numerous websites resulting in over $1.7 billion in damages. In 2001, he was sentenced to eight months in youth custody.

  - *Data encryption methods*. Data is encrypted by turning the information into gibberish. Then the data is uncoded by authorized users.[78] Data-encryption techniques may be unique to an individual company and to its products. The Data Encryption Standard (DES) of the U.S. National Institute of Standards and Technology is a more general data-encryption technique. Using this system, banks and other businesses can freely exchange and decrypt coded data even when the computer systems used in the exchange differ substantially.

  - *Screen blanking*. Screen blanking lacks the sophistication of some of the other methods we have described. It depends upon a relatively simple technology that causes video monitors to go blank after a set period of non-use. Hence, data-entry stations left unattended cannot be casually viewed by other people.

CP Photo/Andre Forget

*Wilful Destruction of Data* As computer systems grow in complexity, they challenge the inventiveness of sophisticated "hackers" or computer buffs. Some hackers are tempted to try their skills at invading highly protected systems. Such top-level invaders typically leave some sign of their accomplishment. It may be something as simple as a message that appears in printed documents or on the screens of legitimate users. Hackers may also introduce a set of hidden instructions that cause a computer to destroy its data or alter its software instructions. The sophisticated but destructive computer programs involved in this modern kind of vandalism are called computer viruses. Viruses spread from one computer to another through disk swapping or over data lines that link one machine to another.

As society becomes more dependent upon computers, the damage potential of viruses increases. **Computer viruses** were brought to public attention in 1988 when the "Pakistani" virus (also called the "Pakistani brain" virus) became widespread in personal and office computers across North America.[79] The Pakistani virus had been created by Amjad Farooq Alvi and his brother Basit Farooq Alvi, two cut-rate computer software dealers in Lahore, Pakistan. The Alvi brothers made copies of costly software products and sold them at low prices mostly to Western shoppers looking for a bargain. Through a convoluted logic, the brothers hid a virus on each disk they sold in order to punish buyers for seeking to evade copyright laws. A more serious virus incident affected sensitive machines in NASA, nuclear weapons labs, federal research centres, and universities across the United States in late 1988.[80] The virus did not destroy data. Instead, it made copies of itself and multiplied so rapidly that it clogged machines and effectively shut them down within hours after it invaded them. Robert Morris, creator of the virus, was finally sentenced in April 1990 to 400 hours of community service and three years' probation and was fined $14 000.[81] Since then, many other virus attacks have made headlines, including the infamous Michaelangelo virus in 1992, and the intentional distribution of infected software on an AIDS-related research CD-ROM distributed about the same time; the Kournikova virus in 2000; the Sircam, Nimda, and Code Red worms—all of which made their appearance or were substantially modified by their creators in 2001—and, more recently, the 2003 Blaster and W32.Welchia worms.

*Data Manipulation* Data manipulation may be the most serious kind of computer crime. People who are able to effect unauthorized entry into computer files are often also able to modify the data they contain. Students who access university administrative computers in order to change the records of their grades is an example of data manipulation. Other skilled operators may transfer funds between private accounts, download trade secrets, hide the evidence of embezzlement, or steal customer lists. The hit movie *The Net* depicted a scenario in which a computer user enters a web of intrigue after accidentally discovering clandestine messages on the internet. Computer experts have warned of the real-life potential for international terrorism through computer sabotage.[82]

What may be the largest computer crime in history (in dollar amounts) happened rather early in the computer age. In 1984, a ring of employees at Volkswagen's Wolfsburg, West Germany headquarters modified files in the company's computers to hide the theft of US$600 million.[83] Some experts say that banks around the world routinely transfer over US$4 trillion a day through electronic media.[84] Such huge amounts are an incentive to technologically sophisticated criminals.

Software piracy is another major concern in the computer industry. A 1998 survey found that about 40 per cent of business software applications used in Canada in 1996 were illegal copies. Converted to dollars, software theft and manipulation cost more than $2.5 billion in sales and some $670 million in taxes. In Canada, a Business Software Alliance has formed in an effort to combat software theft. Despite the attempts of software companies to make copying software difficult, the copying trend does not appear to be declining.[85] These and other forms of computer crime reflect the seriousness of such hi-tech crimes and call for better enforcement practices.

## Combatting Computer Crime

Computer criminals are generally young, well-educated, aggressive, and technically sophisticated.[86] They commit computer crimes for various reasons. Some seek personal riches, while others are attracted to computer crime by the technical challenge it represents. A study of computer felons showed that they saw themselves as pitted against the computer.[87]

**computer viruses**
Small computer programs that are designed to secretly invade systems and modify either the way in which they operate or alter the information they store. Viruses are destructive software that may effectively vandalize computers of all sizes.

The computer criminal is the type of person who would probably resist the temptation to commit most other types of crimes. Because the offence committed is against a machine, however, this otherwise conformist type of person may deny that he or she has committed a crime.

Computer criminals are highly skilled, and the crimes they commit are often difficult for the technically uninitiated to detect. Many large corporations employ experts to detect unauthorized access to data-processing equipment, and a growing cadre of consultants serve the computer-security needs of smaller companies. Police departments have been hard-pressed to keep pace with the growing sophistication of computer equipment and the criminals who prey upon it. Among law enforcement agencies, expertise in computer crime investigations is rare. As noted above, the RCMP has limited resources to combat computer crime. Others, however, must rely upon personnel minimally trained in computer crime investigation. Given the wide range of expertise demanded of today's law enforcement personnel, it is probably unrealistic to expect detectives to be experts in the investigation of computer crime. In 1992, a Calgary-based security company began to specialize in network security. M-tech employs "professional (or ethical) hackers" who are paid to try to break into the computer security systems of major businesses in order to pinpoint security weaknesses.[88]

# TERRORISM

**terrorism** A violent act or an act dangerous to human life in violation of the criminal laws of Canada or of the provinces to intimidate or coerce a government, the civilian population, or any segment thereof, in furtherance of political or social objectives. While we usually think of terrorism as involving bombings, kidnappings, and hijackings, other forms of terrorism might include attacks on the information systems of financial institutions and threats to reveal trade or industry secrets. Crimes that lack the ideological component necessary to qualify as terrorism can be described simply as murder, vandalism, blackmail, and so on.

Relying on systematic but unpredictable violence, **terrorism** poses a unique threat to law enforcement and criminal justice officials. Although there have been comparatively few terrorist incidents in Canada, most Canadians have experienced a heightened awareness of the threat posed by terrorists since the September 11, 2001 attacks on the World Trade Center in New York and the Pentagon in Washington, D.C. Most reports indicate that our criminal justice system will continue to be buffeted by the expanding power of politically oriented endemic groups with radical agendas.[89] Throughout the 1970s and 1980s, increasing domestic terrorism in Canada required more criminal justice resources, as there have been a number of incidents involving racists and reactionary groups including the neo-Nazis and white supremacists such as the Heritage Front. In addition, there have been a number of incidents involving ethnic separatist and left-wing radical organizations. However, one difficulty when dealing with terrorism, which is sometimes referred to as political crime, is the lack of a clear definition. For example, at the turn of the century, the "Sons of Freedom," a small, radical group of Doukhobors whose lifestyle habits at that time were considered inappropriate in Canadian society (e.g., protesting nude in public), were deemed political terrorists. Similarly, the insurrection of the Front de Libération du Québec (FLQ) was also seen as a form of state terrorism. Even the Squamish Five, who in 1983 bombed a number of buildings as a form of protest connected to saving the environment, were branded by the media as terrorists.

It was, however, the bombing of Air India flight 182 in June 1985 that brought the issue of terrorism to the forefront in Canada. The flight originated in Toronto and was en route to Bangkok and Delhi when illegally planted bombs planted by Sikh fundamentalists exploded. The bombing resulted in the deaths of 329 people.

As of mid-October 2003, the trial is still ongoing against two people accused of the bombing: Ajaib Singh Bagri and Ripudaman Singh Malik. The Crown has opted to proceed to trial in the B.C. Supreme Court by direct indictment, without the need for a preliminary inquiry. A third suspect in the bombing, Inderjit Singh Reyat, pled guilty to manslaughter in February of 2003 and will likely testify against his co-accused when their trial commences in September 2003. Both of the accused have elected to be tried without a jury.[90] Although this bombing was not directed at any Canadian group, the fact that Canada was indirectly involved in a major terrorist act caused Canadians to realize that international terrorism was knocking on the domestic door. In November 1998, Sikh newspaper publisher Tara Singh Hayer, from Surrey, British Columbia, was found assassinated. The RCMP has concluded that the murder appears to be linked to the 1985 Air India bombing, and has charged Ajaib Singh Bagri with an earlier 1988 attempt on the life of Hayer. With the growing problems of domestic and transnational terrorism, future crime-fighting initiatives will be greatly affected by the threat posed by terrorists in Canada.

The aftermath of the September 11, 2001 terrorist attack on the Pentagon in Washington, D.C.

The Al-Qaeda attacks on the World Trade Center in New York City and the Pentagon have involved Canada for a number of reasons. Twenty-five Canadians, most of whom were living and working in New York City, died in the attacks on the World Trade Center. Suspected terrorists who are connected to Al-Qaeda have been known to reside in Canada in the past. Canada's close proximity and large undefended border with the United States makes our country a possible entry point for terrorists targeting the U.S. in the future. Border security has increased and intelligence-gathering agencies in Canada and the United States have worked incessantly to identify potential terrorists residing in or travelling to North America.[91] The terrorism infrastructure operating on this continent may be deeper than what was previously thought.[92] The United States and Canada have relatively lax security, according to Philip Jenkins, a counterterrorism expert. "In Europe," says Jenkins, "if you leave a bag at a railroad station, it will be blown up [for security reasons] when you come back 30 minutes later. Here, it will be taken to lost and found."[93] However, Canada has taken aggressive steps to counter the risk of terrorism. Recognizing the growing international nature of terrorist activities, since 1963 Canada began working co-operatively with other countries to combat terrorism. Since then, these countries have signed 11 International Conventions that are designed to counter specific acts of terrorism ranging from unlawful seizure of aircraft to the 1994 Convention on the Safety of the United Nations and Associated Personnel.

The current situation leads many observers to conclude that the Canadian justice system is not fully prepared to deal with the threat represented by domestic and international terrorism. Prior intelligence-gathering efforts focused on such groups have largely failed, leading to military intervention in places such as Afghanistan. Such failures are at least partially understandable, given that many terrorist organizations are tight-knit and very difficult for intelligence operatives to penetrate.

## Rules of Terrorism

According to criminologist Gwynn Nettler, any terrorism, either domestic or international, has six characteristics.[94] They are:

- *No rules.* There are no moral limitations upon the type or degree of violence that terrorists can use.

- *No innocents.* No distinctions are made between soldiers and civilians. Children can be killed as easily as adults.

- *Economy*. Kill 1, frighten 10 000.
- *Publicity*. Terrorists seek publicity, and publicity encourages terrorism.
- *Meaning*. Terrorist acts give meaning and significance to the lives of terrorists.
- *No clarity*. Beyond the immediate aim of destructive acts, the long-term goals of terrorists are likely to be poorly conceived or impossible to implement.

## BOX 15.3    Theory into Practice

## The Threat of Nuclear Terrorism

At the close of the 1980s, as the Soviet Union disintegrated, the ability of Russian authorities to retain control over Cold War stockpiles of weapons-grade nuclear materials was seriously compromised. Evidence of such lack of control quickly surfaced. A few years ago, for example, German police asked Stuttgart's State Center for Environmental Affairs to examine a gritty substance confiscated from the garage of an accused counterfeiter in the small town of Tengen-Weichs in southwestern Germany. They were surprised to find that the material was superpure plutonium 239—a key ingredient needed in the manufacture of atomic bombs. Officials at the European Institute for Transuranium Elements, where the plutonium was sent for further analysis, were able to determine through the identification of "chemical footprints" unique to the material that it had come from one of three top-secret Russian nuclear weapons laboratories—each of which had been among the most strictly guarded sites in the former USSR.

Destruction of 30 000 nuclear warheads under arms control agreements now in effect between the United States and Russia has further loosened controls over bomb-grade plutonium. And there is plenty of money available to reward nuclear smugglers. While the average Russian worker in the country's top-of-the-line nuclear facilities is paid only $160 per month, experts estimate that oil-rich Middle Eastern countries controlled by fanatical and dictatorial regimes are willing to pay as much as $150 million for the plutonium needed to make one bomb—an amount that can be smuggled out of a secure area in a briefcase or even the pocket of an overcoat.

The implications for Western nations concerned with controlling the spread of nuclear terrorism may be particularly dire. On a trip to Russia several years ago, FBI director Louis Freeh told senior law enforcement officers there that, "[o]ne criminal threat looms larger than ... others: the theft or diversion of radioactive materials in Russia and Eastern Europe." While Russian officials denied that any material has disappeared, they eagerly accepted Freeh's offer of U.S. aid in helping to prevent nuclear smuggling.

In the post-Soviet era, however, other officials are more willing to speak openly. Deputy chief of St. Petersburg's organized crime unit Vladimir Kolesnik, whose unit has been making at least four arrests per year of Russians trying to sell stolen nuclear material, says: "The problem is that security standards have slackened, and virtually everybody who has access to nuclear materials could steal something."

Of crucial concern to security experts are what weapons makers call "pits," or baseball-sized plutonium spheres, the end result of an exacting, highly technical, and very expensive manufacturing process. Anyone with even a rudimentary knowledge of bomb making can build an atomic bomb capable of wiping out a large city using stolen plutonium "pits." Pits can also be manufactured by processing plants operating in many places throughout the world from even small amounts of plutonium, weighing a gram or less. Hence, the continued pilfering of minute quantities of weapons-grade plutonium and the resale of such materials on a worldwide black market could soon lead to the construction of powerful terrorist weapons. As one writer explains, "Nuclear weapons in the hands of extremists willing to use them would produce terrorism of a wholly new magnitude. The central logic of terrorism is to maximize horror and shock, producing a blaze of publicity and attention for the cause it represents. By that measure, the crudest of fission bombs set off in a modern city, vaporizing entire blocks, would make the crimes of [traditional terrorists] rank as little more than pinpricks."

## QUESTIONS FOR DISCUSSION

1. What potential consequences does nuclear terrorism hold for the Canadian criminal justice system?

2. Is nuclear smuggling an activity with which Canadian law enforcement agencies are equipped to deal? If not, how might they be better equipped?

---

*Sources:* Jackson, J.O. (1994, July 28). Proliferation: Nightmare in a Vial of Dust. *Time, Inc.*, online; Komarow, S. (1994, August 17). Nuclear Smuggling: A Bomb Waiting to Go Off. *USA Today*, p. 6A; Nelan, B.W. (1994, August 26). Formula for Terror. *Time, Inc.*, online.

*Controlling Terrorism*

Terrorism represents a difficult challenge to all societies. The open societies of the Western world, however, are potentially more vulnerable than are totalitarian regimes. Democratic ideals in the West restrict police surveillance of likely terrorist groups and curtail luggage, vehicle, and airport searches. Press coverage of acts of terrorism encourages copycat activities by other fringe groups or communicates information on workable techniques. Laws designed to limit terrorist access to technology, information, and physical locations are stop-gap measures at best.

There are no signs that international terrorism will abate anytime soon. If diplomatic and other efforts fail to keep terrorism at bay, the criminal justice system may soon find itself embroiled in an undeclared war waged on American soil that may spill over into Canada. The system, whose original purpose was to resolve disputes and to keep order among the citizenry, cannot be expected to adequately counter well-planned, heavily financed, covert paramilitary operations. As long as terrorists can find safe haven in countries antagonistic to the rule of international law, their activities will continue. In addition, counterterrorist measures need to be based on the recognition that for some terrorist groups, retaliation is an open invitation to strike back even harder. In November 1998, from his jail cell in France, Carlos the "Jackal" called upon all his fellow terrorists to murder "one American or Zionist" for every day he spent in jail.[95] Until all nations of the world are willing to work together to ensure the safety of people everywhere, there can be little hope that the problem of terrorism will be solved. As Nettler has observed, "[t]errorism that succeeds escalates."[96]

# Terrorism and Technology

The technological sophistication of state-sponsored terrorist organizations is rapidly increasing. Handguns and even larger weapons are now being manufactured out of plastic polymers and ceramics. Capable of firing Teflon-coated armour-piercing bullets, such weapons are extremely powerful and impossible to uncover with metal detectors. Evidence points to the black-market availability of other sinister items, including liquid metal embrittlement (LME). LME is a chemical that slowly weakens any metal that it contacts. It could easily be applied with a felt-tipped pen to fuselage components in domestic aircraft, causing delayed structural failure.[97] Backpack-type electromagnetic pulse generators may soon be available to terrorists. Such devices could be carried into major cities, set up next to important computer installations, and activated to wipe out billions of items of financial, military, or other information now stored on magnetic media. International terrorists, along with the public, have easy access to maps and other information that could be used to cripple the nation. The numerous, extremely high-voltage (EHV) transformers on which the nation's electric grid depends, for example, are entirely undefended, but their locations can be pinpointed easily on available power network maps.

It is now clear that at least some terrorist organizations have at their disposal weapons of mass destruction, which the firepower and tactical mobility of law enforcement agencies cannot hope to match. The prospect of nuclear terrorism is a reality. The collapse of the Soviet Union at the close of the 1980s led to very loose internal controls over nuclear weapons and weapons-grade fissionable materials held in the former Soviet republics. Evidence of this continues to surface. In 1997, for example, German police were surprised to find that the gritty substance confiscated from the garage of an accused counterfeiter in the small town of Tengen-Weichs in southwestern Germany was the superpure plutonium 239, a key ingredient in the manufacture of atomic bombs. Officials were able to determine, through the identification of "chemical footprints" unique to the material, that it had come from one of three top-secret Russian nuclear weapons laboratories that had been among the most strictly guarded sites in the former Soviet Union.[98] Experts say that oil-rich Middle Eastern countries controlled by fanatical and the dictatorial regimes are willing to pay as much as US$100 million for the plutonium needed to make one bomb—and this amount of plutonium can be smuggled out of a supposedly secure area in a briefcase or even the pocket of an overcoat.

Another new kind of terrorism, called cyberterrorism, is lurking on the horizon. Cyberterrorism involves high technology, especially computers and the internet, in the planning and carrying out of terrorist attacks. The term was coined in the 1980s by Barry Collin, a senior research fellow at the Institute for Security and Intelligence in California. This term refers to the convergence of cyberspace and terrorism.[99] It was later popularized by a 1996 RAND report that warned of an emerging "new terrorism," meaning the way terrorist groups organize and the way they use technology. The report warned of a coming "netwar," or "infowar," consisting of coordinated cyber-attacks on America's economic, business, and military infrastructure.[100] A year later, FBI agent Mark Pollitt offered a working definition of cyberterrorism, saying that it is "the premeditated, politically motivated attack against information, computer systems, computer programs, and data which results in violence against noncombatant targets by subnational groups or clandestine agents."[101]

Scenarios describing cyberterrorism possibilities are imaginative and diverse. Some have suggested that a successful cyberterrorist attack on air-traffic control systems might cause airplanes to collide in midair, or that an attack upon food- and cereal-processing plants that would involve drastically altering the levels of certain nutritional supplements might sicken or kill a large number of our nation's young children. Other such attacks might cause the country's power grid to collapse or might muddle the records and transactions of banks and stock exchanges. Possible targets in such attacks are almost endless. Although no large-scale and disruptive acts of cyberterrorism have yet been reported, the fact that critical systems are potentially vulnerable to such attack was demonstrated by a recent exercise conducted by the U.S. National Security Agency (NSA).[102] Code-named Eligible Receiver, the simulated exercise targeted the U.S. Pacific command in Hawaii, which oversees 100 000 U.S. troops. The attackers were able to penetrate military computers and divert supplies, disrupt troop movements, and control critical Department of Defense computer systems.

The Canadian Security Intelligence Service identifies the possibility of cyberterrorism as part of a disturbing trend:

> The growing dependence of states on computer-based communications and technologies is leading to a world in which future conflicts could involve activities in cyberspace and attacks on a state's information infrastructure—now commonly referred to as information operations. Canada is concerned about its vulnerability to this threat because it relies heavily upon information technologies. Given that teenage hackers can compromise networks using basic skills and tools available on the Internet, the concern centres on what can be accomplished by terrorist groups or states possessing information, far greater resources, and motivation.[103]

To assist in developing protection for America's critical infrastructure, President George W. Bush created the Office of Homeland Security in 2001, making its director a cabinet member. Similarly, in an effort to protect vital interests from future acts of terrorism, the U.S. government is said to be considering the idea of building a whole new internet of its own. Dubbed GOVNET, the service would provide secure voice and data communications by remaining physically and electronically separate from existing internet router and gateways. The idea for GOVNET was first offered by Richard Clarke, President Bush's cybersecurity adviser in 2001. "We'll be working ... to secure our cyberspace from a range of possible threats, from hackers to criminals to terrorist groups, to foreign nations, which might use cyber war against us," Clark said.[104]

# TECHNOLOGY AND THE
# *CHARTER OF RIGHTS*

As governments tackle terrorist organizations and sophisticated organized crime networks, they turn to increasingly sophisticated technological innovations. When agencies of the justice system use cutting-edge technology, it inevitably provokes fears that citizens' rights will be abrogated in favour of these crime control initiatives. Individual rights, including the right to privacy and the protection afforded by the principles of fundamental justice, require constant reinterpretation as technology becomes more sophisticated. However, because some of the technology available today is so new, few court cases have yet to directly address the issues involved. Even so, it is possible to identify areas that hold potential for further dispute.

One of the most revered protections in the *Canadian Charter of Rights and Freedoms* is freedom of expression. Section 2(b) of the *Charter* reads, "Everyone has the following fundamental freedoms: ... freedom of thought, belief, opinion and expression, including freedom of the press and other media of communication...." The dissemination of pornography, and particularly child pornography, via the internet, has been a matter of some concern for approximately the last 10 years. In the early 1990s, Canada's *Criminal Code* was amended to provide specific protection for children from being involved in the production of pornography. Section 163.1 of the *Criminal Code* provides for imprisonment of up to five years for persons found guilty of possessing child pornography, and imprisonment for up to 10 years for those convicted of distributing child pornography. Opponents of this provision have claimed that criminalizing the possession or distribution of child pornography is unconstitutional because it restricts the free expression of the people who create, produce, possess, and distribute child pornography.

In 2001, in the landmark case of *R. v. Sharpe*, the Supreme Court of Canada upheld the constitutional validity of the child pornography provisions in the *Criminal Code*, with minor exceptions.[105] The Court granted an exception to permit the accused to possess self-created expressive material held by the accused alone for his or her own personal use. Otherwise, the *Criminal Code* offence of printing or publishing child pornography, while violating section 2(b) of the *Charter*, was justified under section 1 of the *Charter* as a justifiable limit on the freedom of expression.

With the advent of the internet, the scope for the distribution of offensive materials has expanded in ways not possible to envision a generation ago. Police efforts to curtail the commission of crime through this medium are frustrated by the huge scope of the web and the huge resources required to police it. On January 13, 2003, rock star Peter Townshend was arrested in a wide-ranging, multinational criminal investigation into child pornography on the internet.[106] His arrest was part of a worldwide sting resulting in over 4000 searches and many arrests.

Contemporary "super-sleuth" technologies, which provide investigators with the ability to literally hear through walls (using vibration detectors), listen to conversations over tremendous distances (with parabolic audio receivers), record voices in distant rooms (via laser readings of windowpane vibrations), and even look through walls (using forward-looking infrared devices, or FLIR, that can detect a temperature difference of as little as about one-tenth of one degree Celsius. The law-enforcement application of FLIR for certain kinds of investigative activity has been effectively banned by the Ontario Court of Appeal's 2003 ruling in *R. v. Tessling*.[107] Although not every one of the super-sleuth technologies mentioned here has undergone high-court scrutiny, the *Tessling* case indicates the direction that courts may likely take with regard to other such technologies. The court in *Tessling* addressed the use of helicopter-mounted FLIR technology for detecting the emanation of heat from a house suspected of being a marijuana-growing operation. The Court of Appeal held that the "FLIR represents a search because it reveals what cannot otherwise be seen and detects activities inside the home that would be undetectable without the aid of sophisticated technology."[108] Where the government uses the device to explore details of a private home that would previously have been unavailable without physical intrusion, the surveillance amounts to an unreasonable "search and seizure," in violation of section 8 of the *Charter*. Such searches are presumptively unreasonable without a warrant.

The *Charter* also protects the right of everyone to "life, liberty, and security of the person." These rights may only be deprived if the government does so in accordance with the principles of fundamental justice. What may be the greatest potential threat to the principles of fundamental justice comes not from the physical sciences, but from psychology, sociology, and other social scientific approaches to the study and prediction of human behaviour. Social science research generally involves the observation of large numbers of individuals, often in quasi-experimental settings. Many studies produce results of questionable validity when applied in other settings. Even so, the tendency has been for social scientists to create predictive models of behaviour with widely acclaimed applicability. Worse still, legislatures and criminal justice decision makers have often been quick to adopt them for their own purposes. Behavioural models, for example, are now used to tailor sophisticated law-enforcement investigations such as those based on police criminal-profiling programs. A behavioural model is a way of looking at how the prototypical person with particular characteristics acts. For example, behavioural profilers often distinguish between organized and disorganized killers. Based on crime scene characteristics, they place the suspect into one or the other category. This narrows the field of investigation to those suspects who fit the supposed characteristics. The justice system's growing use of behavioural models demonstrates a growing faith in the reliability of the social sciences, but it also holds the danger of punishment in anticipation of, not the actual committing of, a crime. In other words, identifying the characteristics of a person most likely to be associated with a particular type of crime is a relatively small step to take; a problematic result would arise if one were to isolate (punish) this person before he or she does anything wrong.

The major threat from social sciences to individual rights comes from the tendency they create to prejudge individuals based upon personal characteristics rather than facts—a process associated with racial profiling. Persons designated as dangerous as the result of a scientifically based conceptual profile may be subject to investigation, arrest, conviction, and harsh sentences, primarily on the basis of identified characteristics thought to be

## BOX 15.4  Theory into Practice

### B.C.'s Hate Crime Team: Responding to a Significant Future Crime Problem?

In 1996, British Columbia's government created a Hate Crime Team.[1] Its role is to coordinate investigations into hate and race crimes in the province by working with local police, sharing experiences and information, and communicating results from a centrally maintained database.

The team includes representatives from the RCMP, municipal police departments, the Ministry of Public Safety and Solicitor General (Criminal Justice, Policy, Planning and Legislation, Police Services) and the Ministry of Community, Aboriginal and Women's Services (The Settlement and Multiculturalism Branch). There are also full-time police officers, a community coordinator, and support staff on the team.

The team's mandate includes maintaining a system for tracking and analyzing data on hate-related offences, including hate propaganda offences and other offences where hate is a motivating factor. The officers on the team collect relevant information on hate/bias incidents occurring in the province, and track relevant reports on a centralized database. The Hate Crime Team prepares status reports for public distribution, summarizing the activities of the team, including the level and nature of hate and bias incidents identified by police and other community groups. It adopted the following working definition of a hate crime, based upon section 718.2 of the *Criminal Code*:

A hate/bias crime is a criminal offence committed against a person or property which is motivated by the suspect's hate, prejudice or bias against an identifiable group based on race, national or ethnic origin, language, colour, religion, sex, age, mental or physical disability, sexual orientation or any other similar factor.

Hate and bias offences are committed against individuals or groups because of their personal characteristics such as race, religion, ethnicity, sexual orientation, or disability. These offences strike at the very cohesiveness of a multicultural society. Hate crimes are specifically committed to harm and terrify not only a particular victim but the entire group of which the victim is a member.

The hate and bias crime provisions of the *Criminal Code* can be separated into two categories:

1. Hate propaganda offences where the offender advocates genocide or communicates hatred of any identifiable group. The relevant areas of the *Criminal Code* are sections 318 and 319.
2. Any other offence motivated by hate or bias, where the sentencing judge must consider this motivation as an aggravating factor. Examples are:
   (a) assault—"gay bashing"
   (b) mischief—spray painting a place of worship with racial or prejudicial comments
   (c) threatening—letter or other threatening communication with biased or prejudicial overtones.

Hate and bias crimes are offences involving intimidation, harassment, physical force, or threat of physical force against a person, family, property, or supporter. There is no specific offence of committing a crime motivated by hate and bias. Hate and bias criminal offences such as assault or damage to property arise because they are motivated by hate of, or bias against, people because of who they are, not for what they have done. When criminal activity is motivated

associated with certain kinds of misbehaviour. In effect, some social scientific models could produce unveiled forms of discrimination. This is especially true when the predictive factors of a behavioural model are mere substitutions for race, ethnicity, or gender.

As an example, some early studies of domestic violence tended to show that, among other things, the typical offender was male, was unemployed or had a record of spotty employment, was poorly educated, and was abused as a child or came from a broken home. Because many of these characteristics also describe a large proportion of the nation's black and aboriginal populations, more so than whites, this "model" may create a hidden tendency to accuse minority males of such offences—and sometimes to suspect them even when there is no direct evidence implicating them.

With these considerations in mind, social scientific models may nonetheless prove to be useful tools. The most acceptable solution would treat individuals on a case-by-case basis, looking to the general predictive models of social science only for guidance once all the facts become known.

Modern technological procedures appear to make self-incrimination a possibility, even in the absence of any verbal statements. Legislation requires, for example, that suspects must submit to blood alcohol tests under certain circumstances, and that samples

by bigotry and intolerance of others, it is regarded as a serious matter.

In 1996, in response to the public concerns regarding hate crimes, Parliament amended the *Criminal Code*, adding section 718.2 (a)(i), which makes "bias, prejudice or hate" an aggravating factor in the severity of the penalty imposed upon an offender. Several recent B.C. cases have resulted in courts applying section 718.2 against hate- and bias-motivated offenders.

For example, in *R.* v. *Miloszewski* (1999),[2] a provincial court judge sentenced five individuals convicted of manslaughter in the death of Nirmal Singh Gill. The five accused had been intent on vandalizing cars in a parking lot adjacent to a Sikh Temple in Surrey one evening. A 65-year-old caretaker at the temple came upon three of the accused in the parking lot and was attacked. Gill was later discovered badly beaten and taken to hospital where he died of his injuries. The trial judge applied section 718.2, sentencing the five accused to severe prison terms ranging from 15 to 18 years each.[3]

Not all incidents of hate-motivated bigotry or intolerance are dealt with as criminal offences. There are other avenues for dealing with their occurrence. The federal and provincial human rights codes prohibit discriminatory practices in a variety of contexts, such as publications, employment, residential tenancy, and the use of public facilities. Discrimination is typically prohibited on the basis of race, colour, ancestry, place of origin, religion, marital status, family status, physical or mental disability, and sex or sexual orientation. B.C.'s Human Rights Code (s. 7) prohibits the publication, issue or display of discriminatory material in the form of statements, publications, notices, signs, symbols, emblems, or other representations the expression of which indicate discrimination or an intention to discriminate against a person or a group or class of persons, or that is likely to expose them to hatred or contempt because of the race, colour, ancestry, place of origin, religion, marital status,

family status, physical or mental disability, sex, sexual orientation, or age of that person or that group or class of persons. While B.C.'s Human Rights Code does not contain an offence provision, the Human Rights Tribunal in B.C. accepts, screens, and mediates complaints arising from breaches of this code. Failed attempts at mediation can result in the Human Rights Tribunal conducting hearings into complaints. The Tribunal has the authority to order the discrimination to stop and to order other remedies for the victim of discrimination. Furthermore, the B.C. *Civil Rights Protection Act* might provide a remedy for hate crimes.[4] It defines a "prohibited act" as any conduct or communication interfering with the civil rights of a person or class of persons by promoting hatred or contempt, or superiority or inferiority, based on colour, race, religion, ethnic origin, or place of origin. A "prohibited act" is a civil tort, actionable without proof of damage. The Act has yet to be tested, despite being in force since 1981.

## QUESTIONS FOR DISCUSSION

1. Do provincial and federal efforts adequately address the issue of hate crimes in B.C.? Should other provinces consider enacting a *Civil Rights Protection Act*?

2. Should hate motivation be considered an aggravating factor in sentencing? Is this likely to have any effect on reducing the incidences of hate-motivated crime in our society? If so, how?

[1]See the B.C. government's website and the webpage "End Hate Crime," accessible at time of writing at **www.pssg.gov.bc.ca/end_hate_crime/policy_guide/intro.htm**
[2]*R.* v. *Miloszewski*, [1999] B.C.J. No. 2710 (B.C.P.C.), appeals as to sentence dismissed *R.* v. *Miloszewski*, [2001] B.C.J. No. 2765 (B.C.C.A.).
[3]For another recent examples of the application of section 718.2 in B.C., see: *R.* v. *Gabara*, [1997] B.C.J. No. 3090 (B.C.P.C.).
[4]*Civil Rights Protection Act*, R.S.B.C. 1996, c.49. Note: Although this law has been in force since 1981, it does not appear to have ever been applied.

of breath, semen, hair, and tissue may be taken without consent when the sampling procedures comply with statutory requirements. Technological advances over the next few decades are anticipated to increase the potential for incriminating forms of non-testimonial evidence.

In late 2001, the White House in the United States announced that it would try some captured Al-Qaeda leaders in military tribunals created especially for that purpose. These trials would raise questions regarding the right of individuals to public trials, and the right to trial by an impartial jury. In the years ahead, Canada will no doubt have similar issues to confront.

## SUMMARY

Old concepts of criminality, and of white-collar crime in particular, have undergone significant revision as a result of emerging technologies. Science fiction–like products, already widely available, have brought with them a plethora of possibilities for new high-stakes crimes, including computer crimes and "cybercrime." The well-equipped technologically advanced offender in tomorrow's world will be capable of committing property crimes involving dollar amounts undreamed of only a few decades ago. At the same time, the ability of law enforcement agencies to respond to everyday crimes will be enhanced by the advantage of cutting-edge technology.

Terrorism, a significant criminal justice issue in its own right, brings with it the threat of cyberterrorism and the potential for attacks upon information-management segments of our nation's critical infrastructure. Attacks by cyberterrorists could theoretically shut down or disable important services like electricity, food processing, military activity, and even provincial and federal governments.

Barring global nuclear war or world catastrophe, advances in technology will continue to occur. Citizens of the future will regard as commonplace much of what is only fantasy today. Gradual lifestyle modifications will accompany changes in technology and result in taken-for-granted expectations foreign to today's world. Within that changed social context, the "reasonableness" of technological intrusions into personal lives will be judged according to standards tempered by the new possibilities that technology has to offer.

Coming social changes, combined with powerful technologies, threaten to produce a new world of challenges for criminal justice agencies. Domestic and international terrorism, widespread drug running, and changing social values will evolve into a complex tangle of legal and technological issues that will confront the best law enforcement minds of the future. The Canadian criminal justice system will continue to be buffeted by the expanding power of politically oriented domestic and international groups with radical and unlawful agendas. Only through a massive infusion of funds to support the purchase of new equipment and the hiring and training of technologically sophisticated personnel can tomorrow's law enforcement agencies hope to compete with technologically adept criminals.

## DISCUSSION QUESTIONS

1. How has technology affected the practice of criminal justice over the past 100 years?

2. What future benefits and threats to the practice of criminal justice can you imagine emanating from technological advances that are bound to occur over the next few decades? What new forms of cybercrime do you envision?

3. What are the major differences between the concepts of "white-collar crime" and "occupational crime"? How have advances in technology created new opportunities for white-collar or occupational criminals? What is the best hope of the criminal justice system for coping with such criminal threats?

4. Has criminal law kept pace with the opportunities for dishonest behaviour created by advancing technology? What modifications in current laws defining criminal activity might be necessary in order to meet the criminal possibilities inherent in technological advances?

5. Why is terrorism a law enforcement concern? How is terrorism a crime? What can the Canadian criminal justice system do to better prepare itself for future terrorist crimes?

6. What is cyberterrorism? How do advances in technology increase the likelihood of cyberterrorism?

7. What threats to civil liberties do you imagine advances in technology might create? Will our standards as to what constitutes admissible evidence, what is reasonable privacy, and so on, undergo a re-evaluation as a result of burgeoning technology?

# WEBLINKS

www.safecanada.ca
**Public Safety**
This website is the Government of Canada's official site devoted to public safety concerns, including matters pertaining to computer safety, and national security concerns, such as terrorism issues.

www.csis-scrs.gc.ca
**Canadian Security Intelligence Service**
The official government website of the national intelligence-gathering agency responsible for, among other things, maintaining intelligence on terrorist threats to Canada.

www.terrorism.com
**The Terrorism Research Center**
The Terrorism Research Center is dedicated to informing the public of the phenomena of terrorism and information warfare. This site features essays and thought pieces on current issues, as well as links to other terrorism documents, research, and resources.

www.fbi.gov/terrorinfo/terrorism.htm
**FBI War on Terrorism**
The FBI's website contains information on efforts to combat terrorism in the U.S. This site includes a list of the most wanted terrorist suspects.

www.csfs.ca
**Canadian Society of Forensic Science**
The CSFS is a non-profit organization, created to maintain professional standards in the forensic sciences. Its website provides links to many other interesting websites about the various forensic sciences.

www.cybercrime.gov
**Cybercrime**
The official website of the U.S. Department of Justice, pertaining to law and policy governing cybercrime in the U.S.

# Notes

## Chapter 1

1. Across the globe, high alert. (2001, September 12). *Vancouver Sun*, p. A8.

2. Chretien condemns "evil assault on innocents." (2001, September 12). *Vancouver Sun*, p. A10.

3. Brodeur, J. and Viau, L. (1994). Police Accountability in Crisis Situations. Ch. 12 in Macleod, R.C. and Schneiderman, D. (eds.). *Police Powers in Canada: The Evolution and Practice of Authority*. Toronto: University of Toronto Press.

4. Fisher, L. (1996, July 8). Bizarre Right from Day 1. *Maclean's*, pp. 14–15.

5. B.C. Bishop Guilty of Rape. (1996, August 5). *Maclean's*, p. 27.

6. See also: Harris, M. (1991). *Unholy Orders: Tragedy at Mount Cashel*. Toronto: Penguin Books.

7. Law Commission of Canada. (2000). *Restoring Dignity: Responding to Child Abuse in Canadian Institutions*. Ottawa: Minister of Public Works and Government Services.

8. Harris, M. (1986). *Justice Denied: The Law Versus Donald Marshall*. Toronto: Macmillan.

9. *R. v. Marshall* (1982), 66 C.C.C. (2d) 499 (N.S.C.A.).

10. Hickman, T.A., Chair. (1989). *The Royal Commission on the Donald Marshall Jr. Prosecution*. Halifax: Province of Nova Scotia.

11. Karp, C. and Rosner, C. (1991). *When Justice Fails: The David Milgaard Story*. Toronto: McClelland & Stewart.

12. Makin, K. (1993). *Redrum the Innocent*. Toronto: Penguin Books.

13. Hamilton, A.C., Associate Chief Justice and Sinclair, C.M., Associate Chief Judge. (1991). *Report of the Aboriginal Justice Inquiry of Manitoba: The Justice System and Aboriginal People*, Vol. 1. Winnipeg: Queen's Printer; and Hamilton, A.C. and Sinclair, C.M. *Report of the Aboriginal Justice Inquiry of Manitoba: The Deaths of Helen Betty Osborne and John Joseph Harper*, Vol. 2. Winnipeg: Queen's Printer.

14. Ibid., Vol. 1, p. 610.

15. Jackson, M. (1983). *Prisoners of Isolation: Solitary Confinement in Canada*. Toronto: University of Toronto Press.

16. Ibid., pp. 48–49.

17. Ibid., pp. 185–203. See also: Jackson, M. (2002). *Justice Behind the Walls: Human Rights in Canadian Prisons*. Toronto: Douglas & McIntyre.

18. *The American Heritage Dictionary on CD-ROM*. (1991). Boston: Houghton Mifflin.

19. Boyle, C. (1994). The Battered Wife Syndrome and Self-Defence: Lavallee v. R. Ch. 14 in Hinch, R. (ed.). *Readings in Critical Criminology*. Scarborough, ON: Prentice-Hall.

20. Fletcher, G. P. (1988). *A Crime of Self-defense: Bernhard Goetz and Law on Trial*. New York: The Free Press.

21. The systems model of criminal justice is often attributed to the frequent use of the term "system" by the U.S. Presidential Commission in its report *The Challenge of Crime in a Free Society* (Washington, D.C.: U.S. Government Printing Office, 1967).

22. One of the first published works to utilize the non-systems approach to criminal justice was the American Bar Association's *New Perspective on Urban Crime* (Washington, D.C.: ABA Special Committee on Crime Prevention and Control, 1972).

23. Skolnick, J. H. (1966). *Justice Without Trial* (p. 179). New York: John Wiley.

24. Canadian Centre for Justice Statistics. (2002). *Canadian Crime Statistics 2001* (p. 66). Ottawa: Minister of Industry.

25. Canadian Centre for Justice Statistics. (2002). *Graphical Overview of the Criminal Justice Indicators 2000–2001* (p. 25). Ottawa: Minister of Industry.

26. See *R. v. Brydges* (1990), 53 C.C.C. (3d) 330 (S.C.C.).

27. Ericson, R.V. and Baraneck, P.M. (1982). *The Ordering of Justice: A Study of Accused Persons as Dependants in the Criminal Process* (p. 157). Toronto: University of Toronto Press.

28. *R. v. Hebert* (1990), 57 C.C.C. (3d) 1 (S.C.C.).

29. Packer, H. (1968). *The Limits of the Criminal Sanction*. Stanford, CA: Stanford University Press.

30. For an excellent history of policing in the United States, see: Farris, E.A. (1982, November). Five Decades of American Policing: 1932–1982. *The Police Chief*, pp. 30–36.

31. Carte, G.E. August Vollmer and the Origins of Police Professionalism. *Journal of Police Science and Administration*, Vol. 1, No. 1 (1973), pp. 274–281.

32. Gaines, L.L. (1987). Criminal Justice Education Marches On! In Muraskin, R. (ed.). *The Future of Criminal Justice Education*. New York: Criminal Justice Institute, Long Island University, C. W. Post Campus.

33. For a review of the development of criminology programs in Canada, see: Hackler, J. C. (1994). *Crime and Canadian Public Policy* (pp. 11–17). Scarborough, ON: Prentice Hall.

## Chapter 2

1. Bird, H. (1985). *Above the Law: The Tragic Story of JoAnn Wilson and Colin Thatcher* (p. 11). Toronto: Key Porter Books.

2. Colin Thatcher lost his final appeal to the Supreme Court of Canada in 1987: *R. v. Thatcher* (1987), 32 C.C.C. (3d) 481.

3. As quoted in Hagan, F. (1982). *Research Methods in Criminal Justice*. New York: Macmillan. From E. Webb et

al. (1981). *Nonreactive Measures in the Social Sciences* (2nd ed., p. 89). Boston: Houghton Mifflin.

4. Grainger, B. Data and Methodology in the Area of Criminal Justice. Ch. 2 in Kennedy, L.W. and Sacco, V.F. (eds.). (1996). *Crime Counts: A Criminal Event Analysis*. Toronto: Nelson Canada.

5. Martin, M. and Ogrodnik, L. (1996). Canadian Crime Trends. In Kennedy, L.W. and Sacco, V.F. (eds.). *Crime Counts: A Criminal Event Analysis*. Toronto: Nelson Canada.

6. Savoie, J. (2003). Homicide in Canada, 2002. *Juristat*, Vol. 23, No. 8, p. 5.

7. Wallace, M. (2003). Crime Statistics in Canada, 2002. *Juristat*, Vol. 23, No. 5.

8. Besserer, S. and Trainor, C. (2000). Criminal Victimization in Canada, 1999. *Juristat*, Vol. 20, No. 10, p. 12.

9. Wallace, M. (2003). Crime Statistics in Canada, 2002, note 7, p. 16.

10. Kong, R. (1998). Canadian Crime Statistics, 1997. *Juristat*, Vol. 18, No. 11, p. 15.

11. Wallace M. (2003). Crime Statistics in Canada, 2002, note 7, p. 16.

12. Gomme, I. (1993). *The Shadow Line: Crime and Deviance in Canada*. Toronto: Harcourt Brace. Citing the Canadian Urban Victimization Survey (1985); Kinnon, D. (1981). *Report on Sexual Assault in Canada*. Ottawa: Canadian Advisory Council on the Status of Women.

13. Savoie, J. (2003). Homicide in Canada, 2002, p. 1. See note 6.

14. These and other statistics in this section are derived primarily from Savoie, Homicide in Canada. See note 6.

15. *Crime Counts: A Criminal Event Analysis*, note 4, p. 66.

16. Bureau of Justice Statistics (BJS). (1988). *Report to the Nation on Crime and Justice* (2nd ed., p. 4). Washington, D.C.: U.S. Government Printing Office.

17. Ibid.

18. Ibid.

19. Silverman, R.A. and Kennedy, L.W. (1993). *Deadly Deeds: Murder in Canada*. Scarborough, ON: Nelson Canada.

20. See Rossmo, D.K. (1995). Geographic Profiling: Target Patterns of Serial Murderers (pp. 8–20). Unpublished doctoral dissertation. Simon Fraser University, Burnaby, BC.

21. Johnson, H. (1996). Sexual Assault. Ch. 8 in Kennedy, L.W. and Sacco, V.F. *Crime Counts: A Criminal Event Analysis*. Toronto: Nelson Canada.

22. Flowers, R.B. (1987). *Women and Criminality: The Woman as Victim, Offender and Practitioner* (pp. 33–36). Westport, CT: Greenwood Press.

23. Integration and Analysis Program. (1999). Sex Offenders. *Juristat*, Vol. 19, No. 3, p. 12.

24. Hotton, T. (2001). Spousal Violence After Marital Separation. *Juristat*, Vol. 21, No. 7.

25. Groth, A.N. (1979). *Men Who Rape: The Psychology of the Offender*. New York: Plenum Press.

26. Flowers. *Women and Criminality*. p. 36.

27. Canadian Centre for Justice Statistics. (2002). *Canadian Crime Statistics 2001* (p. 54). Ottawa: Minister of Industry.

28. Wallace, M. (2003). Crime Statistics in Canada, 2002, pp. 16 and 19.

29. Kowalski, M. (2000). Break and Enter, 1999. *Juristat*, Vol. 20, No. 13, p. 5.

30. Canadian Centre for Justice Statistics. (2002). *Canadian Crime Statistics 2001* (p. 16). Ottawa: Minister of Industry.

31. Greenberg, P. Break and Enter. Ch. 9 in Kennedy and Sacco. *Crime Counts*.

32. Federal Bureau of Investigation (FBI). (1984). *Uniform Crime Reporting Handbook* (p. 28). Washington, D.C.: U.S. Department of Justice).

33. Insurance Bureau of Canada. Vehicle Information Centre's website: How Cars Measure Up – Model Years 1999 and 2000. **http://www.vicc.com/english/ MeasureUp00.htm**. Accessed July 18, 2002.

34. Savoie, J. (2002). Crime Statistics in Canada, 2001, p. 11.

35. See Kennedy, L.W., Silverman, R.A., and Forde, D.R. (1988). *Homicide From East to West: A Test of the Impact of Culture and Economic Inequality on Regional Trends of Violent Crime in Canada*. Edmonton: Centre for Criminological Research, University of Alberta.

36. Hackler, J.C. (1994). *Crime and Canadian Public Policy*. Scarborough, ON: Prentice Hall.

37. Short, J. and Nye, F. (1958). Extent of Unrecorded Juvenile Delinquency: Tentative Conclusions. *Journal of Criminal Law, Criminology and Police Science*, 49:296–302.

38. Kennedy, L.W. and Dutton, D.G. (1989). The Incidence of Wife Assault in Alberta. *Canadian Journal of Behavioural Science*, 2(1):40–54.

39. Other Canadian surveys include Vaz, E. (1965). Middle Class Delinquency: Self Reported Delinquency and Youth Culture. *Canadian Review of Sociology and Anthropology*, 2:52–70; LeBlanc, M. (1975). Middle Class Delinquency. In Silverman, R. and Teevan, J.T. (eds.). *Crime in Canadian Society*. Toronto: Butterworths; Hagan, J., Gillis, A.R., and Chan, J. (1980). Explaining Official Delinquency: A Spatial Study of Class Conflict and Control. In Silverman, R.A. and Teevan, J.J. (eds.), *Crime in Canadian Society* (2nd ed.). Toronto: Butterworths; Gomme, I.M., Morton, M.E., and West, W.G. (1984). Rates, Types, and Patterns of Male and Female Delinquency in an Ontario County. *Canadian Journal of Criminology*, 26:313–324; Gomme. (1986). Strain and Adult Crime: The Use of Self Report Measures. Paper presented at the annual meeting of the Academy of Criminal Justice Sciences, Orlando Florida; LeBlanc, M. and M. Frechette. (1989). *Male Criminal Activity From Childhood Through Youth: Multilevel and Developmental Perspectives*. New York: Springer-Verlag.

40. Solicitor General Canada. (1983). Victims of Crime. *Canadian Urban Victimization Survey*. Ottawa: Solicitor General Canada.

41. For a convenient summary of the Canadian Urban Victimization Survey, see Evans, J. and Himelfarb, A. (1992). Counting Crime. Ch. 3 in Linden, R. (ed.).

*Criminology: A Canadian Perspective* (2nd ed., pp. 79–85). Toronto: Harcourt Brace. A more detailed compilation is available from the Solicitor General's publications, which were published after the survey:

Solicitor General Canada. (1983). Victims of Crime. *Canadian Urban Victimization Survey*. Ottawa: Solicitor General Canada.

Solicitor General Canada. (1984). Reported and Unreported Crimes. *Canadian Urban Victimization Survey*. Ottawa: Solicitor General Canada.

Solicitor General Canada. (1984). Crime Prevention: Awareness and Practice. *Canadian Urban Victimization Survey*. Ottawa: Solicitor General Canada.

Solicitor General Canada. (1985). Cost of Crime to Victims. *Canadian Urban Victimization Survey*. Ottawa: Solicitor General Canada.

Solicitor General Canada. (1985). Female Victims of Crime. *Canadian Urban Victimization Survey*. Ottawa: Solicitor General Canada.

Solicitor General Canada. (1985). Criminal Victimization of Elderly Canadians. *Canadian Urban Victimization Survey*. Ottawa: Solicitor General Canada.

Solicitor General Canada. (1986). Household Property Crimes. *Canadian Urban Victimization Survey*. Ottawa: Solicitor General Canada.

42. Chard, J. (1995). Factfinder on Crime and the Administration of Justice in Canada. *Juristat*, Vol. 15, No. 10, p. 9.

43. Hotton, T. (2001). Spousal Violence After Marital Separation. *Juristat*. Vol. 21, No. 7.

44. Johnson, H. (1996). Violent Crime in Canada. *Juristat*, Vol. 16, No. 6.

45. Dauvergne, M. and Johnson, H. (2001). Children Witnessing Family Violence. *Juristat*, Vol. 21, No. 6.

46. Locke, D. and Code, R. (2001). Canada's Shelters for Abused Women, 1999–2000. *Juristat*, Vol. 21, No. 1.

47. BJS, *Report to the Nation on Crime and Justice* (2nd ed., p. 27).

48. Savoie, J. (2002). Crime Statistics in Canada, 2001. p. 3.

49. Hackett, K. (2000). Criminal Harassment. *Juristat*, Vol. 20, No. 11.

50. Ibid.

51. Wiggins, M.E. (1988, April). Societal Changes and Right Wing Membership. Paper presented at the Academy of Criminal Justice Sciences Annual Meeting, San Francisco, California.

52. Holden, R. (1988, April). God's Law: Criminal Process and Right Wing Extremism in America. Paper presented at the annual meeting of the Academy of Criminal Justice Sciences, San Francisco, California.

53. Wiggins, M.E. (1986). Rationale and Justification for Right-Wing Terrorism: A Politico-Social Analysis of the Turner Diaries. Paper presented at the annual meeting of the American Society of Criminology, Atlanta, Georgia, October 1986.

54. 8 Accused of Plotting Los Angeles Race War. (1993, July 16). *The Austin American-Statesman*, p. A1; FBI: L.A. Race War Plot "Despicable." (1993, July 16–18). *USA Today*, p. 1A.

55. Corelli, R. (1995, August 14). A Tolerant Nation's Hidden Shame. *Maclean's*, pp. 40–43.

56. *R. v. Lelas* (1990), 58 C.C.C. (3d) 568 (Ont.C.A.).

57. *R. v. Simms* (1990), 60 C.C.C. (3d) 499 (Alta.C.A.).

## Chapter 3

1. Black, H.C., Nolan, J.R., and Nolan-Haley, J.M. (1990). *Black's Law Dictionary* (6th ed., p. 884). St. Paul, MN: West.

2. Ibid.

3. Wolfgang, M. (1987). *The Key Reporter*. Phi Beta Kappa, vol. 52, no. 1.

4. Roman influence in England had ended by A.D. 442, according to: Brinton, C., Christopher, J.B., and Wolff, R.L. (1967). *A History of Civilization* (3rd ed., Vol. 1, p. 180). Englewood Cliffs, NJ: Prentice Hall.

5. Abadinsky, H. (1988). *Law and Justice* (p. 6). Chicago: Nelson-Hall.

6. Burns, E.M. (1969). *Western Civilization* (7th ed., p. 339). New York: W. W. Norton.

7. Ibid., p. 533.

8. Brinton, Christopher, and Wolff. *A History of Civilization* (p. 274).

9. Aquinas, Thomas. (1983). *Summa Theologica*. Notre Dame, IN: University of Notre Dame Press.

10. *R. v. Morgentaler* (1988), 37 C.C.C. (3d) 449 (S.C.C.).

11. *Borowski v. AG for Canada* (1989), 47 C.C.C. (3d) 1 (S.C.C.).

12. *Daigle v. Tremblay*, [1989] 2 S.C.R. 530 (S.C.C.).

13. Rheinstein, M. (ed.). (1954). *Max Weber on Law in Economy and Society*. (Cambridge, MA: Harvard University Press.

14. Mill, John Stuart. (1859). *On Liberty*. London: Parker.

15. Walker, N. (1980). *Punishment, Danger, and Stigma: The Morality of Criminal Justice*. Totowa, NJ: Barnes & Noble.

16. Law Reform Commission of Canada. (1976). *Our Criminal Law, Report No. 3* (p 28). Ottawa: Information Canada.

17. Holmes, Oliver Wendell. (1881). *The Common Law*. Boston: Little, Brown.

18. Pound, R. (1968). *Social Control Through the Law* (pp. 64–65). Hamden, CT: Archon.

19. As found in Chambliss, W. and Seidman, R. (1971). *Law, Order, and Power* (pp. 154, 141–142). Reading, MA: Addison-Wesley.

20. Ibid., p. 140.

21. Ibid.

22. Ibid., p. 51

23. Ibid.

24. *R. v. Hydro-Quebec* (1997), 118 C.C.C. (3d) 97 (S.C.C.).

25. *R. v. Swain* (1991), 63 C.C.C. (3d) 481 (S.C.C.).

26. *RJR MacDonald Inc. v. Canada (Attorney General)* (1995), 100 C.C.C. (3d) 449 (S.C.C.).

27. A Calgary city bylaw governing the advertising of sex for sale on the streets was struck down in *R. v. Westendorp* (1983), 2 C.C.C. (3d) 330 (S.C.C.).

28. Carter, L.H. (1984). *Reason in Law* (2nd ed.). Boston: Little, Brown.

29. *Doern* v. *Phillips Estate*, [1995] 4 W.W.R. 1 (B.C.S.C.).

30. See MacAlister, D.M. (1999). Financial Compensation for Victims of Crime: Tort Damages as Restorative Justice? Unpublished Master of Arts thesis, School of Criminology, Simon Fraser University, Burnaby, B.C.

31. See Ch. 6 in Bogart, W.A. (1994). *Courts and Country: The Limits of Litigation and the Social and Political Life of Canada*. Toronto: Oxford University Press.

32. The Florida Supreme Court upheld the principle that retail gun dealers have a legal duty to refrain from selling firearms to intoxicated purchasers in this case: *Kitchen* v. *K Mart*, 697 So 2d 1200 (1997).

33. Davis, R. and Mauro, T. (1995, April 12). Judge OKs Suit Against Gun Maker, *USA Today*, p. 3A. While several recent cases in the United States have held gun manufacturer's immune from such suits, the issue is still unresolved in Canada. See: Kasindorf. (2001, August 7). Makers Can't be Sued for Gun Misuse: Court Says California Ruling Reverses Rare Victory for Crime Victims. *USA Today*.

34. See Verdun-Jones, S. (1997). *Criminal Law in Canada: Cases, Questions and the Code* (2nd ed., pp. 4–5 and Ch. 5). Toronto: Harcourt Brace.

35. See note 31.

36. Hackett, K. (2000, November). Criminal Harassment. *Juristat* Service Bulletin. Vol. 20, No. 11. Ottawa: Minister of Industry.

37. Holmes, O. W. (1881). *The Common Law*. Vol. 3.

38. *R.* v. *Ruzic* (2001), 153 C.C.C. (3d) 1 (S.C.C.).

39. The same is not true for procedures within the criminal justice system, which can be modified even after a person has been sentenced and, hence, become retroactive. See, for example, the U.S. Supreme Court case of *California Department of Corrections* v. *Morales* (1995), which approved of changes in the length of time between parole hearings, even though those changes applied to offenders already sentenced.

40. Black, Nolan, and Nolan-Harley. *Black's Law Dictionary* (6th ed., p. 343).

41. Justice Gale in *R.* v. *Widdifield* (1961), 6 Crim.L.Q. 152 (Ont.H.C.J.).

42. Chief Justice Culliton delivered the judgment of the court: *R.* v. *Smith* (1979), 51 C.C.C. (2d) 381 (Sask.C.A.).

43. See for example, the recent Supreme Court of Canada discussion of criminal negligence in the motor vehicle context in *R.* v. *Waite* (1989), 48 C.C.C. (3d) 1 (S.C.C.).

44. See for example: *R.* v. *Wright* (1979), 48 C.C.C. (2d) 334 (Alta.C.A.); *R.* v. *Browning* (1976), 34 C.C.C. (2d) 200 (Ont.C.A.); *R.* v. *Hilton* (1977), 34 C.C.C. (2d) 206 (Ont.C.A.); *R.* v. *Meloche* (1975), 34 C.C.C. (2d) 184 (Que.C.A.); *R.* v. *Lechasseur* (1977), 38 C.C.C. (2d) 319 (Que.C.A.); *R.* v. *Allard* (1990), 57 C.C.C. (3d) 397 (Que.C.A.); *R.* v. *Leblanc* (1991), 4 C.R. (4th) 98 (Que.C.A.); *R.* v. *Baltzer* (1979) 27 C.C.C. (2d) 118 (N.S.S.C.App.Div.);

45. For a discussion of competing psychiatric experts from the perspective of a practising forensic psychiatrist, see Semrau, S. and Gale, J. (2002). *Murderous Minds on Trial: Terrible Tales from a Forensic Psychiatrist's Case Book*. Toronto: The Dundurn Group.

46. Klofas, J. and Weischeit, R. (1987, March). Guilty but Mentally Ill: Reform of the Insanity Defense in Illinois. *Justice Quarterly*, Vol. 4, No. 1, pp. 40–50.

47. See *R.* v. *George* (1960), 128 C.C.C. 289 (S.C.C.).

48. See *R.* v. *Daviault* (1994), 93 C.C.C. (3d) 21 (S.C.C.).

49. See section 33.1 of the *Criminal Code*.

50. See *R.* v. *Parks* (1992), 75 C.C.C. (3d) 287 (S.C.C.).

51. *R.* v. *Stone* (1999), 134 C.C.C. (3d) 353 (S.C.C.).

52. As reported in Binder, A. (1988). *Juvenile Delinquency: Historical, Cultural, Legal Perspectives* (p. 494). New York: Macmillan.

53. *Facts on File, 1978*. (1979) New York: Facts on File.

54. *R.* v. *Lavallee* (1990), 55 C.C.C. (3d) 97 (S.C.C.).

55. *R.* v. *Ruzic*, see note 38.

56. *R.* v. *Coyne* (1958), 124 C.C.C. 176 (N.B.C.A.).

57. *R.* v. *Cancoil Thermal Corp. and Parkinson* (1986), 27 C.C.C. (3d) 295 (Ont.C.A.).

58. *Facts on File, 1987*. (1988) (New York: Facts on File).

59. *The Queen* v. *Dudley and Stephens* (1884), 14 Q.B.D. 273, at p. 286.

60. *Perka* v. *The Queen* (1984), 14 C.C.C. (3d) 385 (S.C.C.).

61. *R.* v. *Jobidon* (1991), 66 C.C.C. (3d) 454 (S.C.C.).

62. See *R.* v. *B(TB)* (1994), 93 C.C.C. (3d) 191 (P.E.I.C.A.) and *R.* v. *M(S)* (1995), 97 C.C.C. (3d) 281 (Ont.C.A.).

63. *R.* v. *W(G)* (1994), 90 C.C.C. (3d) 139 (Ont.C.A.).

64. See *R.* v. *Cey* (1989), 48 C.C.C. (3d) 480 (Sask.C.A.) and *R.* v. *Leclerc* (1991), 67 C.C.C. (3d) 563 (Ont.C.A.).

65. McCloskey, P.L. and Schoenberg, R.L. (1988). *Criminal Law Deskbook* (Section 20.03[13]). New York: Matthew Bende.

66. *R.* v. *Cleghorn* (1995), 100 C.C.C. (3d) 393 (S.C.C.).

67. *R.* v. *Shubley* (1990), 52 C.C.C. (3d) 481 (S.C.C.).

68. See *Kienapple* v. *The Queen* (1974), 15 C.C.C. (2d) 524 (S.C.C.).

69. McCloskey and Schoenberg, *Criminal Law Deskbook*, Section 20.02[4].

70. *R.* v. *Power* (1994), 89 C.C.C. (3d) 1 (S.C.C.).

71. *R.* v. *Crneck, Bradley and Shelley* (1980), 55 C.C.C. (2d) 1 (Ont.H.C.J.).

72. *R.* v. *O'Connor* (1995), 103 C.C.C. (3d) 1 (S.C.C.).

73. Quigley, T. (1997). *Procedure in Canadian Criminal Law* (pp. 351-352). Toronto: Carswell's.

74. See *R.* v. *Mack* (1988), 44 C.C.C. (3d) 513 (S.C.C.).

75. *R.* v. *Barnes* (1991), 63 C.C.C. (3d) 1 (S.C.C.).

76. See *R.* v. *Askov* (1990), 59 C.C.C. (3d) 449 (S.C.C.) and *R.* v. *Morin* (1992), 71 C.C.C. (3d) 1 (S.C.C.).

77. Adams, L. (1995, August 22). Simpson Trial Focus Shifts to Detective with Troubling Past. *Washington Post* online.

78. Nationline: Execution. (1995, June 21). *USA Today*, p. 3A.

79. Paciocco, D. (1999). *Getting Away with Murder: The Canadian Criminal Justice System*. Toronto: Irwin Law.

80. Ibid., pp. 320–321.

81. Ibid.

82. Ibid., p. 313.

83. Morse, S.J. (1995, Winter–Spring). The "New Syndrome Excuse Syndrome." *Criminal Justice Ethics*, pp. 3–15.

84. American Psychiatric Association. (1994). *Diagnostic and Statistical Manual of Mental Disorders* (4th ed). Washington, D.C.: APA.

## Chapter 4

1. A Reminiscence of a Bow-Street Officer. (1852, September). *Harper's New Monthly Magazine*, Vol. 5, no. 28, p. 484.

2. Sutor, A.P. (1976). *Police Operations: Tactical Approaches to Crimes in Progress* (p. 68). St. Paul, MN: West, citing Peel.

3. For a good discussion of the development of the modern police, see Reid, S.T. (1987). *Criminal Justice: Procedures and Issues* (pp. 110–115). St. Paul, MN: West, and Wrobleski, H.M. and Hess, K.M. (1993). *Introduction to Law Enforcement and Criminal Justice* (4th ed.). St. Paul, MN: West.

4. *Statute of Westminster*, 3 Edward I 1275, c. 9.

5. *Statute of Winchester*, 13 Edward I 1285, c. 1-6.

6. For a good discussion of the system of policing that evolved in England, see: Critchley, T.A. (1972). *A History of Police in England and Wales 900–1966* (2nd ed.). Montclair, New Jersey: Patterson Smith.

7. Pelham, Camdem. (1887). *Chronicles of Crime*, Vol. 1 ( p. 59). London: T. Miles.

8. See, for example, Marquis, G. (1994). Policing in Nineteenth-Century Canada. Ch. 1 in *Policing Canada's Century*. (Toronto: University of Toronto Press); Talbot, C.K., Jayewardene, C.H.S., and Juliani, T.J. Policing in Canada: A Developmental Perspective. (1984) *Canadian Police College Journal*, Vol. 8, pp. 218–288; Juliani, T.J., Talbot, C.K., and Jayewardene, C.H.S. (1984). Municipal Policing in Canada: A Developmental Perspective. *Canadian Police College Journal*, Vol. 8, pp. 315–385.

9. For a discussion of early policing efforts in Newfoundland, see Harnum, E.J.A. (1972, January). Newfoundland Constabulary. *Canadian Police Chief*; Fox, A. (1971). *The Newfoundland Constabulary*. St. John's: Robinson, Blackmore Printing and Publishing.

10. Senior, H. (1997). The Canadian Police Perspective. Ch. 10 in *Constabulary: The Rise of Police Institutions in Britain, the Commonwealth and the United States*. Toronto: Dundurn Press.

11. Stonier-Newman. L. (1991). *Policing a Pioneer Province: The B.C. Provincial Police 1858–1950*. Madeira Park, B.C.: Harbour Publishing.

12. See Robertson, D.F. (1978). The Saskatchewan Provincial Police, 1917–1928. 31 Saskatchewan History 1–11; and Anderson, F.W. (1972). *Saskatchewan's Provincial Police*. Aldergrove, B.C.: Frontier Publishing.

13. For a good discussion of the history of the RCMP's role in contract policing for the provinces, see: Macleod, R.C. The RCMP and the Evolution of Provincial Policing. Ch. 3 in MacLeod, R.C. and Schneiderman, D. (1994). *Police Powers in Canada: The Evolution and Practice of Authority*. Toronto: University of Toronto Press.

14. Dickson, J.A. (1987). Reflexions Sur Law Police en Nouvelle-France. *McGill Law Journal*, 497–22, 32. See also Lamontagne, G. (1972, October). Some Quebec Police History, *Canadian Police Chief*, Vol. 61(4), 28–30; Kelly, W. and N. (1976) *Policing in Canada*. Toronto: Macmillan; Juliani, T.J., Talbot, C.K., and Jayewardene, C.H.S. (1984). Municipal Policing in Canada: A Developmental Perspective. *Canadian Police College Journal*, Vol. 8 No. 4, 315–385.

15. Senior, E.K. (1988). The Influence of the British Garrison on the Development of the Montreal Police, 1832 to 1853. In Macleod, R.C. (ed.). *Lawful Authority: Readings in the History of Criminal Justice in Canada*. Toronto: Copp, Clark Pitman Ltd.; and also Senior, H. (1997). Police in Montreal. Ch 4. in *Constabulary: The Rise of Police Institutions in Britain, the Commonwealth and the United States*. Toronto: Dundurn Press.

16. See Ch. 2 in Stenning, P.C. (1982). *Legal Status of the Police*. Ottawa: Ministry of Supply and Services Canada.

17. Talbot, Jayewardene, and Juliani, in note 6.

18. Owings, C. (1969). *Women Police*. Montclair, NJ: Patterson Smith.

19. Seagrave, J. (1997). *Introduction to Policing in Canada*. Scarborough: Prentice Hall. See also Linden, R. (1980). *Women in Policing: A Study of the Vancouver Police Department*. Ottawa: Solicitor General of Canada.

20. Ibid. Seagrave. *Introduction to Policing in Canada*.

21. Linden, R. (1983). Women in Policing: A Study of Lower Mainland RCMP Detachments. *Canadian Police College Journal*, Vol. 7(1), pp. 217–229.

22. *From Social Worker to Crimefighter*, p. 25.

23. Kelly, N. and Kelly, W. (1973). *The Royal Canadian Mounted Police: A Century of History*. Edmonton: Hurtig Publishers.

24. President's Commission on Law Enforcement and Administration of Justice. (1967). *The Challenge of Crime in a Free Society*. Washington, D.C.: U.S. Government Printing Office.

25. See Ch. 4 in Griffiths, C.T., Whitelaw, B., and Parent, R. (1999). *Canadian Police Work*. Toronto: ITP Nelson.

26. Deaken, T.J. (1986, November.)The Police Foundation: A Special Report. *FBI Law Enforcement Bulletin*, p. 2.

27. Kelling, G.L. et al. (1974). *The Kansas City Patrol Experiment* Washington, D.C.: The Police Foundation.

28. Krajick, K., quoting Dr. George Kelling. (1978, September). Does Patrol Prevent Crime? *Police Magazine*.

29. Bieck, W. and Kessler, D. (1977). *Response Time Analysis*. Kansas City, MO: Board of Police Commissioners. See

also McEwen, J.T. et al. (1984). *Evaluation of the Differential Police Response Field Test: Executive Summary.* Alexandria, VA: Research Management Associates; and Sherman, L. Policing Communities: What Works? In Tonry, M. and Morris, N. (eds.). (1986). *Crime and Justice: An Annual Review of Research* (Vol. 8). Chicago: University of Chicago Press.

30. Ibid., p. 8.

31. Krajick. Does Patrol Prevent Crime?

32. Ibid.

33. Chaiken, J., Greenwood, P., and Petersilia, J. The Rand Study of Detectives. In Klockars, C.B. and Mastrofski, S.D. (1991). *Thinking About Police: Contemporary Readings* (2nd ed.). New York: McGraw-Hill.

34. Griffiths, C.T. et al. *Canadian Police Work,* above, note 23.

35. Sherman, L.W., Rogan, D.P., and Shaw, J.W. (1994, November). *Research in Brief.* The Kansas City Gun Experiment—NIJ Update.

36. Sherman, L.W. and Berk, R.A. (1984, April). *Minneapolis Domestic Violence Experiment.* Police Foundation Report #1. Washington, D.C.: Police Foundation.

37. National Institute of Justice. (1987, January–February). *Newport News Tests Problem-Oriented Policing.* National Institute of Justice Reports. Washington, D.C.: U.S. Government Printing Office.

38. Adapted from Deaken. The Police Foundation. See note 24.

39. Besserer, S. and Tufts, J. (1999, December). Justice Spending in Canada. *Juristat,* Vol. 19, No. 12. Ottawa: Minister of Industry.

40. Ibid.

41. Ibid.

42. Ibid.

43. Ibid.

44. R.S.C. 1985, c. R-10 as amended.

45. See "Organization of the RCMP" at the RCMP's website: **www.rcmp-grc.gc.ca/html/organi_e.htm**

46. Royal Canadian Mounted Police. *2000/2001 Performance Report, Royal Canadian Mounted Police.* Available at: **www.rcmp-grc.gc.ca/dpr/performance01e.pdf**

47. Middleton, G., Staff Reporter. (1997, July 27). They're Pulling the Profit Rug Out From Under Pot Growers. *The Province.* p. A9.

48. Palango, P. (1997, July 28). Fighting White-Collar Crime, the RCMP Can No Longer Get its Man: Mountie Misery. *MacLean's,* pp. 10–15 at p. 11.

49. Griffiths, C.T. and Verdun-Jones, S.N. (1994). *Canadian Criminal Justice.* (2nd ed.). Toronto: Harcourt Brace.

50. Statistics Canada. (1996, January). Police Personnel and Expenditures in Canada–1994. *Juristat,* Vol. 16 No. 1, p. 13.

51. Marquis, G. (1993). *Policing Canada's Century.* Toronto: University of Toronto Press.

52. Oppal, W. (1994). *Policing the Gap: Policing and the Community (Report of the Commission of Inquiry into Policing in British Columbia).* Victoria, B.C.: Attorney General.

53. Vancouver Police Department's website: **www.city.vancouver.bc.ca/police**

54. See note 50.

55. Jain, H.C. An Assessment of Strategies of Recruiting Visible-Minority Police Officers in Canada: 1985–1990, Ch. 8. in Macleod, R.C. and Schneiderman, D. (1994). *Police Powers in Canada: The Evolution and Practice of Authority.* Toronto: University of Toronto Press.

56. See note 50.

57. Vancouver Police Department's Recruiting Unit's website: **www.city.vancouver.bc.ca/police/recruiting**

58. Juliani, T.J., Talbot, C.K., and Jayewardene, C.H.S. (1984). Municipal Policing in Canada: A Developmental Perspective. *Canadian Police College Journal,* Vol. 8 No. 4, pp. 315–385 at p. 320.

59. Talbot, C.K., Jayewardene, C.H.S., and Juliani, T.J. (1984). Policing in Canada: A Developmental Perspective. *Canadian Police College Journal,* Vol. 8 No. 3, pp. 218–288 at p. 265.

60. Ontario Provincial Police Annual Business Plan 2002.

61. Ibid; Sûreté du Québec Rapport d'activité 2000–2001.

62. *Private Security: Report of the Task Force on Private Security* (p. 4). (1976). Washington, D.C.: U.S. Government Printing Office.

63. Campbell, G. and Reingold, B. (1994, March). Private Security and Public Policing. *Juristat,* Vol. 14 No. 10. Ottawa: Statistics Canada, 1994.

64. Cunningham, W.C., Strauchs, J.J., and Van Meter, C.W. (1990). *The Hallcrest Report II: Private Security Trends 1970–2000.* McLean, VA: Hallcrest Systems.

65. Forecast Survey: Executive Summary. (1990, January). *Security.*

66. Kelly, W. and N. (1976). *Policing in Canada.* Toronto: Macmillan of Canada.

67. Chang, D.H. and Fagin, J.A. (eds.). (1985). *Introduction to Criminal Justice: Theory and Application* (2nd ed., pp. 275–277). Geneva, IL: Paladin House.

68. George Smiley Joins the Firm. (1988, May 2). *Newsweek,* pp. 46–47.

69. Ibid.

70. For more information on ESI, see Davis, E.D. (1988, Fall). Executive Protection: An Emerging Trend in Criminal Justice Education and Training. *The Justice Professional,* Vol. 3, no. 2.

71. More than a Bodyguard. (1986, February 10). *Security Management.*

72. A School for Guards of Rich, Powerful. (1986, April 21). *The Akron Beacon Journal.* Ohio.

73. National Institute of Justice. (1985). *Crime and Protection in America: A Study of Private Security and Law Enforcement Resources and Relationships* (p. 42). Executive Summary. Washington, D.C.: U.S. Department of Justice.

74. Ibid., p. 60.

75. Cunningham, Strauch, and Van Meter. *Hallcrest II* (p. 299).

76. Ibid., p. 301.

77. Ibid. (italics added).

78. Ibid., p. 117.

79. National Institute of Justice. *Crime and Protection in America* (p. 12).

80. Ibid., p. 12.

81. Above, note 50 (Oppal report) at p. F-14.

82. For additional information, see: Deegan, J.G. (1987, March). Mandated Training for Private Security. *FBI Law Enforcement Bulletin*, pp. 6–8.

83. Cunningham, Strauchs, and Van Meter. *Hallcrest II* (p. 147).

84. Oppal Commission, 1994, p. F-32 – F-33.

85. National Institute of Justice. *Crime and Protection in America* (p. 37).

86. Ericson, R.V. and Haggerty, K.D. (1997). *Policing the Risk Society*. Toronto: University of Toronto Press.

## Chapter 5

1. Guildford Couple to Sue RCMP. (1996, January 24). *The Now*, p. 3.

2. Ogle, D. (1996). *Police Leadership and Management Development: Course Manual*. Halifax: Henson College, Dalhousie University.

3. For the elements of this definition that draw upon the now-classic work, see: Wilson, O.W. (1950). *Police Administration* (pp. 2–3). New York: McGraw-Hill.

4. Seagrave, J. (1997). *Introduction to Policing in Canada*. Scarborough: Prentice Hall.

5. Wilson, J.Q. (1968). *Varieties of Police Behaviour: The Management of Law and Order in Eight Communities*. Cambridge, MA: Harvard University Press.

6. Radelet, L.A. (1980). *The Police and the Community*. Encino, CA: Glencoe.

7. President's Commission on Law Enforcement and Administration of Justice. (1967). *The Challenge of Crime in a Free Society*. Washington, D.C.: U.S. Government Printing Office.

8. Bittner, E. Community Relations. (1976). In Cohn, A.W. and Viano, E.C. (eds.). *Police Community Relations: Images, Roles, Realities* (pp. 77–82). Philadelphia: J. B. Lippincott.

9. Ibid.

10. Hale, C. (1981). *Police Patrol: Operations and Management* (p. 112). New York: John Wiley.

11. Souryal, S. (1977). *Police Administration and Management* (p. 261). St. Paul: West.

12. Weston, P.B. (1976). *Police Organization and Management* (p. 159). Pacific Palisades, CA: Goodyear.

13. Hale. *Police Patrol*.

14. Seagrave. *Introduction to Policing in Canada*. See also: Griffiths, C.T. and Verdun-Jones, S.N. (1994). *Canadian Criminal Justice* (2nd ed.). Toronto: Harcourt Brace.

15. Moore, M.H. and Trojanowicz, R.C. (1988, November). Corporate Strategies for Policing. *Perspectives on Policing*, No. 6. Washington, D.C.: National Institute of Justice.

16. Ibid., p. 6.

17. The Community Policing Consortium. (1995). What Is Community Policing?

18. The Community Policing Consortium. (1995). Community Policing Is Alive and Well (p. 1).

19. Kelling, G.L. (1981). *The Newark Foot Patrol Experiment*. Washington, D.C.: Police Foundation.

20. Trojanowicz, R.C. (1983). An Evaluation of a Neighbourhood Foot Patrol Program. *Journal of Police Science and Administration*, Vol. 11.

21. Bureau of Justice Assistance. (1994). *Understanding Community Policing: A Framework for Action* (p. 10). Washington, D.C.: BJS.

22. Now in its third edition: Trojanowicz, R.C., Kappeler, V.E., and Gaines, L.K. (2002). *Community Policing* (3rd ed.). Cincinnati, Ohio: Anderson.

23. Moore and Trojanowicz. *Perspectives on Policing* (p. 8).

24. See the following: Skolnick, J.H. and Bayley, D.H. (1988). *Community Policing: Issues and Practices Around the World*. Washington, D.C.: National Institute of Justice; and Skolnick, J.H. and Bayley, D.H. Theme and Variation in Community Policing. In Morris, N. and Tonry, M. (eds.). (1988). *Crime and Justice: An Annual Review of Research* (Vol. 10, pp. 1–37). Chicago: University of Chicago Press.

25. Ibid.

26. Goodbody, W.L. (1995, April 30). What Do We Expect New-Age Cops to Do? *Law Enforcement News*, pp. 14, 18.

27. Murphy, C. The Development, Impact and Implications of Community Policing in Canada. Ch. 2 in Chacko, J. and Nancoo, S. (eds.). (1993). *Community Policing in Canada*. Toronto: Canadian Scholars' Press.

28. Normandeau, A. and Leighton, B. (1990). *A Vision of the Future of Policing in Canada: Police Challenge 2000: Background Document*. Ottawa: Solicitor General, Ministry Secretariat, Police and Security Branch.

29. Dicks, R., Superintendent, Officer in Charge of Burnaby Detachment, RCMP. See **www.city.burnaby.bc.ca/ cityhall/departments/pblcsf_rcmp.html**

30. See: Seagrave. *Introduction to Policing in Canada* (Chs. 10 and 11).

31. Generally, see: Chacko, J. and Nancoo, S. (eds.). (1993). *Community Policing in Canada*. Toronto: Canadian Scholars' Press. For a good critique of community policing, and of the current state of American policing in general, see: Sparrow, M.K., Moore, M.H., and Kennedy, D.M. (1990). *Beyond 911: A New Era for Policing*. New York: Basic Books.

32. Dantzker, M. and Mitchell, M. (1996). *Understanding Today's Police*. Scarborough: Prentice Hall.

33. Colebourn, J. (1996, September 16). Community Policing a Waste: RCMP. *The Province*, p. A4.

34. Goodbody, W.L. (1995, April 30). What Do We Expect New-Age Cops to Do. *Law Enforcement News*, p. 18.

35. Ibid.

36. Sparrow, M.K. (1988). Implementing Community Policing. *Perspectives on Policing*, No. 9. Washington, D.C.: National Institute of Justice.

37. L.A. Police Chief: Treat People Like Customers. (1993, March 29). *USA Today*, p. 13A.

38. Wasserman, R. and Moore, M.H. (1988, November). Values in Policing. *Perspectives in Policing*, No. 8 (p. 7). Washington, D.C.: National Institute of Justice.

39. Oppal, W.T. (1994). *Closing the Gap: Policing and the Community*. Commission of Inquiry into Policing in British Columbia. Victoria, B.C.: Attorney General.

40. Ibid.

41. Davis, K.C. (1975). *Police Discretion*. St. Paul, MN: West.

42. McKenna, P.F. (2000). *Foundations of Community Policing in Canada*. Toronto: Prentice-Hall.

43. Goldstein, H. (1979, April). Improving Policing: A Problem-Oriented Approach. *Crime & Delinquency*, Vol. 25, p. 236.

44. Goldstein, H. (1990). *Problem-Oriented Policing*. New York: McGraw-Hill.

45. For a further discussion in the Canadian context, see: Griffiths, C.T., Parent, R.B. and Whitelaw, B. (2001). *Community Policing in Canada*. Toronto: Nelson Thomson Learning.

46. Bayley, D.H. and Shearing, C.S. (1996). The Future of Policing. *Law & Society Review*, Vol. 30, no. 3, p. 585.

47. Ibid.

48. For a critique of Bayley and Shearing, see: Jones, T. and Newburn, T. (2002). The Transformation of Policing? Understanding Current Trends in Policing Systems. *British Journal of Criminology*, Vol. 42, p. 129.

49. Cohen, H. (1987, Summer/Fall). Overstepping Police Authority. *Criminal Justice Ethics*, pp. 52–60.

50. Davis, K.C. (1975). *Police Discretion*. St. Paul, MN: West.

51. Sykes, G. (1986, December). Street Justice: A Moral Defense of Order Maintenance Policing. *Justice Quarterly*, Vol. 3, no. 4, p. 505.

52. Skolnick, J.H. (1996). *Justice Without Trial: Law Enforcement in a Democratic Society*. New York: John Wiley.

53. Westley, W.A. (1970). *Violence and the Police: A Sociological Study of Law, Custom, and Morality*. Cambridge, MA: MIT Press; Westley, W.A. (1953). Violence and the Police. *American Journal of Sociology*, Vol. 49, pp. 34–41.

54. Niederhoffer, A. (1967). *Behind the Shield: The Police in Urban Society*. Garden City, NY: Anchor Press.

55. Barker, T. and Carter, D.L. (1986). *Police Deviance*. Cincinnati, OH: Anderson.

56. For example, see: Brown, M. (1981). *Working the Street: Police Discretion and the Dilemmas of Reform*. New York: Russell Sage Foundation.

57. Vincent, C. (1990). *Police Officer*. Ottawa: Carleton University Press.

58. Bennett, R. and Greenstein, T. (1975). The Police Personality: A Test of the Predispositional Model. *Journal of Police Science and Administration*, Vol 3, pp. 439–445.

59. Teevan, J. and Dolnick, B. (1973). The Values of the Police: A Reconsideration and Interpretation. *Journal of Police Science and Administration*, pp. 366–369.

60. Griffiths, C.T. and Verdun-Jones, S.N. (1994). *Canadian Criminal Justice* (2nd ed.). Toronto: Harcourt Brace.

61. Sherman, L. and Langworthy, R. (1979). Measuring Homicide by Police Officers. *Journal of Criminal Law and Criminology*, Vol. 4, pp. 546–560; Sherman, L.W. et al. (1986). *Citizens Killed by Big City Police, 1970–1984*. Washington, D.C.: Crime Control Institute.

62. Samaha, J. (1988). *Criminal Justice* (p. 235). St. Paul, MN: West.

63. Prenzler, T. and Mackay, P. (1995, Winter-Spring). Police Gratuities: What the Public Thinks. *Criminal Justice Ethics*, pp. 15–25.

64. For example, see: Clark, G. (1996, March 21). Volunteer's Steaming After Police Fire Him for Sipping Free Hot Chocolate. *The Province*.

65. Barker and Carter. *Police Deviance*.

66. While Canadian data on police deviance is scant, a 1995 survey of 6982 police officers conducted in New York City revealed that 65 per cent did not classify excessive force as deviant police behaviour. Likewise, 71.4 per cent of responding officers said that accepting a free meal is not a corrupt practice. Another 15 per cent said that the use of illegal drugs should not be considered corruption, as in the following: Nationline: NYC Cops—Excess Force Not Corruption. (1995, June 16). *USA Today*, p. 3A.

67. *Knapp Commission Report on Police Corruption*. (1973). New York: George Braziller.

68. Daley, R. (1978). *Prince of the City: The Story of a Cop Who Knew Too Much*. Boston: Houghton Mifflin.

69. McAlary, M. (1987). *Buddy Boys: When Good Cops Turn Bad*. New York: G. P. Putnam's Sons.

70. Ibid.

71. Ogilvie, C. (1996, March 5). Senior Cop Stole Cash. *The Province*, p. A4; Ogilvie, C. (1996, May 17). Never Meant to Keep Drug Money: Narc. *The Province*, p. A13.

72. Stanfield, R.T. (1996). *Issues in Policing: A Canadian Perspective*. Toronto: Thompson Educational Publishing.

73. Mewett, A.W. and Manning, M. (1994). *Mewett and Manning on Criminal Law* (3rd ed.). Toronto: Butterworths, p. 625.

74. Sutherland, E.H. and Cressey, D. (1970). *Principles of Criminology* (8th ed.). Philadelphia: J. B. Lippincott.

75. It was an RCMP reinvestigation that disclosed initial wrongdoing in the Donald Marshall incident, arising out of an investigation initially conducted by the municipal police agency in Sydney, Nova Scotia.

76. Marin, R.J. (1997). *Policing in Canada: Issues for the 21st Century* (p. 48). Aurora, Ont: Canada Law Book.

77. National Institute of Law Enforcement and Criminal Justice. (1978). *Controlling Police Corruption: The Effects of Reform Policies, Summary Report*. Washington, D.C.: U.S. Department of Justice.

78. See the "The Officer Down Memorial Page - Canada"

webpage at **www.odmp.org/canada** for a list of police officers killed while on duty.

79. See the review of the trial and sentencing at CBC Manitoba's webpage at: **www.winnipeg.cbc.ca/indepth/strongquill/**

80. See the "The Officer Down Memorial Page—Canada" webpage at **www.odmp.org/canada**

81. Ibid.

82. Ibid.

83. Collecting and Handling Evidence Infected with Human Disease-Causing Organisms. (1987, July). *FBI Law Enforcement Bulletin*.

84. Hammett, T.M. (1988). Precautionary Measures and Protective Equipment: Developing a Reasonable Response. *National Institute of Justice Bulletin*. Washington, D.C.: U.S. Government Printing Office.

85. *National Institute of Justice Reports*, No. 206. (November/December 1987).

86. Utton, T. (2001). Blood Borne Viruses and Associated Risks to Police. *RCMP Gazette*, Vol. 63, No. 3, pp. 37–38.

87. Taking Aim at a Virus: NYPD Tackles AIDS on the Job and in the Ranks. (1988, March 15). *Law Enforcement News*, p. 1.

88. Krantz, L. (2002). *The 2002 Jobs Rated Almanac*. New York: St. Martin's Griffin.

89. Victor, J. (1986, June). Police Stress: Is Anybody Out There Listening? *New York Law Enforcement Journal*, pp. 19–20.

90. Ibid. ??

91. Logan, M. (1995). A Systems Application to Stress Management in the RCMP. *RCMP Gazette*, Vol. 57, pp. 11–12.

92. Ibid.

93. Ibid.

94. Swanson, C.R., Territo, L., and Taylor, R.W. (1988). *Police Administration: Structures, Processes, and Behaviour* (2nd ed.). New York: Macmillan.

95. *Malley* v. *Briggs*, 475 U.S. 335, 106 S.Ct. 1092 (1986); *Biscoe* v. *Arlington* (1984), 80–0766, *National Law Journal*, May 13, 1985.

96. *Vallery* v. *Poe et al.* (1971), 23 D.L.R. (3d) 92 (B.C.S.C.).

97. See: Ceyssens, P. (1994). Legal Aspects of Policing. Saltspring Island, BC: Earlscourt Legal Press, 3–151.

98. The only case that appears to address the matter is the first trial judgment in *Berntt* v. *Vancouver (City)*, [1997] 4 W.W.R. 505 (B.C.S.C.). A new trial was ordered by the B.C. Court of Appeal (unreported decision, June 1, 1999, Vancouver Registry CA 023026).

99. *Persaud* v. *Donaldson* (1997), 143 D.L.R. (4th) 326 (Ont.Gen.Div.).

100. *Crossman* v. *The Queen* (1984), 9 D.L.R. (4th) 588 (F.C.T.D.).

101. *McTaggart* v. *Ontario*, [2000] O.J. No. 4766 (Ont.Sup.Ct.); *Klein* v. *Seiferling*, [1999] 10 W.W.R. 554 (Sask.Q.B.); *Dix* v. *Canada (Attorney General)*, [2002] A.J. No. 784 (Alta.Q.B.). On police civil liability in the Canadian context, see: Ceyssens, P. (1994). *Legal Aspects of Policing*. Saltspring Island, B.C.: Earlscourt Legal Press.

102. *Tennessee* v. *Garner*, 471 U.S. 1 (1985).

103. *Graham* v. *Connor*, 490 U.S. 386, 396–397 (1989).

104. Ibid.

105. Above, note 103.

106. NACOP Questions Delay in Federal Use of "Imminent Danger" Standards for Deadly Force. (1995, October 19). National Association of Chiefs of Police press release.

107. Chappell, D. and Graham, L.P. (1985). *Police Use of Deadly Force: Canadian Perspectives* (p. 96). Toronto: Centre of Criminology, University of Toronto, p. 96.

108. Fyfe, J. (1978). *Shots Fired: An Examination of New York City Police Firearms Discharges*. Ann Arbor, MI: University Microfilms.

109. Fyfe, J. (1981, March). Blind Justice? Police Shootings in Memphis. Paper presented at the annual meeting of the Academy of Criminal Justice Sciences. Philadelphia.

110. It is estimated that American police shoot at approximately 3600 people every year. See: Geller, W. (no date). Deadly Force. Study guide. Crime File Series. Washington, D.C.: National Institute of Justice.

111. Cohen, A. (1980, July). I've Killed That Man Ten Thousand Times. *Police Magazine*.

112. For more information, see: Auten, J. (1986, Summer).When Police Shoot. *North Carolina Criminal Justice Today*, Vol. 4, no. 4, pp. 9–14.

113. Ibid.

114. Hayeslip, D.W. and Preszler, A. (1993). NIJ Initiative on Less-than-Lethal Weapons. *NIJ Research in Brief*. Washington, D.C.: National Institute of Justice.

115. Ibid.

116. As quoted by Siegfried, M. (1989, Spring). Notes on the Professionalization of Private Security. The Justice Professional.

116. Kerr, J. (2002). RCMP Approves Taser Use Across Canada. *RCMP Gazette*, Vol. 64, No. 1, p. 20.

117. Flanagan, T.J. and Maguire, K. (1990). *Sourcebook of Criminal Justice Statistics—1989* (p. 16). Washington, D.C.: U.S. Government Printing Office.

118. Normandeau and Leighton. *A Vision of the Future of Policing in Canada: Police Challenge 2000: Background Document*.

119. See: Farris, E.A. (1982, November). Five Decades of American Policing, 1932–1982: The Path to Professionalism. *The Police Chief*, p. 31.

120. Ibid., p. 34.

121. Oppal, W. (1994). *Closing the Gap: Policing and the Community, the Report, Vol. 1* (p. E-26). Victoria: Policing in British Columbia Commission of Inquiry.

122. Ibid., pp. xxii–xxiii.

123. Wilson, O.W. and McLaren, R.C. (1977). *Police Administration* (4th ed., p. 259). New York: McGraw-Hill.

124. Ibid., p. 270.

125. Jain, H.C. An Assessment of Strategies of Recruiting Visible-Minority Police Officers in Canada: 1985–1990. Ch. 8 in Macleod, R.C. and Schneiderman, D. (eds.). (1995). *Police Powers in Canada: The Evolution and Practice of Authority* (p. 142). Toronto: University of Toronto Press.

126. Ibid.

127. Swol, K. (2002, February 12). *Police Resources in Canada, 2001*. Ottawa: Canadian Centre for Justice Statistics.

128. Walker, G. (1993) *The Status of Women in Canadian Policing: 1993*. Ottawa: Solicitor General of Canada.

129. Linden, R. and Fillmore, C. An Evaluation Study of Women in Policing. In Hudson, J. and Roberts, J. (eds.). (1993). *Evaluating Justice* (Ch. 5). Toronto: Thompson Educational Publishing.

130. Ibid, pp. 115–116.

131. Seagrave, J. (1997). *Introduction to Policing in Canada* (p. 96). Scarborough: Prentice Hall.

132. Bennett, C.L. (1991, March). *Interviews with Female Police Officers in Western Massachusetts*. Paper presented at the annual meeting of the Academy of Criminal Justice Sciences, Nashville, Tennessee.

133. For example, see: Jacobs, P. (1991, March). Suggestions for the Greater Integration of Women into Policing. Paper presented at the annual meeting of the Academy of Criminal Justice Sciences, Nashville, TN; Epstein, C.F. (1988). *Deceptive Distinctions: Sex, Gender, and the Social Order*. New Haven, CT: Yale University Press.

134. Garrison, C.G., Grant, N.K., and McCormick, K.L.J. (no date). Utilization of Police Women. Unpublished manuscript.

135. The Police Foundation. (1990) *On the Move: The Status of Women in Policing* Washington, D.C.: The Foundation.

## Chapter 6

1. *Ethier* v. *Vols* (1989), 76 Sask.R. 164 (Sask.Q.B.), at p. 167.

2. *Hunter* v. *Southam* (1984), 14 C.C.C. (3d) 97 (S.C.C.).

3. Fridman, G.H.L. (1989). *The Law of Torts in Canada* (Vol. 1, p. 11).

4. See: Linden, A.M. (1993). *Canadian Tort Law* (5th ed., pp. 608–618). Toronto: Butterworths; Klar, L.N. (1991). *Tort Law* (pp. 372–376). Toronto: Carswell.

5. See Linden, note 4, at p. 611.

6. See Linden, note 4, at p. 617.

7. See Klar, note 4, at p. 72.

8. See Klar, note 4, at pp. 73–74, citing *Braithwaite* v. *South Durham Steel Co.*, [1958] 1 W.L.R. 986.

9. See Klar, note 4, at p. 73.

10. Ceyssens, P. (1996). Legal Issues in Policing: Course Manual (pp. 60–61). Halifax: Henson College, Dalhousie University.

11. Ceyssens, P. (1994). *Legal Aspects of Policing* (pp. 3–41-3–42). Saltspring Island, B.C.: Earlscourt Press.

12. *R.* v. *Kokesch* (1990), 61 C.C.C. (3d) 207.

13. *R.* v. *Evans* (1996), 104 C.C.C. (3d) 23.

14. *Robson* v. *Hallett* (1967), 2 All E.R. 407 (H.L.).

15. *R.* v. *Johnson* (1994), 4 M.V.R. (3d) 283 (B.C.C.A.).

16. *R.* v. *Tricker* (1995), 96 C.C.C. (3d) 198 (Ont.C.A.).

17. Sopinka J. in *Evans* at p. 30, Major J. at p. 40.

18. Sopinka J. in *Evans* at p. 40.

19. Sopinka J. at p. 30.

20. Per Sopink J. at p. 31.

21. Per Sopinka J. at p. 31.

22. *Hunter* v. *Southam Inc.* (1984), 14 C.C.C. (3d) 97 (S.C.C.).

23. *R.* v. *Kokesch* (1990), 61 C.C.C. (3d) 207 (S.C.C.).

24. Per Major J. at p. 42.

25. Per Major J. at p. 42.

26. *Robson* v. *Hallett* (1967), 2 Q.B. 939 (H.L.).

27. *Halliday* v. *Nevill* (1984), 155 C.L.R. 1 (Austrl.H.C.).

28. *R.* v. *Johnson* (1994), 72 W.A.C. 102 (B.C.C.A.).

29. *R.* v. *Bushman* (1968), 63 W.W.R. 346 (B.C.C.A.).

30. *Robson* v. *Hallett* (1967), 2 Q.B. 939 (H.L.).

31. *Kay* v. *Hibbert* (1977), Crim.L.R. 226 (Q.B.).

32. Ceyssens, note 11 at pp. 3–42-3–43.

33. *McArdle* v. *Wallace* (1964), Crim.L.R. 467 (Q.B.).

34. Ceyssens, see note 11, at p. 3–44.

35. Ceyssens, see note 11, at p. 3–44.

36. Numerous cases, both English and Canadian, are cited for this proposition by Ceyssens. See note 11 at p. 2–13.

37. *R.* v. *Custer*, [1984] 4 W.W.R. 133 (Sask.C.A.).

38. Ceyssens, see note 11, discusses the case law in this regard, at pp. 2–14-2–16.

39. See Ceyssens, note 11, at p. 2–7.

40. *Thomas* v. *Sawkins* (1935), 2 K.B. 249 (K.B.D.).

41. *McLeod* v. *Commissioner of Police of the Metropolis* (1994), 4 All E.R. 583 (Eng.C.A.).

42. *R.* v. *Feeney* (1997), 50 D.L.R. (3d) 753.

43. *R.* v. *Macooh* (1993), 22 C.R. (4th) 70.

44. *Entick* v. *Carrington* (1765), 10 St.Tr. 1029.

45. Ibid, at p. 1073.

46. *Lamb* v. *D.P.P.* (1989), 154 J.P. 381 (Q.B.D.).

47. *Charter of Rights and Freedoms*, section 24.

48. *R.* v. *Therens* (1985), 18 C.C.C. (3d) 481.

49. *Chromiak* v. *R.* (1979), 49 C.C.C. (2d) 257.

50. *R.* v. *Collins* (1987), 33 C.C.C. (3d) 1 (S.C.C.).

51. *R.* v. *Burlingham* (1995), 97 C.C.C. (3d). 385 (S.C.C.).

52. *Nix* v. *Williams* (1984), 104 S.Ct. 2501.

53. Ibid.

54. *R.* v. *Stillman* (1997), 113 C.C.C. (3d) 385 (S.C.C.).

55. Stuart, D. Eight Plus Twenty-Four Two Equals Zero. (1998), 13 C.R. (5th) 50; Stuart, D. (1999.) The Unfortunate Dilution of Section 8 Protection. *Queen's Law Journal*, Vol. 25(1), p. 65.

56. *R. v. Edwards* (1996), 45 C.R. (4th) 377 (S.C.C.).

57. *R. v. Lawrence and Belnavis* (1998), 10 C.R. (4th) 65 (S.C.C.).

58. *R. v. M.(M.R.)*, [1998] 3 S.C.R. 393.

59. *R. v. Ruiz* (1991), 68 C.C.C. (3d) 500 (N.B.C.A.), affirmed [1993] 3 S.C.R. 649.

60. Brockman, J. and Rose, V.G. (2001). *An Introduction to Canadian Criminal Procedure and Evidence* (2nd ed.). Toronto: Nelson Canada.

61. For a look at U.S. developments in this area, see: Kingston, K.A. (1987, December). Look But Don't Touch: The Plain View Doctrine. FBI Law Enforcement Bulletin, p. 18; and *Horton v. California*, 110 S.Ct. 2301, 47 Cr.L. 2135 (1990).

62. Sauls, J.G. (1987, March). Emergency Searches of Premises, Part 1. *FBI Law Enforcement Bulletin*, p. 23.

63. *R. v. Godoy*, [1999] 1 S.C.R. 311.

64. *R. v. Storrey* (1990), 53 C.C.C. (3d) 316 (S.C.C.).

65. Ibid at p. 324.

66. Law Reform Commission of Canada. (1991). *Recodifying Criminal Procedure* (p. 2). Ottawa: LRCC.

67. Some of England's earliest legislation, including the *Statute of Westminster, 1275* and the *Statute of Winchester, 1285* ensure that members of the public are responsible for bringing offenders to justice.

68. Law Reform Commission of Canada. (1985). *Arrest, Working Paper 41* (p. 30). Ottawa: LRCC.

69. *R. v. Whitfield* (1970), 1 C.C.C. 129.

70. *Halsbury's Laws of England* (p. 342). (1955). London: Butterworths.

71. LRCC. See note 68, at p. 31.

72. Salhany, R. (1989). *Canadian Criminal Procedure* (5th ed.). Aurora: Canada Law Book.

73. LRCC, note 68 above, at pp. 32–33.

74. *R. v. Esposito* (1986), 24 C.C.C. (3d) 88 (Ont.C.A.).

75. *R. v. Bazinet* (1986), 25 C.C.C. (3d) 273 (Ont.C.A.).

76. Allman, A. (1994). Further Perspectives on Section 10(b) of the *Charter*: A Reply to Gold. *Criminal Reports*, Vol. 25, 4th, p. 280.

77. Salhany. See note 72, at p. 39.

78. *R. v. Moran* (1987), 36 C.C.C. (3d) 225 (Ont.C.A.).

79. *R. v. Voss* (1989), 50 C.C.C. (3d) 58 (Ont.C.A.).

80. *R. v. Cunningham* (1979), 49 C.C.C. (2d) 390 (Man.Co.Ct.).

81. The Supreme Court of Canada has stated that the arrest power conferred by section 495 (1)(b) in the *Code*, which governs where a peace officer "finds [an accused] committing [a crime]," is validly exercised where the police officer apparently finds the person committing an offence. The validity of the arrest does not depend upon a subsequent conviction for the offence for which the person is being arrested: *R. v. Biron* (1975), 23 C.C.C. (2d) 513.

82. However, if the police believe a summary conviction offence has been committed, they may stop the offender in order to demand his or her identity for the purpose of preparing process to compel the offender to attend court to answer to the charge. The offender's failure to co-operate results in the offence of obstruction under s. 129 of the *Criminal Code*, a hybrid and therefore arrestable offence: *R. v. Moore* (1979), 43 C.C.C. (2d) 83 (S.C.C.).

83. *R. v. Lefebvre* (1982), 1 C.C.C. (3d) 241 (B.C.Cty.Ct.).

84. Ibid. at p. 245.

85. *R. v. Howell* (1981), 78 Cr.App.R. 31.

86. *Hayes v. Thompson* (1985), 18 C.C.C. (3d) 254 (B.C.C.A.).

87. See *Criminal Code*, section 810.

88. *Cloutier v. Langlois* (1990), 53 C.C.C. (3d) 257.

89. *Gottschalk v. Hutton* (1921), 36 C.C.C. 298 (Alta.C.A.).

90. *R. v. Morrison* (1987), 58 C.R. (3d) 63 (Ont.C.A.).

91. *R. v. Miller* (1987), 38 C.C.C. (3d) 252 (Ont.C.A.).

92. *R. v. Caslake*, [1998] 1 S.C.R. 51.

93. *R. v. Simpson* (1993), 79 C.C.C. (3d) 482 (Ont.C.A.).

94. Ibid, 20 C.R. (4th) 3.

95. *R. v. Lal*, unreported ruling on admissibility of evidence (B.C.S.C., December 23, 1996, CC940845, Vancouver Registry). Conviction upheld (B.C.C.A., October 22, 1998, CA 023104, Vancouver Registry).

96. *R. v. Hufsky* (1988), 40 C.C.C. (3d) 398 (S.C.C.).

97. *R. v. Ladouceur* (1990), 56 C.C.C. (3d) 22 (S.C.C).

98. *R. v. Mellenthin* (1992), 69 C.C.C. (3d) 481 (S.C.C.).

99. *R. v. Ladouceur* (2002), 165 C.C.C. (3d) 321 (Sask.C.A.). Note that this is a different case from that found at note 97, which arose out of Ontario.

100. *R. v. Debot* (1989), 52 C.C.C. (3d) 193 (S.C.C.).

101. *R. v. Turcotte* (1987), 39 C.C.C. (3d) 193 (Sask.C.A.).

102. *R. v. Berger* (1989), 48 C.C.C. (3d) 18 (Sask. C.A.).

103. *Bisaillon v. Keable* (1983), 7 C.C.C. (3d) 385 (S.C.C.) and *R. v. Scott* (1990), 61 C.C.C. (3d) 300 (S.C.C.).

104. *R. v. Leipert* (1997), 112 C.C.C. (3d) 385 (S.C.C.).

105. *R. v. Bazinet* (1986), 25 C.C.C. (3d) 273 (Ont.C.A.).

106. *Koechlin v. Waugh and Hamilton* (1957), 118 C.C.C. 24 (Ont.C.A.).

107. *Ibrahim v. The King* (1914), A.C. 599.

108. *R. v. Ward* (1979), 44 C.C.C. (2d) 498 (S.C.C.).

109. *R. v. Horvath* (1979), 44 C.C.C. (2d) 498 (S.C.C.).

110. *R. v. Clarkson* (1986), 50 C.R. (3d) 298 (S.C.C.).

111. *R. v. Whittle* (1994), 92 C.C.C. (3d) 11 (S.C.C.).

112. *R. v. Oickle*, [2000] 2 S.C.R. 3.

113. *R. v. Hebert* (1990), 57 C.C.C. (3d) 1 (S.C.C.).

114. *R. v. Broyles* (1991), 68 C.C.C. (3d) 308.

115. *R. v. Gray* (1991), 66 C.C.C. (3d) 6 (Ont. C.A.).

116. See for example, *R. v. Moore* (B.C.C.A., July 3, 1997, CA 021420, Vancouver Registry), *R. v. Roberts* (B.C.C.A. April 2, 1997, CA 021174, Vancouver Registry), and *R. v. Miller* (1991), 9 CR (4th) 347 (Ont. C.A.).

117. *R. v. Mack* (1988), 44 C.C.C. (3d) 513.

118. *R. v. Barnes* (1991), 63 C.C.C. (3d).

119. *R.* v. *Manninen* (1987), 34 C.C.C. (3d) 385.

120. *R.* v. *Brydges* (1990), 53 C.C.C. (3d) 330 (S.C.C.).

121. *R.* v. *Clarkson* (1986), 25 C.C.C. (3d) 207 (S.C.C.).

122. *R.* v. *Black* (1989), 50 C.C.C. (3d) 1 (S.C.C.).

123. *R.* v. *Matheson* (1994), 92 C.C.C. (3d) 434 (S.C.C.).

124. *R.* v. *Morrison* (1987), 35 C.C.C. (3d) 437.

125. *R.* v. *Golden* (2001), 159 C.C.C. (3d) 449 (S.C.C.).

126. *R.* v. *Greffe* (1990), 55 C.C.C. (3d) 161 (S.C.C.).

127. *R.* v. *Monney* (1999), 133 C.C.C. (3d) 129 (S.C.C.)

128. *R.* v. *Duarte* (1990), 53 C.C.C. (3d) 1 (S.C.C.).

## Chapter 7

1. Russell, P.H. (1987). *The Judiciary in Canada: The Third Branch of Government* (p. 256). Toronto: McGraw-Hill Ryerson.

2. See: Townshend, C.J. (1899). Historical Account of the Courts of Judicature in Nova Scotia. *Canadian Law Times*, p. 25; McKeown, Justice. (1917). The First Supreme Court of New Brunswick. *Canadian Law Times*, p. 830; MacKinnon, F. (1951). *The Government of Prince Edward Island*. Toronto: University of Toronto Press; Noel, S.J.R. (1971). *Politics of Newfoundland*. Toronto: University of Toronto Press.

3. Russell, P.H. (1986). *The Judiciary in Canada* (p. 256–257); see also: Salhany, R.E. (1986). *The Origins of Rights* (p. 110). Toronto: Carswell; Neatby, H, (1937). *The Administration of Justice Under the Quebec Act*. Minneapolis: University of Minnesota Press; Banks, M.A. The Evolution of the Ontario Courts, 1788–1981. In Flaherty, D.H. (ed.). (1983). *Essays in the History of Canadian Law, II*. Toronto: The Osgoode Society.

4. Williams, D.R. (1977). *The Man for a New Country: Sir Mathew Begbie*. Sidney: Gray's Publishing; Farr, D.M.L. (1967). The Organization of the Judicial System in the Colonies of Vancouver Island and British Columbia, 1849–1871. *University of British Columbia Law Review*, p. 1.

5. Russell. *The Judiciary in Canada*. See also: Harvey, H, (1934). The Early Administration of Justice in the Northwest. *Alberta Law Quarterly*, p. 1.

6. Carrigan, D.O. (1991). *Crime and Punishment in Canada: A History* (p. 316). Toronto: McClelland and Stewart.

7. Ibid., p. 317.

8. Laskin, B. (1969). *The British Tradition in Canadian Law*. London: Stevens.

9. Stenning, P.C. (1982). *Legal Status of the Police: A Study Paper Prepared for the Law Reform Commission of Canada* (p. 45). Ottawa: Minister of Supply and Services.

10. Carrigan, D.O. *Crime and Punishment in Canada: A History* (p. 308).

11. Russell, P.H. *The Judiciary in Canada: The Third Branch of Government* (p. 205).

12. Carrigan, D.O. *Crime and Punishment in Canada: A History* (p. 355), citing Dennison, Colonel G.T. (1920). *Reflections of a Police Magistrate* (p. 10). Toronto: Musson.

13. Russell, P.H. *The Judiciary in Canada: The Third Branch of Government* (p. 258).

14. Ibid., at p. 260.

15. See: Hogg, P.W. (1992). *Constitutional Law of Canada* (3rd ed., Ch. 19). Toronto: Carswell.

16. Ibid., pp. 202–204.

17. See: Law Reform Commission of Canada. (1989). *Toward a Unified Criminal Court*. Ottawa.

18. See: Gall, G.L. (1995). *The Canadian Legal System* (4th ed., pp. 192–194). Toronto: Carswell.

19. Henderson, T.A., Kerwin, C.M., Guynes, R., Baar, C., Miller, N., Saizow, H., and Grieser, R. (1984). *The Significance of Judicial Structure: The Effects of Unification on Trial Court Operations*. Washington, D.C.: National Institute of Justice.

20. Thomas, M. Adult Criminal Court Statistics, 2000/01, *Juristat*, Vol. 22, No. 2, p. 3.

21. Ibid., p. 6.

22. Henderson et al. *The Significance of Judicial Structure: The Effects of Unification on Trial Court Operations*.

23. McCormick, P. (1994). *Canada's Courts* (p. 157). Toronto: James Lorimer & Co.

24. Antoniadis, J. (ed.). (1998). *The Canadian Law List 1998*. Aurora, Ont.: Canada Law Book.

25. Russell, P.H. *The Judiciary in Canada: The Third Branch of Government* (p. 283).

26. Morton, F.L. (1992). *Law, Politics and the Judicial Process in Canada* (2nd ed.). Calgary: University of Calgary Press.

27. See further: Gall, G.L. *The Canadian Legal System* (4th ed., pp. 261–279); Friedland, M.L. (1995). *A Place Apart: Judicial Independence and Accountability in Canada* (pp. 240–243). Ottawa: Canada Communications Group,

28. McCormick, P. and Greene, I. (1990). *Judges and Judging* (p. 43). Toronto: James Lorimer and Company.

29. McLintock, B. (1998, June 30). B.C. Provincial Court Judges Receiving Hefty Pay Raises. *The Province*, p. A3.

30. Doob, A., Baranek, P.M., and Addario, S.M. (1991). *Understanding Justices: A Study of Canadian Justices of the Peace* (p. 34). Toronto: Centre of Criminology, University of Toronto.

31. Lewis, M. (1993, May). No Peace for the Justices. *Canadian Lawyer*, pp. 28–30.

32. *Ell* v. *Alberta*, 2003 SCC 035.

33. Millar, P.S. and Baar, C. (1981). *Judicial Administration in Canada* (p. 6). Kingston and Montreal: McGill-Queen's University Press.

34. Rubin, H.T. (1976). *The Courts: Fulcrum of the Justice System* (p. 198). Pacific Palisades, CA: Goodyear.

35. Friedland, M.L. *A Place Apart: Judicial Independence and Accountability in Canada* (Ch. 9).

36. Ministry of Attorney General's website, "British Columbia – Integrated Justice System (JUSTIN)": **www.ag.gov.bc.ca/justin/how_justin_works.htm**.

37. Wright, M. (1991). *Justice for Victims and Offenders* (pp. 104 and 106). Bristol, PA: Open University Press.

38. For a discussion of the importance of the reference power in Canada's political system, see: Cheffins, R.I. and Johnson, P.A. (1986). *The Revised Canadian Constitution: Politics as Law.* Toronto: McGraw-Hill Ryerson; Monahan, P. (1987). *Politics and the Constitution: The Charter, Federalism and the Supreme Court of Canada.* Toronto: Carswell; Conklin, W.E. (1989). *Images of a Constitution.* Toronto: University of Toronto Press.

39. Hogg. *Constitutional Law of Canada* (3rd ed.). (pp. 222–225).

40. Friedland, M.L. (1965). *Detention Before Trial.* Toronto: University of Toronto Press.

41. See the discussion in Chapter 2 of: Law Reform Commission of Canada. (1988). *Compelling Appearance, Interim Release and Pretrial Detention.* Working Paper 57. Ottawa.

42. *R. v. Morales* (1992), 17 C.R. (4th) 74 (S.C.C.) and *R. v. Pearson* (1992), 17 C.R. (4th) 1 (S.C.C.).

43. Delisle, R.J. and Stuart, D. (1996). *Learning Canadian Criminal Procedure* (4th ed., pp. 246–247). Toronto: Carswell.

44. Ericson, R.V. and Baranek, P.M. (1982). *The Ordering of Justice: A Study of Accused Persons as Dependants in the Criminal Process* (p. 61). Toronto: University of Toronto Press.

45. Koza, P. and Doob, A.N. (1974–75). The Relationship of Pre-trial Custody to the Outcome of a Trial. *Criminal Law Quarterly,* Vol. 17, pp. 391–400; Koza, P. and Doob, A.N. (1974–75). Some Empirical Evidence on Judicial Interim Release. *Criminal Law Quarterly,* Vol. 17, pp. 258–272.

46. Kellough, G. "Getting Bail": Ideology in Action. In O'Reilly-Fleming, T. (ed.). (1996). *Post-Critical Criminology* (Ch. 8). Scarborough: Prentice Hall.

47. Hamilton, A.C. and Sinclair, C.M. (1991). *Report of the Aboriginal Justice Inquiry of Manitoba: Vol. 1 The Justice System and Aboriginal People.* Winnipeg: Government of Manitoba.

48. See further: Brockman, J. and Rose, V.G. (1996). *An Introduction to Canadian Criminal Procedure and Evidence* (pp. 84–85). Scarborough: Nelson Canada; Quigley, T. (1997). *Procedure in Canadian Criminal Law* (Ch. 11). Toronto: Carswell.

49. *U.S.A.* v. *Shephard* (1976), 34 C.R.N.S. 207 (S.C.C.).

50. *Criminal Code,* Section 577.

51. Canadian Intergovernmental Conference Secretariat. (2002, November 4–6). Federal-Provincial-Territorial Meeting of Ministers responsible for Justice. News release. Calgary, Alberta/ Online at: www.scics.gc.ca/cinfo02/830768004_e.html.

52. Verdun-Jones, S.N. and Hatch, A.J. (1985). *Plea Bargaining and Sentencing Guidelines* (p. 3). Ottawa: The Canadian Sentencing Commission.

53. Cohen, S.A. and Doob, A.N. Public Attitudes to Plea Bargaining. *Criminal Law Quarterly,* Vol. 32, pp. 85–109 at p. 86.

54. Law Reform Commission of Canada. (1989). *Plea Discussions and Agreements.* Working Paper 60 (p. 7). Ottawa: Law Reform Commission of Canada.

55. Cohen, S.A. and Doob, A.N. Public Attitudes to Plea Bargaining. *Criminal Law Quarterly,* Vol. 32, pp. 85–109.

56. Ericson, R.V. and Baranek, P.M. *The Ordering of Justice: A Study of Accused Persons as Dependants in the Criminal Process,* p. 143.

57. Boland, B., Logan, W., Sones, R., and Martin, W. (1988, May). *The Prosecution of Felony Arrests, 1982.* Washington, D.C.: U.S. Government Printing Office.

## Chapter 8

1. *Legal Services Society Annual Report 2001/02.* (2002). Vancouver: Legal Services Society.

2. Linden, S.B. (2002, February 26). Why We Must Save Legal Aid. *Globe and Mail,* p. A21.

3. The Information Service of the Canadian Bar Association. "Legal Aid." Retrieved December 12, 2002 at **www.cba.org/ CBA/Advocacy/legalAidAdvocacyResourcekit/ Ashorthistoryoffederalfundingforlegalaid.asp**

4. Department of Justice. "Legal Aid." Retrieved December 12, 2002 at **canada.justice.gc.ca/en/ps/pb/legal_aid.html**.

5. Integration and Analysis Program. (1997). *Justice Spending in Canada* (p. 7). *Juristat: Canadian Centre for Justice Statistics.* Ottawa: Ministry of Industry.

6. See, for example: Eisenstein, J. and Jacob, H. (1977). *Felony Justice: An Organizational Analysis of Criminal Courts.* Boston: Little, Brown and Company; Ulmer, J.T. (1997). *Social Worlds of Sentencing: Court Communities Under Sentencing Guidelines.* Ithaca, NY: State University of New York Press; Flemming, R.B., Nardulli, P.F., and Eisenstein, J. (1993). *The Craft of Justice: Politics and Work in Criminal Court Communities.* Philadelphia: University of Pennsylvania Press.

7. See, for example: Clynch, E.J. and Neubauer, D.W. (1981). Trial Courts as Organizations. *Law and Policy Quarterly,* Vol. 3, pp. 69–94.

8. Russell, P.H. and Ziegel, J.S. (1991). Mulroney's Judicial Appointments and the New Judicial Advisory Committees. *University of Toronto Law Journal,* Vol. 41, pp. 4–37.

9. Canadian Judicial Council. (2001). *Canadian Judicial Council Annual Report 2000–2001* (pp. 2–4). Ottawa: Canadian Judicial Council.

10. Ibid., p. 6.

11. Ibid., p. 6.

12. Canadian Judicial Council. (1996). *Canadian Judicial Council Annual Report 1995–1996* (p. 30). Ottawa: Canadian Judicial Council.

13. Judge's Slur Cited. (1996, March 6). *The Province,* p. A12.

14. Gall, G.L. (1995). *The Canadian Legal System* (4th ed., p. 284). Toronto: Carswell.

15. See section 99 of the *Constitution Act, 1867.*

16. The procedure is set out in the federal *Judges Act,* Part II.

17. Canadian Judicial Council. *Canadian Judicial Council*

*Annual Report 1995–1996* (p. 30).

18. Judge-Picking Panel Eyed. (August 15, 1995). *The Province*, p. A8; *The Globe and Mail* (1990, February 16).

19. Gall, G.L. *The Canadian Legal System* (4th ed., pp. 279–301).

20. Ibid., p. 300.

21. Ibid., pp. 279–301.

22. See: Friedland, M.L. (1995). *A Place Apart: Judicial Independence and Accountability in Canada* (pp. 105–113). Ottawa: Canadian Judicial Council.

23. Brockman, J. and Rose, V.G. (1996). *An Introduction to Canadian Criminal Procedure and Evidence* (pp. 17–18). Scarborough: Nelson Canada.

24. Stenning, P.C. (1986). *Appearing for the Crown: A Legal and Historical Review of Criminal Prosecutorial Authority in Canada* (pp. 239–242). Cowansville, Que.: Brown Legal Publications.

25. Ibid., at p. 239, quoting with translation from *Boucher* v. *The Queen*, [1955] S.C.R. 16 at p. 21.

26. Per Viscount Sankey in *Woolmington* v. *D.P.P.*, [1935] A.C. 462 (H.L.) at p. 481.

27. See: Law Reform Commission of Canada. (1990). *Controlling Criminal Prosecutions: The Attorney General and the Crown Prosecutor* (Ch. 3). Working Paper 62. Ottawa: Law Reform Commission of Canada; Stenning, P.C. *Appearing for the Crown: A Legal and Historical Review of Criminal Prosecutorial Authority in Canada* (Ch. 11); and Stuart, D. Prosecutorial Accountability in Canada. In Stenning, P.C. (ed.). (1995). *Accountability for Criminal Justice: Selected Essays*. Toronto: University of Toronto Press.

28. This charge approval process, referred to as "charge screening," is carried out by Crown prosecutors in British Columbia, Quebec, and New Brunswick: see Brockman, J. and Rose, V.G. *An Introduction to Canadian Criminal Procedure and Evidence* (p. 101).

29. Thomas, M. (2002). Adult Criminal Court Statistics, 2000/01. *Juristat Service Bulletin*, Vol. 22, No. 2, p. 6.

30. Province of British Columbia, Ministry of Attorney General, Criminal Justice Branch. *Crown Counsel Policy Manual* (p. 1). (1991, January 1.) File No. 55100-00, No. QUA 1.

31. See for example, the federal government's policy manual on line at: **http://canada.justice.gc.ca,** which sets out the charge approval standard as a "reasonable prospect of conviction."

32. *R.* v. *Stinchcombe* (1991), 68 C.C.C. (3d) 1 (S.C.C.).

33. *Nelles* v. *Ontario*, [1989] 2 S.C.R. 170.

34. Stuart, D. Prosecutorial Accountability in Canada. In Stenning, P.C. (ed.). *Accountability for Criminal Justice: Selected Essays* (p. 341).

35. Spohn, C., Gruhl, J., and Welch, S. (1987). The Impact of the Ethnicity and Gender of Defendants on the Decision to Reject or Dismiss Felony Charges. *Criminology*, Vol. 25, no. 1, pp. 175–191.

36. Stuart, D. Prosecutorial Accountability in Canada. In Stenning, P.C. (ed.). *Accountability for Criminal Justice: Selected Essays*, p. 353.

37. Ibid.; see also Edwards, J., LL.J. The Office of Attorney General — New Levels of Public Expectations and Accountability. In Stenning, P.C. (ed.), *Accountability for Criminal Justice: Selected Essays*.

38. MacAlister, D. (2000). *Accountability of Crown Prosecutors Under the Canadian Charter of Rights and Freedoms*. Unpublished LL.M. thesis, Queen's University.

39. Ibid. See also: MacAlister, D. (2000). Does the Residual Category for Abuse of Process Still Exist? *Criminal Reports* (5th series), Vol. 28, p. 72.

40. Canadian Bar Association. (1988). *Code of Professional Conduct* (p. 37). Ottawa: Canadian Bar Association.

41. Manes, D. and Silver, M. (1993). *Solicitor-Client Privilege in Canadian Law*. Markham: Butterworths.

42. Tufts, J. and Sudworth, M. (2003). *Legal Aid in Canada: Resource and Caseload Statistics*. Ottawa: Minister of Industry.

43. Carlson, D-L. (1993, April). Legal Aid Lineup: Wanting So Much More, Canada: Delivery in Dispute. *Canadian Lawyer*, pp. 19–21.

44. See: Brantingham, P.L. (1985). Judicare Counsel and Public Defenders: Case Outcome Differences. *Canadian Journal of Criminology*, Vol. 25, pp. 67–81; British Columbia Ministry of the Attorney General. (1991). *Legal Aid Models: A Comparison of Judicare and Staff Systems*. Victoria: Ministry of the Attorney General; Zapf, M. (1992). B.C. Bar Raps Discussion Paper on Public Defender Feasibility. *Lawyer's Weekly*, Vol. 11, p. 21; Mossman, M.J. (1993). Towards a Comprehensive Legal Aid Program in Canada: Exploring the Issues. *Windsor Review of Law and Social Issues*, Vol. 4, p. 1.

45. See Brantingham (note 44) and Carlson (note 43).

46. Legal Services Society. (2002, October). "Guidelines for Legal Aid" Pamphlet.

47. See: Cardwell, M. (1994). Legal Insurance in Big Demand from Quebec Consumers. *Lawyers Weekly*, Vol. 13, p. 48; Onyshko, T. (1991). Ontario Considering Public Pre-Paid Legal Insurance. *Lawyers Weekly*, Vol. 11, p. 21.

48. See the interesting discussion in *Fundamentals of the Criminal Justice System* (2nd ed.) by Donald A. MacIntosh (Toronto: Carswell, 1995, pp. 180–181).

49. Greenspan, E.L. The Role of the Defence Lawyer in Sentencing. In Boydell, C.L. and Connidis, I.A. (1982). *The Criminal Justice System* (p. 202). Toronto: Holt, Rinehart and Winston.

50. *R.* v. *Parks* (1992), 75 C.C.C. (3d) 287 (S.C.C.).

51. *R.* v. *Mohan* (1994), 29 C.R. (4th) 243 (S.C.C.).

52. Peterson, J.L. (1987). Use of Forensic Evidence by the Police and Courts. *Research in Brief* (p. 3). Washington, D.C.: National Institute of Justice.

53. Semrau, S. and Gale, J. (2002). *Murderous Minds on Trial*. Toronto: Dundurn Press.

54. Paciocco, D. and Steusser, L. (1996). *The Law of Evidence* (p. 222). Concord, Ont.: Irwin Law; Salhany, R.E. (1996). *The Practical Guide to Evidence in Criminal Cases* (4th ed., p. 187). Toronto: Carswell.

55. Section 644(2) of the *Criminal Code*.

56. Each province has its own jury legislation; for B.C., see the *Jury Act*, R.S.B.C. 1996, c. 242.

57. *R. v. Sherratt* (1991), 3 C.R. (4th) 129 (S.C.C.).

58. *R. v. Williams*, [1998] 1 S.C.R. 1128. See commentary by Gil McKinnon in "The Unbiased Juror," *The Vancouver Sun*, July 4, 1998, p. A23.

59. Speaking from a personal experience, one of the authors was himself the victim of a felony some years ago. His car was stolen in Columbus, Ohio, and recovered a year later in Cleveland. He was informed that the person who had taken it was in custody, but he never heard what happened to that person nor could he learn where or whether a trial was to be held.

60. Section 650 of the *Criminal Code*.

61. Renner, K.E. and Warner, A.H. (1981). The Standard of Social Justice Applied to an Evaluation of Criminal Cases Appearing Before the Halifax Courts. *The Windsor Yearbook of Access to Justice*, Vol. 1, pp. 62–80.

62. *Re Southam Inc. and The Queen* (1983), 3 C.C.C. (3d) 515 (Ont.C.A.).

63. See section 486 of the *Criminal Code* and also *R. v. Barrow* (1989), 48 C.C.C. (3d) 308 (N.S.S.C.).

64. *Dagenais v. Canadian Broadcasting Corporation* (1994), 34 C.R. (4th) 269 (S.C.C.)

65. Ibid., at p. 298.

66. *Canadian Broadcasting Corporation v. New Brunswick (Attorney General)* (1996), 110 C.C.C. (3d) 193 (S.C.C.).

67. Cauchon, D. (1993, March 10). Federal Courts Camera-Less. *USA Today*, p. 2A.

68. See discussions in: Gall,G. (1996). *The Canadian Legal System* (4th ed., p. 165). Toronto: Carswell; Boyd, N. (1998). *Canadian Law: An Introduction* (2nd ed., pp. 145–146). Toronto: Harcourt, Brace.

69. *Chandler v. Florida*, 499 U.S. 560 (1981).

70. Ibid.

71. Canadian Judicial Council. (1995). *Annual Report, 1994–1995* (pp. 34–35). Ottawa: Canadian Judicial Council.

72. See, for example, the B.C. Provincial Court's Criminal Caseflow Management Rules, which are online at: **www.provincialcourt.bc.ca/printthispage/criminalcaseflowmanagementrules.html**.

73. Gertz, M.G. and True, E.J. (1985). Social Scientists in the Courtroom: The Frustrations of Two Expert Witnesses. In Talarico, S.M. (ed.). *Courts and Criminal Justice: Emerging Issues* (pp. 81–91). Beverly Hills, CA: Sage Publications.

74. *R. v. Askov* (1990), 59 C.C.C. (3d) 449 (S.C.C.).

75. *R. v. Morin* (1992), 71 C.C.C. (3d) 1 (S.C.C.); a companion case, *R. v. Sharma* (1992), 71 C.C.C. (3d) 184 (S.C.C.) was handed down at the same time and contained some supplementary discussion on the appropriate conditions under which pretrial delay could be tolerated.

76. *R. v. Collins* (1995), 74 D.L.R. (4th) 355; 99 C.C.C. (3d) 385 (S.C.C.); a companion case, *R. v. Pelfrey*, was resolved at the same time as the *Collins* case, being resolved in the same manner, and for the same reasons as those given in *Collins*.

77. See the discussion of Baar's research in Chapter 2, "Approaches the Guaranteeing Trial Within a Reasonable Time," in the following: Law Reform Commission of Canada. (1994). *Trial Within a Reasonable Time: A Working Paper Prepared for the Law Reform Commission of Canada*. Ottawa: Public Works and Government Services Canada.

78. *R. v. Askov* (1990), 74 D.L.R. (4th) 355, at p. 396.

79. Schmitz, C. (1990, November 2). "Speedy Trial" Decision Sends Shock Wave Through Courts. *The Lawyers Weekly*, Vol. 10, No. 25, p. 1.

80. *R. v. Morin* (1992), 71 C.C.C. (3d) 1 (S.C.C.), at p. 7.

81. Mandel, M. (1994). *The Charter of Rights and the Legalization of Politics in Canada* (rev. ed., pp. 225–228). Toronto: Thompson Educational Publishing.

82. Ibid., p. 227.

83. Law Reform Commission of Canada. *Trial Within a Reasonable Time: A Working Paper Prepared for the Law Reform Commission of Canada*.

84. See, for example, the Supreme Court of Canada's decision in *R. v. Sherratt* (1991), 63 C.C.C. (3d) 193.

85. The procedure governing challenges is laid down in Part XX of the *Criminal Code*, in particular, sections 626–644.

86. For an excellent discussion of the jury selection procedure, see Chapter 20, "Jury Trials," in the following: Quigley, T. (1997). *Procedure in Canadian Criminal Law* (pp. 423–444). Toronto: Carswell.

88. *R. v. Sherratt* (1991), 63 C.C.C. (3d) 193 (S.C.C.).

88. In *R. v. Parks* (1993), 84 C.C.C. (3d) 353 (Ont.C.A.), leave to appeal to the Supreme Court of Canada refused.

89. The Court in *R. v. Williams* (1998), 124 C.C.C. (3d) 481 held to the same effect in regard to questioning about alleged racist attitudes in the community towards aboriginal Canadians.

90. Ibid.

91. Although the words *argument*, *statement* and *address* are sometimes used interchangeably in alluding to opening remarks, defence lawyers are enjoined from drawing conclusions or "arguing" to the jury at this stage in the trial. Their task, as described in the section which follows, is simply to provide information to the jury as to how the defence will be conducted.

92. See section 572 of the *Criminal Code*,.

93. See sections 276–277 of the *Criminal Code*.

94. See *R. v. Seaboyer* (1991), 66 C.C.C. (3d) 321 (S.C.C.).

95. *R. v. Crosby* (1995), 98 C.C.C. (3d) 225 (S.C.C.).

96. See subparagraph 686(1)(b)(iii) of the *Criminal Code*.

97. See *R. v. Bevan* (1993) 82 C.C.C. (3d) 599 (S.C.C.), and *R. v. S.(P.L.)* (1991) 64 C.C.C. (3d) 193 (S.C.C.).

98. *R. v. Avon* (1971), 21 D.L.R. (3d) 442 (S.C.C.).

99. Ibid., at p. 445.

100. Ibid., at p. 446.

101. Leading questions may, in fact, be permitted for certain purposes, including the purposes of refreshing a witness's memory, impeaching a hostile witness, introducing non-disputed material, and helping a witness with impaired faculties.

102. See: Paciocco, D. and Steusser, L. (1996). *The Law of Evidence* (p. 221); Delisle, R.J. (1996). *Evidence: Principles and Problems* (p. 333). Toronto: Carswell.

103. Section 132 of the *Criminal Code* makes perjury an indictable offence subject to a maximum penalty of 14 years in prison.

104. Section 486(2.1) of the *Criminal Code*.

105. *R. v. Levogiannis* (1993), 85 C.C.C. (3d) 327 (S.C.C.).

106. Ibid.

107. *R. v. Khan* (1990), 59 C.C.C. (3d) 92 (S.C.C.).

108. See Delisle, R.J. *Evidence: Principles and Problems* (pp. 531–532).

109. *R. v. B.(K.G.)* (1993), 79 C.C.C. (3d) 257 (S.C.C.), commonly referred to as *K.G.B.*

110. *R. v. U.(F.J.)* (1995), 42 C.R. (4th) 133 (S.C.C.).

111. *R. v. Conway* (1997), 121 C.C.C. (3d) 397 (Ont.C.A.)

112. *Criminal Code*, section 651.

113. *R. v. G. (R.M.)* (1996), 110 C.C.C. (3d) 26 (S.C.C.).

114. Rothwax, H.J., Judge. (1996). *Guilty: The Collapse of Criminal Justice*. New York: Random House.

115. Elwork, A., Sales, B.D., and Alfini, J. (1982). *Making Jury Instructions Understandable*. Charlottesville, VA: Michie.

116. Juror Hardship Becomes Critical as McMartin Trial Enters Year 3. (1989, May 15). *Criminal Justice Newsletter*, Vol. 20, pp. 6–7.

117. Too Scared to Testify. Guess Says Gill Rubs Salt in Wound. Sister's Poem Lost in Her Tears. (1998, June 21). *The Province* (Vancouver), pp. A1, A3, and A20, respectively.

118. See, for example: Berkson, L. and Carbon, S. (1978). *Court Unification: Its History, Politics, and Implementation*. Washington, D.C.: U.S. Government Printing Office; Henderson, T. et al. (1984). *The Significance of Judicial Structure: The Effect of Unification on Trial Court Operators*. Alexandria, VA: Institute for Economic and Policy Studies; Law Reform Commission of Canada. (1989). *Towards a Unified Criminal Court*. Working Paper 59. Ottawa: Law Reform Commission of Canada.

119. See, for example: Kenneth Carlson, et al. (1977). *Citizen Court Watching: The Consumer's Perspectives*. Cambridge, MA: Abt Associates.

120. See, for example: Cook, T.J. and Johnson, R.W. et al. (1982). *Basic Issues in Court Performance*. Washington, D.C.: National Institute of Justice.

121. See, for example: Wildhorn, S. et al. (1977). *Indicators of Justice: Measuring the Performance of Prosecutors, Defense, and Court Agencies Involved in Felony Proceedings*. Lexington, MA: Lexington Books.

122. Canadian Judicial Council. *Canadian Judicial Council, Annual Report, 1995–1996*.

## Chapter 9

1. Corelli, R. (1997, December 15). Latimer and the Law. *Maclean's*, Vol. 110, No. 50, pp. 49–51.

2. Dube, F. (1998, November 24). Court Says Latimer Must Serve 10 Years. *National Post*, p. A1.

3. *R. v. Latimer* (2001), 150 C.C.C. (3d) 129 (S.C.C.).

4. For a thorough discussion of the philosophy of punishment and sentencing, see the following: Garland, D. (1990). *Punishment and Modern Society: A Study in Social Theory*. Chicago: University of Chicago Press; Ellis, R.D. and Ellis, C.S. (1989). *Theories of Criminal Justice: A Critical Reappraisal*. Wolfeboro, NH: Longwood Academic; Sumner, C. (1990). *Censure, Politics, and Criminal Justice*. Bristol, PA: Open University Press.

5. The requirement for punishment is supported by the belief that social order (and the laws that represent it) could not exist for long if transgressions went unsanctioned. For a further discussion of just deserts theory, see: Von Hirsch, A. (1976). *Doing Justice: The Choice of Punishments*. New York: Hill and Wang. See also the more recent work by this architect of just deserts theory: Von Hirsch, A. (1993). *Censure and Sanctions*. Oxford: Clarendon Press.

6. See section 235 of the *Criminal Code* that sets life as the mandatory, that is, minimum) term for those convicted of first- or second-degree murder. Parole ineligibility is covered in sections 745 and 745.1.

7. Back to the Chain Gang. (1994, October 17). *Newsweek*, p. 87.

8. For an excellent review of the new get-tough attitudes influencing sentencing decisions in the U.S., see: Wicharaya, T. (1995). *Simple Theory, Hard Reality: The Impact of Sentencing Reforms on Courts, Prisons, and Crime*. Albany: State University of New York Press.

9. See, for example: Hockenbury, D.H. and Hockenbury, S.E. (1997). *Psychology* (p. 209). New York: Worth Publishers; Myers, D.G. (1992). *Psychology* (p. 241). New York: Worth Publishers.

10. Ibid., p. 225 and p. 247, respectively.

11. For a thorough review of the literature on deterrence, see: Paternoster, R. (1987, June). The Deterrent Effect of the Perceived Certainty; Paternoster, R. (1987, June). Severity of Punishment: A Review of the Evidence and Issues. *Justice Quarterly*, Vol. 4, no. 2, pp. 174–217.

12. Bedau, H.A. (1978, November). Retributivism and the Theory of Punishment. *Journal of Philosophy*, Vol. 75, pp. 601–620.

13. Hart, H.L.A. (1968). *Punishment and Responsibility: Essays in the Philosophy of Law*. Oxford: Clarendon Press, 1968.

14. Gendreau, P. and Ross, R.R. (1987, September). Revivification of Rehabilitation: Evidence from the 1980s. *Justice Quarterly*, Vol. 4, no. 3, pp. 349–408.

15. Bonta, J., Wallace-Capretta, S., and Rooney, J. (1998, October). *Restorative Justice: An Evaluation of the Restorative Resolutions Project*. **www.sgs.gc.ca/epub/cor/ e199810b/e199810b.htm**

16. Bazemore, G. and Umbreit, M.S. (1994, October). *Balanced and Restorative Justice: Program Summary* (foreward). Washington, D.C.: OJJDP.

17. Bonta et al. *Restorative Justice: An Evaluation of the Restorative Resolutions Project.*

18. Ibid.

19. Hogarth, J. (1971). Sentencing as a Human Process Toronto: University of Toronto Press.

20. Oklahoma Rapist Gets 30,000 Years. (1994, December 23). United Press International wire services. Southwest edition.

21. See sections 718.1 and 718.2 of the *Criminal Code*. The restraint principle holds that an offender should not be sentenced to incarceration if a less restrictive alternative is appropriate in the circumstances. The proportionality principle limits the amount of punishment imposed to the amount of harm inflicted in the commission of the crime. The totality principle requires the sentencing judge to ensure that sentencing to consecutive sentences does not result in a sentence that is in aggregate overly harsh or unduly long.

22. *Basic Facts About Corrections in Canada: 1997 Edition.* (1997). Ottawa: Solicitor General Canada.

23. Canadian Sentencing Commission. (1987). Department of Justice. *Sentencing Reform: A Canadian Approach.* Catalogue Number J2-67/1986E. Ottawa: Minister of Supply and Services Canada.

24. For a thorough consideration of alleged disparities, see the following: Kleck, G. (1981). Racial Discrimination in Criminal Sentencing: A Critical Evaluation of the Evidence with Additional Evidence on the Death Penalty. *American Sociological Review*, No. 46, pp. 783–805; Kleck, G. (1985). Life Support for Ailing Hypotheses: Modes of Summarizing the Evidence for Racial Discrimination in Sentencing. *Law and Human Behavior*, No. 9, pp. 271–285.

25. National Council on Crime and Delinquency. (1996). *National Assessment of Structured Sentencing.* Washington, D.C.: BJA.

26. Ibid.

27. Ibid.

28. For an early statement of this problem, see the following: Zimring, F.E. (1974). Making the Punishment Fit the Crime: A Consumers Guide to Sentencing Reform. In Hawkins, G. and Zimring, F. E. (eds.). *The Pursuit of Criminal Justice* (pp. 267–275). Chicago: University of Chicago Press.

29. Alschuler, A.W. (1979). Sentencing Reform and Prosecutorial Power: A Critique of Recent Proposals for Fixed and Presumptive Sentencing. In Messinger, S.L. and Bittner, E. (eds.). *Criminology Review Yearbook* (Vol. 1, pp. 416–445). Beverly Hills, CA: Sage Publications.

30. Ibid., p. 422.

31. Link, C.T. and Shover, N. (1986, September). The Origins of Criminal Sentencing Reforms. *Justice Quarterly*, Vol. 3, No. 3, pp. 329–342.

32. For a good discussion of such issues, see: Toch, H. (1988, June). Rewarding Convicted Offenders. *Federal Probation*, pp. 42–48.

33. Daubney Committee. (1998). *Taking Responsibility: Report of the Standing Committee on Justice and Solicitor General on its Review of Sentencing, Conditional Release and Related Aspects of Corrections.* Ottawa: Queen's Printer.

34. Much of the material in this section is derived from the following: Parent, D., Dunworth, T., McDonald, D., and Rhodes, W. (1997, January). Mandatory Sentencing. *NIJ Research in Action Series.* Washington, D.C.: NIJ.

35. In mid-1996, the California Supreme Court ruled that the U.S. three-strikes law was an undue intrusion on judges' sentencing discretion.

36. Pierce, G.L. and Bowers, W.J. (1981). The BartleyFox Gun Laws Short-Term Impact on Crime in Boston. *Annals of the American Academy of Political and Social Science*, Vol. 455, pp. 120–132.

37. Loftin, C., Heumann, M., and McDowall, D. (1983). Mandatory Sentencing and Firearms Violence: Evaluating an Alternative to Gun Control. *Law and Society Review*, Vol. 17, pp. 287–318; Loftin, C. and McDowall, D. (1984). The Deterrent Effects of the Florida Felony Firearm Law. *Journal of Criminal Law and Criminology*, Vol. 75, pp. 250–259; Joint Committee on New York Drug Law Evaluation. (1978). *The Nations Toughest Drug Law: Evaluating the New York Experience, a project of the Association of the Bar of the City of New York, the City of New York and the Drug Abuse Council, Inc.* Washington, D.C.: U.S. Government Printing Office.

38. McDowall, D., Loftin, C., and Wiersema, B. (1992, Summer). A Comparative Study of the Preventive Effects of Mandatory Sentencing Laws for Gun Crimes. *Journal of Criminal Law and Criminology*, Vol. 83, no. 2, pp. 378–394.

39. Greenfeld. Prison Sentences and Time Served for Violence.

40. Bureau of Justice Statistics. (1995). Prison Sentences and Time Served for Violence. Rockville, MD: Bureau of Justice Statistics.

41. Martello, T. (1994, April 26). Truth in Sentencing. The Associated Press wire services. Northern edition.

42. Eisenstein, J. and Jacob, H. (1977). *Felony Justice* Boston: Little, Brown.

43. Petersilia, J. (1983). *Racial Disparities in the Criminal Justice System.* Santa Monica, CA: The Rand Corporation.

44. Ragona, A.J. and Ryan, J.P. (1983). *Beyond the Courtroom: A Comparative Analysis of Misdemeanor Sentencing Executive Summary.* Chicago: American Judicature Society.

45. Kuklinski, J.H. and Stanga, J.E. (1979). Political Participation and Government Responsiveness: The Behavior of California Superior Courts. *American Political Science Review*, Vol. 73, pp. 1090–1099.

46. Hogarth, J. (1972). *Sentencing as a Human Process.* Toronto: University of Toronto Press.

47. Ibid., p. 382.

48. Klein, S.B., Turner, S., and Petersilia, J. (1988). *Racial Equality in Sentencing.* Santa Monica, CA: The Rand Corporation.

49. Williams, T. (1999). Sentencing Black Offenders in the

Ontario Criminal Justice System. Ch. 12 in Roberts, J.V. and Cole, D.P. *Making Sense of Sentencing*. Toronto: University of Toronto Press.

50. Ibid.

51. See the discussion in *R. v. Gladue*, [1999] 1 S.C.R. 688. Note also: Canfield, C. and Drinnan, L. (1981). *Comparative Statistics: Native and Non-Native Federal Inmates – A Five Year History*. Ottawa: Correctional Service of Canada; Hagan, J. (1975). Law, Order and Sentencing: A Study of Attitude in Action. *Sociometry*, Vol. 38, pp. 375–384; Moyer, S., Billingsley, B., Kopelamn, F., and La Prairie, C. (1987). *Native and Non-Native Admissions to Federal, Provincial and Territorial Correctional Instiutions*. Ottawa: Ministry of Solicitor General.

52. La Prairie, C. (1996). *Examining Aboriginal Corrections in Canada*. Ottawa: Ministry of Solicitor General, Corrections Policy Branch.

53. Contrast these publications: Jackson, M. (1989). Locking Up Natives in Canada. *U.B.C. Law Review*, Vol. 23, p. 205; and La Prairie, C. Sentencing Aboriginal Offenders: Some Critical Issues. Ch. 10 in Roberts, J.V. and Cole, D.P. *Making Sense of Sentencing*.

54. Dioso, R. and Doob, A.N. (2001). An Analysis of Public Support for Special Consideration of Aboriginal Offenders at Sentencing. *Canadian Journal of Criminology*, Vol. 43, No. 3 (2001), pp. 405–412.

55. Palys, T. and Divorski, S. (1986). Explaining Sentencing Disparity. *Canadian Journal of Criminology*, Vol. 28, No. 4, pp. 347–362.

56. Roberts, J.V. and Birkenmayer, A. (1997). Sentencing in Canada: Recent Statistical Trends. *Canadian Journal of Criminology*, Vol. 39, no. 4, pp. 459–482.

57. Smith, A.B. and Berlin, L. (1976). *Introduction to Probation and Parole* (p. 75). St. Paul, MN: West. See also: Carter, R.M. and Wilkins, L.T. (1967). Some Factors in Sentencing Policy. *Journal of Criminal Law, Criminology and Police Science*, Vol. 58, pp. 503–514.

58. Rosecrance, J. (1988, June). Maintaining the Myth of Individualized Justice: Probation Pre-sentence Reports. *Justice Quarterly*, Vol. 5, no. 2, pp. 237–256.

59. Ibid.

60. For a good review of the issues involved, see the following: Davis, R.C., Lurigio, A.J., and Skogan, W.G. (1997). *Victims of Crime* (2nd ed.). Thousand Oaks, CA: Sage; Sebba, L. (1996). *Third Parties: Victims and the Criminal Justice System*. Columbus, OH: Ohio State University Press.

61. Finn, P. and Lee, B.N.W. (1988, August). *Establishing and Expanding VictimWitness Assistance Programs*. Washington, D.C.: National Institute of Justice.

62. MacAlister, D. *Financial Compensation for Victims of Crime: Tort Damages as Restorative Justice?* Unpublished M.A. (Criminology) thesis. Burnaby, B.C.: Simon Fraser University. Discussed by: Boei, W. (2003, May 21). Suits Target Those with Deep Pockets. *The Vancouver Sun*, p. B4; and Pankratz, D. (2003, May 21). Number of Civil Cases Soars Along with the Award Amounts. *The Vancouver Sun*, p. B6.

63. McCormack, R.J. Review of: Elias, R. (1993). *Victims Still: The Political Manipulation of Crime Victims*. Newbury Park, CA: Sage. In *Justice Quarterly*, Vol. 11, no. 4 (December 1994), pp. 725–727.

64. *Coelho v. British Columbia* (1995), 41 C.R. (4th) 324 (B.C.S.C.).

65. Villmoore, E. and Neto, V.V. (1987, August). Victim Appearances at Sentencing Under California's Victims Bill of Rights. National Institute of Justice. *Research in Brief*.

66. Atkinson, R. (1995, March 22). Seles Says Attacker Has Ruined My Life: Retrial of Parche Aims At Tougher Sentence. *The Washington Post*.

67. Atkinson, R. (1995, April 4). Suspended Sentence Upheld for Seles Attacker. *The Washington Post*.

68. Davis, R.C. and Smith, B.E. (1994, September). The Effects of Victim Impact Statements on Sentencing Decisions: A Test in an Urban Setting. *Justice Quarterly*, Vol. 11, no. 3, pp. 453–469.

69. The Supreme Court of Canada permits the use of a starting point approach by provincial appeal courts: *R. v. McDonnell* (1997), 114 C.C.C. (3d) 436. The Alberta approach was first clearly outlined in *R. v. Sandercock* (1985), 22 C.C.C. (3d) 79 (Alta.C.A.), and was recently considered and supported in *R. v. G.(D.W.)* (1999), 244 A.R. 176 (Alta.C.A.).

70. Belanger, B. (2001) Sentencing in Adult Criminal Courts, 1999/00. *Juristat*, Vol. 21, no. 10.

71. Grimes, C. (1997). Adult Criminal Court Statistics, 1995–96. *Juristat: Canadian Centre for Justice Statistics*. Ottawa: Minister of Industry. In this report, Grimes found that 97.6 per cent of adult cases involving federal offences were processed in the provincial courts, with only 2.3 per cent being processed in superior courts.

72. *R. v. Luxton*, [1990] 2 S.C.R. 711.

73. *R. v. Goltz*, [1991] 3 S.C.R. 485.

74. *R. v. Morissey*, [2000] 2 S.C.R. 90.

75. *R. v. Latimer* (2001), 39 C.R. (5th) 1 (S.C.C.).

76. *R. v. Wust* (2000), 143 C.C.C. (3d) 129 (S.C.C.).

77. Hillsman, S.T., Mahoney, B., Cole, G.F., and Auchter, B. (1987, September). Fines as Criminal Sanctions, National Institute of Justice. *Research in Brief*, p. 1.

78. Belanger, B. Sentencing in Adult Criminal Courts, 1999/00. *Juristat*, Vol. 21, no. 10, p. 14.

79. Ibid., p. 7.

80. Hillsman, S.T., Sichel, J.L., and Mahoney, B. (1983). *Fines in Sentencing* (p. 2). New York: Vera Institute of Justice.

81. Ibid.

82. *R. v. Proulx*, [2000] 1 S.C.R. 61.

83. *R. v. Knoblauch*, [2000] 2 S.C.R. 780.

84. Johnson, H.A. *History of Criminal Justice* (pp. 30–31). Cincinnati, OH: Anderson.

85. Ibid., p. 31.

86. Ibid., p. 36.

87. Yemeni Court Upholds Crucifixions. (1997, August 31). The Associated Press wire services.

88. Ibid., p. 51.

89. Koestler, A. (1957). *Reflections on Hanging* (p. xi). New York: Macmillan.

90. Ibid., p. 15.

91. Severy, M. (1989, July). The Great Revolution. *National Geographic*, p. 20.

92. Hatch, A.J. (1995). Historical Legacies of Crime and Criminal Justice in Canada. Ch. 7 in Jackson, M.A. and Griffiths, C.T. (eds.). *Canadian Criminology: Perspectives on Crime and Criminality* (2nd ed.). Toronto: Harcourt, Brace.

93. Capital Punishment Research Project. University of Alabama Law School.

94. U.S. Department of Justice. (1995). *Capital Punishment, 1993*. Washington, D.C.: U.S. Government Printing Office.

95. Willing, R. (1997, May 14). Expansion of Death Penalty to Nonmurders Faces Challenges. *USA Today*, p. 6A.

96. Death Penalty Information Center's website. The statistics in this paragraph were drawn from "Death Row Inmates by State." Accessed November 16, 2001 at **www.deathpenaltyinfo.org/DrowInfo.html#year**

97. Snell, T.L. (2001). Capital Punishment 2000 (p. 1). Washington, D.C.: Bureau of Justice Statistics.

98. *McCleskey* v. *Zandt*, 499 U. S. 467, 493–494 (1991).

99. *Coleman* v. *Thompson*, 501 U.S. 722 (1991).

100. *Schlup* v. *Delo*, 115 S.Ct. 851, 130 L.Ed. 2d 808 (1995).

101. *Felker* v. *Turpin, Warden*, 117 S.Ct. 30, 135 L.Ed. 2d 1123 (1996).

102. Asseo, L. (1996, April 19). Terrorism Bill. The Associated Press wire services. Northern edition.

103. Phillips, A. (1998, November 30). Death Closing In. *MacLean's*, pp. 42–46.

104. O'Hara, J. (1998, December 21). A Man With Nine Lives. *MacLean's*, pp. 30–31.

105. *Kindler* v. *Canada (Minister of Justice)* (1991), 67 C.C.C. (3d) 1 (S.C.C.); *Reference re: Ng Extradition (Can.)* (1991), 67 C.C.C. (3d) 61 (S.C.C.).

106. Ibid. See also *United States of America* v. *Jamieson* (1996), 104 C.C.C. (3d) 575 (S.C.C.), affirming a decision of the Quebec Court of Appeal, (1994), 93 C.C.C. (3d) 265.

107. *U.S.A.* v. *Burns*, [2001] 1 S.C.R. 283.

108. Ogilvie, C. (1996, February 1). Sting Details Come to Light. and Horwood, H. (1996, February 1). Mounties "tricky, not dirty." *The Province*, p. A5.

109. *U.S.A.* v. *Burns*, (2001)(S.C.C.).

110. Brillon, Y., Louis-Guerin, C., and Lamarche, M.-C. (1984). *Attitudes of the Canadian Public Towards Crime Policies*. Montreal: Centre International de Criminologie Comparee, University de Montreal.

111. See Seagrave, J. (1987). The Death Penalty: Will Canada Restore This punishment. *Canadian Journal of Criminology*, Vol. 29, pp. 405–419.

## Chapter 10

1. Verdun-Jones, S.N. and Keltner, A. (eds.). (1981). *Sexual Aggression and the Law: Selected Papers from a Seminar on Sexual Aggression and the Law, Vancouver, Canada, October 16–17, 1981*. Vancouver, B.C.: Simon Fraser University.

2. Daubney, D. (1988). *Taking Responsibility: Report of the Standing Committee on Justice and Solicitor General on Its Review of Sentencing, Conditional Release and Related Aspects of Corrections* (pp. 1–2). Ottawa: Supply and Services Canada.

3. U.S. President's Commission on Law Enforcement and Administration of Justice. (1967). *The Challenge of Crime in a Free Society* (p. 166). Washington, D.C.: U.S. Government Printing Office.

4. Smith, A.B. and Berlin, L. (1976). *Introduction to Probation and Parole* (p. 75). St. Paul, Minn.: West.

5. Augustus, J. (1972). *John Augustus, First Probation Officer: John Augustus' Original Report of His Labours—1852*. Montclair, N.J.: Patterson-Smith.

6. Smith and Berlin. *Introduction to Probation and Parole* (p. 77).

7. Hamai, K. et al. (1995). *Probation Around the World: A Comparative Study*. London: Routledge.

8. Belanger, B. (2001). Sentencing in Adult Criminal Courts, 1999/00. *Juristat Service Bulletin*, Vol. 21, No. 10, p. 4.

9. Ibid., p. 7.

10. Ibid.; see also section 732.2(2)(b) of the *Criminal Code*.

11. Hendrick, D. and Farmer, L. (2002). Adult Correctional Services in Canada, 2000/01. *Juristat Service Bulletin*, Vol. 22, No. 10, p. 18.

12. Ibid., p. 18–19.

13. Section 732.1(2) (a)–(c) of the *Criminal Code*.

14. See section 742.1 of the *Criminal Code*, brought in by the Sentencing Reform Bill C–41 in 1996.

15. *R. v. Proulx*, [2000] 1 S.C.R. 61.

16. Belanger. Sentencing in Adult Criminal Courts, 1999/00. Above note 8, p. 11.

17. Hendrick and Farmer. Adult Correctional Services in Canada, 2000/01. Above note 11, pp. 18–19.

18. Ibid., p. 1.

19. Ibid., p. 8.

20. Section 742.3(1) of the *Criminal Code* imposes these requirements. Offenders are permitted to leave the jurisdiction if prior written permission is obtained from the court or the offender's supervisor.

21. Academic commentary supports the use of the conditional sentence in this manner to fill a gap in the Canadian criminal justice system's ability to adequately respond to the needs of mentally disordered offenders, see: Roberts, J. and Verdun-Jones, S. (2002). Directing Traffic at the Crossroads of Criminal Justice and Mental health: Conditional Sentencing After the Judgment in Knoblauch. *Alberta Law Review*, Vol. 39, No. 4, pp. 788–809.

22. Canada. National Parole Board's website, accessible at time of printing at **www.npb-cnlc.gc.ca/paroldef.htm**

23. Cole, D.P. and Manson, A. (1990). *Release from Imprisonment: The Law of Sentencing, Parole and Judicial Review* (p. v). Toronto: Carswell.

24. Reed, M. and Roberts, J.V. (1998). Adult Correctional Services in Canada, 1996–97. Canadian Centre for Justice Statistics, *Juristat*, Vol. 18, No. 3, p. 9.

25. Goldenberg, C.H. (1974). *Parole in Canada: Report of the Standing Senate Committee on Legal and Constitutional Issues* (pp. 15–16). Ottawa: Information Canada.

26. Hendrick, D. and Farmer, L. (2002). Adult Correctional Services in Canada, 2000/01. Above note 11, p. 20. At the national level, see the following: National Parole Board. (July 2002). *Performance Monitoring Report 2001–2002* (p. 27). Performance Measurement Division: National Parole Board.

27. Minor-Harper, S. and Innes, C.A. (1987). Time Served in Prison and on Parole, 1984. U.S. Bureau of Justice Statistics Special Report.

28. Taylor-Butts, A. (2002). Justice Spending in Canada, 2000/01. *Juristat Service Bulletin*, Vol 22, No. 11, p.1.

29. Correctional Service of Canada. "Basic Facts About Federal Corrections." Accessible at time of printing at **www.csc-scc.gc.ca/text/faits/facts07-content03_e.shmtl**

30. Hendrick and Farmer. Adult Correctional Services in Canada, 2000/01. Above note 11, p. 1.

31. Correctional Service of Canada. "Basic Facts About Federal Corrections." Above note 29.

32. *The Corrections and Conditional Release Act*, S.C. 1992, c. 20, s. 133(2) allows for conditions on parole to be set under the *Corrections and Conditional Release Regulations*, S.O.R./92-620. These may be found in section 161 of the *Regulations*.

33. The Effectiveness of Felony Probation: Results from an Eastern State. (December 1991). *Justice Quarterly*, pp. 525–543.

34. Correctional Service of Canada. "Basic Facts About Federal Corrections." Above note 29. The Correctional Service of Canada indicates that there is a direct relationship between the level of security classification and the cost of housing an inmate such that the higher the security rating, the greater the cost. Historically, women's institutions have been particularly expensive in Canada.

35. Ibid.

36. Finn, P. and Parent, D. (1992). *Making the Offender Foot the Bill: A Texas Program*. Washington, D.C.: National Institute of Justice.

37. Reed, M. and Roberts, J.V. (1998). Adult Correctional Services in Canada, 1996–97. *Juristat*, Vol. 18, No. 3, p. 10.

38. Ibid., p.10.

39. Cole and Manson. *Release from Imprisonment: The Law of Sentencing, Parole and Judicial Review*. p.174.

40. *Re Moore and the Queen* (1983), 4 C.C.C. (3d) 206 (Ont.C.A.).

41. *R. v. Wilmott*, [1967] 1 C.C.C. 171 (Ont.C.A.).

42. *Swan v. Attorney General of British Columbia* (1983), 35 C.R. (3d) 135 (B.C.S.C.), p.136.

43. *Howarth* v. *National Parole Board* (1974), 18 C.C.C. (2d) 385 (S.C.C.).

44. Above note 43, at p. 399.

45. *Harlow v. Clatterbuick*, 30 C.L.R. 2364 (VA S.Ct. 1986); *Santangelo v. State*, 426 NYS 2d 931 (1980); Welch v. State, 424 NYS 2d 774 (1980); and *Thompson v. County of Alameda*, 614 P. 2d 728 (1980).

46. *Tarter v. State of New York*, 38 CLR. 2364 (NY S.Ct. 1986); *Grimm* v. *Arizona Board of Pardons and Paroles*, 115 Arizona 260, 564 P. 2nd 1227 (1977); and *Payton v. United States*, 636 F. 2d. 132 (5th Cir.).

47. del Carmen, R.V. (1986). *Potential Liabilities of Probation and Parole Officers*. Cincinnati, Ohio: Anderson.

48. See, for example, the U.S. case: *Semler v. Psychiatric Institute*, 538 F. 2d 121 (4th Cir. 1976).

49. Human Resources Development Canada. (1998). "Probation and Parole Officers and Related Occupations, National Occupation Classification: 4155." Accessible at time of writing at **www.ns.hrdc-drhc.gc.ca/english/lmi/occsums/4155.htm**.

50. Canadian Criminal Justice Association. (1985). Parole Field Services. *Manual of Standards* (p. 6). Ottawa: Canadian Criminal Justice Association.

51. U.S. National Advisory Commission on Criminal Justice Standards and Goals. (1973). *Task Force Report: Corrections*. Washington, D.C.: U.S. Government Printing Office.

52. Levine, J.P., Musheno, M.C., and Palumbo, D.J. (1986). *Criminal Justice in America: Law in Action* (p. 548). New York: John Wiley.

53. Correctional Service of Canada's website: **www.csc-scc.gc.ca**. Accessed April 1998.

54. Inciardi, J. (1987). *Criminal Justice* (2nd ed., p. 638). New York: Harcourt Brace Jovanovich.

55. Austin, J., Jones, M., and Bolyard, M. (1993). *The Growing Use of Jail Boot Camps: The Current State of the Art*. Washington, D.C.: National Institute of Justice.

56. Sentencing Project. (1990). *Changing the Terms of Sentencing: Defense Counsel and Alternative Sentencing Services*. Washington, D.C.: The Project.

57. Petersilia, J. (1987). *Expanding Options for Criminal Sentencing*. Santa Monica, Calif.: The Rand Corporation.

58. Ohio Revised Code, 2946.06.1, July 1965.

59. Greenfield, L. (1986). *Probation and Parole, 1984*. Washington, D.C.: Bureau of Justice Statistics and U.S. Government Printing Office.

60. Ontario. (1996). Ministry of the Solicitor General and Correctional Services. Strategic Policy and Planning Division. Research Services Unit. *Utilization of Strict Discipline Programs for Young Offenders in Ontario: A Review and Preliminary Analysis: Submission to the Strict Discipline Committee Hearings, January 31, 1996*. Toronto: Ministry of the Solicitor General and Correctional Services.

61. MacKenzie, D.L. and Ballow, D.B. (1989, May/June). Shock incarceration programs in state correctional jurisdictions. *NIJ Reports*, pp. 9–10.

62. National Institute of Justice.(1995). *Multisite Evaluation of Shock Incarceration*. Washington, D.C.: NIJ.

63. MacKenzie, D.L., et al. (2001). *A National Study Comparing the Environments of Boot Camps with Traditional Facilities for Juvenile Offenders*. Washington, D.C.: NIJ.

64. Clark, C., Aziz, D.W., and D.L. MacKenzie. (1994). *Shock Incarceration in New York: Focus on Treatment* (p. 8). Washington, D.C.: National Institute of Justice.

65. Oregon Boot Camp is Saving the State Money, Study Finds. (1995, May 1). *Criminal Justice Newsletter*, pp. 5–6.

66. Section 732 of the *Criminal Code*.

67. Levine, J.P. et al. (1986). *Criminal Justice in America: Law in Action* (p. 549). New York: John Wiley.

68. Erwin, B.S. and Bennett, L.A. (1987). New Dimensions in Probation: Georgia's Experience with Intensive Probation Supervision. National Institute of Justice Research in Brief.

69. Ibid., p. 2.

70. North Carolina Department of Correction. (1988). *Intensive Supervision Manual* (pp. 3–5). Raleigh, N.C.: Division of Adult Probation and Parole.

71. Petersilia, J. (1988). House Arrest. In *Crime File Study Guide*. National Institute of Justice.

72. Ekstedt, J.W. and Jackson, M.A. (1997). *The Keeper and the Kept: Introduction to Corrections in Canada* (p. 43). Toronto: ITP Nelson.

73. Ibid., p. 98.

74. Ibid., p. 298.

75. Ibid.

76. Ibid.

77. Renzema, M. and Skelton, D.T. (1990). *The Use of Electronic Monitoring by Criminal Justice Agencies, 1989*. Washington, D.C.: National Institute of Justice.

78. Bureau of Justice Statistics. (2000). *Correctional Populations in the United States, 1997*. Washington, DC: BJS.

79. Gomme, I.M. (1992). From Big House to Big Brother: Confinement in the Future. In McCormick, K.R.E. and Visano, L.A. (eds.). *Canadian Penology: Alternative Perspectives and Research*. Toronto: Canadian Scholars' Press.

80. Ekstedt and Jackson. *The Keeper and the Kept: Introduction to Corrections in Canada* (p. 311).

81. A useful background reference for electronic monitoring in Canada is found in: Schulz, K. (ed.) (1995). *Electronic Monitoring and Corrections: The Policy, the Operation, the Research*. Burnaby, B.C.: Simon Fraser University, Criminology Research Centre and Public Policy Program, Continuing Studies.

82. Petersilia. House Arrest.

83. Berry, B. (1985). Electronic Jails: A New Criminal Justice Concern. *Justice Quarterly*, 2(1), pp. 1–22; Lilly, J.R., Ball, R.A., and Lotz, Jr., W.R. (1986). Electronic Jail Revisited. Justice Quarterly, 3(3), pp. 353–361.

84. Petersilia. House Arrest.

85. Brook, P. (1997). (1997, February). The Pedophile Next Door. *Chatelaine*.

86. Ibid.

87. U.S. Center for Effective Public Policy. (1995). Abolishing Parole: Why the Emperor Has No Clothes. Washington, D.C.: The Center.

88. O'Leary, V. and Clear, D. (1984). *Directions for Community Corrections in the 1990s*. Boulder, Colo.: National Institute of Corrections.

## Chapter 11

1. Pelham, C. (1887). *Chronicles of Crime: A Series of Memoirs and Anecdotes of Notorious Characters*. (pp. 28–30). London: T. Miles and Co.

2. Kafka, F. (1948). *The Penal Colony: Stories and Short Pieces*. Translated by Willa and Edwin Muir. New York: Schoken Books.

3. This section owes much to the following publication: Barnes, H.E. and Teeters, N.K. (1959). *New Horizons in Criminology* (3rd ed.). Englewood Cliffs, N.J.: Prentice Hall.

4. See Correctional Service of Canada's website. "Abolition of Corporal Punishment 1972," accessible at time of writing at **www.csc-scc.gc.ca/text/pblct/rights/50yrs/50yrs-05_e.shtml**

5. See *Youth and the Law* v. *Canada (Attorney General)* (2000), 146 C.C.C. (3d) 362 (Ont.S.C.J.) and *R.* v. *Poulin*, [2002] P.E.I.J. No. 88 (Q.L.)(P.E.I.S.C.).

6. Barnes and Teeters. *New Horizons in Criminology* (p. 292).

7. Morris, N. and Rothman, D.J. (eds.). (1995). *The Oxford History of the Prison: The Practice of Punishment in Western Society* (p. 53). New York: Oxford University Press.

8. Barnes and Teeters. *New Horizons in Criminology*.

9. Prince Edward Island government's website. "The Pillory and Stocks," accessible at time of writing at **www.edu.pe.ca/gray/pei/crime**

10. Ekstedt, J.W. and Griffiths, C.T. (1988). *Corrections in Canada: Policy and Practice* (2nd ed., p. 21). Toronto: Butterworths.

11. Heath, J. (1963). *Eighteenth-century Penal Theory*. London: Oxford University Press.

12. Morris and Rothman. *The Oxford History of the Prison: The Practice of Punishment in Western Society* (pp. 4–85).

13. Wood, A.E. and Barker Waite, J. (1941). *Crime and Its Treatment: Social and Legal Aspects of Criminology* ( p. 488). New York: American Book Co.

14. Semple, J. (1993). *Bentham's Prison: A Study of the Panopticon Penitentiary* (p. 72). Oxford: Clarendon Press.

15. A detailed examination of the development of penal policy in Great Britain can be found in the following: Radzinowicz, L. and Hood, R. (1986). *A History of English Criminal Law and Its Administration from 1750, Volume 5: The Emergence of Penal Policy*. London: Stevens & Sons.

16. Bozovic, M. (ed.). (1995). *The Panopticon Writings: Jeremy Bentham*. London: Verso.

17. Semple. *Bentham's Prison: A Study of the Panopticon Penitentiary*.

18. Ibid., pp. 9–10.

19. Other references that are useful for a better understanding of Bentham's panopticon theories are: Himmelfarb, G. (1968). The Haunted House of Jeremy Bentham. In *Victorian Minds*. New York: Knopf; Fry, M. (1948). Bentham and English Penal Reform. In Keeton, G.W. and Schwarzenberger, G. (eds.). *Jeremy Bentham and the Law: A Symposium*. London: Stevens; Webb, S. and Webb, B. (1922). *English Prisons under Local Government*. London: Longmans, Green.

20. Semple. *Bentham's Prison: A Study of the Panopticon Penitentiary* (p. 313).

21. Ibid., p. 9.

22. Although some writers hold that the Quakers originated the concept of solitary confinement for prisoners, there is evidence that the practice already existed in England prior to 1789. John Howard, for example, describes solitary confinement in use at Reading Brideswell in the 1780s.

23. Williams, V. (1979). *Dictionary of American Penology: An Introduction* (p. 200). Westport, Conn.: Greenwood.

24. Barnes and Teeters. *New Horizons in Criminology* (p. 348).

25. Williams. *Dictionary of American Penology: An Introduction* (p. 29).

26. With regard to cost, supporters of the Pennsylvania system argued that it was less expensive than the Auburn style of punishment because it led to reformation much faster than did the New York style.

27. Williams. *Dictionary of American Penology: An Introduction* (p. 30).

28. See particularly: Smandych, R.C. (1991, April). Beware of the "Evil American Monster": Upper Canadian views on the need for a penitentiary, 1830–1834. *Canadian Journal of Criminology*, 33(2), pp. 125–147.

29. Ekstedt and Griffiths. *Corrections in Canada: Policy and Practice* (2nd ed., p. 32).

30. Ibid., p. 66. See also: Shoom, S. (1966, July). Kingston Penitentiary: The Early Decades. *Canadian Journal of Corrections*, 8, 215–220; Curtis, D. et al. (1985). *Kingston Penitentiary: The First Hundred and Fifty years, 1835–1985*. Ottawa: Supply and Services Canada; Chunn, D.E. (1981). Good Men Work Hard: Convict Labour in Kingston Penitentiary, 1835–1850. *Canadian Criminology Forum*, 4, pp. 13–22.

31. Beaumont, G. de and Tocqueville, A. de. (1833). *On the Penitentiary System in the United States, and its Application in France*. Philadelphia, Penn.: Carey, Lea and Blanchard.

32. Goff, C. (1999). *Corrections in Canada*. Cincinnati, OH: Anderson Publishing.

33. Dickens, C. (1850). *American Notes, and Reprinted Pieces* (p. 122). London: Chapman and Hall.

34. For a review of the early history of Kingston Penitentiary, and the federal penitentiary that evolved after Confederation, see the following: Griffiths, C.T. and Cunningham, A. (2000). *Canadian Corrections*. Toronto: Nelson; Erdahl, A. History of Corrections in Canada. In Winterdyk, J.A. (ed.). (2001). *Corrections in Canada: Social Reactions to Crime*. Toronto: Prentice Hall; Goff, C. (1999). *Corrections in Canada* (see note 32).

35. As cited in Barnes and Teeters. *New Horizons in Criminology* (p. 428).

36. Morris and Rothman. *The Oxford History of the Prison* (p. 292). See note 7.

37. Connors, S.B. (1982). John Woodburn Langmuir and the Development of Prisons and Reformatories in Ontario, 1868–1882. M.A. thesis. Queen's University.

38. Strange, C. (1983). *The Velvet Glove: Maternalistic Reform at the Andrew Mercer Ontario Reformatory for Females 1874–1927*. M.A. thesis in history. University of Ottawa.

39. Ekstedt and Griffiths. *Corrections in Canada: Policy and Practice*. (2nd ed., p. 41).

40. Professor Griffiths and Alison Cunningham note that very little changed in Canadian prisons during the early part of the twentieth century. See: Hawkins, G. (1983). Prison Labor and Prison Industries. In Tonry, M. and Morris, N. (eds.). *Crime and Justice: An Annual Review of Research* (Vol. 5, pp. 85–127). Chicago: University of Chicago Press. See also the following regarding the contrasting American developments during this time, reflecting the growth of prison industry: Melossi, D. and Pavarini, M. (1981). *The Prison and the Factory: Origins of the Penitentiary System*. Totowa, N.J.: Barnes and Noble.

41. Archambault, J. (1938). *Report of the Royal Commission to Investigate the Penal System of Canada*. Ottawa: King's Printer.

42. Palmer, B.D. (1980, May). Kingston Mechanics and the Rise of the Penitentiary, 1833–1836. *Social History*, XIII, pp. 7–32.

43. See, for example: Baehre, R. (1994). Prison as Factory, Convict as Worker: A Study of the mid-Victorian St. John Penitentiary, 1841–1880. In Phillips, J., Loo, T., and Lewthwaite, S. (eds.). *Essays in the History of Canadian Law* (Volume V, Crime and criminal justice). Toronto: The Osgoode Society; Berkovits, J.G. (1994). Prisoners for Profit: Convict Labour in the Ontario Central Prison, 1874–1915. In Phillips, Loo, and Lewthwaite (eds.). *Essays in the History of Canadian Law*).

44. Ekstedt and Griffiths. *Corrections in Canada: Policy and Practice* (p. 201).

45. Gandy, J. and Hurl, L. (1987). Private Sector Involvement in Prison Industries: Options and Issues. *Canadian Journal of Criminology*, 29, pp. 185–204.

46. John Howard Society of Alberta. (2002). "Inmate Industries," accessible at time of writing at **www.johnhoward.ab.ca/PUB/respaper/indust02.htm**

47. Correctional Service of Canada. (2002). CORCAN Annual Report 2001/2002. Accessible at time of writing at **www.csc-scc.gc.ca/text/prgrm/corcan/pblct/annual_report/01-02/ar_01_02_e.pdf**.

48. Ibid.

49. John Howard Society of Alberta. "Inmate Industria." **www.csc-scc.gc.ca/text/prgrm/corcan/pblct/annual_report/01-02/ar_01_0**.

50. Macdonald, G. (1982). *Self-sustaining Prison Industries*. Vancouver, B.C.: Institute for Studies in Criminal Justice Policy, Simon Fraser University.

51. CORCAN's website, accessible at time of writing at **www.corcan.ca**

52. For an interesting examination of the success of a specific CORCAN location see, Getkate, M. (1993). Insights into Innovative Correctional Industry: A Case Study of COR-CAN at Warkworth Institution. Research report No. 32. Ottawa: Correctional Service of Canada

53. Motiuk, L. and Belcourt, R. (1996, January). CORCAN Participation and Post-release Recidivism. *FORUM on Corrections Research*, 8(1). See also: Gillis, C., Motiuk, L., and Belcourt, R. (1998). *Prison Work Program (CORCAN) Participation: Post Release Employment and Recidivism*. Correctional Service of Canada Publication No. R-69. Ottawa: Correctional Service of Canada.

54. Oregon Begins to Implement Full Employment for Inmates. (1995, March 15). *Criminal Justice Newsletter*, 26(6), pp. 1–2.

55. Gillis, C. (2002). Understanding Employment: A Prospective Exploration of Factors Linked to Community-Based Employment Among Federal Offenders. Doctoral Dissertation. Carleton University, 2001. *Forum on Correctional Research* 14(1), 3–6.

56. See John Howard Society of Alberta. (2002). "Inmate Industries." See note 46.

57. The MacGuigan Report: Subcommittee on the Penitentiary System in Canada. (1977). *Report to Parliament by the Subcommittee on the Penitentiary System in Canada*. Ottawa: Supply and Services Canada.

58. Ibid.

59. Ibid.

60. An excellent and thorough review of the discipline of "correctional psychology" is found in the following: Watkins, R.E. (1992). *An Historical Review of the Role and Practice of Psychology in the Field of Corrections*. Research Report, No. 28. Ottawa: Correctional Service of Canada.

61. Chalke, F.C.R. (1972). The General Program for Development of Psychiatric Services in Federal Correctional Services in Canada. Ottawa: Advisory Board of Psychiatric Consultants.

62. Ekstedt and Griffiths. *Corrections in Canada: Policy and Practice* (2nd ed., pp. 52–3).

63. Ibid., p. 54.

64. Ibid., pp. 205–207.

65. Goff, C. *Corrections in Canada* (p. 81). See note 32.

66. Griffiths, C.T. and Cunningham, A. (2000), *Canadian Corrections*, above note 34, p. 56.

67. Ibid.

68. McNamara, D.E.J. (1978). Medical Model in Corrections: requiescat in pace. In Montanino, F. (ed.). *Incarceration: The Sociology of Imprisonment*. Beverly Hills, Calif.: Sage Publications.

69. Robinson, D., Porporino, F.J., Millson, W.A., Trevethan, S., and MacKillop, B. (1998). A One-Day Snapshot of Inmates in Canada's Adult Correctional Facilities. *Juristat*, Vol. 18, No. 8. Ottawa: Minister of Industry.

70. The summary of the Correctional Service of Canada's inmate programming is derived from the webpage "Correctional Programs." Accessible at time of writing at **www.csc-scc.gc.ca/text/prgrm/corr_e.shtml**

71. Outerbridge, W.A. (1972). Report of the task force on community-based residential centres. Ottawa: Information Canada.

72. Ekstedt and Griffiths, *Corrections in Canada: Policy and Practice* (2nd ed., p. 257).

73. Correctional Service of Canada. (1998). A Primer on Community Corrections and Criminal Justice Work in Canada. Ottawa: Correctional Service of Canada and the Canadian Training Institute.

74. Visano, L. Community-Based Corrections. In Winterdyk, J. (ed.). (2001). *Corrections in Canada: Social Reactions to Crime*. Toronto: Prentice Hall.

75. Ibid.

76. Ibid., p. 299.

77. See "History of Parole in Canada - Part 7" and "The National Parole Board During the Last Decade." Accessible at time of writing at **www.npb-cnlc.gc.ca/about/part7_e.htm**.

78. Ekstedt and Griffiths. *Corrections in Canada: Policy and Practice* (2nd ed., p. 272).

79. Private Family Visits. (2002, June 3). Standard Operating Practices (700–12). Commissioner of the Correctional Service of Canada.

80. Correctional Service of Canada. (1996). *1995 National Inmate Survey: Final Report*. Ottawa: Correctional Service of Canada.

81. Recidivism can be defined in various ways, according to the purpose it is intended to serve in a particular study or report. Recidivism is usually defined as rearrest (versus reconviction) and generally includes a time span of five years, although some U.S. Bureau of Justice Statistics studies have used six years and other studies one or two years as definitional criteria.

82. Various advocates of the "justice model" can be identified. For a detailed description of the two models, see: Pizzi, M.A., Jr. (1986, July 7). The Medical Model and the 100 Years War. *Law Enforcement News*, pp. 8 and 13; MacNamara, D.E.J. (1978). Medical Model in Corrections: requiescat in pace. In Montanino, F. (ed.). Incarceration: The Sociology of Imprisonment. Beverly Hills, Calif.: Sage Publications.

83. U.S. Bureau of Justice Statistics. (1988). *Annual Report, 1987* (p. 70). Washington, D.C.: U.S. Bureau of Justice Statistics.

84. Ibid.

85. Ibid.

86. Greenfeld, L. (1985). Examining Recidivism. Bureau of Justice Statistics Special Report. Washington, D.C.: U.S. Government Printing Office.

87. National Parole Board. "Parole Decision-Making: Myths and Realities," accessible at time of writing at **www.npb-cnlc.gc.ca/whatsn/myths053001_e.htm#mytheight**

88. Martinson, R. (1974). What Works: Questions and Answers about Prison Reform. *Public Interest*, No. 35, pp. 22–54. See also: Lipton, D., Martinson, R.M., and Wilkes, J. (1975). *The Effectiveness of Correctional Treatment: A Survey of Treatment Evaluation Studies*. New York: Praeger.

89. Sechrest, L., White, S., and Brown, E. (eds.). (1979). *The Rehabilitation of Criminal Offenders: Problems and Prospects*. Washington, D.C.: The National Academy of Sciences.

90. Palmer, T. (1975, July). Martinson Revisited. *Journal of Research in Crime and Delinquency*, 12, pp. 133–152.

91. Gendreau, P. and Ross, R.R. (1979, October). Effective Correctional Treatment: Bibliotherapy for Cynics. *Canadian Journal of Criminology*, 29, pp. 463–489.

92. See: Corrections Population Growth. (1997). *First Report on Progress for Federal/Provincial/Territorial Ministers Responsible for Justice*. Fredricton, New Brunswick. Discussed in Motiuk, L. Managing Prison Population Growth, Delivering Effective Community-Based Corrections and Treating Drug-Related and Female Offenders. In UNAFEI (United Nations Asia and Far East Institute for the Prevention of Crime and the Treatment of Offenders). (2001). *Annual Report for 1999 and Resource Material Series No. 57* (pp. 248–262). Fuchu, Tokyo, Japan: UNAFEI. Note also: Reed, M. and Roberts, J. Adult Correctional Service in Canada, 1997–98. *Juristat*, Vol. 19, No. 4.

93. Hendrick, D. and Farmer, L. Adult Correctional Services in Canada, 2000/01. *Juristat*, Vol. 22, No. 10, p. 4.

94. U.S. Bureau of Justice Statistics. (1995). Correctional Populations in the United States: Executive Summary.

95. Correctional Service of Canada's webpage "Institutional Profiles," accessible at time of printing through the "Regions and Facilities" web page at **www.csc-scc.gc.ca/text/regions/regions_e.shtml**

96. Hendrick, D. and Farmer, L. (2002) Adult Correctional Services in Canada, 2000/01. *Juristat*, Vol. 22, No. 10, p. 1.

97. Ibid., p. 4.

98. Correctional Service of Canada. (1995). *C.S.C. National Inmate Survey*. Ottawa: Correctional Service of Canada.

99. Adapted from U.S. Department of Justice. (1988). *Report to the Nation on Crime and Justice* (2nd ed., p. 108). Washington, D.C.: U.S. Government Printing Office.

100. *Rhodes* v. *Chapman*, 452 U.S. 337 (1981).

101. Lieber, J. (1981, March 8). The American Prison: A Tinderbox. *The New York Times Magazine*.

102. John Howard Society of Alberta. (1996). *Prison Overcrowding* (p. 2).

103. Christie, N. (2000). *Crime Control As Industry: Towards Gulags, Western Style* (3rd ed.). New York: Routledge.

104. See Jackson, M. (1983). *Prisoners of Isolation: Solitary Confinement in Canada*. Toronto: University of Toronto Press.

105. *Magrath* v. *The Queen* (1977), 38 C.C.C. (2d) 67 (Fed.Ct.T.D.)

106. *McCann et al.* v. *The Queen* (1975), 29 C.C.C. (2d) 337 (Fed.Ct.T.D.).

107. Zinger, I., Wichmann, C., and Andrews, D.A. (January 2001). The Psychological Effects of 60 Days in Administrative Segregation. *Canadian Journal of Criminology*, 43, pp. 47–83.

108. Jackson, M. (January 2001). Commentary #3: The Psychological Effects of Segregation. *Canadian Journal of Criminology*, 43, pp. 109–116.

109. Roberts, J.V. and Gebotys, R.J. (January 2001). Commentary #1: Prisoners of Isolation: Research on the Effects of Administrative Segregation. *Canadian Journal of Criminology*, 43, pp. 85–97.

110. Grassian, S. (1983). Psychopathological Effects of Solitary Confinement. *American Journal of Psychiatry*, 140(11), pp. 1450–1454; Grassian, S. and Friedman, N. (1986). Effects of Sensory Deprivation in Psychiatric Seclusion and Solitary Confinement. *International Journal of Law and Psychiatry*, 49, p. 49; Committee for the Prevention of Torture. (1997). *Report to the Government of the Czech Republic on the Visit to the Czech Republic from 16–26 Feb 1997*, accessible at time of printing at **www.cpt.org**; Foley, K. (2001). Solitary Confinement: A Violation of International Law? *e-Valuate* (online journal), 3(1), accessible at time of printing at **www.law.ecel.uwa.edu.au/elawjournal**

111. Correctional Service of Canada. (1997). "Task Force Report on Administrative Segregation – Commitment to Legal Compliance, Fair Decisions and Effective Results – March 1997," accessible at time of printing at **www.csc-scc.gc.ca/text/pblct/taskforce/toc_e.shtml**

112. Jackson, M. (2002). *Justice Behind the Walls: Human Rights in Canadian Prisons*. Vancouver: Douglas & McIntyre. Note: Accessible at time of writing at **www.justicebehindthewalls.net/02_publications_00.html**

113. See Langley-Abbotsford MP Randy White's website at **www.randywhite.ca**, accessible at time of writing, with its link to "Behind the Bars," also accessible at time of writing at **www.behindthebars.ca** for a just deserts critique of Canada's federal penitentiary system.

114. Discussed in Chapter 9, Sentencing.

115. Broder, D.S. (1994, March 24). When Tough Isn't Smart. *Washington Post* online.

116. Fletcher, M.E. (1996, April 21). Study Tracks Blacks' Crime Concerns. *Washington Post*, p. A11. See also: Furillo, A. (1996, March 31–April 2). Three Strikes: The Verdict's In (three-part series). Sacramento Bee, p. A1; and LaCouse, D. (1996). How Three strikes Has Fared in Washington State. Seattle, Wash.: Washington Institute for Policy Studies.

117. Wunder, A. (1995, March). Corrections Systems Must Bear the Burden of New Legislation. *Corrections Compendium*.

118. Greenberg, D. (1975). The Incapacitation Effect of Imprisonment, Some Estimates. *Law and Society Review*, 9, pp. 541–580. See also: Cohen, J. (1983, December). Incapacitating Criminals: Recent Research Findings. *National Institute of Justice, Research in Brief*.

119. For information on identifying dangerous repeat offenders, see: Chaiken, M. and Chaiken, J. (1987). *Selecting*

*Career Criminals for Priority Prosecution, Final Report.* Cambridge, Mass.: Abt Associates.

120. For a collection of readings both supporting and criticizing the incapacitation strategy, see: von Hirsch, A. and Ashworth, A. (eds.). (1998). *Principled Sentencing: Readings on Theory and Policy* (2nd ed.). Oxford: Hart Publishing, pp. 88–140.

121. Monahan, J. (1981). *Predicting Violent Behavior: An Assessment of Clinical Techniques.* Beverly Hills, Calif.: Sage Publications.

122. Van Dine, S., Conrad, J.P., and Dinitz, S. (1979). *Restraining the Wicked: The Incapacitation of the Dangerous Offender.* Lexington, Mass.: Lexington Books.

123. Bonta, J. and Motiuk, L.L. (1996). *High-risk Offenders in Canada: A Paper Presented at the 104th Annual Convention of the American Psychological Association* in Toronto, Canada. See also: Bonta, J. et al. (1996). *The Crown Files Research Project: A Study of Dangerous Offenders.* Ottawa: Solicitor General Canada.

124. *Basic Facts About Federal Corrections.* (2001). Ottawa: Solicitor General of Canada.

125. Hendrick, D. and Farmer, L. (2002). Adult Correctional Services in Canada, 2000/01. *Juristat,* Vol. 22, No. 10.

126. The *Constitution Act, 1867* divides responsibility for prisons between the federal and provincial governments. Section 91(28) gives the responsibility for "Penitentiaries" to the federal government, while s. 92(6) gives the provinces responsibility over "Reformatory Prisons." The Act does not create the two-year rule, which appears to be a rule embodied in custom that arose prior to Confederation.

127. Hendrick and Farmer. Adult Correctional Services in Canada.

128. Ibid.

129. Ibid.

130. Beck, A.J. and P.M. Harrison. *Prisoners in 2000.* (Washington, DC: Bureau of Justice Statistics, 2001).

131. Ibid.

132. Ibid.

133. Hendrick and Farmer. Adult Correctional Services in Canada, 2000/01. p. 21. See note 93.

134. Hendrick and Farmer.Adult Correctional Services in Canada, 2000/01. p. 4. See note 93.

135. Ibid.

136. Approximately 63 per cent of new offenders in Canadian correctional institutions test at or below a grade 8 level in mathematics and language. Solicitor General of Canada. "Programs for Offenders," accessible at time of writing at **www.csc-scc.gc.ca/text/prgrm/corr_e.shtml**

137. Ibid., p. 54.

138. Ibid.

139. *Basic Facts About Federal Corrections.*

140. Correctional Service of Canada. (1997, March 31). Employment Strategies Division.

141. Basic Facts About Federal Corrections. (2001). "What Kinds of Programs Are Available to Offenders?" accessible at time of writing at **www.csc-scc.gc.ca/text/faits/facts07_e.shtml**

142. Hendrick, D. and Farmer, L. (2002). Adult Correctional Services in Canada, 2000/01. See also: Robinson, D., Porporino, F.J., and Millson, W.A. (1998). A One-Day Snapshot of Inmates in Canada's Adult Correctional Facilities. *Juristat,* Vol. 18, No. 8.

143. Located in the following: Antigonish, Cape Breton, Colchester, Cumberland, Guysborough, Halifax, Kings, Lunenburg, and Yarmouth.

144. Among some of the many available resources: Anderson, F.W. (1960, April). Prisons and prison reform in the old Canadian west. *Canadian Journal of Corrections,* 2, pp. 209–215; Newfoundland. Corrections Study Committee. (1973). Report of the Newfoundland Corrections Study Committee. St. John's: The Committee; Coles, D. (1979). Nova Scotia Corrections: An Historical Perspective. Halifax, N.S.: Communications Project on Criminal Justice, Correctional Services Division; James, J.T.L. (1979, January). Gaols and Their goals in Manitoba, 1870–1970. *Canadian Journal of Criminology,* Vols. 20–21, pp. 34–42; Kellough, D.G. et al. (1980). The Politics of Incarceration: Manitoba, 1918–1939. *Canadian Journal of Sociology, 5* (Summer), pp. 253–271; Oliver, P. (1984). From Jails to Penitentiaries: The Demise of Community Correction in Early Ontario. *Correctional Options,* 4, pp. 1–10. **Also** Doherty, D. and Ekstedt, J.W. (1990). *Conflict, Care and Control: The History of the Corrections Branch in British Columbia 1848–88.* Burnaby, B.C.: Simon Fraser University Institute for Studies in Criminal Justice Policy; **and** Skinner, S., Driedger, O., and Grainger, B. (1981). *Corrections: An Historical Perspective of the Saskatchewan Experience.* Regina: Canadian Plains Research Center, University of Regina.

145. See, for example: Manitoba. Review Commission on Adult Corrections (1983). Report on Headingly Correctional Institution. Winnipeg, Manitoba: Department of Community Services and Corrections.

146. A valuable resource for research is found in: Smandych, R.C., Matthews, C.J., and Cox, S.J. (1987). *Canadian Justice History: An Annotated Bibiliography.* Toronto: University of Toronto Press.

147. See Ontario. Commission to enquire into the prison and reformatory system of Ontario. (1891). *Report of the Commission to Enquire into the Prison and Reformatory System of Ontario.* Toronto: Warwick and Sons.

148. Shapiro, B.B. (1978). *Report of the Royal Commission on the Toronto Jail and custodial services* (4 vols.). Toronto: Queen's Printer for Ontario.

149. Shapiro's report (see note 148) on the Toronto jail, for example, contains a number of "briefs" that look at the history of the Toronto jail, as well as, the role of correctional officers, including their recruitment, selection, and training.

150. Canadian Criminal Justice Association. (1985). *Manual of Standards: Prisons.* Ottawa: Canadian Criminal Justice Association.

151. The Correctional Service of Canada publishes a series of "Research Reports," as well as "Research Briefs" and a periodical entitled "Forum on Corrections Research." All

of these publications are significantly important to the development of good correctional practices.

152. Solicitor General Canada. (1998). Towards a Just, Peaceful and Safe Society: The Corrections and Conditional Release Act Five Years Later. Consultation Paper. Ottawa: Public Works and Government Services of Canada.

153. U.S. Department of Justice. (1995, May 1). The Nation's Jails Hold Record 490,442 Inmates. Press release.

154. *Basic Facts About Federal Corrections*. See note 124.

155. *Basic Facts About Federal Corrections*. See note 124.

156. Mills, W.R. and Barrett, H. (1990, September/October). Meeting the Special Challenge of Providing Health Care to Women Inmates in the '90's. *American Jails*, 4(3), p. 55.

157. Ibid.

158. American Correctional Association. *The Female Offender: What Does the Future Hold?*(p. 14).

159. Correctional Service of Canada. (1994). "Correctional Program for Federally Sentenced Women." Accessible at time of writing at **www.csc-scc.gc.ca/text/prgrm/ fsw/fsw18/toce_e.shtml**

160. The videotape, which was taken as part of a standard protocol for events requiring the intervention of the CSC emergency response team, was aired on the CBC's public affairs program *The Fifth Estate* on February 21, 1995.

161. Arbour, L. (1996). Report of the Commission of Inquiry into Certain Events at the Prison for Women in Kingston. Ottawa: Canadian Communications Group. See also: Manson, A. (1996). Scrutiny from the Outside: The Arbour Commission, the Prison for Women and the Correctional Service of Canada. *Canadian Criminal Law Review*, Volume 1, pp. 321–338.

162. Correctional Service of Canada. (1994, January). Forum on Corrections Research, Vol. 6, No. 1. This issue included several valuable articles, for example: Shaw, M. Women in Prison: A Literature Review; Scarth, K. and McLean, H. The Psychological Assessment of Women in Prison; and Vachon, M.M. It's About Time: The Legal Context of Policy Changes for Female Offenders.

163. Griffiths, C.T. and Nance, M. (eds.). (1980). The Female Offender: Selected Papers from an International Symposium. Vancouver, B.C.: Criminal Research Centre, Simon Fraser University. See also: O'Sullivan, E. (1907). Women Offenders in Canada. American Prison Association Proceedings, pp. 245–251; Freedman, E.B. (1981). Their Sisters' Keepers: Women's Prison Reform in America: 1830–1930. Ann Arbour, Mich.: University of Michigan Press. Adelberry, E. and Currie, C. (1987). Too Few to Count: Canadian Women in Conflict with the Law. Vancouver, B.C.: Press Gang Publishers.

164. Mills and Barrett. Meeting the Special Challenge of Providing Health Care to Women Inmates in the '90's.

165. Ibid.

166. Zupan, L.L. (1991, January/February). Women Corrections Officers in Nation's Largest Jails. *American Jails*, pp. 59–62.

167. Ibid., p. 11.

168. Correctional Service of Canada. "Women Correctional Officers in Male Institutions," accessible at time of writing at **www.csc-scc.gc.ca/text/pblct/rights/50yrs/ 50yrs-10_e.shtml**

169. Zupan, L.L. (1991, March). Women Corrections Officers in Local Jails. Paper presented at annual meeting of the Academy of Criminal Justice Sciences, Nashville, Tennessee.

170. Ibid., p. 6.

171. Zupan, L.L. (1991, January/February). Women Corrections Officers in Nation's Largest Jails. *American Jails*, pp. 59–62.

172. Zupan, L.L. and Menke, B.A. (1991). The New Generation Jail: An Overview. In Thompson, J.A. and Mays, G.L. (eds.). *American Jails: Public Policy Issues* (p. 180). Chicago: Nelson–Hall.

173. Ibid.

174. Sigurdson, H.R., Watson, B., and Funke, G. (1990, Winter). Empowering Middle Managers of Direct Supervision Jails. *American Jails*, p. 52.

175. Johnson, B. (1994, March/April). Exploring Direct Supervision: A Research Note. *American Jails*, pp. 63–64.

176. Sigurdson, H. (1985). *The Manhattan House of Detention: A Study of Podular Direct Supervision*. Washington, D.C.: National Institute of Corrections. For similar comparisons, see: Conroy, R., Smith, W.J., and Zupan, L.L. (1991, November/December). Officer Stress in the Direct Supervision Jail: A Preliminary Case Study. *American Jails*, p. 36.

177. Dawe, B. and Kirby, J. (1995, March/April). Direct Supervision Jails and Minimum Staffing. *American Jails*, pp. 97–100.

178. Nelson, W.R. and Davis, R.M. (1995, July/August). Popular Direct Supervision: The First Twenty Years. *American Jails*, p. 17.

179. Fuqua, J.W. (1991, March/April). New Generation Jails: Old Generation Management. *American Jails*, pp. 80–83.

180. Sigurdson, Wayson, and Funke. Empowering Middle Managers.

181. McCulloch, D.J. and Stiles, T. (1990, Winter). Technology and the Direct Supervision Jail. *American Jails*, pp. 97–102.

182. McCampbell, S.W. (1990, November/December). Direct Supervision: Looking for the Right People. *American Jails*, pp. 68–69.

183. May II, R.L., Peters, R.H. and Kearns, W.D. (1990, September/October). The Extent of Drug Treatment Programs in Jails: A Summary Report. *American Jails*, pp. 32–34.

184. See, for example, Dietler, J.W. (1990, July/August). Jail Industries: The Best Thing That Can Happen to a Sheriff. American Jails, pp. 80–83. In 2000–01, the combined cost of federal and provincial corrections for adults in Canada was almost $2.5 billion: Taylor-Butts, A. (2002). Justice Spending in Canada, 2000/01. *Juristat*, Vol. 22, No. 11, p. 14.

185. John Howard Society of Alberta. (2002). *Inmate Industries*.

186. American Correctional Association. (1991). *Manual of Standards for Adult Local Detention Facilities* (3rd ed.). College Park, Md.: ACA.

187. Kerle, K. (1987, Spring). National Sheriff's Association Jail Audit Review. *American Jails*, pp.13–21.

188. Thompson, J.A. and Mays, G.L. (1991). Paying the Piper But Changing the Tune: Policy Changes and Initiatives for the American Jail. In Thompson, J.A. and Mays, G.L. (eds.). *American Jails: Public Policy Issues* (pp. 240–246). Chicago: Nelson-Hall.

189. For a more detailed discussion of this issue, see: Robbins, I. (1988). *The Legal Dimensions of Private Incarceration*. Chicago: American Bar Foundation.

190. Hackett J.C., et al. Contracting for the Operation of Prisons and Jails. National Institute of Justice. Research in Brief (June, 1987), p. 6.

# Chapter 12

1. See, Morris, N. and Rothman, D.J. (eds.). (1995). *The Oxford History of the Prison: The Practice of Punishment in Western Society*. New York: Oxford University Press.

2. Reimer, H. (1937). Socialization in the Prison Community. *Proceedings of the American Prison Association, 1937* ( pp. 151–155). New York: American Prison Association.

3. Clemmer, D. (1940). *The Prison Community*. Boston: Holt, Rinehart, Winston.

4. Sykes, G.M. (1958). *The Society of Captives: A Study of a Maximum Security Prison*. Princeton, N.J.: Princeton University Press.

5. Cloward, R.A. et al. (1960). *Theoretical Studies in Social Organization of the Prison*. New York: Social Science Research Council.

6. Cressey, D.R. (ed.). (1961). *The Prison: Studies in Institutional Organization and Change*. New York: Holt, Rinehart and Winston.

7. Hazelrigg, L. (ed.). (1969). *Prison Within Society: A Reader in Penology* (preface). Garden City, N.Y.: Anchor Books.

8. Stastny, C. and Tyrnauer, G. (1982). *Who Rules the Joint? The Changing Political Culture of Maximum-security Prisons in America* (p. 131). Lexington, Mass.: Lexington Books.

9. Goffman, E. (1961). *Asylums: Essays on the Social Situation of Mental Patients and Other Inmates*. Garden City, N.Y.: Anchor Books.

10. The concept of prisonization is generally attributed to Clemmer, *The Prison Community*, although Quaker penologists of the late 1700s were actively concerned with preventing "contamination" (the spread of criminal values) among prisoners.

11. Sykes, G.M and Messinger, S.L. (1960). The Inmate Social System. In Cloward, R.A. et al. *Theoretical Studies in Social Organization* (pp. 5–19). New York: Social Science Research Council.

12. Ibid., p. 5.

13. Wheeler, S. (1961, October). Socialization in Correctional Communities. *American Sociological Review*, Vol. 26, pp. 697–712.

14. Sykes. *The Society of Captives* (p. xiii).

15. Stastny and Tyrnauer. *Who Rules the Joint?* (p. 135).

16. Ibid.

17. A recent Canadian study of correctional culture is summarized in the following: Page, D.M., Stasiak, E., and McKerrell, N.T. (1997). Analysis of Workplace Cultures and Environments in Correctional Services. In American Correctional Association. *The State of Corrections: Proceedings of the American Correctional Association Annual Conferences, 1996.* (pp. 25–36). Philadelphia/Nashville. Fredericksurg, VA: ACA.

18. Kelly, P.W. (1995, November/December). Prisons as Gladiator Schools. *RCMP Gazette*, Vol. 37, No. 11 & 12, pp. 21–26.

19. Sykes. *The Society of Captives*.

20. See, for example, Zamble, E., Porporino, F. and Kalotay, J. (1984). *An Analysis of Coping Behaviour in Prison Inmates*. Ottawa: Ministry of the Solicitor General of Canada.

21. Clemmer. *The Prison Community* (pp. 294–296).

22. Davis, A.J. (1968, December). Sexual Assaults in the Philadelphia Prison System and Sheriff's Vans. *Trans-Action*, Vol. 6, pp. 8–16.

23. Lockwood, D. (1978). Sexual Aggression Among Male Prisoners. Unpublished dissertation. Ann Arbor, Mich.: University Microfilms International.

24. Bowker, L. (1980). *Prison Victimization*. New York: Elsevier.

25. Ibid., p. 42.

26. Ibid., p. 1.

27. Toch, H. (1977). *Living in Prison: The Ecology of Survival* (p. 151). New York: The Free Press.

28. Irwin, J. (1970). *The Felon*. Englewood Cliffs, N.J.: Prentice Hall.

29. Caron, R. (1978). *Go-boy! Memoirs of a Life Behind Bars*. Toronto: McGraw-Hill Ryerson.

30. A superb, and frightening, example of the "mean dude" can be found in the following: Butterfield, F. (1996). *All God's Children: The Bosket Family and the American Tradition of Violence*. New York: Avon Books. In this work, Butterfield describes the criminal career of Willie Bosket, who had the honour of being the most dangerous inmate in the history of the New York penal system.

31. Lombardo, L.X. (1981). *Guards Imprisoned: Correctional Officers at Work* (pp. 22–36. New York: Elsevier.

32. Ross, R. (ed.). (1981). *Prison Guard/Correctional Officer: The Use and Abuse of the Human Resources in Prisons*. Toronto: Butterworths.

33. An important contribution to the "professionalization" of correctional workers was made through several briefs submitted to the Royal Commission on the Toronto Jail and Custodial Services. See: Shapiro, B.B. (1978). *Report of the Royal Commission on the Toronto Jail and Custodial Services, Volume 2 ("Briefs")*. Toronto: Queen's Printer for Ontario.

34. Morgenbesser, L. (1983, Winter). NY State Law Prescribes Psychological Screening for CO Job Applicants. *Correctional Training* (p. 1). Newsletter of the American Association of Correctional Training Personnel.

35. See the Justice Institute of British Columbia's website, accessible at time of writing at **www.jibc.bc.ca/corrections/progCourses/AdCorrOff.htm**

36. Griffiths, C.T., and Cunningham, A. (2000). *Canadian Corrections*. Toronto: Nelson.

37. Ibid., p. 181.

38. Stastny and Tyrnauer. *Who Rules the Joint?* (p. 1).

39. Useem, B. and Kimball, P. (1989). *States of Siege: U.S. Prison Riots, 1971–1986*. New York: Oxford University Press.

40. For a discussion of the riot and its antecedent events, see: Griffiths, C.T. and Cunningham, A. *Canadian Corrections* (pp. 166–170).

41. Going Behind the Prison's Walls. (2001, December 16). *The Calgary Herald* (Alberta), p. A10.

42. Dawson, L. (2001, November 20). Report Explains Prison's Flaws. *The Valley Times*, p. A1.

43. For a discussion of violence in Canadian prisons, see the following: Ishwaran, S. and Neugebauer, R. (2001). Prison Life and Daily Experiences. In Winterdyk, J. (ed.). *Corrections in Canada: Social Reactions to Crime*. Toronto: Prentice Hall.

44. A good Canadian source can be found in the following: Meier, L.F.M. (1982). Predictors of Prison Disturbances. M.A. thesis. University of Saskatchewan.

45. Report of the Attorney General on the February 2 and 3, 1980 Riot at the Penitentiary of New Mexico (two parts). (1980, June and September 1980).

46. See, for example: American Correctional Association. (1981). Riots and Disturbances in Correctional Institutions. College Park, Md.: ACA; Braswell, M. et al. (1985). Prison Violence in America. Cincinnati, Ohio: Anderson; and Conant, R. (1968, Summer). Rioting, Insurrectional and Civil Disorderliness. American Scholar, Vol. 37, pp. 420–433.

47. Blumenthal, H. (2000). Gangs and Violence: A Continuing Concern. *Let's Talk* (Vol. 3). Accessible at time of writing at: **www.csc-scc.gc.ca/text/pblct/letstalk/2000/vol3/index_e.shtml**

48. Griffiths and Cunningham. *Canadian Corrections* (p. 166).

49. Union Lauds Alta. Appeal of Inmate Knife Ruling. (2002, November 7). CTV News. Accessible at time of writing at **www.ctv.ca/servlet.ArticleNews/story/CTVNews/1036671790601_76/?hub=TopStories**

50. See the following: Ormond, D.M. (1933). Report to the Superintendent of Penitentiaries re Kingston Penitentiary Disturbance. Ottawa: Kings Printer; Canada. Correctional Investigator. (1976). Report of Inquiry: Millhaven incident, 3rd November 1975. Ottawa: The Investigator; Moore, B. (1978). Report of His Honour Benjamin Moore, Commissioner. Saskatchewan [dealing with a riot at the Prince Albert Correctional Centre on June 21 & 22, 1977]; Culhane, C. (1979). Barred from prison. Vancouver, B.C.: Pulp Press [dealing with a riot at New Westminster institution]; Canadian Correction Service. (1982). Report of the Inspector-General's Special Inquiry into Riot, Archambault institution, July 1982. Ottawa: Correctional Service; Canada. Correctional Investigator. (1984). Report on Allegations of Mistreatment of Inmates of Archambault Institution Following Events that Occurred on July 25th, 1982. Ottawa: The Investigator; Caron, R. (1985). Bingo! Toronto: Methuen [an "insider's" account of the riot in Kingston Penitentiary].

51. Dillingham, S. and Montgomery, R. (1985). Prison Riots: A Corrections Nightmare since 1774. In Braswell et al. *Prison Violence in America* (pp. 19–36).

52. Fox, V. (1982). Prison Riots in a Democratic Society. *Police*, Vol. 26, no. 12, pp. 35–41.

53. Cressey, D.R. (1972). Adult Felons in Prison. In Ohlin, L.E. (ed.). *Prisoners in America* (pp. 117–150). Englewood Cliffs, N.J.: Prentice Hall.

54. See, Needham, J.P. (1977). *Neutralization of Prison Hostage Situations*. Huntsville, Texas: Sam Houston State University, Institute of Contemporary Corrections and the Behavioral Sciences; Porporino, R., McGee, R.A., and Joseph, R. (1984). *Countermeasures to Prison Violence: A Survey of Correctional Jurisdictions*. Ottawa:Ministry of the Solicitor General of Canada Secretariat.

55. See, Useem, B., Graham Camp, C., and Camp, G. (1996). *Resolution of Prison Riots: Strategies and Policies*. New York: Oxford University Press.

56. Robinson, D., Porporino, F.J., and Millson, W.A. (1998). A One-Day Snapshot of Inmates in Canada's Adult Correctional Facilities. *Juristat*, Vol. 18, No. 8, p. 5.

57. *Basic Facts About Corrections*. (2001). Accessible at time of writing at **www.csc-scc.gc.ca/text/faits/facts07_e.shtml**.

58. Hendrick, D. and Farmer, L. (2002). Adult Correctional Services in Canada, 2000/01. *Juristat*, Vol. 22, No. 10, p. 11.

59. See: Reed, M. and Morrison, P. (1997). Adult Correctional Services in Canada, 1995–96. *Juristat*, Vol. 17, No. 4; Incarceration Population Trends. See the Correctional Service of Canada's website: **www.csc-scc.gc.ca/text/prgrm/fsw/statistical/stat_e-06_e.shtml**, accessible at time of writing.

60. Arbour, The Honourable Louise. (1996). *Commission of Inquiry into Certain Events at the Prison for Women in Kingston* (p. 202). Ottawa: Public Works and Government Services Canada.

61. See the various institutional headcounts at **www.csc-scc.gc.ca/text/region/regions_e.shtml**, accessible at time of writing.

62. Belanger, B. (2001). Sentencing in Adult Criminal Courts, 1999/00. *Juristat*, Vol. 21, No. 10, p. 15.

63. Crew, B.K. (1991, March). Sex Differences in Criminal Sentencing: Chivalry or Patriarchy? *Justice Quarterly*, Vol. 8, No. 1, pp. 59–83.

64. Arbour. *Commission of Inquiry into Certain Events at the Prison for Women in Kingston* (p. 201).

65. Correctional Service of Canada. "Profile of Women Offenders, March 2001," at **www.csc-scc.gc.ca/**

**text/prgrm/fsw/profiles/nomax_e.shtml**, accessible at time of writing.

66. Ibid.

67. Correctional Service of Canada. "The Transformation of Federal Corrections For Women," at **www.csc-scc.gc.ca/text/pblct/choix/index_e.shtml**, accessible at time of writing.

68. Ibid.

69. Arbour. *Commission of Inquiry into Certain Events at the Prison for Women in Kingston* (pp. 218–225).

70. Berzins, L. and Cooper, S. (1982). The Political Economy of Correctional Planning for Women: The Case of Bankrupt Bureaucracy. *Canadian Journal of Criminology*, Vol. 24, pp. 399–416. See also: Kendall, K. (1993). *Literature Review of Therapeutic Services for Women in Prison*. Ottawa: Ministry of the Solicitor General of Canada, Corrections Branch.

71. Strange, C. (1983). The Velvet Glove: Maternalistic Reform at the Andrew Mercer Ontario Reformatory for Females 1874–1927. M.A. thesis in history. University of Ottawa.

72. Ross, R. and Fabiano, E. (1985). *Correctional Afterthoughts: Programs for Female Offenders*. Ottawa: Ministry of the Solicitor General of Canada.

73. Morton, J.B. (1997). Effective Initiatives: What Works with Women Offenders. In American Correctional Association. *The State of Corrections: Proceedings of the American Correctional Association Annual Conference 1996* (pp. 235–244). Philadelphia/Nashville. Fredericksurg, VA: ACA.

74. See, for example: Lambert, L.R. and Madden, P.G. (1974). The Vanier Centre for Women: Research Report No. 1: An Examination of the Social Milieu. Toronto: Ontario Ministry of Correctional Services.

75. Important Canadian resources include the following: The Task Force on Federally Sentenced Women. (1990). *Creating Choices: Report of the Task Force on Federally Sentenced Women*. Ottawa: Correctional Service of Canada; Chunn, D. and Gavigan, S. (1991). Women and Crime in Canada. In Jackson, M. and Griffiths, C. (eds.). *Canadian Criminology: Perspectives on Crime and Criminality*. Toronto: Harcourt, Brace Jovanovich; Shaw, M. (1991a). *The Federal Female Offender: Report on a Preliminary Study*. Ottawa: Ministry of the Solicitor General Canada, Corrections Branch; Shaw, M. (1991b). *Survey of Federally Sentenced Women: Report to the Task Force on Federally Sentenced Women*. Ottawa: Ministry of the Solicitor General Canada, Corrections Branch; Shaw, M. (1992). *Paying the Price: Federally Sentenced Women in Context*. Ottawa: Ministry of the Solicitor General Canada, Corrections Branch; Johnson, H. and Rodgers, K. (1993). A Statistical Overview of Women and Crime. In Adelberg, E. and Currie, C. (eds.). In *Conflict with the Law* (pp. 95–166). Vancouver, B.C.: The Press Gang; and Loucks, A. and Zamble, E. (1994). Some Comparisons of Female and Male Serious Offenders. *Forum on Corrections Research*, Vol. 1, pp. 22–28.

76. Ward, D. and Kannenbaum, G. (1966). *Women's Prison: Sex and Social Structure*. London: Weidenfeld and Nicolson.

77. Heffernan, E. (1972). *Making It in Prison: The Square, the Cool and the Life*. London: Wiley-Interscience.

78. Giallombardo, R. (1966). *Society of Women: A Study of Women's Prisons*. New York: John Wiley.

79. Shaw, M. (1992). *Paying the Price: Federally Sentenced Women in Context*. Ottawa: Solicitor General Canada.

80. Walford, B. (1987). *Lifers: The Story of Eleven Women Serving Life Sentences for Murder*. Montreal: Eden Press.

81. Giallombardo. *Society of Women* (p. 162).

82. For a summary of such studies (including some previously unpublished), see Bowker. *Prisoner Victimization*. (p. 86).

83. Giallombardo. *Society of Women* (p. 162).

84. Dobash, R.P., Dobash, P.E., and Gutteridge, S. (1986). *The Imprisonment of Women*. Oxford: Basil Blackwell.

85. Heffernan. *Making It in Prison*.

86. Harris, J. (1988). *They Always Call Us Ladies*. New York: Scribners.

87. The Lady on Cell Block 112A. (1988, September 5). *Newsweek*, p. 60.

88. Ibid.

89. Ibid.

90. Scarsdale Diet Doctor's Killer Given Clemency. (1992, December 30). *USA Today*, p. 3A.

91. Bowker. *Prison Victimization* (p. 53).

92. Giallambardo. *Society of Women*.

93. A detailed summary of the Commission's recommendations can be found in the report, pp. 251–259. See Arbour. *Commission of Inquiry into Certain Events at the Prison for Women in Kingston*.

94. American Correctional Association. (1990). Task Force on the Female Offender. *The Female Offender: What Does the Future Hold?* (p. 39). Washington, D.C.: St. Mary's Press.

95. *McCann* v. *The Queen*, [1976] 1 F.C. 570 (F.C.T.D.). See also: Jackson, M. (1983). *Prisoners of Isolation: Solitary Confinement in Canada*. Toronto: University of Toronto Press.

96. *Solosky* v. *The Queen*, [1980] 1 S.C.R. 821.

97. Conroy, John W. (1991). *Canadian Prison Law* (3 vols., looseleaf). Toronto: Butterworths.

98. Ibid., p. 24.

99. Price, R. (1974). Bringing the Rule of Law to Corrections. *Canadian Journal of Corrections*, Vol. 16, pp. 209–224.

100. Campbell, M.E. (1997). Revolution and Counter-revolution in Canadian Prisoners' Rights. *Canadian Criminal Law Review*, Vol. 2, pp. 285–329.

101. Jacobs, J. (1980). The Prisoners' Rights Movement and Its Impacts, 1960–1989. In Tonry, M. and Morris, N. (eds.). *Crime and Justice: An Annual Review of Research*, Vol. 6, pp. 429–470.

102. *Solosky* v. *The Queen*, [1980] 1 S.C.R. 821.

103. In *R.* v. *Big M Drug Mart*, [1985] 1 S.C.R. 295, the Supreme Court of Canada ruled that freedom of religion includes a right to "be free to hold and to manifest whatever beliefs and opinions his or her conscience dictates, provided inter alia only that such manifestations do not

injure his or her neighbours or their parallel rights to hold and manifest beliefs and opinions of their own."

104. *Dettmer* v. *Landon*, 617 F. Supp. 592, 594 (D.C. Va. 1985).

105. *Re Maltby et al. and AG Saskatchewan et al.* (1983) 2 CCC (3rd) 153 (Sask.Q.B.).

106. *Bryntwick* v. *Yeomans and Rousseau* (1983), 1 C.C.C. (3rd) 131.

107. *Block* v. *Rutherford*, 486 U.S. 576 (1984).

108. *R.* v. *Olson*, [1996] 2 F.C. 168.

109. Bill C-220 was first introduced in 1995 (as Bill C-205) by Scarborough Southwest MP Tom Wappel. The proposed legislation would amend the Copyright Act and redefine the phrase "proceeds of crime" to include any work that describes a criminal act by someone convicted of that act. The Crown would be empowered to seize the proceeds. It appears that this bill will not pass through the Senate.

110. *R.* v. *Miller*, [1985] 2 S.C.R. 613.

111. *Cardinal* v. *Director of Kent Institution*, [1985] 2 S.C.R. 643.

112. Ibid.

113. See *Solosky* v. *The Queen*, [1980] 1 S.C.R. 821.

114. See the U.S. case *In re Harrell*, 87 Cal. Rptr. 504, 470 P.2d 640 (1970).

115. *Corrections and Conditional Release Regulations*, S.O.R./92-620, s. 86.

116. Ibid., pp. 105–106.

117. *Farmer* v. *Brennan*, 114 S.Ct. 1970, 128 L.Ed. 2d 811 (1994).

118. Ibid.

119. *Ruiz* v. *Estelle*, 679 F.2d 1115 (5th Cir. 1982).

120. *Newman* v. *Alabama*, 349 F. Supp. 278 (M.D. Ala. 1972).

121. Adapted from the American Correctional Association. (1987). *Legal Responsibility and Authority of Correctional Officers: A Handbook on Courts, Judicial Decisions and Constitutional Requirements*. College Park, MD: ACA.

122. In the U.S. context, see: *U.S.* v. *Ready*, 574 F.2d 1009 (10th Cir. 1978); *Katz* v. *U.S.*, 389 U.S. 347, 88 S.Ct. 507, 19 L.Ed. 2ed 576 (1967); and *Hudson* v. *Palmer*, 468 U.S. 517 (1984).

123. *Weatherall* v. *Canada (Attorney General)*, [1993] 2 S.C.R. 872.

124. Correctional Investigator (2002) *Annual Report of the Correctional Investigator, 2001–2002* Ottawa: Public Works and Government Services Canada.

125. Marron, K. (1996). *The Slammer: The Crisis in Canada's Prison System*. Toronto: Doubleday Canada Ltd.

126. Lines, R. (2002). *Action on HIV/AIDS in Prisons: Too Little, Too Late*. Montreal: Canadian HIV/AIDS Legal Network.

127. Ibid.

128. Cauchon, D. (1995, March 31). AIDS in Prison: Locked Up and Locked Out. *USA Today*, p. 6A.

129. Hammett. *AIDS in Correctional Facilities* (p. 29).

130. Kleiman, M.A.R. and Mockler, R.W. (1987, Summer/Fall). AIDS, the Criminal Justice System, and Civil Liberties. *Governance: Harvard Journal of Public Policy*, pp. 48–54.

131. Hammett, T. (1988) *AIDS in Correctional Facilities: Issues and Options* (3rd ed., p. 37). Washington, DC: National Institute of Justice.

132. At the time of this writing, California, Wisconsin, Massachusetts, New York, and the District of Columbia were among such jurisdictions.

133. Crawford. (1994, November). Health Care Needs in Corrections: NIJ Responds. *National Institute of Justice Journal*, p. 31.

134. See Court Allows Restriction in HIV-Positive Inmates. (1994, December 1). *Criminal Justice Newsletter*, Vol. 25, No. 23, pp. 2–3.

135. Cauchon. AIDS in Prison.

136. Ibid.

137. Hammett. *AIDS in Correctional Facilities* (pp. 47–49).

138. Bryan, D. (1994, September). Inmates, HIV and the Constitutional Right to Privacy: AIDS in Prison Facilities. *Corrections Compendium*, Vol. 19, No. 9, pp. 1–3.

139. Crawford. Health Care Needs in Corrections: NIJ Responds.

140. Uzoaba, J.H.E. (1998). *Managing Older Offenders: Where Do We Stand?* Ottawa: Research Branch, Correctional Service of Canada.

141. Wikberg, R. and Foster, B. (1989). The Longtimers: Louisiana's Longest Serving inmates and Why They've Stayed So Long. Paper presented at the Annual Meeting of the Academy of Criminal Justice Sciences, Washington, D.C.

142. Uzoaba, J.H.E. (1998) *Managing Older Offenders*.

143. Wikberg and Foster. The Longtimers. p. 51.

144. Chaneles, S. (1987, October). Growing Old Behind Bars. *Psychology Today*, p. 51.

145. Bland, R.C., Newman, S.C., Thompson, A.H., and Dyck, R.J. (1998). Psychiatric Disorders in the Population and in Prisoners. *International Journal of Law and Psychiatry*, 21(3), pp. 273–279.

146. Brink, J.H., Doherty, D., and Boer, A. (2001). Mental Disorders in Federal Offenders – A Canadian Prevalence Study. *International Journal of Law and Psychiatry* 24(4–5), pp. 339–356; see also Motiuk, L. and Porporino, F.J. (1991). *The Prevalence, Nature and Severity of Mental Health Problems Among Federal Inmates in Canadian Penitentiaries, Report No. 24*. Ottawa: Research and Statistics Branch, Correctional Service of Canada.

147. Toch, H. (1982). The Disturbed Disruptive Inmate: Where Does the Bus Stop? *The Journal of Psychiatry and Law*, Vol. 10, pp. 327–349.

148. Some particularly relevant references include the following: Blanchette, K. and Motiuk, L.L. (1996). Female Offenders With and Without Major Mental Health Problems: A Comparative Investigation. *Correctional Service of Canada Research Report, No. R-46*. Ottawa: Correctional Service of Canada; Endicott, O.R. (1991). Persons with Intellectual Disability Who Are Incarcerated for Criminal Offences: A Literature Review. *Correctional Service of Canada Research Report, No. R-14*. Ottawa: Correctional Service of Canada;

and Porporino, F.J. and Motiuk, L.L. (1992). The Prison Careers of Offenders with Mental Disorders. *Correctional Service of Canada Research Report No. R-33.* Ottawa: Correctional Service of Canada.

149. Lampert, R.O. (1987, Spring). The Mentally Retarded Offender in Prison. *The Justice Professional*, Vol. 2, No. 1, p. 61.

150. Ibid., p. 64.

151. *R. v. Knoblauch*, [2000] 2 S.C.R. 780. See also the commentary on this case: Roberts, J.V. and Verdun-Jones, S. (2000). *Alberta Law Review*, 39(4), pp. 788–809.

152. See Arbour. *Commission of Inquiry into Certain Events at the Prison for Women in Kingston.* Recommendation #13, p. 257.

## Chapter 13

1. Ferguson, E. (1998, November 21). Friends of Slain Youth demand changes to YOA. *Calgary Herald*, p. B4.

2. Canadian Centre for Justice Statistics. (1994). *Juristat*, Vol. 14, No. 14, p. 12.

3. Teen Tormented by Relentless Teasing. (1997, November 28). *Calgary Herald*, p. A21. Six teens involved in the initial beating were convicted of assault causing bodily harm. Subsequently, the girl and boy involved in the final acts of killing, Kelly Ellard and Warren Glowatski, who were 15 and 17 at the time, were tried in adult court for second-degree murder. Both were convicted and sentenced to life terms; however, Ellard has since been released on appeal, and is the subject of a new trial, as in: New Trial Ordered in Virk Slaying: Appeal Court Overturns Ellard Murder Conviction. (2003, February 23). *Times Colonist (Victoria)*.

4. Savoie, J. (2002). Crime Statistics in Canada, 2001. *Juristat*, Vol. 22, No. 6.

5. Foot, D. (1996). *Boom, Bust and Echo* (p. 24). Toronto: Macfarlane, Walter & Ross.

6. Springer, C.E. (1987). *Justice for Juveniles* (2nd printing, p. 50). Washington, D.C.: Office of Juvenile Justice and Delinquency Prevention.

7. See Fox, S. (1972). Juvenile Justice Reform: An Historical Perspective. In Sanford Fox, *Modern Juvenile Justice: Cases and Materials* (pp. 15–48). St. Paul, MN: West.

8. 4 Whart. 9 (Pa., 1839).

9. Fox. Juvenile Justice Reform. p. 27.

10. Platt, A. (1977). *The Child Savers: The Invention of Delinquency* (2nd ed.). Chicago: University of Chicago Press.

11. Carrigan, D.O. (1998). *Juvenile delinquency in Canada: A history*. Toronto: Irwin.

12. Carrigan. *Juvenile delinquency in Canada: A history*.

13. Carrigan. *Juvenile delinquency in Canada: A history* (p. 42).

14. L. DeMause (ed.). (1988). *The History of Childhood*. NY: Peter Bedrick.

15. Carrigan. *Juvenile delinquency in Canada: A history* (p. 43).

16. Johnson, T.A. (1975). *Introduction to the Juvenile Justice System* (p. 3). St. Paul, MN: West.

17. Ibid., p. 29.

18. Carrigan. *Juvenile delinquency in Canada: A history*.

19. Carrigan. *Juvenile delinquency in Canada: A history* (p. 121).

20. Carrigan. *Juvenile delinquency in Canada: A history*.

21. Matza, D. (1964). *Delinquency and Drift*. NY: John Wiley.

22. Lundman, R. (1984). *Prevention and Control of Juvenile Delinquency* (p. 99). NY: Oxford Press.

23. Generally, see Winterdyk, J. (ed.). (1997). *Juvenile justice systems: International perspectives*. Toronto: Canadian Scholars' Press.

24. For a general review, see Reid, S. and Reitsma-Street, M. (1993). In O'Reilly-Fleming, T. and Clark, B. (eds.). *Youth injustice: Canadian perspectives* (Ch. 4). Toronto: Canadian Scholars Press.

25. Caputo, T. (1993). In O'Reilly-Fleming and Clark. *Youth injustice: Canadian perspectives* (Ch. 4). See note 24.

26. Paul, D. (1996, June 17). Violence with a youthful face.

27. Sykes, G.M., and Matza, D. (1957). Techniques of Neutralization: A Theory of Delinquency. *American Sociological Review*, Vol. 22, pp. 664–666.

28. Wolfgang, M., Figlio, R., and Sellin, T. (1972). *Delinquency in a Birth Cohort*. Chicago: University of Chicago Press.

29. Wolfgang, M., Thornberry, T., and Figlio, R. (1987). *From Boy to Man, From Delinquency to Crime*. Chicago: University of Chicago Press.

30. Lab, S.P. (1988). Analyzing Change in Crime and Delinquency Rates: The Case for Cohort Analysis. *Criminal Justice Research Bulletin*, 3(10):2.

31. Greenbaum, S. (1994, Spring/Summer). Drugs, Delinquency, and Other Data. *Juvenile Justice*, Vol. 2, No. 1, pp. 2–8.

32. Going "Wilding": Terror in Central Park. (1989, May 1). *Newsweek*, p. 27.

33. Angry Teens Explode in Violent Wilding Sprees. (1989, April 27). *USA Today*, p. 1D.

34. della Cava, M.D. (1989, April, 27). The Societal Forces That Push Kids Out of Control. *USA Today*, p. 6D.

35. Cavan, R.S. (1969). *Juvenile Delinquency: Development, Treatment, Control* (2nd ed., p. 152). Philadelphia: J. B. Lippincott.

36. Durham III, A.M. (1988). Ivy League Delinquency: A Self-report Analysis. *American Journal of Criminal Justice*, 12(2): 188.

37. Blumstein, A., Farrington, D.P., and Moitra, S. (1985). Delinquency careers: Innocents, desisters and persisters. In *Crime and Justice: An Annual Review of Research* (Vol. 6). Tonry, M. and Morris, N. (eds.). University of Chicago Press, Chicago.

38. Torture Killing. (1993, January 29). *USA Today*, p. 3A.

39. See Caspi, A., McClay, J., Moffit, T.E., Mill, J., Martin, J., Craig, I.W., Taylor, A., and Poulton, R. (2002). Role of Genotype in the Cycle of Violence in Maltreated Children. *Science*, 297, pp. 851–854.

40. Gottfredson, M.R. and Hirschi, T. (1990). *A General Theory of Crime*. Stanford, CA: Stanford University Press. Hirschi's

original theory can be found in: Hirschi, T. (1969). *Causes of Delinquency*. Berkley, CA: University of California.

41. Youngsters "totally out of control." (1993, April 14). *Calgary Herald*, p. A7.

42. Paul, D. (1997, June 17). Violence with a youthful face. (Online).

43. Lazaruk, S. (2003, March 4). Students Cope with Pressure, Stress. The (Vancouver) Province. Accessible at time of writing at **www.canada.com/vancouver/theprovince/specials/generation_next/stories**

44. Ibid.

45. See, for example, Thrasher, F.M. (1927). *The Gang* Chicago: University of Chicago Press; and Foote Whyte, W. (1943). *Street Corner Society, the Social Structure of an Italian Slum*. Chicago: University of Chicago Press.

46. Durham III, A.M. (1988). Ivy league delinquency: A self-report analysis. *American Journal of Criminal Justice*, 12(2):188.

47. Perry, P. (1996). Adolescent substance abuse and delinquency. In J. Winterdyk (ed.). *Issues and perspectives on young offenders in Canada*. Toronto: Harcourt-Brace.

48. Adalf, E.M. and Paglia, A. (2001) *Drug Use Among Ontario Students, Findings From the OSDUS (1977–2001)*. Toronto: Centre for Addiction and Mental Health. Accessible at time of writing at **www.camh.net/research/pdfs/osdus2001_DrugReport.pdf**

49. Ibid.

50. Ibid.

51. Ibid., p. 20. Although this section focuses on illegal drugs, there is a growing body of evidence indicating the problems of prescription drug abuse among youth. The 2001 survey conducted among Ontario students in grades 7 through 13 found that approximately 12 per cent had experimented with prescription drugs.

52. Ibid., p. i.

53. Ibid., p. iv.

54. Telephone conversation with the Street Crimes Unit. (1995, June 20). Los Angeles County Sheriff's Department.

55. Ibid., p. 153.

56. Demuro, P., Demuro, A., and Lerner, S. (1988). *Reforming the California Youth Authority: How to End Crowding, Diversify Treatments, and Protect the Public—Without Spending More Money*. Bolinas, CA: Commonweal Research Institute.

57. Held, M. (1998). Drugs, crime, and youth. Accessible at **www.dmci.org/g8/newg8web/newweb/…/positionp/youth_crime/paper_math.html**

58. Savoie, J. (2002). Crime Statistics in Canada, 2001. *Juristat*, Vol. 22, No. 6, at p. 12.

59. Ibid.

60. Carrigan, *Juvenile delinquency in Canada: A history* (p. 180).

61. Carrigan, *Juvenile delinquency in Canada: A history* (p. 181).

62. Sprott, J.B., Doob, A.N., and Jenkins, J.M. (2001). Problem Behaviour and Delinquency in Children and Youth. *Juristat*, Vol. 21, No. 4.

63. Carrigan, *Juvenile delinquency in Canada: A history* (p. 90).

64. Kennedy, L. and Baron, S. (1993). Routine activities and a subculture of violence: A study of violence on the street. *Journal of Research in Crime and Delinquency*, 30(1): 275–290.

65. Gang members ordered to trial. (1998, Nov. 5). *Calgary Herald*, A5.

66. Bernard, 1949 cited in Campbell, A. (1990). *The girls in the gang* (2nd ed.). NY: Basil Blackwell.

67. Shephard, M. (October 24, 1998). Teen Gangs, Fear in Our Schools. *Toronto Star*. Accessed on March 7, 2003 at **www.tamiltigers.net/tamilcanadian/canada9855.html**

68. Gordon, R.M. (1993). *Incarcerated Gang Members in British Columbia: A Preliminary Study* Victoria, BC: Ministry of Attorney General.

69. Gordon, R.M. (2000). Criminal Business Organizations, Street Gangs and "Wanna-be" Groups: A Vancouver Perspective. *Canadian Journal of Criminology*, Vol. 42, pp. 39–60.

70. Ibid. at p. 51.

71. Ibid. at p. 53.

72. Young, M. (1993). *The History of Vancouver Youth Gangs: 1900–1985*. Unpublished M.A. Thesis. Burnaby, BC: Simon Fraser University, School of Criminology.

73. Huff, R. (1998, October). *Comparing the criminal behavior of youth gangs and at-risk youth* (p. 1). Washington, DC: National Institute of Justice.

74. Ibid., p. 1.

75. Sedlak, A.J., Finkelhor, D., Hammer, H., and Schultz, D.J. (2002). *NISMART: National Estimates of Missing Children: An Overview*. Washington, D.C.: Office of Juvenile Justice and Delinquency Prevention. Accessible at time of writing at **www.ncjrs.org/html/ojjdp/nismart/01/index.html**

76. See "Our Missing Children," accessible at time of writing at **www.ourmissingchildren.ca**

77. National Missing Children Services. (2002). *Canada's Missing Children Annual Report 2001*. Ottawa: Minister of Public Works and Government Services Canada.

78. Runaway statistics. Accessible on December 7, 1998 at **www.child.cyberseach.org/opgohome/stats.htm**

79. Runaway children and the Juvenile Justice and Delinquency Prevention Act: What is its impact? (n.d.). *Juvenile Justice Bulletin*, p. 1. Washington, D.C.: Office of Juvenile Justice and Delinquency Prevention.

80. MacLaren, B. (1996). Runaway and Homeless Youth in Canada. In Winterdyk, J. (ed.). *Issues and Perspectives on Young Offenders in Canada*. Toronto: Harcourt Brace.

81. U.S. Attorney General, *America's Missing and Exploited Children*, p. 19.

82. National Committee for Prevention of Child Abuse. (1986). *Child Abuse: Prelude to Delinquency*. Washington, D.C.: Office of Juvenile Justice and Delinquency Prevention.

83. Wells, M. (1989). *Canada's law on child sexual abuse: A handbook*. Ottawa: Ministry of Justice.

84. Carmichael, K. (1998, May 28). 580 CFRA:news Talk Radio. Accessed at **cfra.com/1998/05/28/37195.html**

85. Fitzgerald, R. (1997). Assault against children and youth in the family, 1996. *Juristat*, Vol. 17, No. 11. See also *Sex Offender Registry Act*, S.B.C. 2001, c. 21 (not in force).

86. Federal Government Introduces Legislation for National Sex Offender Registration System. (2002, November 11). Solicitor General Canada news release and backgrounder. Accessed March 8, 2003 at **www.sgs.gc.ca/publications/news/20021211_2_e.asp**

87. National Committee for prevention of Child Abuse. (1986). *Child Abuse: Prelude to Delinquency?* Washington, D.C.: Office of Juvenile Justice and Delinquency Prevention.

88. Caspi, A., McClay, J., Moffitt, T.E., Mill, J., Martin, J., Craig, I.W., Taylor, A., and Poulton, R. (2002). Role of Genotype in the Cycle of Violence in Maltreated Children. *Science*, Vol. 297, pp. 851–854.

89. Zingraff, M.T., Leiter, J., Myers, K.A., and Johnson, M.C. (1993). Child maltreatment and youthful problem behavior. Criminology, 31(2): 173–202.

90. Wells, R.H. and Willis, C.L. (1988). The police and child abuse: An analysis of police decision to report illegal behavior. *Criminology*, 26(4): 695–715.

91. *Alberta* v. *K.B.*, [2000] A.J. No. 876 (Alta.P.C.F.D.).

92. *Alberta* v. *K.B.*, [2000] A.J. No. 1570 (Alta.Q.B.).

93. Talaga, T. (1998, July 11). Teen's life shattered in a few hours. *Toronto Star*. Accessible at **www.thestar.com**

94. Talaga, T. (1998, July 11). Police role under fire in student suicide. *Toronto Star*. Accessible at **www.thestar.com**

95. Teen age suicide. (1998). Accessible at **www.soonet.ca/starla/suicide**

96. Jones, M.A., and Krisberg, B. (1994). *Images and reality: Juvenile crime, youth violence and public policy*. Washington, D.C.: Office of Juvenile Justice and Delinquency Prevention.

97. Ministry of the Solicitor General of Canada. (1985). *Programs Branch user report*, No. 1985-06. Ottawa.

98. Wright, K.N. and Wright, K.E. (1994). *Family life, delinquency, and crime: A policymaker's guide: research summary*. Washington, D.C.: Office of Juvenile Justice and Delinquency Prevention.

99. J.R. Harris. (1998). *The nurture assumption*. NY: Free Press. In 1998, Harris received the George A. Miller Award from the American Psychological Association for her work.

100. For an introduction to the meaning and significance of an *interdisciplinary* approach to the study of crime and criminality, see: Barak, G. (1997). *Integrating Criminologies*. Boston: Allyn and Bacon, or Winterdyk, J. (2000). *Introduction to criminology: An integrated and interdisciplinary approach*. Scarborough: Prentice-Hall.

101. Adapted from Schmalleger, F. 1998. *Criminal justice today: An introductory text for the 21st century* (5th ed.). Upper Saddle River, NJ: Prentice-Hall.

102. Ibid.

103. For further details on the historical evolution of youth justice law in Canada, see Alvi, S. (2000). *Youth and the Canadian Criminal Justice System*. Cincinnati, OH: Anderson Publishing.

104. See the discussion of the various models of youth justice in Canada in Tanner, J. (2001). *Teenage Troubles: Youth and Deviance in Canada* (2nd ed., pp. 223–224). Toronto: Nelson.

105. *Youth Criminal Justice Act*, S.C. 2002, c. 1, s. 3.

106. See the Department of Justice's discussion of the YCJA, accessible at the time of writing at **canada.justice.gc.ca/en/ps/yj/repository/6legisln/6000001a.html**

107. See section 2 of the YCJA.

108. *R. v. M.(M.A.)* (1986), 32 *C.C.C.*(3d) 567 (B.C.C.A.).

109. *R. v. S.( S.)*, [1990] 2 S.C.R. 254.

110. For a comparison of various jurisdictions, see: Bala, N.M.C., Hornick, J.P., Snyder, H.N., and Paetsch, J.J. (eds.). (2002). *Juvenile Justice Systems: An International Comparison of Problems and Solutions*. Toronto: Thompson Educational Publishing; and Winterdyk, J. (ed.). (2002). *Juvenile Justice Systems: International Perspectives* (2nd ed.). Toronto: Canadian Scholars' Press.

111. *R. v. L.(R.)* (1986), 52 C.R. (3d) 209 and *R. v. B.(S.)* (1989), 76 Sask.R. 308 (Sask.C.A.).

112. deSouza, P. (2002). Youth Court Statistics, 2000/01. *Juristat*, Vol. 22, No. 3.

113. Thomas, M. (2002). Adult Criminal Court Statistics, 2000/01. *Juristat*, Vol. 22, No. 2.

114. The Supreme Court of Canada recently discussed the stigmatizing effects of the young offender label in *Re F.N.*, [2000] 1 S.C.R. 880.

115. The YCJA provides for exceptions to the no-publication rule in a variety of circumstances, discussed in Bala, N. (2003). *Youth Criminal Justice Law*. Toronto: Irwin Law, at pp. 384–388.

116. deSouza, P. (2002). Youth Court Statistics, 2000/01. p. 6.

117. Ibid., p. 7.

118. See *The Parental Responsibility Act*, S.M. 1996, c. 61, *Parental Responsibility Act*, S.O. 2000, c. 4, and *Parental Responsibility Act*, S.B.C. 2001, c. 45.

119. See s. 1 of the B.C. *Parental Responsibility Act*.

120. See Tanner. *Teenage Troubles*, Chs. 3–6.

121. Marinelli, J. (2002). Youth Custody and Community Services in Canada, 2000/01. *Juristat*, Vol. 22, No. 8, p. 3.

122. Ontario Ministry of Public Safety and Security. "Young Offenders: Project Turnaround," accessible at time of writing at **www.mpss.jus.gov.on.ca/english/corr_serv/young_off/project_turn.html**

123. U.S. Surgeon General. (2001). *Youth Violence: A Report of the Surgeon General*. Washington, DC: Department of Health and Human Services, Chapter 5. Accessible at time of writing at **www.surgeongeneral.gov/library/youthviolence/default.htm**

124. Brennan, R. (2003, February 7). Mould Closes Boot Camp for Teens. *The (Toronto) Star*. Accessed on June 20,

2003 at **www.oacas.org/whatsnew/newsstories/03/feb/7mould.pdf**

125. Marinelli, J. (2002). Youth Custody and Community Services in Canada, 2000/01. p. 7.

## Chapter 14

1. Japanese Parliament Approves Wiretap Law. (1999, August 13). Associated Press wire service. This legislation became effective in 2000.

2. Fackler, M. (1998, February 27). Coverage of Brutal Murder Ignites Media Debate in Japan. Associated Press wire service.

3. Sakurai, J. (1997, June 28). Arrest Made in Japan Beheading. Associated Press wire service.

4. Kambayashi, S. (1997, June 29). Beheading Arrest Shocks Japan. Associated Press wire service.

5. Japanese Ministry of Public Management. (2002). Home Affairs, Posts and Telecommunications. *Japan Statistical Yearbook 2002*. Tokyo: Japan Statistics Bureau.

6. Juvenile Crime. *Mainichi Daily News*. Accessed February 2, 2000 at **www3.justnet.ne.jp/matudasy/ikai/eng-news3.html.**

7. Violent Crime Stalks Japan's Youth. *BBC News – Asia-Pacific*. Accessed January 30, 2002 at **www.news.bbc.co.uk/hi/world/asia-pacific/1377781.stm**

8. Lilly, R. (1986, March/April). Forks and Chopsticks: Understanding Criminal Justice in the PRC. *Criminal Justice International*, p. 15.

9. Adapted from Kalish, C.B. (1988). International Crime Rates. A Bureau of Justice Statistics Special Report. Washington, D.C.: BJS.

10. Ibid.

11. Ibid.

12. Ibid.

13. Hockstader, L. (1995, Feb, 27). Russia's War on Crime: A Lopsided, Losing Battle. *The Washington Post* online.

14. Walmsley, R. (1995). *Developments in the Prison Systems of Central and Eastern Europe*, HEUNI papers no. 4. Helsinki, Finland.

15. China: The Hope and the Horror. (1989, Sept.). *Reader's Digest*, p. 75.

16. This section draws heavily upon Leng, S-C. and Chiu, H. (1985). *Criminal Justice in Post-Mao China: Analysis and Documents*. Albany: SUNY at Albany Press.

17. Various authorities give different dates for the ending of the Cultural Revolution. We have chosen 1973 because it represents the date at which military control over law enforcement finally ended.

18. *China Mainland Magazine*. (1968, September 3). p. 23.

19. Central Political-Judicial Cadre's School. *Lectures on the General Principles of Criminal Law in the People's Republic of China* (Peking, 1957), as cited by Leng and Chiu, *Criminal Justice in Post-Mao China*, p. 21.

20. On Questions of Party History. (1981, July 6). *Beijing Review*, Vol. 24, No. 27, p. 20, as quoted in Leng and Chiu, *Criminal Justice in Post-Mao China*.

21. Leng and Chiu. *Criminal Justice in Post-Mao China* (p. 42).

22. China uses technology to tackle soaring crime. (1994, Dec. 18). Reuters online.

23. Ibid.

24. Zhou, Z. (1987). An Introduction to the Present Legal System of the People's Republic of China. *North Carolina Criminal Justice Today*, Vol. IV, No. 6: 8–15.

25. Lilly, R. (1986, March/April). Forks and Chopsticks: Understanding Criminal Justice in the PRC. *Criminal Justice International*, pp. 14–15.

26. Ibid., p. 14.

27. Leng and Chiu. *Criminal Justice in Post-Mao China* (p. 75).

28. The rate in Canada, 8913 per 100 000 people, refers to *Criminal Code* offences without traffic-related offences.

29. Pomfret, J. (1999, January 21). Chinese Crime Rate Soars as Economic Problems Grow. *Washington Post*, p. A19; Ysiheng, D. (1997, Feb.). Haves and have nots: one of the factors causing crime in China. *Crime and Justice International*, 23–25.

30. Ibid.

31. Shenzen Cracks Down Hard on Piracy. (2002, January 24). *People's Daily* (China).

32. China Cracking Down on Piracy of DVDs. (2001, November 26). *People's Daily* (China).

33. Lim, B.K. (1995, February 23). China Declares War on Organized Crime. Reuters online.

34. Statistics on arrest, conviction, and imprisonment in China are taken from the following: Elegant, R. (1988, October 30). Everyone Can be Reformed. *Parade*, pp. 4–7.

35. Leng and Chiu. *Criminal Justice in Post-Mao China*.

36. Forney, M. Bad company: Lost in a moral vacuum, Chinese youth are dropping out of mainstream society and turning to crime. "Time ASIA – China's Next Cultural Revolution." Accessed on November 4, 2002 at **www.time.com/time/asia/features/china_cul_rev/gangs.html**

37. Entao, Z. (1987, January/February). A Perspective on Drug Abuse. *Criminal Justice International*, pp. 5–6.

38. Zhou. An Introduction to the Present Legal System of the People's Republic of China. p. 13.

39. Ibid.

40. For more information, see the following: Zhang, L. et al. (1996, June). Crime Prevention in a Communitarian Society: *Bang-Jiao* and *Tiao-Jie* in the People's Republic of China. *Justice Quarterly*, Vol. 13, No. 2, pp. 199–222.

41. Ibid.

42. Leng and Chiu. *Criminal Justice in Post-Mao China* (p. 64).

43. Elegant. Everyone Can Be Reformed. p. 5.

44. Amnesty International, "The Death Penalty," accessed January 8, 2002 at **www.web.amnesty.org/rmp/dplibrary.nsf/other?openview**

45. Amnesty International. (1997, Oct. 2). At least 1000 people executed in "Strike Hard" campaign against crime. Amnesty International online: **www.amnesty.org**

46. Executions an Every Day Event in China. (1995, March 17). Reuters online.

47. Ibid.

48. Elegant. Everyone Can Be Reformed. p. 6.

49. Ibid.

50. Constitution. People's Republic of China. Article 13.

51. Miller, E.E. (1987). Corrections in the People's Republic of China. In *International Corrections: An Overview* (pp. 65–71). College Park, MD: American Correctional Association.

52. Wu, H. (1991, September 23). A Prisoner's Journey. *Newsweek*, p. 30.

53. Miller. Corrections in the People's Republic of China. pp. 65–71.

54. Sanders, J. and McAninch, T. (1994, November/December). A Communist Prison Experience. *American Jails*, p. 87.

55. Elegant. Everyone Can Be Reformed. p. 5.

56. Souryal, S.S., Potts, D.W., and Alobied, A.I. (1994). The Penalty of Hand Amputation for Theft in Islamic Justice. *Journal of Criminal Justice*, 22(3), pp. 249–265.

57. Saney, P. (1983). Iran. In Johnson, E.H. (ed.). *International Handbook of Contemporary Developments in Criminology* (p. 359). Westport, CT: Greenwood.

58. This section owes much to the following: Lippman, M. (1987). Iran: A Question of Justice? *Criminal Justice International*, pp. 6–7.

59. Imam-Jomeh, S. (1995, August 22). Iran Court Sentences Man to Death for Bank Fraud. Reuters online.

60. The Penalty of Hand Amputation for Theft in Islamic Justice. (1994). *Journal of Criminal Justice*, 22(3):249–265.

61. For additional information on Islamic law, see Adel Mohammed el Fikey. (1986). Crimes and Penalties in Islamic Criminal Legislation. *Criminal Justice International*, pp. 13–14; Souryal, S.S. (1987). Shariah Law in Saudi Arabia. *Journal for the Scientific Study of Religion*, 26(4):429–449.

62. Weber, M. (1967). In Rheinstein, M. (ed.) *On Law in Economy and Society* (translated from the 1925 German edition). New York: Simon & Schuster.

63. Ibid.

64. The Penalty of Hand Amputation for Theft in Islamic Justice. See note 60.

65. England and Wales use two primary sources for collecting crime data. The British Crime Survey was introduced in 1982, and information for this survey is collected every two years. Information about police-recorded crimes has been collected since 1857 and is published every six months.

66. Information for this section was obtained from the Home Office, "Research Development and Statistics" webpage, accessible at time of writing at **www.homeoffice.gov.uk/rds/index.htm**.

67. Wheatley, A. (1994, October 6). Howard Promises Crackdown on Crime. Reuters online.

68. Home Office. *The Crime and Disorder Act, Introductory Guide*. Accessed March 23, 2000 at **www.homeoffice.gov.uk/adact/cdaint2.htm**

69. The information in this section is derived from "Q&A: Anti-terror bill." BBC News online. Accessed December 15, 2001 at **newsvote.bbc.co.uk/hi/english/uk_politics/newsid_1708000/1708097.stm**

70. Stead, P.J. (1985). *The Police of Britain* (p. 94). New York: Macmillan.

71. Home Office. (2002). "Police Service Strength." Accessed February 2, 2003 at **www.homeoffice.gov.uk/rds/pdfs2/hosb1002.pdf**

72. Police and Magistrates Court Act Aids British Service. (1995, May/June). *Criminal Justice International*, p. 7.

73. Exceptions might include the Transport Police who supervise the operation of the nation's ports and secretive intelligence-gathering agencies such as "M.I.5."

74. An Interview with Sir Kenneth Newman, Commissioner of the Metropolitan Police. (1986, November/December). *Criminal Justice International*, p. 17.

75. New Intelligence Service Begins Operation. (1992, July/August). *Criminal Justice International*, p. 3.

76. For a discussion of the curriculum at Bramshill, see the following: Rowe, D. (1986, November/December). On Her Majesty's Service: Policing England and Wales. *Criminal Justice International*, pp. 9–16.

77. Hyder, K. (1995, May/June). Beware LA Law. *Criminal Justice International*, pp. 10–11.

78. "Crime Fighters: Justice, The Forensic Science Service." BBCi, online. Accessed on February 2, 2003 at **www.bbc.co.uk/crime/fighters/fss.shtml**

79. Stead. *The Police in Britain* (p. 147); Criminal Justice System online. "Magistrates Court." Accessed February 2, 2003 at **www.cjsonline.org/working/lcd/magistrates.html**; (U.K.) Court Service. "The Magistrates' Court." Accessed February 3, 2003 at **www.courtservice.gov.uk/you_courts/criminal/introduction/magistrates.htm**

80. Terrill, R. (1997). *World Criminal Justice Systems* (3rd ed.). Cincinnati, OH: Anderson.

81. Fairchild, E. (1993). *Comparative criminal justice system*. Belmont, CA.: Wadsworth.

82. HM (Her Majesty's) Prison Service. "Statistics: Prison Population." Accessed February 3, 2003 at **www.hmprisonservice.gov.uk/statistics/dynpage.asp?Page=18**

83. Home Office. Research and Statistics Department. "Prison Population Brief, England and Wales: October 2002" Accessed February 3, 2003 at www.homeoffice.gov.uk/rds/pdfs2/prisoct02.pdf

84. McConville, S. Some observations on English prison management. In *International Corrections*, p. 37.

85. Gannon, M. (2001). Crime Comparisons Between Canada and the United States. *Juristat*, Vol. 21, No. 11.

86. Statistical information in this section comes from the FBI's website at **www.fbi.gov**. Accessed on February 20, 2002.

87. Reaves, B.A. and Hart, T.C. (2000). *Law Enforcement Management and Administrative Statistics, 1999: Data for Individual State and Local Agencies with 100 or more Officers.* Washington, DC: Bureau of Justice Statistics.

88. DeFrances, C.J. (2002). Prosecutors in State Courts, 2001. *Bureau of Justice Statistics Bulletin.* Washington, DC: U.S. Department of Justice.

89. Death Penalty Information Center. "State by State Death Penalty Information." Accessed February 6, 2003 at **www.deathpenaltyinfo.org/firstpage.html**

90. Death Penalty Information Center. "Death Row Inmates by State and Size of Death Row by Year." Accessed February 6, 2003 at **www.deathpenaltyinfo.org/DRowInfo.html**

91. Death penalty Information Center. "Race and the Death Penalty." Accessed February 6, 2003 at **www.deathpenaltyinfo.org/race.html**

92. Bureau of Justice Statistics. "Prison Statistics." Access February 6, 2003 at **www.ojp.usdoj.gov/bjs/prisons.htm**. See also: Harrison, P.M. and Beck, A.J. (2002). *Prisoners in 2001.* Washington, DC: U.S. Department of Justice.

93. Ibid.

94. Hendrick, D. and Farmer, L. (2002). Adult Correctional Services in Canada, 2000/01. *Juristat*, Vol. 22, No. 10, p. 1.

95. Friday, P. (1983). International Organization: An Introduction. In Johnson, E.H. (ed.). *International Handbook of Contemporary Developments in Criminology* Westport, CN: Greenwood Press. (p. 31).

96. Ibid., p. 32.

97. Mueller, G.O.W. (1983). The United Nations and Criminology. In Johnson, E.H. (ed.). *International Handbook of Contemporary Development in Criminology*, Westport, CN: Greenwood Press. pp. 74–75.

98. Clark, R. (1994). *Formulation of standards and efforts at their implementation.* Philadelphia: University of Pennsylvania Press.

99. Mueller, G.O.W. (1998, June). The United Nations' role in global crime control. *Crime and Justice International*, pp. 5, 26.

100. Clarke, R. *Formation of standards and efforts at their implementation* (pp. 71–72).

101. International News. (1995, June). *Corrections Compendium*, p. 25.

102. Resolutions adopted on the reports of the Third Committee at the Forty-sixth Session of the United Nations General Assembly.

103. Dawoud, K. (1995, May 6). "U.N. Crime Meeting Wants Independent Jail Checks." Reuters online.

104. Robinson, L., address given at the Twelfth International Congress on Criminology, Seoul, Korea, August 28, 1998.

105. Gelbard, R.S. (1996, April 2). Foreign Policy after the Cold War: The New Threat – Transnational Crime. Address at St. Mary's University. San Antonio, Texas.

106. Starr, B. (1998, September 14). "A Gangster's Paradise." ABC News online. Accessed January 22, 2000 at **more.abcnews.go.com/sections/world/dailynews/russiacrime980914.html**

107. Ibid.

108. Bonner, R. and O'Brien, T.L. (August 19, 1999). Activity at Bank Raises Suspicions of Russia Mob Tie. *New York Times*, p. 1A.

109. McKeena, P.F. (1998). *Foundations of policing in Canada* (pp. 52–53). Scarborough, ON.

110. Boisseua, P. (1998, December 31). Killer wants deal for cash, lawyer says. *Calgary Herald*, p. A3. For a detailed account of this fascinating case, see the following. Cairns, A. (1998). *Nothing sacred: The many lives and betrayals of Albert Walker.* Toronto: Seal Books.

111. INTERPOL at Forty. (1986, November/December). *Criminal Justice International*, pp. 1, 22.

112. Drug smugglers frustrate Interpol sleuths. (1997, March). *Crime and Justice International*, p. 19.

113. Europol Will Not Solve All EU's Crime Ills. (1995, July 3). Reuters wire services.

114. Much of the information in this section is derived from the website for the Coalition for the International Criminal Court at **www.iccnow.org**, and from the "Rome Statute of the International Criminal Court" at **www.un.org/law/icc**

115. *Convention on the Prevention and Punishment of the Crime of Genocide*, U.N. General Assembly Resolution 260 (III), December 9, 1948.

116. There are actually a number of Geneva Conventions, the most pertinent being the *Geneva Convention Relative to the Treatment of Prisoners of War*, 75 U.N.T.S. 135 (in force October 21, 1951), and the *Geneva Convention Relative to the Treatment of Civilian Persons in Time of War*, 75 U.N.T.S. 973 (in force October 21, 1950).

117. The conference was officially known as the Conference of Plenipotentiaries on the Establishment of an International Criminal Court. *Plenipotentiaries* is another word for "diplomats."

# Chapter 15

1. Saunders, P. (2003, January 13). The Missing Women of Vancouver. CBC News Online. Accessible as of time of writing at **www.cbc.ca/news/features/bc_missingwomen.html**.

2. National Law Enforcement Technology Center. (1995, April 7). Electronic press release.

3. Shubin, L.D. Research. (1984). Testing, Upgrade Criminal Justice Technology. *National Institute of Justice Reports.* Washington, D.C.: U.S. Government Printing Office, pp. 2–5.

4. Dinitz, S. (1987). Coping with Deviant Behavior Through Technology. *Criminal Justice Research Bulletin*, 3(2).

5. See, for example, the following: Karper, L.P., Bennett, A.L., Erdos, J.J., and Krystal, J.H. (1995). Antipsychotics,

Lithium, Benzodiazepines, Beta-Blockers. In Hillbrand, M. and Pallone, N.J. (eds.). *The Psychobiology of Aggression: Engines, Measurement, Control* (pp. 203–222). New York: The Hayworth Press.

6. See, for example, Tancredi, L.R. and Weistub, D.N. (1986). Forensic Psychiatry and the Case of Chemical Castration. *International Journal of Law and Psychiatry*, 8:259.

7. Schweri, M.M., Deutsch, H.M., Massaey, A.T., and Holtzman, S.G. (2002). Biochemical and Behavioral Characterization of Novel Methylphenidate Analogs. *Journal of Pharmacology and Experimental Therapeutics*, 301(2): 527–535.

8. Soderman, H. and O'Connell, J.J. (1945). *Modern Criminal Investigation* (p. 41). New York: Funk and Wagnalls.

9. Invented by Lambert Adolphe Jacques Quetelet (1796–1874), Belgian astronomer and statistician.

10. For a summation of Bertillon's system, see *Signaletic Instructions* (New York: Werner, 1896).

11. Foote, R.D. (1974). Fingerprint Identification: A Survey of Present Technology, Automated Applications and Potential for Future Development. *Criminal Justice Monograph Series*, 5(2):3–4.

12. Soderman and O'Connell. *Modern Criminal Investigation* (p. 57).

13. Ibid.

14. Galton, F. (1892). *Finger Prints*. London: Macmillan.

15. Foote. Fingerprint Identification, p. 1.

16. Griffiths, C., Whitelaw, B., and Parent, R.B. (1999). *Canadian Police Work*. Scarborough: Nelson.

17. U.S. Congress, Office of Technology Assessment. (1988). *Criminal Justice: New Technologies and the Constitution: A Special Report*. Washington, D.C.: U.S. Government Printing Office.

18. Wilson, F. and Woodard, P.L. (1987). Department of Justice, Bureau of Justice Statistics. *Automated Fingerprint Identification Systems—Technology and Policy Issues*. Washington, D.C.: U.S. Department of Justice.

19. Ibid., p. 27.

20. Griffiths et al. (1999).

21. Kurre, D.G. (1987, December). "On-line exchange of fingerprint identification data." *FBI Law Enforcement Bulletin*, pp. 14–16.

22. RCMP Forensic Laboratory Services. Accessible on February 7, 2003 at **www.rcmp-grc.gc.ca/labs/labs.htm**.

23. *R. v. McNally*, [1989] O.J. No. 2630 (Ont.Dist.Ct.).

24. For up-to-date statistics, see the National DNA Data Bank's website, accessible at time of printing, at **www.nddb-bndg.org**

25. Holmgren, J. (1997). *Beyond the Walls of the Laboratory: An Analysis of Defence Counsel's Access to DNA Evidence within the Canadian Criminal Justice System*. M.A. Thesis, School of Criminology, Simon Fraser University, Burnaby, B.C.

26. Clay, J. (1996, April/May). Privacy or protection? *Law Now*, 21–22.

27. *R. v. F.(S.)* (2000), 141 C.C.C. (3d) 225 (Ont.C.A.).

28. Holmgren, J. and Winterdyk, J. (1994, April). DNA typing: Does it have a place in our legal system? *Law Now*, 18–20.

29. See the collection of articles on DNA testing and databanks brought together by David Lazer (ed.). (2002). *The Technology of Justice: DNA and the Criminal Justice System*. Cambridge, MA: John F. Kennedy School of Government, Harvard University. Available online, and accessible at time of writing, at **www.ksg.harvard.edu/dnabook**

30. "Police DNA Powers 'To be Extended.'" (2003, March 27). *BBC News* online. Accessible June 20, 2003 at **newswww.bbc.net.uk/2/low/uk_news/politics/2890047.stm**

31. Griffiths et al. *Canadian Police Work* (p. 358).

32. Ibid.

33. Ibid.

34. Ibid., p. 360.

35. LeDoux, J.C., and McCaslin, H.H. (1988, June). Computer-based training for the law enforcement community. *FBI Law Enforcement Bulletin*, pp. 8–13.

36. See, for example: Hormann, J. S. (1995, July). Virtual Reality: The future of law enforcement training. *FBI Law Enforcement Bulletin*, pp. 7–12.

37. Rodriguez, M.L. (1988, December). The acquisition of high technology systems by law enforcement. *FBI Law Enforcement Bulletin*, p. 10.

38. Tafoya, W.L. (1986, September/October). Law enforcement beyond the year 2000. *FBI Law Enforcement Bulletin*, pp. 33–36.

39. Ibid.

40. See Rodriguez. The acquisition of high technology systems by the law enforcement, pp. 11–12.

41. Cyberterrorism specialists gather in Chicago. (1998, September). *Crime and Justice International*, pp. 7–8.

42. Akre, B.S. (1995, February, 10). Internet-torture. The Associated Press online.

43. Ibid.

44. Schaefer, J., and George, M. (1995, June 22). Internet User's charges dismissed U.S. criticized for pursuing U-M case. *Detroit Free Press* online.

45. Cribb, R. (1998, July 25). Surfer stumbles on credit card cache. *Toronto Star* online.

46. Duncan, M. (1996). Old laws, new crimes, and a shrinking planet. *RCMP Gazette*, 58(10):25.

47. Coleman, J.W. (1989). *The criminal elite: The sociology of white collar crime* (2nd ed., p. 2). New York: St. Martin's Press.

48. Sutherland, E.H. (1940, February). White-collar criminality. *American Sociological Review*, p. 12.

49. This definition combines elements of Sutherland's original terminology with the definition of "white-collar crime" as found in the *Dictionary of Criminal Justice Data Terminology* (2nd ed.). (1981). Washington, D.C.: Bureau of Justice Statistics. It recognizes the fact that the socio-economic status of today's "white-collar criminals" is not nearly so high as Sutherland imagined when he coined the term.

50. Tennis, anyone? Ivan Boesky does time. (n.d.). *Business Week*, p. 70.

51. Hagan, F.E., and Benekos, P.J. (1990). The biggest white collar crime in history: The great savings and loan scandal. Paper presented at the annual meeting of the American Society of Criminology, Baltimore, Maryland.

52. Ibid.

53. Cox, J. Gold Dust or Bust. (1997, April 17). *USA Today*, p. 1B.

54. Francis, D. (1998). *Bre-X: The inside story*. Toronto: Key Porter.

55. Sutherland, E.H. (1945, April). Is white collar crime crime? *American Sociological Review*, pp. 132–139.

56. *White Collar Crime*. (1987). A Bureau of Justice Statistics *Special Report*. Washington, D.C.: BJS.

57. Carrigan, D.O. (1991). *Crime and punishment in Canada*. Toronto: Macllan & Stewart.

58. Pizzo, S., Fricker, M., and Muolo, P. (1989). *Inside job: The looting of America's savings and loans*. New York: McGraw-Hill.

59. See Geis, G. and Meier, R.F. (eds.). (1977). *White collar crime* (2nd ed.). New York: The Free Press.

60. The venture survey: Crime and your business. (1986, February). *Venture* magazine, p. 26.

61. Ibid.

62. Ibid.

63. Green, G.S. (1990). *Occupational crime*. Chicago: Nelson-Hall.

64. Ibid., p. 16.

65. Ibid.

66. Coleman, J.W. *The criminal elite: The sociology of white collar crime* (p. 9).

67. Ibid.

68. Chambliss, W.J. (1988). *Criminology* (p. 64). New York: Macmillan.

69. Mokhiber, R. and Weissman, R. (1997, December). Beat the devil. *Multinational Monitor*, 1–16. (Available online.)

70. See Snider, L. (1993). *Bad business: Corporate crime in Canada*. Scarborough, ON: Nelson.

71. Bradford, T. (1995, May 19). $12 million high-tech heist one of the largest ever. *USA Today*, p. 3A.

72. In 1998, Miramax began making a film on the Mitnik story based on Tsutomu Shimomura's book about how he caught Mitnik. The film is called *Takedown*.

73. Computer crime costs millions. (1998, June 24). *Ottawa Citizen*. (online: **www.ottawacitizen.com**).

74. Software Publishers Association (SPA) and the Business Software Alliance. (1997, May 7). SPA's website. "Global Study Shows Increase in Software Units Pirated." Accessed May 7, 1997 at**www.spa.org/piracy/releass/96pir.htm**

75. Computer crime cost millions. (1998, June, 24). *Ottawa Citizen*. (Online).

76. Bronskill, J. (1998, December 14). Mounties ill-equipped to fight white-collar crime, says report. *Calgary Herald*, p. A9.

77. For a recent list of suggested computer crime categories, see: Carter, D.L. (1995, July). Computer crime categories: How techno-criminals operate. *FBI Law Enforcement Journal*, pp. 21–26.

78. For information on specific software programs used for data encryption, see Chiang, T. (1987, December). Data encryption: Computer security with data encryption programs. *Profiles*, pp. 71–74.

79. Invasion of the data snatchers! (1988, September 26). *Time*, pp. 62–67.

80. Virus infects NASA, defense, University Computer Systems. (1988, November 4). *The Fayetteville Observer-Times* (North Carolina), p. 19A.

81. *Raleigh News and Observer*. (1990, April 27).

82. Crime in the computer age. (1988, January 25). *MacLean's Magazine*, pp. 28–30.

83. Ibid.

84. Ibid., p. 29.

85. Cribb, B. (1998, October 23). Software piracy: Study paints software theft by the numbers. *Toronto Star*. (online).

86. Bequai, A. (1978). *Computer crime* (p. 4). Lexington, MA: Lexington Books.

87. Ibid.

88. Knapp, S. (1998, June 28). Hackers find the cracks in systems. *Calgary Herald*, p. TL16.

89. Smythe, P. (1996). Terrorism in Canada: Recent trends and future prospects. *RCMP Gazette*, 58(10):18–22.

90. Updates on the Air India Flight 182 investigation are provided by the province of British Columbia and the RCMP at, accessible at time of writing, at **www.ag.gov.bc.ca/airindia/index.htm** and **www3.telus.net/airindiataskforce**

91. For a summary of the efforts of the Canadian Security Intelligence Service, see their website, accessible at time of writing, at **www.csis-scrs.gc.ca/eng/operat/ct_e.html**

92. Canadian Security Intelligence Service. (2000). *International Terrorism: The Threat to Canada*. Ottawa: Canadian Security Intelligence Service. Also accessible at time of writing at **www.csis-scrs.gc.ca/eng/misdocs/200004_e.html**

93. Wouldn't be hard to hit U.S. target. (1993, June 2527). *USA Today*, p. 1A.

94. Nettler, G. (1982). *Killing one another*. Cincinnati, OH: Anderson.

95. MacIntyre, B. (1998, Nov. 13).Carlos the Jackal asks terrorists to avenge his death. *Calgary Herald*, p. A10.

96. Nettler, G. *Killing One Another* (p. 253).

97. See Emerson, S. (2002). *American Jihad: The Terrorists Living Among Us* NY: The Free Press.

98. Wilson, C. (1997, June 30). Two Accused in Nuke Sale Sting. Associated Press wire service.

99. Collin, B. (1997, March). The Future of Cyberterrorism. *Crime and Justice International*, pp. 15–18.

100. Arquilla, J. and Ronfeldt, D. (1996). *The Advent of Netwar*. Santa Monica, CA: RAND.

101. Pollitt, M.M. (1997, October). Cyberterrorism: Fact or Fancy? *Proceedings of the 20th National Information Systems Security Conference*, pp. 285–289.

102. Denning, D.E. (1999). Activism, Hactivism, and Cyberterrorism: The Internet as a Tool for Influencing Foreign Policy. Paper presented at the Internet and International Systems: Information Technology and American Foreign Policy Decisionmaking Workshop, San Francisco, December 10.

103. Canadian Security Intelligence Service. (2002, August 9). *Counter-Terrorism: Backgrounder Series No. 8*. Ottawa: Canadian Security Intelligence Service.

104. U.S. Plans New Secure Government Internet. (2001, October 11). Associated Press wire service.

105. *R. v. Sharpe* (2001), 150 C.C.C. (3d) 321 (S.C.C.).

106. United States Postal Inspection Service News Release. "U.S. Postal Inspectors' Child Pornography Sting Operation Results in More than 4,000 Searches Worldwide." (2003, January 14). Accessible on February 9, 2003 at **www.usps.com/postalinspectors/nr_sting.htm**

107. *R. v. Tessling* (2003), 171 C.C.C. (3d) 361 (ont. C.A.).

108. Ibid., para. 68.

# Glossary

**abuse of process** The use of powers, legitimately conferred on an individual, for purposes other than those originally intended, such as for personal gain. It may also include the illegitimate use of powers granted to the individual to achieve organizational goals such as detaining and prosecuting offenders.

**abused children** Children who have been physically, sexually, or mentally abused. Most provinces also consider that a child is abused when they are forced into delinquent activity by a parent or guardian.

**adversarial system** The two-sided structure under which Canadian criminal trial courts operate, which pits the prosecution against the defence. In theory, justice is done when the most effective adversary is able to convince the judge or jury that his or her perspective on the case is the correct one.

**aggravating circumstances** Those elements of an offence or of an offender's background that could result in a harsher sentence under the determinate model than would otherwise be called for by sentencing guidelines.

**appeal** Generally, the request that a court with appellate jurisdiction review the judgment, decision, or order of a lower court and set it aside (reverse it) or modify it.

**appellate jurisdiction** The lawful authority of a court to review a decision made by a lower court.

**arraignment** The hearing before a court having jurisdiction in a criminal case, in which the identity of the defendant is established, the defendant is informed of the charge(s) and of his or her rights, and the defendant is required to enter a plea.

**arrest** Taking a suspect into physical custody by authority of law, usually for the purpose of charging the person with a criminal offence. Technically, an arrest occurs whenever a person's freedom to leave is curtailed by a law enforcement officer.

**arson** The burning or attempted burning of property with or without intent to defraud. Some instances of arson are the result of malicious mischief, while others involve attempts to claim insurance monies. Still others are committed in an effort to disguise other crimes, such as murder, burglary, and larceny.

**assault** The unlawful intentional inflicting, or attempted or threatened inflicting, of injury upon a person by another. Historically, "assault" meant only the creation of an imminent threat to inflict injury on another person. A completed act constituted the separate offence of battery. Under most modern penal codes, however, attempted and completed acts are put together under the generic name "assault."

**bail** The money or property pledged to the court or actually deposited with the court to effect the release of a person from legal custody.

**bailiff** (also **sheriff**) The court officer whose duties are to keep order in the courtroom and to maintain physical custody of the jury.

**ballistics** The analysis of firearms, ammunition, projectiles, bombs, and explosions.

**booking** A law enforcement or correctional administrative process officially recording an entry into detention after arrest and identifying the person, place, time, and reason for the arrest, and the arresting authority.

**break and entry** The unlawful entry of a dwelling house, or other building or structure, railway vehicle, vessel, aircraft or trailer, or a pen or enclosure for fur-bearing animals. Such entry is unlawful if it is for the purpose of committing an indictable offence.

**capital punishment** Another term for the death penalty. Capital punishment is the most extreme of all sentencing options.

**caseload** The number of probation or parole clients assigned to one probation or parole officer for supervision.

**case law** That body of judicial precedent, historically built upon legal reasoning and past interpretations of statutory laws, which serves as a guide to decision making, especially in the courts.

**Chief Justice** Court administrators acting as coordinating personnel who dictate budgeting of operating funds, and court docket administration.

**circumstantial evidence** Evidence that requires interpretation or which requires a judge or jury to reach a conclusion based on what the evidence indicates. From the close proximity of a smoking gun to the defendant, for example, the jury might conclude that she pulled the trigger.

**civil death** The legal status of prisoners in some jurisdictions who are denied the opportunity to vote, hold public office, marry, or enter into contracts by virtue of their status as incarcerated felons. While civil death is primarily of historical interest, some jurisdictions still place limits on the contractual opportunities available to inmates.

**civil law** That portion of the modern law that regulates contracts and other obligations involving primarily personal interests.

**clearance rate** A traditional measure of investigative effectiveness that compares the number of crimes reported and/or discovered to the number of crimes solved through arrest or other means (such as the death of a suspect).

**closing argument** An oral summation of a case presented to a judge, or to a judge and jury, by the prosecution or by the defence in a criminal trial.

**cohort** A group of individuals sharing similarities of age, place of birth, and residence. Cohort analysis is a social scientific technique by which such groups are tracked over time in order to identify unique and observable behavioural traits that characterize them.

**comes stabuli** Non-uniformed mounted early law-enforcement officers in medieval England. Early police forces were small, and relatively unorganized, but made effective use of local resources in the formation of posses, the pursuit of offenders, and the like.

**common law** A body of unwritten judicial opinion that was based upon customary social practices of Anglo-Saxon society during the Middle Ages.

**community-based corrections** A sentencing style that represents a movement away from traditional confinement options and an increased dependence upon correctional resources that are available in the community.

**community corrections** (also called **community-based corrections**) A sentencing style that represents a movement away from traditional confinement options and an increased dependence upon correctional resources that are available in the community.

**community policing** A collaborative effort between the police and the community that identifies problems of crime and disorder and involves all elements of the community in the search for solutions to these problems.

**comparative criminologists** People who study crime and criminal justice on a cross-national level.

**comparative criminal justice** The study of criminal justice issues from an international perspective.

**computer crimes** Any crimes that take advantage of computer-based technology in its commission. This definition highlights the manner in which a crime is committed, more than it does the target of the offence. Hence, the physical theft of a computer, or of a floppy disk, would not be a computer crime, while the use of computer software to analyze a company's security operations prior to committing a robbery might be.

**computer viruses** Small computer programs that are designed to secretly invade systems and modify either the way in which they operate or alter the information they store. Viruses are destructive software that may effectively vandalize computers of all sizes.

**conflict model** A perspective on the study of criminal justice that assumes that the system's subcomponents function primarily to serve their own interests. According to this theoretical framework, "justice" is more a product of conflicts among agencies within the system than it is the result of co-operation among component agencies.

**concurrent sentence** A sentence that is one of two or more sentences imposed at the same time after conviction for more than one offence and to be served at the same time; or, a new sentence imposed upon a person already under sentence(s) for a previous offence(s), to be served at the same time as one or more of the previous sentences.

**conditional sentencing** Sentencing an offender, who is deemed not to be a danger to the community, to a period of imprisonment for less than 2 years, to be served in the community rather than in a provincial prison. Such sentences place strict conditions on the offender, such as requiring them to remain in their home for the duration of the sentence.

**consecutive sentence** A sentence that is one of two or more sentences imposed at the same time, after conviction for more than one offence, and that is served in sequence with the other sentences or a new sentence for a new conviction, imposed upon a person already under sentence(s) for previous offence(s), which is added to a previous sentence(s), thus increasing the maximum time the offender may be confined or under supervision.

**consensus model** A perspective on the study of criminal justice that assumes that the system's subcomponents work together harmoniously to achieve that social product we call "justice."

**corporate crimes** Violations of a criminal statute by a corporate entity or by its executives, employees, or agents acting on behalf of and for the benefit of the corporation, partnership, or other form of business entity.

**corruption** Behavioural deviation from an accepted ethical standard.

**courtroom work group** Professional courtroom actors, including judges, prosecuting lawyers, private defence counsel, public defenders, and others who earn a living serving the court.

**crime** An act committed or omitted in violation of a law forbidding or commanding it for which the possible penalties for an adult upon conviction include incarceration, for which a corporation can be penalized by fine or forfeit, or for which a juvenile can be adjudged delinquent or transferred to criminal court for prosecution.

**crime control model** A criminal justice perspective that emphasizes the efficient arrest and conviction of criminal offenders.

**criminal court system** The court system that entails lower-level provincial trial and appellate courts, and the Supreme Court of Canada.

**criminal harassment** Engaging in certain acts that the offender knows, or ought to know, will cause another person to fear for their safety or the safety of another known to them. Relevant acts include following the victim, repeatedly communicating with them, watching their home or place of work, and threatening members of the victim's family. Criminal harassment is commonly referred to as stalking.

**criminal law** That branch of modern law that concerns itself with offences committed against society, members thereof, their property, and the social order.

**criminal justice** The criminal law, the law of criminal procedure, and that array of procedures and activities having to do with the enforcement of the criminal law. Criminal justice cannot be separated from social justice because the kind of justice enacted in our nation's criminal courts is a reflection of basic Canadian understandings of right and wrong.

**criminalistics** The use of technology in the service of criminal investigation; the application of scientific techniques to the detection and evaluation of criminal evidence.

**criminalists** The term applied to police crime scene analysts and laboratory personnel versed in criminalistics.

**criminology** The scientific study of crime, its causes, its prevention, and society's response thereto, including the rehabilitation and punishment of offenders.

**Crown prosecutor** (also **Crown counsel**) A public official, licensed to practise law, whose job it is to conduct criminal proceedings on behalf of the Crown against an accused person. Also called a Crown attorney.

cybercrime Crime committed via computers. Another term for computer crime.

data encryption methods Methods used to encode computerized information.

date rape Unlawful forced sexual intercourse with a female against her will that occurs within the context of a dating relationship.

defence counsel (also defence lawyer) A licensed trial lawyer hired or appointed to conduct the legal defence of an individual accused of a crime and to represent him or her before a court of law.

defences (to a criminal charge) include claims based upon personal, special, and procedural considerations that the defendant should not be held accountable for their actions, even though they may have acted in violation of the criminal law.

delinquency A pejorative term that refers to young persons' actions or conduct in violation of criminal law, status offences, and other misbehaviour.

delinquent children Under the JDA, children who had engaged in activities that would be considered crimes if the children were adults. Under the YCJA, the term "young person" is applied to such a child in order to avoid the stigma that comes from application of the term "delinquent."

dependent children Children who have no parent(s) or whose parent(s) is (are) unable to care for them.

design capacity The number of inmates a prison was architecturally intended to hold when it was built or modified.

determinate sentencing (also called structured sentencing) A model for criminal punishment that sets one particular punishment, or length of sentence, for each specific type of crime. Under the model, for example, all offenders convicted of the same degree of burglary would be sentenced to the same length of time behind bars.

deterrence A goal of criminal sentencing that seeks to prevent others from committing crimes similar to the one for which an offender is being sentenced.

direct supervision Describes temporary confinement facilities that eliminate many of the traditional barriers between inmates and correctional staff. Physical barriers in direct supervision jails are far less common than in traditional jails, allowing staff members the opportunity for greater interaction with, and control over, residents.

directed patrol A police management strategy designed to increase the productivity of patrol officers through the application of scientific analysis and evaluation of patrol techniques.

discoverability A test applied to determine whether derived evidence obtained following a Charter violation should be admitted. Admission may result if the Crown can show that the police probably would have discovered the evidence regardless of the Charter violation.

discretion The exercise of choice, by law enforcement agents, in the disposition of suspects, in the carrying out of official duties, and in the application of sanctions.

dispute resolution centres Informal hearing infrastructures designed to mediate interpersonal disputes without need for the moral formal arrangements of criminal trial courts.

dissociation Isolating a prison inmate within the penal setting, often referred to as solitary confinement. Dissociation may be used as punishment to maintain discipline within the institution (punitive dissociation), or administratively as a prison management tactic to protect an inmate from the general population or to insulate the general prison population from an inmate's influence (administrative dissociation).

direct evidence Evidence that, if believed, directly proves a fact. Eyewitness testimony (and, more recently, videotaped documentation) account for the majority of all direct evidence heard (or viewed) in the criminal courtroom.

DNA profiling Using biological residue found at the scene of a crime to make genetic comparisons, with the ultimate goal of identifying criminal suspects.

due process A legal principle that requires fair procedure to be applied in judicial proceedings, sometimes referred to as procedural due process. The legal principle is capable of a broader meaning that allows judges to require the content of the law to be fair, sometimes referred to as substantive due process.

due process model A criminal justice perspective that emphasizes individual rights at all stages of justice system.

emergency search A search conducted by the police without a warrant, which is justified on the basis of some immediate and overriding need—such as public safety, the likely escape of a dangerous suspect, or the removal or destruction of evidence.

entrapment An inducement to crime by agents of enforcement.

ethnocentrism The phenomenon of culture-centredness, by which one uses one's own culture as a benchmark against which to judge all other patterns of behaviour.

European Police Office (Europol) The integrated police-intelligence gathering and dissemination arm of the member nations of the European Union.

evidence Anything useful to a judge or jury in deciding the facts of a case. Evidence may take the form of witness testimony, written documents, videotapes, magnetic media, photographs, physical objects, and so on.

exclusionary rule The understanding, based on Supreme Court precedent, that incriminating information must be seized according to constitutionally sound procedure, or it may not be allowed as evidence in criminal trials.

expert witness A person who has special knowledge and skills recognized by the court as relevant to the determination of guilt or innocence. Expert witnesses may express opinions or draw conclusions in their testimony—unlike lay witnesses.

federal court system The three-tiered structure of federal courts, involving the Federal Court of Canada, the Federal Court of Appeal, and the Supreme Court of Canada.

felonies Criminal offences punishable by death, or by incarceration in a prison facility for at least one year.

first appearance (also initial appearance) An appearance before a provincial court judge that entails the process whereby the charge is read to the accused. At this stage in the criminal justice process, bail may be set or pretrial release arranged.

**fruit of the poisoned tree doctrine** A legal principle that excludes from introduction at trial any evidence later developed as a result of an originally illegal search or seizure.

**forensic anthropology** The application of anthropological principles and techniques in the service of criminal investigation.

**general deterrence** A goal of criminal sentencing that seeks to prevent others from committing crimes similar to the one for which a particular offender is being sentenced by making an example of the person sentenced.

**grievance procedure** Formalized arrangements, usually involving a neutral hearing board, whereby institutionalized individuals have the opportunity to register complaints about the conditions of their confinement.

**hacker** A computer hobbyist or professional, generally with advanced programming skills. Today the term "hacker" has taken on a sinister connotation and includes those hobbyists who are bent on illegally accessing the computers of others, or who attempt to demonstrate their technological prowess through computerized acts of vandalism.

**hands-off doctrine** An historical policy of non-intervention with regard to prison management, which American courts tended to follow until the late 1960s. For the past 30 years, the doctrine has languished as judicial intervention in prison administration has dramatically increased, although there is now growing evidence of a return to a new hands-off doctrine.

**hearsay** Something that is not based on the personal knowledge of a witness. Witnesses who testify, for example, about something they have heard are offering hearsay by repeating information about a matter of which they have no direct knowledge.

**hearsay rule** The long-standing evidentiary rule is that hearsay cannot be used in court. Rather than testimony based upon hearsay being accepted, the trial process asks that the person who was the original source of the hearsay information be brought into court to be questioned and cross-examined. Exceptions to the hearsay rule may occur when the person with direct knowledge is dead or otherwise unable to testify.

**high-technology crimes** Violations of the criminal law whose commission depends upon, makes use of, and often targets, sophisticated and advanced technology.

**home confinement** House arrest. Individuals ordered confined to their homes are sometimes monitored electronically to be sure they do not leave during the hours of confinement (absence from the home during working hours is often permitted).

**Hudud crimes** Serious violations of Islamic law regarded as offences against God. Hudud crimes include such behaviour as theft, adultery, sodomy, drinking alcohol, and robbery.

**illegally seized evidence** Evidence seized in violation of a Charter-protected right or freedom. Most illegally seized evidence is the result of police searches conducted without a proper warrant, or of improperly conducted interrogations.

**incapacitation** The use of imprisonment or other means to reduce the likelihood that an offender will be capable of committing future offences.

**inchoate offence** One not yet completed. Also, an offence that consists of an action or conduct that is a step towards the intended commission of another offence.

**indeterminate** Refers to a model of sentencing that allows for subsequent discretion regarding the eventual release date. Release is contingent upon the offender's eventual rehabilitation, which is thereby promoted through this sentencing approach.

**indictment** A formal, written accusation submitted to the court by a prosecutor, alleging that a specified person(s) has committed a specified indictable offence(s).

**individual rights** Those rights guaranteed to criminal defendants by the Charter of Rights and Freedoms (especially sections 7 through 14) facing formal processing by the criminal justice system. The preservation of the rights of criminal defendants is important to society, because it is through the exercise of such rights that the values of our culture are most clearly and directly expressed.

**individual rights advocates** Those who seek to protect personal freedoms within the process of criminal justice.

**public order advocates** Those who suggest that, under certain circumstances involving criminal threats to public safety, the interests of society should take precedence over individual rights.

**information** A document sworn before a judge or justice alleging an offence or offences has/have occurred. The charge document containing specific allegations against the accused.

**intensive probation supervision** A form of probation supervision involving frequent face-to-face contacts between the probationary client and probation officers.

**intermittent sentence** One which requires that a convicted offender serve weekends (or other specified periods of time) in a confinement facility, while undergoing probation supervision in the community.

**INTERPOL** An acronym for the International Police Association. INTERPOL began operations in 1946 and today has 137 member nations.

**Islamic law** A system of laws, operative in some Arab countries, which is based upon the Muslim religion and especially the holy book of Islam, the Koran.

**judge** An appointed public official who presides over a court of law and who is authorized to hear and sometimes to decide cases and to conduct trials.

**judicial review** The power of a court to review actions and decisions made by other agencies of government.

**jural postulates** Propositions developed by the famous jurist Roscoe Pound, who holds that the law reflects shared needs without which members of society could not co-exist. Pound's jural postulates are often linked to the idea that the law can be used to engineer the social structure to ensure certain kinds of outcomes (such as property rights embodied in the law of theft do in capitalistic societies).

**jurisprudence** The philosophy of law; the science and study of the law.

**jurisdiction** The territory, subject matter, or persons over which lawful authority may be exercised by a court or other justice agency, as determined by statute or constitution.

**jury selection** The process whereby, according to law and precedent, members of a particular trial jury are chosen.

**juror** A member of a jury, selected for jury duty, and required to serve as an arbiter of the facts in a court of law. Jurors are expected to render verdicts of guilt or innocence as to the charges brought against an accused, although they may sometimes fail to do so (as in the case of a hung jury).

**just deserts** As a model of criminal sentencing, one which holds that criminal offenders deserve the punishment they receive at the hands of the law, and that punishments should be appropriate to the type and severity of crime committed.

**justice** The principle of fairness; the ideal of moral equity.

**law** A rule of conduct, generally found enacted in the form of a statute, which proscribes and/or mandates certain forms of behaviour. Statutory law is often the result of moral enterprise by interest groups that, through the exercise of political power, are successful in seeing their valuative perspectives enacted into law.

**lay witness** An eyewitness, character witness, or any other person called upon to testify who is not considered an expert. Lay witnesses must testify to facts alone and may not draw conclusions or express opinions.

**legalistic style** A style of policing marked by a strict concern with enforcing the precise letter of the law. Legalistic departments, however, may take a "hands-off" approach to otherwise disruptive or problematic forms of behaviour that are not violations of the criminal law.

**Mediation Committees** Chinese civilian dispute resolution groups found throughout the country. Mediation Committees successfully divert many minor offenders from handling by more formal mechanisms of justice.

**mens rea** The state of mind that accompanies a criminal act. Also, guilty mind.

**mental disorder defence** A personal defence that claims that the person charged with a crime did not appreciate what he or she was doing, or that the accused did not know that what he or she was doing was wrong, because the person was suffering from a disease of the mind at the time of the offence.

**mitigating circumstances** Those elements of an offence or of an offender's background that could result in a lesser sentence under the determinate model than would otherwise be called for by sentencing guidelines.

**motor vehicle theft** The unlawful taking, or attempted taking, of a self-propelled road vehicle owned by another, with the intent to deprive him or her of it permanently or temporarily. The stealing of trains, planes, boats, construction equipment, and most farm machinery is classified as theft, not as motor vehicle theft, under the UCR reporting program.

**murder** Usually the intentional killing of a human being. Murder is a generic term that, in common usage, may include first- and second-degree murder.

**neglected children** Children who are not receiving the proper level of physical or psychological care from their parent(s) or guardian(s), or who have been placed up for adoption in violation of the law.

**new police** Also known as the Metropolitan Police of London, formed in 1829 under the command of Sir Robert Peel. Peel's police became the model for modern-day police forces throughout the Western world.

**normlessness** A criminological term first developed by Emile Durkheim, it refers to a pervasive sense in a society that the traditional norms and values have broken down and that society is lacking in cohesion and necessary regulation by formal and informal control mechanisms.

**nothing works doctrine** The belief, popularized by Robert Martinson in the 1970s, that correctional treatment programs have little success in rehabilitating offenders.

**occupational crime** Any act punishable by law that is committed through opportunity created in the course of an occupation that is legal.

**original jurisdiction** The authority of a given court over a specific geographic area or over particular types of cases. We say that a case falls "within the jurisdiction" of the court.

**opening statement** The initial statement of a lawyer (or of a defendant representing himself or herself) made in a court to a judge, or to a judge and jury, describing the facts that he or she intends to present during trial in order to prove his or her case.

**operational capacity** The number of inmates a prison can effectively accommodate based upon management considerations.

**opportunity theory** A perspective that sees delinquency as the result of limited legitimate opportunities for success available to most lower-class youth.

**parens patriae** A common-law principle that allows the state to assume a parental role and to take custody of a child when he or she becomes delinquent, is abandoned, or is in need of care that the natural parents are unable or unwilling to provide.

**Parliament** The British legislature; the highest lawmaking body of the United Kingdom composed of the House of Commons and the House of Lords.

**parole** The status of an offender conditionally released from a prison by discretion of a paroling authority prior to expiration of sentence, required to observe conditions of parole, and placed under the supervision of a parole agency.

**parole revocation** The administrative action of a parole board removing a person from parole status in response to a violation of lawfully required conditions of parole.

**Pennsylvania style** (also **penitentiary**) A form of imprisonment developed by the Pennsylvania Quakers around 1790 as an alternative to corporal punishments. The style involved solitary confinement and encouraged rehabilitation.

**Auburn system** (also **congregate but silent system**) A form of imprisonment developed in New York state around 1820 that depended upon prisons with large populations, where prisoners were held as a group, and required to be silent. This style of imprisonment was a primary competitor with the Pennsylvania style.

**peremptory challenge** A means of removing unwanted potential jurors without the need to show cause for their removal. Prosecutors and defence lawyers routinely use peremptory challenges in order to eliminate from juries individuals who, although they express no obvious bias, may be thought to hold the potential to sway the jury in an undesirable direction.

**perjury** The intentional making of a false statement as part of the testimony by a sworn witness in a judicial proceeding on a matter relevant to the case at hand.

**plain view** A legal term describing the ready visibility of objects that might be seized as evidence during a search by police in the absence of a search warrant specifying the seizure of those objects. In order for evidence in plain view to be lawfully seized, officers must have a legal right to be in the viewing area and must have cause to believe that the evidence is somehow associated with criminal activity.

**plea** In criminal proceedings, a defendant's formal answer in court to the charge contained in information, or an indictment that he or she is guilty or not guilty of the offence charged, or has a special plea to make to the offence.

**plea bargaining** The negotiated agreement between defendant and prosecutor, as to what an appropriate plea and associated sentence should be in a given case. Plea bargaining circumvents the trial process and dramatically reduces the time required for the resolution of a criminal case.

**police culture** (also **subculture**) A particular set of values, beliefs, and acceptable forms of behaviour characteristic of Canadian police, and with which the police profession strives to imbue new recruits. Socialization into the police subculture commences with recruit training and is ongoing thereafter.

**police ethics** The special responsibility for adherence to moral duty and obligation inherent in police work.

**police management** The administrative activities of controlling, directing, and coordinating police personnel, resources, and activities in the service of crime prevention, the apprehension of criminals, the recovery of stolen property, and the performance of a variety of regulatory and helping services.

**police professionalism** The increasing formalization of police work, and the rise in public acceptance of the police that accompanies it. Any profession is characterized by a specialized body of knowledge and a set of internal guidelines that hold members of the profession accountable for their actions. A well-focused code of ethics, equitable recruitment and selection practices, and informed promotional strategies among many agencies contribute to a growing level of professionalism among Canadian police agencies today.

**police working personality** All aspects of the traditional values and patterns of behaviour evidenced by police officers who have been effectively socialized into the police subculture. Characteristics of the police personality often extend to the personal lives of law enforcement personnel.

**police–community relations (PCR)** An area of emerging police activity that stresses the need for the community and the police to work together effectively and emphasizes the notion that the police derive their legitimacy from the community they serve. PCR began to concern many police agencies in the 1960s and 1970s.

**pre-sentence report** The examination of a convicted offender's background prior to sentencing. Pre-sentence examinations are generally conducted by probation/ parole officers and submitted to sentencing authorities.

**precedent** A legal principle that operates to ensure that previous judicial decisions are authoritatively considered and incorporated into future cases.

**preliminary hearing** The proceeding before a judicial officer in which it is decided whether there is sufficient evidence to warrant committing a case for trial in a superior court.

**prima facie** A Latin term meaning "at first sight" or on the face of the matter. This term indicates that the situation must involve sufficient evidence to establish a fact, absent any evidence to rebut the fact. In essence, the evidence must be the minimum amount of evidence necessary to avoid having a case dismissed.

**principles of fundamental justice** The basic tenets and principles upon which the legal system is founded.

**prison** A state or federal confinement facility having custodial authority over adults sentenced to varying terms of confinement.

**prison argot** The slang characteristic of prison subcultures and prison life.

**prison subculture** The values and behavioural patterns characteristic of prison inmates. Prison subculture has been found to have surprising consistencies across the country.

**prisonization** The process whereby newly institutionalized individuals come to accept prison lifestyles and criminal values. While many inmates begin their prison experience with only a modicum of values supportive of criminal behaviour, the socialization experience they undergo while incarcerated leads to a much wider acceptance of such values.

**private protective services** Independent or proprietary commercial organizations that provide protective services to employers on a contractual basis. Private security agencies, which already employ about half again as many people as public law enforcement, are expected to experience substantial growth over the next few decades.

**probation** A sentence of imprisonment that is suspended. Also, the conditional freedom granted by a judicial officer to an adjudicated adult or juvenile offender, as long as the adult or juvenile meets certain conditions of behaviour.

**problem-oriented policing** A style of policing that assumes that many crimes are caused by existing social conditions within the community, and that crimes can be controlled by uncovering and effectively addressing underlying social problems. Problem-solving policing makes use of other community resources such as counselling centres, welfare programs, and job-training facilities. It also attempts to involve citizens in the job of crime prevention through education, negotiation, and conflict management.

**procuratorate (also procuracy)** A term used in many countries to refer to agencies with powers and responsibilities similar to those of prosecutors' offices in Canada.

**property crime** An offence category that, according to the UCR Program, includes break and enter, theft, fraud, and possession of stolen property. Since citizen reports of criminal incidents figure heavily in the compilation of "official statistics," the same critiques apply to tallies of these crimes as to the category of violent crime.

**prosecutorial discretion** The decision-making power of prosecutors, based upon the wide range of choices available to them, in handling of criminal defendants, scheduling cases for trial, accepting bargained pleas, and so on. The most important form of prosecutorial discretion lies in the power to authorize a charge, or not to authorize a charge, against a suspect.

**provincial/territorial court systems** Provincial judicial structures. Most provinces have at least three court levels, generally referred to as lower level provincial courts, superior courts, and a provincial court of appeal.

**public defender** A lawyer employed by a government agency or sub-agency, or by a private organization under contract to a unit of government, for the purpose of providing defence services to indigents.

**rated capacity** The size of the inmate population a facility can handle, according to the judgment of experts.

**real evidence** Evidence consisting of physical material or traces of physical activity.

**reasonable grounds** A legal criterion residing in a set of facts and circumstances that would cause a reasonable person to believe that a particular other person has committed a specific crime. Reasonable grounds refers to the necessary level of belief that would allow for police seizures (arrests) of individuals and searches of dwellings, vehicles, and possession.

**recidivism** The repetition of criminal behaviour. In statistical practice, a recidivism rate may be any of a number of possible counts or instances of arrest, conviction, correctional commitment, and correctional status changes, related to counts of repetitions of these events within a given period of time.

**recognizance** Refers to the pretrial release of a criminal defendant on their written promise to appear. No cash bail is required; however, a debt to the Crown is created should the accused fail to attend court for trial.

**reference power** The ability of a court to answer questions pertaining to the constitutional validity of laws or policy when requested to do so by the executive branch of government.

**regulations** Enactments of a body subordinate to a legislative body. Such enactments carry the force of law.

**rehabilitation** The attempt to reform a criminal offender. Also, the state in which a reformed offender is said to be.

**restitution** A court requirement that an alleged or convicted offender pay money or provide services to the victim of the crime or provide services to the community.

**restoration** A goal of criminal sentencing that attempts to make the victim "whole again."

**restorative justice** A sentencing model that builds upon restitution and community participation in an attempt to make the victim "whole again."

**retribution** The act of taking revenge upon a criminal perpetrator.

**revocation hearing** A hearing held before a legally constituted hearing body (such as a parole board) in order to determine whether or not a probationer or parolee has violated the conditions and requirements of his or her probation or parole.

**robbery** The unlawful taking or attempted taking of property that is in the immediate possession of another, by force or the threat of force. Armed robbery differs from unarmed or strong-armed robbery with respect to the presence of a weapon.

**rules of evidence** Rules of court that govern the admissibility of evidence at a criminal hearing and trial.

**scientific jury selection** The use of social-scientific techniques to gauge the likelihood that potential jurors will vote for conviction or acquittal.

**scientific police management** The application of social scientific techniques to the study of police administration for the purposes of increasing effectiveness, reducing the frequency of citizen complaints, and enhancing the efficient use of available resources.

**search incident to an arrest** A warrantless search of an arrested individual that is conducted to ensure the safety of the arresting officer(s), the public, to prevent escape, and to secure evidence. Because an individual placed under arrest may be in the possession of weapons or aids to escape, courts have recognized the need for arresting officers to protect themselves and others by conducting an immediate and warrantless search of an arrested individual and the immediate surrounding area without the need for a warrant. Because evidence may be disposed of by a suspect, a power to search the arrestee and the immediate area for evidence also arises at the time of arrest.

**security of tenure** The protection of judicial independence, embodying the notion that judges cannot be removed from office except in cases of judges breaking the "good behaviour" requirement.

**self-defence** The protection of oneself or one's property from unlawful injury or the immediate risk of unlawful injury; the justification for an act that would otherwise constitute an offence, that the person who committed it reasonably believed that the act was necessary to protect self or property from immediate danger.

**sequestered jury** A jury that is isolated from the public during the course of a trial and throughout the deliberation process.

**service style** A style of policing that is marked by a concern with helping rather than strict enforcement. Service-oriented agencies are more likely to take advantage of community resources, such as drug treatment programs, than are other types of departments.

**sexual assault** A form of assault in which the sexual integrity of the victim is violated. This includes, but is not limited to, forcible rape, in which an offender engages in sexual intercourse with a victim, by force and against the will of the victim, or without legal or factual consent.

**sheriff** The elected chief officer of a county law enforcement agency, usually responsible for law enforcement in unincorporated areas and for the operation of the county jail.

**shock incarceration** A sentencing option that makes use of "boot-camp" type prisons in order to impress upon convicted offenders the realities of prison life.

**shock probation** The practice of sentencing offenders to prison, allowing them to apply for probationary release, and enacting such release in surprise fashion. Offenders who receive shock probation may not be aware of the fact that they will be released on probation, and may expect to spend a much longer time behind bars.

**social control** The use of sanctions and rewards available through a group to influence and shape the behaviour of individual members of that group. Social control is a primary concern of social groups and communities, and it is the interest that human groups hold in the exercise of social control that leads to the creation of both criminal and civil statutes.

**social disorganization** A condition that is said to exist when a group is faced with social change, uneven cultural development, maladaptiveness, disharmony, conflict, and lack of consensus.

**social ecology** An approach that focused on the misbehaviour of lower-class youth, and saw delinquency primarily as the result of social disorganization.

**social justice** An ideal that embraces all aspects of civilized life and is linked to fundamental notions of fairness and to cultural beliefs about right and wrong.

**specific deterrence** A goal of criminal sentencing that seeks to prevent a particular offender from engaging in repeat criminality.

**split sentence** A sentence explicitly requiring the convicted person to serve a period of confinement in a local, state, or federal facility followed by a period of probation.

**statutory law** Written or codified law. The "law on the books," as enacted by a governmental body or agency having the power to make laws.

**status offences** Acts or conduct declared by statute to be offences, but only when committed by or engaged in by a young person. Current legislation has moved away from the notion of status offences, penalizing acts that would be crimes if committed by an adult.

**status offenders** In the past, children who committed an act that was contrary to the law by virtue of the young persons' status as children. Purchasing cigarettes, buying alcohol, and truancy were examples of such behaviour.

**strategic policing** A style of policing that retains the traditional police goal of professional crime fighting, but enlarges the enforcement target to include non-traditional kinds of criminals such as serial offenders, gangs and criminal associations, drug distribution networks, and sophisticated white-collar and computer criminals. Strategic policing generally makes use of innovative enforcement techniques, including intelligence operations, undercover stings, electronic surveillance, and sophisticated forensic methods.

**subpoena** An order issued by a court requiring an individual to appear in court and to give testimony. Some subpoenas mandate that books, papers, and other items be surrendered to the court.

**summons** An order issued by a judge or justice commanding a person charged with an offence to attend court at a particular time and location in order to be dealt with, according to law.

**surety** The requirement that a person other than the accused sign for the accused's release, thereby indebting that individual to the Crown should the accused fail to appear for court.

**suspicionless search** A search conducted by law enforcement personnel without a warrant and without suspicion. Suspicionless searches are only permissible if based on an overriding concern for public safety.

**system of criminal justice** The aggregate of all operating and administrative or technical support agencies that perform criminal justice functions. The basic divisions of the operational aspects of criminal justice are law enforcement, courts, and corrections.

**tazir crime** A minor violation of Islamic law, regarded as an offence against society, not God.

**team policing** The reorganization of conventional patrol strategies into "an integrated and versatile police team assigned to a fixed district." Source: Souryal, S. (1977). Police Administration and Management (p. 261). St. Paul, MN: West.

**terrorism** A violent act or an act dangerous to human life in violation of the criminal laws of Canada or of the provinces to intimidate or coerce a government, the civilian population, or any segment thereof, in furtherance of political or social objectives. While we usually think of terrorism as involving bombings, kidnappings, and hijackings, other forms of terrorism might include attacks on the information systems of financial institutions and threats to reveal trade or industry secrets. Crimes that lack the ideological component necessary to qualify as terrorism can be described simply as murder, vandalism, blackmail, and so on.

**testimony** Oral evidence offered by a sworn witness on the witness stand during a criminal trial.

**the medical model** A theoretical framework for the handling of prisoners, which held that offenders were "sick" and could be "cured" through behavioural and other appropriate therapies.

**tort** A private or civil wrong or injury. A breach of duty to an individual that results in harm to that person.

**total institutions** Enclosed facilities, separated from society both socially and physically, where the inhabitants share all aspects of their lives on a daily basis.

**trial** The examination in a court of the issues of fact and law in a case, for the purpose of reaching a judgment of conviction or acquittal of the defendant(s).

**undisciplined children** Children who were beyond parental control, as evidenced by their refusal to obey legitimate authorities such as school officials and teachers.

**verdict** In criminal case processing, a formal and final finding made on the charges by a jury and reported to the court, or by a trial judge when no jury is used.

**victim assistance programs** Organized programs that offer services to victims of crime, for example, crisis intervention and follow-up counselling, and that help victims secure their rights under the law.

**victim impact statements** The court may use this victim- or survivor-supplied information to make a sentencing decision.

**violent crime** An offence category that, according to the Uniform Crime Reports (UCR), includes homicide, attempted homicide, sexual assault, other sexual offences, abduction, robbery, and assault. Because the UCR depends upon reports (to the police) of crimes, the "official statistics" on these offences are apt to inaccurately reflect the actual incidence of such crimes.

**warehousing** A policy of keeping offenders locked up in prison, usually for lengthy periods of time, without providing any form of treatment, using their labour productively.

**warrant** Any of a number of writs issued by a judicial officer, which direct a law enforcement officer to perform a specified act and afford protection from damages if he or she performs it.

**watchman style** A style of policing marked by a concern for the maintenance of order. This style of policing is characteristic of lower-class communities, where police informally intervene in the lives of residents in order to keep the peace.

**white-collar crime** Non-violent crime for financial gain committed by means of deception by persons having professional status or specialized technical skills during the everyday pursuit of their business endeavours.

**writ of habeas corpus** The writ that directs the person detaining a prisoner to bring the prisoner before a judicial officer in order for the officer to determine the lawfulness of the imprisonment. writ of certiorari The writ that allows a court to review the record of a decision handed down by an inferior court or tribunal, typically looking for an error of law.

**work release** A prison program in which inmates are temporarily released into the community in order to meet job responsibilities.

**youth justice philosophy** A way of thinking about the approach society should take to responding to crime committed by young people. The philosophy of a youth justice system may be embodied in its guiding principles.

**youth justice system** Government agencies that function to investigate, supervise, adjudicate, care for, or confine youthful offenders and other children subject to the jurisdiction of the Youth Justice Court.

# Case Index

# Name Index

# Subject Index

general deterrence, 286
General Social Survey (GSS)
    described, 28–29, 48–49
    family violence, 50
    fear-of-crime data, 51–52
    1999 data, 49
    problems with, 49–50
    sampling methods, 49
    *vs.* UCR Program, 50, 51
    victimization rates, 49
    violent ex-partners, 39
Geneva Conventions, 557*n*
geoprofiling, 503
gin riots, 98–99
*Go-boy!* (Caron), 392
GOVNET, 516
grand jury, abolishment of, 235, 478
Great Britain. *See* England and Wales
grievance procedure, 409–411, 410
guilty pleas, 17
gun control, 38
guns. *See* firearms
*habeas corpus*, 406, 408
*habeas corpus* appeals, 310
hacker, 508, 509, 511
*Hallcrest* report, 123
*Hallcrest II*, 123
Halsbury's Laws of England, 194
hands-off doctrine, 405
"hanging judge," 290
harm, 79
harmless error rule, 270
Hate Crime Team (B.C.), 518–519
hate crimes, 56–58, 518–519
Headingly riot, 397
healing circles, 288
health care security, 122
hearsay, 273
hearsay rule, 273
high-technology crime, 510
    *see also* cybercrime
HIV. *See* AIDS
home confinement, 341–342
home invasion, 41
homeless youth, 438–439, 452–453
homicide
    and age, 35
    alcohol and, 36
    causes of death, 35–36
    classification, 34
    crime statistics, 33–37
    *Criminal Code* classification of, 34
    culpable *vs.* nonculpable, 34
    first-degree murder, 34
    infanticide, 34

    manslaughter, 34
    mass murders, 36–37
    meaning of, 34
    murder, 34
    police killings, 150–151
    reporting of, 31
    second-degree murder, 34
    strangers and, 36
homicide rates
    in Canada, 1961-2001, 34
    geographical distribution, 34–35
    stability of, 34
Homicide Survey, 30
homosexuality
    in policing, 167
    in prison, 391–395
House of Lords, 479
houses of refuge, 425–426
*Hudud* crimes, 469–471
hung jury, 275
hybrid offences, 76, 230
illegally seized evidence, 187
impaired driving, 44
impaneling the jury, 266–267
implied licence from occupier, 178–180
incapacitation, 285
incarceration. *See* prison sentences
inchoate offences, 76
incident-driven policing, 108
*Income Tax Act*, 71
incriminating statements, 202
indeterminate sentencing, 290, 303–305
    *see also* Canadian sentencing model
indictable offences, 75–76, 230
indictment, 16
individual officers, and discretion, 142–143
individual rights
    in Chinese justice system, 464
    courts' role, 20
    defined, 5
    police spot checks, 207
    *vs.* public order perspective, 7–8
    recognition, in *Charter*, 4
    right to counsel, 207–208
    right to privacy, 209
    right to silence, 14, 20
    right to trial by jury, 17
    right to trial in a reasonable time, 91, 262–264
    roots of, 4
    waiver of, 208
individual rights advocates
    defined, 4
    goals of, 7–8
    offenders, treatment of, 8–9
    wrongful convictions, 8

infancy, as defence, 81–82
infanticide, 34
infected evidence, 151–152
informants, 201–202, 205
information, 16
initial appearance, 229
inmate rights. *See* prisoners' rights
inmate types, 392–394, 403
innovative defences, 91–93
Integrated National Security
    Enforcement Teams (INSET), 7
intensive probation supervision (IPS),
    341
intermediate sanctions
    advantages of, 337
    electronic monitoring, 341–343
    home confinement, 341–342
    intensive probation supervision
        (IPS), 341
    intermittent sentencing, 340, 498
    questions about, 343
    shock incarceration, 338–339
    shock probation/shock parole,
        337–338
    split sentence, 337
intermittent sentence, 340, 498
*International Bill of Human Rights*, 485
International Criminal Court, 489–491
international criminal justice organiza-
    tions
    contemporary information on, 484
    Europol, 489
    history of, 484
    International Criminal Court,
        489–491
    International Society for
        Criminology, 484
    INTERPOL, 487–489
    table of, 485
    and transnational crime, 486–487
    United Nations, 485–486
International Criminal Tribunal for the
    Former Yugoslavia, 491
international perspective
    China, 463–468
    comparative criminal justice, 462
    comparative criminologists, 462
    crime data, problems with,
        462–463
    England. *See* England and Wales
    ethnocentrism, 462
    firearms death rates, 476
    incarceration rates, selected coun-
        tries, 480
    Islamic criminal justice, 468–471
    Japan. *See* Japan
    United States. *See* United States;
        United States criminal justice

162

adjournment, 264
arrest of judgment, 265
ban publication, 265
change of venue, 264
close trial to public, 265
determine fitness to stand trial, 265
discovery, 264
exclude evidence, 264
mistrial, 265
motion, defined, 264
particulars, 265
quash indictment/information, 264
severance of counts, 264
severance of defendants, 264
*prima facie*, 176–177
Prince George Youth Custody Centre, 429
*Prince of the City* (Daley), 147
principles of fundamental justice, 19
prison argot, 389, 390
prison code, 389
prison environment syndrome defence, 92
Prison for Women, 404
prison industry, 357–358, 383
prison issues
AIDS, 413–414
elderly offenders, 414–416
mentally ill inmates, 416–417
systemic racism, 414
prison life
deprivation model, 391
functions of prison society, 390–391
gang membership and, 398
homosexuality in prison, 391–395
importation model, 391
inmate types, 392–394
prison argot, 389, 390
prison code, 389
prison rape, 392
prison subcultures, 388–390
from prisoner's perspective, 404
prisonization, 389
research on, 388
riots, 397–399
social structure of, 391
staff, 394–397
total institutions, 388
women in prison. *See* women in prison
prison programs. *See* correctional rehabilitation programs
prison rape, 392
prison riots
causes of, 397–398
described, 397

gang members and, 398
riot control, 399
stages in, 398–399
prison sentences
boot-camp prison programs, 338–339
concurrent sentence, 302
consecutive sentences, 302
dangerous and long-term offenders, 303–305
indeterminate sentences, 303–305
mandatory minimums, 302–303
maximum length of incarceration, 302
pre-sentence custody, 303
shock incarceration, 338–339
statistics, 301
two-year rule, 303
prison staff. *See* correctional officers
prison subcultures, 388–390
prisoner types
colonist, 393
female inmates, 403
hedonist, 393
legalist, 393
mean dude, 392–393
opportunist, 393
radical, 393
realist, 394
religious, 393–394
retreatist, 393
prisoners' rights
access to media, 408
administrative segregation, 406–407
civil death, 405
communications, 407
discipline, 411
grievance procedure, 409–411, 410
hands-off doctrine, 405
legal access to the courts, 408
legal assistance, 408
legal basis of, 405–406
medical care, 408–409
privacy, 409
religious practice, 407–408
Standard Minimum Rules for the Treatment of Prisoners (UN), 485
visitation, 408
writ of certiorari, 406
writ of *habeas corpus*, 406
prisonization, 389
prisons
*see also* correctional institutions
American influence, 352–355
Auburn system, 353–354
Australian influences, 355–356
Bentham's panopticon writings, 351–352

defined, 348
emergence of, 351–355
evolution of, in Canada, 352
humanization of, 352–355
Irish influences, 356–357
Pennsylvania style, 353
Philadelphia model, 353
today's prisons. *See* correctional institutions
*Privacy Act*, 410
privacy rights
diminishing protection against searches, 209
prisoners and, 409
*vs.* public interest, 203
private criminal lawyer, 249
private justice system, 122–123
private law, 73–74
private policing. *See* private protective services
private prisons, 384, 385
private protective services
*Charter*, application of, 124
defined, 120
development of private policing, 121–122
growth in, 121
integration with public security, 125–126
legitimacy of, 123–124
mandatory training programs, 122
private justice system, 122–123
professionalization of, 123–124
salaries, 121
statistics, 120
training programs, 124
private security. *See* private protective services
Privy Council, 217, 218
probation
advantages of, 329–330
conditions, 321–322, 323
defined, 319
described, 18–19
disadvantages of, 330–331
extent of, 320–321
future of, 344
history of, 320
legal framework, 332–336
*vs.* parole, 325
postcard probation, 336
revocation hearing, 332
serious offenders and, 320–321
shock probation, 337–338
statistics, 321–322
young offenders, 455
probation officers, 334–336
problem-oriented policing, 108, 139–140

procedural defences
        abuse of process, 90–91
        described, 89
        double jeopardy, 89–90
        entrapment, 91
        estoppel, 90
        trial in a reasonable time, denial of, 91
procedural law
        described, 73
        sources of, 71
procuratorate, 465
professional bail bondsmen, 234
professional courtroom actors. *See* court-room work group
professional jury system, 278
professional misconduct, 269
professionalization
        of correctional officers, 396–397
        of private protective services, 123–124
Program of Research on the Causes and Correlates of Juvenile Delinquency, 431
prohibition order, 307
Project Turnaround, 339, 457
property crime, 31
proportionality principle, 290
prosecutorial discretion, 244–246
prosecutors
        abuse of discretion, 246–247
        charge approval standard, 245
        defined, 243
        federal offences, 243
        liability, immunity from, 246
        multiple charge decision, 246
        police department advisor, 244
        presentation of evidence, 244
        professional responsibility, 247
        prosecutorial discretion, 244–246
        provincial offences, 243
        quasi-judicial function of, 244, 245
        role of, 243
        sentencing recommendations, 246
prostitution-related offences, 42–43
*Protection of Children Involved in Prostitution Act* (Alberta), 442
provincial appellate courts, 219–221
provincial correctional institutions, 360, 375–378
provincial court administration, 223–224
provincial courts, 219
provincial government, and constitutional powers, 69–70
provincial-level agencies
        legislative authorization, 114
        responsibility, 115

role of, 114
*Provincial Offence Act* (B.C.), 181
provincial/territorial court systems
        administration, 223–224
        authority for, 218
        British Columbia court system, 221–223
        at Confederation, 217
        court reform, 218–219
        development of, 215–218
        differences in, 218–219
        illustration of, 216
        justice of the peace, 217
        levels, 218
        magistrates courts, 218
        post-Confederation, 217–218
        provincial appellate courts, 219–221
        provincial courts, 219
        superior courts of criminal juris-diction, 219
provocation, 88
public defender model, 250–251
public humiliation, 350
Public Inquiry into the Administration of Justice and Aboriginal People, 8, 105
public law, 68–69
public order
        advocates, 4
        *vs.* individual rights perspective, 7–8
        roots of, 4
public prosecutor. *See* prosecutors
*public Safety Act, 2002*, 6
publication bans, 260, 265, 451
punishment, 79
        *see also* early punishments; sentencing
purposes of the law, 66–68
quashing indictment/information, 264
quasi-criminal law, 74–75
*Quebec Act* (1774), 102
Quetelet system, 496
racial prejudice, and challenges for cause, 266, 267
*Railway Act*, 72
RAND Corporation study, 107
rape. *See* sexual assault
rape shield provisions, 269
rated capacity, 369
RCMP. *See* Royal Canadian Mounted Police (RCMP)
*RCMP Act*, 110
real evidence, 269
reasonable grounds
        defined, 16

at preliminary hearing, 16
reasonable person, 78
recidivism, 366, 367–368
recognizance, 16, 233–234
recruitment. *See* police recruitment
redirect examination, 272
reference power, 228
reform schools, 426
refusal of medical attention, 154
Regional Reception Centre (RRC), 366–367
regional variations in reported crime, 43–44
regionalization of policing agencies, 117–118
regulations, 74
regulatory agencies, 75
rehabilitation, 287
release
        conditional release. *See* parole
        judicial interim release, 16, 230–235
        parole. *See* parole
        pretrial release by police, 229–230
        recognizance, 16, 233–234
        statutory release, 328
        work release, 365
religious practice, and prisoners' rights, 407–408
reported crime. *See* UCR Program
*res judicata*, 90
research on prison life, 388
restitution, 307
restoration, 287–289
restorative justice, 299
restraint principle, 290
retained counsel, 249
retribution, 284
retributive justice, 299
*Return to the Teachings: Exploring Aboriginal Justice* (Ross), 288
reverse sting operations, 207
Revised Statutes of Canada (R.S.C.), 71
riots in prisons, 397–399
robbery
        crime statistics, 40
        described, 40
        firearms use during, 40
        home invasion, 41
Rochester Youth Development Study, 431
Roman law, 62–63
*Rome Statute of the International Criminal Court*, 489–491
Royal Canadian Mounted Police

broader offence, 37
crime statistics, 37–40
cultural myths, 37
date rape, 38
decrease in rate, 38
defined, 52
by ex-partners, 39
nonreporting of, 39
prison rape, 392
rates per 100,000 population, 1978-2001, 38
underreporting, 37
victims of, 40
sexual offender programs, 363
sheriff, 97, 253
shock parole, 337–338
shock probation, 337–338
"show cause" hearings. *See* judicial interim release
silence, right to, 14, 20
situational defences
accident, 87
alibi, 89
compulsion under threats, 86–87
consent, 89
described, 85
duress, 86–87
mistake, 87
necessity, 88
provocation, 88
self-defence, 86
sleepwalking, 84–85
slippery slope perspective, 146
social control, 4
social disorganization, 430
social ecology, 430
social engineering, 68
social justice
defined, 9
ideal, and conflict, 11–12
social policy
and crime data, 27
new crime concerns, 52
socialization mode, 425
*The Society of Captives* (Sykes), 391
*Society of Women: A Study of Women's Prisons* (Giallombardo), 401
software piracy, 508, 511
solitary confinement, 8–9, 369–371, 405, 406
sources of law
case law, 61
Code of Hammurabi, 61–62
common law, 63
the Constitution, 64
Justinian Code, 63
Magna Carta, 63

*mala in se*, 66
*male prohibita*, 66
natural law, 64–65
Roman law, 62–63
statutory law, 61
Special Handling Unit (SHU), 366–367
special provincial constables, 124–125
specific deterrence, 286
split sentence, 337
spontaneous statements, 273
spot checks, 207
spousal abuse, 11–12, 498
spree killers, 36–37
squeegee kids phenomenon, 452–453
"stand mute," 17
Standard Minimum Rules for the Treatment of Prisoners (UN), 485
*stare decisis*, 72–73
*State of Prisons* (Howard), 351
statements
confessions. *See* confessions
dying declaration, 273
K.G.B. statements, 273
past recollection recorded, 273
spontaneous statements, 273
status offences, 428
status offenders, 428
*Statute of Westminster* (1285), 98
statutory law, 61, 71
statutory release, 328
stay of proceedings, 90
strategic policing, 134
street kids, 438, 452–453
*Street Terrorism Enforcement and Prevention Act* (U.S.), 441
stress
among police officers, 153–154
post-shooting stress reactions, 160, 161
reduction, 154
strip searches, 208–210
structured sentencing
aggravating circumstances, 291
critiques of, 292–293
described, 291
determinate sentencing, 291
fundamental underlying purpose, 293
mitigating circumstances, 291
subcultures
police subculture, 138
*see also* police culture
prison subcultures, 388–390
subpoena, 256
substance abuse programs, 364
substantive law, 71

suicide, among teens, 442
*Summa Theologica* (Aquinas), 64
summary conviction offences, 75, 230
summons, 14
superior courts of criminal jurisdiction, 219
Supreme Court of Canada
appointment of justices, 228
*Charter*, and judicial review, 228
on child pornography, 517
crime control *vs.* due process, 190
decisions, effect of, 20
described, 226
on exclusion of evidence, test for, 184
on extradition of individuals facing death penalty, 312–314
on extreme intoxication, 84
as final avenue of appeal, 219
functions of, 228
growth of, 228
horizontal law, 73
judicial review, 228
justices of, 227
limited original jurisdiction, 228
power of, 227
on prisoners' rights, 405
reference power, 228
restructuring proposals, 229
rule creation, role in, 189
on search and seizure, 176–177, 191
on sexual assault, as broader offence, 37
on silence, right to, 20
Sûreté du Québec, 138
surety, 233
survivalist groups, 55–56
suspicionless search, 200
Swackhamer Commission Report, 410
system of criminal justice, 12–13
systemic racism, 414
"target plant" investigation technique, 205
the Taser, 160
Task Force on Federally Sentenced Women, 550*n*
*Tazir* crimes, 471
team policing, 134
technology
ballistics, 497
*Charter of Rights and Freedoms*, 516–520
child pornography, 517
clearing houses, 502–503
computer-aided investigation, 503
computer-based training, 503–504
and courtrooms, 276

court system, 483
crime rates, 481
federal law enforcement agencies, 113
federal policing, 482
felonies, 482
indeterminate sentencing jurisdictions, 290
local level policing agencies, 482–483
misdemeanours, 482
modern criminal law in, 481–482
policing, 482–483
public defender model, 250–251
sentencing, 483–484
state level policing agencies, 482–483
*United States Code*, 481
*USA Patriot Act*, 483, 491
*Violent Crime Control and Law Enforcement Act*, 483
*Universal Declaration of Human Rights* (UN), 490
UNOJUST, 485
vagrancy laws, 77
vehicle stops, 200–201
verdict, 274, 275
vicarious liability, 156
victim assistance programs, 256, 299
victim impact statements, 300
victimization
    fear of, 51–52, 54
    risk, 33
    surveys, 48, 49
victimless crimes, 79, 143
victims
    cross-examination, 258
    major issue, 498
    non-reporting, reasons for, 39
    non-reporting of crimes, 28, 32
    restoration, and healing, 289
    restorative justice, 299
    rights of, 4
    role in criminal trial, 257–258
    and sentencing process, 298–300
*Victims of Crime Act*, 256
*Victims Still: The Political Manipulation of Crime Victims* (Elias), 300
violence
    during break and entry, 41
    family violence, 50
    in line of duty, 150–151
    and media, 54
    prison riots. *See* prison riots
    spousal abuse, 498
    in women's prisons, 403–405
    and young persons, 434–436
Violence Against Women survey, 38

Violence Prevention Program, 362
violent crime, 31
*Violent Crime Control and Law Enforcement Act* (U.S.), 310
Violent Crime Linkage Analysis System (ViCLAS), 503
viruses, 509, 511
visible minorities
    deadly use of police force against, 159
    police recruitment of, 165–166
    prosecutors' tendencies against, 246
    racial prejudice, and challenges for cause, 266, 267
    and suspicions of police, 139
    systemic racism, 414
    women in prison, 401
*A Vision of the Future of Policing in Canada: Police-Challenge 2000* (Normandeau and Leighton), 137
visitation, and prisoners' rights, 408
vocational educational programs, 361
voyeurism, 499
Wales. *See* England and Wales
Walker-Mill perspective, 67
warehousing, 365–369
warrant
    defined, 14
    for DNA evidence, 500
    expiry date, 304
    search warrant provisions, 181
    searches under authority of, 181–182
    telewarrant, 181
Washington State Penitentiary, 390
watchman style of policing, 131
white-collar crime, 506–508
willful destruction of data, 511
witnesses
    children as, 272
    compensation, 256
    competency, 270
    cross-examination, 256, 271
    defendant's testimony, 270
    dying declaration, 273
    exclusion of witnesses, 265
    expert witness, 254–255
    hearsay rule, 273
    K.G.B. statements, 273
    lay witnesses, 256
    oath, 256
    past recollection recorded, 273
    perjured testimony, 271–272
    responsibility of, 256
    and self-incrimination, 271
    spontaneous statements, 273
    subpoena, 256

testimony of, 270–272
victim assistance programs, 256
women
    glass ceiling, in corrections, 381
    and mentoring, 167
    in policing, 103, 166–167
    in prison. *See* women in prison
    prosecutors' tendencies against, 246
    sexual assault. *See* sexual assault
    spousal abuse, 498
    and violent ex-partners, 39
    working in corrections, 380–381
women in prison
    aboriginal offenders, 401
    chivalry factor, demise of, 400
    drug abuse, 380
    drug offences and, 400
    facilities for, 379–380
    HIV/AIDS, incidence of, 413
    kinship groups, 369
    mothers, 401
    offence types, 400
    offender characteristics, 400–401
    organized families, 401
    overcrowding, 400
    programs, 401, 402
    rising numbers, 399
    social structure, 401–403
    statistics, 399
    types of female inmates, 403
    violence, 403–405
*Women's Prison: Sex and Social Structure* (Ward and Kassebaum), 401
work release, 365
workhouses, 350–351
World Trade Center attacks, 3, 6–7
writ of *certiorari*, 406, 408
writ of *habeas corpus*, 406, 408
wrongful convictions, 8
young offenders
    *see also* children; *Youth Criminal Justice Act*
    *Charter*, impact of, 444
    comparison of legislation over time, 446
    delinquency, 424
    rate of youths charges, 422
    self-report surveys, 47
    significant court decisions, 443–444
    statistics, 421–422
    strict discipline program, 339
*Young Offenders Act*, 421, 428, 446
young persons
    *see also* children; young offenders
    abuse, other forms of, 440–442
    alcohol abuse, 433–434
    drug abuse, 433–434, 435